$MRP = \frac{\Delta TR}{\Delta \text{input}}$ marginal revenue product (also $MRP = MR \times MPP$)

$MCF = \frac{\Delta TC}{\Delta \text{input}}$ marginal cost of a factor

$\frac{MPP_l}{P_l} = \frac{MPP_k}{P_k}$ condition for least cost combination of inputs

$\frac{MRP_l}{P_l} = \frac{MRP_k}{P_k} = 1$ condition for maximum profit

MCL marginal cost of labour (same as MCF except specifically for labour)

w wage rate, the price of labour

i interest rate (r is also frequently used for the interest rate)

r rate of return (also frequently used for the interest rate)

t time period

R absolute amount of return (as opposed to the rate of return)

$PV = \sum_{t=1}^{n} \left(\frac{R_t}{1+i}\right)^t$ present value of a stream of future income

C consumption

I investment

G government spending on goods and services

M imports (also used for money supply)

X exports

$X_n = X - M$ net exports equal exports minus imports

N frequently used to denote the level of employment

N_b the number of consumers behind demand

N_s the number of suppliers behind supply

AS aggregate supply

AD aggregate demand

$C = C(Y)$ consumption function (also $C = C(Y_d)$)

$S = S(Y)$ savings function (also $S = S(Y_d)$)

AE aggregate expenditure

$MPC = \frac{\Delta C}{\Delta Y_d}$ marginal propensity to consume

$MPS = \frac{\Delta S}{\Delta Y_d}$ marginal propensity to save

$MPC + MPS = 1$ all disposable income is either saved or consumed

MPE marginal propensity to expend (the slope of the expenditure function)

$APC = \frac{C}{Y_d}$ average propensity to consume

$APS = \frac{S}{Y_d}$ average propensity to save

$\frac{1}{1 - MPE}$ the multiplier

T taxes

rr required reserves ratio

$\frac{1}{rr}$ deposit multiplier

M money supply (also used for imports)

V velocity of money

$M \times V = P \times Q$ equation of exchange

L demand for money

C. MICHAEL FELLOWS

Mount Royal College, Calgary

GREGORY L. FLANAGAN

Mount Royal College, Calgary

STANFORD SHEDD

University of Calgary

ROGER N. WAUD

University of North Carolina, Chapel Hill

Economics in a Canadian Setting

HarperCollinsCollegePublishers

Executive Editor: John Greenman
Project Coordination: Donna DeBenedictis
Project Editor: Arlene Grodkiewicz
Design Supervisor: Wendy Ann Fredericks
Text Art: Academy ArtWorks, Inc.
Cover Design: Kay Petronio
Cover Illustration: ©Thomas Lochray/ The Image Bank
Production Manager: Valerie Sawyer
Compositor: Publication Services, Inc.
Printer and Binder: R. R. Donnelley & Sons Company
Cover Printer: The Lehigh Press, Inc.
Color Insert Printer: R. R. Donnelley & Sons Company

ECONOMICS IN A CANADIAN SETTING

This work is also published in two volumes entitled MICROECONOMICS IN A CANADIAN SETTING and MACROECONOMICS IN A CANADIAN SETTING.

Library of Congress Cataloging-in-Publication Data
Economics in a Canadian Setting/ C. Michael Fellows . . . [et al.].
    p. cm.
  Includes index.
  ISBN 0-06-046097-0
   1. Economics—Canada.   I. Fellows, C. Michael.
  HB171.5.C269 1993
  330'.0971—dc20   92-34692
                              CIP

93 94 95 96 9 8 7 6 5 4 3 2 1

Brief Contents

Detailed Contents

v

TWO
The Price System and the
Organization of Economic Activity   111

THREE
Market Structure, Pricing,
and Government Regulation   227

FIVE
Macroeconomic Concepts and Measurement   491

FIVE
Macroeconomic Concepts and Measurement 491

Preface

The primary purpose of *Economics in a Canadian Setting* is to provide students at the first year level of their studies with economic theory useful in analyzing real-world events and problems in a Canadian context. This book is based on Roger Waud's *Economics* which, through five American editions, has successfully provided a well-structured text to assist students in learning the basics of the discipline by incorporating explicit objectives, explaining key concepts clearly, and illustrating them with practical examples. This text endeavours to maintain these characteristics while developing them in a Canadian setting.

The Text's Aims and Approach

Many students today face pressures from financial obligations, family responsibilities, and work-related activities. In addition, reduced funding per capita for postsecondary institutions has led to larger class sizes and reduced availability of instructors and instructional assistants to provide individualized guidance for students.

Over our collective six decades of instructing at Mount Royal College and at the University of Calgary, we have become increasingly concerned over instructional materials used by first- and second-year students of economics. Some principles texts appear to place a premium on terse prose or glitzy presentation. Unfortunately, there may be a tradeoff between the visual impact of a book and its careful development of the basic intellectual arguments of the theory it is presenting. While visually pleasing, some texts become overly busy and create peripheral noisiness resulting in students suffering information-extraction problems. Some other texts seem to concentrate too much on the finer points of upper-level research in the discipline, instead of providing students with a basic discussion tailored to the needs and capabilities of the students who will use the book.

With these challenges in mind, *Economics in a Canadian Setting* has been deliberately structured to guide students in their progression through first-year economic theory. It may seem obvious, and therefore an odd claim to make about a textbook, but this book places emphasis on a thorough, well-sequenced explanation of basic theory. We believe it is a claim which must be highlighted. *Economics in a Canadian Setting* follows the course set out by Waud's American editions, and its bestselling Australian version, to provide a tool that is well-structured and easy for students to use. Like its Australian and American counterparts, it focuses on the basic steps necessary for students to learn to use the theory to analyze real-world economic events. Students deserve a text that gives them the power to understand, analyze, and assess unfolding economic events. *Economics in a Canadian Setting* provides students with the means and encourages them to attain this goal, and this book and supplementary materials will provide students at the first year level with a package that will introduce them to the world of economic analysis in a realistic way that is sensitive to their needs in the 1990s. It will also provide students with the same sense of pleasure and wonder that we ourselves remember feeling from our own first encounter with economics.

Structure of the Book

Economics in a Canadian Setting begins by presenting a thorough discussion of the terminology used in economics to help students establish a solid foundation for understanding the discipline of economics. This beginning is sustained throughout the text as the theory is subsequently developed and refined, new terms are highlighted and defined, and all terms are collected in a complete glossary at the back of the book. Additionally, Part One, the introduction, lays out the major focus of the discipline through the presentation of the basic economic problem—scarcity (Chapter 2) and the circular flow of income (Chapter 3). The role and limitations of government as one of the primary agents in economic decision making is integrated in the discussion. This perspective is maintained throughout the text and enhanced through the Policy Perspectives feature. Supply and demand theory is included in the introduction, since this knowledge is essential to both microeconomics and macroeconomics. Microeconomics follows the introduction and is followed by macroeconomics. We have chosen this progression for two reasons—it appears to be the normal practice in the majority of Canadian colleges and universities, and we feel that macroeconomics must have a firm microeconomic foundation. Nevertheless, it is not necessary to follow this order. Chapters 19 to 32 could precede Chapters 5 to 18, ending the course with Chapters 33 and 34.

Microeconomics

The microeconomics chapters include Chapter 5 through to Chapter 18. In general they constitute a traditional approach to microeconomics with some important differences. We have devoted all of Chapter 5 to elasticity because we view it as one of the most useful and applicable areas of economics. In this chapter we have included both point and arc measures of elasticity. We have included the calculation of cross-price and income elasticity as well as price elasticity of demand and supply. The sections are presented, though, in a manner that allows the instructor to use only the section on price elasticity without loss of continuity.

We have devoted Chapter 6 to the discussion of consumer theory. In this chapter, we include sections on the intuitive description of demand—income and substitution effects; a section on the traditional utility theory; and a section on indifference theory. We attempt to show the inherent commonality of these approaches in a final comment. We have not relegated any of this analysis to an appendix as is often done because we do not wish to prejudice the value placed on one particular method of explanation. Again, the three sections allow the instructor to choose the level of explanation (of demand in this case) depending upon, his or her judgment of what is sufficient in a first year course in economics. In a short course the chapter could be skipped entirely without loss of continuity.

The discussion of market structures in Part Three is conventional, covering the four models—perfect competition, monopoly, monopolistic competition, and oligopoly. This section includes two entire chapters on public policy and regulated markets. Chapter 13 includes a thorough discussion of the development and the current state of competition policy in Canada. Chapter 14 discusses government regulation with regards to market shortcomings. Although it is recognized that some instructors will not have time to include these chapters in their curriculum, we feel it would be an advantage for the student to have a source to refer to when considering the role of government and competition policy in Canada in a political environment emphasizing the advantages of a market economy. These chapters are written in a manner that should require little formal class presentation and could be assigned for reading.

The economic approach to current concerns about the environment is addressed throughout the text starting in Chapter 1 with the introduction of "bads," continuing with the production possibility example of pollution control devices in Chapter 3, in applications of supply and demand in Chapter 7, in Chapter 14 with the discussion of market failures, and in many Policy Perspectives.

Macroeconomics

The macroeconomics section includes Chapter 19 through Chapter 34. The general approach differs from many first year approaches to macroeconomic theory. We have developed the theory from the perspective that the sequence of topics presented by most second-year textbooks in macroeconomics is the preferred sequence, but the mathematical rigour of flexible-price models is unnecessary to a first-year course. We develop an open-economy, flexible-price macroeconomic model framed in static analysis that parallels most intermediate courses, while maintaining a first-year level of rigour and focus. This approach allows for inclusion of the Lucas Critique and rational and adaptive expectations models without the need to move into mathematical modeling that is beyond the level of most introductory students.

Part Five introduces aggregate measurements and the conceptual scope of macroeconomics. Chapter 19 develops a conventional and up to date investigation of national income accounting which introduces students to the methods and intellectual eccentricities of measuring output and its distribution. Chapter 20 focuses on the measurement and social problems endemic in changes in the general price level, fluctuation and instability in the output level, and increases in the unemployment rate.

In Part Six, Chapters 21 through 23 develop an open-economy, fixed-price expenditure model with implicit excess capacity, including analysis of the multiplier effects of changes to autonomous expenditure and fiscal policy using both the aggregate expenditure approach and the withdrawal–injections approach. To introduce the student to the mechanics of macroeconomic modeling, the simple two-sector model developed in Chapter 21 is incrementally adjusted in the subsequent chapters by adding sectors. Parameters, such as the marginal propensity to consume, are left unchanged throughout the development in these three chapters. In this way as exports, government expenditure, taxes, and the marginal propensity to import are incorporated, the student can readily compare the last solution with the next to see the impact of the changing scope of analysis. After the mechanics and mathematics of the fixed-price model are explored, Chapter 25 investigates the impact of the public debt and the various views of the appropriate budgetary stance of fiscal policy.

The text is designed so that after the development of the expenditure model the instructor can choose either of two routes through the further exploration of the macroeconomic model, depending on the desired level of rigour and the breadth of concepts to be included at the first-year level. The first route is more comprehensive, progressing sequentially from Chapters 26 through 34. The sequence includes a full development of the flexible-price, open-economy model with information extraction problems and a longrun and shortrun analysis. The less demanding route skips Chapters 26 and 27, proceeding directly into monetary theory and monetary policy in Chapters 28 through 31 before finishing with an investigation of growth theory in Chapter 32 and international economics in Chapters 33 and 34.

In the more comprehensive route, the development of longrun and shortrun static models of aggregate demand and aggregate supply avoids a mathematical treatment of macroeconomic comparative statistics, concentrating instead on the logic of the model. The emphasis on the logic of the model allows for a full investigation of the transformation of the open-economy, fixed-model developed in Part Six into a flexible price environment including discussions of interest rate, exchange rate, and price level crowding-out, as well as issues in public policy effectiveness. Because of the lack of emphasis on mathematical process we are able to develop a broader discussion of the aggregate supply curve, including discussions of the information extraction problem, policy credibility issues, and a comparison of rational expectations and adaptive expectations in a static framework that is understandable to first year students. At this time this approach appears to be rather a unique feature for a first-year economics book.

Pedagogical Features

Full-Color Capsule Review Inserts

A major pedagogical feature in this text are full-color sections on key ideas in microeconomics and macroeconomics inserted into the two parts of the text. These self-contained, 8-page inserts include graphs, charts, and brief restatements of basic concepts. They are designed for reviewing or recalling some of the most important ideas in economics.

Checkpoints

Checkpoints appear in every chapter, usually at the end of major sections. At each Checkpoint students are signalled to stop and answer a series of questions about the concepts presented in the previous section—to stop and assess their mastery of the concepts before proceeding to the next section. The Checkpoints surmount the problem of waiting until the end of the chapter to ask questions about points of theory which are necessarily understood before subsequent theory is undertaken. In many places in economic theory (such as demand analysis, profit-maximization rules, the development of aggregate expenditure, the multiplier and exchange rate determination) students can waste a great deal of time if the original interpretation is not correct and end up quite frustrated by compounding a misinterpreted portion of the theory as they confront subsequent arguments. Therefore the Checkpoints provide a very valuable tool for students to improve the efficient use of their time while progressing through the theory by initiating immediate checks on their grasp of a concept and giving them immediate feedback through the Hints and Answers to Checkpoints at the end of the book.

Learning Objectives

Learning objectives are listed and set off from the main text near the beginning of each chapter. They outline a plan of study for the chapter, as well as providing an overview of what is to be done and the sequence in which it will occur. After completing the chapter, and before major assignments and examinations, students can review the objectives as a way of organizing their study notes.

Policy Perspectives

Another important feature of this book is its Policy Perspectives. These are a series of discussions of contemporary economic questions. Each chapter contains one or more Policy Perspectives which relate chapter content to current Canadian and international events. Ultimately, a basic education in economics should not only prepare students for subsequent work at more advanced levels, but should foster the ability and desire to apply the theory in disentangling and interpreting the important economic issues encountered through daily exposure to the mass media and individual circumstances. The Policy Perspectives provide effective vehicles for assisting beginning students in seeing how and why economics is useful and important in analyzing complex social phenomena.

Key Terms and Concepts

Precise use and understanding of the technical vocabulary of economics is unavoidable and, as in most introductory level study in other disciplines, it constitutes a necessary part of building the skills to formulate effective concise analysis in the discipline. Words that have several meanings in common usage often require a more precise meaning when used in economics. Such words, along with other important economic terms, appear in boldface type in the text when they are first introduced, and their accompanying definitions are highlighted in italics. The Key Terms and Concepts list at the end of each chapter highlights the new terminology presented in the chapter. These terms and concepts along with their definitions are also reproduced in the Glossary at the back of the book.

Summaries

The Summaries at the end of each chapter are fairly comprehensive and correspond to the chapter objectives. They tie together the main concepts developed in the chapter as well as alert students to areas that may require re-reading.

Questions and Problems

Questions and Problems at the end of each chapter are tailored to the objective statements at the beginning of that chapter. They are generally more complex and extensive than the Checkpoints. Some are almost case-study applications of the theory. Many may be readily used for class discussion or essay questions on examinations. Answers to the end of chapter Questions and Problems, as well as answers to Policy Perspective questions, are provided in the Instructor's Manual. In this way the instructor can determine the appropriate timing and method of providing the answers to the students.

Figures, Graphs, and Tables

Liberal use of Canadian data from *Statistics Canada*, *The Department of Finance*, and other real-world sources is included in the figures, graphs, and tables throughout the text. In some cases hypothetical data are used to illustrate particularly difficult concepts. In these cases we have indicated that hypothetical data are being employed. Throughout the development of the aggregate expenditure model, the same hypothetical values are employed for the marginal propensities and autonomous values for consumption and investment over the two-chapter development of the model. This allows students to get a feel for the impact of each additional component of expenditure as it is introduced.

The captions describing each graph and figure generally begin with a brief summary statement followed by a reasonably complete description of what is protrayed. The captions are a more concise presentation of the more complete description of the concept appearing in the main text. The use of complete but concise descriptions of the concepts within the figures and graphs provides another fast review and study aid for students when reviewing the material prior to examinations.

Supplements and Teaching Aids

The text is supplemented by the following learning and teaching aids: a student Study Guide, an Instructor's Manual, Transparency Masters, two extensive Test Banks in both printed and computerized form, and a Computer Managed Learning System to operate with Campus America educational software for application on Digital computer systems.

Study Guide

Economics in a Canadian Setting has a coordinated Study Guide developed by R. A. Devlin of the University of Ottawa. Each Chapter in the Study Guide corresponds to a chapter in the textbook. At the beginning of each Study Guide chapter there is a list of the learning objectives from the text, followed by a synopsis of the chapter's contents. Matching key terms and concepts appear next, followed by a series of multiple-choice and true-false questions. The Study Guide chapter concludes with several problems and exercises, with each problem covering a major concept area from the text chapter. The answers to questions, problems, and exercises are provided in the Study Guide. As is the text, the Study Guide is published in one- and two-volume editions.

Instructor's Manual

Each chapter of the Instructor's Manual lists the learning objectives and provides a summary and a discussion of important concepts in the corresponding chapter of the textbook. The Instructor's Manual also contains answers to all end-of-chapter Questions and Problems and Policy Perspectives questions from the textbook.

Test Banks

A computerized multiple-choice Test Bank 1 containing over 3,000 questions has been adapted to *Economics in a Canadian Setting* by Stephen Rakoczy of Humber College. Test Bank 2 includes approximately 1,200 non-multiple-choice questions—true and false, matching, short answer, and essay—produced by Gregory Flanagan and Michael Fellows at Mount Royal College. These questions have been thoroughly student-tested and integrated with the text.

Computer Managed Learning System

The Computer Managed Learning System is available for application with Campus America educational software. This system is based on an approach that allows the instructor to prescribe a structured, self-paced course for individual students. Course maps for a one-semester course in microeconomics and a one-semester course in macroeconomics, which were written by the text authors, are tailored to the learning objectives of this textbook. These course maps provide on-line testing, feedback, student progress reports, learning and study management, automated record keeping, and grade determination for the objective components of a course of study in both microeconomics and macroeconomics. The course maps and on-line materials have been thoroughly student-tested and are available to adopters of this text for use with Campus America LMS or LMX software. For more information, contact Gregory Flanagan, Mount Royal College, 4825 Richard S.W., Calgary, Alberta, Canada, T3E 6K6. (Email address: gflanagan@mtroyal.ab.ca)

Transparency Masters

All key figures and graphs are available to adopters as a set of transparency masters.

Additional Course Materials

As an aid to those who feature more work with computers in their introductory economics courses, HarperCollins has available a variety of software packages to support study in microeconomics and macroeconomics. Although not coordinated with *Economics in a Canadian Setting*, a laser disk is also available to provide a video display of 15 animated segments of moving functions, with overvoice, for major economic concepts. Contact your HarperCollins representative for more complete details.

Final Note

Both as authors and also as instructors of first year economics courses, we are sincerely interested in the providing quality instructional materials for students studying economics in Canadian postsecondary institutions. As this book is based on Roger Waud's *Economics,* it has benefited from the progression through five highly successful American editions and the development of the Australian Edition. This text has also undergone a thorough Canadian review process. We have worked very closely with the publisher and have incorporated many suggestions from the reviewers of the Canadian manuscript. We welcome any comments or observations that you have about the strengths and weaknesses you see in our textbook and its supporting instructional materials. We also would welcome any suggestions that you have concerning amendments to the textbook or the supporting materials which would improve the usefulness of the package for you and your students.

Acknowledgments

Many people have provided helpful comments and made contributions to *Economics in a Canadian Setting* throughout the course of its development. We would like especially to thank the hundreds of students at Mount Royal College and the University of Calgary who used draft copies of both the microeconomic and macroeconomic manuscripts. The following students were particularly helpful: Denise Chenger, Heather Cook, Lana Dale, Wayne Federation, Richard Fix, Jennifer Koivuneva, Lara Middleton, and Debra Wilson.

We would also like to thank the following individuals who reviewed drafts of the manuscript or offered assistance in other ways:

Denis Bélanger, Institut d'Economie Appliquée, École des Hautes Études Commerciales
Horst K. Betz, University of Calgary
Chris J. Bruce, University of Calgary
Emanuel Carvalho, University of Waterloo
Jeffrey R. Church, University of Calgary
Rose Ann Devlin, University of Ottawa
Arnold Frenzel, Wilfred Laurier University
L. Fric, King's College, University of Western Ontario
James D. Gaisford, University of Calgary
Hugh Grant, University of Winnipeg
R. Quentin Grafton, University of Ottawa

William J. Ives, Southern Alberta Institute of Technology
William A. Kerr, University of Calgary
Ronald D. Kneebone, University of Calgary
Robert K. Kunimoto, Mount Royal College
Robert N. McRae, University of Calgary
V. Nallainayagam, Mount Royal College
V. C. Olshevski, University of Winnipeg
Stephen Rakoczy, Humber College
Debbie Rasmussen, Agriteam Canada Consulting Ltd.
Steven Renzetti, Brock University
Peter W. Sinclair, Wilfred Laurier University
Leon P. Sydor, University of Windsor
Bruce W. Wilkinson, University of Alberta
Elizabeth A. Wilmar, University of Calgary
Ian A. Wilson, St. Lawrence College

In addition, we would also like to thank our former instructors who introduced us to economic theory when we were beginning students, our families for their patience over the past few years, and John Greenman at HarperCollins for his support of this project.

C. Michael Fellows
Gregory L. Flanagan
Stanford Shedd

To the Student

You don't have to have taken a course in economics to be aware of the economic problems confronting Canada and the world. Newspapers, radio, and television bombard you daily with evidence of the importance of understanding economic phenomena. The media is constantly making us aware of the rate of inflation, unemployment, the federal government deficit, the level of interest rates, the value of the international exchange rate on the Canadian dollar, and possible reasons for a provincial government to consider giving subsidies or tax concessions to some firm or industry. At a different level, the paying of tuition fees or financing of living expenses while attending college or university or the reasons for a change in the price of some favourite product have given you personal experience in dealing with economic phenomena. In short, every member of society who has ever bought or sold something or worked for or hired someone has experience in the subject of economics. Nonetheless, the formal study of economics as an academic discipline is, like psychology, matrix algebra, or physics, a rigourous subject. It should be studied in the same way that you would study other rigourous subjects in the social sciences or sciences—a little bit every day.

- Before reading a chapter, survey the learning objectives that appear at the beginning of the chapter. They will give you a brief outline of what you are about to read and of the authors' aims in presenting the material. After completing each chapter you should go back and review the learning objectives to see that you have grasped the concepts and principles developed in the chapter.

- In most chapters, your attention will be drawn at some point to a Policy Perspective, a feature where basic economic principles are applied to a current problem or policy to enable you to see how the principles can be used to better analyze and understand actual economic phenomena. You should discover that the analytical method of thinking about economic problems, which at first seems somewhat abstract to students, is a powerful tool for understanding and controlling economic events in the real world.

- When reading this book, read for understanding, not speed. Each chapter is broken into major sections that focus your attention on important concepts. Within each major section you will encounter a Checkpoint—a brief series of questions that enable you to test your understanding of what you have just read. You should always stop and measure your progress by trying to answer the questions in these Checkpoints. The answers to the Checkpoint questions appear at the end of the textbook to give you feedback as you study the book.

- Economics is a problem-analyzing discipline. To provide you with the opportunity to apply the principles you are learning and to develop the analytical skill that will be tested on exams, the text has problems and questions at the end of each chapter. Try to solve these after you have completed the chapter. It is recommended that you tackle some of the questions immediately after completing the reading of the chapter and solve some at a later date as part of your overall review of the material prior to major tests and exams.

Finally, bear in mind that the concepts and principles studied in each chapter are typically used again and again in subsequent chapters. Mastering the material as you go makes the chapters that follow that much easier. We wish you success in your study of economics.

C. Michael Fellows
Gregory L. Flanagan
Stanford Shedd

PART ONE

Introduction

Chapter 1

Economics and Economic Issues

Economics is a subject that touches on all peoples' lives whether they are conscious of it or not. One has only to pick up a current newspaper to see how extremely important this subject is. Economics is also a fascinating subject to study, as a considerable number of the major issues and conflicts of the past revolved around economics. Human history and human aspirations are often contingent upon economic matters. How will the study of economics help you? First, a knowledge of economics will help you to analyze economic issues that are reported daily in the press and on television. Second, it will give you the analytical structure to appreciate the developments of the past, as economic development affected social and political history. Third, the study of economics will provide you with the analytical skills that will sharpen the way you perceive the world. Although the laws of economics may not be as absolute as the law of gravity, they will help you to better understand and distinguish the facts and opinions that surround contemporary economic issues. As a result, you will be able to come to intelligent, informed conclusions when faced with both day-to-day problems and questions of national policy.

How do the ideas of economists influence the way politicians, business leaders, and other decision makers confront economic issues and questions of economic policy? Consider the answer offered by one of the most famous economists of the twentieth century, John Maynard Keynes:[1] "The ideas of economists, both when they are right and when they are wrong, are more powerful than is commonly understood. Indeed, the world is ruled by little else. Practical men, who believe themselves to be quite exempt from any intellectual influences, are usually the slaves of some defunct economist. Madmen in authority, who hear voices in the air, are distilling their frenzy from some academic scribbler of a few years back."

---

[1]John M. Keynes, *The General Theory of Employment, Interest, and Money* (New York: Harcourt Brace Jovanovich, 1964), p. 383.

Economy and Economics

The word **economy** typically brings to mind ideas of efficiency, thrift, and the avoidance of waste by the careful planning and use of resources. We might say that some job was done with an economy of motion, meaning that there was no unnecessary effort expended. The word *economy* comes from the Greek *oikonemia*, which means the management of a household or state. In this sense, we often speak of the American or of the Chinese economy; of a capitalist or socialist economy; of a free-market or planned economy; or of an industrialized or underdeveloped economy. The term *economy* refers to *any particular system of organization, usually national, for the production, distribution, and consumption of commodities and services people use to achieve a certain standard of living or well-being.*

The term **economics**, on the other hand, is not so simple. It covers such a broad range of meaning that any brief definition is likely to leave out some important aspect of the subject. Most economists would agree, however, that economics is a social science concerned with the study of economies and the relationships among them. *Economics is the study of how people and society choose to employ scarce productive resources to produce commodities and services and distribute them for consumption among various persons and groups in society.* This definition touches upon several important concepts—choice, scarcity, resources, production, consumption, and distribution—with which we will be concerned both in this chapter and throughout the book.

Before reading any further you should understand that, whatever it is, economics is not primarily a vocational subject such as accounting, marketing, or

---

LEARNING OBJECTIVES

After reading this chapter, you will be able to:

1. Define the terms *economy* and *economics.*
2. Define the terms *macroeconomics* and *microeconomics.*
3. Define and give examples of the different categories of resources.
4. Define and give examples of commodities, goods, services, free goods, and bads.
5. Describe and illustrate the connections between and among resources, production, goods, distribution, and consumption.
6. Distinguish between and give examples of positive and normative statements.
7. Define and distinguish between inductive and deductive methods.
8. Identify the basic elements—variables, assumptions, hypothesis, and prediction— that make up any economic theory.
9. Define and explain *ceteris paribus.*
10. Distinguish between endogenous and exogenous variables.
11. Explain cause and effect relationships and state what fallacy is often committed where they do not occur.
12. Explain and give examples of the fallacies of composition and division.
13. Distinguish between qualitative and quantitative analysis.
14. Explain the role of economic theory and analysis in economic policy making.

---

management. Nor is it primarily intended to teach you how to make or spend money, though it may help. Economics studies problems from society's point of view rather than from the individual's. It is likely you will find the study of economics helpful in whatever career you choose. Moreover, it should make you a more knowledgeable and able citizen.

Macroeconomics versus Microeconomics

Economists often use the terms *macroeconomics* and *microeconomics* to distinguish between different levels of economic analysis. In **macroeconomics**, we are concerned with the workings of the whole economy or large sectors of it. These sectors include government, businesses, and households. For the purposes of analysis, the smaller agents that make up these large sectors are often lumped together and treated as one unit. For example, the consumer sector may be treated as though it were one large household, and the business sector might be considered to be one large business. Macroeconomics deals with such issues as economic growth, unemployment, recession, inflation, stagflation, and monetary and fiscal policy.

Microeconomics, on the other hand, focuses on the individual agents that make up the whole of the economy. Here we are interested in how households and businesses behave as individual units, not as parts of a larger whole. Microeconomics studies how a household spends its money. It also studies the way in which a business determines how much of a product to produce, how to make best use of the factors of production, what pricing strategy to use, and so on. Microeconomics also studies how individual markets and industries are organized, what patterns of competition they follow, and how these patterns affect economic efficiency and welfare.

The Language of Economics

As is the case with many subjects, the terminology used in economics often seems strange to the beginning student. Physicists talk about neutrons, quarks, and hysteresis; football coaches talk about fly patterns, wishbone offenses, and flex defenses. To make sense of a typical news item about economic issues, you must first be familiar with the language of economics. One particular difficulty in the learning of economics is that economists frequently use common, everyday words to mean something more precise than is generally expected in everyday conversation. For instance, when one says someone has a lot of money, common usage suggests that one means a person who owns a lot of things such as cars, houses, buildings, stocks, bonds, cash, and so on. In economics, however, it is generally accepted that "money" means only holdings of currency and demand deposits at a bank. When something else is meant by money, it is spelled out exactly what other items are included in the definition. It should be noted that economics is not about money per se, although money is important for the functioning of modern economies. To start learning what economics is about, it is best to focus by thinking about "real" things. Money is convenient as a common denominator to measure the value of the real things economics is concerned with. Certain basic terms, such as *money*, will come up again and again throughout this book. The following definitions will help you to understand and use these terms correctly.[2]

Economic Resources

Economic resources, also called the *factors of production* or *inputs to production*, are all the natural, produced, and human resources that are used in the production of goods. These resources may be divided into two broad categories: nonhuman resources (capital and land) and human resources (labour).

Capital

Capital is an example of a term that is sometimes used to mean one thing in everyday conversation and another in economics. We often speak of capital when referring to money, especially when we are talking about the purchase of equipment, machinery, and other productive facilities. It is more accurate to call the money used to make such a purchase, **financial capital**. An economist uses the term *capital* to mean all the human-made aids used in production. **Capital** (sometimes called investment goods), consists of such things as machinery, tools, buildings, transportation and distribution facilities, and inventories of unfinished goods. **Investment** is the production of new capital goods. A basic characteristic of capital goods is that they are used to produce other goods. For example, electricity is produced from the use of capital goods such as boilers, turbines, fuel storage facilities, poles, and miles of wire. Note that the context of use often determines whether a good is capital. For example, two otherwise identical automobiles coming off an assembly line are defined differently depending on their use. If the one is bought for personal use it is a consumption good, if the other is used by a taxi company it is a capital good used in the production of transportation services. Capital is scarce relative to the desire for the output of goods and services made with the use of capital. In short, *capital is a good used to produce other goods*.

Land

To an economist, **land** is made up of all natural resources that are used in production. Such resources include water, forests, oil, gas, mineral deposits, and so forth. What makes them natural is that they are found in a state of nature, untouched by humans. Land resources are scarce and, in many cases, are rapidly becoming more scarce. An important distinction with regards to land resources is the difference between renewable and nonrenewable resources. Renewable resources, although scarce, should be sustainable over time with proper man-

---

[2]There will be many more terms used throughout the text that will be defined at the point they are introduced. A glossary of terms is provided at the end the book, and all terms in boldface type are collected there.

agement. Nonrenewable resources will be depleted with time although this can be offset with recycling programs. The time pattern of use becomes a critical question in the use of nonrenewable resources, while with recycling, energy sources become the vital issue. *Land is all natural resources used in production.*

Labour

Labour is a very broad term that covers all the different mental and physical capabilities and skills possessed by human beings that can be used to produce goods and services. Labour is scarce relative to the desire for the output of goods and services made with the help of labour. Labour consists of the services provided by welders, carpenters, masons, dentists, scientists, teachers, managers, and so forth. The term **manager** embraces a host of skills related to the planning, administration, and coordination of production. A manager may also be an **entrepreneur**.[3] This is the person who comes up with the ideas and takes the risks that are necessary to start a successful business. The founders of companies are entrepreneurs, while those running them are more accurately called managers. At this level of abstraction, all of these human services are termed labour. There is, for example, no management-labour distinction such as might be found in a labour relations text. *Labour is the physical and mental skills and capabilities possessed by humans and used in the process of production.*

Economic Goods

An **economic good** is any item that is both desired and scarce. A **free good** is something that is desired but is plentiful and therefore is not scarce. In general, economic goods may be classified as either commodities or services. **Commodities** are tangible items such as food, clothing, cars, or household appliances. (*Tangible* means, quite literally, that the item is able to be touched.) Commodities do not have to be consumed immediately when they are produced—that is, they may be stored for future use. **Services** are intangibles (that is, nontouchables) such as shoeshines, haircuts, doctor examinations, business consultations, and so on. They generally cannot be stored or transferred. For example, I cannot give you my haircut (a service), but I can give you my coat (a commodity). Such distinctions are not always clear. For example, the economic good—electricity might be called a service by some who say it is intangible and a commodity by others who note that it can be stored in a battery. Most often, an economic good is simply referred to as a good. You have heard of the output of the economy referred to as "goods and services." This is done largely to remind us of the existence of services. On the other hand, an **economic bad** is any item that is undesired. Economic bads are often outputs of production as well; an example is pollution. *Economic goods (and bads) are the output of the production process.*

---

[3] Some authors make a distinction, with entrepreneurial skills as a separate resource category. This is useful if profit is seen as strictly a return to the short-term entrepreneurial (innovation) function.

Checkpoint* 1-1

When categorization schemes are created many items cannot be easily placed, for example, the platypus is difficult to categorize in the animal schema. This is true for many items used in production that are difficult to place in the categories of resources—land, labour, and capital. In which categories would you place: dairy cattle, trees in a tree farm, chickens, electrical power, gasoline, and money?

*Answers to all Checkpoints can be found at the back of the text.

Whether they are commodities or services, all economic goods share the quality of being **scarce**. That is, there are not enough of them to supply everyone's needs and desires. As a result, people have to forgo something in order to obtain them, and what they forgo is the opportunity cost of the good.[4] A properly functioning market system will convert this opportunity cost into a **price**. As we will see in Chapter 4, the price of the good is determined to a large extent by the number of people who desire and are able to pay for a particular good, together with what it costs producers to provide it.

Economic Processes

Processes are at work in the economy that are at the core of the economic well-being of the society's individuals. Central to the concept of an economy are the notions of production, distribution and consumption. The fundamental concern in all economic analysis is with the efficiency of these processes in optimizing human goals.

Production

The creation of goods that provide well-being to members of society is called *production*. **Production** is carried out by combining economic resources in various ways in order to obtain something else. *The process of production is the conversion of resources to useful final products in the form of economic goods or capital.* Resources are the inputs to production, while economic goods are the output. Capital has the distinction that it is both an input and an output of production. Nonrenewable land resources are continually being reduced (although more are being discovered and added to *known* reserves, by definition no more are being produced), but the capital stock in a country such as Canada has been growing over time, thereby offsetting the demise of the overall resource stock. The consequence of this raises an important theme that runs through economics—resource substitutability. A recent example of this is the substitution of insulation for heating fuels to provide the good of warm buildings. The mixture of resources is not as important as the goods that can be produced in the economy.

Distribution

Distribution means *the shares of the total product of the economy that go to different individuals, or groups, in society as their incomes.* Incomes are most often in the form of money wages received for labour services rendered to firms. In addition, many individuals receive income from the ownership of capital and land resources. In the latter case these incomes may come in the form of real goods provided by government for free (this does not make them free goods) but financed by revenues generated from taxes or from rent royalties earned by the collective (government) ownership of land resources. Remember that economics

---

[4]The concepts of scarcity and opportunity cost are fundamental to economics and will be discussed at greater length in Chapter 2.

is ultimately concerned with real things; therefore, distribution is the question of who gets the goods (real income) produced in the economy. We all have a personal interest in our own incomes and the *fairness* of income shares in general. The distribution issue has generated much controversy (with ideology always in the forefront of the debate) and it is therefore one of the most interesting aspects of the study of economics. A large amount of **redistribution** of incomes takes place in Canada through taxes and transfers.

Consumption

Consumption is the end purpose of the economy; the use of goods by the individuals or households in society. Consumption does not necessarily imply the using up of the good. For example the consumption of a car, a durable good, may take place over a ten-year period, and even at the end of the car's useful life, most of it still exists physically. Services are goods that are consumed at the instant of use. People desire goods because these goods provide some form of satisfaction. A refrigerator provides satisfaction by keeping food cold. A stereo system provides satisfaction by giving us entertainment. Because an economic good gives us satisfaction, we say that it is useful to us. As a result, economists refer to the well-being or satisfaction a good yields as its **utility**. The common essence that all goods (an enormous number and variety) provide through consumption is utility.

Economic Agents

We have to make economic decisions in our day-to-day lives, as resources are scarce and we cannot do everything we would like to. We classify individuals and groups as economic agents according to what motivates their behaviour. Economic **agents** are the decision makers in the economy and are distinguished by the motivations behind their decisions. Individuals, of course, do not neatly fit into any one category; they often play many different roles in the economy—as consumer, producer, or government official or other decision maker.

The Firm

Resources of land, capital, and labour are brought together in a production unit that is referred to as a business or a **firm**. The firm uses these resources to produce goods, which are then sold. The money obtained from the sale of these goods is used to pay for the resources. Payments to those providing labour services are called **wages**. Payments to those providing land resources to the firm are called **rent**. Payments to those providing capital (those who own stocks and bonds) are called **interest**. The firm's goal or motivation is assumed to be to maximize profit[5] in a market economy or to fulfill the targets for output in a centrally planned economy. Note that in a market-based economy an individual could act as both a firm and a household.

---

[5]There are other theories of the motivations behind business firms' actions, but profit maximization is the best single indicator.

The Household

The agents whose well-being is the ultimate measure of the efficiency of an economy are the individuals who compose that society. Sometimes the individual is the smallest entity considered, but more generally the **household** is the smallest decision-making unit of concern. Of course many households in Canada are comprised of one individual. The household's goal or motivation in terms of economics is assumed to be that of maximizing its utility, subject to the household's income.

The Government

Government refers to the public agents at all levels. In Canada, government comprises at least three levels: municipal or local, provincial, and federal governments—each with different and overlapping responsibilities. In general, when economists refer to government, they mean some authority with extra economic powers (the law) to regulate production and consumption, tax and redistribute income, or generally intervene in the workings of the economy. The term *government* as used in economics, in this general sense, does not refer to any particular partisan government in power at a specific time. From this perspective of government, it is assumed that the motivation of government is the collective well-being of the citizens.[6] Determining the collective interest is one aspect of welfare economics. As this is a normative exercise, it leaves considerable room for different ideological interpretations of what the collective interest is.

The Foreign Sector

Most economies are not closed, that is, they are interactive with other economies. In order to analyze the effects of this interaction, we require a sector separate from the agents described in the previous section. The **foreign sector** aggregates all the transactions between the firms, households, and governments within the domestic economy and those of other countries. Foreign exchange rates—the value of one currency in the denomination of another—and the balance of payments accounts are important in the analysis of the foreign sector.

Gross Domestic Product

Gross Domestic Product will be discussed in Chapter 19, but because this measure is so extensively used throughout economics it will be defined here. **Gross Domestic Product (GDP)** *is the total dollar value of all the final goods produced by all the firms in the economy in one year.* Note that final goods are distinguished from goods still in the process of production—intermediate goods—that are incorporated in other goods. An example would be the steel or the tires used in the

---

[6]More conservative views of government's motivation abound that dispute this assumption that government is altruistic. Some suggest instead that government is a *leviathan.* There is also empirical evidence that strongly suggests that governments do not necessarily act to enhance the public well-being, but to maximize the probability of being reelected.

production of a car. We would not want to double count these products by adding them once when produced and sold to the car manufacturer and again when the car is sold to an individual.

In order to make meaningful comparisons of the GDP for various years, economists often use *real* GDP, which is GDP adjusted so that it only reflects changes in quantity of output, not changes in prices. When the real GDP goes down, we say that the economy is in a *recession*. A severe recession is called a *depression*, although there is no general agreement as to how to decide exactly when a recession becomes a depression.

Inflation and Unemployment

The economic health of an economy of which GDP is only one measure, is directly affected by two other important factors, **inflation** and **unemployment**. These concepts will be discussed at length later on in the text. For the purposes of this chapter they are briefly introduced here. Inflation is an ongoing general rise in prices. The steeper this rise, the faster the decline of a dollar's purchasing power. The unemployment rate measures the percentage of the total number of workers in the labour force who are actively seeking employment but are unable to find jobs. The higher the unemployment rate, the more the economy is wasting labour resources by allowing them to stand idle.

The Method of Economics

Methodology is the method by which a discipline such as economics accumulates knowledge and has confidence in it. Methodology is a very difficult area of study.[7] If the entire concept of how we know anything for sure is foreign to you, take refuge in the fact that many practicing economists (and scientists) never give methodology a second thought. Also those that get too involved in it can suffer from what Joseph Schumpeter has termed *methodological hypochondria*. What you should glean from this section is some understanding of the methodological issues and at least an awareness of the terms one encounters in this field.

Economic Reality and Economic Theory

Economic reality—making a living, paying the rent, shopping for food, paying taxes, and so forth—forces us to deal with a large and confusing swarm of facts, figures, and events. The activities of households, firms, and governments all have a direct effect on our economic lives. In order to make some sense out of the world around us, we all have formulated some economic theories, even without being aware of doing so.

---

[7]For a thorough introduction and survey of the field see Mark Blaug, *The Methodology of Economics, or How Economists Explain* (Cambridge, U.K.: Cambridge University Press, 1980).

POLICY PERSPECTIVE

The First Modern Economist: Adam Smith (1723–1790)

Adam Smith is often thought of as the founder of modern economics. There are others who it could be argued have a better claim to the title, but Smith, in his great work, *The Wealth of Nations** was the first to identify and document, in a systematic and thorough way, the importance of the evolving market system. Although it would not look very much like a modern economics textbook to today's reader, Smith's book contained a solid production and distribution theory (complete with a host of economic policy prescriptions), and most terms introduced in this chapter can be found in it.

The leading theme of *The Wealth of Nations* is economic development and this has been a major preoccupation of economists ever since. As the title states, the work is concerned with how a nation expands its wealth or income over time. One of Smith's most significant contributions to economic thought was his explanation of the importance of the division of labour and its relationship to economic development. In his famous description of operations in a pin factory, Smith shows how output can be greatly increased by dividing tasks into small segments, each performed by specialists who require little training. But Smith's vision of these gains goes well beyond the simple specialization within a firm, and recognizes the social division of labour with a vast network of interrelations among specialized producers willing to trade.

This division of labour, from which so many advantages are derived, is not originally the effect of any human wisdom, which foresees and intends that general opulence to which it gives occasion. It is the necessary, though slow and gradual, consequence of a certain propensity in human nature which has in view no such extensive utility; the propensity to truck, barter and exchange one thing for another. [p. 13]

An important theme in Smith was the value of enlightened self-interest, which has been characterized as *the invisible hand*. An advocate of economic freedom, Smith generally accepted the idea of *natural liberty* taught by the Scottish philosopher Francis Hutcheson, which implied the removal of restrictions of all kinds. Such a theory well suited the rising commercial class in Western Europe, particularly in England, which found government regulations irksome. Freedom allowed the natural instincts provided by a wise providence (in other words, self-interest) to prevail and provide the drive to turn the wheels of trade and commerce.

As Smith saw it, it would be foolish to assume that people satisfy the needs of others simply as a result of feelings of altruism. On the contrary, the baker, the brewer, and the candlestick maker each undertakes to satisfy the needs of others as a means of satisfying his or her own

needs. By seeking to fulfill personal needs, each individual is helping to increase the wealth of society:

He generally, indeed, neither intends to promote the public interest nor knows how much he is promoting it. By preferring the support of domestic to that of foreign industry, he intends only his own security; and by directing that industry in such a manner as its produce may be of the greatest value, he intends only his own gain; and he is in this, as in many other cases, led by an invisible hand to promote an end which was no part of his intention. [p. 423]

Although he preached the doctrine of *laissez faire* (the role of government should be minimized), it is a mistake to overemphasize this view in Smith. The list of failures in a *laissez-faire* system, which Smith documents and offers policy advice on, found in *The Wealth of Nations* is of sufficient length to deter us from viewing Smith as a naive advocate of *natural liberty*. As well, Smith was aware that the self-interest of a small number of industrial producers could lead to collusion (high prices) against the interests of consumers and against the general welfare. Smith offers much more and it is because of this that he stands out as preeminent in the history of economic thought.

*Adam Smith, *An Inquiry into the Nature and Causes of the Wealth of Nations* (New York: Random House, 1937).

How to hold down inflation is a topic about which practically everyone has a theory. One individual, having just filled out an income tax return, might say, "If we don't curb all this government spending, inflation will get worse." The owner of a small business, on the other hand, might feel that "if something isn't done to break up the big unions and big corporations, we'll never bring inflation under control." Based on observations of the way certain groups, organizations, and institutions function, each individual has focused on the relationship that appears to be most relevant to an explanation of inflation. From these examples, we can say that an **economic theory** is an attempt to describe reality by abstracting and generalizing its basic characteristics.

What is needed though is a method to separate uninformed opinion—nonscience from a disciplined and testable view—science. In this way, we can gain confidence in our understanding and can reject inaccurate and false views, refine the theories available, and develop new ones as required. Economists often refer to an economic theory as a law, principle, or model. Each of these terms may be taken to mean the same thing.

Positive and Normative Statements

Before we proceed with economic theory proper, an intelligent discussion of economic methods and issues requires that we distinguish between positive and normative statements. For example, take the statement from above that "a decrease in the unemployment rate will lead to an increase in inflation." This is a statement that may be supported or refuted by examining data. As such, we can say it is a **positive statement**. Positive statements tell us what is, what was, or what will be. "It rained last Thursday" and "The sun will rise in the east tomorrow" are positive statements.

But now let's change our statement about inflation and unemployment slightly. Let's say that "it is better to decrease unemployment and live with the resulting increase in inflation than to allow a large number of people to go without jobs." This is a **normative statement**. A normative statement is an opinion or value judgment. Those of you who are looking for jobs would probably agree with this statement. But if your grandparents are retired and living on fixed incomes, they would likely disagree. Since they are not seeking employment, an increase in the number of jobs available would in no way compensate them for a rise in prices. As far as they are concerned, it would probably be better to slow the rise in prices. This could lead to an increase in unemployment, which would make all job seekers very unhappy. The dispute between these two groups cannot be settled by facts alone. Normative statements tell us what should be (normative means "establishing a norm or standard"). Although normative statements often have their origin in positive statements, they cannot be proven true or false by referring to objective data. For example, I may make the normative statement, "You should study economics." This statement may have its origin in the positive statement, "Studying economics increases your productivity and income." We could disagree forever over the first statement, but statistical studies could be brought to bear on any dispute over the second.

In any discussion about economic issues, as soon as voices rise you can almost be certain that the discussion has shifted from logic and fact to value judgment and opinion. However, don't forget that value judgments and opinion often parade in the clothes of logic and fact. In the case of normative state-

Checkpoint 1-2

Pick out a short
news item in today's
paper and make a
list of all the positive
statements and a list
of all the normative
statements. Examine
the normative
statements and try to
determine what kinds
of positive statements
they may be based on.

ments, everyone is entitled to his or her opinion, although it would be hoped in a democratic system, where everyone has an equal vote, that an individual's normative opinions would be made upon careful thought and analysis. In the instance of positive statements, there should be a means to resolve any difference of opinion through recourse to the facts, although this is not always the case. Note that to say a statement is positive does not imply anything about its being true.

Unfortunately, a given statement we encounter is not always so clearly positive or normative and these differences become blurred. It should also be mentioned that positive and normative types of thinking can become blurred into one another in the normative decisions of choosing variables in a model or setting forth relationships between variables or in interpreting the results of empirical work. Much of what goes on in the name of positive economics today involves a large amount of ideology. Nonetheless these distinctions help clarify ones thinking when it comes to economic theory and policy.

Scientific Method

The purpose of science is to separate false or erroneous views from the truth. Unfortunately the "truth" is a difficult thing to pin down. A couple of issues are of importance here. First is the question as to whether there is one scientific method or whether a social science such as economics should have a different methodology from sciences such as physics. Introspection is possible in the social sciences, as they deal with human behaviour, of which the researcher has personal experience. If we accept this view, it might go far to explain the emphasis on the deductive method, or *apriorism*, in the early history of economic thought.[8] The second major issue involves the verification versus falsification of theory. Early in the development of economic theory it was believed necessary to prove or verify theories to be true. This is now considered to be impossible. The best we can do is construct theories that can potentially be falsified—that is, they are subject to empirical testing.[9] If the evidence, so far, does not refute a theory, then "so far so good." This means nothing is ever claimed to be true, it is only that at present there is no better theory. In the future it is likely to be improved upon or replaced. In this way modern economic theory evolves. In addition to the tentative nature of any one theory, competing theories exist side by side, neither theory having been clearly refuted by the evidence, while each gives different insights into a problem. When a theory has not been refuted for a substantial period of time, it is sometimes referred to as a law. This does not, however, change the provisional nature of the theory.

The inflation-control theories of the individuals just referred to share two common features: (1) Each is based on observation of facts or events, and (2) each makes a prediction or description about the consequences of certain events. We can now add to our definition of an economic theory by saying the following: An economic theory provides an explanation of observed phenomena that may be judged by its ability to predict the consequences of certain events. Although

[8] For a critical review, see Homa Katouzian, *Ideology and Method in Economics* (New York: New York University Press, 1980).

[9] This is the legacy of Karl Popper. See, for example, *The Logic of Scientific Discovery* (New York: Harper & Row, 1934).

economics is not a science like chemistry or physics, it does make use of the scientific method, in its broadest sense, of relying upon observations in arriving at and testing theories.

Induction versus Deduction

The aspects of the scientific method that we are most concerned with here are induction and deduction. **Induction** *is the process of formulating a theory from a set of observations. It is reasoning from specific observations to draw a generalization.* For example, observing many incidents of objects falling to the ground we are led to a generalization—the theory of gravity.

Deduction *is the process of predicting future events by means of a priori (before experience) judgment. It is reasoning from the logic of the general to predict the specific circumstance.* The theory of gravity, a generalization, leads you to predict that if you throw a ball in the air it will come back down. The predictions made by deduction are tested by observing facts or events to see if what was predicted actually takes place. If not, the theory will have to be changed to conform with reality, and the whole process begins again. For example, suppose that there is an increase in government spending, the crucial event in the first individual's theory, but we do not observe the predicted increase in inflation. Following the scientific method, we must either modify or discard the theory because of its failure to predict correctly. The process of induction and deduction is never-ending, since all theories must be retested continually in light of new facts and events. Modern economic methodology incorporates a mixture of the deductive and inductive, but there is greater emphasis within the discipline to formulate, at least potentially, refutable hypotheses and describe under what conditions they would be refuted.

Constructing a Theory

Our income tax–payer and our small business owner did not really use the scientific method in drawing up their theories. But now let's see how an economist would go about formulating a theory. The approach outlined here will be illustrated by many of the economic models in the rest of the text. It will save considerable effort in learning the specific models if you spend some time mastering this general approach.

Elements of Economic Theory

Every formal statement of a theory has four basic elements:

1. It has a statement of specific variables.
2. It has a set of assumptions about other variables that may be relevant.
3. It has a hypothesis about the way the specific variables are related.
4. It has one or more predictions or descriptions.

Variables.   All theory is concerned with variables. We call these *variables* because they can take on different values, that is, they are subject to change. For example, in a theory of gravity, mass and distance are two important variables. The principal variables of a model are called **endogenous** variables. *Endo* is from

Greek and means "inside," so think of it as "inside" the model variables. Intervening variables that affect the model from outside are termed **exogenous** variables. *Exo* means "out." Assumptions are often a way of *fixing* some variable at a certain value and thereby making that variable exogenous to the problem at hand. To illustrate with an example: Suppose I hypothesize that your consumer expenditures are dependent upon your income this year and I assume the interest rate is 20 percent. Your income and expenditure are the endogenous variables of this model. The interest rate is exogenous, yet important. If the interest rate falls to 10 percent, it will likely affect your purchases (allowing you to finance that car you wanted).

Another but different distinction is **stock** versus **flow** variables. For an analogy, think of a lake with a river flowing into and out of it. The lake has a stock of water—so many millions of litres. The river is a flow of water—so many thousands of litres *per minute*. Flow variables always have a per-time-unit dimension. Examples from economics are the variables capital and investment. Capital is a stock variable, while investment is a flow. The capital stock of a country is the accumulated amount of machinery, buildings, roads, and so on that exist at a given time period, while investment is the measure of current production of these things *per year*. If in our analogy investment is the river flowing into the lake and capital is the lake, then depreciation is analogous to the river flowing out of the lake. Depreciation is the flow variable measuring the amount of capital used up or worn out over one year. If the investment (flow) exceeds depreciation (flow) in a given year, then the capital (stock) will be greater at the end of the year.

Assumptions.   Assumptions establish the starting point and are made for many purposes. One type of assumption that is made is to propose what motivates the particular agent's behaviour—for example, it is assumed a firm wishes to maximize profit. Other types of assumptions might restrict the range of variables or limit the conditions under which the theory is to apply. Mathematical assumptions are often made in order to make the theory more convenient to apply—for example, relationships between two variables are often assumed to be linear because straight-line functions are relatively easy to use. Where necessary, methods are adopted that allow the assumptions to change or be dropped. Generally, the more assumptions that are made the simpler (the more abstract) the theory is to work with. However, there is usually a trade-off between the simplicity gained and the ability to analyze more complex situations.

The theory that two objects will fall at equal velocity regardless of their mass when dropped from the same height is based on the assumption that other influencing variables, such as friction, will remain the same. The assumption of holding all other variables constant is referred to as **ceteris paribus** and is a feature of all economic theories. Logically enough, the term is Latin for "all other things remaining the same." This assumption is important when we come to the point of testing our theory. Real-world events may not turn out as the theory says they should. We must be sure to find out whether this is because the theory is wrong or because something other than a principal (endogenous) variable has changed, thus violating the *ceteris paribus* assumption. Thus the observation of a feather and a steel ball falling at *different* speeds does not refute the theory of gravity. The earth's atmosphere, where the air resistance would have a different effect on each item, is an intervening (exogenous) variable. The prediction of the theory—equal velocity—would not hold without the *ceteris paribus* assumption. In economics this assumption is both crucial and controversial. Unlike the example where a controlled laboratory experiment may actually hold the intervening variable— friction—constant, the economics "laboratory" can never be suspended. Economic theory is, therefore much harder to present in a manner that could be easily falsified (at least potentially), as one can never be sure the deviation from prediction wasn't caused by a change in an exogenous variable that one was assuming constant for the moment. Economic theory proposes a tendency of one variable to change in a certain way with changes in another—*if* all other things remain constant. It is because of this feature that economic theory since Alfred Marshall has been referred to as "tendency laws."[10]

Hypothesis.   A **hypothesis** is a statement of the way we think the variables in question relate to one another; it is a statement of behaviour and usually implies causation; and it is the heart of any theory. If the causation is such that one variable increases when the other decreases (or vice versa), this is known as an **inverse relationship**, since the variables are changing in opposite ways. If the variables change in the same way (an increase in one leads to an increase in the other or a decrease in one leads to a decrease in the other), we say that they have a **direct relationship**.

Prediction.   Here we move directly into the realm of the real world. The purpose of theory is to be able to understand the world (although in an abstract way) sufficiently well and/or to predict what will occur before it happens. Theories that explain are usually harder to develop than those that only predict. If theory can predict accurately, then humans can either prepare for that which is not preventable or modify the conditions (policy) to prevent the thing from happening that would have occurred otherwise. This is true for sciences such as physics and social sciences such as economics. The Great Depression brought about a reasonably general social consensus that paved the way for greater government intervention in the economy in order to prevent the massive economic hardship that had occurred. For example, Keynes in *The General Theory* professed a theory that explained the depression and could therefore be used to predict its causes. Intervention removed the causes preventing the reoccurrence of massive unemployment from the period after the Second World War through to the early 1970s. The occurrence of stagflation (high levels of both inflation and unemployment) from the mid-1970s on could *not* be explained using this theory. This underlines the variability of social theory. The underlying social conditions upon which this theory was based may have changed. Problems usually motivate the search for theoretical explanations and social problems change with human development and history.

Checkpoint 1-3
Surveys of young people have found that they believe it will be less likely for them, compared to their parents, to own a single-family home. Describe this belief (or prediction) in the form of a model itemizing the important variables, the assumptions, and the hypothesis(es). Does this perspective seem as believable when structured in this way? How would you "test" the model?

How Exact Is Economic Theory?

Since economic theory tries to explain and predict human behaviour, you probably wonder how it is possible to be very exact. Economic theory cannot be as

---

[10] Marshall's *Principles of Economics* was first published in 1890, ran through eight editions during his lifetime, and was used as a textbook well after. Marshall's analysis was pervaded by the *ceteris paribus* assumption and opened up questions about this approach that have defied conclusive resolutions. Modern econometric analysis is in large part the search for techniques that solve this problem.

exact as Newton's three laws of motion. But economic behaviour is on average more predictable than the behaviour of many subatomic particles currently studied in high-energy physics. If economic behaviour weren't predictable, stores wouldn't hold sales, banks wouldn't need vaults and security guards, and traffic tickets wouldn't carry fines. When we look at the behaviour of a large group of individuals, the on-average similarity of the behaviour of the majority of them dominates the unusual behaviour of the few. Economics theory is unlikely to be quantitatively exact but can give qualitative predictions. Although implicit in much previous theory, Samuelson first drew explicit attention to the notion of qualitative analysis.[11] He argues that it is rarely possible to specify the quantitative magnitude of a change occurring in an endogenous variable when an exogenous variable changes, but we can often determine the sign (plus or minus) of a change. Remember that if the sign is positive, there is a direct relationship between the variables; and if negative, there is an inverse relationship. Thus, qualitative analysis, although not exact, can tell us a great deal about the underlying relationships and often all we need to know.

The economics profession is becoming more quantitative with the increasing application of econometrics. **Econometrics** *is concerned with the systematic study of economic phenomena using observed data.*[12] The use of abundant quantitative data in econometrics does not mean economics is approaching any greater degree of precision. The quality of data, the inability to hold certain variables constant, and the complexity of the interrelationships of data prohibit great exactitude in economics. But the increasing reliance on actual observations is a positive development towards improving the application of economic theory in addressing or correcting economic problems.

Common Pitfalls to Economic Reasoning

In order to analyze an economic issue or problem correctly, we must avoid certain common pitfalls of economic reasoning. One of the most common fallacies arises from the difficulty of distinguishing between cause and effect. Another is commonly known as the *fallacy of composition.*

Cause and Effect

A key interest of economics is to determine how events in the real world can be explained and even predicted. In other words, we are looking for causes. We want to be able to say with reasonable certainty that if A happens, B will be the result. Unfortunately, it is not always easy to tell if some event was the cause of another event, or if it just preceded it in time. The situation is especially tricky when event B regularly follows event A. In economics there are many times when it is very difficult to tell whether A caused B or B caused A. Perhaps there is no causal relationship between B and A at all, but both occur together because event C always causes both A and B to happen. A fire causes smoke and light, but smoke doesn't cause light and light doesn't cause smoke. People in high-income

---

[11]Paul A. Samuelson, *Foundations of Economic Analysis* (Cambridge, MA: Harvard University Press, 1948).

[12]This definition is taken from an advanced level textbook: Aris Spanos, *Statistical Foundations of Econometric Modelling* (Cambridge, U.K.: Cambridge University Press, 1986) p. 3.

POLICY PERSPECTIVE

Why Economists Disagree— The Role of Ideology

Put two economists in the same room and what do you get? An argument, or so it would seem to many people. Why do economists seem to disagree so much? How can the Nobel Prize be awarded in economics and how can economics be regarded as a science if different economists can come up with such dissimilar answers when confronted with the same policy issue? Unlike chemistry and physics, economics is a *social* science; and the nature of a social science is to explore human behaviour, which is inherently and inextricably linked to important ethical issues, the societies humans live in, and the questions of who shall get what and how. Such questions invariably raise issues of value judgment about what is a "good" and "just" society, that is, issues of political ideology. The way different economists view an issue and the nature of their policy recommendations are usually coloured by their particular ideological orientation.

At the risk of oversimplification, there are five broadly recognizable political ideologies that provide different viewpoints on almost any economic issue. These different viewpoints may be termed, on a spectrum from the right to left, the new right, conservative, liberal, social democrat, and radical positions. The spectrum can be roughly characterized by an emphasis on the individual on the part of the right and an emphasis on the social character of the human on the part of the left. Therefore, for example, the right emphasizes the necessity of incentives for maximum production in the form of differences in income while the left emphasizes greater equality of income distribution as

people are inherently creative and productive and an individual's contribution to the total social product cannot be separated out.

THE NEW RIGHT VIEW

The ideology of the new right is rooted in two basic propositions. First, individual rights and the freedom of consenting parties to enter into private contracts (such as between buyer and seller) must be preserved to the greatest extent possible. Second, a competitive market system is central to the proper organization of society. Proponents oppose any "unnatural" interference in the marketplace and view the growth of big government as the greatest threat to economic progress and individual freedom. The government's proper role includes the following: to maintain law and order; to define and preserve property rights; to see that contracts are enforced; to provide a legal system to settle disputes; to provide services not naturally provided by the market, such as national defense. In short, they believe that government, the ultimate monopoly, should not do for people what they are capable of doing for themselves. Where government goes beyond these bounds, not only is individual freedom threatened, but otherwise well-intended government policies can cause or worsen economic problems. For example, proponents would claim that minimum-wage laws intended to improve the lot of low-paid workers actually hurt them in general and that a government-enforced minimum wage higher than that otherwise determined by the market provides greater income for some workers but reduces the quan-

tity demanded of those workers who are poorest, typically the unskilled and disadvantaged.

THE CONSERVATIVE VIEW

Modern conservative ideology is similar to that of the new right, only somewhat less doctrinaire. Conservatives generally favour free enterprise and believe in competition within the economy through free trade. They support reducing the size of the public sector through deregulation and privatization— holding the view that the private sector will provide such services more effectively. When in government, they have focused their attention on minimizing inflation, with an expectation that minimum government intervention will reduce unemployment. Social welfare and education are not expenditure priorities, but neither are they targeted for reduction. Conservatives would add to the role of government the need to supplement private charity and the family, to aid children and others handicapped for reasons beyond their control, and to deal with some problems not naturally solved by markets alone, such as environmental pollution.

THE LIBERAL VIEW

Compared to conservatives and social democrats, liberals are somewhat more difficult to pin down to a representative position. While liberals are defenders of the principle of private property and private enterprise, they do not view these as endowed with categorical rights to the extent conservatives do. Compared to conservatives, liberals are more prone to believe

continued on next page

that individual property rights and the right to act freely in the marketplace must be constrained by concern for the general social welfare. Hence, government intervention in the economy, and even occasional direct regulation of certain industries and markets, is more acceptable to liberals than to conservatives. Liberals would argue that the benefits to the whole society of such intervention outweigh the infringements on individual liberties and property rights that government action might entail. Liberal economists and conservative economists both rely on the same tools of supply and demand analysis to explain markets and the behaviour of the economy. They don't always differ so much on how to describe what is happening as they differ over how and whether government should intervene to affect the outcome.

THE SOCIAL DEMOCRAT VIEW

Supporters of the social democrat position traditionally favour government intervention in the econ-omy as a way of ensuring equal opportunity and more equitable incomes for all citizens. While accepting that the private sector has a role to play in the economy, they believe that the public sector should be actively involved in the provision of certain goods such as health care, public education, and public housing. Proponents generally support greater government regulation in such areas as health and safety and environmental protection. Other policy positions include full employment with more equal distribution of income and wealth, financed with equitable taxation through a progressive personal and corporate income tax without loopholes. Social democrats propose increased democratic process in social institutions. Many Canadians associate social democrats with big government, labour unions, and welfare. In actuality the social democrat spectrum on public policy positions ranges from those who favour a moderate level of government intervention to those who advocate broad government planning of the economy.

THE RADICAL VIEW

To understand the radical position, it is necessary to recognize the central role played by Marxist analysis, although there are many radicals who would reject a close association with Marxism. While it is impossible to do justice to the Marxist critique of capitalism in this short space, in brief, Marx essentially viewed capitalism as a system by which the capitalist class, those who own the means of production, are able to dominate and exploit the working class. According to Marx, the dominant capitalist class shaped private values, religion, the family, the educational system, and political structures all for the purpose of production for private profit. Marxist analysis does not separate economics from politics and society's value system. The bourgeois democracies of the Western world are viewed as simply the tools for the dominant capitalist interests. For a Marxist, the problem with the capitalist system is the system itself, and no resolution of the problem

continued on next page

brackets tend to have better health and more education than people in low-income brackets. Possibly they were born with a hardier constitution and more than the average amount of energy. These factors would enable such people to attend school more regularly and have a greater capacity for work. If so, it is possible that high income and education are no more causally related than smoke and light, but that being born with a hardy constitution causes both. On the other hand, it may be that higher education causes higher income, which makes it possible to afford a better diet and better medical care. *The rather common fallacy of concluding that A caused B simply because A occurred before B is known as the* **fallacy of false cause**.[13]

Fallacy of Composition

Common sense will tell you that if you find yourself in a burning building, you should get out as fast as you can. However, if the burning building is a crowded movie theater and each individual in it tries to get through the door

---

[13] Also referred to as the *post hoc, ergo propter hoc* fallacy.

is possible without changing the system. Coupled with this Marxist heritage, modern radicals are motivated by what they see as the failings of present-day liberalism. Liberal pursuit of policies for general social improvement are viewed as attempts to protect only some interest groups. And those who *really* benefit under liberal programs are seen as being those who have always gained. Corporate power continues to grow and the same elitist groups rule who have always ruled. Furthermore, conservative and liberal goals to improve the national well-being are also perceived as contributing to the exploitation of the disadvantaged and less-developed nations, and continuing the militarization of the economy.

POLITICAL PARTIES

It is difficult to characterize political parties in Canada along this spectrum. The three major parties crowd the center of the spectrum. The liberal view is usually espoused by Canadians who support the Liberal Party, but crosses over into those on the right in the New Democrats and to those on the left in the Progressive Conservatives. However, Progressive Conservatives would span the spectrum from liberal to the new right, Liberals span across the conservative, liberal, and social democrat views, while the New Democrats range from the liberal into the radical. Fringe parties of the right and left are more ideologically pure but therefore appeal to fewer people. Those on the extreme left (radical) and extreme right (new right) are the least satisfied with the status quo. The new right viewpoint is reactionary, wanting to return to a time past when government involvement in the economy was at a minimum. The radical viewpoint wishes to restructure society towards an utopian ideal. The large level of involvement in the economy of Canadian governments and the policies implemented by them appear to be less affected by the particular parties in power than by international economic conditions and societal needs.

We all have personal views based on our experience and knowledge that lead us to be conservative, liberal, and so on, on particular issues. Economists are also caught up in this debate over values, both personally and professionally. When considering any economist's analysis of an economic issue, it is helpful to know his or her ideological orientation—to know "where he or she is coming from." But no matter what viewpoint he or she is motivated by, the methods of economic analysis should bring clarity to the issue.

For Discussion

- What do you think a social democrat would say about the new right and conservative view of minimum-wage laws?
- Describe what each of the five viewpoints would have to say about universal social programs in Canada.
- Among the ten major economic policy goals, how do you think the five viewpoints would differ in the relative importance they would attach to achieving those goals that we argued tend to conflict with one another?

---

at the same time, the results are likely to be tragic. What is good advice for you as an individual is not good advice for the group as a whole. *The false assumption that what is true for a particular part of the whole is also true for the whole itself is called the* **fallacy of composition**. (The whole is made up, or composed, of two or more individual parts.)

We can see how this fallacy works on an economic level if we consider the following example. If you are unemployed and have a mortgage on your house, you might be wise to sell the house. You can use the money obtained from the sale to pay off the mortgage and buy a cheaper house. In this way you can eliminate the burden of monthly mortgage payments. But if everyone on your block decides to do the same thing, the glut of houses on the market may drive prices down so low that you may not be able to get enough money to pay off the mortgage and buy a new house. What makes good economic sense for the individual does not necessarily make good economic sense for the whole economy. We will see other examples in this book where what is true at the microeconomic level is not necessarily true at the macroeconomic level.

In judging what is true for the whole of society, we must not go to the opposite extreme and assume that what is true for the whole is also true for the individual parts. Such an assumption is known as the **fallacy of division.**

Checkpoint 1-4

Think of some examples where confusions about cause and effect might arise. Can you think of a fallacy of composition that frequently occurs when a crowd watches a hockey game?

For example, while it is true that society as a whole may benefit from a highly competitive marketplace, some individual firms with weak management skills may go bankrupt.

Economic Policy

Economic theories have by and large evolved as responses to problems. In other words, necessity has been the mother of invention. But theory is only a tool, a way of looking at economic reality. It does not provide ready-made solutions to problems. John M. Keynes, a highly regarded policymaker as well as theorist, has reportedly said:

> The theory of economics does not furnish a body of settled conclusions immediately applicable to policy. It is a method rather than a doctrine, an apparatus of the mind, a technique of thinking, which helps its possessor to draw correct conclusions.

Economic policy is concerned with finding and implementing solutions to economic problems and intervening where it is deemed to be in the collective interest. While policymakers use economic theory to help them, they must go beyond it as well. They must consider the cultural, social, legal, and political aspects of an issue if they are to formulate a successful policy. Making economic policy involves making value judgments such as those we explored when we looked at the conflict between unemployment and inflation. Therefore, it also includes important philosophical aspects relating to ethics and social justice. These are normative judgments, and an economist has no special claim over anybody else to making these types of judgments. Policy is a political question, and in a democratic country it must be determined by the citizens through leadership, debate and the political process. The goal should be the collective good as determined collectively. Economics can inform this political process with regards to efficiency and the inevitable trade-offs encountered.

Economic Analysis and Economic Policy Making

While economic theory and analysis may not always be able to tell policymakers what they should do, it usually can tell them what they shouldn't do. An understanding of economic principles can keep us from both pursuing unwise policies and chasing conflicting goals. A few examples will illustrate how this is so.

An Unwise Policy.   The printing of money by a central bank in order to finance the expenditures of a government has long been considered by economists to be an unwise move. Despite their warnings, however, history is a graveyard of fallen governments that have yielded to this temptation. Somehow it always seems easier to turn on the printing press than to raise taxes. After World War I, the German government printed money at such a clip that the rate of inflation reached several thousand percent per week! At this point the *deutschemark* ceased to have any value at all as a medium of exchange. No one would accept it in payment for goods or services. Faith in the government's ability to manage was seriously shaken. The resulting political instability may have contributed in some degree to the rise of Adolf Hitler and the Nazi party. More recently, the same temptation to use the printing press is occurring in Russia and the value of the ruble has almost collapsed.

Conflicting Goals.   In the conflicting goals category, an election year is often marked by talk of achieving full employment and reducing inflation—both at the same time. Full employment in Canada today is usually defined as an unemployment rate of roughly six percent.[14] Almost everyone would agree that a one-percent rate of inflation is low. But almost any economist will tell you that these two goals conflict with each other. A six-percent unemployment rate goal is probably not compatible with a one-percent inflation rate goal. Research findings, while not final or always clear-cut, might indicate that a six-percent unemployment rate is possible only if we are willing to accept a five-percent inflation rate. On the other hand, in order to cut inflation to one percent, we might have to live with an unemployment rate of ten percent. This serves to remind us that an economy's behaviour can only be modified within limits. (You can't expect a large bus to take corners like a sports car, or a sports car to carry 50 passengers.) Economic analysis can help us to form realistic policy objectives that don't conflict with one another.

The conflict between goals can be illustrated further by looking at the case of Unemployment Insurance (UI). Compensation in the form of UI payments to those who cannot find work has a number of social benefits. Many cannot find work through no fault of their own, as unemployment is a social ill for which insurance is appropriate. If benefits were not provided, the unemployed would not have as large consumption expenditures and businesses would lay off more people as their goods did not sell, and so on and so on. On the other hand, UI may reduce the incentives to work and prolong or increase the very unemployment it is meant to provide assistance from. The Unemployment Insurance Commission (UIC), as a policymaker, has to choose between assisting those who cannot find jobs and maintaining incentives such that people will choose jobs available appropriate to their abilities.

Special Interests, and the Role of the Economist

Making economic policy forces us to choose among alternatives that have different consequences for different groups. Each of us is a member of one or more special interest groups. As students and educators, we might find it in our interest to pay special attention to any proposed legislation that affects education and institutions of learning. Similarly, labour unions are concerned about legislation on right-to-work laws and the powers and rights of unions to help one another enforce strikes and deal with strikebreakers. Business interests are also concerned with labour legislation, but their stands on such matters are usually opposed to those of labour. Farmers and consumers are both concerned with agricultural policy, but once again their interests are often in conflict. Resolution of these conflicts typically involves choices such as those we have discussed in

---

[14]This is measured statistically using a survey approach where individuals are asked: "Are you available for work and actively looking for work?" Critics have suggested that this technique means the "unemployed" claim they would work at an *unspecified* job at an *unspecified* wage—the unemployment rate is meaningless.

connection with the inflation-unemployment trade-off. That is, we must make choices that are matters of value judgment. As we have noted, economists have no special calling to make subjective judgments as to what particular group should gain at another's expense. Economists probably do their greatest service to policymaking when they take the goals of all parties concerned as given and confine themselves to exploring and explaining which goals are compatible and which conflict, and what economic consequences will result from different policy actions.

Major Economic Policy Goals in Canada

A list of economic policy goals that most economists, policymakers, and citizens feel are important in Canada would probably look like this:[15]

1. *Price stability:* In recent years this has meant controlling inflation, which is necessary for a stable money value. (John Crow, the current governor of the Bank of Canada, considers this the most important problem.)
2. *Full employment:* Most economists would take this to mean keeping the unemployment rate down but not at zero. Although the target percent is controversial, six percent might be described as full employment. Unemployment indicates lost production as well as income and self-esteem lost to the individuals unemployed.
3. *Economic growth:* This means an increasing GDP, the creation of new jobs for a growing population, and continued growth in the standard of living for the average citizen (or GDP per capita).
4. *Economic security:* This means provision of an adequate standard of living for those who are unable to work either because of age, illness, and other handicaps beyond their control or because there are simply not enough jobs for all who want them.
5. *Equitable income distribution:* As well as individual disparity of incomes, regional disparity in Canada is a major national concern. To solve income disparities, the Canadian approach has been to make regional and personal transfer payments, use a progressive income tax system, and supply social services by a delivery system based on need, rather than income. An example of the latter is the Medicare system. Maintaining universality of social programs has recently become an important issue.
6. *An equitable tax burden:* Taxes have become more prominent with the recent introduction of tax reform. There is a concern that our tax system favours those, typically in higher income brackets, who are in a position to take advantage of various loopholes in our tax laws to avoid or greatly reduce their "fair share" of the tax burden. The goods and services tax (GST), implemented in 1991, is a regressive tax. Initially, it was also inflationary.
7. *Balance of payments:* This is a goal orientated to Canadian interaction with other economies—the foreign sector. The objective is to "pay" for imported goods through a balance of exports of Canadian-made goods in exchange. The balance of payments depends on the exchange rate—the purchasing power of the Canadian dollar outside Canada.

---

[15] Most of these goals were explicitly outlined in the *Economic Council of Canada, First Annual Review* (1964) and updated in the *Twenty-Second Annual Review* (1984).

Recent chronic trade imbalances reflect our monetary policies, which have made Canadian goods less competitive with foreign goods. Fluctuations in exchange rates can lead in turn to domestic inflation, unemployment, or reduced growth rate.

8. *Efficiency:* Competition in business is considered the means to obtaining the efficient production of wealth. This goal is both of concern to the internal Canadian economy and our trading arrangements. For the improvement of competition inside Canada the *Competition Act* (1986) was enacted as (the long-in-coming revision of) the *Combines Investigation Act*. After considerable controversy and over an election fought mainly on this issue, the *Free Trade Act* (1988) was enacted, purportedly to improve efficiency and increase domestic competition by allowing unfettered American entry.

9. *Environmental quality:* Canadians across the country are increasingly calling for less pollution and waste from present production and consumption processes and a cleanup of past environmental damage.

10. *Economic freedom:* This is the idea that businesses, consumers, and workers should be given much freedom in their economic activities.

Many of these goals are compatible. For example, goals 2, 3, and 4 all seem compatible in the sense that if we achieve goals 2 and 3, we will very likely enhance economic security, goal 4. And goals 4, 5, and 6 appear compatible and may be furthered by similar policies. We have already pointed out how economic experience has suggested that goals 1, 2, and 7 may not be compatible, and that there appears to be a trade-off between the achievement of one at the expense of the other. Goal 10 can raise serious difficulties when collective interests require coercion of individuals, so goals 4, 5, 6, 7, 8, and 9 may conflict on this issue. Many of the individual goals cited may be incompatible with others, requiring trade-offs. This only emphasizes the main contention of economics—there are opportunity costs involved whenever we make a choice.

Economic Analysis and the Economist

The examples we have considered illustrate why economic analysis is useful in formulating economic policy. In summary, economic analysis (1) helps to predict what the consequences of any policy action are likely to be; (2) indicates from among several ways to achieve a given goal which ones are most efficient in that their side effects are least detrimental, or possibly even helpful, to the achievement of other goals; (3) suggests which goals are compatible with one another and which are not; and (4) indicates what the likely trade-offs are between goals that are not mutually compatible.

If economic analysis does nothing else but keep policymakers from pursuing foolhardy policies, this alone is justification for its use as a policy tool. When economists go beyond the exercise of economic analysis summarized by points 1 to 4, they join the ranks of the various parties to any policy dispute. Their opinions and programs are then properly treated as those of a special interest group. Since economists, just like everyone else, usually do have opinions on matters of value judgment, they often use their economic expertise in support of a cause. In the end, therefore, the burden of separating objective economic analysis from value judgment must rest with you, the citizen. This fact alone should justify the time you devote to the study of economics.

Summary

1. Economics is a social science concerned with the study of how society chooses to use its scarce resources to satisfy its unlimited wants. Economics studies the many issues and problems associated with this process from the social point of view. The economy is the focus of the study of economics. An economy is composed of economic agents attempting to do the best they can with the resources available to them.

2. Economic analysis has been divided into two broad areas. Macroeconomics is concerned with the functioning of the whole economy or large sectors within it. Microeconomics focuses on individual units such as households and firms.

3. Goods are produced by using economic resources. Economic resources are of two basic kinds—human resources (labour) and nonhuman resources (capital and land). Economic resources are also referred to as the factors of production.

4. Goods include commodities, the tangible goods and services the intangible goods. A few goods are "free," that is not scarce. Some outputs of production are "bads"—the undesirable consequences of production or consumption.

5. Resources are combined in production to produce goods which are distributed in the form of income for consumption to provide utility to humans.

6. Discussions of economic issues make use of two kinds of statements. Positive statements are statements of fact. Normative statements, which may be based on positive statements, are statements of opinion.

7. In an effort to explain how things work, economic analysis makes use of the scientific method. This method uses induction to formulate a theory from observation of facts and events. The theory is then used to predict future events (deduction).

8. Every economic theory or model has four basic elements: (1) a statement of variables, (2) a set of assumptions, (3) a hypothesis, and (4) one or more predictions about future happenings. Economic theories may also be called economic laws, principles, or models. Economic theory is exact to the extent that economic behaviour is predictable.

9. Variables in a model are distinguished as either endogenous—determined inside the model, or exogenous—determined outside the model.

10. The *ceteris paribus* assumption is significant in economics. It means "all other things are equal" (that is, only the endogenous variables in the model are changing—the exogenous variables are constant).

11. In economics, it is important to determine whether one event is the cause of another event or simply preceded it in time. To conclude that one thing caused another solely on the basis that one preceded the other is to commit the fallacy of false cause.

12. The assumption that what is true of the parts is true of the whole is known as the fallacy of composition. The assumption that what is true of the whole is true of the parts is known as the fallacy of division.

13. Qualitative analysis can predict the direction of change that might occur from some event. Quantitative analysis is more specific in its predictions, as it includes the magnitude of a change as well as direction. Economics constitutes powerful qualitative analysis but is often less precise in its quantitative analysis.

14. Economic policymakers use economic theory and analysis to help them formulate ways in which to solve the problems posed by economic reality. In most cases, the solution to these problems involves resolving a conflict between special interest groups. Such a resolution usually depends upon value judgments, and economists are no more qualified than anyone else to make such judgments. Economic analysis is most useful in determining the possible consequences of various policies.

Key Terms and Concepts

agents	exogenous	land
assumptions	fallacy of composition	macroeconomics
capital	fallacy of division	manager
ceteris paribus	fallacy of false cause	microeconomics
commodities	financial capital	normative statement
consumption	firm	positive statement
deduction	flow	prediction
direct relationship	foreign sector	price
distribution	free good	production
econometrics	government	redistribution
economic bad	Gross Domestic Product	rent
economic good	household	scarce
economic policy	hypothesis	scientific method
economic resources	induction	services
economics	inflation	stock
economic theory	interest	unemployment
economy	inverse relationship	utility
endogenous	investment	variables
entrepreneur	labour	wages

Questions and Problems

1. Explain in your own words what economics is about.
2. Why might economics be called a social science instead of a social study?
3. Why is it that economists, who supposedly use scientific methods when analyzing economic issues, are so often in disagreement?
4. Pick out a story from the financial and business section of today's newspaper and find instances in which a concept or subject is mentioned or discussed that is related to one or more of the economic terms introduced in this chapter.
5. Label each story in question 3 either microeconomics or macroeconomics and justify why.
6. Explain to a friend that a good that is free is not necessarily a free good.
7. Draw a diagram of an economy showing the relationship between resources, production, and the distribution of goods. Where does capital fit in? How do you illustrate an intermediate good? Where do the "bads" go?
8. Open today's newspaper to the financial and business section. Pick a story at random and calculate the ratio of positive statements to the total number of statements in the story. Now go to the financial and business editorial section and do the same.
9. Search a current newspaper or magazine for an article with a clear hypothesis.
   a. State the variables and distinguish between the endogenous and exogenous variables.

b. Can you identify the assumptions being made?

c. Is there an implied or stated prediction?

d. Are the predictions qualitative or quantitative?

e. Can you find any logical fallacies in the article?

10. Think about the following experiment. Suppose you were to run an ad in your local paper this week stating that you own a vacant 1-hectare lot and that somewhere on the lot is buried a metal box containing $100. You state that any and all are welcome to come dig for it and that you will give the $100 to whoever finds it during the coming week. How many people do you think will show up to dig? Suppose, instead, you had said the box contained $300? How many diggers do you think would show up during the same week? Estimate how many would show up during the same week if the reward were $200, $400, or $500. Now construct a graph that measures dollars of reward on the vertical axis and number of diggers on the horizontal axis. Find the points representing each combination of dollars and diggers and draw a line connecting them.

a. Is the relationship you observe between the size of the dollar reward and the number of diggers an inverse relationship or a direct relationship?

b. What led you to hypothesize the relationship you did between the size of the dollar reward and the number of diggers?

c. If you actually ran the ads over the course of a year and tabulated the number of diggers who showed up for each reward, plotted the results, and found a relationship opposite to the one you had predicted, what would you conclude about your theory? Might the season of the year during which you ran each ad have had something to do with the difference between your theory and what actually happened? Suppose that when you ran the $500 reward ad, it rained for the whole week the offer was good. Suppose that for the $400 reward ad it was sunny for the first two days and rained the next five. Suppose that for the $300 reward ad, it was sunny for the first three days and rained the next four. Suppose that for the $200 reward ad, it was sunny for the first five days and rained the next two. Finally, for the $100 reward ad, suppose that it was sunny the whole week. How do you think the curve obtained by plotting the combinations of dollar reward and number of diggers might look now? Looking back at the first curve you drew, how important do you think your "other things remaining the same" assumption was?

d. Suppose your original curve was based on the assumption that it was always sunny. If instead it was always raining, where would the curve be—to the left or to the right of the original curve?

e. Suppose your original curve was based on the assumption that there was substantial unemployment. If instead there was no unemployment, where would the curve be—to the left or to the right of the original curve?

f. What would you predict would happen if you raised the amount of the reward money to $1,000?

g. Can you, as my economic policy advisor, recommend how I might clear off and dig up a 1-hectare lot that I own in town?

h. Do you think people respond to economic incentives?

i. Do you think human behaviour is predictable?

Chapter 2

Scarcity, Choice, and the Economic Problem

In this chapter we will focus on the basic economic problem that has always confronted individuals and societies and the fundamental questions it poses. Then we will look into the ways economies may be organized to answer these questions. The answers are related to the issues of how well off people are, how much they work, and how choices about these matters are to be made. The basic economic problem has been succinctly characterized this way: "The poor have little, —beggars none; the rich too much,—enough not one."[1]

As was noted in Chapter 1, the economic resources of land, labour, and capital exist only in limited amounts. Therefore there is a limit to the quantity of economic goods that can be produced. Despite this limit on production, people's desire for goods is considered unlimited. Some writers have argued it may be possible to attain a level of abundance that would satisfy everybody's appetites for all things, but such a state has rarely, if ever, existed.[2] One only has to consider the standard of living in a rich nation such as Canada to realize that there is hardly a person who could not draw up a list of wanted goods far exceeding his or her means to obtain them. What would you do if suddenly you had an extra hundred dollars? There are probably a number of things that you want, some of which you could now afford. If you felt completely without want, you might give the money to charity. But on the one hand, people derive utility from giving to charity as they feel someone else's needs are greater than their own; and on the other hand, charity exists because some other group or person has unsatisfied needs or wants.

---

[1] Ben Franklin, *Poor Richard's Almanack* (1732–1757).

[2] See Mashal Sahlins, *Stone Age Economics* (New York: Aldine, 1972) for a description of a society that met this blissful state of affairs, not through great abundance but through restricting desires. "The hunter, one is tempted to say, is 'uneconomic man.' . . . His wants are scarce and his means (in relation) plentiful." (p. 13)

The Economic Problem

In human endeavours that have economic aspects there is a basic problem common to all. This basic problem can be best understood within the interrelated concepts of scarcity, opportunity cost, and choice.

Scarcity.   The interrelationship of limited resources and unlimited wants underlies the basic economic problem. This relationship defines **scarcity**. *Something is scarce if there is not enough of it available for all desired uses.*[3] Scarcity is a relative concept—that is, something is scarce only in relation to the possible uses to which it could be put. The fact that something is limited in availability is not sufficient for it to be scarce. Because of relative scarcity, we are forced to make choices that entail opportunity costs.

Choice.   When we, individually or socially, cannot have or do all we would like to do (unlimited wants) with our means (limited resources), then choices must be made. The question of how to rank various needs and wants, given the necessity of choice, has occupied much energy in the social sciences. In economics the general approach to this problem of ranking is simple: Individuals indicate their desires through their demands for goods—that is, their willingness to pay for these goods. One reason this approach is simple is that distinctions such as need/want are not necessary; another is that the information needs for social-political decision makers are minimized.

LEARNING OBJECTIVES

After reading this chapter, you will be able to:

1. Define and explain *scarcity*.
2. Explain why the combination of limited resources and unlimited wants makes choice necessary.
3. Define, explain, and give examples of opportunity cost.
4. Outline and explain the production possibility frontier (PPF) model.
5. Illustrate, using the PPF model, the concepts of scarcity, opportunity cost, and choice.
6. Define, explain and distinguish between unemployment and underemployment of resources.
7. Explain and distinguish between the terms *productive* and *economic efficiency*.
8. Explain economic growth and illustrate it with the PPF model.
9. Demonstrate how the selection of an output combination on today's production possibilities frontier affects the location of tomorrow's frontier.
10. Formulate the three basic questions posed by scarcity that every society must answer.
11. Define or explain the concept of a market.
12. Distinguish, by characteristics, between a pure market economy, and a command economy.

---

[3] Remember from Chapter 1, if something is in such abundance that there is enough for all possible uses, then it is termed a *free good*. Also note that a scarce resource such as urban air is not free, although it may have a price of zero.

Opportunity Cost.   If, because of scarcity, choices between desirable ends must be made, then in every choice made something else is given up. In our ranking of priorities, the next best thing that could have been chosen, but was not, is a measure of the opportunity cost of the thing actually chosen. The opportunity cost of a given choice is the value of the next best alternative that could have been chosen instead. Opportunity cost is the value of the forgone alternative. A simple example should make clearer the concepts of scarcity, choice, and opportunity cost.

A Simple Example

Robinson Crusoe[4] is a fictional character shipwrecked on a deserted island. His situation is useful for discussing the nature of the choices of an individual abstracted from social relations.[5]

As Crusoe lives alone (before Friday appears on page 292), he has to be self-sufficient. He produces only two goods: corn (for food) and wood (for building and furniture). His limited resources are his labour (his ability to grow corn and cut wood) and the natural resources available on his small island. The nature of Crusoe's economic problem can be illustrated by use of a **production possibilities frontier (PPF)**. *A production possibilities frontier is a curve representing the maximum possible output combinations of goods that can be produced with a fixed quantity of resources.* Crusoe's production possibilities frontier is the downward-sloping straight line in Figure 2-1. Later we will see that the frontier may not be a straight line.

Scarcity is illustrated: The PPF shows the maximum possible combinations of quantities of corn and wood that Crusoe can choose to produce in a year if he fully utilizes his fixed (limited) resources in the most efficient way he knows, given the amount of time he allocates to production. By maximum we mean that Crusoe cannot produce any combination of corn and wood represented by points lying to the right of or above his PPF, shown by the line from *a* to *e* in Figure 2-1. For example, he cannot choose to produce a combination of 27 bushels of corn and 15 cords of wood, point *f*. He simply doesn't have enough resources. On the other hand, Crusoe can produce any combination lying to the left or below the frontier—for example, a combination consisting of 15 bushels of corn and 5 cords of wood, point *g*. But why would he want to? That would be an inefficient use of his fixed resources if he has a use for more of both goods (unlimited wants). Efficient resource utilization will always enable Crusoe to produce a greater amount of both goods than he gets at a point such as *g*.

Opportunity cost is illustrated: If Crusoe is utilizing his resources efficiently, he will always choose to produce a combination of goods represented by a point on his PPF. Five of these possible combinations are indicated by points *a*, *b*, *c*, *d*,

---

[4]Daniel Defoe, *Robinson Crusoe* (Cambridge, MA: The Riverside Press, 1909).

[5]This approach is for exposition only and is not meant to imply individuals' decisions are made outside of their social context. Scarcity is a social concept. Robinson Crusoe's situation is artificial, and had he had no hope of being found his personal decisions about survival would have been irrelevant, as he likely wouldn't have bothered.

FIGURE 2-1 **Crusoe's Production Possibilities Frontier**

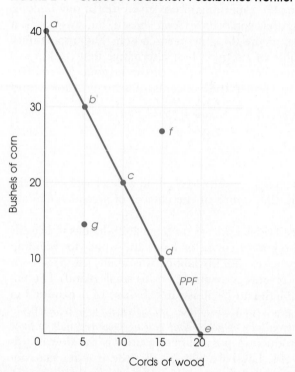

Crusoe's production possibilities frontier is represented by the downward-sloping straight line *ae*. Each point on the frontier represents some maximum-output combination of bushels of corn and cords of wood that Crusoe can choose to produce annually if he fully utilizes his fixed resources as efficiently as possible. Crusoe cannot produce any combinations represented by points to the right or above the frontier, such as *f*. He simply doesn't have enough resources—namely, stamina and ability to grow corn and chop wood. Crusoe can produce any combination represented by points to the left or below the frontier, such as *g*. But he wouldn't want to because that would entail an inefficient utilization of his resources.

and *e*. For example, if Crusoe chooses combination *b*, he will grow 30 bushels of corn and chop 5 cords of wood during the coming year. Alternatively, he may choose combination *c*, consisting of 20 bushels of corn and 10 cords of wood. All he has to do is devote less of his fixed resources to corn growing and use the resources released from that activity to chop more wood. If Crusoe chooses to produce combination *c* instead of *b*, he has to give up 10 bushels of corn (the difference between 30 and 20). However, he gains 5 cords of wood (the difference between 10 and 5). Conversely, if he chooses combination *b* instead of *c*, he gives up 5 cords of wood and gains 10 bushels of corn.

As long as Crusoe is using his resources efficiently (on the line in Figure 2-1), if he wants to produce more of one kind of good, he must of necessity produce less of the other. We say he must *pay an opportunity cost*. The opportunity cost equals the amount of one good that must be given up in order to have more of another. We see from Crusoe's PPF in Figure 2-1 that he has to *give up* 2 bushels of corn in order to get an additional cord of wood (a move downward along his PPF). Conversely, in order to get an additional bushel of corn (a move upward along his PPF) he has to *give up* half a cord of wood. Hence, the opportunity cost of a cord of wood is 2 bushels of corn and the opportunity cost of a bushel of corn is half a cord of wood. These can be calculated as the ratios of the changes (Δ) between any of the points on Figure 2-1. The opportunity cost of a cord of wood is:

$$\frac{\Delta C}{\Delta W} = \frac{10}{5} = 2 \text{ bushels of corn per cord of wood.}$$

The opportunity cost of a bushel of corn is:

$$\frac{\Delta W}{\Delta C} = \frac{5}{10} = .5 \text{ cord of wood per bushel of corn.}$$

Choice is illustrated: When Crusoe uses his fixed resources efficiently, he is always forced to choose between an output combination with more wood and less corn and a combination with less wood and more corn. If he could have more of both or more of one without having to sacrifice any of the other, there would be no "hard" choice because nothing would have to be given up. Unfortunately, Crusoe's limited resources always forced him to give up something—that is, to pay an opportunity cost—whenever he made a choice. A choice requires that one opportunity be given up to gain another. The concept of a PPF, the existence of opportunity costs, and the need for choice are just as relevant for an entire economy as they were for Crusoe. This can be presented formally as a model of the whole economy.

> ### Checkpoint* 2-1
>
> What is the opportunity cost to Crusoe of choosing combination *d* instead of combination *c* in Figure 2-1?
> Of choosing combination *b* instead of combination *d*? Of choosing combination *d* instead of combination *b*?
>
> *Answers to all Checkpoints can be found at the back of the text.*

The Production Possibilities Frontier Model

In Chapter 1 the construction of a theory or model was discussed. The PPF model will illustrate this process. The first step is to determine the relevant variables. For the PPF these are the resources (land, labour, and capital), technology, and economic goods. The second step is to specify the assumptions. The initial assumptions of the PPF model are that technology and resources are fixed (in the shortrun) and the economy is operating efficiently. In the third step, one or more hypotheses are stated about the way the variables are related. In the PPF model, the output levels of the goods are determined and limited by the fixed resources and technology. This relationship is called a *production function* (discussed at length in Chapter 8). In the fourth step, one or more predictions or descriptions of the economy are made. For the PPF model, we will consider these at length.

Scarcity, Production, and Efficiency

Given that resources are limited but that at the same time people's wants are unlimited, the problem that faces any economy is how to use scarce resources and organize production so as to satisfy society's wants to the greatest extent possible. This means that the available resources must be used efficiently such that the maximum output can be obtained from the resources at hand. There are two major problems that can prevent a society from achieving **productive efficiency.** The possible sources of inefficiency are **unemployment** and **underemployment** or **resource misallocation.**

Unemployment.   Maximum productive efficiency cannot be achieved if available resources are not fully used. This holds true for both human and nonhuman resources. As long as there are workers looking for work and unable to find it, or as long as plant capacity remains unused, maximum productive efficiency cannot be achieved. Notice that we stress that in order to have productive efficiency, all *available* resources must be employed. Some parts of the population may not opt to make themselves available for employment (for example, students and retired workers). It is also true that certain kinds of land are prohibited by law from use for certain types of production activity. However, whenever there are available resources standing idle, there are fewer *employed* inputs into the economy's productive process and, therefore, there is a lower output of goods to satisfy society's wants.

Underemployment or Resource Misallocation.   If certain available resources are used to do jobs for which other available resources are better suited, there is underemployment, or misallocation of resources. For example, if cabinetmakers were employed to make dresses and seamstresses were employed to make cabinets, the total amount of cabinets and dresses produced would be less than if each group were employed in the activity for which it was trained. Similarly, if British Columbia's apple orchards were planted with wheat while Saskatchewan's farms were planted with apple trees, the same total land area would provide the country with substantially less of both crops than is the case with the current arrangement. Resource underemployment also results whenever the best available technology is not used in a production process. A house painter painting with a toothbrush and a farmer harvesting wheat with a pocketknife are both underemployed. The point is that resources are used inappropriately, not that society is coping with a lack of suitable resources. Whenever there is resource underemployment or misallocation, a reallocation of resources to productive activities for which they are better suited will result in a larger output of some or all goods and no reduction in the output of any.

Unemployment, underemployment, or misallocation of resources leads to the economy realizing a point inside of the frontier, failing to achieve productive efficiency.

Production Possibilities Trade-Off

When an economy's available resources are fully and efficiently employed, the economy will be on the PPF. In this case, producing more of one kind of good will of necessity mean producing less of another. The amount of reduction in the production of one good that is necessary in order to produce more of another is the opportunity cost.

Let us illustrate this concept by focusing on the issue of the cost of cleaning up environmental pollution. Suppose that the output of an economy may be divided into two categories: pollution control devices (scrubbers[6]), and bundles of all goods other than scrubbers. Each bundle will contain one of every good produced in the economy *except* for a scrubber. Each bundle may be thought of

---

[6]Scrubbers are specifically cleaning devices integrated into smokestacks to remove pollutants from the waste gasses. In this example the term is used to refer to any mechanism to reduce pollution.

as a good but because each contains many individual goods, we will call each bundle a **composite good**. If we are to have a cleaner environment, we will need to use scrubbers in many production processes that cause pollution. How do we measure the cost to society of providing these devices?

In answering the question of how we are to measure the cost to society we will make certain assumptions, as follows:

1. The existing state of technology will remain unchanged for the period in which we are examining this issue.
2. The total available supply of resources (land, labour, and capital) will also remain unchanged. However, these resources may be shifted from producing scrubbers to producing bundles of all other goods, and vice versa.
3. All available resources will be fully and efficiently employed (there will be no unemployment or underemployment in the economy).

With the existing supply of resources and level of technology, society must make some hard choices. Given that resources are fully employed, whatever combination of bundles and scrubbers the economy might choose to produce, any other combination will necessarily contain more of one and less of the other. If the economy chooses to produce more scrubbers, it will have to give up a certain number of bundles; if it chooses to produce more bundles, it will have to give up a certain number of scrubbers and will therefore be exposed to more pollution. Just as in Crusoe's world, something must always be given up in order to gain something else. In short, there's no free lunch; you can't get something for nothing. You have to pay an opportunity cost.

Some of the possible combinations of bundles and scrubbers that the economy can choose to produce per year when all resources are fully employed are listed in Table 2-1. If this economy were to devote all of its resources to producing bundles of all other goods, it would be able to produce 80 million bundles per year and no scrubbers (combination *a*). But with this combination, the economy would be doing nothing at all about pollution. In order for society to do something about pollution, the economy would need to be moved away from combination *a* towards combination *e*. To do this, resources would have to be shifted out of the production of bundles and into the production of scrubbers.

TABLE 2-1   Possible Combinations of Scrubbers and Bundles of All Other Goods That May Be Produced in a Full-Employment Economy
(Hypothetical Data)

Product	Production Possibilities (Output per Year)				
	a	*b*	*c*	*d*	*e*
Scrubbers (in thousands)	0	50	80	100	110
Bundles (in millions)	80	60	40	20	0

How much of a shift in this direction society might choose to make would depend on the degree of concern about pollution.

Because economic resources are scarce, a full-employment economy, which is already producing at a maximum capacity, cannot produce more of *both* bundles and scrubbers. To produce more of one, it must give up producing some of the other. The cost of producing more of one is the opportunity cost, which is equal to the amount of the other that must be given up. For example, by choosing combination *b* in Table 2-1 *instead* of combination *a*, society must forgo the opportunity of producing 20 million bundles of all other goods (the difference between 80 million and 60 million). The opportunity cost of the 50 thousand scrubbers is therefore 20 million bundles. The opportunity cost of choosing *c instead* of *a,* or the opportunity cost of having 80 thousand scrubbers, is 40 million bundles, the difference between the number of bundles associated with combination *a* and the number associated with combination *c.* Whenever scarcity forces us to make a choice, we must pay an opportunity cost. This cost is measured in terms of forgone alternatives.

Note that *all* costs are opportunity costs. These costs are monetized in a modern economy. If you buy a note pad for a dollar, you forgo the opportunity of spending that dollar on something else. Since the pad cost you one dollar, you now have one dollar less to spend on all other goods (unless you have an infinite supply of money, which is impossible).

The Economy's Production Possibilities Frontier

To derive our hypothetical economy's production possibilities frontier, we must first locate all the points on a graph that represent the possible scrubbers/ bundles combinations listed in Table 2-1. If we then connect the points, the result looks like Figure 2-2. The curve slopes downward because when the available resources are fully employed, more scrubbers can be produced only by producing fewer bundles.

On and Off the Frontier

Each point on the PPF represents a maximum-output combination for the economy when its available resources are fully employed. The term *frontier* is used because it is not possible for the economy to produce any combination of scrubbers and bundles represented by a point above or to the right of the curve. For example, a combination of quantities of scrubbers and bundles represented by the point *f* in Figure 2-2 is not possible. If available resources are not being used efficiently—they are either unemployed or underemployed, the economy will only be able to produce output combinations represented by points inside the frontier, such as point *g.*

Increasing Opportunity Costs

Figure 2-2 illustrates how graphs plotted from economic data can make the relationship between two economic variables immediately obvious. In Figure 2-2 we are struck at once by the change in the trade-off between bundles and

FIGURE 2-2   The Production Possibilities Frontier

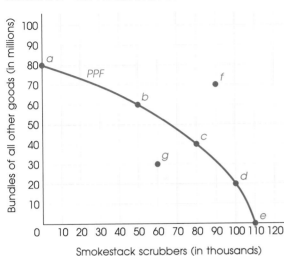

Smokestack scrubbers (in thousands)

Each point on the downward-sloping curve represents some maximum-output combination (scrubbers and bundles) for an economy whose available resources are fully employed. Because no combination to the right or above the curve is possible, it is called the *production frontier.* Point *g* represents a combination of scrubbers and bundles produced when the economy is operating inefficiently due to unemployment or under-employment of economic resources. Point *f* represents a combination that cannot be produced given available resources and technology.

scrubbers as we move from combination *a* to *b* to *c* and so on to *e*. When we move from *a* to *b*, a sacrifice (or cost) of 20 million bundles allows us to have 50 thousand scrubbers. However, a move from *b* to *c*, which costs another 20 million bundles, allows us to have only an additional 30 thousand scrubbers. The additional quantity of scrubbers obtained for each succeeding sacrifice of 20 million bundles continues to get smaller as we move from *c* to *d* to *e*.

The reason for the deteriorating trade-off is that economic resources are more adaptable to some production processes than to others. As more and more resources are shifted from the production of bundles into the production of scrubbers, we are forced to use factors of production whose productivity at making scrubbers is lower and lower relative to their productivity at making bundles. For example, when we move from *a* to *b*, a large number of engineers and scientists might be moved from bundle production to the highly technical production of scrubbers. As we continue moving from *b* to *e*, it becomes harder and harder to find labour resources of this nature. When moving from *d* to *e*, only the labour least suited for producing scrubbers will be left—poets, hod carriers, and so forth. The decrease in the number of additional scrubbers obtained for each additional sacrifice of 20 million bundles as we move from *a* to *e* is a common economic phenomenon referred to as **increasing costs**.

To illustrate this phenomenon more clearly, we divide the number of bundles that must be sacrificed by the additional number of scrubbers obtained by moving from one combination to the next. In the move from *a* to *b*, we see that it costs 20 million bundles to obtain 50 thousand scrubbers, or 400 bundles per scrubber. In the move from *b* to *c*, we see that it costs 20 million bundles to obtain 30 thousand scrubbers, or 666.6 bundles per scrubber. The move from *c* to *d* costs 1,000 bundles per scrubber. The move from *d* to *e* costs 2,000 bundles per scrubber.

We are accustomed to measuring costs in dollars—so many dollars per unit of some good. Since dollars merely stand for the amounts of other goods they

Checkpoint 2-2

In Table 2-1 what is the opportunity cost of choosing combination *c* instead of *d*; *b* instead of *c*; or *a* instead of *d*? Consider the movement from *e* to *a* in Figure 2-2 and represent the law of increasing cost measured in terms of scrubbers.

can buy, we have simply represented the cost of scrubbers in terms of bundles of other goods. *Increasing costs occurs when moving along a PPF. The opportunity cost per additional unit of a good obtained rises due to the difference in the productivity of resources when those resources are used in different production processes.* In the simple example of Robinson Crusoe, the PPF exhibited constant costs. At any point on Crusoe's PPF the opportunity cost was 2 bushels of corn for each cord of wood. That is, it was constant at 2 : 1.[7]

Economic Efficiency

Almost everyone supports environmental protection, but how much are we willing to pay for it in terms of other goods and services not produced? Another way to phrase the question is, What are the optimum or efficient amounts of environmental quality and bundles of other goods? The production possibilities frontier shows us the nature of the choices and the associated costs that must be considered when answering this question. The economist can say objectively that society would be making an inefficient use of resources if it decided to produce a combination of goods inside the frontier. Similarly, an economist can say objectively that a combination above or to the right of the frontier is not possible in the shortrun. For example, in an economy such as that summarized in Table 2-1, it must be pointed out to those who would like to produce 80 thousand scrubbers that they cannot simultaneously produce 80 million bundles.

The first step in achieving **economic efficiency** is to be on the frontier, achieving productive efficiency. Productive efficiency is necessary but not sufficient for economic efficiency. Society must also choose which single combination is the *best*. This is a political and ethical decision based upon the subjective values people hold, in this example, with respect to environmental quality and other goods. Economists as members of society can contribute to this decision, but their views in this decision hold no special weight. The nature of this social decision and of the institutions that determine the outcome are the prominent themes of the rest of the book.

Economic Growth

The PPF in Figure 2-2 is based on the assumptions of a given state of technology and a fixed quantity of resources. What happens if these assumptions are relaxed, if there is a change in technology or in the quantity of resources? The *potential* total output of the economy will change. Hence the PPF will shift position.

The economy's population and labour force tend to grow over time. So too does its stock of capital—the quantities of machines, buildings, highways, factories, and so forth. In addition, there are always advances in the state

---

[7]Note also that the slope (the rise over the run) of Crusoe's PPF is -2, or $-2/1$, indicating the 2 for 1 trade-off. The concave shape of the PPF for scrubbers and bundles of all other goods exhibits increasing costs. If we take a tangent to any point on this curve, the slope of the tangent will indicate the opportunity cost at that point. Note that the slope of the tangents taken will increase as we move from the top (NE) of the curve to the bottom (SW).

of technology. *The growth in the economy's resources and improvements in techno-logical know-how cause* **economic growth**—*an increase in the economy's ability to produce output.* This economic growth shifts the economy's PPF outward (up and to the right) as shown in Figure 2-3. As a result, the economy can produce more of both scrubbers and bundles when its available resources are fully employed.

Choice of Product Combination: Present versus Future

We are all aware that choices made today are an important determinant of the choices available to us tomorrow. Therefore, it should not surprise us that an economy's present choice of a point on its PPF influences the future location of that frontier. To demonstrate why this is so, suppose we divide the total output of an economy into two categories—consumption goods and capital goods. Consumption goods are such things as food, clothing, movies, tennis balls, records, and so forth. Capital goods are such things as machinery, tools, and factories; they enable us to produce other goods, including more consumer goods or more capital goods. An increase in the quantity and quality of capital goods contributes significantly to economic growth, which means there is an expansion in the longrun of the economy's capacity to produce all goods.

Now, let's suppose that the PPF for our economy in 1994 is as shown in Figure 2-4, where capital goods are measured on the horizontal axis and con-

FIGURE 2-3 **Economic Growth Means That the Production Frontier Shifts Outward**

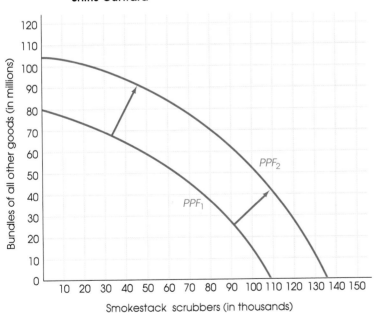

Growth in the economy's available resources and technological know-how shifts the production possibilities frontier outward. This allows the economy to produce more of both scrubbers and bundles—that is, to have economic growth.

FIGURE 2-4 **Present Choices Affect Future Production Possibilities Frontiers**

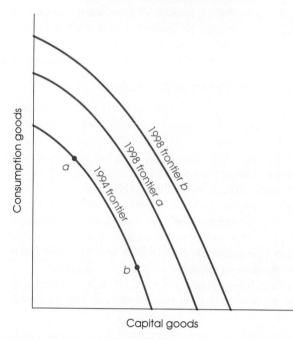

If the economy chooses point *a* on its 1994 frontier, it emphasizes consumption goods production; if it chooses point *b*, it favors capital goods production. Therefore, choice *a* gives rise to less economic growth or a smaller outward shift in the frontier (to 1998 frontier *a*) than does choice *b* (to 1998 frontier *b*).

sumption goods are measured on the vertical axis. If the economy chooses point *a* on its 1994 frontier, it will produce an output combination consisting mostly of consumption goods. Alternatively, if it chooses point *b* on the frontier, the economy will produce a combination predominantly made up of capital goods. All other things remaining the same, we can expect the economy's future (1998) PPF to be farther out if it chooses point *b* on its 1994 frontier than if it chooses point *a*. That is, the choice of point *a* on the 1994 frontier will give rise to 1998 frontier *a*, whereas choosing point *b* will give rise to 1998 frontier *b*. The reason is that choice *b* produces more capital goods, the kind of goods that contribute to economic growth, whereas choice *a* produces fewer such goods. We hasten to add, however, that this does not mean *b* is a better or poorer choice than *a*. After all, we must remember that choice *b* means our having fewer consumption goods to enjoy in 1994 relative to the number resulting from choice *a*.

Basic Problems for Any Economy

Given an economy's available resources and technology, we have seen how the production possibilities from which it may choose can be characterized by a production possibilities frontier. A frontier exists for any economy, whatever its form of government. It is possible to estimate an economy's frontier (although the abstract nature of the model makes it difficult). A knowledge of what is possible

POLICY PERSPECTIVE

Defense Spending–How Much Does It Cost?

In recent years there has been debate about whether or not Canada is spending enough on defense. An important aspect of this debate is the cost of national defense. As with any good or service, we can only have more defense goods and services (more guns, ships, and the services of soldiers) by giving up nondefense goods and services (such as automobiles, golf carts, and the services of house painters). The opportunity cost of more defense is measured by the amount of the necessary sacrifice of nondefense goods and services. This is illustrated by the economy's hypothetical production possibilities frontier in Figure P2-1, which shows the maximum-output combinations of defense and nondefense goods and services the economy can choose to produce when available resources are fully employed. If point *a* is chosen the economy would produce the quantities 0*D* for defense (horizontal axis) and 0*N* for nondefense (vertical axis). However, if policymakers decide that more defense is needed, say an additional amount equal to *DD'*, then it would be necessary for the economy to move to point *b* by giving up a quantity of nondefense goods and services equal to *NN'*—that is, the (opportunity) cost of the increased defense. *The additional cost NN' is the additional "spending" on increased defense.*

Some perspective on the actual cost of national defense in Canada is provided by measuring defense

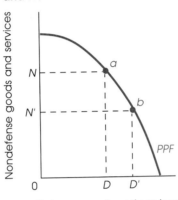

FIGURE P2-1 Production Possibilities Frontier for Defense and Nondefense Goods

spending as a percentage of GDP (gross domestic product), the economy's total annual output of final goods and services. Such a percentage tells us what portion of the dollar value of total output is given over to the production of defense goods and services. In terms of opportunity cost, it is the portion of total output that otherwise could have gone into the production of nondefense products—that is, the goods and services given up in order to produce defense products. In 1989, defense spending amounted to 11 billion dollars or 1.7 percent of GDP. This compares with an estimated expenditure of 7.8 percent of GDP in the United States in 1989. Since 1990, defense spending (not including the Gulf War

expenditures, which were financed by special warrants) has increased in Canada while U.S. spending has fallen. We have not been able to realize the "peace dividend" due to the end of the cold war because of our inability to close military bases in Canada, our greater need to modernize our equipment, and the greater demand for participation in United Nations peacekeeping activities in the 1990s.

Here we have focused on the economic way to measure the cost of national defense. The question of how much national defense we should have depends on one's perceptions of a number of issues such as the level of international tensions and their implications for war or peace, the degree to which we should be responsible for the defense of our own sovereignty, our responsibilities to contribute to United Nations peacekeeping efforts, and other military matters. Thus how much we should spend on defense depends on our estimate of the potential benefits of national defense. But that is a different, and far more controversial, issue.

For Discussion

- What would the opportunity cost be of choosing point *a* instead of point *b* in Figure P2-1?
- Why might it be said that economic growth would reduce the intensity of the debate between those who want more defense spending and those who don't?

is necessary in order to answer a number of important questions that any economy, be it that of Russia or Canada or Haiti, must face. These questions confront socialist and capitalist, command and market, developed and underdeveloped economies alike. These questions are:

1. What and how much should be produced?
2. How should production be organized?
3. For whom should goods be produced?

What and How Much Should Be Produced?

We could draw up an incredibly large list of goods that could be produced in Canada, including everything from needles and thread to public transportation vehicles and kidney dialysis machines. Some of the goods on the list, although possible to produce, might not be desired by anybody. Other goods, such as various kinds of food, might be desired by nearly everyone. Given its respective list, each country has to decide what goods and how much of each to produce.

In the economy summarized in Table 2-1, the answer to the question "What should be produced?" was "scrubbers and bundles of all other goods." The question "How much?" really asks what point on the PPF should be selected. The answer to this question must be decided by society's tastes and priorities. Thus, the answer is a value judgment. The people in one country, seeking rapid economic growth and industrialization, may feel little concern about the environmental impact of these processes. They might not want to divert resources to producing scrubbers. In another country, however, people who have experienced growth and industrialization, might be more aware of the adverse environmental impact of this development and therefore might be more willing to divert a larger share of resources to producing scrubbers. Whether the cost of protecting the environment is outrunning the benefits will depend on who is assessing the benefits.

Who makes the decisions about what and how much should be produced? The answer varies greatly from one economy to another. In a country such as China,[8] these decisions are made by a central planning bureau of the government. In Canada, the United States, and countries of Western Europe, decisions about the allocation of resources are largely made by individuals through the pricing system, or market mechanism. Even in these countries, however, the political process has legislated government intervention in many decisions. For example, in Canada utility companies set rates subject to approval by provincial government regulatory agencies. Similarly, decisions about pollution control have to a considerable degree been made through government action. Government intervention is desirable in certain cases because society has decided that the resource allocations made by free markets have not always been satisfactory. Pollution control is one such case. National defense is another.

---

[8] As of this writing, China was changing its perspective on the merits of central planning and moving to the greater use of markets to determine the answers to these questions.

How Should Production Be Organized?

In discussing the PPF, we emphasized that to be on the frontier it is necessary to use economic resources in the most productively efficient way. Once society has determined what goods to produce, the amount of each of those goods it will be able to produce will depend on how available resources are allocated to various productive activities. If we try to grow apples in Saskatchewan and raise wheat in British Columbia, we are not going to have as much of either as we would if those land resources were used the other way around. In addition, even when resources are allocated to their most productive activities, the most efficient known productive processes must be used. Harvesting wheat in Saskatchewan by hand and apples in B.C. with combines is still not going to give us as much wheat or apples as is technologically possible. Ideally, society should allocate available resources to productive activities and use known productive techniques in such a way that no reallocation of resources or known techniques could yield more of any good without yielding less of another. This is true of any combination of goods represented by any point on the PPF.

This ideal is easy enough to understand and describe. But it may have struck you by now as a little like being told that the way to make money in the stock market is to buy low and sell high. You can understand that perfectly, and wouldn't disagree, but a moment's reflection will lead you to ask the inevitable question: "Yes, but how do I *know* when a stock is at its low and when it is at its high?" Similarly, an economy isn't connected to a big video screen with a picture of its PPF and a cursor that can be moved around by a mouse until society has got itself right at the desired spot on the frontier. Society cannot see the economy's PPF, nor is it a simple matter of moving the mouse to move onto it. So how should an economy go about organizing its available resources in order to use them most efficiently? How will the most efficient production techniques be determined? What regulating mechanisms or management techniques can be used to ensure that the appropriate kinds and necessary amounts of resources will be directed to industries producing desired goods? Any economy, be it centrally planned or completely market oriented, wants to be on its PPF. The question is, how does it get there? Answering this question is in large part what economic analysis is all about.

For Whom Should Goods Be Produced?

For whom should the output of the economy be produced? Put another way, how should the economy's total output be distributed among the individual members of the economy? Should it be distributed to individuals according to their productive contribution to the making of that output? If so, how is an individual's contribution determined in the complex production processes of modern societies? Or should we take from each according to his or her ability and give to each according to his or her need? If people receive strictly according to their productive contributions, it's clear that some people are going to be terribly poor. On the other hand, if there is no relationship between an individual's productive contribution and the reward received for it, the incentive for effort may be reduced. If able and productive members of society do not have an incentive to produce, the total output of the economy will not be as large. If the total pie is smaller, there simply will be less to go around.

All societies must wrestle with this problem. They must decide how to distribute output in such a way as to encourage the productive members to work to their abilities and at the same time try to maintain a minimum standard of living for all. In short, the society must decide what degree of income inequality can be tolerated given these conflicting goals. The range of opinion on this is wide indeed and can fire the most heated debates. It is a matter of politics, cultural values, and moral issues. It involves both positive and normative dimensions.

In addition to solving this problem, all economies must decide how much of the total output should be used for collective purposes by government and how much should be used by individual households. This, of course, raises questions about how taxes should be levied and who should pay them. It raises questions about how much of the decision-making process for allocation of resources should be in the hands of the government rather than of the private sector (households and businesses). And in a country like Canada, where a large proportion of the resources are owned collectively by governments, how should the revenue from these resources be used or distributed to the populace?

Full Utilization of Resources

Economic efficiency requires that we be on the PPF (productive efficiency) and be at the "right" point as determined by the society. In our discussion of productive efficiency and the problem of how to organize production, we emphasized that an economy can fall short of its PPF if resources are misallocated or if the best production techniques known are not used. Another kind of productive inefficiency, also noted earlier, occurs whenever available resources are allowed to stand idle. This kind of inefficiency will also keep an economy from operating on its PPF. In the twentieth century, mixed capitalist economies, such as Canada's, have had frequent periods of recession. Recessions occur when significant amounts of labour and other available resources have been idle, or unemployed. During the depression of the 1930s, the estimated unemployment rate reached levels of 20 percent with an average over the decade of about 13 percent.[9] The actual rate of unemployment may have been considerably higher than this. In capitalist economies we often refer to the recurring pattern of increasing and decreasing unemployment associated with decreasing and increasing output as **business fluctuations**, or **business cycles**.[10]

In the industrialized economies of the Western world, the problem of eliminating, or reducing, unemployment of labour and other available resources is a high priority of economic policy. In Canada, it is the accepted responsibility of the federal government to promote full employment, maximum production and growth, and price stability. These were the first three major economic policy goals discussed in Chapter 1.

---

[9]See M. C. Urquhart and K. A. H. Buckley, *Historical Statistics of Canada* (Toronto: Macmillan, 1965).

[10]Centrally planned economies have not been free from the problem of fluctuations in their production of output. The underlying reasons for these are different, and for ideological reasons the problems have been described differently.

Unemployment of economic resources is similar in its effects to the underemployment of economic resources that results from their misallocation to inappropriate activities or when the best known techniques of production are not used. Both unemployment and underemployment cause the economy to produce at a point inside its production possibility frontier. However, the appropriate ways to deal with these two problems are quite different. The underemployment problem requires an answer to the question of how to organize production. Remedies there require establishing ways to see to it that the most efficient methods of production are used. For example, Saskatchewan is planted with wheat and not apples, and harvesting combines instead of scythes are used to cut the wheat. These kinds of problems are generally studied in microeconomics.

Remedies for the unemployment problem generally take the form of ensuring that there is enough demand for goods and services to require the full utilization of all available resources to meet that demand. You might think it strange that resources could be idle at all, and that it could be due to a low demand for goods. After all, don't people work in order to earn income to buy goods? Unfortunately, in a money-using economy, producing many kinds of goods, a person's offer of labour services in one place is quite removed from his or her desired purchase of goods in another. A line of unemployed job seekers at a steel mill's gate does not mean that each wants to work in direct exchange for a ton of cold rolled steel to be carried home at the end of the day. The mill manager's plans to produce steel and hire workers are affected quite differently by a line of job-seeking, unemployed steelworkers than they are by a line of customers wanting to place orders. It is not obvious that if workers were employed in the back, customers would materialize out front to purchase their output. This is true even though the workers would most likely use their earned money to buy a multitude of items requiring steel. All firms in the economy, producing all kinds of goods, are in the same situation as the steel mill. Clearly, when there are unemployed labourers and other resources in the whole economy, it is a result of the totality of these situations. The remedies for this sort of problem are studied in macroeconomics.

Change, Stability, and Growth

All economies are subject to change. The underlying causes of change are sometimes quite predictable. Population growth, improved education and training, and the improvement in technology are main contributors to economic growth. These kinds of change are fairly steady and ongoing. Population growth in underdeveloped countries is typically higher than in more industrialized countries. It is so high, in fact, that it makes it very difficult to increase the standard of living even when GDP is increasing. The growth in the number of people to be fed makes it hard to divert resources from agricultural production to the capital formation needed for industrialization. This applies not just to the formation of physical capital but also to the investment in human capital needed to provide the level of literacy and skills required of the labour force in an industrialized economy. In other countries, such as Australia, it is felt that the rate of population growth is too low to spur the kind of economic growth desired. Depending on the particular economy, the level of population growth can pose a problem by being either too high or too low. In China, birth control measures are a primary policy concern. In Australia, population policy has been aimed at creating incentives to encourage immigration from abroad and the settlement of the vast interior of the continent.

Other kinds of change are often less predictable and pose severe problems for maintaining stable economic processes in a country. A major cause of instability in industrialized Western economies during the 1970s and early 1980s was the increase in inflation. Since the Second World War, the general direction of prices in Canada has been upward. But during the 1970s the rate of inflation increased considerably (to double digits) and with it the unemployment rate. As well, interest rates became volatile, with the real rate (actual minus the inflation rate) sometimes falling below zero. This kind of variation creates uncertainty among consumers and businesses. Consumers often become more cautious about making major purchases, such as of housing and automobiles. Businesses and labour unions spend more time negotiating about cost-of-living clauses in contracts. Economists are in broad agreement that price instability is an undesirable source of change in the economy.

Every economy has to contend with various kinds of change at one time or another. Some changes are thought to be desirable, such as the growth in technological knowledge. It is also desirable that the economy have the ability to adapt quickly to changes in consumer tastes. Other kinds of change, including inflation, recession, and external shocks to the economy—such as those caused by the Arab oil embargo or the foreign exchange rate swings of the 1980s—are on everybody's bad list.

About some forms of change we have mixed feelings. A prime example in Canada in recent years is economic growth. We like it to the extent that it provides employment and an increase in goods and services. On the other hand, we do not wish it to be accompanied by increases in pollution, congestion in urban areas and on highways, and what many feel is a growing rootlessness and depersonalization of our way of life. A major problem to be solved by an economy is how to adapt to various kinds of change so as to maximize the benefits derived from the desirable aspects of change and to minimize the losses caused by the undesirable aspects.

> ### Checkpoint 2-3
> Do you think the questions of what to produce and for whom to produce it are of a normative or a positive nature? Why?

The Variety of Economic Systems

There is a wide variety of ways of organizing an economy to answer the basic questions we have discussed in this chapter. How an economy deals with the basic problem of scarcity—that is, the questions it poses—is also an expression of a vision of the relationship between the individual and society. The way in which a society chooses to organize its economy is therefore to a large extent a reflection of its cultural values and political **ideology**. It was in recognition of this fact that the subject of economics was originally called *political economy* and that political economy still exists as a discipline in its own right. Almost any debate over the relative merits of various types of economic systems cannot avoid dealing with the different political ideologies on which they are based. In this section we will consider two basic types of economic systems without dwelling at any length on their political and ideological implications. Nonetheless, it should be kept in mind that these implications are usually regarded as matters of considerable importance.

Pure Market Economy, *Laissez-Faire* Capitalism

Laissez-faire is a French expression that means: "let (people) do (as they think best)" or noninterference. Especially in matters of economics, it means allowing people to do as they please without governmental regulations and controls. The ideological basis of a *laissez-faire* economic system is the belief that if each economic agent is allowed to make free choices in pursuit of his or her own best interests, the interests of the group as a whole will be best served. This is the *invisible hand* notion credited to Adam Smith and based on a large number of independent producers and consumers freely competing (see the first Policy Perspective in Chapter 1).

What are the main features of a **pure market economy** based on *laissez-faire* **capitalism**? The means of production are privately owned by private citizens and private institutions. Private property is the rule. Government ownership is generally limited to public buildings and other facilities needed by the government in order to provide such things as national defense, a judicial system, police and fire protection, and public schools and roads. There is freedom of choice for consumers, businesses, and all resource suppliers. Consumers may purchase what they want subject only to the limits of their money incomes—there is consumer sovereignty. Businesses are free to purchase and utilize resources to produce whatever products they desire and to sell them in markets of their choice—there is free enterprise. Suppliers of resources such as labour, land, and financial capital are likewise free to sell them in whatever markets they please. The major constraint on businesses and resource suppliers is imposed by the marketplace, where consumer sovereignty dictates what goods and services can and cannot be produced and sold profitably. Freedom of choice and all market activities are subject to the minimum legal limits consistent with maintaining law and order and with enforcing contracts entered into freely by consenting parties.

The Market Mechanism

The mechanism that serves to coordinate the activities of consumers, businesses, and all suppliers of resources is the market. A **market** *is a mechanism or institution for bringing together information concerning characteristics of a specified product— such as price, quantity, and other qualities—to be shared by potential buyers and sellers of that particular good.* The answers to the questions of what and how much to produce are determined by the signals communicated between buyers and sellers via the interacting network of markets and prices. The potential buyers of a good make contact with the sellers or suppliers in the market. A price must then be determined such that suppliers will provide just the quantity of the good that buyers wish to purchase. On the buyers' (demand) side of the market, the level of the price determines who will buy the good and how much will be bought. On the suppliers' side of the market, the price level determines who will supply the good and how much will be supplied. If buyers want more than is being supplied at the prevailing price, they will signal their desires for more by bidding up the price. Suppliers will then respond by providing more of the good. If at the prevailing price sellers are providing a larger quantity of the good than buyers demand, prices will be bid down. This will be a signal to sellers to reduce the quantity of the good they supply to the market. In this way prices serve as the communicating link between buyers and sellers in a market economy.

Markets Determine What, How, for Whom

The markets for different goods are interrelated because the alternative to using one good is to use another. If the price of beef is felt to be too high, one alternative is to buy poultry. And if the price of poultry is likewise thought to be too high, another alternative might be to buy pork. Hence, the amounts of these goods buyers will demand will depend on the price of beef relative to the price of poultry and pork. Similarly, suppliers will be induced to supply those goods that are selling for the highest prices relative to the prices of other goods. Changes in the price in one market will set up a chain reaction of adjustments in quantities demanded and supplied in related markets. For example, other things being equal, an increase in demand for new housing will cause an increase in the wages of architects, bricklayers, carpenters, furniture sales personnel, and so on. This will induce labour resources to move from other activities into those that now appear relatively more rewarding. All markets in the economy are interrelated to varying extents in this way. It is the "invisible hand" of the marketplace that determines the allocation of resources, *what* goods will be produced, and *how much* of each.

Competition among suppliers of goods and labour services will ensure that the most efficient and productive will charge the lowest price for any good and thus make the sale to buyers. Hence, the forces of the marketplace will cause labour and other resources to flow into those occupations and uses for which they are best suited. This is the way a market economy determines *how production should be organized*.

For whom are goods produced in a market economy? Obviously, for whomever is willing and able to pay the price for them. And who are these people? Those who are able to sell their labour services and any other resources they own that can be used in the production of other goods. The emphasis is on competition and a reward structure oriented towards the most efficient and productive. The vision of the individual's relation to society that underlies pure market, *laissez-faire* capitalism has sometimes been characterized as an ideology of the survival of the fittest. All are free to go into any line of work or business they choose, to take any risks at making as much or losing as much money as they care to. The individual is entitled to all the rewards of good decisions and good luck but must bear the full consequences of bad ones. There is nothing necessarily "fair" about the distribution of income from this process. The equity of the distribution of income generated from a market system has always been a contentious issue in economic and political discussion.

Resource Utilization

How fully do pure market systems utilize their available resources? This is difficult to evaluate, because history provides few, if any, examples of a pure market economy without any form of government intervention. However, many of the industrialized economies of the Western world have a significant portion of their economic decisions determined by market forces. This was even more so in the nineteenth century and the twentieth century prior to World War II. The Great Depression, which afflicted these nations during the 1930s, together with the record of previous decades, suggests that pure market economies have difficulty keeping their available resources fully employed all the time.

Change, Stability, and Growth

As regards change, stability, and growth, economies that most closely approximate pure market, *laissez-faire* capitalism have achieved some of the highest standards of living in the world. Such systems seem particularly well suited to responding to the changing tastes of consumers. They are also able to develop new products and bring new technologies to the everyday use of the masses. From the standpoint of stability, fluctuations in economic activity as measured by GDP, employment, and the behaviour of prices have always been a source of concern in such economies. Obviously, one would be hard pressed to find a pure form of this type of economy today. In the late eighteenth century, at the beginning of the Industrial Revolution, England and the United States came pretty close. Nonetheless, there are still many economies today where markets play a dominant role. The concept of pure market, *laissez-faire* capitalism may be viewed as one extreme on a spectrum of ways of organizing an economy.

The Command Economy

In the **command economy,** also called the *planned economy*, the government answers the questions of how to organize production, what and how much to produce, and for whom to produce. These answers take the form of plans that may extend for as far as 5 to 20 years into the future. In such a planned economy, the government literally commands that these plans be carried out.

Government Command

Typically, the government in a command economy owns the means of production, as in the former Soviet Union or the Republic of China, but this is not always so. In Nazi Germany the government controlled and planned the economy, but ownership remained largely in private hands. Even in command economies the government may allow markets to operate in certain areas of the economy—if it is consistent with, or helpful to, the achievement of other planning objectives. China allows this to some extent in its agricultural sector, for example. In a command economy, all forms of labour, including management, are essentially government employees. The situation in China is rapidly changing and recently private firms have been allowed to hire labour.

Planning What, How, and for Whom

The underlying rationale for a command economy is the belief that the government knows best what is most beneficial for the entire economy and for its individual parts. In a command economy there are differences between what consumers may want and what the planners have decided to produce. If planners do not want to devote resources to television sets, consumers simply will go without them. Once the plan for the entire economy has been drawn up, each producing unit in the economy is told *what* and *how much* it must produce of various goods to fulfill its part of the plan. This determines each unit's need for labour, capital equipment, and other inputs. Obviously, it is not easy to coordinate centrally all the component parts of the plan to ensure that the right kinds and amounts of labour, capital, and other inputs are available to each producing unit so that each may satisfy its individual plan. *How to organize production* is quite a task for central planners overseeing the economy of an entire nation. Managing General Motors, Canadian Pacific, or IBM pales in comparison.

For whom is output produced? Centrally planned economies typically provide for all citizens, regardless of their productive contribution to the output of the economy. However, planners cannot avoid the fact that human nature does respond to material incentives. As a result, government-determined wage scales vary from one occupation or profession to the next, depending on where planners feel there are shortages or surpluses of needed labour skills. This, of course, depends on how authoritarian the government wants to be in allowing people to pick and choose their occupations or professions.

Resource Utilization

Full utilization of available resources presumably does not pose a problem in a command economy. Remember that by full utilization we mean that there are no available resources standing idle. This is a different issue from whether or not resources may be underemployed due to poor planning. In the former Soviet Union planners had continual difficulty in meeting their agricultural goals. If they thought their goals were reasonable, their relatively frequent shortfalls from these goals suggested that the resources devoted to agriculture were not as efficiently employed as possible, even allowing for setbacks caused by bad weather.

Change, Stability, and Growth

How do planned economies deal with *change* and *growth*? Obviously, in a planned economy, growth and many kinds of change can be engineered by the central planning bureau to a large extent. If the government wants to increase economic growth, the central planning agency will draw up plans devoting a larger share of the economy's resources to the production of capital goods. On the other hand, critics argue that authoritarian control, a large bureaucratic structure, and centrally dictated goals put a damper on individual initiative and innovation. Because of this, it is argued that technological discovery and change are inhibited. Such discoveries and changes are considered major factors in economic growth, which critics feel is weak in planned economies. The *stability* of planned economies depends on how well the government is able to set realistic goals and structure the appropriate plans to attain them. If goals are too ambitious, and if the amount of reorganization in the economy is too great for the time allowed, the loss of economic stability can be severe. And as witnessed by the revolutions in the Eastern Bloc countries in 1989 and 1990, the failure to provide a reasonable mix of consumer goods can contribute to the dissatisfactions of the populace, although in many of these countries political repression was the dominant factor in the overthrow of these regimes.

Summing Up

The planned, or command, economy may be viewed as representing the other extreme on the spectrum of economic organization from that of pure market, *laissez-faire* capitalism. No two economies in the world are exactly alike, but each may be thought of as lying somewhere on the spectrum between the two extremes we have described. Most fall under the very broad category of the **mixed economy,** which represents all the cases in between. The point is that all modern economies have to grapple with the economic problem posed by scarcity and the consequent need for choice. In the next chapter we will examine the nature of the mixed economy.

Summary

1. While available economic resources are limited, human wants are virtually unlimited. This creates the fundamental problem of scarcity.

2. Scarcity means we cannot do everything that we would like to do, so we have to make choices between the potential alternatives that are feasible.

3. When we have to make choices, the alternative that we choose to do has an opportunity cost measured by the value of the next best thing that we could have chosen instead.

4. The production possibilities frontier is a curve connecting the maximum possible output combinations of goods for a fully employed economy with fixed resources and technology. In this situation, the production of more of one kind of good is possible only if the economy produces less of another. The cost of having more of one good is the amount of the other that must be given up. This cost is called the opportunity cost of a good.

5. The production possibilities frontier model illustrates scarcity because the frontier depicts a limit to what can be produced with the available resources. It illustrates choice in that only one point on the PPF is achievable at any one time and it illustrates opportunity cost by the negative slope. This indicates that a movement from one point to another on the curve entails a gain in one product only by giving up some of the other.

6. Unemployment exists whenever some available resources are idle. Underemployment (or resource misallocation) exists if certain available resources are employed to do jobs for which other available resources are better suited. Underemployment also exists whenever the best available technology is not used in a production process. Every economy must concern itself with maintaining full employment of its resources (avoiding unemployment). This has frequently been a problem for the industrialized economies of the West.

7. When there is no unemployment or underemployment of available resources, an economy is able to produce the maximum amount of goods possible. Productive efficiency occurs when there is no unemployment or underemployment of resources. When producing this maximum, the economy is said to be on its PPF. Economic efficiency requires that the economy be productively efficient and that the "right" combination of goods be chosen given the desires of the population.

8. Economic growth occurs when an economy's available supply of resources is increased or when there is an increase in technological know-how. As a result, the PPF expands outward.

9. The output combination chosen on today's frontier affects the amount of capital goods that will be available tomorrow. Therefore, today's choice will affect the location of tomorrow's PPF.

Checkpoint 2-4

Describe the likely process of selecting a point on the PPF of Figure 2-2 (that is, the combination of scrubbers and bundles) for a pure market economy and a planned, or command, economy. For each of these two kinds of economies, what difference do you think it makes, in terms of the point chosen on the frontier, if they are industrially underdeveloped as compared to the likely outcome if they are industrially advanced?

10. Any economy, whatever its political ideology, must answer certain questions that arise because of the basic economic problem of scarcity. Every economy must decide what and how much to produce, how to organize production, and for whom output is to be produced. The answer to the question of what to produce determines the nature and location of the PPF. The answer to the question of how much to produce determines the point chosen on the frontier. How to organize production determines whether the chosen point on the frontier will be reached. For whom to produce is largely determined by ideological orientation as to the proper mix of free markets, government regulation, and central planning. Every economy must also deal with change. The stability of an economy depends very much on how well it is able to adjust to change. An important kind of change is economic growth.

11. A market is a mechanism for bringing together all the information about a good in order for buyers and sellers to agree on a price and transact an exchange.

12. There are two basic kinds of economies, or ways of organizing the process of deciding what and how much, how, and for whom to produce. Each kind presumes a particular relationship between the individual and the state. They are basically distinguished by the amount of government intervention they permit in the decision-making process of the economy.

   a. *Pure market, laissez-faire capitalism.* Individual economic agents are given free choice in all economic decisions, which are completely decentralized. There is no interference by government in the form of regulations or controls. Markets and prices are the sole coordinating mechanisms for allocating resources and organizing production.

   b. *Command, or planned, economy.* An authoritarian government decides what and how much, how, and for whom to produce. Government typically owns the means of production, plans economic activities, and commands that these plans be carried out. The underlying rationale is that the government knows best what is most beneficial for the entire economy and its individual parts.

Key Terms and Concepts

business cycles
business fluctuations
command economy
composite good
economic efficiency
economic growth
the economic
    problem

ideology
increasing costs
laissez-faire
    capitalism
market
mixed economy
opportunity
    cost

production possibilities
    frontier (PPF)
productive efficiency
pure market economy
resource misallocation
scarcity
underemployment
unemployment

Questions and Problems

1. Think about the following situation in terms of the concept of opportunity cost. If you choose not to go to college, suppose your best alternative is to drive a truck for $12,000 per year. If you choose to go to college, suppose that you must pay a tuition fee of $2,000 per year and buy books and other school supplies amounting to $400

per year. Suppose that your other living expenses are the same regardless of which choice you make. Suppose you choose to go to college. What is the opportunity cost of your college diploma?

2. Using the production possibilities table for computers and jet airplanes from:

Product	Production Possibilities (Output per Year)				
	a	b	c	d	e
Computers (in thousands)	0	25	40	50	55
Jet airplanes (in thousands)	40	30	20	10	0

   a. Plot the production possibilities frontier for the economy characterized by this table.
   b. Demonstrate increasing costs using the data in this table.
   c. Suppose technological progress doubles the productivity of the process for making computers and also of that for making jet airplanes. What would the numbers in the production possibilities table look like in that case? Plot the new production possibilities frontier.
   d. Suppose technological progress doubles the productivity of the process for making computers but there is no change in the process for making jet airplanes. What would the numbers in the production possibilities table be now? Plot the new production possibilities frontier.
   e. Suppose technological progress doubles the productivity of the process for making jet airplanes but there is no change in the process for making computers. What would the numbers in the production possibilities frontier be now? Plot the new production possibilities frontier. Why is it that, despite the fact that there is no change in the productivity of producing computers, it is now possible at any given level of production of jet airplanes to have more computers?

3. Consider a production possibilities frontier for consumer goods and capital goods. How would the choice of a point on that frontier affect the position of tomorrow's frontier? Choose three different points on today's production possibilities frontier and indicate the possible location of tomorrow's frontier that is associated with each.

4. Construct your own production possibilities frontier by putting a grade point scale on the vertical axis to measure a grade in your economics course and the number of waking hours in a typical day (say 16) on the horizontal axis. Out of those 16 hours per day, how many do you think you would have to give over to study to get a D? a C? a B? an A? Plot the frontier determined by these combinations.

5. Construct a production possibilities frontier with capital goods on one axis and consumer goods on the other. Show different growth outcomes depending on the initial point chosen on this frontier. Explain the reasons for the different shifts. If the initial point chosen was where the capital output was zero, what do you think would happen to the frontier, assuming all other things remain constant?

6. Compare and contrast the ways in which the two types of economies we have discussed deal with the three basic questions or problems any economy faces.

7. Choose a number of countries and place them on a continuum from a pure market economy to a pure command economy. Explain why you place them where you do. What economic factors other than their place on this continuum differentiates them?

Chapter 3

The Mixed Economy

In a mixed economy the answers to the questions what and how much to produce, how to organize production, and for whom to produce are determined by a mixture of private enterprise and a reliance on markets modified by government involvement in many areas of the economy. In some mixed economies, government intervention extends even to the ownership of certain industries—such industries are called **nationalized industries**. Hence, a mixed economy may involve not only a mixture of private and public decision making but a mixture of private and public ownership as well. The degree and growth of government involvement in the Canadian economy are debated at length by the public and politicians as well as economists.

The role of government varies from one mixed economy to the next, reflecting the varying political decisions on this issue in different countries. Nonetheless, there are certain characteristics common to all mixed economies. They all have markets where the exchange of goods and services takes place using money as the medium of exchange. They generally have a large degree of free enterprise stemming from their history of economic development. Countries that most commonly come to mind are Canada, the United States, Great Britain, the Scandinavian countries, France, Germany, Italy, Australia, New Zealand, and Japan.[1] Finally, they all have felt the need to modify capitalism and the workings of free markets through government intervention.

In this chapter we will give a brief overview of some of the main characteristics of mixed economies such as our own, since most of the analysis in the rest of this book will focus on mixed economies. To develop an overview of an economy we will use the **circular flow model** to illustrate the role of markets, money, incomes, profits, and government in such an economic system. The discussion will be restricted to a "closed" economy—that is, one without interactions with

---

[1]These countries and the Netherlands, Belgium, Austria, Luxembourg, Ireland, Greece, Switzerland, Portugal, Spain, and Turkey together comprise the Organization of Economic Cooperation and Development (OECD).

foreign countries. Later in the text, foreign sector interactions (trade) will be added to the model developed here. The purpose of this overview is for you to gain some feel for the economic system as a *whole* before we turn to analyzing each separate part.

In a capitalistic, mixed economy like that of Canada, money is used by households, businesses, and government to buy and sell goods and resources in markets, to pay and collect taxes, and to borrow and lend in financial markets. The flow of goods and resources in exchange for money, the flow of money to fulfill tax obligations to government and to redistribute income from one group to another, the flow of money from lenders to borrowers in exchange for borrowers' IOUs, and the expenditure of the borrowed funds on goods can all be envisioned schematically in a flow diagram. This chapter will develop the circular flow diagram in steps.

The Pure Market System

Before we introduce government into the model, we will outline a simple pure market (*laissez-faire*) system. Of course, no economy could function without a minimum of government, so this is an extreme abstraction. For the moment, we will also ignore the existence of financial markets. Only two groups of agents will be included in this model—households and firms. Figure 3-1 illustrates the relationships between these two groups—the right-hand box represents households and the left represents firms.

Markets

The central mechanism in a mixed economy is the system of markets. Why do markets exist in the first place? Why are goods traded? What is it that leads

---

LEARNING OBJECTIVES

After reading this chapter, you will be able to:

1. Explain why people specialize in what they produce and trade for what they need in markets.
2. Define, describe, and locate in the circular flow diagram the goods and resource markets, the money and real flows, and the different agents—households and firms.
3. Explain how money makes trading much easier and therefore promotes specialization and trade.
4. Define and differentiate *normal profit* and *economic profit*.
5. Explain the role of profit in the creation and allocation of capital.
6. Discuss the importance of incentives to economic efficiency.
7. Describe and locate in the circular flow diagram the financial markets.
8. List and explain the reasons for government involvement in a mixed economy.
9. Define and explain *public goods* and *externalities*.
10. Give reasons why government production may not be economically efficient.
11. Explain the interconnecting economic relationships between households, businesses, and government as characterized in the circular flow diagram.
12. Describe how a mixed market economy determines answers to the questions of what, how, and for whom to produce.

FIGURE 3-1   **The Exchange Flows Between Businesses and Households**

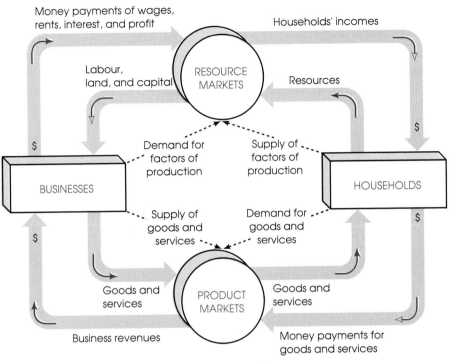

In a money-using economy, businesses obtain the resources (land, labour, and capital) necessary for production from households in exchange for money payments (wages, rents, interest, and profit) as indicated in the upper flow channel. These payments are income to the households, which spend it on goods and services produced by businesses. This is indicated by the money payments made to businesses in exchange for goods and services in the lower flow channel. Businesses use the money proceeds from sales to purchase the resources in the upper flow channel, thus completing the loop.

---

people to go to market? The answers lie in the fact that each of us is better at doing some things than at doing others.

Specialization and Markets

Because people have differing abilities, we tend to specialize. Specialization gives rise to the need for trade, and trade creates markets. Money makes trade easier and therefore encourages specialization and a more extensive development of markets.

If each of us specializes in that particular thing he or she is best at, the whole economy is able to produce more of everything than if each of us tries to be self-sufficient. Of course when each of us specializes in producing one thing, we become dependent on others for the production of everything else. When there is specialization, most of what a person produces is a surplus that must be traded for the other things that person wants. Hence, the greater is the **specialization of labour** in an economy, the greater is the need for trade. And as trade becomes more important to the functioning of an economy, markets in all kinds of goods and services become more commonplace.

A **market** *is an institution that facilitates the exchange between buyers and sellers of some commodity, service, or resource.* The price and quantity exchanged is the information conveyed by a market. In the simple circular model the innumerable markets found in any real modern economy will be reduced to two types: the goods market and the resources market. These are shown as circles in Figure 3-1. The circle at the top of the exchange flow diagram represents the resource markets, where land, labour, and capital are exchanged. The bottom circle represents the goods markets, where all economic goods, which include commodities and services, are exchanged. Although we are representing all markets in circle spaces in the diagrams, markets in the real economy are not confined to specific geographical space or physical locations.

Exchange Flows in the Economy

The flows connecting households and firms and passing through the goods and resource markets are the real flow of goods and resources, and the counterflow of money payments. These flows are illustrated in Figure 3-1, and the reasons for the necessity of both are discussed later.

Trade in a Barter Economy

In a **barter economy** goods are traded for goods. Suppose you are a member of an economy in which each individual specializes in the production of a particular good. Like everyone else, you produce more of your particular good than you need for yourself and trade the surplus for other goods. Suppose you specialize in chopping wood and today you decide to go shopping for a pair of sandals. Your problem is twofold. You must first find someone who has sandals to trade. Second, while you may encounter several such people, you must find among them one who wants to acquire chopped wood. In other words, you are looking for an individual who coincidentally has sandals to trade *and* also wants chopped wood. We say, therefore, that in order to have a trade, it is necessary to have a **coincidence of wants.**

At this point you might ask, "Is it not possible that someone who has sandals to trade, but no need for chopped wood, might accept the wood and then trade it for something he or she does want?" Yes, it is possible, but very inconvenient. If that person accepts the wood, the problem of finding a coincidence of wants has really just been transferred from you to him or her.

In short, the difficulties involved in finding a coincidence of wants tend to discourage specialization and trade in a barter economy. Given the effort and time that must be spent just to find a coincidence of wants, many individuals in a barter economy find it easier to be more self-sufficient and produce a greater variety of items for their own consumption. To this extent, the gains from specialization and trade cannot be fully realized.

A prominent characteristic of most markets with which you are familiar is that goods are traded for money. The more an economy is characterized by specialization of labour, the less likely it is that we will observe goods being traded directly for goods. The fundamental reason for the invention and existence of money is that it makes specialization and trade much easier.

Money as a Medium of Exchange

How does the use of money allow us to get around these difficulties? Money eliminates the need for the coincidence of wants. If the economy uses money to carry on trade, you can sell your chopped wood to whoever wants it and accept money in exchange. Whether the purchaser produces something you want or not is irrelevant. As long as you can use the money received to buy what you want, you are satisfied. We say money serves as the **medium of exchange**.

At different times and in different societies, the medium of exchange used as money has taken many forms: beaver pelts, precious stones, gold coins, currency, and chequable bank accounts. Whatever its form, money's common characteristic is that it must be acceptable to people because they believe they can use it as buyers. Because money eliminates the need for a coincidence of wants, it promotes specialization and trade, and thereby makes possible the gains that stem from specialization and trade. The incentive for societies to use money as a medium of exchange derives directly from these gains. The introduction of money into a barter economy essentially causes that economy's production possibilities frontier to shift outward.

It should be remembered that what is important is the "real" goods exchanged and not the money. The real flows of goods and resources are illustrated in Figure 3-1 by the counterclockwise arrows. The factor services of land, labour, and capital flow from the households to the firms. The firms convert these resources into goods through the production process. The goods flow through the goods markets to the households (the distribution process). In effect, the real goods are the payments to the households for the use of their real resources. Households obtain utility from the use of the goods (the consumption process).

To facilitate these transactions, an opposite flow of money payments takes place. In Figure 3-1 this is illustrated by the clockwise arrows. The flow to households from firms going through the resource markets is comprised of the money incomes to households: rent for land, wages for labour, interest for capital. This flow also constitutes the firms' costs. The money flow from households to firms is comprised of the payments for goods or the firms' revenues.

Markets and Profits

One of the items in the income flow to households from firms is profit. An economy using money with extensive markets fosters specialization among workers and in the methods of production. Specialization leads to the development of more sophisticated production processes, typically requiring large amounts of investment in capital goods. In a capitalistic economy, where the productive units or firms are privately owned either by those who run them or by shareholders, sizable amounts of funds, or financial capital, must be raised by the owners in order to acquire capital goods. Willingness to commit funds to such investments depends on both interest and *profit*. The amount of profit is determined in the markets where the good produced (by the capital) is sold.

In a capitalistic economy profit also provides an incentive for entrepreneurial activity. The entrepreneur described in Chapter 1 is a key factor in the creation and organization of *new* production techniques and the founding of firms that employ these techniques to satisfy the demands for *new* products and continually changing markets.

Checkpoint 3-1*

Suppose there are three people, A, B, and C, and that A specializes in producing lumber, B in catching fish, and C in growing wheat. Each has a surplus of what he or she produces. Suppose that A would like to get some wheat from C, but C doesn't have any desire for A's lumber. Suppose that C would like to get some fish from B, but B doesn't want any of C's wheat. And suppose that B would like to get some lumber from A, but A doesn't want any of B's fish. Describe how trade would have to be carried on under a barter system if each lives alone on an island 20 miles from each of the others and each has a boat. By comparison, describe how trade would be carried on if A, B, and C used money.

Answers to all Checkpoints can be found at the back of the text.

Normal Profit

In economics, profit is a controversial and difficult concept to grasp. For some the word holds positive connotations as the goal for being in business; its acquisition is an indicator of success. For others the mention of the word conjures up images of exploitation and robber barons carving out their pound of flesh from the downtrodden. But what is a "reasonable" profit, or what economists call a **normal profit?** When we say that a firm is earning a normal profit, what must be the relationship between its total sales revenue and its total costs? In order to answer these questions, recall that we emphasized in the previous chapter that all costs are opportunity costs because resources are scarce and have alternative uses. Our discussion of the production possibilities frontier indicated that if resources are used to produce one good, they are not available to produce other goods. The cost of the one good is thus equal to the alternative goods that must be forgone in order to produce it. This notion of cost is directly applicable to the individual firm.

All the resources, including capital and entrepreneurial skills, that a firm needs in order to produce its product have alternative uses in the production of other products by other firms. Hence, the costs of production for a firm are all those payments it must make to all resource suppliers in order to bid resources away from use in the production of alternative goods. When the firm's total sales revenue is just sufficient to cover these costs, all resources employed by the firm are just earning their opportunity costs. When the capital owners are being compensated just enough to keep them from leaving and going into some other line of productive activity, that amount of compensation is called an *interest payment*. When those people providing entrepreneurial skills or risk capital are being compensated just enough to keep them from leaving and going into some other line of productive activity, that amount of compensation is called a *normal profit*. In some firms the entrepreneur provides capital as well as his or her skills. In such a situation normal profit will include a return for both inputs, as they cannot often be distinguished. *Normal profit, then, is a cost of production and, like wages and interest, a necessary incentive for resources to go to the production of goods.* If a firm makes a profit in excess of normal profit, the excess is termed **economic profit**. *Economic profit is the difference between the revenue received from sales and the opportunity costs of all the resources used by the firm.*

Profit and the Allocation of Resources

Changes in the levels of profits that are earned in different markets play an important role in the efficient allocation of resources in a dynamic, changing economy. Suppose that a market for a new product develops or that there is a sudden increase in demand for an existing product. Firms that are first to enter the new market or that are already in a market when demand rises will find they can earn greater than normal, or economic, profits. This happens because demand so exceeds the existing production capacity that prices considerably in excess of cost can be charged. Economic profits serve as a signal to entrepreneurial skills and financial capital used in other areas of the economy that they can earn more by moving into the new and expanding markets. Resources will continue to move into these areas so long as economic profits exist. Eventually, enough resources will have moved into these markets and increased capacity sufficiently that these economic profits will no longer exist. In this way economic profits serve to allocate resources to those areas of the economy where they are most in demand. Similarly, of course, below-normal profits (economic losses) in one area of the economy will cause entrepreneurial skills and capital to move out of that line of productive activity and into those areas where they can earn their opportunity cost.

Profits provide an incentive for capital and entrepreneurial skills to flow to producers of new products or to producers who innovate cheaper production processes. If profits were not allowed to exist, it would effectively remove the incentive for anybody to provide the financial risk capital and entrepreneurial skills necessary for the creation of physical capital goods or the innovative effort necessary to create new technology and supply new markets.[2] On the other hand, persistent longrun economic profits in a mature industry indicate a failure of competition in that industry. Economic profits derived from situations where competition in the marketplace is nonexistent or inhibited are generally considered not to be in the economy's best interest. The role and desirability of profits in mixed economies will undoubtedly always be a much-debated issue. Unfortunately, much of the debate is often the result of confusion over the meaning, or meanings, of the word *profit*. And even if the meanings were clear, it is very difficult in practice to separate the payments of interest, normal profit, and economic profit from the cost and revenue income statements for any given firm. These issues are considered at length in microeconomics under costs, perfect competition, and monopoly.

Checkpoint 3-2

Imagine you are going into business for yourself. Itemize the specific resources you will need and develop a hypothetical income/expense statement for your first year of operation. In this statement, categorize the returns to the factors of production. How did you determine interest? Wages? Profit? If your business generates profit, what kind is it? Will it persist?

The Exchange Flows with Financial Markets

The exchange flows shown in Figure 3-1 are oversimplified in several respects. For one thing, businesses produce and sell goods to one another—capital equipment, for example.

Households and Businesses Borrow and Save

We also know that households do not typically spend all their income on goods and services, nor do businesses always pay out all their sales revenue for the current use of land, labour, and capital. Households save part of their income, usually by putting it in banks and other financial institutions. Similarly, businesses save part of their sales revenue, usually in the form of **retained earnings.** Like households, businesses put savings in banks and other financial institutions. Often they use their savings to purchase bonds and other forms of IOUs issued by parties that want to borrow money. Banks and other financial institutions perform the function of taking the savings of households and businesses and lending this money to borrowers who in turn use it to buy goods and services. When businesses, and sometimes households,

---

[2]This was a central theme of J. A. Schumpeter (1883–1950). See, for example, *The Theory of Economic Development* (Cambridge, MA: Harvard University Press, 1934) and *Capitalism, Socialism and Democracy* (New York: Harper and Brothers Publishers, 1950).

use their savings to buy bonds and IOUs directly without the assistance of the intermediary role played by banks and other financial institutions, the effect is the same—savings are loaned to borrowers.

The Role of Financial Markets

The markets that perform the function of taking the funds of savers and lending them to borrowers are called **financial markets.** The households and businesses that lend their savings to borrowers through these financial markets receive compensation in the form of interest payments. Financial markets serve the function of taking the funds from the savings flows of businesses and households and lending them to borrowers at interest rates mutually agreeable to both lenders and borrowers. Who are the borrowers? Other businesses and households. What do they do with the borrowed funds? Spend them on goods and services. In effect, financial markets take the savings, or the flow of funds provided by those businesses and households that do not want to spend them on goods and services, and put them in the hands of those that do want to spend them on goods and services.

Flow Diagram with Financial Markets and Savings

The role of financial markets can be represented in diagram form by making some changes in Figure 3-1. Figure 3-2 reproduces Figure 3-1 with the addition of savings flows and financial markets. Note that not all of the sales revenue of some businesses is immediately paid out in wages, rents, interest, and profit. Some is retained and saved, and it flows from businesses into the financial markets as indicated by the counterclockwise arrow labeled "Business savings." (It should be emphasized that these savings are still owned by the stockholders of the businesses, who have provided financial capital.) Similarly, some households do not spend all of their income on goods and services. Income that is not spent is saved and flows into financial markets as indicated by the clockwise arrow labeled "Household savings."

The financial markets in the lower part of the diagram lend out the savings of businesses and households to other businesses and households that want to borrow funds. These borrowers do not borrow money and make interest payments on their loans just for the privilege of holding the money. They use it to buy goods and services from businesses, as indicated by the upward-directed arrow labeled "Expenditures on goods and services by borrowers." These goods and services are part of the flow labeled "Goods and services," indicated by the counterclockwise arrow running from businesses to households. The business borrowers purchase goods and services from other businesses.

The main point is this: The flow of money that is diverted away from further expenditure on goods and services by saving is redirected through the financial markets into the hands of those who will spend it on goods and services. In performing this function, financial markets play a crucial role in capitalistic, market-oriented economies. Because there is no government economic intervention indicated in Figure 3-2, it may be interpreted as representing an economic system of pure market, *laissez-faire* capitalism.

FIGURE 3-2 **Exchange Flows with Savings and Financial Markets**

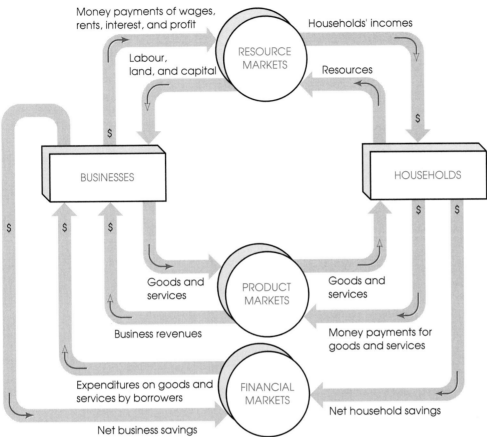

This diagram elaborates on Figure 3-1 by adding the net savings flow from households and businesses. These feed into the financial markets, where they are loaned to borrowers at some mutually acceptable rate of interest. The borrowers then spend the funds on goods and services produced by businesses. The financial markets thus serve to redirect the savings money flows, otherwise diverted from expenditure on goods and services, back into the hands of those who will spend them on goods and services. Figure 3-2 may be viewed as representing a pure market, *laissez-faire* capitalist economy.

Government's Role in the Mixed Economy

There are two broad concerns in the functioning of a market economy that require the involvement of government—efficiency and equity. A market economy could not operate efficiently without at least some government. As a minimum, government is required in order to maintain the conditions for a market system to function. These are the requirements for contracts to be honoured—criminal and civil law, the police, and the judiciary. In addition to this, intervention is required on efficiency grounds because the "invisible hand" of the market often fails to work and the "invisible foot" takes over. Where market failures exist, some

POLICY PERSPECTIVE

Should Profit Be the Only Objective of Business?

Do businesses have obligations to society beyond making a profit? On one side of the issue it is argued that the *only* responsibility of business is to make profits because society's interests are best served by business pursuing that goal alone. Alternatively, the other side of the issue holds that businesses should act according to higher moral principles to prevent damage to society that might otherwise result from a single-minded pursuit of profit. In the extreme, this view holds that it amounts to murder for profit when businesses produce and advertise cigarettes, market automobiles that are not adequately safe in a crash, and dump toxic wastes in the air and waterways. Are there not moral principles that should inhibit such behaviour even at the cost of forgone profit opportunities?

THE ONLY PROFITS VIEW

The view that profit should be the sole objective of business points out that corporate managers in today's world are responsible to the corporation's stockholders (the owners), who expect them to do everything within the law to earn the owners a maximum return (profit) on their investment. The *only profits* view argues that if a corporate executive takes an action that the executive feels is socially responsible and that action reduces profit, then the executive has spent (in effect, stolen) the owners' money. This violates a fundamental tenet of our political economic system—that no individual shall be deprived of property without his or her permission. Corporate executives who want to take socially responsible actions should use their own money, supporting special interest groups, charities, or political parties and causes that promote the social actions they desire. (Corporate boards with the support of the shareholders may approve "socially responsible" objectives.)

THE PROFITS PLUS OTHER CONCERNS VIEW

According to the *profits plus other concerns* view, business firms do have a moral responsibility not to design products or engage in behaviour (for example, deceptive advertising) that they have reason to believe will seriously injure or possibly kill people. Money is a means to an end, and not the sort of end that justifies acting immorally to get it. The *profits plus other concerns* view also argues that if profit is the sole objective of business, then the associated abuses and immoral

continued on next page

form of government intervention may be necessary to correct these failures in order to bring about a more efficient economy.

Equity as well as efficiency is a concern. Equity has many connotations, but generally government is expected to intervene when the public perceives some "unfair" or inequitable outcome from market results. The well-being of the society depends on more equitable income distribution than would occur from an unfettered market system where people would receive only the incomes obtained from what they had to offer in the resource markets. Humanistic values call for a vision of human beings beyond that of seeing them as mere inputs to the production process.

The degree of government involvement is controversial in mixed economies. Most people would probably agree with the objective of achieving economic efficiency, but the issue of equity is highly contentious. And, as in many areas of economics, there is often a trade-off between efficiency and equity. From the economic point of view, the rationale for government involvement depends upon a clear idea of what degree of equity provides the greatest benefit to Canadians. This is a normative question dependent on the views of all Canadians. In a parliamentary system such as Canada, people vote for individuals and parties who

POLICY PERSPECTIVE CONTINUED

behaviour that result will lead the public to impose greater government regulation on business activity. Increased government intrusion in the private sector will cause economic inefficiency as well as pose potential threats to individual freedoms. Therefore, it is argued, in the longrun it is in the best interests of business (and of all of us) to pay heed to moral principles while pursuing profit. Otherwise, society will increasingly use the government and political processes to correct perceived abuses.

HOW DO YOU GET SOCIALLY RESPONSIBLE BUSINESS BEHAVIOUR?

Is it really possible for firms to be socially responsible and survive in a competitive market? Won't firms that incur additional costs to make a safer product or avoid polluting the environment, say, put themselves at a competitive disadvantage vis-à-vis less socially responsible rival firms and be driven out of business? It depends on the nature of the socially responsible behaviour firms engage in. Firms that make products that get a reputation for being

unsafe, for example, will lose sales to the safer products of rivals—in other words, irresponsible firms will be disciplined by the market, while the more socially responsible firms will be rewarded.

On the other hand, socially responsible firms that voluntarily incur costs to prevent environmental pollution are likely to lose out to less socially responsible rivals because pollution control efforts do not show up in product quality where they would be rewarded by the market. Therefore, government regulation to protect the environment may be the only solution to pollution control problems, while the discipline of the market may be a more reliable and efficient way to enforce product safety. Even on the issue of product safety, however, the question is "how many injuries and lost lives does it take for the market to react against an unsafe product?" Where the public has answered "too many," government regulation has been called for, giving rise to numerous federal and provincial regulatory bodies such as the Canadian General Standards Board, Health and Welfare Canada,

and the Canada Labour Relations Board.

THE ROLE OF HUMAN NATURE

What if human nature is such that it is only realistic to expect that the main goal of business is profit? Then the relevant questions are: (1) What kinds of socially irresponsible business behaviour will be curbed by the discipline of the market, and what kinds will not? (2) Where market discipline is of questionable effectiveness, are the costs of government regulation (in terms of an increased threat to individual freedom as well as an increased tax cost) less than the costs (such as injury and loss of life) that trigger market discipline?

For Discussion

- Motorcyclists are required to wear crash helmets. Why might you expect a helmet manufacturer to differ from a motorcycle company on the two views about profit in this case?
- In Canada it is legal to sell alcoholic beverages but not marijuana. How might this distinction be justified?

represent the "best" package of government programs or present the ideological perspective on intervention that the voter prefers. The party with a majority of members elected forms the government and determines the programs that constitute their particular view of the social well-being.[3] These programs are administered through the bureaucracy of ministry departments and government agencies.[4] There is, therefore, always a good deal of controversy over the appropriate role of government versus that of markets in determining what, how, and for whom to produce.

Government, whether it is local, provincial, or federal, performs four main functions in a mixed economy: (1) It provides the legal and institutional structure in which markets operate; (2) it intervenes in the allocation of resources in

---

[3]Governments, in the sense of the party in power, come and go, while much of the government bureaucracy motors on under its own momentum. Existing policies and programs may be difficult to displace by short-term changes in the political party in power at the moment. As well, much of the policy in place has developed in an ad hoc fashion without the explicit ideological direction implied here.

[4]For an outline and analysis of administrative agencies in Canada see *Parliament and Administrative Agencies*, Law Reform Commission of Canada (study paper), 1982.

areas of the economy where public policy deems it beneficial to do so; (3) it redistributes income; and (4) it seeks to provide stability in prices, economic growth, and economic conditions generally. Of course, government actions in any one of these spheres almost invariably have implications for the others, and all of the functions involve balancing the equity-efficiency trade-off.

Legal and Institutional Structure for Markets

Even in pure market, *laissez-faire* capitalism, the government must provide for the legal definition and enforcement of contracts, property rights, and ownership. It must also establish the legal status of different forms of business organizations—from the owner-operated small business to the large corporation. It must provide a judicial system so that disputed claims between parties arising in the course of business can be settled. Government must also provide for the regulation of the supply of money, the maintenance of a system of measurement standards, and the maintenance of a police force to keep order and protect property.

You will find little disagreement anywhere as to the need for government to provide this basic legal and institutional structure. Since the turn of the century, however, the legal sanctions and constraints on the functioning of markets and the economic relationships among business, labour, and consumers have become more complex. In Canada, government has taken an active role in trying to maintain competition in markets. *The Competition Act* of 1987 was enacted after lengthy debate about the degree of competition in Canada. This act replaced the outdated and often ineffectual *Combines Investigation Act*. These laws are essentially aimed at preventing market domination by one or a small number of large firms and protecting buyers and sellers from unfair and predatory trade practices. These laws also make it illegal for firms in any particular market to collude in setting prices or to conspire to restrict competition.

On occasion governments also intervene to ensure monopoly profits. For example in the introduction of the *Drug Patent Act* of 1988, the need for profits to conduct drug research was hotly debated. Patent rights, licenses, and charters all prevent competition from eroding the profits of firms who hold these. Ostensibly the rationale for these limits on competition is that without profit protection not enough research, development, and innovation would occur.

Government intervention in the marketplace through the creation and change of certain aspects of the legal and institutional structure—regulation—has often proved beneficial. In other instances, it has not.

In Canada federal regulatory policy created and administered through parliament and its agencies has recently come under close scrutiny. The federal Conservative government pushed forward the *Agenda for Economic Renewal*, which stated that "government has become too big." Acting on the *Agenda* the Government undertook a sweeping review of the federal regulatory structure. The outcome, the Federal Regulatory Reform Strategy, was launched in the spring of 1986 and much new legislation was enacted,[5] the most controversial item of this legislation being *The Free Trade Act* of 1989.

---

[5] For details see *Regulatory Reform: Making It Work,* The Office of Privatization and Regulatory Affairs, 1988.

Resource Allocation

In addition to the legal and institutional regulatory environment, government affects resource allocation in our economy through its spending activities, its tax policies, and its own production of certain goods and services.

Government Spending

In Canada more than half of all output is produced and sold in markets. The quantity and variety of goods and services represented by this output are the result of decisions made by numerous firms and consumers—the private sector of our economy. The rest of the economy's output is the result of government (public sector) expenditure decisions. This includes all levels of government—namely, federal, provincial, and local. Though much of this output of goods and services is produced by private businesses, it is done under government contract and reflects government decisions about what to produce and for whom—highways for motorists, schools for students, and military hardware for national defense are just a few examples.

Taxation

Another way in which the government affects the allocation of resources is through its power to levy taxes. For example, we have already noted that changes in profit affect the incentive to create new capital goods. From our discussion of the production possibilities frontier in the previous chapter, we know that there is a trade-off between producing capital goods and producing goods for present consumption. In order to produce more of one kind of good, it is necessary to obtain the resources to do so by cutting back on production of the other. By changing the rate of taxation of profit, the government changes the incentive to produce capital goods relative to the incentive to produce goods for current consumption. For instance, suppose the government increases taxes on profits. This might discourage the production of capital goods relative to consumer goods.[6] Some resources might therefore be reallocated from capital goods production to consumer goods production. This is but one example of the way in which the government can affect the allocation of resources through tax policy.

The point is that any tax on the public takes wealth away from individuals and therefore away from what they would choose to do with it and puts it into the hands of the government to be spent on what is collectively determined, thereby changing the overall allocation of resources from what it would have been. In Canada tax revenues equal 33 percent of the GDP. This is below the average for all OECD countries which is 38 percent. In addition the government obtains revenues from productive activities, fees, fines, and sales equal to 6.5 percent of GDP.

---

[6]Individuals may actually save more with a fall in the net return if it is a certain sum of wealth they desire at a future date. The response of individuals to the net return (after tax) on savings and investment is an empirical question and the evidence to date is ambiguous. The net result depends on the relative sizes of the income and substitution effects of saving/investing, as these have opposite effects. These effects are analyzed in microeconomics.

Government Production of Goods and Services

Another way that the government affects resource allocation is by producing goods and services directly. There are certain kinds of goods and services that would not be produced at all if the choice were left up to the market mechanism, even though it might be acknowledged by everybody that such goods provide benefits (above their costs) for all. Such goods are called **public goods.** *An essential feature of a public good is that it cannot be provided to one person without providing it to others.* If the government provides a dam to protect your property from floods, the benefits accrue to your neighbour as well. Public goods are *not* subject to the **exclusion principle.** Any good whose benefits accrue only to those who purchase it is said to be subject to the exclusion principle. The exclusion principle applies to goods produced and sold in a market economy. You cannot consume the hamburger that I buy and eat, for example. If one can have a good without paying for it, then there is no way for producers to charge and receive a price to cover the costs of producing it. Hence, there will be no incentive for firms to produce the good in a market economy. If I build a lighthouse, there is no way I can exclude any ship at sea from benefiting from its beacon. Hence, there is no way I can charge ships at sea for its service, so I won't build it, despite the fact that shipping companies all agree that the reduction in their total economic losses due to shipwrecks far exceeds the cost of providing lighthouses. Similarly, it is difficult to produce privately and sell the services of a dam, national defense, cloud seeding, weather reports, and clean air. *Another feature of a public good is that once it is provided for one citizen, there is no additional cost to providing it for others.* This is really just another aspect of the fact that when a public good provides benefits to one, it unavoidably provides benefits to others. It costs no more to protect one ship at sea than to protect several with the same lighthouse.

A related concept to public goods is that of **externalities**. *An externality occurs when a transaction between two individuals affects a third individual or group not participating in the transaction.* The effect on the third party may be beneficial, in which case it is termed an *external benefit*, or the effect may be negative to the third party, in which case it is called an *external cost*. An example of an external cost would be a steel firm producing air pollution that raises the costs of a laundry downwind. The steel firm and its customers are the first and second parties, respectively, involved in the transaction; the laundry is the third party, bearing an external cost to the others' exchange.

There are many goods that are not by nature public goods that the government provides anyway. Examples of goods and services that can be privately produced and sold in markets but that are provided by local, provincial, or federal government are education, Medicare, police and fire protection, sewage treatment, garbage collection, bridges, and toll roads. In most of these cases, it is usually argued that there are substantial social benefits, and that if their provision were left strictly to private producers and markets, less of these goods would be produced than is desirable due to considerable external benefits in their production.

Canada is a large, sparsely settled country with most of the population having closer geographical links to the United States than to other parts of the country. To overcome this tendency, nation building has been an argument for the provision of a number of goods by the public sector. These goods include radio and television broadcasting provided by the Canadian Broadcasting Corporation (CBC), telecommunications (Telecom Canada), railroads (Canadian National Railways and Via Rail), air transport (Air Canada), mail (Canada Post), and the Trans-Canada Highway, as well as other goods. These goods—mostly communications and transportation services—have been deemed necessary in order to keep Canada linked together from east to west, reducing the (less-expensive) north-south tendencies.

Both public goods and externalities indicate failures of the market system for which government intervention may be a remedy. Much current research in economics considers whether government can improve the situation—that is, a market failure is not sufficient to warrant government intervention, the intervention must also improve the social outcome. Another line of research is an attempt at decentralized mechanisms that will provide the appropriate incentives for the agents to correct the problems (externalities) directly.

Another reason for public production recently advocated in Canada was the introduction of a nationalized firm into an oligopolist industry (a few firms competing). Petro-Canada was an example. The idea was to operate a competing firm without the objective of profit maximization in order to drive industry price down to a competitive level where no economic profit was made in the industry.[7] This was seen as an alternative to price regulation, where price regulation would be difficult to administer. Petro-Canada also had other mandates under the now scrapped National Energy Program, such as security of energy supply to Canadians for the future.

The idea to use a public company in this way was a novel and interesting one.[8] Unfortunately it was never achieved. In the initial years Petro-Canada maintained industry prices in order to accumulate the revenues necessary for expensive takeovers of existing companies. After the election of a Conservative federal government in 1984, Petro-Canada was directed to follow the industry price and maximize profits. Under this mandate it was no better or worse than other firms in the industry. Its one advantage was that the profit returned to the federal government as revenue for use in Canada, whereas in this foreign-dominated industry the profits might otherwise eventually leave Canada. Once Petro-Canada's mandate was changed, the controversy concerning its legitimate role as an instrument of government policy resurfaced. The present government, treating the firm as a profit maximizer, has decided to return the firm to private control because the government no longer feels the firm should serve the goals it was originally set up to accomplish.

> **Checkpoint 3-3**
>
> Is the postal service a public good or not? Why or why not? Should Canada Post be subsidized or should it run on a cost recovery basis? Should it be privatized (sold to private agents)? Should the legislation giving Canada Post a monopoly on letter delivery be changed?

Income Redistribution

In virtually all modern, industrialized, mixed economies there are specific government policies aimed at alleviating the hardships of poverty. If people cannot earn some minimal standard of living in the marketplace, it is generally agreed that they should be given economic assistance in some form. Whatever form

---

[7]Another reason the government chose to organize Petro-Canada was to have a window on the oil industry in order to acquire better information on the size of future oil reserves. The estimates of the oil companies had a tendency to vary with their self-interest at the particular moment.

[8]The idea is credited to Edward Clark, a Harvard Ph.D. graduate in economics who was assistant deputy minister in the the Ministry of Energy when the National Energy Program was developed under the Liberal Government of Pierre Trudeau.

it takes, this assistance makes it necessary to redistribute income from those judged to have enough to those who do not. One obvious way to do this is for the government simply to levy heavier income taxes on people in higher income brackets and transfer the money collected to those in lower brackets.

Many government transfers of income and wealth among citizens do not necessarily redistribute from the rich to the poor. For example, Family Allowance (FA) payments go to all parents regardless of income. Old Age Security (OAS) is a noncontributory pension plan—individuals do not make direct contributions to it. OAS payments are paid to any resident of forty years over 65 years of age; a multimillionaire is eligible for these benefits, and even the lowest-paid worker is obliged to pay the social security taxes used to finance these benefits. (Low-income seniors receive extra benefits in the form of Guaranteed Income Supplement payments.) Although a contributory plan, the Canada Pension Plan (CPP) redistributes as well. CPP payments to retired workers are financed by payroll taxes paid by all citizens presently working as well as by their employers. The controversy over universality is about these payments made to certain categories of people independent of their income.

Government has played a growing role in income redistribution since World War II. Federal government income outlays take the form of payments to individuals, corporations, and provincial and local governments. The payments to provincial governments include transfer payments in the form of Established Program Funding for education, Medicare, social security, and equalization to offset regional disparities. The payments to individuals include benefits to retired workers, the disabled, unemployment insurance benefits, and payments to those eligible for various welfare and special assistance programs. These payments are often referred to as *income maintenance programs* because they effectively maintain minimum income levels for the recipients. Various subsidies are also given to businesses in order to affect their location, employment, and other policies. All of these payments represent an income redistribution from taxpayers to those receiving the payments.

A good deal of the transfer of income and wealth among citizens takes the form of direct government provision of goods and services for free or at prices below cost to the citizens who use them. These are not included in the payments just described. The costs of providing such goods and services are covered by tax revenue, much of which is collected from citizens or corporations who may not themselves use these governmentally provided goods and services. Public education, Medicare, parks and recreation areas, roads, bridges, trains, airports, and public libraries are but a few examples. Again, a wealthy person might choose to use these facilities, while someone with a much lower income might use them little or not at all, even though he or she pays taxes used to subsidize the government provision of such goods and services.

Another way in which the government affects income distribution is by direct intervention in the marketplace. Well-known examples of this are governmentally enforced price supports and supply management programs in agricultural and energy markets and minimum-wage laws in labour markets. Farm price supports reflect a desire to maintain the income levels of farmers. Minimum-wage laws reflect a desire to see to it that laborers' wage levels ensure some minimum standard of living. In the case of agriculture, such direct market intervention has been criticized for unjustly favouring special interests and distorting resource allocation. It has also been charged that minimum-wage laws aggravate unemployment and contribute to poverty rather than alleviate it. This occurs by making low-value labour too highly priced for firms to hire people at minimum wage. Some argue that a direct income supplement would be more appropriate for low-wage workers.

A large amount of redistribution also takes place through the subsidization of businesses. The rate of growth in business subsidies in recent years substantially outweighs any growth in income supplements to individual Canadians. Many of these subsidies are indirect, in the form of "tax expenditures." A tax expenditure occurs when the government, for some reason, forgoes tax revenue by providing a tax deduction or credit—a tax break. Tax expenditures have been growing at a faster rate than regular government expenditures. In 1950, corporate tax raised as much revenue as personal income taxes, with corporate taxes contributing 46.4 percent of government revenues and personal income taxes contributing 47.8 percent. Since then there has been an increasing reliance on personal income taxes with corporate taxes contributing less than 13 percent and personal taxes contributing 85 percent of government revenue in 1989.

Economic Stabilization

In the previous chapter we noted the difficulties that market-oriented economies have avoiding recessions in economic activity, fluctuations in employment and GDP, and unacceptable levels of inflation. In most capitalistic mixed economies, a good deal of responsibility for avoiding these difficulties has been vested in the federal government. Government expenditure and tax changes aimed at smoothing out fluctuations in economic activity unavoidably affect resource allocation, income distribution, and even the competitive market structure of industries in which the government buys goods and lets contracts for public projects. By changing the levels of interest rates, monetary policy has similar effects on resource allocation and income distribution. The role of government as a stabilizer is taken up in macroeconomics.

Controversy About the Role of Government

In recent years there has been a growing skepticism about the ability of government to provide services to the public, give direction to the economy, and supply solutions to a number of social problems. This has led to a critical examination of how government functions in our economy, a search for the reasons why once optimistic expectations about the government's role have often not been fulfilled.

It should be emphasized that none of the following criticisms of the way government functions is necessarily a criticism of individual politicians and government bureaucrats. They respond to rewards and incentives just like people in other walks of life. These criticisms are directed at the ways in which the reward and incentive structures of our political and governmental institutions are not always geared to provide goods and services or collect the rents from publicly owned natural resources in the most economically efficient manner.

Efficiency in Government

Critics of government involvement in the economy argue that government bureaucracies by their nature do not have the built-in incentives for efficiency that exist in the typical business firm. The reward of profit and the threat of loss are absent. Moreover, it is typically difficult to measure either output or performance. It is often impossible for a government bureaucrat to show how and where he or she has saved the taxpayers money. How can one tell how efficiently the Department of Defense or a city school system is being operated? If efficient performance is hard to demonstrate, it is likely to be unrecognized and unrewarded, so why try so hard? Similarly, an inefficient performance is equally hard to detect. Because the relationship between taxpayer dollars and benefits produced is hard to establish, the incentives for efficiency are weak. The annual Auditor General's report on the blunders in government programs takes on tragic-comic proportions.

Special Interest Legislation

Special interest groups often push hard for legislation that provides special benefits for them and possibly little or no benefit for anyone else. These interest groups often get their way even when it may not serve the broader public interest. Why?

Suppose some special interest group presses for a program that will cost an individual taxpayer only a dollar. The total cost of the program may be tens of millions of dollars, but as far as the individual taxpayer is concerned, the extra dollar of taxes will hardly be noticed. For the individual taxpayer it is scarcely worth the effort to become informed about the program. However, those in the special interest group may stand to benefit substantially, so they have very strong feelings about whether the program is approved or not. Consequently, a politician who doesn't work for the special interest group's program stands to lose the group's vote in the next election and possibly a helpful financial contribution to his or her campaign as well. On the other hand, a vote for the program will probably cost the politician few if any votes among the other voters. So, the politician supports the interest group's program, whether it is in the broader public interest or not. In Canada in recent years we have seen this work in reverse. It has become very hard to reduce or discontinue a program. Those who presently benefit from a given program lobby on its behalf, even when the conditions and rationale for the program's existence have changed markedly.

Bias Toward Current-Benefit, Hidden-Cost Projects

Many politicians act morally and responsibly in their decisions about government policy, but because politicians must worry about getting reelected, there is a natural tendency for them to favour projects and programs that have immediate, highly visible benefits and less visible costs. An objective economic analysis of project A might show it to be more worthwhile than a number of other projects. But suppose project A's benefits are spread over a distant future, while tax increases will be required to cover its immediate costs. Project A is therefore likely to lack support, while other economically less worthwhile projects that have more immediate benefits and less visible costs will be pushed forward. Environmental protection projects are often of this type.

Rent Capture

A related problem in Canada of mismatched incentives occurs when many natural resources are owned publicly. The rent from publicly owned resources should go to the owners—the general public. These resources must be managed by politicians who do not necessarily gain in any improved electoral prospects when they impose royalty taxes (rent payments to land resources) on public resources. Companies benefiting by low royalties are likely to be much more supportive of the politicians who push for lower royalties. By imposing appropriate royalties on public resources, politicians only gain in that they have a proportionate share of the public benefit, while with low royalties they stand to gain more personally. Many instances of this occur—for example, low stumpage fees on harvested trees in British Columbia or royalty holidays on oil in Alberta.

Resource Utilization

How good are mixed economies at maintaining a full utilization of their available resources? The Great Depression of the 1930s, which plagued the industrialized economies of the West, led these countries to call for more government involvement in the future. In this way, these economies hoped to avoid another episode of such dramatic underemployment of resources. The ideas put forward at that time by the British economist John Maynard Keynes provided a rationale for how government intervention could prevent such a calamity. Income tax reductions and increased government expenditures to offset the fall in expenditures by businesses and consumers were among the recommended measures to be used. Most economists today are of the opinion that such government intervention would be appropriate and effective in averting another Great Depression. However, there is considerable debate and skepticism among economists as to whether such intervention has been either practicable or effective in alleviating the periodic recessions that have occurred in the postwar period.

Change, Stability, and Growth

Government intervention is justified, at least in part, as a means of promoting stability, growth, and those kinds of change that are considered desirable. How well mixed economies have succeeded is a matter of continuing debate among economists.

With regard to economic growth and stability, many economists argue that greater growth and stability have been promoted by government intervention. Others say, "Not so, the increasing growth of government has stifled the private sector with heavy personal income and corporate profits taxes." In addition, they argue, government policies have been a major cause of inflation. Debates over the pros and cons of mixed economies and the appropriateness or folly of government intervention in different areas of the economy are unending. A failure in a part of the economy to reach an efficient equitable outcome might suggest intervention, but before proceeding it is also necessary to show that government action will improve the net result. As government involvement has its own costs, the search for decentralized solutions to correct failures may be promising. We will encounter these issues again and again throughout this book.

The Exchange Flows Among Businesses, Households, and Government

To characterize a capitalistic, mixed economy in a flow diagram it is necessary to bring government into the picture. This has been done in Figure 3-3. (The term *government* as used here includes federal, provincial, and local governments.)

Government Expenditures, Taxes, and Transfers

To carry out its functions, government must hire labour and other resources owned by households. This is indicated by the counterclockwise arrow running from households to government labeled "Labour and other resources." The money payments by government for these resources are indicated by the clockwise arrow running from government to households labeled "Transfer and factor payments." The factor payments are made to cover wage, rent, and interest payments to households in exchange for labour services, buildings, and land rented to the government, and the capital provided through household holdings of government bonds. These factor payments are viewed as expenditures by the government and as income by the households. Transfers also include tax refunds. Income subsidies represent government payments to households of social insurance benefits and other benefits provided by public assistance programs and are viewed as income by the households receiving them.

To help finance its operations, the government must collect taxes from households in the form of income taxes, property taxes, and sales taxes. These tax payments by households to the government are represented by the clockwise arrow running from households to government labeled "Income and other taxes." The government also collects taxes from businesses in the form of corporate profits taxes, property taxes, and sales taxes. These tax payments to government are represented by the clockwise arrow running from businesses to government labeled "Business taxes." There is yet one other way in which government can finance its operations. That is by issuing and selling new government bonds in the financial markets. The money proceeds from these sales can be used in the same ways as tax proceeds.

The government uses receipts from bond sales along with the tax receipts from businesses and households in part to make the transfer and factor payments to households already mentioned. The government also uses these receipts to purchase goods and services from businesses. These include anything from paper clips and staples to jet airplanes and the construction of dams, highways, and buildings by private contractors. The payments for these items are represented by the clockwise arrow running from government to businesses labeled "Payments for goods and services." The provision of goods and services in exchange for these payments is indicated by the counterclockwise arrow running from businesses to government labeled "Goods and services."

FIGURE 3-3 Exchange Flows with Savings and Financial Markets and Government

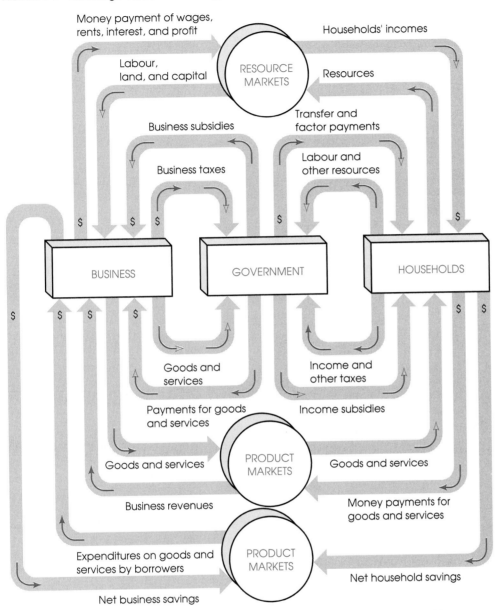

This diagram elaborates on Figure 3-2 by adding government, which is financed by taxes from businesses and households. Government uses tax proceeds to make transfer payments to households as well as to hire labour and purchase other resources from households. Government also uses tax revenue to purchase goods and services from businesses. In this way government reallocates resources and redistributes income. Also, by varying tax rates and the level of its expenditures, government can affect the size of the flows in the flow channels—that is, the level of economic activity. Figure 3-3 may be viewed as representing a closed capitalistic, mixed economy.

Government Affects Resource Allocation and Income Distribution

The taxes paid by businesses must come out of their sales revenues, while those paid by households must come out of their income. By increasing or decreasing the amount of these taxes, government can divert a larger or smaller share of the sales revenues of businesses and the income receipts of households into activities determined by government expenditures, as opposed to the market activities determined by business and household expenditures. This is an obvious way in which government affects resource allocation. Similarly, it can be seen that the government affects income distribution through the redistribution of tax proceeds to households in the form of transfer payments and income subsidies.

Government Affects the Level of Economic Activity

By changing its expenditure and tax policies, government can affect the level of overall economic activity, as represented by the flows in Figure 3-3. Consider two extreme examples. Suppose government increases income taxes on households but does not spend the increased tax proceeds. This obviously takes income from households that would otherwise have been spent on goods and services or saved and put in the financial markets, where it could have ultimately been used by some borrower to buy goods and services. Hence, the volume in the lower two flow channels of Figure 3-3 would be reduced. This would lead to a drop in sales by businesses and a consequent drop in some or all of the categories of business saving, business taxes, and income earned by households, as measured by businesses' money payments of wages, rent, interest, and profit in the upper flow channel of Figure 3-3.

Alternatively, suppose government increased expenditures on goods and services but did not raise taxes to finance these expenditures. Suppose, instead, that it financed them by simply printing money.[9] The result would be that businesses would experience an increase in the dollar volume of sales. This would lead to an increase in some or all of the categories—business saving, business taxes, and income earned by households.

Changes in the expenditure plans of businesses and households can also lead to changes in economic activity as represented by the flows in Figure 3-3. Stabilization policy is aimed at changing all or some combination of government expenditures, tax rates, and the money supply in such a way as to offset undesirable changes in the level of economic activity that may result from changes in business and household expenditure plans.

The flow diagrams are very simplified pictures of the economy. Much detail is omitted. Nonetheless, they give some idea of how the mixed economy's various decision-making units—businesses, households, and government—are linked together to form an interlocking, interdependent system.

Checkpoint 3-4

How would the flow diagram in Figure 3-3 have to be changed if it were to describe an economy such as China's?

---

[9] In Canada the government does not literally print money, but it achieves the same effect by getting the Bank of Canada to create new government bank deposits in exchange for new bonds from the government.

Summary

1. Individuals have different abilities for performing different tasks. Because of this, individuals have an incentive to specialize in production and to trade in markets the surplus, their output in excess of their own need, for the other goods they want but don't produce themselves. This incentive stems from the fact that specialization and trade make possible a larger output of goods and services than is possible if each individual tries to be self-sufficient—that is, if there is no specialization and trade.

2. The circular flow diagram illustrates the flow of goods from businesses to households through the goods market, the flow of resources from the households to the firms through the resource markets, and the counterflows of money—revenues to the firms for goods and incomes to the households for their resources.

3. There is an incentive to use money as a medium of exchange because it eliminates the need for the coincidence of wants, which is necessary for trade to take place in a barter economy. Because of this, money promotes specialization and trade, and thus makes possible a larger output of goods and services than is possible within the context of a barter system of trade.

4. A firm's costs are all those payments it must make to all resource suppliers in order to bid resources away from use in alternative lines of production of goods. Among the resources used by the firm are financial capital and entrepreneurial skills. When they are being compensated just enough to keep them from leaving and going into some other line of productive activity, we say that they are earning a normal profit. If they are earning more than this we say they are earning an economic profit.

5. Under competitive conditions economic profits will draw resources to those areas of the economy where they are most in demand. Below-normal profits in one area of the economy will cause entrepreneurial skills and financial capital to move out of that line of productive activity and into others where they can earn their opportunity cost.

6. Economic incentives for efficiency include the payments to households for the use of their resources—land, labour, and capital. These incentives promote the efficient use of the limited resources available in the economy by giving the greatest reward in the form of profitable prices for the products most desired by the households.

7. Financial markets bring together those who wish to save with those who wish to borrow. In the circular flow diagram, the financial markets receive the money flow not directly spent by households and businesses and transfer it into spending of those households and businesses that wish to borrow.

8. At minimum in any economy, government typically has a basic responsibility for maintaining law and order, regulating the nation's money supply and financial markets, and providing for the national defense, the judicial system, and uniform standards of time, weight, and measurement. In mixed economies government reallocates resources in instances where it is felt that the market mechanism gives unacceptable or undesirable outcomes; often strives to maintain competitive conditions in markets not naturally conducive to them; redistributes income in accordance with some norm of equity and concern for those who can't work or earn a minimally adequate income; and

attempts to maintain economic stability with reasonably full employment of resources.

9. One of the main reasons for the provision of goods by government is the failure of markets to provide optimum levels of certain goods. If a good is a "public good," then the exclusion principle doesn't hold and private firms cannot profitably produce the good, even though society would obtain a net benefit from its production. If externalities arise in a market then there may be too much or too little of a good produced given the social benefits and costs of its production.

10. There are several reasons why the government might not be a very efficient producer of goods and services. Government bureaucracies have a weak incentive structure due to the difficulty of measuring their output and judging their performance. Politicians often support special interest legislation because it wins them votes from interest groups without losing the votes of the remainder of the public. Politicians are subject to an incentive structure biased toward the adoption of projects and programs with highly visible immediate benefits and well-hidden costs. The incentive for politicians to capture rent from public lands is weak. Controversy also surrounds the government's intervention in the marketplace, which is sometimes intended to promote competition through antitrust policy and occasionally to rescue large corporations from bankruptcy.

11. A mixed economy and the basic economic links between its three groups of agents—businesses, households, and government—can be given a skeletal representation in a flow diagram. Such a diagram can show the flows of resources and of goods and services in exchange for money; the flows of savings into the financial markets, where they are loaned to borrowers and spent on goods and services; and the flows of taxes, transfers, and expenditures linking the government to businesses and households.

12. A mixed economy answers the questions of what, how, and for whom to produce primarily by the interaction of households and firms through the markets using economic incentives. Government intervenes in order to redistribute income more equitably, to provide for the production of certain goods such as defense, the criminal justice system, and public goods, to regulate certain aspects of the markets, to maintain the money supply, and to collect taxes in order to pay for these expenses of government.

Key Terms and Concepts

barter economy	externalities	normal profit
circular flow model	financial markets	public goods
coincidence of wants	market	retained earnings
economic profit	medium of exchange	specialization of labour
exclusion principle	nationalized industries	transfer payments

Questions and Problems

1. We have discussed specialization in terms of its economic advantages. From the labourer's standpoint, what are some of the disadvantages of specialization often heard about in the modern industrialized world?

2. We have noted that it might be possible that someone who has sandals to trade, but no need for chopped wood, might nonetheless accept the chopped wood and then later trade it for something else. In a situation such as this, where there is a lack of coincidence of wants, do you think that the sandal maker would be more, or less, willing to accept strawberries than chopped wood (given that the sandal maker wants neither and must trade them for something he or she does want)? Why? Compared to a situation where there is a coincidence of wants between a woodchopper and sandal maker, how do you think the terms of the exchange (the amount of wood needed to purchase a pair of sandals) would be different if the woodchopper wanted sandals but the sandal maker didn't want chopped wood?

3. Elaborate on the following statement: "Profits can, of course, be immoral—if they are exploitive, for example, or result from price-fixing schemes or monopolies. But most profits...are an essential and beneficial ingredient in the workings of a free-market economy."

4. Describe the nature of the role of profit that the author of the following statement must have in mind. "Today, profits, far from being too high, are still too low to ensure the nation's continued economic health. Canada in recent years has fared badly in terms of new industrial investment per capita..."

5. "Despite general agreement about the need for tremendous amounts of new capital, there is no consensus about how the money should be raised. Liberal economists generally favour more generous individual tax cuts...to stimulate consumer buying, which, in turn, creates heightened economic activity. Conservative economists... would prefer federal policies that would enable companies to keep more of their earnings either through higher depreciation allowances for the purchase of new equipment or a further lowering of the corporate tax rate."

   In Figure 3-3, where would liberal economists' policies affect the flow diagram as contrasted with those of conservative economists?

6. Describe a market where an externality occurs. Is it a consumption externality or a production externality or both? How do you think a government could rectify this externality?

7. Describe what you think would change in Canada if the government reduced its role in the economy to provision of the legal system and defense. In your view would this be an improvement or a worsening in the utilization of resources?

8. Your tuition fees cover a fraction of what it costs to provide your education. What are the arguments for raising tuition fees to equal the costs? What are the arguments for lowering tuition fees to zero?

9. Without looking at the diagrams in the chapter, draw and label all the monetary flows between business firms, households, and government and the resource, goods, and financial markets. Then check your diagram with Figure 3-3.

Chapter 4

Demand, Supply, and Price Determination

Demand and supply affect our everyday lives in numerous ways. Some of these effects are quite dramatic, especially when they have a negative impact, and this is usually when we hear about them. But most of the effects that supply and demand have on our lives are not dramatic, and thus we take little notice of them. When something is running smoothly, it is not news. Many markets function so efficiently in determining prices that accurately match the demands of consumers with the supplies of goods and services from producers that there is nothing to report. Simply put, the system works. Adam Smith's (1776) insight was recognition of the fact that prices determined by demand and supply could coordinate the economic activities of millions of people. Every day each of us uses a variety of goods and services in an effort to satisfy our wants—we buy food, we buy clothing, we buy newspapers. The typical consumer hardly gives a thought to the role that markets play in making these things possible.

In this chapter we will focus on the laws of demand and supply. We will examine the concepts of demand and supply in some detail, and we will consider how demand and supply interact to determine the equilibrium price at which the quantity of a good or resource supplied is just sufficient to satisfy the demand for it. In addition to getting a better understanding of how individual markets work, we will begin to see how a *system* of markets allocates resources through market-determined prices.

Demand Theory

In this section we want to examine in detail the law of demand and how the demand curve is determined. We will see how individual demand curves can be combined to give the market demand curve, which represents the entire market demand for a particular product, resource, or service. Finally, we will examine the important distinction between shifts in the position of a demand curve and movements along it.

Law of Demand

The **law of demand** *is a theory or model about the relationship between the quantities of a good a buyer is both willing and able to purchase per period of time at each alternative price that might be charged for the good.* Notice that we emphasize the ability to pay for the good as well as the desire or willingness to have it. Your ability to pay is as important as your desire for the good, because in economics we are interested in explaining and predicting actual behaviour in the marketplace. Your desires for goods can never be observed in the marketplace because you can't buy more than you are *able* to pay for. At a given price for a good, we are only interested in the amount demanded by the buyer that can effectively be backed by a purchase. The law of demand hypothesizes that the lower is the price charged for a good, resource, or service, the larger will be the quantity demanded per unit of time. Conversely, the higher is the price charged, the smaller will be the quantity demanded per unit of time—all other things remaining the same.

For example, the law of demand predicts that the lower the price of steak, the more steak you will desire and be able to purchase per year—all other things remaining the same. The law of demand is repeatedly confirmed by observed

---

LEARNING OBJECTIVES

After reading this chapter, you will be able to:

1. Formulate and explain the law of demand.
2. Define and differentiate the demand schedule and curve, and graph a demand curve from a demand schedule.
3. State and explain the five determinants of demand.
4. Define and distinguish between *substitute, complementary,* and *unrelated* goods.
5. Define and distinguish between *normal* and *inferior* goods.
6. Distinguish between individual and market demand curves and construct the market demand curve from the individuals' demands.
7. Demonstrate and distinguish the difference between shifts in the position of a demand curve and movements along a fixed demand curve.
8. Formulate and explain the law of supply and graph a supply curve from a supply schedule.
9. State and explain the five determinants of supply.
10. Demonstrate and distinguish the difference between shifts in the position of a supply curve and movements along a fixed supply curve.
11. With the use of a graph, show how demand and supply interact to mutually determine equilibrium price and equilibrium quantity (also called *equilibrium*).
12. Explain, and illustrate with supply and demand graphs, a shortage situation and a surplus situation.
13. Using comparative statics, demonstrate how changes in the exogenous variables disturb the existing market equilibrium and result in the establishment of a new market equilibrium.

behaviour in the marketplace. Businesses have sales (i.e., they cut prices), and the amounts of a good they sell per period increases. If the price of steak goes up, the amount purchased per unit of time decreases. Why is this? There are two basic reasons. First, for most goods, there are other goods that may be used to satisfy very nearly the same desires—these goods are called *substitutes*. For example, when the price of steak goes up, if the prices of pork chops, lamb chops, and hamburger remain unchanged, then all these kinds of meats are now *relatively* cheaper compared to steak. Hence, buyers will purchase more of them and less of steak. Second, if the price of something we are buying regularly changes, it is *as if* our income has changed. For example, if the price of going to the movies falls we may feel more wealthy and go to more movies than before.

Individual Demand

The inverse relationship between the price of a good and the quantity of the good demanded per period of time can be depicted in a table, as a graph, or in algebraic terms. Suppose we consider an individual's demand for hamburger. Table 4-1 shows the number of kilograms of hamburger that the individual will demand per month at each of several different prices. This table is referred to as a **demand schedule**. Note that the higher the price, the smaller the quantity demanded per month. Conversely, the lower the price, the greater the quantity that will be demanded per month. Why? Again, because the higher the price of hamburger, the greater the incentive to cut back on consumption of it and eat other kinds of food instead—assuming that all other things remain the same. *Relative* to hamburger, other kinds of food become cheaper to eat as the price of hamburger rises. Conversely, more hamburger will be demanded when successively lower prices are charged for it, since it will become less and less expensive relative to other kinds of food.

The Demand Curve (Constructing a Graph)

So far, we have been using words to explain how the law of demand works. But when we come to the point of relating the theory to data obtained through research, the use of graphs is of considerable help. In the case of the law of demand, we noted that we would be looking at two variables, price and quantity demanded. In economics, it is customary to use the vertical axis to measure

**TABLE 4-1   An Individual's Demand for Hamburger
(Hypothetical Data)**

Price per Kilogram ($)	Quantity Demanded (Kilograms per Month)
5	1.0
4	2.0
3	3.0
2	4.5
1	6.5

price. Quantity demanded, therefore, is measured along the horizontal axis. What does this mean in terms of our investigation into the demand for hamburger? We now have to find out what numbers to use on each axis. In other words, we must determine how much hamburger is demanded at various prices. Let's suppose that our research into the hamburger demand of one consumer comes up with the data given in Table 4-1. We can now label the vertical axis "Price per kilogram" and the horizontal axis "Quantity demanded (in kilograms per month)," as shown in Figure 4-1. (These labels correspond to the column headings in Table 4-1.) We divide the vertical axis evenly into units representing $1 increases in price. We divide the horizontal axis evenly into units representing one-kilogram increases in quantity demanded. Our next task is to find the points on the graph corresponding to the quantity demanded per month and the price per kilogram of hamburger for each of the five pairs of numbers given in Table 4-1. If we plot these price and quantity combinations on the graph, we obtain the **demand curve** D shown in Figure 4-1. Economists frequently represent the demand for a good by use of a demand curve.

Demand Determinants: The Other Things That Remain the Same

When we draw a demand curve such as that in Figure 4-1, we emphasize the way in which the price of a good determines the quantity of it demanded. The price of the good is thereby singled out as the determining factor. This is done by assuming all other things are said to be equal, or remain the same—the *ceteris paribus* condition. *The important point is this: Movement along the demand curve means that only the price of the good has changed and this change has caused a change in the quantity demanded. All other things are assumed to remain unchanged.* What are these other things? They include (1) the prices of all other goods, (2) the individual's income, (3) the individual's expectations about the future, (4) the individual's preferences, and (5) the total number of consumers. A change in one or more of these other things will change the data in Table 4-1. Therefore, the position of the demand curve in Figure 4-1 will be shifted. Such a shift in the demand

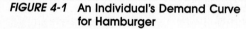

FIGURE 4-1   **An Individual's Demand Curve for Hamburger**

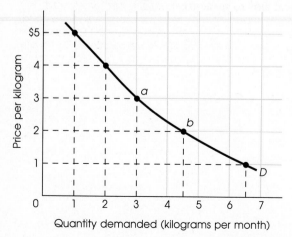

Quantity demanded (kilograms per month)

The individual's demand curve for hamburger is plotted here using the data from Table 4-1. The curve slopes downward from left to right reflecting the law of demand, which says that the quantity demanded of a good by an individual will increase the lower is its price. A change in the price of the good causes a change in the quantity demanded and is represented by a movement along the demand curve. For example, if the price changes from $3 per kilogram to $2 per kilogram, the quantity demanded increases from 3 to 4.5 kilograms per month. This is represented by the movement from *a* to *b* along the demand curve *D*.

curve is called a *change in demand*. A movement along a fixed demand curve is referred to as a *change in the quantity demanded*.

Prices of All Other Goods

We may classify all other goods according to their relationship to the good for which the demand curve is drawn, say good *X*. Other goods are either substitutes for *X*, complements of *X*, or basically unrelated to *X*.

Substitute Good.   A good is a substitute for *X* to the extent that it can satisfy similar needs or desires. Different substitute goods will, of course, vary in the extent to which they satisfy the needs or desires that *X* does. T-bone steak is a closer substitute for sirloin steak than are lamb chops, although both T-bone steak and lamb chops typically would be regarded as substitutes for sirloin steak. *When the price of a substitute good for good X rises, the demand curve for good X will shift rightward.* This is so because when the price of the substitute rises, it becomes cheaper to use *X* instead of the substitute good. For example, suppose initially that the demand curve for hamburger is *D* in Figure 4-2. Now suppose the price of a substitute, chicken, rises. This will cause the individual's demand curve to shift rightward from *D* to D_1. This means that at *any* given price of hamburger (measured on the vertical axis of Figure 4-2), the demand for hamburger (measured on the horizontal axis) will now be larger as a result of the increase in price of chicken.

The opposite is also true. When the price of a substitute for good *X* falls, the demand curve for good *X* will shift leftward. This shift occurs because when the price of the substitute *falls*, it becomes relatively more expensive to use *X* instead of the substitute good. For example, a fall in the price of chicken causes a leftward shift of the demand curve in Figure 4-2, such as from *D* to D_2. Note that substitutes need not be obvious. Home insulation is a substitute for heating fuels. If fuel prices rise, homeowners may buy more insulation.

FIGURE 4-2   Shifts in an Individual's Demand for Hamburger

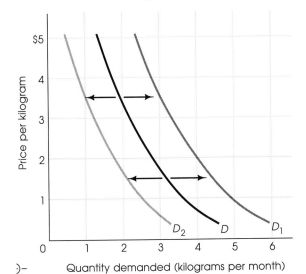

The position of the demand curve is given by the determinants of demand. These are the prices of all other goods, the individual's money income, the individual's expectations about the future, and the individual's preferences. Changes in any of these will cause a change in demand, which is represented by a shift in the demand curve either rightward or leftward. *Warning:* Do not confuse the concept of a *change in demand*, represented by a shift in the demand curve, with the concept of a *change in the quantity demanded*, represented by movement along a fixed demand curve such as that described by the movement from *a* to *b* in Figure 4-1.

Complementary Good.   A good is a complement to good X (or a *complementary good*) to the extent that it is used jointly with good X. For example, gasoline and tires are complements to each other. So are hockey skates and hockey sticks, compact disks and CD players, and salad dressing and lettuce. *When the price of a good that is a complement to good X falls, the demand curve for good X will shift rightward.* This shift occurs because the complementary good is now less expensive to use and therefore more of it will be demanded. More of good X will be demanded as well, because it is used jointly with the complement. For example, a complementary good to hamburger is hamburger buns. If the price of the buns falls, the cost of a hamburger in a bun will be less. This will cause the demand curve D for hamburger to shift to the right in Figure 4-2—to a position such as D_1 for instance. At *any* given price of hamburger, the demand for hamburger will be greater.

The opposite is also true. When the price of a good that is complementary to good X rises, the demand curve for good X will shift leftward. The complementary good is now more expensive to use, and therefore less of it will be demanded. Less of good X will be demanded because, again, it is used jointly with the complement. In Figure 4-2 a rise in the price of hamburger buns will cause D to shift leftward to a position such as D_2. It should be noted that goods are either complements or substitutes depending on these relationships between the price of one good and the demand for the other, *not* because someone suggests they should be consumed jointly or in substitution for one another.

Finally, some goods are basically *unrelated* to good X in that it would be very difficult to classify them as either substitutes or complements for X. In this sense toothpaste seems basically unrelated to garden clippers, or pears to combs, or tennis balls to ballpoint pens. Changes in the prices of goods unrelated to good X do not shift the demand curve for X.

Income

Another variable assumed constant when we move along an individual's demand curve is the individual's money income. How does a change in the individual's income affect the individual's demand curve for a particular good? The answer depends on the nature of the good. Basically we may distinguish between two types of goods in this respect: normal goods and inferior goods.

Normal Good.   A normal good is one that most people typically want more of as their income goes up. Such things as household appliances, travel, and medical services are examples. An individual's demand curve for a normal good will shift rightward when the individual's income rises. Conversely, when the individual's income falls, the demand curve will shift leftward.

Inferior Good.   An inferior good is one that an individual will demand more of at lower income levels than at higher income levels. For example, it has been observed that poor people tend to eat more potatoes and bread than do people in higher income brackets. Evidence suggests that people tend to cut back on their consumption of such foods as their income rises above a certain level. An individual's demand curve for an inferior good will shift leftward as income rises. Conversely, as an individual's income falls, the individual's demand curve for an inferior good will shift rightward.

Suppose that the individual in Figure 4-2 is a student and that hamburger is a normal good. If the student's income were to rise as a result of an increase in a scholarship stipend, the student's demand for hamburger would rise from D to D_1.

Expectations

Among the other things assumed equal or constant when we move along an individual's demand curve are the individual's expectations about all things relevant to his or her economic situation. For example, suppose that the individual expects the price of hamburger to be higher in the future. The individual therefore wants to buy more now, at a relatively lower price, and store it in order to avoid paying a higher price for it later. As a result, the demand curve D shifts rightward to a position such as D_1 in Figure 4-2.

Preferences

Preferences are another thing assumed constant when we move along an individual's demand curve. If a person suddenly develops a sweet tooth, that person's preferences will have changed. This will be reflected in a rightward shift in that person's demand curve for candy. Conversely, several painful sessions at the dentist might cause you to lose your preference for candy. In that event your demand curve for candy would shift leftward.

Market Demand: The Sum of Individual Demands

The **market demand curve** for a good is obtained by summing up all the individual demand curves for that good. To illustrate the simplest possible case, suppose that there are only two individuals who have a demand for hamburger. The first individual's demand is that given in Table 4-1. These numbers are repeated in Table 4-2, along with the second individual's demand for hamburger at each of the five prices listed. The market demand, or total demand, for hamburger is the sum of the quantities demanded by each individual at every price. The sums obtained in this way at each of five of these prices are shown in the last column of Table 4-2. Using the data from Table 4-2, we construct the individual demand curves in Figure 4-3, along with the market demand curve, which is the summation of these individual demand curves.

TABLE 4-2   The Market Demand for Hamburger: Two Individual Buyers (Hypothetical Data)

Price per Kilogram	First Individual's Demand		Second Individual's Demand		Total Market Demand
$5	1.0	+	.5	=	1.5
4	2.0	+	1.5	=	3.5
3	3.0	+	2.5	=	5.5
2	4.5	+	3.5	=	8.0
1	6.5	+	4.5	=	11.0

Quantity Demanded per Month (in kilograms)

FIGURE 4-3 The Sum of the Individual Demand Curves Gives the Market Demand Curve

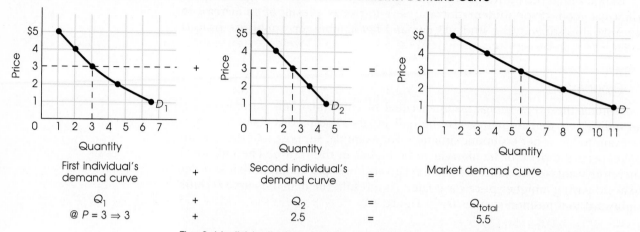

First individual's   +   Second individual's   =   Market demand curve
demand curve   demand curve

Q_1 + Q_2 = Q_{total}

@ $P = 3 \Rightarrow 3$ +   2.5   =   5.5

The first individual's demand curve D_1 and the second individual's demand curve D_2 are constructed from their individual demand data in Table 4-2. The market demand curve D is equal to the sum of the individual demand curves and is constructed from the total market demand data in Table 4-2.

For example, at a price of $3 per kilogram the quantity demanded by the first individual is 3 kilograms and the quantity demanded by the second individual is 2.5 kilograms. Therefore, the total quantity demanded at $3 for these two individuals is 5.5 kilograms. In general $Q_1 + Q_2 = Q_{total}$ at each price level.

Number of Buyers

Because market demand curves are the sum of individual demand curves, they are subject to the same determinants and are affected in the same way as the individual curves are by changes in those determinants. There is one additional determinant of a market demand curve, however, and that is the number of individual demand curves or buyers that enter into the summation. An increase in the number of buyers in the market will cause the market demand curve to shift rightward. Conversely, a decrease will cause it to shift leftward.

Changes in Quantity Demanded versus Shifts in Demand

Warning: One of the most common areas of confusion in economics concerns the distinction between movement along a demand curve versus shifts in the position of the demand curve. Movement along a demand curve represents a change in the price of the good under consideration and the associated change in the quantity of the good demanded, and nothing else. All other determinants of demand (the exogenously determined variables) are assumed to remain the same. For example, when the price of hamburger is changed from $3 to $2 per kilogram in Figure 4-1, the quantity of hamburger demanded increases from 3 kilograms to 4.5 kilograms per month. This is represented by the movement from point *a* to point *b* along the demand curve *D*. By convention, when we simply refer to *a change in the quantity demanded of a good*, we mean *a movement along a fixed demand curve*, such as that from *a* to *b* in Figure 4-1.

Checkpoint 4-2

If the price of peas were to rise, what do you think this would do to the demand curve for lima beans? If the price of pretzels were to fall, what do you think this would do to the demand curve for beer? What would it do to the demand curve for pretzels? Would we say that there is a change in the demand for pretzels or a change in the quantity of pretzels demanded? If the price of hamburger buns went up, what do you think this would do to the demand curve for hamburgers?

In contrast, a change in any other variable that is a determinant of demand will cause the position of the demand curve to change in the manner shown in Figure 4-2. By convention, when we simply refer to *a change in demand* we mean *a shift in the position of the demand curve.* When the demand curve for a good shifts rightward, more of that good will be demanded at every possible price. When the demand curve for a good shifts leftward, less of that good will be demanded at every possible price. A change in demand results from a change in one or more of the five determinants of demand.

Summary of Demand

We can summarize the previous discussion of demand theory quite concisely using algebraic notation.[1] The demand schedule and demand curve for some good X can be stated in algebraic form as:

$$Qd_X = f(P_X) \text{ceteris paribus}$$

This statement is quite general, saying only that the quantity demanded of some good X depends upon its price. If individuals were asked what they would be willing and able to buy at alternative prices, we could collect this data in a *demand schedule* like the one depicted in Table 4-2.[2] This could be graphed to obtain *demand curves* like those depicted in Figure 4-3. The inverse relationship between P_X and Qd_X is illustrated by the negative slope:

$$\text{Slope} = \frac{\Delta Qd_X}{\Delta P_X} < 0$$

However, the demand for X is dependent on the other determinants as well as on the price of X. When we asked people what they would buy at alternative prices, they answered knowing their own income, preferences, prices of related goods, and their current expectations. This more complex relationship can be expressed as:

$$D_x = F(P_X, P_c, P_s, Y, E_B, \textit{Pref}, N_B)$$

This statement lists all of the determinants of demand. In the statement $Qd_X = f(P_X)$, the other things that are assumed to remain the same are (1) prices of all other goods—complements (P_c) and substitutes (P_s), (2) money income (Y), (3) buyers' expectations (E_B), (4) preferences (*Pref*), and (5) the number of buyers (N_B). If we were to ask the same individuals what quantities they would buy at alternative prices *after* any of these other variables had changed, then we would obtain a different demand schedule and curve—the demand curve will shift. The predicted shifts for an *increase* in any of the other (exogenous) variables are depicted in Table 4-3. For an exercise, fill in Table 4-3 for a *decrease* in any of these exogenous variables.

---

[1] For those students who prefer the verbal description of demand theory, this section is not necessary for a thorough understanding of the theory. It is offered here, as a concise formulation of the previous (rather lengthy) discussion, for the more mathematically inclined student.

[2] Surveys are not usually conducted in order to find demand curves because what people say they will do is often not reliable, and we are interested in their actual demand. Demand curves are usually estimated from actual sales data.

TABLE 4-3   Summary of Shifts in a Demand Curve Caused by Increases in the Exogenous Variables

Increase in	Sign of Demand Change	Shift in the Demand Curve
P_s	+	Rightward
P_c	−	Leftward
Y (Normal good)	+	Rightward
Y (Inferior good)	−	Leftward
E_B	?	Depends on situation
$Pref$	+	Rightward
N_B	+	Rightward

Supply Theory

Given that there are demands for goods, what is the nature of the process that determines how those demands will be met? To answer this question we must first have an understanding of the law of supply and of the concept of a supply curve and its determinants.

Law of Supply

The law of supply is a statement about the relationship between the quantities of a good a supplier is willing and able to offer for sale per period of time at each of the different possible prices at which that good might be sold. For example, we say to our supplier: "Suppose the good can be sold at a price of such and such dollars per unit. How many units of the good would you be willing and able to produce and offer for sale per unit of time?" The supplier answers and we write down the number of units along with the price we quoted to the supplier. Then we repeat the question exactly *except* that now we quote a somewhat higher price. We observe that the higher is the price, the larger is the quantity the supplier is willing and able to supply for sale per unit of time. And, of course, the lower is the price, the smaller is the quantity that is offered. This observed relationship is the **law of supply.** *The law of supply states that suppliers will supply larger quantities of a good at higher prices than at lower prices, ceteris paribus.*

The Supply Curve

Suppose that a supplier whom we have been questioning produces hamburger. Table 4-4 lists some of the answers that the supplier gave in response to our questions. This table is a **supply schedule.** If we plot the data of Table 4-4 on a graph, we obtain this supplier's supply curve. As in Figure 4-1, we measure the price per unit (a kilogram) on the vertical axis and the number of units (kilograms) on the horizontal axis. The resulting curve S is shown in Figure 4-4. We have plotted only the five price and quantity combinations. At all the possible prices in between, we presumably could have filled in the whole curve as shown by the solid line connecting the five plotted points. You may view the supply curve in different ways. **The individual supply curve** *indicates the quantities of the*

TABLE 4-4 An Individual Supply of Hamburger
(Hypothetical Data)

Price per Kilogram ($)	Quantity Supplied (kilograms per month)
5	1,200
4	1,100
3	900
2	600
1	200

good the supplier is willing to provide per period of time at different possible prices, ceteris paribus. Or alternatively, we may say it shows what prices are necessary in order to give the supplier the incentive to provide various quantities of the good per period of time.

The shape of the supply curve clearly shows that as the price of the good rises, a supplier supplies more of the good; as the price falls, a supplier supplies less of the good. There is a direct relationship between the price of the good and the quantity supplied. Why is this? Movement along a supply curve always assumes that all other things will remain the same. Among other things, the prices of all other resources and goods are assumed to remain the same, including the prices of the inputs used by the supplier. Thus, the profit that can be earned from producing a good will almost certainly increase as the price of the good rises. The supplier has a greater incentive to produce more of the good. This is one basic reason why a supply curve slopes upward to the right. Another is the fact that beyond some point most production processes run into increasing production costs per unit of output. This is because certain inputs such as plants and equipment cannot be increased in a short period of time. Hence, as the

FIGURE 4-4 **An Individual Producer's Supply of Hamburger**

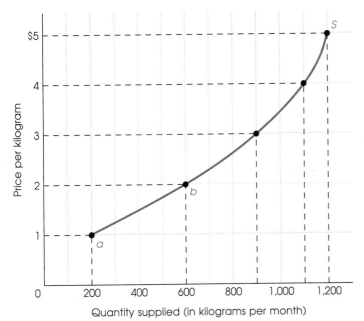

An individual producer's supply curve for hamburger is plotted here using the data from Table 4-4. The curve slopes upward from left to right reflecting the law of supply, which says that suppliers will supply more of a good the higher is its price. A change in the price of the good causes a change in the quantity supplied and is represented by a movement along the supply curve. For example, if price changes from $1 per kilogram to $2 per kilogram, the quantity supplied increases from 200 kilograms per month to 600 kilograms per month. This is represented by the movement from *a* to *b* along the supply curve *S*.

producer increases output by using more of the readily variable inputs, such as labour and materials, fixed plant and equipment capacity causes congestion and bottlenecks. Productive efficiency drops, and the cost of additional units of output rises. Therefore, producers must receive a higher price to produce these additional units.

Consider the individual producer's supply curve for hamburger shown in Figure 4-4. Assuming that the prices of all other resources and goods are constant, if the price per kilogram is raised from $1 to $2, it becomes relatively more profitable to produce hamburger. In this instance, the price increase is just sufficient to make it worthwhile to employ the additional resources necessary to increase production from 200 kilograms per month to 600 kilograms per month. This is indicated by the move from point *a* to point *b* on the supply curve. Similarly, successively higher prices make it even more profitable to produce hamburger, and the quantity supplied of hamburger will be even larger.

Suppose that there are 100 producers of hamburger, each of whom has a supply curve identical to that of Figure 4-4. At each price per kilogram listed in Table 4-4, the quantity of hamburger supplied by the sum of all producers is simply 100 times the amount supplied by one producer. Using these data, Figure 4-5 shows the market or industry supply curve S for hamburger. Note that the units on the horizontal axis of Figure 4-5 are a hundred times larger than those on the horizontal axis of Figure 4-4.

Supply Determinants: The Other Things That Remain the Same

When we draw a supply curve such as *S* in Figure 4-5, we emphasize the way in which the price of the good determines the quantity of it supplied. As with a demand curve, the price of the good is singled out as the determining factor and

---

FIGURE 4-5   Shifts in the Market Supply Curve for Hamburger

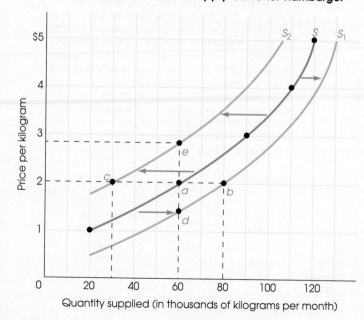

Quantity supplied (in thousands of kilograms per month)

The position of the supply curve is established by the determinants of supply. These are the prices of factors of production, technology, the prices of other goods, the number of suppliers, and the suppliers' expectations about the future. Changes in any of these will cause a change in supply, which is represented by a rightward or leftward shift in the supply curve.

Warning: Do not confuse the concept of a *change in supply,* represented by a shift in the supply curve, with the concept of a *change in the quantity supplied,* represented by movement along a fixed supply curve such as that described by the movement from *a* to *b* in Figure 4-4.

all other things are assumed to be unchanging. These other things—the exogenously determined variables—include (1) the prices of resources and other factors of production, (2) technology, (3) the prices of other goods, (4) the suppliers' expectations, and (5) the number of suppliers. If one or more of these things change, the supply curve will shift.

Prices of Resources

As we saw in Chapter 1, all production processes require inputs of labour services, raw materials, fuels, and other resources and goods. These inputs to a production process are frequently referred to as the **factors of production.** The supplier of a good has to purchase these factors in order to produce the good.

Suppose now that the price of one or more of the factors of production should fall—that is, one or more of the input prices that were assumed to be constant when we drew S now changes to a lower level. Hence, at each possible price of the good, suppliers will find it profitable to produce a larger amount of the good than they were previously willing to supply. The supply curve will therefore shift rightward to a position such as S_1 in Figure 4-5. Conversely, if one or more of the input prices should rise, the cost of production will now be higher and producers will not be willing to supply as much at each possible price of the good. The supply curve will therefore shift leftward to a position such as S_2 in Figure 4-5.

For example, if producers could sell hamburger for $2 a kilogram, they would be willing to supply 60,000 kilograms of hamburger per month. This price and quantity-supplied combination is represented by point a on the market supply curve S in Figure 4-5. Suppose that the price of one or more inputs falls so that the market supply curve shifts rightward to S_1. Now a price of $1.50 per kilogram is sufficient to induce suppliers to produce 60,000 kilograms of hamburger per month, as indicated by point d on S_1. However, because they are receiving $2 per kilogram, they are encouraged to expand output even more until they have moved up the supply curve S_1 from point d to point b. Here they are producing 80,000 kilograms per month. At point b, the price of $2 per kilogram is just sufficient to induce producers to supply this quantity of hamburger per month.

Alternatively, suppose that the price of one or more inputs should rise so that the supply curve shifts leftward from S to S_2. Now a price of $2.80 per kilogram is necessary to induce suppliers to produce 60,000 kilograms of hamburger per month, as indicated by point e on S_2. However, if producers are receiving only $2 per kilogram, they will reduce output until they have moved back down the supply curve S_2 from point e to point c, where they will produce 30,000 kilograms per month. Once again, at point c the price of $2 per kilogram is just sufficient to induce suppliers to produce this level of output and no more.

Prices of Other Goods

Along a fixed supply curve, it is also assumed that the prices of other goods, which the firm could produce, are unchanged. Why do we distinguish between the prices of other goods the firm might produce and the prices of factors of production? The prices of factors of production refer only to the goods used in the production of the good for which the supply curve is drawn. The prices of other goods we now refer to are all the other goods not used in the production of the good for which the supply curve is drawn.

Factors of production are attracted to those production activities where they are paid the highest prices. The higher is the price that the producer gets for the good produced with those factors, the greater will be his or her willingness to pay high prices for those factors. Hence, if the price of milk rises relative to the price of hamburger, farmers will use less of their pastureland for grazing beef cattle in order to make it available for grazing dairy cattle. The opportunity cost of using pasture to produce the beef used in hamburger has effectively risen because the value of that pasture in its alternative use of producing milk has risen. Factors must be paid their opportunity cost if they are to be retained in a particular productive activity. That is, the price that must be paid a factor input must be at least as high as what it could earn in an alternative activity or the factor will be transferred into another line of business. As the price of pastureland will go up because of its increased value in milk production, the cost of using it in beef production will rise. The supply curve for hamburger will then shift leftward, such as from S to S_2 in Figure 4-5. To induce hamburger producers to supply any given quantity of hamburger, the price of a kilogram of hamburger will have to be higher. Why? Because it is necessary to cover the increased cost of pastureland, which is now more expensive to use because of its increased value in production due to the rise in the price of milk.

Technology

Any production process uses some form of technology, whether it involves digging gardens in suburban Toronto with shovels or producing energy-efficient housing in Saskatoon. The term **technology** refers to the production methods used to combine resources of all kinds, including labour, to produce goods and services. The history of the human race is in no small way a history of the advancement of technology.

This advancement has been characterized by an increase in the ability of humans to produce goods through an increase in productivity. Productivity is often measured as output produced per labour hour used in the production process. Increases in productivity are then taken to mean increases in output per labour hour. Because technological advance increases productivity, it lowers the cost of producing goods, *ceteris paribus*. Suppose, for example, that there is a technological advance in the technique used to produce hamburger, such as the development of electric meat grinders. This lowers the cost of producing hamburger. Suppose that the position of the supply curve in Figure 4-5 is at S before the technological advance. The advance will cause the supply curve to shift rightward to a position such as S_1. At every level of output the price necessary to induce suppliers to produce that output level will now be lower, because costs will be lower. Remember that whenever we speak of movement along a fixed supply curve, the state of technology is assumed to be unchanged.

Number of Suppliers

When we constructed the market or industry supply curve S in Figure 4-5, we did it by assuming that there were a hundred identical individual suppliers, each with a supply curve like that shown in Figure 4-4. Summing the individual supply curves horizontally gave us the market supply curve S. If there had been more suppliers, the market supply curve would have been further to the right at a position such as S_1. It follows from these observations that when more suppliers enter the industry, the aggregate supply curve will shift to the right. When suppliers leave the industry, it will shift to the left. When we speak of movement along a market supply curve, it is assumed that the number of suppliers does not change.

Suppliers' Expectations

The term *suppliers' expectations* refers to the expectations suppliers have about anything that they think affects their economic situation. For example, if garment manufacturers expect a strike to stop their production in a few months, they may attempt to supply more now so that stores can build up their inventories to tide them over—the garment industry's supply curve would shift rightward. If suppliers of a good expect its price to be higher in a few months, they may be less willing to offer it now because they expect to be able to sell it at a higher price later—the industry's supply curve would shift leftward in the current market because of this future price expectation. Changes in expectations will cause the supply curve to shift in one direction or the other, depending on the particular situation. However, for any movement along a supply curve, expectations are assumed to remain unchanged.

Changes in Quantity Supplied versus Shifts in Supply

Warning: Along with our earlier warning about the demand curve, another common confusion in economics concerns the distinction between movement along a supply curve versus shifts in the supply curve. Movement along a supply curve illustrates the change in the amount firms are willing and able to offer for sale because of a change in the price of the good, *ceteris paribus*. By convention, when we simply refer to *a change in the quantity of a good supplied*, we mean *a movement along a fixed supply curve*, such as that from *d* to *b* on *S* in Figure 4-5.

A change in one or more of the five determinants of supply discussed earlier will cause the supply curve to shift in the manner shown in Figure 4-5. By contrast, movement along a fixed supply curve always assumes these five things remain unchanged. By convention, unless we say otherwise, when we simply refer to *a change in supply*, we mean *a shift in the position of the supply curve*. When the supply curve for a good shifts rightward, more of that good will be supplied at every price. When the supply curve shifts leftward, less of that good will be supplied at every price. A change in supply results from a change in one or more of the five determinants of supply.

Summary of Supply

To summarize supply theory to this point, we can state the supply schedule and supply curve for some good *X* in algebraic form as:

$$Q_{SX} = f(P_X) ceteris \ paribus$$

This statement is quite general, saying only that the quantity supplied of some good *X* depends upon its price. If individuals were asked what they would be

---

Checkpoint 4-3

If wages go up, what effect will this have on the supply curve *S* in Figure 4-5? If someone develops an improved process for fattening cattle to be used to make hamburger, what effect will this have on the supply curve *S* in Figure 4-5? Suppose that the price of lamb were to rise. Would we refer to the effect of this on *S* in Figure 4-5 as a "change in the supply" or as a "change in the quantity supplied" of hamburger? Explain the economic process by which farmland used to produce wheat becomes converted into factory property for the production of VCRs.

**TABLE 4-5   Summary of Shifts in a Supply Curve Caused by *Increases*
in the Exogenous Variables**

Increase in	Sign of Supply Change	Shift in the Supply Curve
P_Y	?	Depends on the good Y
C	−	Leftward
E_S	?	Depends on the situation
Tech	+	Rightward
N_S	+	Rightward

willing and able to sell at alternative prices, we could collect this data in a *supply schedule* like the one depicted in Table 4-4. This in turn could be graphed to obtain the *supply curve* depicted in Figure 4-4. The direct relationship between P_X and Qs_X is illustrated by the positive slope:

$$\text{Slope} = \frac{\Delta Qs_X}{\Delta P_X} > 0$$

The supply for X is dependent on the other determinants as well as the price of X. When we asked producers what they would sell at alternative prices they answered knowing the prices of resources, prices of other goods, the technology appropriate to the production of the good or service they are offering, and their own income and other expectations. This relationship can be expressed as:

$$S_x = F(P_X, P_Y, C, E_S, Tech, N_S)$$

This statement lists all of the determinants of supply including the number of suppliers (N_S). In the relationship of quantity supplied to the price, $Qs_X = f(P_X)$, the other things that are assumed to remain the same are (1) prices of all other goods (P_Y), (2) prices of resources (C), (3) seller's expectations (E_S), (4) technology (*Tech*), and (5) the number of sellers (N_S). If we were to ask the same individuals what quantities they would offer for sale at all alternative prices *after* any of these other variables had changed then we would obtain a different supply schedule and curve—the supply curve will shift. The predicted shifts for an *increase* in any of the other (exogenous) variables are depicted in Table 4-5. For an exercise fill in Table 4-5 for a *decrease* in any of these exogenous variables.

Market Equilibrium: Interaction of Supply and Demand

As any armchair economist knows, supply and demand are fundamental to economic analysis. Like the two blades of a pair of scissors, both are necessary before any useful result can be achieved. Supply and demand interact mutually to determine the price at which the quantity sellers are willing and able to supply exactly equals the quantity buyers are willing and able to buy at that price. When the price and quantity are established, the market is said to be *in equilibrium*. In equilibrium there is no tendency for the price and quantity to change.

Equilibrium Price and Quantity

To see how equilibrium price and quantity are determined in a market, consider again our hypothetical example of the market demand and supply for hamburger. Table 4-6 contains the market supply schedule on which the market supply curve S of Figure 4-5 is based. It also contains the market demand schedule that determines the market demand curve for hamburger. In this case, the market demand schedule has been obtained by supposing that there are 20,000 individual buyers in the market. Each of these buyers is assumed to have an individual demand schedule like that given in Table 4-1. (That table contained the data for the individual demand curve of Figure 4-1.) The market quantity demand data of Table 4-6 thus equals 20,000 times the individual quantity demand data given in Table 4-1.

Market Adjustment: Price Above Equilibrium Price

Observe in Table 4-6 that at a price of $5 per kilogram suppliers would supply the market 120,000 kilograms of hamburger per month, column (2). Buyers, however, would only demand 20,000 kilograms per month, column (3). At this price, there would be an **excess supply** over demand, or a **surplus** of 100,000 kilograms of hamburger, column (4). A price of $5 per kilogram serves as a relatively strong incentive to suppliers on the one hand, and a relatively high barrier to buyers on the other. If suppliers produce the 120,000 kilograms, they will find that they can sell only 20,000. They will be stuck with 100,000 kilograms. This surplus will serve notice to suppliers that $5 per kilogram is too high a price to charge. They will realize that the price must be lowered if they want to sell more hamburger, column (5), as the law of demand would predict. If they continue to produce 120,000 kilograms per month in the belief that they can sell that much for $5 per kilogram, unwanted inventories will grow due to the continuing surplus. Competition among suppliers will cause the price to be bid down as each tries to underprice the others in order to sell their individual surpluses. Of course, the longer they attempt to put this off, the higher their storage costs and the higher the risk that the product will spoil.

Initially, suppliers attempt to correct this situation through competitive price cutting, and the price eventually falls to $4 per kilogram. At this price, how-

TABLE 4-6   Market Demand and Supply for Hamburger
            (Hypothetical Data)

(1) Price per Kilogram ($)	(2) Total Number of Kilograms Supplied per Month	−	(3) Total Number of Kilograms Demanded per Month	=	(4) Surplus (+) or Shortage (−)	(5) Price Change Required to Establish Equilibrium
$5.00	120,000	−	20,000	=	+100,000	Decrease
4.00	110,000	−	40,000	=	+70,000	Decrease
3.00	90,000	−	60,000	=	+30,000	Decrease
2.50	78,000	−	78,000	=	0	No change
2.00	60,000	−	90,000	=	−30,000	Increase
1.00	20,000	−	130,000	=	−110,000	Increase

ever, the quantity supplied will still exceed the quantity demanded [see columns (2) and (3)]. Though smaller, the surplus amounts to 70,000 kilograms of hamburger per month, column (4). This will cause individual suppliers to continue to try to underprice one another in their competitive attempts to get rid of their individual surpluses, and the price in the market will continue to fall, column (5).

At $3 per kilogram, the quantity supplied will still exceed the quantity demanded, but the surplus that cannot be sold will have fallen to 30,000 kilograms of hamburger, column (4). Nonetheless, this will still signal that price must fall further, column (5). Only when price has been reduced to $2.50 per kilogram by the competition among suppliers will they be induced to produce and supply a quantity that is just equal to the quantity that will be demanded at that price—78,000 kilograms per month, columns (2) and (3). No unsold surplus will be produced, column (4), and there will be no incentive to change price any further, column (5). Market equilibrium will prevail. **Market equilibrium** *is established at the price where the quantity demanded by the buyers of the good is just equal to the quantity supplied by the sellers.* The price and quantity at which market equilibrium occurs are called the **equilibrium price** and **equilibrium quantity**, respectively. In equilibrium the forces of supply and demand are in balance. Price and quantity will have no tendency to change. They are at rest.

The process just described and the equilibrium achieved are readily visualized with the aid of a market demand curve and a market supply curve. Using the supply and demand schedule data given in Table 4-6, the market supply curve and demand curve for hamburger are drawn in Figure 4-6. This is done in exactly the same manner used to obtain the demand and supply curves drawn in the previous figures in this chapter. Equilibrium occurs at the point where the market demand and supply curves intersect, corresponding to the equilibrium

---

FIGURE 4-6   **The Market Demand and Supply Determine the Equilibrium Price and Quantity for Hamburger**

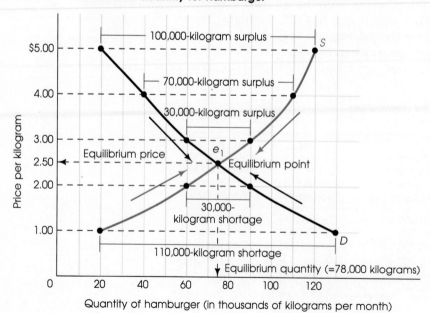

The determination of the equilibrium price and quantity is indicated by the intersection of the market demand curve D and the market supply curve S at e_1. The equilibrium price is $2.50 per kilogram and the equilibrium quantity is 78,000 kilograms. At prices above the equilibrium price, there will be surpluses as indicated. These surpluses will cause a competitive bidding down of price, thereby reducing the quantity supplied and increasing the quantity demanded until they are equal and equilibrium is achieved. At prices below the equilibrium price, there will be shortages as indicated. These shortages will cause a competitive bidding up of price, thereby increasing the quantity supplied and decreasing the quantity demanded until they are equal and equilibrium is achieved.

price of $2.50 and the equilibrium quantity of 78,000 kilograms of hamburger bought and sold per month. It is readily apparent from the diagram that at prices above $2.50 the quantity supplied exceeds the quantity demanded. Competition among suppliers attempting to underprice one another in order to get rid of their surpluses will cause the price to be bid down. This price cutting will cease when the equilibrium price is reached—the price at which quantity demanded equals quantity supplied.

Market Adjustment: Price Below Equilibrium Price

Suppose we consider an initial price below the equilibrium price, say $1 per kilogram. The situation in the market for hamburger is now reversed. The price inducement for suppliers to produce hamburger is relatively low, so they produce relatively little. Because the price to buyers is relatively low, the quantity demanded is relatively high. From Table 4-6 the total quantity supplied is 20,000 kilograms per month, column (2), while the total quantity demanded is 130,000 kilograms per month, column (3). Thus, there is now an **excess demand** for, or **shortage** of, hamburger. Buyers cannot purchase as much as they want at this price. The shortage amounts to 110,000 kilograms, column (4).

There is not enough hamburger to go around at $1 per kilogram. Buyers begin to bid up the price, column (5) as they compete with one another by letting suppliers know that they are willing to pay more to get the inadequate supply increased. As the price of hamburger is bid up, suppliers are encouraged to devote more resources to the production of hamburger, in accordance with the law of supply. At the same time, as the price rises, buyers will begin to reduce the quantity of hamburger that they demand, in accordance with the law of demand. When the price has risen to $2 per kilogram, the quantity demanded still exceeds the quantity supplied [see columns (2) and (3)], but the shortage has been reduced considerably—to 30,000 kilograms, column (4). Nonetheless, the buyers will continue to bid the price up, column (5), as they compete with one another for a supply of output inadequate to satisfy demand. Only when the price has been bid up to $2.50 per kilogram will market equilibrium prevail. The shortage is then eliminated, and there is no further incentive for the price to be changed.

This process of adjustment to equilibrium is illustrated in Figure 4-6. At prices below $2.50 per kilogram, quantity demanded clearly exceeds quantity supplied and a shortage will exist. Competitive bidding by buyers attempting to secure some of the inadequate supply will cause the price to rise. As the price rises, suppliers are induced to buy more inputs and produce more hamburger. The quantity demanded, on the other hand, will fall as buyers are increasingly discouraged from purchasing hamburger as the price rises. Again, this process will eventually lead to the equilibrium point where the demand and supply curves intersect to determine the equilibrium price and quantity.

The Nature of Market Equilibrium

Whether the price is initially above or below the equilibrium level, market forces operate to cause adjustment to equilibrium. If the process starts from above the equilibrium price level, we may envision buyers moving down the demand curve D and suppliers moving down the supply curve S, as adjustment

POLICY PERSPECTIVE

The Market for University Professors

Salaries of university professors, and in fact salaries in general, rose in the period between 1969 and 1990. This is certainly not surprising. That salaries are higher today than two decades ago is not the lesson, though. The salary scales at the University of Calgary and at most other Canadian universities have changed in another important way. In 1969, the highest salary a professor could earn in any given rank was lower than the lowest salary in the next higher rank. For example, as Table P4-1 shows, an associate professor could earn no more than $18,550. All full professors earned at least $18,600. There was no overlap in salaries between ranks. However, by 1990 the situation had become very different, as

illustrated in Table P4-2. Not only could an associate professor earn more than a full professor, but an assistant professor could earn more than a full professor.

Historically universities operated on the assumption that all faculty members were equally valuable and therefore entitled to equal pay. However, the market takes a different view. Faculty members in some disciplines have more possible alternative sources of employment than do faculty members in other disciplines—that is, different discipline training has differing opportunity costs. For example, there are numerous jobs for individuals with graduate training in engineering, computer science, management—even economics. Private indus-

try and government employ large numbers of people with Ph.D.'s in these and related disciplines. On the other hand, there are relatively few jobs outside of universities and colleges for people with Ph.D.'s in English, history, and classics. The alternative employment opportunities for professors in areas such as engineering shifts the demand curve for these disciplines to the right. Figure P4-1 illustrates the market for new Ph.D.'s in English and the market for new Ph.D.'s in engineering.

In Figure P4-1, frame (a), the market for new Ph.D.'s in English is in equilibrium at y_a. In Figure P4-1, frame (b), the market for new Ph.D.'s in engineering is in equilibrium at y_b. Under the old system there was a problem with setting starting salaries. If universities set the starting salary at y_a, the market for English professors was in equilibrium, but there was a shortage of engineering professors. At y_a not enough engineering students were willing to enter the teaching profession; most would opt for nonacademic careers. On the other hand, if universities set the starting salary

TABLE P4-1   Salaries by Rank for Academic Year 1969–1970

Rank	Minimum	Maximum
Instructor	$ 7,750	$10,250
Assistant professor	10,300	13,750
Associate professor	13,800	18,550
Full professor	18,600	Unlimited

TABLE P4-2   Salaries by Rank for Academic Year 1990–1991

Rank	Minimum	Maximum
Instructor	$27,490	$54,674
Assistant professor	35,312	62,973
Associate professor	42,810	79,433
Full professor	55,866	Unlimited

continued on next page

takes place. If the process starts from below the equilibrium price level, buyers move up D and suppliers up S. There is only one price at which the quantity supplied is equal to the quantity demanded. At equilibrium, every buyer who is still willing and able to pay the price will buy exactly the quantity each demands; and every supplier who is still willing and able to offer the product for sale at that price, will sell exactly the quantity each desires to supply. At the equilibrium price the demand intentions of buyers are consistent with the supply intentions of suppliers. When these intentions are actually carried out in the form of buyers' bids to purchase and suppliers' offers to sell, they mesh perfectly. In equilibrium, the decisions of buyers are not frustrated by shortages and the decisions of sellers are not frustrated by surpluses. Since shortages lead to price rises and surpluses

---

POLICY PERSPECTIVE CONTINUED

at y_b, the market for engineering professors was in equilibrium, but there was a surplus of English professors. (In a labour market, a surplus means that there are unemployed workers.) The relatively high salaries would attract more students into graduate work in English than would be required to fill all the academic positions.

In practice, universities tended to set the starting salary at the lower level but then hire new professors in engineering and other higher-paying disciplines at salaries well above the minimum. However, this practice only postponed the problem. It meant that new engineering professors quickly arrived at the top of the range for their rank. They often did not have the publications and experience that were normally associated with a higher rank. However, if they were not promoted, they tended to leave the university to take better-paying jobs in industry and government. Either the university had to lower its standards for promotion or it would face shortages of engineers. The solution to this problem was to create overlapping salary scales such as those illustrated in Table P4-2. Individuals could then be hired at salaries appropriate to their discipline and still be promoted only after they had the necessary experience and status within the profession to warrant the higher rank.

FIGURE P4-1 **Demand and Supply for English and Engineering Professors**

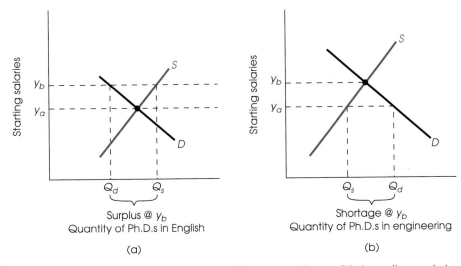

Frame (a) shows the market for English professors, and frame (b) shows the market for engineering professors. Equal starting salaries create problems if the equilibrium salaries are different for different disciplines.

---

to price reductions, the absence of shortage or surplus will mean price will neither rise nor fall. The market is in equilibrium.

The market has provided a solution to society's problem, necessitated by scarcity. It has rationed scarce goods to the highest bidders and has excluded those unwilling or unable to pay. It has provided this function in a decentralized way with a minimum of administrative trouble and cost. Where the market works (and it doesn't work for all goods), it is effective and efficient. However, it should be noted that only those with the ability to pay the equilibrium price will have their demands met, and although efficient, market-determined rationing is not always equitable.

Changes in Supply and Demand—Comparative Statics

In the previous section, we have seen how a market would ultimately reach an equilibrium price and quantity through a *dynamic* adjustment of prices and quantities over time. After this adjustment process, the amount demanded by consumers was just equal to the amount producers would sell at the equilibrium price. Remember that both the demand and supply curves were drawn assuming all other variables remained the same. Because the process of adjustment takes time, these other variables change as well and the whole analysis gets quite complex. To get around this problem, we often assume the market has achieved equilibrium and then analyze how the equilibrium changes when one or more of the other (exogenous) variables change. We then compare the new equilibrium with the old. This comparison is called *comparative static analysis* or **comparative statics** for short. In this type of analysis we are not interested in the dynamic process illustrated in Table 4-6 and Figure 4-6.

For example, suppose that the market for hamburger is initially in the equilibrium position depicted by the intersection of the demand and supply curves shown in Figure 4-6. These curves are reproduced as D and S in Figure 4-7. We know from our discussion of the determinants of supply and demand that any change in one or more of these variables will cause either the supply curve or the demand curve or both to shift. Such a shift will eliminate the existing market equilibrium at e_1 and establish a new equilibrium price and output combination in the market.

FIGURE 4-7   An Increase in Demand for Hamburger

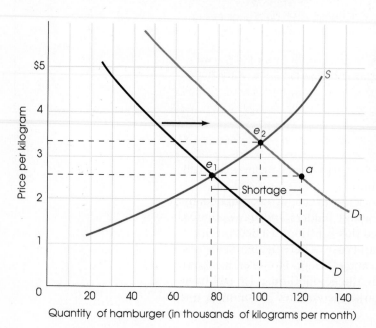

The market is initially in equilibrium, where market demand curve D intersects market supply curve S at e_1. At this point, the equilibrium price is $2.50 per kilogram and the equilibrium quantity is 78,000 kilograms. The increase in demand is indicated by the rightward shift of the market demand curve from D to D_1. This initially gives rise to the shortage of 42,000 kilograms indicated. Competitive bidding among frustrated buyers pushes the price up until market equilibrium is established at e_2. The new equilibrium price is $3.30 per kilogram and the new equilibrium quantity is 100,000 kilograms.

A Change in Demand

Suppose that for one or more of the reasons discussed earlier, the demand for hamburgers increases. For example, this may be due to a rise in the price of hot dogs, P_s, a decrease in the price of soft drinks, P_c, a rise in the incomes of consumers, Y (assuming hamburger is a normal good), a change in preferences, *Pref*, expectations of a future shortage, E_B, a rise in the population, N_B, or any combination of these factors taken collectively. Consequently, the market demand curve for hamburger will shift rightward to D_1 as shown in Figure 4-7. At every possible price, the quantity demanded will now be larger.

In particular, at the initial equilibrium price of $2.50 per kilogram the quantity demanded will increase from 78,000 to 120,000 kilograms per month. At this price, the quantity demanded will now exceed the quantity suppliers are willing to provide, resulting in a shortage amounting to 42,000 kilograms of hamburger. This shortage is the difference between point a on D_1 and the initial equilibrium point e_1 on the supply curve S in Figure 4-7. As a result of this shortage, buyers will tell sellers that they are willing to pay a higher price for hamburger in order to get some. When the price is eventually bid up high enough, equilibrium will once again be established at point e_2, where the demand curve D_1 intersects the supply curve S. The new equilibrium price is $3.30 per kilogram, and the new equilibrium quantity bought and sold is 100,000 kilograms per month. An increase in demand, represented by a rightward shift in the demand curve, will increase both price and quantity, assuming that other things remain the same. (Supply is one of the things that remain unchanged, as is represented by the unchanged position of the supply curve.)

It is interesting to note that the expectation of an increase in the price of hamburger is in fact sufficient to cause an actual price increase. Eventually price rises enough to ration or cut back the quantity demanded (a movement from a to e_2 along D_1) at the same time causing an increase in the quantity supplied (a movement from e_1 to e_2 along S). This increase in quantity supplied is sufficient to restore equilibrium in the market and to eliminate the shortage.

A Change in Supply

Similarly, any decrease in supply (caused, for example, by an increase in the costs of production) would cause the supply curve to shift leftward. Again, consider the initial equilibrium, this time as shown in Figure 4-8. (The demand curve D and the supply curve S are in exactly the same position as D and S in Figure 4-7.) At every possible price, suppliers will now reduce the quantity of hamburger that they are willing and able to supply. In particular, at the initial equilibrium price of $2.50 per kilogram, they will now be only willing to supply 50,000 kilograms of hamburger per month. However, at this price buyers will continue to demand 78,000 kilograms per month. The quantity demanded therefore exceeds the quantity supplied, and there is now a shortage amounting to 28,000 kilograms, represented by the distance between points b and e_1. Again this causes the price to be bid up. When the price reaches $3 per kilogram, the quantity demanded will again equal the quantity supplied. Equilibrium in the market will once more be restored. The equilibrium point is now at the intersection of D and S_1 indi-

FIGURE 4-8   A Decrease in the Supply of Hamburger

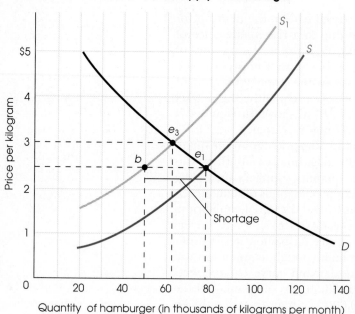

The market is initially in equilibrium, where market demand curve D intersects market supply curve S at e_1. This gives an equilibrium price of $2.50 per kilogram and an equilibrium quantity of 78,000 kilograms. The decrease in supply is indicated by the leftward shift of the market supply curve from S to S_1. This initially gives rise to the indicated shortage of 28,000 kilograms, represented by the distance between points b and e_1. Competitive bidding among frustrated buyers pushes the price up until market equilibrium is established at e_3. The new equilibrium price is $3 per kilogram, and the new equilibrium quantity is 62,000 kilograms per month.

cated by e_3. At the new equilibrium price of $3 per kilogram, the equilibrium quantity bought and sold is 62,000 kilograms per month. A decrease in supply, represented by a leftward shift in the supply curve, will increase price and decrease quantity, assuming other things remain the same. (Demand is one of the things that remain the same, as represented by the unchanged position of the demand curve.)

Both Supply and Demand Change

Suppose that the demand for hamburger and the supply of hamburger have been affected at about the same time. To analyze the consequences for the market for hamburger in our example, we must consider the rightward shift in the demand curve of Figure 4-7 together with the leftward shift in the supply curve of Figure 4-8. This combination of shifts is shown in Figure 4-9. Again, the market supply curve S and the market demand curve D are the same as shown in Figures 4-7 and 4-8, and the initial equilibrium point determined by their intersection is again shown as e_1. The rightward shift in the demand curve from D to D_1 is caused by an increase in demand (the same as that shown in Figure 4-7). The leftward shift in the supply curve from S to S_1 shows the decrease in supply (the same as that shown in Figure 4-8). At the initial equilibrium price of $2.50 per kilogram, the quantity demanded increases from 78,000 to 120,000 kilograms per month. At the same time, the quantity suppliers are willing to supply falls from 78,000 to 50,000 kilograms per month. The shortage now is equal to the sum of the shortages shown in Figures 4-7 and 4-8. Specifically, there is now a shortage amounting to 70,000 kilograms of hamburger, the difference between point a on D_1 and point b on S_1. To restore equilibrium, price will have

FIGURE 4-9 Combined Effects of an Increase in Demand and a Decrease in Supply for Hamburger

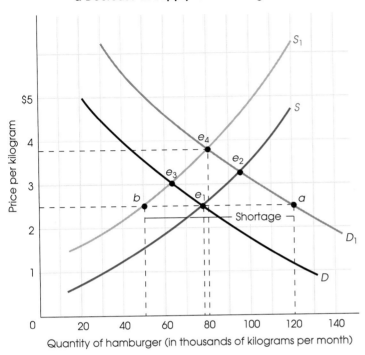

The combined effects of the increase in demand in Figure 4-7 and the decrease in supply in Figure 4-8 are shown here. Starting from the initial equilibrium determined by the intersection of D and S at e_1, the market demand curve shifts rightward to D_1 while the market supply curve shifts leftward to S_1. The new equilibrium price is $3.80 per kilogram, and the new equilibrium quantity is 80,000 kilograms per month. Notice that the new equilibrium price is higher than that established when either the increase in demand or decrease in supply is considered separately, as in Figures 4-7 and 4-8. The new equilibrium quantity is larger (given the relative sizes of the demand and supply curve shifts shown here).

to be bid up until the quantity of hamburger demanded once again equals the quantity suppliers are willing to provide. This occurs where the demand curve D_1 intersects the supply curve S_1 at e_4. The new equilibrium price is $3.80 per kilogram, and the equilibrium quantity bought and sold is now 80,000 kilograms of hamburger per month.

Note that when the leftward shift of the supply curve is considered together with the rightward shift of the demand curve in Figure 4-9, the resulting rise in price is greater than when either shift is considered alone, as in Figures 4-7 and 4-8. This is readily apparent from Figure 4-9. When only the demand shift was considered, the new equilibrium point was e_2. When just the supply shift was considered, the new equilibrium point was e_3. When the effect of both shifts is considered, the new equilibrium point is e_4, which occurs at a higher price than at either e_2 or e_3.

In general, when demand increases and supply decreases, as in Figure 4-9, the equilibrium price will rise; however, the equilibrium quantity may increase, decrease, or even remain the same. Whether equilibrium quantity is unchanged, larger, or smaller depends on the relative size of the shifts in the two curves. In the hypothetical example of Figure 4-9, the relative sizes of these shifts are such that the new equilibrium quantity associated with e_4 is slightly larger than the initial equilibrium quantity associated with e_1. If the leftward shift of the supply curve had been somewhat larger, or the rightward shift of the demand curve somewhat smaller, or both, the new equilibrium quantity might have been somewhat less than the initial equilibrium quantity.

POLICY PERSPECTIVE

Housing Policy—How It Affects the Demand for Housing

Housing has always been important to Canadians, and the quality of housing in Canada is among the highest in the world. Considerable Canadian social policy has been directed towards home ownership. These policies ensure high standards at prices affordable to most Canadians. Over sixty percent of private dwellings are owner-occupied, and about one half of these owners have no mortgage. Housing policy has also played an important part in the economy. A wide range of government programs offer financial support and incentives to housing builders and buyers.

THE EFFECT OF A RECESSION

Housing starts—the quantity of housing units on which construction has begun—vary closely with the level of gross domestic product (GDP) and national income. Housing starts dropped substantially with the 1981–1982 recession, picked up again to a peak in 1987, declined slightly in 1988 and 1989, and then dropped significantly with the recession in 1990 and 1991. By the beginning of 1992 they had fallen to the lowest rate since the 1981–1982 recession. However, our interest here is not with the macroeconomic aspects of housing policy, although these are important, but with how the market demand for housing is affected through public policy. Figure P4-2, frame (a) illustrates the effect upon demand that results from a fall in income due to a recession, *ceteris paribus*. As housing is a *normal* good, the demand shifts leftward from D_0 to D_1. In order to keep the analysis simple, we are assuming that the supply of housing, S in Figure P4-2, is unaffected.

continued on next page

FIGURE P4-2   Interaction of the Demand and Supply for Housing

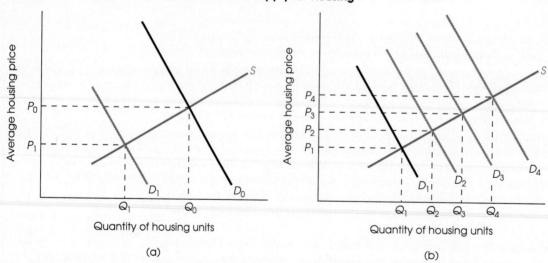

(a)

(b)

In frame (a), demand falls from D_0 to D_1 with the decline in household incomes due to the recession. Frame (b) depicts the predicted changes in demand due to the policy initiatives of the government in early 1992.

HOW GOVERNMENT AFFECTS THE DEMAND FOR HOUSING

Governments can affect the number of housing starts, and therefore the level of national income, through a number of microeconomic polices.

The government biases personal investment toward ownership of housing through the tax system. Taxation policy has affected home ownership by not taxing the shelter services that a home provides, thereby giving home ownership a tax advantage over renting. For example, suppose a person rented a home worth $120,000 at $1,000 per month and invested $120,000 in bonds at 10 percent generating $12,000 per year income. At an average tax rate of 30 percent the net return on the bonds would only be $8,400 $(12,000 - .3 \times 12,000)$. If the person bought the home, the $12,000 rental "income" would not be taxed. Home ownership is the better investment. In addition, if the value of the home appreciates, there is no tax on the capital gain. The capital gain attained through the sale of one's principal residence is not taxed, thus making, in many cases, home ownership the "best" personal investment. This tax policy provides for a larger demand for housing than would otherwise exist if all income were taxed at the same rate.

Most new home buyers also require a mortgage in order to finance the purchase. A mortgage is the service of lending money for a current real estate purchase to be paid back with future income. The price of this service is the interest paid. In this sense a mortgage is a complementary good to the home purchase. Canadian public policy affects the demand for housing by changing the price and availability of its complement good—mortgages.

Expenditure on housing is the largest single budget item for most Canadians. Yet many Canadians do not have easy access to the private financial markets, even though it would be advantageous for them to borrow on future earnings in order to purchase a home. The government created the Canada Mortgage and Housing Corporation (CMHC) in order to provide financing for Canadians who might otherwise not be able to obtain financial capital. CMHC is administered through the National Housing Act. In 1989, CMHC helped finance 150,000 homes and another 12,000 home buyers were assisted by private financing insured by CMHC.

In early 1992, in order to stimulate house sales, a policy change reduced the necessary down payment for CMHC mortgages from 10 percent to 5 percent. The effect of this policy is illustrated in Figure P4-2, frame (b). The demand for housing shifts from D_1 to D_2. This increase in demand would raise the price of housing from P_1 to P_2 and the quantity supplied would rise from Q_1 to Q_2 due to the price increase (a movement along the supply curve).

Interest rates were also reduced in early 1992. As mortgage rates are the price of the housing's complement—mortgages, housing demand would rise as the interest rate fell. Figure P4-2, frame (b) illustrates this effect with the shift in demand from D_2 to D_3. The rise in demand with the fall in interest rates again increases housing prices and induces an increase in the quantity supplied.

A third policy change was introduced with the federal budget of February 1992. This budget program allows an individual to remove up to $20,000 from their accumulated Registered Retirement Savings Plan (RRSP) without a tax penalty if the money is used toward the purchase of an owner-occupied home. Any amount withdrawn would have to be repaid to the RRSP over a period of 15 years without interest. By making these tax-free savings available for the purchase of housing, it is expected that demand would be shifted further to the right as illustrated by the shift from D_3 to D_4 in Figure P4-2, frame (b). The new price will depend on the shape of the housing supply curve, but the new equilibrium quantity clearly increases, thereby increasing housing construction and thus aggregate income and employment.

For Discussion

- The government appears to put great emphasis on home ownership in Canada. What benefits do you think there are for society in having a high number of housing starts? Are these benefits always consistent with stimulating private ownership? Would the same economic goals be achieved by having the government build public housing? Why or why not?

- What effect would a fall in the average price in the resale home market have on new housing starts? Do you think an increase in the number of resale homes sold would affect aggregate income and employment?

Summary

1. The law of demand asserts that the lower (higher) is the price charged for a good, the larger (smaller) will be the quantity demanded—*ceteris paribus.*

2. The law of demand may be represented in a demand schedule or graphically by a demand curve that slopes downward left to right on a graph, with price measured on the vertical axis and quantity measured on the horizontal axis. Any point on a demand curve tells us the quantity of a good buyers desire to purchase per some specified unit of time at the price associated with that point.

3. In addition to the price of the good for which the market demand curve is drawn, the other determinants of market demand are (1) the prices of all other related goods, complements and substitutes, (2) money income, (3) expectations, (4) preferences, and (5) the number of buyers in the market.

4. Goods can be related in two ways: They are either complements or substitutes. Complementary goods are consumed together, and if the price of one goes up, the demand for the other good will fall. With goods that are substitutes for each other, a price increase in one good will produce an increase in the demand for the other.

5. When a consumer's money income changes, the consumer's demand will shift. The direction of the shift will depend on whether the good is normal or inferior. If the good is normal, the consumer's demand will increase with an increase in income and decrease with a decrease in income. If the good is inferior, the consumer's demand will decrease with an increase in income and increase with a decrease in income.

6. The market demand curve for a good is obtained by summing the demand curves for all individuals in the market. As each individual is willing and able to purchase a different quantity at each price, the market demand is the sum of all these individual quantities at each price. Graphically, this amounts to a vertical summation of the individual demand curves.

7. A change in one or more of the determinants of demand will cause the market demand curve to shift either rightward (an increase in demand) or leftward (a decrease in demand). A shift in the demand curve is referred to as *a change in demand.* It is to be distinguished from *a change in the quantity demanded,* which refers to a movement along a fixed demand curve. The latter can only occur because of a change in the price of the good for which the demand curve is drawn.

8. The law of supply asserts that suppliers will supply larger quantities of a good at higher prices for that good than at lower prices, *ceteris paribus.* This law may be represented in a supply schedule or graphically by a supply curve that slopes upward from left to right on a graph, with price measured on the vertical axis and quantity measured on the horizontal axis. Any point on a supply curve tells us the quantity of a good suppliers are willing to produce and desire to sell per period of time at the price associated with that point.

9. Along with the price of the good for which the supply curve is drawn, the other determinants of supply are (1) the prices of resources and other factors of production, (2) the prices of other goods which the firm might

have produced instead of this product, (3) technology, (4) the number of suppliers, and (5) the suppliers' expectations.

10. A change in any of the determinants of supply will cause the supply curve to shift either rightward (an increase in supply) or leftward (a decrease in supply). Such a change is called *a change in supply*. It is to be distinguished from *a change in the quantity supplied*, which is a movement along a fixed supply curve due to a change in the price of the good for which the supply curve is drawn.

11. Supply and demand interact to adjust price until that price is found where the quantity of the good demanded is just equal to the quantity supplied. This is the equilibrium price and quantity, which is represented by the intersection of the supply and demand curves. When this point of intersection is established, we have market equilibrium.

12. Changes in supply and demand, represented by shifts in the supply and demand curves, will upset equilibrium and cause either shortages or surpluses. This will set in motion competitive price bidding among buyers and sellers that will ultimately restore market equilibrium, most typically at new levels of equilibrium price and quantity.

13. An increase (decrease) in demand will lead to an increase (decrease) in equilibrium price and quantity, *ceteris paribus*. An increase (decrease) in supply will lead to a decrease (increase) in equilibrium price and an increase (decrease) in equilibrium quantity, *ceteris paribus*. When both supply and demand change, the effect on equilibrium price and quantity depends on the particular case.

Key Terms and Concepts

comparative statics	excess supply	normal good
complementary good	factors of production	shortage
demand curve	inferior good	substitute good
demand schedule	law of demand	supply curve
equilibrium price	law of supply	supply schedule
equilibrium quantity	market demand curve	surplus
excess demand	market equilibrium	technology

Questions and Problems

1. Classify each of the following goods according to whether *in your opinion* it is a normal or inferior good: shoes, beer, leather gloves, life insurance, auto insurance, stereo equipment, pet dog, radial tires, rice, fishing gear.

2. Classify each of the following pairs of goods according to whether you think they are substitutes, complements, or basically unrelated to each other: ham and eggs, meat and potatoes, Toyotas and BMWs, ice skates and swimsuits, coffee and tea, butter and margarine, apples and oranges, knives and forks, saltshakers and hats, skis and lift tickets, NHL playoff tickets and beer.

3. Suppose that today's weather forecast states that chances are 9 out of 10 there will be rain all during the coming week. What effect do you think that this will have on the demand curve for each of the following: umbrellas, baseball tickets, electricity, taxi rides, parking space in shopping centers, camping equipment, books, and headache tablets?

4. What do you predict would happen to the market demand curve for oranges in Canada as a result of the following:
   a. A rise in average income.
   b. An increase in the birthrate.
   c. An intensive advertising campaign that convinces most people of the importance of a daily quota of natural vitamin C.
   d. A fall in the price of orange juice.
   e. A fall in the price of grapefruit.
5. What will happen to the supply of cars if each of the following should occur? Explain your answers.
   a. An increase in the price of trucks.
   b. A fall in the price of steel.
   c. The introduction of a better assembly line technique.
   d. An increase in the price of cars.
6. If goods are expensive because they are scarce, why aren't rotten eggs high priced?
7. What will be the effect on the supply curve of hogs from a fall in the price of corn? What will be the effect on the supply curve of corn from a fall in the price of hogs?
8. What effect do you think an advertising campaign for coffee would have on each of the following, *ceteris paribus:* the price of coffee, the price of tea, the quantity of sugar bought and sold, the price of doughnuts, the quantity of sleeping pills bought and sold, the price of television advertising time on the late show?
9. Suppose that you read in the paper that the price of gasoline is rising along with increased sales of gasoline. Does this contradict the law of demand or not? Explain.
10. Suppose that there is a strike in the steel industry. Other things remaining the same, what do you predict will happen to the price of steel, the price of automobiles, the quantity sold and the price of aluminum, the price of aluminum wire, the price and quantity of copper wire sold, and the price of electricity? At each step of this chain spell out your answer in terms of the relevant shift in a demand or supply curve. What do you think of the characterization of the economy as a chain of interconnected markets?
11. Suppose that we were to look at some data on the buggy whip industry collected at about the time the automobile industry was rapidly moving out of its infancy. What would you make of the finding that many buggy whip manufacturers were getting out of the business, yet the price of buggy whips was not falling? Demonstrate your analysis diagrammatically.
12. During an energy crisis it is not uncommon to see automobiles lined up for blocks waiting to buy gas.
   a. Demonstrate diagrammatically what happens in the gasoline market when an energy crisis hits.
   b. Given the long lines of cars observed waiting to buy gas, do you think that the equilibrium price of gas prevails at that time?
13. Given that the demand and supply for product X is:

$$Qd_X = 120 - .5P_X$$
$$Qs_X = 20 + 3.5P_X$$

Find:
   a. Equilibrium price P.
   b. Equilibrium quantity Q.
   c. The excess demand at $P = 20$.
   d. The excess supply at $P = 35$.
   e. Suppose that a tax increase on inputs through the introduction of the GST causes supply to change to $Qs'_X = 10 + 3.5P_X$. Explain whether this represents an increase in supply or a decrease.
   f. Given the new supply in (e), what is the new equilibrium price and quantity?

PART TWO

The Price System and the Organization of Economic Activity

Chapter 5

Elasticity

Public transit authorities frequently find they are operating at a loss. Revenues obtained from riders fall short of covering the costs of providing the service. As a public transit system's costs and capacity are largely fixed in the short-run, raising the price of a ride *appears* to be the prudent solution to the problem of how to increase revenue. We do know from demand theory that at a higher price fewer people will use the service, but more precise knowledge is needed. What transit authorities need to know is the "sensitivity" of their ridership to price increases. Will the increase in price offset the decrease in ridership? Will revenues increase with a rise in price or actually decrease, defeating the objective of the authorities? How would you go about measuring the sensitivity of public transit demand to a fare increase? The appropriate measure to use is known as *price elasticity of demand*.

In this chapter we will examine the important and very practical concept of elasticity, which gives us a measure of the responsiveness of one variable to changes in another. In particular we are interested in the responsiveness of quantity to a change in price in demand and supply analysis. Elasticity measures will build on the tools of supply and demand analysis that we first developed in Chapter 4, allowing us to analyze in greater detail some familiar but controversial economic issues.

Brief Review of Supply and Demand

Before beginning our discussion of elasticity, let's briefly review the basics of demand and supply developed in Chapter 4. The *law of demand* says that, in general, people will demand a larger quantity of a good at a lower price than at a higher price. The law of demand is represented graphically by a downward-sloping demand curve, such as D_0 in Figure 5-1, frame (a). The *law of supply* says that, in general, a larger quantity of a good will be supplied at a higher price than at a lower price. The law of supply is represented graphically by an upward-sloping supply curve, such as S_0 in Figure 5-1, frame (a).

The intersection of the market demand curve D_0 and market supply curve S_0, frame (a) of Figure 5-1, determines the equilibrium price p_e and quantity q_e. At the equilibrium price the market is said to be *in equilibrium* because the quantity demanded is exactly equal to the quantity supplied. At any price above the equilibrium price, the quantity supplied exceeds the quantity demanded, so there is a surplus. This surplus will push the market price down to the equilibrium level. At any price below the equilibrium level, the quantity demanded exceeds the quantity supplied and there is a shortage. The shortage will push the market price back up to the equilibrium level.

Movement along a demand curve means that the price of the good has changed causing a change in the quantity of the good demanded. Only a change in price can cause a movement along the demand curve. All other things are assumed to be constant, or unchanged. Among these other things are (1) the prices of all other goods, (2) income, (3) buyers' expectations, (4) preferences, and (5) the number of buyers in the market. A movement along a demand curve is referred to as a *change in the quantity demanded.* If one or more of the other things change, then the demand curve will shift in the manner shown in frame (b) of Figure 5-1. Such a shift in the demand curve is called a *change in demand.* Note that when demand increases, the demand curve shifts rightward, such as to D_1, thereby increasing both the equilibrium price and the equilibrium quantity. When demand decreases, such as to D_2, both equilibrium price and equilibrium quantity decrease.

As with a demand curve, movement along a supply curve means that only the price of the good and, as a result, the quantity of the good supplied change. Among all other things assumed to be constant, or unchanged, are (1) the prices of resources and other factors of production, (2) technology, (3) the prices of other goods, (4) the number of suppliers, and (5) the suppliers' expectations. Movement along a supply curve is referred to as a *change in the quantity supplied.*

LEARNING OBJECTIVES

After reading this chapter, you will be able to:

1. Define the concept of elasticity and explain what information it adds to demand and supply theory.
2. Calculate the coefficient of price elasticity of demand using the point elasticity method.
3. Calculate the coefficient of price elasticity of demand using the arc elasticity method.
4. Interpret the coefficient of price elasticity of demand.
5. Distinguish between the constant slope and changing elasticity along a straight-line demand curve.
6. Explain the relationship between total revenue and price elasticity along a demand curve.
7. List and explain the determinants of the price elasticity of demand.
8. Calculate the coefficient of price elasticity of supply and explain its determinants.
9. Calculate the coefficient of cross price elasticity of demand and interpret it.
10. Calculate the coefficient of income elasticity of demand and interpret it.

FIGURE 5-1   **Demand and Supply Determine Equilibrium Price and Quantity in the Market**

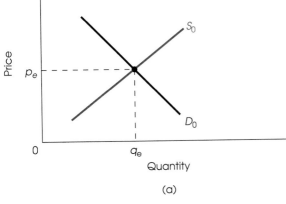

(a)

The intersection of the supply and demand curves S_0 and D_0, respectively, determine the equilibrium price p_e and quantity q_e in the market, frame (a). A rightward shift of the demand curve to D_1, frame (b), increases both the equilibrium price and quantity. A leftward shift to D_2 decreases equilibrium price and quantity. A rightward shift of the supply curve to S_1, frame (c), reduces equilibrium price and increases equilibrium quantity. A leftward shift of the supply curve to S_2 reduces equilibrium quantity and increases equilibrium price.

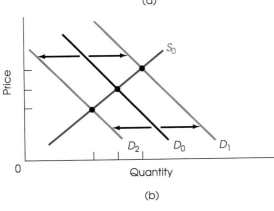

(b)

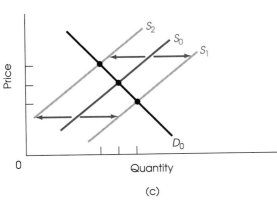

(c)

If one or more of the other things change, the supply curve will shift as shown in frame (c) of Figure 5-1. This is referred to as a *change in supply*. An increase in supply is represented by a rightward shift in the supply curve, such as to S_1, thereby reducing equilibrium price while increasing equilibrium quantity. When supply decreases, such as to S_2, equilibrium price rises while equilibrium quantity decreases.

Price Elasticity—The Responsiveness of Quantity to Price Change

What does it mean when someone says that consumers have demonstrated that they are very responsive to price changes? In other words, how responsive is *very* responsive? In economic analysis, we find it helpful to use a specific quantitative measure of the degree of responsiveness of quantity demanded to a change in price. We call this measure the **price elasticity of demand** to indicate that the measure is in reference to changes in the price of the product and not some related good's price change. Similarly, the **price elasticity of supply** is used to measure the degree of responsiveness of quantity supplied to a change in price. The price elasticity of demand, or supply, is measured as the ratio of the percentage change in quantity demanded, or supplied, to the percentage change in price. Price elasticity therefore measures the percentage change in quantity (demanded or supplied) per one-percent change in price.

Price Elasticity of Demand

The responsiveness of the quantity of a good demanded to a change in its price is reflected in its demand curve. This is illustrated in Figure 5-2. At a price of p_0 the quantity demanded is q_0. Suppose that the price is lowered from p_0 to p_1. If the demand curve looks like D_1, the quantity demanded increases from q_0 to q_1. On the other hand, if the demand curve looks like D_2, the quantity demanded increases from q_0 to q_2. For the exact same change in price the change in quantity demanded is greater for the demand curve D_2, than it is for D_1. The

---

FIGURE 5-2   **Change in Quantity Demanded in Response to a Price Change**

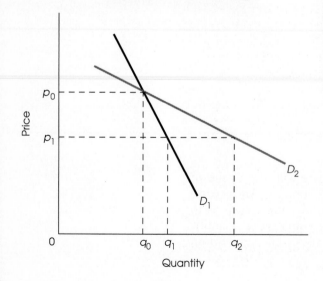

Suppose the price of a good is initially p_0 and the quantity demanded is q_0. If the demand curve is D_2, the quantity demanded increases from q_0 to q_2 in response to a fall in price from p_0 to p_1. However, if the demand curve is D_1, the quantity demanded increases by a smaller amount, from q_0 to q_1. For the exact same change in price, the change in quantity demanded is greater for the demand curve D_2 than it is for D_1. For this price change, we say that the demand curve D_2 is *more elastic* than the demand curve D_1.

reason is that for this price change the demand curve D_2 is flatter, or more horizontal, than the demand curve D_1. Hence, for this price change we say that the demand curve D_2 is *more elastic* than the demand curve D_1. Our graphical example—Figure 5-2—gives us a feel for the origin of the term *elasticity*, but a precise measure of price elasticity cannot be obtained by looking at a demand curve or a supply curve. Indeed, we shall see that the appearance of such curves is not a reliable indicator of the price elasticity of demand or supply.

Coefficient of Elasticity

We measure the responsiveness of quantity demanded to a change in price in percentage terms. This avoids the problem of units. The number arrived at as a result of these calculations is called the **coefficient of price elasticity** (η_d). The coefficient is thus a simple number that will need to be interpreted—it has no units of measure (that is why it is called a coefficient). We obtain this number using the formula:

$$\eta_d = \frac{\text{Percentage change in quantity demanded}}{\text{Percentage change in price}}$$

The sign of the coefficient of price elasticity of demand is negative because the sign of the change in price is opposite to the sign of the associated change in quantity along a demand curve. Remember, this is so because price and quantity demanded are inversely related according to the law of demand. In practice, the absolute value of η_d determines the price elasticity (the minus sign is usually ignored).

Armed with the coefficient of price elasticity, we may now give a more precise meaning to the concept of elasticity by defining the terms *elastic* and *inelastic*. Demand is elastic when the coefficient of elasticity η_d is greater than 1. Put another way, we can say that **elastic demand** exists if a given percentage change in price results in a larger percentage change in quantity demanded. Conversely, **inelastic demand** exists when the coefficient of elasticity is less than 1. We can also say demand is inelastic if a given percentage change in price results in a smaller percentage change in quantity demanded. Suppose that the price of salt per kilogram increased from .10 to .12 and the quantity demanded decreased from 500 tonnes per month to 450 tonnes per month. The coefficient of price elasticity would be .5. A 20 percent increase in price resulted in only a 10 percent decrease in quantity demanded ($\eta_d = 10\%/20\% = .5$). In the special case where the percentage change in price results in an equal percentage change in quantity demanded, we say that demand is **unit elastic** or *of unitary elasticity*. In this case the coefficient of price elasticity equals 1. Put another way, if the price of a good falls by one percent and the quantity demanded increases by one percent, demand for that good is unit elastic.

The coefficient of price elasticity of demand for most goods falls between two extreme values—of zero and infinity. At one extreme, the quantity of a good demanded does not change at all in response to a change in price. In this case we say that demand is **perfectly inelastic** ($\eta_d = 0$), and the demand curve for the good is perfectly vertical. This case is illustrated in Figure 5-3, frame (a). At the other extreme is a good for which demand is zero when price is above a certain level but unlimited when price is at or below that level. We then say that

FIGURE 5-3   Extremes of Elasticity—Zero and Infinity

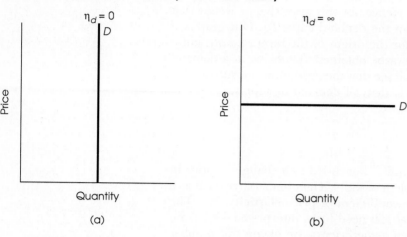

At one extreme, the quantity of a good demanded does not change at all in response to a change in price. Perfectly price-inelastic demand ($\eta_d = 0$) is a vertical demand curve in frame (a). At the other extreme, the demand is zero when price is above a certain level, but unlimited when price is at or below that level. Perfectly price-elastic demand ($\eta_d = \infty$) is horizontal at that price level in frame (b).

the demand for that good is **perfectly elastic** ($\eta_d = \infty$), and the demand curve is perfectly horizontal at that price level. The case of a perfectly elastic demand is illustrated in Figure 5-3, frame (b).

Calculating Point Elasticity

Suppose that we wanted to calculate the price elasticity of demand for tickets to the Grey Cup game at *B. C. Place* (maximum seating capacity—60,000). The demand curve for tickets is shown in Figure 5-4. Let's begin by computing the elasticity for the price change between points *a* and *b* on the demand curve. At point *a*, the price of $60 per ticket has an associated quantity demand of 25,000 tickets. We will use this as our base point. At point *b*, the price of $50 per ticket has an associated quantity demand of 30,000 tickets. We must therefore compute the percentage change corresponding to a $10 change in the price of a ticket and the percentage change corresponding to the associated 5,000-ticket change in the quantity of tickets demanded. Using the formula for the coefficient of elasticity, our calculations for the price elasticity of demand would be

$$\eta_d = \frac{\%\Delta q}{\%\Delta p} = \frac{\frac{q_2 - q_1}{q_1}}{\frac{p_2 - p_1}{p_1}} = \frac{\frac{\Delta q}{q_1}}{\frac{\Delta p}{p_1}}$$

If $p_1 = \$60$, and $q_1 = 25,000$ and $p_2 = \$50$, and $q_2 = 30,000$; then

$$\eta_d = \frac{\frac{5,000}{25,000}}{\frac{10}{60}} = 1.2$$

Alternatively, suppose that we use point *b* as our reference point. Fifty dollars per ticket and 30,000 tickets would be the base price and quantity from which we would compute the percentage change corresponding to a $10 change in the price of a ticket and the percentage change corresponding to the associated 5,000-ticket change in the quantity of tickets demanded. Now $p_1 = \$50$, and

FIGURE 5-4   Demand for Tickets to the Grey Cup

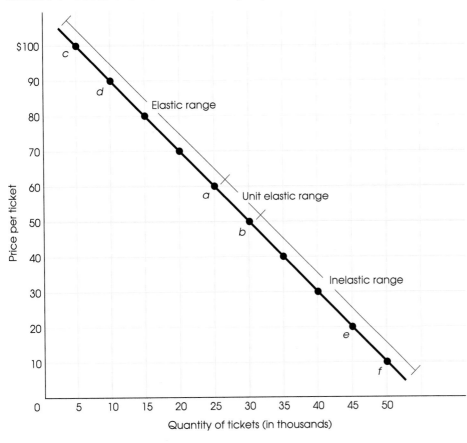

The elasticity of a demand curve is typically different over different ranges. For this hypothetical demand curve for tickets to the Grey Cup, the coefficient of elasticity is 6.33 over the range c to d and gets progressively smaller as we move down the curve from left to right. The curve is unit elastic over the range a to b and becomes progressively more inelastic below this range. The coefficient of elasticity over the range e to f is .16. Note, however, that the *slope* of this demand curve is the same over all ranges because the curve is linear (a straight line). From this example, we can see why the slope of the curve over any range is not a good indicator of the elasticity over that range.

$q_1 = 30,000$ and $p_2 = \$60$, and $q_2 = 25,000$. Our calculations for the price elasticity of demand would now be

$$\eta_d = \frac{\frac{5,000}{30,000}}{\frac{10}{50}} = .83$$

In both these calculations we have used the ratio of two percentage changes. Note that we have used the *standard* method for calculating percentage changes—(change/original). These two calculations result in considerably different values of the price elasticity of demand despite the fact that they are based on the same change along the same demand curve. Moreover, in this particular instance, the first calculation indicates that demand is elastic, while the second indicates it is inelastic. This conflict is somewhat unsatisfactory. How can we resolve it?

One way to deal with the measurement is to make the calculation from the actual direction of change that occurred. If price went down (for instance, in our example from \$60 to \$50), then use the first calculation. If price went up, use the second calculation. The actual direction of change would then determine the point elasticity measured. One advantage of using the point elasticity calculation

Checkpoint* 5-1

The Calgary Stampede raised the entrance fee from $7.00 in 1991 to $7.50 in 1992. The attendance between opening day and the final Saturday was down to 1,010,878 in 1992 from 1,055,630 in 1991. From this information, calculate the coefficient of price elasticity of demand using the point method. Do you think this is a reliable estimate of elasticity? Why? If not, what else should you take into consideration? The last day (Sunday) of the Stampede in 1991 had an attendance of 111,169. In 1992 the Stampede board cut the entrance fee to $4.00. Using the coefficient you calculated previously, what do you predict the 1992 Sunday attendance to be?

*Answers to all Checkpoints can be found at the back of the text.

is that the coefficient calculated will only depend upon the initial price and quantity used. It will not matter how large or small the range between the second point is.

At this point you should be warned against thinking that the price elasticity of demand is the same over all ranges of a straight-line demand curve. Although it is possible to construct demand curves for which the coefficient of price elasticity is the same over all ranges, such curves are not typical for this level of analysis. The shape of the demand curve is assumed when it is estimated from actual data. A straight-line demand curve is used as a reasonable assumption over the range of demand data used, but, and here is the catch, price elasticity coefficients will be different for every point along a straight-line demand curve when they are calculated using the point elasticity measure.

Arc Elasticity—A Variation Using the Midpoints Formula

If an elasticity measure that does not depend upon direction is desired (there is no original price and quantity), then a different calculation is needed. This calculation is based on the midpoint between, for example, points a and b in Figure 5-4. The conventional way to do this is to use the averages of the two quantities and the two prices as base points when computing the percentage changes in quantity and price, which are then used to calculate the coefficient of price elasticity. The average of the two quantities associated with points a and b is $(25,000 + 30,000)/2$, which equals 27,500. The average of the two prices is $(\$60 + \$50)/2$, which equals $55. The percentage change in quantity is therefore $(5,000/27,500) \times 100$, or 18.2. The percentage change in price is $(10/55) \times 100$, or 18.2. The calculation of the coefficient of price elasticity is now:

$$\eta_d = \frac{\frac{5,000}{27,500}}{\frac{10}{55}} = \frac{18.2}{18.2} = 1$$

In general then, we may restate our formula for the coefficient of price elasticity so that it reads

$$\eta_d = \frac{\frac{\text{Change in quantity}}{\text{Sum of quantities}}}{2} \div \frac{\frac{\text{Change in price}}{\text{Sum of prices}}}{2}$$

or

$$\eta_d = \frac{\%\Delta q_d}{\%\Delta p} = \frac{\frac{q_2 - q_1}{\frac{q_1 + q_2}{2}}}{\frac{p_2 - p_1}{\frac{p_1 + p_2}{2}}} = \frac{\frac{\Delta q}{\text{average } q}}{\frac{\Delta p}{\text{average } p}}$$

This new formula measures the **arc elasticity**. The basic difference between point and arc elasticity measures is in how the percentage changes are calculated. Instead of the standard percentage change—the difference over the original—we take the difference over the average of the two numbers. The number calculated is used to represent the price elasticity over the *range* of prices and quantities as in the range between points a and b.

Variation in Price Elasticity Along a Demand Curve

Consider again the straight-line demand curve in Figure 5-4, which is fairly typical of those used. Using the arc elasticity formula, we can determine the coefficient of price elasticity for the range c to d by making the following calculations:

$$\eta_d = \frac{\frac{5,000}{15,000}}{2} \div \frac{\frac{10}{190}}{2} = 6.33$$

We have already seen that for the range a to b, η_d has a value of 1. The value of η_d over the range from e to f is

$$\eta_d = \frac{\frac{5,000}{95,000}}{2} \div \frac{\frac{10}{30}}{2} = .16$$

It is apparent that this demand curve is very elastic at the highest price levels and becomes less and less elastic as we move to lower price levels. At price levels below the a to b range, the demand curve is inelastic and becomes more so as we move to yet lower price levels. Price elasticity on any downward-sloping straight-line demand curve is higher in the upper-left part of the demand curve because the base quantity level from which the percentage change in quantity is computed is small. On the other hand, the base price from which the percentage change in price is computed is large. When we compute the coefficient of price elasticity, a relatively large percentage change in quantity is divided by a relatively small percentage change in price. This gives an elastic demand over this range. In the lower right part of the demand curve, the situation is just the opposite. The base quantity level from which the percentage change in quantity is computed is large, while the base price level from which the percentage change in price is computed is small. When we compute the coefficient of elasticity, a relatively small percentage change in quantity is divided by a relatively large percentage change in price to give a coefficient of elasticity less than 1. This indicates an inelastic demand.

If prices are low, we are less likely to respond to changes in the price, as the price is less significant ($\eta_d < 1$). But if prices are relatively high, we are more likely to be responsive to price changes ($\eta_d > 1$). Why this is so should become more clear, as we shall see later, when we consider the determinants of price elasticity.

Slope and Elasticity

Typically then, for a straight-line demand curve, the coefficient of price elasticity will change as one moves up or down the demand curve. It is easy for beginning students of economics to confuse the slope of a demand curve over some range with the elasticity of demand over that range. Slope and elasticity are different concepts. The **slope of the demand curve** over some range is defined as the change in price over that range divided by the associated change in quantity demanded: Slope $= \Delta p / \Delta q$. This is obviously not the same as the coefficient of price elasticity.

The slope of a straight-line demand curve, such as that in Figure 5-4, is the same over its entire length. For every $10 change in price, the associated change in quantity of tickets demanded is always 5,000. We have already seen, however, that the price elasticity is decidedly different between the ranges *c* to *d*, *a* to *b*, and *e* to *f*, for example. This illustrates how misleading it can be to judge the price elasticity of demand by looking at the slope. While the slope of the demand curve can be readily observed from the appearance of the demand curve over any range, the elasticity cannot.

By contrast, consider the demand curve in Figure 5-5. The slope over the range *a* to *b* is clearly steeper than that over the range *c* to *d*. The slopes over both of these ranges are clearly steeper than the slope over the range *e* to *f*. Yet this demand curve has been constructed so that it is unit elastic throughout its length. The coefficient of price elasticity of this demand curve is always equal to 1, whether it is calculated for the range *a* to *b*, *b* to *c*, *c* to *d*, *d* to *e*, or *e* to *f*.

Price Elasticity and Total Revenue

There is a definite relationship between **total revenue** and the price elasticity of demand. The *total revenue is equal to the quantity of the good sold multiplied by the price per unit*. The way total revenue changes as we move along a demand curve tells us how price elasticity changes along the demand curve. Conversely, the way price elasticity changes along a demand curve is useful in predicting how total revenue changes.

Consider again the demand curve in Figure 5-4, reproduced in Figure 5-6. At point *c*, total revenue is equal to the price per ticket of $100 multiplied by the 5,000 tickets demanded at that price, or $500,000. At point *d*, total revenue is equal to $90 per ticket times 10,000 tickets, or $900,000. Hence, if price is lowered from $100 to $90 per ticket, total revenue increases. We have already observed that demand is elastic over this range, which means that the percentage

---

FIGURE 5-5   Unit Elastic Demand Curve

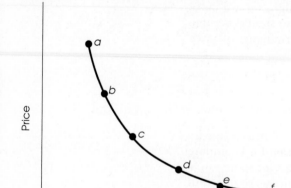

This demand curve is unit elastic (the coefficient of elasticity equals 1) throughout its length. However, the slope varies throughout its length. The slope is very steep over ranges along the upper left portion of the curve, such as *a* to *b*, and becomes progressively flatter as we move down along the demand curve from left to right. This again illustrates why it is misleading to judge the elasticity of a demand curve over any range by its slope over that range.

FIGURE 5-6   Relation Between Elasticity of Demand and Total Revenue

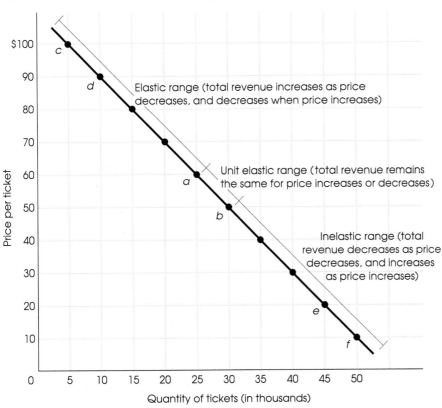

Total revenue (equal to the price per ticket times the number of tickets demanded at that price) gets progressively larger as we move down the demand curve from left to right over the elastic range. Total revenue reaches its maximum over the unit elastic range and gets progressively smaller as we move down the demand curve over the inelastic range. As we move up the demand curve from right to left, total revenue rises to a maximum at the unit elastic range and then falls continuously thereafter. Use the numbers in the diagram to convince yourself of the validity of these statements. Also note in Figure 5-5 that because the demand curve has the same elasticity throughout its length, total revenue is the same at all points on it.

change in quantity is greater than the percentage change in price. In other words, when the price of tickets is lowered from $100 to $90, the loss in revenue due to the reduction in price is more than offset by the gain in revenue due to the increase in the quantity of tickets sold. Conversely, if the price per ticket is raised from $90 to $100, total revenue falls because the gain in revenue due to the increase in price is more than offset by the loss in revenue due to the reduction in the number of tickets sold. *In the elastic portion of a demand curve, an increase in price results in a decrease in total revenue and a decrease in price results in a increase in total revenue. Revenue and price move in opposite directions.*

Now consider the behaviour of total revenue over the range *e* to *f* on the demand curve of Figure 5-6. At point *e*, total revenue is equal to the price per ticket of $20 multiplied by the 45,000 tickets demanded at that price, or $900,000. At point *f*, total revenue is equal to $10 per ticket times 50,000 tickets, or $500,000. Therefore, if price is lowered from $20 to $10 per ticket, total revenue decreases. Recall that demand is inelastic over this range, which means that the percentage change in quantity is less than the percentage change in price. Hence, when the price is lowered from $20 to $10 per ticket, the loss in revenue due to the reduction in price is larger than the gain in revenue due to the increase in the quantity of tickets sold. Conversely, if the price per ticket is raised from $10 to $20, total revenue rises from $500,000 to $900,000 because the gain in revenue due to the increase in price more than offsets the loss in

TABLE 5-1   Price Elasticity and Revenue Relationships
(The Effects of a Price Increase on Quantity Demanded and Total Revenue)

Type of Price Elasticity	Effect on Q_d	Effect on Total Revenue
Perfectly elastic	Decreases without limit	Decreases to zero
Elastic	Decreases by greater percent	Decreases
Unit elastic	Decreases by same percent	Unaffected
Inelastic	Decrease by a smaller percent	Increases
Perfectly inelastic	Unaffected	Increases same percentage

Checkpoint 5-2

We have already calculated the coefficient of price elasticity for the ranges *c* to *d*, *a* to *b*, and *e* to *f* along the demand curve in Figure 5-4. Using the midpoints formula, calculate the coefficient of price elasticity along this demand curve for the ranges $90 to $80, $80 to $70, $70 to $60, $50 to $40, $40 to $30, and $30 to $20. What do you observe about the elasticity of demand as we move down the demand curve from left to right? The Grey Cup game is usually "sold out." Let's assume that total revenue is at its maximum. Where do you think the demand curve actually is—to the right or to the left of the hypothetical demand curve shown in Figure 5-4? Could the price elasticity of the demand curve in the range lying directly above the 60,000-ticket point on the horizontal axis be inelastic? Why or why not?

revenue due to the decrease in the number of tickets sold. *In the inelastic portion of a demand curve, an increase in price results in an increase in revenue and a decrease in price results in a decrease in revenue. There is a direct relationship between price and revenue.*

Over the range *a* to *b* the demand curve of Figure 5-6 is unit elastic. At point *a* total revenue is $1,500,000, which is determined by a price of $60 per ticket multiplied by 25,000 tickets. Total revenue is also $1,500,000 at point *b*, where the price of $50 per ticket is multiplied by 30,000 tickets.[1] Thus, whether price is lowered from $60 to $50 or raised from $50 to $60, total revenue remains unchanged. This is so because the percentage change in price in one direction, over this range, is exactly the same as the percentage change in quantity in the other direction over the same range. The change in revenue due to the change in the price per ticket is exactly offset by the change in revenue due to the change in the opposite direction of the quantity of tickets sold. In the range of a demand curve that is unit elastic, a change in price, up or down, has no effect on total revenue. (Note that because the demand curve of Figure 5-5 is unit elastic throughout its length, total revenue remains the same no matter what price is charged.)

Usually the easiest way to estimate whether a demand curve is elastic, inelastic, or unit elastic over a certain range is to examine the change in total revenue as price and quantity vary over that range. Always remember the following: *Along the elastic portion of a demand curve, total revenue and price move in the opposite direction. Along the inelastic portion of a demand curve, total revenue and price move in the same direction. And at unit elasticity revenue does not change if price changes.* These relationships are summarized in Table 5-1. With these rules in mind, in Figure 5-6 you should be able to convince yourself that total revenue from Grey Cup ticket sales is at a *maximum* when tickets are priced at the midpoint between $50 and $60 ($55). As a consequence, revenue would be maximized when the stadium would be only about half full!

---

[1] Note though that at a price of $55 total revenue is $1,512,500. A consequence of using arc elasticity over a range of prices.

What Determines Price Elasticity of Demand?

There are three main determinants of the price elasticity of demand for a good: (1) the degree of substitutability with other goods, (2) the size of the portion of buyers' income typically devoted to expenditure on the good, and (3) the length of time over which demand conditions are considered.

Degree of Substitutability.   In Chapter 4 it was argued that the demand curve for a good typically slopes downward from left to right because there are other goods that to varying degrees can be used as substitutes. Hence, if its price goes up, a good becomes more expensive relative to its substitutes. Therefore, less of that good and more of the substitute goods will be demanded. Conversely, if its price goes down, the good becomes less expensive relative to its substitutes. More of that good and less of its substitutes will be demanded. The demand curve for a good will be flatter the more close substitutes it has and the more perfect is their degree of substitutability for that good. Conversely, the demand curve for a good will be steeper the fewer close substitutes it has and the less perfect is their degree of substitutability for that good. Now, how is the degree of substitutability related to the price elasticity of demand?

Before answering this question, we should first be clear about the terminology commonly used to describe the degree of steepness, or slope, of a demand curve. Recall that you cannot judge whether a demand curve is elastic or inelastic over a certain range simply by looking at it. However, when slopes of demand curves (those shown in Figure 5-2, for example) are compared, it is common practice to say that the steeper demand curve is "less elastic" than the flatter demand curve. Alternatively, we can say that the flatter demand curve is "more elastic" than the steeper demand curve. The terminology "more," or "less," elastic is often used even when comparing two demand curves over a price range where they are both inelastic. This terminology is accurate as long as it is understood to mean that the "more elastic," or flatter, demand curve has a higher coefficient of price elasticity than the "less elastic," or steeper, demand curve over the same price range. This means that the comparison is only valid for a change in price away from a point of intersection of the demand curves. For example, for the price change from p_0 to p_1 in Figure 5-2, demand curve D_1 is less elastic than D_2.

In summary, abiding by these conventions of usage, the following statements can be made about the appearance of demand curves. We can say that the flatter a demand curve is over any given price range, the more elastic is demand over that range. Conversely, the steeper a demand curve is over any given price range, the less elastic is demand over that range. The more close substitutes a good has and the more perfect is their degree of substitutability for that good, the greater is the price elasticity of demand for that good. Conversely, the fewer close substitutes a good has and the less perfect is their degree of substitutability for that good, the smaller is the price elasticity of demand for that good.

There are many fairly close substitute wines for the red table wine discussed in the Policy Perspective. It is not surprising that our calculations of the coefficient of price elasticity based on the number cited should suggest that demand for that particular wine is fairly elastic (although market demand for wine in general or for all alcoholic beverages is not very elastic). By contrast, there are few, if any, substitutes for an artificial heart valve. Therefore, demand for artificial heart valves is probably quite inelastic.

Checkpoint 5-3

Suppose that utility companies in Brampton and Kitchener say they are finding it difficult to produce all the electricity their customers are demanding. Let us suppose that we were able to obtain information on electricity demand in Kitchener and the data indicate that the demand in this city is less sensitive to changes in price than the demand in Brampton. What sort of shape do you think the demand curve for electricity in Brampton would have compared with the demand curve for electricity in Kitchener? In which city would an increase in price most relieve the strain on the utility companies? Why? If the utility companies raise the price, what effect will time have on the price elasticity of demand?

POLICY PERSPECTIVE

A Sales Analysis of the Demand for Wine

The concept of elasticity can be a practical tool in the business world for providing useful information about markets. Suppose, for example, that you are a consultant hired by the Ontario Grape Growers' Association to analyze the wine sales of an especially large local winery. The members of the association are always keenly interested in how their largest customer is doing in general, and in what kind of sales policies association members should adopt in dealing with the winery in particular. The grape growers want you to give them some idea of how responsive their customers' wine sales are to price changes.

In the course of researching the problem, you discover that the winery recently cut the price of its red table wine from $7.50 a bottle to $6.50 a bottle. You also find out that before the price cut, the wine had been selling at a rate approximately equal to 1,000 cases per month. After the price cut, sales climbed to more than 4,000 cases per month.

You decide to use arc elasticity to calculate the coefficient of price elasticity of demand. The average of the two sales quantities is (1,000 + 4,000)/ 2, which equals 2,500. The average of the two prices is ($7.50 + $6.50)/ 2, which equals $7. Using these two pieces of information, you now calculate the percentage increase in the quantity (number of cases) of wine sold per month, and the percentage reduction in the price per bottle that led to the increase in wine sales. Since you are using percentages it makes no difference whether you measure the quantity in terms of cases or bottles, or whether you measure price as price per case or price per bottle. The percentage change in quantity is therefore (3,000/2,500) × 100, or 120. The percentage change in price is (1/7) × 100, or 14.3. The calculation of the coefficient of price elasticity of demand is

$$\eta_d = \frac{\frac{3,000}{2,500}}{\frac{1}{7}} = \frac{.12}{.143} = 8.4$$

You now interpret your findings for the grape growers association by telling them that wine sales of the winery's red table wine increase 8.4 percent for each 1 percent reduction in the price of the wine. You also point out that the winery must have increased its total revenue by lowering the price of its red table wine from $7.50 to $6.50 per bottle. Why? Your calculated coefficient of price elasticity of demand for this price change is greater than 1. Therefore, the demand curve for the red table wine is elastic over the range corresponding to this price cut, and hence total revenue must have increased. A calculation of total revenue from the rough quantity data also shows that this is so. At a price of $7.50 per bottle, roughly 1,000 cases of wine were sold per month. Assuming 12 bottles to the case, total revenue was $90,000 per month (equal to 12,000 × $7.50). When price was lowered to $6.50 per bottle, the total quantity sold increased to 4,000 cases per month and total revenue increased to $312,000 per month (equal to 12 × 4,000 × $6.50).

For Discussion

- What should your findings suggest to the grape growers' association about the likely significance of the effect on the demand for grapes by the winery as a consequence of the winery's decision to lower the price of its red table wine?
- Do you think that your reported findings would encourage, or discourage, the members of the association from lowering the price they charge the winery for grapes in an attempt to increase the sales revenue from grape sales? Why?

Size of Expenditure.   If you went to the store to buy a number of things, chances are that the number of matchbooks you might purchase would be little affected by whether they cost $.02 or $.03 a book. If they cost $.03 and you were pretty sure they could be had elsewhere for $.02, you probably wouldn't feel it was worth the cost and hassle (the opportunity cost of your time, for example) to make a special trip just to buy a few matchbooks for $.02 apiece instead of $.03. This is probably true even though the latter price is 50 percent higher than the former. The percentage of your total income spent on matches is small. For this reason, your demand for matches is probably fairly inelastic. On the other hand, suppose you were shopping for a new automobile. Price differences of two or three hundred dollars among similar models would likely send you shopping all over town, even though such differences might amount to less than 1 or 2 percent of the purchase price. Therefore, your demand for a particular model and make of automobile is probably fairly elastic—almost certainly more so than your demand for matchbooks. What this illustrates is the following: *In general, the demand for a good will tend to be more elastic the larger is the portion of your income required to purchase that good.*

Time. It is costly and time-consuming for buyers to gather information about the prices and types of different goods and the degree to which they may serve as substitutes for one another. Moreover, when goods are consumed jointly (complements), the immediate effect of a price change on the quantity demanded of one good may be small because one cannot adjust the consumption of its complement quickly. But over time the consumer can change the amount consumed of the complementary good. As a result, it takes time for buyers to adjust their consumption habits in response to price changes that alter the relative expensiveness of different goods. For example, if the price of gasoline increases there may be little change in the quantity bought immediately after this price change. However, as time passes and consumers' cars need replacing, they may switch, for example, away from 6-litre-engine Buicks to 2-litre-engine Nissans in response to the price increase in gasoline. Hence, the demand curve for gasoline will be flatter in the longrun than in the shortrun. This means that the longrun demand curve will be more elastic throughout its length than the shortrun demand curve. Suppose that D_1 in Figure 5-7 represents the demand curve for a good that holds for a month and D_2 represents the demand curve that holds for a month. It is obvious that a fall in price from p_0 to p_1 results in a larger increase in the quantity demanded after a month (q_0 to q_2) than after a week (q_0 to q_1). *The price elasticity of demand for a good is greater in the longrun than in the shortrun because buyers have more time to adjust to a change in price.*

FIGURE 5-7 Effect of Time on the Elasticity of Demand

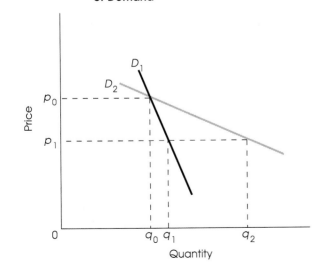

When the price of a good changes, it takes time for all buyers to become aware of the change (time to shop around, for example) and to adjust their consumption habits. The demand curve D_1 for a particular good holds for a shorter period of time, say a week, than does the demand curve D_2, which holds over a longer period of time, say a month. The demand curve D_2 is more elastic than D_1. When price falls from p_0 to p_1, the quantity of the good demanded increases from q_0 to q_1 after a week according to the demand curve D_1, but by the larger amount from q_0 to q_2 after a month according to the demand curve D_2.

Price Elasticity of Supply

The notion of price elasticity is also applicable to supply. The formula is basically the same, but now we are interested in the change in the quantity supplied:

$$\eta_s = \frac{\text{Percentage change in quantity supplied}}{\text{Percentage change in price}}$$

The arc elasticity formula used to calculate the price elasticity of demand is also used to determine the price elasticity of supply. The formula in this case is

$$\eta_s = \frac{\%\Delta q_s}{\%\Delta p} = \frac{\frac{q_2 - q_1}{\frac{q_1 + q_2}{2}}}{\frac{p_2 - p_1}{\frac{p_1 + p_2}{2}}} = \frac{\frac{\Delta q}{\text{Average } q_s}}{\frac{\Delta p}{\text{Average } p}}$$

Supply is the more elastic the larger is the change in the quantity of output produced by suppliers in response to a given change in price. Figure 5-8 shows an inelastic supply curve S_1 and an elastic supply curve S_2. Consider a change in price from p_0 to p_1. The increase in quantity supplied would be from q_0 to q_1 for the inelastic supply curve S_1, a smaller increase than from q_0 to q_2 for the elastic supply curve S_2. **Elastic supply** exists when the coefficient of price elasticity is greater than 1. **Inelastic supply** exists when the coefficient of elasticity is less than 1. A supply curve is unit elastic if the coefficient equals 1. The coefficient of price elasticity of supply will have a positive sign, but as with demand, we are more concerned with the numeric value.

FIGURE 5-8 **Elasticity of Supply**

The greater the elasticity of supply, the larger the change in quantity in response to a change in price. If price increases from p_0 to p_1, the increase in quantity supplied will be from q_0 to q_1 for the inelastic supply curve S_1. The same price increase will result in a larger increase in supply, from q_0 to q_2, for the elastic supply curve S_2.

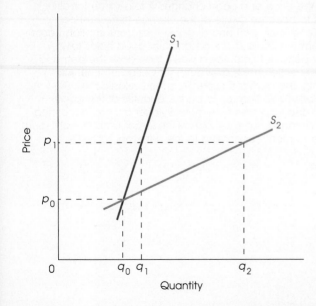

POLICY PERSPECTIVE

Oil Demand Adjustment to Price Change

The price of oil rose nearly twentyfold in the decade following the 1973 OPEC (Organization of Petroleum Exporting Countries) oil embargo. We might expect such a large price increase to reduce the demand for petroleum products substantially. But how much time does it take? The oil embargo provided a unique opportunity to study this question.

Prior to 1973, two decades of falling relative prices (prices in terms of other goods) for oil and petroleum products led firms and consumers to acquire large stocks of energy-using durable goods—houses, factories, commercial buildings, motor vehicles, and machinery and equipment. The large increase in the price of oil in 1973 from $3.65/bbl to $4.50/bbl and in 1974 to $9.00/bbl suddenly made existing stocks of housing and building much more costly to heat and stocks of motor vehicles and machinery and equipment much more expensive to operate. However, Canadian firms and consumers were stuck with these durable goods in the shortrun, no matter what the price of the oil. *In the shortrun the demand for oil is quite inelastic.* It took years to complete the adjustment to substitute sources of energy and to replace existing durable goods with durable goods that are more energy efficient, provide new public rapid transit systems, retrofit existing housing stock with improved insulation, and replace high-energy machinery technologies with improved energy-efficient techniques.

The price elasticity of demand for oil, like that of some other goods, is larger in the longrun than in the shortrun. Over the longrun, oil consumers have more time to seek out alternative energy sources, develop and build durable goods that are more energy efficient, and generally change their energy consumption habits. Hence, as illustrated in Figure P5-1, the shortrun demand curve for oil, D_s, is less elastic than the longrun demand curve, D_l. Therefore, if OPEC raises the price of oil from p_e to p_o, for example, the quantity of oil demanded falls from q_e to q_s—a shortrun adjustment corresponding to a move from point a to point b on D_s. However, as time passes and buyers are able to make all the oil-saving adjustments to the

FIGURE P5-1   The Elasticity of Demand for Oil Increases with the Passage of Time

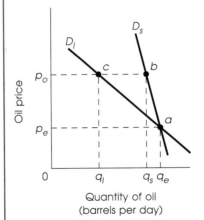

higher price p_o, the demand curve shifts from D_s to D_l and the quantity of oil demand falls from q_s to q_b corresponding to point c on D_l.

There is some evidence on how long the adjustment process might take. For example, studies of gasoline demand find the estimated 1-year price elasticity of demand to lie between .2 and .4. That is, a 10 percent rise in the real price of gasoline causes a 2 to 4 percent reduction in consumption after 1 year—perhaps due mainly to such factors as increased car pooling and shorter vacation trips. The estimated 5-year elasticities are higher, ranging between .6 and .8. Over a 5-year period, consumers appear to adjust by buying more-fuel-efficient cars, moving closer to work, and generally changing fuel consumption habits. The result is that a 10 percent gasoline price rise reduces consumption about 6 to 8 percent. Note, however, that even the 5-year price elasticity of demand is still inelastic. This suggests that the ultimate adjustment to OPEC oil price increases took considerably longer, perhaps a decade or more.

For Discussion

- What do the price elasticity estimates for gasoline demand imply about the behaviour of gasoline sales revenue when gasoline prices increase?
- Do you think that the demand for oil would be more or less elastic for an oil price decrease than it would for an oil price increase? Why?

What Determines Elasticity of Supply?

There are two main determinants of the elasticity of supply of a good: (1) the degree of substitutability of factors of production among different productive activities, and (2) time.

Degree of Substitutability.   When the price of a good rises, it becomes profitable to produce more of it. We examined the reasons why this is so when we discussed the law of supply and the nature of the supply curve in Chapter 4. The increase in the quantity of a good that can be supplied in response to an increase in its price depends, in part, on the ease with which needed factors of production can be induced away from other uses. And this in turn will depend on how readily factors may be adapted from use in other lines of production to production of the good in question.

For example, land that can be used equally well to produce canola or wheat will be easily converted from wheat to canola production if there is an increase in the price of canola (assuming that the price of wheat remains unchanged, of course). The greater is the degree of substitutability of land between wheat and canola production, the larger will be the increase in the quantity of canola supplied in response to any given increase in its price. Consequently, the supply curve for canola will be flatter, or more elastic, the greater the potential for use of the land for other crops. Similarly, if the price of canola should fall, land will be readily taken out of canola production and converted to wheat production. The quantity of canola supplied will be noticeably reduced. On the other hand, if the price of handcrafted artwork were to rise, the quantity produced might increase very little because of the difficulty of finding additional craftspeople. The substitutability of labour between other activities and this one is low. Similarly, a fall in the price of artwork might lead to little reduction in the quantity supplied because the craftspeople like their work so much they are willing to take a considerable cut in wages rather than do something else. The supply curve for handcrafted artwork might therefore be quite steep, or inelastic.

The greater the degree of substitutability of factors of production between the production process of one good and the production processes of other goods, the greater the elasticity of supply of that good.

Time.   The relationship between time and the elasticity of supply is closely related to the degree of substitutability. The more time there is, the more factors of production can be shifted from one productive activity to another. In the canola–wheat example, if the price of canola rises, it will not be possible to increase the quantity of canola supplied during the first week. After the price rise, time will be needed to convert the land to growing canola. As time passes, it will be possible to convert more and more land and other resources to canola production.

In general, in economics we differentiate the market period, the shortrun, and the longrun. The notion of time here is *functional* not chronological—that is, it depends on each individual firm's ability to vary its inputs over time and is useful specifically because it allows us to deal with the different kinds of response possible as a result of price stimuli.

The **market period** is *a period of time during which none of the factors of production can be changed. It is sometimes called the momentary supply.* In the market period,

FIGURE 5-9 **The Effect of Time on the Elasticity of Supply**

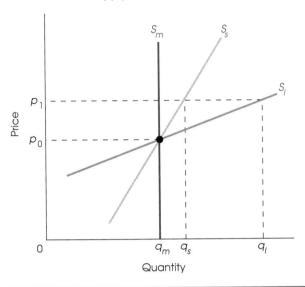

The more time suppliers have to respond to a change in price, the greater will be the change in the quantity of output that they supply. Suppose that price rises from p_0 to p_1. In the very shortrun, or market period, all factors of production are fixed, and it is therefore impossible to change the quantity produced and supplied. Hence, the supply curve is perfectly inelastic, or vertical, like S_m. In the shortrun, some factors of production, such as plant and equipment, are fixed, while some, such as labour, may be changed. Therefore, the supply curve is more elastic, like S_s, and the quantity of output supplied can be increased from q_m to q_s. In the longrun, all factors of production can be changed, the supply curve is even more elastic, like S_l, and the quantity of output supplied can be increased an even larger amount from q_m to q_l.

production is perfectly inelastic but supply may have some elasticity because firms can hold inventory. Only in the upward direction, and after some threshold price, is it impossible to change the quantity of output supplied in response to a change in price. Therefore, at this point, the supply of a good for a market period is perfectly inelastic. The vertical supply curve of a good in a market period appears as S_m in Figure 5-9.

In the **shortrun**, *the quantities of at least some of the factors of production available for the production of a good are given, or fixed. Hence, the shortrun is a period of time that is not long enough to allow the quantities of all factors of production to be changed.* In the shortrun, some factors of production such as labour can be changed. Therefore, it is possible to change the quantity of output supplied to some extent, within the physical capabilities of the fixed plants presently in existence, in response to a price change. Supply may still be inelastic but it is not perfectly inelastic as in the market period. The supply curve for a good in the shortrun appears as S_s in Figure 5-9. In the **longrun** *there is sufficient time to change the quantities of all factors of production.* In the longrun, all factors of production may be changed. Thus, the change in quantity of the good supplied in response to a price change can be much greater than in the shortrun. Supply is more elastic and the supply curve appears as S_l in Figure 5-9. In summary, if price rose from p_0 to p_1 in Figure 5-9, the quantity of the good supplied would remain at q_m in the market period, would increase from q_m to q_s in the shortrun, and would increase from q_m to q_l in the longrun.

Checkpoint 5-4

When we calculate the coefficient of price elasticity for the change in quantity supplied that results from a change in price, we automatically get a positive number. Hence, we don't need to adopt a convention of ignoring the minus sign as we do when we calculate the coefficient of price elasticity for demand. Why is there this difference between the coefficient of elasticity for supply and that for demand?

Other Elasticity Measures

We have shown with demand and supply price elasticities that elasticity is a very useful quantitative measure of the responsiveness of some variable to changes in another. As was mentioned at the beginning of the chapter, this measure can be used to measure the degree of responsiveness between changes in any two variables. Two of the more useful elasticity measures in economic analysis are **cross price elasticity** and **income elasticity** of demand.

Cross Price Elasticity of Demand

Chapter 4 discussed the relationships between goods. If goods are consumed jointly they are referred to as *complements*. If two goods can be used in place of each other, they are referred to as *substitutes*. The shift in demand for one good when the price of another changed was also discussed in that chapter. Cross price elasticity is a more precise way of measuring these relationships between goods. It measures the responsiveness of the quantity demanded of one good, A, to a change in the price of a different good, B. The cross price elasticity of demand is measured as the ratio of the percentage change in demand for good A to the percentage change in price of good B. It thus predicts by how much, in relative percentage terms, the demand for A shifts to the left or right when p_B increases by one percent. The formula for the arc measure of cross price elasticity is:

$$\eta_{D_A}^{p_B} = \frac{\%\Delta D_A}{\%\Delta p_B} = \frac{\frac{D_2 - D_1}{\frac{D_1 + D_2}{2}}}{\frac{p_2 - p_1}{\frac{p_1 + p_2}{2}}} = \frac{\frac{\Delta D_A}{\text{average } D_A}}{\frac{\Delta p_B}{\text{average } p_B}}$$

For example, the price of butter may increase from \$2.00 to \$2.25 causing a shift in the demand for margarine. This is illustrated in Figure 5-10. The quantity of margarine bought at the current price of \$1.50 increases from 1,150

FIGURE 5-10   Cross Price Elasticity

The demand for margarine shifts from D_0 to D_1 because of the increase in the price of a substitute—butter. The quantity demanded of margarine at a price of \$1.50 increases from 1,150 tonnes to 1,200 tonnes per month. The coefficient of cross price elasticity is +.36.

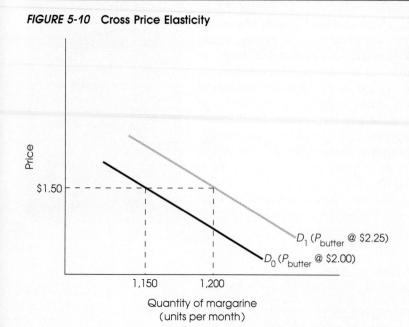

tonnes per month to 1,200. To calculate the cross price elasticity, using the preceding formula:

$$\eta_{D_A}^{p_B} = \frac{\frac{50}{2350}}{2} \div \frac{\frac{.25}{4.25}}{2} = +.36$$

The sign of the elasticity coefficient is important in this calculation. The quantity of margarine bought *increased* with an *increase* in the price of butter. Therefore a plus (+) sign indicates that these goods are substitutes. If the quantity of one good decreased with the increase of the price of a related good, the sign on the coefficient of cross price elasticity would be negative (−), indicating that the goods were complements.

Income Elasticity of Demand

In Chapter 4, the relationship between the demand for a good and consumer income was discussed. If a good is normal, then the demand curve shifts to the right if consumers' incomes increase, *ceteris paribus*. And if the demand curve shifts leftward with an increase in incomes, then the good is an inferior good. Income elasticity is a more precise way of measuring the responsiveness and direction of changes in demand due to income changes. It measures the responsiveness of the demand of the good to a change in income. Income elasticity of demand is measured as the ratio of the percentage change in quantity demanded to the percentage change in income. The formula for the arc measure of income (Y) elasticity of a good X is

$$\eta_{D_X}^{Y} = \frac{\%\Delta D_X}{\%\Delta Y} = \frac{\frac{D_2 - D_1}{\frac{D_1 + D_2}{2}}}{\frac{Y_2 - Y_1}{\frac{Y_1 + Y_2}{2}}} = \frac{\frac{\Delta D_X}{\text{average } D_X}}{\frac{\Delta Y}{\text{average } Y}}$$

For example, consumers' income may increase from \$300 to \$350 causing a shift in the demand for a normal good. This is illustrated in Figure 5-11. The quantity bought at the current price increases from 5 units per week to 6. To calculate the income elasticity, we use the formula just given:

$$\eta_{D_X}^{Y} = \frac{\frac{1}{11}}{2} \div \frac{\frac{50}{650}}{2} = +1.18$$

Again, the sign of the elasticity coefficient is important in this calculation. The quantity of the good bought *increased* with an *increase* in incomes. Therefore a plus (+) sign indicates this good is normal. If the quantity of the good decreased with an increase in incomes, the sign on the coefficient of income elasticity would be negative (−), indicating the good was inferior.

Summary of Elasticity Measures

Table 5-2 summarizes the information obtained from calculating different elasticity measures. The top part of the table indicates the information obtained from the *sign* of the specific elasticity coefficient calculated. The lower part of

FIGURE 5-11   Income Elasticity

The demand curve for a normal good shifts from D_0 to D_1 because of the incease in consumer's income. The quantity demanded of the good at a price of $1.00 increases from 5 to 6 units per week. The coefficient of income elasticity is $+1.18$.

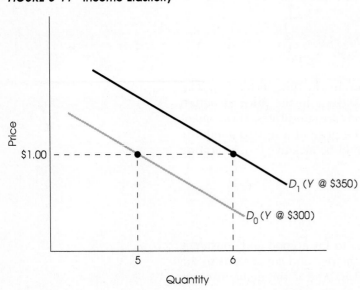

the table illustrates a continuum from zero to infinity. If we take the absolute value of any specific elasticity coefficient that we have calculated and place it on the continuum, we can tell how much one variable responds to another. Elasticity measures are simple quantitative measures that are relatively easy to calculate from accessible market data and provide economists, business people, and policy makers with a wealth of information about the various goods and services traded in the market.

TABLE 5-2   Summary of Elasticity Measures

Type of Elasticity	Sign	Information
Price elasticity	+	Supply
	−	Demand
Cross Price Elasticity	+	Substitutes
	−	Complements
Income Elasticity	+	Normal
	−	Inferior

Absolute Value of the Coefficient of Elasticity $|\eta|$

0		1		∞
perfectly inelastic	inelastic	unit elastic	elastic	perfectly elastic

Summary

1. Elasticity measures the degree of responsiveness of one variable to changes in another. It is measured by the coefficient of elasticity, which is the percentage change in one variable divided by the percentage change in the other. This measure is particularly useful in supply and demand analysis and gives us greater quantitative information about the supply and demand functions.

2. Price elasticity of demand is the degree of responsiveness of the quantity of a good demanded to a change in its price. The coefficient of price elasticity is the percentage change in quantity demanded divided by the percentage change in price. One method of calculating it is to use the point elasticity measure. This method uses standard percentage changes—the difference over the *original*. With this method, a different value for elasticity is obtained depending on which point on the demand curve one starts with. Direction of movement on the demand curve matters.

3. Another method of calculating elasticity avoids the problem of direction. In the calculation of the percentage changes, the average of two points is used instead of the standard method of calculating percentage changes using the original point. With this method one obtains the same elasticity number regardless of which point one starts from. This is called the *arc elasticity method* and uses the midpoint formula.

4. When the coefficient of price elasticity is greater than 1, demand is said to be *elastic*. When the coefficient approaches infinity, demand is perfectly elastic (horizontal). When the coefficient is less than 1, demand is said to be *inelastic*. When it approaches zero, demand is perfectly inelastic (vertical). The quantity demanded is less responsive to price change when demand is inelastic than it is when demand is elastic.

5. The elasticity of demand changes over different parts of a straight-line demand curve with constant slope. Therefore, it can be misleading to judge the elasticity of demand along a certain part of a demand curve by the slope, or flatness or steepness, of the demand curve along that part. The slope changes along a constant-price-elasticity demand curve.

6. Whether a demand curve is elastic or inelastic along a certain range can be determined by observing how total revenue changes along that range as price changes. If total revenue moves in the opposite direction to price, demand is elastic; if total revenue moves in the same direction as price, demand is inelastic.

7. The main determinants of the price elasticity of demand for a good are the degree of substitutability with other goods, the size of the portion of a buyer's income that must be devoted to expenditure on the good, and the length of time over which demand conditions are considered. Demand will usually be more elastic the greater is the degree of substitutability with other goods, the larger is the portion of a buyer's income that must be devoted to expenditure on the good, and the longer is the length of time over which demand conditions are considered.

8. The concept of price elasticity is also applicable to supply. Supply is more elastic the larger is the change in the quantity of output produced by suppliers in response to a change in price, the greater is the degree of substi-

tutability of factors of production among different productive activities, and the longer is the time period over which supply is considered.

9. Cross price elasticity measures the responsiveness of changes in the demand for one good with changes in the price of another. If the sign of the calculated coefficient is positive, the two goods are substitutes. If the sign is negative, the goods are complements. The larger the absolute value of the coefficient the greater is the degree of responsiveness (elasticity) of one good's demand to the price of the other.

10. Income elasticity measures the responsiveness of changes in the demand for a good with changes in consumers' incomes. If the sign of the coefficient is positive, the good is normal. If the sign is negative, the good is inferior. The larger is the absolute value of the coefficient the greater is the degree of responsiveness of the good's quantity demanded to income changes.

Key Terms and Concepts

arc elasticity
coefficient of elasticity
cross price of elasticity
elastic demand
elastic supply
income elasticity
inelastic demand

inelastic supply
longrun
market period
midpoints formula
perfectly elastic
perfectly inelastic
point elasticity

price elasticity of demand
price elasticity of return
shortrun
slope of demand curve
total revenue
unit elastic
variation

Questions and Problems

1. Classify the following goods and services according to whether you think that the demand for them over a period of a year is elastic or inelastic: gasoline, margarine, kidney dialysis machines, Molson's Canadian beer, haircuts, electricity, chocolate ice cream, appendectomies, trash disposal, fire insurance, funeral services, services of medical doctors, and postal service.

2. Classify the following goods and services according to whether you think the supply of them over a period of a year is elastic or inelastic: Rembrandt paintings, advice, soft drinks, suspension bridges, medical services, used cars, corn, hand soap, matches, cactus plants, 5-year-old wine, and oil tankers.

3. Suppose that you owned a lake that had fish in it and you could charge people a daily fee for the privilege of fishing in your lake. That is, payment of the fee, or price, for a daily fishing right would entitle anyone to fish all day for one day with one fishing pole.

   a. If you knew that the market demand for fishing rights was unit elastic, how would you decide what price to charge for a fishing right—a price that would result in the sale of one right, two rights, more, or none at all? Why?

   b. Suppose that neighbours down the road also own a lake. Observing your activity, they decide to start selling fishing rights to their lake. How will this affect the elasticity of the demand curve for fishing rights in your lake? Will you raise or lower the price you charge for a fishing right?

4. Suppose that in the early part of next year there is a severe cold spell and parts of the country experience gas shortages. Suppose that the price of natural gas is free to rise at that time.

a. What do you predict will happen to the dollar volume of gas sales relative to the number of cubic feet of gas actually sold?

b. Suppose you read in the paper that households are reported to be keeping their thermostats at 22 degrees Celsius but many businesses and factories are cutting back operations considerably. What do you conclude about the household demand for gas relative to the commercial demand?

5. Suppose that the demand curve for a good shifts rightward while the supply curve shifts leftward. Rank the following sets of conditions according to the size of the change in price you would predict as a result of the shifts: demand curve elastic and supply curve inelastic, demand curve inelastic and supply curve inelastic, and demand curve elastic and supply curve elastic.

6. Suppose that the demand curve for a good shifts rightward and the supply curve remains fixed. Rank the following sets of conditions according to the size of the change in quantity you would predict as a result of the shift: supply curve inelastic and demand curve inelastic, supply curve elastic and demand curve inelastic, and supply curve inelastic and demand curve elastic.

7. Suppose that the supply curve for a good shifts leftward and the demand curve remains fixed. Rank the following sets of conditions according to the size of the change in quantity you would predict as a result of the shift: supply curve elastic and demand curve inelastic, supply curve inelastic and demand curve elastic, and supply curve inelastic and demand curve inelastic.

8. Find the following coefficients of elasticity of demand from the following changes:

a. the price elasticity of demand;

Price	Quantity Demanded
$24	125
$26	150

b. the income elasticity of demand (and classify good X as normal or inferior);

Income	Demand for X
$300	140
$250	150

c. the cross price elasticity of demand (and state the relationship between goods A and B).

Price of B	Demand for A
$30	120
$35	130

Chapter 6

Consumer Theory of Demand

In Chapter 4 we studied the law of demand—the belief that individuals will buy more of a good the lower its price, all other things remaining constant. In this chapter we will investigate further the logic behind this consumer behaviour.[1] Consumer behaviour is an exciting area of research in diverse subject areas such as psychology and marketing as well as in economics. For different reasons, these disciplines study the motivation behind consumer behaviour. Whatever motivates consumers, the decisions of the individual, family, or household are of crucial importance to the economy. The performance of a market-oriented economy, such as Canada's, is ultimately judged by its responsiveness to consumer desires.

The approach economists have developed to explain consumers' behaviour relies on a particular notion of consumer rationality. To economists, consumers are seeking to obtain the most satisfaction from the limited resources at their disposal. This satisfaction, obtained from the consumption of commodites, is *subjective*, depending on the particular individual. You may have very different feelings, and therefore preferences, about drinking beer than do your friends. If everyone's preferences are individual, how can we generalize about consumer behaviour in any meaningful way? Even though preferences are personal, there is something common to each individual's or household's preferences that allows a systematic, although limited, analysis. This analysis supports the general expectation of downward-sloping demand curves studied in Chapter 4.

In this chapter we will study consumer behaviour from three approaches. The first, a verbal argument, is a simple explanation of the income and

---

[1]There is also a large body of empirical evidence to support the law of demand. If one were convinced by this alone, it might be unnecessary to study consumer theory (the logic of this behaviour), and one could continue on to the next chapter. If nothing else, the theory is of interest for its insights into how economists develop models of rational behaviour. We think the theory has more to offer. It explains not only the behaviour but the effects of policy initiatives on demand *before* they are initiated, in many cases preventing expensive mistakes that could only be noted *after* the fact if one relied on empiricism alone.

substitution effects of a price change. The second approach, utility theory, is an older—some would say obsolete—method of describing demand behaviour. The third, indifference analysis, is a modern rigorous analytical approach to understanding consumer behaviour. The three approaches can lead to the same view of consumer behaviour. We will illustrate the similarities of the approaches at the end of the chapter.

Substitution and Income Effects and Consumer Demand

Up to now we have based our view that demand curves slope downward from left to right on simple common sense and casual observation of the economic world around us. If pushed further, we might reason that if the price of a good is reduced, it will now take a smaller portion of our budget to buy the same quantity of it. This means that more of our budget is now available to purchase more of other goods, as well as more of the good whose price has fallen. Therefore, a price reduction increases real income (purchasing power) and increases the quantity demanded of the good. This increase in quantity demanded, due to an increase in purchasing power caused by a price reduction, is termed the **income effect.** In addition to this effect, we would also expect the quantity demanded of a good whose price has fallen to increase, because that good is now cheaper relative to all other goods. Hence, consumers would substitute more of that good for others. When the price of a good falls, the increase in quantity demanded due to a substitution of this good for other (now relatively more expensive) goods is termed the **substitution effect.** For example, you may go out to purchase a new suit of clothes and find that, because of a sale, you can buy what you want for 30 percent less than you expected. You may buy two suits instead of one as: (1) you feel more prosperous—the income effect; and (2) you substitute clothes for some other goods you were going to buy that now appear relatively more expensive— the substitution effect.

LEARNING OBJECTIVES

After reading this chapter, you will be able to:

1. Explain the law of demand using the concepts of income and substitution effects.
2. Define *utility, marginal utility, total utility,* and *global utility.*
3. Demonstrate understanding of the law of diminishing marginal utility.
4. Explain the condition for unconstrained utility maximization.
5. Explain the "paradox of value."
6. Define and explain consumer's equilibrium using utility theory.
7. Derive a demand curve using utility theory.
8. Develop, graph, and explain an indifference curve and indifference map.
9. Develop, graph, and explain a budget line.
10. Define and calculate consumer's equilibrium using indifference analysis.
11. Derive a demand curve using indifference analysis.
12. Discuss how the three methods of explaining consumer behaviour can be combined in one model.

In general, any change in the price of a good (up or down) may be said to have a substitution effect and an income effect on that good—all other things, such as the consumer's preferences and money income, remaining the same. The substitution and income effects of a change in price for a particular good provide a somewhat fuller explanation of why the demand curve for a good slopes downward from left to right. Another explanation for the shape of a demand curve is based on the concept of utility.

Utility Theory and Consumer Demand

The Concept of Utility

In Chapter 1 we noted that people desire goods because they provide some sort of satisfaction or service. A movie provides entertainment, which gives satisfaction. An apple or a glass of milk provides not only satisfaction but nourishment, which serves to sustain life. The service or satisfaction a good yields is often referred to as the *utility* that the consumer gets from the good. Utility is not to be restricted to usefulness. A concert may not be considered as useful as a screwdriver, but one may feel there is more utility in the form of satisfaction associated with the former than with the latter. **Utility** *is the satisfaction, enjoyment, or usefulness obtained from consuming a good.* Utility is the common *essence* acquired from all goods.

Utility is a subjective response. It is not possible to compare the utility I get from eating a candy bar with the utility you get from eating one. The issue of how much more you enjoy a candy bar than I do is not something that can be settled by objective measurement, as is the case in a dispute over which one of us is taller, for example. However, the concept of utility has been used by economists to provide an explanation for the shape of a consumer's demand curve for a good. This can be done because it is possible to envision an individual consumer making comparisons of the different levels of utility that he or she associates with different kinds and quantities of goods.

Total Utility.   Suppose that we consider the utility that a particular (hypothetical) individual gets from eating chocolates over some given period of time, say a day. This is known as **total utility**. The basic measure of utility, or satisfaction, is called a *util*. The relationship between the amount of chocolates consumed and the amount of associated utility is shown in Table 6-1. The utility associated with eating the first chocolate is 10 utils. If the individual eats another chocolate, the total utility from eating the two chocolates is 19 utils. If the individual were to eat 10 chocolates, the total utility would amount to 55 utils. The data for total utility and chocolate consumption from Table 6-1 are plotted in Figure 6-1, frame (a). This graph clearly shows that total utility increases as the number of chocolates eaten increases. However, total utility reaches a maximum at 10 chocolates. If the individual eats 11 chocolates, the total utility doesn't change. The last chocolate neither adds to nor subtracts from satisfaction. If a twelfth chocolate is consumed, it doesn't go down well and total utility decreases to 54 utils.

TABLE 6-1   One Individual's Total Utility and Marginal Utility from Eating Chocolates During a Day (Hypothetical Data)

Number of Chocolates per Day	Total Utility (Utils)	Marginal Utility (Change in Utility per Additional Chocolate)
1	10	
		9
2	19	
		8
3	27	
		7
4	34	
		6
5	40	
		5
6	45	
		4
7	49	
		3
8	52	
		2
9	54	
		1
10	55	
		0
11	55	
		−1
12	54	

Marginal Utility.   A more useful consideration from an economist's point of view is the way total utility changes with the consumption of each additional chocolate. *The change in total utility that occurs with the consumption of an additional unit of a good is the* **marginal utility.** Marginal utility refers to the increment, or addition, to total utility associated with one more unit of the good consumed. The marginal utility associated with eating chocolate for our hypothetical individual is shown in the third column of Table 6-1. For example, if the individual has had one chocolate already, the marginal utility associated with eating a second is 9 utils. This brings the total utility to 19 utils. The marginal utility of a third chocolate is 8 utils, which brings the total to 27 utils, and so forth. Observe that as the consumer eats more chocolates, the marginal utility associated with eating one more chocolate gets smaller and smaller. This is shown in the graph of marginal utility in Figure 6-1, frame (b).

Law of Diminishing Marginal Utility

The important thing to note about marginal utility is that it decreases as more of the good is consumed over a given period of time. It is, of course, possible that the second or third unit of a good consumed may add more to total utility than the first. (For some chocolate eaters this may be true.) But for almost any good one can think of, marginal utility will eventually begin to fall as more and more of the good is consumed over a given period of time and one's appetite

FIGURE 6-1   Total Utility and Marginal Utility

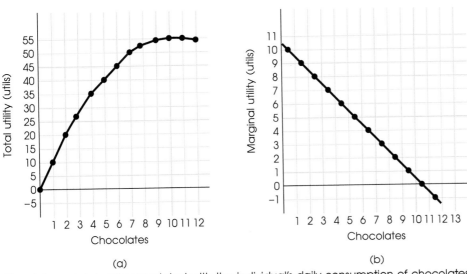

(a)   (b)

The data on total utility associated with the individual's daily consumption of chocolates from Table 6-1 are graphed in Figure 6-1, frame (a). Frame (b) is a graph of the data on marginal utility from the same table. Total utiltiy clearly rises as the individual eats more chocolates, but at a diminishing rate. The slowdown is clearly shown by the graph of the additional, or mariginal, utility [frame (b)] that the individual realizes from each additional chocolate eaten. The fact that it slopes downward from left to right illustrates the *law of diminishing marginal utility.*

for that good becomes satiated. Even the marginal utility associated with the consumption of salted peanuts eventually begins to fall.

Economists assume this behaviour of marginal utility to be so universal that they call it the **law of diminishing marginal utility.** *The law of diminishing marginal utility states that, given the consumer's preferences, the marginal utility associated with the consumption of any good over a given period of time will eventually begin to decrease as more of the good is consumed.* This law is demonstrated by the downward-sloping marginal utility curve in Figure 6-1, frame (b), for example. The law simply reflects the widely observed fact that the more a person has of a good, the less satisfaction or utility is derived from having one more unit of the good.

The "Paradox of Value"

The discovery of the law of diminishing marginal utility was quite significant in the history of economic ideas. Early economists were puzzled by the fact that prices were high for diamonds—relatively useless ornaments—while water, upon which life itself depended, was inexpensive or even free (any resource that is not scarce is free). The solution to this paradox was found in the notion of diminishing marginal utility. Diamonds are relatively scarce, and although their total utility is low, an extra diamond gives a high marginal utility. People are therefore willing to pay a high price. Water, on the other hand, is relatively plentiful, and although the total utility from water is high, another litre is not worth much. Therefore people are not willing to pay much for it. The law of diminishing marginal utility explains the paradox. The immediate value we place on a good depends both on how much we have of it and on what marginal utility an additional unit provides to us. If we have a lot of something we may value an additional unit very little, no matter how important overall the thing is to us. If we have very little of something we may place a high value on obtaining some of it, no matter how unimportant it may be in the scheme of things.

How the Consumer Allocates Expenditures Among Goods

No consumer has an unlimited budget. Therefore, it is necessary to make choices—more of one good can be obtained only by purchasing less of another. (Of course, a consumer could save some of their income.) For our purposes, the consumer's total budget is the amount the consumer is willing and able to spend in a given time period. This amount could be more or less than the consumer's current income, as he or she can either save current income or borrow on future income. A consumer does not usually maximize the total utility from one good unless it is free or the consumer is unconstrained by a budget. Given a limited budget, the individual consumer's problem is how to allocate expenditure of that budget among goods so as to make total satisfaction, or global utility, as large as possible. **Global utility** *is the sum of the total utilities obtained from the consumption of a number of goods.* Given a limited budget, how does a consumer determine what combination of goods should be purchased in order to realize the greatest possible satisfaction? A simple example will help us to understand the answer to this question.

Determining the Utility-Maximizing Combination of Goods—A Simple Example

Let's consider a consumer who has a total daily budget of $11. Suppose that there are only two goods, X and Y, say food and clothing. The utility that a consumer gets from the two goods is shown in Table 6-2. Column (2) gives the total utility obtained from the consumption of the quantity of food, good X, indicated

TABLE 6-2   Utility, Marginal Utility, and Marginal Utility per Dollar Obtained from Goods X and Y* (Hypothetical Data)

Food (Good X): Price = $1				Clothing (Good Y): Price = $2			
(1) Quantity of Good X	(2) Total Utility from X (Utils)	(3) Marginal Utility (Utils)	(4) Marginal Utility per Dollar (MU/Price)	(5) Quantity of Good Y	(6) Total Utility from Y (Utils)	(7) Marginal Utility (Utils)	(8) Marginal Utility per Dollar (MU/Price)
1	10	10	10	1	22	22	11
2	19	9	9	2	42	20	10
3	25	6	6	3	58	16	8
4	29	4	4	4	70	12	6
5	31	2	2	5	78	8	4
6	30	1	1	6	80	2	1

*It is assumed that the marginal utility of either good is unaffected by the quantity of the other good consumed.

in column (1). Column (3) shows the marginal, or additional, utility derived from the consumption of each successive unit of X. Similarly, columns (6) and (7) show the total and marginal utility, respectively, derived from the consumption of clothing, good Y. For each good the law of diminishing marginal utility is reflected in the fact that marginal utility declines [columns (3) and (7)] as more of the good is consumed.

The consumer's preferences or feelings about goods X and Y, as reflected in the utility data of Table 6-2, combined with the prices of the two goods, will determine the combination of X and Y that maximizes the consumer's global utility, given a fixed budget of $11 per day. In order to see how the consumer chooses this combination, the marginal utility data of columns (3) and (7) must be expressed as marginal utility per dollar spent. This makes it easier to compare the additional utility obtainable by spending a dollar on one of the goods with the additional utility obtainable by spending that dollar on the other good. We expect that a consumer would purchase the next unit of the good that provided her with the highest marginal utility per dollar. Suppose the price of a unit of food (P_X) is $1, while that of a unit of clothing (P_Y) is $2. The marginal utility per dollar spent on X, column (4), is found by dividing the marginal utility data in column (3) by $1. Similarly, the marginal utility per dollar spent on Y, column (8), is found by dividing the data in column (7) by $2.

Using this model of behaviour, we can now predict how the consumer would go about spending a daily income of $11 on goods X and Y. Remember, the consumer's objective is to allocate expenditures on X and Y in such a way as to achieve the highest possible level of utility. Think of it as the consumer buying utility not goods. Comparing columns (4) and (8), the consumer should first purchase 1 unit of good Y because its marginal utility of 11 utils per dollar is higher than X's. The consumer still has $9 to spend. At this point the consumer could get the same marginal utility per dollar, 10 utils, from 1 unit of X or 1 unit of Y. So the consumer buys both of them. The consumer now has 1 unit of X, 2 units of Y, and $6 yet to spend. Comparing columns (4) and (8) again, the consumer next should buy a second unit of X, since its marginal utility per dollar is greater than that of a third unit of Y. Observe that, once this has been done, the marginal utility per dollar of a third unit of Y exceeds that of a third unit of X. Hence a third unit of Y is purchased. Now the consumer has 2 units of X, 3 units of Y, and $3 left to spend. The consumer is indifferent as to the choice between a third unit of X and a fourth unit of Y, since each yields 6 utils per dollar spent. However, the consumer has just enough money left to buy each of them.

The consumer has now spent the whole daily income of $11 to obtain a combination consisting of 3 units of X and 4 units of Y. Note that this combination is such that the marginal utility derived from the last dollar spent on each good is the same. This combination gives the consumer the highest global utility possible, given a budget of $11. Global utility equals 95 utils, the sum of the 25 utils derived from the 3 units of X, column (2), plus the 70 utils derived from the 4 units of Y, column (6). There is no other combination that can be purchased for $11 that will give the consumer as much global utility. For example, $11 could purchase a combination consisting of 1 unit of X and 5 units of Y — global utility equals 88 utils. Or $11 could buy 5 units of X and 3 units of Y, giving a global utility of 89 utils. Notice that for either of these combinations it is *not true* that the marginal utility derived from the last dollar spent on each good is the same.

The rule that emerges from our example of picking the combination of goods that maximizes utility is the following: *To maximize global utility the consumer will spend a given budget to buy that combination of goods such that the marginal utility derived from the last dollar spent on each good is the same.*

Why the Rule Works

We can get additional insight into why the rule works by restating it more concisely. The marginal utility (*MU*) per dollar spent on *X* is equal to the *MU* of good *X* divided by the price of *X*, column (4) of Table 6-2. The *MU* per dollar spent on *Y* is equal to the *MU* of good *Y* divided by the price of *Y*, column (8) of Table 6-2. The utility-maximizing rule says that the consumer would spend a given budget to buy that combination of *X* and *Y* that makes the marginal utility of the last dollar spent on *X* equal to the marginal utility of the last dollar spent on *Y* or, more concisely,

$$\frac{MU \text{ of good } X}{\text{Price of } X} = \frac{MU \text{ of good } Y}{\text{Price of } Y}$$

For the optimum combination of 3 units of *X* and 4 units of *Y* in Table 6-2, obtained by spending the $11 of budget, this equality is met:

$$\frac{6 \text{ utils}}{\$1} = \frac{12 \text{ utils}}{\$2}$$

If this equality is not satisfied, it is always possible to increase global utility by buying less of the good having the lower marginal utility per dollar and redirecting the money saved to buy more of the good with the higher marginal utility per dollar.

For instance, suppose that our consumer in Table 6-2 spent the $11 budget to buy a combination consisting of 5 units of good *X* and 3 units of good *Y*. Then the marginal utility derived from the last dollar spent on *X* is 2 utils, column (4) of Table 6-2, which is less than the marginal utility of 8 utils, column (8) of Table 6-2, derived from the last dollar spent on *Y*. The equality is not satisfied:

$$\frac{2 \text{ utils}}{\$1} < \frac{16 \text{ utils}}{\$2}$$

The consumer's global utility could be increased if she purchased a smaller amount of *X* and a larger amount of *Y*. To see why, suppose that the consumer reallocates expenditures by taking $2 away from expenditure on *X* and instead spending that $2 on more *Y*. This reduces consumption of *X* by 2 units (from 5 units to 3 units) and the utility derived from *X* by 6 utils—the sum of 2 utils plus 4 utils in column (3) of Table 6-2. The additional $2 of spending on *Y* increases consumption of *Y* by 1 unit (from 3 units to 4 units), and the utility derived from consumption of *Y* rises by 12 utils, column (7) of Table 6-2. The net gain in utility resulting from this reallocation of expenditures is 6 utils: Global utility increases from 89 utils—equal to 31 utils, column (2), plus 58 utils, column (6)—to 95 utils—equal to 25 utils, column (2), plus 70 utils, column (6).

The utility-maximizing rule works because whenever the marginal utility derived from the last dollar spent on good *Y* is greater than that derived from the last dollar spent on *X*, the increase in utility obtained by consuming more *Y* is greater than the decrease in utility that results from consuming less *X*. The marginal utility per dollar spent on *Y* decreases as the marginal utility diminishes when more Y is purchased, and the marginal utility per dollar spent on X increases as the consumer reduces the consumption of X. As the consumer continues to reallocate expenditures from X to Y, at some point the marginal utility of the last dollar spent on X is brought into equality with the marginal utility of the last dollar spent on Y. The rule is satisfied. At this point utility cannot be increased more by any further reallocation of expenditure.

Why a Demand Curve Slopes Downward

We are now in a position to see how utility theory explains demand. Recall that movement along a demand curve means that no other determinants of demand change. Only two things potentially change—the price of the good and the quantity of the good demanded. All other things remain unchanged, including the consumer's income and all other prices. Assume that the consumer whose preferences are reflected in the utility data of Table 6-2 is maximizing the global utility obtainable from a daily income of $11 by purchasing 3 units of X and 4 units of Y. Hence, we already have one point on the consumer's demand curve for Y: Given an income of $11 and a price of $1 per unit of the other good X, the quantity of Y demanded at a price of $2 is 4 units.

Suppose now that the price of Y is lowered to $1 per unit, all other things remaining unchanged. This means that the data for the marginal utility per dollar in column (8) will double. In fact, these data will be identical to the data in column (7). The combination of 3 units of X and 4 units of Y no longer gives the consumer the largest possible utility. Applying the utility-maximizing rule, the consumer will now purchase the combination consisting of 5 units of X and 6 units of Y. Here the marginal utility derived from the last dollar spent on X will equal the marginal utility derived from the last dollar spent on Y, 2 utils per dollar. Lowering the price of Y from $2 per unit to $1 per unit has caused the quantity of Y demanded to increase from 4 units to 6 units.

This analysis based on utility theory gives the basic proposition of the law of demand: *A decrease in the price of a good will result in an increase in the quantity of that good demanded by the consumer, given that the consumer's budget and the prices of all other goods are held constant.* If this is true for each consumer, it will also be true for all of them taken together. Hence, the market demand curve will slope downward, from left to right. Note that this result depends on the law of diminishing marginal utility.

> ### Checkpoint* 6-1
>
> Suppose that
>
> $$\frac{MU \text{ of } X}{\text{Price of } X} > \frac{MU \text{ of } Y}{\text{Price of } Y}$$
>
> Explain why and how the consumer's expenditures out of a fixed budget will be reallocated until
>
> $$\frac{MU \text{ of } X}{\text{Price of } X} = \frac{MU \text{ of } Y}{\text{Price of } Y}$$
>
> Why can we expect the demand curve for X to slope downward?
>
> *Answers to all Checkpoints can be found at the back of the text.

Indifference Analysis and Consumer Demand

There is a fundamental objection to using the law of diminishing marginal utility to explain the existence of downward-sloping demand curves. It is the fact that utility cannot be measured in the way we measure distance, weight, and height. To measure these things we use **cardinal** numbers. A cardinal number system uses all the properties of arithmetic—for example, $2 + 2 = 4$ and 4 is twice as much as 2. Alternatively, an **ordinal** number system indicates order only. The magnitude of the number is not important. For example, when you rate something from first to tenth, first is better than tenth, but not necessarily ten times as good. An alternative explanation of demand curves that doesn't require a cardinal measurement is based on the concept of a consumer's preferences using indifference curves.

In this approach to consumer behaviour we first rank different combinations of goods according to a consumer's preferences. Then we consider the set of combinations of goods the consumer can afford, given the prices of the goods and her income. We then combine this information in order to locate the most preferred combination that is also affordable. This selected combination of goods is referred to as the *consumer's equilibrium*. The consumer would have no reason to change from this equilibrium combination of goods unless some variable such as the price of a good, the consumer's preferences, or the consumer's income changed.

Preferences

We can initially avoid the notion of utility with cardinal values by discussing the consumer's choice in terms of her preferences. Suppose that there are two goods available, X and Y, and that we want to find out how a particular consumer feels about consuming various combinations of these two goods. We might begin by saying to the consumer, "Suppose that you have 4 of X and 5 of Y. Tell us what other combinations of X and Y would give you exactly the same satisfaction." Another way of putting this would be to say, "What other combinations of X and Y would leave you feeling no better off and no worse off than you do when you have 4 of X and 5 of Y?" Yet another way of saying exactly the same thing would be, "Tell us the other combinations you find equally satisfying as 4 of X and 5 of Y—that is, the combinations you feel *indifferent* as to whether you have one of them or the combination consisting of 4 of X and 5 of Y." How do we find this set of bundles to which the consumer is indifferent if given a choice?

Utility theory considered the satisfaction derived from each good separately. The indifference approach considers goods in bundles. A **bundle** *of goods is some combination of all the possible goods from which a consumer expects to derive satisfaction.* For our purposes we have assumed the consumer has only two goods—good X and good Y—and that having more of any good is better than having less of it. Then one bundle—for example, c of Figure 6-2, frame (a)—includes 4 units of X and 5 units of Y. What we need to do is rank *all* the possible bundles of X and Y in order of the consumer's preference for them. We will start arbitrarily with the bundle c. Note in Figure 6-2 the grid lines through point c. As any bundle in the NE quadrant has at least more of one good and no less of the other, then these bundles, assuming the consumer is not satiated, must be preferred to c. Similarly, any bundle in the SW quadrant must be less preferred than c, as these bundles have less of both goods or less of one and no more of the other good.

In ordering the bundles according to preferences we have already accomplished quite a lot. But the ordering of bundles in the NW and SE quadrants is still ambiguous as these quadrants include bundles with more of one good and less of the other as compared to c. In Figure 6-2, frame (b), a line is drawn from bundle g to bundle h. Note that h is preferred to c, but c is preferred to g from our previous analysis. Therefore there *must* be some bundle, say b, somewhere along the line gh to which the consumer would be indifferent if given a choice between it and c. If we continue this reasoning ad infinitum we will "discover" a set of bundles through the NW and SE quadrants around c that includes bun-

FIGURE 6-2   **Development of an Indifference Curve**

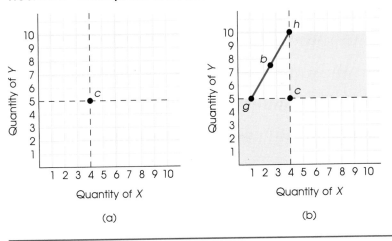

In frame (a) an arbitrary combination of goods X and Y is chosen and grid lines are drawn through the point c, dividing the space into four quadrants. The NE quadrant includes all bundles preferred to c and the SW quadrant includes all bundles less preferred to c. In frame (b) the line *gh* contains some bundle along it, such as *b*, to which the consumer is indifferent if given the choice between it and bundle c.

dles which are equally attractive to the consumer because he or she expects to obtain equal amounts of satisfaction from each bundle.

The Concept of an Indifference Curve

Through the process just described, suppose that this particular consumer télls us five other combinations of X and Y among which she is indifferent. These bundles together with the combination of 4 of X and 5 of Y are listed in Table 6-3. The list of all the bundles represented is called an **indifference schedule.** The first two columns of Table 6-3 list six of the combinations from this schedule. The essential characteristic of an indifference schedule is that the consumer feels indifferent as to which particular bundle of X and Y is consumed. This is because this consumer gets exactly the same satisfaction from any one

TABLE 6-3   **Consumer's Indifference Schedule for Two Goods, X and Y**

Combination	Indifference Schedule (Combinations of X and Y)	Marginal Rate of Substitution Between X and Y $\Delta Y / \Delta X$
a	2, 10	
		$-3/1 = -3.0$
b	3, 7	
		$-2/1 = -2.0$
c	4, 5	
		$-1/1 = -1.0$
d	5, 4	
		$-1/2 = -0.5$
e	7, 3	
		$-1/3 = -0.3$
f	10, 2	

FIGURE 6-3   A Consumer's Indifference Curve

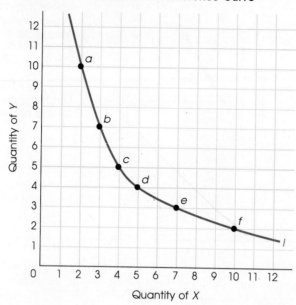

The consumer's indifference curve represents all possible combinations of the goods X and Y that give the consumer equal satisfaction.

bundle as from any other. These bundles are also plotted as the points *a*, *b*, *c*, *d*, *e*, and *f* in Figure 6-3. The consumer could list many more combinations until there is a set of points forming the curve connecting bundles *a* through *f*. The preceding discussion shows that these points when plotted will always fall on a negatively sloped curve. This curve is called an *indifference curve*. An **indifference curve** *is a line in commodity space indicating all bundles of two goods which give a particular consumer the same level of satisfaction.*

A given indifference curve, such as the one illustrated in Figure 6-3, divides *all* the bundles represented in the space into three groups: those preferred to *c*—the bundles to the right of line *af* ; those less satisfying than *c*—the bundles to the left of line *af* ; and those as desirable as *c*—the bundles on the line *af*.

Marginal Rate of Substitution

There is a particularly important point to note about the indifference schedule and its graphic representation, the indifference curve. Starting from any combination or point, if the consumer is given an additional amount of one good, a certain amount of the other must be taken away if the consumer's level of satisfaction is to remain unchanged. The amount taken away is the maximum amount of the one good that the consumer is willing to part with in order to have an additional unit of the other good. It is just the amount that will leave the consumer feeling as well off, but no better off than, as before. *The rate at which the consumer is just willing to substitute good Y for good X so as to leave her level of satisfaction unchanged is called the* **marginal rate of substitution** (*MRS*).

For the consumer of Table 6-3, the marginal rates of substitution between the combinations *a* through *f* are shown in the third column. For example, between the combinations *a* and *b*, the consumer would be just willing to give up 1 unit of X in exchange for 3 units of Y—a move from b to a. Alternatively, the consumer would be just willing to give up 3 units of Y in exchange for 1 unit of X—a move from a to b. The MRS measures the necessary change in good Y with a change in good X if the consumer is to remain equally well off.

$$MRS = \frac{\Delta Y}{\Delta X}$$

Note that the MRS is always negative, indicating that one good is reduced with an increase in the other along an indifference curve.

Diminishing Marginal Rate of Substitution.   Another important characteristic of the indifference schedule and the indifference curve illustrated in Figure 6-3 is that the marginal rate of substitution between X and Y gets smaller the larger is the amount of X the consumer has relative to the amount of Y. For example, suppose that the consumer initially has combination a. If the consumer is given one more unit of X, it is necessary to take away 3 units of Y to maintain the same level of satisfaction at combination b. Continuing in the same fashion from point b to c, to d, to e, and to f, observe that to maintain the same level of satisfaction the amount of X that the consumer is willing to give up per additional amount of Y becomes less and less. This characteristic of the behaviour of the marginal rate of substitution along an indifference curve is referred to as the **diminishing marginal rate of substitution.** It reflects the assumption that the more of good Y a consumer has *relative* to good X, the more of good Y the consumer is willing to part with in order to get an additional unit of good X.[2] It plays a role in indifference theory very similar to the role played by the law of diminishing marginal utility in utility theory.

The Consumer Has Many Indifference Curves

The indifference curve of Figure 6-3 represents only one of a family of indifference curves that characterize the *particular* consumer's feelings of satisfaction derived from consumption of the two goods X and Y. All points on it represent combinations of the goods X and Y that give the consumer the *same* level of satisfaction—a level of satisfaction that is but one among many possible levels of satisfaction. Each of the other possible levels of satisfaction also has an associated indifference curve.

This is illustrated in Figure 6-4. The indifference curve I_1 is exactly the same as the one in Figure 6-3. We are talking about the same particular consumer. Assume that the consumer is at point e on I_1, a combination consisting of 7 units of X and 3 units of Y. Suppose that the consumer was given 4 more units of Y while still keeping 7 units of X. The consumer would then have combination h, consisting of the same amount of X as combination e but more Y. Since at h the

---

[2]In our "discovery" of the indifference curve, all we showed was that an indifference curve must be negatively sloped. The particular shape of the curve in Figure 6-3 suggests more. It shows the widely held view that variety is preferred to extremes. Graphically this means that a point on a straight line drawn from points a and f, such as $5X$ and $7Y$, must be preferred to both bundles a and f, as it entails greater variety. Therefore, a bundle to which the consumer is indifferent compared to a and f must be to the left of this straight line—for example, bundle c.

FIGURE 6-4   **The Consumer's Indifference Map**   The consumer has an unlimited number of in-difference curves, each of which represents a different level of satisfaction.

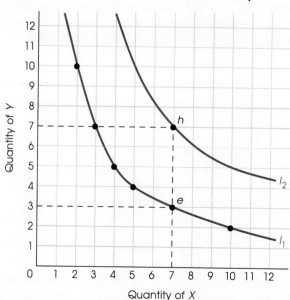

consumer has more of the one good and the same amount of the other as at e, the consumer must feel better off (or feel a higher level of satisfaction) at h than at e. Since the consumer experiences the same level of satisfaction at all points on I_1 as at e, it follows that the consumer feels a higher level of satisfaction at point h than at any point on the curve I_1.

Now suppose that we again ask the consumer to tell us other combinations that give exactly the same level of satisfaction as that at point h. We would then be able to derive the indifference curve I_2 in exactly the same way that we derived the indifference curve I_1. Because the level of satisfaction associated with point h is greater than that associated with any point on I_1, it follows that any point on I_2 represents a higher level of satisfaction than any point on I_1.

Proceeding in this manner, it would be possible to derive an unlimited number of indifference curves, or the **indifference map,** for this particular consumer. Each indifference curve represents a unique and different level of satisfaction. Therefore, they can never intersect with one another. If they did, we would have the logical absurdity that the consumer experiences two different levels of satisfaction from the same bundle of goods. Any indifference curve represents a higher level of satisfaction than the curves that lie to the left and below it.

In the example shown in Figure 6-4, I_2 represents a higher level of satisfaction than I_1. Note, however, that it is not necessary to measure something like utility to establish this. The consumer simply *prefers* combinations on I_2 to those on I_1, because the consumer feels better off on I_2 than on I_1. All that is involved is an ordering. Combinations on I_2 are ranked above those on I_1. No mention is made or need be made about a measure of *how much* better combinations on I_2 are than those on I_1.

If we chose another consumer and established that consumer's indifference map in the same way, we would find that it looks somewhat different from that for the consumer of Figures 6-3 and 6-4. As with fingerprints, no two consumers' preferences are perfectly identical. But the general shapes, running from NW to SE on the graph of combinations of goods X and Y, must be the same for all consumers—given the logic of rational choice. It is this characteristic of indifference curves that allows us to generalize about consumer behaviour, even though it is true all consumers are different.

The Budget Constraint

Consumer's indifference curves reveal how a particular consumer *feels* about having different quantities of the goods X and Y. The question of what combinations of X and Y the consumer can actually afford is a wholly separate issue. The answer depends entirely on the size of the consumer's budget—what a consumer has set aside to spend and the prices of the goods X and Y.

Suppose, for example, that the consumer has a budget of $50 and that the price of X is $10 per unit, while the price of Y is $5 per unit. The budget constraint, or limit, that this puts on the consumer is depicted in Table 6-4 and in Figure 6-5, frame (a). If the consumer's entire budget of $50 is spent on X, 5 units of X can be purchased—line f in Table 6-4 and point f in Figure 6-5, frame (a). At the other extreme, if the consumer spends the entire $50 on Y, 10 units of Y can be purchased—line a in Table 6-4 and point a in Figure 6-5, frame (a). The consumer can, of course, spend the $50 so as to have some of both goods. For example, the consumer could purchase 8 units of Y and 1 unit of X (line b and point b), or 6 units of Y and 2 units of X (line c and point c), or 4 units of Y and 3 units of X (line d and point d), or 2 units of Y and 4 units of X (line e and point e). If the two goods can be purchased in fractions of a unit, then any combination of X and Y lying along a straight line connecting these points can be purchased.

This line is called the **budget constraint,** or **budget line**. *The budget constraint is a line in commodity space showing all possible combinations of goods that a consumer can obtain at given prices by spending a given budget.* The consumer can spend his or her budget on either X or Y or some combination of the two goods, as long as the amount spent in total is no more than the total budget. Therefore the consumer's expenditures, $P_X Q_X + P_Y Q_Y$, must be less than or equal to the budget (B). The budget constraint can be stated as

$$P_X Q_X + P_Y Q_Y = B$$

The slope of this line in X–Y commodity space is just equal to the price P_X

TABLE 6-4   Budget Constraint and Possible Combinations of X and Y Purchased

Combination	P_x × Units of X	+	P_y × Units of Y	=	Budget Constraint
a	$10 × 0	+	$5 × 10	=	$50
b	$10 × 1	+	$5 × 8	=	$50
c	$10 × 2	+	$5 × 6	=	$50
d	$10 × 3	+	$5 × 4	=	$50
e	$10 × 4	+	$5 × 2	=	$50
f	$10 × 5	+	$5 × 0	=	$50

FIGURE 6-5   The Budget Constraint

The budget constraint shows all the possible combinations of goods X and Y that the consumer may purchase with a given budget and for given prices of X and Y.

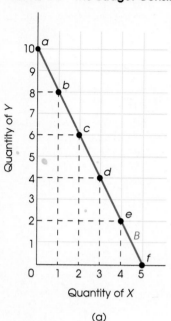

(a)

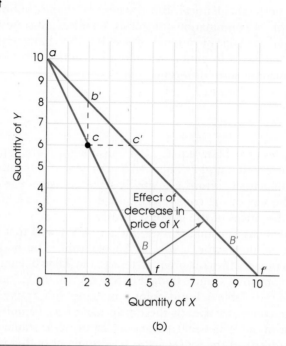

(b)

of the good on the horizontal axis divided by the price P_Y of the good on the vertical axis:[3]

$$\text{Slope of budget constraint} = -\frac{P_X}{P_Y}$$

In the example of Figure 6-5, frame (a), this slope is calculated as

$$-\frac{\$10}{\$5} = -2$$

If the price of good X decreased from $10 to $5, the slope of the budget constraint would then equal -1. The budget constraint would be pivoted counterclockwise about point a to the position depicted in Figure 6-5, frame (b), by the straight line connecting the points a and f'. Whatever combination of goods the consumer selected on the old budget constraint, he or she can now select combinations on the new budget constraint that contain more of both goods. For example, if previously the consumer selected point c, he or she can now select a combination anywhere between b' and c' on the new budget constraint.

If the consumer's budget doubled from $50 to $100, the budget constraint would shift outward to a position parallel to its initial position. It would connect the point at 10 on the horizontal axis to the point at 20 on the vertical axis. The consumer can buy twice as much as previously. *For a given size budget, decreases (increases) in the price of a good cause the budget constraint to pivot outward (inward) about the point on the axis of the good whose price has not changed.* A price decrease allows the

---

[3] In standard straight-line notation ($Y = a + bX$), b is the slope of the line. If the budget constraint, $P_X Q_X + P_Y Q_Y = B$ is rewritten as $Q_Y = B/P_Y - (P_X/P_Y)Q_X$, the slope is $-P_X/P_Y$.

consumer to buy more goods, a price increase fewer goods. *For given prices, a budget increase (decrease) causes the budget constraint to shift outward (inward) parallel to itself.* A budget increase (decrease) means the consumer can buy more (fewer) goods.

The Consumer's Optimum Combination

The consumer's objective is to purchase a combination of X and Y that puts him or her on the highest affordable indifference curve, given the size of his or her budget. By doing this, the consumer will achieve the highest affordable level of satisfaction.

The consumer's indifference map reveals how she feels about various combinations of quantities of the goods X and Y. It is a *subjective* matter reflecting the consumer's tastes. On the other hand, the consumer's budget constraint reflects the *objective* facts of the world that impinge on the consumer's decisions—the amount of money available for expenditure and the prices of the goods. These constraints cannot be ignored—like them or not. They tell what is possible as opposed to what is desirable.

To reconcile the consumer's tastes and desires with what he or she can afford, the consumer's budget constraint and indifference map must be brought together. In this way the consumer determines from among all the attainable combinations of X and Y most desirable in the sense that it maximizes his or her feeling of satisfaction. How this is done is shown in Figure 6-6, which combines the consumer's indifference map with the budget constraint of Figure 6-5, frame (b). The price of both good X and good Y is $5 per unit, and the consumer is as-

---

FIGURE 6-6 The Consumer's Optimum Purchase Combination

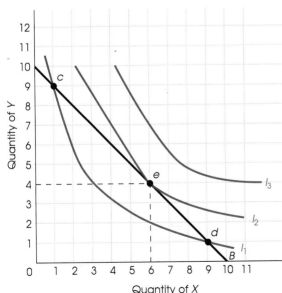

If the consumer has a budget of $50 and the price of both X and Y is $5 per unit, the consumer can purchase any combination given by the budget constraint B. For example, the consumer could spend the $50 to purchase combination c or d. The level of satisfaction associated with d is represented by the indifference curve I_1. The consumer can do better than this, however, by selecting the combination of 6 units of X and 4 units of Y represented by point e. Point e lies on the highest indifference curve it is possible to reach by moving along B. It is therefore the combination of goods X and Y that gives the consumer the highest level of satisfaction allowed by his or her budget constraint.

sumed to have a budget of $50. Of the unlimited number of indifference curves that make up the consumer's indifference map, three are shown in Figure 6-6.

Of all the affordable combinations of the two goods X and Y along the consumer's budget constraint B, which one will the consumer choose? For example, if either combination c or d were chosen, the consumer would experience the level of satisfaction associated with the indifference curve I_1. However, since the consumer's objective is to achieve the greatest level of satisfaction possible, neither of these combinations would be the optimum choice. The reason is that it is possible to get to a higher indifference curve. If combination e is chosen, the consumer will be on the highest affordable indifference curve I_2, and thereby will achieve the highest affordable level of satisfaction. It is the highest possible given the budget constraint.

Note that the optimum combination e is the point where B and I_2 touch each other. This is known as the *point of tangency*, where the slope of the budget line is equal to the slope of the indifference curve. As the marginal rate of substitution MRS measures the slope of the indifference curve and the slope of the budget line is $-P_X/P_Y$, the optimizing combination is where

$$-\frac{P_X}{P_Y} = MRS$$

All indifference curves below I_2 have two points in common with the budget constraint B. The highest affordable indifference curve has only one point in common with it—the point of tangency. Any combination of X and Y on an indifference curve above I_2, such as I_3, is unattainable given the budget constraint. *The point of tangency of an indifference curve with the budget constraint determines the optimum purchase combination. It is optimum in that the consumer realizes the highest affordable level of satisfaction. At this combination the consumer will be in equilibrium.* That is, the consumer will choose this combination continually, *ceteris paribus*. In Figure 6-6 this combination consists of 6 units of X and 4 units of Y. Of course when something changes, such as the consumer's income, the price of X or price of Y, or preferences, then the consumer will adjust purchases to a new tangency point between the budget line and indifference curves.

From Indifference Curves to Demand Curves

Figure 6-7, frame (a), shows again the consumer's budget constraint B and the two indifference curves I_1 and I_2 from the consumer's indifference map. If the consumer has a budget of $50 and the prices of X and Y are each $5 per unit, the consumer will buy combination e, consisting of 6 units of X and 4 units of Y. Suppose that the price of X rises from $5 per unit to $10 per unit, while the price of Y remains $5 per unit and the consumer's budget is still $50. The budget constraint would pivot clockwise from B to B'. The consumer is now constrained to purchase one of the possible combinations along B'. That combination of X and Y that maximizes the consumer's satisfaction by putting him or her on the highest possible indifference curve is at point g, the new equilibrium point after the price change. At g the consumer will purchase 6 units of Y and 2 units of X. Hence, the doubling of the price of X, with the price of Y and the consumer's income staying the same, has caused the consumer to reduce his or her quantity demanded for X from 6 units to 2 units.

FIGURE 6-7   Effect of a Price Change and Derivation of Demand

In frame (a), if the consumer has a budget of $50 and the prices of X and Y are each $5 per unit, the consumer's optimum purchase combination is e (6 units of X and 4 units of Y). If the price of X were to rise from $5 to $10 per unit, the budget line would pivot clockwise from the position B to B'. The consumer's optimum purchase combination would then be g (2 units of X and 6 units of Y). Conversely, if the price of X had fallen from $10 to $5 per unit, the quantity of X purchased would increase from 2 units to 6 units, while the quantity of Y purchased would decrease from 6 units to 4 units. In frame (b), the demand curve D is derived from the points of tangency between the consumer indifference curves and budget constraints of frame (a).

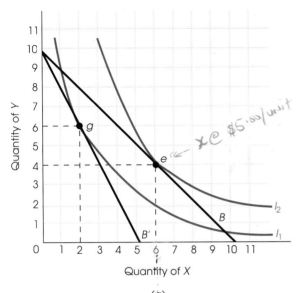

(a)

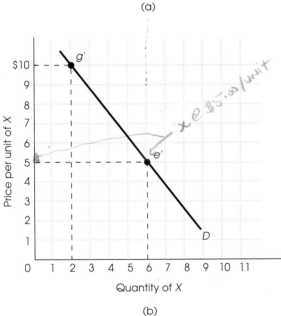

(b)

Suppose that we plot the price of X, (P_X), on the vertical axis and the quantity of X demanded, (Q_X), on the horizontal axis as in Figure 6-7, frame (b). Given the price of Y of $5 per unit and the consumer's budget of $50, if the price of X is $5 per unit, the quantity of X demanded is 6 units, point e in Figure 6-7, frame (a). Corresponding to point e in Figure 6-7, frame (a), we have point e' in Figure 6-7, frame (b). If the price of X is increased to $10 per unit and the price of Y and the consumer's budget remain the same, the quantity of X demanded decreases to 2 units, point g of Figure 6-7. Corresponding to point g of Figure 6-7, frame (a), we have point g' in Figure 6-7, frame (b). If we continued to vary the price of X while holding the price of Y and the consumer's budget constant in Figure 6-7, frame (a), we could derive the entire demand curve D for good X in Figure 6-7, frame (b).

Thus, by the use of indifference curves, we can derive a downward-sloping demand curve by plotting the equilibrium quantities of one good (X in this case) with the changes in its price. Unlike the utility theory approach, it is not necessary to measure *how much* a consumer likes a certain quantity of a good. All that is required is that the consumer be able to tell which combinations of goods are regarded as equivalent and which combinations are preferred to others. The indifference analysis approach thereby gets around the problem that utility cannot be measured. This problem is the major shortcoming of the utility theory approach in explaining why a demand curve slopes downward left to right.

A Model Using the Three Approaches to Consumer Theory

So far we have discussed three approaches to understanding the law of downward demand. These were (1) the use of simple substitution and income effects of price changes; (2) utility theory, including the law of diminishing utility; and (3) indifference analysis. We can combine these approaches by converting the indifference map to a utility function and then using this and the budget constraint concept to separate the income and substitution effects that occur with a change in the price of a good.[4]

A movement from one point to another along an indifference curve represents a change in the amounts of good X and good Y that a consumer would have. But this movement would not change the level of satisfaction the consumer received. The bundles on an indifference curve all provide the same level of utility to the consumer. For example, a movement from bundle c to bundle d on U in Figure 6-8 must indicate a zero change in utility. The change in utility occurring from a change in the amount of good X must be just offset by the change in utility occurring from a change in Y. The overall change in utility is zero. As we have seen in utility theory, a change in utility with a small change in consumption of the good is the marginal utility of the good. The sum of the changes in utility must equal zero along an indifference or utility curve. Therefore the change in the amount of X times the marginal utility of X would just equal the negative of the change in the amount of Y times the marginal utility of Y. In symbols:

$$MU_X \times \Delta X + MU_Y \times \Delta Y = 0$$

rewriting this:

$$MU_X \times \Delta X = (-MU_Y \times \Delta Y)$$

---

[4]Although this section is more difficult technically, we hope that it will help the student see the common foundation of the previously discussed methods of analysis of consumer behaviour. This section could be skipped without loss of continuity.

FIGURE 6-8   Movement Along an Indifference Curve

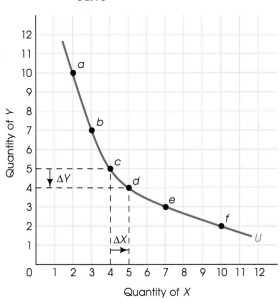

The change in utility with a change in the quantity of X is just offset by the change in utility with a change in the quantity of Y. This leaves the consumer equally well off at d as at c. Therefore, the marginal utility of X times the change in X plus the marginal utility of Y times the change in Y equals the change in utility and as the change in the utility is zero, $MU_X \Delta X = -MU_Y \Delta Y$ and $MU_X / MU_Y = -\Delta Y / \Delta X$.

and dividing each side by ΔX,

$$MU_X = MU_Y \times \frac{\Delta Y}{\Delta X}$$

then dividing each side by MU_Y,

$$-\frac{MU_X}{MU_Y} = \frac{\Delta Y}{\Delta X}$$

Note from the discussion of the marginal rate of substitution (MRS) that

$$MRS = \frac{\Delta Y}{\Delta X}$$

therefore,

$$MRS = -\frac{MU_X}{MU_Y}$$

In equilibrium the consumer chooses the combination of X and Y where the budget line is tangent to the indifference curve. As the MRS measures the slope of the indifference curve and the slope of the budget line is $-P_X/P_Y$, the equilibrium occurs where

$$-\frac{MU_X}{MU_Y} = -\frac{P_X}{P_Y}$$

Now rearranging the terms gives

$$\frac{MU_X}{P_X} = \frac{MU_Y}{P_Y}$$

POLICY PERSPECTIVE

1991 Newsmaker of the Year: The GST

The federal government imposed a new tax of 7 percent on most commodities and services starting on January 1, 1991. This very visible tax replaced a federal tax of 13.5 percent on manufactured goods which was essentially hidden. The manufacturer's sales tax (MST) was considered harmful to manufacturers, especially exporters in Canada.

In picking the GST as newsmaker of the year, the editors of the *Canadian Global Almanac* observed that "no national hero or villain did nearly as much in 1991 to galvanize public opinion and focus its attention as did a new tax–the GST."* No one particularly likes taxes, but the GST was exceptionally unpopular, and two million Canadians signed a petition against the tax before its approval in the House of Commons. The GST bill only received Senate approval after Prime Minister Brian Mulroney used a little-known statute to increase the size of the senate and fill it with Conservative appointees. The *Almanac* editors go on to say: "The tax and the lengths to which the government went to ensure its passage, was a major factor in lowering pub-

*Toronto: Global Press, 1992, p. 10.

lic support for the federal government and in increasing cynicism towards politicians at all levels."

THE ADVANTAGES OF GST

Leaving politics aside, and applying economic analysis to the issue, what might be the advantages of the GST over its precursor the MST? In Figure P6-1, frame (a), a representative consumer's indifference map is drawn with a service on the X-axis and a commodity on the Y-axis. The initial budget constraint, B, is drawn assuming there are no taxes on either good. The initial consumer's equilibrium will occur at point e. If a tax is imposed on the commodity, only the commodity's price, P_c, will rise and the budget constraint will pivot inward, as indicated by the budget B'. The new equilibrium will occur at e'. There is both a substitution effect and an income effect due to this price increase. If we increased the consumer's income in order to allow him to buy the same pretax combination, e, he would have budget B''.

But the consumer would not buy e at this price ratio. He would buy the new equilibrium combination at e'', a combination with less of the commodity and more of the ser-

vice than the original combination of e.

In Figure P6-1, frame (b), the same initial situation is depicted as in frame (a). In this case both goods are taxed at the same rate, so the budget line shifts downward, parallel to the original, to B^* and the new equilibrium occurs at e^*. If the consumer is given sufficient extra income to compensate him for the tax, the new budget line would shift back to the original at B and the equilibrium would coincide with the initial equilibrium at e.

In both cases, imposing taxes makes the consumer worse off, reducing his utility to a lower level. But the MST-type tax, which only taxes one type of product, also distorts the consumer's purchases away from the taxed good, due to the substitution effect. This is indicated in Figure P6-1, frame (a), by what happens when we compensate the consumer's income for the tax, thereby eliminating the income effect. The consumer substitutes the service for the commodity at the higher relative commodity price. There is no substitution effect if the two goods are taxed

continued on next page

This is exactly the equilibrium condition that we obtained in the utility approach to consumer theory.

Now the income and substitution effects approach can be reconsidered within indifference analysis. In Figure 6-9, the effects of a price change have been separated into the substitution effect and income effect. The price of good X has fallen from $10 to $5, causing the budget line B to pivot outward on the X axis from 5 units of X to 10 units on B'. The consumer chooses 2 units of X at budget B and 6 units of X at budget B'. To separate the two effects, the consumer's budget is reduced sufficiently that he or she can just purchase the original bundle g at the new price ratio as indicated by B''. The slope of this

---

proportionally as in Figure P6-1, frame (b), and therefore less distortion is caused by the GST-type tax.

THE DISADVANTAGES OF GST

The case just made suggests that GST is better than an MST, as it is less distortionary. It does not make the case that this is necessarily the best type of tax to implement. What are the disadvantages of sales taxes? A progressive tax charges those with higher incomes a greater proportion of their income in tax. Commodity taxes are often regressive in that lower-income earners pay a greater propor-

tion of their income in tax than do those with higher incomes. Second, the inevitable demands for exemptions occur, bringing back the distortions outlined earlier, when some goods are taxed and others are not. Third, and probably most significant, commodity taxes are very expensive to administer. The implementation of the GST in Canada required the creation of a new costly bureaucracy. As well, some of the administrative costs were hidden by shifting them onto the businesses, which were required to collect the tax. These increased business costs inevitably have an impact on prices

and distort the cost of producing goods. Finally, the timing of the implementation of the GST occurred in a recession, and may have contributed to macroeconomic problems and to cross-border shopping.

For Discussion

- Food items are commonly exempted from sales tax, and this holds true for the GST. What arguments can you make for including food items in the GST? For excluding them?
- If sales taxes are costly to implement, can you suggest a way to implement a tax on expenditures through the income tax?

FIGURE P6-1   **GST versus MST—The Effects upon Consumer Choice**

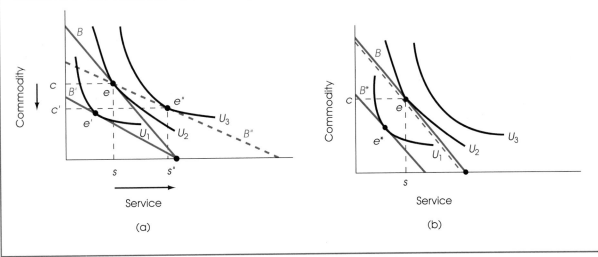

(a)   (b)

---

dashed line, B'', is the same as B'. The consumer is as well off in real terms as before the price change (he or she can afford the same bundle). Will the consumer buy this bundle? No. He or she will be better off by buying less Y and more X. This is the *substitution effect* of the price change. At the new price ratio the consumer chooses 5 units of X, an increase of 3 units. The change from 2 units to 5 units is attributed to the substitution effect. But the reduction of the consumer's budget was artificial—the consumer would only experience the price change. We know that in equilibrium the consumer will purchase 6 units of X at the new price. Therefore, the movement from point f to e is due to the *income effect* of the price change. The change from 5 to 6 units of X, an increase of 1 unit, is attributed to the income effect.

FIGURE 6-9   Price and Income Effects

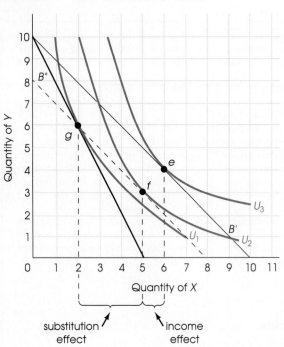

P_X has fallen from $10 to $5, the budget line B pivots outward on the X axis from 5 units of X to 10 units on B'. The consumer chooses 2 units of X at budget B (point g) and 6 units of X at budget B' (point e). The consumer's budget is reduced to budget B'' parallel to B' with the same price ratio and through the original point g. The equilibrium at this budget is 5 units of X (point f). The change in X from 2 to 5 units is due to the substitution effect, and the change from 5 to 6 units is due to the income effect.

As discussed less formally at the beginning of the chapter, the income and substitution effects of a price reduction result in the consumer purchasing more of the good at a lower price and vice versa. This explains downward-sloping demand. There is one consideration to be aware of, though. The income effect will be opposite to our example if the good was inferior. As was explained in Chapter 4, an inferior good's demand decreases with an increase in income. Similarly, for an inferior good the "income effect" of a price decrease would cause a reduction in the quantity of X chosen compared to the level that would be chosen if the substitution effect alone were involved. In general, though, the income effect of a price change in any one good we buy is small compared to the substitution effect. Therefore, even if the income effect is opposite to the substitution effect (an inferior good), it does not usually alter the general outcome that more is demanded at lower prices and vice versa.

Summary

1. Income and substitution effects of price changes provide explanations for the law of demand. Because of the income effect, we expect that when the price of a good declines, the consumer's budget can buy more of the good whose price has fallen, as well as more of all other goods. Due to the substitution effect, we would also expect the quantity demanded for the good whose price has fallen to increase, because that good is now cheaper relative to all others. The income and substitution effects of a price increase cause the quantity demanded for the good whose price has risen to fall.

2. The theory of utility provides a second explanation of the law of demand. This theory assumes that the amount of utility a consumer gets from a good can be measured. The extra utility a consumer receives from consuming one more unit of a good in a given time period is called marginal utility. The satisfaction received from consuming a number of units of a good is referred to as total utility. The satisfaction received from consuming a number of goods in a given time period is referred to as global utility. The theory of utility expects that consumers wish to get the most utility possible with their limited income.

3. The measurement of utility is the basis for the law of diminishing marginal utility, which says that the more of a good a consumer has, the smaller the addition to total utility provided by an additional unit of the good.

4. A person who is consuming one good and is not constrained by a budget (the good is free) will consume only the number of units of the good, in a given time period, that make him or her satiated. The total utility will be maximized where the marginal utility is zero.

5. The "paradox of value," a long-standing puzzle about prices and value, was solved by the discovery of the law of diminishing marginal utility. The price of a good could be explained by the extra utility obtained by the last unit consumed instead of by the worth of the good, as indicated by the total utility the good provides.

6. The law of diminishing marginal utility can be used to show how the consumer's global utility is maximized when the consumer spends a given size budget in such a way that the marginal utility derived from the last dollar spent for each good is the same.

7. Assuming that the consumer's budget is spent in accordance with the utility-maximizing principle, it is possible to derive a downward-sloping demand curve for each good.

8. Indifference curves reflect the consumer's tastes or preferences about goods. The indifference map orders all the bundles in commodity space according to the consumer's preferences. Although subjective, the general shape of the curves and the map will be the same for all consumers.

9. The size of the consumer's budget and the prices of goods are objective facts that determine the consumer's budget constraint or budget line. This line shows the bundles affordable to the consumer.

10. By bringing the consumer's indifference map, which consists of all the consumer's indifference curves, together with the consumer's budget constraint, it is possible to determine the optimum affordable combination of goods. This bundle is optimum in the sense that it is the one, from among all affordable combinations, that gives the consumer the greatest satisfaction.

11. By varying the price of one good while holding the size of the consumer's budget and the price of the other good fixed, it is possible to derive the demand curve for a good from the tangency points of the consumer's indifference curves and budget constraints. Hence, the existence of a downward-sloping demand curve can be explained without resorting to the measurement of utility.

12. The three approaches to consumer behaviour can be combined into one method that illustrates that consumer equilibrium under utility theory and indifference analysis are the same and each change in quantity demanded due to a price change can be separated into substitution and income effects.

Key Terms and Concepts

budget constraint (budget line)	indifference curve	ordinal
bundle	indifference map	"paradox of value"
cardinal	indifference schedule	preferences
diminishing marginal rate of substitution	law of diminishing marginal utility	substitution effect
global utility	marginal rate of substitution	total utility
income effect	marginal utility	utility

Questions and Problems

1. I buy caviar each month at a price of $2 per gram and pay monthly for water at a price of $.01 per 50 litres. I get 2,000 utils from the last gram of caviar I eat and 50 utils from the last 50-litre bath I take. Am I maximizing my utility or should I change the combination of caviar and water I consume per month? If so, how should I reallocate my expenditures between these two goods?

2. Suppose a consumer gets the following utility, shown in the table, from drinking beer and eating nuts:

Cans of Beer	Total Utility (Utils)	Bags of Nuts	Total Utility (Utils)
1	12	1	10
2	30	2	19
3	46	3	27
4	58	4	34
5	68	5	40
6	76	6	45
7	83	7	49
8	88	8	52
9	91	9	54
10	92	10	55

   a. What are the marginal utilities associated with drinking beer and eating nuts?
   b. If the price of beer is $1 per can and the price of nuts is $.50 per bag, what combination of beer and nut consumption will maximize the consumer's utility from consuming beer and nuts, given that the consumer has $8 for such expenditures? What if the consumer has $9.50?
   c. If the price of nuts falls to $.25 per bag and the price of beer remains $1 per can, what is the optimum combination of beer and nut consumption, given that the consumer has $4.75 to spend?
   d. If the price of beer falls to $.50 per can and the price of nuts remains at $.25 per bag, what is the optimum combination of beer and nut consumption, given that the consumer has $3.25 to spend?
   e. What is the optimum combination of beer and nut consumption if the consumer has an unlimited expense account for such consumption activities?

3. Draw one of your possible indifference curves between the following goods:
   a. Brand X salt and brand Y salt.
   b. Right-hand gloves and left-hand gloves.
   c. Red apples and yellow apples.
   d. Bread and water.

4. Suppose that there is a change in the tastes of a consumer, one of whose indifference curves is shown in Figure 6-3. Suppose that this consumer develops a stronger preference for good X relative to good Y. How do you think this will change the indifference curve shown in Figure 6-3?

5. Consider again the consumer budget constraint shown in Figure 6-5, frame (a). Show how each of the following will affect the budget constraint:
   a. The consumer's budget is reduced from $50 to $30.
   b. The consumer's budget is increased from $50 to $80.
   c. The price of Y is increased from $5 per unit to $10 per unit.
   d. The price of X is reduced from $10 per unit to $5 per unit and the consumer's budget is reduced to $35.

6. In Figure 6-3, suppose that the consumer's tastes change in such a way as to increase the consumer's preference for good Y relative to good X.
   a. How would this affect the optimum combination purchased by the consumer?
   b. Using Figure 6-7, frame (a), show how this would affect the position of the demand curve in Figure 6-7, frame (b).

7. Suppose that the consumer's budget was increased from $50 to $60. Using Figure 6-7, frame (a), show how this would affect the position of the demand curve in Figure 6-7, frame (b).

Chapter 7

Applications of Demand and Supply

In previous chapters we developed the fundamental concepts of supply and demand. These concepts can be used to examine a wide variety of economic issues. In this chapter we will apply these concepts to an analysis of how government price regulation affects markets—in particular, as illustrated by price ceilings such as rent controls, and price floors such as supports in agriculture. We will also examine how the existence of sales and excise taxes affects markets and how the burden of paying these taxes is distributed between buyers and sellers. Finally, we will consider the consequences when some of the costs and benefits associated with certain goods are not always borne solely by those who directly buy and sell them. Our application of the concepts of demand and supply to these issues illustrates why the great British economist Alfred Marshall (1847–1924) defined economics as the "study of mankind in the ordinary business of life."[1]

Price regulation occurs whenever the government establishes laws imposing an upper limit or a lower limit on the price at which a particular good or service can be bought or sold. An upper limit is called a **price ceiling.** Price ceilings are often referred to as *price controls.* A legally imposed lower limit on a price is called a **price floor**, or a *price support*. The model of supply and demand developed in Chapter 4 predicts that a free market will achieve an equilibrium price where the quantity demanded equals the quantity supplied and the market will clear. When a price ceiling is placed below the equilibrium market price or a price support is placed above it, serious economic consequences follow. You should understand these consequences because they are often prevalent in the economy around you. Supply and demand analysis predicts that price ceilings lead to shortages and price supports cause surpluses in the markets where they are imposed. These surpluses and shortages typically attract news media attention.

---

[1] Alfred Marshall, *Principles of Economics*, 8th ed. (London: Macmillan, 1964), p. 1.

FIGURE 7-1   Effect of a Price Ceiling on a Market

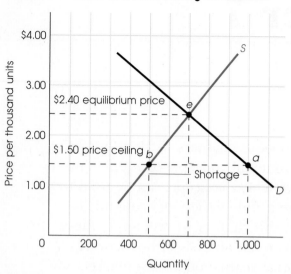

The demand curve D and supply curve S determine an equilibrium price of $2.40 per unit. However, if a price ceiling of $1.50 per unit is imposed, market forces created by the interaction of buyers and sellers are prevented from eliminating the resulting shortage (the horizontal distance between points a and b) because buying and selling at prices above the ceiling is prohibited by law.

Price Regulation—Price Ceilings

In many cases governments impose price ceilings in the economy. Let's examine how such ceilings affect the way a market functions. Consider the effect of the price ceiling imposed on the market illustrated in Figure 7-1. The demand curve D and the supply curve S are shown in Figure 7-1 (the data are hypothetical). If the market forces created by the interaction of buyers and sellers are allowed to work, equilibrium will be established at point e, the intersection of D and S. The equilibrium price would be $2.40, and the equilibrium quantity would be 700 per month. However, the government-imposed price ceiling makes it illegal to sell at a price greater than $1.50. At this price, suppliers only supply 500 per month, while buyers want to purchase 1,000 per month. The shortage amounts to 500 per month, the difference between point a on D and point b on S.

LEARNING OBJECTIVES

After reading this chapter, you will be able to:

1. Define *price ceiling, price floor,* and *black market.*
2. Explain and illustrate graphically how price ceilings affect resource allocation.
3. Describe the reasons for imposing price ceilings and the problems of enforcing them.
4. Explain and illustrate graphically how a price floor affects resource allocation.
5. Describe the reasons for price supports and how they are maintained.
6. Demonstrate awareness of the agriculture industry and apply economic analysis to this industry.
7. Demonstrate the relationship between the concept of tax incidence and the elasticity of demand and supply.
8. Explain the concept of market externalities and the external, or spillover, costs and benefits they cause.

Because the price cannot be higher than $1.50, there is no way to induce suppliers to devote more resources to the production of a larger quantity. If price is not allowed to rise above $1.50, there is no way to cut back the quantity that buyers want to purchase. Given the behaviour of sellers and buyers, the market is stuck with a shortage. The result of this low price is to discourage producers from supplying more while leading consumers to demand a larger quantity of the product.

Price Ceilings and Nonprice Rationing

Price ceilings have been used in market economies extensively during war. Governments have to divert a vast amount of resources to producing war goods, such as weapons and equipment and supplies, to support troops. At the same time, the civilian labour force is typically fully employed, working long hours and making high wages. The economy is on its production possibilities frontier.

If the civilian labour force is allowed to spend the high wages in the marketplace, there typically will be a large demand for consumer or peacetime goods—automobiles, television sets, clothing, food, housing, and so on. These demands conflict and compete with the demands of the government for resources needed to conduct the war effort. In short, the government must do something to ensure that the economy operates at a point on its production possibilities frontier where more wartime goods and fewer peacetime goods are produced than would occur if the civilian labour force were allowed to spend its wages freely. The choices are illustrated on the production possibilities frontier illustrated in Figure 7-2. Point *a* indicates the choice consumers would make if allowed to, while the government needs to move the economy to point *b* in order to conduct the war.

One solution is to impose heavy income taxes on these wages and thereby divert some of the civilian spending power into the hands of the government

---

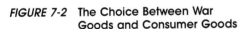

FIGURE 7-2 **The Choice Between War Goods and Consumer Goods**

The production possibilities frontier illustrates the choices between war goods and consumer goods. If consumers could freely make the choice, the economy would seek point *a*, but the government wants the economy to operate at point *b*. It may achieve this through taxes or through price ceilings and rationing.

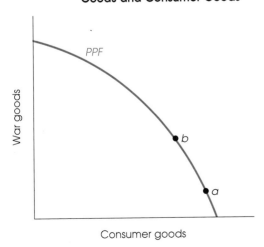

FIGURE 7-3   **A Price Ceiling Causes a Shortage**

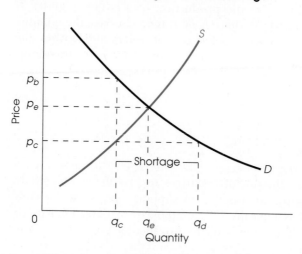

A freely working market with demand curve *D* and supply curve *S* determines an equilibrium price p_e and quantity q_e. If a price ceiling of p_c is imposed on the market, suppliers are only willing to supply the quantity q_c, while buyers demand the larger quantity q_d.

for use in buying wartime goods. If this is the only method used to achieve this objective, however, a major war effort may require such high taxes that there will be a negative impact on workers' incentives to put in the extra hours required for the war effort. To avoid the necessity of having such high taxes, price ceilings and rationing may be used to aid in diverting resources to the war effort, with the sale of victory bonds being used to absorb the excess demand.

Price Ceilings Divert Resources

How do price ceilings divert resources? This is illustrated in Figure 7-3. If market forces were allowed to operate freely, the equilibrium price and quantity would be p_e and q_e, respectively. However, with the imposition of a price ceiling at p_c (which is below p_e), suppliers would only be willing to produce and supply a quantity of the good equal to q_c. Since q_c is less than q_e, fewer of the economy's resources will be devoted to producing this good. The resources that would have been used to produce the additional units of the good between q_c and q_e are now available for the production of wartime goods. However, we know that at the price ceiling of p_c, buyers will demand an amount q_d that is greater than the amount q_c actually supplied. Obviously, since there is less of the good available than buyers want, the demands of all buyers cannot be satisfied. There is now a shortage equal to the difference between q_d and q_c. Since the rationing mechanism of a rising price is not allowed, some nonprice rationing device is needed to portion out the limited supply. One possibility would be to distribute the quantity q_c on a first-come, first-served basis. This would mean some of those, possibly many, who are willing to pay the ceiling price p_c would end up getting none of the good. Another possibility would be to let suppliers distribute the available quantity as they see fit. This would most likely favour the suppliers' close friends, family, and longtime customers. The rest of those willing to pay the price p_c for the good would again go without.

FIGURE 7-4   Effect of a Supply Elasticity on Released Resources

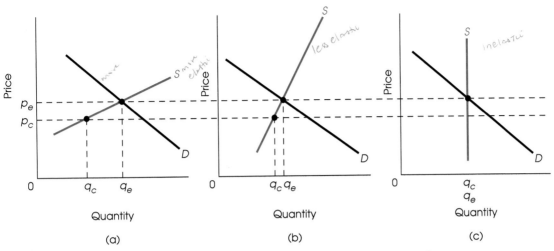

Different elasticities of supply are illustrated. Frame (a) illustrates a relatively elastic supply curve, (b) a less elastic supply, and (c) a perfectly inelastic supply. At the ceiling price p_c the quantity supplied is q_c, and the difference between q_e and q_c is directly related to the resource released for war goods production. The difference between q_e and q_c is less the lower is the elasticity of supply, so fewer resources would be released as the elasticity of supply declines.

Rationing with Ration Coupons

Since these kinds of solutions to the problem seem inequitable and unjust, the government can resort to the use of the **ration coupon.** Each coupon is a claim to a unit of the good. The government could print up just the amount of coupons that will lay claim to q_c units of the good and then distribute the coupons among those who want to buy the good on the basis of so many units per person. If the good were a food item, for example, a family of four would be entitled to a certain number of coupons and a family of two could have half that amount. Hence, all who want to buy the good at price p_c would be assured of getting some, though often not as much as they might want. They present their coupons to the supplier and pay the price p_c per unit of the good, but receive no more than the amount of the good their coupons allow.

Note that a price ceiling's effectiveness in cutting back on the quantity of a good produced, and thereby releasing resources for use in a war effort, depends on the elasticity of the supply curve. The less elastic the supply curve is, the less effective a price ceiling will be in achieving this objective. Indeed, if the supply curve were perfectly inelastic (or vertical), the quantity supplied would not be reduced at all. The effect of the relative elasticity of supply on the amount of released resources is illustrated in Figure 7-4. Frame (a) illustrates a relatively elastic supply curve. At the ceiling price p_c the quantity supplied is q_c, and the difference between q_e and q_c is directly related to the resources released for war goods production. With a relatively less elastic supply, as illustrated in frame (b), the difference between q_e and q_c is less, so fewer resources would be released. With the perfectly inelastic supply shown in frame (c), the price ceiling would not change the quantity supplied from that at q_e.

Black Markets

So far, we have been looking at the way in which a system of price ceilings and ration coupons should work in theory. How close it comes to this ideal in reality will depend on how vigorously the system is policed. The demand curve in Figure 7-3 tells us that there are many buyers who are willing to pay more than the ceiling price in order to get some of the good. Hence, there are profits to be made by those suppliers who are willing to risk breaking the law by selling the good at prices above the ceiling price. Even if they don't expand output beyond q_c, which they might well do, there is a great temptation to charge a price as high as p_b and reap large profits. *A market where goods are illegally traded at prices above their ceiling prices or below their floor prices is known as a* **black market.**

It should also be noted that some consumers may profit from the existence of rationing. There typically will be consumers who don't want any of a commodity at the ceiling price or as much of the commodity as their coupon allotments would entitle them to. On the other hand, there will be other consumers who would like to buy more than their coupon allotment of a commodity at or above the ceiling price. Although it is illegal, there is an incentive for those with un-needed coupons to sell them to those who want more of the commodity. When suppliers sell a commodity at a price above the ceiling price to individual buyers in amounts exceeding those buyers' coupon allotments, the purpose of the ceiling is violated. Given the incentive provided by the economic profits from black market activity, a system of price ceilings without adequate enforcement, may end up being more fiction than fact. The bureaucracy needed to administer the price ceilings and coupon rationing system in Canada during World War II is an example.

Rent Control

Rent control is an example of a price ceiling on the rent that may be charged tenants of rental housing. In some cities, such as Toronto and Vancouver, rental units have been subject to some sort of rent regulation. Those who advocate rent control often argue that it ensures a minimum standard of housing for everyone. It is applied in order to make housing affordable to those whose incomes may not be sufficient for increased rent payments. Also, rent controls can be justified because, in a growing urban area, a portion of the rent payment is a pure economic profit that depends on the high demand for housing units alone, and is not due to the costs of providing the housing. This economic profit that high demand confers on landlords (or pure economic rent)[2] is an "unearned" income, and exists solely because of having built early in an increasing demand area. The desirability of redistributing income from landlords to tenants through rent control is a normative political issue that is debated. Whether rent control is the *best* way to achieve the goal of income redistribution is a different issue. Other consequences occur than income redistribution. Rent controls may keep rents lower than they would be in the shortrun, but in the longrun they reduce the availability of rental units and put upward pressures on rents.

---

[2] Pure economic rent will be discussed in Chapter 17.

Rent controls cause rental housing shortages in the areas where they apply. On the supply side, since rents are not allowed to rise above the price ceiling, there is no incentive to expand the quantity of existing rental units to alleviate this shortage. On the demand side, families are encouraged to consume more housing services than they would if the housing market were free of rent controls. For example, a couple may retain a four-bedroom apartment after children are grown because it is cheap and alternative housing may not be rent controlled. When rents are prevented from rising with the costs of current production, the return on the investment for new rental buildings is below market levels prevailing in other lines of productive activity. This discourages the flow of new financial capital into the production of new rental buildings. It may also lead to a decrease in upkeep and maintenance of old buildings and thereby to neighbourhood decay. This may result in a fall in property values and hence in property taxes that can be collected from rental buildings. This increases the tax burden on commercial and industrial property and owner-occupied single-family dwellings. To the extent that this discourages the location of new businesses and families in the area and encourages those already there to leave, the process of neighbourhood decay continues and further erodes the tax base.

The history of rent control well illustrates how a price ceiling imposed on one market can have wide-ranging social and economic implications for other areas of the economy. It also shows how a policy supposedly aimed at achieving the objective of helping the poor may in fact only create conditions, in this case slums, that are at odds with that objective. Moreover, there are ways to evade rent controls, so poorer people may not be able to afford housing legally subject to rent control anyway. For example, a rent-controlled apartment may be available only if the prospective tenant agrees to buy the existing furniture or to make some other type of side payment. This type of "extra billing" through legal methods violates the intent of the ceiling.

Public Production

Rationing in conjunction with a price ceiling can reduce the quantity demanded to equal the quantity supplied when a price ceiling is imposed. Alternatively, public production of a good can increase the quantity supplied to equal the quantity demanded at the ceiling price. For example, in Toronto, both the municipal and provincial governments have produced public housing units while maintaining rent controls. If in Figure 7-3 a rent ceiling is imposed at p_c, the private market will provide q_c housing units. The shortage between the quantity demanded at this price, q_d, and the quantity supplied, q_c, can be alleviated by the public provision of $q_d - q_c$. This solves the shortage but has other social implications. Economists generally advocate supplementing the incomes of the poor, letting the individuals decide what to choose to spend it on rather than producing goods directly.

Price Regulation—Price Floors

A governmentally imposed price floor has just the opposite effect of a price ceiling. *A price floor or support imposes a lower level below which a price is not allowed to fall.*

Checkpoint* 7-1

Suppose that the government removed the ceiling on tuition fees so that the price of education could rise above the current level. Predict what the length of the lines of students would look like as compared to the way they look now, given that ceilings are imposed? Demonstrate your answer diagrammatically. Describe the allocation mechanism now used to deal with the problem of distributing limited seats in universities and colleges under controlled tuition fees.

Answers to all Checkpoints can be found at the back of the text.

The most common reason for imposing a price support on a good or service is to bolster the income of suppliers above the level that would otherwise prevail in a freely operating market. This is the main motivation for government price supports for farm products—namely, to bolster farm incomes. Similarly, proponents of minimum-wage legislation argue that the incomes of the poor are raised by putting a floor under wages—a price support that applies to the sale of labour services.

The effect of a price support on a market is illustrated in Figure 7-5. When the market forces created by buyers and sellers are allowed to operate freely, the equilibrium price p_e and quantity q_e will prevail. Suppose, however, that the government decides to establish a price support p_s above the equilibrium price p_e. At the price p_s buyers will demand the quantity q_d, corresponding to point c on the demand curve D. However, sellers will supply a larger quantity q_s, corresponding to point a on the supply curve S. Hence the quantity supplied will exceed the quantity demanded, giving rise to excess output, or a surplus, equal to the horizontal distance between points a and c (also represented by the distance between q_s and q_d on the horizontal axis).

Minimum-wage legislation is an example of a price floor. A minimum wage of p_s would give rise to a surplus of labour. This surplus represents workers who would be willing to work at the minimum wage p_s but who would not be hired at this wage. Black markets may also arise with price floors. The minimum wage may be avoided by firms hiring on salary, or hiring an "independent" operator who is a self-employed agent. Although legal, this violates the intent of the minimum-wage law.

FIGURE 7-5   Price Supports Cause a Surplus

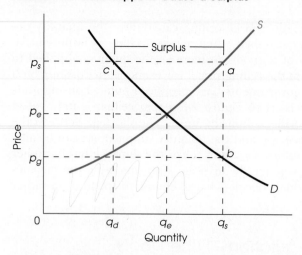

A freely working market with demand curve D and supply curve S determines an equilibrium price p_e and quantity q_e. However, if price is supported at the level p_s, buyers will demand the quantity q_d, while suppliers will supply the larger quantity q_s. The result will be the indicated surplus.

Agriculture and Price-Support Schemes

Scheme 1: Direct Payment.   One way to establish a price support is for the government to tell producers it will guarantee them a price of p_s per unit of output. They would then be allowed to produce accordingly and sell the output for whatever price the market will bear. The government simply pays the producers the difference between the price they receive in the market for each unit sold and the higher price p_s guaranteed by the government. Knowing that they are guaranteed a price p_s for every unit sold, producers will supply the amount q_s. In the marketplace, buyers will be willing to pay a price of p_g to purchase this quantity. The total revenue received by suppliers from the market will then be p_g times the number of units sold q_s. This is represented by the rectangular area $0q_sbp_g$ in Figure 7-5. When the government pays suppliers the difference between the market price p_g and the support price p_s per unit sold, suppliers will receive an additional amount of revenue from the government. This additional amount is equal to the rectangular area p_gbap_s in Figure 7-5. Direct payments have been the single most important vehicle of Canada's agricultural price-support system. Direct payments have taken two forms in Canada: deficiency payments based on a predetermined minimum price level, and ad hoc payments.

The National Tripartite Stabilization Programs for beef, pork, lamb, and sugar were designed and introduced in the late 1980s. In 1990/91, the Gross Revenue Insurance Program (GRIP) was introduced for some grain crops. These programs provide deficiency payments to farmers whenever prices (or gross margins in some cases) fall below a target price level. When this occurs, the producer receives a payment for the difference between the target price and the market price of the commodity. These target prices create a floor price to the producer. This does not prevent the market price from falling below the target price. However, when it does, the stabilization program supplements the market price, which brings the net price received by the producer back up to the floor price. In this case, the farmer's revenue comes from two separate sources—the market place and the stabilization program. When the market price is equal to or higher than the target price, no stabilization payments are triggered. The producer then receives a price higher than the target price, and all of the revenue comes from the marketplace. Ad hoc payments are made randomly, in response to special needs resulting from drought or, in recent years, international market events. These payments are often announced after a poor season in response to the lobbying efforts of Canada's farm groups. These ad hoc payments have totaled approximately three billion dollars since 1986.

Scheme 2: Floor Prices.   The government makes it illegal for a service to be bought or sold at a price below p_s. At price p_s the quantity q_s will be supplied to the market, corresponding to point a on supply curve S. But only the smaller quantity q_d will be purchased, corresponding to point c on demand curve D. Hence, there is a surplus, as indicated in Figure 7-5. Prohibition of lower-price transactions has been used in the milk, poultry, and egg industries since the early 1970s. For each of these groups, a minimum farm price is established that will allow farmers to cover their costs of production. Knowledge of the demand facing the product is used to determine the quantity at which this price would be attained. This scheme is combined with scheme 3 so that total production is limited to the amount, q_d, that will force the market price up to the minimum price desired for that product. Since the total production must be limited to q_d, the production of each individual farmer must also be restricted. To accomplish this, each farmer wishing to produce chicken, eggs, or milk must obtain a quota, which gives the right to produce only a certain amount.

Scheme 3: Output Restriction.
Another way the government can maintain the price floor p_s is to make it illegal for suppliers to produce any more than the quantity q_d. It might do this by assigning each individual supplier a production quota such that the sum of all suppliers' quotas does not exceed q_d. Given the demand curve D, buyers would be willing to pay suppliers a price of p_s per unit for this quantity. Such a scheme would require an elaborate administrative and enforcement apparatus. This apparatus would be needed because the temptation for suppliers to exceed their quota would be great, given that a price of p_s lies above the supply curve at an output level of q_d.

Scheme 4: Government Purchase.
Another alternative is for the government to buy up the surplus. At a price level of p_s, suppliers would want to supply a quantity of the good equal to q_s, while buyers would demand the smaller quantity q_d. This would create an unsold surplus equal to the amount by which q_s exceeds q_d. The government steps in and buys up this surplus at a price p_s per unit and thereby takes it "off the market." Unless the government buys up the surplus, it will be impossible to maintain the price at the level p_s. Price would have to fall to p_g before buyers in the market would be willing to purchase the quantity q_s. But then suppliers would suffer a loss equal to p_s minus p_d per unit of output. By standing ready to buy and store the surplus at a price of p_s, the government ensures that that price will prevail in the marketplace. The government must spend an amount equal to the rectangular area $q_d q_s ac$ to do this. Note that the size of the surplus that results from the establishment of a price support above the equilibrium price is larger the more elastic are demand and supply.

Government purchase of agricultural commodities has not been extensively used in Canada. When price-support programs were first introduced for eggs, a floor price was established but no restrictions were placed on production. The floor price raised the farm price of eggs above the equilibrium level. The quantity supplied, as predicted in Figure 7-5, increased while the quantity demanded decreased. As a result, there was a great surplus of eggs available on the market. The government purchased these eggs and put them into storage where they promptly began to rot. Eventually, the eggs had to be destroyed, which caused some very bad press for the government of the day. As a result of the egg fiasco, the output restrictions described earlier were introduced into the price-support program for eggs and, subsequently, milk and poultry products. Hence, these programs are referred to as "supply management" systems.

Scheme 5: Demand Promotion.
Yet another way to maintain the price level at p_s would be to somehow get the demand curve D to shift out until it intersected the market supply curve S at point a. This would result in a market equilibrium price of p_s and quantity q_s.

POLICY PERSPECTIVE

Farm Support Problems and Resource Allocation

Agriculture is an important sector of the Canadian economy. In 1990, the value of primary agricultural production was 3.7 percent and the value added through the processing sector was another 7.5 percent. In total, 7.5 percent of the work force is involved in agriculture: 3.5 percent in primary production and 4 percent in food processing and distribution. About 900,000 people live on farms in Canada. In response to the needs of the agricultural industry, many government price-support programs have been used.

The major concern around any form of subsidization is the impact on resource allocation. Support programs do two things. First, they increase the profits of the enterprise relative to other en-

terprises. Second, they frequently reduce the risk associated with the enterprise. As a result, producers are attracted to the subsidized commodity and more resources are allocated to its production than would be without the support program.

RESOURCE ALLOCATION CONSEQUENCES

The consequences of this resource allocation can be quite serious. Marginal land tends to be brought into production. This land is typically fragile and prone to erosion. Wildlife habitat is destroyed in the process as trees are cut down and wetlands are drained. There tends to be less diversification in the types of crops grown. As a result, both the ecology and the economy are

less diversified and more prone to certain risks.

Another consequence is what is referred to as the "capitalization of benefits." The subsidy results in increased profits, which allow farmers to pay more for land, buildings, and other factors of production. This increases the farmers' costs of production and eats away at the benefits of the subsidy. Often, all the benefits of the subsidization disappear into higher prices for the factors of production and the farmer is no better off than before.

A third consequence in the long-run is the much higher productivity growth in agriculture versus the growth in demand. Coupled with low income elasticities on food items in North America and parity pricing, this makes prices unresponsive to productivity changes and general demand conditions, distorting the allocative function of the market.

INCOME REDISTRIBUTION

A second concern surrounding policy is the impact on income distribution. This concerns both the farmers receiving the benefits and the consumers who pay. When program benefits are paid on the basis of acreage or volume of production, the biggest farmers receive large sums of money even though they may have adequate incomes without any subsidization. When the cost of the program is borne by the consumer, as with supply management programs, the poorest members of our society are forced to pay higher prices for food. This is in effect a regressive form of

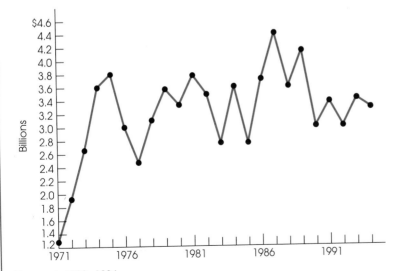

FIGURE P7-1 Realized Net Farm Income, Canada

Forecast: 1992-1994

continued on next page

POLICY PERSPECTIVE CONTINUED

taxation, since the poorest people spend a greater percentage of their income on food than anyone else. Although, in defense of farmers, we must point out that Canadians spend less than 15 percent of their income on food—one of the lowest rates in the world.

Often there seems to be a confusion between the problems of agriculture and those of rural poverty. Ironically, price-support programs have benefited the efficient, larger farmer (who least needs help) more than they have those farmers who are counted among the rural poor. Prudent policy would seem to suggest that the problem of rural poverty be dealt with as an issue separate from agricultural policy.

Finally, subsidization can affect international relations. The presence of subsidies has spawned several countervailing duty battles between Canada and the United States since the middle of the 1980s. Recently, our supply management programs have come under fire from the General Agreement on Tariffs and Trade (GATT) because we limit the amount of milk, eggs, and poultry products that can be imported into Canada.

CURRENT PROBLEMS IN CANADIAN AGRICULTURE

Despite all of the attempts at price and income stabilization in the agricultural sector, the Canadian farm sector is in a terrible income crisis. The depressed levels of commodity prices experienced in the 1980s have driven farm incomes downward. Furthermore, income is expected to improve only slightly by 1994.

The cyclical nature of most agricultural enterprises results in an accompanying cycle of fluctuating income levels and asset values. The 1980s witnessed two major peaks in the grain markets, once in 1984 and again in 1988. The high commodity prices and incomes available at these times encouraged higher prices for land and other productive assets, particularly in Western Canada, where farm income is strongly influenced by grain prices.

Set against these fundamentals, two important trends were developing: major trade disputes spearheaded by the United States and the European Common Market (EC), and high levels of interest rate subsidization at the provincial level. Grain markets normally peak only briefly, followed by a sharp decline to lower levels. The decline from the last grain rallies in 1988 have been greatly compounded by the trade war between the U.S. and the EC. The "beggar thy neighbour" subsidy battles carried out between these two have pushed grain prices to ten-year lows and, in real terms, prices as low as during the 1930s.

Figure P7-1 illustrates the decline in realized net income experienced in Canada since the mid-1980s and forecast values to 1994. The federal and provincial governments have responded to this distress with the development of new support programs and ad hoc payments. The total amount of money transferred to the farm community through direct government payments rose dramatically during the 1980s. Figure P7-2 shows the rapid increase in direct payments during the last decade. Direct payments reached a peak in the late 1980s and then fell significantly in 1990. Forecasts to 1994 indicate that there will be a resurgence in payments, with a new maximum being reached in 1992.

Direct payments have constituted an increasing proportion of realized net income (profits). Direct payments as a percentage of realized net income has represented over 70 percent of realized income for six of the last seven years. In 1988, direct payments accounted for over 90 percent of realized net income. Based on current forecasts, direct payments will exceed realized net income in 1992. In simple words, this means

FIGURE P7-2   **Total Net Direct Payments, Canada**

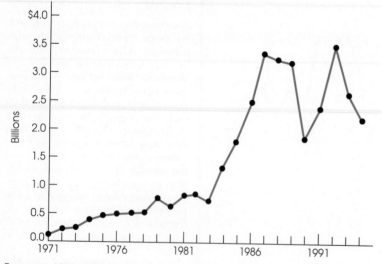

Forecast: 1991–1994

continued on next page

POLICY PERSPECTIVE CONTINUED

that in recent years farmers have earned far more money through government payments than they were able to from the land.

Figure P7-3 depicts the percentage of realized net income provided through direct payments. This decline in farm income should be reflected in a decline in the price of productive assets such as land. However, this adjustment will be complicated by the presence of, or shadows of, additional government policies. Nearly every province has subsidized agricultural interest rates to some degree. While this policy is intended to lower farm production costs, it usually serves only to encourage producers to bid up the price of land and other productive assets. When farm income decreases, as it has, many farmers find their overpriced land too expensive to maintain. The net effect will be to escalate the decline in land values in the future. Those provinces which most heavily subsidized interest rates will find the adjustment process the most painful.

FUTURE CONDITIONS

The outcome of the GATT negotiations would change the conditions of Canadian agriculture. The ongoing GATT negotiations seem to represent an on-again, off-again global love affair with trade liberalization. Once again, the negotiations seem to teeter on the edge of collapse. The outcome could result in two entirely different scenarios for Canadian agriculture.

If the negotiations remain on track and if GATT pursues Article 11 regarding import restrictions and Canada's supply managed industries, major structural changes in incomes and asset values will occur in dairy and poultry. These adjustments will have a regional impact, since these industries are concentrated in Ontario and Quebec. The impact on the grain-based sectors of agriculture, notably Western Canada, will not be so clear, as it does not follow that the decline in the supply managed industries will be immediately or equally offset by

improved grain prices and higher volumes of trade.

If the negotiations remain stalemated, Canadian supply managed industries will be able to maintain their structure, at least in the short-run. The grain sector would then continue to deal with suppressed price levels and declining market share until one of two things occur; the treasuries of the U.S. and the EC run dry, or a fundamental adjustment in supply and demand shocks grain prices out of their current morass.

To summarize, the main argument against government price supports over the longrun is that they give rise to surplus production, requiring the use of productive resources that could otherwise be used in alternative activities. In short, price supports encourage too many farmers and too much land (and other inputs) to stay in agriculture—resources that unregulated market forces would otherwise encourage to leave. Thus, the release of resources to other productive activities made possible by the tremendous growth in agricultural productivity is not fully realized. Over the longrun this productivity growth has no doubt been passed on to consumers in the form of lower food prices to some extent. However, price-support programs keep such price reductions from being as large as they might be.

For Discussion

- If a decision was made to eliminate price supports, do you think that it would be better to do it in 1 year or over a 5-year period? Why?
- How would the effectiveness of a demand-promotion scheme to support a price depend on the elasticity of supply?
- What other productive activities, do you think, might agricultural resources flow to if price supports were eliminated?

FIGURE P7-3   **Direct Payments to Realized Net Income**

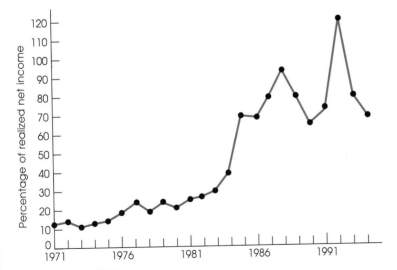

Forecast: 1991–1994

Demand promotion is an important activity for many agricultural commodity organizations across Canada, including many marketing boards. Often, the terms *supply management* and *marketing board* are used interchangeably. However, this is not quite correct, since not all marketing boards are involved in supply management. Dozens of marketing boards exist across Canada whose purpose, among other things, is to promote the consumption of specific agricultural commodities. The "Get Cracking," "Butter It," and "If it ain't Alberta, it ain't beef" advertising campaigns are all examples of commodity associations and marketing boards attempting to increase the demand for their product.

The federal and provincial governments are also active in demand promotion. Government budgets have funded research into such things as the use of corn derivatives for biodegradable grocery bags, the distilling of feed grains into ethanol, and the development of the canola plant through biogenetics. Additionally, the extension of long-term credit to foreign purchasers of grain helps maintain Canadian market share in the world grain markets. Trade missions, funded by government, allow commodity groups and others to attract foreign markets.

Policies Compared

Each of the price-support policies described increases the price received by the farmer. These increased revenues must represent increased costs for some other market participant. In the case of our deficiency payment programs, the market price of the commodity is not changed. The difference between the target price and the market price is made up through government deficiency payments. The producers pay premiums to belong to these programs. However, the producer usually pays only one third of the total cost, while the federal and provincial governments pick up the other two thirds. Hence, the taxpayers contribute to increasing farm incomes. With minimum-price programs, such as the supply management programs, the market price is forced to a higher level by cutting back production. Under these programs, the government does not contribute. Consumers carry the entire cost of the program.

Government purchases increase the market price of the commodity by shifting the demand curve to the right. This causes consumers to pay more than they would at the equilibrium price. In addition to this, the taxpayers must bear the costs of the purchases made by the government, any storage costs incurred, and, in some cases, further costs for transportation, processing and disposal. When ad hoc payments are made, the market price is not affected. The costs of ad hoc payments are borne entirely by the taxpayers. Demand promotion may be financed either by commodity associations or by the government. In the case of the former, the producers pay for the programs. Frequently, the funds are raised by deducting a small fee from every unit of the commodity sold.

Perspective on Agricultural Policy

Price-support schemes like those just outlined have been used extensively by the government in agricultural markets to deal with the "farm problem." Canadian agricultural policy over the past 30 years has been shaped, at least in part, by strong political pressures in favour of price supports. Agricultural interest groups have lobbied for the idea that farmers should be paid prices for their products that bear the same relationship to other prices that farm prices did in the 1909–1914 era, the "golden age" of agriculture. This concept is known as **parity.** Simply put, it means that if the price received for a bushel of wheat in 1909 was such that a farmer could buy a shirt with that amount of money, then he should be able to buy a shirt with the money he receives for a bushel of wheat now. We know, however, that in a dynamic, changing economy it is unrealistic to expect the prices of different goods to bear the same relationship to one another over long periods of time. This is particularly true of the relationship between the prices of farm products and the prices of other goods.

Productivity Growth Exceeds Demand Growth

Agriculture has experienced a much larger rate of productivity growth than the rest of the economy—twice the rate of the industrial sector since 1930. On the other hand, the growth in demand for agricultural products has not been as great as the growth in demand for most other goods and services. In an economy that has reached the level of affluence that Canada has over the last 50 or 60 years, the demand for basic necessities such as food and fiber does not grow at a rate as high as that for industrial products and other services. (A person can only eat so many good meals a day.) Increases in income levels are spent more than proportionally on other goods and services, and the rate of growth of the population, or new mouths to feed and bodies to clothe, has not been large enough to offset this fact.

The result has been that the capacity to supply the typical agricultural product has grown more rapidly than the demand for it. Hence, over the longrun, its freely determined market price would be expected to fall in the manner depicted in Figure 7-6. There the market price falls from p_s to p_b to p_c over time because the demand curve shifts rightward from D_0 to D_1 to D_2 at a less rapid rate than the supply curve shifts from S_0 to S_1 to S_2. Meanwhile, the demand and supply curves for other goods and services typically have shifted rightward at rates that have caused their freely determined market prices either to rise or at least to fall less rapidly.

In order to maintain agricultural prices at a parity level with the prices of other goods, it has been necessary for the government to support agricultural prices at levels above those that would prevail in a freely working market. Given that the demand curve for agricultural goods is shifting rightward at a less rapid rate than the supply curve, the surplus resulting from such a policy can be expected to become ever larger, as shown in Figure 7-6.

Probably no industry in the economy has had research and development subsidized with public funds more than agriculture has. Political pundits and others have wryly observed that it's a shame the tremendous growth in agricultural productivity that resulted has not given the public the lower food prices their taxes have made possible.

Checkpoint 7-2
Suppose that the government wants to maintain a price support for wheat. You are called on for your advice as to which type of price-support program would cost taxpayers less money to run, scheme 1 or scheme 4. Analyze this issue, first assuming that the demand and supply curves for wheat are relatively inelastic and then assuming that they are both relatively elastic. Remember to consider storage costs in your analysis.

Sales and Excise Taxes

Sales and excise taxes are levied on goods in the markets where they are bought and sold. **Sales taxes** apply to a broad range of goods, while **excise taxes** are levied

FIGURE 7-6   Longrun Growth in Supply and Demand in Agriculture

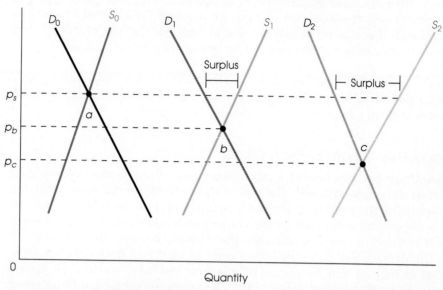

The rapid rate of growth of productivity in agriculture has caused production capacity to increase at a faster pace than the rate of growth of demand. The supply curve for agricultural products has, therefore, shifted rightward over time at a more rapid rate than the demand curve has. Hence, over the longrun, the freely determined market price would be expected to fall—say from p_s to p_b to p_c—as the demand curve shifts rightward from D_0 to D_1 to D_2 at a less rapid rate than the supply curve shifts from S_0 to S_1 to S_2. Under these conditions, maintenance of a price support at p_s will result in an ever-growing surplus as indicated.

on particular goods. Retail sales taxes are used by the federal government (GST) and all provincial governments (PST), except Alberta, as a source of revenue and are applied to most goods and services (with some exceptions). Excise taxes are imposed by both levels of government on specific goods such as tobacco, liquor, and gasoline. If a sales or excise tax is calculated as a percentage of price, it is called an **ad valorem tax.** If either is calculated as a fixed amount of money per unit of the good sold, it is called a **specific tax.** *Sales and excise taxes amount to the government's legal claim on a portion of the price paid for each unit of a good sold.* They may be thought of as driving a wedge between the price buyers pay for a unit of the good and the amount that suppliers receive for it. This wedge is illustrated in Figure 7-7. Because of this wedge, the price paid for the good by the buyer, p_b in Figure 7-7, is higher than the price received by the supplier, p_s. The amount of revenue received by the supplier is lower than is the case in the absence of the tax. In Figure 7-7 the amount received in the absence of the tax is $0p_eq_e$ and with the tax is $0p_sq_s$. The quantity bought and sold is reduced from q_e to q_s. The way the burden of these taxes is divided is called **tax incidence**: that is, what portion of the tax or wedge is paid by the buyer in the form of a higher price per unit, and what portion is paid by the supplier in the form of a lower revenue received per unit of the good sold.

FIGURE 7-7 The Tax Wedge Created Between Suppliers and Buyers

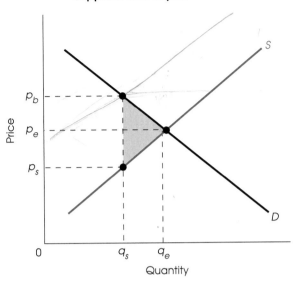

In the absence of a tax, the demand curve D and supply curve S determine an equilibrium price p_e and quantity q_e. The implementation of an excise or sales tax creates a "wedge" (the shaded area) between the price suppliers receive, p_s, and the price buyers pay, p_b. The revenue that suppliers receive is reduced from $0p_eq_e$ to $0p_sq_s$.

Tax Incidence and Elasticity of Demand and Supply

Who bears the greater incidence or brunt of the tax? The answer to this question depends on the elasticity of the demand and supply curves.

Elasticity of Demand

Suppose that the market supply and demand curves for a 24-bottle case of beer are S and D_e in Figure 7-8, frame (a). Their intersection gives an equilibrium price of $20 per case and an equilibrium quantity of 5,300 cases per month. Now what would happen if the government decided to impose a specific excise tax of $10 on each case of beer sold? Would the price of a case of beer rise from $20 to $30? The answer is no. Here's why.

Suppose that the tax is collected from suppliers. Now, in addition to the costs of producing a case of beer, the supplier must also pay the government $10 on each case produced. This effectively means that the cost of supplying a case of beer is now $10 more than before the tax was imposed. Suppliers in frame (a) of Figure 7-8 were willing to supply 5,300 cases per month at a price of $20 per case before the tax was imposed. This $20 was just sufficient to compensate them for the cost of producing a case of beer, including at least a normal profit. But now when suppliers have to pay a tax of $10 per case, they will have to receive a price of $30 per case in order to be willing to supply 5,300 cases of beer per month—$20 in order to receive the same per unit price as before plus an additional $10 compensation for the tax they now pay. Similarly, whatever quantity of output we consider, suppliers must now receive $10 more per case for them still to be willing to supply that quantity after the imposition of the $10 tax. The

FIGURE 7-8   Demand Elasticity and the Incidence of an Excise Tax

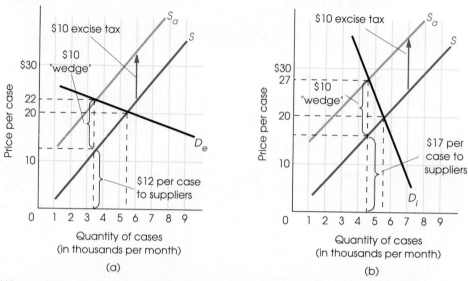

When demand is elastic, as in frame (a), the imposition of an excise tax forces up the price to buyers by less than it forces down the amount suppliers are able to keep, after the government has been paid the tax. In frame (b), the supply curve is the same as in frame (a), but the demand curve is inelastic. The imposition of the same excise tax forces the price up to buyers by more than it forces down the amount suppliers are able to keep after tax payment. The incidence of the tax bears heaviest on suppliers when demand is elastic, frame (a), and heaviest on buyers when demand is inelastic, frame (b).

supply curve is therefore shifted upward by $10 from its before-tax position S to its after-tax position S_a.

How does this affect the market equilibrium price and quantity of beer bought and sold? Given the supply curve, it depends on the elasticity of demand. In frame (a) of Figure 7-8 demand is relatively more elastic than in frame (b). Consider the situation shown in frame (a). The new equilibrium point now occurs at the intersection of S_a and D_e. This means that the new equilibrium price is $22 per case and the new equilibrium quantity is 3,300 cases per month. The price paid by buyers has risen by only $2, from $20 to $22. Of this $22, $10 goes to the government to pay the excise tax. After this "wedge" is paid, suppliers receive $12 per case—$8 less than previously. Therefore, the incidence or burden of this tax is such that buyers pay $2 of it per case and suppliers $8. The incidence of the tax bears more heavily on the suppliers.

What if demand were less elastic? In Figure 7-8, frame (b), the supply curve is the same as in Figure 7-8, frame (a), but the demand curve D_i is relatively less elastic than the demand curve D_e in frame (a). The initial equilibrium price and quantity determined by the intersection of S and D_i is the same as before ($20 and 5,300 cases per month). However, now when the government imposes the $10 excise tax, shifting the supply curve up to S_a, the new equilibrium price is $27 per case and the new equilibrium quantity is 4,600 cases per month. In this

---

POLICY PERSPECTIVE

Can Excise Taxes Stop People from Smoking?

Smoking is singled out as the largest cause of premature deaths, killing at least 40,000 Canadians a year, mainly through heart disease and lung cancer. Since the early 1960s the federal Ministry of Health and Welfare and its provincial counterparts have been cranking out statistics and alarming reports on the health risks of smoking. The government has imposed compulsory health warnings on cigarette packs and obtained "voluntary" agreements from tobacco companies to curb advertising, including a ban on television ads. In addition, excise taxes on cigarettes have steadily increased. These vary from province to province, as both the federal and provincial governments levy taxes on cigarettes. Cigarette consumption has fallen steadily with these policies: from 41 percent of the population in 1966, to 37 percent in 1975, to 33 percent in 1981, to 30 percent in 1986, and to 26 percent in 1991.

In 1991 the federal government imposed another increase in excise taxes on cigarettes, in addition to implementing the GST, sending the price of a pack of cigarettes to $6.00 and higher. At that point, the various treasuries took about 75 percent of the retail price of a pack of cigarettes in excise tax. Canadians are paying up to three times more for cigarettes than Americans. Subsequent to these increases in the excise tax, tobacco companies reported a 10 percent drop in sales. Although some of this fall in sales may be due to cross-border shopping and increased smuggling, a survey estimated that almost a million smokers had quit after the last round of increases.

For Discussion

- Suppose that prior to the 1991 increases in the excise tax on cigarettes the price of a pack was $5.00. Is the demand for cigarettes in Canada elastic or inelastic?
- On the basis of the survey reported, give a rough estimate of how high the price of a pack of cigarettes would have to be pushed by an excise tax in order to completely eliminate smoking in Canada.
- If the demand is inelastic, is increasing the price an efficient way to reduce the number of smokers? Would it be more effective if demand is elastic?

---

instance the price paid by buyers has risen by $7 (from $20 to $27). Out of this $27, $10 once again goes to the government to pay the excise tax. This time, the wedge between the price paid per case by buyers and the amount received by suppliers leaves suppliers with $17 per case—$3 less than before the tax was imposed. Hence, in this instance, where demand is less elastic, the incidence of the tax is such that buyers are burdened with $7 of it per case and suppliers with only $3. The incidence of the tax now bears more heavily on the buyers. In sum, the example of Figure 7-8, frames (a) and (b), illustrates the following fact about the tax incidence of an excise tax or a sales tax: *In general, given the elasticity of supply, the less elastic is demand, the greater is the burden of the incidence of the tax on buyers, and the smaller is the burden of the incidence on suppliers.*

Finally, note also that the greater the elasticity of demand [compare frames (a) and (b) of Figure 7-8], the larger is the reduction in the quantity of the goods produced and sold due to the imposition of the tax, given the elasticity of supply. Hence, if the government's primary purpose is to raise revenue from such taxes, it should impose them on goods and services that have the most inelastic demands. For example, the total tax revenue obtained from the imposition of the $10 tax in Figure 7-8, frame (a), is $33,000 per month ($10 × 3,300 cases per month). In Figure 7-8, frame (b), it is $46,000 per month ($10 × 4,600 cases per month).

Elasticity of Supply

How does the elasticity of supply affect the way in which the incidence of the tax is distributed between buyers and suppliers? *Given demand, the less elastic is supply, the greater is the burden of the incidence of the tax on suppliers and the smaller is the burden of the incidence on buyers.* This is illustrated in Figure 7-9. The supply curve in Figure 7-9, frame (a), is more elastic than that in Figure 7-9, frame (b). Of the total excise tax of $10 per case in Figure 7-9, frame (a), buyers pay $7 while suppliers pay only $3. However, in the case of the less elastic supply curve in Figure 7-9, frame (b), suppliers bear the heaviest incidence of the tax, paying $7 per case while buyers pay only $3.

Subsidies

The same analysis used to examine the effects of an excise tax in Figures 7-8 and 7-9 can be applied to a study of the effects of government subsidies. A **subsidy** can be thought of as the reverse of an excise or sales tax. While such taxes take money away from buyers and suppliers, a subsidy gives them money.

For example, suppose that the government wanted to encourage beer production because it would promote economic development and help alleviate

FIGURE 7-9   Supply Elasticity and the Incidence of an Excise Tax

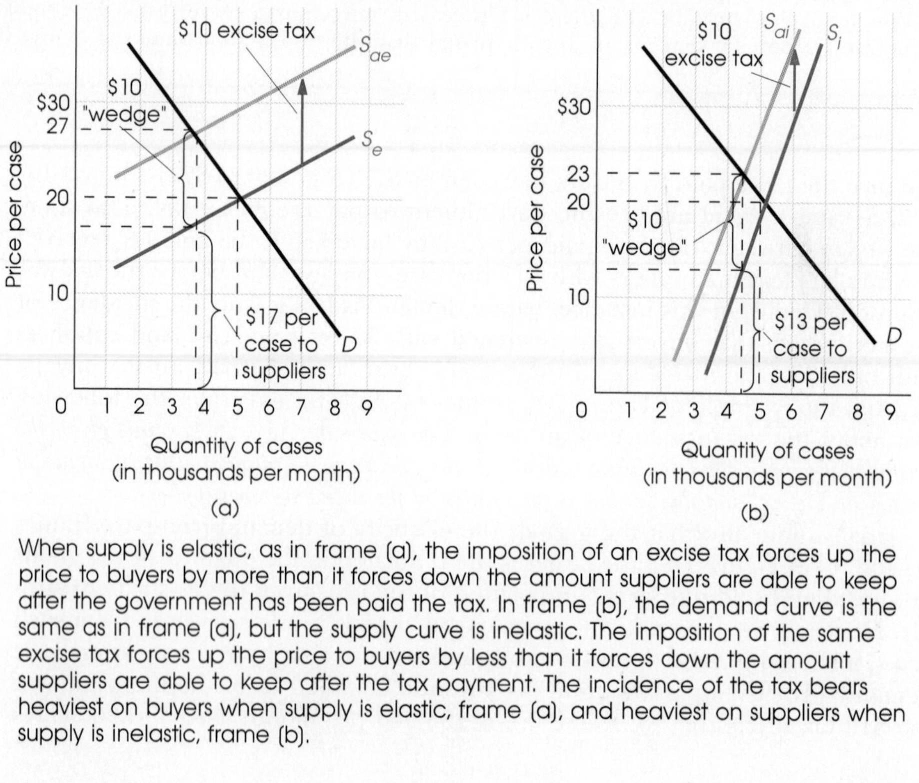

When supply is elastic, as in frame (a), the imposition of an excise tax forces up the price to buyers by more than it forces down the amount suppliers are able to keep after the government has been paid the tax. In frame (b), the demand curve is the same as in frame (a), but the supply curve is inelastic. The imposition of the same excise tax forces up the price to buyers by less than it forces down the amount suppliers are able to keep after the tax payment. The incidence of the tax bears heaviest on buyers when supply is elastic, frame (a), and heaviest on suppliers when supply is inelastic, frame (b).

poverty in certain parts of the country suited to barley growing. Let's assume that the market supply curve is initially S_a in Figure 7-8, frame (a), with the equilibrium price and quantity determined by its intersection with D_e. Now suppose the government decides to pay suppliers a subsidy of $10 per case. This effectively reduces suppliers' costs by $10 per case of beer. The supply curve is therefore shifted down by this amount from S_a to S. The price of a case of beer falls to $20 per case, and the quantity supplied and sold rises from 3,300 to 5,300 cases per month, as determined by the intersection of S and D_e. A *subsidy typically has the effect of reducing price and increasing quantity supplied.* The extent of the price reduction and the quantity increase depends on the elasticity of the demand and supply curves. This can be seen by examining Figures 7-8 and 7-9.

Externalities—External Costs and Benefits

We have already seen in Chapter 4 how the intersection of the demand and supply curves for a good determines the equilibrium price and quantity, as shown in Figure 7-10. To the right of the intersection, the supply curve is above the demand curve. This means that if suppliers produced an amount q_1 that is larger than the equilibrium quantity q_e, buyers would not be willing to pay a price high enough to cover the costs of supplying the additional units of output from q_e to q_1. Buyers do not value the additional benefits, represented by the area aq_eq_1b under the demand curve over the units of output from q_e to q_1, as highly as the value of the resources needed to produce them. The value of these resources is measured by their opportunity cost represented by the area aq_eq_1c under the supply curve over the units of output from q_e to q_1. Resources would

FIGURE 7-10   **The Optimum Quantity of Output**

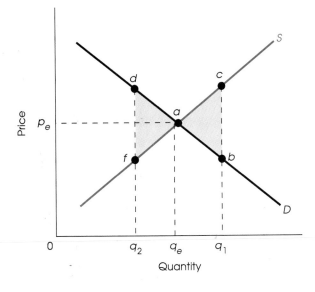

If suppliers produced an amount q_1 that is larger than the equilibrium quantity q_e, buyers would not be willing to pay a price high enough to cover the costs of supplying the additional units of output from q_e to q_1. To produce these extra units would be a waste of society's resources because buyers do not value the additional benefits as highly as the resources needed to produce them. Resources would be overallocated to this activity. If suppliers produced an amount q_2 that is less than the equilibrium quantity q_e, buyers would be willing to pay a price that is more than enough to cover the costs of supplying additional units of output from q_2 to q_e. To produce the smaller quantity of output q_2, would be an underallocation of resources to this activity. The optimum quantity is therefore q_e.

be overallocated to this activity in the sense that the cost to society of producing the units of output from q_e to q_1 exceeds their value to society by an amount represented by the triangular area abc. Therefore, it would be economically inefficient to produce the output beyond q_e.

On the other hand, if suppliers produced an amount q_2 that is less than the equilibrium quantity q_e, buyers would be willing to pay a price that is more than enough to cover the costs of supplying additional units of output beyond q_2. This is reflected by the fact that the demand curve is higher than the supply curve to the left of the intersection. Producing the smaller quantity of output q_2 would be an underallocation of resources to this activity because buyers value the additional benefits from the extra units of output from q_2 to q_e (represented by the area dq_2q_ea under the demand curve) more than the value of the resources needed to produce them. (Once again, the value of these resources is measured by their opportunity cost as represented by the area fq_2q_ea under the supply curve.) If suppliers produce no more than the quantity q_2, society forgoes the excess of the value of the benefits over the costs represented by the triangular area dfa. The equilibrium quantity q_e determined by the intersection of the demand and supply curves is the only one for which buyers are just willing to pay a price p_e sufficient to cover the cost of the last unit produced. The value of the benefits of this last unit are just equal to the value of the resources needed to produce it. The equilibrium quantity q_e is therefore the optimum quantity.

However, what if all the costs associated with producing the good are not paid by the firms who supply it? For example, when air and water are polluted by the production process, society at large typically bears the cost of either cleaning it up or suffering the higher health care and other costs that it may entail. In such cases these costs are not reflected in the market supply curve for the good.

Similarly, what if the benefits associated with a good extend to others besides the buyers of the good? In this case, the total benefits may not be fully reflected in the demand curve for that good. Consider, for example, the purchase by farmers of fencing to keep their livestock from wandering. The fencing protects their investment in livestock, a private benefit that they derive directly. Society at large also benefits, however. There is a reduction in safety hazards, such as livestock wandering onto highways, and a reduction in crop loss caused by livestock wandering into other farmers' wheat and corn fields. However, the market demand curve for fencing reflects only the value of the private benefits to the buyers of fencing, in this case the owners of the livestock.

Costs and benefits that fall on others besides the buyers and sellers of a good are often called **externalities,** or *external costs* and *benefits*. Frequently they are also referred to as *spillovers, neighbourhood effects,* or *external economies* and *diseconomies. All these terms refer to the fact that these costs and benefits fall on others besides the buyers and sellers directly involved in the transactions of the particular market for the good.*

External Costs

Suppose that a particular industry pollutes the environment when it produces its product, but the cost of cleaning up the environment or suffering the consequences is borne by others. Since the firms in the industry do not have to pay the cleanup cost, this cost is not included in the market supply curve S shown in Figure 7-11. It is an external cost borne by others not directly involved in the purchase or sale of the product. Given the market demand for the product, represented by the demand curve D, the equilibrium quantity produced and sold would be q_n and the equilibrium price p_n.

However, what if the firms in the industry had to pay the cleanup costs associated with the production of each unit of output? These costs would be added in, just like an excise tax, along with the other production costs to give the market supply curve S_a, which includes all costs. Because of this, S_a lies above S. The equilibrium quantity produced and sold when firms pay all costs associated with production would be q_o, an amount smaller than q_n. The equilibrium price would be p_o, which is higher than p_n. The incidence of this added cost would be distributed between suppliers and buyers of the good in the same way as an excise tax, rather than falling on other parties who do not buy or sell the good.

Hence, when there are external costs associated with a good, costs not paid for by the buyers and suppliers of a good (sometimes called *spillover costs*), a greater quantity of output is produced and sold than is optimum. This is shown in Figure 7-11, where the supply curve S_a, which includes all costs, lies above the demand curve D for all units of the good from q_o to q_n. This means that the value of the benefits to buyers of this additional quantity of the good is less than the value of all the resources used to produce it by an amount represented by the triangular area abc. *When there are external costs—that is, costs of production not borne by the immediate buyers and suppliers of a good—there is an overallocation of resources to the production of that good. Therefore, more of it is produced and sold than is optimal.*

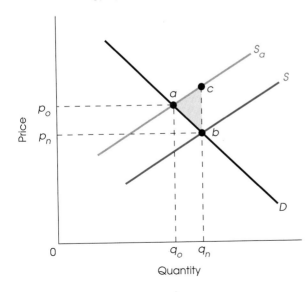

FIGURE 7-11 Externalities and the Allocation of Resources

The presence of externalities in the form of spillover costs means the *market* supply curve S lies below the supply curve S_a, which includes all costs associated with production of the good. As a result, there is an *overallocation* of resources to the production of this good. Therefore, the market equilibrium quantity q_n exceeds the optimum quantity q_o. Because buyers and suppliers don't pay all the costs of production, the market equilibrium price p_n is below the price p_o, which covers all costs.

External Benefits

The market demand curve for a good reflects the value of the benefits of that good that accrue directly to those who buy it. If the good also provides externalities in the form of benefits to others who do not buy the good, these spillover, or external, benefits are not reflected in the market demand curve. The market demand curve for fencing reflects the value of its benefits to the farmers who buy the fencing to protect their investment in their livestock. It does not reflect the benefits of this fencing to motorists who drive on highways adjacent to cattle fields or to farmers who raise crops next door to cattle farms. Similarly, those who get vaccinated against communicable diseases to protect their own well-being also generate benefits for others. For example, they reduce the spread of contagious diseases.

Since the market demand curve for these kinds of goods and services does not reflect the value of these social, or spillover, benefits, it must lie below a demand curve that is drawn to include them. Figure 7-12 shows a hypothetical market demand curve D and supply curve S for flu shots. If the value of the spillover benefits to society at large from these shots is added on, we get the demand curve D_a, which includes the value of all benefits and therefore lies above D. The market equilibrium quantity of flu shots supplied and purchased is q_n (determined by the intersection of S and D). However, the existence of externalities in the form of social benefits means that this is less than the optimum quantity q_o (determined by the intersection of S and D_a). As a result, the demand curve D_a lies above the supply curve S for the additional flu shots from q_n to q_o. This means that the value of all the benefits to society from having these additional flu shots is greater than the cost of supplying them by an amount represented by the triangular area adf. When there are external, or spillover, benefits associated with a good, too few resources are allocated to the production of that good and less of it is produced and sold than is optimum.

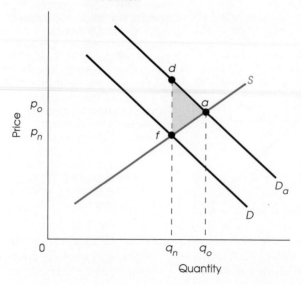

FIGURE 7-12   Spillover Benefits and Resource Allocation

The presence of externalities in the form of spillover benefits means that the market demand curve D lies below the demand curve D_a, which reflects all benefits associated with the consumption of a good. As a result, there is an *underallocation* of resources to the production of this good, so that the market equilibrium quantity q_n is less than the optimum quantity q_o.

POLICY PERSPECTIVE

Acid Rain—A Spillover Cost

As a practical matter of public policy it is not always easy to identify an external, or spillover, cost. An example is provided by the recent concern that acid rain is causing major damage to the lakes, soil, and forests of eastern Canada and the northeastern United States. Acid rain may also cause human health problems.

Scientists in Canada have been aware of acid rain since the late 1960s. Circumstantial evidence links the cause of acid rainwater to sulfur dioxide and nitrogen oxide emissions. The main sources of sulfur dioxide are from coal-fired power stations and ore smelters in the heavily industrialized regions in Ontario and the midwestern and northeastern United States. The main sources of nitrogen oxides are automobile exhaust and the burning of other fuels. More than half of the acid rain in Canada comes from the United States. (Much of our sulfur dioxide emissions travel to Europe.) The sulfur dioxide emissions are thought to interact with moisture in the air to form sulfuric acid, which then falls on lakes and forests whenever it rains or snows. If sulfur dioxide emissions are indeed the culprit, then it is a clear case of identifiable industries creating spillover costs for society at large. The Canadian and American governments could mandate and enforce sulfur dioxide emission controls and thereby internalize the costs to the polluters and those who buy their products.

A study by the U.S. National Resource Council of the National Academy of Sciences, generally interpreted as supporting the "acid rain" thesis, concedes that the magnitude of the changes in alkalinity has been "too large to be caused by acid deposition alone and may result from other human activities or natural causes." The study notes that sulfur dioxide emissions in the northeastern United States "have fluctuated near current amounts since the 1920s," but it never answers the question of why lakes weren't "dying" much earlier. Several other studies point to the acidity problems caused by nature itself. A Hudson Institute report observes that "the humus layer in the eastern watershed usually makes any water contacting it much more acidic than the incident rainfall." Western lakes, by contrast, don't have an acid rain problem, in part because of the region's differing forest soils.

In 1980 estimates suggested about 8 million tonnes of acid rain emissions were being deposited on eastern Canada. Various strategies have been proposed to stop emissions that contribute to acid rain.

The Canadian acid rain abatement program established in 1985 targeted for a reduction by 1990 of sulfur dioxide emissions to one half of that of 1980, 2 million tonnes from Canada and 2 million tonnes from the United States. The *Canadian Environmental Protection Act* of 1988 requires industries and government to reduce or control emissions generated by industrial activity. In 1990 amendments were made to the *U.S. Clean Air Act* to meet this target. A Canada–United States agreement—the Air Quality Accord—was signed in 1991 committing both countries to reducing acid rain emissions to a combined level of 3.2 tonnes annually.

For Discussion

- Many studies show that acid rain adversely affects our environment. If research does definitively show that sulfur dioxide is the primary causal factor in acid rain, do you think that it would be better to levy an excise tax on polluters to cover costs of environmental damage or to impose limits on measured sulfur dioxide emitted from smokestacks, thereby requiring business firms to incur the cost of installing smokestack scrubbers? Why?

Externalities and Government Policy

How can the external costs that arise in the markets for certain kinds of goods be internalized to those markets? That is, how can we ensure that such costs are borne by the buyers and sellers directly involved in the transactions in those markets rather than by others? Similarly, what might be done to encourage a greater production of goods that have external benefits? We cannot give an exhaustive account of all the possible proposals for dealing with these questions. However, the following are often used or suggested by policymakers.

Policy and External Costs

Policies must be devised to make the suppliers and buyers in the market, rather than third parties who are not the immediate buyers and sellers of the good, bear the external costs. Corrective policy must somehow internalize these costs in the market where they occur. When the externalities associated with a good are external benefits, policies are needed that will encourage the production of a quantity of the good more in line with a demand that takes account of the value of all the good's benefits to society.

One way to deal with external costs is to pass laws that make their cause illegal. For example, a provincial or municipal government might pass laws against dumping untreated industrial wastes in rivers or pouring toxic smoke or particulate matter into the air. If the laws are backed up by sufficiently stiff fines, jail terms, and court actions against offenders, producing firms will take it on themselves to incur directly the costs of installing waste treatment and smoke abatement equipment as part of their production facilities. This means that the market supply curves in industries where there are external costs would shift upward as in Figure 7-11. The firms or suppliers in those industries are forced to pay those costs directly. The incidence of these additional costs would be distributed among the buyers and suppliers in proportions determined by the elasticities of demand and supply just as in the case of an excise tax.

Laws against external costs may not always be easy to enforce or use the resources efficiently, however. Detection of offenders and a determination of the extent of their violation of the law can be difficult. Many different firms using a number of different production processes typically add to air pollution over a metropolitan area. Simply checking the air quality rarely gives a clear picture of who contributed what and how much to the situation. The condition of the water in rivers downstream from these areas raises the same kinds of problems for detection. How often do you read or hear of oil spills and oil slicks where the source is unknown and untraceable? There may be many smokers but none willing to step forward and lay claim to the cigar and cigarette butts, especially when a fine is to be levied. Note that using the coercive force of law will not in general be economically efficient. If pollution is reduced to zero through enforcement of the law, the marginal cost of pollution will be zero but the marginal benefit of the clean water or air will not be zero. This will create an underallocation of public resources, as the use of these resources as carriers of effluent are not used to an optimum level. The optimum level of use is where the marginal benefit of the carrier is equal to its marginal cost.

In such situations, it may be easier and more effective to simply levy excise taxes on those goods the production of which is known to give rise to spillover costs. This effectively shifts the market supply curves for these goods upward as in Figures 7-8 and 7-9. The tax revenues collected in this fashion can then be used by the government to finance cleanup operations such as waste treatment plants. In any event, such taxes have the effect of making the buyers and sellers in those markets bear the cleanup costs, while at the same time adjusting output so that it is closer to the optimum level.

Checkpoint 7-4

Some provinces have had laws requiring that all automobiles pass a safety inspection once a year. The inspections are typically made by privately owned service stations licensed by the province to make the inspections and certify whether a car is safe or not. What does this law do to the demand for service maintenance? If you always keep your car in tip-top shape, why might you still favour this law despite the fact that the inspection costs you $10.

Policy and External Benefits

How might the government encourage an increase in the production of those goods that give rise to external benefits? That is, how can it encourage the market depicted in Figure 7-12 to increase output from q_n to q_o? One way is to increase demand by giving buyers purchasing power in a form that can only be used to buy the particular good.

Commodity discount coupons could be used as a strategy to implement this. The coupons could be designated for particular commodities with positive externalities. There may be many reasons for having such programs. These coupons could be provided to target groups of people (for example, coupons for landscaping plants given to those who live along major urban thoroughfares). Retailers accept the coupons from buyers, and the government gives these businesses money in exchange for the coupons. This effectively increases the demand for the commodity with positive externalities on the part of people eligible to receive the coupons. This increase is reflected in the shift of the demand curve from D to D_a in Figure 7-12. Improved resource allocation occurs as the public benefits are internalized in the private market decision.

Another way the government might increase the output of a good with positive externalities would be simply to pay a per unit subsidy to suppliers (the reverse of an excise tax). This would shift the supply curve downward and increase output in the manner already discussed in connection with subsidies.

Summary

1. A price ceiling is a government-imposed maximum price that may be charged by law for a good. It must be set below the equilibrium price in order to have any effect. A price floor is a minimum price that may be charged by law for a good. It must be set above the equilibrium price in order to have any effect. A black market occurs if goods or services are traded illegally at prices above a government-imposed ceiling price or below a floor price.

2. Government-imposed price ceilings result in the quantity demanded at the ceiling price exceeding the quantity supplied at that price. The pressure on price to rise to bring the quantity demanded equal to the quantity supplied (equilibrium) is prevented. A shortage of the good is created at the legal ceiling price.

3. Price ceilings are often used to affect resource allocation during wartime. Rent control is an example of the use of price ceilings to ensure lower prices for goods that are considered necessities. As there is an incentive for sellers to charge the higher price that consumers are willing to pay, strict enforcement measures are needed if the product is not to be traded in a black market. Rationing schemes are often used to ensure that all buyers who are also willing to pay the ceiling price are able to get some of the good. Price ceilings can have wide-ranging economic and social implications.

4. Government-imposed price floors result in an excess of quantity supplied over quantity demanded, or a surplus, at the support price. The downward pressure on price to bring the market to equilibrium is circumvented. Like price ceilings, these, too, can have wide-ranging economic and social implications.

5. Price-support programs have been used to support agricultural prices at various times. In order to support agricultural prices at a level above that of market equilibrium, the government must do one of the following: buy and store surpluses, impose limitations on production, pursue policies that promote demand, or pay producers the difference between the support price and the lower price that producers receive in the market. In the case of labour services, governments impose price floors in the form of minimum-wage laws. In both cases the objective is to raise certain groups' incomes from what they would be if the market were free to determine them.

6. The agriculture industry in Canada has had different types of government support over a number of decades, yet the crisis in agriculture appears to be getting worse rather than better. Productivity gains have outstripped demand increases, support programs have increased the farm debt problem and stimulated the cultivation of marginal lands, and U.S. and EC subsidy programs have worsened the trade possibilities. Allowing the market forces more freedom, over an adjustment period, may be on the horizon.

7. Sales and excise taxes are the government's legal claim on a portion of the price paid for a unit of a good. They affect the equilibrium price and quantity in the market where they are imposed. The more elastic is the demand for a good, the smaller is the portion of the tax paid by buyers and the larger is the portion paid by suppliers—the tax incidence is shifted onto suppliers. The more elastic is the supply for a good, the smaller is the portion of the tax paid by suppliers and the larger is the portion paid by buyers—the tax incidence is shifted onto buyers.

8. Whenever the production and purchase of a good gives rise to costs or benefits that fall on parties other than the immediate buyers and sellers of the good, external, or spillover, costs and benefits are said to exist. When there are external costs associated with the production of a good, a greater than optimum quantity of the good is produced. When there are external benefits, a less than optimum quantity of the good is produced. Policies are needed to internalize external costs in the markets where they occur and to encourage a greater production of goods that have external benefits.

Key Terms and Concepts

ad valorem tax	price ceiling	sales taxes
black market	price floor	specific taxes
exise taxes	price support	subsidy
externalities	ration coupon	tax incidence
parity	rent control	

Questions and Problems

1. It has been observed that when rent controls are imposed, owners of apartment buildings often convert them to condominiums (apartments that are owned by the occupant rather than rented). Can you explain this phenomenon?

2. Some have observed that in a way it is fortunate that the demand for agricultural products is relatively inelastic. They point out that the cost to government (and hence

the taxpayer) of trying to support agricultural prices might otherwise have been larger than it has been all these years. Can you explain what these observers have in mind?

3. If an effective price ceiling were imposed on butter, what would happen to the price of margarine?

4. Suppose that a green tax were applied to energy-using consumer goods in order to reduce pollution over the eastern part of continent.
   a. What would have to be true of supply elasticities in these consumer goods industries to make this a very effective way of achieving this objective?
   b. What sort of demand elasticity conditions would make such a policy more effective?
   c. What would be the sort of supply and demand conditions that would cause you as a policymaker to shy away from imposing this tax on certain industries to achieve your objective?

5. Suppose the (enlightened) objective of an excise tax on cigarettes is to reduce consumption and save lives, and not to raise revenues. If the price of cigarettes was raised by an excise tax but smokers were reimbursed the taxes they paid, would smokers buy fewer cigarettes? Why?

6. If consumers are to be the full beneficiaries of an excise tax cut, what would have had to be true in the industries where the excise taxes were cut?

7. Suppose that an excise tax is levied on the output of television sets. What effect do you think that this would have on the prices charged by movie theaters and the prices of TV dinners?

8. Suppose that the government decides it wants to formulate a tax policy that will "kill two birds with one stone." It wants to eliminate spillover costs in the markets where they occur and significantly increase tax revenues at the same time. Suppose that it decides to impose excise taxes on those markets. What would have to be true in those markets if the government is to be reasonably satisfied with the results?

9. Suppose that antipollution laws are passed and effectively enforced in a certain region. In those markets where there are externalities in the form of spillover costs, what must be true of the elasticities of supply and demand curves if it is correctly claimed that the incidence of the burden, or cost of "cleaning up," bears more heavily on buyers? What must be true if the incidence of the burden falls more heavily on suppliers?

10. In Alberta, the 1915 prohibition referendum prohibited the production and sale of alcoholic beverages in the province. What were the supporters of the act implicitly saying about their estimate of the size of the external costs associated with the production of liquor, wine, and beer? Draw a diagram of the market supply curve and demand curve for alcoholic beverages in Alberta. Where do you think that promoters of prohibition (assuming they had economic efficiency as their objective) would place the supply curve S_a that includes *all* costs? That is, where do you think that the supply curve would hit the vertical axis in relation to where the market demand curve hits that axis?

Chapter 8

The Firm and Costs of Production

Suppose you are handed the following news item and asked for your opinion on it.

"Bad news for the nation's business firms appears to be looming on the horizon at year-end report time. According to the latest available surveys, many Canadian companies will be reporting annual earnings for this year that are significantly lower than they were expected to be only a couple of months ago."

"The director of research for a large brokerage house in Toronto has offered the following explanation of the effect of this year's slowdown in the economic growth rate on company profits. According to this analyst, when a company's volume of sales for the year turns out to be lower than was budgeted, its fixed costs, which include such items as depreciation, interest, and overhead, must be spread over a smaller volume of sales. This cuts into the company's profits per unit of sales."

Clearly, if you are going to give an opinion on this news item you need to know something about business firms and their costs of production.

In the last few chapters we discussed the essential concepts of supply and demand and the way they interact to form a market. However, in order to understand the way our economy is organized to produce goods, the determinant of supply, we need to study the basic agent of production—the firm. In fact, you may well spend most of your working life working for, managing, or owning and running a firm. In that case, you will have to become very familiar with the subjects of this chapter—the way firms are organized, the nature of production processes, and the costs of production. Subsequent chapters will analyze the way firms decide how much to produce and what price to charge for their product on the basis of their costs of production and the demand for their product.

The Firm

In Chapter 1 we said that a firm in the private sector uses factors of production to produce goods that are sold for the purpose of making a profit. We need to expand on this definition here. A **firm** *is a business organization that owns, rents, and operates equipment, hires labour, and buys materials and energy inputs. It organizes and coordinates the use of all these factors of production for the purpose of producing and marketing goods and services.*

The concept of a plant is related to but distinct from that of a firm. A **plant** is a facility where production takes place. A factory, a store, a mine, a car wash—each of these is a plant. A firm owns and operates one or more plants. Some firms own several plants, each of which does the same thing. For example, The Hudson's Bay Company and Canadian Tire are firms that own many retail stores. Firms that consist of such combinations are said to be **horizontally integrated.** On the other hand, a firm may own several plants, each of which handles a different stage in the production process. Automobile companies such as Ford and General Motors own iron mines, steel mills, stamping plants, electronics factories, and assembly plants. A firm that combines plants in this way is said to be **vertically integrated.** Of course, firms can be horizontally and vertically integrated at the same time. Each of the automobile companies has a number of assembly plants located around the world, for example.

Another kind of firm, which you probably have heard a lot about in recent years, is the conglomerate. A **conglomerate** is a firm that produces a wide variety

---

LEARNING OBJECTIVES

After reading this chapter, you will be able to:

1. Define and distinguish the *plant*, the *firm*, and the *industry* (or *market*).
2. Define the three legal forms of the firm: *proprietorship*, *partnership*, and *corporation*; state the differences between them; and explain the advantages and disadvantages of each.
3. Distinguish between the public, private, crown, and cooperative forms of a corporation.
4. Define and distinguish the different time frames: shortrun and longrun.
5. Explain and apply the law of diminishing returns.
6. Define, apply, and describe the characteristics of the production functions: total product or quantity of output Q, average product AP, and marginal product MP.
7. Define *opportunity cost*, *implicit costs*, and *explicit costs*, and distinguish between them.
8. Define and distinguish between *accounting profit*, *normal profit*, and *economic profit*.
9. Define and distinguish between *fixed* and *variable* costs and between *total cost*, *average total cost*, *average variable cost*, *average fixed cost*, and *marginal cost*.
10. Identify and explain the relationships between shortrun cost curves and show how the law of diminishing returns affects the behaviour of these cost curves.
11. Explain the relationship between the firm's shortrun and longrun average total cost curves and graph the longrun AC (envelope curve).
12. Discuss how the shape of the longrun AC is explained by economies and diseconomies of scale and explain the minimum efficient scale or longrun capacity (MES).

of different goods and services for sale in a number of largely unrelated markets. A conglomerate is usually formed by a parent firm, or holding company, that acquires a number of already existing firms. Often these firms keep their original trade names and are referred to as subsidiaries of the controlling parent firm. There are many large conglomerates in Canada— for example, Canadian Pacific, Power Corporation, and the Edper Investments (The Bronfman group).[1]

An **industry** is composed of a number of firms producing the same or similar products. The market structure is usually defined by the the number of firms composing an industry. It may appear easy to define an industry, but from an economic standpoint isolating a specific market may not be easy. One approach would be to consider an industry composed of firms producing products that have a high cross price elasticity (indicating close substitutes). This may mean IBM personal computers are in the same market as secretarial services, which on the surface seems absurd. The alternative—for example, lumping all watches in one market—might seem natural, but is a $10,000 Rolex watch in direct competition with a $50 Timex? Defining the market for any one industry is more difficult than it initially seems, but is an interesting aspect of economic analysis.

The diversity of firms in size and organization is astounding. At one extreme are giants such as General Motors of Canada,[2] which may realize sales of $20 billion annually and employ tens of thousands people. At the other extreme are numerous small barbershops, restaurants, and corner groceries. It is common in Canada for fifty thousand new businesses to be started in a single year and almost as large a number to fail. These large numbers testify to the strength of the urge to go into business for oneself, accepting the risk of one's wealth and security of income that is inherent in business enterprise.

Legal Forms of the Firm

So far, we have been concerned with the firm in terms of what it does, how it is organized, what it produces, and how big it is. But a firm is also a legal entity that operates subject to certain obligations and constraints under the law. Just what these are depends on the legal form the firm takes. There are three basic legal forms for a firm: the proprietorship, the partnership, and the corporation.

The Proprietorship

In the form of organization called a **proprietorship,** there is a single owner (or family), the proprietor, who makes all decisions and bears full responsibility for everything the firm does. The majority of small firms in Canada are of this type. Farms, small retail stores, barbershops, trades contractors, and medical and law practices are very often sole proprietorships. Under the law, the firm and the individual are considered the same.

The main advantage of this type of firm is that the owner has full control over the firm. A second advantage is the small amount of "red tape" necessary to enter into this type of legal form of business. Often all Revenue Canada requires

---

[1] See Statistics Canada, Industrial Organization and Finance Division, *Inter-corporate Ownership* (Ottawa: Minister of Supply and Services, 1990).

[2] The largest firm in Canada is a 100 percent owned subsidiary of a much larger multinational giant.

is a quarterly statement of income and expenses, along with the remittance of employee income and payroll taxes, and collection of GST and PST. Local and provincial licenses are generally inexpensive and easily obtained, depending on the nature of the business.

There are three main disadvantages, however. One is that the resources of the firm are limited by the amount of financial capital the owner either possesses or can borrow. Second, the owner has unlimited liability. This means that he or she is fully liable for all debts and obligations of the firm. If the firm gets into financial difficulty, or is sued, and does not have adequate funds to pay its debts, the owner's personal property and funds may be seized by the firm's **creditors**, that is, those to whom the firm owes money. The third disadvantage is that the proprietor must be able to do the many different tasks necessary for managing the firm's operation. This also puts severe limits on the size of the firm.

The Partnership

A **partnership** is formed whenever two or more individuals get together and agree to own and operate a business jointly. The partnership has two potential advantages over a proprietorship. First, because there is more than one owner, the partnership's financial resources may be larger and its ability to borrow greater than is typically the case for a proprietorship. Second, management and other tasks may be divided up among partners, thereby permitting greater specialization and efficiency of operation than is possible for a proprietorship.

There are some important disadvantages to a partnership, however. First of all, the partners each have 100% unlimited liability. Therefore, each risks all personal as well as all business assets on the management decisions of the others. Sometimes, in order to get more money in the firm without forcing the investor to bear the full risks of partnership, a limited partnership status is granted. A **limited partner** or silent partner risks only the money directly invested in the firm. A limited partner's personal assets cannot be seized to satisfy the firm's debts and obligations. In return for this arrangement, a limited partner does not participate in the management of the firm or engage in business on behalf of the partners.

Another disadvantage of a partnership is that if a partner dies or leaves, the partnership arrangement must be dissolved and reorganized. This can interrupt the business operations of the firm for a time.

Even with these disadvantages, there are thousands of partnerships in Canada. They are common in law and other professions, where the client's trust is a large factor in doing business. The partners' unlimited liability for one another's actions is thought to promote the client's trust in the firm. Even in these areas, partnerships are changing to the corporate form of organization.

The Corporation

Unlike proprietorships and partnerships, a **corporation**, or limited company, has a legal identity separate and distinct from the people who own it. In contrast to proprietorships and partnerships, a corporation can, in the course of doing business, enter into all manner of contracts that are legal obligations of the corporation but not of its owners. The owners are therefore said to have **limited**

liability. In essence this means that a corporation can be sued but not its owners. In the event of failure to meet its debts, pay its bills, or deliver goods and services it has contracted to produce, the limits of financial liability extend only to the assets of the corporation. They do not extend to the personal assets of its owners—those who own shares of stock in the corporation. A stockholder's financial liability is limited to the amount of money invested in the firm through the purchase of stock.

The corporate form of business was a major innovation of seventeenth century Britain. The great trading companies that were formed, such as the Hudson's Bay Trading Company and the East India Trading Company, allowed for the amassing of large sums of finance capital that otherwise would not have been possible if each individual investor had been liable under a partnership arrangement. It is interesting to note that Adam Smith considered this a retrograde development, as it separated the responsibility of individuals from the behaviour of the businesses they were involved in. In recent history, Canadian courts have also come to a dim view of this separation when it has been used by corporate executives to disavow responsibility for such things as environmental damage done by the firm or the loss of assets of the investors and customers of financial institutions that were poorly managed and failed.

There are four basic types of commercial corporations: private, public, cooperative, and crown. A **private corporation** is one that does not sell shares to the public. The shares are held by a small number of shareholders—fifty or less. An example in Canada is Eatons. The main reason for this form of incorporation is to keep the firm's financial information private. A **public corporation** trades shares on public stock exchanges like The Exchange in Toronto and the Vancouver Stock Market. These firms must meet regulatory requirements, produce annual reports, and disclose other financial information in order to raise financial capital through share sales in the stock market. **Cooperatives** are common in Western Canada and Quebec. These corporations differ from private and public corporations in two ways: first, voting on the firm's policies is by membership—one vote per member—not by share ownership; and second, the return to each member is dependent on patronage—the more one uses the co-op the greater the refund—instead of the dividend payments normal to a public corporation. A **crown corporation** is a company that is independent of government (is not part of the bureaucracy) but whose sole shareholder is a government.[3]

Advantages of the Corporation

The chief advantage of setting up a firm as a corporation instead of as a proprietorship or partnership is that it makes it much easier to raise money for investment in the firm. Because their liability is limited, numerous investors, large and small, are willing to invest their money in an incorporated firm. Such firms are therefore able to raise the large amounts of money needed to finance the large plants and complex production processes used in a highly industrialized economy. In exchange for their money, investors receive ownership of

---

[3]In the recent trend to privatization, some crown corporations, such as Air Canada and Petro-Canada, have been partially sold off to the public through share sales in the stock market, but the government is still the major shareholder.

shares, or stock, signifying their equity interest in the firm. These shares entitle them to vote for a board of directors who are responsible for the overall supervision of the firm and the hiring of its top-level managers. The investors are also entitled to share in the company's profits, which are called **dividends** when they are paid out. Profits not paid out, called **undistributed profits,** also belong to the shareholders. They are usually reinvested in the firm's operations.

Organized stock exchanges make it relatively easy for investors to acquire or sell shares in corporations. Investors can reduce their risks by owning shares in several firms that are engaged in widely different businesses without having to become directly involved in the management of any of them. All of these considerations make it easier for investors to share in the monetary returns from enterprise without having to bear the risks and shoulder the management responsibilities associated with either a proprietorship or a partnership.

Because the shares in a corporation can be easily bought and sold, change of ownership does not cause disruptions in operations the way it does in either a proprietorship or a partnership. This gives the corporation a life of its own apart from its owners. This continuity of existence makes long-range planning easier and also increases the ability of the incorporated firm to borrow money. Note the longevity of the Hudson's Bay Company which was first incorporated in 1670.[4]

Disadvantages of the Corporation

Despite all these positive features of corporations, there are some disadvantages. While considering them, bear in mind that corporations account for over 80 percent of the output produced by all firms in Canada and that many sectors of the economy that were traditionally proprietorships, such as farming, are also changing to the corporate form. The emergence of the corporation as the dominant form of organization suggests that its advantages far outweigh its disadvantages.

Compared to a proprietorship or partnership, a stockholder in a corporation often has little meaningful influence over the board of directors and management policy. Even though each share of common stock entitles the owner to one vote (except in a co-op), a large corporation may have so many shares outstanding that most investors can't hope to own enough of them to have a significant voting bloc.[5] As a result, ownership and control can become separated to a much larger extent than is possible in a partnership. In a proprietorship, of course, the two functions are one and the same.

The personal income that a proprietor or the members of a partnership receive as the income from their business can be taxed at rates as high as 50 percent (federal and provincial combined). Profits of corporations may be taxed as much as 38 percent. However, dividends to stockholders, which are paid out

[4] It did not actually incorporate at this time, as the creation of the company predated such laws. It was granted a special royal charter, which served as the prototype for later legislation. It moved its corporate headquarters to Canada (Winnipeg) in 1970.

[5] An alternative point of view is that as shares become dispersed, an individual with a small overall share of the stock can gain control of a company, holding power over its policies in much greater proportion to his or her equity. In Canada, owners of many holding companies wield substantial economic power through minority holdings in numerous companies.

of the profit remaining after payment of this tax, are then taxed at personal income tax rates. Corporate profits are potentially subject to double taxation, while those of proprietorships and partnerships are not. It has been argued this would constitute an unfair discrimination against the owners (stockholders) of corporations. Therefore the principle of *tax integration* is applied, whereby an individual is given a credit for any tax paid by the corporation on dividends he or she received, such that the effective tax rates are approximately equal between income earned from a business regardless if it is incorporated or not.

Costs, Revenue, and Profit

In Chapter 2 we saw that all costs are opportunity costs due to the fact that resources are scarce and have alternative uses. The production possibilities frontier shows that if resources are used to produce one good, they are not available to produce other goods. The **economic cost** of a good is therefore the alternative goods that must be forgone in order to produce it. This notion of cost is directly applicable to the individual firm.

The resources that a firm needs in order to produce its product have costs attached to them because they have alternative uses in the production of other products by other firms. Economists generally divide these costs into two groups, *explicit costs* and *implicit costs*. Added together, they equal the firm's opportunity costs.

Explicit Costs

Some of the resources the firm needs must be purchased or hired from outside the firm and must be obtained by a direct monetary payment. Such resources typically include electricity, fuel, materials, labour, insurance, and so forth. The payments that must be made for these resources are considered **explicit costs.** If we consider the case of a family-owned convenience store, for example, explicit costs might include property taxes, maintenance costs, payments to wholesalers for goods to be sold in the store, and the salary of a stock clerk.

Implicit Costs

Some resources needed by the firm are actually owned by the firm itself. Such resources include the managerial skills and financial resources of the owners. In the case of managerial skills, the cost of such resources is the payments they could have received were they employed in their next best alternative. Similarly, the cost of financial resources is the return they would have received were they invested in their next best alternative. Since these resources are not obtained by direct monetary payments, their costs are considered to be **implicit costs.**

Returning once again to the convenience store, let's assume that the grocers own the store outright, use their own funds to finance inventories, and put 80 hours a week into running the store. The implicit cost of such resources would include the rent the grocers could receive if they leased the building to another firm, the interest or dividends their money could earn if invested elsewhere, and the salaries they could earn if they were employed in another business. To the degree that they undertake risk, it may also be necessary to earn a return on their investment in excess of what they would earn on their assets in alternative uses. This "premium for risk" is also an implicit cost, one that can be quite high in some businesses.

Accounting Profit, Economic Profit, and Normal Profit

There are three distinct notions of profit, each of which is based on a different way of measuring the costs of the firm in relation to its revenues. These three types of profit are *accounting profit, economic profit,* and *normal profit.*

Accounting profit is determined by subtracting the firm's explicit costs from its total revenue or total sales receipts. This notion of profit does not consider any implicit costs.

$$\text{Accounting profit} = \text{Total revenue} - \text{Explicit costs}$$

Economic profit is the difference between the total revenue obtained from the firm's sales and the opportunity costs of all the resources used by the firm. As we have already seen, the opportunity costs of all the resources used by the firm are the total of all explicit and implicit costs. The sum of these costs is referred to as the **total cost**. If the calculation of economic profit results in a value of zero, then these opportunity costs are just being covered by sales receipts. Since all resources are therefore receiving just the amount they could get in their best alternative uses, there is no incentive for any of them to move to another firm. If economic profit were zero for each and every firm in the retail grocery industry, there would be no firms going out of business and leaving the industry. Therefore, economic profit is considered a residual earning, unnecessary in order to keep the firm in business. Economic profit is sometimes referred to as *above-normal profit* or *pure profit.*

$$\text{Economic profit} = \text{Total revenue} - (\text{Explicit costs} + \text{Implicit costs})$$

Normal profit is what the firm is said to earn when economic profit is zero. In that case, all resources employed by the firm are just earning their opportunity costs. *When the financial capital and the managerial skills used by the firm are being compensated just enough to keep them from leaving and going into some other line of productive activity, it is said that they are earning a normal profit.* In the case of the grocery store, the grocers' managerial skills, their own funds invested in the business, and the building they own and use for the store are receiving a normal profit. That is, sales receipts are just sufficient to pay all explicit costs with enough left to cover the implicit costs of the resources owned by the firm's owner.

Note that, in this instance, financial capital includes the grocers' own funds put directly into the business, to purchase inventories, *plus* the money value of the building they own and use in the business. Whether these funds are tied up in inventories or in buildings, they constitute the financial capital required to run a retail grocery business. The inventories and building necessary to do business are merely the physical capital counterpart to the financial capital. The grocers did not need to use their own funds in this way. Instead, they could have rented the building from someone else and borrowed the funds necessary to acquire inventories. It makes no difference whether the grocers provide the financial capital or borrow and rent it from other parties. If the financial capital is not compensated at a rate of return equal to that which it could earn in its next best alternative plus any risk premium, it will not be made available for use in the grocery business.

When economic profit is positive, the managerial skills and financial capital used by the firm are earning more than a normal profit. Similarly, when economic profit is negative, these resources are earning less than a normal profit.

The Shortrun and the Longrun

In Chapter 5 we noted that in economic analysis it is frequently useful to make a distinction between the shortrun and the longrun. *By the **shortrun** we typically mean a period of time short enough so that the amounts of at least one of the factors of production used by the firm cannot be changed, while others can be varied. The shortrun does not refer to a set period of time.*

In a barbershop it takes little time, perhaps a week, to install another chair and find another barber to increase the production of haircuts. For a barbershop, therefore, the shortrun may be as little as a week. It may also take only a week or two to lease some space and get started in many small businesses. Canadian Pacific Railway, on the other hand, needs considerably more time to add more rolling stock or blast a new tunnel through the mountains and hire a work force to run more trains. The shortrun for Canadian Pacific may be years or even decades. Obviously, the actual length of time of the shortrun will depend on the kind of firm and industry we are talking about.

*By the **longrun** we mean a period of time long enough that the amounts of all factors of production used by the firm can be changed.* In other words, the longrun is the amount of time it takes for a new firm to get started and operating or for an existing firm to shut down, dispose of its assets, and go out of business. In our example of a barbershop, the longrun may be any time period longer than a week or two. For CP it may be any time period longer than two or three years. The difference between the behaviour of the firm's costs in the shortrun and the longrun is very significant in the analysis of the firm, as we shall see.

> ### Checkpoint* 8-1
>
> How is a stockholder's status in a corporation different from a limited partner's status in a partnership? In what sense is a normal profit really an economic cost? Suppose that there are two grocery stores that are sole proprietorships, that each has the same levels of sales, and that each realizes zero economic profit. Can you think of reasons why their accounting profits might be different?
>
> *Answers to all Checkpoints can be found at the back of the text.*

Production in the Shortrun

In the shortrun, as we have just noted, some of the firm's factors of production are fixed. Therefore, the firm's level of output during this period can be altered only by changing the quantities of the factors of production that are not fixed—the variable factors. We need to examine the way output typically changes when these variable factors change. This in turn will allow us to examine how the firm's costs vary when output is changed in the shortrun.

To simplify matters somewhat, we will analyze the output and costs of a firm that has only two factors of production—capital and labour. In the shortrun, we will assume that capital (plant and equipment) is the **fixed factor.** Labour (number of labourers) will be the **variable factor.** Our analysis would be more complicated if we considered a firm that had several fixed factors and several variable factors. Since the conclusions would be the same, however, we will choose the simpler case for analysis.

Let's consider a firm that makes chairs. Given its fixed stock for capital, the firm can vary the quantity of chairs produced only by changing the quantity of labour it uses. The data on quantity produced and labourers employed are given in Table 8-1. At this stage we are only considering the relationship of inputs to outputs. Although it has economic consequences, this is essentially an engineering problem, not an economic one. Later we will transform this data, using given prices of inputs, into the costs of production—the economics of production. From this table, we can see that the total quantity of chairs produced, or **total product**, column (2), gets larger as more labourers are employed, column (1). At first glance, we might be tempted to assume that the way to expand the quantity of output indefinitely is simply to keep adding more workers. However, a closer look will show us that this is not the case.

Law of Diminishing Returns

Let's begin by assuming that the firm's fixed capital stock is idle and no labour is employed—hence, there is no output. Now consider how total output changes with the addition of each successive labourer. The increase in output *per* each additional labourer is called the **marginal product** (*MP*) and is calculated as

$$\text{Marginal product} = \frac{\text{Change in total product}}{\text{Change in labour}}$$

TABLE 8-1   Chair Production and the Law of Diminishing Returns

(1) Variable Input (Number of Labourers Used)	(2) Total Product (Quantity of Chairs Produced per Week)	(3) Marginal Product (Change in Output of Chairs)	(4) Average Product (Quantity of Chairs per Worker)
0	0.0		
		+1.0	
1	1.0		1.0
		+2.0	
2	3.0		1.5
		+3.0	
3	6.0		2.0
		+4.0	
4	10.0		2.5
		+3.0	
5	13.0		2.6
		+2.0	
6	15.0		2.5
		+1.5	
7	16.5		2.3
		+1.0	
8	17.5		2.2
		+0.5	
9	18.0		2.0
		0.0	
10	18.0		1.8

The employment of the first labourer (where none had been working before) increases total output from zero up to 1 chair, column (2). Thus, the
marginal product of the first labourer is 1, column (3). Adding a second
labourer increases total output by 2 chairs, from 1 up to 3 chairs, column
(2). The marginal product of the second labourer therefore equals 2, column
(3). The marginal product continues to increase until 4 labourers have been
hired, the marginal product of the fourth labourer being equal to 4, column (3). Hence, up through the employment of 4 labourers, the addition to
total output attributable to each successive labourer gets larger and larger—in
other words, the marginal product, column (3), increases as the first labourers
are employed. This occurs because the plant and equipment are difficult to
operate effectively with just a few labourers. As more are added, each is able to
specialize at fewer tasks and the production process runs more smoothly.

However, after 4 labourers are employed, the marginal product of each successive labourer employed gets smaller. Total output continues to get larger, column (2), but by smaller and smaller amounts, column (3). For instance, while
the fourth labourer has a marginal product of 4, the fifth labourer's marginal
product is 3, the sixth's is 2, and so on. Why is this so? As more labourers are
added, at first the marginal product increases, but eventually the marginal product decreases when the plant is operating in its design range. To use the fixed
factor (the plant) efficiently requires a minimum level of variable factor (labour).
If the plant is operated past its design range, the marginal product will be negative and output will fall as the plant is overcrowded. It is assumed no manager
would hire the (costly) variable input—labour—to the point that output actually
declines. Table 8-1 ends where marginal product is zero and total product is at
a maximum of 18 chairs.

In Figure 8-1, frame (a), the total quantity of chairs produced [Table 8-1, column (2)] is plotted on the vertical axis. The number of labourers employed in
the production process [Table 8-1, column (1)] is plotted on the horizontal axis.
*The graph showing the relationship between the number of labourers employed and the
total quantity of output produced (total product), given the fixed quantity of capital, is the*
shortrun production function. In Figure 8-1, frame (b), the marginal product
[Table 8-1, column (3)] is plotted on the vertical axis and, as in frame (a), the
number of labourers is plotted on the horizontal axis. (Note that the marginal
product data are plotted midway between the labour levels for which they are
computed.) The marginal product graph clearly shows how the marginal product rises until 4 labourers are employed and then begins to decline as labourers
are added beyond this point. Its shape illustrates the **law of diminishing returns**. *This law states that as more and more of a variable factor of production, or input
(such as labour), is used together with a fixed factor of production (such as capital), beyond
some point the marginal product begins to fall.*

Comparison of frames (a) and (b) of Figure 8-1 clearly shows that total product is increasing as long as marginal product is positive. When marginal output
falls to zero, total output reaches its peak. There are increasing returns to the
variable input when marginal product is rising and diminishing returns when it
is declining. These production functions were drawn for our hypothetical case
of chair manufacturing. What is important about these graphs is their characteristic shapes. Although the production function shown is a specific example,
the evidence suggests that the shape of this production function is a universal
characteristic of production with a fixed input.

FIGURE 8-1 **The Law of Diminishing Returns**

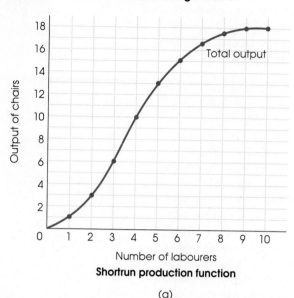

Number of labourers

Shortrun production function

(a)

Frame (a), based on the data from columns (1) and (2) of Table 8-1, shows how larger quantities of total output (vertical axis) can be produced by using larger quantities of labour, the variable input (horizontal axis), given a fixed amount of capital. As more labour is added, total output at first rises by ever-larger amounts, up to 4 labourers, and then rises by ever-diminishing amounts until it reaches a maximum at 9 labourers. In frame (b)—using the data columns (3) and (4)—the graph of marginal product shows how the increase in total output associated with each additional labourer at first rises and then declines as more labour is used. Average product rises as long as marginal product exceeds it and declines when marginal product is below it, so marginal product intersects average product where the latter is a maximum.

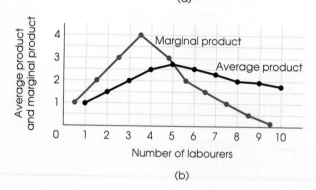

Number of labourers

(b)

Another measure of production is **average product** (*AP*). *The average product is the output produced per unit of variable input hired.* It is calculated as

$$\text{Average product} = \frac{\text{Total product}}{\text{Labour}}$$

In the example of chair production the average product per labourer is shown in Table 8-1, column (4). The average product equals total output, column (2), divided by the corresponding quantity of labour, column (1). Average product is also plotted in Figure 8-1, frame (b), along with marginal product. Note that as long as marginal product is greater than average product, average product must rise, and when marginal product is less than average product, average product must fall. It necessarily follows that the marginal product graph crosses the highest point on the average product graph [corresponding to 5 units of labour, frame (b) of Figure 8-1]. This is simply a property of the mathematics of averages. If the marginal product of one more labourer is greater than the average product of all previous labourers, then the additional labourer's contribution will raise average product. On the other hand, when the marginal product of one more labourer is less than the average product, the additional labourer's contribution will cause average product to fall. The principle can be illustrated by analogy: The average height of the people in a room will be raised whenever an additional (marginal) person enters who is taller than the average of those already in the room. Similarly, the average height is lowered whenever someone enters whose height is below the average.

Costs of Production

The production function needs to be transformed into cost functions in order for economic analysis to proceed. This is done by taking the given prices for the inputs and calculating the costs of the output these inputs produce. It is important to note that the prices paid for the fixed and variable inputs are being held constant when we construct the cost functions from the production function. In the example data of Table 8-2 the fixed input has a price of $50 and each unit of variable input, labour, has a price of $50.

TABLE 8-2   Shortrun Cost Schedules for a Firm Producing Chairs (Hypothetical Data)

(1) Number of Labourers (L)	(2) Quantity of Output per Week (Q)	(3) Total Fixed Cost (TFC)	(4) Total Variable Cost TVC $TVC =$ Wage $\times L$ (Wage = $50 per Week)	(5) Total Cost TC $TC =$ $TFC +$ TVC	(6) Average Fixed Cost AFC $AFC =$ $\dfrac{TFC}{Q}$	(7) Average Variable Cost AVC $AVC =$ $\dfrac{TVC}{Q}$	(8) Average Total Cost ATC $ATC =$ $\dfrac{TC}{Q}$	(9) Marginal Cost MC $MC =$ Change in TC Change in Q
0	0	$50	$0	$50				
								$50.00
1	1	50	50	100	$50.00	$50.00	$100.00	
								25.00
2	3	50	100	150	16.66	33.33	50.00	
								16.66
3	6	50	150	200	8.33	25.00	33.33	
								12.50
4	10	50	200	250	5.00	20.00	25.00	
								16.66
5	13	50	250	300	3.84	19.23	23.07	
								25.00
6	15	50	300	350	3.33	20.00	23.33	
								33.33
7	16.5	50	350	400	3.03	21.20	24.24	
								50.00
8	17.5	50	400	450	2.86	22.80	25.71	
								100.00
9	18	50	450	500	2.78	25.00	27.78	

Total Cost in the Shortrun

Table 8-2 shows the chair firm's shortrun cost schedule. That is, the table indicates the various measures of the firm's costs—columns (3), (4), and (6)–(9)—that are associated with each level of output, column (2), and the corresponding input of labour, column (1). First, consider the relationship between the total output of chairs, column (2), and total cost, column (5), and its two components, total fixed cost, column (3), and total variable cost, column (4).

Total Fixed Cost (TFC)

In the shortrun the firm is saddled with its **total fixed cost,** the costs that do not vary with output or the costs of its unchangeable, or fixed, factors of production. The property tax on its land and buildings, the interest payments on the money it borrowed to finance purchase of plant and equipment, and the opportunity cost of its own money invested in such facilities, measured as the return that money could earn if it were invested elsewhere, are all fixed costs in the shortrun. (Total fixed cost is often referred to as "overhead" or "sunk" costs.) In the shortrun, total fixed cost is always the same no matter what level of output the firm produces—which is what is meant by the term *fixed*. This fixed cost is assumed to be *sunk*—that is, it is not recoverable if the firm goes out of business. Therefore, the firm incurs the fixed cost even if it produces nothing.

Suppose that for the firm making chairs the total fixed cost attributable to its fixed factor, capital, amounts to $50 per week. This cost, column (3), is the same no matter what quantity of chairs is produced per week, column (2). It is plotted in Figure 8-2 to give the total fixed cost curve *TFC*.

FIGURE 8-2   Total Cost Equals Total Variable Cost Plus Total Fixed Cost

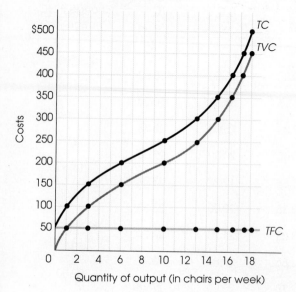

Quantity of output (in chairs per week)

Total fixed cost *TFC* is the cost of the firm's fixed factors and is the same no matter what the level of production. Therefore, the *TFC* curve is horizontal. Total variable cost *TVC* is the cost of the firm's variable factors. The shape of the *TVC* curve shows that variable cost rises at a decreasing rate up to some point and at an increasing rate beyond, reflecting the law of diminishing returns. The total cost *TC* is the sum of total variable cost and total fixed cost and is therefore parallel to the *TVC* curve, lying above it by the amount of the total fixed cost. The points on the curves shown here are plotted from the data of Table 8-2.

Total Variable Cost (TVC)

The costs that the firm can vary in the shortrun by changing the quantity of the variable factors of production, and hence the quantity of output produced, make up the **total variable cost.** Payments for utilities (natural gas, fuels, electricity),[6] materials, and labour are all variable costs.

In the case of the chair firm, the only variable cost is that due to the variable factor labour. Suppose each labourer is paid $50 per week. Multiplying the number of labourers (L) in column (1) by this wage therefore gives the TVC in column (4) that is associated with each quantity (Q) of chairs produced, column (2). The total variable cost is plotted in Figure 8-2 to give the total variable cost curve TVC.

Note that if the graph in Figure 8-1, frame (a), is turned around so that the vertical axis measuring Q becomes the horizontal axis and the horizontal axis measuring L becomes the vertical axis, we get the TVC curve of Figure 8-2 by simply multiplying the number of labourers by the weekly wage of $50 per labourer. Hence, we see that the TVC curve reflects the law of diminishing returns in that it first rises at a decreasing rate and then rises at an increasing rate as the production of chairs is increased.

Total Cost (TC)

The firm's **total cost** is the sum of its total fixed cost and its total variable cost at any given level of output. For the chair firm, total cost TC, column (5), is the sum of TFC, column (3), and TVC, column (4). The total costs are plotted to give the TC curve of Figure 8-2. For each output level Q, the associated point on the TC curve lies directly above the associated point on the TVC curve by an amount equal to TFC. The distance between these points is equal to the amount of the total fixed costs. This reflects the fact that because total fixed costs are constant, the variation in total costs is due entirely to the changes in total variable costs when the level of output is changed.

It can also be seen from Table 8-2 and Figure 8-2 that when output is zero, TFC and TC are one and the same. This simply reflects the fact that when nothing is produced, no labour is used and so there are no variable costs.

> **Checkpoint 8-2**
>
> How would the curves in Figure 8-2 be affected if total fixed cost was increased from $50 to $75? How would these curves be affected if wages rose from $50 to $75 per week? Show the effects of such changes graphically.

Average Costs in the Shortrun

Now consider columns (6), (7), and (8) of Table 8-2. These columns represent average fixed cost, average variable cost, and average total cost.

Average Fixed Cost (AFC)

The **average fixed cost** at any given output level is calculated by dividing total fixed cost by that output level. In symbols this becomes

$$AFC = \frac{TFC}{Q}$$

---

[6]Some portion of these may be fixed—for example, even if output is zero, some heating may be necessary simply to prevent rupture of water lines due to freezing.

This equation may also be interpreted as the firm's total fixed cost per unit of output produced. For the firm of Table 8-2, the *AFC* shown in column (6) is obtained by dividing the *TFC* in column (3) by the *Q* of column (2). Looking at column (6), we can see that *AFC* falls as *Q* is increased. This happens because *TFC* is the same no matter what the output level. Therefore, the larger the output level, the more these overhead costs are spread out. This is clearly shown in Figure 8-3, where the *AFC* data of column (6) are plotted to give the *AFC* curve.

Now we can understand what is meant by a news item commenting on declining business profits with the statement: "When a company's volume of sales for the year turns out to be lower than was budgeted, its fixed costs, which include such items as depreciation, interest, and overhead, must be spread over a smaller volume of sales." The lower is the level of output, the larger is the average fixed cost. Given the price at which a unit of output is sold, the larger is the portion of the price that must go to cover the per unit fixed costs.

Average Variable Cost (AVC)

The **average variable cost** at any given output level is calculated by dividing total variable cost by that output level. In symbols this becomes

$$AVC = \frac{TVC}{Q}$$

In Table 8-2 the *AVC* shown in column (7) is obtained by dividing the *TVC* of column (4) by the *Q* of column (2). The figures from column (7) are plotted in Figure 8-3 to give the *AVC* curve.

Notice that *AVC* at first falls as *Q* increases and then rises. This happens for the same reason that *TVC* is shaped the way it is. Because the *AVC* data are

---

FIGURE 8-3   The Average and Marginal Cost Curves

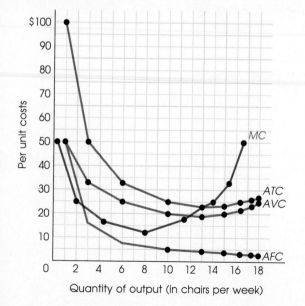

Quantity of output (in chairs per week)

The *AFC* curve here is plotted from the data in column (6) of Table 8-2. *AFC* falls as the total product Q is increased because the overhead costs are spread out. The *AVC* curve is plotted from the data in column (7) of Table 8-2. *AVC* first falls as Q increases and then rises, reflecting the law of diminishing returns. The *ATC* curve is plotted from the data in column (8) of Table 8-2. Since *ATC* equals *AFC* plus *AVC*, the *ATC* curve may be viewed as the sum of the *AFC* and the *AVC* curves. Hence, at any output level the distance between the *ATC* curve and the *AVC* curve equals *AFC*. Marginal cost (*MC*) is the change in total cost associated with the production of an additional unit of output (Q). Equivalently, marginal cost is the change in total variable cost associated with the production of an additional unit of output. The *MC* curve is plotted from the data in column (9) of Table 8-2. The *MC* curve always crosses the *AVC* and *ATC* curves at their bottommost points.

derived from the TVC data and TVC reflects the law of diminishing returns, so does AVC.

Average Total Cost (ATC)

The **average total cost** at any given output level is obtained by simply dividing total cost by that output level. It is also known as the *unit cost* or simply the *average cost* and is calculated as

$$ATC = \frac{TC}{Q}$$

However, since $TC = TFC + TVC$, we see that

$$ATC = \frac{TFC + TVC}{Q}$$

And knowing that

$$\frac{TFC}{Q} = AFC$$

and

$$\frac{TVC}{Q} = AVC$$

we can say that

$$ATC = AFC + AVC$$

The data for ATC are shown in column (8) of Table 8-2. At any output level, it can be seen that the figure in column (8) can be obtained by dividing the figure in column (5) by that in column (2), or alternatively by adding the figures in columns (6) and (7). The data in column (8) are plotted in Figure 8-3 to give the ATC curve. At any output level, the distance between the ATC curve and the AVC curve equals AFC.

Because ATC is the sum of AFC and AVC, the diagnosis given in the news item referred to earlier could be carried even further. Observe that as output falls to low enough levels, ATC, or average total cost per unit, rises as shown in Figure 8-3. Given the price per unit of output, this means a larger portion of the price is required to cover average total cost per unit. Hence, a smaller portion is left for profit. The news item most likely means accounting profit when referring to "profits per unit of sales."

Recall from Figure 8-1, frame (b), how the marginal product [Table 8-1, column (3)] rises until 4 labourers, the variable input, are employed. Since the additional output produced with each successive labourer rises, the variable cost *per unit* of output declines with AVC, reaching a minimum at 13 units of output, Figure 8-3. AVC rises beyond this point because the marginal cost is higher than the average variable cost, pulling up the average. At low levels of output, production is relatively inefficient and costly because plant and equipment are difficult to operate effectively with just a few labourers. The plant is not operating in its design range. Variable costs per unit of output are therefore relatively high.

Checkpoint 8-3

Suppose that total fixed cost falls by $10. Show how this will affect average fixed cost, average variable cost, and average total cost in Table 8-2 and Figure 8-3. Suppose that the weekly wage of a labourer increases from $50 to $60 per week. Show how this will affect average fixed cost, average variable cost, and average total cost in Table 8-2 and Figure 8-3.

As labour is increased and output expands, variable cost per unit of output declines as the production process becomes more cost efficient due to greater specialization and better utilization of the firm's capital equipment. But at some output level (13 units in Figure 8-3), as more of the variable input labour is added to the fixed input (capital), diminishing returns set in. AVC increases beyond this point.

Our discussion indicates that the characteristic shape of the average product AP curve in Figure 8-1, frame (b), is mirrored in the bowl shape of the AVC curve in Figure 8-3. Thus, the characteristic shapes of the production functions determine the characteristic shapes of the cost functions. Glance ahead to see how this is illustrated more directly in Figure 8-4.

Marginal Cost in the Shortrun

Marginal cost MC is one of the most important concepts in economics. *The extra cost of producing one more unit of output is the* **marginal cost**. Since total cost changes with output only because total variable cost changes, marginal cost may be viewed equivalently as either the addition to total cost or the addition to total

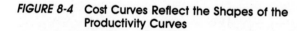

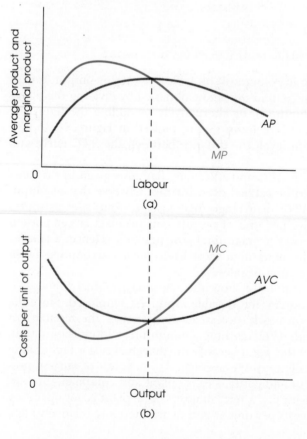

FIGURE 8-4   Cost Curves Reflect the Shapes of the Productivity Curves

The hump shapes of the AP and MP curves, frame (a), are mirrored in the bowl shapes of the AVC and MC curves, respectively, in frame (b). When MC is falling, it reflects the fact that MP is rising. MC reaches a minimum when MP is at its maximum. MC rises when MP falls. A similar relationship holds between AVC and AP.

variable cost associated with the production of an additional unit of output. Therefore, we can say that

$$MC = \frac{\text{Change in } TC}{\text{Change in } Q} = \frac{\text{Change in } TVC}{\text{Change in } Q}$$

Marginal Cost and the Law of Diminishing Returns

Marginal cost for our hypothetical chair firm is given in column (9) of Table 8-2. Since labour is the only variable factor, TC and TVC change only because of the change in the employment of labour. Starting from a zero level of output, the marginal cost of the first chair produced is $50, which is just the change in TVC, column (4). It is also the change in TC, column (5), divided by one chair, the extra output that results from hiring $50 worth of labour. The successive changes in total output Q, column (2), associated with the employment of each additional labourer, column (1), vary according to the law of diminishing returns, as indicated by the marginal product figures in column (3) of Table 8-1. [Note that columns (1) and (2) of Table 8-1 are the same as columns (1) and (2) of Table 8-2.] This is reflected in the data for MC, column (9) of Table 8-2, which is computed as the change in TC divided by the change in Q or the marginal product associated with the employment of each additional labourer.

Since the marginal product of labour *increases* up to the point where 4 labourers are employed, and since the increase in cost associated with each additional labourer is always the same ($50), marginal cost *decreases* over this range. However, beyond this point, the marginal product of labour begins to *decrease* with the employment of each additional labourer. Again, since the increase in cost due to each additional labourer is always $50, marginal cost *increases* from this point on.

The marginal cost data of column (9) are plotted in Figure 8-3 to give the MC curve. (Note that the MC data are plotted midway between the output levels for which they are computed.) *The shape of the MC curve clearly reflects the fact that MC falls when the marginal product of the variable factor (labour) rises, and that MC rises when the marginal product of the variable factor falls.* The hump shape of the marginal product MP curve in Figure 8-1 is mirrored in the bowl shape of the MC curve in Figure 8-3. This is shown more directly in Figure 8-4.

The Relationship Between Marginal and Average Cost

As with the production functions, we are more interested in the characteristic shapes of the cost curves than with the specific example. Looking at columns (7), (8), and (9) of Table 8-2, we can see that, starting from a zero level of output, AVC and ATC fall as output increases so long as MC is lower than AVC and ATC. This is true up to the point where 5 labourers are employed, producing 13 units of output. Beyond the point where MC is greater than AVC, AVC begins to rise. Notice that for some levels of output MC is greater than AVC but less than ATC. Over this range ATC is declining as output increases, while AVC is increasing. MC continues to rise as output increases, until MC is greater than ATC. Beyond that output, both ATC and AVC rise with increases in output. This relationship is reflected in Figure 8-3 by the fact that the AVC and ATC curves decline over the range where the MC curve is below them and increase over the range where the MC curve is above them. From these observations we note the following: *The MC curve passes through the AVC and ATC curves at their minimum points.*

The reason for this relationship between the marginal cost, MC, and the average costs, AVC and ATC, is the law of diminishing returns and the spreading of the fixed cost, as we have already discussed. When the addition to total cost (the marginal cost) associated with the production of another unit of output is greater than ATC, ATC rises. Conversely, if the marginal cost of another unit is less than ATC, ATC will fall. Hence, ATC declines as long as MC is below ATC. When MC is above ATC, ATC rises. Therefore, at the output level at which MC rises from below ATC to just above it, ATC ceases to decline and begins to rise. It follows that ATC reaches its lowest point at the output level at which MC crosses ATC. Exactly the same argument applies to AVC. There is no such relationship between MC and AFC, however. This is so because AFC depends upon TFC, and since TFC is unaffected by changes in TVC, AFC declines continuously as output changes no matter what the behaviour of MC.

The Significance of Marginal Cost for the Firm

The importance of marginal cost is that it tells the firm exactly how much it will cost to produce an additional unit of output. Conversely, it tells the firm the reduction in cost that will result if it reduces production by a unit of output. Average variable and average total cost do not give this kind of information because they are based on the cost of *all* output produced.

As we shall see repeatedly in the next few chapters, the firm's output decision in the shortrun is always made at the margin. The answer to the question of whether we should produce an additional unit of output will be found by comparing the cost of producing that additional unit (the marginal cost) with the additional revenue received from the sale of that unit.

Production and Costs in the Longrun

The longrun in economic analysis is a period of time long enough for the firm to be able to change the quantities of *all* its factors of production. As with the shortrun, the period of time called the longrun is different for different firms and industries. A barbershop or a beauty parlor can change all its factors of production, go into business, or go out of business more quickly than a steel company. Hence, the longrun for barbershops and beauty parlors is a shorter period of calendar time than is the longrun for a steel company.

All Factors of Production Are Variable in the Longrun

When all factors of production are variable, there is, of course, no longer a distinction between variable and fixed costs. In the longrun the only relevant average cost concept is the longrun average total cost (or just average cost), because when all factors are variable, so are all costs. In order to understand average cost in the longrun, we must first look at how changes in plant size affect costs and output.

Checkpoint 8-4

Notice that in Table 8-2, columns (7) to (9), the *change* in average variable cost between successive output levels is always less than the change in the marginal cost. Notice also that the same is true of the change in average total cost only *after* the point at which 3 labourers are employed and 6 units of output are produced. Why is this so? If diminishing returns are larger than is the case in Table 8-2, how would the MC curve of Figure 8-3 be affected?

Changes in Plant Size

The firm can change the entire plant in the longrun to meet its production needs. For any given output level there is an optimum-size plant—one that entails lower per unit production cost (or average total cost) than any other. Each possible plant size can be represented by its shortrun ATC curve.

Let's see how different plant sizes and their shortrun ATC curves are usually related to different output levels. Starting from a zero output level, larger and larger plant sizes typically have lower and lower ATC curves at successively higher output levels up to some point. Beyond a certain output level, however, successively larger plant sizes give rise to successively higher ATC curves. This is illustrated for three possible different plant sizes in Figure 8-5. The lowest point on the ATC curve for the smallest plant (plant 1) occurs at 700 units of output. For the next larger plant (plant 2), the lowest point on its ATC curve occurs at a larger level of output, 1,800 units, and is obviously lower than that of plant 1. The lowest point on the ATC of the largest plant (plant 3) occurs at 2,700 units of output and is clearly higher than that of plant 2.

Points a and b of Figure 8-5 are of particular interest. If the firm produces less than 900 units of output, plant 1 is the best plant size to use because it has the lowest per unit costs for output levels less than 900. This is clear from the fact that to the left of point a the ATC curve for plant 1 lies below that for plant 2. If the firm produces between 900 and 2,400 units of output, plant 2 is the best plant size to use because it has the lowest per unit costs for this range of output. This is reflected in the fact that the ATC curve of plant 2 lies below that of plant 1 to the right of a, and below that of plant 3 to the left of b. If the firm produces more than 2,400 units of output, plant 3 is the best plant size to use because it has the lowest per unit costs for this range of output. This is apparent from the fact that the ATC curve of plant 3 lies below that of plant 2 to the right of point b.

Longrun Average Cost

The observations we have just made about the firm's selection of the optimum plant size to produce different output levels suggest the nature of the firm's

---

FIGURE 8-5   Average Total Cost Curves for Three Possible Plant Sizes

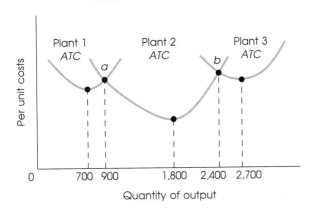

In the longrun the firm can change the size of its plant. Starting from a zero output level, successively larger plants typically have lower and lower ATC curves up to some output level and then successively higher ATC curves beyond. If these are the only three possible plant sizes, the longrun AC curve consists of the segment of plant 1's ATC curve up to point a, the segment of plant 2's ATC curve between points a and b, and the segment of plant 3's ATC curve from point b on.

longrun average cost curve, sometimes called the firm's *planning curve*. *The long-run AC curve shows the lowest per unit cost at which it is possible to produce a given output when there is enough time for the firm to adjust its plant size.* In Figure 8-5 the longrun *AC* curve consists of the segment of plant 1's *ATC* curve up to point *a*, the segment of plant 2's *ATC* curve between *a* and *b*, and the segment of the *ATC* curve for plant 3 from point *b* on.

While only three possible plant sizes are shown in Figure 8-5, a firm may in fact have an almost unlimited number from which it may choose. The larger is the number of possible plant sizes, the smaller will be the part of each plant's *ATC* curve used to make up the longrun *AC* curve. This is illustrated in Figure 8-6. Here, two more possible plant sizes and their associated shortrun *ATC*s have been added to the three shown in Figure 8-5. With the addition of *ATC* curves for plants 4 and 5, it can be seen that the segments *a'a*, *aa''*, *b'b*, and *bb''* of the three original shortrun *ATC* curves are no longer parts of the longrun *AC* curve. They are replaced by the segments *a'a''* and *b'b''* of the *ATC* curves associated with the two additional possible plant sizes.

As more and more possible plant sizes are considered, the segments of their associated *ATC* curves that are part of the longrun *AC* curve become smaller and smaller. The longrun *AC* curve is a smooth *envelope* curve, made up of all the points of tangency with all of the possible shortrun *ATC* curves. This curve

---

FIGURE 8-6   The Longrun Average Cost Curve

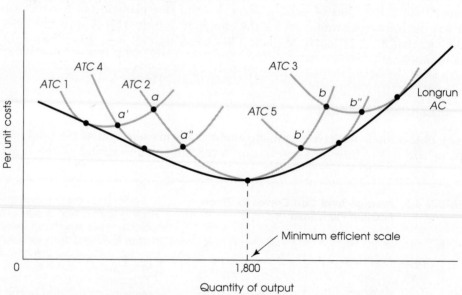

Two more possible plant sizes with shortrun *ATC* curves *ATC* 4 and *ATC* 5 are shown here together with the shortrun *ATC* curves for the three plant sizes shown in Figure 8-5. The segment of the plant *ATC* curves that now make up the longrun *AC* curve are the segment of the smallest plant's *ATC* curve from *a'*, the segments *a'a''*, *a''b'*, *b'b''*, and the segment of the largest plant's *ATC* curve from *b''* on. Given an unlimited number of possible plant sizes, the longrun *AC* curve is made up of all the points of tangency with the unlimited number of shortrun *ATC* curves. As output increases, the firm realizes economies of scale along the falling portion of the longrun *AC* curve and diseconomies of scale along the rising portion.

appears as a heavy line in Figure 8-6. Only five of the unlimited number of shortrun ATC curves that make up the longrun AC curve are shown. Note that only the minimum point of the longrun AC curve at, 1,800 units of output, is tangent to the minimum point of a shortrun ATC curve. At output levels below 1,800 units, the points of tangency occur to the left of the minimum points on the shortrun ATC curves. At output levels above 1,800 units, the tangency points occur to the right of the minimum points on the shortrun ATC curves.

It is clear now why the longrun AC curve is sometimes called the *planning envelope curve*. At any output level the associated point on the longrun AC curve is a point on a shortrun ATC curve corresponding to the plant size that is the most efficient for producing that output level. Therefore, if the firm plans to produce a certain output level, the longrun AC curve tells it the best-size plant to construct. It is best in the sense that the planned output level may be produced at the lowest possible per unit cost.

Economies and Diseconomies of Scale

Why, with some production processes, do the shortrun ATC curves associated with successively larger plant sizes become steadily lower up to some output level and then begin to rise, giving the longrun AC curve the shape shown in Figure 8-6? The reason is *not* the law of diminishing returns, which assumes that some of the factors of production are fixed. That law only explains the U-shape of the shortrun ATC curve associated with a particular plant size. It does not apply here because, in the longrun, all factors are variable. Hence, the reasons for the U-shape of the longrun AC curve must lie elsewhere. We will find them by examining what economists call *economies* and *diseconomies of scale*.

Economies of Scale

Economies of scale are the decreases in the longrun average total cost of production that occur when the firm's plant size is increased, as represented by the declining portion of the longrun AC curve. Economies of scale can occur for a number of reasons.

Specialization of Factors of Production.   In a small firm, labour and equipment must be used to perform a number of different tasks. It is more difficult for labour to become skilled at any one of them and thereby realize the gains in productivity and reductions in per unit costs that specialization permits. In the same way, management functions cannot be as specialized in a smaller firm. Supervisors may have to devote time to the screening of job applicants, a task usually handled more efficiently in a larger firm by a personnel department. Executives may have to divide their attention among finance, accounting, and production operations—functions that could be handled more proficiently by departments specializing in each of these areas in a larger firm.

Similarly, machinery and equipment cannot be used as efficiently when they have to be switched back and forth between tasks. Moreover, in many types of production processes, the most efficient types of production facilities are practicable only at high levels of output. It is very expensive to build custom-

Checkpoint 8-5

It has been said that a firm's longrun AC curve really represents nothing more than a collection of blueprints. In what sense is this true? When a plant operates at a point to the left of the minimum point on its shortrun ATC curve, it is said to be *underutilized*. Assuming an unlimited number of plant sizes make up the longrun AC curve of Figure 8-6, why is it always cheaper at any given output level less than 1,800 units to underutilize a larger plant than to overutilize a smaller one? Similarly, why is it always cheaper at any given output level greater than 1,800 units to overutilize a smaller plant than to underutilize a larger one?

POLICY PERSPECTIVE

Economies and Diseconomies of Scale and the Number of Firms in an Industry

The number of firms in an industry is an important determinant of the degree of competition that exists among firms in that industry, a major concern of anticombine policy, which we will study in Chapter 13. In general, competition will be more intense if there are more firms, other things being equal. The existence of economies and diseconomies of scale is an important determining factor of how many firms there are in an industry.

Consider the three different longrun *AC* curves shown in Figure P8-1. In frame (a), economies of scale are relatively small and diseconomies of scale set in relatively quickly as output is increased. In frame (b), economies of scale are again quickly exhausted, but there is a considerable range of

output over which the longrun *AC* curve is flat before diseconomies of scale set in. In frame (c), economies of scale are realized over a much larger range of output before diseconomies of scale set in.

Given the consumer demand facing an industry, there is likely to be a greater number of smaller-sized firms in the industry if the typical firm's longrun *AC* curve is like that of frame (a) than if it is like that of either frame (b) or frame (c). On the other hand, if the typical firm's longrun *AC* is like that of frame (c), the industry is more likely to be composed of a smaller number of larger-sized firms. This is so because firms will not realize minimum per unit costs until they push production to relatively higher output levels. The in-between case de-

picted in frame (b) suggests the possibility of an industry composed of firms more varied in size, each of which realizes similar levels of minimum per unit costs.

For Discussion

- If there were a decline in demand for an industry's product, which one of the longrun *AC* curves in Figure P8-1 would probably entail the least number of firms having to go out of business? Why? Would fewer jobs be lost?
- Which one of the longrun *AC* curves in Figure P8-1 would be a disadvantage to Canadian producers given the small Canadian market compared to Japan, the United States, or the European Common Market? How would "free trade" change this?

FIGURE P8-1   **Three Different Types of Longrun Average Total Cost Curves**

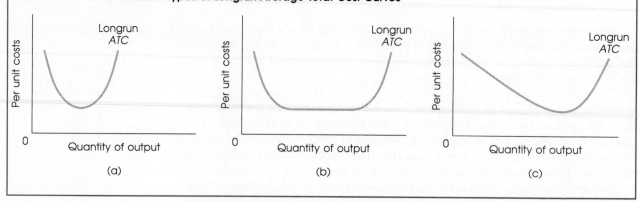

made cars by hand, but it would be equally or more expensive to use a large General Motors assembly plant to build just 100 Chevrolets per year. However, if the plant is used to build 100,000 cars per year, the highly specialized techniques of the assembly line allow the cost per car to be greatly reduced. The gains obtained by the specialization of factors of production in larger-size plants are referred to as **increasing returns to scale.**

Volume Discounts on the Prices of Materials and Other Inputs Used in Production.
Often the suppliers of raw materials, machinery, and other inputs will charge
a lower price per unit for these items if a firm buys in large quantities. When
a firm produces at high output levels, it needs a large volume of inputs and
can take advantage of the associated price discounts to reduce its per unit costs.
These are referred to as **pecuniary economies**.

Economic Use of By-products.   The production of many types of goods gives
rise to by-products that also have economic value. Large-scale firms are often
able to recycle "waste" by-products that smaller-size firms simply have to throw
away because it is not economical to do anything else with them. For example,
a small sawmill may simply throw away sawdust and old wood scraps. A large
lumber-processing firm often finds the volume of these waste products large
enough to make it economical to package sawdust and sell it as a sweeping
compound for cleaning floors and hallways in large buildings. The wood scraps
may be packaged, processed, and sold as kindling wood and artificial logs for
home barbecues and fireplaces. In this way, the sale of by-products effectively reduces the per unit costs of producing lumber in large volume. For
the same reasons, large oil firms often produce a host of petroleum by-
products, and meat-packing firms produce fertilizers, glue, leather, and other
by-products of meat production. The lower costs a firm achieves by spreading costs between a number of products are referred to as **economies of
scope**.

*The Growth of Supporting Facilities and Services Is Encouraged by the Firm's Large
Scale of Operation.*   As a firm's scale of operations gets larger, it often becomes
worthwhile for other firms and local governments to provide it with services.
If a firm builds a large plant in a particular area, an improvement in highways
and expanded transportation services may soon follow. Smaller suppliers, who
find a large part of their sales going to the larger firm, may move closer to the
larger firm to reduce transportation costs. All of these developments result in
lower per unit costs for the large firm. These cost reductions are called **external
industry economies**.

Diseconomies of Scale

Diseconomies of scale refer to the increasing longrun average cost of production represented by the rising portion of the longrun *AC* curve. When the
firm produces at output levels greater than those corresponding to the minimum point on the longrun *AC* curve, the upward pressure on per unit costs
due to diseconomies of scale more than offsets the downward pressure resulting
from economies of scale.

Diseconomies of scale are largely a result of the firm growing so large that it
becomes cumbersome to manage. Once the firm gets beyond a certain size, the
problems of efficiently coordinating a large number of plants and diverse operations become more complex. Central management must communicate with
many more areas of the firm and process more information in order to keep tabs
on what's going on. This often means that more authority must be delegated
to middle and lower management levels. The increased chances of misguided
decisions, combined with central management's difficulty in monitoring all

operations, may result in inefficiencies that cause the per unit costs of output to rise.

Diseconomies of scale can be avoided by replication of lower-cost plants. Instead of producing the larger plant with costs such as ATC 3 in Figure 8-6, operate two smaller plants with ATC 2. In this way AC can be kept at the lowest level possible.

Minimum Efficient Scale

The **minimum efficient scale** (**MES**) is the smallest level of output that achieves the lowest average cost possible. In Figure 8-6 the minimum efficient scale occurs at 1,800 units of output. Graphically it occurs at the minimum point of the longrun average cost curve and separates the ranges of output where economies and diseconomies occur.

Summary

1. A plant is the smallest unit of production; a firm is the legal form of production organization; a firm may have more than one plant. An industry is the collection of firms producing the same or similar product for one market.

2. The three primary legal forms of the firm are the proprietorship, the partnership, and the corporation. While proprietorships and partnerships are more numerous, the corporation is the dominant form of large business enterprise. This is so mainly because it is the only legal form of business organization that affords owners the protection of limited liability. This feature enhances the corporation's ability to raise capital.

3. Corporations take on many forms. A public corporation has shares that are traded on a public stock exchange or market. A private corporation is one whose shares are held by a small number of people and are not traded publicly. The public corporation must disclose more information than the private one. A crown corporation is one whose shares are owned solely by a government. And a cooperative is a corporation that gives patronage refunds instead of dividends to its shareholders and whose members each have a vote, regardless of how many shares they hold.

4. The firm's behaviour is analyzed in two distinct time dimensions. In the shortrun, some of a firm's factors of production, such as its plant, are fixed. Its level of output can be varied only by changing the quantities of its variable factors, such as its labour. In the longrun, there is sufficient time for the firm to vary all its factors of production, including the size of its plant.

5. In the shortrun, the law of diminishing returns describes the changes in output that result as increasing amounts of a variable input are applied to a fixed input. It says that the additions to total output, called the marginal product, associated with the addition of each successive unit of the variable factor will begin to decline beyond some point.

6. In the shortrun, total product, marginal product, and average product have characteristic relationships to variable input termed production functions. The graph of the total product at first rises at an increasing rate and then rises at a diminishing rate to some maximum as the variable input is in-

creased. Correspondingly, the marginal product at first rises and then declines to zero as the variable input is increased.

7. Whether resources are owned directly by the firm or must be hired from outside, their cost is the money payment they could have received if employed in their next best alternative use. The firm's costs include explicit costs, which are the payments to resource suppliers outside the firm, and implicit costs, which equal the compensation that resources already owned by the firm could earn in alternative uses outside the firm. Implicit costs include a normal profit from the entrepreneurial skills and financial capital supplied by a firm's owners. These costs are the opportunity cost of producing the product.

8. Profit takes on many meanings and these need to be distinguished in economic analysis. Accounting profit is the difference between the firm's total revenue and its explicit costs. Normal profit is the return to the firm's own resources necessary to keep these resources in this line of production. Economic profit is the difference between the firm's total revenue and all costs—explicit and implicit. It is a residual that is unnecessary to keep the firm in business.

9. Total fixed cost TFC includes all the firm's costs that do not vary with output in the shortrun. The firm is saddled with fixed cost no matter what level of output it produces. Total variable cost TVC includes all the firm's costs associated with the factors that are variable in the shortrun. Total variable cost changes with the level of the firm's output. At any output level the firm's total cost TC equals the sum of total fixed and total variable costs.

10. Average fixed cost AFC equals total fixed cost divided by the output level. It falls continuously as the output level is increased. Average variable cost AVC equals total variable cost divided by the output level. As output is increased, AVC first falls and then rises, reflecting the law of diminishing returns. Average total cost ATC equals the sum of average fixed cost and average variable cost. It falls and then rises as output increases. Marginal cost MC is the increment to total cost resulting from the production of an additional unit of output. As output increases, MC first falls and then rises, reflecting the law of diminishing returns. It cuts the AVC and ATC curves at their lowest points respectively.

11. Because all factors of production are variable in the longrun, so are all costs. When the firm has sufficient time to adjust the size of its plant, it will select the plant size that has the lowest shortrun ATC curve at the desired output level. For this reason the longrun AC curve is composed of segments of all the shortrun ATC curves. It is sometimes called a planning curve. The longrun AC curve is U-shaped, its declining portion reflecting economies of scale and its rising portion reflecting diseconomies of scale.

12. Economies of scale result from increased specialization of the factors of production, price discounts on volume purchases of inputs, more economical use of by-products, and the growth of supporting firms and services. Diseconomies of scale result from the increased difficulty of managing large-scale operations once the firm has grown beyond a certain size. Economies and diseconomies of scale play a major role in determining the size and number of firms in an industry. In general, given the demand for an industry's product, the larger the economies of scale, the greater will be the size and the

smaller the number of firms in an industry. Conversely, when economies of scale are few, in general the size of firms will be smaller and the number of firms will be larger in the industry. The minimum efficient scale (MES) is the level of output that achieves the lowest longrun average cost.

Key Terms and Concepts

accounting profit
average fixed cost (*AFC*)
average product (*AP*)
average total cost (*ATC*)
average variable cost (*AVC*)
conglomerate
cooperatives
corporation
creditors
crown corporation
diseconomies of scale
dividends
economic cost
economic profit
economies of scale
economies of scope

explicit costs
external industry economies
firm
fixed factor
horizontally integrated
implicit costs
increasing returns to scale
industry
law of diminishing returns
limited liability
limited partner
longrun average cost (*AC*)
marginal cost (*MC*)
marginal product (*MP*)
minimum efficient scale (MES)

normal profit
partnership
pecuniary economies
plant
private corporation
proprietorship
public corporation
shortrun production function
total cost (*TC*)
total fixed cost (*TFC*)
total product
total variable cost (*TVC*)
undistributed profits
variable factor
vertically integrated

Questions and Problems

1. Suppose you examined the costs of each of the firms in a random collection of sole proprietorships and compared them with the costs of each of the firms in a random collection of corporations. Among which group would you generally expect implicit costs to be a larger proportion of economic costs? Why?

2. Rank the following firms according to the maximum length of calendar time you think would constitute the shortrun: retail shoe store, road construction company, real estate brokerage firm, shoeshine stand, nuclear power company, and oil refinery. Suppose that the demand for the goods and services produced by these businesses were to increase tenfold. Rank the industries represented by each of these types of business according to the speed with which you think each would exhibit a complete supply response.

3. Describe how the law of diminishing returns works in each of the following situations, taking care to identify the product and classify the fixed and variable factors in each case:
   a. Preparing for a final exam.
   b. Insulating a house.
   c. Looking for a parking spot within walking distance of a downtown store at 3:00 P.M. on a weekday.
   d. Controlling crime in a big city.
   e. Convincing somebody to give you a job.
   f. Cleaning up the environment.
   g. Protecting the population against nuclear attack.
   h. Protecting yourself from heart attack.
   i. Getting to the other side of town as fast as possible.

j. Discussing the weather.

k. Increasing unemployment benefits to help unemployed people get by financially while looking for jobs.

4. For each of the firms in problem 2, describe the nature of their fixed and variable costs. Is there any relationship between your cost description and how you ranked the firms in your answer to problem 2? Why?

5. Consider the fixed, variable, and total costs of a thermal electric power generating company. How are its TFC, TVC, TC, AFC, AVC, ATC, and MC curves affected by the following changes?

a. An increase in interest rates.

b. An increase in wages.

c. A decrease in property taxes.

d. An increase in the price of coal, oil, and nuclear fuel.

e. A decrease in the purity of the water it takes in for use in its boilers.

f. Imposition of an excise tax on electricity sales collected by the government from the company.

g. A tax on plant size to cover the city's water cleanup costs.

h. Passage of an antipollution law.

i. An increase in premium rates for hazard insurance.

6. Following is a simple production function for making lemonade where the fixed factor is the stand, glasses cooler, lemonade mix, and cash box. The variable factor includes the labour. Calculate the marginal and average products. The factor prices are these: the fixed factor is $100 and the variable factor is $10 per unit. Calculate the cost schedule and graph the cost functions for TFC, TVC, TC, AFC, AVC, ATC, and MC.

Variable Input	Total Quantity of Lemonade Servings Produced	Marginal Product	Average Product
0	0		
1	40		
2	90		
3	126		
4	150		
5	165		
6	179		

7. Because of technological progress, there have been considerable increases in economies of scale in farming in the past 50 years. How do you think that this has affected population shifts between urban and rural areas, all other things remaining the same?

8. As an economics student, what do you think were the major pros and cons of merging the Army, the Navy, and the Air Force into *one* large military organization?

Market Structure, Pricing, and Government Regulation

Chapter 9

Perfect Competition

What is the nature of a market or industry that has a large number of small firms in it? How does a firm behave differently if it is one of a large number of small firms each selling the same product as compared to how it would behave if it were the only firm in an industry in which it sold a unique product with no substitutes? How does the behaviour of a firm change if it goes from being the only firm in an industry to being one of a few large firms able to serve the market? For purposes of economic analysis, how is the farm near Rostern, Saskatchewan, or a drycleaner in Toronto, or a pizza joint in Vancouver, different from the only gas station at Saskatchewan River Crossing, Alberta, or a public utility such as Ontario Hydro or TransAlta Utilities, or a large firm like Irving Oil, Eatons', Inco, or Steinberg's? Finally, will these behaviours be influenced by government intervention to regulate prices? If the government does regulate, can it improve the efficiency of the use of society's resources, and if so what criteria would be used to judge this?

Building the analytical framework to answer these questions will form the direction of the next three chapters of the text. To answer these questions it is important to be able to identify the different market structures used by economists to classify firms.

Market Structures

In economics, **market structure** or what is sometimes called *industrial organization* depends on four characteristics: the ability of the firm to influence the price of its own product, the number and relative size of buyers and sellers in the market, the similarity of the sellers' products, and the ease with which firms can enter and leave the industry. For purposes of description and analysis, economists use these four identifiers to specify four basic types of market structure: perfect (or pure) competition, monopoly, monopolistic competition, and oligopoly. Like the aeronautical engineer's model of the real aircraft, each of these is an abstract characterization of a type of real market.

Perfect Competition in Theory and Reality

In this chapter we will focus on perfect competition. In many respects economists consider this kind of market structure an ideal form of economic organization for providing goods and services to consumers as efficiently as possible. For this reason it is often used as a standard or norm against which other forms of market structure are compared, as we shall see in the next three chapters.

The Four Characteristics of Perfect Competition

What kind of characteristics of an industry or a market promote the existence of perfect competition? Basically there are four: (1) There are many firms, (2) All firms sell a homogeneous product, (3) Each firm is a price taker, and (4) There is freedom of entry into and exit from the industry by firms.

There Are Many Firms

"Many firms" does not mean any specific number. Rather, there are enough firms so that any one firm's contribution to total industry supply is so small that whether a firm produces at full capacity or not at all, market price will not be noticeably affected.

All Firms Sell a Homogeneous Product

The important thing here is that the product of one firm is considered by the buyer to be the same as that of any other firm. Therefore, in the mind of

---

LEARNING OBJECTIVES

After reading this chapter, you will be able to:

1. Define the concept of market structure and classify firms on the basis of market structure characteristics.
2. List and explain the characteristics of perfect competition.
3. Explain and graph the revenue curves for a firm in a perfectly competitive market.
4. State the relationship between the perfectly competitive demand curve facing the firm and the demand curve of the industry.
5. Show how cost and revenue considerations lead the perfectly competitive firm to decide whether or not to produce in the shortrun.
6. Explain the marginal cost–marginal revenue criterion for choosing the profit-maximizing output level.
7. Discuss the conditions for shortrun shut down in a perfectly competitive market.
8. Explain the longrun adjustment process in a perfectly competitive industry.
9. Discuss the nature of the longrun industry supply curve.
10. Explain why a perfectly competitive world would be both production efficient and allocatively efficient.
11. Explain some of the criticisms of perfect competition.

the buyer, each firm's product is viewed as a perfect substitute for the product of any other firm in the market. This ensures that no buyer has any economic incentive to pay any firm a higher price for the product than is charged by other firms.

An important implication of product homogeneity in a perfectly competitive industry is that there is no incentive for firms to engage in nonprice competition. Nonprice competition is encouraged by differences in the products of different firms that can be exploited by advertising and other types of sales promotion. When no such differences exist (and buyers know it), advertising by individual firms will yield them no market advantage over other firms.

Price Takers

In perfect competition each firm, or seller, in a market or industry is a **price taker**. Each firm is unable to affect its price by altering the amount of product that it offers for sale. This is because its production of output is such a small portion of total industry supply that it has no appreciable effect on market supply. The firm can change its level of production and sales without having any noticeable effect on the price of the good it sells. The firm is therefore a price taker because it must accept the sales established in the market as given.

Ease of Entry into and Exit from the Industry by Firms

There are no significant financial, legal, technological, or other barriers to new firms entering the industry or existing firms leaving it. Weak barriers to entry put pressure on firms in the industry to operate as efficiently as possible because otherwise new, more efficient firms can easily enter the industry and replace them.

Summary of Perfectly Competitive Characteristics

Let's summarize how these four characteristics promote the existence of perfect competition. Because there are many small firms (characteristic 1), the output of any one firm is an insignificant share of the market supply. Since the firm's product is indistinguishable from the product of any other firm in the market (characteristic 2), there is no incentive for buyers to pay a higher price for it than for the product of any other firm. Thus, any one firm's output is an insignificant share of the market supply. The individual firm therefore cannot influence the going market price by changing its level of production (characteristic 3). Finally, the easy entry of new firms (characteristic 4) implies that any attempt to increase price by the existing firms will result in new firms entering the industry. This will increase supply and force the price down.

It may have occurred to some students that we have implicitly assumed that buyers and sellers are perfectly informed about the prices of all market transactions. This is correct—the assumption that buyers and sellers have perfect knowledge is an implicit assumption used in perfect competition. We do not explicitly make this assumption part of the market characteristics because it will be used in other market structures as well and consequently it is of little use in distinguishing between perfect competition and the other market structures.

Does Perfect Competition Exist?

By this time you may be suspicious that there is no market that meets all the characteristics of perfect competition. Your skepticism is understandable. It would be hard to find an industry that has a market structure *perfectly* exhibiting all four characteristics. However, there are industries or markets that come close.

Competition in Agriculture

Some segments of the agricultural sector behave very much like perfectly competitive markets. For example, there are over 300,000 farming operations in Canada. A farmer in southern British Columbia or southern Ontario who plants green beans may think of himself or herself as a large operation and may even be the only operator in the area to plant green beans instead of wheat. Such farmers may think of themselves as large operators, but they may still be more accurately analyzed by treating them as if they were a perfect competitor. The farmer may well face competition from imported green beans when customers decide to buy fresh vegetables in the local grocery store. Alternatively, if a farmer is seeking the best price for his or her product he or she may consider selling the green beans to an exporter who will certainly face competition when selling the beans in foreign markets. Suppose that a farmer has planted 200 hectares of green beans and that the total area planted in North America is 20,000,000 hectares, then even assuming that the farmer gets the same yield per hectare as the North American average, the individual will contribute roughly 1/1,000,000 (or 1/10,000 of 1 percent) of the total amount of green beans produced. It certainly seems reasonable to believe that whether any one farm produces or not will have little if any noticeable effect on the market price of green beans. And in the market for green beans it is unlikely that one farm's green beans can be distinguished from another's—the product is homogeneous. These considerations (many firms and a homogeneous product) strongly suggest that the typical farmer is a price taker in the green bean market. Further, they suggest that because the theory captures the essence of the market behaviour, it is a useful tool in analyzing some types of production behaviour in that market.

While the green bean market has many characteristics of a perfectly competitive market, even here there is one characteristic that is missing—ease of entry into the industry. Purchasing a farm (or even a few hectares for most of us) poses a rather sizable financial barrier. Even if farmland is rented, typically one must purchase expensive farm equipment to run a modern farm. Nonetheless, many markets, especially agricultural markets, come close to satisfying the characteristics of the perfectly competitive market model. For this reason the model serves as a useful instrument for analyzing the behaviour of many agricultural markets in general.

A Standard for Market Structure

The concept of perfect competition provides a useful standard against which other market structures may be compared. It allows economists to estimate what would happen in a market where consumer sovereignty is given free reign under competitive conditions. In many respects it also exemplifies the most efficient way to allocate scarce resources among unlimited wants, a matter we will examine at the end of this chapter. In this way, perfect competition is a theoretical idealization of several important notions in economics. Perfect competition provides the simplest starting point for studying the nature of price and output determination by the firm and the role that the cost concepts of the previous chapter and the consumer sovereignty idea of Chapter 2 play in this process.

Market Demand and the Demand Curve Facing the Firm

It is important to understand the relationship between the demand curve facing the individual firm and the market or industry demand curve. It is also important to understand the relationship among total, average, and marginal revenue functions of the perfectly competitive firm.

The Market Demand Curve and the Demand Curve Facing the Individual Firm

When we say that the perfectly competitive firm is a price taker, or that it cannot affect the price at which it sells its product, we are saying something about the shape of the demand curve as seen by the individual firm. Specifically, this demand curve is horizontal (perfectly elastic) at the level of the prevailing market price over the range of output that the firm can feasibly produce.

Such a demand curve looks like the one in Figure 9-1, frame (a). In this example, we assume that the firm's highest feasible output level is 1,200 units. The industry demand and supply curves for the entire competitive market are shown in Figure 9-1, frame (b). Their intersection determines the equilibrium market price p_e and equilibrium market quantity, Q_e, which in this case is 1 million units of output.

The demand curve facing the firm is perfectly elastic for two reasons. First, the firm's product is indistinguishable from that of any other firm in the industry. Hence, if the firm were to raise its price above p_e, it would sell nothing, since buyers can get the same product at the price p_e from other firms. Second, since the individual firm's output capacity is insignificant compared to that of the entire industry, the firm could effectively sell all it could produce at the market equilibrium price p_e. Under these conditions there is clearly no incentive for the firm to try to attract increased numbers of customers by lowering the price of its product below the market (equilibrium) price.

Two important points are clearly illustrated in Figure 9-1, frames (a) and (b). First, because the individual firm provides such a small fraction of the total industry output (about 1/1,000 in this example), it has no effect on the market-determined price p_e. The actions of all firms taken together, however, do affect market price, and therefore the market demand curve D is downward sloping even though the demand curve d, facing the individual firm, is perfectly horizontal. Second, although price is *determined* by the interaction of all buyers and sellers in the market as represented in frame (b), this price p_e is essentially given to, and beyond the influence of, any individual firm as is shown in frame (a). Again, this simply reflects the fact that the individual firm's contribution to total output is of no influence as far as the whole market is concerned. The 1,200

FIGURE 9-1 **Relationship Between a Competitive Demand Curve Facing the Firm and the Competitive Industry's Demand Curve**

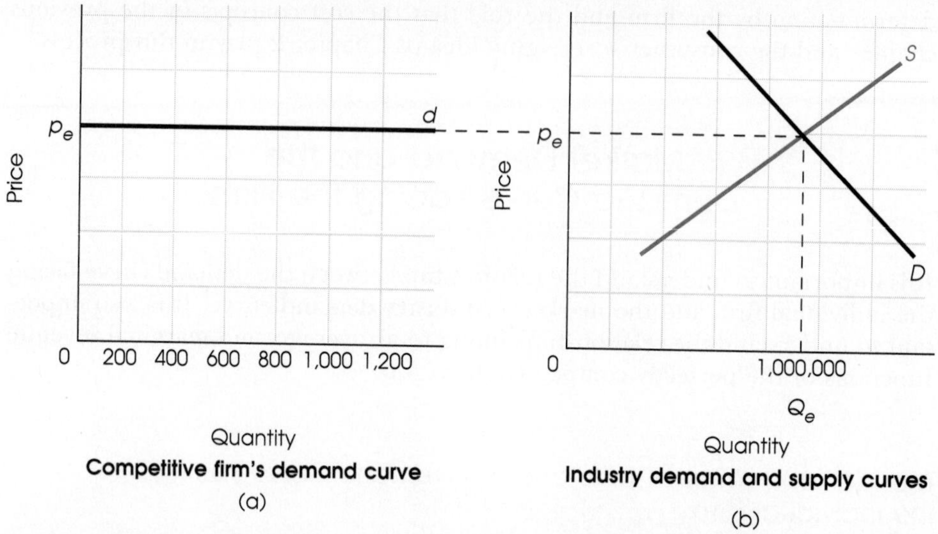

Quantity
Competitive firm's demand curve
(a)

Quantity
Industry demand and supply curves
(b)

Because the industry demand curve D is downward sloping, the production of all firms taken together can affect the market price in frame (b). The market equilibrium price p_e is determined by the intersection of the market demand curve D and market supply curve S representing the output of all firms—in this case 1,000,000 units. Because the individual competitive firm can only contribute a small fraction (about 1/1,000) to this total, its actions cannot affect price. Therefore, its demand curve is perfectly elastic, or horizontal, at the market-determined price level p_e, as shown in frame (a).

units on the horizontal axis of frame (a) are hardly bigger than a dot on the horizontal axis of frame (b).

Total, Average, and Marginal Revenue of a Perfectly Competitive Firm

A demand curve may be looked at from two different viewpoints. On the one hand, it shows the quantity of a good that consumers will purchase per period of time at different prices. On the other, it shows the price, or revenue, per unit that a seller can receive for different quantities of output per period of time. We now want to consider the second interpretation from the standpoint of the perfectly competitive firm. Total revenue equals quantity sold multiplied by the selling price.

In economics, **total revenue** is defined as *the sum of all revenues which a firm receives from sales of its output.* This is similar to the concept of operating revenues in accounting but different in at least one respect. In accounting, the objective of studying revenue is often to assess the financial health of the firm or to determine such things as the taxes owing to the government. In economics, the purpose of studying revenue is to see how production decisions or pricing decisions will affect the ability of the firm to gain the maximum profit.

Suppose that the market price is $10. Since the firm's level of production does not affect this price, it can sell any amount of output it can produce. Total

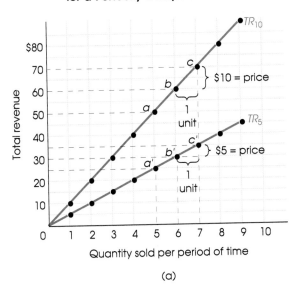

FIGURE 9-2   The Total Revenue Curve, Marginal Revenue Curve, and Demand Curve for a Perfectly Competitive Firm

The perfectly competitive firm's level of production does not affect price. In frame (a), the total revenue curve would look like TR_{10} if price is $10 per unit, or TR_5 if it is $5 per unit. The perfectly competitive demand curve facing the firm is the same as its marginal revenue curve and is perfectly elastic (horizontal). When price is $10, the demand curve associated with TR_{10} in frame (a) is d_{10} in frame (b). When price is $5, the demand curve associated with TR_5 in frame (a) is d_5 in frame (b).

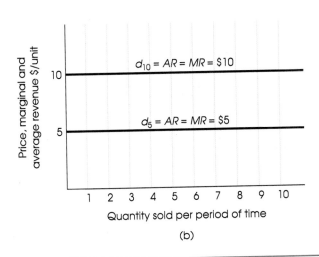

revenue equals quantity sold multiplied by the selling price of $10 per unit. The relationship between total revenue and quantity sold, for a given price of $10 per unit, is shown by the total revenue curve TR_{10} in Figure 9-2, frame (a). For example, when 5 units (measured on the horizontal axis) are sold at a price of $10 per unit, total revenue (measured on the vertical axis) is $50. This is represented by point a on TR_{10}. If an additional unit is sold, making a total of 6, total revenue rises by an amount equal to the price of $10. Total revenue is then $60, as represented by point b on TR_{10}. Similarly, if one more unit is sold at the given price of $10 per unit, bringing the total to 7 units, we move from point b to point c on TR_{10}, where total revenue is $70.

$$TR = p_e \times q$$

Suppose that the market price were to fall from $10 to $5 per unit. This would cause the total revenue curve to pivot clockwise about the origin from the position TR_{10} to TR_5. If the firm now sells 5 units of output, total revenue will be $25, as represented by point a' on TR_5. The sale of 6 units would bring a total revenue of $30, point b' on TR_5. The sale of yet one more unit at the given price of $5 would bring total revenue to $35, point c' on TR_5.

Notice that the TR curves in Figure 9-2, frame (a), are straight lines. Their slopes are $10 per unit of output on TR_{10} and $5 per unit of output on TR_5, no matter what the output level. Because of this, starting from the origin, average revenue per unit sold is the same no matter what total quantity of output is sold. For example, at point a on TR_{10}, average revenue per unit sold equals the total revenue of $50 divided by 5 units sold, or $10 per unit. At point b, average revenue equals $60 divided by 6 units sold or, again, $10 per unit. Similarly, at point c, $70 divided by 7 units sold gives an average revenue of $10 per unit.

For a perfectly competitive or any firm operating as a price taker, average revenue is constant for all output levels. **Average revenue** is *always equal to the price per unit of output.*

$$AR = \frac{TR}{q}$$
$$= \frac{p_e \times q}{q}$$
$$= p_e$$

For TR_{10} the average revenue AR, which equals price per unit (or $10), is plotted in Figure 9-2, frame (b). Hence, average revenue is represented by the perfectly competitive demand curve facing the firm d_{10} when price equals $10 per unit. Similarly, for TR_5, the average revenue AR, which equals price per unit (or $5), is represented by the perfectly competitive demand curve facing the firm d_5. **Marginal revenue** *is the addition to total revenue resulting from the sale of one more unit of output.*

$$MR = \frac{\Delta TR}{\Delta q}$$

Since the perfectly competitive firm is a special case with the price constant regardless of how many units the firm sells, the marginal revenue received from selling one more unit always equals the market price. This is reflected in the fact that the TR curves in Figure 9-2, frame (a), are straight lines. Along TR_{10} each additional unit sold increases total revenue by $10. Hence, at every level of output, marginal revenue equals average revenue and equals price. We see, therefore, that if the marginal revenue of $10 per unit is plotted against output in frame (b), it is the same as the demand curve, d_{10} facing the perfectly competitive firm. If price per unit were $5, then the marginal revenue curve would be the same as the demand curve d_5 at the level of $5 per unit in frame (b).

Note that $AR = MR$ at all output levels *only* for firms operating as price takers such as in perfect competition.

$$MR = AR = p_e$$

In each of the other three forms of market structure that we will discuss, monopoly, monopolistic competition, and oligopoly, the condition that AR equals MR does not hold.

The Competitive Firm in the Shortrun

In the shortrun, the competitive firm's plant is fixed. It can only change the quantity of output it produces by changing its variable inputs, such as labour, materials, electricity, and other energy inputs.

We assume that the firm's objective is to use an amount of the variable inputs together with its fixed plant to produce and sell a quantity of output that will maximize its economic profit or, if necessary, minimize its losses.

If total revenue is greater than *total cost* (the sum of total variable cost plus total fixed cost), the firm will make an economic profit. If it is less, the firm will experience a loss. (Remember that total cost includes the opportunity cost of the firm's own resources, which is often referred to as *normal profit*.)

The way in which the firm seeks to maximize profits or minimize losses may be looked at in two ways. It may be seen either as a process of comparing total revenue and total cost or, equivalently, as a process of comparing marginal revenue with marginal cost. Both approaches will be explained here in order to demonstrate the relationship between them. However, economists typically rely on the marginal revenue–marginal cost approach. Both approaches may also be used to study a firm's behaviour in the context of the other three market structures (monopoly, monopolistic competition, and oligopoly) as well.

Should the Firm Produce in the Shortrun?

In the shortrun, as was explained in Chapter 8, the firm is saddled with its fixed costs regardless of whether it produces or not. If it produces nothing, variable costs will be zero, but it will still have to pay its fixed costs and it will suffer a loss equal to its fixed costs. Hence, the first question that the firm has to answer is whether or not it can reduce the size of this loss, or better yet make a profit, by employing variable factors to produce and sell some quantity of output. The firm's first question in the shortrun is whether to produce or not.

The answer to this question depends on the following considerations. Variable costs are incurred only if the firm produces some quantity of output. Suppose the total revenue received from the sale of this output is greater than the total variable cost of producing it. In this case, the excess of total revenue over total variable cost will offset some or possibly all of the fixed cost. Hence, it pays the firm to produce something. Even if the excess doesn't fully offset the fixed cost, the loss realized by the firm if it produces something will be smaller than its loss, which is its fixed cost, if it produces nothing. Better yet, if the firm's total revenue exceeds its total variable cost by an amount that is greater than its total fixed cost, then it will earn an economic profit. *The firm should produce in the shortrun if the loss it incurs is less than its fixed cost or, better yet, if it can earn an economic profit.*

There are clearly three possible situations that may arise in the shortrun.

1. The firm's total revenue from the sale of its output exceeds its total cost, the sum of its total variable and total fixed cost, and it earns an economic profit by producing.
2. The firm's total revenue exceeds its total variable cost and thus offsets some of its total fixed cost as well. The loss incurred by producing is

therefore less than the firm's total fixed cost, which is the loss if the firm remains idle.

3. The firm's total revenue is not sufficient to cover the total variable cost to which production gives rise. In this case, the loss (equal to total fixed cost) of remaining idle is less than the loss of producing (equal to total fixed cost plus the amount by which total variable cost exceeds total revenue).

In the first two cases, it pays the firm to produce, and therefore the second question the firm must answer is how much to produce. In the third case, the firm obviously should not produce at all. In the first case, the firm will answer the question by choosing that output level that maximizes economic profit. In the second case, the firm will answer by choosing that output level that minimizes losses. This is also essentially the choice it makes in the third case, when it chooses an output level of zero. Assuming given cost data for a hypothetical perfectly competitive firm, we will now consider how the answer to the question of how much to produce is determined in each of these cases. In each case we will examine how the firm can answer the question from the viewpoint of total revenue and total cost, as well as from the viewpoint of marginal revenue and marginal cost.

Maximizing Economic Profit

Table 9-1 contains the total, average, and marginal cost data, as well as the price, total revenue, and marginal revenue data, for a hypothetical perfectly

TABLE 9-1   Output, Revenue, and Costs of a Profit-Maximizing, Perfectly Competitive Firm (Hypothetical Data)

(1)	(2)	(3)	(4)	(5)	(6)	(7)	(8)	(9)	(10)
	Total Costs		Total Costs (TC)	Average and Marginal Costs			Price and Revenues		
Quantity of Output (Q)	Total Fixed Cost (TFC)	Total Variable Cost (TVC)	$TC = TVC + TFC$	Average Variable Cost (AVC) $AVC = TVC/Q$	Average Total Cost (ATC) $ATC = TVC/Q$	Marginal Cost (MC) $MC = \Delta TC/\Delta$ in Q	Price = Marginal Revenue $p = MR$	Total Revenue $TR = p \times Q$	Profit (+) or Loss $\pi = TR - TC$
0	$10	$ 0	$10					$ 0	−$10
1	10	6	16	$6.00	$16.00	$ 6	$9	9	−7
2	10	10	20	5.00	10.00	4	9	18	−2
3	10	14	24	4.66	8.00	4	9	27	+3
4	10	19	29	4.75	7.25	5	9	36	+7
5	10	26	36	5.20	7.20	7	9	45	+9
6	10	37	47	6.16	7.83	11	9	54	+7
7	10	60	70	8.57	10.00	23	9	63	−7

competitive firm that wants to maximize its economic profit. (All data in Table 9-1 are measured per some period of time, such as a month.)

Total Cost and Total Revenue Approach

The firm's total cost data and its associated output levels appear in columns (1) to (4). The price p at which the firm can sell its output is always $9 per unit, column (8). The firm's total revenue TR, column (9), from sales at each output level is obtained by multiplying this price by output, column (1). Profit or loss, column (10), equals the difference between total revenue TR and total cost TC, column (4).

Examination of profit π, column (10), shows that the answer to the question as to whether the firm should produce or not is yes. If the firm remains idle (output level of zero), it will incur a loss of $10, the amount of its TFC, column (2). The table shows us it can do much better than this, however. Profit, column (10), clearly shows that the firm can realize a maximum economic profit of $9. This figure is achieved by producing an output of 5 units. The answer to the second question of how much the firm should produce is therefore 5 units.

The reason for this answer is demonstrated graphically in Figure 9-3, frame (a). Given the price of $9 per unit, the total revenue curve TR_9 is obtained in exactly the same way that we obtained the TR curves in Figure 9-2. The total cost curve TC is plotted from the data in columns (1) and (4) of Table 9-1. The total variable cost curve TVC is plotted from the data in columns (1) and (3). (This is exactly the same procedure we used to obtain the TC and TVC curves of Figure 8-2 in the previous chapter.) The shape of the TC and TVC curves reflects the law of diminishing returns. At each output level, the vertical distance between TR_9 and TC equals the loss or profit π given in column (10) of Table 9-1.

At output levels of 1, 2, and 7 units the firm realizes losses. This is reflected by the fact that the TC curve lies above TR_9. At about $2\frac{1}{3}$ units of output the firm reaches a **break-even point**, $\pi = 0$ with TR_9 equal TC. At output levels beyond this point the firm makes a profit because TR_9 lies above TC. Another break-even point ($\pi = 0$) occurs at about $6\frac{1}{2}$ units of output, beyond which the firm again experiences losses. The maximum profit, equal to $9, is represented by the maximum vertical distance between TR_9 and TC, which occurs at 5 units of output.

Marginal Cost and Marginal Revenue Approach

An alternative way of viewing how the firm decides how much to produce is to consider the relationship between marginal cost and marginal revenue. As with the total cost and total revenue approach, the marginal cost and marginal revenue approach is applicable to all firms whether they are perfectly competitive or operate in a market structure of monopolistic competition, oligopoly, or monopoly. The perfectly competitive firm is different from the others in one important respect, however. Only for the perfectly competitive firm is it true that price p always equals marginal revenue MR, as we have shown earlier in this chapter.

How does the firm use this method to determine how much to produce? The firm must compare the marginal cost (the addition to total cost) associated with the production of one more unit of output with the marginal revenue (the

FIGURE 9-3   Maximizing Profit in a Perfectly Competitive Firm

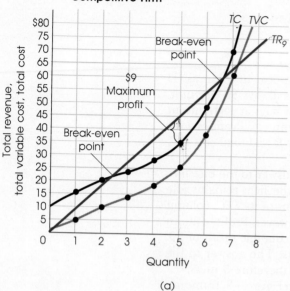

(a)

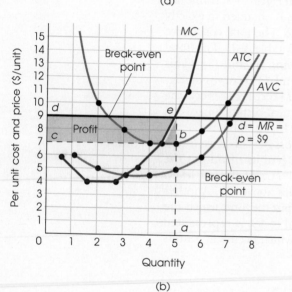

(b)

TR minus *TC* equals profit and is represented by the vertical distance between TR_9 and *TC* at any output level, frame (a). The maximum distance between these two curves represents the maximum profit of $9, which occurs when 5 units of output are produced and sold. The profit-maximizing level of output as shown in frame (b) occurs where $MC = MR$, represented by the intersection of the *MC* curve with the $d = MR = p = \$9$ curve at point e.

addition to total revenue) received from the sale of that unit. If the marginal cost is less than the marginal revenue, the firm will add to profit or reduce its loss by producing and selling an additional unit of output because the increase in total revenue will exceed the increase in the total cost. It may be easier to understand this by considering the marginal profit gained by the firm if it produces an additional unit and sells it. The **marginal profit** *is marginal revenue minus marginal cost.* In the **profit-maximizing** case, this excess of marginal revenue over marginal cost is zero. The firm should continue to increase production as long as the marginal revenue from each additional unit produced exceeds the marginal cost of producing that unit (as long as marginal profit is positive). If the marginal revenue from the last unit produced is less than the marginal cost of producing it, the production and sale of an additional unit will reduce the firm's profit or increase losses. In the profit-maximizing case, this means that at profit-maximizing output if an additional unit were produced it would create a negative marginal profit. It therefore "does not pay" to produce that unit. Hence, the firm should produce output up to the point where the marginal revenue of an additional unit of output is exactly equal to the unit's marginal cost. In short, the firm should produce output up to the point where the marginal profit is zero.

Consider the hypothetical perfectly competitive firm of Table 9-1. Starting from zero output level, when the firm increases production to the successively higher output levels of column (1), it incurs the associated marginal cost MC shown in column (7). The MC of column (7) falls at first and then rises as production is increased, which reflects the law of diminishing returns. The marginal revenue MR in column (8) always equals the price of $9, for the reasons discussed earlier in connection with Figure 9-2. Note that MC is always less than MR up through the production of 5 units of output. However, if the firm produces a sixth unit of output, the associated MC will be $11. This is larger than the MR of $9 associated with the sale of the sixth unit. Hence, it will not generate positive marginal profits for the firm to produce more than 5 units of output. Similarly, the firm will not maximize profit if it produces less than this amount. If it produces less, it will forgo the addition to profit associated with producing and selling additional units of output. Indeed, it can be seen from column (10) that the firm realizes its maximum possible profit of $9 when it produces 5 units of output. This is the same result we obtained when we used the total cost–total revenue approach. The marginal cost–marginal revenue approach is depicted graphically in Figure 9-3, frame (b). The MC curve is plotted from the data in column (7) of Table 9-1. The demand curve facing the firm d is perfectly elastic (horizontal) at the price $p = MR = \$9$, the data in column (8) of Table 9-1. That MC is less than MR up through the production and sale of 5 units of output is demonstrated by the fact that the MC curve lies below the MR curve, or demand curve d, up to this point. Beyond 5 units of output, the MC curve lies above the demand curve d.

Comparison of the Total and Marginal Approaches

We know from the total cost and total revenue graph in Figure 9-3, frame (a), that the firm realizes its maximum profit of $9 at 5 units. This can also be seen in Figure 9-3, frame (b), by looking at the average total cost curve, ATC, which is plotted using the data in Table 9-1, column (6). At 5 units the average total cost is $7.20, which is represented by the distance $0c$, which equals ab. Total cost can then be computed as the 5 units multiplied by $7.20, which gives a total cost of $36. This is represented by the rectangular area $0abc$ in frame (b). For comparison, remember that total cost is also represented by the vertical distance directly above 5 units up to the TC curve in frame (a). The price per unit of $9 is represented by the distance $0d$, which equals ae. Total revenue from the sale of 5 units of output equals 5 multiplied by ae in frame (b). Remember that in frame (a), total revenue is represented by the vertical distance directly above 5 units up to the total curve TR_9. Since total economic profit equals total revenue minus total cost, it is represented by the difference between the areas of the rectangles $0aed$ and $0abc$. Hence, the total economic profit of $9 is represented by the area of the rectangle $cbed$ in frame (b). Remember that in frame (a) total economic profit is represented by the vertical distance between TR_9 and TC.

An alternative way of arriving at the total economic profit is to multiply the economic profit per unit by the number of units. Economic profit per unit is represented by the vertical distance cd, which equals be, in Figure 9-3, frame (b). It equals the average revenue per unit (which is the price p) minus the ATC per unit, $9 minus $7.20, or $1.80. Multiplying this by 5 units gives a profit of $9.

Note that the break-even points in Figure 9-3, frame (a), where the TC curve intersects the TR_9 curve, correspond to the points at which the ATC curve intersects the d curve at the same output levels in Figure 9-3, frame (b). At output levels in between these break-even points, the firm's economic profits are positive. This is shown in frame (b) by the fact that average total cost per unit, as represented by the ATC curve, is less than average revenue per unit, as represented by the demand curve d. (Remember that average total cost, like total cost, includes an allowance for normal profit.) At output levels less than the lower break-even point and greater than the upper break-even point, the firm realizes a loss. This is indicated by the fact that the ATC curve lies above the demand curve d.

We may summarize our results for the marginal cost–marginal revenue approach as follows: To maximize economic profit the firm should produce up to that level of output where marginal cost equals marginal revenue.[1] The perfectly competitive firm is a price taker and therefore price is the same as marginal revenue. The perfectly competitive firm maximizes profit by producing up to the point where marginal cost equals price.

For most sets of data, such as those in Table 9-1, there is typically no whole number level of output at which marginal cost MC is exactly equal to marginal revenue MR, where marginal profit is zero. In that case, the firm should produce output up to the point where the MR associated with the last unit produced is greater than the MC associated with that unit.

Checkpoint 9-2

Use the data in columns (1), (6), and (8) of Table 9-1 to convince yourself that profit is maximized at 5 units of output. Use these data to lightly sketch in the rectangular areas representing total profit in Figure 9-3, frame (b), for output levels of 3, 4, and 6 units. Can you see that the rectangular area representing total profit at 5 units of output is larger than any of these?

Minimizing Loss: "Hanging in There"

If the firm's total revenue is less than its total cost for all levels of output, the best the firm can do is minimize its loss. If total revenue exceeds total variable cost, the firm will offset some of its total fixed cost. Hence, the loss that results from producing under this circumstance is less than total fixed cost, which would be the loss if the plant were to remain idle. The output and cost data from columns (1) to (7) of Table 9-1 are reproduced in columns (1) to (7) in Table 9-2. The firm is still perfectly competitive, but now it is assumed that the market price is $6 instead of $9. Therefore, the revenue data in columns (8) to (10) of Table 9-2 are different from those in columns (8) to (10) of Table 9-1.

Total Cost and Total Revenue Approach

When price is $6 per unit, the firm's TR, column (9), is less than TC, column (4), at all levels of output, column (1). Therefore, the firm cannot avoid losses,

---

[1] This is true whether the firm is perfectly competitive, a monopolist, monopolistically competitive, or an oligopolist, as we shall see in subsequent chapters.

TABLE 9-2   Output, Revenue, and Costs of a Loss-Minimizing, Perfectly Competitive Firm (Hypothetical Data)

(1)	(2)	(3)	(4)	(5)	(6)	(7)	(8)	(9)	(10)
	Total Costs		Total Costs (TC)	Average and Marginal Costs			Price and Revenues		
				Average Variable Cost	Average Total Cost	Marginal Cost	Price = Marginal Revenue	Total Revenue	Profit (+) or Loss
Quantity of Output (Q)	Total Fixed Cost (TFC)	Total Variable Cost (TVC)	TC = TVC + TFC	(AVC) AVC = TVC/Q	(ATC) ATC = TC/Q	(MC) MC = $\Delta TC/\Delta Q$	$p = MR$	$TR = p \times Q$	$\pi = TR - TC$
0	$10	$ 0	$10					$ 0	−$10
						$ 6	$6		
1	10	6	16	$6.00	$16.00			6	− 10
						4	6		
2	10	10	20	5.00	10.00			12	− 8
						4	6		
3	10	14	24	4.66	8.00			18	− 6
						5	6		
4	10	19	29	4.75	7.25			24	− 5
						7	6		
5	10	26	36	5.20	7.20			30	− 6
						11	6		
6	10	37	47	6.16	7.83			36	−11
						23	6		
7	10	60	70	8.57	10.00			42	−28

column (10). If the firm were to produce nothing, the loss at a zero output level would be $10—just equal to its *TFC*, column (2). Examination of column (10) shows that the firm can do better than this by producing. In fact, if it produces and sells 4 units of output, it will minimize its loss, to $5. Another way of seeing this is to compare columns (9) and (3) and note that *TR* exceeds *TVC* by the largest amount at 4 units of output. Hence, this output level provides the largest excess of *TR* over *TVC* to offset the *TFC* that the firm is saddled with in the shortrun.

This situation is depicted graphically in Figure 9-4, frame (a). *TC* and *TVC* are plotted from the data in columns (1), (3), and (4) of Table 9-2. They are, of course, exactly the same as the *TC* and *TVC* curves of Figure 9-3. However, the *TR* curve TR_6 is less steeply sloped than TR_9. This reflects the fact that as total output is increased, total revenue rises more slowly with output when price is $6 per unit than when price is $9 per unit. The *TC* curve now lies above the *TR* curve TR_6, reflecting the fact that total cost exceeds total revenue at all output levels. Nonetheless, the TR_6 curve lies above the *TVC* curve at output levels from 2 to 5 units, so that producing at any of these output levels will always result in some excess of *TR* over *TVC*, which offsets some part of *TFC*. The vertical distance of TR_6 above *TVC* is a maximum at 4 units of output. At this level of output the vertical distance of *TC* above TR_6 is a minimum. It equals the minimum loss of $5.

Marginal Cost and Marginal Revenue Approach

Looking at the perfectly competitive firm from the marginal cost and marginal revenue standpoint in the loss-minimizing case, we focus on columns (7) and (8)

FIGURE 9-4   Minimizing Loss in a Perfectly Competitive Firm

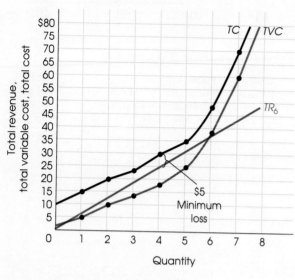

(a)

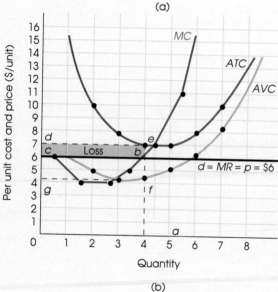

(b)

TC is greater than *TR* at all output levels, frame (a), so that the firm experiences a loss represented by the vertical distance between *TC* and TR_6 at any output level. The minimum distance between these two curves represents the minimum loss of $5, which occurs when 4 units of output are produced and sold.

The loss-minimizing level of output occurs at 4 units, where *MC* = *MR* in frame (b). The loss realized at this output level is represented by the rectangular shaded area *cbed* in frame (b).

of Table 9-2. These are the *MC* and *MR* data, respectively. For the first unit of output produced, the *MR* equals the price of $6 and just covers *MC*, which is also $6. However, if the firm increases output, it finds that *MC* will be less than *MR* up through 4 units of production. If the firm were to produce 5 units of output, the *MC* of the fifth unit would be $7, or $1 more than the *MR* of $6 received from the sale of the fifth unit. Thus, the marginal loss of the fifth unit would be $1 or (wording it another way) the marginal profit of the fifth unit would be negative $1—hence, the loss-minimizing output level we came up with by the total cost and total revenue method.

The marginal cost–marginal revenue approach is depicted graphically in Figure 9-4, frame (b). The *AVC*, *ATC*, and *MC* curves are plotted from the data in columns (5), (6), and (7) of Table 9-2. They are exactly the same as the AVC, ATC, and MC curves of Figure 9-3. However, by comparison with Figure 9-3, frame (b), the demand curve d is now at the level of the lower price of $6 per unit. The MC curve intersects the $MR = d$ curve at point b. This corresponds to the loss-minimizing output level of 4 units.

It should be noted that the loss-minimizing level of output does not necessarily correspond to the lowest level of ATC (the lowest point on the ATC curve). ATC at the loss-minimizing level of output of 4 units is $7.25 [Table 9-2, column (6)]. ATC at 5 units of output is in fact lower, $7.20. Similarly, in the profit-maximizing case, the profit-maximizing level of output is not necessarily the one associated with the lowest level of ATC. For example, suppose that price was $12. By looking at column (7) of Table 9-2, we can see that the profit-maximizing rule of producing up to the point where $p = MR = MC$ would lead the firm to produce 6 units of output. But by looking at column (6) we can see that this does not correspond to the lowest level of ATC.

Comparison of the Two Viewpoints

Total revenue can be calculated by multiplying the output of 4 units, the distance 0a in Figure 9-4, frame (b), by the price of $6, the distance $0c = ab$, to give a TR of $24. This is represented by the rectangular area 0abc in Figure 9-4, frame (b). This area corresponds to the vertical distance up to the TR_6 curve at 4 units of output in Figure 9-4, frame (a). To get total cost, multiply 4 units of output by the ATC of $7.25 [from Table 9-2, column (6)], which is the distance $0d = ae$. The resulting TC of $29 is represented by the rectangular area 0aed in Figure 9-4, frame (b). This corresponds to the vertical distance up to the TC curve at 4 units of output in Figure 9-4, frame (a). The firm's loss of $5 is represented by the shaded rectangular area cbed, which is the difference between 0aed and 0abc in Figure 9-4, frame (b). This area corresponds to the vertical distance between the TC curve and the TR_6 curve at 4 units of output in Figure 9-4, frame (a).

The firm chooses to produce rather than shut down in the loss-minimizing case because TR exceeds TVC, as represented by the vertical distance of the TR_6 curve above the TVC curve at 4 units of output in Figure 9-4, frame (a). TVC can be calculated by multiplying 4 units of output by the AVC of $4.75 [from Table 9-2, column (5)], the distance $0g = af$ in Figure 9-4, frame (b). This gives the TVC of $19, which is represented by the rectangular area 0afg. Therefore, in Figure 9-4, frame (b), the amount by which TR exceeds TVC is represented by the difference between 0abc and 0afg, which is the rectangular area gfbc. If the firm produces nothing, it incurs a loss equal to the total fixed cost. Since $TFC = TC - TVC$, this loss is represented by the difference between the rectangular areas 0aed and 0afg. This difference is the rectangular area gfed in Figure 9-4, frame (b), which is equal to $10. This area corresponds to the vertical distance between the TC and TVC curves in Figure 9-4, frame (a). Figure 9-4, frame (b), makes it clear that the loss, represented by cbed, that results when the firm produces 4 units of output, is less than the loss, represented by gfed (equal to TFC), that results if it remains idle. This is so because the amount by which total revenue TR exceeds total variable cost TVC offsets total fixed cost TFC (equal to gfed) by the amount gfbc.

When its total revenue is at least as great as total variable cost but not larger than total cost, the firm should produce up to that level of output where

Checkpoint 9-3

Use the data in columns (1), (6), and (8) of Table 9-2 (which assume that price equals $6) to convince yourself that loss is minimized at 4 units of output. Use these data to lightly sketch in the rectangular areas representing loss in Figure 9-4, frame (b), for output levels of 2, 3, and 5 units. Can you see that the rectangular area representing total loss at 4 units of output is smaller than any of these? Also, use the data from columns (1), (5), and (8) to lightly sketch in the rectangular areas representing the excess of TR over TVC in Figure 9-4, frame (b), for output levels of 2, 3, 4, and 5 units. Can you see that the rectangular area representing this excess at 4 units of output is larger than any of these?

marginal cost equals marginal revenue in order to minimize its losses.[2] Since price equals marginal revenue in the case of the perfectly competitive firm, it should produce up to the point where price equals marginal cost when the object is to minimize losses.

Finally, summing up both cases, we can state the following: As long as the firm has decided to produce, it will maximize profit or minimize loss by producing up to that output level where marginal cost equals marginal revenue. For the perfectly competitive firm this means producing up to the point where marginal cost equals price.

Shortrun Shut Down—Temporarily Closing the Doors

When the firm's total revenue is not even large enough to cover its total variable cost, it will minimize its loss by producing nothing at all. Its loss will then equal its total fixed cost. Note that in the shortrun this does not mean that the firm goes out of business, but rather that it simply remains idle. (Of course, in the longrun all factors are variable and therefore so are all costs. So if demand does not improve, the firm will go out of business in the longrun.)

The shutdown case for a perfectly competitive firm is depicted in Table 9-3 and Figure 9-5. The cost data in columns (1) to (7) are the same as those in Tables 9-1 and 9-2. All the cost curves in Figure 9-5 are the same as those in Figures 9-3 and 9-4. However, the firm can now only sell its output at a price of $4 per unit, column (8).

---

[2]Like the earlier rule for profit maximization, the loss-minimizing rule applies whether the firm is perfectly competitive, a monopolist, monopolistically competitive, or an oligopolist.

TABLE 9-3   Output, Revenue, and Costs of a Profit-Maximizing, Perfectly Competitive Firm (Hypothetical Data)

(1)	(2)	(3)	(4)	(5)	(6)	(7)	(8)	(9)	(10)
	Total Costs		Total Costs (TC) TC = TVC+ TFC	Average and Marginal Costs			Price and Revenues		
Quantity of Output (Q)	Total Fixed Cost (TFC)	Total Variable Cost (TVC)		Average Variable Cost (AVC) AVC = TVC/Q	Average Total Cost (ATC) ATC = TC/Q	Marginal Cost (MC) MC = $\Delta TC/\Delta Q$	Price = Marginal Revenue $p = MR$	Total Revenue $TR = p \times Q$	Profit (+) or Loss $\pi = TR - TC$
0	$10	$ 0	$10					$ 0	−$10
						$ 6	$4	4	−11
1	10	6	16	$6.00	$16.00				
						4	4	8	−12
2	10	10	20	5.00	10.00				
						4	4	12	−12
3	10	14	24	4.66	8.00				
						5	4	16	−13
4	10	19	29	4.75	7.25				
						7	4	20	−16
5	10	26	36	5.20	7.20				
						11	4	24	−23
6	10	37	47	6.16	7.83				
						23	4	28	−24
7	10	60	70	8.57	10.00				

FIGURE 9-5   Shutdown Case, Perfectly Competitive Firm

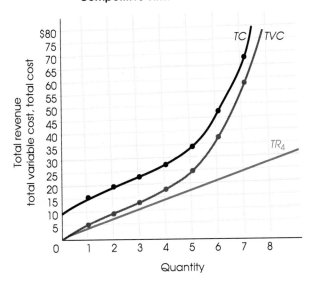

(a)

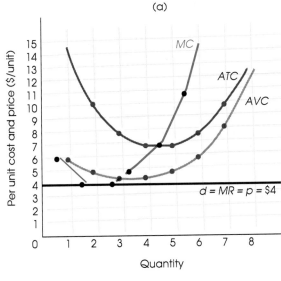

(b)

The vertical distance between the *TC* and *TVC* curves in frame (a) is the same at all output levels because it equals *TFC*. The distance by which the *TVC* curve lies above the TR_4 curve at all output levels represents the additional loss the firm incurs if it produces nothing. The minimum loss will then be the *TFC* of $10.

This situation is represented in frame (b) by the fact that the demand curve *d* is at the price level, or average revenue level, of $4, which is below the *AVC* curve at all output levels. Average revenue per unit is not sufficient to cover *AVC* per unit at any output level.

Total Cost and Total Revenue Approach

By looking at column (10), we can see that the firm's loss is clearly minimized by producing nothing. This is represented in Figure 9-5, frame (a), by the fact that the *TR* curve TR_4 [plotted from the data in columns (1) and (9)] now lies below the *TVC* curve at all levels of output above zero. The vertical distance between *TVC* and TR_4 at each output level represents the loss in addition to that due to the total fixed cost, which is represented by the vertical distance between *TC* and *TVC*. The sum of these two sources of loss at each output level is represented by the vertical distance between *TC* and TR_4, which equals the amounts shown in column (10) of Table 9-3.

Checkpoint 9-4

For 4 units of output, sketch in the rectangle in Figure 9-5, frame (b), that corresponds to the vertical distance between the TVC and TR_4 curves in Figure 9-5, frame (a). What does this rectangle represent? Also, for 4 units of output, sketch in the rectangle in Figure 9-5, frame (b), that corresponds to the vertical distance between the TC and TR_4 curves in Figure 9-5, frame (a). For 4 units of output, sketch in the rectangle that represents TFC.

Marginal Cost and Marginal Revenue Approach

The data in columns (7) and (8) of Table 9-3 tell us that MC is greater than MR at all levels of output except at 2 and 3 units of output, where $MC = MR$. However, for the first unit of output, MC is greater than MR. This means that the firm would not cover its AVC per unit, column (5), even if it did produce 2 or 3 units of output. This is so because the average revenue per unit, column (8), which is its price (also equal to MR for the perfectly competitive firm), is less than AVC, column (5), at all levels of output. This is clearly demonstrated in Figure 9-5, frame (b), by the fact that the demand curve d lies below the AVC curve at all levels of output.

Summary of the Shortrun

If price exceeds average variable cost for some range of output, the perfectly competitive firm should produce at that output level where $MC = p$ in order to maximize profit or minimize loss. If price is less than average variable cost for all levels of output, the firm will minimize loss if it produces nothing.

The Firm's Marginal Cost and Shortrun Supply Curve

We have seen that the perfectly competitive firm maximizes profit or minimizes loss by adjusting its production to that level of output where marginal cost equals price. This was shown in Figures 9-3, frame (b), 9-4, frame (b), and 9-5, frame (b). In other words, as long as price is equal to or greater than average variable cost, the perfectly competitive firm adjusts output by moving along that part of its marginal cost curve that lies above its average variable cost curve. This part of that curve conforms precisely with the definition of a supply curve. As you may recall from our earlier definition of a supply curve, a supply curve indicates the amount of a good a supplier is willing and able to offer for sale per period of time to the market at different possible prices.

The relationship between the supply curve and the marginal cost curve for a hypothetical perfectly competitive firm is shown in Figure 9-6, frame (a). At a price of p_1 the firm is just able to cover its average variable cost. It therefore produces 60 units of output, the level of output at which its MC curve intersects its MR curve MR_1. MR_1, of course, is the same as the demand curve d_1 facing the firm at the price level p_1. If price were to rise to p_2, the firm would increase its production to 73 units, the point at which its MC curve intersects $MR_2 = d_2$. And if price were to rise to p_3, MC would equal MR at the point where the MC curve intersects $MR_3 = d_3$. The firm would then produce 92 units of output. *That rising range of the perfectly competitive firm's marginal cost curve that lies above its average variable cost curve is its* **shortrun supply curve.**

Shifting the Firm's Shortrun Supply Curve

In our explanation of comparative statics in Chapters 5 and 6 we discussed the factors that could cause a market supply curve to shift. The market supply will

FIGURE 9-6   Shortrun Equilibrium for a Perfectly Competitive Firm and Industry

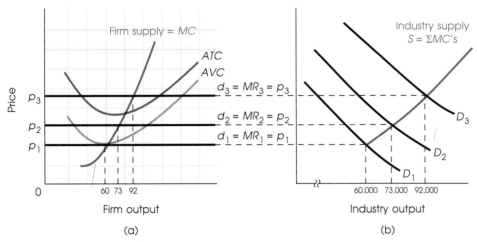

(a)   (b)

The perfectly competitive firm's supply curve is that part of its MC curve that lies above its AVC curve, as shown in frame (a). The industry supply curve S shown in frame (b) is obtained by summing the quantity of output that each firm will produce at each price in frame (a).

The intersection of the industry demand curve and the supply curve in frame (b) determines the equilibrium market price and output level. Since each firm supplies a fraction equal to 1/1,000 of this output, the firm cannot significantly affect market price. The demand curve facing the firm is therefore horizontal at the market-determined price.

shift to the right if new firms enter the market, and it will shift to the left if firms leave the industry. Most of our analysis of the difference between shortrun equilibrium and longrun equilibrium later in the chapter will concentrate on whether firms are entering or exiting the industry. There is another reason for the market supply curve to shift left or right. If each individual firm is willing and able to profit maximize at a higher level of output, then each individual supply curve has shifted to the right and the market supply curve will shift to the right.

Assume the marginal costs facing a firm decrease—that is, the marginal cost curve shifts down at each output level. The firm, faced with these reduced marginal costs, will maximize profit at a higher level of output for any given price. This will shift the supply curve for the individual firm to the right and will shift the market supply curve to the right as well. The factors that could cause a decrease in the marginal cost of producing a given unit of output are a decrease in the price per unit of the variable factor or an increase in the marginal product of the variable factor. If labour were a variable factor of production for a given firm, then a decrease in wages or an increase in the marginal product of labour would cause the marginal cost curve to shift down and would shift the firm's supply curve to the right. It is important to notice that the cost of the fixed factor and other fixed costs do not affect marginal cost. Changes to the price of the fixed factor or other periodic changes in other fixed costs do not affect the shortrun supply curve of the firm or the market supply curve. Conversely, a shift to the left in the position of the firm's shortrun supply curve and the shortrun market supply curve can be caused by an increase in marginal cost.

This in turn can result from an increase in the price per unit of the variable factor or a decrease in the marginal product of the variable factor.

The Industry Supply Curve

Suppose that there are 1,000 firms like that in Figure 9-6, frame (a), which together make up the perfectly competitive industry. The industry supply curve S is the sum of all the individual firms' supply curves. These supply curves are the same as their marginal cost curves (Σ may be read "sum of"), as shown in Figure 9-6, frame (b). For example, in Figure 9-6, frame (a), at a price of p_1 each individual firm supplies 60 units of output. Therefore, the total amount supplied by 1,000 such firms is 60,000 units at a price of p_1, as shown in frame (b). At a price of p_2, each individual firm supplies 73 units of output, frame (a). The total amount supplied by the industry is 1,000 times this amount or 73,000 units, frame (b). Finally, if price were p_3, each individual firm would supply 92 units, frame (a), and the total industry supply would be 92,000 units, frame (b). At each price level the industry supply curve is constructed by summing the amounts each individual firm will supply, as indicated by the firm's marginal cost curve above its AVC curve.

At a price below p_1, firms are not able to cover their average variable costs and therefore will produce nothing. Hence, the industry will supply nothing at a price below p_1, as indicated by the fact that the industry supply curve in Figure 9-6, frame (b), does not extend below this level.

Firm and Industry Equilibrium

Checkpoint 9-5

Suppose that there is a rise in the cost of raw materials used by the firms in the industry depicted in Figure 9-6. How would this affect the firm's cost curves in frame (a)? How would it affect the industry supply curve in frame (b)? If the industry demand curve were at D_1, what would happen to firm and industry output? If the demand curve were D_3, what would happen to price? What would happen to firm and industry output?

We have seen in earlier chapters how market supply and demand interact to determine equilibrium price and quantity for an industry. Earlier in this chapter, when looking at Figure 9-1, we saw that in a perfectly competitive industry, the perfectly competitive firm contributes such a small fraction of total industry supply that it cannot affect the market price. The competitive demand curve facing the firm is therefore perfectly elastic (horizontal). Putting these considerations together with the perfectly competitive firm's cost curves and the industry supply curve, we can examine the relationship between the competitive industry equilibrium and the competitive firm equilibrium in the shortrun.

This relationship can be seen by examining the relationship between frames (a) and (b) of Figure 9-6. When the market demand for the industry's output is given by the market demand curve D_1 in frame (b), its intersection with the industry supply curve S determines the equilibrium price level p_1 and industry output of 60,000 units. A typical firm, frame (a), in the industry therefore faces the horizontal demand curve d_1 at the price level p_1 and supplies 60 units of output. These 60 units are equal to 1/1,000 of the industry total. Since the firm is just covering its AVC at this price (the demand curve d_1 is tangent to the AVC curve at its lowest point), if the industry demand curve were to shift to a position lower than D_1, firms would decide to produce nothing at all. On the other hand, if the industry demand curve shifted to D_2 in frame (b), the intersection of industry supply and industry demand would determine a price of p_2, and the industry would supply 73,000 units of output. The typical firm, frame (a), would now face a demand curve d_2. It still would not be able to cover its total costs because d_2 lies below the ATC curve. But it would minimize losses by producing to the point where marginal cost equals marginal revenue. This point is indicated by the intersection of the firm's MC curve with its $d_2 = MR_2 = p_2$ curve at 73 units of output. Hence, in the shortrun, when the industry demand curve is at positions such as D_1 or D_2, firms in the industry are operating at a loss.

What happens if industry demand shifts outward to a position such as D_3 in frame (b)? Equilibrium price is now p_3, and industry output is now 92,000 units. The typical demand curve facing the firm in frame (a) would now be shifted up to the position d_3. To equate marginal cost and marginal revenue, the typical firm would increase output to 92 units. Since p_3 is above the ATC curve at this point, the firm would be maximizing profit. Hence, with industry demand at D_3, firms in the industry are now realizing profits instead of losses.

The Competitive Firm and Industry in the Longrun

In the longrun all factors of production are variable. In perfect competition this means that it is possible for new firms to enter the industry and for existing firms to leave the industry or go out of business. What is the nature of this adjustment process, and how does it determine the longrun industry supply curve?

Longrun Adjustment

We will first examine the longrun adjustment process by considering what happens when there is an increase in industry demand. We will then look at what happens when there is a decrease in demand. Remember that in the longrun the firm can vary the amounts of all of its factors of production, but we assume that the prices of the factors of production do not change and that technology is held constant.

Demand Increases: Excess Profit Induces Firms to Enter Industry

Suppose initially that the demand and supply curves for the perfectly competitive industry are in the positions D_1 and S_1 as shown in Figure 9-7, frame (b). Their intersection determines the equilibrium price p_1 and equilibrium industry output of 80,000 units. Suppose that there are initially 1,000 firms in the industry, each like that shown in Figure 9-7, frame (a). The demand curve facing the firm is d_1 at the price level p_1, which of course is also its marginal revenue MR_1. MC equals MR_1 at the point where the MC curve intersects the demand curve d_1. The desire to maximize profit will therefore lead each firm to produce 80 units of output. Notice that initially each firm is just earning a normal profit. This is so because at a price of p_1, each is just covering its average total cost, as represented by the tangency of its ATC curve with the demand curve d_1 in Figure 9-7, frame (a). (Remember that ATC includes the opportunity cost of using the firm's own resources or viewed another way it includes a normal profit.)

FIGURE 9-7   Longrun Adjustment of a Perfectly Competitive Firm and Industry to an Increase in Demand

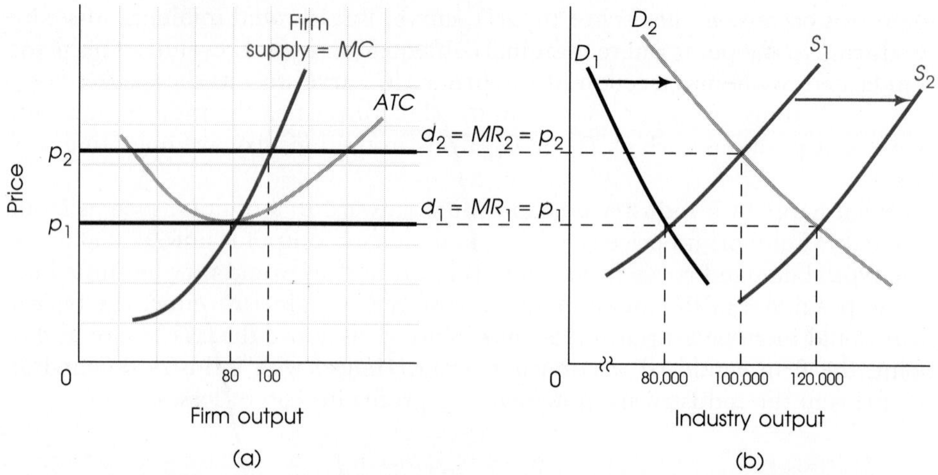

The initial equilibrium position of the perfectly competitive industry is determined by the intersection of the industry demand curve D_1 and the shortrun supply curve S_1 in frame (b). Initially, each firm is just earning a normal profit because at price p_1, each is just covering its average total cost in frame (a).

When the industry demand curve, frame (b), shifts rightward to D_2, price rises initially from p_1 to p_2. At this point, firms are making a profit in excess of normal profit, frame (a). This attracts other firms into the industry, causing the industry supply curve to shift rightward, frame (b).

When enough firms have entered so that the shortrun industry supply curve has shifted to S_2, price will return to p_1. A larger number of firms will now be in the industry in the new equilibrium, each earning a normal profit and facing a demand curve d_1 as in the original equilibrium position in frame (a). Note that the demand curve facing each firm is designated d_1, but it is derived from the intersection of the industry demand curve D_2 and industry supply curve S_2.

Now suppose that there is an increase in industry demand as represented by the rightward shift in the industry demand curve from D_1 to D_2 as shown in Figure 9-7, frame (b). The supply curve S_1 is the shortrun industry supply curve. It is therefore the sum of the 1,000 marginal cost curves of each firm (above AVC), such as MC in Figure 9-7, frame (a). Initially, price rises to p_2 and industry output to 100,000 [the intersection of D_2 and S_1 in frame (b)] because each firm in the industry expands output to 100 units, as determined by the intersection of its MC curve and its now higher demand curve d_2 [frame (a)].

However, at the now higher price of p_2, each firm will be earning a profit per unit in excess of the normal profit. This excess is represented by the vertical distance between the demand curve d_2 and the ATC curve at 100 units of output. It will serve as a signal to other resource suppliers in the rest of the economy that above-normal profits can be earned by starting new firms and entering this industry. As new firms enter the industry, the total number of firms like that in Figure 9-7, frame (a), increases. This increase causes the shortrun industry supply curve in frame (b) to shift rightward.

New firms will continue to enter the industry as long as excess profits exist, since in the longrun all factors of production are variable. As the shortrun supply curve shifts rightward, its intersection with D_2 in frame (b) will occur at lower and lower prices until it has reached the position S_2. At this point, price will have fallen back to the initial level p_1, and each demand curve facing the firm will once again be in the position d_1. Each firm will once again produce and sell 80 units of output, as shown in frame (a). Each firm will again just be earning a normal profit. However, there will now be 1,500 firms in the industry ($\frac{120,000}{80} = 1,500$) producing and selling a total of 120,000 units of output at the price p_1 in frame (b).

Demand Decreases: Losses Induce Firms to Exit

Suppose that we start from the same initial equilibrium we did in Figure 9-7, only now, in Figure 9-8, we will assume that industry demand falls. This is represented by the leftward shift of the industry demand curve from D_1 to D_3, as shown in Figure 9-8, frame (b). The 1,000 firms in the industry each see this decline in demand as a fall in their demand curves from d_1 to d_3 in Figure 9-8, frame (a). The typical firm reduces output by moving down its marginal cost curve to reduce output from 80 units to 60 units. That is, it reduces output until marginal cost again equals marginal revenue at the point where the firm's MC curve intersects its demand curve $d_3 = MR_3 = p_3$. This lower level of output for each individual firm is reflected at the industry level by a fall in industry output from 80,000 to 60,000 units along the industry supply curve S_1, shown in frame (b). Remember that in the longrun all factors are

---

FIGURE 9-8 Longrun Adjustment of a Perfectly Competitive Firm and Industry to a Decrease in Demand

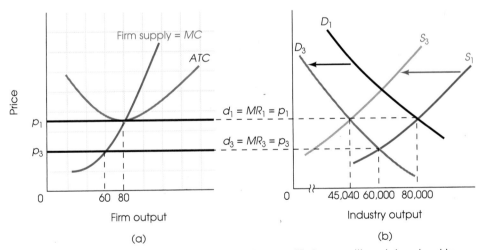

The perfectly competitive industry is initially in the equilibrium position determined by the intersection of the industry demand curve D_1 and the shortrun industry supply curve S_1 in frame (b). Initially, each firm is just earning a normal profit at price p_1 in frame (a).
When the industry demand curve shifts leftward to D_3, frame (b), price initially falls from p_1 to p_3. At this point, frame (a), firms are incurring losses and some begin to go out of business, causing the shortrun industry supply curve, frame (b), to shift leftward. When enough firms have left so that the shortrun industry supply curve has shifted to S_3, price will return to p_1. A smaller number of firms will now be in the industry in the new equilibrium, each again earning a normal profit and facing a demand curve D_1 as in the original equilibrium position, frame (a).

variable and therefore so are all costs. Unlike the shortrun situation, if price is not high enough to cover average total cost, the firm will go out of business.

Since p_3 lies below the ATC curve in Figure 9-8, frame (a), the typical firm is now operating at a loss. Firms will therefore begin to leave the industry because the resources they use no longer earn their opportunity cost. These resources will move to other lines of activity in the economy where they can earn their opportunity cost.

As firms leave the industry, the shortrun industry supply curve will shift leftward until it reaches the position S_3. Here, price once again is p_1 at the intersection of D_3, Figure 9-8, frame (b), and industry output is 45,040 units. The typical firm in the industry will once again face a demand curve d_1. Marginal cost will equal marginal revenue at the point where the MC curve intersects the $d_1 = MR_1 = p_1$ curve at an output level of 80 units [frame (a)]. In the new equilibrium, firms are once again just covering their average total cost, including their opportunity cost. They are again earning a normal profit. There will now be 563 firms in the industry ($\frac{45,040}{80} = 563$) as compared to 1,000 before the fall in demand. Losses have caused 437 firms to go out of business in this industry.

Let us summarize these results. When a perfectly competitive industry is in longrun equilibrium, each firm is operating at the lowest point on its ATC curve. This is the point of tangency with its horizontal demand curve. When the perfectly competitive firm is in longrun equilibrium, price equals marginal cost equals marginal revenue equals average total cost at its minimum. Each firm is just earning a normal profit. That is, economic profit is zero in longrun equilibrium. An increase in demand causes a rise in price, which leads to economic profits (above-normal profits). This attracts new firms into the industry, causing the shortrun industry supply curve to shift rightward until price falls back to the level of minimum average total cost. Once again, each firm operates at the minimum point of its average total cost curve, just earning a normal profit. A decrease in demand causes a fall in price and leads to losses. Firms therefore leave the industry, causing the shortrun supply curve to shift leftward until price rises back to the level of minimum average total cost for the remaining firms in the industry. Each again is just earning a normal profit.

Longrun Industry Supply Curve

The supply curves S_1, S_2, and S_3 in Figures 9-7 and 9-8 are *shortrun* industry supply curves. Along any one of them, the number of firms in the industry is assumed constant, or fixed. For S_1 in Figures 9-7, frame (b), and 9-8, frame (b), there are 1,000 firms, for S_2 in Figure 9-7, frame (b), there are 1,500 firms, and for S_3 in Figure 9-8, frame (b), there are 563. Since we have been considering the longrun adjustment, what is the **longrun industry supply curve** for a perfectly competitive industry? To answer this question, we must consider three distinct situations that may arise; one in which costs are constant, one in which costs are increasing, and one in which costs are decreasing.

The Constant-Cost Case

This is the case we have described in Figures 9-7 and 9-8. Throughout our analysis of the longrun adjustment process, we assumed that the prices of all the factors of production purchased by the firms in the industry remained unchanged, no matter what level of output was produced by the industry. This means that when new firms enter the industry or existing ones leave it, the *ATC* and *MC* curves of all firms in the industry remain at the same level, which is shown in Figures 9-7, frame (a), and 9-8, frame (a).

We observed three different possible positions of the industry demand curve, D_1, D_2, and D_3 in Figures 9-7, frame (b), and 9-8, frame (b), each of which had an associated longrun industry equilibrium. Although the number of firms in the industry associated with each longrun equilibrium varied, the longrun equilibrium position of each firm in the industry was always the same—namely, each produced 80 units of output at the lowest point on its *ATC* curve where its *MC* curve intersected its demand curve $d_1 = MR_1$ at the price level p_1 [Figures 9-7, frame (a), and 9-8, frame (a)].

Suppose that we considered all other possible positions of the industry demand curve *D*. In each case, after all adjustments are completed in the longrun, there would be just enough firms in the industry so that total industry supply would equal industry demand at the price p_1. Therefore, the longrun industry supply curve for the perfectly competitive industry in the constant-cost case is just the horizontal line at the equilibrium price level p_1, as shown in Figure 9-9, frame (a). If you like, you may think of it as consisting of all the points formed by the intersections of all possible industry demand curves with the associated

FIGURE 9-9 Longrun Supply Curves for a Perfectly Competitive Industry—Constant-, Increasing-, and Decreasing-Cost Cases

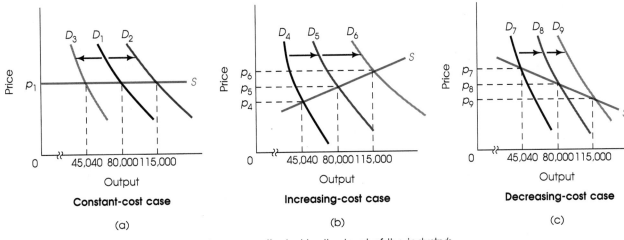

When the prices of inputs to the industry are unaffected by the level of the industry's production, the per unit costs of production are the same at all levels of industry output. Therefore, the longrun industry supply curve is perfectly elastic (horizontal) at the same longrun equilibrium price level no matter what the level of demand, as shown in frame (a).

When the prices of inputs to the industry rise with increases in the level of the industry's production, the per unit costs of production of the firms in the industry rise. Therefore, the longrun industry supply curve is upward sloping in the increasing-cost case as shown in frame (b).

When the prices of inputs to the industry fall with increases in the level of the industry's production, the per unit costs of production of the firms in the industry fall. Therefore, the longrun industry supply curve is downward sloping in the decreasing-cost case as shown in frame (c).

POLICY PERSPECTIVE

Is Perfect Competition an Ideal?—The Case For and the Case Against

The concept of perfect competition has often been held up as an ideal or standard for judging other kinds of industry or market structures. Indeed, it might be said that the principal objective of antitrust policy (to be discussed in Chapter 13) is to see to it that the economy's various industries perform to the greatest possible extent according to standards exhibited by perfect competition. However, while perfect competition has many desirable economic attributes, it has shortcomings as well. We should sharpen our perspective by taking a look at both sides of the picture.

THE CASE FOR PERFECT COMPETITION

The economic case for perfect competition is largely based on the contention that it is the most efficient form of market structure for allocating resources to satisfy consumer wants. At another level, the concept of perfect competition has an appeal that is emphatically more political than economic. Like most issues in economics, these two types of appeal cannot, of course, be entirely separated. But for the purpose of understanding the issues here, we'll consider these two aspects separately.

Perfect Competition as an Effective Allocator of Resources

What does it mean to say that perfect competition is the most efficient way for allocating resources to maximize consumer satisfaction? There are two basic points underlying this argument.

First, when the perfectly competitive industry is in longrun equilibrium, competition forces firms to use a technology that yields the lowest possible ATC curves and to operate at the lowest point on their longrun ATC curves. Because of competition between sellers consumers pay a price equal to this minimum longrun average total cost ATC. This leads economists to say that perfect competition is *production efficient*.

This follows because the existence of many firms producing an identical product means that if any firm tries to charge a higher price, consumers will simply buy from its competitors, so the firm trying to charge more than the going rate will have zero sales. Therefore, each firm is forced by competition to produce at the lowest point on its ATC curve if it wants to stay in business. Hence, the industry produces the good at the lowest possible per unit cost and distributes it to consumers at a price that just covers this cost. Because each firm must use the least-cost technology to survive, there is no way to improve on this situation given the prevailing state of technical know-how. Second, in a perfectly competitive equilibrium (shortrun or longrun), price equals marginal cost, and hence for the last unit of a good purchased, consumers pay a price that just covers the extra cost of producing it.

Given that the industry demand curve is downward sloping, let's suppose that production is not pushed to the point where marginal cost equals price for good A. Then consumers are willing to pay a price

for additional units of A that is greater than the cost of producing these units. When the marginal cost of using society's resources to make an additional unit is just equal to the marginal benefit to society from producing that unit (the marginal benefit will equal the price of the product if the market is operating correctly), then society is said to be *allocatively efficient*. The fact that consumers are willing to pay a price greater than this opportunity cost for the use of these resources in the production of A suggests that society values additional units of A more highly than the alternative goods that these resources could produce. Hence, if production of A is not pushed to the point where marginal cost equals the price of A, there will be an underallocation of resources to the production of A.

On the other hand, let's suppose that the production of A were to be pushed beyond the point where marginal cost equals price. Because marginal cost rises as output increases, the price received for the additional units will be less than their marginal cost. This would indicate that the value society places on these additional units is less than the opportunity cost of the resources needed to produce them. Hence, there will be an overallocation of resources to the production of good A.

What are the implications for consumer satisfaction? When all industries in an economy are in a perfectly competitive equilibrium, each will produce just that quan-

continued on next page

tity of its product so that price will equal marginal cost. In a perfectly competitive equilibrium, there will be no misallocation of resources between the production of different goods, and consumer satisfaction will be as large as possible.

Finally, because there is ease of entry to and exit of firms from perfectly competitive industries, a perfectly competitive economy will quickly reallocate resources to meet changing consumer preferences or supply conditions. This will serve to preserve allocative efficiency over time.

The Political Appeal of Perfect Competition

The notion of an economy characterized by perfectly competitive markets has a special appeal for those who view concentration of power in a few hands as dangerous. Anyone who believes that power groups pose a potential threat to individual rights and personal freedom finds much to recommend the perfectly competitive world.

Markets composed of many buyers and sellers, not one of which is large enough to have a significant impact on price and output, lead to about as much diffusion of power as one could imagine. The forces of keen competition that characterize such markets put a premium on performance. For example, firms that discriminate among workers on grounds other than their ability to perform a job will find themselves at a competitive disadvantage vis-à-vis firms who hire workers solely on the basis of ability. They will soon be out of business.

CRITICISMS OF PERFECT COMPETITION

Perfect competition is not without its critics. The most common criticisms levied against it are that (1) it provides little incentive for innovation, (2) it does not capture spillover costs and benefits, (3) it leads to a lack of product variety, and (4) the

accompanying distribution of income may be "inequitable." All of these charges raise doubts about whether perfect competition is the best form of market organization for maximizing consumer satisfaction.

Let's look at these criticisms individually.

Perfect Competition Provides Little Incentive for Innovation

In a perfectly competitive world, information about technology is readily available to all. In an agricultural market, for example, it would be hard for a farmer to keep a newly developed production technique a secret from competitors for long. As a result, a firm cannot expect to gain much competitive advantage over other firms by developing new technology. The higher than normal profits that the firm might realize would be short-lived as other firms would quickly adopt the new technique and once again compete on an equal footing. Therefore, with little prospect of reaping much gain from technological innovation, there is little incentive for a perfectly competitive firm to devote much effort to such activity.

Since technological innovation is considered essential to the dynamics of economic growth (measured as the rate of increase of output per capita), it is often argued that a perfectly competitive world is lacking in this respect.

Perfect Competition Fails to Capture Spillover Costs and Benefits

We discussed spillover costs and benefits in Chapter 7 (you may need to go back and review these concepts at this point). Clearly, when spillover costs exist, such as water and air pollution, the firm's marginal cost curve does not include them. Producing to the point where marginal cost equals price will therefore mean producing some goods that, in fact, cost

more than the value society places on them. In this case, it can no longer be argued that the existence of perfectly competitive markets leads to the maximization of consumer satisfaction. The same argument holds when there are spillover benefits such as those associated with keeping one's automobile in safe working condition or those associated with the purchase of flu shots.

Perfect Competition Leads to a Lack of Product Variety

This criticism of perfect competition alleges that because a perfectly competitive firm produces a product indistinguishable from that of the other firms in the industry, there may be a dull sameness about a perfectly competitive world. While this may be true, economists are generally not in favour of solving this problem through attempts to create distinctions between the products of different firms when in fact no real difference exists. For example, there is no difference between beet sugar and cane sugar despite advertising to the contrary. Such advertising uses resources that could be used in other activities, with the result that the products advertised cost the consumer more than necessary. Furthermore, the important aspect of homogeneity is that the consumers view the products of different firms as being the same. This presents some practical difficulties for economists because it does not imply that the product is, from a technical point of view, the same product. If consumers view pizza and hamburgers as identical "junk foods" then all restaurants serving both may for all practical purposes be in the same perfectly competitive market. To further complicate things, if the consumers then make a distinction

continued on next page

between speed and having table service, they may view take-out pizza as the same as a drive-in hamburger but they may not view a restaurant that has table service and serves hamburgers as being in the same market as a drive-in burger joint or take-out pizza place! Finally, the sameness of the product is itself determined by the consumers' perceptions and thus may not present any problem of lack of choice, if the consumers' place a premium on difference (for example, they prefer hand-made personalized coffee cups to manufactured thermo-injected plastic coffee holding vessels), then they will regard these items as being substitutes but

no longer in the same homogeneous market.

The Distribution of Income Associated with Perfect Competition May Be Inequitable

A perfectly competitive world provides for an efficient allocation of resources, *given* the existing distribution of wealth or income among members of the economy. If that distribution were different, the allocation of resources provided by the perfectly competitive markets would be different as well, though still efficient by the criterion that price would equal marginal cost in each and every market. However,

society's opinions about an equitable distribution of income are a separate consideration from that of the efficient allocation of resources. The "fairness" of a particular income distribution is a normative issue—disputes over this cannot be settled by an appeal to facts alone.

For Discussion

● Critics claim that perfect competition is not good for economic growth because it doesn't offer enough incentive for innovation. Does the example provided by the agricultural sector of our economy (discussed in Chapter 7) tend to support or refute this claim? Why?

shortrun industry supply curves, such as the intersections of D_1 and S_1, D_2 and S_2, and D_3 and S_3 in Figures 9-7, frame (b), and 9-8, frame (b).

> ### Checkpoint 9-6
>
> What does the notion of opportunity cost have to do with longrun equilibrium in a perfectly competitive industry? What does it mean when we say that firms are just earning a normal profit in longrun competitive equilibrium?

The Increasing-Cost Case

If the resources used by the competitive industry constitute a large enough portion of the total supply of such resources, their prices may rise as the competitive industry purchases more of them. This is particularly true if the supply of these resources is not easily increased. Conversely, when the competitive industry reduces its level of production, and therefore buys fewer of these resources, their prices may fall. For each individual firm in the industry, such as that in Figure 9-8, frame (a), a rise in the prices of its inputs, and hence its unit costs, will be reflected in an upward shift in its ATC and MC curves. Conversely, a decline in input prices, and hence units costs, will be reflected in a downward shift in the ATC and MC curves.

Suppose that we were to consider successively higher levels of industry demand, for example, as represented by the industry demand curve shifting rightward to positions such as D_4, D_5, and D_6 in Figure 9-9, frame (b). When the demand curve shifts from D_4 to D_5, new firms will enter the industry in response to the above-normal profits that are initially realized. As new firms enter, these economic profits will now be eliminated in two ways. First, as we have already seen, economic profits will be reduced by the fall in price that takes place during the adjustment process because of the expanding level of industry output. Second, economic profits will be further reduced by the upward shift of the typical firm's ATC and MC curves, which results from the rise in the price of inputs as industry expansion increases the demand for them. Once the economic profits have been eliminated by these two effects, the industry will be in a new longrun equilibrium position, producing a larger output with more firms. Each will again be operating at the minimum point on its *ATC* curve, but now the typical firm's *ATC* curve will be higher than before. Hence, the larger longrun equilibrium level of industry output is supplied at a higher price.

The longrun perfectly competitive industry supply curve is upward sloping in the increasing cost case, as shown in Figure 9-9, frame (b). As a result, the longrun equilibrium price associated with the successively larger levels of demand represented by D_4, D_5, and D_6 is successively higher (p_4, p_5, and p_6, respectively) at output levels of 45,040, 80,000, and 115,000 units.

The Decreasing-Cost Case

It is also possible as a perfectly competitive industry increases output that the prices it pays for inputs, and hence its per unit costs of production, may decline. This could occur, for example, if some of the industries supplying the inputs to the perfectly competitive industry experienced economies of scale as they produced larger quantities of the inputs. The resulting lower costs of producing these inputs might then be passed along to the perfectly competitive industry in the form of lower input prices. Then the longrun supply curve of the perfectly competitive industry would be downward sloping, as shown in Figure 9-9, frame (c). For the successively larger demands D_7, D_8, and D_9, the longrun equilibrium prices are the successively lower p_7, p_8, and p_9.

Summary

1. To understand how firms behave in pursuit of profits it is necessary to classify them. Economists classify firms into four market structures based on the number and relative size of the firms in the industry, the similarity of the products produced by different firms, the ability of an individual firm to influence the price of its product by varying output, and the ease of entry into the industry by potential competitors.

2. A perfectly competitive industry is made up of many small firms producing a homogeneous product. Because no firm is large enough to affect price, each faces a perfectly elastic (horizontal) demand curve, so the individual firms are price takers. Barriers to the entry and exit of firms to and from the industry are insignificant.

3. The market demand will typically be downward sloping to the right, but because the individual firm supplies such an insignificant portion of the market it cannot influence the price of its own product. Thus the firm faces a perfectly horizontal (perfectly elastic) demand curve.

4. The total revenue *TR* for a perfect competitor is equal to the market price times the quantity the firm sells, $p \times q$. Since p is constant and determined by the market, the total revenue curve is an upward-sloping straight line with a slope equal to the market price.

5. Marginal revenue, *MR*, is the change in total revenue from the sale of one more unit. In perfect competition, because the price remains constant as the firm increases its output, the marginal revenue equals the market price for all levels of output.

6. In the shortrun, the perfectly competitive firm must decide whether or not to produce, and if it does decide to produce, it must then decide how much to produce. This decision process may be viewed from the standpoint of comparing total revenue and total cost or from that of comparing marginal revenue and marginal cost. The firm will produce as long as total revenue exceeds total variable cost or, equivalently, as long as price per unit exceeds average variable cost.

7. If the firm decides to produce, it will maximize profits by producing that quantity of output at which total revenue exceeds total cost by the greatest amount. If total cost exceeds total revenue but total revenue exceeds total variable cost, the firm will minimize losses by producing that output level where total revenue exceeds total variable cost by the maximum amount.

8. From the marginal cost–marginal revenue point of view, the firm will be able to maximize profit, or minimize loss, by producing to the point where marginal cost equals marginal revenue. At this output level the marginal profit is zero on the next unit sold, so total profit is maximized. Following this rule, the firm will maximize profit whenever price exceeds average total cost, or minimize loss whenever price is less than average total cost but greater than average variable cost. When price is less than average variable cost, the firm will shut down.

9. The rising segment of the perfectly competitive firm's marginal cost curve that lies above the average variable cost curve is the firm's shortrun supply curve. Summing the supply curves of all firms gives the shortrun industry supply curve.

10. In longrun equilibrium, a perfectly competitive firm receives a price just equal to the lowest point on its *ATC* curve, so that it just earns a normal profit (economic profit is zero). The existence of greater than normal profit (an economic profit) would attract new firms into the industry, increasing industry supply until competition has forced price to the minimum average total cost level. Conversely, economic losses would lead firms to leave the industry, decreasing industry supply until price has risen to the minimum average total cost level. This longrun adjustment process implies that the longrun industry supply curve is horizontal in the constant-cost case, upward sloping in the increasing-cost case, and downward sloping in the decreasing-cost case.

11. It may be argued that an economy consisting entirely of perfectly competitive markets leads to a maximization of consumer satisfaction. This follows because in longrun equilibrium, competition forces firms to produce with the least-cost technology available, at the lowest possible average per unit cost, and sell to consumers at a price that just covers this cost. In addition, price equals marginal cost, so consumers pay a price that just covers the cost of the last unit of each kind of good produced. Because of the ease of entry and exit of firms to and from industries, a perfectly competitive economy will quickly reallocate resources to meet changing consumer preferences or reflect changing supply conditions. Hence, resources are always efficiently allocated in accordance with consumers' tastes.

12. There are several reservations about whether perfect competition will ensure maximum consumer satisfaction. It is felt that perfect competition provides little incentive for technological innovation, spillover costs and benefits are not captured, there is a lack of product variety, and income distribution may not be "equitable."

Key Terms and Concepts

average revenue	marginal revenue	profit maximizing
break-even point	market structure	shortrun shut down
longrun supply	perfect competition	total revenue
marginal profit	price taker	

Questions and Problems

1. Rank the following industries according to how closely they approximate a perfectly competitive industry, that is, judge them according to the four characteristics of a perfectly competitive industry: automobile manufacturing, electric utilities, barbering, dry cleaning, residential construction, wallpapering, logging, airlines, fruit growing, in-shore fishing, video rental stores, and television set manufacturing.

2. The following industries have some characteristics of a perfectly competitive industry but lack others. In each case, determine what perfectly competitive characteristics they have and what ones they seem to be lacking: petroleum refining, shoeshining, steel production, hairdressing, medical care, sewage disposal, portrait painting, and cattle ranching.

3. Explain how an individual firm can face a perfectly elastic demand for its product when the market demand for that product is inelastic. Can you think of any markets in which the demand at the market level is inelastic and the demand facing the individual firm is almost horizontal?

4. Explain why the firm will profit-maximize or loss-minimize at the output level where its marginal profit is zero.

5. In a perfectly competitive industry, why can the price be below average total cost in the shortrun but not in the longrun?

6. Suppose that a perfectly competitive industry is in shortrun equilibrium. Suppose that the industry demand curve shifts rightward. Thinking in terms of Figure 9-1, what difference does the elasticity of the industry demand curve make to the individual firm?

7. Suppose that the costs of the individual firm in a perfectly competitive industry are those given in columns (1) to (7) of Table 9-1. Suppose that you are told that the industry is in shortrun equilibrium, with total industry production and sales equal to 2,200 units at a price of $8 per unit.
    a. How many firms are there in the industry?
    b. Are they making a profit or are they operating at a loss? What is the amount of the profit or loss per unit?
    c. How will each firm adjust if price falls to $4.60? Why?
    d. Given your answer to part (a), derive the points on the industry supply curve corresponding to each of the following prices: $6, $8, $12, and $23.

8. Will the shortrun equilibrium position stipulated for the firm in Table 9-2 be consistent with a longrun equilibrium position for the perfectly competitive industry made up of such firms? Why or why not?

9. Consider the shortrun equilibrium position of the firm in Table 9-3.
    a. Describe the process of longrun adjustment that this implies for the perfectly competitive industry made up of such firms initially in such positions.
    b. What would the longrun equilibrium price be in this industry?
    c. Suppose that the industry demand curve is downward sloping, starting from a price level of $6.80 on the vertical axis. Would this affect your answer to part (b)? What would be the longrun equilibrium level of output for the industry, given this industry demand curve?

10. One of the concerns often expressed about perfect competition is that it may not provide enough incentive for technological innovation, which is a key to economic growth, measured as growth in income per capita. But we know that in longrun equilibrium perfectly competitive firms are earning a normal profit. How can it be that there is not "enough incentive for technological innovation"?

Chapter 10

Monopoly

We may think of **monopoly** as a form of market structure in which the entire market for a good or service is supplied by a single seller, or firm. This single supplier, called a *monopolist*, is not subject to competition from rival firms. If we classify market structures according to the degree to which individual firms are subject to vigorous competition from rival firms, monopoly would be at the very opposite end of the spectrum from perfect competition.

Because it is generally felt that monopoly so completely lacks the desirable attributes of perfect competition, discussed in the previous chapter, it has become public policy in most countries to eliminate or curb it where possible, or to regulate it where its existence is unavoidable. The Director of Investigations and Research, who is appointed by the Governor General under the provisions of *The Competition Act* of 1986, has the authority to investigate whether a monopoly exists in a particular market. If the director feels that an individual or firm has conspired or agreed "to lessen unduly the facilities for transporting, producing, manufacturing, supplying, storing, or dealing in any product," for the purposes of unreasonably increasing the price of a product or for the purpose of preventing competition, he (or she) can undertake an investigation of the situation. If the investigation produces sufficient evidence of contravention of the *Competition Act* the government may then charge the firm or individual concerned. It is interesting to note that in 1986, changes in the law provided the courts with the ability to convict on circumstantial evidence, and the maximum penalties for being found guilty of indictable offenses under the Act were raised to five years in jail and a maximum fine of ten million dollars. Until the changes of 1986, Canadian law had required the government to meet the same high standards for establishing guilt beyond a reasonable doubt that it would have to meet in laying a charge of murder against an individual. The result was that under the former law there were few successful prosecutions for conspiring to restrict competition in Canada. By contrast, in the United States (although the government can and does charge firms and individuals with offenses under criminal law for restricting competition) much of the law concerning monopoly activities has been under civil law, which has much less strict rules of evidence.

An unregulated industry in which the entire output is controlled by a single firm is almost as rare in the real world as perfect competition. This illustrates how the concept of monopoly, like that of perfect competition, is often used as a benchmark against which an actual, real-world market may be compared. The more closely an actual market approximates a monopoly market structure, the greater is the cause for concern by either the Federal or Provincial Departments of Consumer and Corporate Affairs.

There are many industries, called *oligopolies*, where a few dominant firms are in a position to exert monopoly-type power to varying degrees. Examples that come to mind are the automobile industry dominated by GM, Ford, Chrysler, Honda, and Toyota; the banking industry dominated by five powerful chartered banks; the retail Canadian oil industry, with Imperial Oil, Shell, Petro-Canada, and Irving Oil controlling most of the retailing; and the breweries, with Labatt's and Molson's dominating the industry. In professional sports, the CFL and NHL might be argued to be monopolies.

It will aid our understanding of the functioning of these types of industries, which we will explore in detail in Chapter 12, to study that form of market structure in which there is only one firm. Indeed, in some economic activities, such as the provision of electricity, water, and gas, outright monopolies do exist. In the two chapters following this one, we will see that oligopoly and, to a much lesser extent, monopolistic competition are market structures in which firms have some of the characteristics of a monopoly.

What Makes a Monopoly?

There are three conditions, each of which can give rise to a situation in which one seller, or firm, is able to have sole control over the output of an entire industry—that is, to be the only supplier for a given market. These are (1) the firm's exclusive ownership of a unique resource or particular kind of knowledge,

---

LEARNING OBJECTIVES

After reading this chapter, you will be able to:

1. Explain the characteristics of the form of market organization known as *monopoly*.
2. Define the conditions that make a monopoly possible.
3. Explain the relationship between a downward-sloping demand curve and its associated marginal revenue curve.
4. Demonstrate how the monopolist's profit-maximizing price and output levels are determined by equating marginal cost and marginal revenue.
5. Compare the profit-maximizing price and quantity combination for a monopoly with that for a perfectly competitive firm that has the same costs.
6. Give the reasons why monopoly is considered inefficient as an allocator of resources, inequitable as a distributor of income, and controversial as a promoter of innovation and technological change.
7. Explain the nature of natural monopoly and public utility regulation.
8. List the conditions necessary for price discrimination and the reasons why it pays firms to discriminate.

(2) the existence of economies of scale, and (3) the legal granting of a monopoly by the government. It should be emphasized that these three reasons are the legal sources of monopoly.

Exclusive Ownership of a Unique Resource or Particular Type of Knowledge

A seller, or firm, that has exclusive ownership of a unique resource is in a monopoly position. The unique singing style and voice of a k. d. lang or Celine Dion or the unique artistic talent of an A. Y. Jackson or Roland Gissing give the exclusive owner in each case a monopoly over the market for an unusual but much-demanded product. In these cases, however, we do not describe the singer or artist as a monopolist. The key to understanding monopoly rests on the fact that the firm or individual is supplying something for which there are no close substitutes. It is often alleged that around the turn of the century, the Standard Oil Company controlled almost all sources of oil in the United States, thereby effectively eliminating the possibility of competition from any new firms trying to offer that product. Similarly, the Aluminum Company of America at one time was able to maintain a monopoly position in the aluminum market because it controlled most of the known reserves of bauxite, the ore necessary for the production of aluminum. In both of these examples, as in all cases of monopoly, the product, resource, or intellectual knowledge must be unique enough that no reasonable substitutes exist.

Economies of Scale

We saw in Chapter 8 that large economies of scale cause the firm's longrun average total cost curve to fall over a sizable range as output is increased. In industries where the technology of production leads to economies of scale, the longrun average total cost curve for a single firm may fall over almost the entire range of output covered by the industry demand curve. When longrun average total cost falls in this fashion, it is possible for a firm that gets into this market ahead of others to obtain a competitive advantage. The ever-lower per unit costs it realizes at higher and higher levels of output permit the firm to charge a price lower than the average per unit costs that prevail at lower levels of output. In this way, the firm is able to satisfy the entire market demand at a price below that which potential new rival firms must charge when getting started. Therefore, the established firm is able to keep rivals out of the market and maintain a monopoly position.

An industry in which economies of scale are large enough to lead to such a situation is called a **natural monopoly**. Natural monopolies are common in the markets for electricity, telephone service, and water and sewage treatment—the public utilities that we will discuss in more detail later in the chapter. There are other industries in which economies of scale may not result in monopoly but nevertheless will result in industry domination by a few large firms. The steel, petroleum, and auto industries are examples.

In Canada we have had some examples of natural monopolies created because of economies of scale, although it is often difficult to isolate examples of these from those of other sources of monopoly and there is much overlap. Examples of monopolies created because of economies of scale probably include Ontario-Hydro, Trans-Canada Pipelines, and Alberta Gas Trunk Lines (a subsidiary of NOVA corporation). In each case the firm, once created, had enough capacity to produce 100 percent of the industry need for its good or service, and there is no close substitute for the product. Perhaps the best known example of a natural monopoly in Canada was The Canadian Pacific Railway Corporation between 1887 and the 1950s. Once complete, the railway had sufficient capacity on its main line to meet 100 percent of the bulk commodity movement of products in western Canada for almost 80 years. It was only the advent of long-distance trucking coupled with a long and bitter railway strike in the 1950s that began to weaken this monopoly.

Government-Granted Monopoly

It is sometimes said that the only really secure monopolist is one whose monopoly position is permitted by law or granted by the government. This type of monopoly is another form of exclusive ownership—the exclusive ownership of the right or charter to produce and sell a product or service. The government can grant such monopoly power by issuing patents, licenses, charters, copyrights, or exclusive franchises, as in the case of public utilities.

Patents, Charters, Copyrights, and Licenses

As we noted in our discussion of perfect competition, when efforts made in the area of technological innovation and invention stand small chance of reward, there is little incentive to use resources in such activities. This situation will exist whenever the results of creative effort by one party can be easily adopted or copied and marketed by others. Society as a whole benefits economically, and in other ways, from technological innovation and creative effort. In order to stimulate such activity, it is government policy to grant **patents** to those who develop new inventions and technological processes of all kinds. In Canada, patents grant inventors the exclusive right to market their products for 17 years from the date the patent is granted. This is almost the same as granting the inventor a monopoly, at least for a period of time. Of course, profits earned from a patent monopoly over one product can be used to develop other patentable products. This may lead to the growth of a firm with an ongoing monopoly position in certain markets. The Nobel Plough, Insulin, Alexander Graham Bell's telephone, and his hydro-foil all benefited in this way from the many patents they hold. The government also grants copyrights to writers and composers. **Copyrights** are similar in effect to patents in that they give composers and writers exclusive legal control over the production and reproduction of their work for a certain period of time.

Provincial, municipal, and federal governments grant **licenses** or **charters** in a large number of areas of economic activity. It is illegal to operate in these areas without such a license. Today very few of these licenses give monopoly control over a product or service to any one producer, but they do have the effect of limiting the number of producers in those areas where it is necessary to have a license to operate. It is important to realize that although few of these exclusive monopolies are granted in Canada today, they were nonetheless a very important part of the development of the Canadian economy in the past and have left important features in the character of the Canadian economy. The original charter to the Hudson Bay Company for exclusive rights to trade in and out of the Hudson Bay watershed effectively made one quarter of the North American Continent and all its indigenous peoples the exclusive protected market, and to various degrees the property, of the company. This situation persisted from the late 1600s until the late 1800s. Similarly, the charter granted to the Canadian Pacific Railway guaranteed that no other railway would be permitted to locate track between the CPR main line and the United States border for 20 years after the completion of the railway. Other examples include the exclusive licensing of exploration permits and development permits for lumbering and for mineral extraction by provincial governments and the exclusive licensing of companies to supply goods or services for contracts with various levels of government.

For example, it is necessary to have a provincial license to practice medicine or law. While it may well be true that it is in the public interest to have licensing requirements in these fields, it is also true that the smaller is the number of licenses issued, the larger will be the incomes earned by those to whom they are issued. In order to operate a radio or television station, for example, it is necessary to have a license from the federal government. If only one license is issued in a locality, the effect is to give the radio or television station a monopoly on broadcast advertising in that area. This is potentially a very profitable situation if the population in the area has radios or television sets and is inclined to tune in. Under these circumstances, if you already have a license to sell a particular service, such as medical or legal services, or a particular good, such as liquor, it is in your own economic interest to see that licensing boards set high standards, which has the effect of keeping down the number of competing rivals. Have you ever wondered why in some areas barbers must pass a licensing exam that, among other things, requires them to answer questions about tonsils?

Public Utilities

When economies of scale are so great in an industry that it is a natural monopoly, the monopolist, who ultimately has sole control over output in that industry, is often (but not always) in a position to charge the public a high price and reap large profits. As a matter of public policy, this is considered an undesirable situation, for reasons that we will consider in detail later in the chapter.

On the other hand, it would not be efficient in such cases for several competing firms to supply the market, because the technology of production naturally gives rise to declining per unit costs as output is increased. If several firms shared the market, none would be able to sell enough output to realize the lower per unit cost. Hence, it is desirable to have one firm supply the entire market in order to realize the low per unit costs. But somehow a natural monopoly must be forced to pass such economies on to consumers in the form of lower prices. This is something a freely operating monopolist cannot be expected to do, given the temptation to reap large profits if consumer demand is large enough.

Attempts to deal with natural monopolies have led to the creation of **public utilities**. The technology of providing telephone service, electricity, water, railway transportation, and natural gas is characterized by large economies of scale. In addition, can you imagine having multiple water pipes, gas lines, electric lines, and telephones all hooked up to your home by several different waterworks, gas companies, electric utilities, and telephone companies each competing to sell you their services? In an attempt to give consumers the benefit of economies of scale and at the same time protect them from the undesirable aspects of natural monopolies, the government gives these companies a franchise guaranteeing them the exclusive right to provide their good or service in their region of operation. In return for this legally granted monopoly position, the public utility must agree to allow the price of its product to be regulated and its operations monitored by a government regulatory commission. The purpose of government regulation is to ensure that the legally granted monopoly position is not used to take advantage of the consumer.

Barriers to Competition

Anything that makes it more difficult for a new firm to enter any industry is a **barrier to competition**. The conditions we have been discussing, exclusive ownership, economies of scale, and government-granted monopoly, are such complete barriers that they exclude competitors from the industry. In effect, they ensure the existence of a monopoly.

There are other barriers to competition that by themselves are not usually enough to make an industry into a monopoly, but that nonetheless can contribute to that end. Such barriers tend to keep down the number of firms in any industry in which they occur and thereby reduce competition. As we shall see in the next two chapters, they typically occur in oligopoly market structures. Of course, there are no barriers to competition in perfectly competitive industries.

A little reflection suggests that a firm already established in almost any industry has an advantage over one trying to get started. Accumulated know-how, a labour force that is already experienced and trained, and a management organization that has been molded into a well-coordinated team all tend to give an existing firm an advantage over a newcomer in the industry. An existing firm's proven record of performance and established lines of credit make it easier to get loans from banks and other financial markets. An existing firm typically benefits from consumer familiarity with its product and brand-name recognition resulting from past advertising efforts. All these things usually have to be developed from scratch by a new firm entering the industry.

How a Monopolist Determines Price and Output

How does a monopolist decide how much output to produce? Or, alternatively, how does a monopolist decide what price to charge? In fact, it turns out that the answer to either one of these questions necessarily gives the answer to the other. In this discussion, we will assume that potential rivals are kept out of the market and that the monopolist is not governed by any regulatory commission.

Demand and Marginal Revenue for a Monopolist

We saw in the previous chapter that a firm in a perfectly competitive industry cannot affect the price at which it sells its output. It can, however, sell as little or as much as it wants at the same, given price. It is a price taker, and therefore its demand curve is perfectly horizontal. By contrast, a monopolist is the only firm in the industry. Therefore, the industry demand curve and the monopolist's demand curve are one and the same. A monopolist's demand curve is downward sloping from left to right as a result, and the monopolist can affect price by changing the amount of output.

It should be emphasized that this is not a characteristic unique to a monopoly. Whatever the market structure of an industry, so long as an individual firm in that industry can affect price by changing its level of output, that firm also faces a downward-sloping demand curve. Later, we shall see that this is true of firms in monopolistically competitive as well as oligopolistic industries. In fact, it is only the firm in a perfectly competitive market that faces a perfectly horizontal demand curve. So bear in mind that the following discussion of a downward-sloping demand curve and its associated marginal revenue curve also applies to firms in other market contexts besides monopoly.

Table 10-1 contains hypothetical data on demand and revenue for a monopolist. Observe that the monopolist can sell a larger quantity Q of output, column (1), only by charging a lower price p, or average revenue AR, per unit,

TABLE 10-1   Demand and Revenue Data for a Monopolist (Hypothetical Data)

(1) Quantity of Output (Q)	(2) Price = Average Revenue $p = AR$	(3) Total Revenue (TR) $TR = p \times Q$	(4) Marginal Revenue (MR)
0	$13	$ 0	
			$12
1	12	12	
			10
2	11	22	
			8
3	10	30	
			6
4	9	36	
			4
5	8	40	
			2
6	7	42	
			0
7	6	42	
			− 2
8	5	40	
			− 4
9	4	36	
			− 6
10	3	30	
			− 8
11	2	22	
			−10
12	1	12	
			−12
13	0	0	

Checkpoint* 10-1

A news story reported that the Department of Consumer and Corporate Affairs was conducting a "monopoly investigation into K. C. Irving's activities in the English language newspaper industry in Atlantic Canada." What sorts of things do you think might contribute to a possible monopoly situation in this instance? The North American automobile industry was dominated by General Motors, Ford, and Chrysler from the 1920s to the 1980s. In Canada there was an attempt by Bricklin to enter this industry with a new product. The company failed before it could gain a toehold. What do you think were the nature of some of the barriers to competition that Bricklin was unable to overcome?

Answers to all Checkpoints can be found at the back of the text.

column (2). Total revenue TR, column (3), equals the price p, column (2), multiplied by the quantity Q, column (1). Starting from a zero output level, total revenue TR, column (3), initially gets larger as price is lowered. It reaches a maximum when 6 units of output are sold at a price of $7, or when 7 units are sold at a price of $6, and declines thereafter. This merely reflects a characteristic of a downward-sloping demand curve, which we have already discussed. (For review, reread the discussion of the demand for CFL Grey Cup tickets in Chapter 5.)

Marginal Revenue Declines for a Monopolist

At this point, however, we note a very important difference between a monopoly firm and a perfectly competitive firm. Remember, a perfectly competitive firm can sell each additional unit of output at the same price because its demand curve is perfectly horizontal. Hence, the marginal revenue (the change in total revenue) associated with the sale of one more unit of output is always equal to price for a perfectly competitive firm. Since price doesn't change, neither does marginal revenue. This is not true for a monopolist because a monopolist's demand curve is downward sloping. In order to sell an additional unit of output the monopolist must lower price. And the monopolist not only must accept a lower price for an additional unit sold, but for all the units it sells—in other words, the units that otherwise could have been sold at a higher price.

This means that for a monopolist, marginal revenue is less than price at every level of output. The reason is that when price is lowered to sell an additional unit of output, the resulting change in total revenue equals the sum of two parts, one a plus and the other a minus. One part is the *increase* in total revenue equal to the price received for the additional unit sold. The other part equals the *decrease* in total revenue due to the reduction in price on all other units that was necessary in order to sell the additional unit. For a monopolist, marginal revenue (the change in total revenue) equals the price of the additional unit less the amount of the price reduction on the other units multiplied by the quantity of the other units. Therefore, marginal revenue is less than price at every level of output. It follows from this that since price declines as output increases (because the demand curve is downward sloping), marginal revenue must also decline as output increases.

These relationships among price, total revenue, and marginal revenue are illustrated in Table 10-1. For the first unit of output sold the price, column (2), is $12 but careful observation reveals that marginal revenue was $12 at one half a unit, column (4), so by the point where output equals one unit, marginal revenue has already decreased below $12. To sell two units, price must be lowered to $11. Not only is the second unit sold for $11, but so is the first. Otherwise, the first unit could have been sold for $12, if the monopolist had been satisfied to sell just one unit. Therefore, to sell two units of output, the monopolist has to give up $1 on the first unit while getting an additional $11 from the sale of the second. The change (increase) in total revenue as sales increase from one unit to two units is therefore $10 ($11 minus $1), the marginal revenue shown in column (4). The marginal revenue of $10 is the increase in total revenue from $12 to $22, column (3), resulting from the sale of the second unit of output. Again careful reading of the table reveals that this marginal revenue is assigned at the midpoint of the range over which the increase in output took place. In this case the marginal revenue of $10 is assigned to have occurred at 1.5 units—the midpoint between 1 unit and 2 units. If the monopolist wanted to sell 3 units, price would have to be lowered to $10 per unit. This means that the first two units would have to be sold at $10 per unit as well, instead of the $11 per unit received when only 2 units were sold. The marginal revenue would be equal to the $10 received from the sale of the third unit, less $1 per unit given up on each of the first two units, or $8. Again, the marginal revenue of $8 is recorded in the table at an output of 2.5 units, reflecting that the sale of an extra unit at an output of 2.5 units will lead to additional revenue of $8. You should now be able to convince yourself of the validity of the marginal revenue data in Table 10-1. Note that when output exceeds 6.5 units, marginal revenue becomes negative. Negative marginal revenue is associated with the range over which increases in total output lead to decreases in total revenue.[1]

Relationship Among the Total Revenue, Demand, and Marginal Revenue Curves

The data from Table 10-1 are plotted in Figure 10-1. For each output level in column (1), the associated price is plotted to give the demand curve D in frames (b) and (c). (Demand curves are not necessarily straight lines, but we use them here for simplicity.) Total revenue, column (3), is plotted in frame (a) to give the TR curve.

Comparison of frames (a) and (b) clearly shows that total revenue TR for the monopolist reaches its maximum at 6.5 units of output. Observe that if price is reduced from $7 to $6, frame (b), the quantity of output sold increases from 6 to 7 units, but TR remains unchanged at $42, frame (a). Why is this so? Frame (b) shows us that when price is lowered from $7 to $6, there is a loss in TR of $6 ($1 per unit on the first 6 units). This loss is represented by the shaded horizontal rectangle. However, this loss is just offset by the gain in TR of $6, realized from the sale of the seventh unit. This is represented by the vertical shaded rectangle. Putting it another way, we can say that the marginal revenue MR (the change in total revenue TR) associated with the sale of the seventh unit of output is zero. This is borne out in frame (c), where the MR curve, plotted from the marginal revenue data, column (4) of Table 10-1, crosses the horizontal axis at 6.5 units of output.

Note in frame (a) that at levels of sales less than 6 units TR can always be increased by lowering price, frame (b), and selling an additional unit. Therefore, marginal revenue is always positive up to the sale of the seventh unit. This means that the MR curve in frame (c) lies above the horizontal axis at all output levels less than 6.5 units. Furthermore, starting from a zero level of output, note that TR, frame (a), rises less and less steeply as price is lowered and the number of units sold is increased, frame (b). This is reflected in the fact that the MR curve, frame (c), is downward sloping left to right.

---

[1]The exact relationship between the price and the marginal revenue is found by using the price elasticity of demand coefficient developed in Chapter 5. The equation linking the price to the marginal revenue is

$$MR = P\left(1 + \frac{1}{\eta_d}\right)$$

where η_d is the coefficient of price elasticity of demand and is a negative number.

FIGURE 10-1 Relationship Between the Total Revenue, the Demand Curve, and the Marginal Revenue Curve

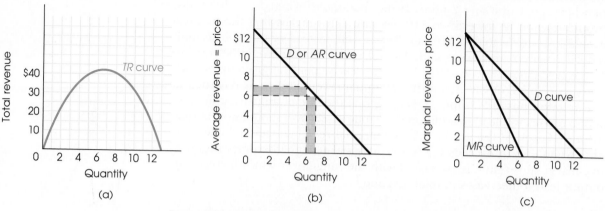

(a)   (b)   (c)

Because the total revenue curve, *TR*, rises at a decreasing rate up to 6.5 units of output in frame (a), the marginal revenue curve, *MR*, is downward sloping and lies above the horizontal axis up to 6.5 units of output in frame (c). It crosses the axis at this point, reflecting the fact that there is no change in total revenue, frame (a), resulting from the sale of the seventh unit of output. This is also represented by the fact that the horizontal shaded rectangular area in frame (b), representing the loss in total revenue on the first 6 units, is just equal to the revenue from the sale of the seventh unit. Because the *TR* curve falls at an increasing rate beyond 6.5 units of output in frame (a), the *MR* curve is downward sloping and lies below the horizontal axis beyond 6.5 units of output in frame (c).

The *MR* curve always lies below the demand curve in frame (c). This is because the marginal revenue from the sale of an additional unit of output is less than the price received for that unit by the amount of the sum of the price cuts on all previous units sold.

Observe that the *D* curve meets the *MR* curve at the vertical intercept in frame (c). Since the price is always greater than marginal revenue, the demand curve *D* always lies above the *MR* curve as we move away from the vertical intercept. Note that at output levels greater than 6.5 units the *MR* curve lies below the horizontal axis. This reflects the fact that the sale of each additional unit beyond this level results in a decrease in *TR* (or, worded another way, *MR* is negative).

Relationship Between Demand and Marginal Revenue Curves—Further Comments

For purposes of illustrating the basic relationship among total revenue, demand, and marginal revenue, we have used rather small numbers when talking about quantity in Table 10-1 and Figure 10-1. It would be more realistic in general to assume that we are dealing with much larger quantities of output. This changes the scale on the horizontal, or quantity, axis so that the number of units is so large that the distance equal to one unit is no larger than a dot. However, the same principles apply: the demand curve and the marginal revenue curve will meet at the same point on the vertical axis, and the marginal revenue curve will have a slope equal to twice the absolute value of the slope of the demand curve. These properties are illustrated in frame (c) of Figure 10-1.

There is another relationship that follows from those discussed in the previous paragraph. For any downward-sloping, straight-line demand curve it will then be true that at any price level, the horizontal distance between the vertical axis and the marginal revenue curve will be exactly half the distance to the demand curve. Note that this means that the marginal revenue curve will cross the horizontal axis exactly halfway between the origin and the point where the demand curve crosses the horizontal axis.

One way to see why this is so, is to recall our discussion of elasticity in Chapter 5. There we observed in Figure 5-5 that a straight-line demand curve is unit elastic exactly at its midpoint. We also observed that at this point total revenue is a maximum. In other words, just to the left of this point, marginal revenue is positive, while just to the right of it, marginal revenue is negative. Therefore, exactly at that point marginal revenue is zero. Hence, where total revenue is a maximum, the marginal revenue curve cuts the horizontal axis.

Monopoly Pricing Policy and the Downward-Sloping Demand Curve

It is very important to be clear about what a downward-sloping demand curve does and does not say about the monopolist's pricing policy. Contrary to the usual belief of the person in the street, it *does not say* that the monopolist can sell a given output at any price desired. It *does not say* that a monopolist can set price at some desired level and *independently* decide how much output to sell at that price, or vice versa. This fallacy is just a variation on the first fallacy. The downward-sloping demand curve *does* say that the monopolist can affect price by changing output or, equivalently, that the monopolist affects output by changing price. But the level of one automatically determines the level of the other due to the shape of the demand curve. Hence, the monopolist's pricing policy is not free of the constraint that selling more means accepting a lower price or that selling a certain level of output means charging no more than a certain price level.

> ### Checkpoint 10-2
> Use the numbers from Table 10-1 to demonstrate the relationship between the elasticity of the demand curve in Figure 10-1, frames (b) and (c), and its associated marginal revenue curve. (You may find it helpful to review briefly the concept of elasticity in Chapter 5.)

Bringing Together Costs and Revenues

To see how a profit-maximizing monopolist determines what output level to produce and what price to charge, we must bring the cost side of the picture together with the demand and marginal revenue side. To make it easier to compare the profit-maximizing behaviour of the monopolist with that of the perfectly competitive firm discussed in the previous chapter, we will assume that the monopolist's costs, shown in Table 10-2, are the same as those we looked at in Table 10-1. For each output level in column (1) of Table 10-2, the monopolist's average total cost, total cost, and marginal cost data are shown in columns (5), (6), and (7), respectively. Columns (2), (3), and (4) repeat the revenue data from columns (2), (3), and (4) of Table 10-1.

TABLE 10-2   Output, Revenue, and Costs of a Monopolist (Hypothetical Data)

(1) Quantity of Output (Q)	(2) Price = Average Revenue $p = AR$	(3) Total Revenue $TR = p \times Q$	(4) Marginal Revenue (MR)	(5) Average Total Cost (ATC)	(6) Total Cost (TC)	(7) Marginal Cost (MC)	(8) Profit (+) or Loss (−) $TR - TC = (3) - (6)$
0	$13	$ 0		$10.00			−$10
			$12			$ 6	
1	12	12		16.00	$16		− 4
			10			4	
2	11	22		10.00	20		2
			8			4	
3	10	30		8.00	24		6
			6			5	
4	9	36		7.25	29		7
			4			7	
5	8	40		7.20	36		4
			2			11	
6	7	42		7.83	47		− 5
			0			23	
7	6	42		10.00	70		−28

The Total Revenue and Total Cost Approach

The monopolist's procedure for choosing that output and price level that maximize profit may be viewed from the standpoint of total revenue TR and total cost TC. Subtracting TC, column (6), from TR, column (3), at each level of output, column (1), we get the profit or loss, column (8), associated with producing and selling that output at the price given in column (2). Column (8) tells us that the monopolist realizes a maximum profit, which equals $7, when 4 units of output are produced, column (1), and sold at a price of $9, column (2).

This is shown graphically in Figure 10-2, frame (a). The TC curve is plotted from the total cost data, column (6), of Table 10-2 and the TR curve is plotted from the total revenue data, column (3). The maximum vertical distance by which the TR curve exceeds the TC curve occurs at 4 units of output. This distance equals the maximum profit of $7.

The Marginal Revenue and Marginal Cost Approach

The marginal revenue and marginal cost approach is an alternative way of determining the output and price combination that maximizes the monopolist's profit. The basic principle behind this selection is exactly the same as that described in the case of the perfectly competitive firm. The monopolist also continues to expand output as long as the marginal cost of producing an additional unit is less than the marginal revenue associated with its sale. The monopolist will produce up to that output level where the marginal cost of the last unit produced is just covered by, or is equal to, its marginal revenue—that is, it will produce up to the output level for which its marginal profit is zero.

Note, however, that the case of the monopolist differs from that of the perfect competitor in two respects. First, marginal revenue for the monopolist is always

FIGURE 10-2   The Relationship Between Revenues and Costs for a Monopolist

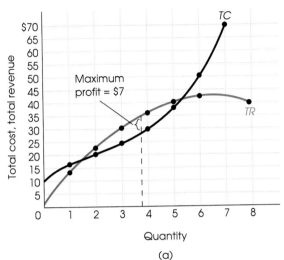

(a)

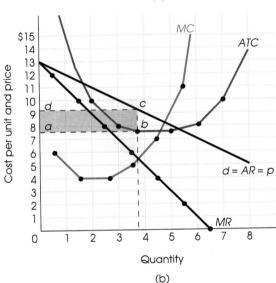

(b)

In frame (a), the profit-maximizing level of output occurs when 4 units of output are sold at a price of $9. This is where the vertical distance between the TR curve and TC curve, which equals total profit, is a maximum.

In frame (b), the profit-maximizing level of output occurs where the MC curve intersects the MR curve, corresponding to 4 units of output sold at a price of $9. The maximum profit of $7 is represented by the rectangular area abcd.

---

less than price. For the perfectly competitive firm, marginal revenue always equals price. Second, marginal revenue for the monopolist falls as output is increased. For the perfectly competitive firm, marginal revenue is the same at all levels of output because price is the same at all levels.

Compare the marginal revenue data, column (4), of Table 10-2 with the marginal cost data, column (7). Observe that MR exceeds MC at all output levels up to and including 4 units. If a fifth unit is produced, however, its MR of $4 is less than its MC of $7. Therefore, according to the marginal cost equals marginal revenue principle, profit will be at a maximum, which equals $7, column (8), when 4 units of output are produced and sold at a price of $9, column (2). This is, of course, the same answer we found by using the comparison of total cost to total revenue approach.

The marginal cost equals marginal revenue approach is shown graphically in frame (b) of Figure 10-2. The ATC and MC curves are plotted from the data in columns (5) and (7) of Table 10-2. (Note that the points on the marginal cost curve are plotted exactly halfway between successive output levels.) The demand curve and its associated MR curve are plotted from the data in columns (2) and (4) of Table 10-2.

That it pays the firm to increase output up to and including 4 units is indicated by the fact that the MR curve lies above the MC curve up to that point. Beyond 4 units of output, the MC curve lies above the MR curve, indicating that marginal cost exceeds marginal revenue. Hence, the monopolist maximizes profit by producing and selling 4 units of output at a price of $9 per unit. The profit-maximizing price is the point on the demand curve that lies directly above the intersection of the MC and MR curves. We have labeled this point c. The profit-maximizing output level of 4 units is the point on the horizontal axis that lies directly below the intersection of the MC and MR curves.

The vertical distance ad = bc, which equals $1.75, is the average profit per unit, so 4 units times $1.75 gives the total profit of $7, represented by the shaded rectangular area abcd. Note that according to Table 10-2, the average profit per unit at 3 units of output is $2, the difference between a price of $10 per unit, column (2), and an ATC of $8 per unit, column (5). However, total profit for 3 units of output at a price of $10 per unit is only $6 (3 units times an average profit per unit of $2). This illustrates the fact that the level of output that maximizes total profit does not necessarily correspond to the one that maximizes average profit per unit.

Suppose that the firm with the cost curves depicted in Figure 10-2 were perfectly competitive instead of a monopolist. Let us assume that its perfectly elastic (horizontal) demand curve is at a level of $9—that is, as a price taker it is given a price of $9. Then, by the $MC = MR = p$ rule we discussed in the previous chapter, it would maximize profit by producing 5 units of output. This is one more unit than would be produced by the monopolist at the same price of $9. The reason for this difference, given that the two firms have identical cost curves, is that marginal revenue equals price is constant at $9 for all levels of output for the perfectly competitive firm but not for the monopolist. For the monopolist, price, and therefore marginal revenue, falls as output increases. Therefore, at a price of $9, marginal revenue is lower for the monopolist than it is for the perfectly competitive firm. This reflects the fact that the monopolist's marginal revenue is reduced by the lower price on all prior units sold.

Losses

Probably the most common image brought to mind by the term *monopoly* is that of a firm making large, even "rip-off" profits. This isn't necessarily the case, however. Consider the monopolist in Figure 10-3. The intersection of the MC and MR curves occurs at the output level Q_l. However, this is a loss-minimizing position. There is no way the monopolist can cover all costs in this case, since the ATC curve lies above the demand curve D at all output levels. Producing the output Q_l and selling it at the price p_l, the monopolist incurs a loss per unit equal to the vertical distance ab. The total loss is represented by the shaded rectangular area. The monopolist is only willing to operate at a loss in the shortrun, and then only so long as it is possible to cover average variable cost.

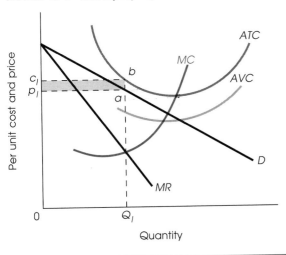

FIGURE 10-3 Monopoly Equilibrium with a Loss

The monopolist here is operating at a loss—a negative economic profit. The intersection of the MC and MR curves dictates the production of Q_l units of output to be sold at the price p_l, a loss-minimizing position in the shortrun. The total loss is represented by the shaded rectangular area.

This condition is met in Figure 10-3 because p_l lies above the AVC curve at the output level Q_l.

The monopolist depicted in Figure 10-2, in contrast to that of Figure 10-3, is earning more than a normal profit. The positive economic profit earned is represented by the shaded rectangular area *abcd* in frame (b) of Figure 10-2. The basic distinction between earning positive economic profit in a monopoly situation and earning it under perfect competition is that, in the longrun, such a profit will attract new firms into the perfectly competitive industry but not into the monopoly industry. Output will be expanded in the competitive industry, and rivalry among firms will cause price to fall until economic profit for each and every firm is driven to zero. In the case of the monopoly, however, barriers to competition prevent this from happening. Therefore, provided costs are low enough and demand high enough, the monopoly is in a position to earn positive economic profit, in this case called *monopoly profit*, almost indefinitely.

Why do we say "almost indefinitely"? Even a monopolist is not protected from longrun advances in technology or changes in consumer demand that may weaken its advantage. A firm that had a monopoly over the buggy-whip market a hundred years ago would have been in an enviable position. But advancing technology and the shift of consumer preferences away from horses and buggies and toward the automobile changed all that. A monopoly over the sale of whale oil would have been more lucrative before the advent of the kerosene lamp, and a monopoly on kerosene lamps would have been more profitable before the development of the electric light. Research and changing technology, the development of substitute products and the expiration of patents on old ones, and the discovery of new resources, supplies, and materials can all lead to the weakening of a monopoly market.

Monopoly versus Perfect Competition

In our study of perfect competition in the previous chapter, we focused on certain questions that are relevant to any market structure. How efficiently does

Checkpoint 10-3

How would an increase in fixed costs affect the equilibrium price and output levels in Figure 10-3? How would such an increase affect economic profit? If the monopolist had to pay a license fee to the federal or provincial government to operate and the fee were doubled, how would that affect the shortrun equilibrium price and output combination of the monopolist? Suppose that the government imposes a price ceiling on a monopolist's product. How might this affect output?

it allocate resources? What sort of incentives does it provide for innovation and technological change? What implications does it have for income distribution? All these questions can be asked about monopoly as well. Since, as we noted in the previous chapter, perfect competition is regarded as a useful standard for market structure, it will be helpful to compare the answers for monopoly with those for perfect competition.

Resource Allocation

Consider a perfectly competitive industry such as that shown in Figure 10-4, frame (a). Here, the industry demand curve D and the shortrun supply curve S determine the equilibrium price p_c and quantity Q_c. Remember that the perfectly competitive industry's shortrun supply curve S is the sum of the portion of the marginal cost curves lying above average variable cost of the individual firms in the industry.

Suppose now that a single firm comes along and buys up all the firms in the competitive industry without affecting the cost curves of any of them. The single firm thus has a monopoly, and its marginal cost curve MC, shown in frame (b) of Figure 10-4, is exactly the same as the supply curve S shown in frame (a). (The cost side of the picture for the industry is assumed to be the same whether it is perfectly competitive or a monopolist. This is done purely for simplicity in comparing a monopoly firm's behaviour to that of a perfectly competitive firm under the same conditions. In no way does it imply that monopoly firms and perfect competitors have the same cost structure. Earlier we pointed out

FIGURE 10-4   Effect of Monopolizing a Competitive Market

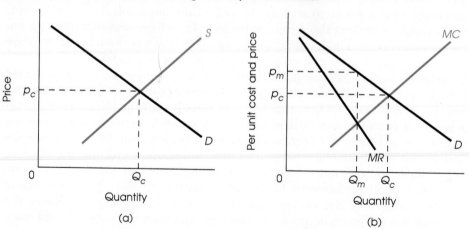

The supply curve S and the demand curve D for a perfectly competitive industry determine an equilibriom price p_c and quantity Q_c in frame (a). In frame (b) it is assumed that a single firm takes over all firms in the competitive industry of frame (a) without affecting costs and becomes a monopoly. The MC curve of the monopolist of frame (b) is therefore the same supply curve S of frame (a). The profit-maximizing monopolist produces the lower output Q_m, to be sold at the higher price p_m. When the market is monopolized, the part of the demand curve over the range from Q_m to Q_c will lie above the MC curve. Unlike perfect competition, there will be consumers willing to pay a price that covers the marginal cost of producing the good who will not be able to get any at that price.

that often the very reason for the existence of a monopoly is that it has economies of scale which would not be available to a firm operating on a more competitive basis. We will look at this situation later.)

The industry demand curve D is unchanged as well, but there will be an important difference between the way the monopolist views D and the way D was viewed by the perfectly competitive firms, each of which was a price taker. The monopoly firm is well aware that it affects price when it changes output. Hence, the profit-maximizing monopolist will use the MR curve associated with D, together with the MC curve, to determine the equilibrium output level Q_m and the price p_m in frame (b). When an industry is a monopoly, consumers pay a higher price for the product and receive less of it than would be the case under perfect competition.

But why do economists generally consider this monopoly equilibrium position to be less desirable than the perfectly competitive one? Economists say there is an inefficient allocation of resources when there are consumers who are willing to pay a price that covers the marginal cost of producing more of the good, but who will not be able to have more at those prices. Under perfect competition, output is produced up to that point, Q_c, where the price, p_c, paid for the last unit produced is just equal to the cost of producing that last unit. In other words, price per unit is equal to marginal cost. In a perfectly competitive market, each and every consumer who is willing to pay a price sufficient to cover the marginal cost of producing the good will have some of the good.

By contrast, if the market is organized as a monopoly, the portion of the demand curve D over the range Q_m to Q_c lies above the MC curve. Hence, there are consumers who are willing to pay a price for the units of output from Q_m to Q_c that exceeds the marginal cost of producing them, but are unable to do so because the monopolist will not produce and sell them at such a price. Whenever there is a monopoly, there will be consumers who are willing to pay a price that equals the marginal cost of producing the good, but who will not be able to have any of the good at that price.

Market Structure and Industry Cost

The preceding discussion assumes that costs are not affected when the perfectly competitive industry becomes a monopoly. It may well be that certain kinds of organizational and technological efficiencies are realized when all the perfectly competitive firms are combined to make a monopoly. If so, the monopolist's MC curve in frame (b) of Figure 10-4 will not be the same as the perfectly competitive industry supply curve S in frame (a).

This is illustrated in Figure 10-5. When the industry is perfectly competitive, equilibrium price p_c and quantity Q_c are determined by the intersection of the industry supply curve S and the industry demand curve D. Suppose that when all the perfectly competitive firms are merged into a single monopoly firm, the increased efficiencies of operation result in a lowering of the per unit costs of production. If the per unit cost reductions resulting from monopolization of the industry are great enough, the monopolist's equilibrium price p_m may be lower than p_c and its equilibrium output Q_m greater than Q_c (corresponding to the intersection of MC and MR), as is shown in Figure 10-5. If, on the other hand, the per unit cost reduction is not great enough to cause the MC curve to intersect MR to the right of point b, corresponding to output level Q_c, monopolization of the industry will result in higher price and lower output levels than would exist

FIGURE 10-5 **Monopolization May Lead to Lower Price and Higher Output**

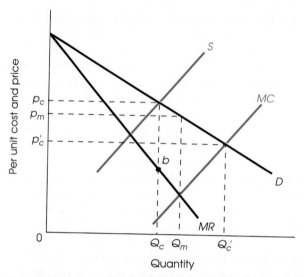

It is possible that monopolization of a perfectly competitive industry will lower per unit costs of production. If monopolization of the industry results in a sufficiently large reduction in per unit production costs, the monopolist's marginal cost curve may assume a position such as MC. Given MC and the marginal revenue curve MR, the monopolist in this case will charge a lower price, p_m, and produce a larger output, Q_m, than occurs when the industry is perfectly competitive with supply curve S. Note, however, that the price equal to marginal cost solution would provide consumers with the yet lower price p_c' and greater output Q_c'.

---

under perfect competition. Which result is more likely can only be answered by examining the facts for a particular industry.

Even though the profit-maximizing monopolist may provide consumers more output at a lower price, there will still be consumers who are willing to pay a price for the good greater than the marginal cost of producing it, but who are unable to get any. This is represented by the fact that the demand curve D over the range from Q_m to Q_c' lies above the MC curve. For this reason, it can be argued that some public policy, or regulation, is needed to promote a result where output Q_c' is produced and sold at a price p_c'.

Incentives for Innovation

In the previous chapter we saw that a perfectly competitive firm must use the most efficient available technology to compete effectively with the multitude of other firms in the industry. But using the best *available* technology is not the same thing as product innovation and development of new, more efficient production techniques. The incentive for a perfectly competitive firm to innovate is small because the prospect of reaping above-normal profits from such activity for any length of time is slight. Firms in the industry can all too readily adopt the innovations of others, thereby quickly eliminating any competitive advantage otherwise realized by the innovating firm. As evidence that perfect competition does not promote innovation, it is often observed that in agriculture most research and innovation comes from large manufacturers of farm machinery and chemicals as well as government-supported experiment stations and departments of agriculture and veterinary medicine at postsecondary educational institutions. Relatively little seems to be initiated in the way of researching and developing new strains of plants and animals or less environmentally damaging low-cost fertilization techniques by the multitude of farms that make agriculture so closely resemble perfect competition.

For a monopoly, the situation would seem to be almost the reverse. Since there are no competing firms in the industry, the monopolist, unlike the competitive firm, is not forced by the existence of many rivals to use the most efficient available technology. This is not to say that it isn't in the monopolist's best interest to do so, since lower costs mean larger monopoly profits. On the other hand, for the more dynamic activity of product innovation and the development of new production techniques, there would seem to be just the incentive for the monopolist that is lacking for the perfectly competitive firm. The development of new technologies or products provides the prospect of above-normal profit for a prolonged, possibly indefinite period of time. In addition, the existence of such profit provides the monopolist with a source of funds to finance technological change and product innovation, a source unavailable to the perfectly competitive firm.

It is sometimes argued, however, that because the monopolist doesn't face the strong competitive threat of rival firms, there is a tendency to stand pat and simply reap the profits from the existing situation. In fact, it has been argued that it is in a monopolist's best interest to protect the existing monopoly situation from the threat of new products and technological change introduced by potential rivals. The monopolist may even buy up and stockpile patents, effectively putting a stop to technological changes and product innovation.

In summary, there is a wide variety of opinion on the pros and cons of monopoly as a market structure that either promotes or inhibits the advancement of product change and production technology. The thrust of public policy, at least that of competition policy, leans toward the view that monopoly most likely inhibits innovation.

Income Distribution

Most economists agree that the existence of unregulated, profit-maximizing monopoly contributes to income inequality. In longrun equilibrium under perfect competition, a great many firms earn a normal profit and the payments to productive factors, including labour, are just sufficient to cover their opportunity costs. By contrast, monopoly gives rise to a much greater concentration of economic power. The potential exists for above-normal, even extraordinary, profit for a prolonged or even indefinite period of time. The owners of a monopoly are potentially in a position to earn much more than what their time and financial capital could earn in the next best alternative use.

If the monopoly is a corporation, the firm reaps the above-average profits and may or may not distribute these profits to the stockholders in the form of dividends, but the stockholders will gain either through above-normal dividends or through relatively high capital gains in the value of their stock. Some economists argue that since stockholders tend to be from middle and upper

POLICY PERSPECTIVE

The Monopoly as Cartel: Why Taxi Rides Can Be Expensive

Monopolies sometimes take the form of a group of firms who effectively agree to collude together to set the price and/or output level of a particular product or service. The group, often called a *cartel*, essentially tries to behave as if it were one large monopoly firm. In Canada, combines laws and *The Competition Act* make it illegal for firms to engage in collusive agreements to fix prices or share markets (provided the government can prove that such action is not in the public interest). Nonetheless, such practices do exist in the taxicab business in some cities.

HOW CAN THERE BE A TAXICAB MONOPOLY?

The crucial ingredient in a taxicab cartel is a city government empowered to issue licenses for operating taxicabs. By restricting the number of licenses issued, the city government can effectively restrict the number of cabs (hence taxicab firms) serving the city market for taxicab rides. The city transit authority or taxi commission may also

have the power to grant different classes of permits so that some facilities (for example, a local airport taxi stand) may be served by only a subgroup of the licensed taxi companies. Without taxicab licensing requirements, the market for taxicab rides would be very much like a perfectly competitive industry in the constant-cost case, as it was in Victorian Britain under the original jitney cabs, as discussed in Chapter 9. There would be unrestricted entry into the industry of firms (taxicabs) producing an essentially homogeneous product (taxicab rides).

This is illustrated in Figure P10-1. The shortrun industry supply curve of passenger kilometres of taxicab service S_c intersects the market demand curve D at point c so that Q_c passenger kilometres are bought and sold at a price (fare) of p_c per kilometre. Taxicabs would earn no more than a normal profit, characteristic of a perfectly competitive market. The longrun industry supply curve is the horizontal line passing through points b an c. (Recall

FIGURE P10-1   Monopolizing the Taxicab Market

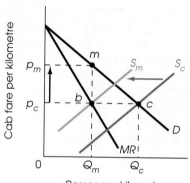

the longrun industry supply curve in the constant-cost case for a perfectly competitive industry, illustrated in Figures 9-7 and 9-8.) However, when the city government has the authority to issue permits (taxicab licenses), it can restrict output (passenger kilometres) and set prices like a monopolist. Restricting the issuance of taxi licenses shifts

continued on next page

income brackets to begin with, the existence of monopoly profit tends to widen the gap between upper and lower income groups.

We hasten to emphasize that the issue of income inequality, and whether a particular income distribution is "good" or "bad," typically generates controversy and deeply felt opinions. It is a normative issue and differences of opinion on the subject are rarely settled by an appeal to facts.

Regulation of Natural Monopolies: Public Utilities

We have already pointed out that where natural monopolies exist, public policy has sought to ensure that the consumer benefits from the low per unit costs of

the shortrun perfectly competitive industry supply curve leftward to the position S_m. S_m is the marginal cost curve of the industry when organized as a monopoly. The intersection of the marginal cost curve S_m with the marginal revenue curve MR at point b determines the equilibrium monopoly output Q_m and price p_m, corresponding to point m on the demand curve D. The cab industry now earns a monopoly profit given by the area $p_c b m\, p_m$. (Recall from the previous chapter that any point on the longrun perfectly competitive industry supply curve given by the horizontal line passing through points b and c represents both the marginal and the average total cost in the longrun.) The monopoly cab fare p_m per passenger kilometre exceeds the perfectly competitive cab fare p_c by the amount bm.

Obviously, taxi owners stand to gain when the government restricts the issuance of taxicab permits, at least those taxi owners who have obtained a permit from the taxi commission. These taxi permit holders benefit directly because of the higher fees in the industry, because of the reduced competition by other firms and because the permit has a capital value that can be sold to another company. Alternatively, the government may set the license fee so high that it effectively taxes the above-normal profits out of the industry. In this case, the government benefits from reducing the supply in the industry.

What has been less obvious from our analysis, which has concentrated on the effect of regulation on the price and availability of service, is why the government would restrict the number of firms in the first place. Often the reason given is that there are personal benefits for politicians and corruption in local administration. In some cities owners have successfully lobbied city officials, through political contributions, for *legal* restraints on trade. The other reason, often overlooked, is that under the old free-market unregulated jitney system, the passenger was not only in a let-the-buyer-beware position but sometimes literally risked his or her life and property getting into a jitney. The public called for protection because it wanted to eliminate unscrupulous and illegal practices. In addition, the cabbies themselves saw the benefits both in terms of higher potential incomes and also, for those drivers who were honest, in having a set of regulations that protected drivers from having to compete with firms whose practices lowered their costs because of illegal actions or inhumane treatment of passengers and horses.

Today the principle of licensing and restricting the number of suppliers in industries that deal with the public (limiting entry into the business), rests on the idea that a local government body, the city, is granting the right to operate while attempting to protect the customers and honest suppliers from the unfair and illegal behaviour likely to occur under unregulated conditions.

For Discussion

- What area in Figure P10-1 represents the loss to society that results from restricting the provision of taxicab service to the quantity Q_m? Why do the taxi owners need city hall to establish their cartel? Why couldn't taxi owners simply agree among themselves to collude to restrict output and charge the monopoly price p_m?
- Why might it be easier for the local government to ensure the safety of the public and protection from taxi drivers taking the "most circuitous straight line" from origin to destination by limiting the number of licenses than by encouraging perfect competition?

production by regulating the price the monopolist can charge. This has resulted in the creation of public utilities. Public utilities are regulated natural monopolies that provide such products as electricity, gas, telephone service, water and sewage treatment, and certain kinds of transportation. How, in principle, should regulators decide what price a public utility should be allowed to charge?

Difficulty with Marginal Cost Pricing

The cost and demand curves for a natural monopoly are depicted in Figure 10-6. The firm's average total cost curve ATC and its marginal cost curve MC fall throughout the range of output covered by the market demand curve D. Of course, as long as the ATC curve is falling, the MC curve must lie below it.

FIGURE 10-6   Fair-Return and Marginal Cost Pricing for a Public Utility

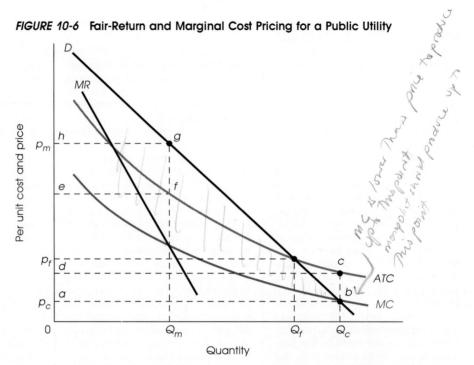

A natural monopoly has continuously declining *ATC* and *MC* curves over the entire range of output covered by the market demand curve *D*. In the absence of any regulatory constraints, the profit-maximizing monopolist would produce an output Q_m. If the government regulation enforced a marginal cost equal to price rule, the utility will produce an output Q_1 to be sold at a price p_1, as determined by the intersection of the *ATC* and *D* curves.

(If you can't remember why, reread the section on marginal and average cost in Chapter 8.)

We have seen before that the most efficient allocation of resources, that which maximizes consumer satisfaction, occurs when output is produced up to the point where price equals marginal cost. It is most efficient in the sense that output is produced up to the point where the price paid for the last unit produced just covers the cost of producing it. For the natural monopolist of Figure 10-6, this occurs where the *MC* curve intersects the *D* curve at point *b* to determine the price p_c and output level Q_c.

This is a much larger output and lower price than the monopolist would choose if left unregulated and allowed to maximize profit. The unregulated, profit-maximizing monopolist would produce the amount Q_m to be sold at a price p_m, as determined by the intersection of the *MC* and *MR* curves. Monopoly profit would equal the rectangular area *efgh*. However, if regulators force the monopolist to produce the amount Q_c to be sold at the price p_c, the monopolist will operate at a loss because the average total cost per unit of output sold will be greater than the price per unit sold by the amount *bc*. The total loss incurred by the monopolist is represented by the rectangle *abcd*. If regulators insist on a marginal cost equals price solution, it will be necessary to somehow subsidize, or pay the monopolist back, by this amount. Otherwise, the firm will go out of

POLICY PERSPECTIVE

How Do You Keep Costs Down? Fooling the Regulatory Commission

What appears easy in principle often turns out to be more difficult in practice. Such is the case with utility regulation, whether regulators attempt to enforce a marginal cost equals price rule or a fair-return price rule.

While utility commissions try to enforce a solution that comes close to that provided by market forces in more competitive industries, it has been observed that regulators are probably more easily fooled than the marketplace. Regulatory commissions are almost invariably at a disadvantage vis-à-vis the firm's management when it comes to knowing what all of the firm's true costs are. They typically have to take management's word for it. No doubt there is a natural temptation for the management of a utility to inflate costs and, as it were, "hide the profits in the costs." More elaborate offices and executive perquisites, padded expense accounts, and trips of questionable necessity are a few examples of how this might be done.

A closely related problem is how to define costs. Let us say, for example, that the regulatory commission took a position that output should

be priced to ensure the utility a fair return of 14 percent on capital. This 14 percent would be calculated as the ratio of profit to invested capital. The question now arises as to how to place a dollar value on the invested capital in order to calculate the rate of return. Should the allowable capital cost be measured in terms of the original purchase price or in terms of the price of replacement today? If its value is given at today's prices, then there is the further question of whether technological change might dictate replacement with somewhat different equipment. This makes cost comparisons even more difficult. Finally, there is even a question of whether the capital investment was justified. It is alleged that sometimes a regulated monopolist will increase the capital investment in its company specifically to increase the assets so that it can apply to the regulatory authority for a price increase.

If management is to receive 14 percent calculated on the basis of whatever the allowable capital cost figure is, sometimes called the **rate base**, then for its part there is little incentive to work to keep the al-

lowable capital cost figure down. In fact, there is a temptation to pad the capital cost figure, since dollar earnings are larger when calculated as 14 percent of a larger number.

Consequently, regulatory commissions are under a heavy burden to formulate allowable cost accounting procedures, equipment procurement practices, and enforceable operating efficiency standards, all in the interest of keeping down the costs of the utility's service to customers.

For Discussion

- If the utility commission regulates the public utility (natural monopoly) in Figure 10-6 by trying to enforce a fair-return pricing rule, where would the utility's managers like the commission to think the *ATC* curve intersects the demand curve, given that the true cost curves are as shown in Figure 10-6?
- Do you think that the way a fair return is actually calculated by a regulated utility company will result in the use of more, or less, capital per unit of labour than would be the case if the utility were unregulated?

business. It can be argued that some segments of the transportation industry fall into this situation. The Canadian government has traditionally subsidized railways. In the case of highways, the cost of one more car using the road, is nearly zero. The government prices most roads at zero and picks up the entire cost.

"Fair-Return" or Average Cost Pricing

In some industries, regulators enforce a marginal cost equals price solution and the government subsidizes the monopolist to cover losses. In other industries the regulatory commissions enforce a **fair-return** or average cost pricing rule. The fair-return concept may be seen as a compromise between the profit-maximizing price output combination chosen by the unregulated monopolist and the marginal cost equals price solution. It is a compromise in the sense that the resulting price and output levels under a fair-return solution will lie somewhere between these two extremes. Hence, the consumer still realizes benefits from the lower per unit costs resulting from the economies of scale of the natural monopoly, while the monopolist is allowed to charge a price sufficient to cover all costs of production including a normal profit, or a fair return on capital.

The fair-return or average cost pricing solution is given by the intersection of the ATC curve with the demand curve D. In Figure 10-6, this determines that the output Q_f will be produced and sold at the price p_f. The price p_f received for each unit sold is just sufficient to cover the average total cost per unit, including a normal profit, or fair return on capital. (Remember that a normal profit is included in the average total cost curve.)

Recall that in longrun competitive equilibrium, price also equals average total cost. While the average cost pricing solution is similar to the perfectly competitive outcome in this respect, it differs in that price does not equal marginal cost as in perfect competition. As a result, there will still be consumers who would be willing to pay a price that is greater than marginal cost for additional units of output, but these units will not be produced. This is represented in Figure 10-6 by the fact that the demand curve D lies above the MC curve over the range of output from Q_f to Q_c.

Monopoly and Price Discrimination

We have seen why a monopolist may be able to earn more than normal profit. Under certain conditions a monopolist may be able to practice price discrimination and thereby realize even greater profit.

Price Discrimination. **Price discrimination** *is the act of a seller charging different prices to different customers when there are no cost differences in supplying the customers.* This is possible whenever different units of the same good or service can be sold at different prices for reasons not associated with cost. We should emphasize that price discrimination can also be practiced by firms that are not monopolists, provided those firms can prevent the resale of their product. However, a monopoly firm is often in a better position to engage in price discrimination by virtue of the fact that it is the only supplier of a particular product with no close substitutes.

Price discrimination is fairly common in our economy. For example, airlines and movie theaters charge different prices for children and adults, dentists may charge different fees to different patients for the same type of procedure, business consultants may charge different customers different fees for essentially the same service, and utility companies charge different rates for businesses and residential users. Why? Because it is more profitable to do so. Let's explore some of the reasons as well as the conditions that make price discrimination possible.

The Ingredients for Price Discrimination

The following conditions contribute to a firm's opportunities to engage in price discrimination.

Resale Not Possible.   The firm must be able to prevent one buyer from selling any of its product to another buyer, or the nature of the firm's product must be such that it is not resalable. For example, it would be almost impossible to charge different prices for bread to different customers. Imagine the grocer charging Jones $1 per loaf and Smith $.75 per loaf. Then Jones could simply have Smith buy enough bread for both of them at $.75 per loaf. However, if a dentist charges Jones more than Smith for a filling, there is nothing Jones can do about it. Jones cannot buy Smith's filling. Obviously, whether a good can be sold from one buyer to another depends on the nature of the good. Services typically cannot be resold. I cannot buy your haircut, and you cannot buy accounting advice intended for me and tailored to my income and circumstances.

Segmentation of the Market.   It must be possible for the firm to segment the market by classifying buyers into separate, identifiable groups. For instance, it is relatively easy to charge one price for adults and another for children. It is also interesting to note that most consumers, businesses, and even governments seem to accept the notion of charging children or seniors or students less than they charge adults for a good, even though it is a form of discrimination on the basis of age and, as such, conflicts with the principle of equal treatment set forth in the *Charter of Rights*. Similarly, utilities charge one price for commercial users of electricity and another for residential users. Often a monopoly can sell its product in country A at one price and in country B at another.

Sometimes it is possible to segment a market according to which unit is sold, the first, second, or tenth. Assuming that there is no cost difference between selling the customer one unit or ten units, it may be possible to gain extra sales, revenue, and profits by charging different prices for the extra units. Often you see advertisements that say, "Buy one jacket at the regular price and you can purchase the second for half price."

Monopoly Control.   If there is only one supplier of a good or service, it is easier for that supplier to engage in price discrimination. Buyers charged discriminatory prices by the monopolist cannot turn to an alternative supplier who might sell to them at a lower price.

Differing Demand Elasticities.   Different buyers have different degrees of willingness to buy a good. Since people are usually as unique in their tastes and preferences for goods as they are in their fingerprints, the shapes of their individual demand curves for a particular good are typically different. Assume that individual A's demand curve for a good is inelastic and individual B's demand curve is elastic. From our discussion of elasticity (Chapter 5), we know that we will get more sales revenue from A by charging A a high price and more sales revenue from B by charging B a low price. Assuming that the good cannot be resold, it clearly pays to charge A and B different prices for the good, to price-discriminate between them. Wherever a market can be segmented according to differing demand elasticities, price discrimination will generate larger total sales revenue than if the good is sold at the same price to all.

Checkpoint 10-4

It has been claimed that monopolists are in a better position than perfectly competitive firms to discriminate against minority groups in their hiring practices. What economic basis is there for this view? If you were a supplier of some input to an industry, would you expect that wining and dining your customers would do more for your sales if they were perfect competitors or if the customers were monopolists? Why?

FIGURE 10-7   **A Price-Discriminating Monopolist**

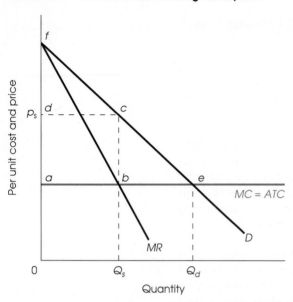

The monopolist depicted here is assumed to have a constant marginal cost *MC* equal to average total cost *ATC*. If the monopolist charges the same price for all units sold, profits are maximized at the price p_s as determined by the intersection of the *MC* and *MR* curves at point *b*.

If the monopolist is able to engage in perfect price discrimination by charging the maximum price buyers are willing and able to pay for each additional unit sold, the demand curve *D* is also the marginal revenue curve. The monopolist would then maximize profit by producing the output Q_d, determined by the intersection of the *MC* and *D* curves at point *e*. The monopolist's profit is then the triangular area *aef*, which is clearly larger than the rectangle *abcd*.

A Price-Discriminating Monopolist; Maximizing Profit

Assume that a firm is a monopolist, is able to identify different buyers according to the price they are willing to pay for its product, and is able to prevent resale of its product. If the monopolist then charged the customers what each individually was willing and able to pay, the monopolist would be engaging in a practice referred to as **perfect price discrimination**.

Examination of the monopolist's downward-sloping demand curve suggests that more profit can be made if the monopolist is able to charge each buyer the full amount he or she is willing to pay, rather than charging all buyers the same price. To see why, in the simplest way, suppose that the monopolist has a constant marginal cost equal to average total cost. That is, the $MC = ATC$ curve is represented by a horizontal line as shown in Figure 10-7. Now, if the monopolist charges a single price for all output produced, then that profit maximizing price would be p_s and the quantity sold Q_s, as determined by the intersection of the *MR* and *MC* curves at point *b*. The monopoly profit is thus represented by the rectangular area *abcd*.

Alternatively, suppose that the monopolist is able to charge each buyer of the good the maximum price that each is willing to pay for the good. That is, assume that all the conditions necessary for price discrimination, as discussed before, are satisfied. The maximum price that each and every buyer is willing to pay for the good is therefore represented by all the points on the demand curve *D*. For example, if the monopolist charges the single price p_s, all the buyers represented by the demand curve over the range from *f* to *c* are getting the good at a price below that which they would be willing to pay for it (except for the last unit sold at point *c*). If instead the monopolist were to charge each and every buyer just what each is willing to pay for the good, the monopolist would make the added profit represented by the area *dcf*.

Carrying this further, if the monopolist charges for each additional unit sold the maximum price that buyers are willing to pay, the addition to total revenue will always be equal to the price received for the last unit. There now will be no offsetting reduction in total revenue—as there is when a single price is charged for all units, which requires reducing the price on all previous units in order to sell an additional unit. Thus, selling each unit for the maximum price buyers are willing to pay means that the demand curve D will also be the marginal revenue curve MR. The monopolist will therefore expand output to Q_d, the point where the MC curve intersects the demand curve D at point e—that is, the point at which marginal cost equals marginal revenue under price discrimination. The total profit is now represented by the triangular area aef. This is clearly larger than the rectangle $abcd$, the profit earned when the monopolist does not discriminate but rather charges the same price p_s for all units sold.

If an electric utility company were not subject to public regulation, it is conceivable that it might be able to behave just like the perfectly price-discriminating monopolist of Figure 10-7. By keeping tabs on customers' electricity meters, it could get a pretty good idea how much electricity each customer would purchase at different prices. Resale of electricity from one customer to another is difficult because customers would have to rig up wiring between their different homes and businesses, something that the electric utility company could easily check on. In most jurisdictions the resale of electricity would also be illegal because the government has granted local monopolies, thus the monopoly supplier, having discovered the wires, could get the resale stopped, another example of the importance of being able to prevent resale. Given these conditions, the utility company could charge different customers different prices for electricity.

Our example of perfect price discrimination is the extreme case where the firm can charge each customer what that customer is willing and able to pay and where resale from one customer to another is not possible. In many cases firms are not in a position to charge perfectly discriminating prices to each individual consumer. This is because the firm may have only incomplete information about each individual customer's willingness to pay a certain price or the customers can, with varying degrees of difficulty, resell the product. Alternatively, there are administrative costs associated with determining and then bargaining with individual customers, which may reduce the benefits to the firm of attempting to charge each different consumer the highest price that customer is willing to pay. As a result of these complications, firms may settle for segregating submarkets of consumers with similar characteristics and charging a different price to each submarket. This imperfect or partial discrimination is based on the same idea as the perfect discrimination just outlined. The only difference is that it is easier and less costly for the firm to administer and it brings in less extra profit.

Checkpoint 10-5

Suppose that all buyers have identical demand curves for a good that is not resalable. If you are the monopoly producer of the good, would it pay to price-discriminate? Why or why not?

Summary

1. Monopoly is a form of market structure in which the entire market for a good or service is supplied by a single seller or firm.
2. For a monopoly to exist there must be large (in effect insurmountable) barriers to competition from potential firms seeking entry to the industry. Such barriers may take a number of different forms, such as exclusive ownership of a unique resource; economies of scale possibly even large enough to create a natural monopoly; and government-sanctioned protection in the form of patents, licenses, charters, copyrights, and franchises. No barrier, with the

possible exception of those that are government sanctioned, is as insurmountable in the longrun as it is in the shortrun.

3. The monopolist's demand curve slopes downward and lies above the marginal revenue curve, unlike that of a perfectly competitive firm, whose demand curve is horizontal and the same as the marginal revenue curve. The profit-maximizing monopolist produces that output and sells at that price at which marginal cost equals marginal revenue. This does not mean that the monopolist always makes an above-normal or positive economic profit, however. If costs are high enough or demand falls, a monopolist may even operate at a loss in the shortrun.

4. Compared to a perfectly competitive firm with the same costs, a monopolist will always produce less and sell at a higher price.

5. Because an unregulated monopolist's profit-maximizing price always lies above marginal cost, there are always consumers who are willing to buy additional units at a price greater than the marginal cost of producing them. However, because the monopolist restricts output, these consumers cannot have these additional units. Compared to a perfectly competitive market, where demand is satisfied for all who are willing to pay a price that covers marginal cost, monopoly results in an inefficient allocation of resources.

6. While many economists agree that monopoly tends to contribute to income inequality, there is far less agreement on whether it promotes or inhibits product innovation and technological advancement. Some argue that the existence or potential of large profit, protected by barriers to competition, provides a great incentive to innovation and the use of improved production methods. Others argue that barriers to competition and the consequent lack of rivals causes the monopolist to be lethargic and disposed to preserve the status quo.

7. Where natural monopolies exist, as in the provision of utility services, charters are often granted to monopolists in exchange for submitting to public regulation, thereby creating a public utility. Either marginal cost pricing or average cost pricing (fair-return) regulations may then be imposed on the utility in order to pass the low per unit cost benefits on to consumers.

8. Where a monopolist can conveniently classify buyers and effectively prevent resale of output, it is possible to price discriminate by selling a good or service at different prices to different buyers. Because different buyers almost always exhibit different degrees of willingness to buy a product, price discrimination is usually more profitable than selling the product at the same price to all.

Key Terms and Concepts

barrier to competition	license	patent
charter	marginal cost pricing	price discrimination
copyright	monopoly	public utilities
fair return	natural monopoly	rate base

Questions and Problems

1. What is the nature and source of monopoly power in each of the following cases: Trans-Alta Utilities, The Montreal Forum, the Mafia, *Porkies II*, Canada Post, The

Canadian Imperial Bank of Commerce, the Ontario Bar Association, your local Blue-box Recycling Program, and your local garbage pick-up?

2. It is often said that in a spectrum of competitive characteristics, monopoly and perfect competition are the extreme opposites. Arrange the following industries according to where you feel they fall on that spectrum: chemical fertilizer manufacturers, automobile manufacturers, electric power producers, dry cleaners, airlines, taxicab services, automobile repair shops, movie theatres, steel producers, newspapers, fish processing plants, and professional hockey teams.

3. If you were a monopolist, would you set price in your demand curve (a) in the elastic portion or (b) in the inelastic portion? Why?

4. If we observed a monopolist who always set price at that point on the demand curve where the elasticity was 1, what might we conclude about the monopolist's variable costs? If this monopolist's fixed costs were cut in half, how would this be reflected in the monopolist's price and output behaviour?

5. Is normal profit part of monopoly profit?

6. Suppose that the government levies a tax on a monopolist equal to 50 percent of all profit in excess of normal profit. How would this affect the profit-maximizing monopolist's choice of price and output combination? Why? How would the price and output combination be affected if such a tax were increased to 75 percent?

7. If all of a monopolist's profit in excess of normal profit were taxed away, would it improve the monopolist's performance as an allocator of resources? Why or why not? Do you think such a tax could be used to reduce income inequality? How?

8. Instead of having public utility regulators enforce either a marginal cost pricing or an average cost pricing rule, what do you think of having them allow a public utility to determine price and output like any profit-maximizing monopolist and then tax away the monopoly profit and distribute the proceeds to consumers in proportion to the amount of output they bought from the utility? From the standpoint of efficient resource allocation, do you think that this would be better or worse than enforcing an average cost pricing rule? Why? Would this be better or worse from the standpoint of income distribution?

9. Once a natural monopoly is turned into a public utility subject to price and output regulation, it is always a difficult task for regulators to keep costs down by enforcing average cost pricing.

   a. Show how this problem would be reflected in the natural monopoly's average and marginal cost curves over time.

   b. In view of your answer to part (a), at which point might it be wiser to drop enforcement of average cost pricing, simply allow the utility to set price like a profit-maximizing monopolist, and then tax away the monopoly profit, redistributing it to consumers in proportion to the quantity each buys from the utility? Demonstrate your answer graphically.

10. For each of the following goods or services, tell whether you think price discrimination is or is not possible and why: airline passenger tickets, custom-tailored clothes, computer software sales, postsecondary educations, monogrammed clothes, haircuts, landscaping services, and telephone service. What role do monopoly considerations play in your answers?

Chapter 11

Monopolistic Competition

Perfect competition and monopoly do not provide a complete description of the kinds of market structures that we observe in the real world. They represent two extremes. The closest example of perfect competition is probably the agricultural sector in our economy. And even there, perfect competition is not an entirely accurate description—acquiring farmland, the necessary machinery, and in some markets the necessary quotas or licenses, sometimes makes entry difficult, for example. At the other extreme, except for your local electric utility company, it is hard to think of many examples of a market completely dominated by one firm. Nonetheless, all industries we observe in the real world exhibit *some* of the characteristics of both perfect competition and monopoly to varying degrees. In this chapter we describe a form of market structure called *monopolistic competition*. It resembles perfect competition in many ways, yet has a few characteristics of monopoly as well.

A monopolistically competitive industry is one in which there are many firms, as in perfect competition, but each of them produces a product that is slightly different from that produced by its competitors. Drugstores, barbershops, dry cleaners, restaurants, gas stations, and many service industries are examples of monopolistic competition. On a spectrum of types of industry structure with perfect competition at one extreme and monopoly at the other, monopolistic competition may be thought of as the one that comes closest to perfect competition.

Characteristics of Monopolistic Competition

Four general characteristics distinguish **monopolistic competition** from other forms of market structure: (1) there are a very large number of firms; (2) each firm's product is slightly different from the others in the industry, so that each firm has a slightly downward-sloping demand curve which makes each firm a price setter with limited power; (3) there is freedom of entry to and exit from the industry; and (4) the firms engage in nonprice competition.

Large Number of Firms.   The number of firms that make up a monopolistically competitive industry may be about the same as that in a perfectly competitive industry. As a result, none of them is large enough to dominate the market. In the garment industry in the United States, for example, there are about 11,600 firms. As an indication of the size of the typical firm, there is an average of about 47 workers per shop. The average annual sales for each is slightly less than $1 million. This means the average firm accounts for only about 1/10,000 of total industry sales. Thinking about it in another way, consider the number of barbershops, drugstores, dry cleaners, restaurants, and newsstands that are found in the typical large city. Finally, think how often you pass an intersection with gas stations on two or more corners.

Product Differentiation.   Unlike perfect competition, in which firms produce an identical product, in a monopolistically competitive industry each firm's product is slightly different from every other's. Why do you usually go to the same barber or eat at a favorite restaurant? Most likely you think your barber "produces" a better haircut or your favorite restaurant serves better food than the others. Some gas stations have better mechanics than others. Some drugstores have a better magazine selection, others a greater variety of cosmetics, and some are simply more conveniently located. In the garment industry, some firms are considered to make certain clothing items better than others. **Product differentiation** is the factor that most distinguishes monopolistic competition from perfect competition.

Because of product differentiation, each firm has a slightly downward-sloping demand curve. Since each firm's product is a close, but not perfect, substitute for every other firm's product, demand is quite elastic, but not perfectly so. In perfect competition, on the other hand, each firm produces exactly the same product. Consequently, the perfectly competitive firm's demand curve is perfectly elastic (horizontal).

Because the monopolistically competitive firm's demand curve is downward sloping, the firm uses the associated marginal revenue curve to select its optimum price and output level in the same fashion as a monopolist. This is the

---

LEARNING OBJECTIVES

After reading this chapter, you will be able to:

1. Define the characteristics of a monopolistically competitive market.
2. Demonstrate how a monopolistically competitive industry adjusts in the longrun to eliminate shortrun profits or losses.
3. Discuss the efficiency of resource allocation under monopolistic competition as compared to perfect competition and understand the significance of product differentiation for this comparison.
4. Explain the role of nonprice competition in the form of advertising and the economic arguments for and against it.
5. Evaluate the incentives for innovation and technological change under monopolistic competition and consider its effects on income distribution.

"monopolistic" aspect of monopolistic competition. "Competition" results from characteristics 1 and 3—that is, the existence of a large number of firms and freedom to enter and exit the market.

Freedom of Entry and Exit.   In a monopolistically competitive industry, firms have the same kind of freedom to enter into and exit from the industry as they do in a perfectly competitive industry. We will explore in greater detail how this characteristic makes for keen competition among firms. For the moment, note that it ensures that in the longrun no monopolistically competitive firm is able to make a greater than normal profit. Freedom of entry and exit means that there are no barriers to competition in a monopolistically competitive industry.

Existence of Nonprice Competition.   Since each firm produces a product similar to but somewhat different from the products produced by every other firm in the industry, there is an incentive for each firm to play up the difference in its product in order to boost its sales. This is known as **nonprice competition** and takes many forms. "Service with a smile," or, "If we forget to clean your windshield, you get a full tank free" are common examples. Beauty parlors may compete with one another by providing background music, better magazine selections, or fancier interior decorating than their competitors. Anything that may serve to distinguish a firm's product from that of its competitors in this way might be tried, so long as the firm feels that the cost of such promotional activity is more than made up for by the resulting increase in sales. Advertising in local newspapers, shoppers' guides, and other media outlets is common. You only have to drive down a typical main street in any town to observe fancy signs beckoning you to come in and try this or buy that.

This type of competition is common among monopolistically competitive firms. By contrast, there is no incentive for this activity in a perfectly competitive industry because one firm's product is indistinguishable from any other's.

Equilibrium in a Monopolistically Competitive Industry

Examination of the preceding characteristics clearly indicates that the most important difference between monopolistic competition and perfect competition is product differentiation. It is this factor that causes the monopolistically competitive firm's demand curve to be slightly downward sloping, and it is this factor that gives rise to nonprice competition.

In terms of the concept of elasticity, the less product differentiation there is among firms in the industry, the more elastic will be the individual firm's demand curve. This follows from our earlier study of the determinants of demand. The more a firm's product is similar to that of other firms in the industry, the more willing consumers will be to switch to that firm's product if it lowers its price, and away from that firm's product if it raises its price. Thus, the greater is the degree of similarity, and therefore substitutability, between a firm's product and those of its competitors, the greater will be the change in its sales resulting from any given change in price. (In the extreme case of perfect substitutability, the firm's demand curve is perfectly horizontal, or infinitely elastic, and we are back in a perfectly competitive world.)

Since the monopolistically competitive firm is able to affect its level of sales by changing its price, it is in this respect similar to a monopoly. It knows that in order to sell an additional unit of output it must lower price, not only on the additional unit, but on all previous units as well. Therefore, like the monopolist but unlike the perfect competitor, the monopolistically competitive firm finds that at any output level price is always greater than marginal revenue. This is reflected in the fact that the monopolistically competitive firm's demand curve lies above its associated marginal revenue curve, exactly as in the case of the monopolist.

Shortrun Equilibrium

The shortrun equilibrium position of a monopolistically competitive firm looks just like that of a monopolist. Of course, the difference is that there are many firms in the monopolistically competitive industry rather than just one, as in a monopoly.

One such firm is shown in Figure 11-1. Two possible shortrun equilibrium positions are shown in frames (a) and (c). Whatever the position of the firm's demand curve and its associated marginal revenue curve, the firm adjusts price and output so that marginal cost equals marginal revenue. This is determined by the intersection of the MC and MR curves (assuming that it can cover

FIGURE 11-1   Equilibrium for a Monopolistically Competitive Firm

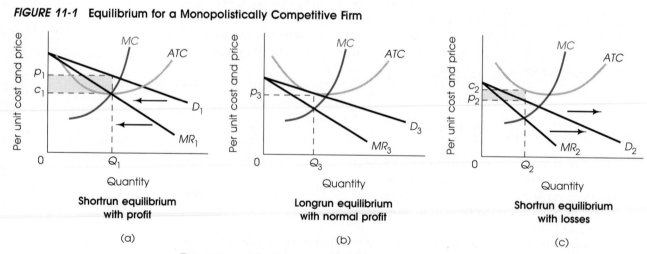

The monopolistically competitive firm in frame (a) is earning an above-normal profit (positive economic profit), equal to the shaded area. Assuming that this firm is representative of the many firms in the industry, the positive economic profits will attract new firms into the industry in the longrun until economic profits are eliminated and each firm in the industry is in a longrun equilibrium position like that shown in frame (b).

Alternatively, suppose that firms in the industry are realizing losses equal to the shaded area for the representative firm in frame (c). Some firms will leave the industry, and those that remain will have a larger share of the market, as represented by the rightward shift in each of their demand curves. This process will continue until the remaining firms are just making a normal profit (zero economic profits), as represented by the longrun equilibrium position shown in frame (b).

its average variable costs). In frame (a), the firm's demand curve D_1 is such that it produces Q_1 to be sold at the price p_1. The resulting profit is represented by the shaded area. In frame (c), demand for the firm's product is weak, and so the entire demand curve D_2 lies below its ATC curve. Assuming that it can cover average variable cost, the best the firm can do is produce Q_2, sell it at the price p_2, and minimize its losses, which are represented by the shaded area.

Checkpoint* 11-1

Can you list the industries that might be considered to be monopolistically competitive? By way of review, explain why the slope of a demand curve is a reflection of the existence of substitutes.

*Answers to all Checkpoints can be found at the back of the text.

Adjustment to Longrun Equilibrium

For a monopolist, frame (a) of Figure 11-1 could represent a longrun equilibrium position. However, for a monopolistically competitive firm, it can only be a shortrun equilibrium position because, unlike the monopoly situation, there is free entry of new firms into the monopolistically competitive industry in the longrun. There are no barriers to competition.

Above-Normal Profits—Entry of New Firms

If each of the many firms in a monopolistically competitive industry is realizing positive economic profits (greater than normal profits), like the one in Figure 11-1, frame (a), new firms will be attracted to the industry in the longrun. As more firms open up for business, the total market for the industry will have to be divided up among more and more firms. Therefore, each firm's share of the whole market will get smaller. This means that the typical monopolistically competitive firm's demand curve and associated marginal revenue curve will shift leftward during this process, as indicated by the arrows in frame (a). New firms will continue to enter the industry as long as positive economic profits exist. Hence, the demand curves of firms already in the industry will continue to shift leftward until the positive economic profits of each have been eliminated and normal profits are just sufficient to cover opportunity cost.

The typical monopolistically competitive firm will finally be in the longrun equilibrium position shown in frame (b). It will produce output Q_3 and sell it at price p_3 as determined by the intersection of MC and MR_3. The price p_3 will just be equal to the average total cost per unit, as indicated by the fact that the demand curve D_3 will be tangent to the ATC curve at this point. The typical firm's total revenue will just equal its total cost, including a normal profit. There will be no incentive for any new firms to enter the industry.

Why is it that in longrun equilibrium the monopolistically competitive firm's demand curve D_3 is tangent to ATC at just that output level Q_3 where $MC = MR$? Note that for any output level greater than Q_3 the price received per unit would be less than the average total cost per unit, as represented by the fact that the demand curve D_3 lies below the ATC curve. The same is true for any output level less than Q_3. Only at output level Q_3 does price just cover average total cost per unit. Given the demand curve D_3 and associated marginal revenue curve MR_3, the best the firm can do is produce and sell Q_3 at price p_3. (This is best in the sense that it is the only output level where the firm does not realize a loss.) Hence, this must be the output level corresponding to the point where marginal cost equals marginal revenue, as represented by the intersection of MC and MR. At any output level greater than Q_3, marginal cost exceeds marginal revenue, represented by the fact that the MC curve lies above the MR curve.

Checkpoint 11-2
Typically waiters and
waitresses have been
paid wages that are
low relative to jobs that
require similar skill
levels and working
conditions. Part of
the reason for these
low wages can be
attributed to the idea
that profit margins
aren't great enough
to pay higher wages.
Using graphs like
frames (b) and (c) of
Figure 11-1, explain
what would happen in
the restaurant industry
if restaurant workers
were to get large wage
increases. What would
happen to price and
output levels? What
effect do you think
that this would have
on the number of
people employed as
waiters or waitresses?

Therefore, it does not pay for the firm to produce output beyond Q_3. For any output level less than Q_3, marginal revenue exceeds marginal cost; the MC curve lies below the MR curve. Hence, it reduces losses or increases profits for the firm to expand output up to the level Q_3.

Losses—Exit of Existing Firms

Alternatively, suppose that each of the many firms in the monopolistically competitive industry is realizing losses, such as the typical firm shown in Figure 11-1, frame (c). In the longrun, if a firm continues to realize losses like this, it will be forced out of business. Therefore, firms will leave the industry. As this process continues, the share of the market left for each of the firms remaining in the industry will grow. Their demand curves and associated marginal revenue curves will shift rightward, as indicated by the arrows in frame (c). This process will continue until enough firms have left the industry so that those remaining are just able to cover costs, including a normal profit. The industry will then be in longrun equilibrium, with the typical firm again in the equilibrium position depicted in frame (b).

Economic Effects of Monopolistic Competition

We can evaluate the economic effects of monopolistic competition by answering some of the same questions we considered in analyzing perfect competition and monopoly. How efficiently does monopolistic competition allocate scarce resources to fill consumer wants? What are the pros and cons on the economic effects of advertising, that often-controversial form of nonprice competition? How much does monopolistic competition promote innovation and technological advancement? What about the effects of such a market structure on income distribution?

Efficiency of Resource Allocation

It is often claimed that monopolistic competition is inefficient because it results in too many firms in an industry, each operating with excess capacity and selling output at a price that exceeds marginal cost.[1] This is illustrated by the monopolistically competitive firm shown in Figure 11-2.

Monopolistic Competition versus Perfect Competition

Because of the downward-sloping demand curve, which results from product differentiation, and because of free entry into the industry, the market forces the typical firm to produce Q_1 and sell it at the price p_1. This corresponds to point a, at which the downward-sloping portion of the ATC curve is tangent to

---

[1]By convention, we say that a firm is *operating at capacity* when it is at the lowest point on its ATC curve. When the firm is operating on the downward-sloping portion of the ATC curve, at a point to the left of the lowest point, we say that the firm has *excess capacity*. When the firm is operating on the upward-sloping portion of the ATC curve, at a point to the right of the lowest point, we say that it is *overutilizing its capacity*.

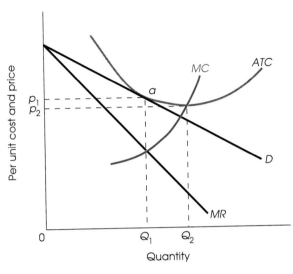

FIGURE 11-2   Efficiency and Equilibrium in Monopolistic Competition

In longrun equilibrium, the monopolistically competitive firm is forced to operate at a point (such as a) along the declining portion of its ATC curve.

the demand curve D. Attracted by above-normal profits, potential competitors have entered freely with the result that so many firms have entered the industry that the typical firm has excess capacity. If the typical firm were able to use this idle capacity, it could produce the larger output Q_2, corresponding to the lowest possible average total cost per unit. The normal-profit, longrun equilibrium position of a monopolistically competitive firm occurs at an output level less than that at which average total cost is a minimum.

It is often argued that consumers' needs could be satisfied at a lower cost with fewer firms if somehow each firm could be forced to operate at the larger output level. This is the level at which average total costs are lowest and corresponds to the minimum point on the ATC curve. There would be fewer corner grocers, barbershops, and gas stations, and each would be more fully utilized.

There are other implications of monopolistic competition that are closely related to the excess capacity issue. In longrun equilibrium, the monopolistically competitive firm produces the output Q_1 and sells it at the price p_1 in Figure 11-2. If you look to the right of this point, you will see that there is a range of the demand curve that lies above the marginal cost curve. This means that under monopolistic competition there are consumers willing to pay a price for the product that exceeds the marginal cost of producing it but who are unable to buy it at such a price. This follows from the fact that for a monopolistically competitive firm the longrun equilibrium price is above marginal cost.

Suppose that the cost curves shown in Figure 11-2 were those of a typical firm in a perfectly competitive industry. In longrun equilibrium the perfectly competitive firm would produce output Q_2 and sell it at price p_2. Price would equal MC as well as the minimum level of ATC. Why? Because, as we saw in Chapter 9, the perfectly competitive firm's demand curve is perfectly horizontal. This means that the demand curve and the marginal revenue curve are one and the same. Moreover, in longrun equilibrium the perfectly competitive firm's demand curve is tangent to lowest point on the longrun ATC curve. The firm produces the output level corresponding to this point because here price equals marginal cost. It is also the output level where the firm produces at the lowest possible level of average total cost.

In terms of Figure 11-2, the perfectly competitive firm would produce output right up to the point where the marginal cost of the last unit produced is just covered by the price consumers are willing to pay for it. Here, p_2 equals MC equals the lowest possible level of ATC. Consumers would pay a price for the good that just covers the lowest possible average total cost of producing it. By contrast, the monopolistically competitive firm produces the smaller output level Q_1 and sells it at the higher price p_1. This price is higher than marginal cost and higher than the lowest possible level of average total cost (the lowest point on the ATC curve).

If the perfectly competitive longrun equilibrium position is taken as the ideal of economic efficiency (for the reasons discussed in Chapter 9), then monopolistic competition falls short of this standard.

Implications of Product Differentiation for Economic Efficiency

In the preceding comparison with perfect competition, monopolistic competition comes out on the short end of the stick. But let's carry the comparison a bit further. After all, under monopolistic competition, it is true that in longrun equilibrium no more than a normal profit is earned, just as in perfect competition. But in addition, it can be argued that monopolistic competition offers the consumer more product variety in the forms of quality, service, information, and other aspects of nonprice competition.

Are the added costs of the product variety and production at less than full capacity necessarily "bad"? The fact that consumers are willing to pay for product differentiation suggests that they think it is a benefit. If consumers want variety, who are economists to say that this is "inefficient and undesirable"? Of course, this is often used as the argument for why monopolistic competition cannot be judged relative to perfect competition. If consumers wanted the restaurant industry to produce only one standard meal to meet their nutritional needs, then although this would ensure that price equals MC equals minimum ATC, the dreary sameness of everyone's diet would be dull indeed. In a society where consumers prefer variety over sameness and are willing to pay the extra cost to have it, it is simply a value judgment (a normative statement) to say that "product differentiation is less desirable than product homogeneity." Comparisons between sameness and variety are like comparisons between apples and oranges. They are different goods.

In order to make the claim that monopolistic competition is inefficient, one must have a standard for comparison, an alternative that is "better." But can monopolistic competition really be compared with the alternative of perfect competition and marginal cost pricing? Perfect competition may be more efficient, but it can only be achieved at the cost of reducing the variety of available products. Is it therefore "better"? Any answer is open to debate.

Pros and Cons of Advertising

If the monopolistically competitive firm is able to differentiate its product from that of its competitors in the right way, it may be able to gain a competitive advantage. Successful product differentiation amounts to tailoring the product to best suit consumer demands. Nonprice competition in the form of advertising serves this goal to the extent that it informs the consumer about differences among products. However, advertising may go beyond the simple conveying of facts when it attempts to tailor consumer demands to goods, rather than simply making consumers aware of the nature of a product. (Much of what we will say here about advertising also applies to oligopolistic market structures, the subject of the next chapter.)

There is a grey area in all this, of course. It is often difficult to distinguish informative advertising from that which simply urges consumers to buy for reasons only superficially related to the product, or even on the basis of claims that may be entirely false. Sometimes the difference between real information and pure hype is pretty obvious. What has "By Appointment to Her Majesty the Queen . . ." really got to do with the taste of a meat sauce or brand of marmalade? Similarly, does it matter to the purchaser of an automobile whether or not a car dealer is "a fun kind of guy"? There are some 15,000 to 20,000 parts in the typical automobile. What does the personality of the car dealer, or images of a four wheel drive vehicle tearing apart a quiet mountain stream tell you about the quality of those parts or how your car will idle in a rush hour traffic jam on the 401 out of Toronto? Since any form of advertising costs something, the question is whether the benefits justify the use of scarce resources in this kind of activity. Is it worth it? This issue is as much debated as it is unsettled.

Is Advertising Informative?

To the extent that advertising provides consumers with knowledge about product prices, quality, alternatives (substitutes), and where particular products can be purchased, it can save the consumer the costs of searching and shopping. Newspaper advertising, particularly classified ads, and shoppers' guides appear to serve this end well. On the other hand, television and radio often provide relatively uninformative types of advertising pitched along lines such as, "you will be more of a man if you buy this" or "more of a woman if you buy that." The "hidden persuaders" of this type of advertising often bear little relation to the realities of the product.

It has been argued that the prohibition of advertising by some trade groups is a practice intended to reduce information that would promote competition and lead to lower product prices. In recent years there have been various court rulings and legislative actions making some of these prohibitions illegal. Removal of such prohibitions has led to increased advertising and lower prices for eyeglasses and dentures, for example. It has also resulted in more advertising by lawyers, providing the public with greater information about the fees charged for different legal services. Such advertising is informative and very likely promotes competition among sellers that results in lower prices to consumers.

Can Advertising Reduce the Costs of Goods?

It is sometimes argued that by increasing sales and therefore revenue, advertising allows firms to introduce new products at lower costs to consumers. This argument is illustrated in Figure 11-3. Suppose that in the absence of advertising, the monopolistically competitive firm has average total cost represented by

FIGURE 11-3   The Effect of Advertising on the Monopolistically Competitive Firm

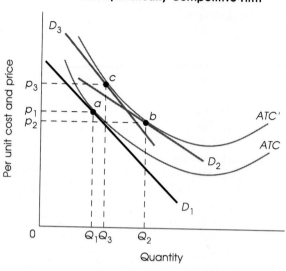

The cost of advertising causes the *ATC* curve to shift upward to the position *ATC'*. If the effect of advertising increases consumer demand for the firm's product in such a way as to shift the demand curve outward to D_2, the new longrun equilibrium position is at point *b*. In that case the firm will produce Q_2 and sell it at the lower price p_2. However, if the demand curve is shifted outward to D_3, the new longrun equilibrium will be at point *c*. Output will then be Q_3 and price will rise to p_3. Since advertising tends to increase product differentiation, product substitutability will likely decrease, making point *c* the more likely outcome. Advertising gives rise to a higher price, p_3.

the *ATC* curve. Given the demand curve D_1, the longrun equilibrium occurs at point *a*, where output Q_1 is produced and sold at price p_1.

Now suppose that the firm advertises. Let's say that advertising costs push the *ATC* curve upward to the position *ATC'*. If the advertising is effective, it should result in increased demand for the firm's product, represented by a rightward shift in the demand curve. If the demand curve shifts to a position such as D_2, then in the new longrun equilibrium the firm will operate at point *b*, producing output Q_2 and selling it at price p_2. This price, which is equal to average total cost, will indeed be lower. The lower price is due to the production of the larger output Q_2, which allows the firm to realize some economies of scale. But what if advertising causes the demand curve to shift rightward to a position such as D_3? The new longrun equilibrium will occur at point *c*. Although a larger output Q_3 is produced, price p_3, which is equal to average total cost, is now higher than initially.

In summary, while it is possible that advertising can lead to reduced costs of production and lower product price, it is obviously possible for just the opposite to happen. Furthermore, the monopolistically competitive firm typically advertises with the intent of making the firm's product more distinguishable or different from those of other firms in the industry. This will decrease the degree of substitutability between its product and those of other firms. Therefore, the demand curve will become less elastic, or more steeply sloped, resembling D_3 rather than D_2. This makes it less likely that advertising will lead to a lower price.

Is Advertising Wasteful?

Advertising that is informative can certainly improve a firm's competitive position. However, much advertising aimed at improving the firm's competitive position is not informative. It merely claims brand X to be superior to brands Y and Z on the basis of doubtful allegations and meaningless comparison tests. In order to defend their market shares, brands Y and Z respond in kind with similar advertising campaigns.

POLICY PERSPECTIVE

How Important Is Advertising to Economic Prosperity?

Total advertising expenditures in the United States usually amount to around 2 percent of GNP, and a similar figure for Canada would be appropriate. In relative terms we can get an idea of the size of the advertising industry and the amount of society's resources committed to it by remembering that Canada's defense spending to meet our NATO and Norad defense commitments amounts to about the same percentage of GDP as does advertising. However, some economists argue that the importance of advertising to the well-being of the economy is much greater than the 2 percent figure would suggest. Basically, they contend that much advertising has the effect of molding consumer tastes to form new demands for new products, often doing this by effectively making existing products appear obsolete.

No doubt the almost steady year-to-year growth in demand experienced by the garment industry is a result of the industry's efforts to bring about fashion changes and new fads in clothing styles. Messages such as "Last year's dresses are simply passé this spring" or "Double-breasted suits are coming back" are part of this effort. In the auto industry, the new models produced every year are usually pushed by advertisement in all possible media outlets. Henry Ford used to say, "You can have any color Ford you want, as long as it's black." The auto industry seems to have learned long ago that it's much better for sales to have a lot more change and variety than this.

Some economists, such as John Kenneth Galbraith, have argued that such "contrived obsolescence," aided and promoted by advertising, is a waste of resources; resources that might be used instead to provide improved school systems, update the sewer systems of cities like Halifax, or provide other badly needed public goods. It is charged that advertising creates a social imbalance between private and public goods because it is used to push private, or consumer, goods "disproportionately" more than public goods.

But who should be the arbiter of consumer tastes and preferences: consumers, advertisers, economists, government regulators? The idea of consumer sovereignty, that in the final analysis consumers decide what and how much, still has its advocates. As evidence in support of this position, cases are often cited where products were rejected by the market, despite large advertising campaigns. Similarly, products that became a market success with little or no assistance from advertising provide further evidence along this line. The maxi skirt flopped despite heavy advertising. The rotary engine Mazda made only a modest and short-lived splash, despite its advertisements. The Volkswagen "bug" was one of the largest successes in automotive history, and for years this sales success came without the aid of any advertisement at all.

For Discussion

- Do you see any potential conflicts between Galbraith's position and the idea of freedom of information? Can you think of examples of attempts by the government to offset the demand-expanding effects of advertising?

As a result of such competitive advertising efforts, the total market for the industry's product may hardly increase at all. Even the market shares of the individual firms may remain unchanged because their efforts merely offset one another. But the *ATC* curves of each will be higher, reflecting the increased advertising costs. A typical participant in such a competitive advertising "war" may simply end up in a position such as point *c* instead of point *a* in Figure 11-3. Some firms may be producing a little more, others a little less. In the end, all that seems certain is that consumers will be paying higher prices for the industry's output to cover the costs of competitive advertising, which may have very little "hard" information content.

However, this may be an unduly harsh judgment. To the extent that this type of advertising persuades consumers to try different brands, they will be exposed to the "true facts" of each firm's product through their own sampling activity.

"Try it, you'll like it" may, at least, result in a "try it and see." Such advertising may result in the acquiring of hard information after all.

In addition to simply splitting up the existing market into smaller segments and increasing the cost of production, advertising may also reduce and distort the availability of other public goods even when they are "free goods." In an attempt to make highway travellers aware of its beautiful view of a lake, a local motel might put up a billboard along a local stretch of highway. In self-defense another motel puts up a billboard beside the first. By the time each hotel, resort, and motel in the area has finished defending its right to have the public made aware of the benefits of staying in it, the highway has become fenced with billboards obstructing the view of the lake!

Finally, the argument that consumers need to be informed through advertising of the relative benefits of a particular product in order to exercise informed consumer sovereignty is often overstated. Some advertising does indeed inform the consumer of the availability and usefulness of products, but "third-party" and "life-style" advertising seeks to do something very different. As was mentioned earlier in the chapter ads that link the product to a famous person, such as personal endorsements by rock stars, actors, or Her Majesty, Elizabeth II, encourage consumers to use a product simply because someone else derives benefit from using it. In a sense this is the very opposite of consumer sovereignty, for it encourages consumers to accept someone else's tastes in preference to their own judgment and choose and use products without critically assessing whether these products are of any value to them personally.

How Significant Is Advertising in Monopolistic Competition?

It should be recalled at this point that in longrun equilibrium the monopolistically competitive firm can only earn a normal profit, just like a perfectly competitive firm, and this is true no matter what form of nonprice competition the firm may engage in. Nonprice competition, such as advertising, can only result in above-normal profits in the shortrun. We have seen how the competitive force of free entry leads to an adjustment process that eliminates them in the longrun. The fact that competitive advantage obtained through expenditures on advertising is fleeting no doubt puts a limit on just how much of this activity is "worth it" to the monopolistically competitive firm. Your barber probably advertises little, perhaps no more than an occasional ad in the neighborhood paper or by helping to sponsor a community hockey team or baseball team for kids. The same is true of service stations, dry cleaners, florists, and car washes. Much of what we have said about advertising applies equally, perhaps more so, to oligopolistic market structures, which is the subject of the next chapter.

Innovation and Technical Change

Does monopolistic competition provide much incentive for innovation and change? Remember that in a perfectly competitive market, free entry of new firms makes it difficult for any firm to reap above-normal profits (positive economic profits), for any length of time. Any positive economic profit earned by the perfectly competitive firm as a result of innovation is eliminated by rivals who quickly copy and adopt the new development, thereby keeping themselves on the same competitive footing with the original innovator. Longrun equilibrium entails nothing more than a normal profit. Since a monopolistically competitive industry is also characterized by free entry and a normal profit in longrun equilibrium, it might be expected that the incentive to innovate is no greater than in perfect competition.

On the other hand, it is possible that product differentiation provides an added spur for monopolistically competitive firms to innovate. Nonprice competition may stimulate product development aimed at further distinguishing the firm's product from those of other firms in the industry. If nothing else, a firm may gain some additional, economic profits in the shortrun through such activity. Here again, however, because such profits are short-lived, the incentive to innovate is definitely limited. For this reason, some economists argue that in monopolistically competitive industries, product innovation and technological change is more cosmetic than real. Since cosmetic change is cheaper, the development of packaging that is more eye-catching may substitute for substantive product improvement. Given the prospect of additional shortrun profit but nothing more, such changes may appear to be "worth it," while the greater expense of real innovation does not.

Some evidence suggests that this is the case. The construction industry is made up of a large number of independent contractors and might well be characterized as monopolistically competitive. Compared to other areas of the economy, the technology of constructing residential housing does not appear to progress very rapidly. (Some might argue that union work rules and outdated building codes have had more to do with unchanging techniques in residential construction than the market structure has.) True, more power tools and motorized equipment are used today. But these were developed by other industries more oligopolistic in structure—the automotive, heavy machinery, and electrical equipment industries.

Income Distribution

In terms of its implications for income distribution, monopolistic competition is very similar to perfect competition. The absence of economic profit in longrun equilibrium means that all factors are just earning their opportunity costs. The presence of a large number of firms means that these normal profits are spread over a large number of people. Many economists argue that this is conducive to a more equal distribution of income.

Reports indicate that average hourly earnings for workers in the textile industry are lower than those for workers in the manufacturing sector. Many of the other industries in the manufacturing sector of the Canadian economy are much more oligopolistic than the textile industry. That is, there are fewer but larger firms. In these industries higher barriers to competition are no doubt a contributing factor to higher wages and larger profits.

Checkpoint 11-3

The publications, *Consumer Reports*, *Lemon Aid*, and *Protect Yourself Magazine* are devoted entirely to objective comparisons among products of various kinds. Sold on newsstands throughout the country, these magazines have been successful products in their own right. What do you think the popularity of these magazines says about advertising? What would be the legal difficulties in having the federal or provincial departments of consumer and corporate affairs regulate advertising so that only informative advertising would be permitted?

Summary

---

1. Monopolistic competition is very similar to perfect competition in that it is a market structure with many firms and an absence of financial, legal, or other barriers to entry into or exit from the industry. It differs from perfect competition in that each firm in a monopolistically competitive industry produces a slightly different variation of the same product. Product differenti-

ation means that each firm's product is a close but not perfect substitute for that of every other firm. This is reflected in the fact that each firm's demand curve is slightly downward sloping.

2. Because of its downward-sloping demand curve, a monopolistically competitive firm makes its price and output decisions in the same manner as a monopolist does. It produces where marginal cost equals marginal revenue and sells at a price above that at which marginal cost equals marginal revenue. However, because of low barriers to competition, the entry and exit of firms to and from the industry allows them to earn only a normal profit (zero economic profit) in the longrun.

3. Compared to perfect competition, monopolistic competition is considered inefficient because in longrun equilibrium price exceeds minimum average total cost of production as well as marginal cost. Hence, consumers are not getting the product at the lowest price permitted by cost conditions, and there are consumers who are willing to pay a price greater than the marginal cost of the product but who are unable to have any of it. However, these alleged shortcomings of monopolistic competition may be offset by the benefits of product differentiation.

4. Product differentiation is the primary means by which monopolistically competitive firms engage in nonprice competition. An important but controversial form of nonprice competition is advertising. To the extent that advertising provides consumers with hard information about prices, factual characteristics of products, and where they can be purchased, it provides them with benefits in the form of reduced search and shopping costs. To the extent that it misleads consumers by distorting facts or making false claims, it only confuses them, wastes resources, and leads to higher product prices.

5. Under monopolistic competition, innovation and technological advancement are limited by the fact that the positive economic profits that may reward such activity are limited to the shortrun. Furthermore, nonprice competition may lead to innovation in the form of product differentiation that is more cosmetic than substantive.

6. Many, but not all, economists argue that monopolistic competition may be conducive to a more equal distribution of income when compared to monopoly because in longrun equilibrium there are many firms, each earning only a normal profit.

Key Terms and Concepts

monopolistic competition   nonprice competition   product differentiation

Questions and Problems

1. Do you think that a monopolistically competitive industry is composed of many firms selling slightly differentiated products (a) at the same price, or (b) each at slightly different prices? Why? Do you think that the cost curves of all the firms must necessarily be identical?

2. Rank the following products according to the degree to which they may be truly differentiated, as opposed to "artificially" differentiated through advertising and packaging: toothpaste, sugar, breakfast cereals, fast food restaurants, retail clothing shops, oil well service companies, fish-packing plants, lumber mills.

3. Suppose that the government forced all monopolistically competitive firms to set price equal to marginal cost. What sort of difficulty would this create in longrun equilibrium? What would you suggest the government do if it insists on enforcing such a policy? (Figure 11-2 will help you to answer this question.)

4. Do you think that advertising makes the longrun equilibrium position of monopolistically competitive firms more, or less, like that of perfectly competitive firms? Why?

5. Rank the following goods according to the degree to which you think their advertising is informative: heavy machinery (advertised in trade journals), perfume, used cars, beer, apartments, new cars, clothing, dairy products, dogs, patent medicine. Give reasons for the rankings you select.

Chapter 12

Oligopoly and Market Concentration

A large part of our economy is made up of industries that are dominated by a few large firms. An industry of this type is called an **oligopoly,** a word of Greek origin that loosely translated means "few sellers." In terms of sheer dollar volume of economic activity, oligopolies dominate industry in Canada.

Our analysis of oligopoly will complete our examination of types of market structures. If we were to order these structures along a spectrum according to their similarities with one another, they would line up as follows: perfect competition, monopolistic competition, oligopoly, and monopoly. Oligopoly is like monopolistic competition because in some industries firms produce a differentiated product. It is like monopoly in that there are barriers to the entry of new firms into the industry and it is possible to make economic profit in the longrun. The market outcome in oligopoly, depending upon the circumstances, can range from being close to the competitive price and output to being close to that of a monopoly. The conditions for oligopoly may give rise to economic profits for a prolonged period of time to firms in the industry. The existence of only a small number of dominant firms may result in cooperative behaviour, such as collusion to set the price where joint profit is maximized. In this case the market situation closely approximates that of a monopoly.

The most important implication of oligopolist conditions is that the firms are interdependent; therefore, if they do not collude they must act and react to competitors strategically. As in sports, card games, and chess, each firm in an oligopoly must act in reponse to the strategies adopted by its competitors. This strategic interdependence makes oligopoly extremely difficult to analyze. Each action made by a firm in an oligopoly must take into account the previous actions and future reactions of its competitors. Therefore, firms require a strategy. To study this behaviour requires a dynamic analysis unlike any brought to bear in previous market structures. For example, Coca-Cola would likely reap large profits in the current time period if it were to reduce its price. But a retaliatory price cut by Pepsi in the next time period may reduce the sum of the profits to Coca-Cola over the two periods. Oligopoly is a complete course in itself and an exciting area of study in which game theory has given important insights into firms' behaviour. In this text we can only touch on some of the theory of oligopoly, but you should bear in mind that oligopoly is the most complicated and varied form of market organization that we will study.

Characteristics of Oligopoly

There are several identifying characteristics of oligopoly that are always present, although to different degrees in different industries. The type of product that the firm produces can be either a homogeneous product or a differentiated product. A small number of dominant firms, but not necessarily a small total number of firms, exist in the industry. Substantial barriers to entry occur, especially economies of scale. The implications of these characteristics are a recognized mutual interdependence among firms, nonprice competition and price rigidity, and the incentive for firms to collude or to merge. As we proceed through this chapter, it will be apparent that these characteristics and their implications are interrelated.

Type of Product

Oligopolies may be divided into two major types. Those that produce undifferentiated, or homogeneous, products are often called **undifferentiated oligopolies.** One firm's product is no different from that of the other firms in the industry. The metals industries—producers of aluminum, steel, and copper—are examples. A manufacturer who uses one of these metals usually orders by exactly

---

LEARNING OBJECTIVES

After reading this chapter, you will be able to:

1. List and explain the characteristics of an oligopoly market.
2. Describe industrial concentration and critically interpret concentration ratios as a measure of oligopoly.
3. List and explain the possible barriers to entry into an industry.
4. Explain how mutual interdependence among oligopolistic firms can lead to price rigidity in oligopolistic industries.
5. Explain and graph the kinked demand and revenue (AR/MR) curves for the oligopolist.
6. Explain how price competition between a few firms (price wars) will lead to the competitive price and output result as illustrated by the Bertrand model.
7. Explain how mutual interdependence among oligopolistic firms can lead to collusive behaviour, price leadership, and joint profit maximization among oligopolistic firms.
8. List the conditions that affect the possibilities for collusive behaviour.

specifying characteristics such as tensile strength and carbon content. There is little if any room for product differentiation. Oligopolies that produce differentiated products, or **differentiated oligopolies,** are more numerous. These include the electrical appliance, automobile, and aircraft industries, among others. Some oligopolies, such as the petroleum industry, often produce identical products but attempt to differentiate them through advertising or complement services. But since all gasolines are characterized by octane rating and other such specified traits, there is little room for true product differentiation. In general, the differentiated oligopolies are in the consumer product industries and the undifferentiated oligopolies are in the producer product industries.

A Few Dominant Firms

What evidence do we have that oligopolistic market structures are widespread in Canada? Many studies have concluded that Canadian industry is highly concentrated. John Porter's *The Vertical Mosaic* (1965), Wallace Clement's *The Corporate Elite* (1975), and Peter Newman's *The Canadian Establishment* (in two volumes, 1975 and 1981), are examples of this literature. **Concentration** occurs in an economy when a small number of firms control a large amount of the assets, sales revenue, and profits generated in the economy. Table 12-1 compares the level of concentration by asset values, sales volume, and profits between the years 1975 and 1985. These data show that the top 25 enterprises account for a third of the industrial assets in Canada, while the top 500 enterprises account for two thirds. Note also that the top 25 enterprises have expanded their share of the total but the largest 500 have maintained their proportion of assets, sales, and profits. A more specific measure by industry of this concentration is the concentration ratio. *The **concentration ratio** is a measure of the extent to which a few firms dominate an industry.*

Concentration Ratios

A variety of types of concentration ratios are used by economists to measure the extent to which a few firms dominate an industry. One of the most commonly used concentration ratios is the sales ratio. The sales ratio for a given industry

TABLE 12-1   Concentration in Canada as Measured by Shares of Total Nonfinancial Assets, Sales, and Profits of the Leading 25, 100, and 500 Enterprises*

	Year	Leading 25	Leading 100	Leading 500
Assets	1975	29.2	46.5	65.0
	1985	33.5	52.0	67.4
Sales	1975	20.8	36.0	53.1
	1985	23.2	38.1	53.2
Profits	1975	22.2	43.1	65.6
	1985	31.5	49.9	67.0

Source: Statistics Canada. *Annual Report of the Minister of Supply and Services under the Corporations and Labour Unions Returns Act* (Ottawa, June 1989), cat no. 61–210.

*Note: Statistics Canada defines an enterprise as a group of companies under common control.

is computed on the percentage of total industry sales accounted for by the four, or eight, largest (in terms of sales) firms in the industry. In principle, the ratio can be based on whatever number of the largest firms an investigator may think is most revealing. Concentration ratios for selected manufacturing industries in Canada are given in Table 12-2.

The closer the concentration ratio of an industry is to zero, the more likely it is that the industry takes on more of the characteristics of monopolistic competition or perfect competition. The closer the ratio is to 100, the more we might expect to find giant firms and barriers to entry nearly as insurmountable as those of a monopoly. This interpretation should not be taken too literally, however. It is obviously tempting to suppose that higher concentration ratios are indicative of less competitive conditions. However, the numbers are only based on dollar sales figures and therefore may conceal some fundamental differences among industries.

Suppose that there are two different industries, each having identical concentration ratios. If one is a differentiated oligopolistic industry and the other is undifferentiated, there is bound to be some difference between the two in terms of the nature and extent of nonprice competition that takes place in each. Competition among firms in the differentiated oligopoly may be more directed toward emphasizing the differences among the products of the different firms (through advertising, for instance). Price competition (who charges the lowest price) may not be as important a factor as in the undifferentiated oligopoly, where buyers perceive less difference among the products of different firms and are more interested in who sells the product at the lowest price. The two industries could have the same concentration ratio, but the nature of their competitive behaviour would be very different, a fact not revealed by a comparison of concentration ratios.

It should also be noted that the industry sales figures used to compute concentration ratios exclude sales of foreign firms competing in Canada. For instance, the three largest firms producing motor vehicles in this country (GM, Ford, and Chrysler) account for about 95 percent of sales *by domestic producers*. At times in recent years foreign cars have accounted for over 30 percent of *all* auto sales (domestic plus foreign makes) in Canada.

In many oligopolistic industries there are a large number of firms that are much smaller in size than the few large firms. Concentration ratios typically do not reveal the existence or extent of this fringe very well. For example, in the brewing industry, where two giants—Labatt's and Molson's—dominate the market, there are a large number of small cottage breweries and brew pubs across the country, yet note the high concentration ratio for breweries in Table 12-2. The sum total of these fringe breweries amounts to less than 3 percent of industry sales. These small brewers tend to strongly differentiate themselves from the large brewers' product, as they cannot compete on price.

Another qualification on the use of the concentration ratio is that in some industries the concentration ratio calculated on a nationwide basis is low. However, the market may be regional or metropolitan in nature, and the concentration ratio measured for the more local market may be high. For example, a few restaurants in a small town may act more like an oligopoly although the concentration ratios for restaurants for all of Canada is low.

Despite the shortcomings of concentration ratios, they do give us a rough indication of the extent to which the few largest firms dominate an industry. Dominance by a few large firms is what basically distinguishes oligopoly from

TABLE 12-2   Concentration Ratio: Sales Ratios for Selected Manufacturing Industries

Industry	Share of Industries Sales Made by Four Largest Firms
Industries with High Concentration	
Glass*	100.0
Tobacco†	100.0
Sugar	100.0
Breweries	97.5
Copper†	95.9
Railroad rolling stock*	94.6
Motor vehicles	94.0
Batteries*	92.2
Aluminum	89.5
Major appliances	86.2
Asphalt roofing	85.9
Distilleries	83.1
Cement	80.5
Shipbuilding and repair	77.6
Abrasives	75.6
Wire	73.8
Leather tanneries	71.9
Petroleum products	68.5
Steel pipe and tubes	57.5
Industries with Low Concentration	
Concrete products	23.7
Boatbuilding and repair	21.3
Logging	20.9
Commercial printing	20.1
Children's clothing	17.4
Sawmills and planing mills	15.7
Signs and displays	14.0
Wooden household furniture	12.8
Other machinery and equipment	12.8
Men's clothing contractors	11.5
Millwork	11.3
Platemaking, typesetting, etc.	10.1
Other plastics fabricating	9.7
Metal dies	8.4
Women's clothing contractors	8.0
Machine shops	7.8

Source: Statistics Canada, *Industrial Organization and Concentration in the Manufacturing, Mining and Logging Industries, 1986* (Ottawa, March 1992), cat no. 31–402.

*These industries are the eight largest firms.

†These industires are the twelve largest firms.

monopolistic competition. For example, in one of the most concentrated industries listed in Table 12-2, motor vehicles (concentration ratio equal to 94 percent), the largest firms are subsidiaries of the first and second largest manufacturing corporations in the world—GM and Ford, respectively. On the other hand, if the concentration ratio of an industry were equal to 2 percent, then most economists would consider that industry to be more an example of monopolistic competition than of oligopoly. A mid-range concentration ratio could lead to endless (and pointless) debate about classification. However, concentration ratios help illustrate what is meant when we speak of a spectrum of market structures extending from perfect competition through monopolistic competition and oligopoly to monopoly.

Barriers to Entry in Oligopoly

Substantial barriers to entry of new firms into oligopolistic industries is the major factor in any explanation of the existence of oligopoly. In general, the larger these barriers are, the fewer will be the number of firms in an industry. Barriers to entry are so crucial to the existence of oligopoly that we will examine them in greater detail. Barriers to entry of new firms into oligopolistic industries can take many forms. Among the most important are economies of scale, cost differences, product recognition, legal restrictions, and product complexity and proliferation.

Economies of Scale

Economies of scale are often so large relative to the size of the total market that it only takes a few firms to supply the whole market. In the case of a natural monopoly, we saw that one firm could supply the entire market because its longrun average total cost curve declined over the entire range of output covered by the market demand curve. An oligopolistic industry is a less extreme form of this situation.

This is illustrated in Figure 12-1, where D represents the industry demand curve for an undifferentiated oligopoly. Given this industry demand curve, the individual firm with the longrun average total cost curve AC realizes sizable economies of scale. This is represented by the fact that its AC curve reaches its minimum point at output level q, which is a sizable share of the total quantity Q demanded at the industrywide price p. Hence, at a price that just covers per unit costs when firms are operating most efficiently, total market demand will only support a small number of such firms.

In the auto industry, for example, there are only a small number of domestic producers, but these firms are of very different sizes. It is often pointed out that there are sizable economies of scale inherent in the production and sale of cars. It is argued that General Motors, with more than 35 percent of the Canadian market, is able to realize these economies of scale more fully than Chrysler and Ford, which between them account for 35 percent of the market (foreign imports and a few small domestic producers account for slightly less than 30 percent).

Economies of scale can be a serious barrier to entry into an oligopolistic industry. This is illustrated in Figure 12-2. Suppose that a firm already in the industry has a demand curve that looks like D_e in frame (a). Since a potential new firm in the industry would be unfamiliar to consumers at first, let us say that its demand curve would look like D_1 in frame (b). But let's suppose that both the new firm and the old firm have the same average total costs, represented by AC. In order to make a go of it, the new firm would have to charge a price no lower than p_1 and produce an output no greater than q_1 as shown in frame (b).

FIGURE 12-1   Economies of Scale Can Lead to Oligopoly

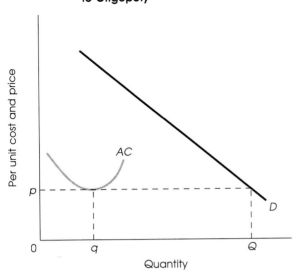

The demand curve D represents the total market demand for the output of an undifferentiated oligopolistic industry. When the typical firm in the industry operates at its minimum per unit cost level of production, it produces an output level q that is a sizable portion of the quantity demanded by the total market. At a price p that would just cover per unit costs when forms are operating most efficiently, total market demand is Q and only a few such firms can be supported by the market.

FIGURE 12-2   Economies of Scale as a Barrier to Entry in Oligopoly

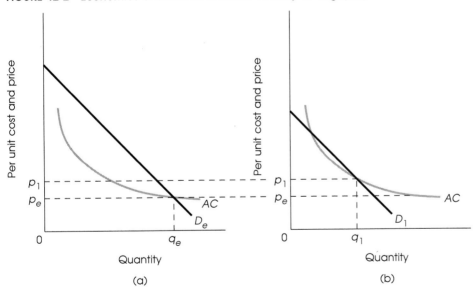

An established firm in the industry has a demand curve D_e, frame (a). It has an average total curve AC, which declines over a large range of output, reflecting the presence of substantial economies of scale. Suppose that a potential entrant to the industry can expect to have the same costs and therefore the same AC curve, but it also expects to have a much lower level of demand, represented by the demand curve D_1, frame (b). If the established firm sets price anywhere below p_1 but above p_e, it can still cover costs and make an above-normal profit. However, because D_1 lies below AC in this price range, the new firm would incur losses and would therefore be discouraged from entering the industry.

If it tried to produce more, it would have to sell its product at a price lower than per unit production costs, as represented by the fact that D_1 lies below AC to the right of q_1. If the new firm did so, it would incur losses.

If the new firm enters, the firm already in the industry knows that its share of the total market will be diminished. Its demand curve D_e, frame (a), would therefore shift leftward. To keep the new firm out, the existing firm can take advantage of its economies of scale by charging a price below p_1. In fact, the existing firm can still make a profit at any price below p_1 so long as it doesn't charge a price below p_e and produce more than q_e. Though the existing firm might be able to maximize its profits for a time by charging a price above p_1, it might feel that such gains would not be worth it given the likely loss in market share to a new entrant attracted by the large profits. By pricing below p_1, the existing firm effectively discourages the new firm from entering the industry. Or the firm may set its price below p_1 because it fears the reaction of the public through government regulation if profits appear excessive. By charging the lower price, the company appears to be a good corporate citizen.

Suppose that there were no economies of scale beyond q_1, and that instead the AC curve either became horizontal or began to rise. Then the firm already in the industry would not be able to charge a price below p_1 without incurring a loss. It would therefore not be able to charge a price low enough to keep out the potential new entrant.

Cost Differences

A potential new entrant into an industry may not have the same AC curve as a firm already in the industry. Even putting aside economies of scale, the costs of production for a new entrant may well be higher than those of established firms for a host of reasons.

Existing firms can have lower costs because of know-how gathered from long experience in the industry. Their management organizations have had time to become more coordinated and effective units. Their labour forces may be more experienced, and their production problems may be fewer. Established firms often can get better credit terms from bankers and suppliers. They may have lower advertising costs due to brand recognition. They also may have patents on production processes that reduce costs. Some new firms may be able to overcome these barriers eventually, but this takes time. As a result, these barriers can discourage the entry of many potential rivals.

A simple example of the potential entrant's problem is shown in Figure 12-3. The potential entrant's AC curve, represented by AC_n, is higher at all levels of output than that of an existing firm, represented by AC_e. For simplicity, we will suppose that the new firm's demand curve can be just like that of an established firm, once it gets going. This curve is represented by D_e. If the established firm didn't have to worry about a possible reduction in its market share as a result of the new entry, it might well charge a price such as p_1 and produce q_1 in order to maximize profits. However, the threat of a potential new entrant leads it to never charge a price greater than or equal to p_L. At any price lower than p_L the potential new entrant is not able to cover per unit costs and is therefore discouraged from entering the industry. The established firm, on the other hand, can still earn a profit at a price below p_L. This is represented by the fact that the demand curve D_e still lies above AC_e to the right of q_L.

FIGURE 12-3   **Cost Differences as a Barrier to Entry in Oligopoly**

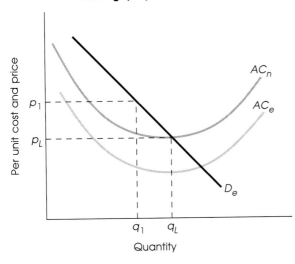

An established firm's AC curve, AC_e, is lower than that of a potential new entrant, represented by AC_n. The established firm can effectively discourage entry of the new firm by setting price below the limit price p_L. This is because the new entrant would have to operate at a loss, while the established firm could still cover costs and earn an above-normal profit, as represented by the fact that D_e lies below AC_n and above AC_e over a range to the right of q_L.

The price p_L is often called a **limit price** because if an established firm never charges a price greater than or equal to p_L, the entry of new firms to the industry will be limited. When a potential new firm is at a disadvantage relative to established firms because of economies of scale, cost differences, or both, existing firms can turn these disadvantages into barriers to entry by keeping the product price low enough. Yet this price may still be high enough to ensure existing firms an economic profit.

Other Barriers to Entry

In oligopolistic industries, capital requirements, control of input supplies, government regulation, product recognition, product complexity, and product proliferation often constitute formidable barriers to entry. The cost of overcoming these barriers can cause the AC of a potential new entrant to be higher than that of an established firm.

Capital Requirements

To operate a firm at its most efficient size in an oligopolistic industry can require many millions, even billions, of dollars' worth of capital. A potential entrant into the airline, automobile, chemical, electrical appliance, petroleum, railroad, or steel industries, to name but a few, needs large amounts of capital and must pay the fixed costs associated with this capital. Such capital requirements are a substantial barrier to entry.

Control of Input Supplies

When existing firms in an industry control important inputs to the production process, potential new firms may face an almost insurmountable barrier to entry. For example, for many years the Alcan Aluminum Company controlled most of the known reserves of bauxite (aluminum ore), thus making it very difficult for other firms to establish much of a market position in the production of aluminum ingots. DeBeers has controlled most of the world's diamond production.

Government Regulation of Entry

Government (municipal, provincial, or federal) sometimes regulates entry into various industries by granting exclusive franchises and by requiring and issuing licenses. The Canadian Radio-television and Telecommunications Commission (CRTC), for example, controls entry into radio and television broadcasting—a station must have a license to operate in any given region of the country. In order to start a commercial bank, a charter must be obtained from the federal government (Regulator of Financial Intermediaries). The federal government defines what a letter is and then licenses only Canada Post to deliver it below a certain (high) price. There are numerous other such examples where the force of law is a barrier to entry.

Product Recognition

A potential new firm typically must introduce its product into a market where the products of existing firms are already well known and established in the minds of consumers. To overcome this lack of product awareness usually requires a sizable advertising campaign. The cost of this campaign may well be higher than the cost of advertising that is needed to maintain the market positions of firms already established.

Product Complexity

Closely related to the problem of product recognition is that of product complexity. For products such as automobiles, television sets, refrigerators, stereo equipment, nuclear power stations, and many others, the very complexity of the item requires that buyers have more information about the product than that provided by mere recognition if they are going to be convinced to buy. Product complexity often extends to such areas as the availability and quality of product service. For example, one of the major hurdles that must be bridged by a new entrant to the auto industry is the establishment of an extensive dealer network through which service and parts can be provided.

Product Proliferation

Product proliferation has proven to be an effective barrier to new entrants in a number of oligopolistic industries. General Motors makes five basic product lines—Chevrolet, Pontiac, Oldsmobile, Buick, and Cadillac. Ford makes three—Ford, Mercury, and Lincoln—and so does Chrysler—Plymouth, Dodge, and Chrysler. Yet when all the variations on these models are considered, the degree of product proliferation is enormous.

Why is this? One reason may well be that product proliferation helps each of the Big Three to preserve its respective share of the auto market from the

Checkpoint* 12-1

Every time the automobile industry changes models, which is about once a year, plants must be equipped with new tools (jigs and presses) in order to deal with new body and engine designs. This retooling is very costly. Some estimates suggest that production costs might be reduced by 20 to 30 percent if the industry did not change models. Hence, it would seem firms could enjoy larger profits if they refrained from model changes. So why do you think there are model changes?

*Answers to all Checkpoints can be found at the back of the text.

inroads of rivals and the entry of new firms into the industry. A potential entrant is not confronted with the prospect of competing with just one kind of automobile, but many. If the entrant successfully takes sales away from Ford's Mercury Cougar, these sales may amount to a small fraction of one percent of the automobile market. This is hardly enough to allow the new firm to realize the economies of scale enjoyed by GM, Ford, and Chrysler. In the 1920s Ford dominated the auto industry by producing the Model T, which offered only slight variations in models and "any color, as long as it's black." GM took a sizable share of the market away from Ford in later years in large part because it offered consumers a greater variety of models. More recently, Delorean, a former vice president of GM, attempted to enter the industry with an innovative stainless steel sports model. After a number of government sponsorships, and technical delays, because of the complexity of offering a new product, the Delorean entered the market after the Big Three had developed more powerful competitors. Simultaneously the market for such vehicles declined, and the Delorean company went bankrupt. A similar story occurred for the Bricklin car, which was sponsored by the province of Nova Scotia.

Implications of Oligopoly Characteristics

The preceding sections outlined the characteristics of an industry that identify it as an oligopoly. In an oligopoly a few firms dominate the industry, there are substantial barriers to entering into the industry, and the industry may have a homogeneous product (like perfect competition) or a differentiated product (like monopolistic competition). When an industry has these characteristics, certain behavioural implications arise. The firms' actions are interdependent, they tend not to compete on price, and there is an incentive for them to collude or merge.

Interdependence

Interdependence *occurs when the actions of one firm affect the behaviour of another firm.* Recognized interdependence among firms in terms of the effects of their individual price and output decisions on one another's sales is a hallmark of oligopoly. Since the number of firms that typically make up an oligopolistic industry is relatively small, price changes and any other kind of competitive behaviour by any one will have noticeable effects on the rest. The firms are interdependent. Each firm in an oligopolistic industry is aware of this, and each has to consider the reaction of the other firms to any price change or other competitive action it might take. A price cut by one firm will usually cause the others to cut prices in order not to lose their shares of the market. Similarly, an advertising blitz by one firm in an oligopolistic industry will usually lead to counter campaigns by the others. Such actions initiated by one firm can result in costly price wars and advertising campaigns that may leave all firms worse off, including the firm that started it all. The fewer the number of firms in an oligopolistic industry, the more significant are the consequences of their actions for one another.

Price Rigidity and Nonprice Competition

Nonprice competition and price rigidity are characteristics of oligopoly closely related to the recognized interdependence among firms. Because attempts to induce customers away from competitors by cutting price can often lead to price wars and lower profits for all, firms have a strong incentive to avoid price competition if possible. This reluctance to engage in price competition causes firms to compete in other ways—to engage in nonprice competition. Consequently, oligopolistic industries are characterized by price stickiness, or even price rigidity.

Nonprice competition among oligopolists often relies heavily on advertising and product differentiation. The competitive advantage that a firm may realize through these activities cannot be as easily matched by rivals as is a price cut. In the automobile industry, for example, model design and skillful advertising are key elements of nonprice competition.

Incentive for Firms to Collude

Collusion *occurs when two or more firms act jointly to set prices and output in order to increase the profit in the industry.* The temptation for firms to collude in setting prices is an understandable aspect of oligopoly behaviour, given that competitive price cutting can so easily lead to lower profits for all. This is particularly true for undifferentiated oligopolists because the absence of product differentiation shuts off an important avenue of nonprice competition. It thereby tends to put more pressure on firms to engage in price competition. Recognizing that their mutual interests are best served by avoiding price wars, the firms in an oligopoly may jointly agree to charge a price that maximizes their collective profits. The tendency for this cooperation was noted in a famous passage over 200 years ago:

> People of the same trade seldom meet together, even for merriment and diversion, but the conversation ends in a conspiracy against the public, or in some contrivance to raise prices.[1]

The more successful the efforts to collude, the more the industry behaves like one giant monopoly firm.

An explicit agreement of this nature is illegal in Canada, the United States, and many other nations. However, firms may still act in a manner that amounts to the same thing by having secret agreements to collude. It can be very difficult to tell whether firms are changing their prices at the same time because they are competing with one another or because they are acting in collusion.

Merger Activity

The incentive for firms to merge is in a way a logical extension of the motives for collusion. If all firms in an oligopolistic industry colluded perfectly together, each would be, in effect, a division of a monopoly. Perfect collusion for joint profit maximization is almost the same as profit maximization for a monopolist.

---

[1] Adam Smith, *The Wealth of Nations* (the Cannan edition) (New York: The Modern Library, 1937), p. 128.

When two firms in an oligopolistic industry merge to become one larger firm, they effectively enter into a perfect collusion. The new, larger firm has a larger share of the total industry market and is therefore a more substantial competitor with the other firms in the industry. In addition, the merger may result in lower per unit production costs through rationalization of production facilities, layoffs, and closures of some of the plant capacity no longer needed to respond to the competitive challenge. This happens because the larger size of the new firm may enable it to realize economies of scale not attainable by each of the two original firms operating separately. Hence, the new firm's profits may be larger than the sum of those earned by the two original firms for two reasons: (1) a perfectly collusive pricing policy takes the place of what may have been a very competitive price relationship between the two original firms, and (2) lower per unit costs unattainable by the two original firms may be realized by the new, larger firm.

Merger of two firms, or the acquisition of one firm by another, can contribute substantially to the increased concentration of market power among a few firms in an industry. Some indication of the extent of merger activity in Canada is provided in Table 12-3. It is noteworthy that mergers have been steadily increasing in Canada. There have been more mergers during the period 1980–1986 than in any prior comparable period. Up until the 1960s, mergers were usually horizontal (among producers of a similar product) or vertical (among buyers and sellers in different stages of the production process). Since the 1960s, many mergers have been of the conglomerate form (combining firms in wholly unrelated lines of production).

How much does this activity contribute to increased industrial concentration? Some evidence suggests that the largest firms, measured by asset size, are the most active in acquiring other firms. And to a greater extent, it is the smaller firms that are most often acquired. These facts suggest that it is just those firms

TABLE 12-3   Number of Mergers in Canada Between 1970 and 1986

Year	Total	Horizontal
1970	427	224
1971	388	215
1972	429	238
1973	352	227
1974	296	158
1975	264	179
1976	313	214
1977	395	261
1978	449	231
1979	511	290
1980	414	220
1981	491	302
1982	576	284
1983	628	352
1984	641	345
1985	714	370
1986	953	383

Source: R. S. Khemani et al., *Mergers, Corporate Concentration and Power in Canada* (Halifax: Institute for Research on Public Policy, 1988).

Checkpoint 12-2
It has been pointed out that concentration ratios provide no information on the relative positions of firms or the amount of turnover among firms at the top. How might such information aid in assessing the implications for competition in industries with high concentration ratios? What do you think are the implications of merger activity for price flexibility?

that might most closely approximate perfectly competitive or monopolistically competitive firms that are most often being absorbed by larger firms. Furthermore, it is most often the largest firms that are getting larger as a result of acquisition activity.

Data on acquisitions tend to hide some important considerations from view. For example, the product line of the acquiring firm compared to the product line of the acquired firm is an important consideration for economists. Competition in the airline industry would certainly be reduced if Air Canada acquired Canadian Airlines International (or vice versa), and some economists would be unhappy about this. Little, if any, concern was expressed when Safeway acquired Woodward's Foods, however, because the implications for competition appeared nowhere near as dire.

Price and Output Determination

The variety of firm behaviours that come under the market structure of oligopoly is clearly much wider than that spanned by perfect competition, monopolistic competition, or monopoly. An oligopoly can be a market consisting of only two firms, of many small firms dominated by a few large ones, or of several large firms. There can also be wide variation in the degree to which the market exhibits each of the characteristics discussed earlier. There may be much product differentiation, as in the automobile industry, or relatively little, as in the metal can industry.

These considerations, coupled with the existence of a recognized interdependence among firms, make it impossible to present a single definitive model of price and output determination for oligopoly as we did for perfect competition, monopoly, and monopolistic competition. A number of models are used to analyze oligopolist behaviour under different strategic assumptions. Instead of developing these somewhat complex models, we will examine some of the explanations economists have offered for the existence of price stickiness and of the tendency for firms to move their prices together when they do change them. We will also examine two models that approximate the extremes of our market structure continuum. The Bertrand model leads to a competitive price outcome. The collusive model leads to a monopoly outcome. The comparison shows why it pays firms to collude and the conditions that are favourable and unfavourable for collusive price behaviour.

Interdependent Price Behaviour

Each firm in an oligopolistic industry is aware that any price change it makes will affect the sales of the other firms in the industry. If a firm lowers price, it will take customers away from its competitors. If it raises price, it will lose some of its own customers to competitors. Other firms typically will not remain passive if they are losing customers to a price-cutting firm but will react to defend their market positions. Hence, in order to know how its sales will be affected by any price change it initiates, a firm has to be able to predict the reactions of its competitors. In short, the true demand and marginal revenue curves facing a firm must take into account the reactions of rivals. But the ability to predict such reactions accurately is limited at best. What are the implications of this for price and output determination in an oligopoly?

The Firm's Demand Curve and Rival Reaction

Figure 12-4, frame (a), shows the demand curve D_n facing an oligopolist based on the assumption that there is no reaction from rivals when the firm changes price. D_r is the demand curve facing an oligopolist based on the assumption that rivals will react to any price change initiated by the firm. Suppose that initially price is p_1, so the firm is at point b on its demand curve. If the firm reduces price to p_2 and rivals do not react by reducing their prices, the relevant demand curve is D_n, and the firm will sell an output level given by the point c'. Its increase in sales will be made up in part of purchases by customers who switch to its product and away from those of other firms in the industry. The rest of the firm's sales increase will be due to the substitutability of its product for similar products of other industries that are now relatively more expensive.

If, instead, other firms in the industry react by cutting their prices, the relevant demand curve will be D_r and the firm will move to point c as price is reduced from p_1 to p_2. The firm experiences a smaller increase in sales, reflecting the fact that its rivals in the industry have matched its price cut and therefore have not lost any customers to it. Nonetheless, the firm does experience

---

FIGURE 12-4 Rivals' Reaction to Price Change and the Kinked Demand Curve

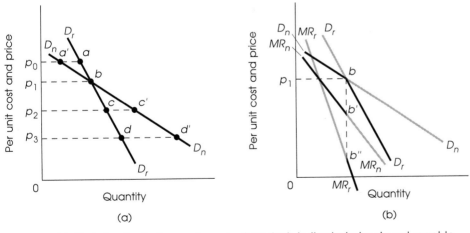

In frame (a), D_n is the firm's demand curve when rivals in the industry do not react to its price changes but keep their own prices unchanged. D_r is the firm's demand curve, drawn on the assumption that rivals match any price change the firm makes. The demand curves D_r and D_n of frame (a) are reproduced in frame (b). If it is assumed that rivals will match any price cut that the firm initiates, but they refrain from matching any price increase, then the relevant parts of the firm's demand gives the kinked demand curve represented by the highlighted part of D_n above point b and the highlighted part of D_r below point b. The marginal revenue curve associated with the kinked demand curve has a gap, or vertical segment, from b' to b''.

some increase in sales, as do the other firms in the industry, because the industry's product is now cheaper relative to the substitute products of other industries. By the same line of reasoning, if the firm had reduced price to p_3 and the other firms in the industry hadn't reacted, the firm would have moved to point d' on demand curve D_n. On the other hand, if the other firms match the price cut, the firm's sales will increase less, as it moves to point d on D_r.

Let's consider it from the opposite direction. Suppose that the firm were to raise its price from p_1 to p_0. If the other firms in the industry don't raise their prices, the firm will lose customers to them and will be at point a' on D_n. However, if the other firms in the industry raise their prices also, the firm will end up at point a on D_r and will not lose customers to them. Its loss in sales, which is now less, will only be to other industries that produce substitute products.

The Kinked Demand Curve

Given that a firm in an oligopolistic industry is initially at a point such as point b in Figure 12-4, frame (a), it is only reasonable to assume that its demand curve for price *decreases* will be D_r. This is the curve that assumes that rivals will react and match any price cuts in order to avoid losing customers to the initiator of the price cut. What about a price *increase* to a level above p_1? Rivals might well refrain from reacting to any price increase the firm initiates. The firm will then lose customers to its rivals in the industry because its product becomes more expensive relative to theirs. Therefore, starting from the initial position at point b, price level p_1, the relevant demand curve for any price increase will be D_n.

The demand curves D_r and D_n are reproduced in Figure 12-4, frame (b), with the relevant parts highlighted. It is clear that if the firm is initially at point b its demand curve is the kinked demand curve formed by the highlighted parts of D_r and D_n, with the kink occurring at point b. MR_n is the marginal revenue curve associated with D_n. The part of the marginal revenue curve associated with the highlighted part of D_n is the highlighted part of MR_n extending down to b'. Similarly, MR_r is the marginal revenue curve associated with D_r. The part associated with the relevant section of D_r is the highlighted part of MR_r starting at point b'' and extending downward. Hence, the marginal revenue curve associated with the kinked demand curve has a gap, or a vertical segment, extending from b' to b'' (indicated by the dashed line) and lying directly below the kink in the demand curve at point b.

The kinked demand curve offers some possible insights as to why prices in oligopolistic industries appear to be slow to change, or sticky. If the existing price is p_1, the firm may be reluctant to lower price because its rivals will follow suit and the resulting gain in its sales will be modest. In fact, it is entirely possible that the segment of its kinked demand curve below point b is inelastic. In that case, any cut in price to a level below p_1 would result in a fall in total sales revenue and any profit the firm might be making. (Point b'' would be at or below the horizontal axis. Why?)

Remember that although we can draw the kinked demand curve and talk as if the firm knows its shape exactly, in reality the firm may be quite uncertain as to the curve's exact shape, because it may be uncertain about the extent of rivals' reactions. Cutting price below the existing level is chancy given that the segment below point b may in fact turn out to be relatively inelastic. Why run the risk of upsetting the applecart by possibly starting a price war that could be disastrous, especially if demand is inelastic below point b?

For similar reasons the firm is reluctant to increase price to a level above p_1. The segment of the kinked demand curve above point b is relatively elastic, as is indicated by the fact that the associated marginal revenue curve above point b' lies well above the horizontal axis. Hence, if the firm raises price but rivals do not follow suit (the kinked demand curve above point b is based on the assumption that they will not), the firm will lose sales to rivals, and total revenue and any profit it may be making will fall.

There is another reason why price may be sticky at the level p_1. It has to do with the gap, or vertical segment, of the marginal revenue curve from b' to b''. Let's assume that the firm arrived at the price p_1 by equating marginal cost with marginal revenue, and that its marginal cost curve is MC_0, as shown in Figure 12-5. Suppose that production costs rise, so that the marginal cost curve shifts upward. Unless costs rise enough to shift the marginal cost curve up above the position MC_2, the firm will have no incentive to change price or output. Similarly, if production costs fall so that the MC curve shifts downward, the firm will have no incentive to change price or output unless the MC curve falls to a position below MC_1. As long as the MC curve lies in the gap in the MR curve, between b' and b'', the firm will not change its level of production or its selling price. *The kinked demand curve provides one possible explanation of why firms in an oligopolistic industry are reluctant to change an established price.*

Checkpoint 12-3

What would cause a firm to move price to a level above the kink in the demand curve, even though the demand curve is elastic above this point and a price rise results in a fall in total revenue? Under what conditions would the firm never reduce price below the level of the kink, no matter what happened to costs?

FIGURE 12-5   Price Rigidity and the Kinked Demand Curve

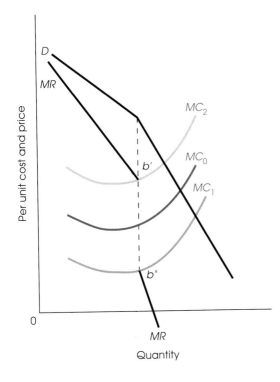

An oligopolistic firm will have no reason to change price or output level as long as any change in production cost is not large enough to push the MC curve above MC_2 or below MC_1. The existence of the vertical segment of the marginal revenue curve associated with the kinked demand curve therefore provides one explanation for price rigidity in oligopoly.

Competitive Price and Output

An early model of markets containing few firms was developed by Augustin Cournot. Cournot assumed each firm recognized that its decisions about its output would affect the price, but he assumed that each firm's decision about output would not affect other firms' decisions. Joseph Bertrand criticized the Cournot model, which was the only model of oligopoly at the time. Bertrand argued that oligopolists would recognize their self-interest and collude on price. Ironically, his argument on the advantages of collusion in effect presents another model of behaviour called the **Bertrand model**, that, under certain circumstances, leads to a competitive price and output. Consider two firms, with the same costs, that are competing on price. Imagine that firm 1 is charging a $p > AC$. Firm 2 might think it can reduce price and its rival will not follow suit. Firm 2 can increase its output and profit by charging a price, p_2, slightly less than p_1 but greater than AC. That firm 1 would not also reduce its price is unlikely. Each firm knows it can generate greater profit by undercutting its competitor, but the competitor reduces price in retaliation. The only price that can occur in equilibrium is $p_1 = p_2 = MC = AC$—the competitive equilibrium. Bertrand used this analysis to show that firms would naturally collude on price, as the consequence of price competition would eliminate profits. How might this type of competition exist in an oligopoly industry?

One way to approximate this outcome is to require sealed bid tenders from the competing firms. It will be apparent to each firm that they might as well submit a bid for the contract at their cost of production, $p = AC$. If their price were higher, the competition could obtain the contract at $p_2 < p_1$ and so on and so on until $p = AC$ is achieved. This is the argument for tendering contracts when dealing with oligopolists. Of course, the incentive still exists for bid-rigging by the firms—a form of collusion.

Oligopoly firms may occasionally enter into price competition if they believe they have a cost advantage over their rivals. A price war may have the effect of driving competitors out of business if their costs are higher. Price wars tend to be short-lived as they lead to lower profits. The gasoline market is a frequent example. Periodically, price wars break out among gasoline retailers. For a time the public enjoys lower gas prices, but inevitably prices go back up. All retailers raise their prices almost simultaneously. The reason for these price wars is the attempt by some one retailer to increase market share at the expense of the others, but as other firms follow suit the inevitable loss of profit results in the firms raising price back to the joint profit maximum.

Collusive Price and Output

Given an oligopolistic firm's uncertainty about rivals' reactions to any price change the firm might initiate, it is naturally fearful that it may start a price war if it lowers price, or will price itself out of the market if it raises price. This sort of situation, often referred to as *noncollusive oligopoly*, is precarious at best. We will give a simple example that illustrates why firms prefer to collude if at all possible. We will then examine conditions both favourable and unfavourable to collusion, as well as a common form of collusion known as *price leadership*.

Why Collusion Pays

The simplest possible form of oligopoly to analyze is the case where there are only two firms in the industry, often called a *duopoly*.

Consider a duopoly in which both firms have identical costs of production and both produce exactly the same product and serve the same market. To make matters even easier, we will assume that marginal cost is the same at all levels of production and that it always equals average cost. All these assumptions are shown in Figure 12-6. Frames (a) and (b) represent the individual firms, and frame (c) represents the entire industry.

Total industry demand is represented by the demand curve D_m. Its associated marginal revenue curve is MR_m, as shown in frame (c). Since each firm produces exactly the same product, it is reasonable to assume that when each charges the same price, each will have exactly half of the total industry demand given by the demand curve D_m. This is shown in frames (a) and (b) of Figure 12-6, where the total industry demand curve D_m is shown for comparison with each firm's demand curve D_f. At any price, note that D_f lies halfway between the vertical axis and the total market demand curve D_m. Hence, at any price the sum

FIGURE 12-6 The Incentive to Collude in an Oligopolistic Industry with Two Firms

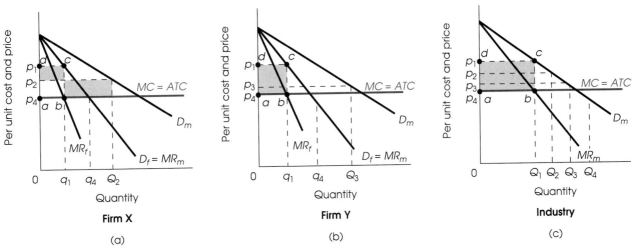

If the two firms in frames (a) and (b) collude so that each charges a price p_1 and sells an output q_1, then they split the total market sales Q_1 and each earns a maximum possible profit—represented by the rectangular area, $abcd$, frames (a) and (b)—equal to half the shaded rectangle $abcd$ in frame (c). In effect, they act as if they were a monopoly firm producing output Q_1 and setting price p_1, where MC intersects MR_m to give the maximum monopoly profit, represented by the shaded rectangle $abcd$ in frame (c).

Suppose that instead of colluding, firm X cuts price to p_2 and takes all market sales equal to Q_2. As a result, firm Y loses all its sales and therefore reacts by cutting price to p_3, whereupon it takes all market sales, equal to Q_3, and firm X loses all *its* sales. This process of price cutting continues until price is driven down to p_4, where it just covers all costs of each firm including a normal profit and each firm produces and sells q_4. The price war is over, and each firm is worse off than when price was initially p_1.

of the quantities demanded from each firm equals the total industry demand. For example, at the price p_4 the quantity demanded from firm X is q_4 and the equivalent quantity, q_4, is demanded from firm Y. The sum of these two quantities, or 2 times q_4, equals the total quantity demanded from the industry at the price p_4—the quantity Q_4 shown in frame (c).

Also note the following: Recall that at any given price the marginal revenue curve always lies exactly halfway between the vertical axis and the straight-line demand curve. Hence, each firm's demand curve D_f, frames (a) and (b), is in exactly the same position as MR_m, the marginal revenue curve associated with the industry demand curve D_m in frame (c). The marginal revenue curves associated with each firm's demand curve D_f are shown as MR_f, frames (a) and (b).

Suppose initially that each firm is charging the price p_1. This is the price that corresponds to the point where $MC = MR_f$ for each firm, as represented by the intersection of the MC and MR_f curves in frames (a) and (b) of Figure 12-6. At this price each firm produces and sells q_1. The sum of their outputs, $2q_1$, equals total industry output Q_1, as shown in frame (c). Note that this result is exactly the same as it would be if both firms colluded to act like a monopoly, or if both firms had in fact merged to form a monopoly firm. In the latter case the intersection of the curve $MC = ATC$ with MR_m determines the profit-maximizing output Q_1 and price p_1 in frame (c). Here the monopoly profit equals the shaded rectangle $abcd$. Producing output q_1 and charging the price p_1 is the best that each firm can do, subject to the existence of the other selling at the same price. Each realizes a profit equal to that represented by the rectangular areas $abcd$ in frames (a) and (b), which added together equal the shaded rectangle $abcd$ in frame (c).

However, if the firms are not colluding in any way, either may be tempted to undercut the price of the other and take the whole market. That is, when one cuts price below that charged by the other, the price-cutting firm's demand curve becomes the industry demand curve D_m. Suppose that firm X tries this by cutting price to p_2. Since the firms produce an identical product, firm Y, still charging p_1, loses all its customers to firm X, which now supplies the entire market the quantity Q_2. For the moment, firm X is making a larger profit than it was initially, since the gain in profit, represented by the larger shaded rectangular area, exceeds the loss in profit, represented by the smaller shaded rectangular area in frame (a) of Figure 12-6. Indeed, this was firm X's motive for cutting price. Firm Y now has no sales at all. Consequently, it reacts by cutting price to p_3, thereby undercutting firm X's price of p_2. Total industry sales Q_3 now go entirely to firm Y, and firm X's sales fall to zero. Firm X now reacts by cutting its price to p_4, and firm Y must do likewise if it is not to lose all its sales. However, neither can cut price below this level because at p_4 both firms are just covering all costs including a normal profit.

Checkpoint 12-4

Is it necessary for both, or just one, of the firms in Figure 12-6 to misjudge the likely reactions of the other in order for events to lead them to the price level p_4?

At this point the price war is over, with each firm selling q_4, or half the total market sales of Q_4 (which is equal to $2q_4$). Each firm is now just making a normal profit. Each is worse off than before the price war started because at the initial price p_1, each was making a profit (in excess of normal profit) represented by the rectangle $abcd$ in frames (a) and (b). The outcome of the competitive price war is a marginal-cost-equals-price solution, just like that in perfect competition. Consumers are better off, but each firm considers itself worse off. At this point the firms may sit down together and mutually agree not to get involved in any more price competition with each other. Both can see that it is in their own best interest to collude and jointly maximize profits by agreeing to keep price at p_1. In effect they agree to split total market sales of Q_1 with q_1 going to each. The moral of the story? Collusion pays, price competition does not.

Conditions For and Against Collusion

It is not usually as easy for firms in an oligopolistic industry to collude as it was in the above example. The following conditions are important determinants of whether or not successful collusion is possible:

1. Barriers to entry serve to keep out potential new firms that are attracted by the economic profits resulting from collusion among established firms in the industry. The greater the threat of entry by new firms, the more reluctant established firms may be about sticking to a collusive agreement because they fear they will lose out in the longrun to market inroads made by new firms. The larger the barriers to entry, the smaller is this threat, and therefore the easier it is to keep a collusive arrangement together, jointly maximizing profits. Keep in mind that making collusive agreements is criminal behaviour. Some (ethical) managers will therefore not engage in collusion regardless of the gains. Others will weigh the gains (profits) against the losses (potential criminal action) to decide whether to collude or not.

2. The number of firms is a most crucial determinant of the risk of collusion taking place. You are no doubt well aware that the larger the number of people involved, the more difficult it is to reach a consensus on anything. The firms in an oligopolistic industry often do not have identical production costs and products. Each really wants to maximize its own profit, and this goal is usually not consistent with the role other firms want to give it in a particular collusive arrangement.

When push comes to shove, each firm in an oligopoly typically sees collusion as a compromise between an arrangement of price and market share it would prefer for itself and that which the other firms are willing to go along with. The more firms there are, the more difficult it is for would-be colluders to arrive at a compromise collusive arrangement satisfactory to all. There is incentive for each to disguise price reductions or give secret price breaks to get customers away from competitors. Each firm is willing to do anything that will improve its sales, so long as the other firms in the collusive arrangement don't find out. The larger the number of firms, the harder it is to police such activities and prevent competitive deviations from the agreement. Too many firms can simply make collusion impossible. This is why attempts at collusion invariably fail in perfectly competitive and monopolistically competitive markets.

3. Product differentiation also reduces the risk of collusive price arrangements occurring. With differentiation, there is more room for disagreement on the appropriate price for one firm's product vis-à-vis the price of another firm's similar, yet somewhat different, product. A Ford and a Chevy are close competitors, yet they are different in many respects, however small. In addition, product complexity makes for nonprice competition in a number of ways, such as extras and add-ons ("bells and whistles"). On the other hand, the more similar each firm's product is to the others', the less room there is for nonprice competition. Each has a more difficult time getting a competitive advantage over the other, and the danger of price competition leading to a price war is greater. This in-

creases the incentive for collusion. Lack of product differentiation in the steel industry is one of the main reasons why steel producers are so concerned about keeping their prices in line with one another.

4. Economic conditions in general affect the willingness of firms to conspire against the public through collusive pricing. When the industry or the whole economy is experiencing a recession, firms are often stuck with excess capacity and fixed costs that are spread over an unusually low volume of output. In an effort to relieve this situation and avoid the necessity of laying off workers, each firm may be more tempted to engage in price cutting to increase sales volume. The perceived profits of collusion are reduced during such periods, and a spirit of competitive pricing is more likely to prevail. By contrast, during an expansionary period, the incentives for price cutting are reduced and collusion on prices and market sharing is more attractive.

5. *The Competition Act* in Canada forbids collusive agreements among firms to fix prices or share markets. If the duopolists of our example in Figure 12-6 were to agree to set price p_1, they would be acting illegally. (We will look at competition policy more closely in the next chapter.) However, open collusion among firms, agreed to either verbally or in writing, is legal in many other countries. A group of firms colluding to set prices or share markets in this fashion is known as a **cartel.** (OPEC, the Organization of Petroleum Exporting Countries, is a cartel that agrees on setting a price at which it will sell oil to the rest of the world.) It is one thing to outlaw collusive agreements and another to keep firms from acting collusively. Firms may enter into secret collusive agreements whose existence is difficult to prove. Rather than getting together in boardrooms or executive offices, executives can make such arrangements during a round of golf or on any other "social" occasion.

Price Leadership

Given that open collusion is illegal in Canada, firms in oligopolistic industries often seek other ways to coordinate their market activities. Each usually has something to gain from any scheme that will reduce the uncertainties that might trigger competitive price cutting. Secret collusive agreements are one answer. Another method that seems prevalent in many industries in Canada is the practice of **price leadership.**

In the absence of any collusive arrangement, firms find it difficult to adjust to changes in overall industry demand. If industry demand is expanding, each firm may want to increase price to take advantage of the potential for higher profit, but each may be fearful that if it does, other firms may not follow and it will lose sales. Suppose, however, that there is some implicit agreement among them that one firm, possibly the largest, will always initiate or lead such moves, and that the rest will follow, on cue as it were. Then, when market conditions dictate that all might benefit by increasing prices together, an "orderly" adjustment can be made. Similarly, the price leader can signal an orderly reduction of prices when industry demand decreases and each would be better off charging a lower price. Not only does the price leader signal the timing and direction of such moves, but the appropriate size of each firm's price change may be gauged by the size of the price leader's move.

At one time or another, the practice of price leadership has been common in such oligopolistic industries as steel and other metal industries, cigarettes, petroleum products, and coal, among others. It is certainly not always clear to

POLICY PERSPECTIVE

The OPEC Cartel—International Collusion in Oil

In 1960 the world's major oil-producing countries banded together to form the Organization of Petroleum Exporting Countries (OPEC).* Their goal was to collude in the pricing and production of oil—that is, to act as a cartel or monopoly. However, OPEC was unable to raise the price of oil during the 1960s because the OPEC countries had conceded too much control over oil production and pricing to American oil companies drilling on OPEC soil. Regaining control of their oil supplies was essential for running a successful cartel, so between 1969 and 1973 the OPEC countries began to withdraw first some and then all of these concessions. They were then able to set world oil prices by acting together to exercise their monopoly-like control over the production of OPEC oil. The 1973 Arab-Israeli war further strengthened the unity and resolve of the Arab OPEC countries. Many believe it provided the spark that led OPEC in October 1973 to impose a 6-month oil embargo on the United States and other nations considered sympathetic to Israel. The abrupt halt in the supply of foreign oil caused the price of oil to quadruple. Prior to the first OPEC embargo of oil exports to the United States and the rest of the world in 1973, oil sold for about $2 U.S. per barrel. By the early 1980s the price had risen to over $35 U.S. per barrel.

CARTEL COLLUSION AND TIME

The length of time needed to adjust to increased oil prices and the short-run inelastic demand for oil served to strengthen the OPEC oil cartel during the 1970s. When the cartel raised the price of oil, its total revenues increased (because demand was inelastic). Under these conditions each cartel member was better off as a result of all members mutual cooperation. Each had a strong incentive to remain united with the others to coordinate production plans and set oil prices. However, the elasticity of demand for oil, like that of other goods, is larger in the longrun than in the shortrun and greater at higher prices as its percentage of the budget increases (see Chapter 5). As time passed, oil substitutes, as diverse as insulation and mass transit systems, were found and more energy-efficient durable goods were produced. On the supply side, the price increase led to increased exploration and development of petroleum (in the North Sea and Mexico) and other energy sources. Consequently, OPEC's total sales revenue ceased growing by 1980.

Generally, when the individual members of a cartel see their revenues decline, each may be tempted to cut prices to grab sales from the others and preserve its share of the market. Such behaviour can destroy the unity of the cartel. By the early 1980s the OPEC cartel was beginning to experience just such a set of problems.

CRACKS IN THE CARTEL

World oil demand began dropping by 1979. In addition, consumers began buying more oil from non-OPEC countries such as Angola, Mexico, Malaysia, Norway, the United Kingdom, and Canada. In 1979, the non-Communist countries consumed an average of 52 million barrels of oil per day, of which 31.6 million came from OPEC. By 1983 OPEC accounted for only about 14 million barrels of the estimated 43 million bar-rels a day being consumed by non-Communist countries. Finally, responding to this drastic reduction in demand, on March 14, 1983, OPEC announced the first price cut in its 23-year history, slashing the price of oil by $5 per barrel—from $34 to $29. OPEC oil revenue peaked in 1980 at $285 billion (U.S.) and by 1983 was $157 billion.

In the 1980s, as demand for OPEC oil continued to diminish, there were coordinated production cuts among OPEC members in order to shore up oil prices. Such coordination became more difficult to achieve, however, and certain OPEC countries cut price while refusing to cut production as the cartel dictated. As a result, in recent years the price of OPEC oil fell to as low as $15 to $20 per barrel. OPEC oil revenues increased prior to the Gulf War of 1991 to $147 billion in 1990, the highest since 1983, but were down to $140 billion in 1991. Since the Gulf War, OPEC has maintained a free-for-all production policy, allowing members to pump as much oil as possible. Expanded output has compensated for lower prices.

For Discussion

- What kinds of barriers to entry into the oil production business were probably most important for the existence of OPEC?
- Which characteristics of the OPEC cartel were conducive to collusion, and which characteristics were not?

*The Organization of Petroleum Exporting Countries (OPEC) consists of the Arab countries of Algeria, Iraq, Kuwait, Libya, Quatar, Saudi Arabia, and the United Arab Emirates and the non-Arab countries of Ecuador, Gabon, Indonesia, Venezuela, Nigeria, and Iran.

an outsider whether observed pricing behaviour in an industry is the result of price leadership or not, especially if the firm acting as price leader changes from time to time. In fact, prices charged by firms in an industry may well move together because they are "locked in competition." Industry representatives would certainly have us believe so.

In the next chapter we will consider the pros and cons of oligopoly as a desirable, or undesirable, form of market structure. We will also take up the subject of competition legislation and public policy toward market organization and industrial concentration.

Summary

1. Oligopoly industries are of two types: Either the firms produce a homogeneous product, or they produce a differentiated product. An oligopoly is an industry dominated by a few large firms, with barriers to entry. The market share of each is large enough that its actions cause reactions among the others. The competitive behaviour of each firm reflects its awareness of this situation.

2. The Canadian economy is highly concentrated overall. Concentration ratios measure the percentage of total industry sales attributable to the largest firms in specific industries. High concentration ratios in many industries indicate that oligopoly is fairly prevalent in the Canadian economy. Evidence suggests that merger and acquisition activity is a significant contributing factor to increased industrial concentration.

3. The occurrence of oligopoly depends heavily on the existence of economies of scale and other substantial barriers to entry. Oligopoly also tends to be characterized by nonprice competition and price rigidity, the temptation for firms to collude, and the presence of incentives for firms to merge.

4. The interdependence of firms is an important implication of oligopoly. Given the many possible types of strategic behaviour among interdependent firms in a wide variety of oligopolistic industries, it has not been possible to put forward a unique theory of oligopoly. Because of the interdependence of the firms, price rigidity is characteristic in oligopolistic industries in which there is no collusion. Given the reluctance to engage in price competition, oligopolistic firms rely heavily on product differentiation, product proliferation, and advertising. It takes rivals more time and it is more difficult for them to match efforts along these lines than it is to match price cuts.

5. The kinked demand curve and its associated marginal revenue curve provide one possible explanation of price rigidity in oligopolistic industries in which there is no collusion.

6. The Bertrand model of competitive pricing in oligopoly results in a price and output that are the same as in the perfect competitive model, where $p = MC = AC$. This result illustrates why oligopolists avoid price competition or price wars.

7. Firms in oligopolistic industries have an incentive to reduce uncertainty about rivals' reactions and to avoid profit-reducing price wars. Therefore, they may collude to set prices and share markets in a manner that maximizes profits for all.

8. Collusion is less likely to occur if there are low barriers to entry, a large number of firms, high product differentiation, weaker market demand, and

a greater likelihood of prosecution for violation of the *Competition Act*. Because explicit collusion is illegal in Canada, firms may enter into secret agreements to collude or they may practice price leadership, a form of implicit collusion.

Key Terms and Concepts

Bertrand model	differentiated	oligopoly
cartel	oligopolies	price leadership
collusion	interdependence	sales ratio
concentration	kinked demand curve	undifferentiated
concentration ratio	limit price	oligopolies

Questions and Problems

1. In what ways is oligopoly similar to monopolistic competition? There are hundreds of companies retailing groceries in Canada, yet the industry is considered an oligopoly. Why?

2. We often hear a lot about price leadership in the petroleum industry. When one of the firms raises (or lowers) prices, the news media typically carry several stories about what the other firms have done by way of reaction on subsequent days. Why do you suppose that we hear very little about this kind of price behaviour in the computer industry?

3. Using the diagram depicting the oligopolistic firm of Figure 12-4, demonstrate the likely effects if the firm steps up its advertising. Demonstrate the likely effects if the firm's rivals step up their advertising.

4. Rank the following industries according to how difficult you think that it would be for firms to collude in each of them (the concentration ratio for each is given in Table 12-2): breweries, batteries, concrete products, and women's clothing contractors. In each case, be careful to take into account all the characteristics of oligopoly mentioned in this chapter as well as the nature of the product, and give the reasons for your ranking.

5. It is sometimes claimed that collusive price behaviour actually stimulates technological change and innovation. What arguments would you offer to support such a claim?

6. As a consumer having to purchase some product produced in a highly concentrated industry (for example, purchasing glass for a new house), consider what the Bertrand model suggests and outline a strategy that would allow you to make the purchase at the lowest possible price.

7. In 1991 the airline industry was in financial trouble and there was discussion about takeovers from foreign carriers or a merger between the two major carriers, Air Canada and Canadian Airlines International, to save the industry. In early 1992, Air Canada and Canadian started a seat sale war to fill vacant seats on scheduled routes, as each was incurring losses. The minister of transport declared a preference for two airlines in order "to maintain competition in the industry." Discuss the merits of the minister's position.

8. It is often stated that a price that matches another price is a competitive price. What are the pros and cons regarding the truth of this statement in an oligopoly industry?

Chapter 13

Market Structure, Public Policy, and Regulated Markets

Previous chapters have examined how competition in a market helps to provide an efficient allocation of resources to maximize consumer well-being. Where monopoly is unavoidable, we have seen how government regulation is used to try to enforce a price and output solution more consistent with a socially efficient outcome similar to the competitive market ideal. In the last chapter we saw how oligopolistic industries may possess pronounced elements of monopoly power, particularly when there is a high degree of industrial concentration. In this chapter we will examine the case for government intervention in these industries with the aim of establishing more competitive conditions.

First we will look at some evidence on the economic effects of oligopolistic market structures and the existence of large firms in Canada. We will then consider how anticombine and competition legislation has evolved and been used to deal with monopoly-type power and other anticompetitive practices in the Canadian economy.

Before we begin, a word on terminology. We are concerned with the issue of the existence of monopoly-type power and how public policy deals with it. Strictly speaking, *monopoly* means that one seller supplies a whole market. We have already seen how public policy regulates the situation by using the public utility concept. As a practical matter, most of the industries where monopoly-type power becomes a matter of concern are oligopolies. Because these industries exhibit many monopoly traits, they are often loosely referred to as monopolies in the press and even occasionally in economics textbooks. **Competition policy** *is largely concerned with deciding when and where monopoly characteristics are pervasive enough in an oligopolistic industry to warrant some kind of legal action to eliminate or at least curb them.*

Economic Effects of Oligopoly and Industrial Concentration

How well does oligopoly allocate scarce resources to unlimited wants? The criteria we have used to try to answer this question for the market structures discussed in previous chapters are relevant here as well. Because oligopolistic industries account for such a large share of the economy's output and typically represent large concentrations of economic power, economists have spent a good deal of effort trying to determine how well oligopoly measures up by these criteria. We will try to summarize some of these findings and their implications in the next few pages.

Efficiency

Clearly, the economic models of oligopoly suggest that profit-maximizing oligopolist firms do not produce at that level of output for which marginal cost equals price. Even if an oligopoly had exactly the same cost curves as a perfectly competitive firm producing the same product, nothing ensures that it would produce at the minimum point on the ATC curve (as the perfectly competitive firm would). If it does not produce that level of output at which per unit costs are lowest, it would not be efficient by this criterion.

This comparison is largely a fiction, however, because of the significant role that economies of scale play in oligopoly. These economies make it unreasonable to suppose that if an oligopolistic industry were reorganized to be perfectly competitive, the resulting perfectly competitive firms would have the same cost curves as the oligopolist. If the steel industry were reorganized in this fashion, it would take thousands of small firms to produce the amount of steel currently produced by a couple of large firms; and none of these small firms would be able to realize the economies of scale that are attained by large steel firms such as Stelco and Dofasco, the dominant firms in the industry. Therefore, per unit costs of production would be higher under perfect competition, even though each firm would be operating at the minimum point on its ATC curve. This cost comparison is illustrated in Figure 13-1. The small firm achieves a minimum cost of c_S on ATC_S at output q_S, while the large firm reaches a minimum cost

---

LEARNING OBJECTIVES

After reading this chapter, you will be able to:

1. Discuss the issues concerning the efficiency of oligopolistic industries.
2. Discuss the potential effect of industrial concentration on technological change and innovation.
3. Briefly relate the evolution of competition law in Canada.
4. Outline the enforcement and administration procedures for the *Competition Act.*
5. Outline the criminal and civil offenses under the *Competition Act.*
6. Discuss the effectiveness of competition policy in Canada.
7. Delineate the various schools of thought on the proper role of competition policy.
8. Briefly describe the regulated industries, the pros and cons of such regulation, and the consequences of deregulation and privatization.

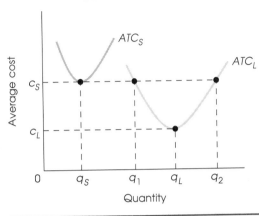

FIGURE 13-1   Cost Efficiency Comparison Between Small and Large Firms with Economies of Scale

A small firm achieves a minimum average cost of c_S on ATC_S at output q_s. When economies of scale exist a large firm can reach a minimum average cost at c_L on ATC_L at q_L. A large number of these small firms in competition would reach an equilibrium price equal to c_S—a price higher than any average cost of the large firm between outputs q_1 and q_2.

at c_L on ATC_L at q_L. A large number of these small firms in competition would reach an equilibrium price equal to c_S ($P = $ minimum ATC)—a price higher than any average cost of the large firm between outputs q_1 and q_2. This means that at the competitive break-even price for the small firm, the large firm would make economic profits at any output between q_1 and q_2.

Technological Change and Innovation

Does oligopoly encourage technological change and innovation? Some economists would say, "Definitely." They argue that oligopoly may well be the most progressive of all types of market structures because it comes closest to the ideal combination of the carrot of profits and the stick of competition.

The possibility of economic profits, protected by substantial barriers to entry, provides an incentive for innovation as well as a ready source of funds to finance innovative activity. In this respect, oligopoly is much the same as monopoly. However, in an oligopolistic industry the existence of rival firms, coupled with a reluctance to engage in price competition, creates unusually heavy pressures to engage in nonprice competition. Such competition may take the form of product development and innovation to spur sales and advances in production techniques to lower production costs. It is argued that since firms are leery of price competition as a means of capturing a larger share of the market and increasing profits, there is more emphasis on technological change and innovation. The competitive advantages that a firm may realize through these activities are not as easily or quickly matched by rivals as is a price cut.

In sum, it may be argued that technological change and innovation are encouraged in an oligopoly because of the existence of potentially high profits, as in monopoly. However, unlike monopoly, in an oligopoly, technological change and innovation are also stimulated by the competitive pressures created by rival firms. Similarly, it may be argued that technological change and innovation in oligopoly benefit from the competitive pressures created by rival firms as in perfect and monopolistic competition, but unlike these forms of market structure, oligopoly does not suffer from a lack of profit incentive.

Checkpoint* 13-1

If an industry was found to have a concentration ratio that could be justified by economies of scale, what do you think its profit rate would be like compared to that associated with a finding that the concentration ratio was larger than could be justified by economies of scale? Why? Would the nature of an industry's product have an effect on the implications you might draw from a finding that its advertising outlays are large and its concentration ratio is high? Why? Compare the automobile and the cigarette industries in this regard.

*Answers to all Checkpoints can be found at the back of the text.

The preceding paragraph sums up briefly the arguments of some economists in support of oligopoly as the form of market structure most favourable to technological progress and innovation. However, other economists argue that to the extent oligopolistic industries are characterized by collusive arrangements of one kind or another, a "live-and-let-live" mentality may develop. As a result, they claim, there is less progressive and innovative behaviour than the existence of several apparently competitive rivals would seem to suggest. It may be that collusive behaviour among oligopolistic firms results in a sort of "shared monopoly" situation. In that case, the implications for innovation and technological change are much more like those of monopoly than those of an oligopoly characterized by the existence of vigorous competition. What does the evidence suggest?

The evidence that has been gathered so far generally does not support the contention that high industrial concentration and very large firm size provide a definite increase in benefits with regard to invention and innovation. Studies suggest that for a large portion of invention and innovation, high concentration ratios and obstructive barriers to entry seem to stifle progress. At the other extreme, very low concentration ratios and high firm turnover in an industry do not appear conducive to technological progress either. Intermediate market structures, tending to the competitive side of the spectrum, seem best.

Profits, Advertising, and Concentration

Economic theory suggests that oligopoly is likely to give rise to economic profits, particularly when firms engage in collusion. There are several aspects to this issue and a certain amount of evidence to support this theory. In our analysis of monopolistic competition in Chapter 11, we discussed the pros and cons of advertising. We pointed out (you might wish to reread that section at this time) that advertising may play an even larger role in oligopoly than in monopolistic competition. In oligopolistic industries, advertising may well contribute to economic profits because it stimulates product differentiation and proliferation. As we said in Chapter 12, product differentiation and proliferation can be formidable barriers to entry and thereby help exclude potential competitors from an industry. This makes it easier for established firms to charge higher prices and realize monopolistic profits.

Advertising outlays tend to be large in increasingly concentrated consumer goods industries and also tend to bear a distinct relationship to above-average profits in those industries. Much of the money goes for national television advertising, which does not provide substantive information about the product.[1]

An Evaluation of Oligopoly

Looking at the great variety of industries that have pronounced oligopoly characteristics, all observers might agree on one point. Namely, all could cite a few

---

[1] For a comprehensive analysis of advertising in our society, see W. Leiss, S. Kline, and S. Jhally, *Social Communication in Advertising* (Toronto: Methuen, 1986).

oligopolistic industries to support the claim that oligopoly is an ideal combination of the carrot of profit, which provides incentive, and the stick of competition, which enforces efficiency. At the same time one could point to a few oligopolistic industries that bear a disturbing resemblance to an unregulated monopoly situation—a shared monopoly. Where the latter situation occurs, or where there are strong overtones of it, economists raise the same kind of concerns about the efficiency of resource allocation, technological progress, income distribution, and the concentration of economic power that we have discussed in the case of unregulated monopoly.

It should be emphasized that this somewhat negative appraisal is not a blanket evaluation of all oligopolistic industries. Rather it is directed at those that appear to fall into the grey area in which the complex of oligopolistic characteristics becomes more noticeably shaded by overtones of monopoly. The small number of firms that dominate an oligopolistic industry have market power—they are the major suppliers, and their decisions largely determine price and output for the entire industry. The smaller is the number of firms that dominate, the more their market power can take on shades of monopoly-type power. We will now consider some of the ways firms achieve and exercise market power.

The Nature and Exercise of Market Power

Market power can be realized and exercised in many ways in an oligopolistic industry.

1. A dominant firm may result from the merger of existing firms or as a result of the acquisition by one firm of the stock or assets of another.
2. Firms may collude (conspire) to maximize profits for all by fixing prices and output at mutually agreed-upon levels. Such price fixing is a practice that works to the advantage of all parties to the agreement, as we saw in the previous chapter.
3. A firm may engage in what is called *predatory behaviour* against competing firms. One type of predatory behaviour is **predatory pricing**, a practice whereby a large firm, operating in many markets, can afford to sell at prices below costs in some markets until smaller competitors in those markets are driven out of business. Once the competition is eliminated, the larger firm is in a monopoly position in those markets.
4. Firms may use exclusive dealing agreements and tying contracts to restrict competition and increase their domination over the market. Some manufacturers enter into **exclusive dealing agreements** with dealers and distributors that restrict the purchase, sale, or use of competing products. The idea is that if a distributor or dealer concentrates on selling one product line—Sony electronics, Ford cars, or Imperial Oil petroleum products—the result will be a more effective job of selling the manufacturer's product. This practice is *sometimes regarded* as a way of increasing market power.

   A firm wishing to expand sales may resort to the use of a **tying contract.** A large firm selling several products that are typically used in conjunction with one another is sometimes in a position to force a buyer wanting product X to buy products Y and Z as well.

5. A firm may obtain an unfair advantage from false or **misleading representation** of its products. This type of behaviour transcends size of business—large and small firms alike can, and have engaged in misleading representation. In any event it distorts the working of (honest) competition to the detriment of the consumer and rival firms and is therefore anticompetitive.
6. Firms may form specialization agreements, where two or more firms each agree to stop production of some product and buy it exclusively from another firm in the agreement.

Each of these six methods of achieving and exercising monopoly-type power has been the object of some section of competition legislation, which we will examine in the next section.

Public Policy Toward Size and Market Power

The policies of the federal government toward firm size and market power have been expressed by means of laws such as the *Competition Act* and its precursor the *Combines Investigation Act*. This body of legislation and associated administrative bureaucracy and procedures is referred to as *competition policy*. Most of the economy is subject to the intent of competition policy. It is generally considered by economists that the intent of competition policy is to reduce the inefficiencies caused by monopoly-type power. In Canada competition policy has been directed more toward the abuse of power resulting from lack of competition than toward maintaining competition in the Canadian marketplace.

Evolution of Canadian Combines Policy [2]

Most Western industrialized nations have legislation restricting corporate concentration and promoting competition. Canada's first competition law was enacted over a century ago in 1889, a year prior to the American *Sherman Act*. The *Sherman Act* was a reaction to the situation in the United States, during the 1880s and 1890s, where there was a great deal of merger activity. Small and large firms alike combined to form "trusts," in which they colluded to restrict output and raise prices. In some industries, huge firms assumed monopoly-type dominance, often as a result of openly predatory behaviour toward rivals. To Americans, it became increasingly clear that some form of antitrust (combines) legislation was needed if the growth of monopoly was to be curbed and more competitive markets were to be maintained.

The situation was somewhat different in Canada. It was not an increase in mergers that upset Canadians. Canadians have always been more tolerant and less distrustful than Americans of large-scale business and even the forming of trusts between otherwise independent businesses.[3] What initiated Canada

---

[2]This section draws heavily from P. K. Gorecki and W. T. Stanbury, *Objectives of Competition Policy 1888–1983* (Montreal, 1984).

[3]See the *Report of the Royal Commission on Corporate Concentration* (Ottawa: Minister of Supply and Services, 1978).

into competition legislation was a reaction to the effects of John A. Macdonald's *National Policy* of the 1870s and 1880s. The purpose of the National Policy was to encourage the development of Canadian industry through high tariffs (25 to 35 percent) while letting in cheap raw materials. This tariff protection sufficiently reduced the price competition from foreign—primarily American—goods on Canadian manufacturers that they were able to considerably increase prices. The first legislation, in 1889, was designed to prevent excessively high consumer prices and coercion by some firms of rival businesses who wished to be free to compete.

The Act of 1889

An Act for the Prevention and Suppression of Combinations Formed for the Restraint of Trade was passed by Parliament in 1889. This first Canadian national anticombine legislation was also the first enacted anywhere in the world. The Act of 1889, though, was not a strong law. For one thing, no provision was made by the federal government for its administration and enforcement. It was expected that the provincial attorneys-general would enforce the law. For another, businesses acting as a combine or trust had to be found to be lessening competition "unlawfully" and "unduly" or a business had to be raising prices "unreasonably" to be in violation of the Act. The inclusion in the Act of these words was a major hindrance to its effectiveness, and attempts were made to eliminate them in proposed reforms of 1890 and 1891. These reforms failed.

Prior to 1900, there was only one prosecution under the Act, and it was unsuccessful. The word, "unlawful," in the act made it logically unenforceable. Instead of strengthening competition legislation, the Liberal government of Sir Wilfred Laurier approached the combine problem by amending the *Customs Tariff Act*, part of the National Policy of 1897. In 1900 the word "unlawful" was deleted from the Act and in 1902 the 1889 Act was incorporated into the *Criminal Code*. There were still only seven prosecutions with five convictions between 1903 and 1910.

The Combines Investigation Act (1910)

In 1910 the federal government introduced a new act into Parliament to deal with the increasing problems of combines. The *Combines Investigation Act* was designed to provide a means to investigate alleged combines in restraint of trade. The terms "merger" and "monopoly" were first incorporated into this act. But the definition of combines—including monopolies, trusts, and mergers—was too broad. These terms were neither specifically nor sufficiently defined until 1935.

The focus of the new act was the protection of the consumer from high prices, and producers (farmers) from low prices. In the Canadian tradition, as distinct from that of the United States, the legislation was not aimed against mergers and combines as such, but at the abuse of the power that could be derived from combinations. This view holds that the harm to the public is the *abuse* of economic power not the attainment of the power (the abuse theory of detriment). The implication is that there are good and bad combines. The difficulty for the law was in making explicit what was illegal if it was not in fact the act of combining.

The Act of 1910 established the first specific mechanisms for enforcement of competition law. Administration and enforcement were to be carried out by the Ministry of Labour, but the mechanism was cumbersome. Unfortunately, the new procedures were ineffective—only one investigation was initiated under the 1910 Act. To a large degree the law was symbolic of the government's wish that business would act morally and not abuse its economic power. It was not meant to prevent that power from arising, nor was it capable of preventing abuse of that power where it existed. As its title suggests, it might *investigate* abuse, but in the end how were the courts to distinguish a "good" from a "bad" combination?

The New Combines Investigation Act (1923)

The *Combines Investigation Act* was replaced by the government of the time with the *Combines and Fair Prices Act* of 1919. As part of this reform, a Board of Commerce was created to administer the Act. Both the Board and this Act were declared unconstitutional in 1921. In 1923, Mackenzie King, then prime minister, introduced the new *Combines Investigation Act*. The purpose of this act was to obtain the benefits of combinations—economies of scale—but prevent the abuses possible from monopoly power. For the first time, provisions aimed at controlling mergers and monopolies "detrimental to the public" were included. It was recognized by many that the purpose of combines was unlikely to be to lower prices but rather to maintain or raise them, so there was a need for more stringent enforcement through the use of the *Criminal Code*. Under this act, prosecutions were still left to the provincial attorneys-general. Not much was done in this "new" act to increase prosecutions. The common belief was that the existence alone of the Act would provide a moral deterrent to the abuse of economic power, and enforcement was not a prime concern.

In 1934 "detriment to the public interest" was redefined to include fixing common prices or monopolizing and controlling or otherwise restraining trade. In 1935 the list of anticompetitive behaviour was extended to include enhancing prices and preventing competition or limiting production. Price discrimination and predatory pricing were made *Criminal Code* violations. The 1935 amendments placed the administration of the *Combines Investigation Act* under a federal agency—the Dominion Trade and Industry Commission—established at the same time. This arrangement, too, was declared unconstitutional in 1937.

The 1937 amendments again placed the administration of the Act under the Ministry of Labour. These amendments restated that the purpose of the legislation was not to prevent or discourage large-scale business or combinations but that investigation and penalties might occur if firms controlled prices to the detriment of the public. Economic power—monopolies, mergers, and trusts—was not illegal per se, but abuse of economic power was. The Act continued to have little practical effect on competition as the questions of just what was meant by "the public interest" and what constituted "unduly" were debated in the courts and Parliament.

In the 1952 amendments, the administration of the Act was removed from the Ministry of Labour and the duties were split between the Director of Investigation and Research and the Restrictive Trade Practices Commission. Resale price maintenance was added as an offense under the *Criminal Code*. By transferring administrative authority to the Director, better enforcement of the act was realized.

The Combines Investigation Act (1960)

In 1960 the *Combines Investigation Act* was substantially amended in order to prevent specific practices of single businesses regardless of size. The emphasis of previous legislation on the abuse of economic power was no longer the focus. Included in the prohibited practices were the use of misleading advertising and deceptive trade practices. The definitions of a "merger" and a "monopoly" were made distinct. A merger was said to have occurred when a person or company acquired a controlling interest in another company. A monopoly was said to occur when one or more persons or companies had at least substantial control over some area of the market. Mergers and monopolies that lessened, or were likely to lessen, competition were included in the list of criminal behaviours, but again the modification that these be detrimental to public interest was included. The courts noted two themes in the legislation—"fair" competition and consumer protection.

Enforcement of the Act didn't substantially improve with these amendments. It is generally agreed that the reformed act was not an effective tool for dealing with the abuses of economic power. There was a lack of successful prosecutions, even in an environment of increasing merger activity and increased concentration. For example, there wasn't a single conviction in a contested merger case.

The process of reforming the Act began in 1966 when the Economic Council of Canada (ECC) was asked to study the current competition laws, their effectiveness, and the need for revisions. This was a significant watershed in competition policy in Canada. Although Mackenzie King, the major framer of the 1910 Act (as minister of labour) and the 1923 Act (as prime minister) had a Ph.D. in economics from Harvard, the ECC report was the first comprehensive study integrating the current economic knowledge of competition theory with the legal aspects of abuse of economic power. In 1969 the ECC published its three-year study, which proposed major reforms. The reform process encompassed such central issues as how to define, determine, and control market power abuse; the adjudication process; and the civil and criminal nature of mergers and monopolies.

A significant reform that was proposed would have made mergers and monopolies subject to civil rather than criminal law. A proposed specialized tribunal would have administered these matters. These and other proposals were introduced in an amending bill in 1973. Business was so strongly opposed to these amendments that the government backed off and proposed that amendments be introduced in two stages. The first stage, stage I amendments, was introduced after further consultation with business and academics. The stage I amendments came into effect in 1976 and made some significant changes. The Act became applicable to services (a major oversight in previous legislation); altered provisions dealing with misleading advertising, resale price maintenance, and conspiracy; made bid-rigging illegal; and made a number of of items reviewable by civil law. This stage of amendments did not address a central concern—the abuse and potential abuse of power resulting from mergers or combines.

Between 1976 and 1984, a number of stage II amendments were proposed and brought forward as bills in the House of Commons. Some of the proposals common to these bills would have made mergers and monopolies civil rather than criminal offenses. The concept of lessening competition or the likelihood of lessening competition significantly (replacing substantially) was proposed. This indicated a shift away from the idea of abuse of power to the notion of competition per se as an offense. A number of factors were proposed for the courts to consider in a judgment of an offense. Provisions were included in defense of monopoly if "gains in efficiency will result in a substantial real saving of resources." There was considerable opposition to these amendments and none were implemented, the last dying on the order paper in the 1984 call for an election.

The Competition Act of 1986

After nearly two decades of reform proposals, some of which were implemented in stage I reform, the passage of the *Competition Act* and the *Competition Tribunal Act* incorporated the stage II amendments, completing in (1986) the reform process.

The Major Changes to Competition Law

The *Competition Act* and the complementary legislation the *Competition Tribunal Act* brought many changes.[4] Under the *Competition Tribunal Act* a tribunal is a replacement for the ordinary court functions previously divided between the Restrictive Trade Practices Commission (RTPC) and the criminal courts. This tribunal has the power to hear and determine cases but does not conduct general inquiries or authorize investigation as the RTPC did. The Tribunal includes up to four judges from the Federal Court and up to eight other lay members, but the chairperson must be a judge. The lay members are chosen by the minister in consultation with experts in economics, industry, commerce, and public affairs. An advantage of this Tribunal is that the lay members and the judges appointed will have or be able to gain expertise in business, economics, and competition policy. By using a tribunal instead of the criminal courts the time to process cases should be much reduced.

Cases that apply to the Tribunal are heard by a panel. Each review panel is chosen from the Tribunal members and includes between three and five members. Every panel is chaired by a judge. If a firm is found guilty in a civil case, the Tribunal may force it to desist from practices that violate the law. The Tribunal will review the civil matters under the Act. By creating a quasi-judicial tribunal, the Act recognizes the input from individuals familiar with economic and business matters in addition to the legal issues involved.

The merger and the abuse of dominant position provisions are some of the most important changes under the *Competition Act*. Previously, mergers were a criminal offense. Criminal prosecution required proof of a violation beyond a reasonable doubt. This posed a major obstacle in prosecutions under the old legislation. The new act makes mergers a civilly reviewable practice and repeals the former criminal provisions. The standard of proof under civil law is the

---

[4]For a thorough discussion of the changes incorporated into the Act, see Robert S. Nozick and Charlotte Neff, *Annotated Competition Act* (Toronto: Carswell, 1987). This work includes the *Tribunal Competition Act* and the *Combines Investigation Act*.

"balance of probabilities" rather than the more demanding "beyond a reasonable doubt."

The Tribunal has the power to approve specialization agreements providing for the reduction of product lines among competitors where these will likely yield efficiency gains that exceed the effects of reduced competition. If approved, a specialization agreement is exempt from the cartel and exclusive dealing provisions of the Act. Crown corporations and governmental agencies that supervise banking and insurance, sectors of the economy that were exempt from the *Combines Act* have been included in the *Competition Act*.[5] Therefore, most of our economy is now subject to competition law.

A new civil prohibition directed against the abuse of dominant position or anticompetitive acts (listed in the Act) replaces the criminal offense of being party to or the formation of a monopoly. Delivered pricing, a form of price discrimination, has been added to the list of civilly reviewable practices.

A strengthening of the cartel provisions allows for conviction of conspiracy on circumstantial evidence without the need for direct evidence of communication between or among parties. Also it is not necessary to prove a cartel has the *intent* to "lessen competition unduly" only that a cartel has the *effect* of lessening competition.

An Overview of the Competition Act

The objectives of the *Competition Act* are as follows:[6]

> Competition is essential for an effective market economy. It encourages productivity, enterprise and efficiency. With competitive forces at work, consumers are provided with quality products, choice, and the best possible price. Increased competition at home should make Canada more competitive abroad.
>
> Today's *Competition Act* provides a framework for business conduct in Canada and encourages competition to:
>
> - promote the efficiency and adaptability of the Canadian economy;
> - expand opportunities for Canadian participation in world markets while at the same time recognizing the role of foreign competition in Canada;
> - ensure that small and medium sized enterprises have an equitable opportunity to participate in the Canadian economy; and
> - provide consumers with competitive prices and product choices.

Administration of the Act

The Act is administered by the Director of Investigation and Research (the Director) and the Competition Tribunal (the Tribunal). The Director is the head

---

[5] Banks were previously regulated under the *Bank Act*.

[6] Director of Investigation and Research, Consumer and Corporate Affairs, *Information Bulletin: An Overview of Canada's Competition Act* (Ottawa: Ministry of Supply and Services, November, 1990).

of the Bureau of Competition Policy, Consumer and Corporate Affairs Canada (the Bureau). The Act applies to both goods and services and to almost all businesses in Canada. Practices that violate the Act may be either criminal or civil offenses. Criminal actions are subject to the *Criminal Code* while civil offenses are reviewable by the Tribunal. The Director may initiate an inquiry into an alleged offense following an application of six adult Canadians, or by the direction of the Minister of Consumer and Corporate Affairs, or on the Director's own initiative. In all cases the Director is responsible for enforcing the Act with the assistance of the resources of the Bureau.

Violations of the criminal provisions of the Act are prosecuted by the Attorney General of Canada. Under criminal law a firm found guilty may be fined, its officers fined or given jail sentences, or both. Court orders forbidding certain activities (**prohibition order**) may also be obtained upon application by the Director. Criminal offenses include conspiracy, bid-rigging, discriminatory and predatory pricing, price maintenance, and misleading advertising or deceptive marketing practices. As these actions are prosecuted by the courts, guilt must be established "beyond a reasonable doubt."

Civil actions are reviewed by the Tribunal. Private firms or individuals who have suffered loss or damage may sue those engaged in anticompetitive behaviour. If a firm is found guilty in a private case, the offending firm may be required to pay the complainant an amount equal to only the total damages. Civil matters include mergers, abuse of dominant position, refusal to deal, consignment selling, exclusive dealing, tied selling, market restriction, and delivered pricing. If a firm is found guilty in a civil case, the Tribunal may force it to desist from practices that violate the Act. Offenses are referred by the Director to the Tribunal for review. These do not require the stricter proof of criminal cases, they need only meet the balance of probabilities test.

In an investigation of an alleged offense, the Director may obtain information about a firm from customers and competitors. Search warrants may be issued, premises searched, and business records (including computer systems) seized. Records and individuals may be subpoenaed by the courts or the Tribunal. Applications for the use of these formal investigatory powers must be made through the courts to be consistent with the charter provisions of the *Constitution Act* of 1982.

Alternatives to prosecution under the Act exist. Written undertakings—a commitment to undertake some action or to refrain from some action—may be used in place of a full inquiry or judicial proceeding. The Director may accept an undertaking if it eliminates or rectifies an uncompetitive behaviour. A consent order is another method to rectify an uncompetitive situation without further proceedings. There is also a "program of advisory options": A firm may submit a plan of action prior to its implementation so that the Director may provide an opinion on any concerns about competitive abuses that the plan may contain. In the case of proposed mergers, "Advanced Ruling Certificates" may be issued when the Director is satisfied that the merger would not violate the intent of the Act. If the merger plan is carried out within one year, the certificate ensures that no review will occur. Some prosecutions are avoided when violations of the law are explained to the firm involved and the firm ceases the behaviour. The existence of the law prevents many firms from engaging in uncompetitive acts. Voluntary compliance with the Act is facilitated by the Bureau through communication and public education.

Criminal Offenses

Criminal offenses fall under the *Criminal Code* and therefore are enforced by the courts with the more onerous requirement in law that a firm must be guilty of criminal behaviour beyond a reasonable doubt.

Conspiracy.   A conspiracy is any agreement or arrangement among firms to set price or restrict entry into the industry that lessens competition unduly. The forming of a cartel or combine is considered a conspiracy under the Act. The courts can infer the existence of an agreement from circumstantial evidence without direct evidence of communication among parties, and the Crown need not prove intent to lessen competition unduly on the part of a cartel that in effect does lessen competition. Penalties now include a fine up to $10 million or up to five years' imprisonment, or both.

Bid-Rigging.   Bid-rigging is an agreement among potential bidders on a contract, public or private, where one or more firms arranges to tender certain prices or not tender at all. It is not necessary for the courts to prove that competition is affected. Violators are subject to a fine at the discretion of the court or up to five years' imprisonment, or both.

Price Discrimination and Predatory Pricing.   Price discrimination occurs when a supplier firm charges different prices to customers that are competing firms (in the same market), for reasons unrelated to cost. Note that there is no provision for price discrimination in the retailing of a product. Predatory pricing is either selling products in one region of Canada at lower prices than other regions or selling products at unreasonably low prices for the purpose of lessening competition substantially or eliminating a competitor. Convictions bring up to two years' imprisonment.

Resale Price Maintenance.   If suppliers attempt to influence retailers to raise their prices or discourage them from lowering prices, the suppliers are engaging in **resale price maintenance**. The supplier cannot discriminate against firms with low-price policies. For a conviction it is only necessary to prove an attempt to influence prices in this manner. Penalties include a fine at the discretion of the court or up to five years' imprisonment, or both.

Misleading Advertising or Deceptive Marketing Practices.   Any representation of a product that is false or substantially misleading is illegal. Misrepresentations of such things as performance, durability, warranty, and regular price are included. Other offenses include: double ticketing, pyramid selling, bait and switch selling, referral selling, and sale above advertised price. Clear disclosure rules apply to promotional contests as well. Penalties include a fine at the discretion of the court or up to five years' imprisonment, or both.

Civilly Reviewable Matters

Mergers.   The *Competition Act* defines a merger as the acquisition or establishment of control over a significant interest in the whole or the part of the business of a competitor, supplier, customer, or other person. Any merger or proposed merger that prevents or lessens, or is likely to prevent or lessen competition substantially is reviewable by the Tribunal. The Act applies to all mergers in Canada, whether large or small, or whether domestic or foreign companies are involved.

Firms must report to the Bureau if the assets acquired, or the gross revenues from sales generated by those assets, exceed $35 million, or in the case of corporate amalgamation $70 million. The firms involved must have total assets or gross annual revenues of $400 million. The merger must wait for up to 21 days before it can proceed, while the Director reviews the application to see whether any competition concerns are involved.

If the Director is concerned that there may be substantial lessening of competition, the merger can be reviewed by the Tribunal any time up to three years after the final transaction. If the Tribunal finds that a merger prevents or substantially lessens competition, it can obtain court orders for the **dissolution** of a firm (breaking it up into smaller firms), or the **divestiture** of properties (selling off assets) obtained through merger. If the merger is only proposed, it may be prohibited. If the merger is likely to bring gains in efficiency, and the gains offset the lessening of competition, the Tribunal will not prevent the merger.

Abuse of Dominant Position.   Abuse of dominant position occurs when one or more persons substantially or completely control a type of business in Canada, or any area thereof, *and* are engaged in anticompetitive behaviour that lessens competition substantially in the market. The Act contains a long list of behaviours that are considered to be anticompetitive. The list is not to be considered all-inclusive—the Tribunal may deem other acts are also anticompetitive.

Other Abuses.   The Act proposes remedies for a number of other abuses of competition. *Refusal to deal* occurs when a supplier refuses a firm adequate supplies because of insufficient competition between suppliers. *Consignment selling* is the practice of a supplier using dealers who only pay for what they sell and may return any unsold products. The offense only occurs if the supplier dealer is using the method to control the price and discriminate between consignees and other dealers. *Exclusive dealing* is the prevention by a supplier of a retailer from carrying a competitive product. *Tied selling* is the act of requiring a customer to purchase one product in conjunction with another product. *Market restriction* is the limiting by a supplier of the resale of a product to a restricted geographical region causing a lessening of competition. *Delivered pricing* is the practice of refusing a customer delivery of a product under the same terms as other customers in the same location. *Specialization agreements* between producers of the same articles occur when each agrees to quit producing one of the products in order to specialize in the other. These agreements are exempted if they result in gains of efficiency that offset their lessening of competition and the agreement is registered with the Tribunal.

The preceding actions will be reviewed as abuses only if they are deemed to lessen competition "substantially." Furthermore, for each abuse there are other conditions that allow for exemption. The remedies under the Act vary from prohibition orders or other orders that in the Tribunal's opinion are necessary to restore or stimulate competition to, in the case of abuse of dominant position, an order of partial divestiture of assets. The Tribunal may take stronger remedial measures in more severe cases.

Evaluation of the Competition Laws

How have the laws drawn up by Parliament been enforced by the courts and other adjudication tribunals? How have they been interpreted by the courts and the administrative bodies? How have they been used to regulate industrial concentration and market structure and to curb anticompetitive business practices or market conduct?

Regulation of Industrial Concentration and Market Structure

Naturally enough, the early anticombines laws had largely been administered and interpreted by prosecuting attorneys and judges. Although these competition laws have been interpreted to suggest that reduction of competition is illegal per se, judges have been aware that the legislation declared illegal only those agreements that "lessen competition unduly" or are to the "detriment of the public." Monopoly-type *behaviour*, rather than the *existence* of the type of market structure that gives rise to such behaviour, has tended to be the target of anticombine action. The legal mind seems to have more inclination to look for *bad market conduct* than for *bad market structure,* structure that leads to monopolistic practices.

Judicial Interpretation—The Abuse Doctrine

The **abuse doctrine** is the concept that market conduct—the abuse of dominant position—rather than share of market control should determine guilt or innocence under the competition laws. Case law shows that abuse doctrine in effect continued to grant large market share immunity from prosecution. "The law does not make mere size an offense. It requires . . . overt acts." This stretched the abuse doctrine so far as to raise the question of how "bad" bad conduct had to be before it violated the law.

For all intents and purposes, these developments in judicial interpretation of the anticombines laws had effectively removed them as barriers to monopolistic tendencies. During much of Canadian history there has been a generally favourable public attitude toward big business. Limited government intervention, as a public policy stance, had been the general perspective of our competition laws to 1976.

The *Combines Investigation Act* in its various manifestations was an ineffective mechanism for dealing with mergers and the existence of monopoly power. In all of its history there had never been a conviction in a contested merger case. Between 1910 and 1976 only one conviction upon a plea of guilty was obtained. The record for monopolistic behaviour was almost as bad. In 16 cases brought to court under the monopoly provisions, only a few convictions resulted. The obstacles to the enforcement of competition were great. It was necessary to prove without a reasonable doubt that competition had been lessened *substantially* to the *detriment* of the public or, in the case of monopoly, that market control was also achieved. The case law under the *Combines Investigation Act* established a number of propositions. Canadian law perceived monopolies as benign. Monopoly power was not per se illegal; the mere existence of a monopoly was not proof of detriment to the public. If entry to the market was not prevented, then lessening of competition through merger or monopoly was not necessarily a detriment to the public. The mere acquisition or elimination of competitors was not illegal if other competitors still existed. Abuse of economic power had to be proved beyond a reasonable doubt.

Effect upon Merger Activity

A **horizontal merger** is a merger between two firms selling the same, or very similar, products in the same market. The merger of two grocery stores would be a horizontal merger. A **vertical merger** is a merger between a supplier and its customer. For example, an oil refining company might merge with an oil pipeline company so that the refining and shipping operations are vertically integrated under one company. A **conglomerate merger** is a merger of companies that operate in completely different markets and produce largely unrelated products. An example would be the merger of a sporting goods company with a computer company and a cosmetics company.

One of the main purposes of anticombines laws was to restrict merger activity. Nevertheless, there has been a large merger movement since World War II. Fewer than 60 mergers per year occurred between 1945 and 1949. The number of mergers increased in the 1960s to an annual average of 250, rising to 500 per year in the late 1970s and early 1980s. From the implementation of the *Competition Act* (1986) to 1990 there have been 3,600 mergers (or an annual average of 900), with a pronounced increase in conglomerate mergers.

In the case of horizontal mergers and vertical mergers, the Competition Tribunal has taken the position that they potentially lessen competition. Still, Canadian competition policy has had little success in blocking vertical and horizontal mergers. It has had no effect on the surge of conglomerate mergers that started in the 1960s and continues to the present. Indeed, there were more major mergers in the period 1980–1990 than in any comparable period in our history, and more than 75 percent were conglomerate mergers.

From the standpoint of competition policy, conglomerate mergers are a relatively new and unfamiliar phenomenon. Part of the difficulty stems from a relative lack of knowledge about their impact on competition and market structure. Though they probably have increased concentration in manufacturing, there is little evidence that conglomerate mergers have lessened competition in individual markets. Because of their relatively large size and the wide range of their activities, they would seem to gain advantages in dealing with suppliers and customers on a reciprocal basis. ("Our branch X will buy supplies from you if you will buy the nuts and bolts you need from our branch Y.") While fears of such arrangements were once a matter of some concern to the Competition Tribunal, investigations have not turned up evidence that they are all that prevalent or significant.

Superior Performance versus Abuse of Power

There is legitimate concern that competition policy runs the risk of punishing firms that have achieved market dominance through superior innovation and efficiency rather than by the use of restrictive or unfair business practices. In

FIGURE 13-2 **The Economic Implications of Legal Mergers**

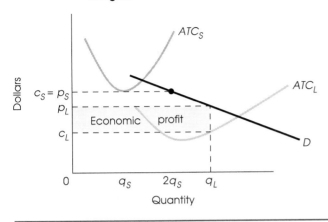

Small firms making zero profit at market price p_S with ATC_S merge to form a single firm with ATC_L. The large firm with market power can charge p_L, which is lower than p_S, and p_L generates an economic profit for the larger firm with ATC_L. The competition laws permit this merger even though competition is reduced because the industry is more efficient.

determining whether competition has been lessened substantially, the Tribunal must consider whether an undesired practice is the result of superior competitive performance. The *Competition Act* will not interfere with a combine that shows increased efficiency by lessening prices. This may allow a firm, even though it lowers price, to obtain economic profits as it becomes more dominant in an industry. This possibility is illustrated in Figure 13-2. For example, if two of the smaller firms with ATC_S merge to form a single firm with ATC_L, thus becoming dominant in the industry, the larger firm with market power can charge p_L which is lower than p_S. But p_L generates an economic profit for the larger firm with ATC_L, while previously the industry may have been making only normal profits at p_S and ATC_S. Is this profit an abuse of dominant position? Economists would argue that it is, but the competition laws allow for this situation to exist. This approach may be pragmatic in many cases. Regulating this industry in order to obtain a price equal to the lowest ATC may cost society more than the benefits obtained.

The Importance of Market Definition

In all issues of monopoly—mergers, combines, and the like—market definition is important. The size of a firm relative to the market is more critical than the size of the firm alone. The question of what forms the immediate substitutes and complements of any product depends on how broadly one defines the market along two dimensions: geographical area and product definition. Markets may have local, national, or international dimensions and may vary considerably in economic significance. For example, restaurant services are often modeled as a monopolistically competitive product. In the *Canadian* market there are hundreds of thousands of individual firms. Even in an *urban* market there are hundreds of restaurants. But there may be only one in some small towns. Should this one restaurant be regulated because of its monopoly power in its market? Similarly, there may be only one producing firm in the Canadian market, but is competition in the *international* market sufficient to keep the firm's market power at a minimum? Secondly, how broadly do we define the product?

What products can be considered close substitutes? Is there a restaurant services market or is there a separate market for pizza and a separate market for hamburgers? The more narrowly we define the market geographically or around a specific product, the more likely for an interpretation of market power.

The Results Under the Competition Act

Since the *Competition Act* has come into force, examination of over five hundred merger cases have been initiated. Many have been abandoned, a small number have concluded with monitoring only, and some mergers were restructered; but so far the Tribunal has rendered only a small number of decisions relating to mergers.

In one case, involving Palm Dairies, the Tribunal refused a consent order. The Tribunal has also issued consent orders that allowed the mergers to proceed on the terms negotiated by the Director and the firms involved. Air Canada's Reservec and Canadian Airlines Pegasus computerized reservation systems were given a consent order to form the single system to be known as Gemini. In the Imperial Oil–Texaco merger a consent order was approved in February 1990 after Imperial Oil addressed the various concerns raised by the Tribunal. Pacific Western Airline (PWA), which operated Canadian International Airlines, was not given a consent order directly, but a lengthy background report accompanied the decision not to challenge the merger with Wardair to form the new Canadian Airline. The PWA–Wardair merger effectively reduced the airline industry to a duopoly. The merger of Molson and Carling O'Keefe breweries was ultimately approved, but it is one that is to be monitored to observe its effects upon the beer market. This merger required the approval of both the Bureau of Consumer and Corporate Affairs and Investment Canada, as the merged firm would be half owned by a foreign company.

An inquiry into the first case of abuse of dominant position was begun in October 1988 by the Tribunal relating to Nutrasweet's alleged anticompetitive acts in the aspartame market.

In early 1992 the first contested merger case went to the Tribunal—the 1990 purchase by Southam Incorporated of 38 local community and real estate papers in British Columbia's lower mainland. The case was important, as the newspaper industry is already highly concentrated and dominated by Southam and Thompson Corporation. Southam beat the challenge in the Spring of 1992, when the Tribunal concluded that the daily and community newspapers do not compete head-on for advertisers. Previous efforts by the Bureau and a number of Royal Commissions over the last 25 years have also failed to halt this increasing concentration.

These results indicate that the approach to mergers and monopoly hasn't changed dramatically under the *Competition Act*. The director has taken a "compliance orientated approach to case resolution." New legal issues are bound to arise with the application of the Act as it is interpreted by the courts.

Regulation of Market Conduct and Business Practices

In addition to regulating industrial concentration and market structure, the competition laws specifically ban certain kinds of market conduct and business practices as outlined previously in the overview of the *Competition Act*. Let's briefly examine some of these and a few recent instances in which they have brought about important court decisions.[7]

Bid-rigging among firms is illegal under the *Competition Act*. In 1988 four firms in the business forms industry were found rigging bids to the Saskatchewan government. The Saskatchewan court of Queen's bench levied fines against these four totalling $1.6 million. As well, two of these firms were also convicted of bid-rigging in Nova Scotia and were fined $200,000 each. It is important for economic efficiency to prosecute this activity. In the previous chapter's discussion of the Bertrand model, we saw that the price outcome of an oligopolistic industry competing through sealed bids was equal to that of a competitive industry, if there is no collusion. It is therefore important for economic efficiency that bid-rigging be prevented in order to maintain competitive pricing in an otherwise (for cost reasons) oligopolistic industry.

Resale price maintenance is outlawed by the Act. In 1989 significant convictions were obtained in regard to gasoline pricing (Shell Canada Products), the soft drink industry (Coca-Cola), and electronics (Toshiba and Commodore Business Machines). Some of these resulted in record fines. Preventing this behaviour is important in order to allow retailers to compete effectively on price, producing greater efficiency in the provision of the retail service component of consumer purchases.

Misleading representations are prohibited under the Act, with criminal sanctions imposed on those convicted. Competition legislation banning this behaviour has been rigorously enforced ever since its first introduction in 1960. Hundreds of convictions have been made with fines reaching as high as $1 million. Thousands of orders have been issued to sellers to stop false advertising that misrepresents goods as to quality, curative power, real price, composition, and origin. Marketing violations are by far the most enforced area under competition policy.

Current Thought on Competition Policy

Anticombine activity has been greater since the late 1960s than it was during the 70 years following the passage of the first *Combines Investigation Act* (1889), yet economists continue to differ considerably on the merits of competition policy.

What are the main schools of thought about competition policy and the direction it should take in the future? Basically, there are three: (1) Large firms and highly concentrated oligopolistic industries are our best hope for future progress and international competitiveness and should be left alone; (2) competition laws should be revised to promote "workable competition"; or (3) we need more active enforcement of the current *Competition Act* and changes in other policies that tend to lessen competition. Let's consider each of these in turn.

---

[7]These cases have been drawn from the *Annual Report of the Director of Investigation and Research, Bureau of Competition Policy, Consumer and Corporate Affairs* (Ottawa: Ministry of Supply and Services, 1990).

Bigness Means Progress

The distinguished economist Joseph Schumpeter (1883–1950) argued that economists were wrong to place so much emphasis on perfect competition as a model of ideal efficiency. He claimed that the incentive for technological change and product innovation comes from the prospects for economic, or monopoly, profit. These prospects are greater when there is monopoly power, not when competitive conditions prevail.

Some proponents of this point of view go on to argue that in many industries modern technology and the efficiencies realized from economies of scale do not go along with a market structure of many firms, the basic ingredient of a highly competitive market. To use competition laws to impose such a market structure in these cases would only result in a loss of efficiency due to a decrease in economies of scale and technological innovation. This point of view has prevailed in our competition law.

Competition Laws Should Promote Workable Competition

This school of thought is somewhat related to the first. According to this view, the concept of perfect competition is an idealization that has few counterparts in real-world market structures. Furthermore, given the existence of mass production technologies and the associated economies of scale, competition policy and laws based on the notion that there must be many firms engaged in fierce price competition may be misdirected.

Proponents of **workable competition** argue that it would be both realistic and more promising to recognize that vigorous competition can take many forms in an oligopolistic industry, including product differentiation and development, innovations in production technology, better customer service, and informative advertising. They say it would be wiser if competition policy focused more on these dimensions of nonprice competition. They say that workable competition exists where competition along these lines is vigorous among existing firms and where there is the potential threat of new entrants to the industry should prices and profits rise too much. Moreover, they claim that workable competition may exist in oligopolistic industries where firm size is large, the number of firms is few, and industry concentration is high. However, critics of the workable competition concept say that it puts too much stress on judging an industry by its market performance. They argue that in effect it would leave competition policy to something like the "abuse of dominant position" philosophy.

A relatively new perspective on workable competition is the notion of a **contestable market**. *A market is contestable if the incumbent firm(s) in the industry are disciplined to keep price low (close to average cost) by the threat of competition through entry.* Entry is not blocked even though there may be few firms or only one in the market. A perfectly contestable market is depicted in Figure 13-3. There are economies of scale in production of the commodity, as is indicated by the falling longrun average cost curve. In this example the *LRAC* curve has a very flat bottom, indicating that there is no difference between the average cost at the current level and the level the existing firm could expect to produce if one more firm were to enter the industry. If the existing firm in the market charges a price above the minimum average cost, thereby making an economic profit, firms would immediately enter and the profit would be lost to competition. This

FIGURE 13-3   A Perfectly Contestable Market

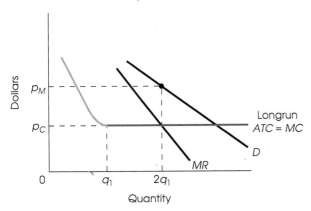

A profit-maximizing firm would produce at $2q_1$ and charge price p_M if entry is blocked. If entry is not blocked then p_C is charged in order to prevent a rival firm's profitable entry.

market situation, if it exists, is extremely significant, as it has long been argued that a firm with large economies of scale would need to be regulated or possibly owned and operated by government in order to achieve socially efficient prices $(P = MC = ATC)$. Contestability provides one means to judge the potential for abuse of power more objectively. Industries containing relatively few firms can be judged by considering the cost relationships and barriers to entry rather than market share and concentration ratios. If a market is contestable, *potential* competition is as effective in keeping price efficient as actual competition, and an unregulated monopoly with economies of scale is less of a problem than it would appear at first glance.

Competition Policy Should Promote Competition More Actively

Proponents of this point of view argue that more resources ought to be devoted to the investigative activities of the Director of Investigation and Research and the Bureau of the Consumer and Corporate Affairs. In addition, they argue that policy changes are needed in several related areas.

Markets Untouched by Competition Policy.   There are groups in our economy that are currently exempt from competition law, and it is claimed, indulge in monopolistic practices. Labour unions are among these groups. Some argue that the market power of large unions may exceed that of all but the largest corporations. The restrictions imposed by unions on the entry of new trainees into the skilled trades is often cited as evidence of this. Trade and professional associations, such as the Canadian Medical Association and the Canadian Dental Association and their provincial counterparts, are often accused of similar practices aimed at restricting entry and limiting the supply of practitioners, thereby keeping their incomes high. Trade practices among lawyers, doctors, dentists, real estate agents,[8] and architects typically bar competitive determination of fees.

[8]In December 1988, the Federal Court of Canada upon recommendation of the Tribunal issued a comprehensive order of prohibition with respect to commissions, services, or practices that will affect all of the real estate industry in Canada.

Yet these groups have remained largely immune from competition policy. All these groups are usually cited as targets for some form of action by those who advocate more vigorous competition policy.

More Dissolution, Divorce, and Divestiture.   Those who favour a more active competition policy often argue that there has been too much reluctance to use the three D's of competition—dissolution, divorce, and divestiture—to break up large firms. These are cited as the most effective ways to break up monopoly power because they attack market structure directly. Once in a great while courts have decided in favour of the separation of the units of a vertical combination (divorce) or the selling of assets (divestiture). The breaking up of a larger firm into several smaller firms (dissolution) is even rarer. The reluctance to do this stems largely from the legal and financial problems involved—the difficulty of "unscrambling an omelet." There is also the fear that the resulting smaller units might not succeed. There have only been a few cases of dissolution, divestiture, and divorcement in 100 years of competition activity.

Public Policy Bias Toward Big Business.   There is a tendency for government policy to lend a helping hand to large businesses in trouble while many small businesses fail every day with little notice. In a competitive marketplace, some less-efficient competitors are bound to fail. Why inefficient large firms should be saved from failure by government protection while small firms are not is a hotly debated question. In recent years, for example, controversy over this issue was spurred by the government's rescue of Chrysler from bankruptcy. Critics of such policy argue that it encourages the notion that there is an added safety feature in bigness—government protection from failure. This may encourage merger activity and management policies that are riskier and less efficient than would be the case without the safety of a government backstop.

Removal of Barriers to Foreign Trade.   One way to increase competition and provide the consumer with a greater variety of products at lower prices is to remove barriers to foreign competition. Such barriers include import tariffs (taxes on imported goods) and quotas (volume limits on the quantity of imported goods). In those areas of the economy in which industrial concentration is high and oligopoly market structure has strong overtones of monopoly power, removal of barriers to direct foreign competition may be the most effective public policy for the maintenance of vigorous competition. The *Free Trade Agreement* with the United States was a movement in this direction, although critics argue that this agreement is more of a protection of continentalist interests than a free-trade agreement.

A Final Comment

It may well be that the mere existence of competition laws serves as a significant deterrent to the exercise and growth of monopoly power. For example, it is sometimes said that General Motors, which in some years has had nearly 35 percent of the auto market, would take over a great deal more of that market if it were not afraid of the competition action that would likely be taken against

Checkpoint 13-3

Why might it be argued that market structure is a more important criterion than market conduct for judging an industry when enforcing competition laws?

it. The deterrent effect of competition laws is difficult to measure. Nonetheless, many economists feel that it is of significant importance to the maintenance of competition and the restraint of monopoly-type power and practices.

The Regulated Industries—Protecting Consumers or the Regulated?

Certain industries such as airlines, trucking, railroads, radio and television broadcasting, and banking are (or have been) regulated by government commissions. More often than not it seems such regulation protects the regulated from competition instead of assuring the benefits of competition to the consumer. Some economists argue that the regulatory agency is often "captured" by the regulated firms and used to fix prices (rates), allocate market shares among firms, restrict entry into the industry, and promote other anticompetitive practices. This is done under the guise of legitimate government regulation, and is otherwise in violation of the competition laws from which some of these industries have been exempt. This type of criticism of regulated industries has given rise to a movement toward **deregulation** in recent years.

The Pros and Cons of Industry Regulation

Regulation legislation as typically stated has as one of its objectives to ensure "fair and reasonable" prices. Those critical of industry regulation generally argue that it tends to create resource misallocation, inefficiency, and therefore higher costs to the public. Regulation critics question the ability of bureaucratic intervention to improve on the market-guided decisions of individuals and firms where the potential for competition exists. Regulation proponents argue that regulation is required in some markets to protect vulnerable consumers, or to pursue social and cultural goals. In addition, they claim that regulation is sometimes necessary to protect firms from periodic bouts of cutthroat competition that threaten their ability to provide reliable service to the public. The examples provided by the industries regulated by the Canadian Radio-television and Telecommunication Commission (CRTC) and the Canadian Transport Commission (CTC) illustrate both sides of the debate.

Regulation of Air Transport

The Canadian Transport Commission was created in 1967 and became the one federal agency overseeing all transportation regulations including railroads, interprovincial highway transport, commodity pipelines, air transport, maritime transport, and initially telecommunications, which was transferred to the CRTC in 1976. Regulation of land transport by railways and highways has been significant in Canada but not to the extent it has been in the United States. Except for the grain freight rates established under the Crows Nest Pass agreement of 1897, railroads have been virtually free of any rate regulation. For all practical purposes highway transport is provincially regulated, with a variation from little regulation in Alberta to comprehensive regulation in Quebec. Trucking regulation in Canada is often alleged to be an example of the capture hypothesis. The CTC's greatest regulatory control was in the air. Advocates of the regulation of airline routes and fares argue that without such controls, rate-cutting competition might invite cost-cutting practices that endanger pubic safety. It is also frequently claimed that regulation is necessary to assure air service to smaller communities.

Critics point out that CTC regulations prevented airlines from charging fares on different routes to reflect differences in costs per passenger mile (due to cost efficiencies associated with time in the air and route travel density). Routes were also assigned by CTC administrators on the basis of noneconomic considerations ("such-and-such community needs air service," says its influential member of Parliament). Critics claim that entry restriction, rate-setting regulations, and other controls served to protect established concerns and labour unions from competition, and consumers ended up paying higher prices due to higher costs.

Regulation of the Airwaves

The CRTC regulates radio and television use of the airwaves and effectively restricts the number of radio and television stations in local areas across the country. Limiting entry to the radio and television industry in this way effectively jacks up profits from advertising revenues and has led to dominance by two major networks—CTV and CBC. Advocates of radio and television regulation say that regulation is necessary to protect the public interest. Opponents argue that it mainly serves to generate economic profits for the radio and television industry while restricting the program menu available to the public. In recent years the advent of cable television networks has brought more competition to the industry.

Movement Toward Deregulation

Since the late 1970s there has been some significant deregulation, reducing controls exercised by the CTC and CRTC, as well as some controls on banking and finance (removal of deposit interest ceilings and restrictions on the provisions of financial services, for example), grain freight rates (in 1983), and oil pricing (in 1985). The deregulation movement has had remarkably wide public and bipartisan political support, yet it has also met resistance from affected special interests, typically the established firms and unions feeling the increased competition.

Deregulation of Telecommunications

Deregulation of the telecommunications industry was to a large extent the result of technological change. In the 1970s the CRTC separated the regulation of transmission services of telephone companies from their provision of equipment. This opened up a whole new competitive industry for supplying telephones and other equipment. In 1979 restrictions on data interconnection were relaxed, allowing companies like CNCP Telecommunications to compete for data transmission and other private-line services. In 1985, though, the CRTC, unlike in the United States, decided that competition for long-distance voice transmission would not be allowed. A high proportion of the fixed costs of providing voice telephone services are covered by long-distance rates. It is felt that if competition existed for long distance, local carriers would have to raise local service rates significantly. Long-distance rates thus subsidize local service, and the CRTC considered this to be appropriate policy. More recently, the CRTC has changed this view and has moved toward deregulation.

Deregulation of Airlines

Until 1959 Trans Canada Airlines (later Air Canada), a crown corporation, had a monopoly on all transcontinental flights. The first moves toward deregulation in the airline industry started in the 1970s when regulations governing international and domestic charter fights were eased, discount fares were allowed, and in 1977 capacity restrictions were removed from Canadian Pacific Airlines, which at the time was the second largest airline in Canada. These actions initiated a large growth in airline business. In 1984 the CTC gave airlines more freedom to set fares and reduced entry restrictions on new airlines and new routes. In 1986 the CTC ceased to exist and was replaced by a national transportation agency with much reduced authority, but retaining some decision-making authority in cases where the public interest is affected. This change virtually eliminated regulation of air travel in Canada. Consequently, many existing carriers altered their routes (both expanding and contracting service on specific routes). At the same time, a number of new long-distance charter carriers entered the industry, bringing most long-distance air fares down. Loss-producing routes were abandoned to new specialized commuter lines (especially in smaller communities on low-volume routes), or the larger carriers adjusted fares upward to reflect real operating costs. Deregulation seems to have resulted in lower fares as the airlines have been allowed to price and operate in response to actual supply and demand conditions. More recently, concentration has been increasing in the industry. Since the PWA–Wardair merger the two dominant firms are Canadian and Air Canada. These two firms have been competing aggressively for the limited market with price reductions, seat sales, traveler's points, and other methods in order to become the sole survivor in an industry with increased concentration and diminished competition.

Summary

1. High industrial concentration can be justified on efficiency grounds if economies of scale in production exist. However, to what extent monopoly-type power, and the economic profits that occur from it, should be allowed in order to achieve reduced costs of production is the social dilemma.

2. Some economists contend that oligopoly provides an ideal combination of the opportunity for profit, which gives incentive to innovation, and the existence of competition, which encourages efficiency. High industrial concentration and large firm size are not consistently related to inventive and innovative activity. There also tends to be a positive relationship between industrial concentration and the amount of advertising, a large part of which is of dubious information content.

3. Public policy, expressed in a series of competition laws, has sought to maintain competition and curb monopoly power in the unregulated part of the economy. The keystone of competition policy is the *Competition Act* of 1986. This act made a number of anticompetitive actions illegal, with criminal sanctions, and made other matters, such as mergers and abuse of dominant position, open for civil review. It exempts labour from antitrust actions.

4. The *Competition Act* is administered by the Director of Investigation and Research under the Bureau of Competition Policy, a division of the Ministry of Consumer and Corporate Affairs. The *Competition Tribunal Act* of 1986 created the Tribunal to adjudicate the civilly reviewable matters under the *Competition Act*. This Tribunal is a quasi-judicial body composed of judges and lay experts in economics, business, and public policy. Criminal code violations are adjudicated by the Justice Department in the courts. The Tribunal is empowered to investigate, hold hearings, issue prohibition orders and consent orders, and grant advanced ruling certificates.

5. Although many anticompetitive behaviours are illegal per se, judicial interpretations of the competition laws have been based on an evaluation of market conduct (the abuse doctrine) and not on an evaluation of market structure. The abuse doctrine comes from the requirement that for a merger or abuse of dominant position to constitute a violation of the law, it must substantially lessen competition to the detriment of the public.

6. Competition policy has not been successful in blocking mergers, but it has been successful in stopping much anticompetitive activity.

7. There are basically three schools of thought on the proper role of antitrust policy: (1) Large firms and highly concentrated industries should be left alone, (2) competition laws should be used to promote "workable competition," or (3) current competition laws should be more actively enforced and changes should be made in other policies that currently dampen competition.

8. There has been a movement toward deregulation in the regulated industries—railroads, trucking, airlines, broadcasting, telecommunication, and banking. Privatization of businesses owned or controlled by the government has also been on the increase. Legislative action in the past 10 years has substantially reduced regulatory powers in a number of matters. In the airline industry, for example, rate setting, route assignments, and entry of new firms have been deregulated. Airports are also being privatized. Deregulation appears to have resulted in increased competition and lower prices—all to the benefit of the public.

Key Terms and Concepts

abuse doctrine	divestiture	prohibition orders
competition policy	exclusive dealing	resale price
conglomerate	agreements	maintenance
merger	horizontal	specialization
contestable	merger	agreements
market	misleading	tying contract
deregulation	representation	vertical merger
dissolution	predatory pricing	workable competition

Questions and Problems

1. Draw a graph illustrating the market demand and marginal revenue curves for a product that has economies of scale in production. Indicate on this graph the competitive price that would occur if a number of firms existed in the industry, each with a small plant. Can you show on this graph a situation where one firm with a large plant could sell the product at a profit-maximizing price that is below the competitive price and still make large economic profits? What does the situation depicted suggest about using competition law to enforce low concentration in this industry?

2. To what extent do you think the abuse doctrine would rely on industrial concentration ratios when examining an industry for possible competition law violations? Suppose an industry has a much higher concentration ratio than can be justified by economies of scale. How might this manifest itself in ways that would violate competition laws under the abuse doctrine? Why?

3. Consider the following news item. The Canadian Bar Association said it will fight a civil competition suit by the Competition Tribunal challenging the ban on advertising by lawyers. The CBA moved to permit limited advertising if provincial bar associations approve, but several provincial bars have rejected the change in the code of ethics. What aspects of the *Competition Act* do you think the CBA's practices may violate?

4. Suppose that you came across an editorial that observed that the Canadian economy might end up completely dominated by conglomerates happily trading with each other in a new kind of cartel system. What is your assessment of this statement?

5. Compare and contrast vertical and horizontal mergers in terms of their likely effects on market structure and the growth of monopoly power. How do the three D's of competition policy deal with these types of merger activity?

6. In the newspaper publishing dispute in British Columbia, the Director argued that the proposed deal would unduly lessen competition and give Southam a stranglehold on newspaper advertising in the region. Southam successfully argued that it would not be able to manipulate advertising rates because the lower mainland papers it recently bought and its own daily papers draw on different sorts of advertisers and face competition from other media. Discuss the definition of the market this decision would imply. Would it affect the concentration ratio for this market?

7. What would each of the various schools of thought on competition policy have to say about the following statement by Edmund Burke: "One of the finest problems in legislature [is] to determine what the State ought to take upon itself to direct by the public wisdom, and what it ought to leave, with as little interference as possible, to individual exertion."

8. A distinguished authority on the economics of competition policy, E. S. Mason, once said: "Market power is the central problem which any effective competition policy must confront." What do you think the proponents of the various schools of thought on competition policy would have to say about this?

Chapter 14

Government Regulation: Dealing with Market Shortcomings

The Canadian economy is a mixed economy—one in which the questions of what and how much to produce, how to organize production, and for whom to produce are answered by a mixture of government regulation and control in some areas of the economy, coupled with a very substantial reliance on private enterprise and free markets in other areas. We have already examined government intervention in areas of the economy where monopoly, oligopoly, and collusion have threatened to diminish competition—a problem that has been attacked through competition legislation and government regulation (often controversial) of some markets. We have also seen how government has attempted to provide a minimum standard of living for all citizens through various social insurance programs, minimum-wage legislation, and various welfare programs. All such forms of government intervention give recognition to the fact that some outcomes of pure market, laissez-faire capitalism are undesirable—that government intervention is sometimes necessary to improve on the results.

In this chapter we extend our analysis of the ways in which freely operating markets may not give satisfactory results. *When the market leads to a less than social optimal allocation of resources, economists say that there has been a* **market failure**. We will consider whether or not government regulation can be expected to improve matters and whether the costs of regulation are justified by the potential benefits. We will then examine the kinds of government regulation that attempt to correct shortcomings of the market mechanism. In particular, we will consider government regulation to protect the environment and to promote better working conditions, product safety, and consumer protection.

Shortcomings of the Market

We can identify four major problem areas for the market. First, markets cannot be depended on to provide certain products (such as national defense and lighthouses), called **public goods**. Second, markets do not always capture the full costs or benefits associated with the production of a particular good or service—these are external or spillover costs and benefits. Third, while markets convey information about prices, they sometimes suffer from a lack of other kinds of information—for example, information about the possible hazards of a complex product such as a new drug. Finally, some goals such as an equitable income distribution or equal employment opportunities sometimes cannot be achieved through the market mechanism; these are *nonmarket goals*. Let us consider each of these market shortcomings in turn. While this chapter is very important, the reader might consider how much of this book deals with how markets work and how little of it deals with how markets fail.

Public Goods

We briefly introduced the concept of a public good in Chapter 3. Here we will elaborate on this concept and distinguish between a pure public good and a near-public good.

Pure Public Goods

A **pure public good** *is a good that cannot be provided to one person without it also being provided to others. That is, it is impossible to prevent joint consumption.* The beacon from a lighthouse is an example often cited. If one ship in the vicinity can see the beacon, so can others. Suppose that a shipping company were to buy and operate a lighthouse. There is no way it could exclude other shipping companies' ships from benefiting from the beacon, even though they contributed nothing

---

LEARNING OBJECTIVES

After reading this chapter, you will be able to:

1. Explain what is meant by the term *market failure* and identify the four types of market failures.
2. Define the terms *public* and *near-public goods* and explain why such goods can lead to a market failure.
3. Define the terms *external* or *spillover costs (benefits)* and explain how such costs (benefits) can lead to a market failure.
4. Explain why full and accurate information is a necessary condition for the efficient functioning of the market.
5. Explain why some goals cannot be achieved through the market.
6. Show how benefit-cost analysis can be used to determine the optimal amount of government regulation.
7. Explain why the total elimination of pollution is not necessarily optimal and describe the government's role in environmental protection.
8. Describe and evaluate government efforts in regulating working conditions, product safety, and consumer advertising and labeling.

to the cost of operating the lighthouse. The other shipping companies would be free riders. *A* **free rider** *is anyone who receives the benefits from a good or service without having to pay for it.*

Markets will fail to supply pure public goods precisely because of the free-rider problem. Since anyone can have all the benefits provided by a pure public good without paying, no one will pay for it. Therefore, private producers will have no incentive to produce it. Hence, despite the fact that a pure public good yields valuable benefits to society, the market mechanism will not provide such a good. Pure public goods must be provided by the government and paid for with tax money or with revenues from the sale of government bonds.[1]

In sum, a pure public good is *not* subject to the exclusion principle. *Any good whose benefits accrue only to those who purchase it is said to be subject to the* **exclusion principle.** Those who do not pay for the good are excluded from its benefits. If you buy a car, your neighbour is excluded from its benefits unless you choose to allow him or her to use it.

What are some other examples of pure public goods? Our legal system is one. Laws that protect you also protect me, but neither of us would be willing to finance the system alone. Another example is national defense. Even if someone is on welfare and pays no income taxes, our national defense system protects that person as much as it protects anyone who pays hundreds of thousands of dollars in income taxes. Neither of these individuals would have any incentive to pay voluntarily for national defense, and, since it is provided, both are free riders. (If it were not provided, neither one individually could really make a significant contribution to it anyway, even though they both might value national defense highly.) The quality of the air we breathe is also a pure public good. If it is clean and free of pollutants for one, it is for all. If many pay taxes to finance the costs of antipollution efforts, those who don't pay taxes share equally in the benefits as well—they are free riders.

The total demand for a public good is *not* the horizontal summation of individual demand. It is the vertical summation. Consider the total demand curve for two different goods, automobiles and one year of service from a lighthouse. Assume that in each case there are ten possible buyers. In the case of the car, each buyer wants 1 unit at a price of $15,000. The total quantity demanded at $15,000 would be 10 units. In the case of a lighthouse each buyer is willing to pay $12,000 for 1 year of service. They only want 1 lighthouse, but together they would be willing to pay $120,000 per year to get the service. We have added the price each is willing to pay for 1 unit, not the quantity that each is willing to buy at a given price. Notice that it would be possible to have the services of a lighthouse if the cost of service for 1 year is $12,000 or less and if 1 firm does not object to providing rival firms with free service. Then that firm could contract for the lighthouse. However, if the service cost more than $12,000 per year, there would have to be a way to organize the market in order to ensure the lighthouse would operate. The simplest way to provide such organization would be to use the taxing power of the government to collect the money and to provide the service. In practice it usually falls to government to do so. Of course, there is no absolute guarantee that the government will provide the economically

---

[1]Note that the government may simply contract with private firms to have the good produced. It is even possible for a private firm to build a lighthouse and operate it at a profit if they could find a single shipping company that would value that lighthouse highly enough to fund its operation.

optimal amount of the public good, but the private sector is very unlikely to provide it at all.

If the legal system, national defense, and environmental protection were not provided by government, they would not be provided at all. For why should any individual producer of these services provide them, knowing that it is not possible to charge free riders for consuming the benefits—and why should any individual pay if he or she can be a free rider? In short, since no one would voluntarily pay for these services, no private producer would find it profitable to provide them. Yet they are important to our society, and so government is authorized to provide them.

Near-Public Goods

Near-public goods *are goods that are consumed jointly but do not completely qualify as public goods for one reason or another.* Examples of near-public goods are athletic events, plays, movies, television and radio broadcasts, parks, and highways (toll roads). Government provision of pure public goods is necessary because of the free-rider problem. However, near-public goods are subject to the exclusion principle. Hence, it is feasible for them to be provided by private producers responding to market demand.

In our economy we see near-public goods provided both publicly and privately. There is CBC Radio and Television, produced and supported by the federal government, there are various provincially funded educational stations, and people in many parts of Canada can receive American public stations, while at the same time there are private broadcasting companies such as CTV, Global, and Moffet. There are parks owned and operated by the government, such as Banff National Park, and privately run theme and amusement parks.

Since near-public goods may be produced privately, why should the government ever produce them? Critics of government provision argue that since consumers get the good at a zero price, there is no way of knowing how much of it to provide. Is the cost of providing more of the good covered by what consumers would be willing to pay if they had to? This question suggests that government provision may result in either over- or underproduction of near-public goods. Society may end up devoting too many or too few resources to such goods. Either case is economically inefficient. Hence, the case for government provision of near-public goods is not as persuasive as the case for government provision of pure public goods.

Externalities

We previously discussed externalities in Chapter 7. Here we will briefly review the concept to provide a basis for our discussion of government regulation. **Externalities** *are any costs or benefits that fall on others besides the buyers and sellers of a particular good or service.* Externalities are often referred to as *external costs* or *diseconomies, external benefits, spillovers, neighbourhood effects,* or *external economies.*

There are numerous examples of external costs. Nonsmokers trapped in a meeting room with smokers cannot avoid inhaling some of the smoke. The health hazard of the smoke is an external cost to the nonsmoker. Similarly, residents in the vicinity of a steel mill bear an external cost when smoke from the mill corrodes the paint on their houses, pollutes the air they breathe, and stunts the growth of the surrounding plant life. If residents feel they must move, then that, too, is an external cost in the form of moving expenses. When Uncle Jake cleans his false teeth ultrasonically, it may cause static on his neighbour's radio. The radio static is an external cost borne by the neighbour. Some electronic heating machines used to make plywood and plastic goods can cause serious interference with frequencies used by airport flight-control towers. The resulting reduction in air passenger safety, possibly leading to airplane crashes, is an external cost borne by airlines and their passengers.

Examples of external benefits are not hard to find either. You may invest considerable time and money caring for your yard. Your neighbour reaps the external benefit of viewing a beautiful lawn and garden without spending a cent. If you buy a flu shot, you protect yourself from sickness, an obvious benefit to you. However, others get an external benefit because they are less likely to catch the flu from you. Similarly, if you spend money maintaining the brakes on your car, you bestow an external benefit on other drivers because your car is now less likely to run into them. A pure public good is an extreme example of a good that provides external benefits to parties not directly involved in the purchase or sale of the good. If a shipping company pays to provide a lighthouse beacon, then nonpaying shippers receive an external benefit because they can use the beacon free of charge—they are free riders, as are all recipients of external benefits. Your university education will bring you a higher income, but it may also bring benefits to others. You will be a more productive worker. You may even be a better citizen.

Society's Loss Due to External Costs

Recall our discussion of external costs in Chapter 7. There we considered an industry (any industry) that pollutes the environment while producing its product. The cost of cleaning up or suffering the consequences is an external cost borne by others. For example, the homeowner who has to paint more often, the individual who develops health problems, the maple sugar producer who suffers a drop in yield. However, this cost is not included in the industry or market supply curve S shown in Figure 14-1. Given the market demand curve D, the equilibrium quantity produced and sold without regard for this external cost is q_n and the equilibrium price is p_n.

Suppose that the firms in the industry had to pay all of the environmental cleanup costs associated with the production of each unit of output. These costs would be added to the firm's other production costs to give the market supply curve S_a, which includes all costs and hence lies above S. The equilibrium quantity produced and sold would now be q_0, an amount smaller than q_n. The equilibrium price would be p_0, which is higher than p_n. In this new equilibrium, the cost of pollution would be borne entirely by the buyers and sellers of the product—it is no longer borne by nonconsenting third parties.

The new equilibrium is optimal from society's standpoint; the old equilibrium is not. Why? Because the external costs associated with a good—that is, costs not borne by the buyers and sellers of the good—foster the production of additional units of output that are not valued as much as the cost of producing them. This can be seen in Figure 14-1 from the fact that the supply curve S_a (which includes all costs) lies above the demand curve D for all units of the good from q_0

FIGURE 14-1   **Society's Loss Due to External Costs**

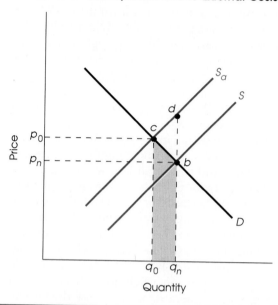

The presence of external costs means that the actual market supply curve S lies below the supply curve S_a, which includes all costs associated with production of the good. The external (or spillover) costs lead to the production of additional units of the good (equal to $q_n - q_0$) that are not valued as much as the cost of producing them. The dollar amount of this excess of costs over value equals the area cbd; it represents society's loss due to external costs when the amount q_n is produced.

to q_n. The dollar value of the total benefits to buyers of this additional quantity $q_n - q_0$ of the good is represented by the area $q_0 q_n bc$. The cost, or dollar value, of the resources used to produce these additional units is represented by the area $q_0 q_n dc$. The dollar amount by which the costs of the additional units *exceed* their benefits is represented by the area cbd. This is society's loss due to external costs (spillover costs).

This loss is a consequence of the fact that output q_n exceeds the optimal output level q_0—resources are overallocated to the production of this good. The price per unit of the good p_n fails to cover the costs of producing the good. Society's loss due to external costs is the result of a market shortcoming— namely, a failure to prevent some of the costs of the good from being borne by nonconsenting third parties.

Society's Loss Due to Missed Opportunities—External Benefits

In our discussion of external benefits in Chapter 7 we saw that if a good provides benefits to others who do not buy the good, these spillover, or external, benefits are not reflected in the market demand curve. For example, the market demand curve for flu shots reflects the value of their benefits to the people who buy them to prevent themselves from contracting the flu. It does not reflect the benefits of the flu shots to those who don't buy them, but who are nonetheless better off due to the reduction in the spread of a contagious disease.

Since the market demand curve for goods and services providing external benefits does not reflect the full value of these benefits, it must lie below a demand curve that is drawn to include them. Figure 14-2 shows a hypothetical demand curve D and supply curve S for flu shots. The market equilibrium quantity of flu shots supplied and purchased is q_n, and the equilibrium price is p_n. If the value of the external (or spillover) benefits to society at large from these flu shots were added on to D, we would get the demand curve D_a. Since D_a

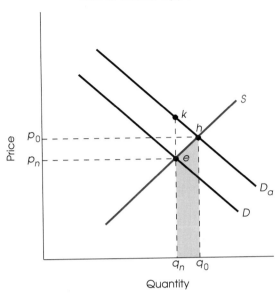

FIGURE 14-2 **External Benefits: Society's Loss Due to Missed Opportunities**

The presence of external benefits means that the market demand curve D lies below the demand curve D_a that includes the value of all benefits associated with the good. Because of the external (or spillover) benefits, the market fails to produce additional units of the good (the quantity $q_0 - q_n$) that are valued more than the cost of producing them. The dollar amount of this excess of benefits over costs equals the area ehk. It represents society's loss because the market produces less than the optimal amount of the good.

includes the value of all benefits, it lies above D. The equilibrium quantity produced and sold would now be q_0, an amount larger than q_n, and the equilibrium price would be p_0, which is higher than p_n.

Why is the new equilibrium, q_0 and p_0, optimal from society's standpoint? Because when external benefits are associated with a good—benefits that accrue to others who don't pay for it—the market will not produce enough of the good. When only q_n units of the good are produced, society forgoes a quantity of goods ($q_0 - q_n$) that it values more than the cost of producing them. This can be seen in Figure 14-2 from the fact that the demand curve D_a (which includes the value of all benefits) lies above the supply curve S between output quantities q_n and q_0. The dollar value of the benefits to society of the additional quantity $q_0 - q_n$ of the good is represented by the area $q_n q_0 hk$. The cost of the resources used to produce these additional units is represented by the area $q_n q_0 he$. The dollar amount by which the total benefits of these additional units *exceed* their cost is represented by the area ehk. This represents society's loss due to the missed opportunity of not having the additional output from q_n to q_0—a loss caused by the failure of the market to capture external benefits.

The loss reflects the fact that output q_n falls short of the optimal output level q_0. Resources are underallocated to the production of this good because the price per unit of the good p_n fails to reflect the full value of the good. *Where there are external costs, the market mechanism tends to encourage overproduction, the provision of goods whose costs exceed the value of their benefits. Where there are external benefits, the market mechanism gives rise to underproduction, the failure to provide goods even though the value of their benefits exceeds their costs.*

Canada and most other industrialized countries have universal medical care systems. These systems are often defended on the grounds of equity. It is unfair for anyone to be denied medical care because of low income. This is a perfectly valid, but clearly normative argument. It is also possible to argue for such programs in part on the basis of external benefits. Universal medical care not only means better health for low-income Canadians, it also protects all other Canadians from exposure to disease from those who in the absence of free health care would go untreated. It also contributes to lower costs to business because of lower absenteeism.

Imperfect Information

The market mechanism may fail to provide adequate information. Information is an economic good; it has value. Consumers spend time and money seeking information about products—how good is the product, how safe, what are the alternatives, how much does the product cost in one store as compared to another? Sometimes the information desired is prohibitively expensive or perhaps unavailable at any price. For example, a new drug may have side effects that are as yet unknown. Buyers must always make decisions to varying degrees on the basis of imperfect information. To what extent is there a conflict between producer and consumer interests where product information is concerned? To what extent is product information a public good? To what extent is the lack of perfect information fit cause for government market intervention?

Conflict Between Consumer and Producer Interests

A buyer who purchases a product repeatedly will become quite familiar with its characteristics by trial and error. Foods, beverages, clothing, haircuts, restaurant meals, and automobile servicing are all goods and services whose producers are very dependent on repeat sales if they are to stay in business. Producers have a considerable incentive to ensure consumer satisfaction, because consumers will become fairly well informed about their products in a short period of time. If brand A soap causes a skin rash or brand B toothpaste tastes bitter, sales will drop off fairly rapidly. However, even repeat-purchase items can have characteristics that consumers may not learn about on their own. For example, it is typically not in the producer's best self-interest to inform consumers about possible health hazards associated with longrun use of a product. Cigarette companies were certainly not pleased when the government of Canada forced them to print health hazard warnings on cigarette packages. There is, then, often a disparity between what consumers would like to know about a product and what producers want them to know.

Products that are only purchased infrequently, or that are too complex for the typical consumer to evaluate knowledgeably tend to allow greater scope for conflict between consumer and producer interest. Suppose that you hire a contractor to build a house. Suppose that 10 years later you discover that faulty foundations are cracking, giving rise to basement flooding during heavy rains. The contractor may have long since become wealthy building subdivisions of homes like yours. The market's failure to provide information that protects home buyers from such calamities is one reason most local governments establish building codes.

Drugs provide another good example of product complexity that is beyond the information-gathering ability of most consumers. Imperfect information concerning these products has given rise to significant government regulation. And sometimes the cost of gathering information is so high that the use of standards set by government regulatory agencies may be a cheap substitute for other, expensive information.

At its worst, the conflict between consumer and producer interests can lead to producer attempts to deceive consumers deliberately. Such deception may take the form of false advertising claims and misleading labeling of products. Subtle manipulation of demand through advertising that appeals to the consumer's ego or emotions is common. Deceptive advertising and labeling amount to attempts to misinform the consumer. It also can be unfair to rival producers who represent their products honestly. The *Competition Act* outlaws such practices, but it is not completely successful in eliminating them. At the same time, a good deal of government activity has been devoted to the provision of additional product information.

Is Product Information a Near-Public Good?

As we already noted, information is an economic good. There is a market for it. Sellers spend money on advertising to spread information about their wares in trade journals, in newspapers, and on radio and television. Consumers spend money to get information from shoppers' guides, newspapers, and magazines. (Recall our discussion of the information content of advertising in Chapters 11 and 12.) There are private organizations that specialize in selling information to consumers. In spite of their efforts, there remains an imbalance between the information available to buyers and sellers.

One example is *Canadian Consumer*, a magazine that contains reports on the results of its own testing of hundreds of products. The American magazine *Consumer Reports* is also widely available in Canada. Such publications provide this information for the price of the magazine; to avoid conflicts of interest, they accept no advertising. The information provided by *Canadian Consumer* is very much in the nature of a near-public good. It cannot be provided to the initial purchaser without possibly providing it to others who do not pay—it is not entirely subject to the exclusion principle. Only the original purchaser must pay the price of the magazine. Anybody can read a copy at the public library for nothing. Obviously, many people could read a single copy, yet the publisher would receive only the purchase price of that one copy. The publishers of such information are unable to capture the full value of the service provided because they cannot keep those who don't pay for the information from getting it.

In short, the external benefits from *Canadian Consumer* are probably considerable. As we saw in Figure 14-2, this means that the market produces less of this information than is optimal from society's standpoint. Hence, it may be argued that government action is appropriate to provide additional product information. Indeed, as will be discussed later, there has been a good deal of government activity in this area.

Nonmarket Goals

Certain of the goals and values of any society are either ill-served or not served at all by the marketplace. For instance, markets do not keep people from harming themselves and each other in ways that society considers unacceptable. Also, freely working markets will reward some and penalize others to extremes that may conflict with society's sense of fairness and justice.

Protecting Individuals from Themselves and Others

Markets are capable of providing many kinds of goods and services that society at large considers harmful to the buyer. The government may declare the production and sale of such products illegal or limit their distribution in some way. For example, the government prohibits the sale of hard drugs such as heroin. Some provinces or municipalities ban the sale of firecrackers. Almost all jurisdictions in North America have legislation requiring motorcycle riders to wear helmets. Similarly the use of seat beats is nearly universally required. Often there is considerable controversy about whether the government is too overbearing in such regulation. It is worth noting that these laws are intended not only to protect those who wear helmets and seat belts, but also to reduce medical costs for everyone.

One of the most notable examples of controversial legislation was prohibition, which banned the production and sale of alcoholic beverages in Canada in the early part of this century. Gradually the anti-dry forces gained the upper hand in one province after another, often using the practical argument that prohibition did not work. This legislation proved to be so unpopular and difficult to enforce that by 1930 only Prince Edward Island was still dry.

People also have to be protected from one another. (Of course, this is a major reason why government and the rule of law exist in the first place.) Government intervention in the marketplace for this purpose includes child-labour laws that protect children from exploitation by establishing a minimum working age. Laws requiring children to have a minimum amount of schooling tend to restrain parents from extracting full-time labour services from their children in the home or on the farm. *The Canadian Human Rights Act* attempts to prevent discrimination against minorities and females in the labour market. It is administered by the Canadian Human Rights Commission. In addition, each of the provinces has similar legislation. Of course, in a broader sense, competition laws, welfare policies, and regulations governing product safety, working conditions, and environmental quality are all intended to protect individuals from one another. All such laws, policies, and regulations, whether provincial or federal, may be regarded as responses to market shortcomings.

Income Redistribution

Freely working markets will reward some and penalize others. Those who are hard-working, able, and lucky may live handsomely by the market. Most people have little sympathy for the able-bodied but lazy whom markets treat sternly. But the impersonal forces of the market are indifferent to the disabled, the handicapped, and others beset by misfortune beyond their control. Society generally takes the attitude that, in such cases, private charitable organizations, government policies, or both should be used to redistribute income from the more fortunate to the less fortunate. (We will examine a number of policies with this goal in Chapter 18, where we will focus on the problems of poverty.)

Some argue that antipoverty efforts are a public good. When you give money to private charity to help alleviate poverty, you bestow external benefits on non-

Checkpoint **14-1**

Some machines used to make plywood are as powerful as large AM radio stations. If not contained by shields, the machines' signals can cause serious interference with frequencies used by airport flight-control towers. Some machine owners are reluctant to install the shields because of their high cost, but a letter from the CRTC informing them that they may be liable for airliner crashes usually gives them an incentive. How is the CRTC's letter to the plywood makers likely to affect the price and quantity of plywood bought and sold? Why?

Answers to all Checkpoints can be found at the back of the text.

givers. That is, the benefits that stem from poverty reduction (a decline in disease, slums, and so forth) accrue to society at large. Hence, each would-be giver is tempted to be a free rider—let the other person do the giving. As illustrated in Figure 14-2, whenever there are external benefits associated with a good, there will be underproduction of the good—in this case, antipoverty efforts.

Government Regulation—A Response to Market Shortcomings

When markets perform inadequately in the ways we have discussed, should government regulations be used in an attempt to attain perfection, or are there trade-offs between the reduction of shortcomings and its costs? How do we know how much government regulation is needed? And what about the possibility that government regulation will make matters worse? We now turn to these questions. In addition, we will also briefly examine four areas of government regulation: protection of the environment, working conditions, product safety, and consumer protection—the last through regulations aimed at preventing deceptive advertising and labeling.

How Much Government Regulation Is Appropriate?

How do we know how much government regulation is needed to correct the undesirable consequences of market shortcomings? Attempts to answer this question are a source of continual, often heated debate among politicians, policymakers, and citizens and special interests affected by regulation. The kind of regulation called for can vary greatly from one type of market shortcoming to another. But in all cases, in determining the appropriate amount of regulation, we must recognize that there is a trade-off between the benefits and costs of regulation. Moreover, we should be aware that any regulation can have perverse effects, outcomes quite the opposite of those intended.

Trade-Offs Between the Costs and Benefits of Regulation

Economics is a study of trade-offs. To have more of one thing we have to give up a certain amount of something else. The cost (or opportunity cost) of having more of one thing is the value of the other things that must be given up. *Rational decisions about the appropriate amount of regulation require recognition of the fact that regulation has costs, too, and that there is a trade-off between the costs and benefits of regulation.*

Consider government regulation to promote safety. Some argue that it is impossible to put a dollar value on human suffering or human life. However, any decision concerning the imposition of safety regulations unavoidably makes such a valuation. For example, advocates of the 90 kilometre per hour speed limit argue that the regulation saves lives. They judge the saving of those lives (along with any fuel savings) to be more valuable than the time that is lost through slower travel. On the other hand, those who advocate increasing the speed limit to 120 kilometres per hour imply that the time saved is worth more than the reduction in suffering and loss of life that results from fewer traffic accidents at the lower speed. Each of the two groups implicitly argues that there is a trade-off between the value of human lives and the value of time.

If human life were priceless, people would not travel in airplanes, work on skyscrapers, build bridges, drive motorcycles, mine coal, or go to war. The question, then, is not whether or not a value can be placed on human life; when society sets any policy or takes any action, it implicitly decides on such a value. The only question is whether that value is acceptable. Most automobiles can go 140 kilometres per hour. But Canadian society values life too highly to make 140 the acceptable speed limit.

Regulation and Perverse Results

It has been said that the road to hell is paved with good intentions. Sometimes, regulations that are motivated by the best of intentions can actually make matters worse. For example, most people would agree on the desirability of some minimum level of qualifications for doctors and health-care facilities. Regulations in Canada stipulate that many medical services may be provided only by a licensed physician. Nurses and paramedics could provide some of these services equally well, but regulations prevent them from doing so. Such regulations tend to restrict the supply of medical care and thus drive up its cost to the taxpayer. In an effort to save money, a provincial government may restrict spending on new facilities and equipment necessary to perform expensive procedures. As a consequence, a patient with a minor cut may be treated by a medical doctor while another patient is put on a long waiting list for open heart surgery. Thus, a regulation aimed at improving the quality of health care drives up its cost to the taxpayer, and perhaps the overall quality of health care declines. Such regulation also has the effect of increasing the income of medical doctors.

Benefit-Cost Analysis

The optimal amount of regulation should be determined in the way we determine the optimal amount of any other good or service. *Regulation should be extended up to the point where the dollar value of the last unit of benefit just equals the cost of obtaining it.* Remember that in calculating the costs and benefits it is important to realize that the process of regulation itself imposes costs on society. A determination of the optimal amount of regulation according to this principle requires a benefit-cost analysis. We will illustrate how benefit-cost analysis can be used to determine the appropriate amount of regulation for environmental protection.

Environmental Protection

Environmental pollution is widespread in industrialized societies. It plagues capitalist, socialist, and communist countries alike. It seems to be an inevitable consequence of economic growth, the increase in the output of goods and services per capita. Industrialization and increased production of goods and services also mean increased production of "bads" and "disservices": noxious waste products that pollute air and waterways; junkyards, slag heaps, smokestacks, derricks, and mining and industrial sites that spoil the landscape; and urban and suburban congestion and noise that cause tension and stress.

The costs imposed on society by these bads and disservices take the form of health and property damage and, generally, an impaired quality of life. Moreover, these costs are external, or spillover, costs—they are borne by parties other than the producers and buyers of the goods whose production causes them. These costs cannot be eliminated, but they can be shifted to the parties who cause them. This is done by internalizing such costs to the markets where they occur.

For example, suppose that the residents in the vicinity of a steel mill incur property damage and health costs as a consequence of air pollution caused by the mill. If the steel mill is required to purchase equipment that eliminates its emission of air pollutants, then the cost of the pollution is shifted to those directly involved in the production and sale of steel. Those who buy and use steel now pay all the costs of producing steel; none of the cost is imposed on people living near the steel mill. The supply curve of steel is shifted leftward as discussed in connection with Figure 14-1. Those who buy steel now pay a higher price, which includes the cost of pollution. (For a discussion of how this cost is distributed between buyers and sellers, see Chapter 9.) Environmental pollution occurs because clean air and clean rivers, lakes, and oceans are public goods. It is impossible to keep the air or water clean for some in a region and not for others. The exclusion principle does not apply.

A firm that *voluntarily* invested in equipment to reduce the amount of pollutants emitted from its smokestacks would not be able to charge for this service. Why? Because those who won't pay will have clean air just the same as those who do. Everyone has an incentive to be a free rider and "let the other guy pay." If the firm charged a higher price for its product to cover the cost of its antipollution efforts, it would lose sales to competitors who did not incur such costs and who therefore could charge lower prices. Environmental protection thus seems to require government regulation. The tough questions are, How much regulation, and in what form?

How Much Pollution Control—Benefits versus Costs

Regulation, like any "product," provides certain benefits and gives rise to certain costs. These benefits and costs vary as the amount of regulation varies. *A* **benefit-cost analysis** *is an examination of the benefits and costs associated with differing levels of output (here the output is regulation) to determine the most effective level according to some criterion.*

To illustrate, let's consider a hypothetical benefit-cost analysis of pollution control in a particular region, as illustrated in Table 14-1. Suppose that as a by-product of its production process, a large company is polluting the air, giving rise to external costs. In the absence of government regulation requiring the company to control its pollution, suppose the company's smokestacks annually emit 100,000 units of pollutant—row (1), column (1) of Table 14-1—causing external costs equal to $1 million of damage (external costs) to the surrounding area—row (1), column (2). The government decides to take action to regulate this pollution. Should government regulators force the company to stop polluting entirely, or should they require only that some portion of the

TABLE 14-1   Benefit-Cost Analysis for Pollution Control
(Hypothetical Data)

	(1) Annual Units of Pollution (Thousands)	(2) Annual Pollution Damage (Thousands of Dollars)	(3) Marginal Benefit of 10,000 Units of Added Pollution Reduction (Thousands of Dollars)	(4) Annual Total Costs of Pollution Reduction (Thousands of Dollars)	(5) Marginal Cost of 10,000 Additional Units of Pollution Reduction (Thousands of Dollars)	(6) Total Benefits Equal Total Reduction in Pollution Damage (Thousands of Dollars)	(7) Net Gain Equals (6) Minus (4) (Thousands of Dollars)
(1)	100	$1,000		$ 0		$ 0	$ 0
(2)	90	900	$100	10	$ 10	100	90
(3)	80	750	150	25	15	250	225
(4)	70	575	175	50	25	425	375
(5)	60	460	115	90	40	540	450
(6)	50	350	110	150	60	650	500
(7)	40	250	100	235	85	750	515
(8)	30	160	90	355	120	840	485
(9)	20	80	80	555	200	920	365
(10)	10	35	45	905	350	665	60
(11)	0	0	35	1,405	500	1,000	−405

pollutant be removed from smokestack emissions? The answer is that regulators should require the company to remove pollutants from smokestack emissions up to the point where the marginal cost of pollution reduction equals the marginal benefit of pollution reduction.

Suppose that the company is required to reduce pollution from 100,000 to 90,000 units—column (1), rows (1) and (2). Pollution damage would be reduced from $1 million to $900,000—column (2), rows (1) and (2)—so that the marginal benefit of pollution reduction is $100,000, column (3). The total cost to the company of reducing pollution this much is $10,000—column (4), row (2)—which is also the marginal cost, column (5), since the company starts from a level of zero pollution expenditures. Total benefits from pollution reduction amount to $100,000—column (6), row (2). This amount of pollution reduction is clearly worthwhile, since the marginal benefit of $100,000, column (3), certainly exceeds the marginal cost of $10,000, column (5). In fact, examination of columns (3) and (5) indicates that the marginal benefits of increasing pollution reduction continue to exceed the marginal cost of such reduction until pollution has been reduced to a level of 40,000 units—column (1), row (7). Reducing pollution from 50,000 to 40,000 units gives rise to marginal benefits of $100,000, which exceeds the marginal cost of $85,000 associated with reducing pollution by another 10,000 units.

It would not be worthwhile to force the company to reduce pollution to 30,000 units—column (1), row (8). Why? Because the required additional, or marginal, cost of $120,000, column (5), would exceed the additional, or marginal, benefit of $90,000, column (3). This would amount to an overallocation of resources to pollution control.

In sum, the marginal benefit–marginal cost rule implies that pollution control should be expanded as long as marginal benefits, column (3), exceed marginal costs, column (5). According to this criterion, the most effective amount of control is at, or as close as possible to, that point where marginal benefits equal marginal costs. Note that this rule maximizes the excess of total benefits over total costs, column (7); that is, it provides the greatest net gain from pollution control—equal to $515,000, column (7), row (7). In our example, government pollution regulations should require that the company not emit more than 40,000 units of pollution annually.

Three important observations should be made at this point.

The Optimal Level of Control.   The total elimination of pollution is not necessarily optimal. We know it is not optimal to reduce speed limits to the point where there are no traffic accidents. The benefit-cost analysis of our pollution control problem (Table 14-1) shows why it is not optimal to eliminate pollution completely. The total annual cost of reducing pollution to zero is $1,405,000—column (4), row (11). The total benefits resulting from the complete elimination of pollution damage equal $1 million—column (6), row (11). The net gain is *minus* $405 million—column (7), row (11)—a loss! In other words, the cost of completely eliminating pollution exceeds the value of the benefits, so it isn't worth it. Complete elimination of pollution would be optimal only if the marginal cost of pollution reduction were always less than the marginal benefits. While this is not true for our example in Table 14-1, it could be the case for certain kinds of pollution problems. In any event, a benefit-cost analysis is necessary to determine the optimal amount of pollution control. *A benefit-cost analysis is required to determine the optimal amount of any form of government regulation.*

Enforcing Pollution Control.   With the benefit-cost data of Table 14-1, government regulators could calculate the optimal pollution level as we have. They could use one of three alternative schemes to enforce pollution control: (a) adopt legislated standards, (b) levy pollution emission taxes, or (c) issue tradeable pollution rights,

1. *Legislated standards.* The government could pass laws empowering government regulators to establish maximun allowable levels of pollution. For instance, regulators could declare it illegal for the company of Table 14-1 to emit pollutants in excess of 40,000 units per year, row (7). If the law were backed by sufficiently stiff fines and possible court action, the company could be compelled to incur the $235,000 cost of abiding by the 40,000 units per year pollution limit. While such an approach is possible, it is likely to prove too inflexible to be efficient in actual practice.

2. *Pollution emission taxes.* The government could also achieve the optimal pollution level by placing a tax on pollution. For example, if the government levies a pollution tax of $90,000 for each 10,000 units of pollutants, the company in Table 14-1 would have an incentive to keep pollution down to the optimal level of 40,000 units. To see why, note that the marginal cost of reducing pollution by another 10,000 units is less than $90,000—column (5), rows (1) to (7)—all the way to the point where pollution has been reduced to a level of 40,000 units. To this point it is cheaper for the company to pay the cost of reducing pollution than to pay the pollution tax. However, the company will find it cheaper to pay the pollution tax on the remaining 40,000 units of pollution. Why? Because the marginal cost of eliminating each successive 10,000 units of

pollution once the pollution level has been reduced to 40,000 units is always greater than the $90,000 tax per 10,000 units of pollution. That is, the last four entries in column (5) are all greater than $90,000.

3. *Tradeable pollution rights.* As stated earlier legislative standards may prove to be too inflexible. Consider the case where there is more one than one firm. Assume that there are only two firms in a jurisdiction. Each firm emits 30,000 units of pollution per year. The government imposes a limit of 40,000 units per year. It assigns pollution rights of 20,000 units to each firm and informs each of them that they must cut their emissions by 10,000 units per year. One firm can meet this target by making relatively minor changes in its production process, which will add only $50,000 annually to its operating costs. The other firm will have to make substantial changes in its production process in order to reduce emissions by the required 10,000 units. These changes will cost $185,000 annually. The first firm could change its energy source to one that is much less polluting at a cost of $100,000 per year. By so doing it could reduce the emissions by 20,000 units per year. But it has no incentive to undertake this change. To do so would increase its costs more than necessary to meet the legislated standards. Higher costs would mean a higher price for its product and therefore reduced sales, particularly if the firm operates in a competitive market. Clearly, the legislation would result in the desired drop in emissions, but at a cost a $235,000 per year ($50,000 for the first firm and $185,000 for the second). A more flexible approach would make use of the fact that the first firm could reduce its emission enough to accomplish the goal on its own for $100,000.

Now assume that the government allows each firm the right to buy additional emission rights or to sell surplus rights. Obviously the second firm, faced with high abatement costs, would be in the market to buy additional rights. It would be willing to pay up to $185,000 for the rights to an additional 10,000 units of emissions. The first firm would be happy to sell those 10,000 units for any price that exceeded the additional $50,000 of costs that it had to incur to affect the change. The actual price at which the trade would occur would have to be negotiated.

The government itself could sell the rights. If it was determined that emission should be held to 40,000 units per year, the government could sell the rights to the highest bidder rather than assign rights and then allow firms to trade them. Either solution would in effect allow the external costs of pollution to be internalized within a market and would therefore result in an economically efficient solution.

You would find it instructive at this point to answer Questions 4 and 5 at the end of this chapter.

Problems of Measurement.   In our discussion to this point, we have assumed that government regulators know the dollar value of the pollution damage associated with each level of pollution. It also has been assumed that they can measure the quantity and nature of the pollution as well as the benefits and costs of preventing it. In other words, we have assumed that the government regulators know all the data in Table 14-1. In reality this is rarely the case. Determining the optimal level of pollution regulation is therefore very difficult in practice. Nonetheless, a benefit-cost analysis forces the analyst to ask the right questions and to seek the information needed for wise decision making.

Government's Role in Environmental Protection

The Canadian government has a long (though not always effective) history of involvement in environmental protection, although such activities have not always been labeled as such. This history dates at least from the late nineteenth century, when the first national parks area was set aside. In part there has been a lack of will to be effective. It has been only relatively recently that there was any significant pressure to deal with the problems of the environment in a systematic way. Even now there are serious obstacles to effective regulations to protect the environment. Not the least of these obstacles is the fact that it is not clear who has jurisdiction over the environment. Is protecting the environment a federal or a provincial responsibility? Constitutionally, the provinces have a substantial claim to jurisdiction. On the other hand, in January 1992 the Supreme Court of Canada ruled in a case involving a dam on the Old Man River in Alberta that the federal government had the right to review large-scale provincial projects. At the same time, most provinces were arguing for increased powers over the environment.

What is clear is that pollution is not restricted by provincial or even international borders. Dams in British Columbia affect the environment in Alberta, acid rain generated in Alberta is carried east by prevailing winds, and so forth. Pollution is not only an externality in the sense that it generates costs that are borne outside the firm, but also in the sense that it may generate costs that are borne outside the political jurisdiction in which it originates. These spillovers can be interprovincial or international. Pollutants dumped by Americans in the Great Lakes can affect Canadian drinking water and vice versa. Acid rain from Ohio falls in Ontario, and acid rain from Ontario falls in the Maritimes and Northern Europe. Unfortunately, effective policies to deal with pollution are likely to be some time in coming. By their nature, they will require political and diplomatic solutions, and economists have little to offer in these areas.

However, economists can provide important insights. Pollution is an external cost, but it is a very real cost. The frequent suggestion that society cannot afford to clean up the environment ignores the fact that externalities are real costs. It is *never* economically efficient to allow significant externalities to exist. They distort the market. In the case of relatively small externalities, the transaction costs of correcting the market failure may exceed the benefit of correcting it, and the distortion can be ignored. Economists have long argued that it is important to internalize external costs. By so doing, society will use its resources more efficiently. Externalities may also affect the distribution of income. Any change in the distribution of income could be judged only in a normative light. In effect, policies that allow pollution tend to redistribute income from individuals in general to those that pollute. Effective pollution control would ensure the distribution of income that would have occurred if there had been no market failure.

Federally, environmental concerns fall under Environment Canada. *The Canadian Environment Protection Act (CEPA)* went into effect in 1988. It is intended to protect Canadians from pollution caused by toxic materials. The CEPA allows for much tougher enforcement than was previously possible. In 1985 Canada established the Canadian Acid Rain Abatement Program. Under it the federal government and the provinces agreed to a permanent ceiling as of the year 2000 of 3.2 tonnes of SO_2. The American *Clean Air Act* of 1990 is

Checkpoint 14-2

In the benefit-cost analysis example of Table 14-1, suppose that the marginal cost of pollution reduction is $70,000 higher at every level—that is, assume every entry in column (5) is larger by $70,000. What would be the optimal level of pollution?

also of interest to Canadians. Canada signed the 1987 International Protocol on Substances that Deplete the Ozone Layer. This Protocol was strengthened at the 1990 meeting in London, England. At that time Canada had reduced its emission of ozone-depleting CFCs by more than the amount required in the 1987 Protocol.

Working Conditions

Can the market effectively deal with problems of occupational health and safety? Those who say yes argue as follows: Workers will take hazardous jobs only if they are offered higher wages to compensate for the increased risk of injury. Employers will reduce work hazards if it costs less than paying higher wages. On the other hand, if paying higher wages is cheaper than reducing hazards, then workers will be compensated for the hazards.

Those who disagree with this argument claim there are factors that hamper the labour market's ability to deal effectively with problems of occupational health and safety. They argue that often there is inadequate information on the relationship between job conditions and health and safety hazards. For example, the effects of many health risks, such as exposure to cancer-causing substances, may not show up for years, or such hazards may not be known during the term of employment. Unsafe or unhealthy working conditions also may give rise to external costs—costs borne by parties other than the employer and employee. For instance, workers exposed to certain substances subsequently may have children with birth defects attributable to this exposure—the children are the injured third parties. Imperfect information and the presence of external costs will tend to inhibit workers from demanding wages adequate to compensate for health and safety hazards. Therefore, employers will not have adequate incentive to incur the costs of reducing work hazards, and, consequently, there will be an underallocation of resources to the maintenance of health and safety in the workplace. It can also be argued that in depressed areas of Canada or in periods of high unemployment workers may be forced to accept any job—even one that they know to be hazardous. It can be argued that these considerations make a case for government regulation of occupational health and safety.

Government Regulation of Workplace Safety Standards

We are sometimes warned that most accidents occur in the home, but many accidents occur at the workplace. In fact more than a million accidents occur at work in Canada each year. Moreover, the majority of these accidents are so severe as to require time off work. Many require hospitalization. In 1989 there were 656,503 disabling injuries that were work related. That represented a 22 percent increase over 1979. During the same period the number of workers only increased by about 19 percent. Most of these disabilities were short-term. However, some were long-term or permanent. In the same year there were 1,164 fatal job-related accidents. This figure was down slightly from 1979 but up substantially from the 889 in 1984. In addition to accidents, workers' health can also be adversely affected by exposure to hazardous materials, high noise levels, computer screens, and repetitive tasks.

As was the case with environmental problems, occupational health and safety falls under both federal and provincial jurisdiction. Provincial labour legislation varies from province to province but in general deals with such areas as minimum wages, working hours, and health and safety. Most federal legislation is consolidated in the Canada Labour Code.

Part I of the Code deals with industrial relations. Part II deals with occupational health and safety. Part III covers labour standards. Part II is intended to ensure a safe workplace and allows for regulations to set standards for health and safety. It allows workers the right to refuse work if they feel their health or safety could be compromised. Safety regulations relate to such matters as ventilation, hazardous materials, protective gear, noise, and radiation. There is also a separate law relating to toxic materials. Special legislation exists for certain particularly dangerous occupations. Part III of the Canada Labour Code sets labour standards. It defines such matters as standard workdays and workweeks, overtime pay, vacation pay, and maternity leave.

In recent years society has become acutely concerned that people could suffer economic hardship because they were discriminated against in the labour market for reasons beyond their control—race, sex, religion, language, or nationality. Both the federal and provincial governments have passed legislation aimed at ensuring equal employment opportunities for all.

Product Safety

Government regulation of product safety is based on the contention that many products are too complex for consumers to make informed purchase decisions. Moreover, as we observed earlier, information is a near-public good in that the market tends to produce less than the optimal amount of information. Product complexity, together with inadequate market provision of information, may lead consumers to underestimate the hazards associated with certain products.

The legal position of the consumer relative to that of the seller has changed substantially during the last century. That position has shifted from one of *caveat emptor*, "let the buyer beware," to one of *caveat venditor*, "let the seller beware." Under the doctrine of *caveat emptor*, buyers bore responsibility for the consequences of their purchase decisions. They could not claim damages from sellers for faulty products. Gradually, legal rules of fraud evolved that allowed buyers to recover damages if they could prove that sellers had misrepresented their products. In addition, negligence rules evolved that held the seller responsible for the costs of injuries caused by product defects that the seller either knew about or should have known about. Recent years have seen a dramatic upsurge in product liability actions against sellers. The government is increasingly deciding that sellers are responsible for the goods they market.

Paralleling the emergence of the doctrine of *caveat venditor* has been an expansion of government regulation to ensure product safety. Once again this is an area of split provincial and federal responsibility, so the situation varies from province to province. Federally, Consumer and Corporate Affairs Canada is responsible for a wide range of legislation. It has four different branches and is basically charged with maintaining fair market practices. It deals with products as varied as children's toys and explosives. It operates under legislation such as the *Hazardous Product Act*, the *Consumer Packaging and Labelling Act* and the *Textile Labelling Act*.

Checkpoint 14-3

Compared to regulations for product safety, do you think that regulation of deceptive advertising serves to enhance or restrict consumer choice?

POLICY PERSPECTIVE

Regulation of Canadian Television Content

In Canada, radio and television broadcasting is regulated by the Canadian Radio-television and Telecommunications Commission (CRTC). It licenses and regulates broadcasters. There are a number of reasons why such regulation is regarded as necessary. In the absence of regulation two broadcasters in nearby cities could operate on the same frequency, or a super-powerful station could be built in a highly populated area, and its signal would block out all other stations. A station could be used to broadcast hate literature or other generally offensive material.

CANADIAN CONTENT REGULATION

The CRTC also requires that radio and television broadcasters fulfil Canadian content regulations. In effect the Canadian government limits the amount of foreign programming which can be broadcast by Canadian stations. Obviously, such restrictions protect Canadian producers of television programs in the same way as a quota on imported shoes or steel would protect firms and workers in those industries. Most of the television programs imported into Canada for rebroadcast are of American origin. Canada and the United States have entered into a free trade agree-

ment. Why is it that Canada is allowed to impose restrictions on American television programs? Actually the Canada–United States Trade Agreement exempts cultural industries, so it is perfectly legal.

A more difficult question is, Why does Canada wish to restrict the importation of foreign programs? Quotas on imported television programs tend to generate employment for Canadian actors, actresses, directors, technicians, and so forth. It may also generate higher profits for Canadian producers, but it seems an unlikely reason to give television (and other cultural industries) special status. It is also possible that the government is trying to control information—a less obvious version of the prereform Soviet effort to jam Western broadcasts in an effort to force its people to listen to and view only Soviet propaganda. This explanation is clearly absurd in view of the democratic and pluralistic nature of Canada.

The generally accepted reason for Canadian content regulations has to do with the nature of television programming. Television programming has public goods aspects. Television can produce external benefits. Good Canadian programs can promote a sense of Canadian identity, and can create Canadian heroines and heros

with which Canadians can identify and thereby develop a pride in Canada and Canadian values. Television can also promote national unity. Canada is a vast country with diverse cultures, regional economies, and social outlooks. A Canadian in one part of the country may find it difficult to understand the problems and aspirations of Canadians in other regions. Most wheat farmers from the prairies lack the time, money, and motivation to investigate the circumstances of the Atlantic fisherman, the Quebec factory worker, or the Bay Street banker, nor are any of those groups likely to spend a week battling grasshoppers in the wheat fields. Television could help to weave an integrated Canadian fabric.

MERIT GOODS

Canadian-content television programming could be considered a merit good. *A* **merit good** *is a good that is better than the buyer realizes.* One could ask, "better in whose view?" In this case the answer is, "the elected government." Clearly the designation of a merit good involves normative economics, as a merit good is a good that is thought to generate positive externalities. In the case of television, the buyers are the businesses that spon-

continued on next page

Summary

1. The market mechanism has several problem areas. It does not provide pure public goods; it gives rise to external costs and benefits in providing certain goods; it provides inadequate amounts of certain kinds of information; and its results are incompatible with some of society's goals. Government intervention, in the form of regulation, may be used in an attempt to correct such faults.

POLICY PERSPECTIVE CONTINUED

sor the programs. The only benefit they see is the increased sales that they realize from the advertising that is carried with the program. They measure this benefit indirectly by using viewer ratings, which estimate the size of the audience. The more viewers, the more sales for the firm. The firms buying commercial time are willing to pay for this benefit. They are not willing to pay for the external benefits that flow from Canadian content. As a consequence, the demand for Canadian programming underestimates its value. This is illustrated in Figure P14-1. D_p is the private demand for Canadian-content programs. D_s represents their social value. D_p is the MRP of commercials. D_s is their MRP plus the externalities. At any price Canadian content will be underconsumed. This is because private purchasers are not willing (nor should they be expected) to pay for the extra social benefits. There has been a market failure. The market has allocated fewer resources to the production of Canadian content than it would have had all the benefits been considered.

The fact that it undervalues Canadian-content programming is not the only problem with the market. Most of the costs of producing television programs are fixed costs. It costs very little more to produce a program that is viewed by 30 million people than to produce a program of the same quality for an audience of 3 million. In theory the marginal cost of one more viewer is virtually zero. Therefore the supply price of a television program in the market cannot be based on

marginal cost, it must be based on some form of average cost pricing. Under these circumstances the cost of American programs will be far less than the cost of Canadian programs of comparable quality.

There are some areas where the demand (based on viewer hours) for Canadian programs will be much higher than for American ones. In the areas of news, current affairs, and sports, Canadians will prefer domestic to imported shows. Who wants to watch the weather forecast for Salt Lake City? However, this preference for Canadian content is likely to be much weaker in the case

of drama, sitcoms, and soap operas. Therefore Canadian stations faced with the choice of showing U.S. or Canadian drama would usually choose American. It is cheaper, and sponsors undervalue Canadian programs. Quotas are intended to redress this situation.

For Discussion

• Quotas are not the only tool used to increase Canadian content. The government of Canada also subsidizes domestic firm production. Explain how this can correct the market failure discussed here.

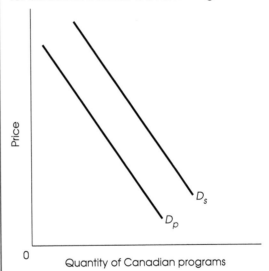

FIGURE P14-1   Social and Private Demand for Canadian-Content Television Programs

If it is assumed that Canadian content is a value, then the market underproduces Canadian programs.

2. Government provision of pure public goods, such as national defense, is necessary because such goods are not subject to the exclusion principle. Near-public goods are jointly consumed, like pure public goods, but they are subject to the exclusion principle, and hence they will be provided by the market.

3. External or spillover costs are costs that are not borne by the economic unit responsible for creating them. Whenever external costs are associated with the market for a good, society suffers a loss because too much of the good is produced. Whenever there are external benefits, a loss occurs because too

little of the good is produced. In either case, government regulation may be used to achieve the optimal output level.

4. Imperfect information is usually a problem in the purchase and sale of products that are not purchased repeatedly or that are complex. The market probably provides less product information than is optimal because such information is like a near-public good.

5. Society has goals and values that are sometimes at odds with market outcomes. Government may ban products that markets will provide but that society deems harmful to those who would buy them. Government regulation is also used to prevent people from exploiting one another in ways society considers unacceptable, and the government plays an ever-increasing role in the redistribution of income to modify the income distribution otherwise provided by market outcomes.

6. Any determination of the appropriate amount of government regulation must recognize that there is a trade-off between the costs and benefits of regulation and that it is possible for regulation to make matters worse rather than better. Benefit-cost analysis is a useful tool for determining the optimal amount of regulation.

7. Environmental pollution imposes external, or spillover, costs, because clean air and clean rivers, lakes, and oceans are public goods. Benefit-cost analysis suggests that total elimination of pollution is usually not optimal. Legislated standards and pollution emission taxes can be used to regulate the amount of pollution and internalize its costs to the markets that cause it. In recent years the federal and provincial governments of Canada have increased their efforts to reduce pollution. Many of those interested in environmental issues feel that they have not done enough.

8. In Canada, government intervention to correct market failures falls to both the federal and provincial governments. A number of agencies regulate economic activities in Canada. They deal with such matters as worker safety, protecting the environment, consumer safety, and the provision of market information.

Key Terms and Concepts

benefit-cost analysis

exclusion principle

externalities

free rider

market failure

merit good

near-public goods

pure public good

Questions and Problems

1. What is the distinction between a pure public good and a near-public good? Classify each of the following as either a pure public good, a near-public good, or neither: a movie, a radio program, a symphony concert, a clean ocean, a haircut, a cable television program, a quiet neighbourhood, a baseball game, a clean lake, a keg of beer, the spectrum of radio waves, international relations, the postal service.

2. It has been observed that community-owned property (such as a public park, roadside, or stadium) tends to be more littered with wastepaper and empty bottles than private property (such as people's yards and driveways). How would you relate this observation to each of the following concepts: public good, external costs, the free-rider problem?

Suggest some product regulations that might reduce this litter. Illustrate the nature of the problem for bottled beverages in terms of either Figure 14-1 or Figure 14-2, indicating how you would measure the size of the external costs on such a graph and the effect of regulations to eliminate the external costs.

3. Why does the market provide less product information than is optimal? Do you think that information in general is likely to be underproduced or overproduced?

4. Suppose that the total amount of pollution damage in Table 14-1 were $1 million greater at every level of pollution–that is, add $1 million to each entry in column (2). A public outcry about the problem leads the local government to hire you as an economic consultant to advise them what to do. Assume that prior to the $1 million jump in pollution damage the government already taxed pollution emissions at the rate of $90,000 per 10,000 units of pollutants. What would you advise the government to do now? Is it possible for pollution damage to get worse even though you always follow an optimal environmental protection strategy?

5. Suppose that there are two firms in a neighbourhood, each emitting 5 units of pollutants in the absence of regulation. Suppose that their marginal costs of eliminating each unit of pollution are as shown in the following table. Without any regulation each firm would emit 5 units of pollution.

Marginal Cost of Eliminating Each Successive Unit of Pollution

Firm	1st	2nd	3rd	4th	5th
Firm A	$100	200	300	400	500
Firm B	$200	400	600	800	1,000

Assume that regulators wish to reduce neighbourhood pollution by a total of 6 units. You are called in as a consultant and asked whether they should set a maximum emission limit of 2 units of pollution per firm or, alternatively, use a pollution emission tax to accomplish their goal. What would you tell them, and why? What does this indicate about the relative merits of maximum emission standards and pollution emission taxes as tools for pollution control?

6. Suppose a plant has a number of safety hazards. How should the plant manager allocate available resources to eliminate these hazards? That is, how should the manager decide the amount of resources to allocate to each problem area?

7. Suppose that employees were allowed to waive their right to work in a "government acceptable" work environment in return for a wage increase. Do you think that the wage increase they would ask for would be greater than or less than the increase that the firm would be willing to grant in return for exemption from federal and provincial standards? Why?

8. What effect would a more vigorous enforcement of consumer product safety standards have on consumer product prices? Why?

9. Suppose that the provincial government in your province was considering more vigorous enforcement of regulations against deceptive advertising of the following products: barbells, diet pills, glue, automobiles, cigarettes, wheat, detergents, eggs, cosmetics, toothpaste, air conditioners, shoes, and thumbtacks. Rank the products according to the size of the effect such vigorous enforcement would be likely to have on sales. Then rank the products according to complexity, and finally according to the degree to which they are repeat-purchase items. What relationships do you observe among the three rankings?

Factor Pricing and Income Distribution

Chapter 15

Production and the Demand for Productive Resources

In this and the next three chapters we focus on the demand for the economy's productive resources. Economists often refer to these resources as *factors of production* or simply as *factors*. We will address a number of important questions. What determines wage rates, and what roles do unions and the structure of labour markets play in this process? What are rent, interest, and capital? Finally, having examined answers to these questions, we will be prepared to turn to the closely related topics of income distribution, poverty, and welfare policy.

Up to now we have focused on the way prices are determined in the markets for the goods and services produced by firms, the markets where households are on the demand side and businesses are on the supply side. We have said little about the determination of the prices of the economic resources that the firm must use to produce these goods and services, the markets where firms are on the demand side and households are on the supply side. The prices of such economic resources as land, labour, capital (plant and equipment), energy, and raw materials are matters of major significance. In this chapter we will look at some of the basic considerations that enter into the determination of these prices.

Why Resource Pricing Is Important

Resource pricing is important basically for two reasons. First, it determines how the economy's limited supply of economic resources is allocated to the various production activities necessary to produce the multitude of goods and services that society wants. Second, it determines how income earned from productive activities is distributed among the citizens of the economy. The first reason bears on the *how* question of the three questions any economy must answer—*what* to produce, *how* to produce it, and *for whom* to produce it (recall the discussion of these three questions in Chapter 2). The second reason bears on the *for whom* question. Let's examine each reason more closely.

Allocation of Economic Resources to Productive Activities

Resource prices are the signalling devices that direct resources to the different industries, firms, and governmental activities that constitute the economy's productive capacity. If the wages paid to machinists in the auto industry rise relative to those paid to machinists in the aircraft industry, this type of labour resource will tend to move away from aircraft production and into auto production. If the price of land for residential use rises relative to that for agricultural use, the rate at which farmland is converted into suburbs will tend to increase. If the rate of return on financial capital invested in physical capital (plant and equipment) in the computer industry rises relative to the rate earned in the steel industry, the rate of new physical capital formation in the computer industry will tend to rise relative to that in the steel industry. If the wages paid to government employees rise relative to those paid to workers in the private sector, labour will tend to flow into the government sector and away from the private sector.

Determination of Income Distribution

Most productive resources in our economy are owned by somebody. In a few cases ownership is not clear, and because of this situation, problems can result. Who owns resources such as the air and offshore fish and minerals? The owners sell the services of their resources and the payments received in exchange constitute their incomes. There are two variables that make up this exchange:

LEARNING OBJECTIVES

After reading this chapter, you will be able to:

1. Explain why resource pricing is important.
2. Demonstrate that the demand for a resource is derived from the demand for the good(s) that it helps to produce.
3. Show that the marginal revenue product curve of a factor constitutes the firm's demand curve for that factor.
4. Explain why the marginal revenue product curve for a factor must be downward sloping.
5. Determine the market demand curve for a factor.
6. Discuss the changes that can cause shifts in factor demand curves.
7. Discuss the substitution and output effects.
8. Explain what determines the elasticity of demand for factors.
9. Explain how a firm can find its least costly combination of resources.
10. Discuss how a firm can use resources in such a way to maximize profits.

---

the quantity of resource services sold and the price at which a unit of the service is sold. A labourer's income depends on the number of labour hours sold and the price (or wage rate) of a labour hour. A landlord's income depends on the number of hectares of land or square metres of floor space rented out and the rental rate per unit. The income that a stockholder in a corporation receives depends on the number of shares owned and the dividends and capital gains earned per share.

Whether we are talking about labourers, landlords, or stockholders, it is obvious that the prices received per unit of the resource service sold enter into the determination of the income they receive. This income in turn determines the share of the economy's output of goods and services that each of them may purchase. Given the implications for the welfare of different groups in the economy that follow from this, it is little wonder that the determination of resource prices is frequently a matter of considerable controversy. What is a "just" wage or a "fair" return? Questions such as these go to the heart of the often emotional issue of income distribution, a subject fraught with normative judgments. We will delve more deeply into various aspects of the roles of labour unions, business, and government, and explore other institutional characteristics of this subject over the course of the three following chapters.

Our discussion in this chapter is concerned with the analysis of factor demand from the viewpoint of the firm. We will be concerned with how it works rather than with normative questions of its implications for the distribution of income among different groups in the economy, a subject to be taken up in a subsequent chapter. The demand for economic resources, or factors of production, is really just a special application of the general principles of demand with which you are already familiar.

Factor Demand Is a Derived Demand

The basic characteristic of factor demand is that it is a **derived demand**. *This means that the demand for any productive factor ultimately depends upon, or derives from, the demand for the final product or products that the factor is used to produce.*

The demand for steelworkers derives from the demand for steel. The demand for steel derives from the demand for the many products that contain steel. The demand for farmland derives from the demand for agricultural products, as does the demand for farm machinery and other capital equipment needed in agricultural production. The demand for high-technology space scientists and engineers is derived from the demand for space vehicles and their support facilities. Examples of derived demand are almost endless.

The demand for any particular productive factor may well derive from its use in the production of several different products. The more narrowly we define a productive factor, the fewer the products from which its demand will be derived. Labour is used in the production of all goods. Barbers are used only in the production of haircuts. Similarly, drill presses are a general category of capital equipment needed in many production processes, but only certain types of presses are used to produce wristwatches. The complexity of explaining *the derived demand* for a productive factor will therefore depend on how broadly or narrowly we define that factor.

Marginal Productivity Theory of Factor Demand

The nature of the demand for a productive factor can be made more precise by determining the productive factor's specific contribution to the making of the final product. Common sense suggests that the larger the contribution the factor makes to the output of a product, the greater will be the demand for the factor. The **marginal productivity theory of factor demand** provides an explanation of why this is so.

To understand the basics of this theory, it is easiest to begin by considering a firm that sells its product in a perfectly competitive market. Hence, the firm is a price taker. As we have seen, this means that the firm can sell as little or as much of its product as it wants at the given market price because it provides such a small portion of total supply that its effect on market price is insignificant. We will also assume that the firm uses one fixed factor (such as capital) and one variable factor (such as labour) of production. That is, the quantity of one factor is fixed and unchangeable, while the quantity of the other factor can be varied. The firm also buys the variable factor in a perfectly competitive market, which means that it can buy as little or as much of that factor as it wants at a given price. In other words, the firm's purchases of the variable factor represent such a small fraction of the total supply of the factor that the firm cannot affect the factor's market price.

Marginal Revenue Product

Suppose the firm has a certain quantity of the fixed factor. Table 15-1 illustrates the way in which the quantity of the variable factor F contributes to

TABLE 15-1   Relationship Between Productive Factor and Marginal Revenue Product, Assuming Perfect Competition in Both Factor and Product Markets

(1) Quantity of Productive Factor (F)	(2) Total Output of Final Product (Q)	(3) Marginal Physical Product (MPP) $MPP = \dfrac{\text{Change in } Q}{\text{Unit change in } F}$	(4) Price of Product (p)	(5) Total Revenue (TR) $TR = p \times Q$	(6) Marginal Revenue Product (MRP) $MRP = \dfrac{\text{Change in } TR}{\text{Unit change in } F}$
0	0			$ 0	
		12			$120
1	12		$10	120	
		10			100
2	22		10	220	
		8			80
3	30		10	300	
		6			60
4	36		10	360	
		4			40
5	40		10	400	
		2			20
6	42		10	420	
		1			10
7	43		10	430	

the production of the firm's final product and therefore to the revenue the firm realizes from the sale of that product. In order to keep the example short, it is assumed that the law of diminishing returns applies from the first unit of variable factor.

As more of the factor F is used, column (1), the quantity of output of final product Q increases, column (2). The increase in total output associated with the addition of one more unit of the factor F to the production process is the **marginal physical product (MPP),** column (3). Columns (2) and (3) measure total output and marginal physical product in terms of physical units, such as the number of tonnes of wheat or the quantity of widgets. Because of the law of diminishing returns, the MPP decreases as more and more of the factor F is added and used together with the given quantity of the fixed factor. The relationship between the quantity of the factor F and the total quantity of output of final product Q, column (2), is the shortrun production function, a concept that we looked at in Chapter 8. Figure 15-1, frame (a), plots the data in columns (1) and (2) of Table 15-1 on a graph. The relationship between the factor F and the marginal physical product (MPP) is illustrated in Figure 15-1, frame (b), using the data in columns (1) and (3) of Table 15-1. (Note that the marginal physical product data are plotted midway between the integers on the horizontal axis. This is so because they represent the changes in total output and total revenue respectively from one unit of the factor to the next.)

FIGURE 15-1   Relationship Between the Shortrun Production Function, the Marginal Physical Product, and the Marginal Revenue Product, Assuming Perfect Competition in Both Factor and Product Markets

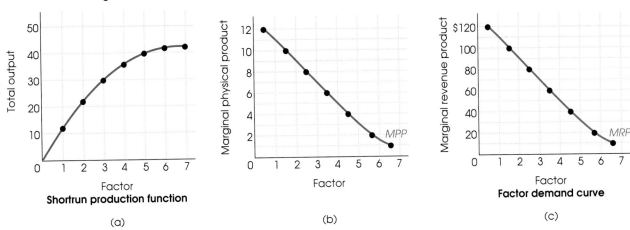

Frame (a) shows the perfectly competitive firm's shortrun production function plotted from the data in columns (1) and (2) of Table 15-1.

Frame (b) is a graph of the marginal physical product, the increase in total output attributable to each additional unit of the variable factor, plotted from the data in columns (1) and (3) of Table 15-1. (Note that it is assumed that the law of diminishing returns applies immediately. If this were not the case, the MPP curve would start sloping up and then, when the law of diminishing returns sets in, it would turn and slope down. Even in that case only the downward-sloping portion of the MPP curve would be relevant.)

Frame (c) is a graph of the marginal revenue product, the increase in total revenue attributable to each additional unit of variable factor, plotted from the data in columns (1) and (6) of Table 15-1.

In order to arrive at the relationship between the quantity of the factor F and the sales revenue it helps to produce, it is necessary to multiply the output of column (2) by the price at which it is sold. Since the firm sells its product in a perfectly competitive market, this price is the same no matter what the output level. Assuming that the price p is $10, column (4), total revenue TR, which equals $p \times Q$, column (4) times column (2), is given in column (5). The increase in total revenue associated with each 1-unit increase in the variable factor F is called the **marginal revenue product (MRP).** This figure is given in column (6). It may be computed either by determining the difference between the successive total revenue figures in column (5) or by multiplying the MPP of column (3), which is the addition to total output Q, by the price p of column (4). The marginal revenue product curve MRP is plotted in frame (c) of Figure 15-1 from the data in column (6) of Table 15-1. Note that it mirrors the MPP curve of frame (b). This is so because MRP may be obtained by multiplying the given final market price p (which does not change with the firm's output under perfect competition) by MPP.

Determining the Quantity of a Factor to Employ

How does the firm decide how much of the variable factor to employ? The principle that is used to answer this question is very similar to the marginal-cost-equals-marginal-revenue rule used to decide how much output to produce.

Employ the Factor Until MCF = MRP

In Chapter 8, we found that the question, How much output should be produced? was answered as follows: Produce that level of output at which *the marginal cost of the last unit produced is just equal to the marginal revenue obtained from the sale of that last unit.* The answer to the question, How much of the variable factor should be employed? is really just a slight variation on the answer to the question, How much output should be produced? This is not surprising if we remember that when the firm produces its optimum output level (the one that maximizes profit), it must of necessity use a certain amount of the variable factor to produce it. This amount is the answer to the question, How much of the variable factor should be employed? In short, we may view the firm's profit-maximizing level of activity either from the vantage point of input or from the vantage point of output. *From the vantage point of input (how much of the variable factor should be employed?), the firm should employ the variable factor up to the point at which the marginal cost of the factor (MCF) is just equal to the marginal revenue product (MRP).*

In other words, it should employ the variable factor up to the point at which the cost of the last unit of that factor employed is just equal to the additional revenue realized from the sale of the additional output produced by that last unit of the factor.

This may be illustrated by use of the data in Table 15-1. Suppose that the price of the factor, its per unit cost to the firm, is $50. Since the firm is a price taker in the factor market, it must pay $50 per unit of the factor no matter how much or how little of the factor it buys—the firm's MCF equals $50 at every level of output. At this price the firm will employ 4 units of the factor. Why is this so? Because the MRP, column (6), exceeds MCF (equal to $50) for every unit of the factor up through 4 units, and falls below it for every additional unit of the factor beyond 4 units. Each additional unit of the factor employed up through the fourth adds more to total revenue than it costs to purchase the factor. Hence, it is profitable for the firm to employ each of these units of the factor. For instance, the addition of the fourth unit of the factor increases total revenue by $60. The marginal cost of the factor (MCF) is $50, which is less than the marginal revenue product (MRP) of $60, column (6). The firm realizes a $10 profit. However, if the firm were to add a fifth unit of the factor, the MCF of $50 would exceed the MRP of $40 realized from the sale of the fifth unit. Hence, the firm would lose $10 on the production and sale of the additional output realized from the employment of the fifth unit of the factor. Similarly, the firm would lose money on each additional unit of the factor employed beyond the fifth. Thus, the firm should employ no more or less than 4 units of the variable factor.

The Factor Demand Curve Is the MRP Curve

The MRP curve of frame (c) of Figure 15-1 is reproduced in Figure 15-2. According to the data in column (6) of Table 15-1, the first unit of the factor F has an MRP of $120. If the price of 1 unit of F is less than this, the firm will hire the factor. The MRP of a second unit of the factor is $100. If the price of the factor is $110, say, then the firm will hire 1 unit but not a second. On the other hand, if the price of 1 unit of the factor is $90, the firm will hire 2 units of F. We can continue this line of reasoning by considering successively lower prices for the factor. Assuming that the factor is divisible into fractional units (so many hours, minutes, and seconds of labour services, for example), the result will be the smooth MRP curve that in effect constitutes the firm's demand curve D_F for the factor. It tells us how much will be demanded at each possible price of the factor.

For example, if the price of the factor is $50 and the firm can buy as much as it wants of the factor at that price, the MCF of the factor is $50 at every level of output. The supply curve of the factor is then S_F, as is shown in Figure 15-2.

FIGURE 15-2 The Marginal Revenue Product Curve Is the Firm's Demand Curve for a Productive Factor

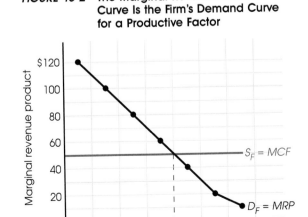

The marginal revenue product curve MRP shown here is the same as that shown in frame (c) of Figure 15-1. Therefore, the MRP curve is the firm's factor demand curve D_F.

If the firm can purchase as much as it wants of the factor at a price of $50, the marginal cost of the factor, or MCF, to the firm is $50 and the supply curve of the factor is S_F. The firm will purchase 4 units of the factor, as determined by the intersection of D_F and S_F, the point where $MRP = MCF$.

The firm will employ 4 units of the factor as determined by the intersection of S_F and D_F, the point where $MCF = MRP$.

Variable Product Price and Factor Demand

The data in Table 15-1 and Figures 15-1 and 15-2 assume that the firm sells its product in a perfectly competitive market. Therefore, the price at which it sells each unit of output is the same no matter how much the firm produces, as is indicated in column (4) of Table 15-1. Since $MRP = MPP \times p$, the *only* reason the factor demand, or MRP, curve of Figure 15-1, frame (c), and Figure 15-2 slopes downward is that MP falls, reflecting the law of diminishing returns. [The fall in MPP is shown in column (3) of Table 15-1 and in Figure 15-1, frame (b).] However, if the firm were an imperfectly competitive firm (a monopolist, an oligopolist, or a member of a monopolistically competitive industry), the price at which it sells its product would vary inversely with the quantity of output it produces. That is, the demand curve for the firm's product would slope downward, reflecting the fact that the price p the firm receives for its product falls as more of that product is supplied to the market. Hence, both MPP and p fall as the firm increases output.

The combined effect of the fall in both MPP and p on total revenue and marginal revenue product is illustrated in Table 15-2. The firm is the same as that in Table 15-1 so that columns (1), (2), and (3) remain unchanged. However, it is now assumed that the demand curve for the firm's product is downward sloping, so that the firm must accept a lower price in order to sell larger quantities of its product, as is indicated in column (4) of Table 15-2. Because of this, total revenue and marginal revenue product, columns (5) and (6), fall more rapidly in Table 15-2 than is the case in columns (5) and (6) of Table 15-1.

TABLE 15-2   Relationship Between Productive Factor and Marginal Revenue Product, Assuming Imperfect Competition in Product Market and Perfect Competition in Factor Market

(1) Quantity of Productive Factor (F)	(2) Total Output of Final Product (Q)	(3) Marginal Physical Product (MPP) $MPP = \dfrac{\text{Change in } Q}{\text{Unit change in } F}$	(4) Price of Product (p)	(5) Total Revenue (TR) $TR = p \times Q$	(6) Marginal Revenue Product (MRP) $MRP = \dfrac{\text{Change in } TR}{\text{Unit change in } F}$
0	0		$10	$ 0	
		12			$108
1	12		9	108	
		10			68
2	22		8	176	
		8			34
3	30		7	210	
		6			6
4	36		6	216	
		4			−16
5	40		5	200	
		2			−32
6	42		4	168	
		1			−39
7	43		3	129	

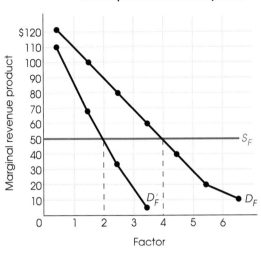

FIGURE 15-3 The Factor Demand Curve of an Imperfectly Competitive Firm and a Competitive Firm Compared

The factor demand curve D_F of the perfectly competitive firm is downward sloping only because MPP falls as more of the variable factor is used, a reflection of the law of diminishing returns. The factor demand curve D_F' of the imperfectly competitive firm lies to the left of D_F and is more steeply sloped because in addition to the fall in MPP, the price of the firm's product falls as more of the factor is used to produce more output.

Using the data in column (6) of Table 15-2, the marginal revenue product curve, which is the same as the firm's factor demand curve for the variable factor, is plotted as D_F' in Figure 15-3. The D_F curve from Figure 15-2 is reproduced in Figure 15-3 for comparison.

Clearly, the factor demand curve D_F' lies to the left of D_F and is more steeply sloped. This is so because D_F' reflects the decline in the price of the firm's product *in addition to* the decline in MPP when more of the factor is used to increase the imperfectly competitive firm's output. The result, as can be seen in Figure 15-3, is that at any price of the factor the imperfectly competitive firm will demand less of the factor than the perfectly competitive firm, all other things remaining the same. For example, at a factor price of $50, the imperfectly competitive firm will demand 2 units of the factor, while the perfectly competitive firm will demand 4 units.

Finally, note that the less elastic is the demand curve for an imperfectly competitive firm's product, the more rapid is the decline in product price as the firm increases output. Therefore, the less elastic is the demand curve for the firm's product, the less elastic will be the factor demand curve.

Market Demand Curve for a Factor

Recall that we get a market demand curve for a good by summing up all the individual demand curves for the good. Similarly, we could obtain the market demand curve for a productive factor by summing up all the individual firms' factor demand curves. As with any demand curve, a movement along the market demand curve for the factor assumes that *only* the price of the factor and the quantity of the factor demanded change. All other things are assumed to remain unchanged. However, this assumption will not hold for the market demand curve for the factor obtained in the usual way we have just described. Let's consider why.

If the price of the factor is lowered, for example, all of the firms in a perfectly competitive industry that use the factor to produce their product will now be able to get it cheaper. This means that the cost of production for the firms in the industry will be lower. The industry supply curve will therefore shift rightward (equivalently it may be viewed as shifting downward). Therefore, the industry's output will increase and the price of its product will decline. But this is one of the prices, along with all others, that was assumed to remain unchanged when we move down the market demand curve for the factor.

Hence, when we lower the price of the productive factor, our assumption that all other things remain unchanged is no longer valid. In particular, the price of the product the factor helps produce is changed. The fall in product price means that each firm's MRP, or factor demand curve, will fall both because MPP falls and because product price p falls. This is exactly the case we have just examined for the imperfectly competitive firm. But it applies as well to the firms in a perfectly competitive industry that use the factor when we allow for the fact that the industry product price falls as they all expand output. Because of the fall in product price, each firm's demand curve for the factor will be steeper, like D_F' rather than D_F in Figure 15-3. Summing up all such D_F' curves, we would get the market factor demand curve. Because it takes account of the fall in product price, it will be steeper than the market demand curve that would be obtained by summing up the individual firm demand curves D_F, which do not take account of the fall in product price.

Shifts in the Demand Curve for a Factor

Up to this point we have only considered movements along a factor demand curve. What causes shifts in the position of a factor demand curve? There are essentially four major reasons for the curve to shift: (1) changes in the demand for the final product, (2) changes in the quantities of other productive factors, (3) technological improvements, and (4) changes in the prices of other factors. Let's consider each in turn.

Changes in the Demand for the Final Product

If there is an increase in demand for the final product that the factor helps produce, firms will need to use more of the productive factor in order to increase production of the final product to meet this demand. This will cause the demand curve for such a factor to shift rightward. Similarly, a decrease in demand for the final product will ultimately result in a leftward shift of the factor demand curve. As demand for the final product decreases, firms will produce less and therefore use smaller amounts of the productive factor. Looking back to Table 15-1, suppose that there is an increase in demand for the final product that causes product price p to rise from \$10 to \$15 in column (4). If you redo the calculations, you will find that for each quantity of the productive factor in column (1), the MRP in column (6) will now be larger. Consequently, the factor demand curve in Figure 15-1, frame (c), and Figure 15-2 will be shifted rightward.

Changes in the Quantities of Other Productive Factors

If the amounts of other productive factors used by a firm are increased while the quantity of one factor remains the same, the marginal productivity of the unchanged factor will increase. For example, suppose that we give one labourer a half hectare of land and some seed but no capital equipment such as a shovel or a hoe. He or she then produces a certain quantity of output. The labourer's productivity will rise considerably if he or she is provided with some capital equipment; it will rise even more if another half hectare of land is added. If the labourer is given more capital equipment in the form of a tractor and plow plus another 100 hectares of land, the labourer's productivity will rise still higher. In terms of Table 15-1, if the firm were to get more of the factor that was assumed to be fixed, the MPP, column (3), of the variable factor would be larger for every amount of that factor shown in column (1). This would mean that the factor demand curve of Figure 15-1, frame (c), and Figure 15-2 would be shifted rightward.

Technological Improvements in Productive Factors

If there is an increase in the productivity of some factors due to technological changes specific to those factors, the productivity of other factors used in conjunction with those factors will be increased as well. For example, if a woodcutter's handsaw is replaced by a power saw, the woodcutter's productivity will increase. Of course, the woodcutter's productivity may be increased even more by added education in the art of woodcutting. In sum, the MPP of a factor may rise either because of improvements in other factors or because of improvements in the factor itself. If the MPP figures in column (3) of Table 15-1 are increased, the MRP figures of column (6) will also be increased. As a result, the factor demand curve of Figure 15-1, frame (c), and Figure 15-2 will be shifted rightward.

Changes in the Prices of Other Factors

We have already noted that there is a certain amount of substitutability among the productive factors used in most production processes. We also know from our study of demand curves that if the price or prices of goods *other* than the one for which the demand curve is drawn change, then the demand curve for that good will shift. We learned that the direction of the shift in the demand curve will depend on whether the other good whose price changes is a substitute or a complement for the good for which the demand curve is drawn. Similar principles apply when we consider a factor demand curve.

Substitute Factors

Given the demand curve for a factor F, let's suppose that the price of a substitute factor S falls. The effect on the demand curve for factor F must be broken into two parts. *First*, because the substitute factor S is now cheaper relative to the factor F, there will be a tendency to substitute factor S for factor F

in the production process. This happens because firms desire to produce their output in the least costly manner. This **substitution effect** alone will reduce the demand for factor F and thereby cause the demand for factor F to shift leftward. *Second*, the reduction in the price of factor S means that the cost of producing the final product whose production requires the use of factors F and S is now lower. This means the supply curve of the final product will be shifted rightward. Hence, there will be an increase in the production of the final product, which will require the use of more of both factors F and S. This **output effect** alone will shift the demand for factor F to the right. Since the output effect and the substitution effect push demand for factor F in opposite directions, the final position of the factor demand curve after a fall in the price of S will depend on which effect is larger. This can only be established by observation on a case by case basis.

Complementary Factors

Just as there is complementarity among some final products, such as between coffee and sugar or ham and eggs, there is complementarity among some factors of production. These are called, logically enough, **complementary factors** of production. Two factors are complements in production if an increase in the amount of one of them used in production requires an increase in the use of the other one as well. Conversely, a decrease in the use of one factor will lead to a decrease in use of the other. For example, to produce cargo transportation service in a city requires trucks (capital) and drivers (labour). If the price of trucks falls, it will be cheaper to provide cargo transportation service. The service can be sold at a lower price and more of it will be used. The demand curve for the factor trucks will therefore shift rightward. Since each truck needs a driver, a complementary factor, the demand curve for drivers will also shift rightward. In the case of complementary factors there is only an output effect, since complementary factors are not substitutes for one another and so cannot be used in place of one another.

Checkpoint 15-2

How do changes in the firm's final product price affect D_F? Why? Use Figure 15-2 to illustrate the effect on employment of the fact reported in a news item that "firms generally have managed to boost their prices even more rapidly than labour costs have risen." How do productivity gains affect the position of the factor demand curve in Figure 15-2? Explain your answer.

Elasticity of Factor Demand

The elasticity of the derived demand curve for a particular productive factor is determined by the nature of the demand for the final product produced with the aid of the factor, as well as by the nature of the production process and costs associated with producing the final product.

Determinants of the Elasticity of Factor Demand

When we consider the effect of a change in the price of a productive factor, we want to know how much the quantity demanded of that factor will change as a result of the change in its price. That is, we want to know the shape of the derived demand curve. This requires an examination of four links between the demand curve for the productive factor and the demand curve for the final product it helps produce. These links are four of the basic determinants of the shape of

the derived demand curve for the productive factor. These determinants are
(1) the elasticity of the demand curve for the final product, (2) the ratio of the
cost of the productive factor to the total cost of producing the final product,
(3) the degree of substitutability of the productive factors used to produce the
final product, and (4) the rate of decline in marginal physical product MPP
that occurs as the firm expands its output by using more of the factor. We will
consider each determinant separately.

Elasticity of Final Product Demand

Suppose that the price of a productive factor is reduced. The price of that
factor is a cost to the firms that use the factor to produce a final product. Hence,
the reduction in the factor's price means that the cost of producing the final
product will be reduced as well. This in turn will lead to a fall in the price of the
final product. Consequently, there will be an increase in the quantity of the final
product demanded. The extent of that increase will depend upon the elasticity
of the demand curve for the final product. The more elastic is the demand, the
greater the increase will be. The larger the increase is in the quantity demanded,
the larger will be the quantity of the final product that will be produced. The
larger is the quantity of the product produced, the larger will be the increase in
the quantity of the inputs needed to produce it. *The greater is the elasticity of the
demand curve for the final product, the more elastic will be the derived demand curve for
a factor used to produce it, all other things remaining the same.*

Ratio of Factor Cost to Total Cost

The meaning of this determinant will become clear if we consider a case in
which only one productive factor is used to produce a final product. If the price
of this productive factor is reduced by 50 percent, the cost of producing the
product will also be reduced by 50 percent, since that cost is exactly the same
as the cost of the productive factor. Alternatively, let us suppose that the cost of
this one productive factor accounts for only 2 percent of the cost of producing
the final product, with the cost of other productive factors accounting for the
remaining 98 percent of the total cost of production. A 50 percent reduction in
the price of this one productive factor will result in only a 1 percent reduction
(50 percent of 2 percent) in the cost of producing the final product. Given the
shape of the demand curve for the final product, the resulting decrease in the
price of the good that results from the reduction in the cost of production will
be greater in the first case than in the second. It follows, then, that the increase
in production of the final product that results in the first case will be greater
than in the second. Consequently, the increase in the demand for the productive
factor will be greater as well. *The larger is the ratio of the cost of a productive factor to
the total cost of producing the final product, the greater will be the elasticity of the derived
demand curve for the productive factor, all other things remaining the same.*

Degree of Factor Substitution

The production of most products typically involves the use of several different productive factors. However, it is often true that there are a number of
different combinations of these productive factors that might be used to produce

a given amount of a product. Ten tonnes of wheat may be grown by use of a number of different combinations of land, labour, and capital equipment. Many labour hours can be combined with a modest amount of capital equipment (such as hoes and sickles) and a certain amount of land. Alternatively, a few labour hours may be combined with more sophisticated capital equipment (such as tractors and combines) and a different amount of land. Generally, if we reduce the amount of one productive factor, we must increase the amounts of one or more of the other productive factors in order to be able to produce the same amount of a product. In other words, there is a certain amount of substitutability among factors used in any production process.

The particular combination of productive factors used to produce a given quantity of a product will depend on the prices of the factors. If the price of one factor falls, it becomes cheaper relative to other productive factors and the firm will tend to use more of it in place of other productive factors. The degree to which this will take place will depend on the degree of substitutability among factors, and this varies with the kind of product produced. For example, the degree of substitutability between labour and capital equipment in the production of wheat is greater than that between these two factors in the production of hothouse orchids. The degree of substitutability between steel and aluminum is greater in the production of automobiles than in the production of airplanes, and greater in either of these than in the production of railroad flatcars. *The greater is the degree of substitutability of a factor for other factors in the production of a final product, the greater will be the elasticity of the derived demand curve for the productive factor, all other things remaining the same.* That is, the greater is the degree of substitutability of a factor for other factors, the larger will be the increase in the quantity demanded of that factor in response to a given reduction in its price.

Rate of Decline in Marginal Physical Product MPP

Finally, note that since $MRP = MPP \times p$, the elasticity of the MRP curve (see Figure 15-2) or of the factor demand curve, D_F, also depends on how much the marginal physical product (MPP) of the variable factor declines as output is increased by using more of the factor. If MPP tends to decline rapidly, then the factor demand curve will decline rapidly, and if MPP tends to decline slowly, the factor demand curve will decline slowly. *The MRP curve, or factor demand curve, will be less elastic the more rapidly MPP declines as the firm expands its output by using more of the factor, and it will tend to be more elastic the less rapidly MPP declines.*

Summary of Determinants of Elasticity of Factor Demand

In summary, the elasticity of the derived demand curve for a productive factor depends upon the following:

1. *The elasticity of the demand curve for the final product.* The greater the elasticity of the demand curve for the final product, the greater the elasticity of the factor demand curve.
2. *The ratio of the cost of the productive factor to the total cost of producing the final product.* The larger is the ratio of the cost of the productive factor

to the total cost of producing the final product, the greater will be the elasticity of the factor demand curve.

3. *The degree of substitutability of the factor for other factors in the production of the final product.* The greater is the degree of substitutability, the greater will be the elasticity of the factor demand curve.

4. *The rate at which marginal physical product (MPP) declines as the firm expands its output by using more of the factor.* The slower is the decline in *MPP*, the greater will be the elasticity of the factor demand curve.

Optimum Use of Several Factors

Our discussion up to this point has assumed that there is only one variable factor of production. In reality, a firm typically uses several variable factors of production. In principle, how does a firm decide how much of each of these factors to employ? In other words, what determines the optimum (or best) combination of inputs of factors to use in the production process? The answer may be arrived at by two closely related methods: the least-cost combination and the maximum-profit combination. For simplicity, we will assume that there are two variable factors of production, both of which are sold in perfectly competitive markets. The analysis, however, readily extends to cases where there are several factors. Clearly the following analysis is relevant to the longrun when all factors of production are variable.

The Least-Cost Combination of Factors

In previous chapters, whenever we have used the concept of a cost curve, it has always been *assumed* that at any output level the corresponding point on the cost curve represents the least possible cost at which that output level can be produced. But how does the firm select that particular combination of factors that minimizes the cost of producing a given output level? Or, in other words, for any given output level, how much of each of the factors should the firm employ if it wants to produce that output level at the least possible cost? The answer is this: *The firm produces a given output level at the least possible cost when the marginal physical product per dollar spent on each factor is the same.*

To convince yourself that this is true, suppose that there are two factors—labour and capital. Suppose that a firm is producing a given level of output with a quantity of capital and a quantity of labour such that

$$\frac{MPP \text{ of capital}}{\text{Price of capital}} = \frac{60 \text{ units of output}}{\$10}$$

and

$$\frac{MPP \text{ of labour}}{\text{Price of labour}} = \frac{30 \text{ units of output}}{\$10}$$

With the price of a unit of labour and the price of a unit of capital each being $10, the firm could produce more output for the *same* total cost by spending

Checkpoint 15-3

Describe what you think the demand curve for rubber looks like in terms of the first three basic determinants listed in the text that link it to the final products in which it is used. Take care to think about the likely relative importance of these final products in terms of the proportion of total rubber output that each uses. List five examples of factor inputs that you think would have very inelastic demand curves, and in each case explain your selection in terms of the first three basic determinants that link it to the goods in which it is used.

$10 less on labour and $10 more on capital. The cutback of 1 unit of labour would reduce total output by 30 units, while the increase of 1 unit of capital would increase total output by 60 units. Hence, by simply shifting $10 away from expenditure on labour and toward expenditure on capital, there will be a net increase in total output of 30 units.

As long as there is a difference between the marginal physical product of capital (MPP_k) per dollar and the marginal physical product of labour (MPP_l) per dollar, the firm can always increase the total output produced for a given total dollar expenditure by reallocating this expenditure away from the factor with the lower MPP per dollar and toward the one with the higher MPP per dollar. As the quantity of labour is reduced and capital increased, we would move up along labour's downward-sloping MPP_l curve while moving down capital's downward-sloping MPP_k curve. In our example we would continue to reduce the quantity of labour used and increase the quantity of capital until

$$\frac{MPP_l}{p_l} = \frac{MPP_k}{p_k} \tag{1}$$

(p_l and p_k are, respectively, the price of a unit of labour and capital.) Once a combination of capital and labour is employed such that this equality holds, it is not possible to increase total output further by reallocating the given total expenditure between the two factors. At this point the maximum possible output is being produced given the total dollar expenditure on factors. Stated the other way around, but equivalently, the quantity of output is being produced with the least costly combination of factors whenever the equality in Equation (1) holds.

Any given output level that a firm might choose to produce typically can be produced with a variety of different possible combinations of factors. However, only that combination which satisfies the equality in Equation (1) allows the firm to produce the given output level at the least possible cost. If the quantities of both the factors of capital and labour are variable, it follows that whenever we say that a firm is producing and selling a level of output that *maximizes* profit, we are implicitly assuming that the equality in Equation (1) holds. If this were not true, it would mean that a less costly combination of the factors exists that could be used to produce that output level, in which case profit could be made larger.

The Maximum-Profit Combination of Factors

Looking at the employment of two or more factors of production from the standpoint of the maximum-profit combination is really just a straightforward extension of the marginal revenue product principle that we have already examined in the case of one variable factor.

Recall that so long as the cost of an additional unit of the factor (the marginal factor cost) is less than the addition to total revenue (the marginal revenue product) resulting from the sale of the additional product produced with the help of that unit, the firm will be able to increase profit by using more of the factor to increase output. The firm will expand output until a point is reached at which the marginal factor cost of using one more unit of the factor is equal to the marginal revenue product realized from the sale of the additional output produced with the aid of that unit. If the factor was labour and it cost the firm p_l per unit, the firm would hire labour up to the point where this price was equal to the marginal revenue product of labour MRP_l, or $p_l = MRP_l$.

The same principle applies if there are two or more variable factors of production. If the firm is a price taker in the market for these factors (it can't affect the prices of these factors), it will be able to increase its profit as long as the MRP of any factor still exceeds the price of that factor. If the firm has two factors, capital and labour, it will maximize profit by employing that quantity of each factor such that

$$p_l = MRP_l$$

and

$$p_k = MRP_k$$

Note that these two expressions may be rewritten as

$$\frac{MRP_l}{p_l} = 1$$

and

$$\frac{MRP_k}{p_k} = 1$$

or

$$\frac{MRP_l}{p_l} = \frac{MRP_k}{p_k} = 1 \tag{2}$$

Relationship Between Least-Cost and Maximum-Profit Approaches

How is the least-cost combination of factors viewpoint, expressed by Equation (1), related to the maximum-profit combination of factors viewpoint, expressed by Equation (2)? Recall that for a firm operating in a competitive market, the marginal revenue product of a factor equals its marginal physical product multiplied by the price p of the product that it helps to produce. That is, we know that $MRP_l = p \times MPP_l$ and $MRP_k = p \times MPP_k$. Hence, if we multiply both sides of Equation (1) by p we get

$$\frac{MRP_l}{p_l} = \frac{MRP_k}{p_k} \tag{3}$$

This looks very much like Equation (2) *except* that this equality can hold even if the ratio of the marginal revenue products of the factors to their factor prices does not equal 1, as is required by the maximum-profit combination of factors point of view expressed in Equation (2). In other words, if the equality in Equation (2) holds, then the equality in Equation (1) must hold as well, but if the equality in Equation (1) holds, that does not necessarily mean that the equality in Equation (2) holds.

What is the meaning of this distinction? Recall that when both labour and capital are factors that the firm can vary in its production process, the equality in Equation (1) must be satisfied at all points along the firm's cost curve. This is so

POLICY PERSPECTIVE

Will Robots Replace Workers?

During the 1980s a strange new word became more commonplace in our vocabulary—*robotics*—a new field dealing with the technology and use of robots in all sorts of practical applications. No longer a science-fiction fantasy, robots are beginning to replace workers in a wide variety of manufacturing operations. They promise greater automation of the office as well. It is becoming so apparent that robots will take over an increasing share of the North American workload that both labour leaders and their rank and file are concerned about job losses due to robots.

Why hire robots? There are lots of reasons. A robot doesn't have good or bad days—only perfect days. A robot does the same task over and over again without mistakes. A robot will work all night without complaint. A robot doesn't require a salary, fringe benefits, or pension. Robots don't go on vacation and they don't call in sick. A robot never talks back or asks for a raise.

THE ECONOMICS OF ROBOTS

Many of the robots used in North America are employed in the auto industry. This is not surprising given that the hourly cost of an auto worker (including all fringes as well as wages) is the highest among all blue-collar workers in North American manufacturing.

When rising wage demands make it more and more difficult to run a manufacturing plant at a profit, robots are increasingly seen as an alternative. Reports suggest that typically an industrial robot purchased for $50,000 can be paid for and operated for about $6 per hour, compared to an average minimum cost in excess of $20 for a human worker. It is not hard to see why it has been predicted that by the year 2000, 45 million factory and office jobs could be affected by automation in some way. Robots simply seem to be a sensible alternative to human workers from a "bottom-line" standpoint.

DISPLACED WORKERS AND FEARS OF UNEMPLOYMENT

The prospect of robots replacing millions of humans in the workplace worries a lot of people. Even the most profit-minded management is concerned that greater efficiency might not mean much if millions of people are thrown out of work by robot technology. There is particular concern that unskilled workers, who have traditionally worked on the lowest rung of Canadian industry, will be lost in the shuffle as businesses rush to buy robots to increase efficiency and match the competition.

There is an old and familiar ring to all this, however. The history of rising living standards is one of technological change eliminating certain kinds of jobs while creating new ones, and improving labour productivity in the process. Can-dlemakers were replaced by makers of kerosene lamps, who in turn were replaced by electricians. Blacksmiths and carriage makers were replaced by auto workers. One farmer today can produce the equivalent of what 50 produced at the turn of the century. The other 49 are now working in other sectors of the economy which, in fact, were able to develop and expand precisely because labour was released from the farm. Automation of manufacturing assembly lines and the office place has been going on for decades—machines have been replacing labourers. The advent of robots is just a continuation of that process. They too are just another kind of capital, a new type of machine. Their development is no more ominous for jobs and employment than the development of the steam shovel for ditch digging, the printing press for reproducing manuscripts, or the automatic cash teller for dispensing money.

For Discussion

- How does the development of robots affect the marginal physical product of capital? Illustrate your answer in a graph.
- Are robots likely to affect the marginal physical product of labour and, if so, how? Are robots likely to affect labour productivity, defined as the average product of labour? If so, why?

because each point on the cost curve represents the least possible cost for which the associated output level can be produced. However, it is entirely possible for the firm to produce and sell a quantity of output that does not maximize profit according to the marginal-cost-equals-marginal-revenue criterion that we studied in previous chapters. Nonetheless, the firm can still be producing that quantity of output at the least possible cost. That is, the equality in Equation (1) will be satisfied and so will the equality in Equation (3), which is simply obtained by multiplying both sides of Equation (1) by the product price p. However, the ratio of the marginal revenue product of each factor to its respective price will not equal 1. The equality in Equation (2) is satisfied *only if* the firm is also producing and selling that level of output that maximizes profit.

Example of Distinction Between Least-Cost and Maximum-Profit Approaches

In summary, the equality in Equation (2) says that in order to maximize profit, the firm should use that least-cost combination of productive factors such that the marginal revenue product per dollar spent on each factor equals 1. For example, suppose that p_l and p_k each equal \$1 and that a firm is producing a level of output such that $MRP_l = MRP_k = \$5$. The equality in Equations (1) and (3) is satisfied—the firm is producing output at the least possible cost. However, Equation (2) is clearly not satisfied. The firm is not maximizing profit. Since the firm can buy an additional unit of each factor at \$1 apiece, and since the MRP of each factor exceeds its price by \$4 (\$5 − \$1), the firm can increase profit by hiring more of the factors and increasing its level of output and sales. It should continue to hire capital and labour until the MRP of each falls to \$1. At that point, the equality in Equation (2) will be satisfied and the firm will produce and sell that quantity of output that maximizes profit.

Summary

1. There are two basic reasons why resource pricing is important: (1) it determines how the economy's limited supply of productive resources, or factors, is allocated to the various production activities necessary to produce the multitude of goods and services society wants, and (2) it is a major determinant of how income earned from productive activities is distributed among the economy's citizens.
2. The demand for a productive factor ultimately derives from the demand for the final product or products that the factor helps to make. The greater the demand for the goods and/or services that the factor helps produce, the greater the demand for the factor itself. For example, an increase in the demand for cars will lead to an increase in the demand for auto workers, steel, and so on.
3. The marginal productivity theory of factor demand says that when a firm is a price taker in a factor market, it will hire the factor up to the point at which the price of the factor just equals its marginal revenue product. Because of this, the marginal revenue product curve of the factor constitutes the firm's demand curve for the factor.
4. Because of the law of diminishing returns, the marginal physical product of a factor falls as additional units of it are used. Consequently, the marginal revenue product curve, or factor demand curve, is downward sloping for this reason alone if the firm is a price taker in the product market. However, if the firm's product demand curve is also downward sloping, the factor demand curve will be downward sloping not only because of the decline in

marginal physical product with the use of additional units of the factor but also because of the decline in product price.

5. The factor demand curves of individual firms can be summed to obtain the market demand curve for a factor. However, when doing so, we should recognize that it is not realistic to assume that the price of the product the factor helps produce remains constant when we change factor price and thereby move along the factor demand curve.

6. Shifts in a factor demand curve are caused by (1) changes in demand for the final product; (2) changes in the quantities of other productive factors; (3) technological improvements in the factor for which the factor demand curve is drawn or in the other factors with which it is combined in the production process, or in both; and (4) changes in the prices of other factors.

7. If two factors X and Y are substitutes in production and there is a change in the price of X, then there will be a substitution and an output effect, each of which pushes the factor demand curve for Y in a direction opposite to the other. The ultimate direction of the shift depends on which effect dominates. On the other hand, if X and Y are complements in production and the price of X rises (falls), then the factor demand curve for Y will shift leftward (rightward), since there is only an output effect between complementary factors.

8. The elasticity of a factor demand curve depends on (1) the elasticity of the demand curve for the final product, (2) the ratio of the cost of the productive factor to the total cost of producing the final product, (3) the degree of substitutability of the productive factor for other productive factors used to produce the final product, and (4) the rate at which the marginal physical product declines as the firm expands output by using more of the factor.

9. To produce any given level of output, the firm's least-cost combination of productive factors is determined by employing that quantity of each such that the marginal physical product per dollar spent on each factor is the same for every factor.

10. To produce that level of output that maximizes profit, the firm should use that least-cost combination of productive factors such that the marginal revenue product per dollar spent on each factor equals 1.

Key Terms and Concepts

complementary factors
derived demand
marginal physical product

marginal productivity
theory of factor
demand

marginal revenue product
output effect
substitution effect

Questions and Problems

1. Specify how each of the following would affect the demand curve for a productive factor X used in the production of a product Y. Where there is uncertainty, explain why.
   a. There is an increase in the demand for Y.
   b. There is a decrease in the number of substitute products for Y.
   c. There is a change in production technology that has the effect of reducing the amount of X used relative to other factors.

d. There is a technological improvement in one of the other factors used with X in the production process.

e. There is a fall in the price of one of the other factors used with X in the production process.

f. There is a decrease in the price of X.

g. There is a natural disaster that destroys some of the other factors used with X in the production process.

2. It is often suggested that minimum-wage legislation reduces job opportunities for young workers and minorities. Using the marginal productivity theory of factor demand and a diagram similar to Figure 15-2, explain why this is likely to be a problem.

3. How is the derivation of the demand curve for a factor by an imperfectly competitive firm similar to the derivation of the market demand curve for a factor?

4. Sometimes it is argued that the way to help poor people is to educate and train them in ways that will increase their productivity. Assuming a perfectly competitive industry, how might this point of view be refuted or buttressed by the marginal productivity theory of factor demand? (Remember that although each firm in the industry is a price taker in the labour market, this does not rule out the possibility that the supply curve of labour to the industry may be upward sloping—even though to the individual firm it appears horizontal as in Figure 15-2.) In assessing this point of view, what difference does it make whether the supply curve of labour to the industry is horizontal or upward sloping?

5. Consider the production and sale of automobiles. Suppose that the price of each of the following items falls by 5 percent: safety glass, copper, aluminum, steel, rubber, synthetic fiber, plastic, and wood.

a. Rank the items according to the degrees of impact that you think the 5 percent price reduction in each has on the price of automobiles. Explain the reasoning underlying your ranking.

b. Rank the items according to their degree of substitutability in the production of automobiles. Explain your ranking.

c. Rank the items according to the elasticity of the automobile industry's demand curve for each of them, and explain the reasons underlying your ranking.

6. Explain why it is possible for a firm to use a least-cost combination of factors and yet still not maximize profit.

7. Consider a firm that uses labour and capital to produce a good for which these two factors have the productivity shown in the following table. Suppose that the good is sold at a price of $1 per unit, and that the price of labour is $1 per labourer and the price of capital is $2 per unit of capital. Assume that the firm is a price taker in both the factor market and the product market.

Number of Labourers	MPP of Labour	Units of Capital	MPP of Capital
1	12	1	20
2	10	2	17
3	8	3	14
4	7	4	7
5	4	5	2
6	2	6	1
7	1	7	0

a. If the firm wanted to produce 88 units of output, what combination of the two factors would allow it to do so for the least cost? Explain the principle by which you arrived at your answer.

b. If the firm wanted to maximize profit, what quantity of output should it produce and what combination of the two factors should it use to produce that quantity? Explain the principle by which you arrived at your answer.

c. If your answers to parts (a) and (b) are both least-cost combinations, why are they different?

d. Suppose that the price of a labourer rises to $8. How would this change your answer in part (b) of this question?

Chapter 16

Wage Determination, Labour Market Structure, and Unions

In the last chapter we examined the marginal productivity theory of factor demand. We showed that it provides a convenient starting point for thinking about the demand for labour. However, there is much more to be explained about the nature of wage determination in today's labour markets. The existence of large unions confronting large corporations to hammer out agreements on wages, fringe benefits, working conditions, hiring, layoffs, grievance procedures, and management versus union prerogatives tends to conjure up images of war games more often than the cut-and-dried interaction of supply and demand curves.

For most households, wages and salaries are the primary source of income. They are therefore the major determinant of most families' standard of living. They are the payment to our most important resource—labour, or what economists often refer to as *human resources*. Little wonder that real-world wage determination has often been accompanied by hostile confrontations and even violence.

In this chapter we will look more deeply into the nature of wage determination, with particular emphasis on the role played by unions and other important institutional factors that have fashioned the modern-day collective bargaining process used by management and labour.

What Are Wages, Salaries, and Earnings?

The terms *wages*, *salaries*, and *earnings* are familiar to all of us. Loosely speaking, they refer to the payments made in exchange for labour services. More particularly, the term *wage* is commonly used to refer to the hourly rate of payment made to blue-collar workers, while *salary* customarily refers to the weekly, monthly, or annual payments made to white-collar workers. The term *earnings* may refer to either wages or salaries, but most often it is used to designate the sum of payments received from the sale of any kind of labour service over some considerable length of time. The term *labour* may refer to any kind of worker, from the floor sweeper to the chairperson of the board, or to doctors, dentists, mechanics, proprietors of self-owned businesses, fire fighters, entertainers, and professional athletes. In general, a **wage** *is the price per unit of labour service*—the price per labour hour, for example. In addition to wages and salaries, workers may also receive other benefits. **Fringe benefits** *include any payment made by an employer for a benefit for the employee.* Common examples of such payments are employers' contributions to pensions plans and employers' payments for medical and dental insurance.

Money Wages versus Real Wages

It is very important in any discussion of wages to keep in mind the distinction between money (or nominal) wages and real wages. *The* **money wage** *is simply the size of the wage measured in dollars and cents. The* **real wage** *is the size of the wage measured in terms of the quantity of goods that can be purchased with it.* The real wage is a more meaningful measure of a worker's wage because it indicates the standard of living that the wage makes available to the worker in terms of purchasing power. For example, suppose that you were offered a job paying a money wage of $40 per hour. Now, suppose that you find out that the price of a loaf of bread has risen to $10, a pair of shoes to $300, and a litre of gas to $5. Similar price increases have also taken place for a host of other commodities. Under these conditions, you would probably decide that an hourly money wage of $40 is not much of a real wage—it simply doesn't allow you to buy very much. Almost unconsciously, we tend to think of a dollar in terms of what it will buy. In other words, we think of its real value, measured in terms of the goods it enables us to have. We do the same thing when quoted a money wage. That is,

---

LEARNING OBJECTIVES

After reading this chapter, you will be able to:

1. Distinguish between money wages and real wages.
2. Summarize the reasons why wages differ across occupations and between workers.
3. Explain the role of market structure in the determination of the wage and employment level in a labour market.
4. Explain how wages are determined in a competitive labour market.
5. Explain how a craft union can raise wages in an otherwise competitive labour market.
6. Explain how a monopsony can lower wages in an otherwise competitive labour market.
7. Explain how wages are determined in a bilateral monopoly labour market.
8. Briefly outline the history of the union movement in Canada.
9. Assess the record of achievement of unionism.

---

we convert it to a real wage by envisioning the quantities of various goods that it will buy.

Converting a Money Wage to a Real Wage

How do we convert a money wage to a real wage? Let's take a simple example. Suppose that the only good in the economy is bread and suppose that your money wage is $10.00 per hour and the price of bread is $1.25 per loaf. Since the real wage is the size of the wage measured in terms of the quantity of goods that can be purchased, your real wage must be 8 loaves of bread. It is the money wage of $10.00 divided by the price of a loaf of bread, which is $1.25. Suppose that next year the price of a loaf of bread rises to $2.50 per loaf. If the money wage remains at $10.00 per hour, the real wage falls to 4 loaves of bread per hour, or $10.00 divided by $2.50. Since the money wage of $10.00 only buys half as many loaves as previously, the real wage has been halved.

In reality there are many goods in our economy. So when economists want to convert a money wage to a real wage, they usually divide the money wage by an index of the general price level. The index of the general price level is constructed in such a way as to measure the cost of the "basket" of goods purchased by a "typical," or "representative," household. [The consumer price index (CPI), which will be discussed in Chapter 20, is such an index.] The real wage obtained in this fashion is a measure of the money wage's purchasing power in terms of such a basket of goods.

For example, the consumer price index had a value of 100 in 1986, a value of 23.9 in 1961, and a value of roughly 119.5 in 1990. This may be interpreted to mean that the price of a basket of goods in 1961 was about 74 percent lower than the price of that same basket of goods in 1986. By 1990, however, the price of that basket had risen until it was five times as expensive as it was in 1961. Another completely equivalent interpretation is that $1 in 1986 had about the same purchasing power in 1986 as $.24 did in 1961. Similarly, it would have taken more than $1.19 in 1990 to have the same purchasing power that $1 had in 1986. Using 1986 as a base year, we can convert a money wage in any year to its equivalent expressed in 1986 dollars. (The selection of 1986 as the base year is arbitrary, but it does correspond to the base year used by Statistics Canada at the time this book was written.) We would then have a measure of the real wage expressed in terms of 1986 dollars. For example, suppose that we convert a money wage of $10 per hour to a real wage expressed in terms of 1986 dollars for each of the years 1961, 1986, and 1990. This customarily would be done by dividing $10 by the consumer price index, expressed as 23.9 for 1961, 100 for 1986, and 119.5 for 1990. (Because the consumer price index is normally expressed in percentage terms, these values are actually .239, 1.00, and 1.195 respectively.) The real wage for 1961 expressed in 1986 dollars would be $41.84 ($10 ÷ .239), for 1986 it would be $10 ($10 ÷ 1.00), and for 1990 it would be $8.37 ($10 ÷ 1.195). Hence, if your hourly money wage (the number of dollars actually paid to you for an hour of work) remained the same at $10, your real wage would have fallen over the years from 1961 to 1990. Assuming a constant money wage of $10, the amount of purchasing power given to you in exchange for 1 hour of work in 1990 would have been less than one fifth of what it was in 1961.

Money Wages and Real Wages Since 1961

The average hourly money wage earned in the manufacturing sector of the Canadian economy for each of the years 1961 to 1990 is shown in Figure 16-1. Also shown is the average hourly real wage in each of these years. The average real wage is obtained by dividing the average money wage for each year by the consumer price index for that year. Clearly the money wage has risen at a faster rate than the real wage. This reflects the circumstance that the general price level also has been rising throughout these years and the purchasing power of the money wage, as measured by the real wage, has not risen as fast. Nonetheless, the rise in the real wage does indicate that the rise in the money wage has been more rapid than the rise in the general price level, except during 1978, 1979, 1980, 1981, 1983, 1985, 1986, and 1988. While the level of real wages in 1990 was substantially higher than it was in 1961, the growth in real wages was in the early part of this period. *In fact, real wages in manufacturing were higher in 1977 than in 1990. This stagnation reflects the generally poor performance of the economy during that period and the fact that the share of total output going to labour fell during that period.*

FIGURE 16-1   Index of the Average Hourly Real Wage and Money Wage in Canadian Manufacturing Since 1961 (1986 = 100)

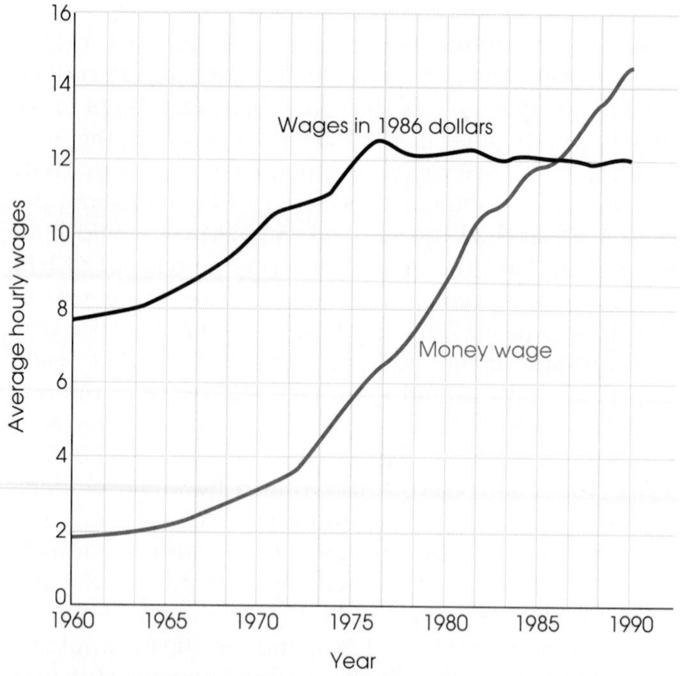

Source: Statistics Canada. 1950–1983; *Canada Yearbook*, various years; 1983–1990 *Canadian Economic Observer*, various years (11-010)

The index of the average hourly real wage shown here is obtained by dividing the index of the average hourly money wage for each year by the consumer price index (CPI) for that year. The rise in the real wage indicates that the rise in the money wage has been more rapid than the rise in the general price level up through the mid-1970s, but remained relatively constant into 1990.

Real Wages and Productivity

In the last chapter we saw how the demand for a factor such as labour depends on its productivity. In particular, the marginal productivity theory of factor demand tells us that if a firm purchases labour services in a perfectly competitive market (the firm can buy as many labour hours as it wants at the given wage rate and sell as many units of its output as its wants at a given price), it will hire labour up to the point where the marginal revenue product (MRP) of labour equals its money wage w. Recall also that the MRP of labour in a competitive market is equal to the marginal physical product of labour (MPP) multiplied by the price p of the product that the labour is used to produce. This may be written

$$w = p \times MPP = MRP \tag{1}$$

Equivalently, by dividing both sides of the equation by p, this may be expressed as

$$\frac{w}{p} = MPP \tag{2}$$

The left side of Equation (2) is the real wage, which is the money wage w divided by the price p. Note that since p is the price of a unit of the firm's product, w/p is the real wage in that it measures the compensation of labour in terms of the number of units of the firm's product. We know from the last chapter that technological progress and an increase in other factors used in combination with labour lead to increases in labour productivity. This in turn is reflected in increases in MPP and rightward shifts in the demand curve for labour. From Equation (2) we can see that such increases in MPP mean that labour's real wage, w/p, will rise when labour productivity increases. This suggests that the rise in the real wage during the 1960s and early 1970s for the manufacturing sector of the Canadian economy shown in Figure 16-1 reflects the growth in demand for labour due to the growth in labour productivity. Of course, the supply of labour has been growing over these years, and we know from supply and demand analysis that this factor by itself would tend to push money wages and real wages down.[1] When the real wage was rising, the growth in labour productivity was great enough to cause the demand for labour to grow at a faster rate than the supply of labour. This is illustrated in Figure 16-2. When the real wage was falling, it could be that the supply of labour rose faster than the demand for labour or that the demand for labour was not increasing.

Sources of Productivity Growth

In the last chapter we noted that increases in labour productivity, or the MPP of labour, may be due to a number of factors. The most obvious is increased years of schooling and job-specific training investment in human capital, which improves labour productivity directly. In addition, labour productivity increases

---

[1]You may convince yourself of this by turning back to Figure 15-2. The marginal cost of the factor MCF in that figure shifts down along D_F. Given the price level p, from Figure 15-1, frame (b), we can see that this means that the MPP of labour falls. From Equation (2), this means that the real wage, w/p, falls.

FIGURE 16-2   Effect on Real Wage of Growth in Labour Supply and Demand

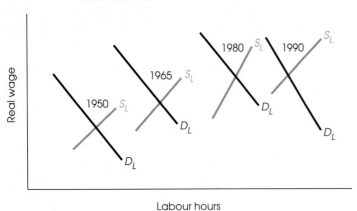

The increase in productivity in Canada has until recently caused the demand for labour to increase at a faster rate than the increase in the supply of labour. Hence, over time the demand curve for labour has shifted farther rightward than the supply curve, thereby causing the real wage to rise.

when labour is combined with new capital equipment embodying the latest advances in technology and scientific knowledge. Output per labour hour on the farm increased greatly when the tractor, with its much greater pulling power, replaced the horse. Somewhat less obvious at first thought, but nonetheless of great importance to the growth of labour productivity, are the improvements in economic organization and other institutional arrangements in our society. The improvement of traffic flows through and around metropolitan areas makes the transport of goods to markets and labour to jobs easier, thereby contributing to increased productivity. Effectively enforced competition laws may well promote the quest for more efficient operation of firms trying to get a competitive edge on rivals. Similarly, the more competitive environment may provide greater incentive to develop and adopt more productive technologies.

Does Technological Progress Create Unemployment and Make Labour Worse Off?

It is clear that it is very difficult to disentangle, identify, and separate out the individual sources of growth in labour productivity. With this in mind it is interesting to consider the common allegation that new machines and technology eliminate jobs and create unemployment, thereby making labour worse off. It is true that this kind of progress may well eliminate certain jobs and cause certain workers to seek other employment, but this is typically, though not always, a shortrun adjustment process. In the longrun, new machines and technology increase labour productivity and thus increase output per labour hour and make possible an increase in real wages. The jobs eliminated release a certain amount of labour and make it available to produce more goods and services previously unavailable. Hence, for a given size of the economy's labour force, it is possible to produce a larger total output. Over the longrun, it is this process that allows the real wage of all workers to rise and thereby results in an increase in the general standard of living. These longrun aggregate gains may not be much consolation to older workers who cannot be retrained to perform the new jobs unless society compensates them out of the general increase in living standard. If this were not the case, Western economies would be much worse off today than they were before the industrial revolution. Actually, Western economies are much better off today because of two centuries of rapid technological change.

For example, even if all of Mexico's labour force were fully employed, the total output of the Mexican economy would be less than that of (a fully employed) Canada. Because labour productivity in Mexico is low, so are real wages. The low productivity is due to a number of factors: a generally high rate of illiteracy and poor health due to low investment in human capital (in the form of education, job training, and medical care); an insufficient quantity of modern physical capital (machines, paved highways, and so forth) to complement the labour force and make it possible to engage in modern production activities; and, of course, political and cultural institutions that are often not conducive to a change in these conditions. Yet if Mexico's labour force were fully employed, this would amount to several million jobs! This example points out that jobs are not the source of an economy's wealth. Rather, it is the high productivity and the high real wages that this high productivity makes possible. It is differences in productivity that explain the differences in real wages among nations.

Why Wages Differ

Why do wages differ from one occupation to another and between individuals in the same occupation? Doesn't it seem unfair that some professional athletes are paid several million dollars a year for playing a game while a coal miner makes but a small fraction of that sum for performing a dangerous, grimy job providing an essential source of energy for the economy? These differences can be explained in terms of supply and demand. Hardly anyone can score goals as well as Brett Hull or catch a football like Rocket Ismail. The supply of that kind of talent is extremely limited and the public's demand to see it displayed is large. While the demand for coal and consequently the derived demand for coal miners is also large, many people possess the ability and willingness to be coal miners. In short, the difference in wages between great professional athletes and coal miners is due to the difference between the size of the supply *relative* to the demand for the services provided in each of these occupations. The supply of great professional athletes *relative* to the demand to see them perform is much smaller than the supply of coal miners *relative* to the demand for their services in producing coal. The high income of professional athletes and entertainers vis à vis coal miners is analogous to the high price of diamonds vis à vis water.

But what are the factors underlying such differences in demand relative to supply in various labour markets, both within and across occupations? Perhaps the best way to identify these factors is to envision the nature of an economy in which there are no wage differences. Suppose that all members of the labour force were exactly alike in ability, skills, and educational background. Each worker could therefore do any job as well as any other worker, whether it were brain surgery, plumbing, playing professional hockey or the violin, or collecting garbage. If, in addition, each labourer were completely indifferent as to choice of job or occupation, the wage would be the same for each and every labourer in a competitive economy. For example, if the wage were higher in one occupation relative to that prevailing in the others, labourers would tend to move into that occupation and out of the others. Then the increased supply of labour to that occupation would push its wage rate down and the decreased

Checkpoint* 16-1

Suppose that someone is concerned that the introduction of new capital equipment will eliminate jobs. To be logically consistent with this point of view, what should this person's position be on a plan to introduce a more efficient traffic flow pattern in and around a large city? Why? What jobs might be eliminated? How will output per labour hour be increased?

*Answers to all Checkpoints can be found at the back of the text.

supply to the others would push theirs up until a uniform wage prevailed once again. Conversely, if the wage in one occupation was lower than that prevailing in others, workers would move from that occupation and into the others until the wage difference was similarly eliminated. Of course, the elimination of wage differences requires that labour be perfectly mobile. If members of the labour force are not perfectly mobile, are not indifferent as to job preference, and are not exactly alike in ability, skills, and educational background, wage differences will exist between occupations, between workers in the same occupation, and between geographic locations. We will now look at each of these factors in turn.

Labour Mobility

One has only to look at the persistently high unemployment rates and low wages in Newfoundland to see that low wages and a lack of jobs do not necessarily cause labour to move. Family ties, old friends, a sense of "roots" or community, the costs of searching for a new job, the costs of moving, lack of knowledge, the structure of unemployment insurance and welfare programs, and a fear of the unfamiliar are all factors that may inhibit labour mobility. These factors do not mean, however, that labour is immobile "at any price." They lead to labour immobility only when the alternatives to the status quo as perceived by a worker are not felt to be worth the cost of change. Often these factors contribute more significantly to immobility among older and less-educated workers. Older workers' working-life horizon is shorter than that of younger workers; they have less chance to recoup the costs of searching out and moving to a new job. This is even more the case when costs of retraining and acquiring new skills are required in order to successfully make such a move.

Labour immobility can also foster high wages. For example, there are institutional constraints on labour mobility that tend to keep wages high in some occupations. Law, medicine, dentistry, teaching school, and a number of other occupations require participants to be licensed before they may legally practice their profession or trade in a given province. Those already licensed typically exercise firm control over the provincial licensing board. Obviously, they are not eager to issue more licenses that would permit an influx of practitioners from other areas of the country and thereby push their wages down. Similarly, craft unions sometimes restrict the mobility of tradespeople. This is not to say that some restrictions on mobility are not necessary to protect consumers from poor service.

Of course, in addition to all these considerations is the fact that demand for different kinds of labour in different parts of the economy is always changing. Indeed, the resulting differences in wage rates between occupations and regions are signals that tell the labour force where more lucrative opportunities exist and when local ones may be drying up. In a dynamic economy where this allocation mechanism is at work, we would naturally expect to see wage differences for this reason alone. Since labour is not perfectly mobile, it takes time for it to move in response to these signals.

Another factor that impedes labour mobility is discrimination by race, sex, and other factors. This takes many forms, from an employer not being willing to hire a member of a particular minority group [Aborigine, Francophone (or Anglophone), black, or immigrant] or sex to barriers to training and education necessary to gain admittance to a particular occupation.

Job Preference and Nonpecuniary Considerations

Even if each labourer were exactly like every other labourer in ability, skills, and educational background, there might be considerable variation in how much each enjoys, or does not enjoy, doing a particular job. Hence, two equally able workers might have to be offered considerably different wages in order to induce them to take a given job.

Many jobs in the economy may differ in the wages they pay in part because of these nonpecuniary advantages or disadvantages associated with them. Working conditions, the degree of danger associated with doing the job, the location, and even the degree of pride or humiliation one may feel in having a particular kind of job are all nonpecuniary considerations. The **nonpecuniary considerations** surrounding a job are the characteristics associated with it that will cause labour to require either a higher or a lower wage, depending on whether the particular characteristics make the job either less or more attractive. Welders who work on skyscrapers get higher wages than welders who work at ground level. The difference is necessary as compensation for the greater danger associated with working at such heights.

Ability, Skills, and Education

The marginal productivity theory of factor demand tells us that the greater the productivity of a factor such as labour, the greater will be the demand for it. Labour's productivity can be enhanced by vocational training, formal education, on-the-job experience, improved health care, and any other form of investment in human capital. Of course, such factors as innate ability and motivation play a large role in determining just how much productivity can be improved by education and specialized training. Very few of us will ever play goal like Patrick Roy, pitch like Roger Clemens, or be scientists like Albert Einstein or Roberta Bondar, no matter how much training and education we receive.

In theory and often in practice, the greater one's productivity in any given occupation, the greater will be one's earnings. The more skilled house painter, the more motivated salesperson, and the more competent manager all have an edge over their less capable co-workers. Their greater productivity will typically mean that the demand for their services is larger. A worker who can do a job more efficiently and quickly than others will produce more output per unit of time and can usually expect to earn more. A barber who can give more haircuts per hour than other barbers will usually earn a higher wage. Where workers are employed on an assembly line, the relationship between productivity and earnings will to some degree be based on the average productivity of the workers rather than the productivity of the individual worker. Unusual talent or skills will not necessarily result in high wages, however. Again, it depends on the relationship between supply and demand. The supply of blacksmiths is much less today than a hundred years ago, but there is less demand for their services. Thus, wages are not particularly high for the few that remain.

Many occupations require a person to have a considerable amount of education in order to become successfully employed. In general, the more rigorous the training and the more prolonged and expensive the required educational process, the higher the level of wages required to induce people into that particular occupation, other things remaining the same. Surgery and architecture

Checkpoint 16-2

Rank the following jobs according to your preference for them, assuming that each pays an hourly wage of $8 per hour: mail carrier, garbage collector, dogcatcher, night watchperson, traffic cop. If the night watchperson's job pays $8 per hour, what hourly wage would each of the other jobs have to pay for *you* to feel indifferent as to which job you take? (The necessary wage of each will typically be different from that of every other.)

FIGURE 16-3   **Relationship Between Education and Earnings**

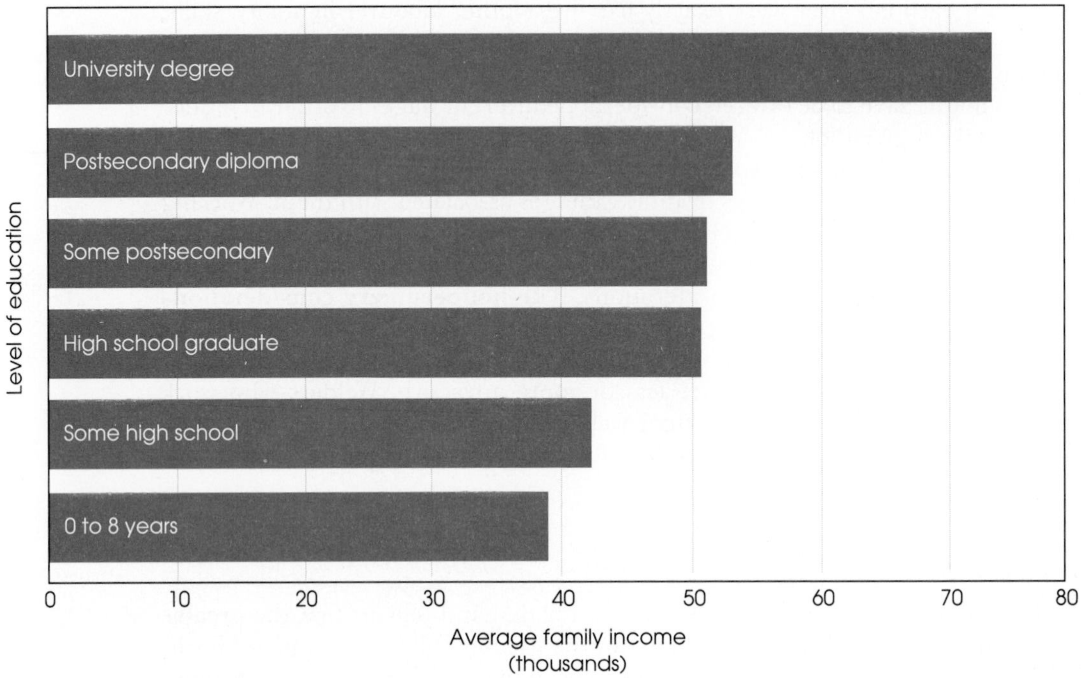

Source: Statistics Canada. *Income Distribution in Canada*, 1990 (13-207)

The earnings of university gradutes tend to exceed those of high school graduates, which in turn tend to exceed the earnings of those who have only completed the eighth grade. (Level of education refers to heads of families for the year 1990.)

are examples of such professions. This consideration, together with the fact that increased training and education tend to increase labour productivity, suggests that higher earnings should be related to higher educational levels. While it is possible that at any given point in time some profession may be overstaffed, and therefore the market can be temporarily depressed, over longer periods the relationship between education and earnings is generally true. The available evidence, as indicated in Figure 16-3, seems to bear this out.

Market Structure and Wage Determination

In previous chapters, we have seen how the equilibrium quantity and price of a final product depend on the structure of the market in which it is bought and sold. Similarly, the wage rate and the quantity of labour services bought and sold in a particular labour market also depend on market structure. We will now consider several important types of labour market structure and the significant role played by unions in some of them.

Wages and Competitive Markets

In a perfectly competitive labour market, so many labourers compete with one another for jobs that no one of them individually is able to affect the wage that he or she receives. The same is true on the buyers' side of this market. There are so many employers that each represents but a small fraction of the entire market—so small, in fact, that no one of them can affect, by its individual hiring and firing decisions, the wage that must be paid for labour services. In aggregate, however, employers in such a labour market will have to pay a higher wage if they want to increase the quantity of labour they hire. Let us make the following assumptions. Employees are all equally qualified to do the work. There are no barriers to employees seeking employment or to employers seeking to hire employees. Finally, both employers and employees have good information about the market. In this section we also are assuming that the product is sold in a perfectly competitive market—that is, all the assumptions given for perfect competition in Chapter 9 are met in the product market.

As long as workers have alternative employment opportunities, it will be necessary to pay a wage high enough to induce them away from their next best employment opportunity in some other area of the economy. As more workers are hired, employers can only compete for those with other employment opportunities by paying them a higher wage.

Figure 16-4 depicts equilibrium in a perfectly competitive labour market, frame (b), and the associated equilibrium position of a typical firm hiring labour

FIGURE 16-4 **A Perfectly Competitive Labour Market**

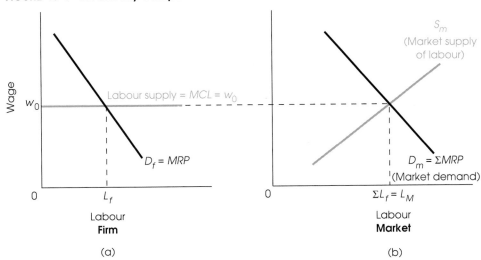

In a perfectly competitive labour market, the supply curve of labour to the typical firm, frame (a), is horizontal (or perfectly elastic) at the money wage w_0. This wage is determined by the intersection of the market demand curve for labour D_m and the market supply curve of labour S_m in frame (b). According to the marginal productivity theory of factor demand, the typical firm hires the quantity of labour L_f, frame (a), determined by the point where the marginal cost of labour (MCL) equals its marginal revenue product (MRP). The market supply curve of labour S_m, frame (b), is upward sloping because if the aggregate of all firms buying labour in this market want more labour, they must bid it away from its alternative employment in other areas of the economy.

in that market, frame (a). This figure might be the market for janitors in Toronto, for example. The market demand curve D_m in frame (b) is the sum of the individual firms' demand curves for labour, such as d_f in frame (a). These demand curves are the marginal revenue product curves (MRP) for labour for each firm. The demand curve d_f is a factor demand curve like those studied in the previous chapter (D_F in Figure 15-2, for example). The market supply curve S_m in frame (b) is upward sloping, reflecting the fact that if all firms want to hire more labour in this market, then they will have to pay a higher wage. The market equilibrium money wage w_0 is determined by the intersection of the market demand and supply curves, D_m and Sm, respectively, in frame (b).

The supply curve of labour for the individual firm, frame (a), is perfectly horizontal at the money wage rate w_0. This reflects the fact that the individual firm cannot influence the wage no matter how little or how much labour it hires. Because of this, the supply curve of labour for the individual firm is the same as the marginal cost of labour (MCL) for the firm. (Each additional unit of labour service adds its price per unit, the wage rate w_0, to the firm's total costs.) As we saw in the previous chapter, the firm will hire labour up to the point at which the marginal cost of that factor equals its marginal revenue product. In this instance, the quantity of labour L_f is determined by the intersection of MCL and d_f in frame (a). This amount represents but a tiny fraction of the total amount hired, L_M, in the entire market, frame (b).

Unions and Wages in Competitive Markets

The labourers in the perfectly competitive labour market we have just described compete with one another for jobs, and each deals directly with his or her employer on all matters concerning the terms of employment. Suppose, instead, that the labourers band together to form a union. A **union** is an organization that all labourers agree will represent them collectively in bargaining with employers over wages and other terms of employment. Labourers agree to this arrangement because in unity there is strength. It is still assumed that there are a large number of employers on the buyers' side of the market, all competing with one another in the hiring of labour.

The usual objective of the union, but typically not the only one, is to put labour in a stronger bargaining position in order to secure higher wages for its members. Other goals may include improving working condition and safety standards, increasing job security, and providing for social activities. There are basically three different ways for unions to promote higher wages for their members: restrict the supply of labour, impose a wage above the equilibrium wage, and support policies that promote increased demand for labour. Professional organizations, while not referring to themselves as unions, often behave in very much the same way.

Restriction of Supply—Craft Unions, Occupational Licensing

In certain occupations that require the development of special skills, training in a craft, or extensive education before one can do the job, it is possible to restrict the supply of labour and thereby increase wages. This is much more difficult in labour markets for unskilled labour because lower educational and skill requirements allow a great many more workers to enter the market to compete for jobs.

For example, workers in the skilled trades, such as bricklayers, electricians, and printers, have often banded together to form **craft unions**. By controlling the length of apprenticeship programs and restricting membership (which is often necessary to get into such programs), unions are able to control the supply of skilled labour in these trades. The more effectively they can do this, the easier it is to force employers to agree to hire only union members. This in turn further strengthens the craft union's ability to restrict the labour supply. The effect of this on the wage rate and the level of employment in such a trade is shown in Figure 16-5, frame (a). Before formation of the craft union, the equilibrium wage is w_0 and the equilibrium level of employment is L_0, as determined by the intersection of the labour demand curve D and supply curve S_0. When the craft union is formed and operating effectively, less labour will be supplied at every wage rate. This causes the supply curve to shift leftward from S_0 to S_1. The new equilibrium wage is now increased to w_1 and the level of employment is reduced from L_0 to L_1.

To work in a number of occupations and professions, it is necessary to have a license—no license, no job. The medical and legal professions are examples. To get a license to practice medicine, one must go through 4 years of medical school (preceded by an undergraduate education), and as many as 7 to 8 more years of internship and residency are required in some specialized fields. Moreover,

FIGURE 16-5   The Effect of Craft Unions and Industrial Unions on Wages and Employment

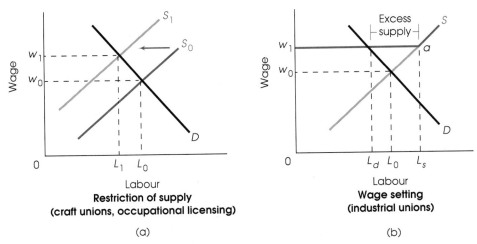

(a)   (b)

Craft unions directly restrict the supply of skilled labour by controlling apprenticeship programs and limiting union membership. As shown in frame (a), this effectively shifts the supply curve leftward from S_0 to a position such as S_1, causing employment to fall from L_0 to L_1 and wages to rise from w_0 to w_1.

In contrast to craft unions, industrial unions attempt to organize all the hourly paid workers, skilled and unskilled, in a given industry. As shown in frame (b), the union then uses the resulting bargaining power to set the wage rate at a level such as w_1, which is above the equilibrium wage rate w_0 that would otherwise prevail in a perfectly competitive labour market, while the amount supplied is L_s. There is thus an excess supply of unemployed union members, represented by the difference between L_s and L_d.

medical schools strictly limit the number of students that are allowed to enrol. While such extensive training can be (and is) defended as being in the public interest, it is nonetheless true that it makes entry into the practice of medicine difficult and therefore restricts the supply of doctors. This tends to push up doctors' wages as shown in Figure 16-5, frame (a). The average income of doctors in Canada is well over $100,000 per year. While entry into the legal profession is less restrictive, a university education followed by 3 years of law school, a period of articling and a passing performance on the bar exam likewise tend to push the supply curve of lawyers leftward, as in Figure 16-5, frame (a). In general, licensing will have this effect on any occupation for which it is required, whatever the merits (likely considerable) of the public interest arguments.

In addition to restricting their own membership levels, almost all unions at various times have supported legislation that serves to restrict the supply of labour generally. Such legislation includes child labour laws, immigration quotas, compulsory retirement at a certain age, and a shorter workweek. A union can also control supply if it can enforce an agreement with employers whereby only union members can be hired. Such an arrangement is called a **closed shop**. Naturally, to be effective the union must be able to limit its membership in some way. An alternative is a **union shop**. It does not restrict hiring to union members, but does require all employees to join the union once they are hired. Clearly the union shop does not restrict supply.

Wage Setting—Industrial Unions

Industrial unions, unlike craft unions, do not restrict their membership to only those workers in a particular trade. On the contrary, they attempt to organize all the hourly paid labourers, skilled and unskilled, in a given industry. Indeed, given the easy substitutability of readily available, nonunion, semiskilled, and unskilled labour, it would be foolish for the union to restrict membership. In effect, by maximizing the size of its membership and getting complete control of the labour supply needed by the industry, an industrial union forces firms in the industry to bargain exclusively with the union over wages and other conditions of employment. Firms unwilling to reach mutually agreeable terms with the union face the threat of being closed down by a walkout or **strike**—the loss of their labour supply—at least until one or the other side gives in.

Armed with this kind of bargaining power, an industrial union is able to set wages above the level that would otherwise prevail in a perfectly competitive labour market. This situation is illustrated in Figure 16-5, frame (b). Without the union, the equilibrium wage would be w_0 and the quantity of labour bought and sold would be L_0, corresponding to the intersection of the demand curve D and the supply curve S. Using its bargaining power, the union is able to push the wage up to w_1. Because the demand curve is downward sloping and the supply curve is upward sloping, the quantity of labour demanded falls to L_d, while the quantity of labour supplied increases to L_s. This gives rise to an excess supply of labour, which is represented by the distance from L_d to L_s. These are workers who would like to have jobs in the industry at this wage but can't—they are involuntarily.unemployed.

Obviously, the higher the union pushes the wage, the larger will be the pool of unemployed workers among its membership. This fact limits the union's ability to push up the wage rate. A large pool of unhappy, unemployed members may lead to defection within the ranks and threaten the very solidarity on which union bargaining strength is based. The more inelastic (steeply sloped) the demand and supply curves, the smaller the rise in such unemployment as the wage is pushed up. Thus, there will be less of an unemployment constraint on the union's ability to push up the wage.

With the wage rate at w_1, the supply curve of labour to the industry is represented by $w_1 aS$. The industry can hire as much labour as it wants up to the quantity L_s. If it wants more than this, it will have to raise the wage, as indicated by the upward-sloping portion of the curve aS.

While both the craft union and the industrial union reduce the level of employment as a result of their efforts to raise members' wages, their methods differ. The craft union pursues policies aimed at directly restricting the supply of labour. This is represented by the fact that the craft union causes the supply curve to be shifted leftward [Figure 16-5, frame (a)], which then leads to a rise in the wage rate. By comparison, the industrial union uses its bargaining power directly to set the wage rate higher [Figure 16-5, frame (b)], which then leads to a fall in employment.

Increasing Labour Demand

When labour unions succeed in raising the wages in a particular labour market either by restricting supply or by direct bargaining, the level of employment in that market is reduced. If instead unions are somehow able to bring about an increase in the demand for the labour services of their members, they will be able to have the "unmixed blessing" of *both* higher wages *and* higher employment. Particularly in the case of industrial unions, this avoids the conflict between getting higher wages for most members while creating unemployment for the rest. This is illustrated in Figure 16-6. If the demand curve for labour can be shifted from D_0 to D_1, the equilibrium wage and level of employment will rise from w_0 and L_0 to w_1 and L_1, respectively.

FIGURE 16-6   Increased Labour Demand Leads to Higher Wages and Increased Employment

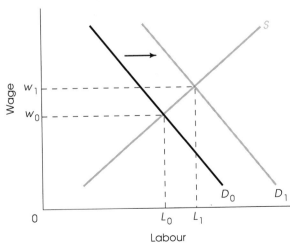

If unions can somehow increase the demand for their labour services, they can have the best of both worlds—higher wages and more employment. A shift in the demand curve for labour from D_0 to D_1 results in an increase in the wage from w_0 to w_1 and a rise in employment from L_0 to L_1.

How can unions cause the demand curve for their labour services to shift rightward? The marginal productivity theory of labour demand tells us that anything that increases labour productivity will cause the demand curve to shift rightward. The International Ladies' Garment Workers' Union (ILGWU) has actually conducted seminars to instruct employers on how assembly line techniques may be used to increase productivity in the garment industry. Another way to increase labour demand in specific industries is to put tariffs and import quotas on imported goods that compete with domestically produced goods, thereby raising the prices of the foreign goods. This tends to increase the demand for domestically produced goods, which are substituted for the now more expensive imported goods. The derived demand for the labour used to produce the domestic goods is thereby increased. Because of this it is not surprising that labour unions frequently join with employers to support tariff legislation that protects their industry from import competition. While this practice may increase the demand for labour in a particular industry, foreign countries can normally be expected to retaliate; therefore, it is unlikely that there would be any general increase in level of employment.

Monopsony—The Monopoly Employer

A **monopsony** is a market structure in which one buyer purchases a good or service from many sellers. It may be thought of as the opposite of a monopoly, in which one supplier sells to many buyers. A labour market in which one employer, the monopsonist, confronts a nonunionized group of labourers competing with one another for jobs, may be characterized as a monopsony. Fish packing plants in the Atlantic provinces and mill towns in the Maritimes and Quebec are often monopsony employers. Many remote mining towns in Canada are excellent examples of monopsony markets. In fact, the "company towns" which are common in Canada provide many examples of monopsony.

Table 16-1 and its graphical representation in Figure 16-7 illustrate how wages and employment are determined in a monopsony labour market. Being

TABLE 16-1   Wage and Employment Determination in a Monopsony Labour Market

(1) Number of Units of Labour Service (L)	(2) Wage Rate = Average Cost of Unit of Labour Service or Supply Price of Labour (w)	(3) Total Cost of Labor (TCL)	(4) Marginal Cost of Labour (MCL)	(5) Marginal Revenue Product of Labour (MRP)
1	$3	$ 3	$ 3	$15
2	4	8	5	13
3	5	15	7	11
4	6	24	9	9
5	7	35	11	7
6	8	48	13	5

FIGURE 16-7   Wage and Employment Determination in a Monopsony Labour Market

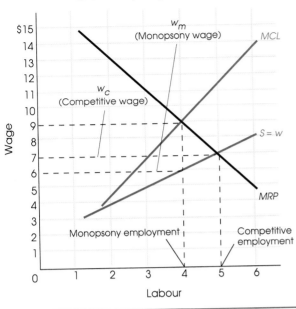

The monopsony firm hires the factoy labour up to the point at which its marginal cost equals its marginal revenue product, $MCL = MRP = \$9$, as determined by the intersection of the MCL and MRP curves. The monopsonist thus hires 4 units of labour at a wage w_m of $6 per unit of labour. By contrast, if the labour market were perfectly competitive, the equilibrium wage w_c would be $7 and the quantity of labour hired would be 5 units, as determined by the intersection of the MRP and S curves. Clearly, the monopsonist pays a lower wage and hires less labour.

the only buyer of labour services in the market, the monopsonist firm must pay a higher and higher wage to employ more and more labour. This is indicated in columns (1) and (2) of Table 16-1 and depicted by the supply curve S in Figure 16-7. The higher wage, or average cost of labour, must be paid not only to the last unit of labour hired but to all those units of labour already employed as well. If this were not done, previously employed labourers would become unhappy, quit, and have to be replaced or rehired at the higher wage paid the last worker employed. (This is very similar to the way a monopolist who wants to sell an extra unit of output in the product market must be willing to take a lower price not only on the extra unit sold but on all other units as well.) Therefore, the additional, or marginal, cost of hiring one more unit of labour is the sum of the wage paid to the additional labourer *plus* the increase in the wage that must be paid to all previously employed labourers, multiplied by the number of such labourers. Equivalently, the marginal cost of labour (MCL), column (4), is simply the increase in the total cost of labour (TCL), column (3), due to the employment of one more unit of labour. Figure 16-7 shows clearly that MCL rises faster than the wage rate, which is governed by the supply curve S.

How much labour will the monopsonist hire? According to the marginal productivity theory of factor demand, the firm will hire labour up to the point at which the marginal cost of the factor equals its marginal revenue product. That is, it will hire labour up to the point at which $MCL = MRP$. Columns (4) and (5) of Table 16-1 tell us that this point is reached when 4 units of labour are hired. At that point, the marginal cost of labour and its marginal revenue product both equal $9. This corresponds to the point at which the MCL and MRP curves in Figure 16-7 intersect. Here the monopsonist will pay labour a wage w_m of $6, the amount necessary, according to the supply curve S—and columns (1) and (2) of Table 16-1—to induce 4 units of labour to offer their services. Note by comparison that if the labour market were perfectly competitive, the equilibrium level of employment would be 5 units of labour at a competitive wage rate w_c of \$7, as given in columns (1), (2), and (5) of Table 16-1 and as represented by the intersection of S and MRP in Figure 16-7. All other things being equal, a monopsonist hires fewer workers at a lower wage rate than would be the case if the labour market was made up of several small employers. When labourers compete with one another for jobs offered by a monopsonist employer, the resulting equilibrium wage and level of employment will be lower than would be the case if the particular labour market were perfectly competitive.

Finally, it should be noted that although the monopsonist firm is a monopoly buyer in the labour market, it may be selling its product in any kind of market structure, ranging over the entire spectrum from perfect competition to monopoly.

Bilateral Monopoly

So far, we have considered a labour market in which the supply of labour is controlled by an industrial union acting as monopoly seller of labour and the demand for labour consists of many employers (firms) competing with one another in the hiring of labour. In that case, we saw that the wage is set by the union as shown in Figure 16-5, frame (b). At the other extreme, we have considered the case of a monopoly buyer of labour services, a monopsonist, and labourers who are not unionized but instead compete with one another for jobs. These labourers receive the monopsony wage as shown in Figure 16-7.

But what happens when there is monopoly power on both sides of the market—that is, when there is a **bilateral monopoly**? Suppose that a large industrial union represents the labour force in the sale of labour to a monopsonist. The monopsonist, or monopoly buyer of labour, may be one large firm or several firms acting in a collusive, oligopoly fashion in the hiring of labour services. A situation very similar to the latter occurs when a union confronts a monopsonist employer to bargain over worker wages and other terms of their employment. A similar example is provided by the provincial medical association and the provincial government bargaining over a fee schedule or a power plant that is the only buyer of coal bargains with a mine that is the only seller.

In order to characterize such a situation, we combine the analysis of the industrial union shown in Figure 16-5, frame (b), with that of the monopsonist shown in Figure 16-7. This is illustrated in Figure 16-8. Given a labour supply curve S and the associated marginal cost of labour curve MCL, the monopsonist would like to hire L_0 units of labour service at a wage of w_m. On the other hand, the industrial union would like to set the wage at w_u when L_0 units of labour services are sold. The union may wish to set the wage higher than this, but then, of course, the employer will hire less than L_0 units of labour service.

There is obviously a discrepancy between the desired wage objective of the union and that of the monopsonist when L_0 units of labour service are employed. This discrepancy is equal to the difference, or gap, between w_u and w_m. When "push comes to shove" and the monopoly hiring power of the employer is set against the monopoly selling power of the union, what mutually agreeable wage level in this gap will finally prevail? The bargaining power of the union typically depends on the willingness and financial ability of its membership to endure the

Checkpoint 16-3

It was reported in a news item that union leaders in the coal mining industry were going to push for higher wages despite the recession in the industry. Using a diagram like that in Figure 16-5, frame (b), for the industrial union analysis, show why the union leaders' objective is more difficult to achieve during a recession than during more normal times. Suppose that it were reported that "to forge a more united management front, one industry group, the Mine Owners Association, is seeking to bring significant numbers of owners together." How would you explain the economic rationale for this move?

FIGURE 16-8 A Bilateral Monopoly Labour Market

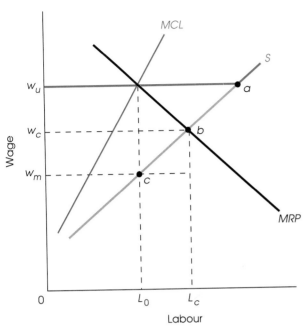

A situation in which there is a monopsonist on the employer side of the labour market and an industrial union on the seller side may be represented by combining the analysis of the industrial union in Figure 16-5, frame (b), with that of the monopsony in Figure 16-7, as shown here. The monopsonist would like to hire L_0 units of labour service at a wage of w_m. The industrial union would like to set the wage at w_u when L_0 units of labour service are sold. The wage that will be mutually agreeable to both sides will lie somewhere between w_u and w_m, depending on the relative bargaining power of the industrial union versus that of the monopsonist.

hardship of a strike. Similarly, the bargaining power of the employer depends on the willingness to incur the loss of business that will result from a shutdown. The greater is the bargaining power of the union relative to that of the employer, the closer we would expect the ultimate wage settlement to be to w_u. Conversely, the greater is the bargaining power of the employer relative to that of the union, the closer we would expect the ultimate wage settlement to be to w_m.

If the union prevails completely on the issue of wages, the supply curve of labour is $w_u a S$. If the employer prevails completely, it is $w_m c S$. Indeed, it is possible for the relative bargaining power of the two sides to be such that the wage settlement occurs at w_c with an amount of labour employed equal to L_0. Generally the labour union has no interest in increasing employment to the competitive level (L_c). However, in some cases unions do bargain for increased levels of employment. The latter goal is most likely to occur if the union has reason to wish to ensure job security—for example, in an industry where new technology may result in job losses. In such a case the union would trade higher wage demands for greater employment opportunities. If the final settlement provided for a wage of w_c with employment at L_c, the outcome would be the same as would result in a perfectly competitive labour market! In sum, the level of the ultimate wage settlement depends on the bargaining power of the union relative to that of the employer, and this varies from one industry and time to the next. *In a bilateral monopoly labour market, at the level of employment corresponding to the intersection of MCL and MRP, the wage level mutually agreeable to the monopoly employer and monopoly union will lie somewhere between the most desired wage w_u of the union and the most desired wage w_m of the employer.*

Growth of Unions in Canada

The history of unions in Canada has been characterized by a long struggle for employer recognition and public acceptance.[2] This struggle has occasionally been marked by violence and disruptive confrontation. But since World War II, confrontation has by and large given way to a spirit of mutual accommodation between management and labour that now generally typifies the widespread practice of collective bargaining. The union–management disputes that make headline news today represent but a very small portion of the many negotiations and settlements. Even when they do merit more than passing mention, it is generally because they involve unions whose activities directly and immediately affect the public, such as postal workers or city bus drivers.

Incentives for Unionization

The advent of the Industrial Revolution in the late 1700s set in motion a fundamental change in the nature of working conditions for an ever-increasing portion of the labour force. Before the Industrial Revolution the labour force was largely engaged in agricultural pursuits. What little industry existed could be characterized as "cottage industry"—spinning, weaving, and other handicrafts typically carried out by households otherwise engaged in farming on the same premises. Such activity, carried out along with farm chores, was usually aimed at satisfying the immediate needs of the family. While the average family was poor by present-day standards, the purpose and rewards of such work were direct and obvious. Moreover, the working conditions and relationships were personal and family oriented, and the work regimen, if long on hours, was loose and varied, involving work indoors as well as in the open air. The employer and arbiter was the head of household, usually oneself or one's parents.

The growth of mass production and factories caused labour to move away from such rural settings and into rapidly expanding towns and cities. There, workers typically found themselves tied to the strict and tedious regimen of machines set on mass-production schedules. They worked long hours in the close confines of poorly ventilated, crowded shops ("sweat-shops") and factories, turning out a product at the command of impersonal market forces. They typically felt themselves oppressed and abused by an authoritarian employer who often appeared as at best nothing more than an unpleasant, unsympathetic stranger to be feared. Monopsony was an apt characterization of many of the labour markets spawned by the new industries. Wages were low, and 12- to 14-hour workdays, six days a week, were common. Living conditions in crowded tenements in sooty, smoke-filled cities were usually as unhealthy and grey as the working conditions. It was one thing to be poor in a cottage industry setting, quite another in a nineteenth-century city.

Spurred by these conditions, workers began to recognize that by acting together they could confront monopolistic employers much more forcefully. In

---

[2] This section draws on Alton W. J. Craig, *The System of Industrial Relations in Canada* (Scarborough, Ont.: Prentice-Hall Canada, 1986).

a real sense, the whole could be much greater than the sum of its parts. In unity there could be strength and "solidarity," an oft-used term in the history of the labour movement. Improved working conditions could be demanded of employers and wages pushed higher, as indicated by our analyses of craft unions, industrial unions, and bilateral monopoly in Figures 16-5 and 16-8.

History of Unionization in Canada

The first attempts to organize by workers in Canada predate Confederation by more than 50 years. Unions in that period were local. The earliest unions developed in Nova Scotia and New Brunswick. Printers, shoemakers and tailors were among the first workers to organize. In the 1850s international unions began to appear in Canada. An example of these early international unions was the Amalgamated Society of Carpenters and Joiners, which was based in Britain. In the 1860s American unions crossed into Canada. Since that time American unions have had a major impact on the Canadian labour movement.

In 1871 the Toronto Trades Assembly was established. This organization was instrumental in the fight for the 9-hour workday and the passage of the *Trade Union Act* and the *Criminal Law Amendment Act* of 1872. These two pieces of legislation were major steps to ensuring the labour movement the right to organize. The Toronto Trade Assembly led to the formation of the Canadian Labour Union (CLU) in 1873. It never succeeded in organizing workers outside Ontario and was relatively short-lived.

The first labour organization to play a dominant national role in Canada was the Knights of Labor. Although an American organization, its philosophy of organizing all workers and promoting political as well as economic ends was well suited to the goals of Canadian workers. It grew rapidly and in the 1880s merged with the Toronto Trades and Labour Council to form the Trades and Labour Congress of Canada (**TLC**), which continued until the formation of the Canadian Labour Congress (**CLC**) in 1956. The TLC quickly affiliated with the American Federation of Labour, with which it shared the crafts union philosophy.

Canadian unions grew rapidly during the early twentieth century. A second national union, this time Canadian, formed in 1902 as the Canadian National Trade and Labour Congress. In 1910 it became the Canadian Federation of Labour (CFL). It was based on a much more nationalistic outlook than was the TLC. This Canadian outlook has played an important and at times controversial role within the labour movement throughout its history. Many regard the formation of the Canadian Labour Congress in 1956 as the beginning of a truly autonomous Canadian labour movement. This independence movement has clearly continued to develop since that time with the growth of the public service unions and the independent Quebec unions, and finally with the separation of the Canadian Auto Workers from their American counterpart in the later part of the 1980s.

Government Policy Toward Labour Unions

Since 1925, unions have generally fallen under provincial jurisdiction. Therefore, public policy with respect to labour varies from province to province.

POLICY PERSPECTIVE

Have Unions Increased Wages?

Figure 16-1 showed us that the average real wage of labour in Canada has risen since 1961. This average real wage represents an average of both union and nonunion workers. Two issues are of interest: (1) the effect of unions on their members' real wages, and (2) the effect of unions on all workers' real wages.

EFFECT OF UNIONS ON MEMBERS' REAL WAGES

Have unions brought about a greater increase in real wages for their members than would have occurred without them? After all, that is one of the major objectives of unionism—to raise members' wages higher than might otherwise be possible. Figures 16-5 through 16-8 indicate ways in which unions achieve this goal.

At first thought you might be tempted to compare the real wages of nonunion workers with those of union workers over time to answer the question about union effectiveness. But it is not as easy as that. There are too many other possible factors that enter into the determination of the behaviour of real wages. For example, suppose that demand for industry A's product is static, neither growing nor declining, while demand for industry B's product is expanding rapidly. As a result, suppose that real wages in industry B are rising more rapidly than in A. A's workers may be unionized and B's not, but union efforts to push up wages in A are

constrained by the unemployment this causes among union members in a static industry. Conversely, if B's workers are unionized and A's are not, how do we know to what extent the more rapid rise in B's real wages is due to faster demand growth for B's product rather than to the efforts of the union? This gives some idea of the difficulties encountered when researching the union effectiveness question. Bearing this in mind, what does research tell us?

Industry studies appear to indicate that unions are often effective in raising real wages somewhat above those paid for nonunion labour. The differential between union and nonunion wages within an industry appears to be not more than 10 percent for the average organized industry. However, in a few industries, such as coal mining, commercial airlines, and construction, the differential may be as much as 25 percent, while in a number of industries there is little wage advantage at all.

EFFECT OF UNIONS ON ALL WORKERS' REAL WAGES

Have unions pushed the average real wage of all workers, union and nonunion, up to a higher level than would have been reached without them? That unions can raise real wages in certain industries is certainly consistent with our theoretical analysis in Figures 16-5 through

16-8. Each of those figures showed how the existence of a union pushes up the money wage for its members. For a given price level p, this means the real wage $w \div p$ must also rise. However, the same type of analysis suggests that unions may not be able to do this for the average real-wage level of all workers—union and nonunion—taken together.

The reason is illustrated in Figure P16-1. Suppose that labour market X, represented by Figure P16-1, frame (a), is unionized by a craft union. This causes the supply curve of labour in that market to shift leftward from S_X to S'_X. The money wage therefore rises from w_0 to w_1 (determined by the intersection of S_X and S'_X with demand curve D_X), so that given the price level, the real wage of union members rises also. Note, however, that the quantity of labour employed in that market falls from L_0 to L_1. The quantity of unemployed labour $L_1 L_0$ must now find employment in some other market. To the extent that these unemployed workers seek work in a nonunionized labour market such as Y, represented by Figure P16-1, frame (b), they will cause the supply curve in that market to shift rightward from S_Y to a position such as S'_Y. Hence, the money wage in that market will fall from w_0 to w_2.

continued on next page

However, there is a considerable degree of consistency across Canada. To begin with, the very right of workers to organize was questioned. Under English common law, a union could be deemed a restraint of trade and as such illegal. Many employers regarded unions as potentially dangerous and dealt with any attempt to organize in a summary manner. Workers were fired and even blacklisted. Sometimes employers forced employees to sign a **yellow-dog contract**. Under

POLICY PERSPECTIVE CONTINUED

Given the price level, the real wage of workers in this market will fall, and the level of employment will rise from L_0 to L_2. The net result is that a smaller number of workers (L_1) is now earning a higher real wage in market X, while more workers (L_2) are earning a lower real wage in market Y.

It is not clear whether a weighted average of the two real-wage levels (each real wage weighted by the proportion of the labour force employed at that real wage) would be higher, lower, or the same as the weighted average of the two real-wage levels prevailing in the two markets before unionization of market X. It all depends on the shapes of the supply and demand curves in the two markets as well as the number of workers employed in each market before and after the supply curves shift.

In view of these theoretical considerations, it is not surprising that research has generally concluded that it is difficult to say that unions have had any discernible impact on the average level of real wages received by workers as a whole.

In some instances union policies may even have inhibited technological change and retarded productive efficiency. This seems to be the case in coal mining, construction, and railroads. To this extent, unions have held back improvements in real wages for the entire labour force. Yet unions often contribute to industrial discipline (reduce labour turnover and absenteeism) and cooperate with management to improve productivity, thereby contributing to raising real wages. On the national level, while there is little evidence that unions have had much effect in causing

money wages to rise more rapidly than they otherwise would have during times of prosperity, they do seem to have been successful in resisting wage reductions during recessions.

For Discussion

- Given the initial equilibrium positions and the indicated shifts in the supply curves shown in Figure P16-1, what kinds of shapes of the demand curves would assure that the weighted average real wage would fall as a result of unionization of market X?
- Given the shapes of the demand curves indicated by your answer to the question above, how difficult do you think that it would be to maintain union solidarity as compared to a situation where the demand curves are shaped as shown in Figure P16-1?

FIGURE P16-1   Effect of a Union on the Average Real Wage of Union and Nonunion Workers

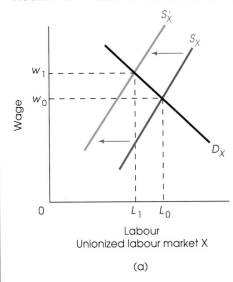

(a)
Labour
Unionized labour market X

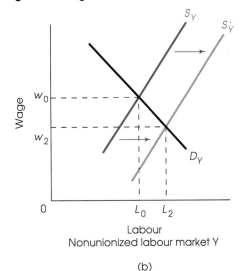

(b)
Labour
Nonunionized labour market Y

a yellow-dog contract workers agreed not to organize. In this early period the federal and provincial governments generally took a hands-off policy, passing neither anti- nor prolabour legislation. The first legislation to provide some aid for labour came in 1900. It established a framework to deal with labour management disputes. In 1907, the *Industrial Dispute Act* accepted the right of workers to organize and bargain collectively. It did not, however, force management to recognize unions. It certainly did not ensure industrial peace. In the years that followed there were many confrontations between labour and management. The worst of these was the Winnipeg general strike of May and June 1919, which resulted in loss of life.

In 1939 amendments to the Criminal Code made it illegal for an employer to take action against employees who unionized. Union membership grew rapidly in the late 1930s and the war years. During the war, government provided unions with further protection. The *Wartime Labour Relations Regulation Act* of 1944 did much to establish workers' right to collective bargaining. Another important gain came just after the war when Mr. Justice Ivan Rand of the Canadian Supreme Court was appointed to settle a strike at Ford Motor Company of Canada. In his ruling he established what has became known as the *Rand Formula*. Under this formula all workers must pay union dues even if they were not members of the union. The last major gain for unions came in the 1960s, when most public service employees were granted the right to strike.

Summary

1. A wage is the price of a unit of labour. The money wage is the size of the wage measured in dollars and cents. The real wage is the size of the wage measured in terms of the quantity of goods that can be purchased with it. The real wage is usually obtained by dividing the money wage by some index of the general price level. The level of real wages is a reflection of labour productivity, which in turn is determined by the amount of capital and other resources, the state of technology, the amount of education and training invested in human capital, and the institutional, social, and political structure of the economy. Real wages have risen in Canada because these factors have caused the demand for labour to grow faster than the supply of labour.

2. Wage differentials exist because labour is not perfectly mobile, workers differ in their job preferences, jobs have nonpecuniary considerations associated with them, and workers differ in ability, skills, and education.

3. The structure of a labour market is as important to an explanation of wage determination as the structure of a product market is to explaining price determination.

4. In a perfectly competitive labour market, a large number of employers compete with one another to hire labour from among a large number of workers competing with one another for jobs. The intersection of the market demand and supply curves for labour determines the equilibrium wage rate and quantity of labour employed. If workers organize a union in such a market, they can push the wage level above the equilibrium level.

5. A craft union is an organization of skilled workers in a particular craft or trade. It raises competitive wages by controlling the supply of labour. An industrial union is an organization that attempts to encompass and represent all workers, skilled and unskilled, in a given industry. It uses its bargaining power to set the wage rate higher than the competitive level. It is limited in its ability to do this by the unemployment that this causes among its membership. The main bargaining weapon of a union is the strike.

6. A monopsony labour market is one in which there is a monopoly buyer of labour services confronting unorganized workers competing with one an-

other for jobs. Because the monopsonist must bid up wages to hire additional labourers and pay the higher wage to all workers employed, the marginal cost of labour curve will lie above the labour supply curve. When the monopsonist hires labour up to the point at which the marginal cost of labour equals its marginal revenue product, less labour will be employed at a lower wage than would be the case if the structure of the market were perfectly competitive.

7. When a monopsonistic employer buys labour services from a union that is a monopoly supplier of labour, the structure of the labour market is that of a bilateral monopoly. The level of the wage that prevails in such a market depends on the bargaining strength of the union relative to that of the employer. No more definite statement can be made about the effect of such a market structure on wages and labour supplied.

8. In the late eighteenth and for most of the nineteenth century, attempts to unionize labour were largely unsuccessful due to the criminal conspiracy doctrine and the antagonism of employers. With the exception of certain craft unions, employers were able to check the growth of unionism by the use of the yellow-dog contract, strikebreakers, blacklisting, lockouts, skull cracking, and the support of the courts. Workers began to organize before Confederation in order to better wages and working conditions. Organization gained momentum after 1870. Canadian unions were heavily influenced by American craft unions. Later, industrial unions developed in Canada. In 1956 craft and industrial unions merged to form the CLC. Since 1900, the federal government has passed a number of laws that strengthen workers' ability to organize and bargain collectively.

9. The evidence from industry studies suggests that unions have been successful in raising the real wages of union workers over those of nonunion workers. However, research has generally concluded that it is difficult to say that unions have had any discernible impact on the average level of real wages received by workers as a whole.

Key Terms and Concepts

bilateral monopoly	money wage	TLC and CLC
closed shop	monopsony	union
craft unions	nonpecuniary considerations	union shop
fringe benefits	real wage	wage
industrial unions	strike	yellow-dog contract

Questions and Problems

1. The index of the general price level is constructed in such a way that it measures the cost of the "basket" of goods purchased by a typical, or representative, household. Suppose that two workers are paid the same money wage, and suppose that this money wage rises by the same percentage as the general price level year in and year out. Why might you expect that the real wages of each of these workers are, in fact, changing at different rates?

2. Explain why the level of real wages is a reflection of labour productivity. How do you think each of the following would affect real wages? How do you think unions representing workers would react?

    a. A law is passed allowing taxpayers an income tax deduction for expenditures on schooling and vocational training.

    b. Restrictions are raised on immigration quotas.

    c. The length of the workday is reduced.

    d. The size of the reward paid workers who have their suggestions—which they have placed in the employee suggestion box—chosen for adoption by the plant is increased.

    e. The tax on oil is increased.

    f. A new oil field is discovered.

    g. Laws are passed restricting the use of coal.

3. In the field of news reporting—radio, television, newspapers—average reporter salaries are quite low compared to the salaries of many other occupations requiring a comparable educational background. Earnings of long-distance truck drivers, for example, are much higher, yet far less schooling is required to do this job. What factors do you think explain these earnings differentials?

4. It is sometimes said that while unions usually oppose automation and the adoption of new capital equipment, ironically they may be a major cause of such technological development. Explain this point of view and its possible relation to the fact that the proportion of blue-collar workers in the labour force has fallen from roughly half at the end of World War II to roughly one quarter today.

5. Compare and contrast the advantages and disadvantages of craft unions and industrial unions as ways of organizing labour. How are the concepts of craft unions and occupational licensing related?

6. How would you characterize the structure of the following labour markets: professional hockey players, truck drivers, household help, the police in a town or city, blue-collar workers in the auto industry, shoe salespersons, fortune tellers, dentists?

7. Suppose that a monopsonist hires nonunion labour. Under what conditions would the monopsonist be able to realize the greater advantage: (a) when the labour supply curve is more elastic or (b) when it is less elastic?

8. Under what conditions would labour potentially be able to realize the biggest wage gains from unionization: (a) when the monopsonist's demand curve for labour is more elastic or (b) when it is less elastic? If the mobility of nonunion workers in a monopsony labour market is very low, how do you think their incentive to unionize would compare to that in a situation where their mobility is very high?

Chapter 17

Rent, Interest, and Capital

Wages for labour, which we looked at in the previous chapter, constitute by far the largest source of income in our economy. They amount to about 70 percent of total income when we consider not only the wages of hourly and salaried workers, but also that form of labour income earned in the professions (by doctors, lawyers, etc.) and by the proprietors and partners in the many forms of unincorporated businesses. In this chapter we will examine two other main sources of income, rent and interest.

No doubt, the terms *rent* and *interest* are already familiar to you from everyday conversation. In this chapter, however, we will introduce the more specific definitions of interest and rent that economists use. The theory of interest rate determination and its relation to the concept of capital is a complex subject. We will touch only on some of its more elementary aspects here.

Economic Rent

For most people the term *rent* brings to mind the monthly payment due on their apartment or the payment made to Budget or Tilden for the use of an automobile. Although we think of rent as a simple payment, we can easily see that it covers a host of costs. The rent on an apartment goes to pay property taxes, insurance, heat, maintenance, mortgage interest or opportunity costs, and other costs connected with the apartment building. Car rental payments go toward all the costs associated with operating a car rental business such as wages for mechanics, rent for counter space at airports, and taxes.

In economics the term *rent*, or *economic rent*, has a much more definite meaning than that often associated with the term in everyday usage. **Economic rent** *is any amount of payment a resource receives in excess of its supply price when there is* *market equilibrium.* The supply price of any resource is the price that the resource must be paid in order to cover its opportunity cost including a normal profit. In other words, it is the price the resource must receive in order to keep it from going into its next best alternative use. If a buyer is willing to pay the supply price, the resource will be supplied to that buyer. The qualifier "when there is market equilibrium" is necessary because resources will often receive *temporarily* higher payments while markets are adjusting to shifts in demand and supply curves.[1]

Economists first developed the concept of economic rent in connection with the nature of the payments received by landlords for the *use* of their land. Subsequently, it came to be recognized that other factors and resources also receive economic rent. First, we will illustrate the meaning of economic rent in the case of land, and then we will examine its meaning more generally for any resource.

Land

The most prominent characteristic of land is that it has a perfectly inelastic supply. It is an essential characteristic of land that its supply is fixed. In economic terms, the supply curve of land is vertical, or perfectly inelastic. Note that it is only the natural resource land that has a perfectly inelastic supply. Improvements to land are a different issue. It is possible to increase the supply of served lots or the fertility of soil. The supply of these improvements is *not* perfectly inelastic, and therefore these improvements do not earn economic rent.

LEARNING OBJECTIVES

After reading this chapter, you will be able to:

1. Define *economic rent.*
2. Explain why rent is viewed as a surplus.
3. Apply the concept of economic rent to land.
4. Explain how the concept of rent can be applied to factors other than land.
5. Explain why rent may be either an implicit or explicit cost.
6. Define *interest.*
7. Explain why savings is necessary if there is to be capital formation and therefore greater productivity by the use of more roundabout methods of production.
8. Explain the relationship between the rate of interest and the level of investment.
9. Explain the relationship between the rate of interest and the level of savings.
10. Discuss the factors that influence capital formation in the longrun.
11. Explain how consumer borrowing affects capital markets.
12. Give the reasons why there are many different interest rates, and explain their role in resource allocation and the important distinction between real and nominal interest rates.
13. Explain how the federal, provincial, and local governments in Canada influence the interest rate.

---

[1]The student is warned that economists do not always define terms in exactly the same way. We are now into an area of economics where a number of terms are used, sometimes in slightly different ways, to refer to rent and related payments. If you pay close attention you should be able to understand.

Economic Rent and Land

Economists first used the term *economic rent* to refer to the payments for the use of land. In early nineteenth-century England, the price of corn (the term used to refer to all grains at that time) rose to such levels that it became a matter of heated public debate as to what to do about it.

On one side of the debate were those who claimed that it was the fault of the landowners. It was argued that they charged farmers such high rents for the use of their land that the farmers in turn had to charge a high price for corn in order to cover their costs. Proponents of this point of view proposed that the government should control the amount of rent that landlords could charge farmers. Central to their position was the belief that high rents *caused* high corn prices.

On the other side of the debate were those who claimed just the opposite— high corn prices *caused* high rents. Perhaps the most lucid proponent of this position was David Ricardo, the renowned classical economist. Ricardo's analysis is illustrated in Figure 17-1. Essentially, he argued that the supply of land available for growing corn was fixed, say at the amount Q, and that it had no other use except the growing of corn. In modern economic terms its supply curve S was perfectly inelastic, or vertical. As with any factor of production, the demand for the land is a derived demand. In this case, the demand curve D is derived from the demand for corn, the final product that the land produces. It was argued that as a result of the Napoleonic Wars, there was a shortage of corn and therefore the price of corn was high. Farmers thus found it very profitable

FIGURE 17-1 Economic Rent for Cornland

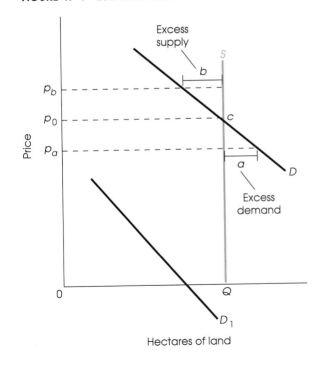

Hectares of land

When there is a fixed supply Q of a factor or resource such as cornland, its supply curve S is perfectly inelastic (vertical). Since the demand for corn is a derived demand, the position of the demand curve for cornland depends on the price of corn. If the price of corn is high, the demand curve for cornland is D and the rent per hectare of cornland is p_0, which is determined by the intersection of D and S. On the other hand, if the price of corn is low enough so that the demand curve for cornland is D_1, landlords will receive a zero rent per hectare for their land.

to produce corn. In competing with one another to obtain the use of the fixed supply of farmland, they bid up its price, or rent.

In modern economic terms we know that the price of the final product determines the position of the derived demand curve for a factor of production (as we discussed in Chapter 15). Hence, the higher the price of corn, the higher the position of the derived demand curve D for land in Figure 17-1. The price, or rent, p_0 per hectare paid by farmers to landlords for the use of their land, is determined by the intersection of D and S.

But what did Ricardo mean when he claimed that high corn prices caused high rents? Essentially, Ricardo assumed that the land had no other use, that it was simply there and the quantity of it available was completely unresponsive to any change in the price, or rent, paid for its use. Landlords simply rented their land to the highest bidder, and they would certainly rather earn something from it than let it lie idle. If the demand curve fell to a position such as D_1 in Figure 17-1, landlords would be offered nothing for the use of their land—its price, or rent, would be zero—yet the amount supplied would still be the same, Q. Historically, free land was not that uncommon. Early settlers to Western Canada were given free land, provided they fulfilled all the requirements, as homesteaders.

If the demand curve was D, then the price, or rent, was p_a and there would be an excess demand for land equal to the distance a. In their attempts to obtain land, farmers would bid the rent up to p_0 as landlords rented it out to the highest bidder. If on the other hand rent per hectare was p_b and the demand curve was still D, there would be an excess supply of land equal to the distance b. Rather than leave this land idle and therefore earning nothing, landlords in competition with one another to rent their land out would lower rent to p_0. In short, land receives whatever rent the demand for it dictates. If demand were low enough, land would be free. The price of corn determines the position of the derived demand curve for land, and landlords react accordingly. The landlords' role is passive. Hence, Ricardo claimed, the price, or rent, of cornland was high because the price of corn was high, not the other way around. Advocates of this point of view argued that the solution to the problem of high corn prices was not to control landlords but rather to lower restrictions on the import of foreign corn. This would increase the supply of corn and lower its price, thereby lowering the demand for cornland and reducing its rent.

Ricardo's analysis generally came to be accepted by economists as correct. It gave rise to the concept of economic rent. Economic rent, once again, is defined as the surplus, or amount of payment to a factor over and above its supply price, or opportunity cost, when there is market equilibrium. In the case of Ricardo's cornland in Figure 17-1, the economic rent per hectare is p_0, the entire rent, or price, paid for the use of a hectare of cornland. This is so because the cornland is presumed to have no other use (its supply price is zero) and therefore can be kept in the activity of corn production even at a zero rent. The total economic rent received by cornland is equal to the rectangular area $0Qcp_0$.

In reality, the determination of rent on land is more complex. Not all land is equally fertile or equally well located. As a result, some land is more valuable than other land. Soil that is more fertile produces higher yields and therefore higher rents. Land in the business districts of large cities can become very valuable because of its location.

Taxing Land's Economic Rent

The economic rent on land has struck many, economists and lay people alike, as an "unearned surplus." When population and incomes grow, the demand for the fixed quantity of land increases. The good fortune of landowners is to sit back and effortlessly watch the economic rents they receive grow accordingly as the demand curve for their land shifts rightward. How many times have you heard of someone who bought a corner lot on some sleepy country crossroads 20 years ago that is now worth a small fortune as commercial property on a busy suburban intersection? It has always appeared to many that economic rent is more a product of good fortune than the fruits of honest work. While the issue is only a part of the more general problem of how to tax in an equitable manner, it is little wonder that land rents should have become a ready target for taxation.

In the latter half of the nineteenth century, Henry George, a printer and self-taught economist, gathered a large following of supporters behind his **single tax movement**. Running on this platform, he was almost elected mayor of New York in 1886. The main objective of George's movement was to finance government by taxing away the unearned increment that landowners receive as economic rent on their land. George and his followers argued that in a growing economy, particularly in urban areas, these economic rents were an ever-growing surplus obtained by landowners without effort. To them it seemed only just that government should be financed by taxing away this surplus—that economic rent rather than the wages of the working person should bear the burden of taxation. Since the land was there as the bounty of nature, George argued that these economic rents rightfully belonged to the public and should be used for public purposes. This position was forcefully advanced in his popular book *Progress and Poverty* (1879).

Aside from its compelling normative appeal to the many of the public's sense of justice, a single tax on land has another advantage over most other forms of taxation—it is neutral in its effects on production incentives and resource allocation. We know, for example, from our discussion of excise and sales taxes in Chapter 7, that taxes typically affect the prices and the quantities bought and sold of the goods and services on which they are levied. The reason this does not happen when a single tax is levied on the economic rent of land is illustrated in Figure 17-2.

The supply of land Q, being fixed, is perfectly inelastic, as indicated by the vertical supply curve S. This, together with the demand for the use of land, represented by the demand curve D, determines an economic rent received by landowners equal to p_0. Now suppose that the government levies a tax amounting to 50 percent of the economic rent received on all land. In other words, 50 percent of any rent payment made for the use of a piece of land must go to the government. This tax is just like the sales or excise taxes we studied in Chapter 7. In particular, recall that when the supply curve is perfectly inelastic, as in Figure 17-2, the entire burden of the tax is borne by the supplier—in this case the landowner.

The position of the demand curve D and its intersection at point a with the supply curve S are unaffected by this tax. It thus follows that the price, or rent, p_0 paid for the use of a unit of land remains the same as before the imposition of the tax. However, after the government has taxed away 50 percent, the portion

FIGURE 17-2 **Landowners Bear the Entire Burden of a Tax on Land's Economic Rent**

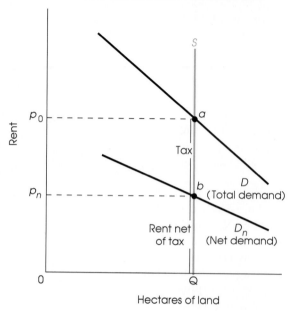

Suppose that the economic rent on land is initially p_0, as determined by the intersection of the demand curve D and the perfectly inelastic supply curve of land S. If the government levies a 50 percent tax on economic rent, D and S are unchanged and so is the rent p_0 paid by farmers and other land users. However, landowners now only receive half of this rent after the government takes its cut. From the landowners' viewpoint, the demand curve for land is effectively D_n, which is the demand after tax, or net demand. The economic rent p_n received by the landowners corresponds to the intersection of D_n and S at b.

actually received by the landowner per unit of land is p_n—the rent net of (or minus) tax. This is represented by the intersection of the net demand curve D_n with the supply curve S at b. The net demand curve D_n is the one effectively facing the landowners after the government has taken its cut out of the economic rent. Any point on the demand curve D_n lies one half the distance below the point vertically above it on D, a reflection of the 50 percent tax.

In sum, the full burden of the tax falls entirely on the landowners and there is nothing they can do about it, despite the fact they don't like it. The quantity of land is fixed and they must take whatever is given to them by demand. Since the quantity of the land Q and the rent paid for it p_0 are the same as before the tax, there is no distortion of resource allocation. This is true because if the rent p_0 paid by farmers or other users is unchanged, it means that the tax does not affect the prices and quantities of any products that use land as a factor of production. This would be true whether the tax is 10 percent, 75 percent, or any other percentage.

Difficulties with a Land Tax

Taxing the economic rent earned by land appeals to many in theory, but it is difficult to carry out in practice. The problem is that rental payments (as opposed to economic rents) cover the costs of other things in addition to the land itself, as we noted at the outset of our discussion of economic rent. For example, how do you separate out that part of the actual rental payment for agricultural land that is made because the land is more productive due to investment in land clearing, drainage canals, and other such productivity-increasing activities? Indiscriminate taxation of rental payments on land would discourage landowners from spending money to make such improvements because, unlike the land itself, the supply of such activities is dependent upon the return they bring in to the owner. To the extent that such indiscriminate taxation of rental payments applies to the portion that goes to pay for other factors besides the land itself, production incentives and resource allocation will be disturbed.

The same problem arises when we consider rental payments made on urban and suburban properties. A part of such payments covers the services of the buildings and facilities that stand on the land. How do you separate this part from the part that is the economic rent for the land? Is it really possible to do so? Rent payments cover the costs of the building and a host of other factors that have to be sorted out to get at the economic rent attributable to the land. To the extent that attempts to tax the economic rent of land in urban and suburban areas also apply to the rental payments on the buildings on this land, the construction of new buildings and the maintenance of existing ones will be retarded. Again, production incentives and resource allocation will be disturbed.

Economic Rent on Other Factors

The concept of economic rent first arose in connection with land. The supply of land was usually assumed to be unchangeable and to have but one use, such as corn growing. Given these assumptions, the supply curve of land is vertical. It is more realistic, however, to recognize that a given piece of land typically has more than one use. For example, farmland can be converted to residential and urban use. The greater the demand for housing, the larger the portion of available farmland that is converted to such use. Hence, the supply curve for land for residential use is upward sloping, left to right, rather than vertical. Because they have alternative uses, this is true of most resources that are used as factors of production. When a factor's supply curve is upward sloping, part of the payment to the factor is economic rent and part is the factor's supply price or transfer earnings. **Transfer earnings** *are that part of the payment to a factor which are required to induce the seller to supply that quantity of the factor.*

This is illustrated for oil in Figure 17-3, frame (a). Like farmland, oil is a factor of production. Some oil is near the surface, easy to find and extract. It would be profitable to produce at relatively low prices. Other oil, which is more difficult to find or extract, will only be supplied at a high enough price to cover the additional cost associated with its production. The higher the price of oil, the more oil can be supplied at a normal profit. As a result the supply curve for oil is upward sloping. The actual price of oil is determined by supply and demand.[2] The price of oil is p_0 in Figure 17-3, frame (a).

The supply price of the least costly oil is at p_1. It is possible for that producer to recover and market that barrel of oil profitably at p_1. However, that producer will be aware that the market price of oil is at p_0, so the firm will not be willing to sell that barrel of oil for any price less than the market price. The difference between p_1 and p_0 is a *bonus*. This bonus is sometimes referred to as as a *producers' surplus* or as *rent*. As in the case of farmland with no other use, this surplus is not required to induce the owner to transfer the use of the resource. Only the

---

[2]The authors caution the reader that the oil industry is *not* perfectly competitive. In spite of that fact, the analysis in this example is useful in explaining rent in general and in the particular case of the oil industry.

FIGURE 17-3   Economic Rent Results When Owners of Factors Differ in Their Willingness to Supply Them

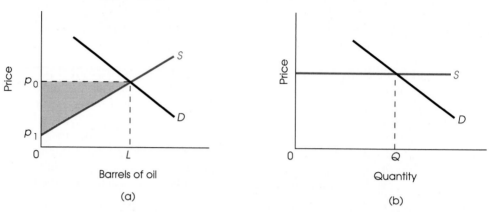

(a)   (b)

In a perfectly competitive market for oil, frame (a), firms differ in their willingness to supply oil and therefore have different supply prices. The upward-sloping supply curve reflects this fact.

The supply price of the first barrel of oil is p_1, so that in market equilibrium the first barrel earns an economic rent equal to the difference between p_0 and p_1. The supply price of each succeeding barrel is higher, but below the market-determined price p_0 that each receives. Hence, each earns economic rent (except the last barrel purchased). The total economic rent earned by suppliers in this market is represented by the shaded area.

If, unlike the situation in frame (a), all owners of a factor have the same supply price, no economic rent will be earned. In that case the supply curve of the factor is horizontal, or perfectly elastic, as shown in frame (b).

payment of p_1 is required to induce the sale of the first barrel of of oil. The total rent received at p_0 is shown by the shaded area in Figure 17-3, frame (a). Other factors with upward-sloping supply curves also receive economic rent that is represented in this manner. Even labour can receive rent. *There are many factors of production that have upward-sloping supply curves because owners differ in their willingness to supply the factor. Therefore, part of the price received for these factors by their owners is economic rent. No economic rent will be received if all owners of a factor have the same supply price.* In that case the supply curve of the factor is horizontal, or perfectly elastic, as is shown in Figure 17-3, frame (b).

Economic Rent as Cost and Surplus

Whether we are talking about resources with perfectly inelastic supply curves, such as any type of land that has only one use, or those with upward-sloping supply curves, such as oil, the nature of economic rent depends on whether you are a buyer or seller. If you are a farmer renting land to grow corn, the economic rent you must pay is a cost of production as far as you are concerned. Similarly, if you are a firm hiring labour, that part of the wages you pay that is economic rent is still a cost to you. From the standpoint of the owner of the productive factor, the economic rent is an excess above supply price, the price at which the owner would be willing to supply the factor anyway. From the owner's vantage point, economic rent is a surplus above that needed to engage the factor in the particular line of productive activity.

Explicit and Implicit Economic Rent

In Chapter 8 we made a distinction between explicit and implicit costs. (You might want to look back over that section at this point.) That distinction is also relevant for economic rent. Landowners might use their land themselves rather than lease it out, as is the case with farmers who farm their own land. Such farmers would be kidding themselves as to how well they are doing if their calculations didn't include the cost of using their own land—that is, its implicit cost, or rent. The implicit rent equals the economic rent the farmers would receive if they were to rent the land out to someone else.

Similarly, an owner who personally manages his or her business would make the same kind of mistake if the wages he or she could make managing some- one else's business were not included as costs. Moreover, the owner should not calculate the opportunity cost of these services as the price for which he or she would be willing to work somewhere else—his or her supply price. Rather, the cost should be calculated as the wage the market would pay for this work. It may well be that this market wage is greater than the owner's supply price. To use the supply price rather than the market wage would leave out the economic rent the owner could earn and therefore understate his or her opportunity costs.

Taxing Rent from Other Factors

Governments often tax all or part of the rent earned from the sale of natural resources. Royalties on oil and natural gas are a common example. Stumpage fees on timber are another. The same principle could be applied to fish stocks, iron ore, or any other resources. If ownership of natural resources is deemed to reside with society in general, then it is clearly appropriate for society acting through its government to collect the rents on such resources. Moreover, the tax is neutral—does not affect production—*as long as it does not exceed the actual rent*. In the oil example in Figure 17-3, the tax must be taken out of the shaped area in frame (a).

Checkpoint* 17-1

It is sometimes said that movie stars and great professional athletes earn large economic rents. Explain this observation. As a proportion of their earnings, how do you think the economic rents earned by presidents of major corporations compare with those of movie stars and great professional athletes? Why?

Answers to all Checkpoints can be found at the back of the text.

Interest and Capital

If you borrow money to pay your tuition or to buy a car or house, you must pay a special price called **interest** for the use of such funds. This aspect of interest is quite familiar to most people. What is not so obvious is the intimate relationship between interest and capital. In Chapter 1 we observed that businesses need capital—plant, equipment, inventories—to produce goods and services, and that they need money, or financial capital, to purchase this productive factor. It is the productivity of the capital that allows businesses to pay the interest necessary to obtain this money.

Why There Is Capital

Recall that capital goods are all goods created by human labour that are used in production. There are goods used to produce other goods. Factories, trucks, drill presses, and computers are a few examples. The economy has limited resources

POLICY PERSPECTIVE

Subsidized Job Training versus Labour's Economic Rent

In the early days of the auto industry, Henry Ford foresaw that the growing industry would need a large and increasing supply of skilled labour—tool-and-die makers, layout designers, and so forth. One way to get more labour into these trades would be simply to allow the increasing demand for such services to raise wages—that is, let the usual market forces of supply and demand solve the problem. Another way would be to subsidize training in these areas and thereby increase the supply of skilled workers. Ford tried the latter route and opened the Ford Trade School.

THE ALTERNATIVES COMPARED

The two alternatives have different implications for employer costs and skilled labour's wages. The difference turns on the issue of economic rent. This is illustrated in Fig-

FIGURE P17-1   Employer's Costs versus Labour's Economic Rent

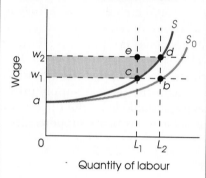

ure P17-1. Suppose that the objective is to increase the quantity of skilled labour from L_1 to L_2. Given the supply curve S for skilled labour, this could be done by raising the wage from w_1 to w_2, a movement from point c to point d on S. Note that this results in a

considerable increase in the economic rent paid labour, which is represented by the shaded area w_1cdw_2. Note also that a large part of this increase in economic rent has to be paid to the quantity of skilled labour L_1 that was already willing to work at the previous wage of w_1. This part of the economic rent increase is represented by the shaded area to the left of the vertical hatched line between points c and e—that is, the area w_1cew_2.

Now let's look at the other alternative—subsidizing the training of skilled labour, as Henry Ford did by setting up the Ford Trade School. This subsidy has the effect of increasing the quantity of skilled labour that is available at any wage level, as represented by the right-

continued on next page

and therefore can produce only so much output per period of time. Thus, if a portion of that output is to take the form of new capital goods, the economy will have to forgo a certain amount of goods that could otherwise be produced for current consumption. We know this from our discussion of the production possibilities frontier in Chapter 2. Moreover, if individuals in society are to be persuaded to sacrifice some current consumption goods in order to produce capital goods, they must perceive some gain or return from doing so.

Capital Productivity and Roundaboutness

The gain from the production of capital goods today essentially derives from the fact that it will make possible a greater production of goods (of all types) tomorrow than would be possible without those capital goods. Ranking in importance with the invention of the wheel was the realization that the most direct way of producing goods was not necessarily the most efficient.

Stone Age people discovered that it was usually more productive to take some time off from hunting game and tilling a plot of ground with bare hands

---

ward shift of the supply curve from S to S_0. This means that the required increased supply of labour L_2 can now be had at the same wage w_1 as before.

Compare the costs of the two alternative ways of increasing the quantity of labour from L_1 to L_2. It can be seen that increasing the available labour simply by raising the wage from w_1 to w_2 along supply curve S means that the employer will have to pay more in total wages than if the employer subsidizes the training of workers. The additional amount of total wages is represented by the rectangular area $w_1 b d w_2$, the largest portion being the additional economic rent represented by the shaded area $w_1 c d w_2$. Remember that this market is the demand and supply of labour services per some unit of time, such as a month or year. If the additional amount of total wages per unit of time is greater than the costs per that same unit of time of subsidizing the operation of the trade school, it will be cheaper for the employer to obtain L_2 labourers by operating the trade school rather than paying a higher wage w_2. If the reverse is true, it will be cheaper

for the employer to simply pay the higher wage.

POLICY IMPLICATIONS

Henry Ford operated the Ford Trade School through the 1930s. Then, with the great surge in the labour union movement after 1935, organized labour in the auto industry recognized what the school was costing them in terms of lower wages, in particular their forgone economic rents. Labour pressure led to the closing of the school.

The same type of issue is still very much alive in Canada today. Policy-makers sometimes advocate various sorts of government-subsidized job-training programs to deal with high unemployment among teenagers and in areas in the Maritimes and Quebec. If a new business were to start up in one of the Atlantic provinces, it would face the problem that while there was an adequate supply of available labour, much of it might not have the appropriate job skills. The firm could hire enough workers by increasing wages. Or it could do as Henry Ford and offer subsidized training. The latter alternative is not without risk. Once trained, the work-

ers could leave their employer and take a job with another firm. Clearly it would be in the firm's interest to have the government offer the necessary training.

One can understand why union members might have mixed feelings about such programs. One can also see why business often seems eager to cooperate with and lend support to these programs. If such programs are funded by the provincial (or federal) government, it means that employers can pay lower wages without incurring the cost of the training. It is important to recognize that while the already trained workers' wages are held down by such programs, many previously unskilled workers gain. Society may gain because of lower unemployment and a generally more productive labour force.

For Discussion

- How would you explain the fact that there are many fellowships and scholarships available for graduate students in physics, chemistry, and other basic scientific disciplines, while there are comparatively very few available for medical students?

---

or sticks and use this time to fashion stone hatchets and crude stone hoes to use in these activities. The first hunting and growing season they did this they had less game and food to consume than usual because of the hunting and crop-tending time lost to toolmaking. But in the next season, aided by their new tools, they were able to kill more game and grow more food than before, when they were hunting and producing only with the aid of sticks. This is a simple example of a roundabout process of production. A **roundabout process** involves taking time and effort away from the direct production of goods for current consumption and instead producing capital goods that will provide a larger subsequent production of goods than would be otherwise possible.

Just as in a Stone Age economy, modern economies, whether centrally planned like that of China or more market oriented like that of Canada, use the same principle of roundaboutness to increase their productivity. By devoting a portion of this year's production to the formation of capital goods instead of consumption goods, the total output of the economy in future years will be larger than if those capital goods were not produced this year. The current sacrifice of consumption to produce capital is rewarded by the gain in future production that is made possible. The larger the prospective gain, the more willing society is to sacrifice current consumption to this end.

Net Productivity of Capital and Its Rate of Return

The expenditure for a new unit of capital is typically referred to as *investment in capital*, or simply **investment**. You may think of capital as an investment in a roundabout process. How do we calculate the net productivity of capital and its rate of return?

First, since capital is only one of the factors of production, we need to know the portion of the total dollar value of the sales of final product attributable to it. By deducting the costs of the other factors of production from total sales, we obtain the dollar receipts of capital. The sum of these receipts over the life of a capital good minus (or net of) the cost of the capital good is a dollar measure of its net productivity. If net productivity is positive, we are usually interested in determining whether the net productivity is large enough to justify investment in the capital good.

In order to do this, we determine the ratio of the dollar measure of the capital good's net productivity to the cost of the capital good and express it as a percentage per year, or **rate of return**. We may then say that the **net productivity of capital** is the annual percentage rate of return that can be earned by investing in it.

For example, in a large, bustling city a taxicab might last a year (after that it becomes scrap). Suppose that a business firm buys a cab for $20,000, employs a cab driver for $30,000 per year, spends $15,000 on gasoline, $4,000 on maintenance, $2,000 on insurance, $2,000 for a license, and $3,000 in taxes. Also, suppose that the firm takes $2,000 per year to compensate it for its management services of running the cab business. Suppose that total receipts from cab fares for the year come to $80,000. Total costs exclusive of the cost of the cab, which is a capital investment of $20,000, are $58,000. Subtracting this from total receipts leaves $22,000, which is what is left to cover the cost of the cab. Subtracting the cost of the cab ($20,000) from $22,000 leaves $2,000. That $2,000 is attributable to the productivity of the capital good, the cab. The net productivity, or rate of return, on this capital good is therefore $2,000/$20,000, which equals .10, or 10 percent.

As we noted earlier, it is necessary to pay interest in order to borrow money. Since the interest on borrowed money must be paid with money, interest is expressed as a percentage rate just like the rate of return on capital. What market interest rate would the firm be willing to pay to borrow the money to buy the $20,000 cab and start its own taxicab business? Certainly not more than 10 percent, because a higher interest rate than this would exceed the rate of return on its investment in the cab and the firm would realize a loss. Any interest rate lower than 10 percent would allow the firm to realize a profit. Rather than borrow the money, the firm might choose to use its own money. But the decision as to whether to invest or not would be no different. The firm would not be willing to invest its own money in the cab if the market interest rate exceeded 10 percent. Why? Because the opportunity cost of doing so exceeds the net productivity, or rate of return, on the cab. It would be better off in this case lending its money out to someone else at the higher interest rate.

Economists frequently use the *present value* of a piece of capital to determine whether it is a good investment. This approach is useful because a firm normally buys capital equipment outright as opposed to leasing it. However, what the firm is buying is the stream of future production which that machine will create over its lifetime. Assume that a firm is considering the purchase of a machine that has a five-year life. That is relatively short for a machine but it keeps the example short. Further assume that this machine will produce net earnings of $10,000 each year for the five years and that it will have a scrap value of $5,000 at the end of the five years. It might seem that the machine has a value of $55,000 to the firm ($10,000 per year times 5 years plus $5,000 scrap value), but this overstates its value. A payment at some future time is always worth less than a payment now. If you have the money now you can invest it and earn interest until the future time. In order to calculate the present value of a $10,000 payment one year from now, it is necessary to discount that payment. It can be discounted by dividing $10,000 by 1 plus the interest rate. If we assume that the current interest rate is 8 percent then the first year's $10,000 return is worth $10,000/(1 + .08) or $9,259.26. Check it out. If you lend $9,259.26 for one year at 8 percent, you will earn $740.74 interest. At the end of the year you will have $10,000. The $10,000 return from the second year is worth $10,000/(1 + .08)^2 or $8,573.39. The term in the denominator is squared because the interest earned is compound. In the first year $8,573.39 earns 8 percent interest ($8,573.39 × 1.08 = $9.259.26). This amount then receives 8 percent interest in the second year. For the third year the $10,000 return must be divided by (1.08)^3, and so forth. In the last year the return is $15,000, the $10,000 net earnings plus the $5,000 scrap value. Therefore, the present value of the machine is

$$\frac{\$10,000}{1+.08} + \frac{\$10,000}{(1+.08)^2} + \frac{\$10,000}{(1+.08)^3} + \frac{\$10,000}{(1+.08)^4} + \frac{\$15,000}{(1+.08)^5} = \$43,330.02 \quad (1)$$

The **present value** of an asset is simply the value today of the stream of future income it produces.[3] A firm will undertake an investment project only if the present value of that project is at least as great as the purchase price of that project. In the example just given, the investment is worthwhile if the purchase price of the machine is no greater than $43,330.02.

The Demand for Capital

The demand for capital derives from its net productivity in the production of goods. Like the demand for any factor of production, this is a derived demand. Recall that the demand curve for labour is its marginal revenue product curve. Similarly, the demand curve for capital may be thought of as its marginal revenue product curve expressed in percentage terms, or what we have called its *net productivity*.

This is illustrated in Figure 17-4, where for simplicity it is assumed that there is only one kind of capital. The demand curve D is made up of the points representing the net productivity of capital (vertical axis) associated with each

---

[3] The formula to calculate present value is

$$PV = \sum_{t=1}^{n} \frac{R_t}{(1+i)^t}$$

where t is the time period in years, R_t is the return in the tth year, and i is the market interest rate.

FIGURE 17-4   **The Demand for Capital Depends on Its Net Productivity**

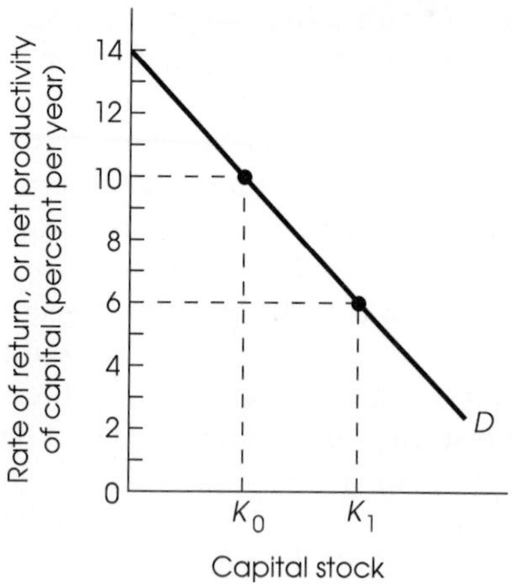

The demand for capital, like that for any other productive factor, is a derived demand. Its demand curve *D* may be thought of as its marginal revenue product curve expressed in percentage terms, or what we have called its *net productivity.* Because of diminishing returns, each additional unit of capital has a lower net productivity than the previous one, as is reflected in the fact that *D* is downward sloping.

additional unit of capital (horizontal axis). The first unit of capital has a net productivity of 14 percent. (The scale on the horizontal axis is such that one unit of capital is no larger than a point.) If the interest rate is higher than this, it will not pay to invest in this unit of capital. Note that each additional unit of capital has a lower net productivity than the previous unit—hence, the demand curve is downward sloping. This reflects the fact that the law of diminishing returns applies to capital just as it does to other productive factors, such as labour. Given the fixed amounts of all other factors, the net productivity of each additional unit of capital decreases as the total quantity of capital is increased.

If the market interest rate is 10 percent, for example, it pays to invest in capital, or undertake those roundabout processes that have a net productivity greater than 10 percent. Once the economy has created all the capital that has a net productivity of 13 percent, it will move on to invest in capital that has a net productivity of 12 percent, and so on, until it has exploited all those opportunities to create capital that have a net productivity, or rate of return, greater than 10 percent per year. Therefore, at an interest rate of 10 percent, the stock of capital demanded will equal K_0. If the market interest rate were 6 percent, the economy would desire to invest in all those capital projects with a rate of return greater than 6 percent, and the stock of capital demanded would equal K_1.

Interest and Saving

We have seen that to produce capital goods it is necessary to give up a certain amount of current consumption. Only by our doing so can a portion of this period's total production take the form of capital goods. The sacrifice of current consumption to the roundabout process of capital formation must be made up for by the prospect of a future gain in order to make the sacrifice worthwhile. In effect, society's ability to produce consumption goods and capital goods is limited by its production possibilities frontier. Economists call this sacrifice of current consumption *saving*. *For the economy as a whole,* **saving** *is defined as not consuming all of this period's production of output.* It is the extent of saving, or refraining from current consumption, on the part of the individual members of the economy that determines the amount of total saving. This total saving is the amount of this period's total production that can be devoted to the output of capital goods, as opposed to the output of goods for current consumption. In an open economy such as the Canadian economy, it is possible that capital formation will come in the form of foreign investment. In other words, foreign citizens will refrain from consumption in order to create new capital in Canada. Naturally, the future return on that capital will accrue to those foreign investors.

People save part of their incomes for many reasons—to provide for old age, to buy a home or a car, to assist their children in obtaining a university education, and so on. The attainment of these goals is the reward these people expect for the sacrifice of current consumption that saving requires. Another very tangible reward is the interest they can earn on their saving. While it is not necessarily always true, it is often assumed that whatever the other reasons for saving, the higher the interest rate received, the larger the reward for saving, and therefore the more people will be induced to save part of their incomes.

The relationship between the interest rate and the total amount of saving (or refraining from current consumption) for the whole economy is illustrated in Figure 17-5. The saving curve S gives the relationship between the interest rate (vertical axis) and the economy's total saving per year, or the dollar amount of that part of the economy's total annual output that may take the form of capital goods. The higher is the interest rate, the larger is the amount each individual will want to devote to saving and hence the greater is the total amount of saving. As a result, the saving curve is upward sloping. For example, at an interest rate of 4 percent, the total amount of saving would equal S_0, while at the higher interest rate of 7 percent, saving would be the larger amount S_1. It is important to note that the interest rate is not the only determinant of the level of saving. Income is an even more important factor in determining saving. However, at any given level of income, higher interest rates will mean more savings. Remember,

FIGURE 17-5   **The Relationship Between the Interest Rate and Saving**

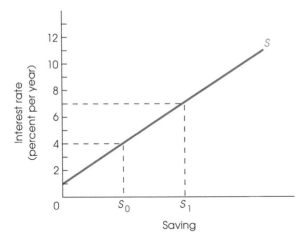

Saving is defined as refraining from current consumption. To this extent, it entails a sacrifice. Among the possible rewards of saving is the rate of interest that can be earned. The higher is the interest rate, the larger is this form of reward and the greater is the incentive to save. The upward-sloping saving curve S reflects this fact.

this chapter is based on the assumption that the level of income and the level of aggregate economic variables remain constant.

Interest Rate Determination

We are now in a position to lay out the basics of the traditional theory of interest rate determination. It is important to realize that this theory assumes that savings is a function of the rate of interest. Alternatively, it can be argued that saving is a function of the level of income and the rate of interest and that the level of income is constant. It is also useful to assume a closed economy (one with no international trade or financial dealings) with no changes in population or technology.[4]

This is illustrated in Figure 17-6. Frame (a) shows the economy's net productivity, or demand curve for capital, which is like that shown in Figure 17-4. Frame (b) shows the economy's saving curve, which is like that shown in Figure 17-5.

It should be emphasized that it is the stock of capital that is measured (in units of capital) along the horizontal axis in frame (a) of Figure 17-6. It takes time, often many years, for an economy to accumulate a sizable capital stock. Suppose that the economy's capital stock is K_0, the accumulation of many years

---

[4]The determination of interest rates is discussed in detail in macroeconomics.

FIGURE 17-6   The Determination of the Interest Rate

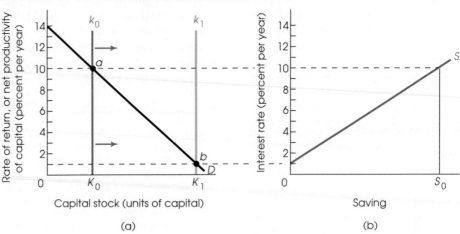

Capital stock (units of capital)   Saving

(a)   (b)

The vertical stock supply curve of capital k_0 intersects D at a point a, where the rate of return on capital, and, therefore, the interest rate, is 10 percent, frame (a). At this interest rate the economy is willing to save (refrain from consuming) S_0 dollars worth of the economy's annual production of output, frame (b). Lent out to investors, this becomes the dollar flow of investment, or expenditure, on new capital goods produced in the current year. As long as the interest rate is high enough to induce saving, capital formation will continue, causing the rightward shift of the vertical capital stock supply curve in frame (a). This will eventually drive down the rate of return on capital, and hence the interest rate, to the point where saving becomes zero. This occurs with a capital stock of K_1, where the supply curve k_1 intersects D at b, frame (a), to determine an interest rate of 1 percent.

of capital formation. This stock is represented by the perfectly inelastic (vertical) stock supply curve k_0. This curve intersects D at a, and the net productivity, or rate of return, on the last unit of this capital stock is therefore 10 percent. Hence, if the economy saves (that is, refrains from consuming) a part of this year's total production of output (a flow measured as so many dollars of output per year) so that this part may take the form of investment in new capital goods, the rate of return on these new capital goods will not be greater than 10 percent. Investors in new capital stock will therefore be willing to pay an interest rate up to 10 percent to induce people to lend them their savings so that the investors can buy newly produced capital goods.

But point a on D represents a shortrun equilibrium. Let us see why. At an interest rate of 10 percent, people will be induced to save an amount totalling S_0 dollars per year, as shown in frame (b) of Figure 17-6. Remember that the horizontal axis of frame (b) measures a *flow*, the dollar flow of saving out of this year's dollar flow of output. Lent out to investors it becomes the dollar flow of investment, or expenditure on new capital goods, produced in the current year. The new units of capital produced in the current year and purchased with this money are then added to the stock of capital K_0. (Assume for simplicity that there is no depreciation, or wearing out, of the existing capital stock, so that new capital isn't used for replacement of old.) Hence, over time the stock of capital will grow and the vertical stock supply curve in frame (a) will move rightward. Its resulting intersection with the capital stock demand curve D at lower and lower points down along D means that the rate of return on capital, and therefore the interest rate, will fall.

As the interest rate becomes progressively lower, it is clear from frame (b) that the amount of saving that makes new additions to the capital stock possible will also decline. Finally, when the capital stock has grown to the size K_1, so that the vertical stock supply curve of capital k_1 intersects D at b, the rate of return on capital and the interest rate will be 1 percent. The flow of saving will be zero, frame (b), and new capital formation will cease. The economy will consume its entire annual production of output, and nothing will be devoted to capital formation. Point b on D, frame (a), therefore corresponds to its longrun equilibrium position. *The existing stock of capital, together with the net productivity or demand curve for capital, determines the interest rate, which in turn determines the amount of saving. The amount of saving is the amount of total output produced that is not devoted to current consumption and that is therefore available for the production of new capital goods, which increase the size of the capital stock.* The longrun equilibrium interest rate is that interest rate at which saving becomes zero and new capital formation therefore ceases.

Why We Never See Longrun Equilibrium

To reach longrun equilibrium, we must move down the demand curve D and realize diminishing returns—because all other things are assumed constant. Of course, the other things, such as technology and population, do not remain unchanged. New inventions and technological progress cause the net productivity of capital to increase. This causes the demand curve D for capital to shift rightward. We know from our discussion in Chapter 15 that when the supply of one factor of production increases, the marginal productivity of other factors is increased. Therefore, increases in the labour supply resulting from population growth also increase the net productivity of capital and, likewise, cause the demand curve D to shift rightward. In a dynamic, growing economy the demand curve for capital will be continually shifted rightward as a result of such ongoing changes. Consequently, the rate of return on capital, and hence the interest rate, never falls to the extent necessary to reach the longrun equilibrium position.

In our discussion of the demand curve D in Figure 17-6, frame (a), it was implicitly assumed that the net productivity, and hence the rate of return on capital, is known to investors in capital with certainty. Any assessment of the net productivity of capital goods or roundabout processes undertaken can at best only be based on educated guesses about the demand for the goods that they will produce in the future. Given this, the demand curve for capital is subject to changes in such guesses, and changes in events will lead to a continual revision of these guesses. Shifts in business optimism about the future, which often occur rapidly, cause sporadic movement in the demand curve D and therefore its intersection with the vertical stock supply curve of capital. The interest rate will move about accordingly.

Historically, the saving habits of the economy have been much more stable than investor willingness to undertake new capital formation. This is not surprising given that saving is a decision made about the disposition of income already in hand (how much of it to save and how much to spend on current consumption) and the fact that savings is influenced by factors other than the rate of interest, while investment in new capital is based to a much greater extent on guesses about events yet to happen. Nonetheless, the saving curve in frame (b) of Figure 17-6 can shift around and thereby affect the rate of capital formation. This in turn will affect the amount of change in the interest rate over time.

Consumption Loans

From time to time some people choose to spend more than their total income on current consumption. To do so, they may draw down their own savings or borrow from others in the economy who save a part of their income. In this case the amount of such borrowed funds that the borrower spends on current consumption is just equal to the amount the lender must refrain from spending on current consumption in order to make the loan. What one consumes, the other doesn't. The aggregate, or sum, of all such consumption loans in the economy therefore does not affect the amount of total expenditure on current consumption. Hence, it does not affect the position of the economy's saving curve in Figure 17-6, frame (b). At any interest rate above 1 percent, total saving is positive. This means that the total amount saved by those not spending all their incomes exceeds the total amount spent by individuals on current consumption in excess of their incomes.

Why There Are So Many Different Interest Rates

Up to now we have talked about "the" interest rate. Economists find this convenient in order to spell out the basic elements of the traditional theory of capital formation. However, a casual observer of the financial pages of any newspaper or the behaviour of the numerous financial institutions in our economy knows that there are, in fact, many different interest rates. These rates correspond to the many different debt instruments issued by borrowers to lenders. These **debt instruments** are the written contracts between borrower and lender specifying the terms of a loan, such as the time period of the loan (or its maturity date), its size, and the rights of the borrower and lender under the agreements. Bonds, bank deposits, commercial paper, credit union shares, and mortgages are all examples of debt instruments. Interest rates on debt instruments differ because of differences in risk, the length of the loan, the marketability of the loan, and the structure of the financial markets.

Risk.   Risk essentially depends on the likelihood that the borrower will default on (be unable to pay back) the loan. The greater this likelihood, the larger the interest rate that will have to be paid to induce lenders to make the loan. A small company in a highly competitive space-age-technology industry will typically have to pay a higher interest rate to borrow money than Canadian Pacific does because there is a higher risk of the small company defaulting on its loan.

Loan Length.   Loan length, or maturity, refers to the duration of time until the loan must be repaid. Naturally the greater the length of time over which the money is borrowed, the greater the possibility that the borrower may run into financial difficulty somewhere down the road. Also, the risk that interest rates will rise, resulting in a decline in the value of the asset, is greater if the term of the loan is longer. Therefore, the interest rate on longer-term loans is usually higher to compensate the lender for these risks.

Marketability.   Marketability, or the liquidity of a loan, refers to the ease with which the lender may sell the debt instrument to someone else before the loan matures. If you write me an IOU for a gambling debt, I will probably be able to sell it to someone else only if I am willing to take considerably less for it than the amount owed. By comparison, the market for an IBM bond is much more extensive and well developed. The chances of selling it for what I paid for it are much greater. Interest rates on less-marketable debt instruments tend to be higher, all other things remaining the same, to compensate the lender for their lower marketability.

Financial Market Structure.   The financial market structure plays much the same role in determining the level of interest rates as product market structure considerations play in determining the price level of goods. A monopoly lender is in a better position to charge a higher interest rate than many lenders competing with one another to make loans.

Interest Rates and Resource Allocation

The existence of many different interest rates on the many different kinds of debt instruments in the economy serves the same kind of resource allocation function as does the existence of many different prices on the many different kinds of goods the economy produces. In reality, there are a large variety of capital investment projects, ranging from a tunnel under the English Channel to starting up a family-owned video rental store. Capital projects differ in their riskiness and life expectancy as well as in their size. Shifts in the demand for the products that capital goods help produce will cause changes in the capital goods' relative net productivity and thus in the interest rates they can pay to attract financial capital.

For example, during the last 50 years the increased demand for airline passenger service relative to that for railroad passenger service increased the net productivity of capital used in the former industry relative to that used in the latter. The interest rates that could be paid to attract financial capital into the building of airplanes and airports thus rose relative to those that could be paid to finance railways, passenger cars, and depots. Consequently, the rate of capital formation in the airline industry rose relative to that in the railroad passenger industry.

The problem of capital allocation has to be solved by every economy. Centrally planned economies such as China resort to some sort of interest rate structure to do this, just as do market-oriented economies such as Canada. The institutional structure surrounding the determination of interest rates, and even the terminology used, differs, reflecting the differences in political and ideological orientation between the two countries.

Nominal and Real Interest Rates

Up to this point it has been assumed that the price level is given—that is, there is no inflation in the economy. (*Inflation* is defined as an increase in the general price level at some percentage rate per year.) Suppose also that lenders are lending money at an interest rate of 5 percent, based on the expectation that there will continue to be no inflation. A lender just willing to lend out $1 worth of purchasing power today is induced to do so by the promise of getting back $1.05 worth of purchasing power next year, or 5 percent more purchasing power than originally loaned. In terms of goods, or "real" terms, the lender will be able to obtain 5 percent more goods today. The annual percentage rate of increase in the lender's purchasing power on money loaned is the **real interest rate**.

Now suppose for some reason that lenders come to expect a rate of inflation of 4 percent per year. They no longer will be willing to lend at a nominal interest rate of 5 percent, but will now charge an interest rate of about 9 percent.[5] Why? Because the dollars they lend out today will be worth 4 percent less in terms of their purchasing power in a year—4 percent less in real terms. Hence, lenders must charge an additional 4 percent in interest to ensure that they will still get back 5 percent more purchasing power than they originally loaned. In short, in order to continue to realize an increase in purchasing power, or a real rate of interest, of 5 percent, it is necessary to charge a nominal rate of interest of about 9 percent. *The* **real interest** *rate is the nominal interest rate corrected for inflation.*

In our example, when the anticipated rate of inflation was zero, the real interest rate and the nominal interest rates were the same, 5 percent. Only when the anticipated rate of inflation equals zero is it true that the nominal interest rate and the real interest rate are equal. The quoted interest rates we observe in financial markets are nominal interest rates. To arrive at the real interest rate, it is necessary to subtract the anticipated rate of inflation from these nominal interest rates. However, as a practical matter, it is difficult to measure accurately the public's anticipated rate of inflation.

---

[5] Actually the appropriate interest rate is 1.092% (1.04% × 1.05 = 1.092%).

The Government and Interest Rates

The government can affect interest rates in many ways. Two major avenues of influence are the federal government's fiscal and monetary policy actions.[6] Fiscal policy affects interest rates through government expenditure and tax policies. For example, if government expenditures exceed tax revenues, then the government must issue bonds to finance the deficit. Government bonds must compete for financial capital alongside private debt instruments and will cause interest rates to rise, other things remaining the same.

Monetary policy, as implemented through the Bank of Canada, affects the amount of money available to accommodate loan demand. If the Bank of Canada limits expansion of the money supply, interest rates will tend to rise, at least in the shortrun, as borrowers' demand for loans grows relative to the rate of growth in the availability of loanable funds through the banking system. On the other hand, if the Bank of Canada increases the availability of funds more rapidly than the rate of growth of loan demand, interest rates will tend to fall, in the shortrun at least. In the longrun, if the Bank of Canada continues to expand the nation's money supply at such a rate, prices are likely to rise correspondingly and cause the public to anticipate an ongoing inflation. As we discussed earlier, this means that nominal interest rates will rise relative to the real interest rate, as lenders attempt to protect themselves against the erosion of the purchasing power of the dollars they loan out.

Provincial and local governments also affect the interest rates by their issuance of bonds to finance schools, roads, and numerous other capital projects (or current spending) necessary to provide public services not covered by current tax revenues.

Open Economy

Interest rates in Canada are often affected by events that occur outside of Canada. If the Federal Reserve Bank in the United States decides to limit the expansion of the U.S. money supply, interest rates in the United States will increase. The Bank of Canada will then be faced with the situation that if they do not take action to raise interest rates in Canada, investors in Canada may find it attractive to invest their funds south of the border. Similarly, lower interest rates abroad may result in foreign funds flowing into Canada. Because there are no restrictions on the movement of money across the Canadian border, it is often difficult for Canada to maintain a "made in Canada" interest rate.

> **Checkpoint 17-2**
>
> How is a university education a roundabout process? How would you measure the net productivity, or rate of return, of such an investment in human capital? If for some reason people became less willing to save, how would this affect the saving curve in Figure 17-6, frame (b)? How would this affect the longrun equilibrium stock of capital? Why? Suppose that there is a sharp increase in the rate of population growth. How will this affect the position of the demand curve for capital in Figure 17-6, frame (a), and the longrun equilibrium stock of capital?

Summary

1. Economic rent is any amount of payment a factor, or resource, receives in excess of its supply price when there is market equilibrium.
2. Rent is a surplus because the payment of rent is not required to ensure the transfer of the factor.

---

[6]The material in this section is dealt with in considerably more detail in macroeconomics. Fiscal policy is discussed in Chapter 23, monetary policy is discussed in Chapter 29, and the international aspects of an open economy are discussed in Chapter 34.

3. Because land has a perfectly inelastic supply and is available whether or not it receives payment, any economic rent received by land may be considered a surplus. Taking this point of view, in the late nineteenth century Henry George initiated the single tax movement, which advocated taxing the economic rent on land to finance government. In theory such a tax would not affect resource allocation. However, in practice it is difficult to distinguish economic rent attributable to land from the return earned on buildings and other capital improvements on the land.

4. Any productive factor—not just land—may earn economic rent. The economic rents of productive factors are a surplus, but they are costs to firms and others who must pay to use them.

5. When factors are used by their owners, their economic rents are implicit. Implicit economic rent is equal to the explicit economic rent that could be received by a factor if its owner hired it out to its next best alternative use. That is, implicit rent for a factor equals its opportunity cost.

6. Interest is the price, expressed as a percentage rate, that is paid for the use of borrowed funds.

7. When an economy saves, it refrains from consuming a portion of its current output. This allows it to undertake roundabout production processes by devoting that portion to the formation of capital goods. The gain from capital formation is the net productivity of capital, measured as the annual percentage rate of return that can be earned by investing in it.

8. Capital's demand curve may be expressed in percentage terms. Plotted on a graph, the stock of capital demanded is measured on the horizontal axis and its annual percentage rate of return on the vertical axis. Any point on the demand curve represents that market interest rate at which it just pays to invest in the associated stock of capital.

9. One of the rewards of saving, among others, is the interest people can earn by lending their savings. Hence, *ceteris paribus*, the higher is the interest rate, the more savings will take place.

10. The existing stock of capital together with the demand curve for capital determine the interest rate, which in turn determines the amount of saving in the economy and hence the rate of new capital formation. The longrun equilibrium interest rate, where saving becomes zero and new capital formation ceases, is never attained because of continual technological change and population growth. Uncertainty, which plays a large role in the assessment of capital's net productivity, and changes in saving habits may also cause the interest rate to fluctuate.

11. A certain amount of lending takes the form of consumption loans. Summing across all borrowers and lenders this nets out, so the economy's total saving at any interest rate is the amount available for capital formation.

12. There are a variety of interest rates in our economy because there are many kinds of loans differing in risk, maturity, marketability, and the structure of the financial market in which the loan is made. These interest rates play the same kind of role in the allocation of resources as do prices in goods markets. Inflation's erosion of the purchasing power of money leads to a distinction between nominal and real interest rates.

13. The federal government affects interest rates through monetary and fiscal policies. Provincial and local governments affect interest rates through their issuance of bonds to finance the provision of local public services and the construction of public facilities such as roads and schools.

Key Terms and Concepts

debt instruments

economic rent

financial market structure

interest

investment

loan length

marketability

net productivity
  of capital

nominal interest rate

present value

rate of return

real interest rate

risk

roundabout process

saving

single tax movement

transfer earnings

Questions and Problems

1. Using the marginal productivity theory of factor demand, explain why some pieces of land receive higher economic rents than others.

2. Why is it often said that the economic rent of land is demand determined, unlike the economic rent of other productive factors? In what way does the levying of a tax on the economic rent of land have different implications for resource allocation than the levying of a tax on the economic rent of other kinds of productive factors?

3. It has been argued that if the economic rent of land is an "unearned surplus" that should be taxed, then so is the economic rent received by anyone who owns an unusual natural talent, such as a great singing voice or an above-average athletic ability. If land is a gift of nature, then so are such unusual abilities, and if land's economic rent should be taxed, it is only just that the economic rent of these abilities should also be taxed. Would you agree with this position? What difficulties might hamper the implementation of such a policy?

4. Suppose that you own some grapevines, and it costs you $20 to turn this year's grapes into grape juice. Suppose that after 1 year you can sell the juice as wine for $22. Assuming there are no other costs, what is the net productivity, or rate of return, on this roundabout process?

5. What is the relationship among the economy's willingness to sacrifice current consumption, the net productivity of capital, interest, and saving?

6. During World War II, many Canadians bought bonds sold by the federal government to help finance the war effort. Years later, these bond owners found that the real interest rate they earned on the bonds was negative. Explain how this could have happened.

7. Rank the following loans according to their riskiness: college tuition loan, mortgage loan, car loan, City of Toronto municipal bond, Brazilian government bond, and Canadian government bond.

Chapter 18

Income Distribution, Poverty, and Welfare Policy

Few issues generate more heated discussion and controversy than those related to income distribution, poverty, and welfare policy. These issues go to the very heart of the questions, For whom is the economy's output produced? What is a "just distribution" of income?

The kind of social order we call "capitalism," constructed on the basis of a market economy, was from its beginnings hostile to any political or "social" definition of distributive justice. The basic premise held by many of its proponents is that a "fair" distribution of income is determined by the productive input of individuals to the economy—"productive" as determined by the marketplace. Specific talents, character traits, and just plain luck enter into the determination of such productivity. Capitalism holds that this market-based distribution of income creates economic incentives that encourage the production of goods and services. Such production provides society's material standard of living, which is not necessarily shared equally by all. Naturally, this system (or for that matter any other system) may shape society in ways not everyone likes. Historically, market-oriented capitalistic societies have been reluctant to concede to any authority the right to overrule the determination of income distribution provided by the marketplace. Many supporters of capitalism would go so far as to argue that the unequal distribution of income that results from a market economy actually benefits everyone—because it increases total output and therefore the size of the share going to those at the lower end of the income distribution.

By contrast, noncapitalist societies historically have adhered to different notions of distributive justice. For some, distribution was (is) based on the individual's contribution to the *society*, not merely to the *economy*. Economic rewards are "socially" justified, as distinct from economically justified. For example, in the

461

Middle Ages the activities of the Church and the clergy were deemed to have a social significance and value that justified compelling ordinary people to provide their economic support. Similarly, the Communist party in the former Soviet Union did not try to defend its budget on economic grounds.

In the world there are not now nor have there ever been pure forms of market capitalism. Similarly there are not and have never been any noncapitalistic societies that do not allow some capitalistic, free-market practices to exist. All noncapitalistic societies recognize to one degree or another the need for differences in rewards, based on individual skills, as a spur to economic activity. Likewise, all capitalistic, market-oriented societies recognize to one degree or another that if the marketplace were the sole judge of the individual's claim to a piece of the economic pie, cruel hardships would befall some.

What can be said about these different concepts of a *good* society and the principles of *fairness* in income distribution by which they operate? In the abstract, the question of which principle of distribution is *better* is a normative issue. It cannot be settled by a mere appeal to facts. A society's judgment about this issue will depend on such things as its traditions, attitudes, social conventions, and history. It is pointless to argue that a society *should* be capitalist or socialist, if the vast majority of its people will not be bound by the different kinds of discipline that each of these systems requires in order to work.

In this chapter we will examine the measurement and determinants of income distribution in Canada. We will also study the economics of poverty, along with various programs and proposals designed to prevent or alleviate it.

Income Distribution

There are many possible ways to look at the distribution of income. Whichever way we choose, however, it is always the case that all the economy's income is ultimately received by households. This happens because households are the ultimate owners and suppliers of all resources (land, labour, and capital) used to produce the economy's output. Another fact that should be kept in mind in any analysis of income distribution is that reported income data usually do not include all the income that households receive. Unearned income (such as gifts and favours), income received in kind such as occurs in a barter transaction (Jane does plumbing for Bill and in exchange he does her bookkeeping), and

---

LEARNING OBJECTIVES

After reading this chapter, you will be able to:

1. Explain the concept of income distribution and show how income inequality is measured.
2. Summarize some of the major determinants of income inequality.
3. Explain the measurement, description, and basic causes of poverty.
4. Describe the social security system, its critics, and its problems.
5. Explain how poverty may be attacked through the labour market and by use of an income tax transfer system.

---

cash transactions for goods and services are all examples of income that *may* go unreported to tax collectors and census takers, our main sources of income data.

Keeping these limitations in mind, we will now look at the two most common ways of analyzing income distribution. These are the functional distribution of income approach and the size distribution of income, or personal distribution of income, approach.

The Functional Distribution of Income

In preceding chapters we have examined both the determinants of wages, rent, interest, and profits, and the earnings of the factors of production—labour, land, and capital. Since all income derives from the sale of factors of production, economists have long been interested in the distribution of income among the owners of these factors—that is, the distribution of income according to the function performed by the factor owned by the income receiver. *The* **functional distribution of income** *approach to the analysis of income distribution characterizes the way income is distributed according to the function performed by the factor owned by the income receiver.*

Rent payments are the money income received by property owners, wages are the money income received by labour, and interest and profits compensate those who provide financial capital and own businesses (either incorporated or unincorporated).

Labour, landowners, and capitalists were the three major social classes in the eyes of nineteenth-century economists such as David Ricardo and Karl Marx. The relatively clear distinctions among these classes perceived in nineteenth-century Europe are considerably more blurred today. It is now common for any given individual to receive income from ownership of at least two, and possibly all three, of these factors. For example, the rise of the corporation as the dominant form of business organization has made it possible for large numbers of the labour force to be capitalists through ownership of shares of corporate stock and the receipt of dividend income. In many cases workers own shares of businesses without even knowing it. For example a worker's pension plan may invest in corporate stock.

The functional distribution of before-tax income in Canada for selected years is expressed in percentage terms in Table 18-1. Wages include salaries, wages, commissions, and other benefits paid to workers. Corporate profits are the profits of incorporated businesses before taxes. Interest includes miscellaneous

TABLE 18-1 Percent Distribution of Net Domestic Income by Type of Income: The Functional Distribution of Income in Canada

Type of Income	1926	1934	1951	1961	1971	1981	1990
Wages	55.9	65.2	58.6	68.4	72.3	69.2	72.6
Corporate profits	11.5	12.0	17.2	13.3	12.0	13.2	8.7
Interest	3.3	4.1	2.4	4.1	5.4	11.4	11.1
Farm income	14.3	5.6	10.2	2.7	2.0	1.3	.6
Nonfarm income	15.1	13.2	11.6	11.5	8.2	4.9	6.9

Note: Columns may not total to 100 percent because of rounding. Income is before tax.

Source: Based on data from Statistics Canada. *Canadian Economic Observer, Historical Statistical Supplement* 1990/91 (11–210)

investment income. Farm income is accrued net income of farm operators from farm production. Nonfarm income is the net income of nonfarm unincorporated business. It includes rent. These categories are the same as those used in the discussion of the national accounts. It is interesting to note that the share of the economy's total income going to employee compensation has increased from 55.9 percent in 1926 to 72.6 percent in 1990. Over the same period the share going to nonfarm unincorporated business income has fallen from 15.1 to 6.9 percent. Farm income has declined even more rapidly, from 14.3 percent in 1926 to only .6 percent in 1990. These trends most likely reflect the declining role of agriculture and the growth of employment in corporations and the government sector, which has expanded significantly over this period. Corporate profits tend to be quite volatile on a year-to-year basis, reflecting the fact that they are what is left over after all other costs have been deducted from sales revenue. The share of interest income has increased in recent years, largely as the result of the generally rising level of interest rates in the 1980s.

Karl Marx predicted that as a capitalist society developed, the capitalist class would become relatively better off and workers relatively worse off. The trends in employee compensation, proprietor's income, and corporate profits shown in Table 18-1 do not appear to support this prediction. Adam Smith and David Ricardo predicted that landlords would become relatively better off and capitalists relatively worse off as society developed. If anything, the data in Table 18-1 seem to suggest that landlords who are included in unincorporated nonfarm business income have lost ground relative to capitalists. However, it should be reemphasized that the distinctions between classes are not as clear today as they appeared to economists a century or more ago.

The Size Distribution of Income

The **size distribution of income** *approach to the analysis of income distribution ranks all families in the economy according to the size of the income received by each, regardless of the source (wages, rent, interest, or profit) of their income.* The size distribution is also referred to as the *personal distribution of income.* It may then be asked what percentage of total income is received by families (or individuals) in different income brackets. For example, what percentage of total income goes to families earning less than $10,000 per year, what percent to families earning $10,000 to $20,000 per year, and so forth? The size of the income brackets is a matter of choice. Alternatively, this approach may ask what percentage of total income is received by the lowest fifth (or quintile) of all families, the second fifth, the middle fifth, and so forth. Any other fraction might be used as well. This type of breakdown for Canada is illustrated for selected years in Table 18-2. It is based on before-tax income.

The size distribution of income approach is thought to be a better indicator of the degree of inequality of income distribution than is the functional distribution of income approach. For example, among those receiving proprietor's income there are rich business people and poor ones, well-to-do farmers and subsistence farmers. Within each classification by type of income in Table 18-1, such income inequalities are hidden from view.

Reliable data on the size distribution of income in Canada is available since the 1950s. However, the earlier data is not completely compatible with the data

TABLE 18-2 Percent of Total Income Received by Quintile for Families in Canada

Quintile	1965	1971	1977	1983	1990
Lowest fifth	6.2	5.6	5.9	6.2	6.4
Second fifth	13.1	12.6	13.1	12.3	12.4
Middle fifth	18.0	18.0	18.5	17.8	17.9
Fourth fifth	23.6	23.7	24.4	24.1	24.0
Highest fifth	39.0	40.0	38.0	39.5	39.3

Note: Columns may not total to 100 percent because of rounding. Total income refers to total before-tax income earned by families.

Source: Statistics Canada. *Income Distribution by Size in Canada*, various years (13–207)

cited in Table 18-2 because it is for nonfarm families only. Examination of the size distribution of income over time in Table 18-2 indicates that there has been relatively little change in the degree of inequality in income distribution since 1965. What evidence there is for the period before 1965 strongly suggests that there was a substantial decrease in the degree of inequality between the 1920s and the 1950s but little change between 1950 and 1965.

Several factors probably contributed to this change. The Great Depression of the 1930s wiped out many fortunes, large and small, along with the high incomes often realized from such wealth. World War II and the accompanying full-employment years of the early and middle 1940s greatly boosted the average worker's pay cheque. The war also brought about a sizable increase in income tax rates. These were progressive income tax rates, so that the larger a household's income, the greater the percentage of that income taken away by income taxes. The effect of this tax structure as an explanatory factor behind the change in before-tax income distribution between 1929 and 1950 is a subject of debate among economists. For example, it is possible that progressive tax rates tend to dampen people's incentive to work harder and make more money, thus reducing the share of before-tax income going to the highest fifth of families. Alternatively, it is possible that the higher taxes reduce the ability of the wealthy to accumulate the large fortunes that generated the high incomes of the earlier period.

While the relative shares going to the different quintiles have remained relatively stable, the absolute differences in incomes between those at the bottom and those near the top have widened. Figure 18-1 traces the upper limit of each of the first four quintiles since 1965. There is a clear widening.

The Lorenz Diagram

A convenient way to represent the degree of inequality in the size distribution of income is to construct a **Lorenz diagram.** This is illustrated in Figure 18-2. The lengths of the horizontal and vertical axes are the same in the Lorenz diagram, and the units of measurement along each are percentages. The percentage of total families in the economy is measured along the horizontal axis, and the percentage of total income is measured along the vertical axis. Suppose that income were distributed equally among all families. This would mean, for example, that 20 percent of all families would receive 20 percent of the

...ges of Income Received by Each Fifth of Families

Shown here are the income ranges for the families in each of the first four quintiles for the period 1965 to 1990.

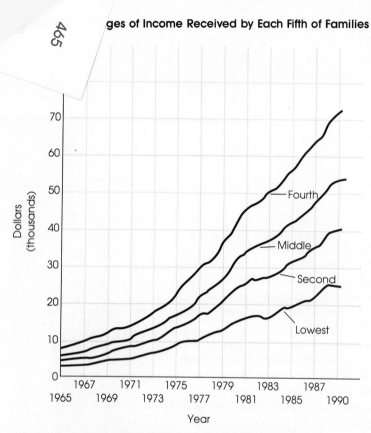

Upper limits for four lowest quintiles

Source: Statistics Canada. *Income Distribution by Size in Canada*, various years (13-207)

FIGURE 18-2 **Measuring Income Inequality with a Lorenz Diagram**

In the Lorenz diagrams shown here the percentage of total families in the economy is measured along the horizontal axis and the percentage of the economy's total income is measured on the vertical axis. The straight diagonal line in a Lorenz diagram corresponds to perfect equality in the size distribution of income. The greater the degree of inequality in the size distribution of income, the more bowed the Lorenz curve will be toward the lower right-hand corner of the diagram. For example, the Lorenz curve based on the data given in Table 18-2 for Canada for 1990 passes through the points a', b', c', and d'.

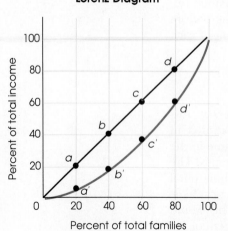

economy's total income, as represented by point a. Similarly, 40 percent would receive 40 percent of total income as represented by point b, and so on. Hence, if each family received exactly the same income as every other, this would be represented by a straight diagonal line passing through points a, b, c, and d, connecting the corners of the square Lorenz diagram.

Because the straight diagonal line represents perfect equality of income distribution, it provides a benchmark against which to compare the degree of inequality in the actual size distribution of income. Using the data in Table 18-2 for 1990, the curve (called the *Lorenz curve*) representing the size distribution of income in Canada passes through the points a', b', c', and d'. Point a' indicates that the lowest 20 percent of families receives 6.4 percent of the economy's total income. Point b' indicates that the lowest 40 percent of families receives 18.8 percent, the sum of 6.4 and 12.4 from Table 18-2. Points c' and d' are obtained in similar fashion.

The greater the degree of inequality in the size distribution of income, the more the Lorenz curve will be bowed toward the lower right-hand corner of the Lorenz diagram. If the Lorenz curve in Figure 18-2 were compared to one for 1929, the one for the earlier year would be clearly nearer to the right-hand corner. It is important to recognize that the straight diagonal line represents absolute equality. It may or may not represent a *fair* distribution of income. Whether or not a more equal distribution of income is more fair or not is a normative question. The Lorenz curve measures the degree of statistical inequality in the distribution of income, not the degree of inequity in the distribution of income. It does, however, involve normative elements. It implies that a dollar's difference in two individual's (family's) incomes is equally important regardless of the level of income. Obviously if the straight diagonal line is taken to be more than a statistical benchmark, it becomes normative.[1]

Checkpoint* 18-1

Table 18-2 and Figure 18-2 are both based on family income, but do not take into consideration the fact that different families vary in size. How could an adjustment be made to handle this factor? They could be based on household income. In that case the income of families and unattached individuals would be mixed together. What do you think that would do to the Lorenz curve? Why?

*Answers to all Checkpoints can be found at the back of the text.

Determinants of Income Inequality

What causes an unequal distribution of income? In many respects an answer to this question is as complex as an answer to the question, Why do people have different tastes and behaviour patterns? Some of the primary factors economists cite as explanations of income inequality are differences in the productivity of labour, market structure, the distribution of wealth, differences in earning power with age, the tax structure, and sheer luck. Let's consider each of these.

Marginal Productivity and Factor Demand

In Chapters 15 and 16 we examined how wages are determined according to the marginal productivity theory of factor demand. We saw that for any job, other things remaining the same, the greater is labour's marginal productivity, the higher is the wage that a labourer is likely to receive, and hence the higher

---

[1] Economists often prefer a numerical index of inequality. One such index is the *Gini coefficient*. It is numerically equal to the ratio of the area between the Lorenz curve and the straight diagonal line to the total area under the straight diagonal line.

will be the labourer's income. (Don't forget that a labourer can be anyone from a floor sweeper to the head of a giant corporation.) It follows that those things that determine a labourer's productivity are important determinants of the size of a labourer's income. They are also important to any explanation of differences in income among labourers.

As we noted in our earlier discussions, natural abilities, character traits, education, and job training are all important determinants of a labourer's productivity. Therefore, we would expect different endowments of these factors among individuals to lead to differences in income. Natural ability certainly makes it possible for Anne Murray to earn a larger income than the typical member of the local choir. Character traits referred to by terms such as "work ethic," "grit," and "stick-to-it-iveness" are difficult to measure but may be very important. Tom Dempsey was born with only one hand and minus a half of one foot, but he holds the National Football League record for the longest field goal (63 yards). Canadian history is replete with rags to riches stories.

Data indicate that there is a definite positive relationship between education and earning power. This relationship is illustrated in Table 18-3. It is tempting to conclude from these data that more education leads to higher income. But we should be wary of concluding that there is a definite cause and effect relationship—because of the *post hoc, ergo, propter hoc* (after this, therefore, because of this) fallacy that we discussed in Chapter 1. The figures in Table 18-3 are based on averages. There are millionaires who have had less than 8 years of schooling just as there are people on welfare who have had 4 or more years of university. Nonetheless, the data are *consistent* with the notion that education, or investment in human capital, increases labour productivity and leads to higher earnings. The higher earnings of the more highly educated are the result of not only higher wages, but also lower unemployment rates.

Market Structure

In our previous discussions of the four basic forms of market structure—perfect competition, monopoly, monopolistic competition, and oligopoly—we touched on some of their implications for income distribution. We noted that economists generally believe that monopoly and oligopoly, with their accompanying economic, or above-normal, profits, lead to a less equal distribution of income than do market structures more aptly characterized as monopolistically or perfectly competitive. We also observed that the evidence suggests that profits tend to be higher in those industries where concentration is higher. Not only are profits

TABLE 18-3   Relationship Between Years of Education and Income for Individuals: 1990

Level of Education	Average Income
0 to 8 years	$13,730
At least some high school	17,749
High school graduation	22,226
Postsecondary certificate or diploma	25,255
University degree	37,098

Source: Statistics Canada. *Income Distribution by Size in Canada*, 1990 (13–207)

higher, but it is likely that wages will also be higher. This source of inequality is particularly applicable to Canada because concentration levels are higher in Canada than in most other countries.[2]

In our study of labour markets in Chapter 16, we saw how the level of the wages depends on market structure. In particular, if there are many firms competing with one another to purchase labour services from a large union, the wage level will be higher than if both sides of the market are perfectly competitive. The wage level will also be higher if the labour market is perfectly competitive than if there is a monopsonistic employer hiring workers from a large body of unorganized labourers competing with one another for jobs. Clearly, the structure of labour markets will have an effect on the relative distribution of income between employers and employees. Professional organizations, such as exist for medicine, law, engineering, and numerous craft unions, which seek higher wages by restricting the supply of labour in their respective fields, also have an effect on income distribution. The existence of these groups tends to increase the incomes of those accepted into their ranks relative to the incomes of those who are excluded.

The Distribution of Wealth

Wealth includes holdings of cash, chequing and savings accounts, real estate, corporate stock, bonds, notes and mortgages, and life insurance. With the exception of cash, all these forms of wealth typically generate income, called *property income*, for their owners. The distribution of wealth in Canada is much less equal than the distribution of income. In 1977 the top 20 percent of families in Canada controlled 64.6 percent of the total wealth. The top 10 percent of families and unattached individuals controlled over one half (50.6 percent) of all wealth. While these proportions may seem very high, they are roughly the same as those for the United States and substantially lower than those for Britain and many other European countries. In 1970 the top 10 percent in the United Kingdom controlled 69.2 percent of the wealth.[3]

The reason that the distribution of wealth in Canada is more equal than the distribution of wealth in Britain is largely historical. Britain and other European countries have a wealthy landed class, the remnant of the feudal system. However, it would be wrong to assume that Canada is a class-free society. In spite of the strong relationship between education and income, it is not always what you know that matters, who you know can also be important. The old school tie from Upper Canada College is far more valuable than the school jacket from a core city public high school. Similarly, the "old boy's network" at the Petroleum Club in Calgary or the Royal Oaks Yacht Club in Victoria will land you a much better job than the "regulars" who have morning coffee at Frank's Truckstop Cafe. As Peter Newman says, there is a Canadian establishment.[4]

---

[2]Lars Osberg, *Economic Inequality in Canada* (Toronto: Butterworth, 1981), pp. 27–28.

[3]For more information on the distribution of wealth in Canada see Gail Oja, "Inequality of Wealth Distribution in Canada: 1970 and 1977," pp. 341–359 and Alan Harrison, "The Distribution of Personal Wealth in Canada, the U. K., and the U. S. A.," pp. 360–380, both in *Reflections on Canadian Incomes* (Ottawa: Economic Council of Canada, 1980).

[4]Peter Newman, *The Canadian Establishment* (Toronto: McClelland and Stewart, 1979).

Differences in Earning Power with Age

It is commonly observed that earning power tends to vary over a worker's life-time. Younger members of the labour force have less work experience and on-the-job training. In professional fields such as law and medicine, younger members simply have not put in the years necessary to develop the contacts and clientele established by their older counterparts. It usually takes business executives and managers a couple of decades to acquire the knowledge and experience that allows them to function at their full potential. The typical worker's earning power appears to increase up through the beginning of middle age and into the fifties. After that it tends to taper off until retirement age is reached. This pattern is illustrated in Table 18-4. The age structure of the population tends to change over time. Because earning power tends to vary with age, it follows that a changing age structure will cause the distribution of income in the economy to change over time, all other things remaining the same.

Tax Structure

On a par with the weather, people probably complain about few things more than taxes. Year in and year out there always seem to be some politicians seeking votes with promises to close tax "loopholes," aspects of the tax laws that frequently give (perfectly legal) special tax breaks, which usually are only useful to those in the highest income brackets. For example a $100,000 exemption from tax on capital gains is not likely to benefit an unemployed fisherman. Many believe that such breaks tend to make it easier for those who are rich to stay rich.

It is often argued that under our present tax structure those in middle income brackets who aspire to climb the economic ladder by work, saving, and capital accumulation have a tough time because too much of their income is taxed away. Indeed, as their incomes rise, a larger and larger percentage is taken because of Canada's progressive income tax rates. On the other hand, it is often argued that families living off the income earned from inherited wealth are the beneficiaries of lenient inheritance and gift taxes. Our discussion of the evidence on the distribution of wealth in Canada seems to lend strength to this point of view. To the extent that these criticisms are valid, our tax structure may well contribute to an unequal distribution of income. In short, one question will continue to be heatedly debated among economists and lay persons alike: "Are our tax laws such that it is easy to stay rich but difficult to become rich?"

TABLE 18-4   Average Household Income by Age of Head of Household: 1990

Age of Head	Average Household Income
Under 24 years	$27,834
25–34 years	45,656
35–44 years	55,694
45–54 years	64,664
55–59 years	56,761
60–64 years	51,270
65 and over	38,749

Source: Statistics Canada. *Income Distribution by Size in Canada*, 1990 (13–207)

Preferences, Luck, and Opportunity

Suppose that everyone were born with identical talents and abilities and given equal access to training and education. It would still be true that income would differ among individuals. Although all would be equally capable of being poets and engineers, those who preferred to be poets might well find their incomes lower than that of those who prefer being engineers. For better or worse, society's demand for poets might be slight relative to the supply, while the demand for engineers might be great relative to the supply. For the most part, differences in preferences will lead to differences in income, all other things being equal.

Good or bad luck, being at the right place at the right time or the wrong place at the wrong time, is also a source of differences in income. Similarly, opportunity or a lack of it has the same effect, a subject we will consider in more depth later in this chapter when we look at the problem of poverty.

Checkpoint 18-2

Using Lorenz curves, show how a progressive tax structure would affect the distribution of after-tax income as compared to the distribution of before-tax income. What effect do you think that the baby boom of the late 1940s and 1950s would have on the Lorenz curves of income distribution for 1970, 1980, 1990, and 2000?

The Economics of Poverty

What is poverty? Is it definable? What are its causes?

Poverty Defined: A Relative Standard

In general, a person is considered to live in **poverty** *if his or her income and other means of support are insufficient to provide for basic needs as defined according to some social norm.* Obviously, different societies, and different people and groups within the same society, may disagree as to what constitutes basic needs. In many underdeveloped countries of the world, tens of millions of people exist on a per capita income of less than $200 per year. (Income data for underdeveloped countries can be misleading, however, because in such countries much trade is carried on by barter and more goods and services are produced in the home and therefore escapes official money measures of economic activity.) In such countries a family of four with an annual income of $15,000 per year generally would be considered rich. In Canada, a family of four with the same income would generally be considered poor. Poverty is relative to what a society considers a decent standard of living.

A family's needs depend on many factors. Probably the most important is the size of the family. The size of the place of residence is sometimes important. Generally, it costs more to live in a large city than in a small town. The 1990 Statistics Canada low income cut-offs are shown in Table 18-5. They allow for different cut-offs based on family size and the size of the place of residence. Obviously they do not allow for special circumstances such as poor health that might affect a family needs.

While Statistics Canada does not refer to them as such, **low income cut-offs** *are sometimes regarded as Canada's "official" poverty lines.* "Official" definitions of poverty are always somewhat arbitrary. In Canada there are other poverty lines. For example the National Council of Welfare annually provides a somewhat higher set of poverty lines. It is based on 50 percent of the average family income in Canada. The merits of any definition are open to debate.

TABLE 18-5   Low Income Cut-Offs (1986 Base) for Family Units: 1990

Family Size	Size of Place of Residences				
	500,000 or more	100,000– 499,999	30,000– 99,999	Less than 30,000	Rural
1 person	$14,155	$12,433	$12,146	$11,072	$ 9,637
2 persons	19,187	16,854	16,464	15,008	13,064
3 persons	24,389	21,421	20,926	19,076	16,605
4 persons	28,081	24,662	24,094	21,964	19,117
5 persons	30,680	26,946	26,324	23,997	20,887
6 persons	33,303	29,248	28,573	26,047	22,672
7 or more	35,818	31,460	30,734	28,017	24,385

Source: Statistics Canada. *Income Distribution by Size in Canada*, 1990 (13–207)

Poverty is often much more than a simple shortage of money. Mere numbers do not tell the complete story. Poverty is also a human condition, as distinct from a statistical condition. When considering the statistics of poverty, bear in mind that there is a social dimension to poverty that cold numbers cannot completely convey. The population living in poverty, particularly in large cities and on Indian reservations, is often demoralized, as evidenced by higher rates of crime, juvenile delinquency, drug addiction, unwanted teenage pregnancy, and alcoholism.

Identifying the Poor

According to the Statistics Canada low income cut-offs, 12.1 percent of the total population of Canada was living in poverty during 1990. This was down from 23.1 percent in 1969 and about 27 percent of the nonfarm population in 1961. However, it was higher than the 11.1 percent of all families living below the cut-offs in 1989. Table 18-6 presents some selected characteristics of the dimensions of poverty in Canada for 1990. The data are mainly for families. As a

TABLE 18-6   Average Family Income in Canada and Selected Characteristics of Families Below Statistics Canada Low-Income Cut-Off in Canada for 1990

Median family income (all families)	$51,633
Low income cut-off, urban family of four	$28,081
Families below low income cut-off	12.1%
Families in Newfoundland	14.3%
Families in Prince Edward Island	10.2%
Families in Nova Scotia	12.0%
Families in New Brunswick	12.7%
Families in Quebec	14.5%
Families in Ontario	9.8%
Families in Manitoba	14.4%
Families in Saskatchewan	14.0%
Families in Alberta	12.9%
Families in British Columbia	11.9%
Families with young (age 24 or less) head	38.4%
Families with aged (age 65 or more) head	8.2%
Families with female head	40.2%
Families with head with 0 to 8 years of school	16.5%
Unattached individuals	34.1%

Source: Statistics Canada. *Income Distribution by Size in Canada*, 1990 (13–207)

benchmark for comparison, note that the average income for all families in 1990 was $51,633.

1. The incidence of poverty in certain regions of Canada is substantially higher than in other regions. Poverty is more prevalent in the Atlantic provinces (particularly Newfoundland) and Quebec. Even within Ontario there are significant pockets of poverty. These regional variations have been a chronic problem in Canada.
2. The incidence of poverty among families with young heads is very high. This fact is consistent with the earlier findings that income is correlated with age. In general, poverty among the young is not regarded as a serious social problem because as young workers gain experience and education, they tend to move out of the ranks of the poor.
3. The incidence of poverty among the elderly is relatively low. However, this has not always been the case. Until improvements in old age assistance programs in the late 1970s, those 65 or over were very likely to be poor. In 1969 over 41 percent of the elderly were below the low income cut-off. In 1975 the proportion was still over 21 percent.
4. The incidence of poverty among families with female heads is an ongoing problem. A family with a female head is more than three times as likely to be poor as the Canadian average. In part this differential is the result that most families headed by females do not have two adult wage earners, whereas many families headed by males do. However, in large part the difference is a result of discrimination against women in the labour market.
5. The incidence of poverty among the less educated is more than one third greater than the overall average. This finding is consistent with the earlier findings that income and education are highly correlated.
6. The incidence of poverty is much higher among unattached individuals than among families. In part this is because unattached individuals tend to be very young or very old.

Causes of Poverty

As you might expect, many of the factors we have already cited as causes of inequality in the distribution of income are also important causes of poverty. A lack of natural abilities, training, education, and opportunity, as well as labour markets that restrict entry, all come immediately to mind. Several other factors should be noted, including poverty itself, lack of political influence, and discrimination.

Poverty as a Cause of Poverty

Poverty can be likened to a vicious circle. It tends to perpetuate itself from one generation of a family to the next. Because a family is poor, it suffers from a lack of dental and medical care, adequate nutrition, and other amenities important to childhood development. A poverty-line income typically cannot provide sufficient fruit, vegetables, meat, and clothing or proper housing conditions. Newspapers, magazines, books, and other sources of cultural and educational enrichment are luxury items that must usually be forgone. All these conditions impair the ability of children in such families to perform in school and keep up with their more prosperous contemporaries. Discouraged in school, and often finding little encouragement in the home to pursue educational endeavours, these children drop out of school or attend only in a perfunctory manner, gaining little from the educational system. They are destined to have job opportunities no better than those of their parents. In short, because they are poor, they are poorly educated. Because they are poorly educated, the job market offers little opportunity for economic improvement. Because of this, they grow up to be poor and form below-poverty-line families of their own. The vicious circle is complete. Serious students of the poverty problem find the evidence on the circle of poverty disheartening. The odds on poverty-stricken families breaking out of this circle appear to be about one in five.

The Silent Poor

Almost every segment of our society has some kind of organized political voice. Labour has its unions. Various industries have their trade associations. There are even associations and societies that look after the well-being of animals. Almost all of these special interest groups contribute to political candidates sympathetic to their causes and points of view. All such groups have resources to devote to enhancing their political visibility and clout. The political voice of the poor is generally weak by comparison.

Living in slums, ghettos, and rural backwaters where they often have little visibility, usually disorganized and unsophisticated in the art of politics, their collective voice is weak at best or most often simply mute. Organizations that collect money on behalf of the poor often divert a good share of these funds to cover their own overhead. Naturally, the public becomes suspicious. Are these organizations merely using the poverty issue and playing on public sympathy as a means of providing income for a bureaucracy of middle class administrators? Perhaps not, but public suspicion that they are does limit their effectiveness.

Discrimination

We have already noted that the incidence of poverty among female-headed families is about three times higher than the national average (see Table 18-6). It was suggested that this differential was in part due to discrimination. However, women are not the only group to be discriminated against in Canada. Blacks, Asians, Francophones, the handicapped, and many others are sometimes affected by prejudice.

If one group can be singled out as the victim of the most severe discrimination, it is the aboriginal peoples of Canada. The following quote from the Fifth Annual Review of the Economic Council of Canada indicates how serious the problem is:

> No discussion of poverty in Canada can avoid making special reference to the Indian, Eskimo, and Métis members of our society. A few simple statistics tell a brutal story. One is that the average life expectancy of an Indian woman in Canada is 25 years. Another is that the infant mortality rate among Eskimos is about 293 deaths per thousand live births, more than 10 times the infant death rate for the population as a whole.[5]

---

[5] Economic Council of Canada, *The Challenge of Growth and Change* (Ottawa: 1968).

This quote from the Economic Council is obviously dated. Unfortunately, the underlying basis of the quote has not changed. The ongoing unrest on reservations is a clear indication of its current relevance.

While discrimination against women is much less severe than discrimination against natives, it affects a far larger group and as such it also represents an important social problem. Table 18-6 indicated that families with female heads were more than three times as likely as families in general to fall below the Statistics Canada low income cut-offs. (Compared to families with male heads, female-headed families are actually almost 4.5 times more likely to be poor.) Why females earn less than males is a complex issue, but there is no question that there is a substantial gap between the earnings of males and females and that a significant proportion of the difference is the result of discrimination. Table 18-7 shows the trend for male and female incomes.

Clearly there has been a narrowing in the gap between female and male workers. However, it is still very great. In 1990 the average male made $11,468 more than the average female. Part of the reason for the difference is that females are more likely than males to work part time. In 1990 full-time male workers averaged $36,863. For the same year, the average full-time female worker earned $24,923, or 67.6 percent of the male earnings. To the extent that female workers *voluntarily* choose to work only part time, part of the total gap cannot be considered discrimination.

Another possible explanation for part of the female–male gap can be found in difference in education. We have already established that there is a positive correlation between the level of education and the level of income. Historically, males have been more likely than females to graduate from university. In 1990, 17.7 percent of full-time male workers were university graduates, while only 14.9 percent of females were. On average, male university graduates who were full-time workers earned $51,772, and comparable females earned $37,236, or 71.9 percent of male earnings. While it is true that males are more likely to be university graduates than are females, for non-university graduates, females tend to be more educated than males. A higher proportion of females complete high school and earn postsecondary diplomas or certificates. On the other hand, it is not simply the level of education that determines income. It also depends on the field. Males have tended to major in better-paying disciplines than females. Males major in medicine, engineering, and management while females major in nursing, English, and sociology. Old barriers are being broken down, but some

Checkpoint 18-3

Colleges and universities have come under fire for not having more aboriginal students. However, some have argued that institutions of higher learning may, in fact, have little control over this situation, because the return on investment in the human capital represented by a college or university education is lower for aborigines than whites. How would you explain the rationale behind this point of view?

TABLE 18-7   Average Earnings by Gender

Year	Female Earnings	Male Earnings	Ratio
1967	$ 2,454	$ 5,323	.461
1971	3,307	7,056	.469
1976	5,785	12,390	.467
1981	9,687	18,115	.535
1986	13,469	23,467	.574
1987	14,221	24,673	.576
1988	15,054	26,236	.574
1989	16,292	27,628	.590
1990	17,141	28,609	.599

Source: Statistics Canada. *Earnings of Men and Women*, 1990 (13–217)

POLICY PERSPECTIVE

Regional Income Disparities

As was noted there are normally two different ways to look at the distribution of income. However, besides considering the functional and size distributions of income, it is possible to consider its distribution in a number of more specific ways. One such way of viewing income distributions is in terms of regions. The discussion on poverty indicated that families who live in Newfoundland and Quebec were substantially more likely to fall below the Statistics Canada low income cut-offs than were families who lived in Ontario. In fact, there are persistent and large differences between the incomes of families and individuals in different parts of Canada. These differences, referred to as *regional disparities*, are illustrated in Table P18-1.

As can be seen in Table P18-1, income in Ontario is well above the national average. The situation in the Maritimes and Alberta has improved while the situation in British Columbia has deteriorated. Otherwise the distribution of income between provinces has not changed much since 1961. There has been some lessening in the degree of inequality but not very much. It might be said that in Canada only three things are certain: death, taxes, and regional income disparities. In 1930 per capita income in the three Maritime provinces (Prince Edward Island, Nova Scotia, and New Brunswick) was 68.5 percent of the national average. In 1961 their per capita income had fallen to 62.0 percent, and in 1990 it was back to roughly where it had been in 1930—little change in spite of 60 years of government programs to lessen regional disparities. The problem of regional inequality is a difficult one. Much has been written on the topic, but it seems safe to say that no one has come up with a cure. However, there are some obvious factors that are important in explaining why regional disparities exist.

UNEMPLOYMENT AND EMPLOYMENT

The Atlantic provinces and Quebec tend to have higher average unemployment rates. In 1990 the national unemployment rate was 8.1 percent. The rate in Newfoundland was 17.1 percent; in Prince Edward Island, it was 14.9 percent; Nova Scotia, 10.5 percent; New Brunswick, 12.1 percent; and in

TABLE P18-1　Per Capita GDP Income by Province for 1990

Province	GDP/pop. 1961	GDP/pop. as a % of National	GDP/pop. 1990	GDP/pop. as a % of National
Newfoundland	$1,118	50.2	15,228	59.7
PEI	1,099	49.4	15,357	60.2
Nova Scotia	1,457	65.5	18,917	74.1
New Brunswick	1,340	60.2	18,232	71.4
Quebec	2,017	90.7	23,225	91.0
Ontario	2,674	120.2	28,862	113.1
Manitoba	2,004	90.1	21,977	86.1
Saskatchewan	1,735	78.0	20,504	80.3
Alberta	2,420	108.8	28,808	112.9
BC	2,480	111.5	25,934	101.6
Canada	2,225	100.0	25,523	100.0

Source: Statistics Canada. *Canadian Economic Observer, Historical Statistical Supplement,* 1990/91 (11–210)

continued on next page

remain. In any case, differences in the quantity and type of education cannot explain anywhere near the total gap between males and females.

One last factor may account for some of the gap. In general, female workers have less experience than male workers. In 1990 13.2 percent of the male workers had 20 years or more of tenure with their present employer. Only 5.4 percent of the female workers had similar length of service.

Still, when all the explanatory factors are considered there is a residue left from the original gap which cannot be explained. This residue represents

POLICY PERSPECTIVE CONTINUED

Quebec the rate was 10.1 percent. Not only were there more workers unemployed in the five eastern provinces, but they also had lower labour participation rates. The national participation rate in 1990 was 67.0 percent, but the five eastern provinces had participation rates ranging from 56.0 percent in Newfoundland to 66.0 percent in Prince Edward Island. Taken together, the higher unemployment rate and the lower participation rate means that a smaller proportion of the population was working in these provinces than nationally. If fewer people are working, per capita income will be lower. Assume that there are only two regions. Each has 10 people. In region A, 60 percent are working. In B only 50 percent are working. Each worker earns $10,000 per year. The total income for A will be $60,000 and the total for B will be $50,000. The per capita income of A will be $6,000 compared to $5,000 for B. A significant portion of the lower income in the five eastern provinces can be attributed to the fact that a lower proportion of the population are employed.

WORKER PRODUCTIVITY

While the lower employment rates can explain a substantial part of the below-average incomes in eastern Canada, they do not completely explain the problem of regional disparities. Not only are individuals less likely to be employed, those who are employed tend to earn lower wages. In 1990 average weekly earnings in Canada were $512.79. In the five eastern provinces average weekly earnings range from a high of $502.02 (97.9 percent of the national average) in Quebec to $419.63 (81.8 percent) in Prince Edward Island. The lower earnings reflect lower worker productivity. Lower productivity may be the result of worker training. Education tends to be highly correlated with productivity. The labour force in some parts of the eastern provinces is less educated than in the rest of Canada. (The level of education varies substantially from province to province and within provinces, so this generalization does not apply universally within the area.)

Worker productivity also depends upon the capital stock. Workers in modern, capital-intensive plants have higher productivity than workers in older or less capital-intensive plants. In general, the capital to labour ratio is lower in eastern Canada than in the rest of Canada and the average age of capital is older. Consequently workers are less productive and are paid less. Many government policies aimed at reducing regional disparities have attempted to increase the level of investment in the poorer regions of Canada.

INDUSTRIAL MIX

Manitoba and Saskatchewan also have low incomes, but they have average unemployment and participation rates. Workers in these provinces tend to be relatively well educated and the capital stock in these provinces tends to be relatively large. Still, these are low-income provinces. This is in large part due to the importance of agriculture in their economies. Returns in agriculture tend to be lower than returns in manufacturing. This is in part due to the more competitive nature of agriculture. It is also an industry with less growth potential. As a society's income rises, the demand for most manufactured goods increases more than proportionally, but the demand for food increases very little. The industrial mix is also important in understanding the problem in the Atlantic provinces. Their dependence on the fisheries and light manufacturing is a factor in their depressed income.

For Discussion

- Wages tend to be lower in depressed regions than in the rest of Canada. This wage gap has resulted in outmigration from the Atlantic provinces to Ontario and the West. As workers leave the Atlantic region what does that do to the supply of labour? What would economic theory predict would happen to wages in that region? What should happen to wages in Ontario and the West as the new workers arrive? Why might workers not migrate even if wages are higher in another region?

discrimination. Much of this discrimination is the result of occupational segregation. Because females find entry into many better-paying occupations made difficult, they tend to be crowded into a limited number of "female" jobs. This crowding increases the supply of workers in these positions and forces down the wage rate. It is often said that female workers are crowded into *pink-collar ghettos*. While progress is being made, there is still substantial discrimination against women.

Social Programs

As a result of illness, injury, death, retirement, or unemployment, a family or individual may suffer a drastic loss of income and consequent unavoidable economic hardships. The Great Depression of the 1930s dramatized this problem for large numbers of people. In an effort to provide families and individuals with some protection against such calamities, Parliament has passed a substantial body of social legislation. There are a number of programs in Canada that taken together provide a safety net for residents. These programs generally have at least some federal government involvement. In many cases they are essentially federal programs although they constitutionally may be under provincial jurisdiction. Many of these programs redistribute income.

Old Age Programs

In Canada the public provision of pensions dates back to before the Great Depression. *The Old Age Pensions Act* of 1927 was the beginning of public pensions in Canada. This act established a joint federal-provincial pension plan. The two levels of government shared the cost. The plan was *means tested* and paid a maximum monthly benefit of $20. To be eligible for a means-tested program, an individual must demonstrate (usually on the basis of income) a need for the benefit. Old age security has evolved over the years into the three-part system that is in place today. The three parts are Old Age Security (OAS), Guaranteed Income Supplement (GIS), and Canada Pension Plan (CPP). In Quebec, the CPP is replaced by the Quebec Pension Plan (QPP).

Old Age Security (OAS) is a universal plan (not means tested) for all Canadian residents at age 65. As of April 1, 1991, it paid $362.37 monthly to an unattached individual or $724.74 for a married couple. OAS payments are indexed every quarter. The payments received under OAS are taxable income. In addition to the standard old age pensions, spouse's allowances are available to spouses of OAS recipients and widow(er)s of former recipients who are between 60 and 64. In the April 1989 budget speech, the federal government proposed ending the universal nature of OAS payments. However, as of the time this book was written this proposal had not been made law.

Guaranteed Income Supplement (GIS) is a means-tested plan intended to augment the income of seniors with little or no other source of income than OAS. The maximum monthly benefit under GIS is $430.65 for an individual or $561 for a couple. Benefits are reduced by $.50 for every dollar of income received other than OAS. Like OAS, GIS is indexed quarterly. In addition there have from time to time been ad hoc increases. GIS payments are not taxable income.

OAS and GIS are both noncontributory programs. Canadian residents automatically qualify for benefits without having to pay into the programs. The **Canadian** and **Quebec Pension Plans (CPP)** and **(QPP)** are different. In order to receive benefits one must have contributed. In the case of employed workers, both the employees and employers contribute to CPP (QPP). In 1990 both contributed 2.2 percent of the employee's salary up to an annual maximum income of $26,100. Self-employed workers must contribute the entire 4.4 percent. The maximum income subject to contributions changes annually to reflect the average industrial wage in Canada. The contribution rates are projected to increase gradually until they reach 2.9 percent from employer and 2.9 percent from employee in 1999. Even with these increases CPP (QPP) will run into problems early in the twenty-first century. In the past, contributions to CPP (QPP) have always exceeded the benefits that had to be paid. As the babyboomers reach retirement age this will no longer be true. As a result, either contributions will have to be increased even more, funds will have to be taken out of general revenue, or benefits will have to fall.

Benefits under CPP (QPP) are based on the individual's accumulated contributions. Consequently benefits for higher-waged workers (up to the average industrial wage) are greater than those for lower-waged workers. Similarly workers with more years of employment receive higher pensions than those with fewer years of employment. Elderly who have never been employed are not eligible for any benefits in their own right under CPP (QPP). This means that many elderly women who worked as housewives are excluded. As of April, 1991, the maximum monthly benefit under CPP (QPP) was $604.86 per month. Basically, CPP (QPP) is designed to replace about 25 percent of a worker's preretirement income. The maximum benefit is 25 percent of the average industrial wage. The benefit payments are indexed. Normally, benefits commence at age 65. CPP (QPP) also pays disability and survivor's benefits.

Some provinces have modest supplemental programs in addition to the federal programs. The government also provides tax relief for individuals who save for their own retirement through contributions to registered employer pension plans and registered retirement savings plans (RRSPs). While such plans do not represent a direct expenditure on the part of the federal or provincial governments, they do represent a cost in terms of taxes not collected. Taken together, all income provision programs ensure that most elderly couples have an income that is above the poverty line. However, many unattached elderly, usually women, do not have incomes high enough to meet the Statistics Canada low income cut-offs. Still, the situation has improved dramatically since the mid-1970s, when about 20 percent of the elderly families and over half of the elderly single individuals lived below the low income cut-offs.

The various levels of government in Canada also provide assistance to the young. The Canadian government transfers money to parents of children in the form of *family allowances* and *child tax credits*. Family allowance is a universal program, but the payments vary from province to province. Family allowance benefits are taxable. Because child tax credits are means tested, they are only paid to low-income families.

In addition to the programs just discussed, which provide cash transfers, there are a number of programs that redistribute income in kind. Income in kind refers to income that comes as goods or services instead of cash. Government expenditures on education and medical care represent redistribution in kind. Naturally, expenditures on education tend to redistribute income to younger Canadians. Expenditures on medical care benefit all Canadians, but particularly the young and the elderly.

Unemployment Insurance

Except for CPP (QPP), all the programs discussed to this point are social assistance programs. They are funded out of general revenue and represent a transfer of income from society in general to a specific group within society. CPP (QPP) is different. It is self-financed. The funding for CPP (QPP) comes from contributions made by workers and employers. These contributions then provide the revenue to pay benefits. [Unless some changes are made, CPP (QPP) will not remain self-financing much after the turn of the century.] The pension portion of CPP (QPP) essentially is a government-sponsored savings program. Payments to survivors and the disabled are insurance benefits. **Unemployment Insurance (UI)** is also a government-sponsored insurance plan.

Payments under UI are not welfare payments. As with CPP (QPP), both the employer and the employee pay premiums. In 1991 the employee paid $2.25 per $100 of insurable income. The maximum insurable income for 1991 was $680 weekly. The employer pays 1.4 times the employee contribution. The employees contribution is tax deductible, and benefits received are taxable income. Unemployed workers receive 60 percent of the average insured earnings based on the qualifying period. Normally, workers must have worked at least 20 weeks during the last year or since last collecting UI benefits, whichever is shorter. In areas of high unemployment, the qualifying period is shortened. The maximum period for which a worker can receive benefits depends upon how many weeks the worker has worked since last receiving UI benefits and the level of unemployment in the area. No worker can receive benefits for more than 50 consecutive weeks. Workers involved in commercial fishing may be eligible for special benefits. A worker may earn up to 25 percent of her or his benefits while on UI. If he or she earns more than 25 percent, benefits are reduced on a dollar per dollar basis for each dollar of earnings over 25 percent. Workers who quit their job without just cause, refuse a suitable job, or are dismissed from their previous job for cause can only receive 50 percent of their maximum insurable earnings. UI pays benefits for workers on maternity leave or who are temporarily ill.

UI has been subjected to substantial criticism. Much of the criticism suggests that UI is too generous and qualification for benefits is too easy. As a result, unemployment rates are higher than they otherwise would be. Because unemployment rates have been higher than anticipated, UI has required additional funding out of general revenue. On the other hand, UI is an automatic stabilizer and as a result it helps ensure that there is not another depression such as occurred in the 1930s.

Workers' Compensation

UI is intended to help workers who are temporarily out of work. It is not intended to deal with workers who suffer injuries related to their work that result in long-term or even permanent disability. Such workers are dealt with under workers' compensation programs. These programs fall under provincial jurisdiction. Ontario and Nova Scotia were the first provinces to introduce workers' compensation. Their programs began in 1915. Today every province has a workers' compensation board. The coverage and level of benefits vary greatly from province to province. All programs are financed through a payroll tax. Generally, premiums are higher for jobs that involve higher risks of injury. Workers' compensation plans generally protect employers against legal action by workers.

A CAPSULE REVIEW

The following eight pages make up a self-contained unit of graphs, charts, tables, and brief statements of key concepts in microeconomics. These pages are designed to be a quick reference section on important ideas in microeconomics. The chapter number given at the center of each item refers to the text chapter where the concept is discussed more fully.

OPPORTUNITY COST

The opportunity cost of a unit of a good is measured in terms of the other goods that must be forgone in order to obtain it.

Chapter 2

THE LAW OF DEMAND

The law of demand says that larger quantities of a good will be demanded at lower prices than at higher prices, *ceteris paribus* (all other things remaining the same).

Chapter 4

THE LAW OF SUPPLY

The law of supply says that suppliers will supply larger quantities of a good at higher prices than at lower prices, *ceteris paribus* .

Chapter 4

MOVEMENT ALONG A CURVE VERSUS SHIFTS IN A CURVE

A *movement along* a demand or supply curve depicts the change in quantity demanded or supplied that results from a change in the price of the good, *ceteris paribus.* If one or more of the other variables change, there will be a *shift* in the curve.

Chapter 4

MARKET DEMAND AND SUPPLY DETERMINE THE EQUILIBRIUM COMBINATION OF PRICE AND QUANTITY OF A GOOD. THE LAWS OF SUPPLY AND DEMAND ARE IMPORTANT BECAUSE TOGETHER THEY EXPLAIN HOW MARKETS WORK.

DETERMINING EQUILIBRIUM PRICE AND QUANTITY

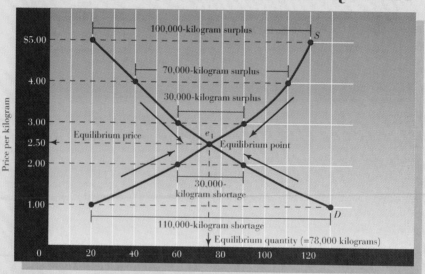

Quantity of hamburger (in thousands of kilograms per month)

The determination of the equilibrium price and quantity is indicated by the intersection of the market demand curve *D* and the market supply curve *S* at e_1. At prices above the equilibrium price, there will be surpluses (unsold hamburger) that cause a competitive bidding down of price, leading producers to reduce the quantity supplied and consumers to increase the quantity demanded until equilibrium is achieved. At prices below the equilibrium price, there will be shortages that cause a competitive bidding up of price, increasing the quantity supplied and decreasing the quantity demanded until equilibrium is achieved.

Chapter 4

PRICE ELASTICITY IS IMPORTANT BECAUSE IT ALLOWS US TO DESCRIBE THE RESPONSIVENESS OF THE QUANTITY DEMANDED OR SUPPLIED OF A GOOD TO A CHANGE IN ITS PRICE AT DIFFERENT POINTS ON THE DEMAND OR SUPPLY CURVE.

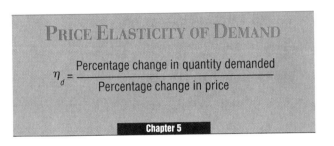

PRICE ELASTICITY OF DEMAND

$$\eta_d = \frac{\text{Percentage change in quantity demanded}}{\text{Percentage change in price}}$$

Chapter 5

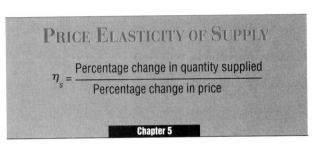

PRICE ELASTICITY OF SUPPLY

$$\eta_s = \frac{\text{Percentage change in quantity supplied}}{\text{Percentage change in price}}$$

Chapter 5

RELATION BETWEEN ELASTICITY OF DEMAND AND TOTAL REVENUE

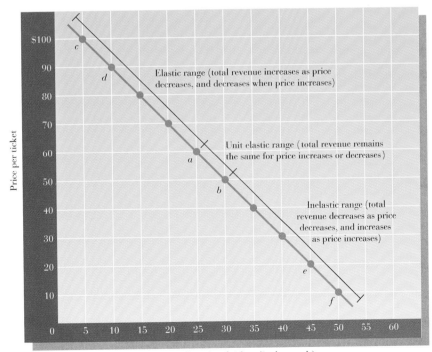

Quantity of tickets (in thousands)

Total revenue (price per ticket times number of tickets demanded at that price) gets larger as we move down the demand curve from left to right over the elastic range. Total revenue reaches its maximum over the unit elastic range and gets smaller as we move down the demand curve over the inelastic range.

Chapter 5

THE LAW OF DIMINISHING RETURNS GOVERNS THE WAY THE FIRM'S VARIABLE COSTS CHANGE AS OUTPUT IS CHANGED IN THE SHORTRUN.

LAW OF DIMINISHING RETURNS

As more and more of a variable factor of production, or input (such as labour), is used together with other fixed factors of production (such as capital), there comes a point beyond which the additional, or marginal, product attributable to each additional unit of the variable factor begins to fall.

Chapter 8

THE LAW OF DIMINISHING RETURNS ILLUSTRATED

Frame (a) shows how larger quantities of total output (vertical axis) can be produced by using larger quantities of labour, the variable input (horizontal axis), given a fixed amount of capital. In frame (b) the graph of marginal product shows how the increase in total output associated with each additional labourer at first rises and then declines as more labour is used. Average product rises as long as marginal product exceeds it and declines when marginal product is below it.

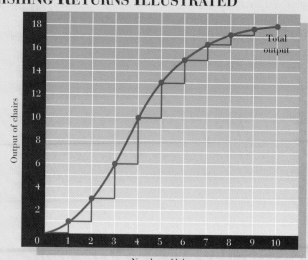

Number of labourers
Shortrun production function
(a)

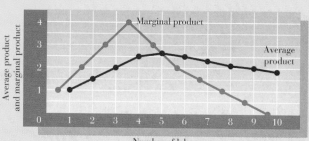

Number of labourers
(b)

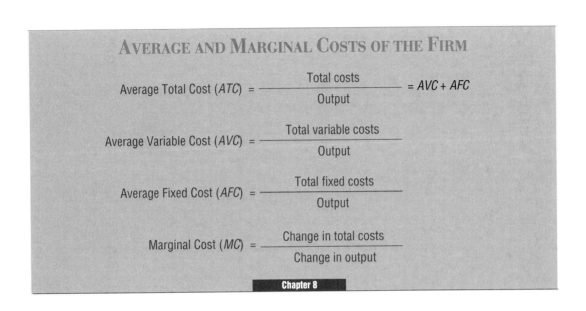

AVERAGE AND MARGINAL COSTS OF THE FIRM

Average Total Cost (ATC) = $\dfrac{\text{Total costs}}{\text{Output}}$ = $AVC + AFC$

Average Variable Cost (AVC) = $\dfrac{\text{Total variable costs}}{\text{Output}}$

Average Fixed Cost (AFC) = $\dfrac{\text{Total fixed costs}}{\text{Output}}$

Marginal Cost (MC) = $\dfrac{\text{Change in total costs}}{\text{Change in output}}$

Chapter 8

COST CURVES REFLECT THE SHAPES OF THE PRODUCTIVITY CURVES

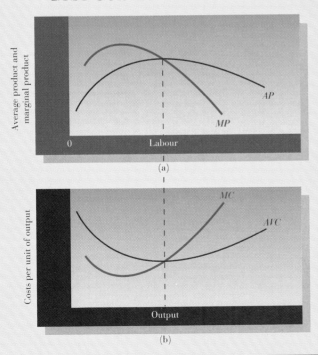

The hump shapes of the *AP* and *MP* curves, frame (a), are mirrored in the bowl shapes of the *AVC* and *MC* curves, respectively, frame (b). *MC* falls because *MP* is rising. *MC* reaches a minimum when *MP* is at its maximum. *MC* rises when *MP* falls. A similar relationship holds between *AVC* and *AP*.

Chapter 8

HOW IS OUTPUT DETERMINED BY THE
COMPETITIVE FIRM IN THE SHORT RUN?

Question
When should the firm produce?

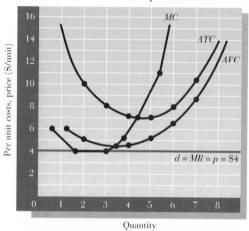

Answer
When price is equal to, or greater than, minimum average variable cost. Here, price is below *AVC*, so the firm should not produce and should shut down.

Chapter 9

Question
What quantity should the firm produce?

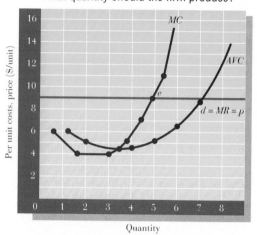

Answer
It should produce that quantity where marginal revenue (price) equals marginal cost, corresponding to 5 units at a price of $9 per unit.

Chapter 9

Question
When will there be economic profit?

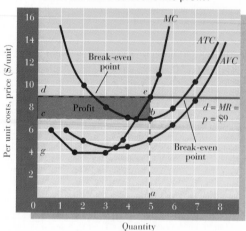

Answer
When price is greater than average total cost. Here, the firm makes an economic profit of $10 producing and selling 5 units at a price of $9 per unit.

Chapter 9

Question
When will the firm produce despite a loss?

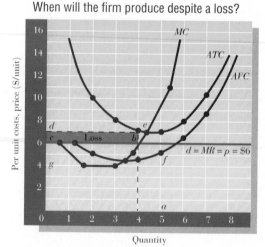

Answer
In the shortrun, whenever price is greater than average variable cost but less than average total cost, the firm will cover some of its fixed costs if it produces. Here, the firm has a loss of $4 producing and selling 4 units at a price of $6 per unit.

Chapter 9

HOW A MONOPOLY DETERMINES
PRICE AND OUTPUT.

RELATIONSHIP BETWEEN DEMAND D, MARGINAL REVENUE MR, AND TOTAL REVENUE TR WHEN THE DEMAND CURVE SLOPES DOWNWARD.

THE MONOPOLIST PRODUCES OUTPUT Q_e WHERE MARGINAL COST MC EQUALS MARGINAL REVENUE MR, CHARGING PRICE P_e, AND EARNING ABOVE-NORMAL PROFIT (SHADED AREA).

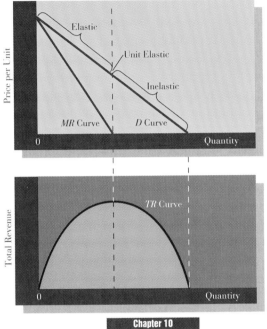

Chapter 10

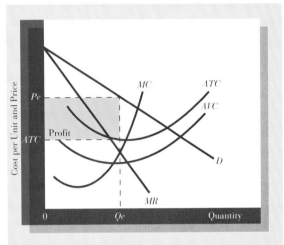

Chapter 10

FOUR BASIC TYPES OF MARKET STRUCTURE

Characteristics	Perfect Competition	Monopolistic Competition	Oligopoly	Pure Monopoly
Number of firms in market:	Very many	Many	Few	One
Firm's ability to alter price by changing output:	None	Limited	Constrained by price setting behaviour of other firms, but considerable if firms collude	Significant
Difficulty of new firm entering market:	Easy, no significant barriers	Reasonably easy	Difficult, significant barriers	Impossible
Product differentiation among firms:	Undifferentiated	Differentiated	Undifferentiated and differentiated	One type product with no close substitutes
Nonprice competition:	None	Some advertising and promotion of product distinctions	Considerable advertising and promotion of brandname and product distinction	Product promotion and public relations advertising
Examples:	Agriculture	Retail stores, dry cleaners, beauty parlors, etc.	Automobiles, steel, most household appliances	Electric utilities, local phone company

Chapters 9-12

HOW A MARKET DETERMINES
WAGES AND EMPLOYMENT LEVELS.

WAGE AND EMPLOYMENT DETERMINATION
IN A PERFECTLY COMPETITIVE LABOUR MARKET

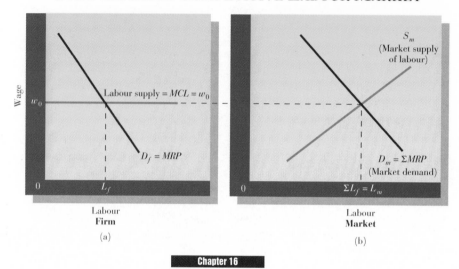

Labour
Firm

(a)

Labour
Market

(b)

WAGE AND EMPLOYMENT DETERMINATION
IN A MONOPSONY LABOUR MARKET

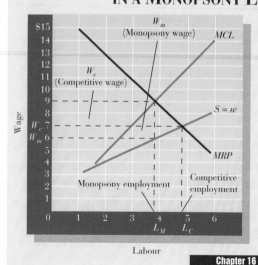

A monopsony labour market results in lower wages and lower levels of employment than in a perfectly competitive labour market.

Labour

Social Assistance

In 1966 the federal government introduced the Canada Assistance Plan (CAP). It provided for equal cost sharing of general and some specific welfare programs between the federal and the provincial governments. While some features of this program have changed over the years, the basics have remained the same. It is still a shared-cost program with the provinces responsible for its administration. General assistance under CAP is always means tested. The conditions for qualification and the level of benefits payable varies substantially from province to province. Social assistance payments tend to go to single parents, individuals with serious health concerns, and long-term unemployed who have exhausted their unemployment insurance benefits.

Welfare programs in Canada (and in many other countries) have been subjected to massive amounts of criticism. Some of the criticism is based on issues of equity or fairness. Are support levels adequate? Is it fair that most individuals work hard to earn a living while others do nothing? Do welfare payments go to those most in need? While these questions may appear to be objective, they do involve a normative element. What is need?

Not all the criticism relates to issues of fairness. There are questions of efficiency as well as questions of equity. Assuming that Canadians have decided who is deserving of income transfers, the government has then to design a program to redistribute income in accord with society's wishes. Then there are positive questions. Is the money actually going to the people who *deserve* it? Is the government minimizing its administrative costs in redistributing the money? Is welfare creating a disincentive to work? Welfare reform will be discussed in a policy perspective later in this chapter.

Health Insurance

As was mentioned earlier, income can be redistributed in kind. Canada has a universal government-funded health insurance program. As with government funding of education, government provision of free medical care involves a redistribution of income in kind. Full health care insurance began in 1968. Health care is a provincial responsibility. However, it is jointly funded by the federal and the provincial governments. The public provision of health care has proven to be an expensive undertaking. Health care costs have risen rapidly in all highly developed countries. This increase is to be expected. Health care has a relatively high income elasticity. While there has been some criticism of Canada's health care program, it has generally been one of the most widely supported social programs. Canada's position as one of the healthiest nations in the world is certainly due in part to the quality of its health care delivery system. In Canada the life expectancy of a female at birth is 81. For the United States, the only major industrial country that lacks a universal government-funded health care program, the life expectancy of a female at birth is 79. In Canada the infant mortality rate is 7 per 1,000 live births. In the United States it is almost 50 percent higher at 10 per 1,000 live births. Moreover, the patchwork of private and public programs in the United States actually cost more per capita than does the Canadian plan.

Checkpoint 18-4

What effect do you think that the social assistance and social insurance programs have on the distribution of disposable income in Canada? What are the possible consequences of such programs on the unemployment rate?

Attacking Poverty: Ways and Means

In addition to existing social assistance and social insurance, other methods have been used or proposed for attacking the poverty problem. One proposal involves attacking the problem through the labour market, either by the use of **minimum-wage laws** that attempt to raise wages of low-paid workers directly or by the use of government-subsidized job-training programs that attempt to increase the employability of the hard-core unemployed and those lacking the skills to earn a decent wage.

The Minimum-Wage Approach

It has been suggested that it is possible to help those workers who are employed, yet earn wages that still leave them poor, by passing minimum-wage legislation. In fact, all provinces in Canada have comprehensive or at least nearly comprehensive minimum-wage legislation. There is also a federal law, but it affects relatively few workers. The minimum-wage concept has been a subject of controversy since its inception. What are the arguments pro and con?

The Case Against Minimum Wage

Many people are of the opinion that the minimum wage contributes to unemployment. Their argument is illustrated in Figure 18-3, frame (a), which shows

FIGURE 18-3   Pros and Cons of Minimum-Wage Legislation

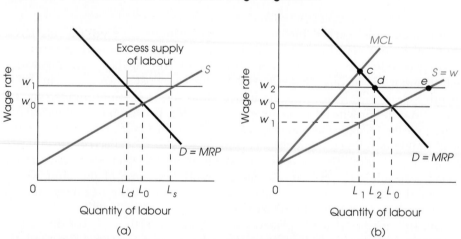

Minimum-wage legislation affects employment differently in different labour markets.
    Frame (a) depicts a perfectly competitive labour market. If minimum-wage legislation sets a minimum wage of w_1, the quantity of labour employed will fall from L_0 to L_d, and the quantity $L_d L_0$ will be thrown out of work.
    Frame (b) depicts a monopsony labour market. In general, if the minimum wage lies anywhere above w_1 up to the level corresponding to point c, both employment and earnings will be higher than they would be without such minimum wage. However, if the minimum wage is set higher than point c, employment will be reduced.

the labour demand curve D (which is also labour's marginal revenue product curve MRP) and the labour supply curve S in a perfectly competitive labour market. When the market is in equilibrium, the wage is w_0 and the quantity of labour employed is L_0. However, suppose that the market-determined wage w_0 is below the legislated minimum-wage level w_1. This means that it is illegal for employers to pay labour a wage as low as w_0 because society feels such a wage is too low.

When employers are forced to pay the minimum wage w_1, they will demand less labour, the quantity L_d, because the demand curve for labour is downward sloping. On the other hand, the quantity supplied of labour will increase to L_s because the supply curve of labour is upward sloping (the higher is the wage, the more workers are willing to work). Consequently, at the minimum wage w_1, there will be an excess supply of labour equal to the difference between L_s and L_d. The quantity of labour actually employed, L_d, is less than the quantity L_0 that would be employed in the absence of the minimum-wage law. The quantity of labour unemployed in this market as a result of the minimum-wage law equals $L_d L_s$. It is true that though a smaller quantity of labour is employed, those who are employed are better off, since they earn a higher wage w_1. Note that some of the unemployed workers at w_1 were previously employed and lost their jobs, while some of the unemployed workers were not previously employed and only decided to enter the labour market because of the higher wage. The former group of unemployed have suffered a welfare loss, the latter are no worse off than they were before the minimum-wage law took effect. *Many who are against minimum-wage legislation argue that while it increases the wages of some workers, it increases unemployment among others. Therefore, they conclude, it is not a very effective method for fighting poverty.*

Actual minimum wages in Canada tend to be substantially below average wages. As a result only a limited number of workers would even consider employment at minimum wage. However, teenagers, disabled workers, and others with relatively limited jobs skills can be affected by minimum-wage legislation. Whether or not, and if so by how much, unemployment is increased by minimum-wage laws is an empirical question. To date there is no definitive study.

The Case for Minimum Wage

Those people who favour minimum-wage legislation argue that the perfectly competitive model of the labour market, shown in frame (a) of Figure 18-3, is not representative of many of the labour markets in our economy. They claim that in a large number of labour markets, employers have a substantial monopsony position in the hiring of labour: They are monopsonists, a concept we discussed in Chapter 16.

The effect of minimum-wage legislation in a monopsony labour market is illustrated in Figure 18-3, frame (b). (This diagram is the same as Figures 16-7 and 16-8.) From our discussion in Chapter 16, you will recall that a monopsonist will hire labour up to the point at which the marginal cost of labour equals its marginal revenue product. This is represented in Figure 18-3, frame (b), by the intersection of the MCL curve and the labour demand curve D (the marginal revenue product curve MRP) at point c. In this situation, the monopsonist will hire L_1 units of labour and pay them a wage equal to w_1.

Again, suppose that society regards such a wage level as substandard, and that minimum-wage legislation makes it illegal for employers to pay a wage less than the statutory minimum. Let us say that this minimum wage is w_2. The marginal cost of labour to the monopsonist is now represented by the line w_2e. Its intersection with the labour demand curve D at point d indicates that the amount of labour the monopsonist will now hire is L_2. The level of employment in this market is now higher than before. Moreover, labour is now earning a higher wage than previously, since the minimum wage w_2 is higher than w_1.

In fact, if the statutory minimum wage lies anywhere above w_1 up to the level corresponding to point c, both employment and earnings will be higher. If, for example, the minimum wage were w_0, the level of employment, L_0, would be the same as that which would prevail in a perfectly competitive equilibrium. Of course, if the minimum wage were above point c, employment would be less than L_1. Minimum-wage legislation would then have the same kind of adverse effect on employment that it does in the perfectly competitive labour market of frame (a) in Figure 18-3. Those who favour minimum-wage legislation argue that many labour markets are monopsonistic. They therefore claim that a statutory minimum wage may not only increase workers' earnings but may increase employment as well—so long as the minimum wage is not set too high. In Canada there are a number of isolated resource towns that proponents of minimum-wage laws might argue have monopsonist employers. Possible examples include a remote mining town in British Columbia and a fish packing plant in a Newfoundland outport.

Even if a firm is not a monopsonist, it is possible that there is a market failure if employees do not have good knowledge of market conditions. (You will recall that good knowledge was one of the conditions required for perfect competition.) Proponents of minimum-wage laws could argue that teenagers and others likely to be affected by such legislation are also likely not to have good knowledge about employment opportunities.

Finally, some proponents would use the purely normative argument that it is morally wrong for anyone to be forced to work for wages that are so low as to leave the worker well below the Statistics Canada low income cut-offs.

Both sides of the minimum-wage debate make telling points. Obviously, whether a statutory minimum wage has beneficial or adverse effects on employment depends on the structure of the particular labour market examined. Minimum-wage legislation definitely raises wages for some workers. It may even raise the wages of some workers who otherwise would be just above the minimum-wage level. But given its uncertain effects on employment, such legislation may make some workers worse off. For example, most studies conclude that the minimum wage contributes to the high unemployment rate among teenagers. However, while the overall effects of minimum-wage legislation is uncertain, it does not seem to be a reliable method for attacking poverty.

Job-Training Programs

A second approach to reducing poverty through the labour market is the use of government-subsidized **job-training programs**. These are aimed at helping the young and unemployed develop the job skills that they need to increase their employability. These programs also aim at improving the job skills of older workers who are below the poverty line even when fully employed because they lack the skills to hold any but low-paying jobs.

FIGURE 18-4 **Increased Labour Productivity Leads to Increased Labour Demand and Higher Wages**

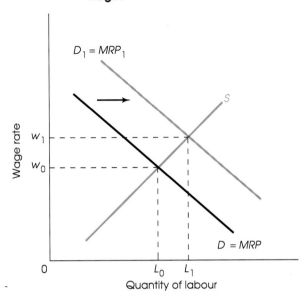

The demand curve D for labour is its marginal revenue product curve MRP. Recall that $MRP = p \times MPP$, or the price p of the final product labour helps to produce times the marginal physical product of labour MPP. The basic intent of the job-training approach to reducing poverty is to increase labour productivity, or MPP, by increasing workers' skills. In the labour market shown here, this causes the labour demand curve D (which equals MRP) to shift rightward to D_1 (which equals MRP_1). Given the supply curve of labour S, this results in an increase in employment from L_0 to L_1 and an increase in the wage rate from w_0 to w_1.

The basic rationale behind this approach is that increasing workers' skills increases their productivity and hence their earning power. This is illustrated in Figure 18-4. Recall from Chapter 15 that the marginal physical product of labour (MPP), together with the price p of the final product that labour helps to produce, determines the position of the marginal revenue product (MRP), or demand curve for labour, $D = p \times MPP$. (You may want to review these concepts in Chapter 15 at this point.) Given the existing state of labour productivity, along with the price of the final product, suppose that the demand curve for labour in the labour market of Figure 18-4 is D (which is equal to MRP). This, together with the labour supply curve S, determines the equilibrium wage w_0 and level of employment L_0. A training program that increases labour's productivity, and hence its MPP, causes the demand curve for labour to shift rightward to a position such as D_1 (which is equal to MRP_1). As a result, workers now receive a higher wage w_1 and, in addition, a larger number of workers, L_1, are employed. Unlike the minimum-wage approach, there is no question about the increase in employment. And along with this increase, workers will receive a higher wage because they are more productive and therefore have more market value in the production process, not because of a statute requiring that they receive a higher wage.

The Job Development Program is an attempt by the federal government to improve the employment skills of the unemployed. The Economic Council of Canada reports that although this program could be improved, it has been effective.[6]

---

[6] Economic Council of Canada, *Transitions for the 90s* (Ottawa: 1990).

POLICY PERSPECTIVE

The Negative Income Tax: Give the Money to the Poor and Cut Out the Bureaucracy

The attacks made on poverty by minimum-wage legislation, job-training programs, and the numerous forms of aid provided by the social assistance and social insurance system have obviously not eliminated poverty. Many have argued that the sheer number of these programs has resulted in overlapping responsibilities and the proliferation of agencies employing tens of thousands of federal and provincial bureaucrats. The result is inefficiency and large payrolls, all of which drive up the costs of helping the poor and providing welfare. Such considerations have led policymakers and economists to propose schemes that simply take income tax revenues from higher income groups and transfer them into the hands of the lowest income groups with a minimum amount of

bureaucratic intervention and loss of funds to bureaucracy payrolls along the way. One such income tax transfer scheme frequently contemplated is the **negative income tax (NIT)**. It was proposed by the Special Senate Committee on Poverty in its 1971 report, *Poverty in Canada*. Since then, numerous individuals and groups have reiterated the call for the development of an NIT. Supporters of an NIT come from the right as well as the left of the political spectrum.

A negative income tax is taxation in reverse on any income that is less than a certain statutory level. If a household's earned income falls below the statutory level, the government gives the household a subsidy, or negative income tax, equal to a certain fraction of the difference between the statutory income

level and the income earned by the household. The negative income tax is financed by income taxes on households with income above the statutory level.

EXAMPLE OF THE NEGATIVE INCOME TAX

For example, suppose that the negative income tax rate is 40 percent and that the statutory income level for a family of four is $25,000. (The actual value of statutory income is arbitrary. It is a policy matter, but $25,000 is close to the low income cut-off for a family of four in a large city.) The way in which the negative income tax would work for earned income below this level is shown in Table P18-2. If a household had no earned income—

continued on next page

TABLE P18-2   Negative Income Tax Scheme (Hypothetical Data)

(1) Statutory Income Level	(2) Earned Income	(3) Statutory Minus Earned Income = (1) − (2)	(4) Negative Income Tax = .40 × (3)	(5) Total Income = (2) + (4)
$25,000	$ 0	$25,000	$10,000	$10,000
25,000	2,500	22,500	9,000	11,500
25,000	5,000	20,000	8,000	13,000
25,000	7,500	17,500	7,000	14,500
25,000	10,000	15,000	6,000	16,000
25,000	12,500	12,500	5,000	17,500
25,000	15,000	10,000	4,000	19,000
25,000	17,500	7,500	3,000	20,500
25,000	20,000	5,000	2,000	22,000
25,000	22,500	2,500	1,000	23,500
25,000	25,000	0	0	25,000

column (2), row (1)—its earned income of zero would be $25,000 less, column (3), than the statutory level of $25,000, column (1). The government would give the household a negative income tax equal to 40 percent of this difference, or $10,000, column (4). The total income received by the household therefore would be $10,000, column (5), which is equal to the household's earned income (zero in this case) plus the amount of its negative income tax—column (2) plus column (4). A family with no earned income at all is thus ensured a minimum income of $10,000. If the family had an earned income of $2,500—column (2), row (2), $22,500 less, column (3), than the statutory level of $25,000, column (1), the government would give the household a negative income tax equal to $9,000, column (4), or 40 percent of $22,500. The total income received by the household, therefore, would be $11,500, column (5), which is again equal to the sum of its earned income and the amount of its negative income tax—column (2) plus column (4). You should check the numbers given by this calculation process for the earned income levels given in rows (3) through (10).

Note that the closer the family's earned income level is to the statutory level of $25,000, the smaller is the negative income tax, column (4), that it receives. If its earned income is $25,000, it receives no subsidy from the government at all. Above this level the household pays income taxes to the government according to the regular income tax schedule. The particular negative income tax scheme shown in Table P18-2 is but one possible example. In general, the statutory income level may be set at any level and so may the negative income tax rate.

IMPORTANT FEATURES OF THE NEGATIVE INCOME TAX

There are several important features of a negative income tax scheme:

1. It provides a guaranteed minimum level of income for households that have no earned income at all.
2. At the same time that it provides financial assistance to low-income households, it does not destroy their incentive to work. This can be seen by examining Table P18-2. Starting from a position of zero earned income, row (1), note that if the household is able to earn $2,500, column (2), the amount of the negative income tax it receives falls by only $1,000, from $10,000 to $9,000, column (4). Therefore, by working it is $1,500 better off—its total income rises from $10,000 to $11,500, column (5). As long as the household's earned income is below the statutory income level, the negative income tax it receives falls by only $.40 for every additional $1 of income it earns. It always pays to earn income under this scheme.
3. The only criterion for deciding whether a household is eligible for assistance is whether its earned income level is below the statutory income level. Other welfare and assistance programs use a multitude of criteria, some of which are so subjective as to put welfare administrators and social workers in the position of playing God to the poor. Many feel that this kind of paternalism is arbitrary and demeaning to those receiving assistance.
4. The negative income tax could be administered by the Revenue Canada using existing machinery for tax collection and income transfer. This might well be more efficient than the elaborate bureaucratic structure now used to administer welfare programs.

CRITICISMS OF THE NEGATIVE INCOME TAX

Despite all these positive features, the idea of a negative income tax has its critics, which is attested to by the fact that it has never made it off the drawing board:

1. There is a conflict between any attempt to provide a minimum guaranteed income level intended only for those at or below the poverty line and at the same time provide an incentive to work. Referring once again to Table P18-2, suppose that $25,000 were regarded as the poverty line for a family of four. In order to maintain the incentive-to-work feature of the negative income tax, it is unavoidable that many households with earned incomes below $25,000 will remain below the poverty line.
2. Many students of poverty argue that it is not realistic to think that by simply handing money to poor people, you can expect to break the vicious circle of poverty. If the head of household is addicted to drinking, drugs, or gambling or is simply irresponsible with money, the benefits to the rest of the household from a money handout may be slight at best. Money handouts without some guidance or change in habits may only reduce poverty by definition, but not in fact.
3. Many citizens object to the negative income tax concept simply because it is such a blatant way of taking income away from one group and handing it over to another. Lower-middle-income workers would find themselves forced to give some of their income over to people with income only a few hundred dollars less than their own.

Summary

1. The distribution of income in an economy goes to the heart of the question, For whom is the economy's output produced? One important measure of this distribution is the functional distribution of income, which shows how the economy's total income is divided among wages, rents, interest, and profits.

2. Another is the size distribution of income, which shows how total income is divided among individuals and families, the ultimate recipients of all factor income.

3. The basic determinants of the observed inequality in the distribution of income are (a) the differences among individuals in ability, education, training, and motivation; (b) the various market structures of the many different markets in our economy; (c) the distribution of wealth among individual households; (d) the age distribution of the population; (e) the economy's tax structure; (f) discrimination; and (g) differences among individual job preferences, luck, and opportunities.

4. In Canada the inequality in the distribution of income lessened between 1929 and the end of World War II. Since that time the distribution of income has remained relatively unchanged, with the lowest one fifth of families receiving about 6 percent of the total income and the highest one fifth receiving slightly less than 40 percent. The inequality in the distribution of wealth is even greater than the inequality in the distribution of income.

5. In 1990 about 12 percent of the Canadian population lived below the poverty line, down from approximately 23 percent in 1969. The incidence of poverty falls most heavily among aborigines, families with a female head, those with limited education, those with young heads, and those living in certain regions. Poverty begets poverty in that families have great difficulty rising above it from one generation to the next. Relative to other groups in our society the poor suffer from a lack of political visibility. Discrimination appears to be a major cause of the higher incidence of poverty among females.

6. Canada maintains a network of social insurance and social assistance programs. While these programs have certainly helped low-income Canadians, they have often been criticized and there is pressure for reform. The most important of the programs are the Canadian and Quebec Pension Plans, Old Age Security, Child Allowance, Unemployment Insurance, and universal health care.

7. Poverty also may be attacked through the job market. Minimum-wage legislation has established statutory minimum wage levels. While this approach provides higher wages for some workers, others may be forced into unemployment, which raises doubts about minimum-wage legislation's overall effectiveness in combating poverty. The job-training approach attempts to increase the employability and wages of poor people by improving their productivity and labour skills.

8. Income tax transfer schemes attempt to combat poverty by taxing higher income groups and transferring the proceeds to lower income groups. Under one such proposal, the negative income tax, the government pays households with incomes below some statutory level an amount equal to some percentage of the difference between the statutory level and the household's earned income. While this approach may be an economically efficient way to fight

poverty, some argue that simply handing money to poor people does not come to grips with the social pathology of poverty.

Key Terms and Concepts

Canadian and Quebec Pension Plans

functional distribution of income

Guaranteed Income Supplement (GIS)

job-training programs

Lorenz diagram

low income cut-offs

minimum-wage laws

Old Age Security (OAS)

poverty

size distribution of income

Unemployment Insurance (UI)

Questions and Problems

1. It has been said that if perfect equality in the distribution of income could be enforced, possibly by means of some kind of redistributive tax scheme, individuals would unavoidably be treated unequally. In what ways might this be so?
2. In the early days of the Russian Revolution, one much-publicized dictum of Communist party ideology held that income distribution would be determined according to the dictum "from each according to his ability, to each according to his need." How are workers' "needs" and "abilities" reflected in a perfectly competitive labour market? How well might the objective of the dictum be achieved in an economy where factors are employed in accordance with the marginal productivity theory of factor demand?
3. Harriet Martineau, a nineteenth-century English writer, once hypothesized that if the government redistributed income in the morning to achieve perfect income equality, by nightfall the rich would once again be back in their comfortable beds and the poor asleep under the bridges. What factors would Martineau most likely stress as the important determinants of income inequality?
4. Suppose that you constructed the Lorenz curves representing income distribution in *each* of the following occupational groups: grade school teachers, gamblers, lawyers, business proprietors, and boxers. How do you think the curves would look relative to one another and why?
5. Historically, the aged have typically had to depend on the young for their support. It was fairly traditional for older people to live with their children, often largely dependent on their offspring's sense of duty and parental respect. As originally conceived, the old age security system could be said to lessen that dependence to some extent. Today some critics of the OAS, CPP, and GIS system say that the old are again becoming dependent on the younger generation for financial support. What is the basis of this contention, and in what sense is it correct?
6. What effects do you think minimum-wage laws would have on employment in each of the following: apple orchards, textile mill towns in the Maritimes, and dry-cleaning businesses?
7. Some argue that minimum-wage laws have effects that are the same as if the age limit of child labour laws were increased. Why is this so and how might job-training programs get around this problem despite the presence of minimum-wage laws? Illustrate your answer graphically.
8. In what way would the size of the negative tax rate affect the incentive of those receiving a negative income tax to seek work?

Macroeconomic Concepts and Measurement

Chapter 19

The Measurement of Domestic Income and Product

This chapter begins our study of macroeconomics. Recall from Chapter 1 that macroeconomics is concerned with the performance of the whole economy or large sectors of it, and with both domestic and international aspects. Macroeconomics attempts to explain why the economy's total output of goods and services fluctuates over time, giving rise to the business cycle with its accompanying upward and downward movements in the unemployment and inflation rates. Finally, macroeconomics is concerned with the potentially helpful as well as possibly harmful role that government plays in these events, including such issues as the government's ability to control inflation, the effectiveness of government policies aimed at smoothing the business cycle, and the size and effects of government budget deficits (the latter an issue of much concern in recent years).

In this chapter we will focus on national income accounting. *National income accounting provides us with aggregate measures of what is happening in the economy.* It is the way we measure the various flows depicted in the flow diagrams of Chapter 3. We will begin by examining the important concept of gross domestic product, or GDP, the most commonly used measure of the economy's total output of goods and services. The rest of the chapter will present the basics of national income accounting, the way we go about keeping track of the economy's performance. In Chapter 20 we will examine the historical record of the Canadian economy in order to gain a perspective on the way the economy behaves, the nature of the business cycle, and the closely related problems of inflation and unemployment.

Why Is National Income Accounting Important?

When you drive your car, you usually keep an eye on the speedometer to see how fast you are going. You check the fuel gauge before starting out to make sure that you have enough gas to reach your destination. The temperature gauge warns you about engine overheating before serious damage is done. Without the information these gauges provide, you could find yourself in a dangerous situation. The same is true with respect to the performance of our economy. National income accounting is the gauge that economists and policymakers use for measuring the performance of the economy.

When our economy plunged into the Great Depression of the 1930s, the general lack of any timely, systematic measurements of what was happening became painfully apparent. This experience spurred the development of today's national income accounting procedures. Armed with relatively recent statistical measurements of the economy's performance, businesses, households, and government policymakers are better informed about what has been happening in the economy and where it appears to be headed. Businesses and households are therefore in a better position to make economic plans. Government policymakers need this kind of information to assess the economy's performance in order to implement timely policies to improve that performance. Shy of this lofty ambition, policymakers need such information at least to avoid policy actions that may harm the economy's performance.

What Is Gross Domestic Product (GDP)?

The most cited measure of the economy's overall performance is its **gross domestic product (GDP).** *GDP is the market value of all final goods and services produced by the economy during a year.* GDP per capita (*GDP ÷ population*) is often used to measure output per person. GDP has several important characteristics. First, it is a flow concept. Second, it is measured in money terms. Third, it only includes goods and services bought for final use, not unfinished goods in the intermediate stages of production that are purchased for further processing and resale within the year. Fourth, GDP has two sides: It may be viewed from the income side or from the expenditure side.

LEARNING OBJECTIVES

After reading this chapter, you will be able to:

1. Define *gross domestic product* (GDP).
2. Identify transactions that are not included in GDP.
3. Differentiate between real and money GDP.
4. Explain how economists avoid double counting when calculating GDP.
5. Explain why GDP is not a measure of social welfare.
6. Identify the components on the expenditure side of GDP.
7. Identify the components on the income side of GDP.
8. Identify and explain the relationships between the various national income accounting concepts.

Until 1986 the most often cited measure of Canadian overall economic performances was **gross national product (GNP)**. GNP includes investment income received from non-residents but does not include investment income paid to non-residents. Table 19-1 illustrates the difference between GDP and GNP for 1990.

The change to GDP brought Canada in line with the practice of most other industrialized countries. The United States is the remaining important exception. The Americans still use GNP. Actually, it is relatively unimportant which measure a country uses. The two measures are generally highly correlated.

GDP Is a Flow

As you will recall from Chapter 1, a flow is a quantity per unit of time, such as so many litres of water running through a pipe per minute. By contrast, a stock is a quantity measured without respect to time, such as the number of litres of water in a tub. GDP is a flow measured as the quantity of final goods and services produced by the economy per year. It is a flow that is measured at an annual rate.

We could measure GDP by giving a complete listing of all final goods and services produced per year. For instance, the number of automobiles, haircuts, toothbrushes, car washes, and so forth. This obviously would be a rather cumbersome list, probably about the size of a large city's telephone directory (even longer if the breakdown of products is very fine). We can't add the quantities of these different goods together to get a meaningful number—you can't add apples and shirts. It is far easier and less awkward simply to summarize all this information by adding up the dollar values of all these goods. Hence, the dollar value of GDP is given as the sum of the price of an automobile times the number of automobiles per year plus the price of a haircut times the number of haircuts per year plus the price of a toothbrush times the number of toothbrushes per year plus the price of a car wash times the number of car washes per year plus..., and so forth. GDP may be viewed either as a flow of numbers of units of final goods and services produced per year or as a flow of the dollar value of these final goods and services produced per year.

The importance of distinguishing between final goods and services produced this year and those produced in other years cannot be overemphasized. Only those produced this year are to be counted in this year's GDP, since it is the production of those products only that requires the current use of resources

TABLE 19-1   The Difference Between GDP and GNP for 1990
(Millions of Dollars)

GDP at market prices	$671,577
Plus investment income received from non-residents	9,255
Minus investment income paid to non-residents	33,208
Equals GNP at market prices	647,624

Source: Statistics Canada. *Canadian Economic Observer*, October 1991 (11–010)

and thus provides jobs for workers and income for other resource owners. Those produced in other years are counted in GDP for the years in which they were produced.

The measurement of GDP requires that we add up all the market transactions representing the purchase and sale of final goods and services. Such transactions measure the dollar value of productive activity that actually went into the production of final goods and services within the economy this year. However, there are many market transactions in our economy that do not involve the purchase and sale of final goods and services produced this year. For the purpose of measuring GDP, these transactions are not counted, and care must be taken not to include them in the measurement of GDP. In addition, it should be recognized that some productive activities that should be included in GDP do not always show up as market transactions.

Productive versus Nonproductive Transactions

Many market transactions that occur in our economy do not represent the production of a good or service. Therefore, we don't want to count them in GDP. The purchase and sale of used goods is an example of such a transaction. If Alice buys Bob's 2-year-old stereo set for $300, this transaction does not involve the purchase of a final good produced this year. When the set was purchased new, 2 years ago, its purchase price was included in GDP for that year. What about a set produced and purchased in February of this year and then resold by the initial buyer a month later? The purchase of the set by the initial buyer would be included in GDP for this year because the set was produced this year. However, it would not be correct to include the resale transaction in GDP, because this would amount to counting the production of the set more than once. The resale of a used good is a transaction that merely represents the transfer of ownership of a previously produced good. It does not represent the production of a new good. Always remember that GDP is a measure of productive activity. You and I could buy and sell the same car back and forth daily, but we have not produced any new cars. If the resale involves a broker, then the broker's commission would represent productive activity and would be included in GDP.

There are also certain types of *financial transactions* in our economy that do not represent any productive activity that adds to the output of final goods and services. Therefore, they are not included in GDP. Such transactions include (1) the trading of stocks, bonds, and other kinds of securities in financial markets; and (2) private and public transfer payments. Again the brokerage on such transactions is included.

1. The trading in stocks and bonds in financial markets amounts to several tens of billions of dollars per year. None of this is counted in GDP, however, because it only represents the trading of paper assets. True, businesses and government often issue new stocks and bonds to raise funds to spend on currently produced final goods and services. But this only amounts to a minute fraction of the total yearly purchases and sales of securities. Funds raised and used to purchase final goods and services are included in GDP when they appear in business firms' accounts recording such purchases.

2. Private and public **transfer payments** are transactions in which the recipient is neither expected to nor required to make any contribution to GDP in return. The transfer of funds from one individual to another, either as a gift, a bequest, or a charitable donation, constitutes a private transfer payment not included in GDP. Also included under private transfer payments are payments out of the principal of private pension funds. Public transfer payments are made to some groups in the economy by the government. Such payments include social insurance, welfare, unemployment, and veterans' benefits. While these payments are not included in GDP, the national income accounts do keep a record of them, as we shall see.

Productive Nonmarket Transactions

If GDP is to measure the economy's production of final goods and services, it is necessary to recognize that not all productive activities show up as market transactions on the business accounting statements used to construct an estimate of GDP. Therefore, it is necessary to impute a dollar value to productive activities not represented by a market transaction and to include this dollar value in the calculation of GDP.

For example, people who live in their own home do not write themselves a rent cheque every month. However, those who do not own their home must make such an explicit rent payment. Both groups receive a currently produced service, the shelter provided by the dwellings, yet only the payments made by renters to landlords show up as a market transaction. The rent on owner-occupied homes must be imputed as the rent payments the owners would have to make if they rented their homes from landlords. These payments could also be looked at as the amount of rent owners could receive if they were to rent their home to somebody else. Such an imputed rent on owner-occupied homes is included in GDP, along with the rent payments made to landlords. In the interest of consistency, the purchase of a new home is treated as a capital investment and not as consumption. Similarly, the value of the food that farm families produce and consume themselves must be imputed and included in GDP.

However, there are a number of productive nonmarket transactions that are not included in GDP. The productive services of homemakers—cooking, housecleaning, and childcare—are not included despite the fact that this constitutes a sizable amount of productive activity. (If you're not convinced, just check the want ads to see what it would cost you to hire a cook, a housekeeper, and a nanny.) Many people repair and remodel their own homes, cars, and a host of other items. Yet the productive services of the do-it-yourselfers are not included in GDP, largely because it is so difficult to estimate and keep track of the total value of such activities in our economy. Also, illegal and underground activities are not counted, and there is some evidence that there has been considerable growth in that economy. The underground economy may actually involve "market" transactions, but these do not occur in the "official market"; they are usually underground to avoid taxes. If one tradesperson exchanges services with another but does not report the income to avoid GST and income tax, real production takes place but is not recorded as part of GDP. Similarly the production of the "I'll do it for less if you pay me in cash" auto mechanic is not recorded.

Value Added—Don't Double Count

We have stressed that GDP only includes goods and services bought for final use. It does not include the unfinished goods in the intermediate stages of production that are purchased by one firm from another for further processing and resale in the same year. The market value of a final good is the full value of the good in that it already includes the value added at each stage of the production process. If we also counted the purchases of the component parts of the good each time they were sold by a firm at one stage of the production process to a firm at the next stage, we would end up counting the market value of the final good more than once. For example, we don't want to count the sale of Canadian Firestone tires to the Ford Motor Company of Canada because the cost of the tires will be included in the price of the cars that Ford sells to final customers. If we did include the sale of tires from Firestone to Ford, the tires would be counted twice in GDP.

These points are illustrated by the example in Table 19-2. Suppose that it costs you $.50 to buy a pad of notebook paper in your local retail store. This pad is a final product, since you intend to use the paper yourself, not to transform it into another product and resell it. The market value of the final product, $.50, equals the sum of the values added at each stage of the production process. How does this work? Firm 5, the retail store that sells the pad of paper to you, must pay $.45 of the $.50 it receives, columns (3) and (4), to Firm 4, the paper manufacturer that provides Firm 5 with the paper. Firm 5 pays out the remaining $.05 in wages, rent, interest, and profit to the factors of production used by Firm 5 to provide the retailing service. This $.05 constitutes the value added, column (5), to the final product by Firm 5 through its provision of these services. Firm 4 must pay $.30 of the $.45 received from Firm 5 to Firm 3, the pulpwood mill, for the pulpwood Firm 4 processes into notebook paper. Firm 4 pays out the remaining $.15 in wages, rent, interest, and profit to the factors of production it uses to process pulpwood into paper. This $.15 is the value added to the final product by the paper manufacturer.

Proceeding back through each stage of production, the pulpwood mill adds value to the final product by processing the logs it buys from the logging com-

TABLE 19-2   Sales Receipts, Cost of Intermediate Products, and Value Added at Each Stage of Production of Notebook Paper
(Cents per Pad of Paper)

	(1) Production State	(2) Product	(3) Sale Price of Product		(4) Cost of Intermediate Product		(5) Value Added (Wages, Interest, Rent, and Profit)
Firm 1	Tree farm	Trees	$.15	—	$ .00	=	$.15
Firm 2	Logging company	Logs	.20	→	.15	=	.05
Firm 3	Pulpwood mill	Pulpwood	.30	→	.20	=	.10
Firm 4	Paper manufacturer	Notebook paper	.45	→	.30	=	.15
Firm 5	Retail store	Retailing service	.50	→	.45	=	.05
Final sale							$.50
							(Final sale price = sum of value added)

pany. And the logging company adds value to the final product by making logs out of the trees it buys from the tree farm. *The* **value added** *to the final product at each stage of production is the difference between what the firm sells its product for and what it pays for the intermediate materials or good it processes at that production stage.* This difference is paid out in wages, interest, rent, and profit to the owners of all the factors of production that provide the productive services that add value to the product at that stage of production. The sum of the values added at each stage of production equals the sale price of the final good or service.

In the example of Table 19-2, the $.50 sale price of the final good, a pad of notebook paper, equals the sum of the value added figures of column (5). If instead we added up the sales figures in column (3) we would get $1.60. This figure overstates the value of the final good because it counts the value added by Firm 1 five times, that by Firm 2 four times, Firm 3 three times, and Firm 4 two times. In order to avoid this double, or multiple, counting, it is necessary to subtract the purchase price of intermediate products to be processed at each stage of production, as indicated by the arrows. This leaves the value added figures of column (5), the sum of which equals the correct value of the final product. For this reason, that is the only figure we want to include in GDP. We do not add in the sales transactions between the first four firms.

It may have occurred to you that the good and services tax is really a value added tax. In fact many countries have very similar taxes called **value added taxes**. The GST, unlike a provincial sales tax, is not simply charged to the consumer when the final good or services is purchased. It is assessed at each stage of production on the value added at that level of production.

Money GDP versus Real GDP

Money GDP is the economy's gross domestic product measured in terms of the prices at which final goods and services actually sell. **Real GDP** is money GDP adjusted to remove the effects of price changes. It is important to understand what this means.

Adjusting GDP for Price Change—A Simple Example

Suppose, for simplicity, that the entire economy produces only one kind of good. Say that good is hamburgers. In any given year the economy's money GDP equals the current price of a hamburger multiplied by the number of hamburgers produced during the year. Any change in money GDP from one year to the next could therefore be due to a change in price or a change in quantity or both. However, we typically are only interested in GDP to the extent that it measures the quantity of output produced.

For instance, suppose that the economy has a dollar GDP of $1,000 in 1992, which results from the production of 1,000 hamburgers that sell at a price of $1 per hamburger. It will be no better or worse off in 1998 with a dollar GDP of $2,000 if that GDP again results from the production and sale of 1,000 hamburgers, at a price of $2 per hamburger. When prices rise over time in this way we have **inflation**—that is, a decrease in the purchasing power of a dollar. It

Checkpoint* 19-1

While the purchase and sale of used cars are not included in GDP, the sales commissions earned by used-car dealers are. Similarly, the purchase and sale of stock on the Toronto Stock Exchange are not included in GDP, but the sales commissions earned by stockbrokers are. Why are the sales commissions generated from these activities included in GDP, while the sales themselves are not? During the last 30 years or so the proportion of working wives in the labour force has increased considerably. What effect does this have on GDP? Construct a hypothetical value added table like Table 19-2 for the production and sale of a loaf of bread.

*Answers to all Checkpoints can be found at the back of the text.

takes $2 to buy one hamburger in 1998 that could have been purchased for $1 in 1992. Similarly, if prices decline over time we have **deflation**, an increase in the purchasing power of a dollar. The task is somehow to adjust the dollar GDP figure so that it only reflects changes in quantity of output produced and not price changes—not inflation or deflation.

Table 19-3 illustrates how national income accountants would make this adjustment for our simple hamburger economy. Suppose that over a 5-year period the current price p of hamburgers rises, as shown in column (2). Suppose also that the quantity Q of hamburgers produced each year is increasing at a rate of 10 percent per year, as shown in column (3). The money GDP for each year equals the current price p times Q, as shown in column (4). Clearly the increase in money GDP (or GDP in current prices) from year to year is much greater than the yearly increase in the physical quantity of hamburgers produced, due to the increases in the current price of hamburgers. Since these money GDP figures are inflated over time by the rising current price of hamburgers, column (2), it is necessary to adjust them so that they only reflect changes in quantities of output produced, and not price changes.

This adjustment is made by constructing a *price index*. In this case the price index would be called the *GDP implicit price index* or simply the *GDP deflator*. A **price index** expresses the current price of hamburgers in each year as a ratio relative to the current price in some base, or benchmark, year. This base year may be chosen arbitrarily. In Table 19-3, the base year is the third year. The price index constructed in this way is shown in column (5). For example, the price of a hamburger in year 1 is two-fifths, or 40 percent, of the price of a hamburger in year 3 ($\frac{\$2}{\$5}$). Hence, if we want to adjust the money GDP of year 1, column (4), to obtain output in terms of year 3 prices, we must multiply the money GDP of year 1 by $\frac{5}{2}$ or, equivalently, divide it by .40, the value of the price index in year 1. Year 1 GDP expressed in year 3 prices is $5,000, column (6). By the same procedure the money GDP of each of the other 4 years may be expressed in terms of year 3 prices to give real GDP, or GDP in constant dollars or prices, column (6). The GDP figures in column (6) are "real" in the sense that their year-to-year change accurately reflects the year-to-year change in the quantity of hamburgers produced in the economy, column (3). The figures in both columns increase at a rate of 10 percent per

TABLE 19-3   Adjusting Money GDP for Price Level Changes to Obtain Real GDP: A Simple Example

(1) Year	(2) Price per Hamburger p	(3) Number of Units (Hamburgers) of Output per Year Q	(4) Money GDP or GDP in Current Prices $p \times Q = (2) \times (3)$	(5) Price Index (2) ÷ Price in Year 3	(6) Real GDP or GDP Constant Prices or Dollars (4) ÷ (5)
1	$ 2	1,000	$ 2,000	$\frac{2}{5}$ = .40, or 40 percent	$5,000
2	3	1,100	3,300	$\frac{3}{5}$ = .60, or 60 percent	5,500
3 = base year	5	1,210	6,050	$\frac{5}{5}$ = 1.00, or 100 percent	6,050
4	7	1,331	9,317	$\frac{7}{5}$ = 1.40, or 140 percent	6,655
5	10	1,464	14,640	$\frac{10}{5}$ = 2.00, or 200 percent	7,320

year. It also may be said that the GDP figures of column (6) are stated in constant dollars or prices in the sense that they are all expressed in terms of the year 3 price of hamburgers.

To conclude, money GDP, or GDP in current prices or dollars, measures the dollar value of final goods and services produced in a given year at the prices at which they actually sold in that year. Real GDP, or GDP in constant prices or dollars, measures the dollar value of final goods and services sold in a given year in terms of the prices at which those goods sold in some base, or benchmark, year.

Money and Real GDP in Canada

Our hamburger economy example greatly oversimplifies the problem of transforming money GDP into real GDP, yet the basic principle of adjustment carries over to the real world. The essential difference, of course, is that a real-world economy typically produces a multitude of different goods, not just hamburgers. This means there are many different prices that may change over time, so the price index used must be constructed as an average (usually a weighted average) of all these prices. An example with three different goods is provided in the Questions and Problems section at the end of this chapter.

Such a price index (called the *GDP deflator*) for the Canadian economy is shown for selected years in column (3) of Table 19-4. The base year is 1986. This column tells us, among other things, that the general level of prices rose by 18.3 percent from 1986 to 1990, that the general level of prices in 1950 was 18.2 percent of that prevailing in 1986, and that prices rose by 650 percent between 1950 and 1990. Money GDP—that is, GDP in current prices or dollars—is shown in column (2). Using exactly the same procedure as in Table 19-3, the money GDP figures in column (2) of Table 19-4 are divided by the price index for the corresponding year in column (3) to give real GDP in column (4). This real GDP is thus expressed in constant 1986 prices or dollars. The behaviour of real GDP

TABLE 19-4   Money GDP and Real GDP in Canada, Selected Years
(Millions of Dollars)

(1) Year	(2) Money GDP (Current Dollars)	(3) Price Index* Base Year 1986	(4) Real GDP (Constant 1986 Dollars)
1950	$ 19,125	18.2	$104,821
1955	29,250	21.7	134,889
1960	39,448	24.0	164,126
1965	57,523	26.5	216,802
1970	89,116	32.8	271,372
1975	171,540	49.0	350,113
1980	309,891	73.0	424,537
1985	477,988	97.7	489,437
1986	505,666	100.0	505,666
1990	671,577	118.3	567,541

Source: Statistic Canada. *Canadian Economic Observer, Historical Statistical Supplement*, 1990/91 (11–210)

*GDP implicit GDP index.

FIGURE 19-1   Gross Domestic Product (GDP) in Current and Constant 1986 Dollars: 1972–1990

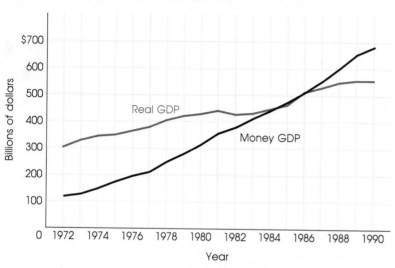

Growth of money and real GDP

Since 1972, GDP in current dollars (money GDP) has grown continuously. However, GDP in constant 1986 dollars (real GDP) reveals that growth in the economy's production of final goods and services has not been as rapid or continuous. While real GDP declined in 1982, GDP in current dollars increased, reflecting the general inflation in prices.

Source: Statistics Canada. *Canadian Economic Observer, Historical Statistical Supplement,* 1990/91 (11 – 210)

Checkpoint 19-2

Using Table 19-3, calculate real GDP in terms of constant year 2 dollars. It is sometimes said that calculating real GDP "inflates" the money GDP data for years before the base year. In what sense is this so? When would this not be true?

in column (4) indicates that the quantity of final goods and services produced by the economy increased more than fivefold between 1950 and 1990. Column (2) indicates that money GDP, the quantity of final goods and services evaluated in current prices, increased by somewhat more than 35 times over this period. This reflects the fact that prices increased more than sixfold, as indicated in column (3). Clearly, if we want a more accurate measure of the economy's productive performance, we must use real GDP, GDP measured in constant dollars, column (4).

The difference in the behaviour of money GDP (GDP in current dollars) and real GDP for the years since 1972 is shown graphically in Figure 19-1. While GDP in current dollars rises continuously throughout these years, largely reflecting the inflation of prices during this period, GDP in constant (1986) dollars generally grows more slowly and even declines in one year (1982). Figure 19-1 clearly indicates that whenever we talk, read, or write about GDP it is important to be clear whether it is money GDP or real GDP that is referred to. There is obviously a difference.

The Two Sides of GDP

Envision a sales counter in any store. On one side stands the customer paying out money in exchange for the good or service that the store provides. On the other side stands the proprietor, giving the customer the good or service in exchange

POLICY PERSPECTIVE

What GDP Does Not Measure

It is easy, and tempting, to look at GDP as a measure of society's well-being. Yet it was never intended to be a measure of social welfare. It is simply an accounting measure of economic activity. While there is certainly reason to believe that an economy is "better off" if it has a large real GDP—more goods and services for all—this is not necessarily so. On the other hand, a society may become better off in ways that GDP simply does not measure. Let's consider some of the "goods" and "bads" that GDP does not measure.

PRODUCT QUALITY

A generation ago, even a multimillionaire couldn't buy the kinds of medicines commonly available to the person of average means today. Yesteryear's automobiles didn't have four-wheel brakes, automatic transmissions, and a host of features commonly built into today's cars. Suppose that you were given an Eaton's catalog for 1950. You could buy from the catalog at the listed price or in person at your local Eaton's store at current prices. Clearly some items would be a better buy in the catalog, but many items would be a better buy at the store. Many items you might want would not even be available in the catalog. From which one would you rather buy kitchen appliances, sports equipment, TV sets, computers, and stereos? Because GDP is a quantitative rather than a qualitative measure, it does not measure product improvement and the development of new kinds of goods.

The GDP in 1950 did not include the kinds of goods that are included in today's GDP. But when their value is measured in dollars alone, yesterday's products are indistinguishable from today's. For this reason changes in real GDP often fail to indicate just how much society's standard of living has changed.

COSTS NOT MEASURED— EXTERNALITIES

GDP does not measure many of the by-products associated with producing the goods and services that are measured by GDP. And many of these by-products are "bads"— smoke, noise, polluted rivers and lakes, garbage dumps, and junkyards. Economists call such "bads" *externalities*. (Externalities were discussed in Chapter 14.) The costs of health problems (both physical and mental) caused by such environmental blight are either not measured at all or do not show up until years after the production of the GDP that caused them. These undesirable by-products tend to increase right along with growth in GDP. If the costs of these bads were subtracted from GDP, the resulting GDP would not appear as large or grow as fast. It would also be a more accurate measure of society's true well-being.

LEISURE AND GDP

For most people a certain amount of leisure is desirable. When people take more leisure, less working time is devoted to producing goods and services. This means GDP will be smaller than it otherwise might be. However, this increase in leisure must add to people's sense of well-being more than enough to offset the forgone output, or else people wouldn't have chosen to take it. Therefore, it would be completely misleading to interpret the reduction in GDP that results from increased leisure as a reduction in society's well-being. For example, the length of the average workweek has been roughly cut in half over the last century. Workers have chosen to take more leisure, and as a result, GDP is not as large as it would be if workers put in as many work hours as they typically did a hundred years ago. However, it would be erroneous to conclude that society is worse off because GDP is not as large as it could be. Why? Because more leisure has been chosen in preference to the additional output.

THE UNDERGROUND ECONOMY

As you already know, not all productive activities are included in GDP. In general, activities are not counted because they are difficult to measure. Included in these are most illegal activities. Of course many illegal activities do not produce any real output. If a thief steals a television set, there is no new production. However, many vice crimes do involve the production of a good or service. The sale of

continued on next page

for the customer's money. Corresponding to every purchase there is a sale, since there are always two sides to every transaction. We know from our discussion of value added that all the money received on the seller's side of the counter ultimately is paid out in wages, rent, interest, and profit as compensation to the owners of the factors of production used to produce and distribute the product.

POLICY PERSPECTIVE CONTINUED

homebrew represents real output just as much as the sale of legally produced alcohol. The sale of cocaine also represents real production, even if society in general does not view cocaine as a "good." The bookmaker's services are not counted, but on-track betting is. The total value of all such activities is hard to estimate, but it is certainly in the billions of dollars annually. In practice, because criminals sometimes find it necessary to launder the illegal earnings, some of this production is counted. When this happens these earnings may be counted as legal production.

Many legal activities also occur as "underground" production. In some cases, while the activity is legal the intent is not. The agents involved wish to avoid the "public" market in order to avoid paying GST and/or income tax. Again, it is hard to estimate the value of such production. It is likely significant, and some feel that with the imposition of the GST it has become more common. Others would argue the opposite. The GST requires reporting at every step in production. If people try to hide their value added from Revenue Canada, they run the risk that someone else will report them rather than pay tax on that value. When citizens successfully hide production from the tax collector, GDP is underestimated and taxes on market-produced goods and services are higher (to make up for the lost revenue).

Most of the home production that takes place is excluded. This production is neither illegal nor taxable. The major component in this category is homemaker production. Some countries actually

estimate the value of homemaker production and include it in their GDP. There are two problems with not counting this production. First, in our market-oriented society we tend to see value in terms of price. If it is free, it is not of value. This minimizes truly worthwhile production, mostly produced by women. Second, it has resulted in an overestimate of the growth of the Canadian economy over the last two decades. As women have moved out of uncounted production in the home and into counted production in the marketplace, no correction has been made for the loss of the value of substantial amounts of home child care, cooking, cleaning, sewing, and so on. Of course, some women continue to do some of

these jobs while they work at a paying job. Some even have husbands who are willing to do their share. Still, there is less home production now than in 1960, and Canada's national accounting does not show this fact.

PER CAPITA GDP AND THE DISTRIBUTION OF OUTPUT

If we divide a side of beef among 5 people, each individual will certainly be better off than if we have to divide it among 10 people. Similarly, in order to assess how well off a nation is, we need to know more than just the size of its annual output (i.e., its real GDP). We

continued on next page

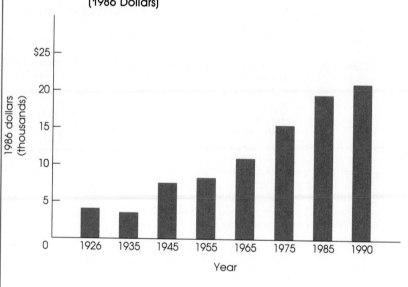

FIGURE P19-1   Growth of Real per Capita GDP in Canada (1986 Dollars)

Source: Statistics Canada. *Canadian Economic Observer, Historical Statistical Supplement,* 1990/91 (11–210)

Therefore, all the money received on the seller's side of the counter is income to all the owners of the factors of production—land, labour, and capital.

We may think of all such counters in the economy across which all final goods and services flow as one big sales counter. The total of all the money flowing across the counter in exchange for all the final goods and services produced

also need to know how that output is divided among its citizens. If it were divided equally among them, then we would simply divide the nation's GDP by its population. This gives **per capita GDP**. Figure P19-1 shows how real per capita GDP (in 1986 dollars) has grown since 1926 in Canada. While there is in fact no economy where GDP is distributed equally among its citizens, per capita GDP gives a simple measure of how well off an economy would be if its GDP were divided up in this fashion. Because an economy's GDP is typically distributed unequally among its citizens, it is necessary to study this distribution in more detail in order to get a

more accurate assessment than that provided by per capita GDP.

COMPOSITION OF GDP

The kinds of goods produced by an economy are completely hidden from view by a GDP figure. One economy could have a $100 billion GDP composed entirely of weapons for war, and another could have a $100 billion GDP composed entirely of sports cars, steak dinners, and fine clothes. These economies would clearly have different kinds of living standards, though you could never tell it from GDP data. GDP alone tells nothing about the composition of the economy's output. For example, the composition

of GDP in Canada has shifted more toward the production of services, as shown by the comparison of personal expenditures on consumer goods and services for Canada for 1947 and 1990 in Figure P19-2.

For Discussion

- Suppose that the portion of an economy's GDP spent on health care increases over time. What considerations would be important in deciding whether this represented an increase in society's well-being or not?
- How do coffee breaks and sick leaves affect GDP? Which sort of time loss affects GDP in the same direction as societal well-being?

FIGURE P19-2 **The Changing Composition of GDP in Canada**

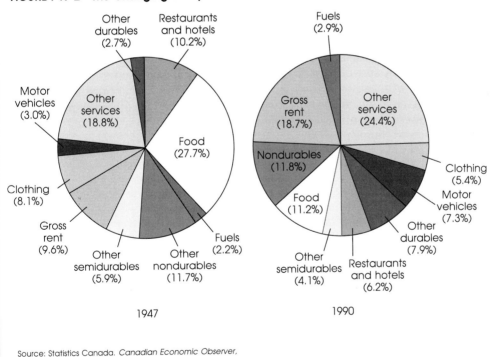

1947

1990

Source: Statistics Canada. *Canadian Economic Observer, Historical Statistical Supplement*, 1991/92 (11 – 210)

in a year is the money GDP. When we view GDP from the buyer's side of the counter, where expenditures are made and goods are taken off the counter, we are viewing GDP from the expenditure, or output, side. This viewpoint is referred to as the *expenditure approach* to GDP. On the other hand, if we look at GDP from the seller's side of the counter, where all the income is received and ultimately distributed to the owners of productive factors, we are viewing GDP from the income, or earnings, or allocations side—called the *income approach* to GDP. These two sides of GDP may be summarized by the following equation, which is always valid:

$$
\left.\begin{array}{l}\text{Total} \\ \text{expenditures} \\ \text{on final goods} \\ \text{and services}\end{array}\right\} = \text{GDP} = \left\{\begin{array}{l}\text{Total income} \\ \text{from production} \\ \text{and distribution} \\ \text{of final output}\end{array}\right.
$$

The left side of this equation may be thought of as representing the lower flow channel (labeled "Goods and services") in Figure 3-2, and the right side as representing the upper flow channel.

In the Canadian national accounts these two sides of GDP are referred to as *GDP—income based* and *GDP—expenditure based*. To understand the elements that go into national income accounting and the basic concepts used in much macroeconomic analysis, we need to look at both ways of viewing GDP in more detail. In fact, this is necessary even if you only want to make some sense out of an everyday news item about the state of the economy.

The Expenditure Approach to GDP

The economy can be divided into four distinct sectors: households, businesses, government, and foreign. Total expenditure on GDP can be divided according to which of these sectors makes the expenditure. Personal consumption expenditures are made by households; private domestic investment expenditures by businesses; government expenditures by provincial, local, and federal governments; and, finally, net exports reflect our trade with foreigners.

Personal Expenditure on Consumer Goods and Services (C)

Personal expenditures on consumer goods and services by households are often simply termed **consumption** or designated C. These are household expenditures on consumer durables such as cars and household appliances, on consumer nondurables such as food and clothing, and on services such as medical care, shelter, beauty treatments, haircuts, and dry cleaning. Also included are imputed household expenditures, such as the value of food that farm families produce and consume themselves. In 1990 consumption by Canadians was $399 billion.

Gross Private Domestic Investment Expenditure (I)

Recall the distinction we made in Chapter 1 between the common usage of the term *investment* and that used by economists. In common usage, people often speak of investing money in stocks and bonds, for example. However, these are only financial transactions representing the purchase of titles of ownership. When economists and national income accountants use the term **investment**, they are referring primarily to business firms' expenditures on new capital goods, goods that are used to produce other goods and services.

The term *private* means that we are referring to expenditures by private business firms, as opposed to government agencies, whereas the term *domestic* means that we are speaking of investment expenditures in Canada. The term *gross* will be explained later. Gross private domestic investment, often designated *I*, includes all final purchases of new tools and machines by business firms, all construction (residential as well as business), and all changes in inventories. Several clarifying remarks are in order.

1. Only *new* tools and machines are included because, as we have already stressed, purchases of secondhand goods are not included in GDP.
2. Residential construction of owner-occupied dwellings is included along with factories and apartment buildings. These dwellings are income-producing assets in the sense that they produce a service, shelter, that could be rented out, just like an apartment or other commercial structure. (You might wonder why cars and furniture, which can also be rented, are included in consumption, since the line of reasoning we've been using suggests that they could be included in investment. The fact that they are included under consumption simply illustrates that there is a certain arbitrariness in national income accounting conventions.)
3. Why are changes in business inventories included in gross private domestic investment? First of all, inventories are included in investment because they are a necessary part of the productive process just like any other capital good. Inventories consist of stocks of raw materials and other inputs, goods in various stages of completion, and finished goods not yet sold. The firm has money invested in inventories just as it has money invested in other capital goods. The basic reason for taking account of inventory changes is that GDP is supposed to measure the economy's output of goods and services during a year. But what do inventory changes have to do with this?

Suppose that the economy's production of output for the year exceeds the quantity of output actually sold during the year. The amount of output not sold must go into **inventories**, that is, stocks of unsold goods. Inventories at the beginning of the year consist of goods produced in previous years (and therefore not included in this year's GDP). Therefore, inventories at the end of the year will be larger by the amount of output produced but not sold this year. So, in order to correctly measure this year's total output, or GDP, we must add this increase in inventories to this year's sales of final goods and services.

Alternatively, suppose the quantity of output sold during the year exceeds the quantity of output produced by the economy. Since this excess of sales over production can only occur by selling goods out of inventories, inventories will be lower at the end of the year than at the beginning. Since inventories at the beginning of the year consist of goods produced in previous years, the sale of those goods should not be included in this year's GDP. Hence, the decrease in inventories must be subtracted from this year's total sales of final goods and services in order to correctly measure this year's total output, or GDP.

In the Canadian national accounts, investment is broken down into two major categories: business fixed capital and business inventories. These two classes of investment are further subdivided. Business fixed capital consists of residential construction, non-residential construction, and machinery and equipment. Inventories consist of farm and non-farm inventories.

Gross versus Net Investment: Depreciation

Capital goods wear out and get "used up" during the course of producing other goods—in other words, they are subject to **capital depreciation**. In the Canadian national accounts depreciation is referred to as **capital consumption allowance**. Machines, tools, and equipment need to be repaired or replaced. Factories and buildings require maintenance. That part of gross private domestic investment expenditures that goes toward these replacement activities simply maintains the economy's existing stock of capital. What is left over represents a net addition to the economy's capital stock and is therefore called **net private domestic investment. Gross private domestic investment** equals replacement investment plus net private domestic investment. For example, in 1990 gross private domestic investment in Canada was about $122 billion. Of this amount about $76 billion was replacement investment. This means that there was roughly $46 billion ($122 billion minus $76 billion) worth of net addition to the capital stock in Canada in 1990.

It should be realized that the government of Canada often uses capital consumption allowances as a tool to encourage investment. The government does this by allowing firms to speed up their deduction of depreciation. This policy means that firms that invest can defer their income tax. It also means that if such a program is in effect at the present time, capital consumption may be less than is indicated in the national accounts. Correspondingly, at other times the official figure may underestimate the amount of depreciation. In effect, the figure for capital cost allowance in the national accounts, which are based on income tax data, may not exactly correspond to an economist's definition of depreciation.

Investment and Capital Formation

To a large extent, the economy's ability to produce goods and services depends on its stock of capital goods. (Land and labour are its other important factors of production.) Growth in the economy's capital stock is therefore important because it contributes to growth in the economy's GDP. When gross investment is greater than replacement investment, net investment is positive and there is growth in the capital stock. When gross investment equals replacement investment, net investment is zero and there is no growth in the capital stock. If gross investment is less than replacement investment, net investment is negative and the economy's capital stock is wearing out faster than it is being replaced. Net investment in Canada has generally been positive, but, during the 1930s there were periods when our capital stock actually decreased.

Government Spending (G)

Government spending, often designated G, includes spending on final goods and services by government at all levels—federal, provincial, and local. Local governments not only include towns and cities, but also school boards, hospital boards,

Dutch elm disease control boards, and so on. Expenditures on services include wages paid to all government employees, civilian and military. We have already noted that government transfer payments are not included in GDP because they are not purchases of current production. These payments are not included in government expenditures for the same reason they are not included in GDP. In the Canadian national accounts, government spending is divided into current expenditures of goods and services, and government investment on fixed capital and inventories. In 1990 total current expenditures on goods and services by Canadian governments were $132 billion. Total government investment was $17 billion.

Net Exports (X_n)

The total expenditures on final goods and services in our economy include those made by foreigners on our output as well as those made by our own residents on foreign goods and services. Foreign purchases of our output are **exports**. Our purchases of foreign output are **imports**. Since GDP is supposed to be a measure of productive activity in our economy, it should only measure the output actually produced domestically. Imports are already counted in C, I, and G. Imports must therefore be subtracted from total expenditures on final goods and services when measuring GDP. Exports are not included in C, I, and G. Since exports represent goods produced domestically, they must be added in. National income accountants do this by simply adding in exports and subtracting out imports. That is, they add in the difference between exports and imports, or **net exports** which are designated X_n.

$$X_n = \text{Net exports} = \text{exports} - \text{imports}$$

Net exports can be either positive or negative depending on whether exports are larger or smaller than imports. In 1990 net exports were positive. Exports were 169 billion dollars and imports were 167 billion.

Summary of the Expenditure Side of GDP

There is one more element in the calculation of the GDP from the expenditure side. Because Statistics Canada does not have exact records of every transaction that occurs in Canada, it cannot make an exact calculation of GDP. As a result, there is always some error involved in the estimate. While this error is not generally believed to be substantial, it does mean that the expenditures approach to calculating GDP does not produce a value exactly equal to the value calculated by the income approach. In order to reconcile the two approaches, a statistical correction factor, *statistical discrepancy*, is included. If the value derived by the expenditures approach was $120 million more than the value derived by the incomes approach, then half of this discrepancy would be subtracted from the expenditure side and half would be added to the incomes side. Although it is very small, this correction must be made because we know in theory both approaches must yield the same result. In 1990, $231 million was subtracted from the expenditure-based side of GDP.

Checkpoint 19-3

Assume that the Department of Finance's chief economist was reported to have made the following observation about GDP growth: "Although the fourth quarter growth rate probably won't exceed the third quarter's, the composition will be better as more growth will come from personal consumption and less from inventory accumulation." Why do you think he or she felt this particular composition of growth in the fourth quarter was better than that of the third quarter?

While this statistical discrepancy term is important in the actual measurement of GDP, it is not relevant to theoretical discussions and will not be included in our models. When GDP is viewed from the expenditure side, it is equal to the sum of personal consumption expenditures C, gross private domestic investment I, government expenditures G, and net exports X_n. In brief, from the expenditure side:

$$GDP = C + I + G + X_n$$

The Income Side of GDP

Now let's consider GDP from the seller's side of the counter. Viewed from this vantage point, GDP is distributed as payments or income to the owners of all the inputs that contribute to its production. These payments consist of wages, interest, rent, and profit. In addition, a certain amount goes to pay indirect business taxes and a portion is provided for capital consumption allowances. The only other elements are the inventory valuation adjustment and the other half of the statistical discrepancy.

Wages and Salaries

Wages and salaries, or employee compensation, consist of all payments to employees for labour services of any kind. In the Canadian national accounts these are referred to as wages, salaries, and supplementary labour income (bonuses and tips come immediately to mind). Also included are employer contributions to the social insurance and to private pension, health, and dental insurance plans, and employer payments in kind, the personal use of a company car, for example. These supplemental benefits to wages and salaries are viewed as part of the necessary wage payments that employers must make to obtain the labour services they want. In 1990 this item in the national accounts was $378 billion.

Interest and Miscellaneous Investment Income

Consistent with the notion that earned income is the payment for the use of productive factors, interest is the payment made by businesses for the use of financial capital. It does not include interest payments by government or consumers. It can be regarded as a payment for the service of capital. The miscellaneous investment income is of relatively little consequence. It also includes some rents in the form of royalties to individuals. In 1990 this entry in the national accounts was $58 billion.

Rents

In the national income accounts, rent includes the income earned by households for the use of their real property holdings such as land and buildings of all kinds. It also includes the imputed rent of owner-occupied dwellings. In addition, it embraces income payments received by households from copyrights, patent rights, and royalties from the use of things such as a famous name or an endorsement by a famous person. In the normal breakdown in the Canadian national accounts, rents are not shown as a separate item. They are included in other categories.

Profits

National income accounts break profit into three categories: corporate profits, accrued income of farm operators from farm production, and net income of nonfarm unincorporated business including rent.

Corporate Profits

Corporate profits are divided into three parts. Part of corporate profits are used to pay corporate income tax. The balance can either be paid to stockholders as **dividends** or be retained as **undistributed corporate profits**. The latter funds are normally reinvested by the firm in new plant and equipment. In theory (and normally in practice) the stockholders will "earn" that part of profits in the form of appreciated stock prices. In 1990 corporate profits before taxes were $45 billion.

Accrued Income to Farm Operators from Farm Production

This rather complicated title indicates the net income of farmers from their farm operation. It is net of operating expenses and the capital consumption allowance on machinery and farm buildings. It includes the imputed value of farm output consumed on the farm and the value of any physical changes in inventories. It does not include any income earned off the farm from nonfarm work. This item amounted to $3 billion in 1990.

Net Income of Non-Farm Unincorporated Business Including Rent

This category refers to the income earned by the owners of unincorporated businesses. Many professionals, such as doctors, lawyers, and accountants, and many other small businesses are not incorporated. After these owner-operated businesses have paid wages, rent, and interest to all the factors of production they hire, what remains out of their total sales revenue is income or profit to the owners—proprietors' income. For 1990 it was $36 billion.

Other Components in GDP—Incomes Based

The preceding items roughly correspond to the factor payments in the circular flow model. However, they do not include all the entries in the income-based approach to GDP. The remaining items are now discussed.

Inventory Valuation Adjustment

The inventory valuation adjustment is necessary because businesses often carry inventories over from one year to the next. In the process they frequently profit because the price of the goods carried over increases in the subsequent year. This increase in value of an existing good does not represent real output; therefore, it must be subtracted from GDP in the year in which it is sold. Naturally if prices fell, the valuation adjustment would be added to the next year GDP. In 1990 inventory valuation adjustment amounted to a negative $145 million.

Indirect Taxes Less Subsidies

Indirect taxes consist of sales and excise taxes and business property taxes. The old manufacturer's sales tax and the GST are included in this element. Because sales and excise taxes are levied on the goods and services businesses produce and not on the businesses themselves, the term *indirect* is used to describe them. Since indirect taxes are paid to the government, they are not a payment or earned income to a factor directly used by the firm to produce a product, as is the case for wages, interest, rent, and profit. Nonetheless, indirect taxes must be paid out of the sales price of the product. For example, suppose that a firm must receive $10 per unit of a good to cover the costs of all the factors used to produce it. If the government levies a 7 percent sales tax, the firm must charge a price of $10.70 to cover both its factor costs and the $.70 it owes the government. Since $10.70 is what must be spent to get a unit of the product (the expenditure side of GDP), the $.70 indirect business tax must be included on the income side of GDP if the two sides are to be equal. This is necessary even though the sales tax is not an item of earned income for any factor of production.

The government sometimes pays subsidies to producers. These subsidies reduce the cost of production and the sale price of the goods and services that the firms receive. Even if the subsidized producer does not pass its savings on to the buyer, these subsidies will show up as higher profits. In calculating GDP by the incomes approach, therefore, indirect taxes less subsidies must be included. Indirect taxes less subsidies were $75 billion in 1990.

Capital Consumption Allowances—Depreciation

We have already discussed the concept of depreciation, or capital consumption allowances. It is the difference between gross investment and net investment. When the economy produces its annual output of final goods and services, part of its capital stock or productive capacity is worn out, or used up in the process. If you produce 10 hammers but wear out 2 hammers in the process, it would be misleading to say that you are 10 hammers ahead. Similarly, after deducting indirect taxes less subsidies from GDP, it would be misleading to say that all of the remainder is income earned by the factors of production in the form of wages, interest, rent, and profit. An allowance must first be made for the capital stock that was worn out in the process—the depreciation of machines, tools, and commercial and residential buildings. Therefore, when GDP is viewed from the income side, in addition to deducting indirect taxes less subsidies, it is also necessary to deduct depreciation, or capital consumption allowances, before we may view the remainder as income earned in the form of wages, interest, rent, and profit. In 1990 depreciation was $76 billion.

TABLE 19-5   The Expenditure Side and the Income Side of GDP: 1990
(Millions of Dollars)

Expenditure or Output Side of GDP		Income or Allocations Side of GDP	
Add:		Add:	
		Wages, etc.	$377,627
Consumption (C)	$398,711	Corporate profits	45,145
		Interest income	57,940
Government (G)	148,891	Farm income	3,348
		Unincorpcorporated business	36,282
Investment (I)	122,156	Inventory valuation	−145
		Indirect taxes less	
Net exports (X_n)	2,050	subsidies	75,103
		Depreciation	76,045
(Statistical discrepancy)	−231	(Statistical discrepancy)	232
Equals GDP	671,577	Equals GDP	671,577

Source: Statistical Canada. *Canadian Economic Observer,* September 1991 (11–010)

Statistical Discrepancy

This is the other half of the statistical correction that was discussed earlier in conjunction with the expenditures approach to GDP. For 1990, $232 million was added to the income-based side of GDP.

Summary of the Two Sides of GDP

Table 19-5 summarizes our discussion of the two sides of GDP. The items on the expenditure, or output, side are on the left, and the items on the income, or allocation, side are on the right. Data for the Canadian economy for 1990 are given to illustrate how the sum of the expenditure items on the left-hand side of the table add up to the sum of the income items on the right-hand side of the table. Each side, of course, sums up to GDP.

Related National Income Accounting Concepts

There are five other important and related national income accounting concepts needed for a complete picture of the basics of national income accounting. These are gross national product (GNP), net national product (NNP), national income (NI), personal income (PI), and disposable income (DI). Each may be viewed as a link between the total sales of final goods and services, or GDP, and the amount of those total sales receipts that households receive. You already are familiar with the relationship between GDP and GNP. This section will introduce you to the other four concepts.

Net National Product (NNP)—GNP Minus Depreciation

We noted earlier that if you wear out 2 hammers while producing 10 hammers, you are 8 hammers "better off," not 10. True, 10 hammers were produced and that quantity is a measure of total productive activity over some period of time. But in order to assess what that productive activity has actually provided, it is necessary to deduct the 2 hammers used up to get the net product of our efforts.

Similarly, GDP is a measure of the economy's total productive activity. But it makes no adjustment to account for the quantity of the year's output that must be used to replace the goods used up in producing this year's output. To do so, we subtract the annual depreciation of the economy's capital stock, or capital consumption allowance, from GNP to get the economy's net national product. **Net national product (NNP)** *measures the dollar value of the economy's annual output of final goods and services after adjustment is made for the quantity of the year's output needed to replace goods used up in producing that output.*

Net national product can be obtained by deducting net foreign investment income and the capital consumption allowance from GDP. Obviously it does not matter whether GDP is obtained by the incomes or the expenditures approach. The calculation is illustrated in Table 19-6.

Net national income (NNI) can be obtained by deducting indirect taxes less subsidies from NNP. NNI is also corrected for any statistical discrepancy. The remaining national income accounting concepts are net domestic income (NDI), personal income (PI), and personal disposable income (PDI). PI and PDI are often used by economists as measures of economic welfare. It is possible to derive the values for these measures from NNI. NDI equals NNI less net investment income from non-residents. (Generally for Canada, this latter value is negative, so we are subtracting a minus or in effect adding the value.) PI equals NDI plus transfer payments. PDI equals PI less personal taxes and transfers to government. However, this is not the method currently used by Statistics Canada to derive these measures. They are derived in Table 19-6 as they are derived in the national accounts.

Personal income (PI) is the income earned and received by households in Canada. Part of net national income does not reach households. The major

TABLE 19-6   **Deriving Gross National Product, Net National Product, Net National Income, Personal Income, and Disposable Income from GDP: 1990 (in Millions of Dollars)**

Gross domestic product (GDP)	671,577
Add: net investment income from non-residents	−23,953
Equals: gross national product (GNP)	647,624
Deduct: capital consumption allowance	76,045
Equals net national product (NNP)	571,579
Deduct: indirect taxes less subsidies	75,103
Statistical discrepancy	232
Equals net national income (NNI)	496,244
Wages, salaries and supplemental labour income	377,627
Add: net income received by farmers from farm production	3,191
Net income from nonfarm unincorporated business income, including rents	36,282
Interest, dividends, and miscellaneous investment income	87,478
Current transfers	85,590
Equals: personal income (PI)	590,168
Deduct: personal taxes and transfer payments to government	135,359
Equals: personal disposable income (PDI)	454,809

Source: Statistics Canada. *National Income and Expenditure Accounts*, January 1992 (13–001)

components that households do not receive are corporate income (or profit) taxes and undistributed corporate profits. On the other hand, households receive some income that is not included in net national income. This income comes in the form of transfer payments. From the standpoint of society as a whole, these do not actually represent income because there is no corresponding real output. However, from the standpoint of the households that receive them, these payments do represent a real improvement in their purchasing power. On the other hand, households cannot control how all of their personal income is spent. Some of their personal income must go to pay personal taxes. **Personal disposable income (PDI)** measures the income over which households have control. It measures their control of resources. For this reason it is probably the best measure of how well off they actually are. Personal income and personal disposable income are both derived in Table 19-6.

The Circular Flow Model Revisited

In Chapter 3 we discussed how the economy could be viewed as a circular flow of income. It is time to return to the concept of the circular flow and to relate it to the national accounts. In the process we will add the rest of the world to our circular flow diagram. Figure 19-2 is a flow diagram of

FIGURE 19-2 Expenditure and Income Flows in the National Accounts

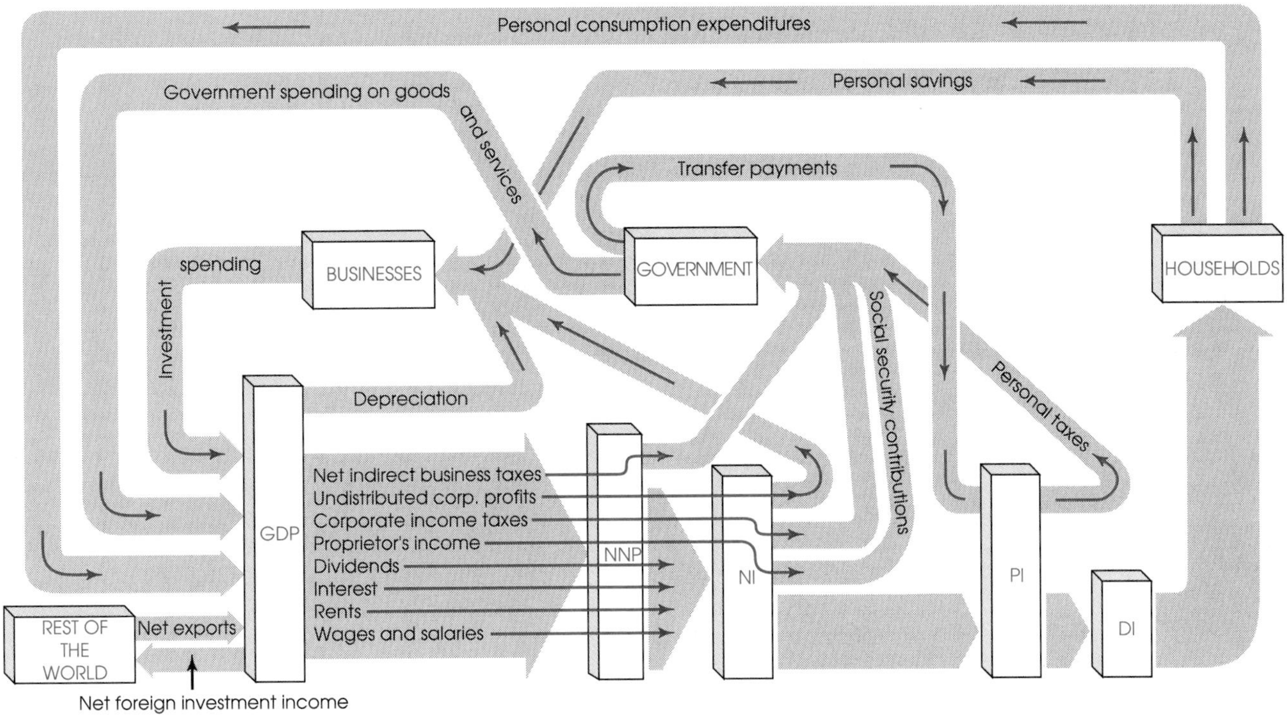

The circular flow diagram presented here elaborates on Figure 3-3 and shows how the actual components of the national accounts are related in the circular flow of the Canadian economy. This figure may be viewed as representing an open, capitalistic, mixed economy.

the economy in terms of the national accounts as discussed in this chapter. Flowing out of the right of the GDP block is the income side of GDP. Flowing into it is the expenditures side. This diagram emphasizes the fact that all expenditures and all income are interrelated. It shows how the expenditure and income sides of GDP are linked to each other. It also clearly shows how income results from expenditures and how income in turn gives rise to expenditures in an ongoing, repetitive process. Figure 19-2 can be used to envision how all the national accounting concepts are related. You are urged to study it carefully.

Summary

1. Gross domestic product (GDP) is the market value of the economy's total output of final goods and services produced during a year.

2. GDP does not include "nonproductive" transactions, such as the purchase and sale of used goods, the trading of stocks and bonds in financial markets, and private and public transfer payments. Certain productive non-market activities are included, such as the imputed rent on owner-occupied housing and the value of food produced and consumed by farm families. However, other activities are not included, such as the services performed by homemakers and the myriad tasks performed by do-it-yourselfers.

3. Money GDP, or GDP in current prices or dollars, measures the dollar value of GDP in a given year in terms of the prices at which final goods and services actually were sold in that year. Real GDP, or GDP in constant prices or dollars, measures the dollar value of GDP in a given year in terms of the prices at which final goods and services sold for in some base, or benchmark, year.

4. When calculating GDP, care must be taken to avoid double, or multiple, counting of intermediate goods.

5. GDP is an accounting measure and was never intended to be a welfare measure. GDP does not reflect changes in the composition of output nor does it take account of the costs of pollution or the benefits of leisure. Per capita GDP is a better indicator of an economy's welfare than GDP alone, but neither really tells us anything about the true distribution of any economy's output among its citizens.

6. When GDP is viewed from the expenditure, or output, side it equals the sum of personal consumption expenditures made by households; gross private domestic investment expenditures made by business firms; government expenditures made by federal, provincial, and local governments; and net exports, the difference between foreign purchases of our goods and our purchases of foreign goods.

7. When GDP is viewed from the income side, it appears as payments, or income, in the form of wages, interest, rent, and profit to the owners of all the inputs that contribute to its production. In addition, a certain amount goes to pay indirect business taxes and a portion is provided for capital consumption allowances.

8. In addition to GDP, there are several other important and interrelated national income accounting concepts: (1) gross national product; (2) net national product, which equals gross national product minus capital consumption allowances or depreciation; (3) net national income, which equals net na-

tional product minus indirect business taxes; (4) net domestic income, which equals net national income plus net investment income from nonresidents personal income; (5) personal income, which equals net domestic income minus income earned but not received (corporate income or profits taxes and undistributed corporate profits) plus income received but not currently or necessarily earned (public and private transfer payments); and (6) personal disposable income, which equals personal income minus personal taxes.

Key Terms and Concepts

capital depreciation
consumption
deflation
exports
gross domestic product
   (GDP)
gross national product
   (GNP)
gross private domestic
   investment
imports

indirect taxes
inflation
inventories
investment
money GDP
net exports
net national income (NNI)
net national product
   (NNP)
net private domestic
   investment

per capita GDP
personal disposable
   income (PDI)
personal income (PI)
price index
real GDP
transfer payments
undistributed corporate
   profits
value added

Questions and Problems

1. Why is GDP a flow?
2. Why are inventories not a flow?
3. When we measure GDP, why is the problem of productive versus nonproductive transactions never an issue in the case of services (as distinct from goods)?
4. How is a transfer payment different from the purchase of a final good? Why is Christmas so "good for business" if gifts are merely private transfer payments?
5. Home milk delivery service used to be more common a generation ago than it is today, yet milk consumption per capita has not changed all that much in the meantime. What effect do you think the gradual decrease in home milk delivery has had on GDP and why?
6. When measuring GDP, what similarity do you see between the problem of double, or multiple, counting and the problem of nonproductive market transactions?
7. It has been argued that the production of goods often gives rise to externalities, such as polluted rivers and air, whose costs to society are not included in the price of the final good. Suppose that the average price of an automobile is $17,000. Suppose additionally that it would cost $1,000 to clean up the air and water pollution associated with the production of an automobile but that neither the auto company nor the buyer of the car has to pay the cost—the "mess" is simply not cleaned up. If the company were forced to clean up the mess, what would be the effect on money GDP? What would be the effect on real GDP? What do you think of the contention that GDP is such a "silly" measure that if allowance were made for the cost of economic "bads," GDP actually would go up?
8. GDP is supposed to measure the economy's output of final goods and services. But in what way and to what extent could it also be said to be a measure of the value of the services of productive factors?

9. The following national income accounting data are for Canada for 1929 (in millions of dollars), the last year before the onset of the Great Depression of the 1930s.

Wages, salaries, and supplemental labour income	$2,928
Government purchases	652
Statistical discrepancy (expenditure based)	−49
Accrued net income of farm operators from farm production	393
Net income of non-farm unincorporated business including rent	770
Business investment	1,230
Inventory valuation adjustment	−15
Indirect taxes less subsidies	711
Interest and miscellaneous investment income	183
Net exports	−16
Capital consumption allowances	726
Statistical discrepancy (income based)	50
Personal consumption	4,583
Current transfers from government	92
Corporate profits before taxes	634

Use the data in the table to answer the following questions about the year 1929. Show your work.

a. Calculate GDP by the incomes approach.

b. Calculate GDP by the expenditure approach.

10. Assume that there are only three goods available in an economy. They are food, shelter, and clothing. In year 1 an average family buys 10 units of food at $20 per unit, 2 units of shelter at $400 per unit, and 1 unit of clothing at $40 per unit. Their cost of living would be 10 × $20 plus 2 × $400 plus 1 × $40 or $1,040. Now assume that in year 2 the prices change so that food costs $21, shelter costs $440 and clothing costs $38. The family's cost of living is now 10 × $21 plus 2 × $440 plus 1 × $38 or $1,128. The consumer price index can be calculated by dividing $1,128 by $1,040 and then multipling by 100. It would be approximately 108.5. There would have been 8.5 percent inflation over the year. Now assume that the prices in the second year are $22 for food, $429 for shelter, and $39 for clothing. Calculate the consumer price index using those assumptions.

Chapter 20

Economic Fluctuations, Unemployment, and Inflation

Economic fluctuations have been a major problem for all industrial economies throughout history. Canada is no exception. Unemployment and inflation are major costs associated with that problem. In this chapter we will concern ourselves with the nature of business cycles and the interrelated problems of unemployment and inflation. Much of our discussion in the following chapters will focus on trying to understand the causes of economic fluctuations, unemployment, and inflation.

How the Level of Economic Activity Changes over Time

Even the most casual observer of our economy is aware that its performance varies greatly over time. Periods of rapid growth alternate with periods of slower growth or even contraction. Periods of expanding business and employment opportunities are followed by periods of increased business failures and rising unemployment. These economic fluctuations, often referred to as **business cycles**, are most commonly recognized by their effects on unemployment, sales, and the level of prices. Of course, the business cycle is reflected in many other measures of economic activity as well.

Growth and Fluctuations

Some idea of the way the Canadian economy moves is conveyed in frame (a) of Figure 20-1 by the graph of real GDP (1986 dollars) since 1926. While the information in this figure is Canadian, the pattern has been very similar for the United States, United Kingdom, and other industrial countries. Two things are obvious: The economy grows over time, but there are irregular fluctuations in its rate of growth from one year to the next. An economy has a long-term growth trend but with cycles around that trend. The size of these fluctuations or cycles is further illustrated by the graph of the annual percentage changes in real GDP over this period of time, as seen in frame (b) of Figure 20-1. The long-term growth trend is also shown in frame (b). Since 1950 these fluctuations have been less violent than those of the 1930s or the 1940s. The size of the fluctuations during the 1930s was a reflection of unstable conditions resulting from the Great Depression and the beginning of World War II. Those of the 1940s came about when the economy was fully converted to a wartime economy during the first half of the decade and then reconverted to a peacetime economy during the second half. It is easy to see from frame (a) of Figure 20-1 why one might describe the economy as climbing a hill and then resting on a plateau before climbing another hill.

The Business Cycle

The fluctuations in real GDP that are more clearly shown in frame (b) of Figure 20-1 are often called *business cycles*. Comparing frames (a) and (b) of Figure 20-1, we can see that the business cycle is a phenomenon quite separate from the growth trend in this aggregate measure of economic activity. The *growth trend* (of roughly 4.1 percent over this period) is represented by the horizontal line in the bottom graph. The business cycles during this period are represented by the irregular but recurrent up and down movement of the saw-toothed solid line about this trend. *Business cycles are irregular but recurrent patterns of fluctuations in economic activity.*

These fluctuations are apparent in aggregate measures of sales, output, income, employment, and a host of other measures over a period of years, quite apart from any longrun trends in these series.

Phases of the Business Cycle

A hypothetical, stylized version of the business cycle, measured in terms of real GDP, is shown in Figure 20-2. The cycle may be viewed as having four phases: a peak, a recession, a trough, and an expansion. The **recession** phase

---

LEARNING OBJECTIVES

After reading this chapter, you will be able to:

1. Define the term *business cycle* and identify its four phases.
2. Explain how different industries and segments of the economy are affected differently by the business cycle.
3. Identify the major determinants of the business cycle.
4. Discuss the various types of unemployment and relate them to the nonaccelerating inflation rate of unemployment.
5. Relate the rate of unemployment to the level of aggregate demand.
6. Define *inflation*.
7. Explain the consequences of anticipated and unanticipated inflation.
8. Relate the consumer price index (CPI) to the cost of living.

FIGURE 20-1   Growth of Real GDP and Rate of Change

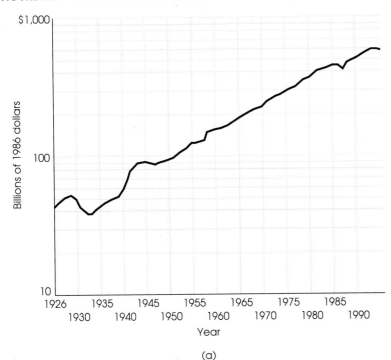

(a)

Frame (a) shows real GDP (1986 dollars) since 1926. It fluctuates about a long-term growth trend. Note that the vertical axis in frame (a) is a logarithmic, or ratio, scale on which equal distances represent equal percentage changes. (Convince yourself by measuring that the distance from 600 to 900 equals that from 1,000 to 1,500.) If real GDP were plotted on an ordinary arithmetic scale, its plot would curve sharply upward, because a given percentage change in a small number would be represented by a smaller distance than the same percentage change in a larger number.

The plot of the annual percentage changes in real GDP shown in frame (b) gives a more vivid picture of the fluctuations in real GDP around the long-term growth trend, the business cycles with their peaks and troughs. These fluctuations have been milder since the early 1950s by comparison with the 1930s and the turbulent war and postwar years of the 1940s.

(b)

Source: Statistics Canada. *Canadian Economic Observer, Historical Statistical Supplement*, 1990/91 (11-210)

FIGURE 20-2 **Phases of the Business Cycle**

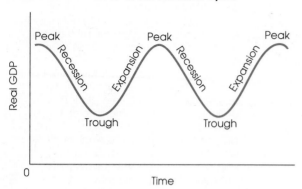

The hypothetical business cycles shown here (measured in terms of real GOP) are idealizations. Actual business fluctuations are never this regular or periodic, and no two are ever quite this similar to each other.

corresponds to the contraction, or slowing down, of economic activity. During this phase typically unemployment rises while sales, income, and investment all fall. An unusually severe recession, such as occurred in the 1930s, is called a **depression**. The Great Depression is obvious in Figure 20-1. The lower turning point of the business cycle is called the **trough**. At this point economic conditions are at a low ebb. The trough is followed by an upturn in economic activity, the **expansion** (or **recovery**) phase of the cycle. During this phase unemployment falls while sales, income, output, and capital formation all rise. The subsequent upper turning point is referred to as the **peak** (or **boom**) phase of the cycle. During this phase, output, income, sales, and capital formation reach their highest levels while unemployment falls to its lowest level. Business and consumer optimism about the future typically rise throughout the expansion phase of the cycle and fall during the recession phase.

Comparison of the real world of Figure 20-1 with the hypothetical one of Figure 20-2 indicates that actual business cycles are not nearly as regular or periodic as the stylized picture presented in Figure 20-2. This is the reason real-world business cycles are often more accurately called *business fluctuations*. No two cycles are ever quite alike. Furthermore, it is not always clear exactly when the economy is passing into another phase of the business cycle.

Seasonal Variation

To get a clearer picture of business cycles, we have seen that it is helpful to abstract from any longrun trend that may be in the data. This is essentially what was done in frame (b) of Figure 20-1. In addition, it is also helpful to adjust the data for **seasonal variation**. For example, general retail sales are typically high in December because of the holidays. On the other hand, sales of a particular good, air conditioners, are typically low at that time of the year but higher during the summer months. From the standpoint of the business cycle we need to know how sales look after allowing for their typical seasonal behaviour. Actual retail sales data typically rise from November to December in a given year. When we allow for the usual seasonal rise in the data at that time of year, we can more accurately determine if the economy is in an expansionary or a recessionary phase.

How do statisticians adjust data to remove seasonal variation? Suppose past monthly sales data indicate that, on average, snowmobile sales in December are

1.9 times as high as average monthly sales over the course of a year. Similarly, suppose that snowmobile sales in June are only .4 times as large as average monthly sales over the course of a year. To remove the seasonal variation from the data, the statistician would divide the December sales figures by 1.9 and the June sales figures by .4. In similar fashion, the sales figures for each month and each good or service would be adjusted by such seasonal adjustment factors. The resulting sales figures are said to be *seasonally adjusted.*

One of the difficulties with seasonal adjustment is that seasonal variation patterns may change over a period of several years. Given that the seasonal adjustment factors are necessarily derived from past data, they are not able to account for these changes in the most recent data. Thus, seasonal adjustment may not be completely accurate in removing seasonal variations from data.

Duration of Cycles

The ups and downs of the Canadian economy can be traced back to before Confederation. The data from 1926 are particularly good. Before that time the government did not keep as complete a record of Canada's economic performance. From Figure 20-1 it is obvious that cycles can vary in length and severity. However, the cycles in the 1950s, 1960s, and 1970s were not as severe or in general as long as those in the 1930s and 1940s. Notwithstanding, the 1982 recession was severe.

Determinants of the Business Cycle

The characteristics of the business cycles of an economy will depend on the shocks that hit it and the way it is put together—that is, the nature of its products, the structure of its markets, and the interconnecting relationship between its industries.

Product Characteristics: Durables and Nondurables

Industries that produce durable goods—steel, machinery, motor vehicles, construction, consumer appliances, and so forth—experience much larger fluctuations in employment, production, and sales over the course of the business cycle than do industries that produce nondurable goods—textiles, food products, agricultural commodities, and so forth. (While food and agricultural products may not vary over the business cycle in the highly consistent manner that steel, new house construction, and automobile manufacturing do, agriculture is in general a very unstable industry.) The major reason for this lies precisely in the difference in the nature of durable and nondurable goods.

When the economy goes into a recession, unemployment rises. Businesses find themselves with idle productive capacity in the face of lagging sales as consumer and business optimism about the future declines. Consumers tend to make the old car or refrigerator last another year, particularly if they are unemployed or faced with increasing job uncertainty. Similarly, businesses make do with existing plant and equipment, especially since some of it is idled by the slowdown in sales and the accompanying buildup of unsold inventories. In short, when times are bad and a cloud of uncertainty shrouds the future,

Checkpoint* 20-1

When we look at the graph in frame (a) of Figure 20-1, it appears that the expansion phase of business cycles is a great deal longer than the recession phase. Would you agree with this assessment? Why or why not? What do you think the monthly seasonal adjustment factors for university textbook sales would look like over the course of a year?

Answers to all Checkpoints can be found at the back of the text.

POLICY PERSPECTIVE

Dating Business Cycle Peaks and Troughs: When Do They Occur?

How do we know when the expansion phase of a business cycle is over and a recession has begun, or when a recession is over and an expansion has begun? Such turning points in the business cycle become easier to recognize the more time passes after their occurrence. However, there is an unavoidable arbitrariness in designating the dates of turning points because economic theory provides no hard and fast criteria.

Many economists and government officials are sympathetic to designations of turning points that focus on the behaviour of real GDP.

For example, a business cycle peak might be said to have occurred and the economy to be in a recession if real GDP does not grow for at least two quarters in a row. One might well ask why the criterion is not one quarter, or three out of four, all of which points out the element of arbitrariness in any definition. Other important factors that economists often take into consideration are the behaviour of the unemployment rate, the rate of investment spending on new plant and equipment, and the rate of capacity utilization in the manufacturing sector (that is, the degree to which

the available stock of capital equipment is being used in production).

For Discussion

- Notice that the recovery shown in Figure P20-1 is much longer than the recession. Why do you think this is likely to be generally true of business cycles?
- The last three quarters in 1986 show virtually no growth. What do you think happened to GDP per capita during that period? Could that period be called a recession?

FIGURE P20-1 **A Business Cycle**

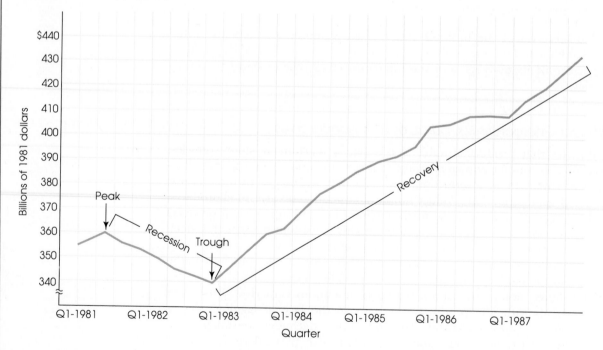

Source: Statistics Canada, *National Income and Expenditure Accounts,*
First Quarter, 1989 (13–001)

The 1982 recession was the worst downturn experienced by Canada since the Great Depression. It is a classic example of a business cycle.

durable goods purchases will tend to be postponed. This is possible precisely because durable goods are durable. This, of course, means that a recession hits the durable goods industries especially hard.

By contrast, nondurable goods purchases cannot be put off nearly as long. People can't postpone eating, brushing their teeth, being sick, or heating their homes. They also seem very reluctant to cut back on smoking and other personal consumption habits. As a result, history shows that during recessions nondurable goods industries do not experience nearly as severe a decline in employment, production, and sales as do the durable goods industries.

On the other hand, during business cycle expansions, durable goods purchases previously postponed are now carried out. Rising sales put increasing demands on productive capacity, and businesses have a greater incentive to buy new equipment and expand plant size. Similarly, consumers have more job certainty, employment, and rising paycheques, and more households are willing to replace the old car and refrigerator with new ones. As a result, durable goods purchases pick up at a faster rate than purchases of nondurables.

The growth in importance of the service sector has also had some impact on the nature of business cycles. Services are in some ways like nondurable goods, as they cannot be stored. If they are essential, buyers will likely continue to demand them even if there is a recession. However many services are not essential. If the family's budget is tight, a haircut can wait or even be done at home.

Regional Variations

Business cycles do not necessarily affect all regions of Canada in the same way. As was mentioned earlier, agriculture is one of the most unstable industries. Other resource-based industries such as fishing, forestry, mining, and oil also tend to be unstable. Weather plays a major role in the ups and downs of agriculture. And not just the weather in Canada is important. A drought in some other part of the world can lead to a boom in the prairie provinces. A bumper crop in Russia can lead to depressed markets for grain. Similarly, the oil industry can be affected by political events in the Middle East or new discoveries of oil in other countries. British Columbia's forest industry can benefit from a foreign housing boom or be hurt by foreign restrictions on cedar shingles. Tourism in the Maritimes could decline because of high gas prices or boom because Americans are afraid to fly to Europe when it is faced with terrorism because of a war in the Middle East. The fact that the different regions of Canada have different economic bases can create policy problems. The economy in the manufacturing-based provinces can be in a boom period while the resource-based provinces are in a recession or vice versa.

Market Structure

Markets in which numerous firms compete with one another in the production and sale of a product tend to reduce prices more sharply in the face of declining demand than do markets dominated by a few large firms that have monopoly power. On the other hand, markets with only a few large producers tend to reduce output and employment more sharply than do markets with numerous competing firms. In short, over the course of the business cycle, markets with only a few large firms adjust to changing demand largely by changing production rather than by changing price. Highly competitive markets with numerous firms adjust largely by changing price rather than by changing output.

Markets in durable goods industries such as steel, electrical machinery, appliances, and automobiles tend to have relatively few large firms. Each of these industries is dominated by less than 10 firms. On the other hand, competitive market structures tend to prevail in nondurable goods industries such as agriculture and wearing apparel. There are literally tens of thousands of farmers and restaurants, for example.

External Factors Affecting the Business Cycle

We have briefly examined a few of the important aspects of the economy's internal, or endogenous, structure that determine how it moves when it is subjected to external shocks. The nature of its products (durable versus nondurable), the structure of its markets (competitive versus monopolistic), and the interconnecting relationships between its industries are all important internal determinants of the economy's motion. In subsequent chapters we will examine other characteristics of the economy's internal structure that are also important determinants of the way it moves. These determinants affect the economy just as weight, size, and center of gravity affect the way a rocking horse moves when given a push.

We have also noted that external circumstances can affect some industries in Canada. However, more needs to be said. Accordingly we will briefly describe a few frequently cited explanatory factors underlying business cycles that are generally regarded as external, or exogenous, causes—like the push applied to a rocking horse. Among these factors are changes in population growth rates, such as the end of the baby boom, and migration trends, such as the wave of 2.6 million immigrants that arrived in Canada between 1903 and 1913; new inventions and technological developments; the discovery of new mineral deposits and energy sources or the reduction of old ones, such as temporarily occurred when OPEC reduced oil exports; the opening up of new land frontiers; and political events and social upheavals, such as wars.

Most of these factors are thought of as exogenous to the workings of the economy. But it is often difficult to make a clear-cut distinction on this score. For example, increases in the population growth rate seem to be encouraged by economic expansion and dampened by recessions. However, this is a two-way street. Increases in the population growth rate tend to stimulate economic expansion, while decreases tend to slow down the growth of demand for goods and services. To the extent that population change is the result of economic factors it could be considered endogenous. Population changes can also result from social changes that have no direct relationship to the economy. The same sort of two-way influences may exist for any of the external factors listed earlier. Unstable economic conditions in post–World War I Germany may have contributed to the rise of Hitler and the advent of World War II, which in turn pulled the Canadian economy out of the depression years of the 1930s. (It is important to realize that, although the war may have provided the stimulus to pull our economy out of the Great Depression, there were far more humane ways to bring about an economic recovery. War may bring economic benefits to some industries or some regions, but it can never be argued that war is economically beneficial in any larger sense.) On the other hand, the hike in oil prices by the OPEC countries in 1973–1974 is viewed by many economists as an exogenous shock to the Western economies that helped trigger the 1974–1975 recession—the second most severe recession in the postwar period. While this hike in oil prices did not affect Canada as much as it did the United States, Japan, and many Western European countries, it did affect us significantly. It affected Canada in part because it led to a reduction in Canadian exports to these countries as their economies contracted.

Finally, the ebb and flow of optimism or confidence about the future—what the great English economist, Lord Keynes, called "animal spirits"—is often cited as a crucial factor in the business cycle. For example, it is sometimes argued that optimism lost touch with reality in the late 1920s. This allegedly led to excessive speculation in land and stocks and to investment in plant, equipment, and apartment and office buildings far beyond what demand warranted. When sober judgment finally set in, the economy was plunged into the deepest and longest depression in our history, and a mood of deep pessimism prevailed. At its depth in 1932, Franklin Roosevelt may have measured the main problem very well when he said, "The only thing we have to fear is fear itself." This quote was as applicable to Canada as it was to the United States. In fact, while there are many other things to be concerned with besides fear itself, it is still applicable to any country today.

Employment and Unemployment

The economy's **labour force** includes all persons age 15 or older (except residents of the territories and Indian reservations, inmates of institutions, and full-time members of the Canadian Forces) who are employed plus all those who are unemployed but actively looking for work. The labour force in our economy amounts to more than half of the population over age 14. Only those individuals who are part of the labour force can be unemployed. The group not in the labour force are not considered unemployed. This group includes full-time students, the retired, and homemakers. These are individuals who voluntarily choose not to be gainfully employed. We will look at those who are in the labour force but who are not working. The unemployed are those individuals who wish to have jobs, but do not. The unemployment rate is the percentage of unemployed in the labour force. Statistics Canada estimates the unemployment rate by polling a sample of Canadians and asking if they are working and if they are seeking employment. Statistically speaking a worker is unemployed if he or she does not have a job, is available to work, and is seeking employment. Many economists would argue that individuals are unemployed if they are not working but are willing and able to work at the going wage rate. In practice the official Statistics Canada definition of unemployment means that individuals can be counted as unemployed if they indicate that they are seeking employment, even though they might not accept a job if it was offered. This situation could exist if individuals had unrealistic wage expectations or did not wish to work but were collecting unemployment insurance and therefore were forced to say that they were willing to accept employment. On the other hand an individual who was willing and able to work at the going wage rate would not be counted as unemployed if she or he had quit looking for employment because he or she knew there were no jobs available. Such individuals are referred to as *discouraged workers*. Depending on whether there are more of the former or the latter individuals in the labour

Checkpoint 20-2

An American economist, Gardner Means, did a study of the percentage drop in product price and the percentage drop in production in each of 10 industries during the onset and downturn of the Great Depression of the 1930s. These industries were textile products, agricultural implements, agricultural commodities, petroleum, motor vehicles, leather, cement, food products, iron and steel, and automobile tires. How do you think they ranked (1) in terms of the degree of price reduction he observed in each of them, and (2) in terms of the degree or output reduction? Industries in Canada tend to be more concentrated than those in the United States. What does this concentration imply for the Canadian economy?

market, the Statistics Canada measure can overestimate or underestimate the true unemployment rate. We will consider such questions as the following: Are there different types of unemployment? Is there such a thing as a normal level of unemployment? What is full employment? What are the costs of unemployment?

Types of Unemployment

A worker may become unemployed in basically three different ways. (1) The worker may quit his or her current job to look for a better job, giving rise to what is called *frictional unemployment*. (2) The worker's current job may be permanently eliminated—the plight of buggy whip makers at the turn of the century—possibly causing *structural unemployment*. (3) The worker's current job may be temporarily eliminated by a recession, thus giving rise to *cyclical unemployment*. Let's look more closely at each of these three types of unemployment.

Frictional Unemployment

Often workers quit one job to look for one that pays better or is more attractive in some other way. (Alternatively, they may be laid off because they are in a particular industry that is declining.) These workers are unemployed for short periods of time while they are between jobs. Suppose, for example, that each worker in the labour force changed jobs once a year and was unemployed for a 2-week transitional period. Suppose also that the number of workers changing jobs at any one time was spread evenly over the year. If this was the only cause of unemployment, then at any time during the year $\frac{2}{52}$, or 3.8 percent, of the labour force would thus be unemployed. If only half of the labour force switched jobs in this manner, the unemployment rate would be 1.9 percent.

Other forms of *frictional unemployment* are due to seasonal layoffs, such as those that affect farm workers and construction workers. New entrants into the labour force with marketable job skills are also frequently unemployed for a brief period of time before finding jobs.

Structural Unemployment

As the term *structural unemployment* implies, this kind of unemployment is due to fundamental changes in the structure of labour demand—specifically, the kinds of jobs that the economy offers. Technological change, the development of new industries and the demise of old ones, and the changing economic role of different regions in the country all mean that new kinds of jobs need to be done and that many old ones cease to exist. The new jobs often require different skills and educational backgrounds than the old ones and are frequently located in different geographic regions.

Workers sometimes find themselves displaced by these structural changes. They may lack the required skills and training needed to gain employment in other areas of the economy. Often they are unwilling or even unable to move away from old friends and familiar neighbourhoods. As a result, they end up among the ranks of the long-term and hard-core unemployed. This is a particular problem among older workers and unskilled workers in declining economic regions such as the outports of Newfoundland, many areas in the Maritimes, the Gaspé, the eastern townships of Quebec, or rural areas in general. Even in generally booming provinces such as Ontario, the unskilled of large cities may face structural unemployment, particularly if they are young and poorly educated or victims of discrimination such as blacks or aborigines. In general, the basic characteristic of the structurally unemployed is their lack of marketable skills (or, in the case of nonwhites, discrimination may play a role).

Cyclical Unemployment

Cyclical unemployment is related to the business cycle. Economists sometimes refer to this type of unemployment as *demand-deficient* or *inadequate demand unemployment*. When the economy's total demand for goods and services rises during the expansion phase of the cycle, employment rises and unemployment falls. During the recession phase of the cycle, total demand for goods and services falls, causing unemployment to rise and employment to fall. Unemployment rates tend to lag behind other variables. That is to say, the unemployment rate does not increase immediately when the recession starts, and unemployment does not decrease immediately when the recovery starts.

Cyclical unemployment looms large in the movement of the unemployment rate. This is illustrated in Figure 20-3, which compares the unemployment rates in four different years. For each year, the unemployment rate is broken into four components: job losers, workers who were laid off or fired; job leavers, workers

FIGURE 20-3 Cyclical Unemployment and the Unemployment Rate

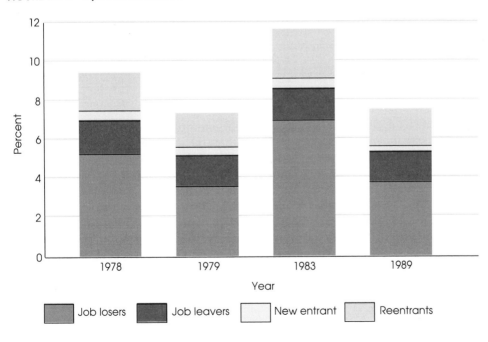

Source: Statistics Canada. *Historical Labour Force Statistics*, 1990 (71–201)

The change in the unemployment rate over the course of the business cycle is largely due to the change in the job-losers component, which reflects cyclical unemployment.

NATURAL RATE

RATE of Employment

os voluntarily; new entrants, workers just entering the labour
force and reentrants, experienced workers who have dropped out of the labour
force for some time but are again looking for work. Two of the years cited, 1978
and 1983, had relatively high unemployment rates. There were significantly
more workers in the job-loser category in these two years than there were in the
low-unemployment years of 1979 and 1989. In fact the percentage of unemployed
workers in the job-loser category in 1983 was nearly equal to total unemployment in 1979
and 1989. Clearly the major source of change in the overall unemployment rate
over the business cycle is this job-loser group. It is interesting to
note that the reentrants category also increased in 1983. This was likely because
when some workers in a family were laid off, other members of the family
went back to work. Often if one spouse loses his or her job, both spouses
seek work.

Free Trade and Unemployment

It is frequently suggested that the U.S.-Canada Free Trade Agreement and the
proposed North American Free Trade Agreement could cause unemployment in
Canada. Often these stories have no basis in fact or are greatly exaggerated. However, there certainly have been some job losses as a result of free trade, and there
will be more in the future. There will also be new jobs created. Essentially, Canada
will lose jobs when the United States (or Mexico) can produce more efficiently, but
gain jobs when Canadian producers are more efficient. In the process, frictional
unemployment will develop as workers move from contracting to expanding industries. Some workers may be too old or immobile to shift, and they will become
structurally unemployed. This latter problem should be minimal because many of
the tariff reductions under the U.S.-Canada Free Trade Agreement were phased
in over time. Other trade agreements usually do the same.

Is Zero Unemployment Desirable—Or, What Is Full Employment?

It is clear from our discussion of frictional unemployment that as long as there
are workers moving from one job to another, the statistical measurement of unemployment will not be zero. Moreover, it is likely that there will normally be a
certain amount of structural unemployment. Some economists believe that these
two types of unemployment constitute a _natural rate of unemployment_ toward which
the economy automatically gravitates in the absence of other disturbances. They
argue that _full employment_ is the level of employment associated with the natural
rate of unemployment. In the early 1960s many Canadian economists would have
accepted that full employment roughly corresponded to a 4 percent unemployment rate—what might be called the _natural unemployment rate_. Since that time the
level of the natural unemployment rate has been revised upward. In recent years
a number of economists have come to think that it may be around 6 percent.

While the term _natural rate of unemployment_ is widely used, it is not a universally
accepted term within the profession. Still, it is clearly true that zero unemployment is unlikely to be attainable or even desirable. However, there is no natural
law that determines the rate of unemployment. The rate of unemployment in
any economy is determined by a variety of institutional, cultural, geographic,
and policy factors. For this reason, unemployment may vary markedly from
one country to another and within any given country from decade to decade.

TABLE 20-1 Comparative Unemployment Rates

Country	1984	1989	July 1990
Canada	11.8%	7.5%	10.4%
France	8.3%	9.4%	9.5%
Germany (West)	8.0%	5.6%	4.6%
Japan	2.6%	2.3%	2.2%
United Kingdom	12.5%	6.4%	9.7%
United States	9.5%	5.5%	6.7%

Source: Statistics Canada. *Canadian Economic Observer*, various dates (11–010)

Table 20-1 lists the unemployment rates in a few major industrial countries. As you can see, there are wide disparities.

The unemployment rate in Japan is substantially lower than the unemployment rates in the other countries cited. In part this might be explained by the tendency of Japanese employers to be more paternalistic than Western employers. Unemployment rates in Canada may be somewhat higher because of the size of this country. A worker who loses a job in one region may find it difficult, if not impossible, to find new employment *quickly* if that employment is 6,000 kilometres away. Given enough time, government policies can influence the level of structural and frictional unemployment. For example, a more generous unemployment insurance program can increase the level of frictional unemployment by allowing workers longer search time to find the best possible job. It is also possible that a generous program will allow a few individuals who are so inclined to avoid working for substantial periods of time. (Whether workers do the former or the latter is a question for positive economics, but whether or not a generous unemployment insurance program is good is a normative question.) A highly efficient nationwide employment service could reduce frictional unemployment. A good vocational education program could reduce structural unemployment by training (or retraining) unemployed workers for available jobs. Thus, there is nothing *natural* about any particular level of unemployment.

While the level of unemployment is ultimately determined by a multitude of institutional, cultural, geographic, and policy variables, there is at any point in time a level of unemployment where there is only structural and frictional unemployment. At that level there is no cyclical unemployment. Imagine an economy in recession. There is inadequate aggregate demand, resulting in cyclical unemployment. As this economy enters into the recovery stage, aggregate demand increases because of increased private and/or government spending. The cyclical unemployment disappears. However, there continues to be frictional and structural unemployment. Further increases in aggregate demand will not further decrease unemployment quickly or painlessly. Quite possibly, further decreases in the unemployment rate would come only in combination with increasing rates of inflation. This level of unemployment could be considered *full employment*, or it could be referred to as *the natural rate of employment*. Some economists prefer to refer to this level of unemployment as the *nonaccelerating inflation rate of unemployment* or **NAIRU**.[1] The argument in favour of this terminology is that it does

---

[1] Inflation will be discussed later in this chapter. Inflation occurs whenever there is an increase in the general price level. The term *nonaccelerating inflation* means that the general price level is increasing at a constant and presumably modest rate.

not imply that there is anything *natural* about this rate of unemployment. Nor does it imply that it is impossible to reduce unemployment below the NAIRU. It does indicate the likely consequences of such a policy. If an economy tries to reduce unemployment below NAIRU by increasing aggregate demand, the rate of inflation will increase.

There is one other term that economists commonly use. Sometimes economists refer to a *target rate* of unemployment. The target rate is normative. It is the rate of unemployment that the government feels it should pursue as a policy goal. This rate might well correspond to the NAIRU. It could be lower, if the society valued the reduction in the unemployment rate more than the problem of increasing inflation. The appropriate target level of unemployment is a policy question.

Measuring Unemployment

The most commonly used definition of **unemployment** states that, to be considered unemployed you must be out of work, looking for a job, and available to take one immediately. Some think this definition is too broad because it doesn't distinguish between those who need jobs to support themselves and their families and those who don't. Hence, some critics say this measure overstates unemployment distress. They point out that a full-time student seeking part-time work, a job-seeking teenager living at home with two working parents, or an individual who could have worked but refused a job because it pays less than he or she wanted counts just as much in this measure of unemployment as does a jobless head of household who has been out of work for several weeks. However, others argue that this measure understates unemployment because it doesn't include discouraged workers who have dropped out of the labour force after a prolonged, unsuccessful search for a job, nor does it include part-time workers who are looking for a full-time job.

Population and Labour Force Growth

Longer-run changes in the size of the labour force relative to the size of the total population have implications for the unemployment rate and the percentage of the working-age population employed. So do longer-run changes in the age and sex makeup of the labour force. If the size of the total population grows faster than the size of the labour force, the number of people demanding goods will grow faster than the number of people who want jobs. Other things remaining the same, this should tend to lower the unemployment rate because more workers will be needed to make the goods. On the other hand, if the size of the labour force grows more rapidly than the size of the total population, the number of people wanting jobs will increase faster than the number demanding goods and services. This will tend to increase the unemployment rate, other things remaining the same.

Since the latter half of the 1960s, the Canadian economy has had to cope with a labour force that has grown at a faster rate than the total population—in other words, the labour force as a percentage of the total population has increased, as shown in Figure 20-4. In part this has been due to the maturing of the post–World War II baby-boom generation, which has swelled the working age population during these years. In addition, the proportion of working age women who have moved into the labour force has increased dramatically.

FIGURE 20-4   Labour Force as a Percentage of Population

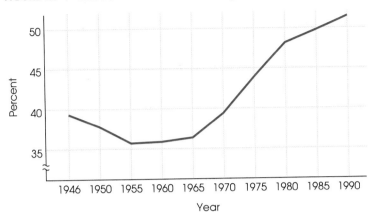

The labour force as a percentage of population fell after the end of World War II as the Canadian economy reconverted to peacetime. It remained relatively constant throughout the 1950s and early 1960s. Since then it has risen substantially. This reflects the maturing "baby-boom" generation entering the labour force, the increased participation of women in the labour force, and the decline in the birthrate since 1961.

Source: Statistics Canada. *Canadian Economic Observer*, various years (11–010); *Canada Yearbook*, various years

Whereas only about 35 percent of the country's population of adult females were in the labour force in the mid-1960s, somewhat more than 58 percent worked or were seeking work in the late 1980s. Taken together, these two trends resulted in much higher labour participation rates. Despite this, the economy did quite well in providing jobs for these people. In the decade 1971–1980 total employment in Canada was up about 32 percent, while population was up about 12 percent. In other words, total employment grew more than two and one half times as fast as the total population. Job creation during the 1971–1980 decade resulted in a growth in employment much greater than at any time in our recent history. Since 1980 employment has continued to grow at a faster rate than population.

On the negative side, many economists argue that the more rapid rate of growth of the labour force relative to that of the total population has contributed to a rise in the level of what should be considered the NAIRU. They believe that the unusually large increase in the number of new job seekers relative to the growth in the population pushes the level of frictional unemployment higher. Another possible factor in a higher natural unemployment rate is the increased flow into the public's pockets of transfer payments—unemployment insurance payments, welfare money, and so on. This may well cause people who are really not trying very hard to find employment to list themselves as unemployed.

The Costs of Unemployment

Labour is an essential factor of production in our economy. Consequently, the greater is the total demand for goods and services, the higher is the level of employment and the lower is the level of unemployment, given the available labour supply. Recall from Chapter 2 that unemployment exists whenever any available factors of production are idle. The term *available* is important.

Unemployment exists among workers whenever there are labourers who make themselves available for work by actively looking for a job but are unable to find one.[2] For society as a whole, unemployment means fewer goods and services are produced: a smaller pie, which means there is less available for all. This is the economic cost of unemployment. As a matter of public policy, unemployment is of particular concern because it also represents hardship for those unemployed. There may also be costs in terms of suicides, family breakups and violence, and generally higher crime rates. How might we measure these costs and hardships?

Economic Cost: The GDP Gap

How can we measure the economic cost of unemployment to society? First, we might estimate the economy's **potential GDP,**[3] or what GDP would be if the economy were at NAIRU. We would then subtract actual GDP from potential GDP to get the **GDP gap**. *The GDP gap is the dollar value of final goods and services not produced because the unemployment rate exceeds some designated level of unemployment.* The GDP gap is therefore a measure of the cost of unemployment.

Economists have attempted to measure the GDP gap. Different economists measure the GDP gap differently because they have different views as to what constitutes the appropriate level of unemployment to use as a standard. To some degree different measures of potential GDP represent different normative views of what is desirable for the economy. A measure (in constant 1986 dollars) of potential GDP and the associated GDP gap—equal to the difference between potential and actual GDP—is shown in Figure 20-5, frame (b). The unemployment rate is shown in Figure 20-5, frame (c). We can see by comparing the two graphs how the GDP gap widens when the unemployment rate rises and narrows when the unemployment rate falls. Indeed, during the early 1970s the unemployment rate was at its lowest levels for the period represented in the graph, and actual GDP exceeded potential GDP (the GDP gap was negative). This reflects the fact that the potential GDP represents not the *maximum* GDP the economy can produce but rather that which it can produce at what is considered a target level of unemployment. At this level of unemployment, the economy is considered to be operating at full employment. When the economy produces above its potential level, productive facilities are being utilized beyond their most efficient capacity levels and there is much overtime employment. The unemployment rate is squeezed below this level.

The GDP gap for the years in which the economy operated below its potential is indicated by the shaded areas in Figure 20-5, frame (b). These areas represent the economic costs of unemployment, measured in constant 1986 dollars. The large costs of the years in the early 1980s reflect the deepest recessions and highest unemployment rates of the postwar years.

---

[2]This is essentially the definition that Statistics Canada uses. Economists sometimes require that a worker must be looking for work and be willing to work at the prevailing wage rate to be considered unemployed.

[3]A discussion on potential GDP can be found in Arthur Okum, "Potential GNP: Its Measurement and Significance" in the *Proceedings of the Business and Economic Statistics Section of the American Statistical Association*, 1962.

FIGURE 20-5   The GDP Gap, the Unemployment Rate, and the Changing General Price Level

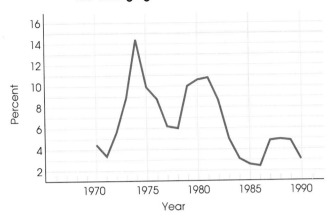

Changes in the GDP deflator

(a)

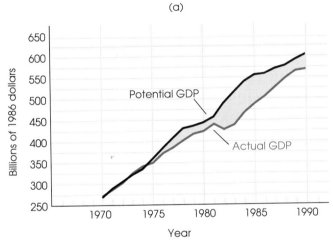

Actual and potential GDP

(b)

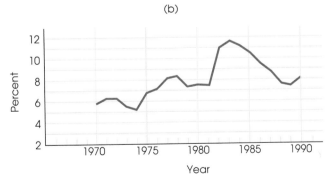

Unemployment rate

(c)

The difference between potential and actual GDP since 1970 is the GDP gap shown in frame (b), expressed in constant 1986 dollars. This gap is a measure of the dollar value of final goods and services not produced because there is unemployment and is therefore a measure of the cost of unemployment. Comparison of the behaviour of the unemployment rate in frame (c) with that of the GDP gap indicates how the GDP gap widens when the unemployment rate increases and narrows when the unemployment rate falls.

While the relationship between inflation and the GDP gap is not as obvious, it is clear that following the narrow GDP gap of the early 1970s, the rate of inflation increased. On the other hand, the rate of inflation dropped following the wide GDP gap of the early 1980s. When viewed in terms of the unemployment rate, rapid inflation followed the low unemployment rate of the early 1970s, while slower inflation followed the high unemployment of the early 1980s.

Sources: GDP deflator, real GDP, and unemployment rates: Statistics Canada. *Canadian Economic Observer, Historical Statistical Supplement*, 1990/91 (11–210). Potential GDP is based on the authors' calculations.

Source: Statistics Canada. *Canadian Economic Observer,* Historical statistical supplement, 1990/91 (11–210)

Other Costs of Unemployment

The burden of unemployment is obviously more severe if you happen to be one of the unemployed than if you are among the employed. And some groups in the labour force tend to have a higher incidence of unemployment than others. For example, in 1983, when our economy experienced its highest rate of unemployment since World War II, the overall unemployment rate for the civilian labour force was 11.9 percent. Yet among males 25 years of age or older, the unemployment rate was 9.2 percent, while among males under 25 it was 22.4 percent. Among those living in the Prairie region, the unemployment rate was 9.7 percent, in Ontario it was 10.4 percent, while in the Atlantic region, it was 15.0 percent and in Quebec it was 13.9 percent. Unemployment rates in Newfoundland and among aborigines were much higher.

Aside from those aspects of unemployment that can be quantified, there is a social pathology associated with unemployment that is more difficult to measure. The unemployed worker often suffers a loss of self-esteem. Medical researchers have reported findings suggesting that anxiety among unemployed workers leads to health problems and family squabbles. Severely prolonged unemployment of family breadwinners often leads to broken homes and suicides. History suggests that high unemployment rates tend to spawn political and social unrest, and that more than one social order has been upset for want of jobs. The high unemployment rates among aboriginal teenagers on reservations have had a lot to do with the sense of hopelessness, desperation, and anger that leads to high crime rates and alcohol abuse.

Checkpoint 20-3

Comparing frames (b) and (c) of Figure 20-5, what appears to be the level of unemployment on which the estimate of potential GDP is based?

Price Changes and Inflation

The burden of unemployment falls most heavily and obviously on those who are unemployed. Although it is often more subtle, inflation affects virtually everybody. Some individuals lose from inflation, while others may actually benefit. *Inflation is a rise in the general level of prices of all goods and services. Inflation therefore reduces the purchasing power of money.*

The term *inflation* is not used when the prices of just a few goods rise. Rather, **inflation** refers to a situation in which the average of all prices rises. Some economists would require that the price increases not only be general but also that they be sustained over a period of time. (Deflation is just the opposite of inflation—that is, the average of all prices falls.) Inflation is not *high* prices, it is *rising* prices. When we discussed the difference between money GDP and real GDP in the previous chapter, we saw that inflation means a dollar will purchase fewer goods tomorrow than it does today.

Recent Experience with Inflation

The annual percentage change in a measure of the general price level (the GDP deflator) for the years since 1970 is shown in Figure 20-5, frame (a). Note that the general price level has gone up, though at different rates, in every year over this period.

It is interesting to compare the size of these percentage increases with the changes in the size of the GDP gap, Figure 20-5, frame (b), and the unemployment rate, Figure 20-5, frame (c). Roughly speaking, the percentage rise in the general price level tended to be smaller in years following an increase in the GDP gap and the unemployment rate—when the economy had more excess capacity. Conversely, the percentage rise in the general price level tended to be greater in the years following lower unemployment rates and smaller GDP gaps. This has long been regarded as the conventional pattern in the relationship among inflation, the GDP gap, and the unemployment rate.

While lower rates of inflation did follow the high unemployment rates and substantial GDP gap of the early 1980s, this period is not typical of past experience in Canada. This period was one of both very high unemployment rates and rapid inflation. This unconventional combination of events gave rise to the term *stagflation,* which means the occurrence of economic stagnation combined with high rates of inflation. In subsequent chapters we will examine explanations of the conventional pattern of the relationship between inflation and unemployment as well as explanations of the pattern known as stagflation.

Anticipated versus Unanticipated Inflation

Inflation is sometimes said to be an effective, continuously operating thief. It steals the purchasing power of your money whether you hold it in your hand, your wallet, your chequing account, or even in the vault of a bank. People have an incentive to protect themselves from inflation just as they have an incentive to protect themselves from theft of any kind. And they will attempt to do so if they anticipate or expect inflation. It is when they fail to anticipate inflation that they are most often hurt by it. Some individuals may not be able to protect themselves from inflation even if they do anticipate it. While this view is widely held, it is important to understand that it is a normative view. Not everyone views inflation as a thief. It is equally valid (and equally a value judgment) to describe unemployment as a thief that robs the unemployed of their livelihood.

Anticipated Inflation and Contracts: Indexing

The terms of a great many economic transactions are stated in *dollars* and are spelled out in a contract to which all parties to the transaction agree. Labour unions and management agree to a labour contract stipulating the hourly wage rate to be paid, along with other conditions of employment—length of work-week, amount of paid vacation, and so on. Loan contracts set out the terms of loans mutually agreed to by borrowers and lenders. These terms include the amount of a loan, the interest rate to be paid by the borrower, and the rights of each party in the event of default. Pension plans, insurance policies, rent leases, construction contracts, and contracts to produce and deliver goods to a customer by a certain date at a certain price are all examples of such contracts.

When one or both parties anticipate inflation, they will attempt to account for it explicitly in the terms of the contract. A landlord who anticipated that there would be six percent inflation would try to ensure that any multiyear lease would provide for an annual rent increase of at least six percent. If it is a labour contract and the union anticipates inflation, it may press for a wage increase large enough to cover the inflation. Alternatively it may press to have a cost of living allowance (COLA) clause in the contract. Such a clause ties wages to the rate of inflation (called **indexing**) by stipulating that if the general price level rises by x percent, then the hourly wage rate must be increased by x percent as well. Suppose that the union fails to anticipate inflation and agrees to a $10 per hour money wage rate over the next 2 years. The onset of a 10 percent rate of inflation would mean that the real, or constant dollar, wage would fall to $9 by the end of the first year. In other words, the money wage of $10 would only have 91 percent of the purchasing power it had at the beginning of the contract. At the end of 2 years the money wage of $10 would only have roughly 82 percent of its original purchasing power. If the union had insisted on a cost of living clause in the contract, the money wage at the end of the first year would be $11. At the end of the second year it would be roughly $12.10. The real wage would then remain $10 in constant dollars. In Canada a substantial proportion of labour contracts do have COLAs. However, the exact percentage of contracts varies greatly from year to year, and they do not necessarily vary with the actual rate of inflation. *It is not only money (cash and chequing accounts) that is subject to decreased purchasing power during periods of inflation, but any contract that is stated in terms of dollars. If the inflation is anticipated, the terms of the contract can be set to protect its real value from the erosion of inflation.*

Gainers and Losers from Unanticipated Inflation

We can see that if inflation is correctly anticipated, people can try to take steps to protect themselves against it. Unfortunately, the world is an uncertain place. What is anticipated is often different from what occurs. The amount of inflation that occurs that is unexpected is called **unanticipated inflation.** Whenever there is unanticipated inflation, there are both gainers and losers.

Creditors versus Debtors.   Suppose that the Regina Bank (the creditor) lends $100 to a Ms. Smith (the debtor), at a 5 percent rate of interest for 1 year. We will assume that the creditor entered into this loan agreement anticipating that there would be no inflation over the year. This means that the Regina Bank was induced to lend $100 of purchasing power by the prospect of getting back $105 of purchasing power 1 year from now. Conversely, Ms. Smith is willing to agree to pay $105 of purchasing power 1 year from now in order to get $100 of purchasing power today.

Suppose that over the course of the year there actually is a 10 percent rise in the general price level, a 10 percent rate of inflation, that was completely unanticipated by the bank. Now when Ms. Smith pays $105 at the end of the year, as stipulated by the loan agreement, this $105 will buy only about $95 worth of goods in terms of original purchasing power. The 10 percent rate of inflation more than offsets the 5 percent rate of interest on the loan. As it turns out, the Regina Bank has given up more purchasing power than it actually gets back. Due to unanticipated inflation, the creditor has suffered a loss. The debtor, on the other hand, ends up paying back less purchasing power than was originally received. Because of unanticipated inflation, Ms. Smith has gained. Her gain in purchasing power is just equal to the bank's loss. The Regina Bank would never have entered into the loan agreement with Ms. Smith had it known that this was going to be the outcome. The debtor in effect has ended up getting a loan on much more favourable terms than would have been possible had the bank correctly anticipated the inflation. If the Regina Bank had correctly foreseen the 10 percent inflation, it would have required 15 percent interest on the loan. Under those terms Ms. Smith would have had to repay $115 in current dollars when the loan was due. This $115 would have represented about $105 in terms of original purchasing power. The bank would have earned a real

5 percent. *Whenever there is unanticipated inflation, there is a redistribution of wealth from creditors to debtors that would not have occurred if the inflation had been anticipated.*

Fixed-Income Groups.   We have noted how a labour union anticipating inflation would like to get a cost of living clause in its union contract. Indeed, all those anticipating inflation would want to ensure that their real income would not be reduced by inflation. For example, many retired people have found that their pension plans do not have a provision for this possibility. The dollar incomes they receive do not rise with inflation, and therefore their real incomes fall. The same thing can happen to any group of individuals in our economy who fail to anticipate inflation or who fail to anticipate it sufficiently. People with fixed dollar incomes lose ground relative to those whose dollar incomes rise right along with any increase in the general price level. The fixed-dollar-income group's claim on a share of the economy's total pie falls relative to those whose dollar incomes keep pace with inflation.

Owners of Fixed-Dollar versus Variable-Dollar Assets.   We have seen that if you lend out money (that is, enter into a loan contract) but fail to anticipate a rise in the general price level, you can end up getting back a smaller amount of purchasing power than you initially bargained for. There are a number of assets that have fixed dollar values that give them this property.

If you put $100 into a savings account at your local bank, you can subsequently withdraw the $100 plus the initially stipulated rate of interest at any time. If in the meantime there is an unanticipated rate of inflation, you will not get back the amount of purchasing power you had counted on. There are several kinds of **fixed-dollar assets**—money, bonds, bank loans to businesses and consumers, and, in general, *any kind of asset that guarantees a repayment of the initial dollar amount invested plus some stipulated rate of interest* (zero in the case of money). Parties who make these kinds of investments without anticipating inflation end up recovering an amount of purchasing power that is less than that for which they had bargained.

On the other hand, there are many assets, **variable-dollar assets,** that *do not guarantee the owner any fixed dollar value that may be recovered*. Such assets are also frequently called *real assets*. If you buy a piece of land, you can sell it at any time, but only at the current market price. The same is true of a share of stock in a corporation (an indirect ownership of a real asset), a painting, a vintage car, a house, or an antique. When there is an inflation, these assets can frequently (but *not* always) be sold at prices that are higher than their original purchase price by an amount that reflects the increase in the general price level. People owning these kinds of assets do not necessarily lose purchasing power as do those holding fixed-dollar assets such as money, savings accounts, and bonds. *An unanticipated inflation will result in a loss of wealth on all holdings of fixed-dollar assets and often in little or no loss of wealth on all variable-dollar assets.* Fixed-dollar-asset holders may thus lose relative to variable-dollar-asset holders. Since many people own some of each kind, whether they are net gainers or losers will depend largely on the relative proportions of the total assets they hold in each.

Unanticipated Inflation and Uncertainty

It is often argued that inflation isn't necessarily bad, provided it occurs at a constant rate that everyone anticipates. Then all parties can make their plans

Checkpoint 20-4

Deflation is the opposite of inflation. There have been periods of deflation, most notably the depression of the 1930s. Explain how an unanticipated deflation would affect the distribution of wealth between creditors and debtors, and between fixed-income groups and non-fixed-income groups. If inflation "steals" money, what does deflation do? Explain what would happen if anticipated inflation did not actually happen.

POLICY PERSPECTIVE

Wage and Price Controls— Sometimes the Magic Works, but Usually It Doesn't

Wage and price controls are governmentally enforced limits on the rate at which wages and prices are allowed to increase. In the extreme case wages and prices may not be allowed to increase at all. (Wage and price controls are also known as *incomes policy*.) Buyers and sellers engaging in transactions at prices and wages higher than the limit are subject to prosecution under the law. During the Second World War, Canada (and most of the other countries involved in the war) enacted wage and price controls. These controls were felt necessary because the war resulted in a very high level of aggregate demand. The government feared that in the absence of such controls the high level of aggregate demand would have created substantial inflation. In fact, during the First World War there had been massive inflation. Naturally, limiting the rate at which prices (and wages) could increase meant that prices (and wages) soon fell below their equilibrium level. As you learned in Chapter 4, if prices are below their equilibrium level there will be shortages. Normally, these shortages will result in higher prices, but with wage and price controls prices cannot increase fast enough to eliminate the shortages, so the shortages become chronic. To limit the quantity demanded of various goods and thereby avoid the shortages, the government also introduced rationing. Rationing meant that con-

sumers could only buy goods if they had the purchase price *and* a rationing coupon. Rationing reduces the actual quantity demanded so that it corresponds to the quantity supplied. The combination of price and wage controls and rationing allowed the Canadian government to ensure the availability of war materials without inflation. The policy was successful because Canadians saw it was necessary to win the war.

The Second World War was not the last time that the Canadian government introduced wage and price controls. In 1975 the Canadian government was worried that there were serious inflationary pressures within the economy. The CPI increased by 10.9 percent in 1974 and 10.8 percent in 1975. Accordingly the government created the Anti-Inflation Board (AIB), which had the power to limit wage and price increases for the next three years. The AIB established relatively liberal targets for wage increases. While it tried to limit wage and price increases, the AIB did not introduce rationing. The rate of inflation did drop to 7.5 percent in 1976, but by the time the AIB was disbanded in 1978 inflation was back at about 9 percent.

Many other countries have also tried wage and price controls policies to deal with inflation since the Second World War. But despite their ready appeal—simply make inflation illegal—controls are diffi-

cult to enforce and can be evaded in ways that render them ineffective inflation fighters. It is one thing to enforce wage and price controls when they are widely supported, as during a war, and a very different thing when they do not have public support.

THE INCENTIVE TO EVADE

The basic reason why controls are hard to enforce is illustrated in Figure P20-2, which shows the demand curve D and supply curve S for a typical market in the economy. (You may want to review briefly the discussion of market demand and supply in Chapter 4.) If the market were allowed to operate freely,

continued on next page

FIGURE P20-2   The Economic Incentive to Evade Price Controls

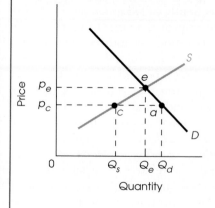

the equilibrium price and quantity would be p_e and Q_e, respectively, corresponding to the intersection of the demand curve D and the supply curve S at point e. However, suppose that price controls make it illegal for suppliers in this market to charge a price higher than p_c. At the price p_c suppliers are only willing to supply the quantity Q_s, corresponding to point c on S, while buyers will demand a quantity Q_d, corresponding to point a on D. With the price held down to p_c, there will be a persistent shortage, equal to Q_d minus Q_s, and frustrated buyers who cannot get as much of the good as they want. Since these buyers are willing to pay a higher price to get more of the good, there is an economic incentive for suppliers to evade the price controls, even though they run the risk of getting caught breaking the law. Obviously, the effectiveness of price controls will depend on how intensively the government polices them to detect evasion.

The same is true of wage controls. Suppose that employers' demand for labour in a particular labour market is represented by the demand curve D in Figure P20-2, while S is the supply curve of labour. If wage controls prohibit employers from paying a wage higher than p_c, there will be a shortage of labour equal to Q_d minus Q_s. Frustrated employers will be tempted to evade the wage control and pay a higher wage in order to get more labour. And, of course, more workers will be induced to offer their services if they can get a higher wage.

ENFORCEMENT AND EVASION

The Canadian economy produces literally millions of different kinds of products varying in complexity from hairpins to icebreakers. To enforce price controls on every one of them would take an army of enforcement agents. We can get some idea of the magnitude of the problem of enforcing wage and price controls by considering a few examples of how such evasion can occur.

Price Control Evasion Through Product Change

Producers can effectively evade controls by changing the product without changing the price. For example, the typical automobile contains around 15,000 different parts. If the price of automobiles is controlled, the producer can substitute a cheaper plastic part for a metal part here, use a little less or a cheaper grade fabric there, and so on. The outside of the car may look the same, but the inside of the car can be changed in numerous ways. While the overall price of the car hasn't increased, the quality and durability of the car that is purchased at that price has been lessened. In a simple product such as a 50-cent pack of gum, the size of the gum sticks could be reduced. Whether the product is simple or complex, changes like these mean that consumers are getting less for their money—and that's inflation, controls or no controls. Such changes mean that reported price data for the consumer price index (CPI) may not rise above control limits. Hence, the rate of inflation measured by the rise in the CPI will appear to slow down as a result of the controls, but product quality changes spurred by the controls make this a false impression. The rate of decline in what you are getting for your money may not have slowed at all. In truth, properly measured, the upward trend in inflation may be unaffected by controls.

Wage Control Evasion— Reducing Actual Work Hours

Evasion of wage controls can take place in a similar fashion. An enforcement agent who periodically inspects company payrolls may find that hourly wages are not in violation of wage controls. However, in competing with one another to hire various kinds of labour services, companies may well resort to giving workers longer lunch and coffee breaks, longer paid vacations, and more paid holidays. While recorded hourly wages may be held in check by the enforcement of wage controls, the amount of hours *actually* worked will be less. Total hours on the job are different than hours actually worked. In effect, the same number of dollars spent on wages is buying fewer hours of actual work. Again, wages per actual hour of work—measured to take account of all these ways of evading controls—will reveal that, in truth, wages are increasing at a rate in excess of that allowed by controls. Another way of evading wage controls is to promote workers. Everyone becomes a supervisor. Like prices, recorded wages may appear to be held in check by controls when, in reality, wages per actual hour worked are rising more rapidly. And the latter is the meaningful measure of inflation. Reported prices and wages can really disguise, even hide altogether, the true rate of inflation.

For Discussion

- Give some examples of products for which it would be difficult to evade price controls through product change.
- How would the degree to which a good is subject to product change affect the observed shortage associated with price control?

and enter into economic transactions on terms that fully take account of the inflation. As long as both parties have equal bargaining power, there will be no gainers and losers, no unplanned redistributions of income and wealth such as occur when there is unanticipated inflation.

When there is uncertainty about what the rate of inflation may be, fear of the consequences of unanticipated inflation may make it harder for businesses and consumers to make plans. This could put a damper on the economy's ability to operate at its potential employment level—that is, to close the GDP gap. Thus for many, one of the major goals of economic policy is price stability. *Price stability is one of the major goals of economic policy for two reasons: (1) It is necessary in order to avoid the arbitrary redistribution of wealth that results from unanticipated inflation, and (2) by reducing uncertainty about inflation, it enhances the economy's ability to operate at its full employment potential.*

The Consumer Price Index

Probably the most commonly used and widely publicized measure of the general level of prices in the economy is the **consumer price index (CPI)** compiled by Statistics Canada. The rate of inflation is often measured as the percentage rate of change in the CPI. Very often the press, politicians, and people in general interpret the CPI as a measure of the "cost of living," and changes in the CPI as changes in the cost of living. However, examination of the way the CPI is constructed reveals that change in the CPI may be a misleading measure of the actual change in the cost of living.

The Market Basket

The CPI is a weighted average of the prices of a market basket of goods and services purchased by an average urban family. The weights are calculated as equal to the proportions of a typical family's expenditures made on food, clothing, housing, medical care, and so on, based on a Statistics Canada survey of urban families during the base period. Statistics Canada is currently using 1986 as its base period.

The following simplified example will help you understand how the CPI and other price indices are calculated. Assume that there are only 4 products. The 4 types of goods and services are food, shelter, clothing, and entertainment. Table 20-2 summarizes the data necessary to calculate the hypothetical price index.

The cost of living in the base year is $(100 \times \$2.00) + (2 \times \$400.00) + (4 \times \$25.00) + (10 \times \$5.00)$ or $1,150. The cost of living in the next year is $(100 \times$

TABLE 20-2 A Hypothetical Price Index

Good or Service	Quantity Consumed in the Base Year	Price in the Base Year	Price in the Next Year
Food	100 units	$ 2.00	$ 2.20
Shelter	2 units	400.00	410.00
Clothing	4 units	25.00	24.00
Entertainment	10 units	5.00	5.25

$2.20) + (2 × $410.00) + (4 × $24.00) + (10 × $5.25) or $1,188.50. The CPI for the new year would be $1,188.50 ÷ $1,150.00 × 100 or 103.3. The price level has risen by 3.3 percent.

One problem with viewing changes in the CPI as changes in the cost of living is immediately obvious. While construction of the CPI for any subsequent year (after 1986) uses the subsequent year's prices for each expenditure category, the weights used are still those for 1986. However, we know that expenditure patterns change over time, a fact that the CPI ignores. Such changes may come because of changes in tastes or because of changes in relative prices. How does this bias the CPI as a tool for measuring changes in the cost of living? When the prices of different goods change relative to one another, consumers tend to spend more on goods that have become relatively cheaper, less on those now relatively more expensive, and, as is shown in Figure 20-6, differences in the amount of price change between different kinds of goods and services have been substantial. By not changing the weights in the CPI to reflect this fact, over time the CPI increasingly overstates the importance of the relatively higher priced goods. Therefore the CPI and changes in it are biased upward (overestimate the increase in the cost of living). To minimize this problem, Statistics Canada changes its base year fairly often.

Changing Composition and Quality of Market Basket

Another problem with the CPI is due to the fact that a number of items consumers buy today were not available in the 1986 period and are therefore not represented at all in the calculation of today's CPI. A somewhat similar problem

FIGURE 20-6   **Percentage Increase in Prices of Major Expenditure Classes of the Consumer Price Index, 1981–1988**

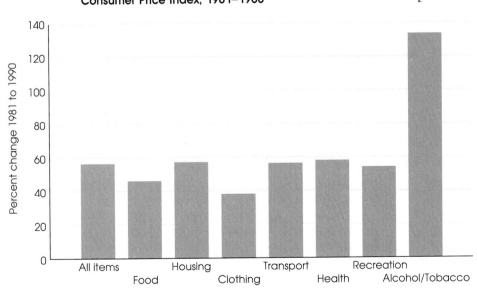

Source: Department of Finance. *Quarterly Economic Review, Annual Reference Tables,* June 1991

arises from the fact that the CPI does not take account of changes in the quality of goods and services. Typically, higher-quality items cost more. For example, a jet plane capable of carrying 120 passengers costs more than yesteryear's propeller-driven aircraft of the same capacity, though the jet aircraft may cut travel time in half. Hence, the price per constant quality unit of a 120-passenger aircraft has not gone up nearly as much as the price of such a plane. Similarly, today's cars are much better than in the past (antilock brakes, airbags, more fuel efficient, stereo sound systems) and much more expensive as well. But again, the price per constant quality unit of cars has not gone up nearly as much (if at all) as the quality-unadjusted price of cars used in the CPI. The lack of adjustment for quality improvement in the goods and services represented in the CPI is another source of upward bias in that price index. Likewise, it fails to indicate that there is inflation when the quality of a product drops, but its price does not.

CPI Overstates Inflation: The Consequences

Because of the preceding considerations, as well as others, the evidence suggests that on balance the CPI overstates the rate of inflation. What are the consequences? The overstatement may itself contribute to inflation because the incomes and wages of many people are indexed to changes in the CPI. For example, we have already noted that a significant percentage of workers are covered by COLA clauses. In addition, the monthly benefits of Old Age Security and some other social insurance benefits are at least partly indexed to the CPI. When prices rise, the money wages and incomes of these groups rise, automatically contributing to a further rise in inflation. Moreover, workers not covered by indexing schemes tend to make wage demands influenced by the behaviour of the CPI. Similarly, firms attempt to adjust their behaviour in setting prices and wages. Also, if lenders anticipate inflation they will demand higher interest payments. Hence, the upward bias in the CPI as a measure of inflation may itself contribute to inflation. In spite of the problems inherent in price indices, Statistics Canada does attempt to minimize the bias in the CPI and other price indices. As a result, the CPI and other indices are very useful measures of inflation over reasonable periods of time.

Where Do We Go from Here?

As noted at the outset, the business cycle, unemployment, and inflation are all interrelated problems. In the following chapters, we will examine how modern economics attempts to analyze their causes. This will require that we become more familiar with the institutional structure of the economy as well as with some tools of economic analysis. Ultimately, we want to grapple with the following sorts of issues: Can government action effectively put a damper on business fluctuations? How do government deficits affect the economy? Is there a trade-off between inflation and unemployment? (That is, can we reduce the amount of one of them only if we are willing to have more of the other?) Why was it that during the 1970s and 1980s our economy was plagued with recessions and their accompanying high unemployment while suffering from inflation at the same time—the problem of stagflation?

Summary

1. The economy grows through time but exhibits fluctuations about its growth trend called business cycles. The four phases of the business cycle—recession, trough, expansion, peak—may vary considerably in magnitude and duration from one cycle to the next, and no two cycles are ever exactly alike.
2. The business cycle affects different industries and segments of the economy in varying degrees. Durable goods industries tend to experience larger fluctuations than nondurable goods industries. These are usually industries with a few large, dominant (oligopolistic) firms that tend to have larger fluctuations in output and employment than in product price. Industries with many small competitive firms tend to show larger fluctuations in product price than in output and employment—typically, these are nondurable goods industries.
3. While many determinants of the business cycle reflect the internal structure of the economy, others are considered exogenous (external). The distinction is not always clear-cut, however.
4. Three basic types of unemployment may be identified: frictional, structural, and cyclical. There are several measures of unemployment along with considerable controversy over which is the most appropriate one. There is reason to believe that the NAIRU for the economy has risen since World War II.
5. The greater is the economy's total demand for goods and services, the greater is the total demand for labour needed to produce them. As a result, the level of employment is higher and the level of unemployment is lower. One measure of the cost of unemployment is the GDP gap—the dollar value of the goods and services not produced when the economy is operating at less than potential output. Though they are often hard to measure, there are also psychological and social costs associated with unemployment. Moreover, the burden of unemployment is quite unevenly distributed among different groups in our economy.
6. Inflation is a rise in the general level of prices of all goods and services. Inflation reduces the purchasing power of money. The effects of anticipated inflation will be accounted for in the terms of economic contracts of all kinds.
7. Unanticipated inflation will result in a loss of purchasing power (wealth and income) among creditors, fixed-dollar-income groups, and fixed-dollar-asset holders. It results in an arbitrary redistribution of income and wealth. Uncertainty about inflation breeds a fear of these consequences of unanticipated inflation, and this inhibits the economy's ability to perform at its full employment potential. For these reasons, price stability is a major goal of economic policy.
8. The consumer price index (CPI) is a measure of the general level of prices in the economy, and as such is often interpreted as a measure of the "cost of living." The CPI most likely slightly overstates the rate of inflation because the market basket weights are changed infrequently, new products are not included, and there is no allowance for the changing quality of the goods included in the market basket.

Key Terms and Concepts

business cycles
consumer price index
  (CPI)
depression
expansion (recovery)
fixed-dollar assets
GDP gap

indexing
inflation
labour force
NAIRU
peak (boom)
potential GDP
recession (contraction)

seasonal variation
trough
unanticipated inflation
unemployment
variable-dollar assets
wage and price
  controls

Questions and Problems

1. Can you give reasons why the average length of business cycle expansions should be longer than the average length of recessions, as indicated in Table 20-1?

2. Suppose that you are an interviewer in an unemployment office. As a practical matter, how would you differentiate the frictionally unemployed, the cyclically unemployed, and the structurally unemployed?

3. Since the early 1960s the growth rate of the total population has been considerably lower than it was during the 1950s and late 1940s—the years of the baby boom. Assuming that the population growth rate remains constant at its present lower level, what are the implications for unemployment in the early part of the twenty-first century?

4. In the event of an unanticipated inflation, which of the following assets would you prefer to own: a stamp collection, savings bonds, cash, a collection of old English coins, common stock, a fast food restaurant, a contract to deliver towels and linen to a hotel chain, a deposit in a savings and loan bank, a mortgage on your neighbour's house? Why?

5. How does inflation affect fixed-dollar-income groups? What does it do to their share of real GDP?

Macroeconomic Theories of Income and Employment

Chapter 21

Classical and Keynesian Theories

In Chapter 19 we saw how we keep tabs on the economy's performance by use of national income accounting. Chapter 20 introduced some of the characteristics of the economy's performance, along with two problem areas of major concern—unemployment and inflation. In this chapter we will see that the classical view holds that competitive markets act as a mechanism that automatically assures continual full employment in a capitalistic economy. By contrast, we will see that the Keynesian view holds that full employment is not guaranteed. Indeed, Keynesians argue that total expenditure might not be sufficient to yield an equilibrium at full employment.

In this chapter we will examine why many economists from Adam Smith's time up through the 1930s believed that capitalistic, market-oriented economies tended naturally to operate at full employment—a view that essentially assumed the economy was always (except for short periods of adjustment) operating at capacity. Then we will see how and why the Great Depression of the 1930s forced a major rethinking on this issue—the Keynesian revolution. This gave rise to the Keynesian income–expenditure theory, an approach that assumes that, because of significant excess capacity, total output could be increased without prices increasing and that the equilibrium level of total income, output, and employment is determined solely by total expenditure. We will examine this approach here and again in the next chapter. Government expenditure and taxation will be introduced into this framework in Chapter 23.

The Classical View of Income and Employment

Classical economists subscribed to the notion that capitalistic, market-oriented economies tended naturally to operate at a full employment output level. The classical economist's faith in this point of view was based on Say's Law,[1] an appealing, yet deceptive, argument.

Say's Law

Simply put, **Say's Law** states that supply creates its own demand. According to Say's Law, people only produce and supply goods and services because they want to acquire the income to buy goods and services. A level of total dollar spending insufficient to purchase the full employment output of goods and services is considered impossible because the total income earned from the production of the economy's total full employment output would be spent to purchase that output.

Classical economists subscribed to two fundamental assumptions about how the economy worked—two assumptions essential to a belief in Say's Law. First, they believed that prices and wages would always adjust quickly to clear markets. Second, they believed that the interest rate would always adjust to equate saving and investment.

Prices and Wages Adjust to Clear Markets

Classical economists argued that if the economy's total expenditure on goods and services declined, flexible prices and wages would quickly adjust downward until the total quantity of goods and services demanded was once again restored to the initial full employment total output level. Let's briefly examine this argument.

LEARNING OBJECTIVES

After reading this chapter, you will be able to:

1. State Say's Law and outline its policy implications.
2. Identify the mechanisms that the classical economists believed would ensure full employment and explain how these mechanisms were thought to operate.
3. Explain why the Great Depression led to a critical reevaluation of the classical position.
4. Identify and discuss the major elements of the Keynesian revolution.
5. Distinguish between the factors that cause movements along versus shifts in the consumption and savings functions.
6. Explain why investment expenditures are more variable than consumption and government expenditures.
7. Discuss the relationship between planned investment and total income and know the factors that affect this relationship.
8. Demonstrate how the 45° line can be used to determine equilibrium in the income–expenditure approach.
9. Explain how the economy will move toward equilibrium if total income is either more or less than the equilibrium level.

---

[1] Initially put forth by the French economist Jean Baptiste Say.

A decline in the economy's total expenditure is reflected in leftward shifts in the demand curves in each of the economy's many product markets. In response, product prices fall and labourers quickly and willingly accept lower wages in order to keep their jobs. This adjustment occurs in every product market in the economy so that each continues to produce and sell the same quantity of output and employ the same amount of labour as before the initial decrease in demand. Therefore, the economy continues to produce the full employment total output level that it did before the downward adjustment of all prices and wages.

Saving and the Income–Expenditure Flow

Our examination of the circular flow diagrams of the economy in Chapter 3, and our discussion in Chapter 19 of how GDP may be viewed either from the expenditure side or the income side, both indicated that

$$\left.\begin{array}{l}\text{Total expenditure}\\\text{on final goods}\\\text{and services}\end{array}\right\} = \left\{\begin{array}{l}\text{Total income from}\\\text{the production and}\\\text{sale of final output}\end{array}\right.$$

For the purpose of simplifying our discussion of this relationship, we will assume that there is no government expenditure or taxation.

Consideration of the total expenditure equals total income relationship immediately suggests a possible problem for a believer in Say's Law. *While it is undeniably true that every dollar of expenditure on goods and services creates a dollar of income, it does not follow that the person receiving the income necessarily spends all of it.*

What happens when households save some of their income? As long as there is a saving leakage from total dollar income, won't total dollar expenditure and total dollar output and income continue to get smaller and smaller? The answer is yes. The continuing fall in total demand that results when households do not spend all their income means that wages and prices must fall continually in order to maintain full employment. Hardly a realistic state of affairs!

The Interest Rate Equates Saving and Investment

But classical economists had an answer to the problem posed by the saving leakage from the income–expenditure flow. *If that part of total income that is saved is just matched by an equivalent amount of investment expenditure by businesses, then the leakage from the income–expenditure flow that results from saving is offset by the injection of investment into that flow.*

But what ensures that the amount of investment expenditures businesses intend to make will be equal to the amount of saving that households intend to do? Classical economists contended that in a capitalistic economy the **interest rate** would always adjust—like the price in any other market—to ensure that the total intended investment in the economy would equal the total intended saving. If the interest rate is viewed as the price of borrowing, businesses will demand more borrowed funds for investment at low interest rates than at high rates. Therefore, the investment curve for the economy slopes downward (like any demand curve), as shown in Figure 21-1. On the other hand, since saving out of income involves a sacrifice by households—the forgone consumption they could have enjoyed—it is necessary to pay households a higher interest rate to

Checkpoint* 21-1

Suppose that the economy is operating at full employment equilibrium. Assume the classical economists' point of view that wages and prices are perfectly flexible. Describe the adjustment process that would occur in product markets in response to an increase in the economy's total demand. When equilibrium is once again restored, will wages and prices be higher, lower, or unchanged? Suppose that the economy is operating at full employment equilibrium and that we take account of the role of saving and investment as envisioned by the classical economists. Suppose that the investment curve in Figure 21-1 shifts leftward, but that for some reason the interest rate cannot fall below the level r_e. Will wages and prices rise, fall, or stay the same? Explain your answer.

*Answers to all Checkpoints can be found at the back of the text.

FIGURE 21-1 Classical Economists Argued the Interest Rate Would Equate Saving and Investment

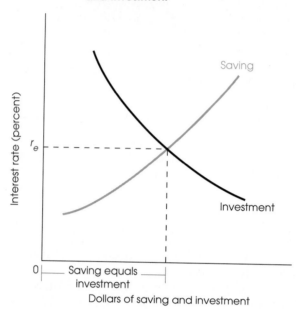

The equilibrium interest rate r_e equates the quantity of dollars demanded for investment by business with the quantity of dollars households are willing to save. According to classical economists, this equality ensured that the economy would operate at full employment.

induce them to save more. Hence, the saving curve for the economy—that is, the supply of dollars available to be loaned out of total income—is upward sloping (like any supply curve), as shown in Figure 21-1.

The intersection of the saving and investment curves in Figure 21-1 corresponds to the equilibrium level of the interest rate r_e. As in any other market, if the price (interest rate) is above this level, the supply of dollars to loan (saving) exceeds the demand for dollars to invest (investment) and price will be bid down to r_e. Similarly, if the price (interest rate) is below this level, demand exceeds supply, and price will be bid up to r_e. Because of the market adjustment of the interest rate, classical economists argued that the savings plans of households would always be equal to the investment plans of businesses.

Classical economists maintained that the economy would operate at its full employment output level without a need for continually falling wages and prices. *Say's Law assumes that the unfettered forces of free markets and laissez faire capitalism will guarantee full employment with price stability. If there are disturbances that cause investment or saving curves to shift, or shifts in demand and supply curves in any other market, adjustments in wages, prices, and the interest rate will always return the economy to a position of full employment equilibrium.*

The classical view of the economy can be represented in terms of the *aggregate demand (AD)* and *aggregate supply (AS)* curves shown in Figure 21-2. The concepts of aggregate supply and aggregate demand will be developed in detail in Chapter 26; for now, an intuitive approach is sufficient. *The aggregate demand curve shows the relationship between the economy's total demand for output and the general price level of that output. The aggregate supply curve shows the relationship between the total output that all firms will produce and the general price level.* In the

FIGURE 21-2   Aggregate Demand and Supply in the Classical View

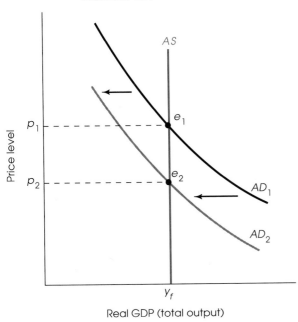

Price level

Real GDP (total output)

The aggregate supply curve AS in the classical view is horizontal at the full employment level of total output y_f (horizontal axis) because prices, wages, and the interest rate always adjust quickly to maintain full employment in response to any change in aggregate demand. For example, if the AD curve shifts leftward from AD_1 to AD_2, the economy's equilibrium price level would fall from p_1 to p_2, while total output would remain at y_f.

classical model, the aggregate supply curve AS is vertical in keeping with the view that prices, wages, and the interest rate will always adjust quickly to ensure the full employment total output level y_f (horizontal axis). Suppose that the AD curve is initially AD_1 so that the economy's price level is p_1, corresponding to the intersection of AD_1 and AS at e_1. If aggregate demand declines, represented by a leftward shift in the AD curve from AD_1 to AD_2, then the economy's price level (the average of all prices, including wages) will fall to p_2, corresponding to the intersection of AD_2 with AS at e_2. The equilibrium output level is still y_f.

Aggregate Demand and Employment: The Income–Expenditure Approach

Classical economists had always acknowledged that capitalistic, market-oriented economies might experience occasional, temporary bouts of unemployment, possibly caused by rapid shifts in the composition of demand or by such things as wars and crop failures. But then came the 1930s. A prolonged depression—the Great Depression—gripped the capitalistic, market-oriented economies of the world. The gap between classical theory and fact was now too great to ignore. In Canada, the unemployment rate was never lower than 9.1 percent in the years from 1931 through 1940. Indeed, at the worst it reached 19.3 percent. Money GDP fell by nearly 50 percent between 1929 and 1933, while gross investment fell by nearly 80 percent.

The Keynesian Revolution

A Cambridge University economist, John Maynard Keynes, offered an explanation that went beyond the bounds of the classical framework and sparked what has come to be called the Keynesian revolution. In 1936 Keynes published his analysis, *The General Theory of Employment, Interest, and Money*, which argued that the inevitability of full employment equilibrium was an unlikely proposition at best and simply wrong in general.

Keynes argued that it is irrelevant whether complete wage and price flexibility would ensure full employment if *in fact* wages and prices are slow to adjust in the real world. During the Great Depression, economists noted that this was true in a number of markets and that wages were particularly slow to adjust downward. Keynes also argued that disposable income—not the interest rate—is the main determinant of saving. Given this, Keynes questioned the ability of the interest rate to equate saving and intended investment as required by Say's Law.

The Keynesian Analysis

In the classical model the equilibrium level of total output (constant dollar total income or real GDP) is determined on the supply side by virtue of the assertion based on Say's Law that the economy tends automatically to operate at full employment, as represented by the vertical *AS* curve at y_f in Figure 21-2. Aggregate demand serves only to determine the price level, which is assumed to adjust quickly to any shift in the *AD* curve.

The Keynesian analysis switches the emphasis from the supply side to the demand side. *Keynesian analysis focuses on how the equilibrium level of total income, output, and employment is determined in an economy that operates at less than full employment and where the price level is not flexible.*

The equilibrium level of total output and employment is completely determined by aggregate demand, as shown in Figure 21-3. The aggregate supply curve *AS* is horizontal at the fixed (inflexible) price level p_0. If the *AD* curve is AD_1, then the equilibrium level of total output is y_1 (horizontal axis), corresponding to the intersection of AD_1 and *AS* at e_1, a level less than the full employment output level y_f. Suppose that aggregate demand falls, represented by a shift from AD_1 to AD_2. Now total output declines (but not the price level, as in the classical model) from y_1 to y_2, and the associated level of employment falls as well (it takes less labour to produce less output). In sum, the levels of total income, output, and employment vary directly with aggregate demand and are completely *demand determined*.

The Income–Expenditure Approach: Determining Aggregate Demand

The upshot of the Keynesian analysis is straightforward. In an economy that operates at significantly less than full employment and where the price level is not flexible, an explanation of the determination of total output, income, and employment requires an explanation of the determination of aggregate demand—why is the *AD* curve where it is and why does it shift? An analysis

FIGURE 21-3   Aggregate Demand and Supply in the Keynesian Analysis

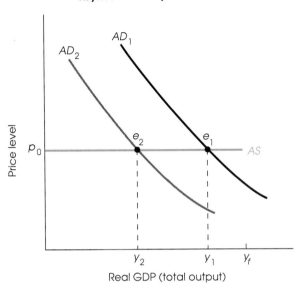

When the price level is not flexible, the aggregate supply curve AS is horizontal at the fixed price level, indicated here as p_0 (vertical axis). Shifts in the aggregate demand curve, such as from AD_1 to AD_2, cause total output and employment to change. Total output, income, and employment are completely demand determined.

known as the *income–expenditure approach* provides an answer to this question. It boils down to an explanation of the behaviour of the four main expenditure categories—consumption C, investment I, government G, and net exports X_n. These four categories constitute the expenditure side of GDP (discussed in the previous chapter), or the left side of the relationship:

$$\left.\begin{array}{l}\text{Total expenditure} \\ \text{on final goods} \\ \text{and services}\end{array}\right\} = \left\{\begin{array}{l}\text{Total income from} \\ \text{the production and sale} \\ \text{of final output}\end{array}\right.$$

In the next section we will examine consumption and investment spending, two of the key components of total expenditure. Then we will see how consumption and investment combine to determine the equilibrium level of total income, output, and employment according to the income–expenditure approach, under the simplifying assumption that government spending and net exports are zero. Throughout our discussion it will be assumed that the price level is unchanging. Ultimately we will want to examine what causes the price and output levels to change at the same time, a more complicated issue that will be taken up in Chapter 24 and subsequent chapters.

Checkpoint 21-2

How would you describe the way saving and investment plans were matched for Robinson Crusoe in his one-man island economy? Could he have an unemployment problem? How well would Say's Law describe the way his economy worked? What is it about modern industrialized economies, as compared to Robinson Crusoe's, that leads to difficulties for Say's Law?

The Consumption and Saving Functions

Consumption is the portion of their disposable income that households spend on goods and services. Personal saving is the remaining part, the portion of disposable income that households refrain from spending. Therefore, whatever explains consumption behaviour must also explain personal saving behaviour.

Consumption and Saving Depend on Income

Keynes contended that the single most important determinant of consumption expenditure and personal saving is the household's disposable income. Repeated statistical studies tend to bear out that claim.

Using hypothetical data, Table 21-1 shows the total amount of consumption, column (2), that the economy's households would plan to do at different levels of disposable income, column (1). The difference between disposable income and consumption is the amount of saving, column (3). This is the amount that households refrain from spending at each level of disposable income. Note that as income increases so do both consumption and saving. All other factors that affect consumption are assumed to be given—that is, fixed and unchanging.

The Consumption Function: Graphical Representation

The income consumption relationship may be represented graphically by measuring consumption expenditures on the vertical axis and disposable income on the horizontal axis. In Figure 21-4, frame (a), both axes are measured in the same units, billions of dollars. The consumption data from column (2) of Table 21-1 and the disposable income data from column (1) are plotted in Figure 21-4, frame (a), to give the consumption curve C. When actual levels of the economy's consumption expenditures are plotted against the associated levels of the economy's disposable income, economists have found a relationship that looks very much like the consumption curve C shown in frame (a).

Note the 45° line that bisects the 90° angle formed by the horizontal and vertical axes of the diagram. Any point on the 45° line corresponds to the same dollar magnitude on either axis. This line serves as a very useful reference for interpreting the relationship among disposable income, consumption, and saving. At any given level of disposable income, the vertical distance between the corresponding point on the consumption curve C and the 45° line represents the amount of saving, or the amount of disposable income households refrain from spending. For example, at a disposable income level of $475 billion (horizontal axis) the vertical distance to the corresponding point on the

TABLE 21-1   Consumption and Saving Schedules
                 (Hypothetical Data in Billions of Dollars)

(1) Disposable Income (DI)	(2) Consumption (C)	(3) Saving (S) $S = (1) - (2)$
$300	$320	−$20
325	335	−10
350	350	0
375	365	10
400	380	20
425	395	30
450	410	40
475	425	50
500	440	60

FIGURE 21-4 The Consumption Function and the Saving Function

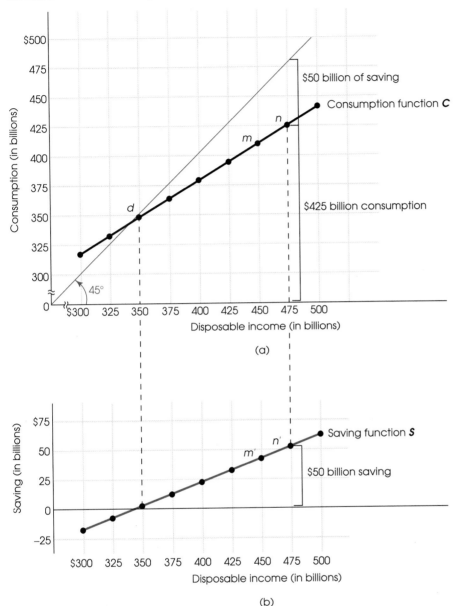

The consumption function C in frame (a) is plotted from the data in columns (1) and (2) of Table 21-1. Note that as disposable income increases, consumption also increases, but by a smaller amount. Movement along the consumption function is caused by a change in disposable income, while all other things that affect consumption are assumed to remain unchanged. The amount of saving at any disposable income level is represented by the vertical distance between the consumption function and the 45° line in frame (a). In other words, what households don't consume they save.

Using the data from columns (1) and (3) in Table 21-1, saving also may by plotted against disposable income, frame (b), to give the saving function S. The saving function slopes upward, reflecting the fact that the level of planned saving rises as disposable income rises.

consumption curve (point n) measures the $425 billion of consumption spending (vertical axis) that takes place at that disposable income level. The vertical distance from that point on the consumption curve up to the 45° line measures the $50 billion of saving that takes place when disposable income is $475 billion.

At point d, where the consumption curve intersects the 45° line, the entire $350 billion of disposable income goes into consumption expenditure. Saving is zero. At disposable income levels greater than $350 billion, saving is positive and is equal to the vertical distance between the 45° line and the consumption curve.

At disposable income levels less than $350 billion, the consumption curve lies above the 45° line and the economy's households spend more than the amount of disposable income. Households are able to spend more than disposable income either by drawing on wealth accumulated in the past or by borrowing. This amounts to negative saving, or dissaving.

The relationship between the level of disposable income and the level of consumption, represented by the consumption curve C, is called the **consumption function**. The term *function* is used here because the level of consumption expenditure is determined by (is a function of) the level of disposable income. *The consumption function shows that as disposable income increases, consumption also increases, but by a smaller amount. Movement along the consumption function is caused by a change in disposable income, while all other things that affect consumption are assumed to remain unchanged.*

The Saving Function: Graphical Representation

What households don't consume out of disposable income, they save. When income increases, consumption increases by a smaller amount because part of any increase in income goes into saving. And saving obviously gets larger as income increases. Another very useful representation of the relationship between disposable income and saving is shown in frame (b) of Figure 21-4. The axes are drawn to exactly the same scale as those in frame (a) of Figure 21-4, except that saving is measured on the vertical axis. The saving function S is plotted from the data in columns (1) and (3) of Table 21-1.

The vertical distance between the saving function and the horizontal axis represents the amount of saving that the economy's households would desire to do at each income level. At any given income level the vertical distance between the saving function and the horizontal axis in frame (b) is the same as the vertical distance between the consumption function and the 45° line in frame (a). This correspondence is pointed out at the $475 billion disposable income level, for example, and is also obvious at the break-even point. *The* **saving function** *displays the relationship between the economy's level of disposable income and the level of desired or planned saving. It slopes upward, reflecting the fact that the level of planned saving rises as income rises.*

Movements versus Shifts in Consumption and Saving

In Chapter 4 we discussed the difference between movement along a good's demand curve and shifts in the position of its demand curve. A similar distinction must be made between movement along a consumption function or a saving function and shifts in these functions.

Movements Along the Consumption and Saving Functions

Movement along a consumption function can only be caused by a change in disposable income, assuming that all other things affecting consumption are unchanged. Of course, for any movement along a consumption function, there is a corresponding movement along the associated saving function. For example, in frame (a) of Figure 21-4, if disposable income rises from $450 to $475 billion, there is a movement along the consumption function from point m to point n and a corresponding movement along the saving function in frame (b) of Figure 21-4 from point m' to point n'.

Shifts in the Consumption and Saving Functions

When any of the other things (besides disposable income) that affect consumption changes, there is a shift in the consumption and saving functions. For example, suppose that the consumption function is initially in the position C_0, as shown in frame (a) of Figure 21-5. The associated saving function is S_0, as shown in frame (b). If the consumption function shifts downward from C_0 to C_1, the saving function then shifts upward from S_0 to S_1. At any given disposable income level, households now consume less and save more. On the other hand, if the consumption function shifts upward from C_0 to C_2, the saving function then shifts downward from S_0 to S_2. In this case, households now consume more and save less at any given disposable income level.

Other Determinants of Consumption and Saving

What are the "other things" that can change and thereby cause shifts in the consumption and saving functions? Three examples are credit conditions, wealth, and expectations about employment, prices, and income.

Credit Conditions.   The easier it is for consumers to obtain credit and the lower the interest rate they pay for it, the more likely they are to borrow from banks and other financial institutions to buy cars, household appliances, and other goods on credit. This would tend to shift the consumption function upward and the saving function downward. Tougher credit conditions and a higher interest rate have the opposite effect.

Wealth.   The size and composition of the stocks of assets (bank accounts, cash, bonds, stocks, houses, etc.) owned by consumers are important determinants of consumer spending. Disposable income is not the only source of funds consumers have. Consumption spending can also be financed by withdrawals from bank accounts or by cashing in other forms of wealth. An increase in wealth would tend to shift the consumption function upward and the saving function downward. A decrease would have the opposite effect.

> ### Checkpoint 21-3
> Suppose that a news item reports that "most forecasters still look for somewhat lower interest rates and expect consumer outlays to remain strong." If the forecasters are right, how will the consumption function shift and why? How will the saving function shift?

FIGURE 21-5 The Consumption and Saving Functions Shift when the "Other Things" Change

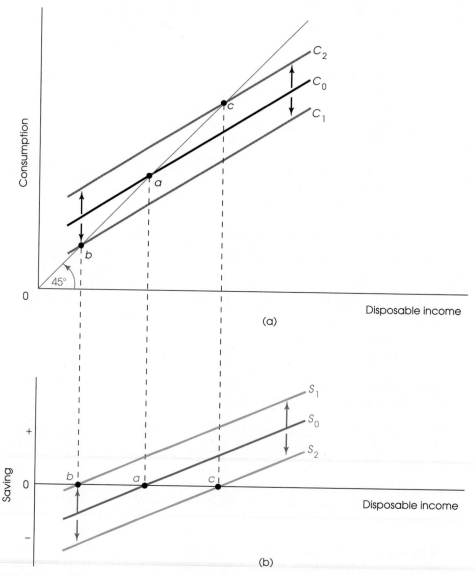

(a)

(b)

Movement along the consumption function or the saving function is due to changes in disposable income. All other things that affect consumption are assumed to be unchanged. When any of these other things change, they cause a shift in the consumption and saving functions. Suppose that the consumption function is initially C_0, frame (a), and the associated saving function then shifts upward from S_0, frame (b). If the consumption function shifts downward from C_0, to C_1, the saving function then shifts upward from S_0 to S_1. At any given disposable income level, households now consume less and save more. Similarly, if the consumption function shifts upward from C_0 to C_2, the saving function then shifts downward from S_0 to S_2. Households consume more and save less at any given disposable income level.

Expectations About Employment, Prices, and Income.   Consumer expectations about the course of the economy play a crucial role in their willingness to spend. For example, if consumers begin to expect lower levels of employment and income, they might try to save more for possible rainy days ahead. The result would be a downward shift in the consumption function and an upward shift in the saving function. Changes in expectations about inflation also affect consumption and saving, but the direction of the shift is not as clear.

Investment and Its Determinants

Of the three major categories on the expenditure side of GDP—consumption, investment, and government—investment expenditures vary the most. This is evident from the graphic representation of these three categories in Figure 21-6. As long as members of households are employed and have a steady source of income, consumption varies little, growing rather steadily through time with the growth of the economy. Government expenditure, although not quite as steady as consumption, has certainly been less variable than investment. What are the main determinants of investment expenditure, and what accounts for its variable behaviour? The fourth component on the expenditure side is net exports. While imports and exports account for a large share of GDP, net exports (exports minus imports) is relatively small because the difference between the two elements tends to be only a few billion dollars.

Investment and Profit

If businesses anticipate that revenue from the sale of goods and services produced with the aid of capital goods will more than cover all costs of production, so that there is a profit, they will invest in the capital goods. Otherwise they won't. A major underlying reason why investment is so variable (as illustrated in Figure 21-6) is the fact that the decision whether or not to invest in capital goods depends on business expectations about future profits.

Forecasting Future Profit

Put yourself in the shoes of an investment decision maker. In order to forecast prospective profits in any meaningful way, you have to forecast the magnitudes of all of the ingredients that will enter into the calculation of profit: sales revenues and the level of costs (wage rates, rents, interest rates, materials prices, utilities payments, various taxes, and tax rate changes). Based on these forecasts, you must come up with your best forecast of the future profits (or losses) likely to result from any investment currently undertaken.

Changing Expectations

Profit forecasts are quite obviously dependent on the current expectations held by businesses about the future. Changes in these expectations cause changes in profit forecasts, which in turn lead to changes in the amount of investment businesses intend to do. Expectations can be very volatile, buffeted by continually

FIGURE 21-6   Consumption, Government, and Investment

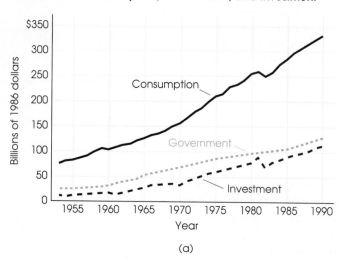

(a)

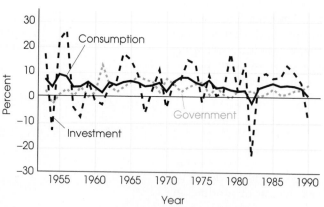

Change from previous year

(b)

Shown in frame (a) are personal expenditures on consumer goods, government current expenditures on goods and services, and gross investment over the period 1953 to 1990. Frame (b) shows the year-to-year percentage change in each of these variables. Investment expenditures have been the most variable of these major components of the expenditure side of GDP during this period. If net exports were included in this graph, they would be generally positive but of very low magnitude; however, the annual rate of change in frame (b) would vary greatly.

Source: Adapted from Statistics Canada. *Canadian Economic Observer, Historical Statistical Supplement,* 1990/91 (11–210)

changing information about markets, government policies, political events, and even the weather.

The Investment Schedule and Its Determinants

When we develop the basic theory of how the economy's level of total income and employment are determined according to the income–expenditure approach, we will need to add the consumption plans of households to the investment plans of businesses to get the economy's total intended, or planned, expenditure on goods and services. In order to do this, we will need to relate the level of businesses' investment spending plans (their intended investment) to income, just as consumption spending plans are related to income by the consumption

FIGURE 21-7 The Investment Schedule

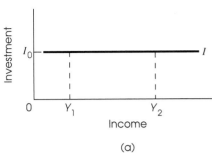
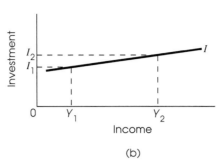

In these diagrams the amount of investment expenditure in the economy is measured on the vertical axis and the economy's total income on the horizontal axis. The investment schedule I shows the total amount of investment businesses desire to make at each level of the economy's total income, all other things remaining the same. In frame (a) desired investment expenditure in the economy equals I_0 no matter what the level of total income. The investment schedule in frame (b) slopes upward on the assumption that business will be more optimistic about profit prospects the higher is the current level of economic activity as measured by total income.

function. To simplify the ensuing discussion we will assume government taxes are zero and make no distinction among DI, PI, NI, NNP, and GDP, because we will ignore all those things that differentiate these measures from one another.

The relationship between income and intended investment is represented by the investment schedule I shown in frame (a) of Figure 21-7. The economy's total dollar income, or total output, is measured on the horizontal axis, and its gross investment expenditures are measured on the vertical axis. As drawn, the investment schedule I shows that businesses in aggregate plan, or intend, to spend an amount equal to I_0 on plant, equipment, and inventories no matter what the level of income in the economy—*all other things remaining the same*. Therefore, the investment schedule I is perfectly horizontal at the level I_0. Our discussion of the determinants of investment, the "other things," will indicate what determines the position of the I schedule and how it may be shifted by changes in these determinants. Remember that the question of what determines investment expenditure in our economy is basically one of what determines the prospects for profit. Some of the more important determinants are the variations in total income, the interest rate, and technological change, including the introduction of new products.

Variation in Total Income

It seems reasonable to believe that the higher is the level of current economic activity, as measured by the level of total income, the more optimistic firms will be about prospects for future profits. This optimism may well encourage them to invest more at higher income levels. If so, the investment schedule I may slope upward as shown in Figure 21-7, frame (b).

The Interest Rate

The funds that businesses use to make investment expenditures on capital goods either must be borrowed from outside the firm or must be generated

FIGURE 21-8   Shifts in the Investment Schedule

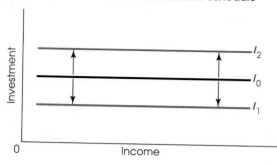

The investment schedule shows the total amount of investment businesses desire to do at each level of income, all
other things that affect investment remaining the same.
If one or more of these other things should change, it will
cause the investment schedule to shift, either upward from
I_0 to a position such as I_2 or downward to a position such
as I_1.

internally in the form of the firm's business saving (also called *retained earnings*).
If the funds are borrowed from outside the firm, the cost of borrowing is the
interest rate that must be paid to the lender. If they are generated internally, the
cost to the firm is the forgone interest the firm could have earned if it had lent
the funds to someone else. In either case the interest rate is the cost of the funds
invested in capital goods. The higher is the interest rate, the more this cost cuts
into profit and reduces the incentive to invest in capital goods. Conversely, the
lower is the interest rate, the larger is the profit and the greater is the incentive
to make investment expenditures.

Since the interest rate is among the "other things" assumed unchanged for
any *movement along* the investment schedule, a change in the interest rate will
cause the I schedule to shift, as shown in Figure 21-8. In sum, increases in
the interest rate shift the investment schedule downward and decreases in the
interest rate shift it upward.

Technological Change and New Products

Technological change often makes existing capital equipment obsolete. Firms
that fail to invest in capital goods that feature the latest technological break-
throughs may find themselves at a competitive disadvantage relative to those
that do. Those that acquire the latest capital first will get a competitive jump on
rivals. Given these carrot and stick incentives, technological change often results
in an upward shift in the investment schedule, such as from I_0 to I_2 in Figure 21-8.

The development of new products opens up new markets. Lured by the
resulting profit opportunities, firms will want to invest in the capital goods necessary to produce these new products. This, too, will cause an upward shift in
the investment schedule.

> **Checkpoint 21-4**
>
> How would an
> increase in the prices
> of new capital goods
> affect the investment
> schedule? How
> do you think the
> investment schedule
> would be affected
> if labour unions
> and management
> in major industries
> throughout the
> country successfully
> negotiated new labour
> contracts without
> resorting to strikes?

Total Expenditure and Total Income: Determining Equilibrium

Now we will see how the consumption function and the investment schedule
combine to determine the economy's equilibrium level of total income, output,
and employment. We will continue to make no distinction between GDP, NNP,

NI, PI, and DI because we assume that there is no government expenditure or taxation, that all saving is personal saving, and that capital depreciation is zero. We also continue to assume that net exports are zero and that the price level is fixed.

The **equilibrium income level** *is the one income level, among all possible income levels, at which the dollar value of the economy's total expenditure on output is just equal to the dollar value of total output that the firms in the economy produce. The equilibrium income level is also the level of total income that will be sustained once it is achieved.* Let's see how the equilibrium income level is determined.

Total Expenditure Equals Consumption Plus Intended Investment

We have examined how the level of consumption expenditure and intended investment expenditure can be shown in a graph with the income level measured on the horizontal axis and desired consumption expenditures [Figure 21-4, frame (a)] or intended investment expenditures (Figure 21-7) measured on the vertical axis. We may now combine these two components to form the economy's total spending, or *total expenditure schedule*. We assume that the only components of total expenditure are consumption and investment.[2]

The hypothetical example of Table 21-2, which is shown graphically in Figure 21-9, shows how this is done. At each level of total income, column (1) of Table 21-2, the economy's households wish to spend an amount given by the associated level of consumption expenditures C shown in column (2). Column (3) of Table 21-2 shows the level of intended or planned investment expenditures I for the entire economy associated with each level of total income in column (1). Our example assumes that the amount of intended investment is the same ($300 billion) no matter what the level of total income. [This pattern of investment could be represented by a horizontal investment schedule like that shown in Figure 21-7, frame (a).] The total expenditure level, column (4) of Table 21-2, is obtained by adding the level of consumption expenditures (column 2) to the intended investment expenditures (column 3). It is represented in Figure 21-9 as

---

[2]Government expenditures and net exports will be introduced in Chapter 23.

TABLE 21-2   Total Expenditure Equals Consumption Plus Intended Investment
(Hypothetical Data in Billions of Dollars)

(1) Total Income	(2) Consumption Expenditure (C)		(3) Intended Investment (I)		(4) Total Expenditure (E) E = (2) + (3)
$ 200	$ 300	+	$300	=	$ 600
400	400	+	300	=	700
600	500	+	300	=	800
800	600	+	300	=	900
1,000	700	+	300	=	1,000
1,200	800	+	300	=	1,100
1,400	900	+	300	=	1,200
1,600	1,000	+	300	=	1,300
1,800	1,100	+	300	=	1,400

FIGURE 21-9   Determining the Equilibrium Level of Total Income

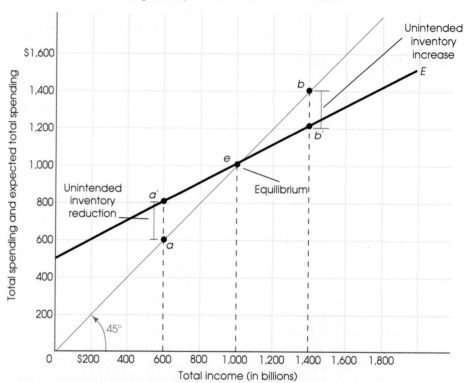

The economy's total expenditure schedule *E* combines with the 45° line to determine the equilibrium level of total income, which equals $1,000 billion, corresponding to the intersection at point e. This level of total income gives rise to a level of total spending that just buys up the total output the economy's businesses produce. Thus, there are no changes in inventories.

At total income levels lower than the equilibrium level, total expenditure is greater than total output. Therefore, unintended inventory reduction is necessary in order to satisfy the excess of total spending over total output. This will lead the economy's businesses to increase total output, causing total income to rise toward the equilibrium level.

At total income levels greater than the equilibrium level, total expenditure is less than total output. There are unintended inventory increases equal to the excess of total output over total spending. Therefore, the economy's businesses will decrease total output, causing total income to fall toward the equilibrium level.

(The data on which Figure 21-9 is based are shown in Table 21-3.)

the economy's *total expenditure schedule E. The economy's total expenditure schedule represents the total that the economy's households and businesses desire to spend on final goods and services at each possible level of total income.*

Total Income Equals Expected Total Spending

Total income is the sum of *all* payments received by the suppliers of all productive factors—land, labour, capital, and all other inputs—used in the production of the economy's total output. Therefore, total income is the dollar value of this total output. The economy's firms produce this total output because they *expect* to sell it. That is, the dollar value of this total output (which equals total income) equals the level of *expected total spending* on final goods and services—the level of *total sales expected by the economy's businesses*, which they therefore produce to meet.

This concept is also represented graphically in Figure 21-9. Expected total spending is measured on the vertical axis and total income on the horizontal axis. Since total income (horizontal axis) is always equal to expected total spending (vertical axis), this relationship may be represented by the already familiar 45° line. Why? Because any point on this line corresponds to a dollar magnitude on either axis that is exactly equal to the corresponding dollar magnitude on the other axis.

For example, suppose that the economy's business firms expect total spending to be $1,000 billion (vertical axis), which corresponds to point *e* on the 45° line. They will then proceed to produce $1,000 billion of total output, an amount just sufficient to satisfy expected total spending. Since this $1,000 billion is the total of all payments for the factors used to produce the total output, it is the level of total income in the economy. Measured on the horizontal axis, a total income level of $1,000 billion also corresponds to point *e* on the 45° line.

Determining the Equilibrium Level of Total Income

We can now see how the economy's equilibrium level of total income is determined. This is the level of total income that will be sustained once it is achieved. To do this we combine the economy's total expenditure schedule *E* with the 45° line that represents the relationship between expected total spending and total income. This combination in Figure 21-9 is based on the hypothetical data of Table 21-3. First we will consider two possible nonequilibrium levels of total income. It will then be readily apparent why the equilibrium level of total income occurs where the total expenditure schedule *E* intersects the 45° line at point *e*.

Unintended Inventory Reduction

Let us suppose that the economy's business firms *expect* total spending (vertical axis) to be $600 billion. This corresponds to point *a* on the 45° line of Figure 21-9. Acting on the basis of this expectation, they produce $600 billion worth

TABLE 21-3   How the Economy's Equilibrium Total Income Level Is Determined
(Hypothetical Data in Billions of Dollars)

(1) Expected Total Spending	(2) Total Income	(3) Total Expenditure (E)	(4) Change in Inventories	(5) Total Income Will Tend to
$ 200	$ 200	$ 600	−$400	Rise
400	400	700	−300	Rise
600	600	800	−200	Rise
800	800	900	−100	Rise
1,000	1,000	1,000	0	Equilibrium
1,200	1,200	1,100	+100	Fall
1,400	1,400	1,200	+200	Fall
1,600	1,600	1,300	+300	Fall
1,800	1,800	1,400	+400	Fall

POLICY PERSPECTIVE

The Great Depression—Attempts to Explain a Paradox

One of the most frightening things about the Great Depression is that no one, especially economists, seemed to have an adequate explanation that might suggest a policy for dealing with it. In almost any city, long lines of unemployed workers could be seen seeking a free meal or some sort of assistance for their impoverished families. Somehow it all seemed a paradox. Why was it that able-bodied workers, who wanted nothing so much as a job in order to buy badly needed food and other goods, could not find work producing these

products? Wouldn't the income they earned give rise to the demand that would justify the production that would give them employment? Couldn't failing businesses see the connection between the lack of customers at the front door and the long line of unemployed workers seeking jobs at the back door? How could this situation go on for so long? These riddles led to a growing fear. Had Karl Marx been right all along—would capitalism fall by its own weight? What was the matter?

WAGE AND PRICE FLEXIBILITY

Many economists of the day, schooled in the classical tradition, argued that the problem lay in a number of markets where wages and prices were "sticky." They contended that in some product markets, large monopolistic firms were not willing to lower product prices as rapidly as was necessary in the face of declining

continued on next page

FIGURE P21-1   Wage and Price Levels in Canada During the Great Depression

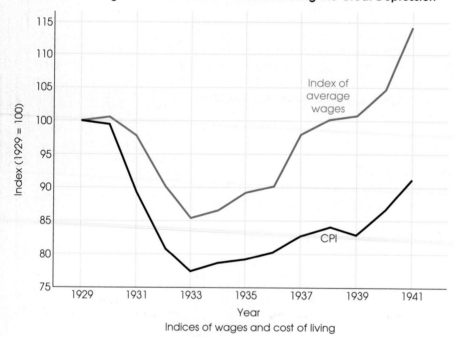

Indices of wages and cost of living

It is true that both wages and prices fell during the early 1930s; however, they did not fall enough to ensure full employment.

Source: Adapted from F. H. Leacy, *Historical Statistics of Canada*, 2nd ed. (Ottawa: Statistics Canada, 1982)

product demand. Similarly, they argued that many unemployed workers were too reluctant to accept lower, or low enough, wages to gain employment. Hence, these economists concluded that classical wage and price flexibility was not allowed to work to bring the economy back to a full employment equilibrium. Even though wages and prices did fall during the Great Depression, as shown in Figure P21-1, they contended that the decline was not far enough or fast enough.

CAN THE INTEREST RATE MATCH SAVING AND INVESTMENT PLANS?

Perhaps the weakest link in the classical argument was the idea that interest rate adjustments would ensure the equality of saving and investment plans.

Many Things Affect Saving

The classical economists' argument that households are induced to save more at high interest rates than at low rates raises some questions. Even if the assertion is true, it may take large changes in interest rates to really affect the level of saving much at all, other things remaining the same. Indeed, many of the "other things" may be much more important determinants of saving plans than is the interest rate.

For example, much household saving is directed toward accumulating the funds needed to make some future purchase—a house, an automobile, a university education, a vacation, and so forth. Saving may also be aimed at providing a "nest egg" for unforeseen emergencies such as job loss, illness, or simply a general sense of security. Saving can also provide for retirement years. Some people may simply want to accumulate enough wealth to be able to live off the interest it can earn. The last mo-

tive has an interesting implication. The higher the interest rate, the less wealth it takes to earn a given level of income. If the interest rate is 5 percent, it takes $10,000 to earn $500 per year. At an interest rate of 10 percent, it takes half that amount, or $5,000, to earn $500 per year. Therefore, if people save in order to accumulate just enough wealth to be able to earn a certain income level from it, the higher is the interest rate the less will be the amount of saving necessary to achieve their goal. Of course, this is just the opposite of the classical proposition that saving will increase when the interest rate increases.

Investment—How Important Is the Interest Rate?

During some years of the Great Depression capital consumption, or depreciation of the economy's capital stock, was actually larger than the amount of gross investment. In other words, net investment was negative. Many economists question whether interest rates lower than those that actually prevailed would have substantially increased investment expenditures in those years. A host of other factors are generally considered to be more important determinants of the level of investment.

For example, the behaviour of retail or final sales may be quite important, as suggested by our discussion of Figure 21-7. The fact that money GDP fell by nearly 50 percent between 1929 and 1933 would seem to have some bearing on the fact that gross investment fell by nearly 80 percent during this same period of time. No matter how low the rate of interest, dramatically falling sales would hardly seem likely to encourage businesses to invest in new plants and equipment or more inventories.

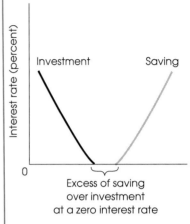

FIGURE P21-2 Even at a Zero Interest Rate, Saving May Not Equal Investment

Regarding the interest rate, Keynes argued that there might well be a lower limit (above zero) to how far it could fall. Without getting into the complexity of his argument, this meant that the interest rate might not be able to fall low enough to match saving and investment plans and ensure full employment. Keynes also noted that even if the interest rate fell to zero, investment plans might still be less than saving plans, as shown in Figure P21-2. The leakage from saving would then lead to a continuing fall in aggregate demand for goods and services.

For Discussion

- Could you envision the paradox described here occurring in Robinson Crusoe's world (one person living alone on an island)? Why or why not?.
- How might a decline in the total income level affect the saving curve S in Figure P21-2?

of total output. Since this represents $600 billion of payments to all the factors used to produce this total output, the economy's total income level (horizontal axis) is $600 billion, which also corresponds to point *a* on the 45° line. However, with a total income of $600 billion, the *actual* level of total spending in the economy will turn out to be $800 billion, corresponding to point *a'* on the economy's total expenditure schedule *E*. But the economy only produced $600 billion worth of total output during the period. Consequently, the only way the total spending of $800 billion can be satisfied is for businesses to sell $200 billion of goods from inventories, stocks of goods produced and accumulated during *past* periods. The amount of this *unintended inventory reduction* is represented by the vertical distance between point *a'* on the economy's total expenditure schedule *E* and point *a* on the 45° line. It is *unintended* because the economy's business firms underestimated what the level of total spending in the economy was going to be.

The fact that the economy's business firms have to sell from inventories tells them that they underestimated total spending. If they were to continue doing this, unintended inventory reduction would also continue. Eventually, perhaps quickly, this would cause them to revise their expectations of total spending upward. The dollar value of total output produced, and hence the level of the economy's total income, would rise accordingly. This adjustment process would continue as long as there was any unintended reduction of inventories.

When and where would the adjustment stop? When unintended inventory reduction ceased—that is, at the income level at which the level of total spending is just equal to that expected. In Figure 21-9 this occurs at a total income of $1,000 billion, corresponding to the intersection of the total expenditure schedule *E* with the 45° line at point *e*. It is therefore the equilibrium level of total income.

Starting from any level of expected total spending—and hence total income—below $1,000 billion, total income will tend to rise until the equilibrium level is reached and there is no longer any unintended reduction of inventories. This is illustrated in Table 21-3. You should check the numbers shown there and relate them to Figure 21-9.

Unintended Inventory Increase

Consider what happens at total income levels greater than the equilibrium level. Suppose that the economy's business firms expect total spending (vertical axis) to be $1,400 billion, corresponding to point *b* on the 45° line in Figure 21-9. They therefore produce that amount of total output, and the economy's total income (horizontal axis) is $1,400 billion. But at that total income level, actual total spending (vertical axis) will turn out to be only $1,200 billion, point *b'* on the economy's total expenditure schedule *E*. This means that $200 billion of the economy's total output will go unsold and therefore end up as an unintended inventory increase. This increase is represented by the vertical distance between points *b* and *b'* in Figure 21-9.

The $1,400 billion level of total income will not be sustained. Why? Business firms will not go on producing more output than they can sell, thereby increasing their unsold inventory. Instead, they will revise their expectations of total spending downward and produce less. As a result, total income will fall to the equilibrium total income level of $1,000 billion, which corresponds to the intersection of the economy's total expenditure schedule E and the 45° line at point e in Figure 21-9. We can now see that, starting from any level of total income greater than the equilibrium level, total income will tend to fall to the equilibrium level. Again this is illustrated in Table 21-3. You should check the numbers in this table and relate them to Figure 21-9.

The economy's equilibrium level of total income gives rise to a level of total spending that just purchases the total output that the economy's businesses desire to produce. In equilibrium there is no change in inventories because total spending just matches the dollar value of total output.

Equilibrium Without Full Employment

Recall that we are assuming that the economy's price level is fixed. Therefore, if total spending and total income change, the entire change is due to a change in the number of actual physical units of output produced by the economy. This requires a change in the amount of labour used in production. Consequently, every level of total income on the horizontal axis of Figure 21-9 corresponds to a different level of total employment. *A major implication of the income–expenditure approach is that the level of employment associated with the equilibrium level of total income need not correspond to full employment, and typically will not.*

For example, suppose that the labour force will be fully employed only when the economy produces the level of total output associated with a total income level equal to $1,400 billion. However, we have already seen that if the economy's total expenditure schedule is E (Figure 21-9), total spending is not sufficient to sustain this level of total income. Consequently, some of the labour force will be unemployed. In general, the lower is the equilibrium level of total income, the higher is the unemployment rate.

> **Checkpoint 21-5**
>
> Give the explanation of what happens in the economy starting at any level of expected total spending and proceeding from columns (1) through (5) in Table 21-3.

Summary

1. Classical economists argued that a capitalistic, laissez faire economy would automatically tend to operate at a full employment equilibrium. This contention was based on Say's Law, which states that supply creates its own demand.
2. The classical argument held that if wages and prices were perfectly flexible, a drop in total demand would result in a downward adjustment in wages and prices sufficient to reestablish a full employment level of total output. In addition, the leakage from the income–expenditure flow due to saving would create no problem because the interest rate would adjust to ensure that saving plans always equalled investment plans.
3. The Great Depression of the 1930s led to a critical reexamination of the classical position. It became obvious that in a number of markets, prices and particularly wages were sticky, or slow to adjust downward. The notion that saving and investment plans could be equated by interest rate adjustments alone was brought into question.
4. The Keynesian revolution led to the development of income–expenditure theory and its basic building blocks—the consumption function, the saving function, and the investment schedule. The consumption function shows the amount households want to consume (spend) and the saving function the amount they want to save (not spend) at each disposable income level. The

investment schedule shows the amount businesses want to invest at each income level.

5. Movements along the consumption and saving functions are caused by changes in disposable income, all other things that influence consumption and saving remaining the same. Changes in one or more of the other things will cause shifts in the consumption and saving functions. Important among these other things are credit conditions, consumer wealth, and consumer expectations about unemployment, prices, and income.

6. Investment expenditures are more variable than the other two major components of the expenditure side of GDP, consumption and government expenditures. The expectation of profit is what determines the level of desired investment expenditure. The variability of investment expenditure results from the difficulty and complexity of forecasting prospective profits combined with the sensitivity of expectations to changes in the economic environment.

7. The investment schedule represents the relationships between the level of planned investment and the level of total income. Several important determinants of profit prospects that can cause shifts in the investment schedule are interest rate changes, technological change, and the development of new products.

8. According to the income–expenditure approach, the equilibrium level of total income, output, and employment occurs where the total expenditure schedule intersects the 45° line. At equilibrium the total income earned from production of the economy's total output corresponds to a level of total spending just sufficient to purchase that total output.

9. At levels of total income less than the equilibrium level, total spending is greater than total output and there is unintended inventory reduction. This leads the economy's business firms to increase total output, so that total income and employment rise toward the equilibrium level. At levels of total income greater than the equilibrium level, total spending is less than total output and there are unintended increases in inventories. The economy's business firms then reduce total output, so that total income and employment tend to fall toward the equilibrium level.

Key Terms and Concepts

consumption function	interest rate	Say's Law
equilibrium income level	saving function	

Questions and Problems

1. According to Say's Law, supply creates demand. Why couldn't this law be stated the other way around—namely, that demand creates supply?

2. Suppose that you were a completely self-sufficient farmer living in the wilderness. What would be the relationship between your saving and investment decisions? What would be the significance of the notion of involuntary unemployment?

3. Explain why wage and price flexibility are not sufficient to restore a full employment equilibrium subsequent to a fall in total demand.

4. Using a diagram like Figure 21-1, illustrate what would happen if there were no positive level of the interest rate that would equate saving and investment plans. Describe what would be happening in the economy in this situation.

5. How do you think the following would affect the consumption and saving functions and why?
   a. Employer-subsidized pension plans for employees are set up throughout the economy.
   b. There is a general decline in the stock market.
   c. The government announces that gasoline will be rationed to consumers starting 3 months from now.
   d. Households anticipate that the rate of inflation is going to rise from 5 percent per year to 15 percent per year during the next 6 months.
   e. Households begin to doubt the financial soundness of the social insurance system, causing concern about the level of future retirement benefits that the system will be able to pay them.

6. What do you think would be the effect on prospective profit of each of the following and how would the investment schedule shift as a result?
   a. Unions demand that employers make larger contributions to employee pension plans.
   b. New sources of natural gas are discovered.
   c. Parliament passes a law allowing larger tax write-offs for research and development costs.
   d. Parliament passes a law mandating stiffer controls on industrial waste disposal.
   e. War breaks out in the Middle East, threatening the destruction of oil fields in the area.
   f. The Prime Minister calls for price ceilings on final products and an increase in social insurance taxes.

7. Compare and contrast the way businesses decide to invest with the way households decide how much to consume, and explain why investment is more variable than consumption.

8. How do you think the position of the total expenditure schedule E in Figure 21-9 would be affected by each of the following?
   a. The expected profitability of business declines.
   b. The interest rate rises.
   c. The wealth of households rises.
   d. Consumer indebtedness rises.

9. Why does total income equal expected total spending? In what sense are inventories a buffer against mistakes in forecasting?

10. In Table 21-3, suppose that the economy's level of total expenditure, column (3), is higher by $100 billion at every level of total income, column (2). What would be the new equilibrium level of total income, and how would columns (4) and (5) be changed? Can you sketch this change in Figure 21-9?

11. Why is it that the unintended inventory increase represented by the vertical distance between b and b' in Figure 21-9 is included in total income, while the unintended inventory reduction equal to the vertical distance between a' and a is not?

Chapter 22

Equilibrium Income in the Keynesian Model

In this chapter we will examine more closely the Keynesian view of the determination of the economy's equilibrium level of aggregate income, output, and employment. First, we will focus on the relationship between investment and saving in the determination of equilibrium. Then we will define and explain the marginal propensity to consume (*MPC*) and the marginal propensity to save (*MPS*). We will use these concepts to explain the important Keynesian concept of the multiplier, which tells us how aggregate income will change in response to an autonomously caused change in aggregate expenditure. Finally, we will define and explain the "paradox of thrift."

We will continue to make no distinction among GDP, NDP, NI, PI, and DI because, for the time being, we will assume that there are no exports, no imports, no government expenditure or taxation, that all saving is personal saving, and that capital depreciation is zero. Finally, we assume that wages and prices are unchanging, an assumption that simplifies the analysis without interfering with the learning objectives in any way. The concepts developed in this chapter will prove very useful to us in the next chapter, where we will introduce exports, imports, government expenditure, and taxation into this framework.

Equilibrium and Realized versus Desired Investment

So far, our discussion of how equilibrium income is determined has focused on the aggregate expenditure schedule *AE* and its relationship to the 45° line. Now, let's look at this relationship more closely. First, we will explicitly recognize that the aggregate expenditure schedule *AE* is equal to the sum of consumption and the level of intended or desired investment, as was shown earlier, in Table 21-2.

TABLE 22-1   Determination of the Equilibrium Level of Aggregate Income, and the Relationship Between Intended Investment, Realized Investment, and Saving
(Hypothetical Data in Billions of Dollars)

(1) Total Income and Output	(2) Consumption Expenditure (C)	(3) Saving (S) S = (1) − (2)	(4) Intended Investment (I)	(5) Total Expenditure (E) or Total Spending E = (2) + (4)	(6) Unintended Inventory Change Equals Total Output Minus Aggregate Expenditure (1) − (5)	(7) Realized Investment Equals Intended Investment Plus Unintended Inventory Change (4) + (6)
$ 200	$ 300	−$100	$300	$ 600	−$400	−$100
400	400	0	300	700	− 300	0
600	500	100	300	800	− 200	100
800	600	200	300	900	− 100	200
1,000	700	300	300	1,000	0	300
1,200	800	400	300	1,100	100	400
1,400	900	500	300	1,200	200	500
1,600	1,000	600	300	1,300	300	600
1,800	1,100	700	300	1,400	400	700

Then we will focus on the relationship between aggregate income and consumption (the consumption function) and aggregate income and saving (the saving function). These relationships were shown earlier in Figure 21-4. Continuing with our hypothetical example, the data from Tables 21-2 and 21-3 are shown again in columns (1), (2), (4), (5), and (6) of Table 22-1.

Also shown is the level of saving, column (3), which is equal to the difference between aggregate income and consumption, column (1) minus column (2). Realized investment, which is equal to the sum of columns (4) and (6), is shown in

---

LEARNING OBJECTIVES

After reading this chapter, you will be able to:

1. Distinguish between actual investment and desired investment, and explain their relationship to saving.
2. Explain the relationship between aggregate income and unintended inventory changes.
3. Identify the relationship between withdrawals and injections at equilibrium income.
4. Describe and explain the paradox of thrift.
5. Solve for equilibrium income using the aggregate expenditure–aggregate income approach.
6. Solve for equilibrium income using the withdrawal–injection approach.
7. Define and explain the average and marginal propensities to consume and to save.
8. Calculate the average propensity to consume, average propensity to save, marginal propensity to consume, and marginal propensity to save given an income schedule and consumption schedule.
9. Define the multiplier.
10. Calculate the multiplier given an aggregate expenditure function.
11. Explain and illustrate why changes in autonomous aggregate expenditure have multiplier effects on equilibrium income.

column (7). These relationships are shown in Figure 22-1, frame (a), which is the same as Figure 21-9 except that the consumption function has been added. This function is the level of consumption expenditure C, column (2), associated with each level of aggregate income, column (1). We will use Figure 22-1 to help us define the concept of realized investment and its relationship to intended

FIGURE 22-1   **Determination of the Equilibrium Level of Aggregate Income, and the Relationship Between Desired Investment, Actual Investment, and Saving**

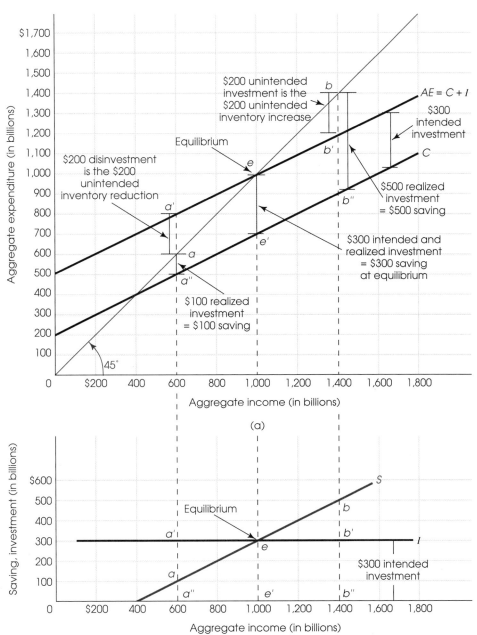

The diagram in frame (a) is the same as that in Figure 21-9 except that the components that make up aggregate expenditure AE, consumption C, and desired investment I are shown explicitly along with the level of saving (which is equal to the difference between consumption C and the 45° line).

The diagram in frame (b) shows an alternative but completely equivalent way to represent the determination of the equilibrium level of aggregate income. It combines the saving function S, corresponding to the consumption function in frame (a), with the investment schedule I, which shows the level of intended investment; the investment schedule I is the same as the vertical distance between the aggregate expenditure schedule AE and the consumption function C in frame (a). The points corresponding to a, e, b, and so forth in frame (a) are similarly labeled in frame (b). The vertical distances between these points have exactly the same interpretation in frame (b) as in frame (a).

investment. We will then examine the relationship between these two types of investment and saving, both when the economy is at its equilibrium income level and when it is not.

Actual Investment and Saving

In Chapter 19 gross private domestic investment was defined as including all final purchases of new tools and machines by business firms, all construction expenditures, and *all changes in inventories*.

Unintended Inventory Depletion

We have seen that when the economy is at an aggregate income level less than equilibrium income, there is an unintended inventory depletion. This change is represented by the vertical distance between the aggregate expenditure schedule *AE* and the 45° line. For example, when aggregate income is $600 billion, Figure 22-1, frame (a), there is an **unintended inventory depletion** of $200 billion, which is represented by the vertical distance between a' and a. The amount of the intended investment, or the investment that business firms desire to do, is $300 billion, which is represented by the vertical distance a' to a'' between the aggregate expenditure schedule *AE* and the consumption function *C*. However, this $300 billion investment expenditure, when combined with $500 billion of consumption expenditure (a sum equal to $800 billion), exceeds the $600 billion of total output produced during the period (corresponding to a point a on the 45° line) by $200 billion. Hence, $200 billion of goods has to be sold from inventory to satisfy this excess of aggregate expenditure over production. The $200 billion decrease, or negative change, in inventories is an offset to the $300 billion of intended investment. This decrease, which is often called a **disinvestment, actual investment**, or **realized investment**, therefore amounts to only $100 billion, which is represented by the vertical distance between point a on the 45° line and point a'' on the consumption function *C*.

Note that this vertical distance between point a on the 45° line and point a'' on the consumption function also represents the amount of saving that households do out of the $600 billion aggregate income. Therefore, it follows that *realized investment is equal to saving*. At any aggregate income level less than the equilibrium level of aggregate income (which is equal to $1,000 billion in our example), intended investment is always greater than realized investment. A comparison of columns (4) and (7) of Table 22-1 for the aggregate income levels, column (1), less than the equilibrium level bears this out. At any of these aggregate income levels, it is also always true that realized investment equals saving—compare columns (3) and (7). You should relate these numbers to Figure 22-1.

Unintended Inventory Increases

We observed that, at aggregate income levels greater than equilibrium income, there are unintended inventory increases represented by the vertical distance between the aggregate expenditure schedule *AE* and the 45° line. For instance, at an aggregate income level of $1,400 billion, Figure 22-1, frame (a), we see a $200 billion **unintended inventory increase**. This increase is equal to the vertical distance between b and b'. Once again the amount of intended invest-ment that the economy's business firms desire to do equals $300 billion. This desired investment is represented by the vertical distance between point b' on the aggregate expenditure schedule AE and the point b'' on the consumption function C. This amount of investment expenditure plus the $900 billion of con-sumption expenditure gives an aggregate expenditure level of $1,200 billion. But this level is $200 billion lower than the $1,400 billion level of total output pro-duced during the period (point b on the 45° line). As a result, unsold goods worth $200 billion remain on shelves and in warehouses as inventory. This $200 billion increase, or *positive change*, in inventory is unintended investment. Therefore, *ac-tual* or *realized investment* amounts to $500 billion, which is equal to the vertical distance between point b on the 45° line and point b'' on the consumption func-tion C. Again, this vertical distance represents the amount of saving, equal to $500 billion, that takes place when the aggregate income level is $1,400 billion. Once more we see that *realized investment is equal to saving*. Indeed, this is true at any aggregate income level greater than the equilibrium level. For example, in Table 22-1 compare columns (3) and (7) for each of the aggregate income levels in column (1) greater than the $1,000 billion equilibrium level. It is also true that at any aggregate income level greater than the equilibrium level, realized invest-ment is always greater than intended investment, as we can see by comparing columns (4) and (7). Again, you should relate these numbers to Figure 22-1.

Equilibrium Income

Now consider the equilibrium level of aggregate income, which is $1,000 billion. It is only here that the level of intended investment is equal to the level of realized investment, in this case $300 billion, which is represented by the vertical distance from e to e' in Figure 22-1, frame (a). This reflects the fact that there is no unintended change in inventory because the $1,000 billion level of total spending just equals the $1,000 billion of total output produced. Again observe that realized investment equals saving, just as at all other levels of total income. But *only at equilibrium is it also true that intended investment equals saving*.

By way of summary (assuming government expenditure and taxes and net exports are zero) we can say that:

1. Actual or realized investment always equals saving no matter what the level of aggregate income.
2. Intended investment equals saving only at the equilibrium level of aggregate income.
3. Realized investment and intended investment are equal only at the equilibrium level of aggregate income. At all other levels of aggregate income, they differ by the amount of unintended inventory change.
4. There is an unintended decrease in inventory at all levels of aggregate income less than equilibrium income.
5. There is an unintended increase in inventory at all levels of aggregate income greater than equilibrium income.

Withdrawals and Injections Interpretation of Equilibrium

In Figure 21-4 we examined the correspondence between the consumption func-tion and the saving function. The saving function S in Figure 22-1, frame (b), corresponds to the consumption function *C* in Figure 22-1, frame (a), in exactly the same manner. The saving function is based on the data from columns (1) and (3) of Table 22-1. Figure 21-7, frame (a), showed us that when the level of intended investment is the same at all income levels, it may be represented by a horizontal investment schedule. Hence, the $300 billion level of intended investment represented by the vertical distance between the consumption function *C* and the aggregate expenditure schedule *AE* in Figure 22-1, frame (a), also can be represented by the investment schedule *I* in Figure 22-1, frame (b). This investment schedule is based on the data from columns (1) and (4) of Table 22-1. The combination of the saving function *S* and the investment schedule *I* in frame (b) of Figure 22-1 is an alternative way, but equivalent to that shown in frame (a), of representing how the equilibrium level of aggregate income is determined. The points corresponding to *a, e, b,* and so forth in frame (a) are similarly labeled in frame (b). The vertical distances between these points have exactly the same meaning in both parts of the figure. However, the combination of the saving function *S* and the investment schedule *I* in frame (b) suggests another interesting interpretation of the determination of the equilibrium level of aggregate income—the withdrawals and injections interpretation.

The Circular Flow

We anticipated the use of the withdrawals–injections approach to equilibrium income in Chapter 21. There we noted that the circular-flow nature of the total-spending-equals-aggregate-income relationship suggests that saving is like a withdrawal from the ongoing flow, while investment is like an injection into that flow. Investment spending by businesses acts to compensate for the saving by households and can prevent a sharp drop in the ongoing level of total spending. This is so because not all of the economy's output is sold to consumers. Some of it is sold to businesses in the form of capital goods; thus, investment spending takes a portion of total output off the market.

Equilibrium income will be the income at which the withdrawal due to saving is just exactly offset by the amount of injection due to intended investment—that is, the level of aggregate income at which intended investment equals saving. This level is represented in frame (b) of Figure 22-1 by the intersection of the saving function *S* and the investment schedule *I* at point *e*, which corresponds to an aggregate income level of $1,000 billion.

Net Withdrawals

At aggregate income levels greater than the equilibrium level, the withdrawal (saving) will be larger than the injection (intended investment). This situation, referred to as **net withdrawals**, can be seen by comparing columns (3) and (4) of Table 22-1, and it is also represented by the fact that to the right of point *e* the saving function *S* lies above the investment schedule *I*. For example, at an aggregate income level of $1,400 billion, point *b″*, the withdrawal from aggregate income due to saving equals $500 billion, which is represented by the vertical distance from *b″* to *b*. However, the injection due to intended investment is only $300 billion, the vertical distance from *b″* to *b′*. This means that of the $500 billion of total output *not* purchased by consumers, only $300 billion is taken off the market through intended investment spending by businesses. The rest, amounting to $200 billion and represented by the vertical distance from *b′* to *b*, is left unsold on shelves and in warehouses as an unintended addition to inventory. This addition to inventory will lead the economy's businesses to reduce production (remember that prices are assumed constant) and thereby cause the level of aggregate income to fall, as we discussed earlier in looking at Figure 22-1, frame (a). Aggregate income will continue to fall until the amount of output consumers refrain from purchasing (that is, the amount consumers save) equals the amount businesses purchase (that is, their intended investment spending). This equality occurs only at the equilibrium aggregate income level of $1,000 billion, the level at which saving and intended investment both equal $300 billion, as represented by the vertical distance between points e' and e in frame (b) of Figure 22-1.

Net Injections

At aggregate income levels less than the equilibrium level, the withdrawal (saving) will be less than the injection (intended investment). This situation, referred to as positive **net injections**, can be seen by comparing columns (3) and (4) of Table 22-1. It is also represented by the fact that the saving function lies below the investment schedule to the left of point e in Figure 22-1, frame (b). For instance, at an aggregate income level of $600 billion, point a, the withdrawal from aggregate income due to saving is only $100 billion, represented by the vertical distance from a to a''. But the injection from intended investment amounts to $300 billion, which is equal to the distance from a' to a''. The difference, amounting to $200 billion, is the excess of aggregate expenditure or spending over total output, which is represented by the vertical distance between a and a'. In order to satisfy this excess demand, producers must sell goods from inventories. But this reduction in inventories will lead the economy's businesses to increase the production of total output. Consequently, the economy's aggregate income will rise, as we discussed earlier in connection with frame (a) of Figure 22-1. Aggregate income will continue to rise, and the amount of withdrawal due to saving will continue to increase until it equals the amount of injection into the circular flow due to intended investment. Again, this equality occurs only at the equilibrium aggregate income level of $1,000 billion, the level at which the saving function S intersects the investment schedule I at point e in frame (b) of Figure 22-1.

Equilibrium Level of Aggregate Income

The equilibrium level of aggregate income, corresponding to the intersection of the saving function S and the investment schedule I, is the only level where the total saving of the economy's households just matches the total investment plans of the economy's businesses. At any other level there will be a discrepancy between the plans of these two groups.

Checkpoint 22-2

Using the data in Table 22-1, suppose that the economy is currently at an aggregate income level of $1,600 billion. Indicate the adjustment process which would occur to bring the economy to its equilibrium level of aggregate output.

Checkpoint 22-3

Using Figure 22-1, explain why there is an unintended inventory increase when injections are less than withdrawals at the current level of aggregate income. Why is it that businesses do not merely decrease their prices when withdrawals exceed injections? What happens to resource use as a result of the expected response by businesses trying to eliminate unintended increases in inventory?

Marginal and Average
Propensities to Consume and Save

Students often confuse the concepts of marginal and average. The distinction between them is important to our understanding of the consumption and saving functions and their role in the theory of income and employment determination.

In particular, the marginal propensity to consume and the marginal propensity to save are needed to understand the important Keynesian concept of the multiplier, as we shall see.

Marginal Propensities to Consume and to Save

The **marginal propensity to consume** (*MPC*) *is the fraction or proportion of any change in disposable income that is consumed:*[1]

$$MPC = \frac{\text{Change in consumption}}{\text{Change in disposable income}}$$

The term *marginal* refers to the fact that we are interested *only* in the *change* in the level of consumption brought about by a *change* in the level of disposable income. Similarly, the **marginal propensity to save** (*MPS*) *is the fraction or proportion of any change in disposable income that is saved:*

$$MPS = \frac{\text{Change in saving}}{\text{Change in disposable income}}$$

These concepts are illustrated in Table 22-2. As we move from one level of disposable income to the next in column (1), the *change* (Δ) in the level of

[1]We have no need in this chapter to distinguish among GDP, NDP, NI, PI, and DI, as noted at the outset. However, at this point we define the *MPC* in terms of disposable income because the distinction between DI and GDP will be important to our use of *MPC* when we introduce exports, imports, government spending, and taxation into the picture in the next chapter.

TABLE 22-2   The Consumption and Saving Schedules, the Marginal Propensity to Consume, and the Marginal Propensity to Save
(Hypothetical Data in Billions of Dollars)

(1) Disposable Income (DI)	(2) Change in DI (ΔDI)	(3) Consumption (C)	(4) Change in C (ΔC)	(5) Saving (S) S = (1) − (3)	(6) Change in S (ΔS)	(7) Marginal Propensity to Consume (MPC) $MPC = \frac{(4)}{(2)}$	(8) Marginal Propensity to Save (MPS) $MPS = \frac{(6)}{(2)}$
$300		$320		−$20			
	$25		$15		$10	.60	.40
325		335		− 10			
	25		15		10	.60	.40
350		350		0			
	25		15		10	.60	.40
375		365		10			
	25		15		10	.60	.40
400		380		20			
	25		15		10	.60	.40
425		395		30			
	25		15		10	.60	.40
450		410		40			
	25		15		10	.60	.40
475		425		50			
	25		15		10	.60	.40
500		440		60			

disposable income ΔDI is given in column (2). The associated *change* in the level of consumption ΔC brought about by the *change* in disposable income ΔDI is given in column (4). The associated marginal propensity to consume (*MPC*) is shown in column (7). In this case, the *MPC* (which is $\Delta C \div \Delta DI$) equals .60. Similarly, the change in the level of saving (ΔS) brought about by the *change* in disposable income (ΔDI) is given in column (6). The associated marginal propensity to save (*MPS*) is given in column (8). In this case, the *MPS* (which is $\Delta S \div \Delta DI$) equals .40.

Suppose, for example, that disposable income rises from $450 billion to $475 billion, an increase of $25 billion, column (2). What do households do with this increase? According to Table 22-2, they consume .60 of it, which is $15 billion, column (4), and save .40 of it, which is $10 billion, column (6). These are the only two things households can do with the increase: consume it or save it. The portion that is not spent is saved. By definition, then, the fraction of the increase in disposable income consumed, *MPC*, plus the fraction saved, *MPS*, when added together, are equal to the whole increase in disposable income. Therefore, *the sum of MPC and MPS must always equal 1:*

$$MPC + MPS = 1$$

The data in Table 22-2 show us that this is true, since

$$.60 + .40 = 1$$

The marginal propensity to consume is represented graphically by the slope of the consumption function. This is shown in frame (a) of Figure 22-2. (Figure 22-2 is the same as Figure 21-4. It is not related to Figure 22-1.) The slope of any line is the ratio of the amount of vertical change in the line to the associated amount of horizontal change. For the consumption function, the vertical change ΔC is associated with the horizontal change ΔDI. The marginal propensity to save is represented graphically by the slope of the saving function. This is shown in frame (b) of Figure 22-2.

If the consumption function is a straight line, then so is the saving function. When the consumption function is a straight line, its slope (*MPC*) has the same value at every point along the line. The same is true of the slope (*MPS*) of the straight-line saving function. The consumption and saving functions of Figure 22-2 are both straight lines. If, however, the consumption function were a curve that was less steeply sloped at higher disposable income levels, then the saving function would be a curve that gets more steeply sloped at higher disposable income levels. In that case the *MPC* would be smaller at higher income levels and the *MPS* would be larger. Draw such consumption and saving functions and illustrate these characteristics.

Average Propensities to Consume and to Save

The **average propensity to consume** (*APC*) *is the fraction or proportion of total disposable income that is consumed:*

$$APC = \frac{\text{Consumption}}{\text{Disposable income}}$$

FIGURE 22-2   The Marginal Propensity to Consume and the Marginal Propensity to Save

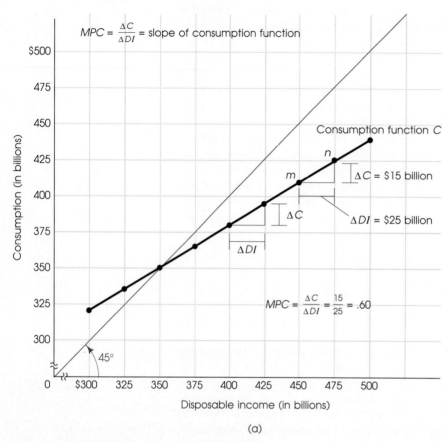

(a)

The slope of a line is the ratio of the amount of vertical change in the line to the associated amount of horizontal change. For the consumption function, the vertical change ΔC is associated with the horizontal change ΔDI, as shown in frame (a). Hence, the slope of the consumption function is

$$\frac{\Delta C}{\Delta DI}$$

which is the marginal propensity to consume, MPC. Similarly, the slope of the saving function is

$$\frac{\Delta S}{\Delta DI}$$

which is the marginal propensity to save, MPS, as shown in frame (b). Both of these functions are straight lines. Therefore, the marginal propensity to consume is the same no matter where it is measured along the consumption function. The same is true of the marginal propensity to save measured anywhere along the saving function. In the examples shown here, which are based on the data in Table 22-2, the MPC equals .60 and the MPS equals .40.

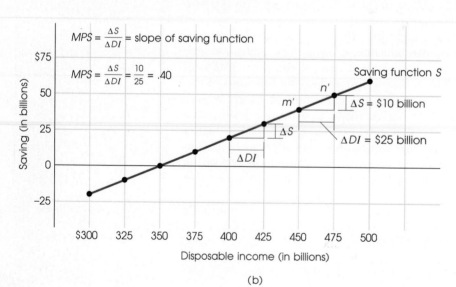

(b)

TABLE 22-3   The Consumption and Saving Schedules, the Average Propensity to Consume, and the Average Propensity to Save
(Hypothetical Data in Billions of Dollars)

(1) Disposable Income (DI)	(2) Consumption (C)	(3) Saving (S) $S = (1) - (2)$	(4) Average Propensity to Consume (APC) $APC = \frac{(2)}{(1)}$	(5) Average Propensity to Save (APS) $APS = \frac{(3)}{(1)}$
$300	$320	−$20	1.07	−.07
325	335	− 10	1.03	−.03
350	350	0	1.00	.00
375	365	10	.97	.03
400	380	20	.95	.05
425	395	30	.93	.07
450	410	40	.91	.09
475	425	50	.89	.11
500	440	60	.88	.12

Note that whereas the *MPC* is the ratio of the *change* in consumption to the *change* in disposable income, the *APC* is the ratio of the *level* of consumption to the *level* of disposable income. The *APC* and the *MPC* are therefore two distinctly different concepts.

Table 22-3 shows the same data in columns (1), (2), and (3) for *DI*, *C*, and *S* as in columns (1), (3), and (5) of Table 22-2. The average propensity to consume for each level of disposable income, column (1), and its associated level of consumption, column (2), is shown in column (4). *APC* equals *C/DI*, which is the consumption data in column (2) divided by the disposable income data in column (1). Note that unlike the *MPC*, column (7) of Table 22-2, the *APC*, column (4) of Table 22-3, declines as disposable income increases.

The **average propensity to save** (*APS*) *is the fraction or proportion of total disposable income that is saved:*

$$APS = \frac{\text{Saving}}{\text{Disposable income}}$$

Again, it should be remembered that the *APS* and the *MPS* are different concepts. While the *MPS* is the ratio of the *change* in saving to the *change* in disposable income, the *APS* is the ratio of the *level* of saving to the *level* of disposable income.

The *APS* of our example is shown in column (5) of Table 22-3. Note that while the *APC*, column (4), falls as disposable income increases, the *APS*, column (5), increases. In other words, if the fraction of total disposable income consumed gets smaller at higher disposable income levels, then it follows that the fraction of total disposable income saved must get larger. Since all disposable income is either consumed or saved, it also follows that

$$APC + APS = 1$$

Checkpoint 22-4

Use a graph to illustrate how the consumption function would have to look if its *MPC* and *APC* are always equal to each other, no matter what the level of disposable income. What would be true of the relationship between the *MPS* and the *APS* of the saving function in this case, and what would the saving function look like? How would the consumption function have to shift for the *APC* to increase and the *MPC* to remain unchanged? Show what would happen to the saving function in this case.

Autonomous Expenditure
Change and Equilibrium Income

Our examination of the business cycle in Chapter 20 indicated that aggregate income, output, and employment are always changing. One of the explanations for the variation of output, income, and employment was the Keynesian interpretation. In this theory, income is moving from one equilibrium to another in response to some change in the autonomous level of aggregate expenditure that shifts the position of the entire aggregate expenditure function. In the simple Keynesian model we are considering in this chapter, where government expenditure, taxation, and foreign trade are ignored, shifts in aggregate expenditure can be caused by shifts in either or both of its components—consumption and intended investment. Such shifts are represented by changes in the position of the aggregate expenditure schedule and result in changes in the equilibrium levels of aggregate income, output, and employment.

Shifts in the consumption and saving functions, the investment schedule, and hence the aggregate expenditure schedule are due to causes *other than* changes in the level of aggregate income. Changes in the level of aggregate income cause *movements along* these curves. Changes in all other things—expectations, wealth, interest rates, and so forth (the list of *factors other than income* that could cause either consumption or intended investment to change is quite extensive, but the three items listed are sufficient for this simple analysis)—cause *shifts or changes in the position* of these curves. In order to keep this extremely important distinction in mind, changes in expenditure that cause the aggregate expenditure schedule to shift are often referred to as *exogenously caused*, or *autonomous*, expenditure changes.

The Paradox of Thrift

You have probably heard sayings such as, "A penny saved is a penny earned," or "We must tighten our belts if we wish to be better off in the future." It seems like good advice for households to save in order to increase their wealth in the future. While these old adages are undoubtedly true for individual families in society, they may not be good advice for the economy as a whole. To presume what is good advice for a family is good advice for the entire economy is a case of the *fallacy of composition*—what is true of the part is not necessarily true of the whole.

Suppose the equilibrium level of aggregate income and output in the economy is $1,400 billion. This level is determined by the intersection of the saving function S_0 with the investment schedule I at point e_0 in frame (a) of Figure 22-3. The level of saving and investment (vertical axis) is $400 billion. Now suppose that the economy's households decide to save more at every level of aggregate income. The result would be an upward shift in the saving function from S_0 to S_1. But look what happens! The equilibrium level of aggregate income and output falls from $1,400 billion to $1,000 billion, as determined by the intersection of S_1 and I at e_1. Furthermore, the amount of saving that actually takes place remains unchanged at $400 billion. A penny saved *may not be* a penny earned. Quite to the contrary, the *attempt* to save more results in no increase in saving and, worse yet, may lead

FIGURE 22-3   The Paradox of Thrift

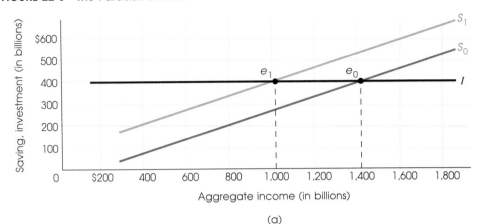

(a)

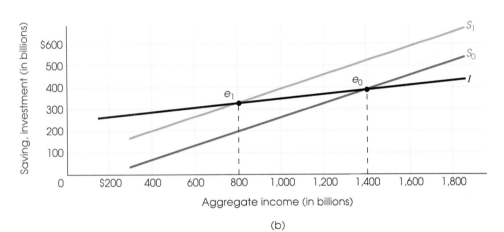

(b)

It may well be good advice for a household to try to save more, but it will be bad for the economy if all households attempt to do so. Suppose that the economy's equilibrium level of aggregate income is initially $1,400 billion, as determined by the intersection of the saving function S_0 and the investment schedule I at point e_0. If the economy's households attempt to save more, the saving function will shift up to the position S_1. Given the investment schedule I in frame (a), aggregate income and output will fall to $1,000 billion, and the amount of saving will in fact remain unchanged at $400 billion. If the level of desired investment varies with the level of aggregate income and output, as shown in frame (b), the attempt to save more actually causes the amount saved to fall!

---

to an actual decline in the aggregate income earned! The **paradox of thrift** *is the attempt by a society to increase its savings at a specific income, resulting in a decrease in aggregate income, output, employment, and, depending on the behaviour of intended investment, either no change at all or a decrease in the actual level of saving.*

This paradox of thrift is even more pronounced if the level of intended investment varies directly with the level of aggregate income, so that the investment schedule I slopes upward as shown in frame (b) of Figure 22-3. Then the same upward shift in the saving function from S_0 to S_1 results in an even greater fall in aggregate income and output, from $1,400 billion to $800 billion, as determined by the intersection of S_1 and I at e_1. Moreover, the amount of saving that

Checkpoint 22-5

Explain the paradox
of thrift in terms of
what happens if the
economy's households
attempt to save less.
Use both frames (a)
and (b) of Figure 22-3.
Suppose a news item
suggests consumers
may attempt to rebuild
their savings that
have dwindled. As
an analyst, what
do you think about
this? What are the
possible implications
for autoworkers and
steelworkers?

actually takes place is now smaller! The attempt by the economy's households to save more leads to the paradoxical result that they end up saving less.

What explains the paradox of thrift? The answer is that the attempt to save more results in a larger withdrawal from aggregate income. At the initial equilibrium level of aggregate income, $1,400 billion in our example, the withdrawal exceeds the amount of intended investment spending. Consequently, the level of aggregate income falls as the economy's businesses cut back the production of total output in order to avoid unintended inventory increases. This fall in total output and income continues until the level of saving, or withdrawal, is once again brought into equality with the level of intended investment, or injection. At this point there is no unintended inventory accumulated and the economy is once again at equilibrium.

The Multiplier

*The **multiplier** is the term used to identify the phenomenon that, whatever the initial cause, an exogenously induced change in aggregate expenditure leads to a larger change in equilibrium income and output.* Given the dollar amount of a shift upward in aggregate expenditure, the change in aggregate income and output will increase by some multiple of the initial increase in aggregate expenditure. This multiple is called the *multiplier*. For instance, if intended investment (or the autonomously determined portion of consumption) rises by $10 billion and the resulting change in aggregate income is $30 billion, the multiplier is 3. If the rise in aggregate income is $40 billion, the multiplier is 4. Let's see why there is a multiplier effect and what determines the size of the multiplier.

Graphical Interpretation of the Multiplier

Suppose that the economy's business firms believe that sales are going to pick up in the coming year and that they are going to need more productive capacity to meet this increase. Let's suppose that investment spending increases from $200 billion to $400 billion.

The effect of this increase on aggregate income and output is shown in Figure 22-4. In this figure the economy is initially in equilibrium at an aggregate income level of $800 billion. This is the level at which the aggregate expenditure schedule AE_0 (which equals $C_0 + I_0$) and the 45° line intersect—point a in frame (a). Equivalently, it is the point at which the investment schedule I_0 and the saving function S intersect—point a in frame (b). A $200 billion autonomous increase in investment from I_0 to I_1 causes the aggregate expenditure schedule in frame (a) to shift upward from AE_0 (which equals $C_0 + I_0$) to AE_1 (which equals $C_0 + I_1$). Equivalently, this is represented in frame (b) by the upward shift in the investment schedule from I_0 to I_1. Each of the diagrams shows that the equilibrium level of aggregate income rises from $800 billion to $1,400 billion—given by the intersection of AE_1 and the 45° line at point b in frame (a) and by the intersection of S and I_1 at point b in frame (b). In other words, the $200 billion increase in investment causes a $600 billion increase in aggregate income and output. This is the multiplier. The value of the multiplier is 3 in this hypothetical example. The multiplier effect also applies for any autonomous decrease in the level of investment spending.

FIGURE 22-4 **Shifts in Aggregate Expenditure Have a Multiplier Effect on Aggregate Income and Output**

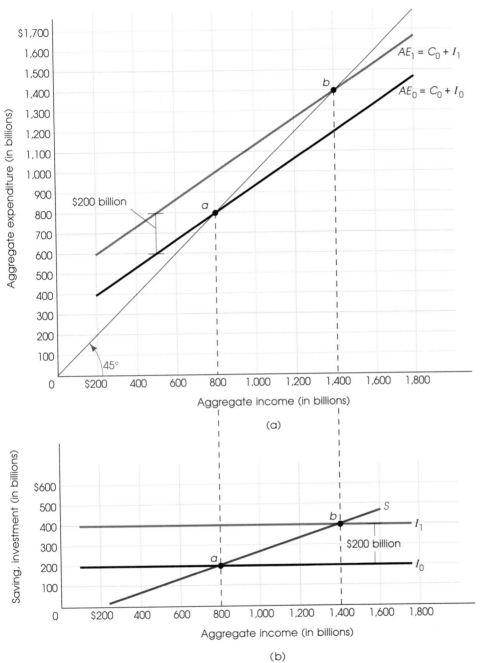

The aggregate expenditure schedule in frame (a) will be shifted by a shift in either or both of its components—the consumption function (hence the saving function) and the investment schedule. If the investment schedule shifts upward by $200 billion from I_0 to I_1, the aggregate expenditure schedule will shift upward from AE_0 (which equals $C_0 + I_0$) to AE_1 (which equals $C_0 + I_1$). Consequently, the equilibrium level of aggregate income and output will rise from $800 billion to $1,400 billion, or by three times the amount of the investment spending increase. This is the multiplier effect. The multiplier equals 3 in this example. Frame (b) shows an equivalent representation of this shift in terms of the investment schedule and the saving function. This diagram indicates clearly why there is a $600 billion increase in aggregate income in response to the $200 billion increase in investment spending. The $600 billion increase in aggregate income gives rise to a $200 billion increase in saving, or withdrawal, that is just enough to offset the initial $200 billion increase in investment, or injection.

A Numerical Interpretation of the Multiplier

We can also provide a numerical interpretation of the example of the multiplier that is illustrated in Figure 22-4. In this example, the marginal propensity to consume (MPC), which is the slope of the consumption function, is 2/3. Hence, the marginal propensity to save (MPS), which is the slope of the saving function, is 1/3. In addition, because we have assumed that the level of intended investment *is not* influenced by the level of aggregate income, the MPC is the slope of the aggregate expenditure curve. We will see now how the slopes of the aggregate expenditure curve, the MPC, and the MPS play a crucial role in the multiplier effect and in the determination of the size of the multiplier.

Consider the data in Table 22-4. Again, we will assume that the economy is initially in equilibrium at an aggregate income level of $800 billion. The table shows how an autonomous increase in investment expenditure of $200 billion has a chain reaction effect on the economy. The autonomous expenditure increase causes an unintended inventory decrease, which as we saw earlier, causes businesses to increase output. This causes increases in both employment and aggregate income. Part of this income increase is spent, causing a further increase in income, part of which is spent, and so on, round after round. At the first round, firms react to the increase in aggregate expenditure by increasing total output by $200 billion. This increased output, of course, is received as increased income, column (1), in the form of wages, rents, interest, and profit by the households who own the factors of production used to produce the increased output. Given an MPC of 2/3, households will spend $133.4 billion of this income increase, column (2), and save $66.6 billion, column (3).

In the second round, firms react to this $133.4 billion increase in aggregate expenditure by increasing total output an equivalent amount. This gives rise to another increase in payments to factors of production and a further rise in aggregate income of $133.4 billion, column (1). In turn, two thirds of this, or $89 billion, is spent, column (2), and $44.4 billion is saved, column (3). This process repeats itself round after round until the additions to aggregate income ultimately become so small that they are insignificant.

Adding up all the round-by-round increases in aggregate income in column (1) gives the total increase in aggregate income and output as $600 billion.

TABLE 22-4   Multiplier Effect of an Expenditure Increase, Round by Round (Hypothetical Data in Billions of Dollars)

Expenditure Round	(1) Change in Income and Output	(2) Change in Consumption $MPC = 2/3$	(3) Change in Saving $MPS = 1/3$
First round	$200.0	$133.4	$ 66.6
Second round	133.4	89.0	44.4
Third round	89.0	59.4	29.6
Fourth round	59.4	39.6	19.8
Fifth round	39.6	26.4	13.2
Rest of the rounds	78.6	52.2	26.4
Totals	$600.0	$400.0	$200.0

This is the same result we saw in Figure 22-4. Why does the expansion in aggregate income end here? The reason is that the $600 billion increase in aggregate income gives rise to a $200 billion increase in the amount of saving, or withdrawal, column (3), that is just enough to offset the initial $200 billion increase in investment, or injection. At this point the economy is once again in equilibrium. Aggregate income has increased by three times the initial increase in investment because the economy's households save one third of any increase in income. The multiplier is 3, just as it was in Figure 22-4.

The Multiplier and the *MPS* and *MPC*

Our example of the multiplier, illustrated in Figure 22-4 and Table 22-4, suggests that the size of the multiplier depends on the size of the *MPS* or its complement, the *MPC*. (Remember that *MPS* + *MPC* = 1, always.)

Recall that the *MPS* is represented by the slope of the saving function [see Figure 22-3, frame (b)]. The *MPS*, or slope of the saving function *S*, in Figure 22-4, frame (b), is 1/3. This means that every $1 increase in saving (vertical movement) corresponds to a $3 increase in aggregate income (horizontal movement). Consequently, when the investment schedule shifts upward by $200 billion from I_0 to I_1, saving likewise rises by $200 billion (vertical axis) and aggregate income rises by $600 billion (horizontal axis). Every $1 of increase in investment spending gives rise to a $3 increase in aggregate income. The multiplier is therefore 3. But this is just the reciprocal of the *MPS* — that is, the value of the *MPS*, which is equal to 1/3 — turned upside down.

When we look at the numerical illustration of our example in Table 22-4, the same conclusion emerges. When the *MPS* equals 1/3, every $1 of increased investment ultimately results in $3 of increased aggregate income — that is, the $200 billion increase in investment spending ultimately results in a $600 billion increase in aggregate income. The multiplier is 3.[2]

In summary, for the simple economy of this chapter (no net exports, no government expenditures, no taxation, and constant prices), *the multiplier is equal to the reciprocal of the MPS*:

$$\text{Multiplier} = \frac{1}{MPS}$$

If *MPS* equals 1/3, for example, then

$$\text{Multiplier} = \frac{1}{1/3} = 3$$

Note that because *MPC* + *MPS* = 1, it is true that *MPS* = 1 − *MPC*, and so we can also say

$$\text{Multiplier} = \frac{1}{1 - MPC}$$

---

[2]If the *MPS* had been 1/2, the ultimate increase would have been $400 billion — so the multiplier would have been 2. If the *MPS* had been 1/4, the increase would have been $800 billion — so the multiplier would have been 4.

Checkpoint 22-6

Using the aggregate expenditure and investment schedules AE_0 and I_0 in frames (a) and (b), respectively, of Figure 22-4, show what the effect would be if there were a $200 billion upward shift in the consumption function. Assuming that the *MPS* is 1/5, show what the effect of a $100 billion *downward* shift in consumption would be in a table like Table 22-4. Also, illustrate this effect graphically, using a figure like Figure 22-4, frames (a) and (b).

Further, because our example assumed that the only component of aggregate expenditure affected by changes in aggregate income was consumption, we can generalize by stating that

$$\text{Multiplier} = \frac{1}{1 - \text{Slope of aggregate expenditure}}$$

The multiplier will be larger the

- smaller is the *MPS* and larger is the *MPC*.
- larger is the slope of the aggregate expenditure curve.

Conversely, the multiplier will be smaller the

- larger is the *MPS* and smaller is the *MPC*.
- smaller is the slope of the aggregate expenditure curve.[3]

Final Notes on the Multiplier

Finally, two important points should be made about our discussion of the multiplier. First, our example assumed that the multiplier was triggered by an autonomous shift in investment spending. Exactly the same results would have followed if the trigger had instead been an autonomous shift in consumption spending, as represented by a shift in the consumption and saving functions. Second, the multiplier is just as applicable to downward shifts in investment or consumption spending as it is to upward shifts.

Summary

1. Actual investment is always equal to saving. Desired investment equals saving only at the equilibrium level of aggregate income. Therefore, desired investment and actual investment are equal at the equilibrium level of aggregate income but differ from each other by the amount of unintended inventory change at all other levels of aggregate income.

2. Desired investment may be viewed as an injection into the circular flow of spending and income, while saving may be viewed as a withdrawal from that flow. At the equilibrium level of aggregate income, the injection of desired investment is equal to the withdrawal due to saving. Graphically, this corresponds to the point on the income axis at which the investment schedule intersects the saving function. At levels of aggregate income greater than the equilibrium level, the withdrawal due to saving exceeds the injection due to desired investment, characterized by an increase in unintended inventory, and aggregate income will tend to fall toward the equilibrium level. At less than equilibrium levels of aggregate income, the withdrawal due to saving is less than the injection from desired investment. This inequality is characterized by decreases in unintended inventory which cause aggregate income to rise toward the equilibrium level.

---

[3]Convince yourself of this by computing the multiplier first when $MPS = 1/2$, hence $MPC = 1/2$, and second when $MPS = 1/4$, hence $MPC = 3/4$.

3. If households try to save more, the economy's aggregate income will fall and the level of saving will be no higher than it was initially, or it may even be lower. This is the paradox of thrift.
4. The marginal propensity to consume (MPC) is the fraction of any change in disposable income that is consumed. This is represented graphically by the slope of the consumption function. The marginal propensity to save (MPS) is the fraction of any change in disposable income that is saved. This is represented graphically by the slope of the saving function. The sum of the MPS and the MPC always equals 1.
5. The average propensity to consume (APC) is the fraction of disposable income that is consumed, and the average propensity to save (APS) is the fraction of disposable income that is saved. The sum of the APC and the APS always equals 1.
6. Changes in autonomous spending, represented by shifts in the aggregate expenditure schedule, cause changes in aggregate income that are several times the size of the initial spending change. This multiplier effect may be triggered by changes in either or both of the components of aggregate expenditure—the consumption function (and therefore the saving function) and the investment schedule. In the simple economy of this chapter, the multiplier equals the reciprocal of the marginal propensity to save.

Key Terms and Concepts

actual investment
autonomous spending
average propensity
   to consume (APC)
average propensity
   to save (APS)
desired investment

disinvestment
marginal propensity
   to consume (MPC)
marginal propensity
   to save (MPS)
multiplier
net injections

net withdrawal
paradox of thrift
realized investment
unintended inventory
   depletion
unintended inventory
   increase

Questions and Problems

1. Why does actual investment always equal saving? When actual investment and desired investment are not equal, why do the levels of aggregate income, output, and employment tend to change?
2. When injections exceed withdrawals, what happens to the economy's level of aggregate income? What is the relationship between desired investment and actual investment in this situation? If the level of aggregate income is falling, what must be the relationship between saving and desired investment? If the level of aggregate income is rising, what must be the relationship between actual investment and saving?
3. Show what happens to the consumption and saving functions as a result of the following:
   a. The MPS decreases.
   b. The APC increases.
   c. The APC decreases and the MPS increases.
   d. The APS and the MPS decrease.
   e. The APC and the MPC increase.
   f. The APC decreases and the MPC increases.

4. Explain the paradox of thrift in terms of Figure 22-1, frame (a). Suppose that the marginal propensity to consume (MPC) decreases because households want to save more out of income so they won't be so hard-pressed for funds when Christmas shopping time rolls around. What do you predict this decrease in MPC will do to ease their budget problems come Christmas?

5. If the saving function shifts downward, what must happen to the investment schedule in order for the aggregate expenditure schedule to remain unchanged? What will happen to the level of employment in this instance? Why will this happen?

6. What happens to the value of the multiplier if the consumption function becomes steeper? What happens to the value of the multiplier if the saving function shifts downward to a position parallel to its initial position? What is the effect on the level of aggregate income in this case?

7. Given the following equations for consumption and desired investment:

$$C = 100 + .8Y$$

and

$$I = 25$$

Find each of the following:

a. What is the equation for savings?

b. If income is $600 find the values for $APC, APS, MPC,$ and MPS.

c. What is the equation for aggregate expenditure?

d. What is the value of consumption if income is $700?

e. What is the size of the undesired inventory buildup or undesired inventory depletion if income is $700?

f. What is the size of the undesired inventory buildup or undesired inventory depletion if income is $1,000?

g. What is the level of equilibrium income?

h. What is the size of the multiplier?

i. If investment were to increase by 5, by how much would equilibrium income increase?

Chapter 23

Government Spending, Taxation, the Open Economy, and Fiscal Policy

The last chapter presented the basic Keynesian explanation of why the equilibrium level of total income may be at an income level less than the full employment level. This chapter integrates first the role of foreign trade and then the influence of government activity into the analysis of the economy. It moves us from a *simple closed economy model*—in which only consumer and investor decisions can affect the levels of total income, output, and employment—to an *open four-sector model*—in which changes in the actions of consumers, businesses, international trading partners, and the government are all influential in determining the level of expenditure, the multiplier, the level of employment, and the level of *aggregate income*, or *GDP*. For simplicity we will assume that wages and prices are inflexible so that the economy's general price level is fixed.

We will begin by investigating the factors affecting the behaviour of exports of Canadian goods and services to foreign countries and imports of goods and services from foreign countries by Canadians. The pattern of behaviour of our exports and imports will then be examined to see how foreign trade changes the size of the multiplier and influences the levels of aggregate income and employment.

Next we will discuss the influence of the government and its pattern of expenditure and revenue generation through taxation. The ability of the government to deliberately manipulate its own spending or taxation in order to influence aggregate income, the level of employment, or the stability of the business cycle through *discretionary fiscal policy* will be explained. *Automatic stabilizers* and their significance will be discussed. The final section of the chapter will examine the difficulties in using discretionary fiscal policy effectively and the limitations of stabilization policy.

In the next chapter we relax the fixed price and fixed wages assumptions. This allows us to develop the aggregate demand (*AD*), aggregate supply (*AS*) model, and then integrate the aggregate demand, aggregate supply model into the aggregate expenditure and aggregate income model that was developed in Chapter 22. The aggregate demand, aggregate supply model will allow us to review the controversial subjects of stagflation and supply-side theory. Within this framework we will examine the possible supply-side effects of fiscal policy as well as some of the major policy proposals of supply-side economics.

We will return to our discussion of the impact of international trade and international financial flows in Part Nine, Chapters 33 and 34. That part will provide more specific detail to the analysis of the effects of international trade on relatively small open economies, such as Canada, than is possible in the initial development of the open economy model in this chapter.

Integrating International Trade into Income Determination

Until now, our analysis of the determination of aggregate income, output, and employment has assumed that the economy is a simple **closed economy**—that is, that it is not involved in international trade. In reality, all economies are *open economies* to some extent because they trade with each other. In relative terms, Canada is one of the more open Western economies. Sweden, Norway, and Austria export and import a larger percentage of their GDP than does Canada, but Canada has higher exports and imports as a proportion of GDP than Germany, France, Japan, the United Kingdom, or the United States. In addition, no other

LEARNING OBJECTIVES

After reading this chapter, you will be able to:

1. Explain how exports affect expenditure and equilibrium income.
2. Explain the effect of imports on the aggregate expenditure function.
3. Explain the effect of imports on the size of the multiplier.
4. Calculate the size of the open economy multiplier, given the marginal propensity to save and the marginal propensity to import.
5. Explain how government spending and taxation affect aggregate expenditure and the equilibrium level of aggregate income.
6. Define *discretionary fiscal policy.*
7. Explain the effect of income taxes on the size of the multiplier.
8. Explain the balanced budget multiplier.
9. Calculate the balanced budget multiplier, given the marginal propensities to save, import, and tax.
10. Distinguish between discretionary fiscal policy and automatic stabilizers.
11. Explain the practical limitations of discretionary fiscal policy.
12. List the automatic stabilizers and describe how they work to moderate the cyclical swings in our economy.

major Western economy is as dependent on one other economy as a market for its exports and a source of its imports. Canada sells approximately 75 percent of its exports to the United States and receives approximately 80 percent of its imports from the United States. By contrast, while Canada is the largest market for American exports, it is only the second largest source of imports to the United States. Furthermore, in Canada approximately 25 percent of all production and 20 percent of all employment has been estimated to be dependent on international trade. In the United States the figures are roughly 5 percent of the value of production and 3 percent of employment, respectively. In spite of the recent signing of the Free Trade Agreement (FTA), which formally links the economic futures of Canada and the United States, it is important to realize that Canada is over 16 times as dependent on its trade with the United States as the United States is on its trade with Canada. The magnitude of Canada's trade dependence and its vulnerability due to the high percentage of trade to one foreign market, make the study and integration of international trade extremely important to the understanding of macroeconomic theory in Canada.

The Impact of Exports and Imports on Aggregate Expenditure

International trade affects the levels of aggregate expenditure, employment, and income in two separate ways. First, exports represent an injection into aggregate expenditure and imports are a withdrawal. If exports exceed imports, there is a net increase in the level of aggregate expenditure and an increase in aggregate income and employment. The second effect involves economic efficiency and the impact of foreign trade here is much broader and longer term. International trade increases the size of the market available to each producer, thereby allowing each nation to specialize in those products in which it has a comparative advantage. This specialization leads to increases in the efficient allocation of resources internationally, and to higher output and income from the same resources on a global level. In this chapter, we will confine ourselves to the idea of exports and imports affecting the composition of aggregate expenditure (without considering the effects of trade on international economic efficiency). Total expenditures on final goods and services in our economy include those arising from **exports**—the purchases of domestic output by non-residents. Hence, exports increase domestic production, incomes, and employment. They may be viewed as an injection into the economy's income stream, just like investment. **Imports**, on the other hand, represent expenditures by the residents of Canada on output produced abroad. Such expenditures are withdrawals from our economy's total income, just like saving. That is, imports also may be viewed as income *not* spent on domestically produced goods and services. As such, unlike exports, imports decrease domestic production, incomes, and employment. Therefore, the net effect of trade on a country's aggregate income, output, and employment depends on whether injections from exports are greater or less than the withdrawals due to imports. In Chapter 19 we saw that net exports X_n equaled exports minus imports. We may say that the effect of international trade on aggregate expenditure, employment, and aggregate income depends on whether net exports X_n is positive or negative. Exactly how does this difference affect the level of aggregate income?

Determinants of Exports and Imports

To determine the effect of net exports on the level of aggregate income we must first consider what determines the volume of a country's exports and imports. Part of this answer, involving resource endowments, economies of scale, and differences in technological efficiency, will have to wait until the detailed analysis in Chapters 33 and 34. However, given all these factors, the demand for a country's exports in foreign markets depends on the foreign country being willing and ready to buy some product and on how expensive the Canadian products appear to foreign customers in relation to products made in their own country. These two different effects become easier to analyze if we treat them separately.

Aggregate Income in Foreign Economies and Canadian Net Exports

In Chapter 22 we pointed out that consumption, which is a large portion of aggregate expenditure, was primarily, although not exclusively, determined by aggregate income. We can extend this idea and say that in foreign countries their desire to purchase goods and services is, in general, directly dependent on their aggregate income. For the moment, holding everything else constant and assuming that Canadian products are able to compete relative to foreign goods, an increase in the aggregate income of a foreign country will increase its aggregate expenditure and some portion of that increase will be for Canadian-made goods and services. Conversely, if the aggregate income of our trading partner were to decrease, this would reduce their level of aggregate expenditure and some of the reduction in expenditure would be reflected in a reduced demand for Canadian-made products. Thus, the exports of one country vary directly with the level of aggregate income of its trading partner. For example, if the GDP of the United States is in the expansion phase of a business cycle, Americans will purchase more goods and services, and some of these will be products produced in Canada. Thus, the volume of Canadian exports to the United States will rise. Conversely, a recession in the United States will lower their demand for Canadian exports; when the United States catches a cold, Canada dies of pneumonia!

Canadian Aggregate Income and Canadian Net Exports

On the other hand, the volume of the exports of a small country, like Canada, will *not* be influenced to any significant extent by its *own* level of aggregate income. This is because the foreign customer typically is not influenced by the levels of Canadian income or production. However, the level of our imports is affected by our level of aggregate income. The higher Canadian aggregate income is, the higher will be our purchases, and some of these purchases will be imports from foreign countries. The increase in imports that results from a one-dollar increase in aggregate income is defined as the **marginal propensity to import**. Because imports are a withdrawal of expenditure out of the Canadian economy, they reduce the level of aggregate expenditure; this in turn will change equilibrium GDP. The size of the multiplier is also affected by the marginal propensity to import. Net exports will decrease as a result of an increase in aggregate income, even when exports themselves are not influenced by income, because imports increase in response to increases in aggregate income. The result of this increase in imports is that aggregate expenditure increases less than it would otherwise have increased as a result of a given increase in income. In short, the respending stream set off by a change in autonomous expenditure is smaller than it would be without imports and consequently the multiplier is smaller. Conversely, as an economy's aggregate income decreases, imports decrease, causing net exports to increase. In summary, net exports vary inversely with respect to changes in aggregate income.

The Canadian Exchange Rate and Canadian Net Exports

The *exchange rate is the price of one currency in terms of another.* For simplicity, we will use the exchange rate as the price measured in our currency needed to purchase one unit of foreign currency. Just as we price the amount of gasoline in Canadian currency, we also price units of foreign currency in Canadian dollars, whether that foreign currency is Japanese yen or American dollars. For example, just as gasoline might be priced at 50.9 cents per litre in Alberta, and slightly higher elsewhere, the Japanese yen might be priced at $.00846 Can. ($1.00 Can. = 118.18 yen), or the Canadian exchange rate on the American dollar might be $1.20 Can. = $1.00 U.S. ($1.00 Can. = $.8333 U.S.). If the Canadian exchange rate increases for a particular foreign currency, *ceteris paribus*, it means that the foreign currency price for Canadian products is decreasing in a foreign country. As Canadian products become less expensive in that foreign market, the demand for them will increase and Canadian exports will increase. Conversely, if the Canadian exchange rate on the U.S. dollar were to decrease, Canadian products would become more expensive for Americans to purchase, and as a result Canadian exports to the United States would decrease. In the same way that the exchange rate affects the attractiveness of Canadian products in foreign markets by changing their price relative to foreign-made products, it also influences the attractiveness of foreign-made products relative to Canadian-made products here in Canada. As the Canadian exchange rate increases, it takes more Canadian dollars to purchase the same foreign product. Canadian consumers see this as an increase in the price of foreign-made products in Canada, and they decrease their demand for imports by reducing product usage or by purchasing Canadian-made products instead of imports. Conversely, a decrease in the Canadian exchange rate on a foreign currency increases imports to Canada.

The Foreign Price Level and Canadian Net Exports

As the general price level in a foreign country increases, *ceteris paribus*, there is a tendency for Canadian products to appear less expensive relative to products made in that foreign country. When this happens, demand for Canadian exports increases. Similarly, as the foreign price level increases, it forces up the price of foreign products in the Canadian economy and Canadians decrease their imports from that foreign country. Since Canadian exports are rising and Canadian imports are decreasing because of the rise in the foreign price level, it is obvious that Canadian net exports tend to increase in response to an increase in the general price level in the economy of a foreign country that trades with Canada. Of course the reverse behaviour also applies. If the foreign country experiences a decrease in its general price level (deflation), or if its general price level rises less rapidly than Canada's general price level, then Canadian exports would decrease and Canadian imports from that country would increase, causing Canadian net exports to decrease.[1]

In summary,

| | Effect on: | | |
Causal variable	Canadian Exports	Canadian Imports	Canadian Net Exports
Foreign GDP_f	Direct	Unaffected	Direct
Canadian GDP	Unaffected	Direct	Inverse
Canadian exchange rate	Direct	Inverse	Direct
Foreign price level	Direct	Inverse	Direct

An economy's net exports vary *inversely* with its *own* level of GDP, but its net exports vary *directly* with the aggregate incomes of a country's trading partners (GDP_f) and *directly* with the general price level of trading partners.

Aggregate Expenditure in an Open Economy

We can now examine exactly how trade affects the economy's aggregate expenditure and its aggregate income, or GDP. We will use the withdrawals–injections approach that we developed in Chapter 22. Suppose initially that exports and imports are zero. Assume that the equilibrium level of GDP is $1,200 billion as determined by the intersection of the aggregate expenditure schedule $C + I$ and the 45° line in Figure 23-1, frame (a). This intersection corresponds to the intersection of the savings function S and the desired investment function I in Figure 23-1, frame (b).

Now assume the citizens of a foreign country decide to purchase $350 billion in products from Canada. As was already explained, the amount that the non-residents wish to purchase from Canada is unaffected by the level of aggregate income, *GDP*, in Canada. This amount of exports X adds another element onto the aggregate expenditure schedule, pushing it vertically upward by $350 billion on goods and services, in Figure 23-1, frame (a). Given that the *MPC* is assumed to equal 2/3, the multiplier is 3. Therefore, GDP increases by $1,050 billion (from $1,200 billion to $2,250 billion), corresponding to the intersection of the aggregate expenditure schedule $C + I + X$ with the 45° line.

This also may be shown in terms of Figure 23-1, frame (b). Here the $350 billion of export earnings X adds another element onto desired investment I to give the *injections* schedule $I + X$. The intersection of $I + X$ with the saving or *withdrawal* function S is the point at which the withdrawals from saving, equal to $550 billion, are just offset by the sum of the injections from intended investment and exports $I + X$, equal to $200 billion plus $350 billion. When we

---

[1]It may have occurred to you that an increase in the price level in Canada decreases net exports in a similar manner to that experienced if there is an increase in the foreign price level. While this is true, the discussion of the influence that a change in the domestic price level has on aggregate expenditure is sufficiently complex that we will deal with it in the next chapter.

FIGURE 23-1   **Exports and the Equilibrium Level of GDP**

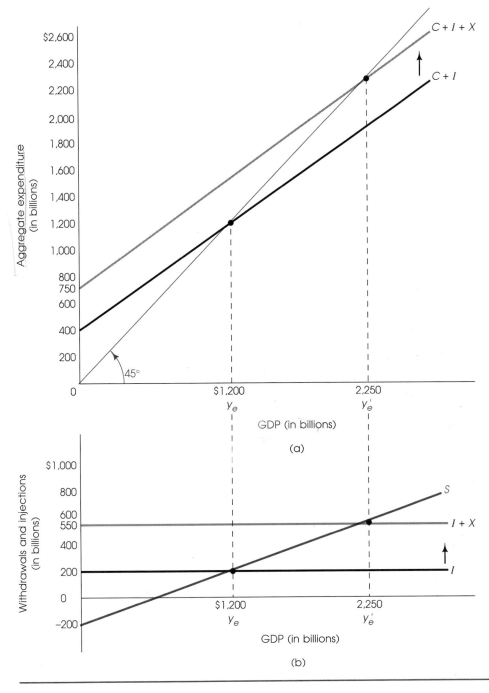

Exports are an injection into the economy's income stream just like investment. When exports of $350 billion are added to investment of $200 billion, the exports of $350 billion cause the total expenditure schedule to shift upward from C + I to C + I + X in frame (a). The equilibrium level of GDP is thereby increased from $1,200 billion, corresponding to the intersection of C + I and the 45° line, to $2,250 billion, corresponding to the intersection of C + I + X and the 45° line.

This can be shown equivalently in terms of withdrawals and injections in frame (b). The $350 billion of exports expenditure adds another layer X onto the injections schedule I to give the I + X schedule. The new equilibrium of GDP at $2,250 billion corresponds to the intersection of the withdrawal function S and the I + X schedule. Here the withdrawal of $550 billion in savings is exactly offset by the $550 billion of injections (investment of $200 billion plus exports of $350 billion).

bring exports into the picture, we see that it is no longer necessary for intended investment to equal saving at equilibrium. What is important is that the total withdrawals from income equal the total injections into it, or that $S = I + X$ in this case. (Note that imports and government activity will modify this later in the chapter, although they will not change the general statement.)

An increase in the level of exports would act just as would an increase in desired investment. It would shift the aggregate expenditure function $C + I + X$, frame (a), vertically upward by the increase in exports and cause income to increase by the multiplier times this increase. Alternatively, using the injections approach, the increased exports will cause the injections schedule $I + X$, frame (b), to shift vertically upward by the amount of the increase in exports and will increase GDP by the multiplier times the increase in exports. Conversely, a decrease in X will cause the aggregate expenditure function, $C + I + X$, frame (a), and the injection function, $I + X$, frame (b), to shift downward and the equilibrium level of GDP to decrease. An increase in the level of exports will cause an increase in the level of GDP, just like upward shifts in the level of intended consumption or intended investment. A decrease in exports will cause a decrease in GDP.

Exports are one aspect of the effect of international trade on aggregate expenditure and equilibrium income. Imports are the other. Suppose that residents of the economy (households and businesses), spend 1/6 of any increase in aggregate income on products imported from other countries. Conversely, anytime aggregate income decreases by $150 billion, residents decrease their purchases of imports by $25 billion. This behaviour emphasizes that imports, unlike exports, are influenced by the level of a country's own GDP. Figure 23-2 demonstrates how this influence works. The equilibrium of Figure 23-1, frame (a), determined by the aggregate expenditure schedule $C + I + X$ is shown again in this figure. Initially GDP equals the income level at which the aggregate expenditure $C + I + X$ intersects the 45° line. When imports are included, the aggregate expenditure function rotates *downward* by the amount of imports at every level of GDP. Since part of every dollar of GDP is directed to imports that do not create a demand for domestic production, imports reduce the level of aggregate expenditure for domestically produced goods and services. Therefore imports *reduce* the level of aggregate expenditure by 1/6 of the value for GDP at every level of GDP.

It follows that the reduction in aggregate expenditure will be reflected in a reduction in equilibrium income and employment. The magnitude of reduction in each is determined by the size of the MPC and the size of the MPM. The MPC and MPM are equal to 2/3 and 1/6, respectively, in this case. Therefore, the level of imports will *increase* and the level of aggregate expenditure will *decrease* by $25 billion for every $150 billion of GDP. The aggregate expenditure schedule is rotated downward from $C + I + X$ to $C + I + X - M$.

Of particular significance is the fact that the slope of the aggregate expenditure function decreases as a result of moving from a closed economy model to an open economy model. The slope of aggregate expenditure now becomes the marginal propensity to consume, MPC, minus the marginal propensity to import, MPM. It should be remembered from Chapter 22 and the earlier part of this chapter that the greater the slope of the aggregate expenditure function, the larger it will make the multiplier. Conversely, the smaller the slope of the aggregate expenditure function, the smaller it will make the multiplier. We will examine this in more detail below but for now we can see that the lower slope of $C + I + X - M$ in Figure 23-2, frame (a), reduces equilibrium from \$2,250 billion to \$1,500 billion.

We get the same result if we take the withdrawals and injections perspective. The equilibrium of Figure 23-1, frame (b), determined by the intersection of the savings function S and the $I + X$ function, is shown again in Figure 23-2, frame (b). In addition to the *withdrawal* due to saving, now at every level of GDP there is an additional withdrawal due to imports, M, equal to 1/6 of the value of GDP. When the imports are added to savings, in Figure 23-2, frame (b), we obtain the withdrawal schedule $S + M$. The equilibrium level of GDP is now \$1,500 billion, determined by the intersection of $S + M$ and $I + X$ in Figure 23-2, frame (b). Here the sum of the withdrawals from GDP, which is equal to saving (\$300 billion) plus imports (\$250 billion), is just offset by the sum of the injections (\$550 billion), which is equal to intended investment plus exports. Again we see that while total withdrawals must be equal to total injections at equilibrium income, $S + M = I + X$, there is no reason to believe that savings will equal investment or that exports will equal imports.

The Open Economy Multiplier

As we saw in Figure 23-2, frames (a) and (b), the impact of *net exports* changes the slope of the aggregate expenditure function and the slope of the withdrawals schedule. The expenditure multiplier could be found by dividing one by the slope of the withdrawal function. Alternatively, the multiplier equals one divided by one *minus* the slope of the aggregate expenditure function. In Figure 23-2 the slope of the withdrawal function became the combined slope of saving *plus* imports.

Mathematically the open economy multiplier can be written

$$\frac{\Delta GDP}{\Delta \text{Exports}} = \left(\frac{1}{MPS + MPM} \right)$$

— marginal propensity to save.

so

$$\text{Open economy multiplier} = \frac{1}{MPS + MPM}$$

The multiplier will be smaller for an open economy than it is for a closed economy. For example, suppose that the MPS is 1/3, then the closed economy multiplier would be 3. Now suppose that this same economy imports \$25 billion more products every time its GDP increases by \$150 billion; this gives it an MPM of 1/6. The open economy multiplier for this economy is only 2. Remember that using the injections–withdrawals approach in the last chapter we pointed out that as a result of an increase in injections, the level of aggregate income must rise until withdrawals increase to equal the new level of injections. In a situation in which withdrawals increase because of a rise in imports as well as a rise in savings, as income increases, income does not rise by as much to produce the necessary rise in withdrawals.

FIGURE 23-2   Exports and Imports and the Equilibrium Level of GDP

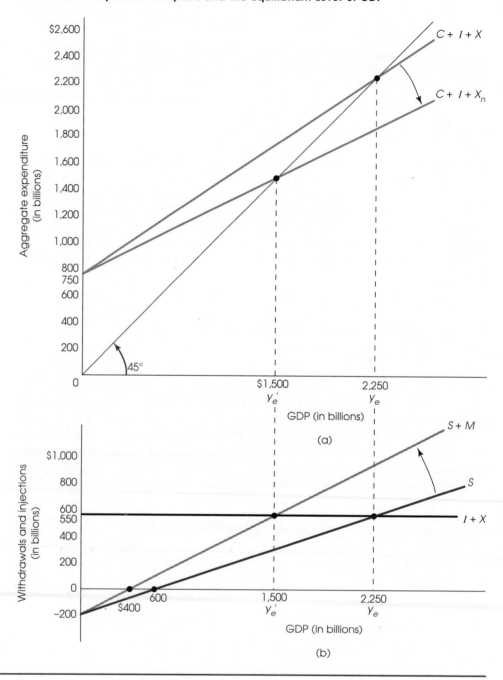

The injections function, $C + I + X$ equals \$550 billion for all levels of GDP as it did in Figure 23-1. Imports are a withdrawal from this economy's income stream just like savings. When the imports, in this case equal to 1/6 of GDP, are added to the saving function, in this case $S = -200 + \frac{1}{3}(GNP)$ we get a *total withdrawal schedule*. Total withdrawals are equal to the sum of the withdrawals from savings S and imports M. An equilibrium is established at a GDP of \$1,500 billion, with injections of \$550 billion just equal to withdrawals of \$550 billion (saving of \$300 billion plus imports of \$250 billion). Once there is more than one type of injection and withdrawal, saving need not equal investment at equilibrium. All that is important is that *total injections* must equal *total withdrawals* at equilibrium.

Using the aggregate expenditure approach in frame (a) of Figure 23-2 we are confronted with a new problem. When we added investment on to consumption to get aggregate expenditure in Chapter 22, investment did not change as GDP increased, therefore $C + I$ was parallel to and above C at all levels of GDP. Therefore, the new aggregate expenditure function was also parallel to the consumption function, which meant that the slope of the aggregate expenditure was equal to the slope of the consumption function, and the slope of the consumption function was MPC. Since imports increase as GDP increases, the aggregate expenditure function adjusted for imports is not parallel to consumption. Therefore, when we subtract imports from aggregate expenditure for an open economy we find that $C + I + X - M$ shares the same intercept as $C + I + X$ but has a smaller slope. Careful inspection shows that the open economy aggregate expenditure curve, $C + I + X - M$ or $C + I + X_n$, lies above $C + I$, but it has a smaller slope and lies below $C + I$ at high GDP. This is because at sufficiently high GDPs, exports are smaller than imports, and as a result *net exports*, $X - M$ are negative, which causes aggregate expenditure to be smaller in the open than in the closed economy.

Assuming exports equal to \$350 billion and imports equal to 1/6 of GDP at all levels of GDP, the open economy expenditure curve $C + I + X_n$ intersects the 45° line at a GDP of \$1,500 billion.

Summary of the Effects of International Trade

International trade makes the aggregate expenditure of the economy dependent on the behaviour of factors within an economy and external to that economy, which affects the economy in several ways. Changes in equilibrium income and employment in the domestic economy may result from changes in aggregate income of a foreign country, changes in the general price level of a foreign country, or changes in the exchange rate between a nation's currency and the currency of a foreign country. This complicates the behaviour of the economy and opens the economy to unexpected benefits and unexpected disadvantages resulting from trade. Finally, we demonstrated that the open economy multiplier is smaller than the closed economy multiplier.

The Government Budget   .

Like any budget, the federal government's budget is an itemized account of expenditures and revenues for a specific fiscal year. In Canada, the federal government's fiscal year begins April 1 and ends March 31. The disbursements, or outlay, side of the budget consists mainly of transfers to persons, including interest payments on government bonds; transfers to other levels of government, including federal provincial revenue sharing, subsidies for education and health care, and equalization payments; transfers and subsidies to corporations; and the expenses of running the institution of the government itself, including defense

Revenues to cover these outlays come largely from direct taxation of persons, indirect tax (sales tax and *GST*), investment income (including profits from crown corporations), rents from crown lands, and direct tax on corporations.

An examination of provincial and local government budgets shows the largest proportion of outlays going to health care and education. Next come expenditures for social services including police, fire protection, the administration of the judicial system, and family counselling; the development of natural resources; and the establishment and maintenance of recreation programs and facilities. The largest proportion of the remaining expenditures goes into highways and roads. The major sources of revenue for provincial governments has been personal and corporate income tax, followed by revenue from the sale and leasing of provincial land (natural resources). The largest sources of revenue to local governments are transfers from senior levels of government, property taxes on land and buildings, and licenses, local business permits, and pet licenses.

Deficits and Surpluses

A government has a **balanced budget** if total expenditures equal total tax revenues. It has a **budget deficit** if expenditures are greater than tax revenues. By convention the *government deficit equals government purchases G minus tax revenue T*. When governments actually release the budget figures, they include transfer payments as disbursements. While this makes sense from an accounting view, it complicates the impact that government has on aggregate expenditure, since transfers, once received by households, form a portion of personal income and part of the transfer becomes consumption, part becomes savings, part becomes imports, and part will even be returned to the government as taxes. It is therefore simpler to treat the government deficit as government purchases of goods and services minus taxes and exclude transfers from the analysis. Similarly, government is said to have a **budget surplus** if expenditures (excluding transfers) are less than tax revenues. In other words, there is a budget surplus if $G - T$ produces a negative number. The federal budget of Canada has shown a continuous string of growing deficits for all years since 1975. A fact that usually surprises students is that this tendency for growing chronic deficits is more recent in Canada than in many Western countries, including the United States. In the three decades prior to the 1980s, Canada's federal government experienced alternating periods of deficit and surplus, with more years of surplus budgets than years of deficit budgets. It also showed no general growth in the public debt in relation to GDP over that period. The deficit figures for more recent years also hide the fact that a large part of the recent increase in federal deficits is because of the high interest paid on Canada government bonds owned by individual Canadians and organizations. If these payments, which in a sense represent a special type of transfer payment from one group of Canadians (taxpayers) to another group of Canadians (owners of government bonds), are excluded from the calculation, it has been estimated that the Canadian government would have been in a surplus budgetary position for every year from early 1950s until the early 1980s. However, the fact that the rise in the government deficit is recent should not detract the student's attention from the fact that since 1984 the deficit has more than doubled and is increasing at the highest rate ever under peacetime conditions.

Checkpoint* 23-1

Consider again the example of Figure 23-1. Suppose that the *MPC* is 4/5 and the *MPM* is 1/5. Explain how the aggregate expenditure schedule is now affected by a $100 billion increase in exports. Give an explanation in terms of the withdrawals and injections approach. By how much do imports increase as a result of the rise in aggregate income caused by the increase in exports? Using the injections and withdrawals approach, explain why saving does not necessarily equal investment at equilibrium in the open economy model.

Answers to all Checkpoints can be found at the back of the text.

Fiscal Policy and the White Paper on Employment and Income of 1945

The Great Depression of the 1930s made many people fearful that the economy might plunge into another depression when peacetime conditions returned at the end of World War II. Being aware of the impact that government intervention and purchases seemed to have had on employment and aggregate income due to their increased responsibilities during the war, many countries began to investigate the possibility of harnessing the fiscal power of the state as a formal permanent tool for promoting economic prosperity in the postwar period. Canada became one of the first countries along with the United Kingdom and the United States to formally adopt a Keynesian interventionist stance for its federal government.

On April 12, 1945, C. D. Howe introduced the *White Paper on Employment and Income to the Parliament of Canada*. This document charged the federal government with the responsibility of using its taxing, spending, and transfer powers to become the "prime factor in the creation and disposition of a major share of the national wealth."[2]

A common ideology ran through the provisions of most of the initiatives undertaken by governments around the world. They accepted the new economic theory developed in the 1930s by John Maynard Keynes. This theory postulates that independent private sector self-interest decisions of consumers and investors acting in conditions of *laissez faire* might cause instability of spending or prolonged periods of either too little or too much aggregate expenditure. The collective effect of these expenditures would cause instability in aggregate income, the general price level, and employment, or they might lead to prolonged periods of excess capacity, stagnant economic activity, and unacceptably high unemployment or inflation. The remedy, according to Keynesian theory, was that the government, acting in the collective public interest, could use its own powers of spending and taxation to prevent these unwanted developments. It was this analysis that brought about a Keynesian fiscal policy agenda for the major Western economies for the next thirty years.

Principles of Discretionary Fiscal Policy

Discretionary fiscal policy *refers to the government's deliberate manipulation of its spending and taxing activities to attempt to smooth out economic fluctuations and ensure maximum employment with as little inflation as possible.* Our discussion of discretionary fiscal policy will be simplified by assuming that the only kind of taxes collected by the government are personal income taxes. This means that personal income, PI, now differs from disposable income, DI. We will continue to make no distinction among GDP, GNP, NNP, NI, and PI. They are all assumed to be the same, what we refer to as *aggregate income* or total income. In our simplified world, GDP differs from DI only by the amount of net taxes T. Initially we will maintain the assumption that prices and money wages are *inflexible*.

---

[2] P. C. Newman, *The Canadian Establishment* (Toronto: McClelland and Stewart-Bantam Limited, 1977), p. 376.

The effect on our analysis of allowing prices and money wages to vary will be considered in the next chapter.

Government Expenditure and Aggregate Expenditure

Suppose initially that government spending and taxation are zero. Assume that the equilibrium level of GDP is $1,500 billion as determined by the intersection of the aggregate expenditure schedule $C + I + X_n$ and the 45° line in Figure 23-3, frame (a). This intersection corresponds to the intersection of the withdrawal function, $S + M$, and the injections function, $I + X$, in Figure 23-3, frame (b). If potential GDP is $1,800 billion, then the economy is plagued by a considerable amount of unemployment when GDP is only $1,500 billion.

The economy can be pushed to potential GDP and unemployment reduced if the government spends $150 billion on goods and services. This amount of government spending G then adds another element onto the aggregate expenditure schedule, pushing it vertically upward by $150 billion to the position $C + I + X_n + G$ in Figure 23-3, frame (a). Given that the MPC is assumed to equal 2/3 and the MPM is assumed to be 1/6 (hence $MPS + MPM$ equals 1/2), the open economy multiplier is 2. Therefore, GDP increases by $300 billion from $1,500 billion to $1,800 billion, corresponding to the intersection of the aggregate expenditure schedule $C + I + X_n + G$ with the 45° line. This also may be shown in terms of Figure 23-3, frame (b). Here the $150 billion of government spending G adds another element onto injections in addition to investment and exports, $I + X$, to give the schedule $I + X + G$. The intersection of $I + X + G$ with the withdrawal function, $S + M$, is the point at which the withdrawals from saving and imports, equal to $700 billion, are just offset by the sum of the injections from intended investment, $I + X$, equal to $550 billion, and government spending, equal to $150 billion. When we bring government spending into the picture, we are reminded of the point made earlier in this chapter that at equilibrium income the total withdrawals from income equal the total injections into it, so that in this case $S + M = I + X + G$. (Note that government expenditures do not have to be financed by taxes, although they can be, as we shall see later.) Of course, a decrease in G will cause the aggregate expenditure function, $C + I + X - M + G$, frame (a), and the injections function, $I + X + G$, frame (b), to shift downward and the equilibrium level of aggregate income to decrease. Increases in the level of government spending will cause increases in the equilibrium level of aggregate income, just like upward shifts in the level of consumption, investment or exports. Decreases in government spending will cause decreases in aggregate income.

Taxation and Aggregate Expenditure

Government spending is one side of fiscal policy. Taxation is the other. Suppose that the government decides to finance its $150 billion expenditure by levying a lump-sum tax of $150 billion. This is a lump-sum tax in the sense that the tax is not related to the level of GDP. Property taxes and poll taxes are regarded as lump-sum taxes. How will this affect the equilibrium level of GDP?

Figure 23-4 demonstrates what will happen. The equilibrium of Figure 23-3, frame (a), determined by the aggregate expenditure schedule $C + I + X - M + G$,

FIGURE 23-3   **Effect of Government Spending on Equilibrium GDP**

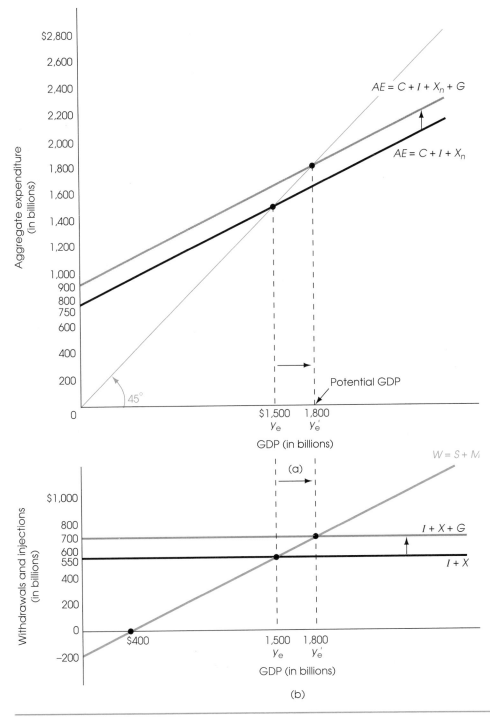

Government spending of $150 billion causes the total expenditure schedule to shift upward from $C + I$ to $C + I + G$ in frame (a). The equilibrium level of GDP is thereby increased from $1,500 billion, corresponding to the intersection of $C + I + X - M$ and the 45° line, to $1,800 billion, corresponding to the intersection of $C + I + X - M + G$ and the 45° line. This can be shown equivalently in terms of withdrawals and injections in frame (b). The $150 billion of government expenditure adds another layer G onto the injections schedule $I + X$ to give the $I + X + G$ schedule. The new equilibrium of GDP at $1,800 billion corresponds to the intersection of the withdrawal function $S + M$ and the $I + X + G$ schedule. Here the $700 billion withdrawal (saving of $400 billion plus imports of $300 billion) is exactly offset by the $700 billion of injections (investment of $200 billion plus exports of $350 billion plus government spending of $150 billion).

FIGURE 23-4   Effect of Government Taxation on Equilibrium GDP

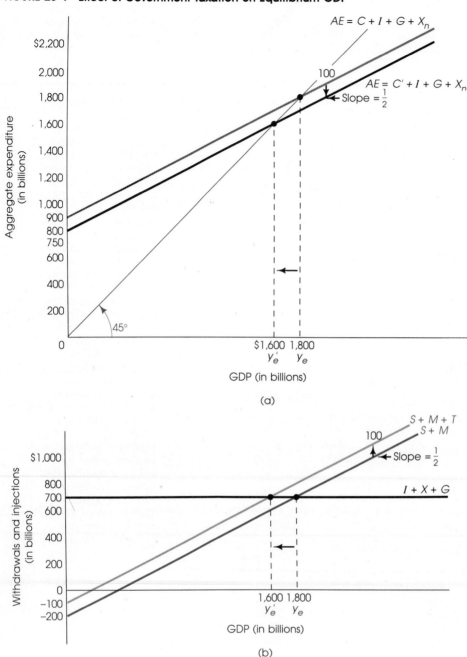

(a)

(b)

Suppose that the government imposes a lump-sum tax of $150 billion. This means that DI will be $150 billion less at every level of GDP. Assuming that the *MPC* equals 2/3 and therefore that the *MPS* is 1/3, and assuming that *MPM* is 1/6, consumption will be $100 billion less at every level of GDP. The consumption function will be shifted downward by this amount. The total expenditure schedule will therefore shift downward by this amount, from $C + I + X - M + G$ to $C_1 + I + X - M + G$ in frame (a). The equilibrium level of GDP will fall from $1,800 billion to $1,600 billion.

In terms of the withdrawals–injections approach of frame (b), with an *MPS* of 1/3 the $150 billion reduction in disposable income will cause saving to be $50 billion less at every level of GDP. Hence, the withdrawal function will be shifted downward by this amount, from $S + M$ to $S_1 + M$. The $150 billion tax withdrawal must be added to the saving and import leakage at every level of GDP to give the total leakage function $S_1 + M + T$. The new equilibrium level of GDP is $1,600 billion.

is shown again in this figure. Initially GDP equals DI. When the government imposes the lump-sum tax, a wedge equal to $150 billion will be driven between GDP and disposable income, DI, at every level of GDP. Since part of every dollar of DI is consumed and the rest saved, it follows that the reduction in DI will be reflected partly in a reduction in consumption and partly in a reduction in saving.[3]

The degree of reduction in each category is determined by the size of the MPC and the MPS. In this case, the MPC and MPS are each equal to 2/3 and 1/3, respectively. Therefore, the $150 billion tax will cause a $100 billion reduction in consumption and a $50 billion reduction in saving at every level of GDP. The consumption function is the only component of the aggregate expenditure schedule affected by the tax. It is shifted down by $100 billion from C to C_1 at every level of GDP. Consequently, the aggregate expenditure schedule is shifted downward by $100 billion from $AE = C + I + X - M + G$ to $AE_1 = C_1 + I + X - M + G$ as shown in Figure 23-4, frame (a). The equilibrium level of GDP therefore decreases from $1,800 billion, to potential GDP at a high employment level, to $1,600 billion. This $200 billion decrease is the result of the multiplier effect times the reduction in consumption due to the tax increase.

We get the same result if we take the withdrawals–injections perspective. The equilibrium of Figure 23-3, frame (b), determined by the intersection of the withdrawals function $S + M$ and the $I + X + G$ function, is shown again in Figure 23-4, frame (b). When the $150 billion lump-sum tax is imposed, DI is reduced by this amount at every level of GDP. With an MPS of 1/3, this means that saving is reduced by $50 billion at every level of GDP, so that the withdrawal function shifts downward by this amount from $S + M$ to $S_1 + M$. In addition to the withdrawal from GDP due to saving and imports, now there is also a $150 billion withdrawal due to taxes T at every level of GDP. Adding this to the withdrawal function gives us the total withdrawal function $S_1 + M + T$. The equilibrium level of GDP is now $1,600 billion, determined by the intersection of $S_1 + M + T$ and $I + X + G$ in Figure 23-4, frame (b). Here the sum of the withdrawals from GDP, which is equal to saving plus imports plus taxes, is just offset by the sum of the injections, which is equal to intended investment plus exports plus government spending. At equilibrium, $S_1 + M + T = I + X + G$.

Whether we look at it from the aggregate expenditure schedule vantage point of frame (a) or from the withdrawals and injections vantage point of frame (b), we see that imposing a tax will cause the equilibrium level of GDP to decrease. Similarly, removing the tax would cause the aggregate expenditure schedule to increase or, equivalently, the $S + M + T$ function to fall, so that the equilibrium level of GDP would increase. An increase in taxes will cause a decrease in GDP. A decrease in taxes will cause an increase in GDP.

The Balanced Budget Multiplier in an Open Economy

Note that the $150 billion of government spending alone *increases* the equilibrium level of GDP from $1,500 billion to $1,800 billion (Figure 23-3). This

---

[3]The observant student may question whether the tax wedge will affect imports as well as saving and consumption. We have simplified the effect of the tax wedge in order to be consistent with our earlier definitions, in Chapter 19, that $DI = C + S$ and our simplifying assumption in this chapter that $GDP = DI + T$. In a more complex analysis the tax wedge would also influence imports and quite possibly investment as well.

represented an increase of two dollars of aggregate income for every dollar increase in government spending, so the full multiplier effect applies. However, the $150 billion lump-sum tax collected to finance the spending *decreases* the equilibrium level of GDP from $1,800 billion to $1,600 billion (Figure 23-4). The increase in tax decreased income only by $1.33 for every dollar increase in the tax. The multiplier effect of an autonomous change in taxes is less powerful in its multiplier effect on aggregate income than an equal-sized autonomous change in government spending. The implication of this phenomenon is that if government spending and taxes are *both* increased by $150 billion, GDP will increase but by only $100 billion.

This illustrates the **balanced budget multiplier**, *which is the number by which a change in government expenditure is multiplied by to estimate the resulting change in GDP if the change in government spending was balanced by an equal change in taxes.* Note that the change in government spending has a smaller effect on GDP when the change in government spending is balanced by an equal change in taxes. However, it still causes GDP to change in the same direction as the change in government spending. In a closed economy in which all spending except consumption is autonomous, the balanced budget multiplier will actually equal one. In open economies, however, the balanced budget multiplier is generally less than one. Even in this circumstance, the level of equilibrium aggregate income will vary *directly* with the change in government spending when government spending and taxes are *both* changed by the *same* amount and in the same direction.

In our present example the increase in GDP is equal to the multiplier times the amount of the government expenditure increase, *minus* the multiplier times the amount by which *consumption* decreases as a result of the tax increase. Similarly, a government expenditure decrease balanced by an equal decrease in taxes will result in a decrease in GDP equal to the multiplier times the net change in aggregate expenditure resulting from the decrease in government spending and the increase in consumption due to the reduced taxes. The balanced budget multiplier equals the open economy multiplier times *MPS*.

What explains the operation of the balanced budget multiplier? Consider our example again. If the government *hadn't* taxed the $150 billion away from the public, what would the public have done with it? Answer: spend only $100 billion of it ($MPC = 2/3$). However, if the government *does take* the $150 billion away from the public by taxation, what does the government do with it? Answer: spend the *whole* $150 billion. Therefore, on balance there is $50 billion more spending and, given a multiplier of 2, an increase in GDP of $100 billion. Therefore the balanced budget multiplier in this case is *less than 1*, which is the normal case for balanced budget multipliers in open economies.

In the example shown in Figures 23-3 and 23-4, GDP must equal $1,800 billion if there is to be full employment. Assuming that we want a balanced government budget, how much would government spending and taxes have to be increased in order to raise GDP from $1,500 billion to $1,800 billion? According to the balanced budget multiplier, both government spending and taxes would have to be raised by $450 billion. Clearly, this must be judged an inefficient method of using discretionary fiscal policy, since it involves changing the government's taxes and government spending by an amount larger than the desired adjustment in the economy's gross domestic product!

Mathematically the balanced budget multiplier for an economy can be written

$$\Delta GDP = \left(\frac{1}{MPS + MPM}\right) \times \Delta G - \left(\frac{MPC}{MPS + MPM}\right) \times \Delta T$$

but since ΔG *must equal* ΔT for the balanced budget, let $\Delta B = \Delta G = \Delta T$ and $1 - MPC = MPS$. Therefore,

$$\Delta GDP = \frac{MPS}{MPS + MPM} \times \Delta B$$

So

$$\text{Balanced budget multiplier} = \frac{MPS}{MPS + MPM}$$

Discretionary Fiscal Policy in Practice

Our analysis of the effects of government expenditure and taxation on the equilibrium level of GDP indicates how discretionary fiscal policy might be used to combat recessions and inflationary booms. Reductions in government expenditures, increases in taxes, or both may be used to reduce the level of aggregate expenditure when economic expansions create excessive inflationary pressures. If the government budget is in deficit to begin with, a reduction in the deficit or possibly its replacement with a surplus will be required to reduce aggregate expenditure. If the budget is balanced to begin with, the creation of a budget surplus will be required to reduce aggregate expenditure. If a surplus exists initially, an even larger surplus will be required.

When the economy is slipping into a recession, increases in government expenditures, reductions in taxes, or both, may be used to increase aggregate expenditure. If the government budget is initially in deficit, these actions will give rise to an even larger deficit. If the budget is balanced to begin with, a deficit will be required. And if a surplus exists initially, the surplus will be reduced or replaced by a deficit. These prescriptions for the ideal exercise of discretionary fiscal policy are not so easy to carry out in practice. Let's see why.

Policies and Priorities

Federal government expenditure and tax programs are formulated in the various ministries, reviewed and accepted by the Priorities and Planning Committee of the Government, passed by the House of Commons and then given Royal Assent. The planning and budgeting affects over $110 billion per year and involves or indirectly affects over 225,000 employees in the public sector.[4] It

---

[4]For students interested in an excellent and up-to-date discussion of the size of the public sector, its machinery for budgeting, and the political problems plaguing attempts to control public spending see Donald J. Savoie, *The Politics Of Public Spending In Canada* (Toronto: University of Toronto Press, 1990).

is a political process affected by many different special interest groups and lobbies, each with a list of priorities that often conflicts with the goals of discretionary fiscal policy. For example, suppose that prudent fiscal policy calls for a reduction in government expenditures to reduce inflationary pressures. Suppose also that nobody wants government expenditures cut that affect his or her region. The other alternative is to increase taxes. Which taxes should be increased, and who shall pay them? Neither politicians nor the public ever likes decreasing government spending, reducing transfer payments, or increasing taxes. Similarly, if governments come to expect that they will not be able to increase taxes once they are cut or believe that they will not be able to reduce a specific type of expenditure once it is in place, they may be reluctant to initiate new timely spending programs when they are needed. Canada appears no less prone to this behaviour than other countries. In the last three federal budgets we have seen proposals to reduce transfers to senior citizens withdrawn from the budget because of political pressure, which forced the government to reverse its position. On the expenditure side, we have seen the proposals to upgrade the Canadian maritime defense capability withdrawn and the implementation of a national child care system delayed because of budgetary considerations.

The politics of working out compromises among various interest groups with conflicting objectives takes time. Hence, the question is whether the Minister of Finance, working with his or her ministerial advisers and the Cabinet, can resolve the various issues associated with an expenditure or a tax bill and pass it in time to counteract either inflationary pressures or a recession.

Forecasting, Recognition, and Timing

The preceding observation aside, it is necessary to be able to forecast the future course of the economy fairly accurately in order to take appropriately timed fiscal actions to head off expected recessions or curb inflationary booms. Forecasting is still more an art than a science, despite the development of large econometric models of the economy. The record of economic forecasters, both in government and out, is mixed at best.

Often it is almost as hard to recognize where the economy is as it is to forecast where it is going. Frequently the economy has been in a recession for several months before economists, policymakers, and other observers have recognized and agreed that this is the case. Part of the problem is the fact that many important measurements of the economy's performance are only available some time (often several months) after the events that they attempt to measure have occurred. For instance, statistics on GDP become available every quarter year, a month or more after the quarter has ended. Another similar problem is that different indicators sometimes give different or conflicting insight into what is happening to the economy. For instance, because of the different ways of calculating the consumer price index (CPI), and the general price deflator for the GDP, it is possible that one might show inflation at the same time that the other shows deflation. The result of this recognition lag is that discretionary fiscal policy tends to be more a reaction to past developments in the economy than an anticipation of those to come. In practice, forecasting and recognition problems combine with political considerations and the sluggishness of democratic decision making to create serious timing problems for discretionary fiscal policy.

Even when a change in government spending or taxes finally takes place, there is often a considerable time lag before its full effect on the economy is realized. Given all these considerations, it is not hard to see how a government spending increase or tax cut intended to offset a recession might be badly timed. Such actions could end up taking place in the expansion phase of the business cycle, *after* the trough of the recession has passed. Rather than reducing the depth of the recession, they would simply add inflationary pressures to the expansion phase of the cycle that follows. Timing problems associated with discretionary fiscal policy can make economic fluctuations worse.

Expectational Changes, Credibility, and the Lucas Critique

In addition to the technical problems associated with fiscal policy, there is a more philosophical problem associated with the use of fiscal policy. Economic agents in the private sector may react differently to the same government action when that action is repeated under different circumstances.

From the turn of the twentieth century onward economists understood that the intervention of the government could influence the size of the economy and direct its pattern of spending. They were also aware that in a social science such as economics it is difficult to predict the reaction of economic agents to a particular type of stimulus such as tax cuts. While this knowledge was well recognized, most economists ignored it or treated it as an esoteric problem of no importance to the practical application of economic policy. As the ideas of John Maynard Keynes gained acceptance, governments began to use discretionary fiscal policy more vigorously. The concern among a small group of economists that the theory did not include changing behaviour by consumers and businesses in response to the repeated initiatives by the government led economists to explore how expectations were formed and how government action affected expectations.

We will delay a thorough investigation of this until the next chapter, but for now we can say that the work of R. E. Lucas helped shed much light on building a useful theory of how expectations are formed and how they affect the usefulness of discretionary initiatives by the government.[5] Lucas's methodology, which is usually referred to as *rational expectations theory*, has two key concepts of immediate interest: first, that expectations are formed on the basis of all the information available to consumers and businesses at the time the decision is made; and second, that for the policy to be effective in the shortrun, the policymaker must be credible—that is, the agents affected by the policy initiative must believe that the policymaker will follow through on the policy and that the policy will be effective.

The results of combining these two simple ideas led to the formation of the **Lucas Critique** *that the effect of any government policy is uncertain because any new policy will cause a change in the information available to the private sector and will result in somewhat unpredictable changes to the various marginal propensities to spend throughout the economy.* The changes in the spending patterns occur because those in the private sector will reevaluate their own expectations about the future and

---

[5]Robert E. Lucas, *Studies in Business-Cycle Theory* (Cambridge, MA: M.I.T. Press, 1989), pp. 104–145.

Checkpoint 23-2

Consider again the example of Figures 23-3 and 23-4, and suppose that the MPC is 4/5 and the MPM is 1/5. Explain how the aggregate expenditure schedule is now affected by a $50 billion decrease in lump-sum taxes accompanied by a $50 billion decrease in government spending on goods and services. Give an explanation in terms of the withdrawals and injections approach. Explain why the balanced budget multiplier in an open economy does not equal 1 if MPM is greater than 0, no matter what the values are of MPC and MPS.

the credibility of the government's policies every time the government initiates a new policy. From the policymaker's point of view this greatly complicates the exercise of public policy. We have explained in this chapter that to change the level of employment and equilibrium income, a policymaker would have to know the marginal propensity to consume and the marginal propensity to import. Then the policymaker would have to adjust taxes or government spending or transfers so that the portion of the adjustment that would be respent through the multiplier will cause aggregate spending to change by just enough to bring equilibrium income to the desired level. What Lucas pointed out is that each time taxes or government spending or transfers are changed, there is some largely unpredictable change in the marginal propensity to consume and the marginal propensity to import. Thus, the marginal propensity to consume, the marginal propensity to import, and the multiplier become much more difficult if not impossible for policymakers to accurately predict ahead of time.

Fiscal Effects of Provincial and Local Governments

Discretionary fiscal policy might be more effective if it represented a coordinated effort of federal, provincial, and local governments. However, there is no body of legislation that requires the different levels of government to coordinate their fiscal policies. If anything, provincial and local governments tend to conduct their fiscal activities in ways that increase, rather than reduce, the fluctuations of the business cycle. This happens partly because provincial and local governments are under more pressure to balance their budgets than is the federal government. Their ability to tax and raise money to finance expenditures rises and falls with the business cycle. This is especially a problem for the smaller provinces and the local governments. In some provinces the law forbids local governments from running deficit budgets without the express approval of the provincial government. Therefore, they tend to spend more heavily on postponable projects such as school building and civic capital projects during periods of general economic prosperity than during recessions.

Automatic Stabilizers: Nondiscretionary Fiscal Policy

Discretionary fiscal policy requires deliberate action by the Government of Canada and Parliament. The decisions to change the level of government spending, taxation, or both must be made on a case by case basis. However, our economy also contains automatic stabilizers. **Automatic stabilizers** *are built-in features of the economy that operate continuously without discretionary political intervention to smooth out the peaks and troughs of business cycles.* They are comparable to a cruise control in an automobile that maintains constant speed for the vehicle within the mechanical ability of the automobile to run at a constant speed. Like the cruise control, the economy's automatic stabilizers don't necessarily eliminate the need for deliberate action. But they do reduce it. Let's look at some of the more important built-in stabilizers and how they work.

Tax Structure

Up to now we have used only lump-sum taxes in our analysis, so that the amount of tax revenue is the same no matter what the level of GDP. In reality, the tax structure of Canada and all modern countries is such that the amount of tax revenue rises when GDP increases and falls when GDP declines. The significance of this for economic stability is illustrated in Figure 23-5. There it is assumed that the level of government and intended investment expenditures is the same at all levels of GDP or, in other words, that the $I + X + G$ schedule is flat.

Frame (a) of Figure 23-5 shows the lump-sum tax case with which we are already familiar. Suppose that the sum of investment, exports, and government expenditure is initially $300 billion, as represented by the $I_0 + X + G$ schedule. The equilibrium level of GDP is $1,200 billion, determined by the intersection of $S + M + T$ and $I_0 + X + G$. If investment spending increases by $100 billion from I_0 to I_1, the $I_0 + X + G$ schedule shifts up to $I_1 + X + G$, and the equilibrium level of GDP increases by $400 billion, from $1,200 billion to $1,600 billion.

Proportional Taxes

Now consider the effect of the same fluctuation in investment, given the same saving function S, when the economy's tax structure is such that tax revenues rise and fall *proportionally* with GDP. This situation is shown in frame (b) of Figure 23-5. The tax revenue at each level of GDP is represented by the vertical distance between the withdrawal function $S + M$ and the new withdrawal function $S + M + T$. This distance gets proportionally larger as GDP increases. With a **proportional tax,** *a given percentage increase (or decrease) in GDP always results in the same percentage increase (or decrease) in tax revenues.* For example, if GDP increases by 10 percent, tax revenues also increase by 10 percent. Given the position of the withdrawal function $S + M$, the larger is the proportional tax rate, the steeper will be the $S + M + T$ function in frame (b).

When the $I + X + G$ schedule is in the position $I_0 + X + G$, the equilibrium level of GDP is $1,300 billion. When the $100 billion increase in investment shifts the schedule up to $I_1 + X + G$, the equilibrium level of GDP increases by $200 billion to $1,500 billion. In short, the same $100 billion fluctuation in investment causes a smaller fluctuation in GDP under a proportional tax structure than under a lump-sum tax structure—a $200 billion versus a $400 billion GDP fluctuation. Why is this?

Recall that taxes, like saving and imports, are a withdrawal that drains off potential spending on goods and services. With a lump-sum tax the tax withdrawal does not change with changes in GDP. But with a proportional tax the withdrawals increase as GDP increases and has an *even greater* braking effect on further rises in GDP. Hence, a rise in injections due to increased investment, exports, government spending, or all three, is offset to a larger extent by an increase in withdrawals under a proportional tax structure than under a lump-sum tax structure. Similarly, a fall in the level of injections results in a more rapid decline in withdrawals under a proportional tax structure. Therefore, GDP does not have to decline as far to reestablish the equality between injections and withdrawals.

FIGURE 23-5 The Tax Structure as an Automatic Stabilizer

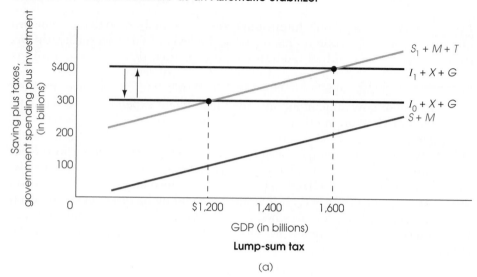

Lump-sum tax

(a)

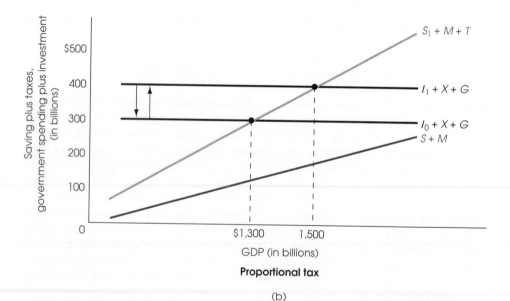

Proportional tax

(b)

Proportional taxes and progressive taxes act as automatic stabilizers because they increase withdrawals when GDP rises and decrease withdrawals when GDP falls. The withdrawals and injections diagrams of frames (a) and (b) all have the same saving function and the same $100 billion $I + X + G$ schedule shifts, but they each assume different tax structures. When taxes are lump-sum, frame (a), a $100 billion shift in the $I + G$ schedule, from $I_0 + X + G$ to $I_1 + X + G$, or vice versa, causes a $400 billion change in GDP. By comparison, the same shifts in the $I + G$ schedule under a proportional tax structure, frame (b), cause a smaller change (equal to $200 billion) in GDP. The same shifts under a progressive tax structure would result in a still smaller change.

The stabilizing effect of the proportional tax structure is greater the larger is the proportional tax rate or the percentage of GDP that is collected in taxes. An increase in the proportional tax rate makes the $S + M + T$ function in frame (b) steeper.[6] This means that the shift in the $I_0 + X + G$ schedule to $I_1 + X + G$, or from $I_1 + X + G$ to $I_0 + X + G$ will cause an even smaller change in GDP. The economy is more stable in that it is less sensitive to such a disturbance.

Progressive Taxes

In reality, tax revenues in our economy tend to rise and fall *more than proportionally* with increases and decreases in GDP because personal and business income is subject to a progressive tax. A **progressive tax** *on income imposes successively higher tax rates on additional dollars of income as income rises.* For example, the first $10,000 of an individual's income might be subject to a 17 percent tax rate, the second $10,000 to a 26 percent tax rate, the third to a 29 percent rate, and so forth. This means that the *fraction* of total income taxed away gets larger as total income rises. By contrast, with a proportional tax rate the *fraction* of total income taxed away is the same no matter what the level of total income. The progressive nature of Canada's tax structure enhances the effectiveness of the tax system as a built-in stabilizer by automatically increasing tax withdrawals more than proportionally as GDP rises and by reducing such withdrawals more than proportionally as GDP falls. Increasing withdrawals during an inflationary expansion has a dampening effect on the economy. Conversely, decreasing withdrawals during a recession tends to buoy up spending.

Unemployment Insurance and Welfare

The Great Depression of the 1930s caused major changes in Canada's attitude toward the poor and unemployed. Until the 1930s, laws governing social assistance to those out of work or the working poor largely reflected the ideas of the *Poor Laws* introduced under Queen Elizabeth I in 1601![7] Since the 1930s unemployment assistance has become an increasingly important automatic stabilizer in our economy. Recessions swell the ranks of the unemployed. Without some form of assistance, laid-off workers must cut back their spending in proportion to the reduction in their earned income. This only makes the recession worse. Paying unemployment insurance benefits and welfare enables those who are not receiving employment income to better sustain their consumption spending and thus cushions the downturn not only for those who receive direct benefits *but also for other members of society who remain employed because of the money spent by those who receive direct benefits.* In theory, unemployment insurance benefits are paid out of a fund established by using the insurance premiums paid by employers and employees receiving coverage under the

---

[6]The slope of the tax curve is, like the slope of the savings curve and the slope of the import curve, given the designation marginal. The marginal propensity to tax or marginal tax rate affects the slope of the withdrawals function and reduces the multiplier.

[7]Minister of Supply and Services Canada. *Welfare In Canada, The Tangled Safety Net, a Report by the National Council of Welfare* (November, 1987), p. 2.

program. In practice, the tax revenue from UIC during periods of economic expansion has entered general revenue and the benefits paid to individuals during the downturns have not been financed directly from the plan. Similarly, the benefits paid to individuals under the Canada Assistance Plan (welfare) have not been financed directly from the plan but come from general revenue (income tax and borrowing). The benefits increase automatically as the economy performs less well (during the trough of the business cycle) as more of the population qualifies for benefits, and the benefits decrease automatically as the economy recovers and less of the population qualifies for benefits. Thus, as aggregate income increases, the *progressive tax system and UIC premiums* increase the withdrawals *more than proportionally* during boom periods, tending to curb excessive inflationary expansions. During recessions, injections into the economy from unemployment benefits and welfare increase and the withdrawals due to taxes and unemployment insurance premiums decrease, and the economy is stimulated on balance. During expansionary periods, withdrawals due to taxes and unemployment insurance premiums tend to exceed injections from unemployment benefits and welfare, and the net effect is to curb inflationary pressures.

Other Automatic Stabilizers

Other automatic stabilizers in our economy include price-support programs for agriculture and fisheries, Established Programs Financing (EPF), and equalization. While each of these programs works differently from a technical point of view, they share the common tendency that they *automatically* increase the flow of funds from the government to the private sector during periods of downturn in the business cycle and tend to hold the flow constant or decrease it during the expansion phase of the business cycle. We will not go into great detail on the technical workings of any of the programs, but a brief investigation will help show the significance of the automatic stabilizers.

The price of many agricultural and fishery products decreases during recessions and increases during inflationary periods. Successive governments have introduced stabilization programs designed to reduce the magnitude of the decrease in incomes caused by the decreases in prices during the trough of the business cycle. Most of these involve a system of quotas or performance criteria under which producers sell their products to the government at some government-determined price or reduce their production in return for a subsidy.

Established Program Financing (EPF) involves the federal government giving transfers to the provinces for a set proportion of the total cost of programs provided by lower levels of government. This support increases automatically as demand for these programs increases during a recession. In periods of expansion the federal government limits the rate of increase on many of these programs to a specified rate that is below the rate of inflation.

Automatic Stabilizers Are a Double-Edged Sword

The same characteristics of automatic stabilizers that make them desirable can also make them very undesirable under certain circumstances. For example, the

Checkpoint 23-3

Suppose that the government spending component of the $I + X + G$ schedules in Figure 23-5 is always equal to \$150 billion, whatever the level of GDP. For each of the cases shown in frames (a) and (b) of Figure 23-5, explain how the government budget changes as a result of the \$100 billion change in investment, both when it represents an increase from I_0 to I_1 and when it represents a decrease from I_1 to I_0. That is, for each case, does the budget remain balanced, go from surplus to deficit or from deficit to surplus, or what? In light of your findings, how might you state the way the automatic stabilization effect works in terms of the government budget? Similarly, what happens to net exports $X - M$ as a result of the increase in investment?

POLICY PERSPECTIVE

Discretionary versus Nondiscretionary Expenditures

While automatic stabilizers tend to smooth out the peaks and troughs of business cycles, they do not eliminate them entirely. Research on the matter suggests that the amplitude of business cycles (the difference in GDP from trough to peak) may be reduced by anywhere from one third to one half as a result of the presence of automatic stabilizers. This means that there may still be a role for well timed discretionary fiscal policy in eliminating that part of the business cycle not smoothed out by the automatic stabilizers.

Discretionary fiscal policy expenditures usually have a different impact on the economy than do the expenditures arising from nondiscretionary fiscal policy. Discretionary government expenditures are typically for goods and services—roads, buildings, trucks, research grants, and so forth. Nondiscretionary government spending usually takes the form of transfer payments, such as old age security, unemployment insurance, welfare benefits, and interest on the government debt. Hidden behind a given dollar figure for government expenditure is a

variety of decisions about the role of government in our economy.

Viewed only in terms of the expansionary impact on the economy, however, government spending on goods and services is more expansionary than transfer payments. For example, suppose that the open economy multiplier equals 2 and that the economy is not operating at full employment. Government spending of $30 billion of goods and services will cause the economy to produce $60 billion of additional output—$30 billion to meet government purchases and $30 billion to meet increased consumption spending by households of $40 billion and increased import spending of $10 billion as a consequence of the multiplier effect. Alternatively, if the government paid out the $30 billion in unemployment insurance benefits, no increase in output would be needed to satisfy government purchase orders. The government would simply hand unemployed workers $30 billion. The unemployed would spend two thirds of this on goods and services (because an open economy multiplier of 2 implies an *MPC* of 2/3), or $20 billion. The operation of the

multiplier effect on this $20 billion expenditure would mean that the economy's total output would increase by $40 billion. In summary, a $30 billion government expenditure on goods and services would cause the economy's total output and aggregate income to increase by $60 billion. But a $30 billion transfer payment would cause total output and aggregate income to rise by only $40 billion.

For Discussion

- In 1952 transfer payments from the federal government were equal to roughly 8 percent of GDP. By the mid-1980s they had risen to about 18 percent of GDP. Over the same period of time federal government purchases of goods and services as a share of GDP fell from 10 percent to the equivalent of about 7 percent. What implications about fiscal policy might you draw from these trends over this time period?

- If the trends reported above had been just the opposite, how do you think the GDP gap would have been affected compared to the way it actually behaved?

tendency of the Canadian tax structure to increase withdrawals when GDP rises helps to curb inflationary pressures when the economy is near full employment. However, if the economy is coming out of the depths of a recession, this same tendency for withdrawals to rise acts as a fiscal drag on economic recovery, preventing the economy from moving to full employment. **Fiscal drag** *may be defined as the tendency for a progressive tax system to automatically vary taxes inversely compared to the desired change required by discretionary fiscal policy to move aggregate income to a desired level.* The increased stability that arises from the automatic stabilizers can as easily keep GDP relatively stable at an *undesirable* level as it can help to prevent undesirable changes in income.

POLICY PERSPECTIVE

The 1988 Federal Budget—Lower Rates and Lost Loopholes

Two factors probably contributed to the tax reform measures included in the federal budget introduced to the public in April of 1988. First, a perceived growing concern about the size of the federal government deficit and interest payments on the public debt by the financial sector, the business community, and international agencies contributed to the sense that the government should be seen to be addressing the deficit. Second, the United States and the United Kingdom had both introduced major tax reform measures in the preceding four years, which had distorted the relationship between taxable earnings in Canada and those earned in the other two countries. While this may be of little significance to the average factory worker or history professor, it may be very important to the tax planning and investment decisions of the transnational companies that make up a large part of the Canadian economy. Unlike that of the United States, the Canadian tax reform was not introduced as a single wide-sweeping change but appears to have been an ongoing process, and the budget of April 1989 moved on several fronts to extend the direction initiated in 1988. The restructuring of the Canadian tax system will involve several stages

and a general tendency to increase the reliance on indirect taxes such as the Goods and Services Tax (GST) and reduced reliance on income tax.

The basic direction of tax reforms through the budgets of 1985 to 1989 has been to lower marginal tax rates (the extra tax paid from an additional dollar of disposable income) but to increase tax revenue by eliminating tax breaks (loopholes) and by reducing the eligibility and the duration of transfer benefits such as UIC. Dozens of special exceptions, write-offs, deductions, and exemptions in past tax legislation designed to encourage investment, savings, energy conservation, and a host of other economic goals were repealed or sharply curtailed. At the same time, the budgets significantly reduced the progressiveness and level of tax rates on personal income. Under the budget of 1987 the number of tax brackets was reduced to three, with progressive marginal tax rates of 17, 26, and 29 percent. The previous income tax structure had 10 brackets with progressive marginal tax rates that ranged from 6 up to 34 percent. Reforms on the corporate tax system between 1985 and 1989 reduced the ability of firms to transfer accelerated de-

preciation allowances, and losses through the payment of dividends to other firms, and introduced a new *large corporation tax* to increase corporate income tax. These measures, combined with the reduced level of tax rates on personal income, were intended to shift some of the overall tax burden from individuals to corporations over a 5-year period. However, it is not expected that these measures will increase the corporate share of total income taxes received by the federal government back up to the levels of the 1970s. In the 1950s corporate income tax provided more tax revenue to the federal government than did personal income tax, and as late as the 1960s corporate tax contributed over fifty percent of federal tax revenue. With the reforms of 1985 to 1989, the corporate income tax share of federal revenue will still be only about one third of federal revenue and still much less than personal income tax.

One of the more interesting aspects of Canada's tax reform is the government's intention to replace the existing federal sales tax with a goods and services tax (GST)—or business transfer tax (BTT), as

continued on next page

Summary

1. The effect of exports on aggregate expenditure and equilibrium income is essentially the same as the effect of investment. With the introduction of more categories of injections and withdrawals, the necessary condition for equilibrium income changes from being the level of GDP at which saving equals investment and becomes instead the level of GDP at which total injections equal total withdrawals.

POLICY PERSPECTIVE CONTINUED

it was originally proposed. This tax was placed on nearly all categories of value-added, including services. While many critics claim that such a tax is difficult to administer and will encourage barter transactions so as to avoid paying the tax, most European countries, New Zealand, and Australia have all introduced this type of tax and they seem to work fairly effectively in generating the expected tax revenues for governments concerned. However, the tax is controversial on other grounds. It is a type of tax that makes it very difficult to ensure that the taxpayer is being taxed according to his or her ability to pay. As late as 1986 the Economic Council of Canada warned that the proposed BTT would be *regressive* (that is, it would decrease as a per-

centage of income as income rose) and that it would tend to shift the tax burden from the wealthy to low-income groups.* The subsequent introduction of the GST in January of 1991 involved measures such as the tax-credit rebate for low-income families to help address some of the concerns, but the overall effectiveness of the GST and the debate over its effect on many aspects of the Canadian economy will go on for many years to come.

The budget of 1988 also included a 3 percent surtax on taxable incomes over $50,000; this made the effective marginal rate 31 percent for taxable incomes above $50,000. In the budget of 1989 this surtax was broadened and increased so that all 13.5 million tax payers would pay 4 percent by July 1, 1989

and high-income earners (taxable incomes of $70,000) would pay an effective surtax of 5.5 percent. In subsequent years the individual surtax will be 5 percent and will affect all 13.5 million tax payers and the high income surtax will add 8 percent tax to taxable incomes over $70,000.

For Discussion

- How do you think the tax reforms that have reduced marginal tax rates have affected the automatic stabilizers of our economy and the size of our multiplier?

*Economic Council of Canada, *Changing Times, Twenty-Third Annual Review* (Minister of Supply and Services Canada, 1986), p. 33.

TABLE P23-1   Comparison of the Number of Tax Brackets on Federal Income Tax Liabilities and Average Federal Tax Rates, by Income Class, 1987 and 1988

1987		1988	
Taxable Income	Marginal Tax Rate	Taxable Income	Marginal Tax Rate
0 –$ 1,320	6%	0 –$27,500	17%
$ 1,320 – 2,639	6	$27,500 – 55,000	26
2,639 – 5,279	17	55,000 and over	29
5,279 – 7,918	18		
7,918 – 13,197	19		
13,197 – 18,476	20		
18,476 – 23,755	23		
23,755 – 36,952	25		
36,952 – 63,347	30		
63,347 and over	34		

Sources: Revenue Canada Taxation, T1 General Schedule 1, 1987 and 1888; Budget Papers, Department of Finance Canada, April, 1989.

2. Imports represent a withdrawal from the spending stream, which is similar to saving. In addition, because imports are influenced by the level of aggregate income, they change the slope of the aggregate expenditure and withdrawals functions. This reduces the size of the open economy multiplier compared to the closed economy multiplier.

3. The government budget is an itemized account of government expenditures and revenues over the course of a year. The budget is said to be balanced, in surplus, or in deficit, depending, respectively, on whether government spending equals, is less than, or is greater than government tax revenues.

4. The *White Paper on Employment and Incomes* of April 12, 1945, proposed that the federal government of Canada has the responsibility for being the primary creator and shaper of national wealth. In interpreting the provisions of this document successive federal governments over a forty-year period accepted the idea that they should use their spending, taxing, and transfer powers to reduce unemployment, to increase real output, to reduce the swings of the business cycle, and to reduce inflation.

5. The equilibrium GDP can be raised by increasing government expenditures on goods and services, increasing government transfer payments to the private sector, lowering taxes, or any combination of these three policies. Conversely, the equilibrium GDP can be lowered by decreasing government expenditures, decreasing transfers, raising taxes, or by doing any combination of these.

6. Like savings and imports, taxes represent a withdrawal from the spending stream. In addition, because taxes reduce the disposable income of households, they affect aggregate expenditure only by the marginal propensity to consume times the change in taxes. Thus the impact of a change in taxes is less powerful in changing aggregate expenditure than an equal change in government spending.

7. If the taxes collected by the government are directly related to the level of income, as in the case of income tax, the slope of the aggregate expenditure will decrease and the slope of the withdrawals functions will increase. This reduces the size of the multiplier compared to an economy in which all taxes are independent of income.

8. According to the balanced budget multiplier, a simultaneous increase in both government expenditures and taxes of a matched, or equal, amount will cause an increase in GDP. The converse is true of a decrease.

9. During a recession a suitable discretionary fiscal policy calls for the Minister of Finance to deliberately stimulate aggregate expenditure by, for example, increasing government spending and reducing taxes. Conversely, an overheated expansion would call for a decrease in government spending and an increase in taxes.

10. Discretionary fiscal policy is hampered by the recognition lag in identifying the current state of the economy, the forecasting problem of anticipating the future, the timing lags due to the slowness of governmental responses in a democratic process, the tendency of those in the private sector to anticipate government policies and to alter their behaviours in somewhat unpredictable ways, and the tendency for provincial and local governments to accentuate contractions and expansions through pro-cyclical fiscal actions.

11. Nondiscretionary fiscal policy relies on the economy's built-in automatic stabilizers. Chief among these are a progressive tax structure, Canada Assistance Program (welfare), Established Programs Financing (education, health care, and so forth) (EPF), equalization, Unemployment Insurance (UIC), and agricultural and other price-support systems. These automatically tend to generate expansionary budget deficits during recessions and budget surpluses that dampen pressures to overheat during expansions. Automatic stabilizers reduce but do not eliminate the need for discretionary fiscal policy.

12. Automatic stabilizers can sometimes slow down the recovery from a recession by creating too much stability and thus hinder rather than help the economy.

Key Terms and Concepts

automatic stabilizers
balanced budget
balanced budget
    multiplier
budget deficit
budget surplus
closed economy

discretionary fiscal policy
exports
fiscal drag
imports
Lucas Critique
marginal propensity
    to import (MPM)

marginal propensity
    to tax (MRT)
    or (MPT)
open economy
    multiplier
progressive tax
proportional tax

Questions and Problems

1. Suppose that the GDP of a large trading partner such as the United States decreases dramatically. How might this affect the level of injections in the Canadian economy? How might it affect the level of withdrawals in the Canadian economy? Show how this would affect the equilibrium level GDP of Canada.

2. At the level of aggregate income where injections equal total withdrawals assume that imports exceed the level of exports. How can this be the equilibrium level of GDP?

3. How is the effect of net exports (positive or negative) on the economy similar to the effect of a government budget deficit or surplus?

4. Suppose that the level of a nation's investment spending fluctuates from year to year. Using a diagram like Figure 23-1, can you explain why the resulting fluctuations in the nation's GDP might be smaller if it imports goods than if it doesn't import? How might the composition of imports—whether the nation imports mostly consumption goods or mostly capital goods—affect your answer?

5. Use the formulas for the open economy multiplier and the closed economy multiplier to investigate which economy tends to have a smaller multiplier. What might this imply about the stability of the two economies if each experiences the same exogenously caused increase in investment?

6. List and explain several reasons why it might be more difficult to use discretionary fiscal policy to combat unemployment in a relatively open economy like Canada than in a less open economy like the United States?

7. Suppose that the government budget is balanced and that the economy is experiencing an inflationary boom. Assuming that the economy's *MPC* is 4/5, compare and contrast each of the following discretionary fiscal actions in terms of their effectiveness in dealing with this situation:
    a. Increase lump-sum taxes by $10 billion.
    b. Decrease government spending by $10 billion.
    c. Decrease both government spending and lump-sum taxes by $10 billion.
    d. Decrease government spending by $16 billion and lump-sum taxes by $20 billion.

8. From 1931 through 1940 the unemployment rate never fell below 14.3 percent, yet the government had a budget deficit in every one of those years. If deficits are expansionary, what were the possible problems? Use a withdrawals and injections graph to illustrate your answer. [Either of the diagrams from Figure 23-5, frames (a) or (b) will do, but show the government spending schedule and the investment schedule separately, as well as their sum.]

9. Assume that there is a $100 billion downward shift in consumption spending. Using the diagrams in frames (a) and (b) of Figure 23-5, what would be the difference in the discretionary change in government spending required to keep the equilibrium GDP from changing, comparing the lump-sum tax case with the proportional tax case? What does this illustrate about the relationship between the role of automatic stabilizers and the need for discretionary fiscal action?

10. A number of economists have argued that discretionary fiscal policy is not well suited to deal with the relatively brief recessions that Canada has experienced since World War II. They contend that it is necessary to rely more on the built-in stabilizers to deal with such recessions. On the other hand, they argue that the relative importance of discretionary versus nondiscretionary fiscal policy is just the reverse in a depression like that of the 1930s. Explain why you would agree or disagree with these economists.

11. Given the following equations for consumption, desired investment, government spending, exports, and imports:

$$C = 100 + .8(Y - T)$$
$$I = 25$$
$$G = 300$$
$$T = 200$$
$$X = 50$$
$$M = 30 + .1Y$$

Find each of the following:
a. What is the equation for aggregate expenditure?
b. If income is $1,000 find the values for C and M.
c. What is the value of equilibrium income?
d. What is the value of consumption at equilibrium income?
e. What is the size of the undesired inventory buildup or undesired inventory depletion if income is $1,000?
f. What is the size of the multiplier?
g. If government spending were to increase by 10 by how much would equilibrium income increase?
h. If taxes were to decrease by 10 by how much would equilibrium income increase?

Chapter 24

The Flexible Price Model and Fiscal Policy

In the previous chapter we explained the open economy model and the basic technical aspects of using discretionary fiscal policy to deal with prolonged periods of unemployment or inflation. In this chapter we will integrate this model with the flexible price environment, which we first discussed in Chapter 19. We will begin by incorporating the effect of changes in the general price level on the components of aggregate expenditure into the determination of equilibrium income and the size of the multiplier effect. In Chapters 22 and 23 we indicated that changes to the general price level might cause changes to the levels of consumption, business investment, and net exports. In the first part of this chapter we will use this knowledge to derive the aggregate demand curve. Once we have investigated the derivation of the aggregate demand curve, we will explore the factors that will cause it to shift.

We will explain how changes in the general price level will affect the willingness and ability of the firms to produce goods and services. This will lead to the derivation of the aggregate supply curve. There is a controversy about the factors affecting the slope of the aggregate supply curve. We will briefly explore the issues surrounding the slope of aggregate supply. The causes of shifts in the aggregate supply curve will be discussed.

By combining a shift in the aggregate demand with a stationary aggregate supply curve we will analyze **demand shocks**. Using this technique we will illustrate how a demand shock can increase output and the price level. Excess aggregate demand can cause increases in both output and the price level, and deficiencies in aggregate demand can lead to high unemployment and a decrease in the price level. These adjustments, coming from the expenditure side of the economy, are usually referred to as *Keynesian* economics.

By reversing the process, we can investigate **supply shocks**. Shifts to the left or upward in the aggregate supply curve can cause increases in the general price level and rises in unemployment and decreases in aggregate income and output. This condition is described as **stagflation**. Conversely, shifts to the right in the aggregate supply curve will tend to increase output and aggregate income, and at the same time decrease inflation and lower the unemployment rate. This analysis, which relies on adjustments to aggregate supply, is generally referred to as *supply-side economics*.

The final section of the chapter will integrate this flexible price perspective with the basic theory of fiscal policy presented in the last chapter. This allows us to discuss some of the recent developments in macroeconomic policy in Canada, the United Kingdom and the United States, usually described as supply-side economics. While there is much controversy surrounding the whole field of supply-side theory, it is an area of macroeconomic theory that has raised serious concerns about the ability of the policymakers to cure traditional macroeconomic problems.

The Aggregate Demand Curve

So far, our analysis of the determination of aggregate income, output, and employment has assumed that wages and the general level of prices are both fixed. We have implicitly assumed that when aggregate expenditure increased, firms would respond to the increased potential for sales by increasing production and offering more goods and services to the market at the existing price level. This means that any change in the dollar value of aggregate income and output is due entirely to a change in the quantity of real output (so many tonnes of wheat, tonnes of steel, shoe shines, medical examinations, and so forth). Now we want to allow for the situation in which *both* the general price level and the aggregate output change at the same time. When the general price level changes it will affect the level of aggregate expenditure by adding one more source of informa-

---

LEARNING OBJECTIVES

After reading this chapter, you will be able to:

1. Derive the aggregate demand curve.
2. Explain why an aggregate demand curve is downward sloping.
3. Explain what factors cause shifts of the aggregate demand curve.
4. Define the aggregate supply curve.
5. Discuss the differences between the aggregate supply curve and individual industry supply curves.
6. Discuss the factors that affect the slope of the aggregate supply curve.
7. Explain what factors cause shifts of the aggregate supply curve.
8. Illustrate the effect of a change in aggregate demand on the general price level and output.
9. Illustrate the effect of a supply shock on the general price level and output.
10. Illustrate the effect of simultaneous demand shocks and supply shocks.
11. Discuss the controversy over when to use demand-side fiscal policy and when to use supply-side fiscal policy.

tion to the items already considered by decision makers when they are deciding how much they want to purchase. This requires that we derive the aggregate demand curve, *AD*.

The Price Level and Aggregate Expenditure

The Real Balance Effect

In Chapter 21 we noted that an increase in the wealth held by households would shift the consumption function upward, while a decrease in wealth would shift it downward. Much wealth held by households consists of fixed-dollar assets such as money, corporate and government bonds, and saving accounts. When the price level rises, the *real value* or purchasing power represented by those fixed-dollar assets decreases, and when the price level decreases the purchasing power of fixed-dollar assets increases. Individuals may own other assets such as houses or stock in companies, which do not have fixed value, but to the extent that financial assets with fixed nominal values (such as Canada Savings Bonds and term deposits at financial intermediaries) make up a sizable portion of their wealth, consumers as a group will experience a loss of wealth if the general price level increases. Hence, an increase in the price level, *ceteris paribus*, decreases the real wealth held by households (the purchasing power of a given dollar amount of wealth), while a decrease in the price level increases it. By reducing real wealth, an increase in the price level will therefore shift the consumption function downward. Conversely, a fall in the price level, by increasing real wealth, will shift the consumption function upward. Since the consumption function is a major component of the aggregate expenditure schedule, as shown in Figure 24-1, any shift in the consumption function will cause the aggregate expenditure schedule to shift and thus cause the equilibrium level of real GDP to change. This inverse relationship between the general level of prices and consumer spending is usually referred to as the *real balance effect*, but it is also described as the *Pigou effect* in honour of A. C. Pigou, who is usually credited with identifying it.

The Interest Rate Effect

In Chapter 21 we explained that an increase in the interest rate would shift the investment schedule and the consumption function downward. This occurs because higher interest rates make investment less attractive due to reduced net expected earnings at higher interest rates, and because higher interest charges force consumers to defer purchases of consumer durables such as cars and appliances, which are frequently purchased using loans. What we wish to explain here is that an increase in the general price level will cause an increase in interest rates. When this is done the link between higher prices and lower aggregate expenditure should become more clear.

An increase in the economy's price level increases the demand for money, which pushes up the interest rate *ceteris paribus*. The full explanation of the determination of the interest rate and the linkage between the general price level and the demand for money and the supply of money will be dealt with in Chapters 28, 29, and 30. At the present it is sufficient to know that an increase in the general price level will increase the demand for money, *ceteris paribus*, and that

FIGURE 24-1   The Relationship Between Aggegrate Expenditure and the Aggregate Demand Curve

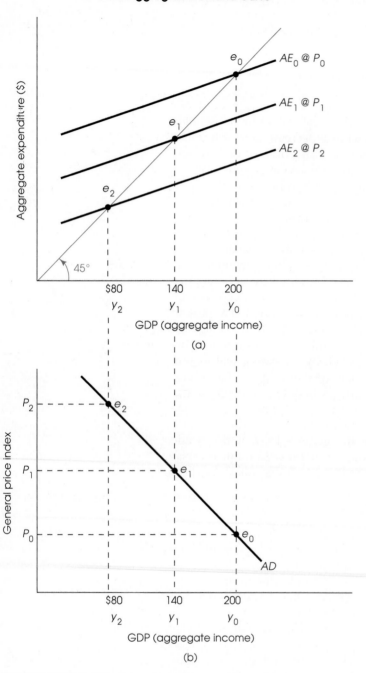

Increases in the economy's price level from P_0 to P_1 to P_2 cause the aggregate expenditure schedule to shift downward from AE_0 to AE_1 to AE_2 and the equilibrium level of real GDP to decline from y_0 at $200 billion to y_1 at $140 billion to y_2 at $80 billion as shown in frame (a). In frame (b) we plot these price levels and their associated levels of equilibrium real GDP to get the points e_0, e_1, and e_2 on the aggregate demand curve AD, corresponding to the points e_0, e_1, and e_2 in frame (a). Note that changes in the price level cause *shifts* in the aggregate expenditure curve that correspond to movements *along* the AD curve.

when there is an increase in demand, there is a tendency for the interest rate to increase. In short, there is a direct relationship between the price level and the interest rate. The decrease in consumer spending on durables and investment spending caused by the higher interest rate makes aggregate expenditure shift down.

Conversely, a lower price level decreases the demand for money and reduces the interest rate. Therefore, an increase in the price level, by pushing up the interest rate, shifts the investment schedule and the consumption function downward. A decrease in the price level, by pushing the interest rate down, shifts them upward. The investment schedule, like the consumption function, is also a component of the expenditure schedule (see Figure 24-1).

The Foreign Purchases Effect

As the general price level in Canada increases, *ceteris paribus*, there is a tendency for foreign products to appear less expensive relative to Canadian products.[1] When this happens, Canadian demand for Canadian products decreases as Canadians purchase more imports instead of Canadian products. Similarly, as the Canadian general price level increases, it forces up the price of Canadian exports in foreign countries, causing foreigners to decrease their demand for Canadian exports. Since Canadian imports are increasing and Canadian exports are decreasing because of the rise in the Canadian price level, it should be clear that Canadian net exports tend to decrease as a result of an increase in the our general price level. Conversely, the reverse behaviour also applies, if Canada experiences a decrease in its general price level (deflation), or if its general price level rises less rapidly than the price level of its trading partners, then Canadian exports would increase and Canadian imports would decrease, causing Canadian net exports to increase.[2]

When the general price level in Canada increases, net exports from Canada will decrease, *ceteris paribus*, causing a shift downward in the aggregate expenditure curve. Conversely, a decrease in the general price level in Canada, *ceteris paribus*, will cause the aggregate expenditure curve to shift upward and thus cause an increase in the equilibrium level of GDP.

A decrease in the general price level, by shifting the consumption function, the investment function, and the net export function upward, causes the aggregate expenditure function to shift upward and causes the equilibrium aggregate real income (GDP) to increase. An increase in the general price level has the opposite effect, causing aggregate expenditure to shift downward and the equilibrium aggregate real income (GDP) to decrease.

---

[1] This relationship can become quite complex, as the attempt by Canadians to purchase foreign products under these circumstances will create pressure for the exchange rate on the dollar to change on international money markets. In Chapter 34 we will study the behaviour of exchange rates, but in this chapter our focus is to investigate the impact of a change in the general price level on aggregate demand. Because of this focus we will assume throughout the chapter that the exchange rate is constant.

[2] The size of the change in net exports that results from a one percent change in Canada's general price level (deflator or CPI) depends on the relative price elasticities of the products exported by Canada and the products imported by Canada. For a review of the concept of price elasticity see Chapter 5.

Derivation of the Aggregate Demand Curve

Figure 24-1, frame (a), shows the determination of the equilibrium level of real GDP by tracing the impact on the aggregate expenditure schedule for three different possible price levels. The aggregate expenditure schedule AE_0 associated with the lowest of the three price levels P_0 determines an equilibrium level of real GDP equal to $200 billion, corresponding to the intersection of AE_0 with the 45° line at point e_0. For a higher price level P_1 the associated aggregate expenditure schedule is AE_1 and equilibrium real GDP is lower, equal to $140 billion, and for a yet higher price level P_2 the associated expenditure schedule, AE_2 and equilibrium real GDP of $80 billion are even lower. Each combination of equilibrium real GDP and its associated price level in frame (a) determines a point on the aggregate demand curve AD in frame (b) of Figure 24-1.

Points e_0, e_1, and e_2 on the AD curve in frame (b) correspond respectively to the points e_0, e_1, and e_2 in frame (a). The negative slope of the AD curve reflects the fact that increases in the price level cause equilibrium real GDP to decrease. Conversely, increases in the general price level will cause real GDP to increase.

The **aggregate demand curve** *shows all the combinations of the general price level and real GDP that create equilibriums for the expenditure side of the economy.* Changes in the price level cause shifts in the aggregate expenditure schedule that change equilibrium real GDP, and correspond to movements along the AD curve. Therefore, movement along the AD curve shows the response of equilibrium real GDP to changes in the price level.

Possible Causes of Shifts in the Position of the AD Curve

In Chapters 22 and 23 we have seen that any autonomous, or exogenously caused, change in consumption, investment, government spending, exports, taxes, or imports will cause the aggregate expenditure schedule to shift and will change equilibrium real GDP. We shall now show that such exogenous changes also cause the AD curve to shift.

We have seen that any change in the price level will cause the aggregate expenditure schedule to shift, but it will cause a *movement along* the AD curve, as illustrated in Figure 24-1. But for a given price level we know that any exogenously caused change to consumption, investment, exports, government spending, or taxes will also cause the aggregate expenditure schedule to shift and equilibrium real GDP to change. (These are the only kinds of cases that have been considered so far in the previous chapters.) Since the price level is given, or unchanged, such a change in real GDP certainly cannot be represented by movement along an AD curve. Therefore, it must be represented by a shift in the position of the entire AD curve.

This is illustrated in Figure 24-2. Suppose that the price level is given as P_0 and that the aggregate expenditure schedule is AE_0 in frame (a) of Figure 24-2. The equilibrium real GDP is y_0, and the point corresponding to e_0 in frame (a) is e_0 on the AD_0 curve in frame (b). Suppose that there is an exogenously caused expenditure increase (an increase in government spending, say) that shifts the aggregate expenditure schedule up from AE_0 to AE_1 and increases equilibrium real GDP to y_1, corresponding to point e_1 in frame (a). Given the price level P_0, the AD_0 curve in frame (b) is shifted rightward to AD_1 and the equilibrium point e_1 on AD_1 corresponds to point e_1 in frame (a).

FIGURE 24-2   **The Relationship Between Shifts in the Aggregate Expenditure Schedule and Shifts in the AD Curve**

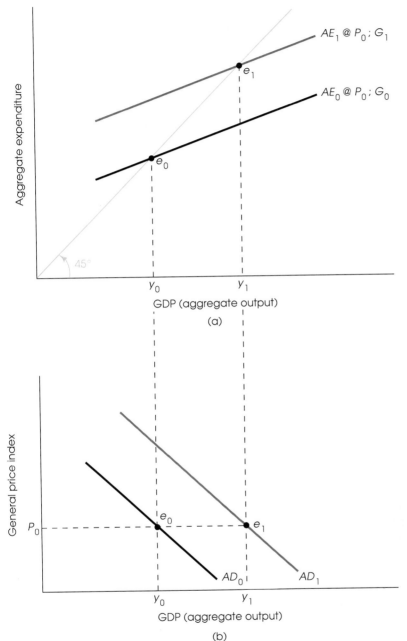

(a)

(b)

Assume a given, or unchanging, price level P_0. Then an exogenous increase in consumption, investment, government, or net export expenditure, or a reduction in tax rates, shifts the aggregate expenditure schedule upward from AE_0 to AE_1 in frame (a). This shift increases equilibrium real GDP from the level associated with point e_0 to that associated with point e_1. Corresponding to the shift from AE_0 to AE_1 in frame (a), the aggregate demand curve shifts rightward from AD_0 to AD_1 in frame (b). Given the price P_0, the points e_0 and e_1 on AD_0 and AD_1 correspond to points e_0 and e_1 in frame (a) and the associated equilibrium levels of real GDP. An exogenous reduction in consumption, investment, government, or net export expenditure, or an increase in tax rates, shifts the aggregate expenditure schedule downward and the aggregate demand curve leftward, given the price level P_0.

The conclusions of Chapters 22 and 23 about the effects of any exogenously caused changes to consumption, investment, net exports, government spending on goods and services, or taxes on the aggregate expenditure schedule can now be stated in terms of their effects on the *AD* curve. In summary:

- The *AD* curve will shift to the right due to any exogenously caused increase in consumption, investment, exports or government expenditure, or any exogenously caused decrease in imports or taxes.
- The *AD* curve will shift to the left due to any exogenously caused decrease in consumption, investment, exports or government expenditure, or any exogenously caused increase in imports or taxes.

The Aggregate Supply Curve

As we indicated in Chapter 21, the economy is equally dependent on what happens to supply conditions as it is on what happens to demand. The willingness and ability of the businesses to produce and offer goods and services for sale is also an obvious and important determinant of the level of equilibrium income and of employment. Just as the general price level influences the decisions of consumers, investors, and foreign customers (as was discussed in the previous section), the effect of changes in the general price level may influence the amount of goods and services offered for sale. In this section we want to incorporate the effect of changes in the general price level into the *aggregate supply* of goods and services. We will concentrate on the shortrun behaviour of aggregate supply in this chapter and then review longrun changes in supply behaviour in Chapter 26.

The Shape of the Aggregate Supply Curve

The supply of products depends on, among other things, the profits that firms expect to receive from the sale of their products. This in turn is influenced by the price each firm expects to receive, the cost per unit of the factors used in production (which include wages, interest, and the prices for strategic commodities such as fuel), taxes, and the level of technology employed. Although the detailed discussion of the factors that influence the amount of product that an *individual firm* will offer for sale at any specific price is part of microeconomics (and is discussed in depth in Chapters 4, and 7 through 12), some discussion of the behaviour of a representative individual firm is necessary to understand how firms in the aggregate behave in response to a change in the general level of prices throughout the economy.

In Chapter 4 we saw that, *ceteris paribus*, firms in one market will offer more for sale in response to an increase in the price of their product. While this is true for any individual firm in a competitive market and is very useful for microeconomic analysis, it would be a fallacy to think that this behaviour is perfectly transferable to macroeconomic analysis. In other words, what is true for an individual firm operating in one market or true for one market within the economy, is not necessarily true for the economy as a whole—the fallacy of composition.

The Information Extraction Problem

The **aggregate supply curve** *is the amount of aggregate output that businesses are willing and able to produce at different average price levels.* The aggregate supply curve is not simply the horizontal sum of the market supply curves in all the markets in the economy at all possible prices. Remember that the general price level P is an index or weighted average of the prices in a wide range of industries such as the GDP deflator or the consumer price index, which were discussed in Chapter 20. The fact that the general price level is not one price applying to one firm presented economists with a difficult problem in trying to build a theoretical model of how the general level of prices affects the amount of products offered for sale. In the mid-1970s, Robert Lucas, Edmond Phelps, Leonard Rapping, and Thomas Sargent managed to provide satisfactory explanations to link the microeconomic behaviour of individual firms to the macroeconomic movement of the general price level and furnished the foundations for the modern theory of aggregate supply. Although some debate still surrounds the exact nature of the linkage between the behaviour of individual firms and the aggregate supply behaviour of the economy, for our purposes in this section, we will develop the shortrun aggregate supply curve based primarily on assumptions from R. E. Lucas's work.[3]

It is not the general price level P that a firm receives when it sells a product, instead the firm receives the price of its own product, p_i. Nor is it the general price level that a firm pays to a specific employee or to a specific input supplier when it purchases inputs. How then does the general level of prices affect the behaviour of any individual firm when it decides what to produce or how much to offer for sale? When an individual firm's price increases, the firm is presented with a problem. It may interpret the increase as a rise in its price relative to all other prices and costs in society (p_r), or it may view the price rise as being nothing more than an increase in its price to keep pace with inflation. Will a firm behave differently in response to an increase in its price if it interprets that increase to be nothing more than keeping up with the prevailing level of inflation in the economy? How does the individual firm extract information from an increase in its price to interpret it as a rise in its price relative to other prices and costs?

To answer the first question, let's see how an individual firm behaves if the general price level P is known and if it is expected to remain constant in the near future. In other words, each firm expects the costs per unit for inputs used in production (wages, interest, rent, and the price of key inputs) to remain constant on average in the near future. Now assume that there is an increase in the price p_i received by each firm when it sells its product.[4] The cause of the increased price is not important at this stage, and we will explore it more fully later. For convenience the price increases could be viewed as the result of some increase in aggregate demand that simultaneously created temporary shortages

[3] Robert E. Lucas, *Studies in Business-Cycle Theory* (Cambridge, Mass.: M.I.T. Press, 1983).

[4] The designation of the firm's price for its own product as p_i may appear confusing but it allows for each firm in the economy to have a price different from all other firms. This notation becomes useful if different firms in the same industry have different prices, as sometimes occurs in oligopoly and monopolistically competitive markets. These market structures are discussed in Chapters 10 and 11. It should be noted that for perfectly competitive markets all firms in the same industry would face the same price, so p_i would be the same for a number of firms.

in a number of markets. The result is that the expected profit from increased production has increased for each firm, and each will respond by increasing its output. If an individual firm's price increases, and if the firm believes that the price increase will lead to increased profits, it will bring forth increased levels of production in the aggregate.

In our simple example, individual firms increase their production because they interpret an increase in the price of their own product p_i as an increase in the price of their product, *ceteris paribus*. It may have occurred to you that when each firm increases its price at the same time, there must have been an increase in the general price level for the whole economy, P. This is correct; when the prices for products making up a sizable portion of the aggregate real output of the economy increase, there is an increase in the general price level. Statistically the exact size of the increase, as measured by any particular price index, such as the GDP deflator or the CPI, depends on the weightings assigned to the various products. In our example, as individual firms' prices increased, this caused the general price level to increase, even though individual firms expected the general level of prices to remain unchanged. Thus, if firms interpret an increase in their own product's price as an increase in their price, *ceteris paribus* they will respond by increasing their production. When this happens, an increase in the general price level P will cause aggregate output Y to move in the same direction as the movement in the general price level. This aggregate supply behaviour is illustrated by the curve AS_1 in Figure 24-3.

By extension, if the general level of prices in the economy is increasing, then a relatively large number of firms will be facing increases in the price of the products that they produce. As long as these firms believe that the price of their output will rise relative to the price of their inputs and other prices in society, they will perceive the increase in the general price level as leading to higher profit margins for them. In turn, they will increase production in response to the increase in their own price. Under these circumstances an increase in production will take place even if each firm does not believe

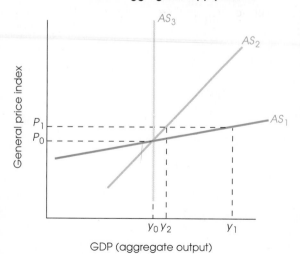

FIGURE 24-3 **The Effect of the Information Extraction Problem on the Slope of the Aggregate Supply Curve**

When the price that an individual firm sells its products for increases, the firm is presented with a problem. It must interpret the increase as either a rise in its price relative to all other prices and costs in society (p_r), or it must view it as nothing more than an increase in its price just to keep pace with inflation. The way a firm interprets the amount of relative price movement coming from a change in the price of its own product is known as the information extraction problem. If there is a very small information extraction problem, firms will view the rise in their own product's price as a rise in their price *ceteris paribus*. As a result they will increase production within the limits of their plant capacity and technology. This is illustrated by AS_1. If the information extraction problem is moderate, firms interpret an increase in their own product's price to be partly caused by an increase in the relative price and partly by an upward movement in the general price level. Their response in increasing output will be less, as shown in AS_2. If firms suffer from a severe information extraction problem, they view the rise as entirely attributable to the increase in the general price level—that is, they believe that their relative price has not changed. In this case they will not change output in response to the rise in price, as shown by AS_3.

that its price is increasing, *ceteris paribus*. All that is necessary for individual firms to be willing to increase output in response to an increase in the price of their own products is that each firm interpret the increase in the price of their product as an increase in the **relative price** of its product, p_r. In other words, a rise in the price that a firm charges will cause output to increase as long as the firm views the increase as a rise in its price relative to the general level of prices throughout the economy and specifically as a rise in its price in comparison to its costs of production. In this example, as in the previous one, the aggregate output will vary directly with the general price level P. Once again, the aggregate supply curve will be positively sloped. However, the firms in this case view only some portion of the price increase facing them as an increase in the relative price of their product, so they will be less responsive in increasing their output than in our earlier example. We can indicate the link between the increase in the individual price and the relative price by saying that the firm accepts only some portion α of the increase in the price of its product Δp_i as the increase in the relative price of its product Δp_r. In a situation where firms view some part of a price increase as being relative and some part of a price increase as simply keeping up with the move in the general price level (where $0 < \alpha < 1$), the aggregate supply will be positively sloped. It will be less responsive than if the firms view all of the increase in the price of their product as a relative price increase. This type of response is illustrated by aggregate supply curve AS_2 in Figure 24-3.

   In AS_1 each firm believed that if they increased their price by 4 ($\alpha = 1$), all other prices would remain constant, resulting in a rise in the relative price of its product p_r by $4 \times \Delta p_i$. By contrast, on AS_2 each firm believes that only three quarters of any increase in the price of its own product Δp_i represents an increase in its relative price Δp_r. In others words, α is three quarters ($\alpha = .75$). Thus if the firm increases its price by 4, it will infer that its relative price will increase by only 3 ($\Delta p_r = .75 \times 4$).

   Now assume that firms interpret any increase in the price of their products as a reflection of the movement in the general level of prices in the economy. These firms expect that when the price of their own product increases, in a very short time, the prices that they pay for their inputs (wages, interest, rent, and the price of important commodities) will all rise by a proportionate amount. Thus, each firm believes that the increase in the price of its own product will not lead to increased profits. Under these circumstances, each firm will not change its production level in response to a change in the price of its product, since it is not expecting the change in its price to be reflected in increased profits. Using the equation, we can substitute $\alpha = 0$. The result is that the firm increasing its price by 4 believes that none of the increase is an increase in its price relative to other prices ($\Delta p_r = 0 \times 4$). If a large number of firms, supplying a relatively large portion of the economy's total production, were to behave this way, then as the price of their products increased or decreased there would be a change in the general price level but it would induce no change in the level of aggregate output, as is shown by aggregate supply curve AS_3 in Figure 24-3.

The Importance of Diminishing Returns

   Even if individual firms interpret all of any increase in the price of their own product's price p_i to be an increase in the relative price of their product p_r, we would expect aggregate supply to have some slight positive slope.

Checkpoint 24-2

Assume that a firm receives a specific price p_i for its product and it pays a specific price p_z for the only input it uses. Explain why a change in the GDP deflator might affect how much the firm is willing to supply at p_i. Do you think that the recent inflation rate might influence the firm's decision? How?

We have already explained that individual firms will be fairly responsive in increasing output when their price changes if they view the increase in their price as entirely relative. Although the output may be responsive, it is not without limit. The amount by which a firm can adjust its output depends on many technical factors as well as the willingness of decision makers to accept the price increase as a rise in the relative price. Although factories and office complexes can often handle a wide range of output, in the shortrun, the amount of capacity that a plant was designed to produce will restrict the physical capability of a firm to expand its output beyond some level without experiencing some cost increases due to overcrowding of production facilities, waiting time for machinery, or shortages of inventory storage space. These diminishing returns and bottlenecks lead to increased cost per unit as output increases. Firms will try to recover the increased costs through higher prices.[5] Thus, assuming that the cost per unit of their inputs has not changed and assuming constant or decreasing returns to scale in the longrun, we expect that firms would increase output only as their price increases even if they interpret all of the increase in the price of their own product to be an increase in the relative price of their product.

Review of Aggregate Supply and Aggregate Demand

To review, the slope of the aggregate supply curve depends on two things. The first is the extent to which firms interpret a change in the price of the product that they supply p_i to be a change in the relative price of their product p_r. The more firms interpret the increase in the price, their own product p_i to be an increase in the relative price of their product p_r, the more horizontal the aggregate supply curve. Conversely, the more firms interpret an increase in the price of their own product p_i to be nothing more than an increase in the general price level, the less they view it as a change in the relative price of their product p_r. If firms interpret a change in the price of their own price as having no effect on the relative price of their product, then the aggregate supply curve will be vertical. In other words, in the equation

$$\Delta p_r = \Delta \alpha p_i$$
$$\text{where } \alpha = 0$$

This is thought to occur if firms have what is described as a serious information extraction problem. Remember, in the shortrun the costs faced by the individual firm do not change (by assumption the input costs are fixed in the shortrun), it is only the individual firm's perception of what will happen to its unit costs and the prices charged by competitors that is changing. When firms see the prices of their own products change, they cannot extract the relevant information about the change in their own prices relative to other prices. This can occur if a country has experienced unpredictable swings in its inflation rates or unpredictable shifts in demand between various industries.

The second thing that affects the slope of the aggregate supply curve is the law of diminishing returns. The more severe the overcrowding and bottlenecks confronted by firms as they try to increase production from existing facilities, the steeper their individual supply responses and the steeper the aggregate supply

---

[5]Students may wish to read the technical reasons for diminishing returns discussed in Chapter 8.

curve. Conversely, the less severe the diminishing returns effects experienced by firms as they expand production, the shallower the aggregate supply curve.

Two Special Cases—The Classical and Keynesian Aggregate Supply Curves

In the last example, the aggregate supply was vertical because firms expected the general price level P to increase in the same proportion as the increase in their own price p_i. There is a similar, although much older, explanation that results in a vertical aggregate supply curve.

Using the logic of Say's Law (explained in Chapter 21), the classical economists of the last century claimed that the economy would naturally gravitate to equilibrium output with full employment. Under these circumstances, most firms would be operating at or close to plant capacity. If demand increased and there was an increase in the price of a large number of products, the majority of firms could not simultaneously expand production. Thus, as prices rose the level of aggregate output would remain constant. Conversely, the classical economists claimed that if there were a decrease in aggregate demand, firms would decrease their prices in order to maintain their sales. This would allow firms to continue to operate at full capacity, spreading their fixed costs over a higher level of output and maintaining lower average costs. This means that in the aggregate, the level of output will not change in response to a change in

---

FIGURE 24-4   Horizontal AS_K and Vertical AS_C

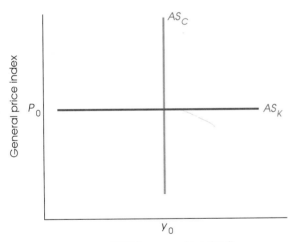

GDP (aggregate output)

Classical economists, using the logic of Say's Law, claimed that the economy would naturally gravitate to equilibrium output at a potential GDP with full employment. Under their circumstances, most firms would be operating at or close to plant capacity. If demand increased and there was an increase in the price of a large number of products, the majority of firms could not simultaneously expand production. Thus, as prices rose the level of aggregate output would remain constant. Conversely, if there were a decrease in aggregate demand, the classical economists claimed that firms would decrease their prices in order to maintain their sales. This results in a vertical aggregate supply curve shown by AS_C. With the Keynesian aggregate supply curve AS_K, it is theoretically possible to have a perfectly horizontal aggregate supply curve. In this case we assume that most firms are operating with a large amount of extra unused plant capacity and they believe the general price level will remain constant in the near future. Firms can respond to increased demand by increasing production without increasing their prices. Thus, the aggregate supply curve under these conditions would be horizontal, as illustrated by AS_K.

the general level of prices in the economy. The resulting **classical aggregate supply curve** was vertical, and is illustrated as AS_C in Figure 24-4.

Because the classical aggregate supply curve was vertical, there was a tendency to call any vertical aggregate supply curve (i.e., AS_3 in Figure 24-3) a classical aggregate supply curve. There is an important theoretical difference between the aggregate supply curve AS_3, discussed earlier, and the classical aggregate supply curve AS_C in Figure 24-4. In the case of the classical aggregate supply curve, the assumption is made that the economy is at full employment. Thus, the economy may have other problems that involve policy initiatives—such as inflation or some problem with interest rates or the exchange rate of the nation's currency on international markets—but it cannot have an unemployment problem. In short, under the assumptions of the classical theory the economy normally reaches equilibrium at potential output with only frictional unemployment, as discussed in Chapter 20.

By contrast the modern derivation of the vertical aggregate supply curve AS_3 was the result of firms believing that a change in their own price Δp_i was nothing more than a rise in the general price level ΔP, so $\Delta p_r = 0$. This will happen anytime firms suffer from a severe information extraction problem and interpret that their relative price has not changed, $\alpha = 0$, so $\Delta p_r = 0 \times \Delta p_i$. Unfortunately, there is nothing to require that the economy will gravitate to full employment in the shortrun under this expectations-based theory. Firms can mistake a change in their price p_i that really is a change in their relative price p_r if the economy is in a state of flux with rapidly changing patterns of demand or if the economy has had volatile and variable inflation in the recent past. This difference between classical theory and modern expectations theory concerning the reason why the aggregate supply curve might be vertical has important implications for the use of government fiscal policy in the shortrun.

In one special case, attributed to John Maynard Keynes, and called the **Keynesian aggregate supply curve** AS_K, it is theoretically possible to have a perfectly horizontal aggregate supply curve. There is not much likelihood of this curve existing in normal circumstances in the economy. Like many other theoretical tools throughout the sciences and social sciences, it serves as a useful abstraction to check the behaviour of other variables. This curve and its behaviour were implicitly used in the analysis of fiscal policy in the last chapter and will be reviewed more explicitly in this chapter before moving to more complex aggregate supply curves.

We have demonstrated earlier that the slope of aggregate supply is affected if a firm's responsiveness to a price increase is affected by its interpretation of the relative price change and the extent to which the firm experiences diminishing returns. Under the special assumption that most firms in the economy are operating with a large amount of extra unused plant capacity and that most firms are not expecting the general price level to increase at all in the near future, the aggregate supply curve will be horizontal. These were in fact the kinds of conditions experienced by many firms during the early years of the Great Depression of the 1930s. In this situation, if there is an increase in aggregate demand (for example, coming from expansionary fiscal policy), then firms can respond to the larger markets that they face by increasing production without increasing their prices. Thus, the aggregate supply curve under these conditions would be horizontal (perfectly elastic with respect to the general price index). This supply curve AS_K is shown in Figure 24-4.

Possible Causes of Shifts of the AS Curve

There are a number of reasons why the *AS* curve can shift. Among the most important are changes in input prices (such as fuel prices), changes in productivity, changes in the availability of resources (the labour force, important natural resources, and the capital stock of the country), and changes in certain kinds of taxes.

The *AS* curve will shift to the right and downward as a result of the introduction of new and better technology and higher resource productivity, increases in the supply of resources (including labour), decreases in the price per unit of resources, decreases in tax rates paid by the firms or their input suppliers, or any increase in the profit that firms can *expect* to earn from a particular activity. Conversely, the *AS* curve will shift to the left or upward as a result of a loss of technology and lower resource productivity, decreases in the supply of resources (including labour), increases in the price per unit of resources, increases in tax rates paid by the firms or their input suppliers, or any decrease in the profit that firms can *expect* to earn from a particular activity.

Changes in Input Prices

We have emphasized that in the shortrun input prices are assumed to remain unchanged. They are among the other things assumed to remain the same when there is movement along the *AS* curve. Our discussion of market demand and supply curves in Chapter 4 suggests immediately that a change in any of those other things, such as input prices, will cause a shift in the *AS* curve.

One particularly important input price is the money wage rate. Given the prices firms are receiving for their products, if workers demand and get higher money wages, firms will find their profits reduced. Consequently, whatever their current output levels, firms will only be willing to continue producing at those levels if they receive higher prices. Therefore, whatever the real GDP, the associated price level will have to be higher if the economy's firms are to continue to produce that level of real GDP. Thus, the *AS* curve will shift up, such as from AS_0 to AS_1 in Figure 24-5.

For example, suppose the economy's firms had been willing to produce the real GDP y_0 at price level P_0 prior to the increase in money wages, corresponding to point a on AS_0. After the money wage increase they will be willing to produce y_0 only if the general price level is P_1, corresponding to point b on AS_1 in Figure 24-5. Equivalently, prior to the money wage increase, the economy's firms were willing to produce a real GDP level y_1 at general price level P_1, corresponding to point c on AS_0. After the increase they are only willing to produce a smaller real GDP level y_0 at the general price level P_1, corresponding to point b on AS_1.

An increase in money wages or any other input price will cause an upward shift in the *AS* curve. A decrease in money wages or any other input price will shift the *AS* curve downward.

Changes in Productivity

Another important item assumed to remain the same along the *AS* curve is technology. An improvement in technology is one of the reasons why labour

FIGURE 24-5   The Effect of an Increase in Input Prices on Aggregate Supply

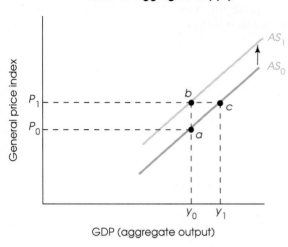

An increase in the price of one or more inputs will cause profits to decrease. Assume that money wages increase. Firms will only be willing to continue producing at their current output levels if they receive higher prices. Therefore, whatever the real GDP, the associated price level will have to be higher if the economy's firm are to continue to produce that level of real GDP. If firms had been willing to produce the real GDP y_0 at price level P_0 prior to the increase in money wages, corresponding to point a on AS_0, after the increase they will produce y_0 only if the general price level is P_1, corresponding to point b on AS_1. Looked at another way, prior to the money wage increase, firms were willing to produce a real GDP level y_1 at general price level P_1, corresponding to point c on AS_0. After the increase they are only willing to produce a smaller real GDP level y_0 at the general price level P_1, corresponding to point b on AS_1.

productivity increases. As a result of improved technology each worker can produce more. Given money wage rates and the prices of other inputs, this means that production costs per unit of output decrease whenever advances in technology increase the productivity of labour. The economy's firms are therefore willing and able to produce and sell their products at lower prices. Moreover, given the size of the labour force and the quantity of the economy's other resources, the maximum amount of output the economy can produce is increased. Consequently, the AS curve shifts downward and to the right, such as from AS_0 to AS_1 in Figure 24-6.

Changes in Labour Force and Capital Stock

If the size of the economy's labour force and its stock of capital increase, there will be an increase in the aggregate real GDP that the economy can produce.

FIGURE 24-6   An Increase in Aggregate Supply

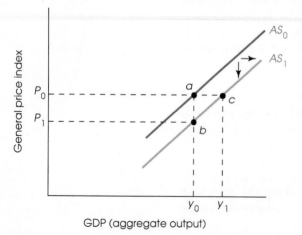

Improvements in technology, increased productivity, increases in the size of the labour force, reductions in the marginal tax rate, or decreases in input prices increase profits at a given output and price combination, point a. Firms are able to produce and sell their products at lower prices. Provided there is sufficient competition, this increased ability to supply will cause output to increase at the same price. The effect is represented by a shift to the right from point a on AS_0 to point c on AS_1. Moreover, if the increased profits set off competitive price cutting among firms, then a given output y_0 that was available at point a at P_0 on AS_0 before the increase in aggregate supply will now be available at a lower price level P_1 at point b on AS_1.

This will cause the AS curve to shift rightward, such as from AS_0 to AS_1 in Figure 24-6.

Note that for any level of aggregate output y_0 the point on AS_0 is higher than the corresponding point on AS_1. This reflects the need for a higher level of prices, P_0 as compared to P_1, in order to produce a given level of real output when the capital stock or the labour force is smaller. This is explained by recalling that when output is increased, individual firms face diminishing returns—production becomes more difficult and costly as the economy gets closer to full capacity. With a larger labour force or more capital stock, these difficulties do not become as severe until higher levels of real GDP are reached.

Changes in Taxes

In the 1970s Arthur Laffer and a number of economists, usually referred to as *supply-siders,* investigated how changes in taxes affect aggregate supply. Supply-siders argue that lower tax rates, particularly lower tax rates on income earned from supplying labour services, give higher after-tax rewards or greater incentives to work, save, and invest. The economy's capacity to produce and supply goods and services is increased if people respond to these incentives. Other things being equal, a decrease in the tax rate will cause the AS curve to shift down and to the right, such as from AS_0 to AS_1 in Figure 24-6. Conversely, supply-siders argue that any increase in tax rates drives a wedge between the cost that firms must pay in order to use a factor of production and the price the resource supplier receives from a firm in return for supplying factor services. If tax rates on income earned by supplying labour increase, this reduces the after-tax compensation for working and, to the extent that income serves as the incentive to supply labour services, causes a reduction of the amount of labour available at each money wage rate. With less labour working at each wage rate, the aggregate output decreases and the AS curve shifts to the left, as illustrated in Figure 24-5.

Macroeconomic Comparative Statics

The analysis of aggregate income determination when there are changes in the aggregate price level is called **macroeconomic comparative statics**.

Our analysis of the determination of aggregate income, output, and employment in Chapters 21, 22, and 23 assumed that production could and would increase or decrease in response to changes in expenditure without there being any changes in the general price level. Implicitly this means that the aggregate supply curve AS was horizontal—the Keynesian aggregate supply. The general price level therefore remained unchanged whenever the AD curve shifted, as in Figure 24-7, which is a reproduction of Figure 21-3. Now we can examine how that analysis is modified when the general price level P can vary with changes in output y.

Figure 24-7 shows the change in real GDP at a given price level in response to an exogenous, or autonomous, expenditure increase (in consumption, investment, government, or export spending) or a decrease in taxes, or imports, which shifts the aggregate expenditure schedule upward and the AD curve rightward. Such a shift is repeated again in Figure 24-8, but now allowing for the price level

FIGURE 24-7   The Relationship Between Shifts in the Aggregate Expenditure Schedule and Shifts in the AD Curve

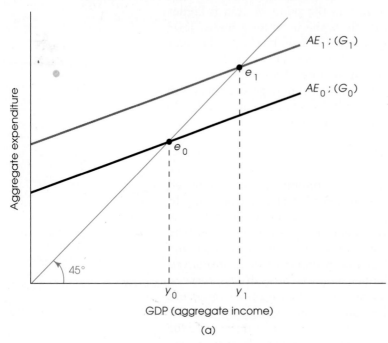

(a)

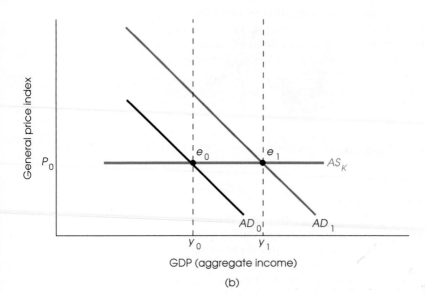

(b)

Assume a Keynesian aggregate supply curve AS_K and an initial equilibrium between AS_k and AD_0 at point e_0. An exogenously caused increase in aggregate expenditure shifts AE_0 to AE_1 in frame (a) and shifts AD_0 to AD_1 in frame (b). This increases equilibrium real GDP from y_0 associated with point e_0 to y_1 associated with point e_1. Given a Keynesian aggregate supply curve AS_K, the general price level remains P_0. Conversely, an exogenously caused reduction in consumption, investment, government spending, or net export expenditure, or an increase in tax rates shifts the aggregate expenditure schedule downward and the aggregate demand curve leftward, resulting in a reduction in real GDP at a constant price level.

FIGURE 24-8   **The Change in Real GDP and the Price Level Due to Exogenous Expenditure Change**

Initially, equilibrium real GDP is y_0 and the equilibrium price level is P_0 at point e_0 in both frame (a) and frame (b). An exogenous expenditure increase shifts the aggregate expenditure schedule upward from AE_0 to AE_0' [arrow 1, frame (a)] and the AD curve rightward from AD_0 to AD_1. If the economy's firms were willing to increase output in response to the increase in aggregate demand at price level P_0, real GDP would increase from y_0 to y_0' [arrow 1, frame (b)], an amount equal to the simple or *fixed-price* multiplier effect. However, because the AS curve is upward sloping, there is instead an excess expenditure schedule to shift downward to AE_1 [arrow 2, frame (a)] and movement up along the AD_1 curve [arrow 2, frame (b)], restoring equilibrium at point e_1 [frames (a) and (b)], at real GDP level y_1, and price level P_1. The multiplier effect on real GDP (equal to the increase from y_0 to y_1) is smaller when the price level rises than it is (y_0 to y_0') when the price level remains unchanged.

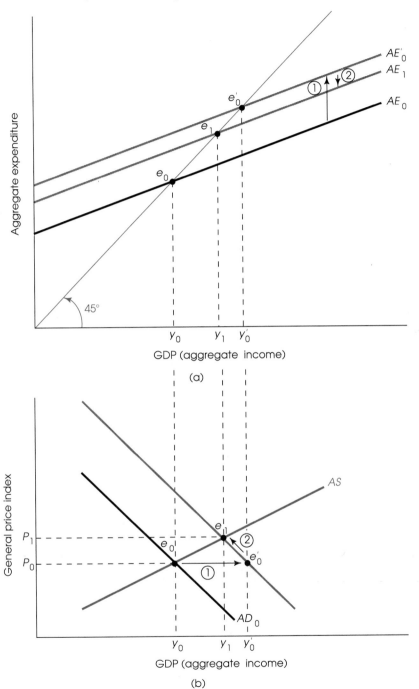

to change along an upward-sloping *AS* curve. The adjustment can be broken into two steps.

Step 1. The aggregate expenditure function *AE* shifts upward from AE_0 to AE_0' in frame (a) of Figure 24-8, causing the *AD* curve to shift rightward from AD_0 to AD_1 as shown in frame (b). If the firms in the economy were willing and able to increase output at the existing general price level P_0 in response to the increase in aggregate demand, real GDP would increase from y_0 to y_0' corresponding to a move from point e_0 to point e_0' The adjustment would be exactly the same as that already described in Figure 24-7. The increase in real GDP from y_0 to y_0' would be equal to the multiplier effect discussed in Chapter 23. Now, however, because the *AS* curve is upward sloping, the firms in the economy are not willing or able to produce a real GDP greater than y_0 at the existing price level P_0. Therefore, at P_0 there is an excess aggregate demand for total output equal to the distance between point e_0 and e_0' in frame (b).

Step 2. The excess aggregate demand causes the general price level to increase. This has two separate effects, a *movement along* the aggregate supply curve to the *right* and a *movement along* the new aggregate demand curve AD_1 to the *left*. The movement along the aggregate supply curve is relatively straightforward and was described earlier. It is the effect of the movement along the aggregate demand curve AD_1 that is of more concern to us. The increase in the general price level will cause the aggregate expenditure function to *shift downward* from AE_0' in frame (a), which causes a *movement along* the AD_1 curve, frame (b), as was previously shown in Figure 23-1. The adjustment is complete once the aggregate expenditure function has shifted down to AE_1 in frame (a), and the general price level has risen to P_1, corresponding to the intersection of AD_1 and AS at point e_1 in frame (b). Compared to the increase in real GDP that occurs when the price level remains unchanged (from y_0 to y_0') real GDP now increases by a smaller amount (from y_0 to y_1) because some of the initial increase in aggregate demand is absorbed or reduced by the increase in the price level.

Consider what would have happened if the aggregate demand curve had intersected a vertical or classical *AS*. Figure 21-2 showed that a shift to the left in aggregate demand from AD_1 to AD_2 resulted in a decrease in the price level with no increase in equilibrium income. Conversely, if aggregate demand were to shift to the right while intersecting a vertical aggregate supply curve, it would cause an increase in the general price level while leaving output constant. The multiplier effect on real GDP is actually zero on a vertical aggregate supply curve and classical aggregate supply curve. The implication of this is significant for two reasons. First, if the economy were on a vertical aggregate supply curve, expansionary fiscal policy of the type we explored in Chapter 23 would be ineffective in increasing GDP and reducing the unemployment. Second, if the economy were on a vertical aggregate supply curve and were also experiencing inflation, reduced government spending or tax increases might reduce the inflation *without* causing any reduction in equilibrium income or employment.

To summarize: If the economy is on a vertical or classical aggregate supply curve, the multiplier effect of an exogenously caused change in aggregate expenditure is zero. When the economy is operating along an upward-sloping aggregate supply curve, an exogenously caused change in aggregate expenditure will have a smaller multiplier effect on equilibrium real GDP than when

Checkpoint 24-3

Explain why exogenously caused changes in aggregate expenditure cause the *AD* curve to shift. What would be the effect on the *AD* curve of a $10 billion increase in government expenditures financed by a $10 billion increase in lump-sum taxes?

the economy is operating along the horizontal or Keynesian aggregate supply curve. Therefore, the size of the multiplier effect varies *inversely* with the slope of the aggregate supply curve.

Fiscal Policy in a Flexible Price Model

Our discussion in Chapter 23 of the effects of government spending, taxation, and budget policy on the economy presented a strictly Keynesian point of view. In particular, according to the Keynesian view, taxes affect only the expenditure side of the economy. By causing a deficit (or surplus) in the government's budget, tax changes increase (or decrease) aggregate expenditure and aggregate demand, thus increasing (or decreasing) aggregate income, output, and employment. Moreover, we have seen that according to the Keynesian analysis, a dollar of government expenditure has a more expansionary impact on the economy than a dollar of tax cuts because the government spends the whole dollar, whereas taxpayers save part of any tax cut.

Tax Rates and Incentives

Supply-side economics stresses cutting income tax *rates*. (Remember, tax rates are not the same thing as tax *revenues*, the amount of money collected from taxpayers.) In particular, supply-siders argue that marginal tax rates are what must be reduced. The **marginal tax rate** is defined as follows:

$$\text{Marginal tax rate} = \frac{\Delta \text{ in tax liability}}{\Delta \text{ in income}}$$

The marginal tax rate indicates how much of an additional dollar of one's income (the marginal or last dollar earned) must be paid in taxes. For example, if the marginal tax rate is .34, 34 cents of an *additional* dollar of income must be given to the government, leaving the individual with 66 cents of after-tax income. Supply-siders argue that a reduction of marginal tax rates will increase work effort, encourage more saving and investment, improve resource allocation, and reduce the amount of resources devoted to tax-avoidance activities. Each of these effects of reduced marginal tax rates will tend to increase the economy's aggregate supply of goods and services. Let's consider why.

Tax Rate Effects on Work Effort

When an individual considers whether or not to work harder or longer, it is assumed by some economists that the relevant question is, What will be the additional after-tax income, or take-home pay, resulting from the additional effort? The larger the marginal tax rate, the smaller the after-tax reward and therefore the less the incentive to work harder or longer. This consideration is relevant not only to people contemplating the merits of additional work effort in their current jobs (more overtime, for example) but also to those contemplating promotion possibilities, career choices, new business ventures, and other forms of innovative work effort. The assumption that higher marginal tax rates reduce the incentive to work and increase the misallocation of society's resources by encouraging resources to seek tax avoidance provides us with an opportunity to investigate the supply-side interpretations of government tax policy.

Suppose that the marginal tax rate on additional income above $30,000 were .95 (a marginal rate similar to the rates prevailing at this income level under the progressive tax structure in Sweden). Few people would want to put in the additional time and effort, acquire the additional training and education, or take on the additional responsibility and risks necessary to earn an income greater than $30,000 if income were the main reward for taking the training or doing the job. Supply-siders argue that higher marginal tax rates encourage people to take more leisure time and work less. This can occur in many ways: a reduction in overtime, earlier retirement, more absenteeism, or less willingness to undertake other innovative (often risky and demanding) forms of work effort. Supply-siders argue that a reduction in the marginal tax rate stimulates work effort and will cause a shift to the right in the position of the aggregate supply curve.

Tax Rate Effects on Investment

Business willingness to invest in capital goods is directly dependent on the after-tax rate of return on the dollars invested in capital goods. A lower after-tax rate of return reduces the expected profit in the future from a given investment project and reduces the after-tax profits that firms receive from current assets. In Canada retained or undistributed corporate profits are, like savings, a major source of funds used to finance capital formation. Therefore an increase in the marginal tax rate that reduced the expected future profits or the present retained profits of businesses would reduce investment. Supply-siders argue that a reduction of marginal tax rates stimulates investment spending, increasing capital formation and thereby increasing the aggregate supply.

Tax Rate Effects on Resource Allocation

High marginal tax rates encourage the creation and use of tax avoidance, and loopholes in the tax law provide legal ways in which payment of taxes at going marginal tax rates can be avoided. We should stress that some tax loopholes may be deliberately created by political decision makers to correct for market failures or to channel spending into particular regions or industries. The prevailing mainstream view in economics is that where tax avoidance occurs simply to avoid high marginal tax rates, this activity causes inefficiency in society's resource allocation in two ways. First, workers and investors direct resources into activities where after-tax rates of return are relatively high only because of the special advantages created by the loopholes. Such tax advantages are available to those investing in Canadian films, the oil exploration industry, and certain types of stocks in Canadian corporations. As a result, it is possible that the economy devotes more resources to these activities than it would under normal market activity. At the same time, it incurs a relatively high opportunity cost in terms of other productive activities not offering such generous tax advantages. The second way the loopholes create misallocation of resources is that seeking out and taking advantage of complicated tax loopholes typically requires the use of trained lawyers and accountants. Higher marginal tax rates make it more worthwhile for potential taxpayers to employ such services in order to avoid taxes. According to the supply-side view it is probable that billions of dollars' worth of highly skilled and educated legal and accounting services are employed annually in this fashion—labour that could be employed in producing other goods and services more useful from society's viewpoint.

Supply-siders argue that reductions in marginal tax rates would reduce the "payoff" from tax avoidance and the misallocation of resources employed in searching for this payoff. They claim that reduced marginal tax rates would lead to a more efficient allocation of resources, thereby increasing the economy's capacity to supply goods.[6] This increased efficiency in resource usage would shift the aggregate supply curve to right.

To summarize, supply-siders argue that reducing marginal tax rates will shift the aggregate supply to the right because it stimulates the work effort, encourages investment because of increases in after-tax profits, and stimulates a more efficient allocation of resources through reducing the payoff from loopholes and reducing the use of resources to engage in tax-avoidance activities.

The Effect of a Tax Rate Reduction

Supply-siders argue that the increase in the economy's supply of total output resulting from reductions in marginal tax rates will put downward pressure on prices and hence help to fight inflation. This proposition can be illustrated in terms of the economy's aggregate supply curve.

Suppose that the economy initially has an equilibrium level of real GDP y_0 and price level p_0 determined by the intersection of AD and AS_0 at point a in Figure 24-9. Suppose that there is a reduction in marginal tax rates. For the moment, let's focus only on the effect on the aggregate supply curve. Since marginal tax rates are now lower, workers, other resource suppliers, and firms will get to keep a larger fraction of the dollars they earn from the sale of the goods and services they produce. Suppliers can supply the same quantity of goods as before, but they can now sell the goods at a lower price and still receive the same after-tax income. The reduction of marginal tax rates could shift the aggregate supply curve AS_0 downward to the position AS_1.

As a consequence of the shift in the AS curve from AS_0 to AS_1 the economy's equilibrium level of real GDP increases from y_0 to y_1 while its equilibrium price level falls from P_0 to P_1, corresponding to the intersection of AD and AS_1 at point b. We now see why supply-siders argue that reducing marginal tax rates could reduce inflation at the same time as it increases employment.

A decrease in the marginal tax rate will produce a downward shift in the position of the aggregate supply curve. If the aggregate supply curve were perfectly horizontal (the Keynesian aggregate supply), there would still be a decrease in the general price index and a rise in equilibrium aggregate output. This is illustrated in Figure 24-9, frame (b). As the marginal tax rate is reduced, the aggregate supply curve shifts from AS_{K_0} to AS_{K_1}. As before, when the aggregate supply was positively sloped, with AD and AS_{K_0}, the equilibrium is at the general price level P_0 and GDP of y_0, point a. After the reduction in the marginal tax

---

[6]Department of Finance, *Goods and Services Tax, Technical Paper* (Ottawa: Department of Finance, August 1989), pp. 29–37.

FIGURE 24-9 **The Supply-Side Effect of a Decrease in the Marginal Tax Rate**

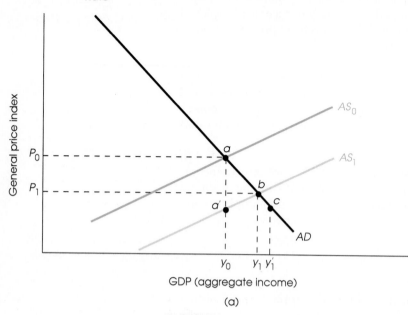

(a)

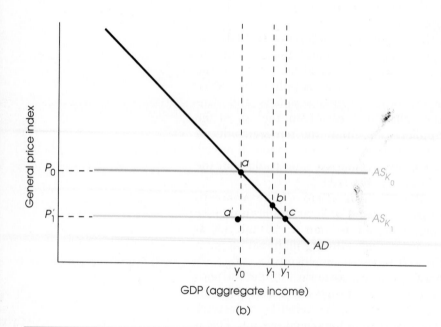

(b)

Assume the economy initially has an equilibrium level of real GDP y_0 and price level P_0 determined by the intersection of AD_0 and AS_0 at point a. Suppose that there is a reduction in marginal tax rates. Firms get to keep a larger fraction of their sales revenue. Consequently, they can supply the same quantity of goods at a lower price and still receive the same after-tax income. The reduction of marginal tax rates shifts the aggregate supply curve downward from AS_0 to the position AS_1 in both frame (a) and frame (b). Given the aggregate demand curve AD, real GDP increases from y_0 to y_1 and its equilibrium price level falls from P_0 to P_1, in frame (a).

If the aggregate supply curve were perfectly horizontal (the Keynesian aggregate supply), there would still be a decrease in the general price index and a rise in equilibrium aggregate output. This is illustrated in frame (b). As the marginal tax rate is reduced, the aggregate supply curve shifts from AS_{K_0}, to AS_{K_1}. The reduction in the marginal tax rate causes the aggregate supply curve to shift down by the same amount as it did in frame (a). Thus equilibrium moves from point a to point c in frame (b). Consequently, the output rises from y_0 to y_1' and the general price level decreases from P_0 to P_1', in frame (b).

FIGURE 24-10   **The Combined Demand-Side and Supply-Side Effects**

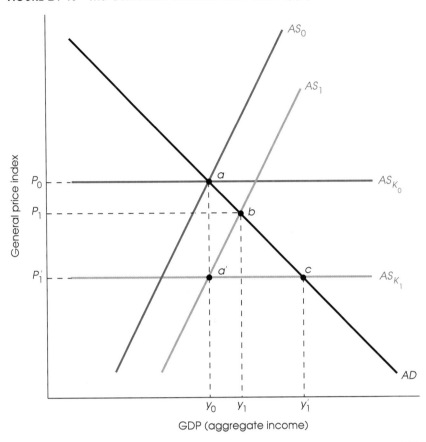

When the marginal tax is reduced, the aggregate supply curve shifts downward to the extent that the tax cut increases the ability of resource suppliers and firms to offer a given quantity for a lower price. Thus, a given reduction in the marginal tax rate will shift the AS curve down by the distance a to a'. This is shown by the shift down from AS_0 to AS_1 and the shift from AS_{K_0} to AS_{K_1}. The price level decreases and the output level increases as a result of the decrease in marginal tax rate in both cases. The magnitude of the effect of the reduction in the marginal tax rate is affected by the slope of the AS curve, however. If the aggregate supply curve is upward sloping, the price level decreases from P_0 to P_1. By comparison, if the aggregate supply curve is horizontal, the price level decreases from P_0 to P_1'. Similarly, in the case where the aggregate supply curve is positively sloped the equilibrium output increases from y_0 to y_1, while in the case of the horizontal aggregate supply curve output increases from y_0 to y_1'.

rate, the new equilibrium is at AD and AS_{K_1}, with a general price level of P_1' at point c.

What is not immediately apparent is that although a reduction in the marginal tax rate has the same general effect on the price index and the level of aggregate output, the magnitude of change is different. In Figure 24-10 we have combined frames (a) and (b) from Figure 24-9. When the marginal tax rate is reduced, the aggregate supply curve shifts downward to the extent that the tax cut increases the ability of resource suppliers and firms to offer a given quantity for a lower price. Thus, a given reduction in the marginal tax rate will shift the AS curve down by the distance a to a'. This is shown by the shift down from AS_0 to AS_1 and the shift from AS_{K_0} to AS_{K_1}. In both cases the price level decreases and the output level increases as a result of the decrease in marginal tax rate. The magnitude of the effect of the reduction in the marginal tax rate is affected by the slope of the AS curve, however. If the aggregate supply curve is upward sloping, the price level decreases from P_0 to P_1. By comparison, if the aggregate supply curve is horizontal, the price level decreases from P_0 to P_1'. Similarly, in the case where the aggregate supply curve is positively sloped the equilibrium output increases from y_0 to y_1, while in the case of the horizontal aggregate supply output increases from y_0 to y_1'.

A decrease in the marginal tax rate causes the aggregate supply curve to shift downward. Conversely, an increase in the marginal tax rate causes the aggregate supply curve to shift upward. Given a downward-sloping aggregate demand curve, a decrease in the marginal tax rate causes a decrease in the general price level and an increase in the output level. When the aggregate supply curve shifts, the size of the resulting change in the general price level and output level are inversely related to the slope of the aggregate supply curve. The steeper the aggregate supply curve, the smaller the changes in the general price level and output level resulting from a given shift in AS.

The graphs and analysis for this section have concentrated on the shift in aggregate supply caused by a change in the marginal tax rate. Remember from our earlier discussion that aggregate supply can shift for a variety of reasons. All these shifts would have effects on the equilibrium general price level and equilibrium output. Any increase in the marginal tax rate would cause the general price level to increase and the level of output to decrease. Similarly, anything else that causes the aggregate supply curve to shift upward [an increase in input prices, a decrease in resource availability (including labour force), or a decrease in factor productivity] will cause an increase in the general price level and decrease in the output level.

A downward shift in the aggregate supply curve will decrease the general price level and increase the level of output. Conversely, any upward shift in the aggregate supply curve will increase the general price level and decrease the level of output. The magnitudes of the changes in the general price level and output level caused by a given shift in aggregate supply will be larger if the aggregate supply curve has a small slope than if its slope is large.

Combining Supply-Side and Demand-Side Effects of Fiscal Policy

We will now combine the demand-side effects of a reduction in marginal tax rates, discussed in Chapter 23 and illustrated in Figure 23-5, with the supply-side effects discussed in this chapter and illustrated in Figure 24-10. Remember that the exact size of the shift of aggregate demand would depend on the size of the change in autonomous expenditure and the size of the multiplier. Similarly, the exact magnitude of the shift in aggregate supply would depend on the amount of impact of diminishing returns as production increases and on the severity of the information extraction problem. For simplicity we will limit our investigation to the directions of movement of the general level of prices and output that result from exogenously caused changes to both aggregate demand and aggregate supply.

On the demand side, a reduction in marginal tax rates will cause the aggregate demand curve to shift to the right from AD_0 to AD_1. On the supply side, the marginal tax rate reduction will cause the aggregate supply curve to shift downward from AS_0 to AS_1. In Figure 24-11 we have represented the effects of this combination of the shift in AS and the shift in AD on output and the general price level. Notice that in both frame (a) and frame (b) the AD curve shifts to the right and the AS curves down. In both cases the real GDP increases, from y_0 to y_1 in frame (a) and from y_0 to y_1' in frame (b). The reduction in the marginal tax rate produces effects on the aggregate demand and aggregate supply curves that, in the shortrun, will reinforce each other in making output

FIGURE 24-11   The Combined Demand-Side and Supply-Side Effect of a Reduction in Marginal Tax Rates

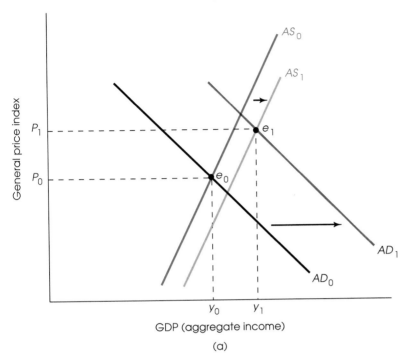

(a)

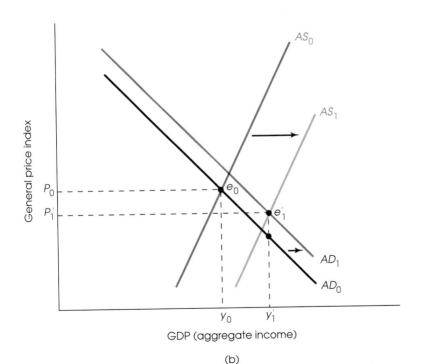

(b)

A reduction in marginal tax rates causes the economy's aggregate demand curve to shift to the right from AD_0 to AD_1 in frames (a) and (b), according to the demand-side view. The reduction in the marginal tax rate also causes the aggregate supply curve to shift downward from AS_0 to AS_1 in both frames (a) and (b), according to the supply-side view. When the AD curve shifts to the right from AD_0 to AD_1, real GDP increases from y_0 to y_1 in frame (a), or y_1' in frame (b). In frame (a) the general price level rises from P_0 to P_1. This is because in frame (a) we have made the shift to the right in the AD large enough to dominate the effect of the downward shift in AS sufficiently large, then the effect of the change in the general price level is reversed. In frame (b) the AS shifts to the right by enough to make the general price level decrease from P_0 to P_1'. A reduction in the marginal tax rate will normally make GDP increase, but the effect on the general price level will depend on the relative responses of AD and AS.

POLICY PERSPECTIVE

The Controversy over Demand-Side and Supply-Side Policy

Economists throughout the world have been working on finding empirical evidence for the responsiveness of aggregate demand and aggregate supply to such things as changes in the marginal tax rate and changes in the level of government spending since the 1950s. The evidence is often conflicting and ambiguous. In the early 1980s there was much optimism about governments in the United States and the United Kingdom using tax cuts and reductions in the size of the public debt to shift the aggregate supply downward. It was believed by many economists and policymakers at the time that a reduction in marginal tax rates and other tax reform would cause a relatively large increase in aggregate supply. It was also argued at the time that the increase in aggregate supply would compensate for any reductions to aggregate demand resulting from decreases in the government deficit that resulted from decreases in government spending on social programs.

The evidence throughout the decade was quite mixed. There was an impressive increase in GDP in the United States, but critics of supply-side theory claimed that this growth was the result of increases in defense spending, not the response to reduced taxes. To complicate things, attempts to reduce the government deficits during the 1980s in the United States, in Canada, and in most OECD countries were not

very effective. We will see in Chapter 25 that increases in the government deficit and growth in the public debt can, under some circumstances, lead to increases in interest rates. Proponents of supply-side theory argued that the reduced tax rates would have worked if the government had followed a low-interest-rate policy. Finally, despite the growth in GDP, the level of unemployment did not decrease by as much as either the Keynesians or the supply-side theorists had predicted.

The situation can be summed up by saying that the flexible price model has opened a new broad dimension to the role of fiscal policy. Economists agree on appropriate shortrun strategies for combatting unemployment or rises in the general price level if the responsiveness of aggregate demand and the responsiveness of aggregate supply resulting from the policy initiative are known. Much of the debate about the appropriate government policy to be followed and its likely effectiveness is really a debate about estimates of the relative responsiveness of aggregate demand and aggregate supply to some specific policy. To the extent that this is the case, research will help reduce the conflict over the years. This does not mean that consensus can be expected at some point in the future.

There will likely remain some fundamental bias by different economists and policy advisors over their willingness to intervene in the

working of the economy and the kinds of policies they favour when intervention takes place. For example, during the 1980s, in addition to their concerns about the technical ability of supply-side theory to reduce unemployment, Keynesians pointed out that a combined policy of decreasing social spending and reducing marginal tax rates would widen the gap between high-income people and low-income people. Many Keynesians opposed the measures, even though they might be effective in increasing employment and output, because of the implied social problems. Putting it another way, this group of Keynesians opposed the supply-side policies proposed at the time because these policies did not lead to an unambiguous improvement in social welfare. Similarly, some supply-side economists have opposed proposals to increase government spending or reduce taxes on specific industries, not simply because they felt that the policies would not work, but because they claimed that the policies would undermine the role of the market in coordinating economic behaviour. They feared that the increased use of the role of government to prevent unemployment might lead to a weakening of the individual initiative in people. The difference in these perspectives reflects a difference in the ethical values and the normative economics surrounding the issue, and it therefore cannot be solved by an appeal to facts.

increase. By contrast, the impact of the reduction in the marginal tax rate on the general price level is more complex. As the aggregate supply curve shifts down it will tend to decrease the general price level; however, the shift to the right of the aggregate demand curve will tend to increase the general price level. In Figure 24-11, frame (a), the shift right in the aggregate demand curve produces a more powerful effect on the general price level than the effect coming from the downward shift in aggregate supply. The result is that the price level rises from P_0 to P_1. By contrast, in Figure 24-11, frame (b), the effect of the downward shift in AS produces a more powerful effect on the general price level than does the rightward shift of AD. The result is that in frame (b) the general price level decreases from P_0 to P_1'.

The situation is therefore much more complex than the simple discussion of fiscal policy indicated in the previous chapter. The exact factors that will make the AS curve shift down by a little amount or a large amount in response to a decrease in the marginal tax rate (or because of some other discretionary action by the government) is not something we will discuss in this textbook. However, it is of great importance to more advanced levels of the discipline. If aggregate demand is relatively insensitive to discretionary actions taken by the government and if the aggregate supply curve is relatively responsive, then increases in output can be achieved by having the government stimulate the economy by giving tax cuts to producers and resource suppliers—the situation shown in Figure 24-10, frame (b). In contrast if the aggregate supply curve is relatively insensitive to discretionary government stimulus and if the aggregate demand curve is relatively sensitive, then increases in output, initiated by the government, could occur and be more easily achieved by policies aimed at directly stimulating demand. These policies might include increased expenditure on social programs, increased transfer payments to individuals, increased government spending for goods and services, or tax cuts aimed at getting consumers to spend more. The consequence would be that higher employment and output would also bring an increase in the general price level.

> **Checkpoint 24-4**
>
> How would a strictly demand-side or Keynesian point of view regarding the effects of an increase in marginal tax rates be modified when supply-side effects are taken into account?

Summary   *Read this*

1. An increase in the economy's price level causes the aggregate expenditure schedule to shift downward and the equilibrium level of real GDP to decrease, while a decrease in the price level shifts the aggregate expenditure schedule upward and increases equilibrium real GDP. The aggregate demand curve AD plots this relationship between the price level and the equilibrium level of real GDP. Movement along the AD curve thus shows the response of equilibrium real GDP to changes in the general level of prices in the economy.

2. The aggregate demand curve is downward sloping to the right because of the real balance effect, the interest rate effect, and the foreign purchase effect.

3. An exogenously caused increase in expenditure or a tax reduction will shift the AD curve rightward. An exogenously caused decrease in expenditure or a tax rate increase will shift the AD curve leftward.

4. The aggregate supply curve is the relationship between the general price level and the amount of output that firms are willing and able to produce. The aggregate supply curve is generally upward sloping to the right. This means that in the shortrun, increases in the general price level will cause increases in aggregate real output.

5. The aggregate supply curve is not the sum of individual supply curves. Firms receive a specific price p_i when they sell their product. Individual firms will increase production within the limits of their capacity in response to an increase in the price of their own product if they view the increase as an increase in their price relative to other prices (p_r). The Keynesian aggregate supply AS_K

is a special case in which the *AS* curve is horizontal. The classical aggregate supply AS_C is another special case, one in which the *AS* curve is vertical.

6. The *AD* and the *AS* curves jointly determine the equilibrium price level and the equilibrium level of real GDP. An exogenously caused expenditure change, or an exogenously caused tax rate change, will have a smaller multiplier effect the steeper the slope of the *AS* curve.

7. Supply-side fiscal policy concentrates on how decreases to the marginal tax rate might increase the after-tax rewards of supplying factors of production including labour effort. These increases to the incentives to supply factors of production and products would shift the aggregate supply curve down and cause an increase in equilibrium output and a decrease in the equilibrium price level.

8. When macroeconomic comparative statics are taken into account, fiscal policy becomes much more complex to analyze. The effectiveness of fiscal policy depends on the responsiveness of aggregate demand and the responsiveness of aggregate supply to the fiscal policy initiative.

9. The controversy over demand-side fiscal policy and supply-side fiscal policy depends on two things. First, there is a debate over the estimates of the responsiveness of aggregate demand and responsiveness of aggregate supply to any particular fiscal policy. Second, the choice of appropriate policy tools is also a normative issue that depends on ethical concerns about the fairness of policy.

Key Terms and Concepts

aggregate demand curve
  (*AD*)
aggregate supply curve (*AS*)
classical aggregate supply
  curve (*AS_C*)
demand shock
foreign purchases effect

information extraction
  problem
interest rate effect
Keynesian aggregate
  supply curve (*AS_K*)
macroeconomic
  comparative statics

marginal tax rate
real balance
  effect
relative price
stagflation
supply-side
  theory

Questions and Problems

1. Explain the derivation of the *AD* curve from the aggregate expenditure schedule.

2. Explain how each of the following would affect the *AD* curve: an exogenously caused increase in consumption expenditure, an exogenously caused reduction in tax rates, a decrease in the price level, an exogenously caused increase in government spending, an exogenously caused decrease in net export spending, an exogenously caused increase in investment spending.

3. Explain how a change in the GDP deflator could cause a movement along an aggregate supply curve. How would the slope of aggregate supply be affected by the information extraction problem?

4. Explain why the combination of a low information extraction problem coupled with a large amount of unused plant capacity might cause a very shallow slope for the aggregate supply curve.

5. Using Figure 24-9 or Figure 24-10, explain why a doubling in the price per barrel of oil in Western economies in 1979 might have contributed to an increase in the price level and increased unemployment in the early 1980s.

6. Suppose that a gradual aging of the population causes the labour force to shrink in relation to the population because of increased numbers of people retiring and thus leaving the workforce. Use Figure 24-9 to predict the effect of this action on the level of GDP, the effect on the price level, and the level of unemployment.

7. Assuming that the economy has a very severe information extraction problem, what is the likely effect of an increase in government spending by $10 billion? How does this compare to the effect of an increase of government spending by $10 billion if the economy were facing a classical aggregate supply curve?

8. Suppose that marginal tax rates on income earned from labour compensation (wages) were reduced. Rank the following as either "much" or "little" in terms of the effect the reduction would have on work effort: self-employed house painter, mail carrier, building contractor, police officer, senator, shoeshine person, barber, mayor, automobile company executive, librarian, realtor, owner of a machine-tool shop, majority stockholder in a chain of department stores, retired farmer with an RRSP.

9. Suppose that the marginal tax rate remained the same for income earned from labour (wages) but the government reduced the marginal tax rate for income earned from nonlabour sources (interest, dividends, and miscellaneous investment income). How would this tax change affect your answers to question 5?

10. Using Figure 24-11, explain the effect of the introduction of increased government spending on health care and education, which increases the participation rate and productivity of labour at the same time that it increases aggregate expenditure.

11. Given the following equations

$$AS : \quad Y = 100 + \alpha P$$
$$AD : \quad Y = 2A_0 - .5P$$

Find each of the following;
a. Assuming $\alpha = 1$, find aggregate supply for $P = 100$, 150, and 200.
b. Assuming $\alpha = 0$, find aggregate supply for $P = 100$, 150, and 200.
c. Assuming $\alpha = .5$, find aggregate supply for $P = 100$, 150, and 200.
d. Construct a graph illustrating the three aggregate supply curves.
e. Construct the graph for AD if $A_0 = 125$.
f. Find the equilibrium income and equilibrium price for each AS curve with AD.

Chapter 25

Budget Policy, Deficits, and the Public Debt

Does the federal deficit really matter? The Mulroney government emphasized its concern over the public debt and the interest paid to finance the public debt during the election campaign of 1988. Finance Minister Michael Wilson even used taxpayer money to pay for a national television advertising campaign during the Stanley Cup playoffs to warn of the possible burden on future generations of Canadians if he did not adopt tough budget measures to reduce the growth rate of the public debt. The ads also pointed out that interest on the public debt could divert tax revenue away from other government responsibilities, crowding out the government's own spending on necessary programs. While we will find out later in this chapter that this particular use of the term *crowding out* is an unusual way to describe crowding out, the finance minister's concern helps us appreciate the need to investigate the deficit, the debt, how the debt is financed, and what crowding out is.

A review of the daily newspapers in any Canadian city over the last decade reveals that the government deficit and the government debt were viewed as major factors contributing to the existence of high interest rates. These high interest rates were in turn blamed for cost-push inflation, and record numbers of bankruptcies of small businesses, farms, and individuals. There were dire predictions in the Canadian media, within the accounting profession, and by economic consultants that borrowing by the federal government to fund the deficit would crowd out productive private sector expenditure. It was claimed that in the longer term these high interest rates would reduce Canada's ability to compete with other countries. In this chapter we will analyze the impact of the government deficit and the cumulative public debt on the conduct of fiscal policy and the impact of the deficit and debt on private sector spending.

Nor is concern about the size of federal government deficits limited to Canada. In Australia, Japan, the United Kingdom, and the United States similar patterns of interest emerged as *real interest rates* rose to very high levels in the 1980s. In most of the industrialized countries of the world citizens and governments expressed misgivings and feelings of foreboding about the growing debts of their governments. There were similar predictions of crowding out of private investment and consumer spending on durables, and there were fears that the deficit would cause high interest rates, which in turn would result in a loss of international competitiveness. Few subjects receive more media attention or spark more public controversy than the federal government's budget, its budget deficits, or the government debt. In this chapter we will examine some of the major issues and concerns raised by these topics.

Budget Policy

Federal government budget policy is the joint result of government spending and tax policy. Budget policymakers have to consider when and how often the budget should be balanced, when it should be in surplus, and when in deficit. These questions have always provoked controversy.

Different Views on Budget Policy

The following represent three of the most often heard views on budget policy. Now that we are familiar with how government spending and taxation can affect the economy, we can consider the economic implications of each of them.

Classical View: Balance the Budget Annually

The classical economists generally believed that government expenditures should be matched by government tax revenues every fiscal year. In short, they believed that the government budget should be balanced annually. As a result of the Great Depression of the 1930s and the loss of faith in the classical theory of full employment, few economists today subscribe to the view that the govern-

---

LEARNING OBJECTIVES

After reading this chapter, you will be able to:

1. Outline the major views of budget policy.
2. Explain the concept of the cyclically adjusted budget and contrast it to the annual budget.
3. Explain the financing effects of budget deficits.
4. Explain government-induced crowding out.
5. Explain the supply-side view on the relationship between tax rate reduction and deficits.
6. Describe the differences between public and private debt.
7. Discuss the burdens of the government debt.
8. Discuss the impact of public debt financing charges on discretionary fiscal policy.

ment should balance its budget on an annual basis, although a growing number of economists express concern that government budgets should be balanced over a period of several years or over the phase of the business cycle. Yet there are many politicians, business leaders, and others who believe that the government budget should be balanced annually. Generally, they view the government budget like the budget of a household or business firm. These people argue that households and businesses that have budget deficits often go bankrupt. Although often used to support the view that governments should run balanced budgets, this scenario is misleading. Few families would try to pay the full cost of a new house out of their current yearly income; they borrow against their future expected income in order to facilitate purchasing something that they could not otherwise afford to pay for out of present income. Similarly, modern financial management theory supports the idea that firms are better run when they use the extra purchasing power available to them from prudent borrowing against their expected future income than they are if they try to pay for everything (including their factory) using only their present income.

One of the fascinating aspects of the theory developed by J. M. Keynes, which we presented in Chapter 23, is the counterintuitive idea that if the government budget is balanced every year, then fiscal policy will add to economic instability rather than reduce it. For example, suppose that the economy is in the expansionary phase of a business cycle. As GDP rises, tax revenues rise at a more rapid rate than does GDP because of a progressive tax structure. Given the level of government expenditures, the increase in tax revenues may well give rise to a budget surplus. In order to keep the budget balanced, the government will have to cut taxes or increase government expenditures or both. However, we have seen that increases in government expenditure as well as reductions in taxes push up aggregate expenditure and shift the aggregate demand curve to the right. This will add to the economic expansion.

On the other hand, suppose that the economy is entering a recession. As GDP declines, tax revenues will decline by a larger fraction than GDP declines, again due to the progressive structure of taxes. Given the level of government expenditure, this may result in a budget deficit. In order to keep the budget balanced, the government will have to increase taxes or reduce government spending or both, but such actions will reduce aggregate expenditure, shift aggregate demand to the left even further, and make the recession worse.

Thus, the annually balanced budget would make the expansion phase of the business cycle larger and could increase the dangers of inflation. Similarly, an annually balanced budget during the recession phase would deepen a recession and increase unemployment. Business cycles would be more severe.

Balance the Budget Cyclically

Another point of view argues that the budget should be balanced over the course of the business cycle. That is, the budget should be balanced over whatever period of time it takes for a complete business cycle. Those who favour this approach contend that balancing the budget in this way will at the same time permit the exercise of a stabilizing fiscal policy. During a recession the government would run a budget deficit by increasing spending and reducing taxes to stimulate the economy. During the expansion and boom phase of the cycle, the government would run a surplus by cutting back its spending and increasing taxes in order to curb inflationary pressures. Ideally, the size of the deficit that occurs in the recession is just matched by the size of the surplus during the boom. The budget is therefore balanced over the business cycle.

In reality, for two reasons it is very difficult to do this. The first reason is that recessions and expansions typically differ from one another in length and magnitude. Therefore, the size of the deficit incurred while fighting the recession is not likely to be the same as the size of the surplus generated by attempts to curb an inflationary expansion. The second reason is that, as we discussed in Chapter 24, it is very difficult to forecast the behaviour of the economy over the phases of the business cycle. A government attempting to stimulate during what it believes to be a contractionary phase of the cycle may find out that it has to run deficits at a later date when the government anticipated it would be back in a surplus position.

Functional Finance

The functional finance point of view contends that the goals of economic stabilization and full employment without inflation should come ahead of any concern about balancing the budget. This means that the budget may have to run in deficit over a period of several years in order to keep employment high or run in surplus to curb inflation. Proponents of functional finance argue that any difficulties associated with ongoing deficits or surpluses are far outweighed by the benefits of high employment without inflation.

Critics of the functional finance approach argue that it throws away the fiscal discipline imposed by a balanced budget objective. Generally, the critics do not argue for slavish pursuit of a balanced budget. Rather, they believe that it should be a rough guideline used to keep inflationary deficit spending under control.

The Cyclically Adjusted Budget

The cyclically adjusted budget is an indicator of which budget policy is being used. Each of the viewpoints on budget policy we have just mentioned has obvious drawbacks. The annually balanced budget may be destabilizing. Balancing the budget over the business cycle is very difficult if not impossible. Functional finance seems to lack any standard for evaluating budget policy performance. Another budget concept, the cyclically adjusted budget has gained popularity among economists and policymakers because it provides a way of judging to what extent fiscal policy is pushing the economy toward potential GDP.[1]

The **cyclically adjusted budget** *is the estimated government surplus or deficit that would exist if the level of government spending were subtracted from the estimated taxes which the government would receive if the economy were operating at potential GDP.* Specifically, government spending on commodities is held constant, transfers are estimated to decrease because of the lower numbers of people who would be eligible to collect unemployment insurance benefits and social assistance at higher GDP, and tax receipts are adjusted to reflect the increased receipts of tax revenue that would automatically flow to the government if the economy were operating at potential GDP.

---

[1]Students wishing to review the definition of potential GDP should see Chapter 20.

The Actual Budget and the Cyclically Adjusted Budget

The *actual* government budget surplus or deficit is equal to the difference between *actual* tax revenues and *actual* government expenditures (including spending on transfers). As was explained in Chapter 23, if $T - G$ is greater than zero, the government has a surplus, and if $T - G$ is less than zero, the government has a deficit. Suppose that actual GDP is less than the potential GDP. Given that the tax structure is progressive, the actual tax revenues are less than the amount that would be collected at the potential GDP level. The actual government budget might well show a deficit, as prudent fiscal policy would say it should during a recession. Injections from government spending exceed tax withdrawals (i.e., there is a net injection). But is this actual budget deficit large enough to combat the recession? How can we tell?

Suppose that we compare this actual level of government spending with the amount of tax revenue that would be collected *if* GDP were at the Potential GDP level. It might turn out that the tax revenue at potential GDP would exceed the actual government spending. In other words, if the economy were at potential GDP, there would be a budget surplus. This means that actual fiscal policy would be a force tending to push GDP down and away from potential GDP and its higher employment level! Clearly, the *actual* budget deficit would not be as large as it should be if fiscal policy was to be oriented toward pushing GDP up to potential GDP.

If actual GDP is less than potential GDP and there is a cyclically adjusted budget deficit, fiscal policy may be viewed as a force contributing to the achievement of potential GDP and a higher employment level. On the other hand, if under these same circumstances there is a cyclically adjusted budget surplus, fiscal policy may be viewed as not sufficiently expansionary for the purpose of achieving a potential GDP. If actual GDP is greater than potential GDP, the existence of a cyclically adjusted budget deficit would suggest that fiscal policy is overly expansionary and is contributing to inflationary pressures. However, if under these same circumstances there is a cyclically adjusted budget surplus, fiscal policy may be viewed as a force favourable to curbing excessive expansion.

Finally, note carefully the following point. Even if the cyclically adjusted budget (deficit or surplus) indicates that the current stance of fiscal policy is contributing to the achievement of potential GDP, it is no guarantee that this goal will be realized. Consumption, investment spending, and net exports may be either so expansionary or so contractionary that an equilibrium at potential GDP cannot be reached or maintained. Put another way, even though the cyclically adjusted budget may be favourable to the achievement of potential GDP, the *size* of the cyclically adjusted budget (deficit or surplus) may not be large enough given the existing level of consumption, investment, and net exports.

Recent Budget Experience

Figure 25-1 compares the difference between actual government spending and actual tax revenues (the actual budget deficit or surplus) with the difference between actual government spending and tax revenues that would have been generated at average sustainable GDP over the business cycle (Canada used this method of adjustment to calculate the cyclically adjusted budget deficit or surplus) for the years since 1975. Observe that in most of these years the actual

FIGURE 25-1   **The Actual Budget and the Cyclically Adjusted Budget (Structure Deficit) Since 1975**
(National Accounts, Calendar Year Basis)

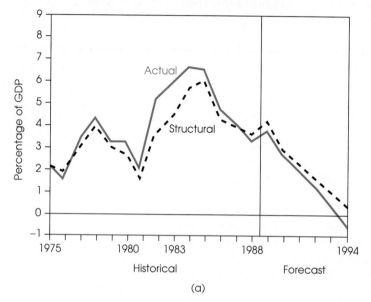

(a)

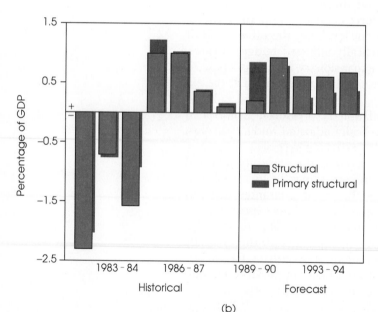

(b)

The actual budget deficit or surplus equals the difference between actual government spending (including transfers). The structural budget deficit or surplus equals the difference between actual government spending and the level of tax revenues that would be collected at the *average* level of economic activity that would be sustained over the cycle. Canada does *not* use the level of tax revenue that could be expected *at potential GDP* as the tax variable to calculate cyclically adjusted deficits, even though this is the convention used by the United Kingdom, the United States, and most other Western economies. The cyclically adjusted budget and structural deficit or surplus are better indicators of how well the government is managing fiscal policy than is the actual budget surplus or deficit. For most of the periods shown here, both the actual budget and the structural budget have shown a deficit, but the actual budget deficit usually has been greater than the structural budget deficit because actual GDP has been below the estimated average GDP over the cycle for much of this period. The fact that the structural budget was in deficit throughout most of this period indicates that fiscal policy was geared toward pushing the economy to potential GDP. The Department of Finance, Canada pointed out that after the economic recovery of 1982 the economy has experienced above-average growth and that the entire deficit during this six-year period was structural.

budget deficit was larger than the cyclically adjusted budget deficit. If one only looked at the actual budget deficit, the expansionary impact of fiscal policy would generally appear more pronounced than is indicated by the cyclically adjusted budget deficits. Nonetheless, the cyclically adjusted budget was in deficit in each of these years, indicating that fiscal policy was expansionary over this period. Largely due to the automatic stabilizers, it was particularly expansionary, as was desirable, during the latter stages of the severe recession that reached its trough at the end of the fourth quarter of 1975 and during the period after the third quarter of 1987 in the run up to the 1988 federal election. It was by contrast, less expansionary than would be expected during the very severe recession that reached its trough in 1981.

> **Checkpoint* 25-1**
>
> Compare Figure 25-1 with Figure 6-5, frame (b), and describe how well fiscal policy has performed in view of the behaviour of the GDP gap since 1975.
>
> *Answers to all Checkpoints can be found at the back of the text.*

The Effects of Financing Government Budget Deficits

Financing a Budget Deficit or a Budget Surplus

By definition, a budget deficit means that tax revenues are less than government expenditures (including transfers). How and where does the government get the funds to finance the difference? There are three ways in which the government can obtain the needed funds: (1) It can borrow the money from the domestic private capital market by selling government bonds; (2) it can borrow the money from foreign capital markets by selling bonds; or (3) it can borrow money from its own central bank, the Bank of Canada. It can also do some combination of all three. In each of the three cases it will run the risk of inflicting undesirable side effects on economy. The expansionary effect on the economy of a budget deficit varies, depending on which method is used to finance the deficit. Similarly, the contractionary effect on the economy of a budget surplus depends on what is done with the surplus. The other concerns about deficits, which we will discuss, include the extent to which they may crowd out (reduce) investment spending and the extent to which they may crowd out exports. Finally, there is even controversy over whether or not deficits can be reduced by raising tax rates.

Domestic Bond Market Financing

Domestic bond market financing *is selling bonds to the Canadian private sector.* Like any other bond, a government bond is a contract whereby the borrower (the government) agrees to pay back the lender (the buyer of the bond) the amount lent plus some rate of interest after some specified period of time. For example, consider a $1,000 government bond that pays a 10 percent rate of interest and promises to pay back the lender after 1 year. At the end of 1 year the lender, or bond buyer, gets back $1,100 (the original $1,000 plus 10 percent of $1,000, or $100) from the government, the bond seller. As with any bond, the only way the government can sell the bond (borrow the $1,000) is by paying a high enough rate of interest to induce people to buy it (lend the $1,000).

The government must sell its bonds in the bond market, in competition with bonds sold by businesses that are trying to borrow funds to finance their investment spending. Government bonds are generally viewed as having a lower risk of default than private sector bonds and therefore usually give the purchaser a lower return than that paid by private bonds. However, if the government is issuing increased amounts of bonds to finance an increased deficit it may have to increase the interest rate paid on the bonds to induce the public to buy this new issue. To the extent that this creates competition between the financing needs of the government and those of the business sector, this will push up the rate of interest. We know from our discussion in Chapter 21 (see Figure 21-8) that this interest rate rise will cause the level of investment spending to fall, as represented by a downward shift in the investment schedule. When a government deficit is financed by selling government bonds, the expansionary effect of the deficit on the economy is somewhat offset by a downward shift in investment spending (if the increased government financing causes a rise in the interest rate).

Foreign Bond Market Financing

Foreign bond market financing *is selling bonds to non-residents.* Like the selling of bonds in the domestic financial market, a government can sell bonds to non-residents. The concepts regarding interest and making the bond attractive relative to other investments that the non-resident investor can take advantage of are essentially the same as those for domestic financing, but a new dimension must be considered when a government elects to finance part of its deficit in foreign markets. The non-residents are likely to lend the government foreign currency and to prefer payments of interest and the repayment of principal in their own foreign currency. When a non-resident purchases a bond using foreign currency, the government will generally have to convert this foreign currency into Canadian money before spending it. Although we will not examine the detailed workings of exchange rates until Chapter 34, we have already seen, in Chapters 23 and 24, that some basic appreciation of the effects of exchange rate fluctuation is essential for understanding the behaviour of equilibrium income, the general price level, and unemployment in an open economy. Although there are different ways of setting the exchange rate between two currencies, we will assume in this chapter that the Canadian exchange rate on the foreign currency under consideration is *flexible*—that is, that the number of Canadian dollars needed to purchase one unit of foreign currency (e.g., one yen) is determined by the international supply and demand for both the yen and the Canadian dollar.

Under this condition, when the Canadian government starts to convert foreign currency (yen) into Canadian dollars on the international financial market, it tends to increase the supply of foreign currency (yen) and also increase the demand for Canadian dollars. This will decrease the Canadian exchange rate on the yen by decreasing the *Canadian dollar price* of the yen. As we discussed in Chapters 23 and 24, if the Canadian exchange rate decreases, Canadian products are less competitive on foreign markets, which reduces net exports. Thus, when the government finances its deficit through the sale of bonds to foreign financial markets, it initially causes the value of the Canadian dollar to increase on international markets. This in turn causes exports to decrease as they become more expensive on foreign markets, causing a crowding out of net exports, which reduces the expansionary effectiveness of the government deficit.

Printing Money

The third way in which the government can finance the deficit is to create the needed money. We will be able to describe how this is done in a modern economy after we have studied how the banking system works in Chapters 27 through 30. For the purposes of this chapter, we will simply assume that if the government sells bonds to the Bank of Canada, the Bank of Canada cranks money out with a printing press to pay the government for the bonds. Using this method means that there is no longer a need to raise the interest rate or change the exchange rate, so there is no crowding out to decrease investment spending or net exports. There is, however, a danger that the increase in the money supply will cause inflation in Canada and that the rise in domestic prices in Canada will cause a decrease in consumption, investment, and net exports as a result of the *real balance effect*, the *interest rate effect*, and the *net foreign purchase effect* (all discussed in Chapter 23).

When the government finances a deficit through the central bank by creating new money, the expansionary effect of the deficit on the economy will be greater than when the deficit is financed by borrowing from the private domestic market or by selling bonds to foreign markets.

Disposing of a Government Budget Surplus

Although it seems strange, the government may collect more tax revenue than it spends. Students may think that analyzing the effects of government surpluses is purely theoretical because budget surpluses have been so rare in the past twenty years. It should be remembered that in the past some provincial governments in Canada and some state legislatures in the United States have had surpluses. Some of these have been quite large. The most notable of these surpluses in North America have been the provincial and state surpluses that led to the creation of the "provincial and state trust funds" in Alberta, British Columbia, and Saskatchewan, in Canada and in Alaska, Montana, Oklahoma, and Texas, in the United States. At the federal level, the Government of Canada had surplus budgets quite frequently in the 1950s and 1960s.

A budget surplus is desirable at the boom phase of the business cycle because it is anti-inflationary, meaning that it dampens inflationary pressures. But the extent of this dampening effect depends on what the government does with the surplus. There are three possibilities. The government can use the surplus to retire (pay off) some of the outstanding government debt held by the domestic private sector, it can redeem (pay back) debt held by non-residents, or it can retire outstanding debt held by the central bank. The repayment of debt owed to the central bank amounts to withdrawing money from the economy.

Suppose that the surplus is used to retire outstanding debt owed to the domestic private sector. Think of the surplus as the net withdrawal—the excess of the withdrawals due to taxes over the injections of government spending. Returning the surplus to the economy by retiring debt offsets this net withdrawal to the extent that it puts money back into the hands of the private sector, which then spends some portion of it. Debt retirement to the domestic private sector thereby reduces the anti-inflationary effect of the budget surplus.

Similarly, if the government were to run a surplus budget for the purpose of reducing inflationary pressures, but then used the surplus to repay outstanding bonds held by non-residents, there would be an increase in the Canadian exchange rate on foreign currency—a decrease in the value of the Canadian dollar on international markets. This occurs because if the government increased the demand for foreign currency and increased the supply of Canadian money on the international market, *ceteris paribus* the Canadian currency price of foreign currency would rise. This would lead in turn to higher net exports and thus reduce some of the intended contractionary impact of the government budget surplus.

If the government uses the surplus to repay debt owed to the Bank of Canada or simply holds the money in idle funds, a method referred to as **impounding**, there is no offset to reduce this net withdrawal. The anti-inflationary effect of a government budget surplus is greater when the surplus funds are used to pay back debt held by the central bank or held idle than when they are used to retire debt.[2]

Crowding Out of Capital Formation and Exports

In recent years there has been increasing concern about the size of federal government budget deficits. While federal deficits were a small percentage of the GDP in the 1960s, so that the net public debt as a percentage of GDP actually decreased between 1952 and 1975, the situation changed dramatically in the latter half of the 1970s and deteriorated further in the 1980s. The size of the deficits and their frequency relative to the number of years of surplus both increased after 1975. In the first half of the 1970s the Canadian government budget deficit averaged .7 percent of GDP, in the second half of the 1970s this increased to 2.4 percent, and in the first half of the 1980s the deficit jumped to almost 3 percent of GDP. In the worst year, 1984–1985, the deficit exceeded 8.6 percent of GDP.[3]

A critical concern often expressed about federal deficits is that they absorb resources that would otherwise be available to build up the economy's capital stock. It is therefore often said that deficits "crowd out" investment in capital formation. We have already noted how this can occur as a consequence of the government financing a budget deficit by issuing bonds. Recall that the resulting rise in the interest rate causes investment spending (hence capital formation) to decline—to be crowded out. The argument may also be illustrated in terms of the relationship that says that the sum of investment I plus exports X plus government spending G must equal the sum of saving S plus imports M plus taxes T, or $I + X + G = S + M + T$. When there is a deficit, government spending G is larger than tax revenue T, which means $S + M$ is larger than $I + X$. Assuming for simplicity that the financing of the deficit is done in a way that does not disrupt the exchange rate, it follows that exports and imports are *not* influenced by the deficit. In this situation the deficit causes the interest rate to rise and there is a decrease in private investment spending on capital formation.

Now suppose that the deficit is financed in a way that does not require a reduction in private capital formation. In other words, suppose that the government used *only* borrowing from foreign capital markets as its method of financing the deficit. In this case, the interest rate may not increase and domestic investment and saving can be considered to be unaffected by the borrowing

---

[2]Note that retiring government debt removes government bonds from the bond market and thus reduces competition with private bonds. This tends to reduce the interest rate and thereby stimulate investment spending. This is another source of stimulus to the economy that occurs when there is debt retirement.

[3]Honourable Michael Wilson, Minister of Finance, *The Fiscal Plan, Controlling the Public Debt* (Department of Finance Canada, April, 1989), pp. 51–108.

to finance the deficit. However, when we consider that injections $I + X + G$ must equal withdrawals $S + M + T$ at equilibrium income, it becomes obvious that if saving and investment are not affected by the deficit, then exports and imports must be affected. As we discussed earlier, when the government finances the deficit through foreign borrowing, the Canadian exchange rate on foreign currency decreases and causes net exports to decrease. Thus, a deficit can "crowd out" net export expenditure instead of crowding out investment. In practice, most open economies experience some crowding out in both ways.

Crowding out *is defined as the reduction in the level of one or more of the components of aggregate expenditure (usually investment or exports) that results from financing a government deficit.* The larger the crowding-out effect, whether because of a higher interest rate or because of a lower exchange rate, the less effective will be expansionary fiscal policy by the government.

For example, suppose that investment I equals $100 billion, exports X equal $150 billion, and government spending G equals $120 billion, so that total injections $I + X + G$ equal $370 billion. In addition suppose that saving S equals $125 billion, imports M equal $145 billion, and taxes T equal $100 billion, for total withdrawals $S + M + T$ equal to $370 billion. But because $I + X + G = S + M + T$ is *always equal*, we can rewrite the statement as $G - T = S - I - X + M$; this can be simplified to $G - T = S - I - X_n$. In other words, the government deficit must equal the combined excess withdrawal of saving minus investment minus net exports. In our example the government budget deficit is $20 ($120 - $100). The value of saving minus investment is $25 ($125 - $100) and net exports equal $5 ($150 - $145). Thus, in this case the trade surplus absorbs only a portion of the withdrawal created by savings being larger than investment. The result is that the high saving rate is able to offset the combined net injection from exports being larger than imports and the government deficit. If the level of saving had been lower or investment had been higher, then to be in equilibrium either net exports would have to be negative or the government would have to run a surplus. In other words, part of the economy's saving S must be used to finance the deficit, part can be absorbed through net exports $X - M$ being greater than zero, and the remaining part is used to finance investment I. What if government spending were larger, say $G = $160? Then the deficit would be larger, $160 - $100 = $60. Assuming no change in savings or net exports, this $60 excess of government spending over tax revenue would have to be financed by reducing investment. Since the government budget deficit has increased by $40, we can see that in the present circumstance investment must decrease by $40, from $100 to $60, as savings are diverted to finance the deficit. Our example illustrates how growing deficits can cause the economy's rate of capital formation to decline due to crowding out. In a similar way we could assume that investment and savings would remain unchanged as the government deficit increased. In this case the increase in the government deficit would crowd out net exports by forcing some combination of a decrease in exports and a rise in imports. When net exports decreased by $40 the economy would be back in equilibrium.

Finally, it should be remembered that in our examples the level of aggregate income was assumed constant as the government deficit increased. Crowding out was illustrated by focusing attention on the decrease in investment or net exports necessary to allow for an increase in the government deficit, since injections must equal withdrawals. From our discussion of the effects of stimulative fiscal policy in Chapter 23 it was noted that an increase in injections (a larger government budget deficit) will cause aggregate income to increase. As income increases it will cause both savings and imports to increase, and therefore some portion of the increase in the government deficit will be absorbed by larger withdrawals rather than reductions in investment. In addition, in Chapter 24 we explained that if aggregate supply were positively sloped, then an increase in aggregate expenditure would cause a shift to the right in aggregate demand. When aggregate demand increases as a result of an increase in the government deficit there will be a pressure for the price level to increase.

The preceding discussion should help to explain why the very large government budget deficits in Canada in the early 1980s were accompanied by relatively low rates of real investment and very rapid rise in foreign borrowing to finance the deficit. In addition it should help to illustrate why many economists and government advisors were concerned that the growing government deficits would lead to increased inflation. In 1981, in fact, the Canadian government exceeded any other country in new foreign bond issues, in 1982 it was second highest, and in 1983 it was the third highest foreign borrower in the world.[4]

The preceding discussion has pointed out that a government deficit can be financed either by a decrease in investment or by a decrease in net exports. Like Canada, the United States experienced large and increasing government deficits during the 1980s; in that country the rate of capital formation declined and its net exports became negative. So rapid was the decrease in the U.S. trade surplus that it went from being the world's richest creditor to being the world's biggest debtor in a period of only five years.

Tax Rates and the Deficit

While a reduction in marginal tax rates may cause an expansion in the economy's capacity to produce goods and services, as discussed in the last chapter, won't it also lead to larger budget deficits due to a decline in tax revenues? Some macroeconomists, such as Arthur Laffer, say no. Using supply-side arguments, these economists point out that the increase in aggregate income and output resulting from a reduction in marginal tax rates may well give rise to an increase in tax revenue despite the reduction in tax rates. This proposition may be characterized in terms of the well-known **Laffer curve** shown in Figure 25-2.

The Laffer curve shows the relationship between the marginal tax rate (vertical axis) and the amount of tax revenue the government receives (horizontal axis). It is easy to establish the two points where the Laffer curve meets the vertical axis. Clearly, if the marginal tax rate is zero, the government will receive no tax revenue, which corresponds to point a at the origin of the graph. At the other extreme, if the marginal tax rate is 1, so that every dollar of income is confiscated by the government, people will have no incentive to work and again tax revenue will be zero, corresponding to point d. If the marginal tax rate is t_1 (roughly .2, say), government tax revenue would equal R_n, corresponding to point b on the Laffer curve. If the rate is increased to t_m, tax revenue rises to R_m, corresponding to point m on the curve. Notice, however, that any further increase in the rate will actually cause the level of tax revenue to decline. At t_2, for

---

[4]Economic Council of Canada, *Steering the Course, Twenty-First Annual Review* (Minister of Supply and Services Canada, 1984), p. 46.

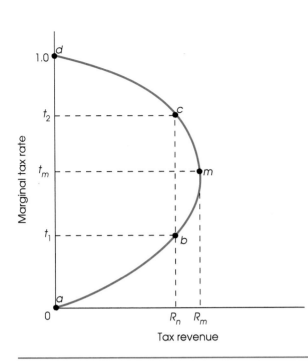

The Laffer curve suggests that tax revenue (horizontal axis) rises as the marginal tax rate is increased up to some rate t_m, corresponding to point m on the curve, where the maximum possible tax revenue is R_m. Tax rates higher than t_m discourage productive efforts so much that aggregate income falls, causing tax revenue to decline. The curve implies that if the marginal tax rate is above t_m, rate reduction will give rise to increased tax revenue. It also implies that for every marginal tax rate above t_m, there exists a lower rate that would generate the same tax revenue.

instance, tax revenue falls back to the level R_n corresponding to point c. Why? Above some marginal tax rate such as t_m, the after-tax rewards for working and capital formation become so low that these productive activities are reduced. The resulting decline in aggregate income is so great that tax revenues decline despite the increased marginal tax rate. For example, suppose that the economy has a proportional tax structure and the marginal tax rate is increased from .3 to .4. If aggregate income declines from $600 billion to $500 billion, tax revenues decline from $200 billion to $125 billion.

Increasing Tax Revenue by Tax Reduction

In the early 1980s, some supply-siders contended that marginal tax rates in Canada, the United Kingdom, and the United States were high enough to put these economies at points such as c on their respective Laffer curves. It was argued that by lowering the marginal tax rate and moving down the curve, tax revenue would increase. For instance, moving from point c down to point m would increase tax revenue from R_n to R_m in Figure 25-2. Moreover, if the supply-siders had been right, a lower marginal tax rate could yield the same level of tax revenue previously realized. For example, in Figure 25-2 the rate t_1 will yield the same tax revenue R_n as the rate t_2.

Where Are We on the Laffer Curve?

Skepticism about the supply-siders' argument that lowering marginal tax rates will lead to increased tax revenues is fairly widespread. Many economists and policymakers agree that, at least from a hypothetical perspective, the proposition may be true in the longrun, after sufficient economic growth. As to the

Checkpoint 25-2

What are the
implications for the
cyclically adjusted
budget concept of
the fact that the
expansionary impact
of a deficit depends
on how it is financed?
Similarly, what are
the implications
for this concept of
the different ways
of disposing of a
surplus? In our initial
crowding-out example,
what would have to
happen to investment
or imports if taxes
were cut to $100?

shortrun, however, many critics argue that a decrease in tax rates cannot have sufficient impact on the economy's supply side to expand income enough to actually increase tax revenues. Many economists seriously question whether Canada has ever been on the upper portion of the Laffer curve. The tax rate reductions, which started with the indexing of personal tax rates to the rate of inflation in 1975 and have been expanded through the introduction of *Registered Retirement Savings Plans (RRSPs)* and other subsequent measures, including the reduction in marginal income tax rates in the 1988 federal budget, suggest that Canadian government budget deficits increase rather than decrease in response to reductions in effective marginal tax rates. This clearly suggests that Canada is on the lower portion of the curve.

In the United States, empirical studies suggest that the economy has never been on the backward-bending upper section of the Laffer curve.[5] A similar study for Sweden, which has much higher tax rates than Canada or the United States, concludes that Sweden is on the upper portion of its Laffer curve.[6]

The Government Debt

The government debt is a subject of controversy and a source of concern to many people. Should we be concerned about it? Who owes what to whom? How can we tell whether the debt is too big or not? What are the burdens of the debt? And what are the implications of continually large deficits for budget policy given that deficits are the source of government debt growth?

What Is the Government Debt?

Since the beginning of World War I the public debt in Canada has increased almost every year in absolute terms (see Figure 25-3). From a value of $2.38 billion in 1926 the net public debt (the gross public debt minus net recorded assets) increased to $292.18 billion by 1988, an increase of over 1,200 percent.[7]

This enormous increase appears to be alarming, and there may be good reasons for concern about this explosion in the debt, but we cannot view the size or the rate of increase of the public debt in isolation. In order to evaluate it we must compare it to other variables to see what may have caused it, if it is a problem, and if so, why it is a problem. In the same way that we might be interested in what caused a rapid increase in the debt of an individual or corporation and we might be interested in the ability of that individual or corporation to repay and service their debt, so we may be interested in the government's ability to repay and service the public debt. In summary, what caused the public debt to grow so large? How does the government finance its debt?

[5]Bruce Bender, "An Analysis of the Laffer Curve," *Economic Inquiry,* July 1984, pp. 414–420. Also see Don Fullerton, "On the Possibility of an Inverse Relationship Between Tax Rates and Government Revenues," *Journal of Public Economics,* October 1982, pp. 3–22.

[6]Charles E. Stuart, "Swedish Tax Rates, Labor Supply, and Tax Revenues," *Journal of Political Economy,* October 1981, pp. 1020–1038.

[7]Department of Finance, *The Fiscal Plan, Controlling the Public Debt* (April 27, 1989), pp. 115–147.

FIGURE 25-3 **The Government Debt**

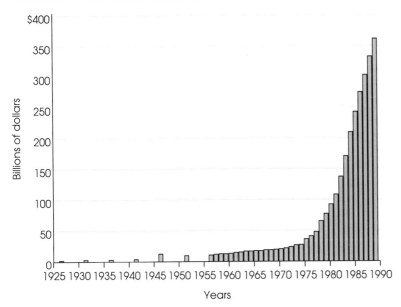

The government debt increased dramatically during the Great Depression of the 1930s, and again during World War II. Between 1952 and 1975 it rose more slowly, and it began to increase very rapidly following the recession of the early 1980s.

Can the government afford to have this much debt? Does the continuous growth in the public debt reduce the government's ability to effectively manage the economy? What negative side effects are felt by the rest of the economy because of this debt?

The size and growth of Canada's net public debt relative to GDP between 1926 and 1988 is shown in Figure 25-4, and the Canadian net public debt relative to the public debt of the other most advanced western economies, the so-called Group of Seven (G-7), is shown in Table 25-1.

Public versus Private Debt

Most of us are accustomed to thinking in terms of private debt—the personal debt people incur when they borrow money to buy a car, a house, or a post-secondary education. The chief fear is that of not being able to pay the debt off as repayments come due. If you cannot, your assets—the car, the house, the furniture (although not the education)—may be seized by those who have lent you money. They may even be able to put a *lien* on your paycheque. A **lien** is a legal claim that allows those to whom you owe money to take a part of every paycheque (direct from your employer) until they have been paid back the amount owed to them by you.

Government, or public, debt is different from private debt in important respects, though it is similar in others. Consider the following hypothetical example. Suppose that the government's debt is held entirely by its own citizens and that each citizen owns the same number of government bonds as every other

FIGURE 25-4   Ratio of Government Debt to GDP and Government Debt to Government Revenues

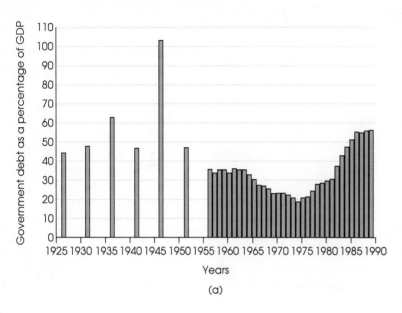

(a)

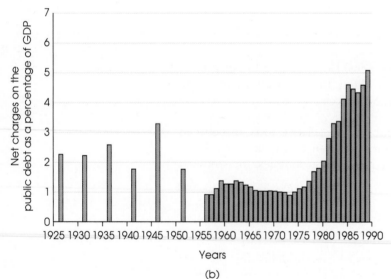

(b)

One measure of the burden of the government debt is its size relative to that of GDP. The net public debt as a percentage of the GDP is shown in frame (a) and the net charges for the debt as a percentage of the GDP are shown in frame (b).

Frame (a) indicates that the public debt was a much higher percentage of GDP at the end of World War II than it is today. However, the upward trend in debt to GDP ratio has made the debt to GDP ratio almost as high as it was in the 1930s.

Frame (b) shows that the net charges on the public debt have increased dramatically since 1978. In 1983 these charges surpassed the previous record percentage and in 1989 they were five times as high in relation to GDP as they had been in 1975. This supports the view that the burden of public debt has increased in recent years but it also changes the perspective of why the burden has risen. Many economists are now supporting the view that it was the high interest rate established by the Bank of Canada's interest rate policy from 1975 to 1992 which has increased the burden of the public debt.

TABLE 25-1   International Comparisons of Government Net Debt, National Accounts Basis, 1975 to 1990

	Weighted Average of G-7[1]	Canada	U.S.	U.K.	France	Germany	Italy	Japan
				(percentage of GDP/GNP)				
General government								
1975	21.9	7.5	22.6	57.0	11.1	1.0	52.0	2.1
1980	22.3	12.3	19.7	47.5	14.3	14.3	53.6	17.3
1981	23.2	10.0	19.3	46.7	14.2	17.4	57.3	20.7
1982	26.1	16.5	22.3	45.9	17.8	19.8	63.4	23.2
1983	28.8	22.5	24.9	46.3	20.0	21.4	68.7	26.2
1984	30.1	26.2	25.8	47.6	21.7	21.6	74.2	26.9
1985	31.8	32.8	27.8	46.6	23.8	21.9	80.9	26.6
1986	33.3	36.7	29.9	45.9	25.3	22.1	85.6	26.6
1987	33.6	37.7	30.3	43.4	26.6	23.0	89.1	25.9
1988[2]	33.2	37.6	30.0	39.1	26.6	23.8	92.0	24.6
1989[3]	32.8	39.0	29.4	35.1	27.0	24.0	95.0	23.5
1990[3]	32.4	40.2	28.6	31.6	27.5	24.7	98.1	22.6
Central government								
1975	—	5.4	24.5	—	7.7	—	—	7.1
1980	—	15.1	23.3	—	11.0	—	—	27.0
1981	—	15.2	23.4	—	10.4	—	—	31.2
1982	—	20.1	27.4	—	13.0	—	—	35.0
1983	—	25.1	31.1	—	15.5	—	—	38.7
1984	—	29.2	33.1	—	17.8	—	—	40.7
1985	—	34.0	36.4	—	20.5	—	—	41.6
1986	—	37.2	39.9	—	22.7	—	—	43.4
1987	—	38.2	41.7	—	23.1	—	—	—
1988[2]	—	38.6	41.8	—	—	—	—	—
1989[3]	—	39.8	41.6	—	—	—	—	—
1990[3]	—	40.8	41.3	—	—	—	—	—

Note: "—" indicates data not available.

[1] 1980–1981 GDP/GNP weights in U.S. dollars.

[2] Estimate.

[3] Forecast.

Source: *The Fiscal Plan, Controlling the Public Debt*, Department of Finance Canada, April 1989, p. 99.

citizen. Since it is the citizens' government, the government debt is the citizens' debt, or what the citizens owe themselves! Suppose that the government decided to pay off the entire debt by levying and collecting a tax of the same size from each citizen. The amount of taxes each citizen would pay the government would be just equal to the amount of money each would receive from the government for the government bonds that each holds. It is the same as if each citizen were to take a set number of dollars out of his or her left pocket and put them back into the right pocket.

What about interest payments on a government's debt held entirely by and distributed equally among its own citizens? Again, suppose that the government levies and collects a tax of the same size from every citizen to pay the interest on the debt. Each citizen would then pay an amount of taxes exactly equal to the interest payments received on the government bond he or she holds. Again, what each citizen takes out of the left pocket matches what is put back into the right pocket.

Obviously, in our hypothetical example the existence and size of the government debt is of no consequence whatsoever. The example shows how different a government, or public, debt can be from a private debt.

Burdens of the Government Debt

Our hypothetical example serves another important purpose. It suggests that any cause for concern about the government debt lies in the fact that *certain of the example's assumptions don't hold in reality.* Because of this, the government debt imposes certain burdens similar to those of a private debt.

Distribution Effects

First of all, government bonds outstanding are not distributed equally among the nation's citizens. Some people hold none and others own a great number. However, any attempt to retire some or all of the debt would have to be financed out of taxes that are paid by taxpayers. It is an obvious but important point to remember that some people who hold government bonds are not taxpayers and some people who pay taxes do not hold government bonds. In addition not all citizens are taxpayers, since some citizens avoid or evade paying any taxes due to either poverty or creative accounting. To the extent that the group paying taxes is different from the group that holds government bonds there would be a transfer payment from taxpayers to bond holders, which would result in a redistribution of income. Some citizens would end up paying out an amount of taxes larger than their holdings of government bonds. These citizens would experience a net loss, since they would pay out more than they would get back. Others would experience a net gain in this transfer. Their tax payment toward the debt retirement effort would be less than their holdings of government bonds.[8]

Interest payments on the government debt have the same distribution effects. These interest payments are transfer payments, financed by taxpayers and paid to those holding government bonds. This transfer payment was approximately $24.5 billion in the fiscal year 1987–1988.[9] The same basis of calculation shows that this transfer cited by the finance minister rose to $40.0 billion in the fiscal year 1989–1990.[10] Making the simplifying assumption that the benefits from increased government spending resulting from the expenditure portion of the government deficit are available to all citizens,

---

[8]Many government bonds are held by pension funds, trust funds, banks, insurance companies, and other businesses. A multitude of citizens either own or have claims on these institutions and therefore own government bonds indirectly. This makes no difference to our argument. The exceptional circumstances concerning government bonds owned by the Bank of Canada or owned by non-residents will be discussed later in this section and in Chapters 27, 28, and 29.

[9]Honourable Michael Wilson, Minister of Finance, *The Fiscal Plan, Controlling the Public Debt* (Department of Finance Canada, April, 1989), pp. 51–108.

[10]Department of Finance. *Quarterly Economic Review*, March 1991.

then a citizen can be regarded as a gainer if the amount received in interest payments exceeds his or her share of the tax payments used to pay interest on the debt. Otherwise the citizen experiences net losses in this transfer. While some economists may argue that these people made a rational choice to invest in other assets rather than in government bonds, this argument overlooks the obvious cases where individuals were not able to invest in any bonds, government or private, but were still in a taxable position.

In summary, the issue of public debt burden may be viewed in terms of the distribution effects of the transfer payments used to retire the debt or pay interest on it. In simplified terms it is a burden to those citizens who experience net losses in this transfer. *For them the burden is similar to that of a private debt.*

Relative Size of Public Debt and GDP

It is difficult to give an accurate statistical measure of the burden created by redistribution effects. Whatever they are, the citizens' ability either to retire the public debt or to pay interest on it is all relative to the citizens' capacity and willingness to pay taxes. A first approximation of this ability is the size of the GDP relative to the size of the debt and to the amount of the interest payments that must be paid on it.

Figure 25-4, frame (a), indicates that since World War II, the government debt has become much smaller relative to the size of GDP. In the immediate postwar years, 1945–1947, the debt was actually larger than GDP. From then until 1974, however, GDP grew at a more rapid rate than did the government debt, until it was roughly three times as large as the government debt. By this criterion the burden of the public debt declined steadily until 1974. Since then, and particularly between 1982 and 1986, the ratio of the debt to the size of GDP has increased, suggesting that the debt burden is increasing.

What about the size of net charges for servicing on the public debt relative to the size of GDP? From 1956 until 1976, these payments amounted to between .9 and 1.16 percent of GDP. Since 1976 they have been accelerating so that in 1989 they were 5.1 percent of GDP. Though this still seems a small fraction of total GDP, the increase is cause for concern as it indicates that the burden is over five times as high as it was in 1976. Increasingly, economists are supporting the view that the major reason for the rapid rise in the burden in terms of the net charges on the debt as a percentage of the GDP is because of the very high interest rates that Canada has experienced in recent years.

Fiscal Integrity and Interest Payments on the Public Debt

Another way of evaluating the burden of the public debt is to compare the size of interest charges on the public debt to the size of government revenue for the current period. Since the payment of interest on the public debt may absorb a portion of tax revenue that could be used to provide needed government services, there is an argument that interest on the public debt crowds out other forms of more useful government spending. This idea overlooks the possibility that taxes may be unusually low because the government has deliberately chosen to finance its spending by borrowing instead of by raising taxes. However, to the extent that taxes form a longrun limit to government fiscal action and the public tends to resist any increase in taxes, it is useful to compare the interest on the public debt to government revenue. In the period from 1952 to 1980 net charges on the public debt amounted to between 5.5 percent and 13 percent of government revenues. In 1980 this figure rose to almost 17 percent of government revenue and has continued this escalation so that for 1989–1990 it absorbed over 22 percent of government revenue.[11] By comparison the interest charges on the public debt were twice as high as the money spent on transfers to senior citizens through old age pensions and over three times as high as payments on national defense to keep over 60,000 people employed in the Canadian Armed Forces!

External versus Internal Debt

Government debt held by residents of Canada is what we as citizens collectively owe to ourselves. The redistribution effects associated with taxation and transfer payments only redistribute the economy's total output domestically. As a nation there would be no loss in aggregate output accruing from this kind of redistribution. That part of government debt held by non-residents (Canadian citizens and foreign citizens who live outside Canada) is another matter. Interest payments on such debt, as well as the retirement of that debt, amounts to a transfer of purchasing power from residents of Canada to non-residents. In other words, a part of the nation's output must be given up to a foreign economy. It may well be that the money originally lent to Canada by non-residents was used to enhance the growth of the economy through government spending to create infrastructure. In such a case, the growth enhances the ability of Canada to increase its output so that it can repay the debt and still increase the standard of living. In this way there may be parallels between a nation borrowing from foreign sources and a firm or individual borrowing to invest. However, the basic point remains that foreign-held debt is like private debt at the time of repayment in that one party must reduce its present purchasing power by virtue of the obligation to pay another.

In Canada the portion of government debt held by non-residents has increased in recent years. During the 1960s and 1970s the amount of Canadian public debt held by non-residents was always below 5 percent of GDP and actually decreased over the period in absolute terms as well as relative to GDP. In the 1980s non-resident debt has increased so rapidly that in 1988 it accounted for over 19 percent of total public debt. While this is still a small portion of the total debt, the increase is somewhat disturbing. Some say it reflects the high degree of openness of the Canadian economy and is due to the unusually high interest rates in Canada compared to those in Europe and Japan.[12]

Is the Debt a Burden on Future Generations?

It is sometimes argued that government debt creation imposes a burden on future generations. Is this true? Debt creation does saddle future generations with the redistribution effects associated with the taxes and transfer payments

---

[11] Based on information in Department of Finance, *The Fiscal Plan, Controlling the Public Debt* (April 27, 1989), pp. 57, 139; *Canadian Economic Observer*, September 1991; and the *Quarterly Economic Review*, March 1991.

[12] Economic Council of Canada, *Steering the Course, Twenty-Fifth Annual Review* (Minister of Supply and Services Canada, 1984), p. 46.

needed to make ongoing interest payments on the debt. To the extent that taxpayers and bondholders are not necessarily the same people, this redistribution of income will be a burden to some members of future generations.

The creation of public debt during times when the economy is operating at potential GDP with full employment *may* represent a burden to future generations, but not necessarily. New government bonds may crowd out bonds being issued by businesses when the economy is producing at maximum capacity. To this extent business may have to cut back on capital expansion for lack of funds. The government gets the funds and uses the resources that would otherwise go to businesses for something else. Suppose that, for political or other reasons, the government spends the funds from its bond sales inefficiently or on something society doesn't want. For example, suppose the government builds an antisubmarine hydrofoil for the navy, which it decides to keep in dry dock for thirty years, or spends for development of a new air superiority all-weather fighter plane, which it then decides to scrap. Present and future generations are *burdened* because of the forgone capital that would have allowed the economy to produce more output now and tomorrow. Note, however, that the government might have raised taxes instead of selling bonds to get the funds for those expenditures which it subsequently decided were inappropriate. *Only* when selling bonds is easier than raising taxes (due to political considerations, say) is it true that creating government debt is a cause of the burden. Even then the real cause is poor fiscal policy.

Creation of public debt can be a blessing under certain conditions. Suppose that the economy is in a depression. Under such circumstances savings may be low or businesses may lack confidence or creditworthiness to borrow for large and important major capital investment. The government can use its fiscal powers to stimulate the creation of capital, whether privately owned or publicly (government) owned. The creation of new capital might be anything: building the Saint Lawrence Seaway, construction of the Welland Canal, creation of hydroelectric generating capacity, development of a plant to convert tar-sand into energy, or any number of other expensive ventures. Prudent fiscal policy would call for increased government spending through direct involvement, increased government subsidies to private investors, or reduced taxes—in short, a deficit. And creating this deficit requires the creation of more government debt.[13] If the government didn't take these actions, the economy would have a longer and deeper recession than otherwise. Goods and services, including capital goods, that otherwise could be produced would not be. This year's forgone production would be forever lost to society. Society would be saddled with *the burden of doing without goods it could have had*—now and in the future.

Deficits and the Growing Government Debt

Whatever the size of a government budget deficit, financing that deficit results in the creation of an equivalent amount of new government debt. One of the

---

[13] Even if the government financed the deficit by creating more money ("printing it"), it would be necessary to create more bonds under modern central banking arrangements, the subject of Chapters 27 through 30.

major concerns about the large deficits of recent years is that they have caused an increase in the rate of growth of the government debt.

Debt Growing Faster than GDP

In contrast to most of the period from 1945 to 1975, since 1975 the rate of growth of government debt has exceeded the rate of growth of GDP, resulting in an increase in the ratio of government debt to GDP, as can be seen from Figure 25-4, frame (a). Given the rate of interest that must be paid on government debt, total interest payments on the debt tend to become an even larger factor in the government's budget as long as the debt grows at a faster rate than GDP. While interest payments on the debt absorbed 4.9 percent of the government budget revenue in 1973, they rose to over 28 percent in 1985 and declined to about 25 percent since 1988.[14] These figures are still well below the 32 percent to 37 percent figures experienced in the 1920s and early part of the Great Depression of the 1930s. More recent measures based on the charges on the public debt as a percentage of total government expenditures indicate that the carrying charges on the debt rose from 10.4 percent of total government expenditures in 1973 to 27.2 percent in 1989. These indications that the burden of the debt continues to rise concern most economists and financial experts because of their transfer effect and the potential for crowding-out effects on investment and exports.

Obviously the rate of growth of government debt cannot exceed the rate of growth of GDP indefinitely. Eventually the interest payments on the debt would take up the whole government budget, leaving nothing for all other government expenditure categories (education, medicare, national defense, old age security payments, and so forth). Even ignoring the displacement of other forms of government spending, the continuous growth in the public debt would eventually force the government to repudiate it—the government would in effect be bankrupt. No doubt political pressures would build up to reduce deficits and curb growth of the government debt long before this point was reached. In this context it is interesting to note that in Canada, government spending for goods and services, measured in real terms after allowing for inflation, has actually declined by 0.5 percent annually since 1984.

Limiting the Growth of Government Deficits

What kind of limit on the size of government deficits is necessary if the growth rate of the government debt is not to exceed the growth rate of GDP? The answer is that the dollar size of the deficit must not exceed the growth rate of nominal GDP multiplied by the dollar size of the government debt. For example, if the debt equals $400 billion and nominal GDP is growing at 5 percent per year, then the deficit should not exceed $20 billion. A $20 billion deficit would require the government to issue (sell) $20 billion of new government bonds, thus increasing the debt by another $20 billion (to $420 billion), or at a 5 percent annual rate. Actual deficits were so large from 1977–1978 through 1987–1988

[14]Department of Finance, *The Fiscal Plan*, 1989, Table 3-1.

Checkpoint 25-3

Suppose that half of the nation's citizens each hold an equal share of the government debt and that all citizens each pay an equal share of the taxes used to pay interest on the debt. Given this situation, how large do you think the total debt could be in relation to GDP before serious unrest might develop? What would government bankruptcy mean in this case?

POLICY PERSPECTIVE

How Did Budget Deficits Get So Large?

A major economic policy issue in recent years has been the alarming size of federal government budget deficits (see Figure 25-1)—the excess of federal government expenditures over receipts. The ballooning of federal deficits during the 1970s and 1980s appears to have been associated with a combination of adverse budgetary developments rather than with a single cause, such as supply-side economic policies, as some critics would have it. An examination of government expenditures and receipts since 1979 is revealing.

CAUSES OF INCREASE IN FEDERAL GOVERNMENT DEFICITS IN THE 1970S AND 1980S

The surge in the size of government deficits during the 1970s and 1980s reflected the rise in total government outlays for transfers to the provinces and for service charges on the federal debt as a share of GDP. There was also a significant decrease in federal tax revenue as a proportion of GDP during the second half of the 1970s and the 1980s.

Federal deficits as a share of GDP are shown in Figure P25-1. They are broken down into two major categories: the primary balance, and net charges on the public debt. The primary balance is essentially the revenue of government from taxes and other earnings minus its expenditure for goods and services and subsidies. By contrast, the net charges on the public debt may be thought of as the interest payments on the government debt. The primary balance was negative and growing in relation to GDP

through the 1970s. In 1980 tax recovery measures taken by the government, including some provisions of the National Energy Program, temporarily reversed this trend. The increases in the primary deficit over this period can be attributed mainly to increases in the federal government's commitments to cost-sharing arrangements with the provinces for health care and education and to the indexing of income taxes in the mid-1970s. In the early 1980s there was a large increase in transfer payments to individuals, largely as a result of the automatic stabilizers of unemployment insurance and social assistance during the economic downturn at that time. Federal expenditures for goods and services have declined as a percentage of GDP since 1984. The chart shows the increase in debt charges on the public debt since 1978. With the exception of a minor downturn in 1983, when interest rates temporarily decreased, the percentage of debt payments to GDP has shown a steady and rapid increase relative to GDP over the period.

GROWTH OF FEDERAL EXPENDITURES

The increase in transfers to the provinces began in the late 1960s, when shifts in the demographic composition of the population took place. There were tremendous increases in the spending for education and health care as the age distribution of the population changed. This was accompanied by increases in the demand for local spending for the provision of social services and infrastructure as the population shifted from rural areas

to urban areas. Under the articles laying out the division of responsibilities for spending and taxation between the federal and provincial governments in the British North America Act of 1867 (BNA Act), which preceded the present Canada Act, most of the increased expenditure involved provincial concerns. The federal government entered into cost-sharing arrangements with the provinces to help ensure that the standards and level of spending per capita were similar for all Canadians, regardless of the province or territory in which they lived. These increased obligations caused a rise in federal transfers to the provinces for expenditures over which the federal government had little or no control. Federal government spending for goods and services for its own areas of responsibility under the BNA Act from 1960 until the middle of the 1980s shows that federal government actually reduced its spending relative to GDP over this period. By contrast, its transfers to the provinces more than doubled as a percentage of GDP over the same period. Traditionally, the federal government has been a creator of real capital in Canada by building transportation and communication infrastructure, but with the rise in its cost-sharing payments to the provinces, the federal government reduced its capital formation expenditures from an average of over 12 percent of GDP in the three decades before the 1960s down to an average of under 8 percent for the 1970s and even less in the 1980s.

continued on next page

POLICY PERSPECTIVE CONTINUED

FIGURE P25-1   **Federal Government Primary Budget Balance and Debt Charges as a Share of GDP**
(Negative Values Are Surpluses)

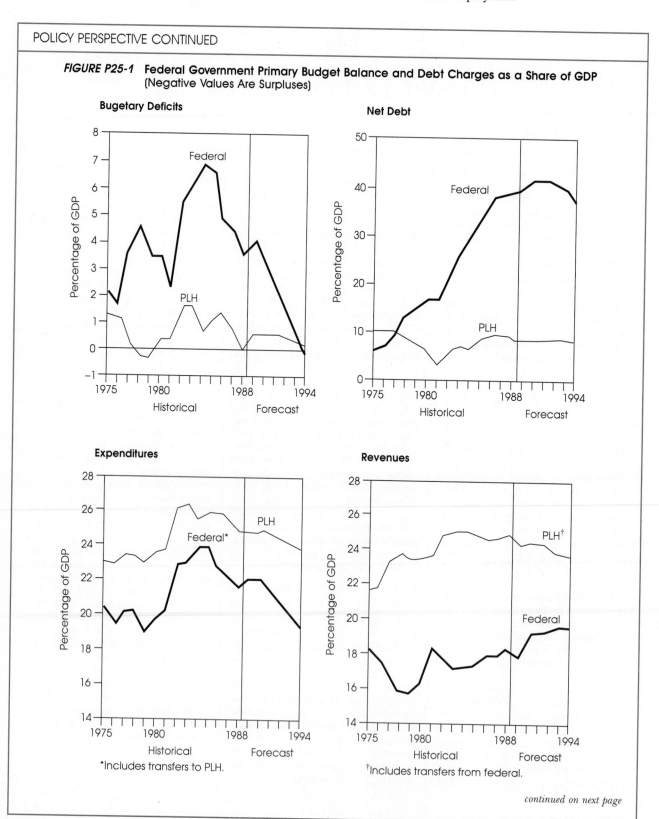

Bugetary Deficits

Net Debt

Expenditures

*Includes transfers to PLH.

Revenues

†Includes transfers from federal.

continued on next page

POLICY PERSPECTIVE CONTINUED

TABLE P25-1 Public Debt Charges in Comparative Terms

	Gross Public Debt Charges as a Percentage of			Net Public Debt Charges as a Percentage of		
	GDP*	Budgetary Revenues	Budgetary Expenditures	GDP*	Budgetary Revenues	Budgetary Expenditures
1926–27	2.5	34.9	39.4	2.4	32.5	36.7
1931–32	2.6	39.9	29.0	2.4	37.0	26.9
1936–37	3.0	32.6	27.5	2.7	30.0	25.3
1941–42	2.1	11.6	9.4	1.8	10.1	8.2
1946–47	3.9	15.5	18.0	3.4	13.2	15.4
1951–52	2.4	12.5	13.7	1.8	9.6	10.5
1956–57	1.6	9.1	9.7	0.9	5.4	5.7
1957–58	1.6	10.0	9.6	0.9	5.8	5.6
1958–59	1.8	12.3	10.5	1.1	7.5	6.4
1959–60	2.1	13.2	11.9	1.4	8.7	7.9
1960–61	2.1	12.5	11.5	1.3	7.9	7.3
1961–62	2.0	12.9	11.2	1.3	8.1	7.1
1962–63	2.1	13.7	12.2	1.4	9.1	8.0
1963–64	2.1	14.0	12.0	1.3	8.8	7.6
1964–65	2.0	12.8	12.3	1.2	7.6	7.3
1965–66	1.9	12.4	12.8	1.2	7.5	7.8
1966–67	1.8	12.1	11.9	1.0	6.8	6.7
1967–68	1.9	12.1	11.3	1.0	6.3	5.9
1968–69	1.9	12.3	11.9	1.0	6.4	6.2
1969–70	2.0	11.9	12.1	1.0	5.8	6.0
1970–71	2.1	12.7	12.1	1.0	6.0	5.7
1971–72	2.2	12.8	11.7	1.0	5.9	5.4
1972–73	2.1	12.0	11.1	1.0	5.4	5.0
1973–74	2.0	11.5	10.5	0.9	4.9	4.5
1974–75	2.1	11.1	10.4	0.9	4.9	4.6
1975–76	2.3	12.6	10.6	1.1	6.0	5.1
1976–77	2.4	13.7	11.6	1.2	6.7	5.7
1977–78	2.5	16.0	12.3	1.3	8.5	6.5
1978–79	2.9	19.1	14.2	1.6	10.8	8.0
1979–80	3.1	20.3	15.9	1.8	11.6	9.1
1980–81	3.4	21.9	17.1	2.0	13.0	10.2
1981–82	4.2	25.2	20.2	2.8	16.7	13.4
1982–83	4.5	27.8	19.1	3.3	20.2	13.9
1983–84	4.5	28.2	18.7	3.4	21.3	14.2
1984–85	5.0	31.7	20.6	4.1	25.7	16.7
1985–86	5.3	33.1	22.9	4.5	28.2	19.5
1986–87	5.3	31.1	22.9	4.4	26.1	19.3
1987–88	5.3	29.8	23.1	4.5	25.1	19.5

*For 1926–1927 to 1960–1961 inclusive, figures are expressed as a percentage of GNP.

Source: *Quarterly Economic Review*, March 1991; and *The Fiscal Plan*, 1989.

The increase in cost-sharing payments to the provinces and the reduction in infrastructure spending on new capital destroyed the idea that, as C. D. Howe had put it, the federal government should be "the prime factor in the creation and disposition of a major share of the national wealth."*

The conversion of the role of the federal government from a fiscally responsible spender in areas

*P. C. Newman, *The Canadian Establishment* (Toronto: McCelland and Stewart-Bantam Limited, 1977), p. 376.

continued on next page

in which it had constitutional authority and responsibility for spending to a conduit for diverting funds from one province to another in accordance with provincial initiatives in expenditure or taxation would have been acceptable fiscal strategy if federal tax revenue had increased as quickly as federal disbursements, but it did not.

FEDERAL RECEIPTS AS A SHARE OF GDP

Federal tax revenues began to grow more slowly than federal obligations for provincial cost-sharing and interest payments on the public debt in the mid-1970s. This trend began in 1974, with the indexation of the personal tax deductions to the inflation rate. Other tax measures designed to reduce the revenue yield to the government from individuals included the introduction of registered retirement and registered home-owner saving plans (RRSPs and ROHSPs) and the less significant provision for exempting an amount of capital gains from tax liability. Further measures to soften the impact of inflation or prevent the automatic growth in tax revenue that would occur under the progressive tax structure as a result of normal growth in nominal aggregate income were not limited to the household sector. Measures introduced to reduce the increase in tax revenue from the business sector included special deductions for investment in the Canadian film industry, publishing industry, and energy sector. There were tax reductions for the creation of multiple unit rental accommodations (MURBs), reductions in the indirect federal sales tax on certain manufactured products, and a provision that allowed a firm with losses to sell its tax credits to another firm. Accelerated depreciation allowances were introduced that reduced corporate tax revenues to the federal government for all firms making

certain types of capital purchases. There was even one measure introduced that allowed yachts and recreational vehicles to be used to reduce an individual's or firm's tax liability.

THE ROLE OF INTEREST RATES AND THE PUBLIC DEBT

We have already discussed the idea that interest payments on the public debt can require a reduction in other government expenditures. Another aspect of the interest on the public debt is that if interest rates increase, the cost of servicing the existing debt will grow. It is even possible, although rare, that if the interest rate grows rapidly enough the increase in the interest payments and carrying charges on the government's existing debt could grow more rapidly than the government's tax revenue, which would result in a growth in both the present deficit and the size of the outstanding total public debt. In other words, if the interest rate increases rapidly enough relative to the normal growth in the economy, then, even if the government decreases its spending on goods and services, the increase in the interest charges might be larger than the increase in tax revenues. As a result, *even if the government were running a surplus on its primary balance, the deficit and public debt could increase.* Some economists argue that this phenomenon occurred in the period between 1986 and 1991.

In the early 1980s the interest rate rose dramatically. This was to some extent a deliberate strategy by the Bank of Canada to reduce inflationary pressure and to stabilize the external value of the Canadian dollar. In relation to GDP, the net charges on the public debt rose to an all-time high of over 4 percent of GDP (see Figure P25-1). While most economists agree that recent deficits and the public debt

are too large in relation to the size of the economy, some financial experts argue that it is interest rates which are too high and that the public debt and the yearly deficits (measured in primary terms) may not be too high in relation to GDP. Further, they point out that every time the interest rates rise by one percent it costs the government roughly an extra $2 billion in added interest payments to finance the debt. Therefore, they argue, unless interest rates can be lowered, the federal government must reduce services and transfer payments to the provinces simply to remain at the same deficit position every time the interest rate is increased.

THE ROLE OF THE BUSINESS CYCLE

Budget developments during the early 1980s were largely a reflection of the business cycle. In the early 1980s almost all industrialized economies experienced a widespread and severe recession. Canada was no exception, and as unemployment rose the automatic stabilizers of unemployment insurance and social assistance increased federal payments to the provinces. Note that government expenditures, and especially transfer payments, typically rise and receipts generally fall relative to GDP during recessions (for the reasons discussed in Chapter 23). The greater severity of the recession of 1981–1982 (relative to other postwar recessions) accentuated the cyclical swing in the deficit during the first half of the 1980s. This pattern was repeated again in 1991–1992 as the economy plunged into a sharp decline. As with the previous recession the government was faced with an unplanned increase in its deficit largely caused by the growth in unemployment insurance, welfare,

continued on next page

and equalization payments to the poorer provinces that were necessary in the face of deteriorating economic activity. Further, the failure of the government to reduce its deficits during the period 1988–1991 meant that once the economy entered a severe downturn in 1991, the government had little fiscal opportunity left to use increased deficits to counteract the declining levels of aggregate expenditure brought on by the recession.

CONCLUSION

In summary, the large increases in deficits during the 1980s and early 1990s were due to a combination of factors: larger transfer payments to the provincial governments and larger transfer payments to individuals because of the recession, abnormally low growth in the tax revenues caused by indexation and other tax reductions, and very high

interest rates set by the Bank of Canada. Two different federal governments had failed to exploit the opportunity to reduce the deficit during the relatively healthy middle years of the 1980s and had failed to reform the locked-in system of federal transfers. In addition, politicians had exploited political advantage by pointing to the deficits incurred by previous governments as a sign of irresponsible economic policy and had created a political climate in which it was difficult if not impossible to gain public support for increased deficits during the recession periods of 1981–1982 and 1991–1992, even if those deficits could be used to increase spending on worthwhile capital formation projects to create infrastructure. In this way the federal government has lost much of its ability to use increased deficits to create infrastructure that might

contribute to the future growth and health of the economy. Instead, federal deficits are being used to finance transfers that do not directly support the growth of capital goods that might enhance the productive capacity of the economy.

For Discussion

- Some claim that if the Bank of Canada would lower interest rates, the deficits of the 1980s and 1990s would stop causing concern. Comment on this point of view using the evidence in Figure P25-1.
- Both Keynesians and supply-siders might argue that raising taxes to reduce the deficit could actually end up making it larger. Explain the likely, but different, reasoning underlying their contention.

that the net government debt grew at an average rate of about 20 percent per year while nominal GDP grew only about one third, at an average rate of about 7 percent per year. Eventually politicians and policymakers are going to have to reduce government deficits or reduce interest rates in order to bring the growth rate of government debt down to or below the rate of growth of nominal GDP. In 1989, The Fiscal Plan of the Department of Finance set the target for the deficit to average about $15 billion by the early 1990s, which would place it low enough to reduce the debt to GDP ratio and reduce the burden of the public debt if that figure can be achieved.[15] Unfortunately the deepening recession of 1991–1992 forced the government to increase its payments for equalization to the poorer provinces and led to increases in disbursements for welfare and unemployment insurance, which increased the deficit and forced delays in the government's schedule for reducing the deficit. The decrease in interest rates in the second half of 1992 provides some hope that refinancing costs will allow the government to reduce the carrying cost of the debt.

Summary

1. Annually balanced budgets might accentuate the business cycle. A cyclically balanced budget policy is difficult to follow because the expansion

---

[15]The Honourable Michael Wilson, Minister of Finance, *The Fiscal Plan, Controlling the Public Debt* (Department of Finance Canada, April, 1989), p. 17.

phase of a business cycle typically differs in length and magnitude from the recession phase. Consequently, functional finance is the budget policy most often followed.

2. Given the actual level of government spending, the cyclically adjusted budget measures what the budget deficit or surplus *would be* if the economy were operating at potential GDP. The cyclically adjusted budget deficit or surplus is a more accurate measure of the impact of fiscal policy than is the actual budget deficit or surplus.

3. A budget deficit has a more expansionary impact on the economy if it is financed by creating new money than if it is financed by borrowing. A budget surplus has less of a contractionary impact on the economy if the surplus is used to retire privately held debt outstanding than if it is simply left to accumulate in the government treasury.

4. One concern about budget deficits is the extent to which they may crowd out investment spending. In terms of the relationship between withdrawals and injections this means that part of the economy's saving must go to finance the deficit, leaving only the remainder to finance investment.

5. A supply-side view holds that it may be possible to reduce deficits by lowering marginal tax rates. It is argued that the resulting increase in total income might yield an increase in tax revenue despite the reduction in tax rates, a proposition that is characterized by the Laffer curve.

6. The government debt, or the stock of government bonds outstanding, was larger than GDP in the immediate post–World War II years. Up through 1975, GDP grew faster than the debt until the debt was only one fifth the size of the GDP. By this criterion the debt became less of a burden over time. In recent years the ratio of government debt to GDP has increased to over one half of GDP, suggesting that the debt burden is increasing.

7. The government debt may be a burden to the extent that the taxes and transfer payments needed to make interest payments on the debt cause a redistribution of income among citizens, to the extent that the debt is held by non-residents, and to the extent that debt creation allows the financing of unproductive or unnecessary government spending.

8. The large budget deficits of recent years have caused the government debt to grow at a faster rate than GDP, raising concern that growing interest payments on the debt will take an increasing share of the government budget. To keep the debt from growing faster than GDP, the dollar size of the deficit must not exceed the growth rate of nominal GDP multiplied by the dollar size of the government debt.

9. The indexing of personal income tax deductions and the evolution of a system of complex tax deductions and allowances have reduced federal tax revenues as a percentage of GDP over a fifteen-year period. The federal government committed itself to cost-sharing programs with the provincial governments over the period from 1965 to 1975. The combination of these two events along with the aging and urbanization of the population caused an increase in the structural federal deficit.

10. If interest rates increase faster than the increase in tax revenues, the burden of interest payments on the public debt relative to GDP can increase even if the government reduces its spending for goods and services.

11. The ballooning of federal government budget deficits during the 1980s and early 1990s was caused by growth in cost-sharing payments to the provinces,

increased transfer payments to individuals, tax rate reductions (to some extent), and unusually high interest rates. During the early years of both the 1980s and 1990s sluggish growth and recession also were factors.

Key Terms and Concepts

burdens of the
    government debt
crowding out
cyclically adjusted
    budget

distribution
    effects
domestic bond market
    financing
external debt

foreign bond market
    financing
impounding
Laffer curve
lien

Questions and Problems

1. Relative to other views on budget policy, it has been said that "functional finance isn't so much a deliberate budget policy as a rationalization for what actually happens." Considering all the difficulties associated with discretionary fiscal policy, as well as the difficulties of pursuing the other budget policies, give an assessment of this statement.

2. It has been argued by some economists that financing government deficits by borrowing may actually result in completely offsetting the expansionary effect of the deficit. What must they be assuming about the degree of difficulty of inducing the public to buy government bonds and the degree of sensitivity of investment spending to interest rate changes? These economists would refer to this as a situation of "complete crowding out," where the real issue is one of *who* will decide how resources are to be used—the government or the private market. Explain.

3. Explain how an increase in the deficit can actually increase the amount of investment in the economy. What must be true about net exports, the relationship between saving and investment, and investor confidence for this to be true?

4. Suppose that the economy's total income equals $500 billion and that income is subject to a proportional tax rate of .5. If the proportional tax rate is reduced to .4, by how much would total income have to rise in order for total tax revenue to increase?

5. In what sense is the public debt "what we owe ourselves"? In what sense and why might this not be true from the standpoint of an individual taxpayer? Why do foreign holdings of our nation's government debt put us in a position like that of an individual who is in debt?

6. If the government debt equals $350 billion and nominal GDP is growing at 4 percent per year, what limit on the size of the government deficit is necessary if the growth rate of the government debt is not to exceed the growth rate of GDP? Does this value change if the interest rate increases?

7. In the early 1970s Canada eliminated the inheritance tax and indexed the basic personal deduction on personal income tax to the rate of inflation. These two measures along with certain tax measures affecting business taxes effectively reduced the marginal income tax rates in Canada. Using supply-side theory explain what effect these tax reductions should have had on the level of equilibrium GDP, the level of unemployment, and the size of the government deficit during the 1970s. Does the fact that the government deficit increased substantially during the later part of the 1970s support the supply-side consequences of the reductions in marginal tax rates?

Chapter 26

Inflation, Unemployment, and Expectations

In the past, mainstream economic theory associated a rising rate of inflation with a declining unemployment rate during the expansion phase of the business cycle. The behaviour of inflation and unemployment during the 1960s certainly conformed to this theoretical relationship. The experience of Canada and other Western economies during the 1970s and 1980s suggests that this relationship between the unemployment rate and inflation rate is more complex than was previously assumed, or that the relationship has entirely broken down. In the mid-1970s unemployment in Canada rose dramatically while the inflation rate remained almost unchanged. This was followed by a period in the late 1970s and early 1980s during which the inflation rate increased markedly but was accompanied by very little change in unemployment. Between 1976 and 1978 a mild increase in inflation was accompanied by a dramatic rise in unemployment, then from 1979 to 1981 there was a dramatic increase in inflation accompanied by a very slight rise in unemployment. From 1984 to 1988 the inflation rate remained almost stable and unemployment declined by almost one third. From 1988 to 1991 the conventional inverse relationship between inflation and unemployment appeared once again.

In this chapter we will begin by investigating whether there is a trade-off between inflation and unemployment, often referred to as the *Phillips curve*. While there has been much controversy over the possible existence of such a curve, that debate has given rise to some interesting new theories of inflation and unemployment. We will examine these developments in economic thinking as well as their implications for macroeconomic policy. We will also look at the changing nature of the unemployment problem, its implications for inflation, and the types of policies necessary to be effective in reducing unemployment and inflation at the same time. Before beginning this agenda, however, it will be useful to briefly review aggregate demand *AD* and aggregate supply *AS*, the distinction between demand-pull and cost-push inflation, and the role of monetary and fiscal policy in the *AD–AS* framework.

Aggregate Demand and Supply Reviewed

Recall from our earlier discussion of aggregate demand and aggregate supply, in Chapter 24, that there are three reasons why the *AD* curve slopes downward to the right: (1) the wealth effect, (2) the interest rate effect, and (3) the foreign purchases effect. The wealth effect contributes to the negative slope of the *AD* curve because a higher price level reduces the purchasing power of consumers' fixed-dollar assets and causes consumers to cut back on the quantity of goods and services they demand. The interest rate effect holds that an increase in the economy's price level drives up the interest rate—the price paid for the use of money. A higher interest rate tends to discourage business borrowing to purchase capital goods and household borrowing to buy certain kinds of consumer goods. The foreign purchases effect contributes to the negative slope of the *AD* curve because a rise in the general level of prices in the economy relative to the price level in other countries makes domestic goods more expensive relative to foreign goods. Canadians therefore buy more imports instead of Canadian goods, and foreigners buy fewer of the now more expensive Canadian exports.

Turning to the *AS* curve, recall that the slope depends on two things: (1) diminishing returns and (2) the extent to which businesses and resource suppliers regard an increase in the price of the item that they are selling as an increase in the relative price of their good or factor service. The more severe the effect of diminishing returns, the more vertical will be the aggregate supply curve. Similarly, the aggregate supply curve will be vertical if resource suppliers or firms believe that an increase in the price of their product is simply a symptom of a rise in the general level of prices. The intersection of the *AD* and *AS* curves determines an economy's equilibrium real GDP and the associated employment level, as well as the equilibrium level of prices.

LEARNING OBJECTIVES

After reading this chapter, you will be able to:

1. Explain the concept of the Phillips curve.
2. Explain the factors that can cause the inflation rate and the unemployment rate to increase at the same time.
3. Define the natural rate hypothesis used in longrun equilibrium.
4. Explain the accelerationist view of the inflation–unemployment trade-off.
5. Discuss the differences between adaptive expectations and rational expectations.
6. Explain the policy ineffectiveness proposition of new classical theory.
7. Explain the new Keynesian view that rational expectations and effective government policy can coexist.
8. Describe how changing demographic factors and institutional factors can change potential income and alter the natural unemployment rate.

Demand-Pull Inflation

Figure 26-1 uses *AD–AS* analysis to show the difference between demand-pull inflation and cost-push inflation. In frame (a) of Figure 26-1 the economy is initially in equilibrium at point e_0, where AD_0 and AS intersect to determine price level P_0 and real GDP level y_0. Suppose that aggregate demand increases so that AD_0 shifts rightward to AD_1—caused by more optimistic business and consumer expectations, for example. Real GDP increases to y_1 (and unemployment declines) while the general level of prices rises to P_1, corresponding to the new equilibrium at e_1. The increase in aggregate demand has caused an increase in

FIGURE 26-1 Demand-Pull and Cost-Push Inflation

When aggregate demand increases, frame (a), causing the price level to rise from P_0 to P_1, we have demand-pull inflation. Real GDP increases from y_0 to y_1 and unemployment is reduced. A cost-push inflation occurs when the aggregate supply curve shifts upward, such as from AS_0 to AS_1, frame (b), pushing up the price level from P_0 to P_2. Real GDP declines from y_0 to y_2 and unemployment rises.

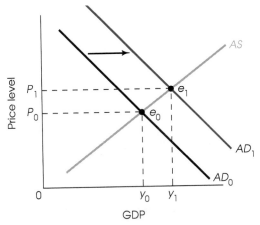

Demand-pull inflation

(a)

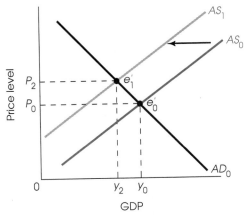

Cost-push inflation

(b)

the employment level, the income level, and the price level. This is demand-pull inflation. Recall also that such an increase in aggregate demand can be caused by an expansionary monetary policy, which occurs when monetary policymakers increase the money supply and ease credit conditions, thereby stimulating business and consumer buying. Similarly, aggregate demand can be increased by an expansionary fiscal policy as we discussed in Chapters 23 and 24. Note that from this point of view policymakers are faced with a trade-off. Expansionary policies can increase the economy's real GDP and reduce unemployment, but only by generating an increase in the general level of prices.

Cost-Push Inflation

Cost-push inflation is illustrated in Figure 26-1, frame (b). Recall that the aggregate supply curve's position reflects costs of production in the economy. Given these costs, the businesses will continue to produce only if they receive prices that cover costs and yield a normal profit. An increase in money wages, energy or raw material prices, or any other input price will raise production costs and hence the prices that the economy's firms receive at any level of real GDP. The aggregate supply curve is shifted upward from AS_0 to AS_1, say, and equilibrium moves from e_0' to e_1'. Real GDP declines from y_0 to y_2 (so that unemployment rises) and the price level increases from P_0 to P_2. The upward shift in the aggregate supply curve has pushed up the price level. This is cost-push inflation. Because output (and employment) declines while the price level rises, this is also referred to as *stagflation* to indicate that the economy is stagnating in terms of real output at the same time that prices are rising.

The Trade-Off Between Inflation and Unemployment

Ever since the late 1950s, economists, policymakers, and politicians have speculated and argued about the existence of a trade-off between inflation and unemployment. Many have claimed that it is possible to reduce unemployment if we are willing to tolerate higher rates of inflation. Conversely, it is often claimed that inflation can be reduced only by incurring higher rates of unemployment. The implication is that there exists a trade-off—namely, we can get higher employment at a cost of more inflation, or less inflation at a cost of greater unemployment.

The graphical representation of this trade-off is known as the **Phillips curve,** after the British economist A. W. Phillips who in 1958 put forward empirical evidence of a similar trade-off for the British economy over the period 1862–1957. Economists have subsequently devoted considerable effort to investigating the possible existence of Phillips curve trade-offs in industrialized countries for the postwar period. The experience with inflation and unemployment during the 1960s, 1970s, and 1980s suggests that such a trade-off is not so simple or straightforward. Indeed, the experience of recent years has raised serious questions about whether such a trade-off even exists.

The Phillips Curve

Recall our discussion of the effects of increased aggregate demand on an upward-sloping aggregate supply curve in Chapter 24. There we saw that increases in aggregate demand cause output and employment to increase, unemployment to fall, and the economy to move closer to potential full employment at potential GDP. This is illustrated again in Figure 26-2, where increases in aggregate demand from AD_0 to AD_1 to AD_2 cause real GDP to rise from y_0 to y_1 to y_2. Note, however, that in this figure the aggregate supply curve is a curved line with the slope increasing as the level of output increases. Therefore, increases in aggregate demand result in ever-larger increases in the general price level (from P_0 to P_1 to P_2) and ever-smaller increases in employment and the quantity of output, or real GDP. Therefore, the ever-larger increases in the general price level are accompanied by ever-smaller reductions in the unemployment rate. Changes in real GDP and unemployment are inversely related. This description characterizes the onset of demand-pull inflation as the economy approaches potential employment. It suggests that we can only have a lower unemployment rate if we are willing to have a higher rate of inflation. This is the essence of the logic underlying the Phillips curve.

Graphical Representation of the Phillips Curve—A Menu of Choices

A hypothetical Phillips curve is shown in Figure 26-3. The annual percentage rate of increase in the price level, the rate of inflation, is measured on the vertical axis, and the unemployment rate is measured on the horizontal axis. The curve slopes downward left to right, a reflection of the fact that a lower unemployment rate can only be achieved by having a higher rate of inflation, and vice versa.

The Phillips curve represents a menu of choices for monetary and fiscal policy. For example, the hypothetical Phillips curve of Figure 26-3 suggests that

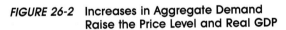

FIGURE 26-2 Increases in Aggregate Demand Raise the Price Level and Real GDP

When aggregate demand increases over the *AS* curve, the resulting rise in the economy's price level becomes ever larger, while that of real GDP becomes ever smaller. This suggests that lower rates of unemployment are accompanied by higher rates of inflation.

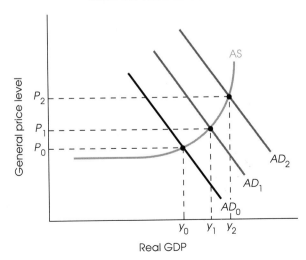

694

Part 6   Macroeconomic Theories of Income and Employment

FIGURE 26-3   The Phillips Curve: The Inflation
and Unemployment Trade-Off
(Hypothetical Example)

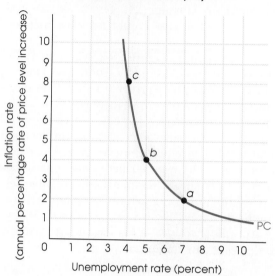

The Phillips curve is downward
sloping left to right, suggesting
that there is a trade-off between
inflation (vertical axis) and
unemployment (horizontal
axis). The curve implies the
hypothetical shape of the
Phillips curve.

if policymakers want to keep the rate of inflation at 2 percent or less, they must be willing to settle for an unemployment rate of 7 percent or more, as represented by point *a* on the Phillips curve. On the other hand, if policymakers are willing to tolerate a 4 percent inflation rate, the unemployment rate can be reduced to 5 percent, point *b* on the Phillips curve. The trade-off between inflation and unemployment, represented by the slope of the curve between points *a* and *b*, is a reduction of 2 percentage points in the unemployment rate in exchange for a 2 percentage point increase in the inflation rate. However, the trade-off worsens between points *b* and *c*. If policymakers want to reduce the unemployment rate from 5 percent to 4 percent, they must be willing to settle for an increase in the inflation rate from 4 percent to 8 percent.

The lower right-hand portion of the Phillips curve suggests that to achieve a zero rate of inflation would require an unacceptably high rate of unemployment. Conversely, the upper left-hand portion suggests that a reduction of the unemployment rate below 4 percent would give rise to prohibitively high rates of inflation. The Phillips curve reminds us that economics is a study of choices, and that every choice has an associated cost. For example, choosing point *b* instead of point *a* means choosing a 5 percent instead of a 7 percent unemployment rate, a reduction in unemployment that is considered desirable. However, the cost of this choice is an additional 2 percentage points of inflation, from a rate of 2 percent at point *a* to 4 percent at point *b* —a move that is undesirable but necessary in order to achieve the lower unemployment rate.

It should be emphasized that the Phillips curve shown in Figure 26-3 is strictly a hypothetical example. The curve could lie to the left or right of the position shown. It might conceivably intersect the horizontal axis at a 10 percent unemployment rate. This would suggest that if we were willing to settle for a 10 percent unemployment rate, to accept it as natural or normal, we could have a zero rate of inflation.

Implications of the Phillips Curve—The Reversibility Issue

One important implication of the Phillips curve is that the economy will usually experience both inflation and unemployment at the same time. In other words, price stability and full employment are not compatible goals of fiscal and monetary policy. Another implication is that the economy can move up along the Phillips curve, reducing the unemployment rate and increasing the rate of inflation. However, the Phillips curve also implies that this process is reversible—that the economy can move back down the curve, as from point *c* to point *b* to point *a*, reducing the rate of inflation and increasing the unemployment rate. This implication is far more questionable and controversial than the others.

It appears to most observers of the Canadian economy that the rate of inflation rises more readily than it falls. Almost all economists would agree that an increase in aggregate demand is likely to lead to an increase in the rate of inflation and a reduction in the unemployment rate, a movement up the Phillips curve. Not as many economists would argue that the economy is likely to follow the same path back down the Phillips curve in response to a decrease in aggregate demand. What does the evidence show?

Is There a Stable Phillips Curve?—The Evidence

Figure 26-4 plots the rate of inflation (vertical axis) and the associated unemployment rate (horizontal axis) for the Canadian economy in each year since 1962. The data strongly suggest that there is not a stable Phillips curve relationship. This figure shows us that periods during which the inflation rate rose and the unemployment rate fell were followed by periods in which the inflation rate fell by less than the previous rise as the unemployment rate increased. Clearly movements up along any hypothetical Phillips curve are not followed by reverse movements back down the same Phillips curve. Even more striking are the instances in which both the inflation rate and the unemployment rate moved in the same direction. Inflation and unemployment both rose over the periods from 1966 to 1968, 1976 to 1978, and 1979 to 1981. In addition there is one period from 1983 to 1985 when unemployment and inflation both fell at the same time! These movements are completely contrary to the proposed shape of the Phillips curve. The data in Figure 26-4 suggest that the economy has experienced an upward spiral in the inflation rate associated with cyclical movements in the unemployment rate. Also, on average, the unemployment rate attainable at any particular inflation rate seems to have increased between the 1960s and 1980s.

Rather than following an inflation against unemployment trade-off relationship explained by the Phillips curve, Figure 26-4 suggests that the economy follows irregular cyclical loops as far as unemployment and inflation are concerned. For example, the first loop appears from 1962 to 1971. The second loop occurs from 1971 to 1976, and a third loop occurs from 1978 to 1989. Note that these loops appear to have shifted upward and outward to the right, indicating that a particular level of inflation is accompanied by higher levels of unemployment as time advances. Much of the rest of this chapter is concerned with possible explanations for the phenomena shown in Figure 26-4.

FIGURE 26-4   **The Canadian Experience with Inflation and Unemployment 1962–1991**

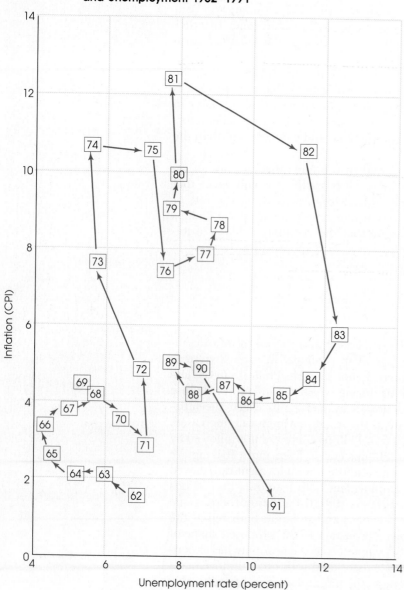

The data suggest that the economy has experienced an upward spiral in the rate of inflation associated with cyclical movements in the unemployment rate. On average, the unemployment rate attributable at any particular inflation rate seems to have increased between the 1960s and 1990s.

Supply-Side Shocks and Stagflation

The concept of the Phillips curve really derives from the notion that increases in aggregate demand tend to increase inflation and reduce unemployment, while decreases in aggregate demand tend to reduce inflation and increase unemployment. However, during the 1970s the Canadian economy suffered a number of severe supply shocks—large increases in the price of imported oil and other fuels, intermittent worldwide food and raw materials shortages, as well as increased wages and interest rates. These shocks have led economists to focus more attention on the role of aggregate supply and its interaction with aggregate demand as an explanatory factor underlying the behaviour of inflation and unemployment.

Recall our discussion in Chapter 24 of cost-push inflation and how it might be represented in terms of the aggregate supply curve, as illustrated in Figure 24-5. There we explained that a cost-push inflation can occur in a number of ways. It might come about because powerful unions force through wage increases that exceed the productivity gains of their members. Businesses then pass on the resulting rise in per unit costs, at least in part, in the form of higher prod-uct prices. Cost-push inflation may also result because a few large firms in key industries exercise their market power to raise profits by increasing the prices they charge for their products. Some economists argue that this cause should be categorized as profit-push inflation, but most include it as simply one of the causes of cost-push. Another source of cost-push inflation, which was common in the 1970s, was the increase in the prices of vital resources, such as energy and other raw materials. Again, such increases cause increases in average costs that push up the prices of almost all goods and services, as reflected by a rise in the general price level. Alternatively, increased costs can be caused by the government through increases in some types of taxation or through increased interest rates. In Figure 24-5, we saw how cost-push inflation is represented by an upward shift of the aggregate supply curve.

Stagflation *is defined as a simultaneous increase in both the rate of inflation and the unemployment rate.* Note that this is contrary to the conventional Phillips curve trade-off. Using the aggregate supply and aggregate demand model, stagflation can result from an upward shift of the aggregate supply curve—a cost-push effect. Stagflation provides a possible framework for analyzing the behaviour of inflation and unemployment from 1966 to 1969, from 1976 to 1978, and from 1979 to 1981, as shown in Figure 26-4. Most economists have used the 1973 to 1974 and 1979 to 1981 episodes, in particular, as examples of the consequence of supply shocks, caused by dramatic increases in the price of petroleum and factor tax rates. These periods are also used as examples of a cost-push type of inflation that creates stagflation.

Two Theories of the Natural Rate Hypothesis

While the simultaneous increase in the inflation and unemployment rates of 1966–1969, 1976–1978, and 1979–1981 were caused by supply-side shocks, the factors underlying the pattern of combinations of inflation and unemployment for other years shown in Figure 26-4 are less clear. Only the years 1962–1966, 1969–1971, and 1988–1989 bear any resemblance to the hypothetical Phillips curve of Figure 26-3, and even these years suggest that the Phillips curve has shifted over time. Moreover, these years were characterized by the expansion of aggregate demand in the economy. Finally, there are periods over which unem-ployment either rose or fell by relatively large amounts, with little or no change in the rate of inflation. These experiences, illustrated by the periods 1974 to

Checkpoint* 26-1

Suppose that the Phillips curve in Figure 26-3 shifts in such a way that unemployment can be reduced with a small increase in the rate of inflation. Sketch how the new Phillips curve might look. Suppose that the Phillips curve in Figure 26-3 rotates so that the economy can have a zero-percent rate of inflation when it has a 9 percent unemployment rate, and yet requires larger increases in the inflation rate for each percentage point of reduction in the unemployment rate. Sketch how such a Phillips curve might look. If the Phillips curve represents a menu of choices, is the policymakers' selection of a point on the curve a normative or a positive issue? Why?

*Answers to all Checkpoints can be found at the back of the text.

1975 and 1984 to 1988, provide a vexing complication that there may be no permanent trade-off between unemployment and inflation. An example of the lack of reversibility back down a stable Phillips curve is illustrated by the recession of 1981–1982. This recession was largely due to a tightening of monetary policy in an attempt to curb what was then regarded by the Bank of Canada and other policymakers as an alarmingly high inflation rate. The consequence was a contraction of aggregate demand. Unfortunately, this resulted in little change in inflation but a rather large increase in the unemployment rate. In general, what the pattern of data represented in Figure 26-4 does suggest is that if there is a Phillips curve it appears to be shifting upward and rotating.

Attempts to explain the data of Figure 26-4 have contributed to the development of the accelerationist view of the inflation–unemployment trade-off. This view essentially holds that the Phillips curve shifts upward if workers begin to expect higher rates of inflation over time and that it will shift downward if workers expect lower inflation. Probably the most dramatic developments in macroeconomic thinking in recent years have been the emergence of adaptive expectations theory by Milton Friedman and Edmund Phelps and the development of rational expectations theory by R. E. Lucas. These theories were initially adopted by the new classical theorists whose conservative views suggested that a *laissez-faire* approach by government would produce the most desirable performance by the economy in terms of unemployment and inflation. The usefulness of the rational expectations approach in particular was soon recognized by proponents of more liberal interventionist government policies including Lawrence Ball, Gregory Mankiw, David Romer, and Janet Yellen. Using rational expectations as their starting point, these theorists developed a more interventionist theory, called *new Keynesian theory*. Today both new classical theory and new Keynesian theory rely heavily on the rational expectations theory developed by R. E. Lucas as the basis of their methodology.

The Accelerationist View—Adaptive Expectations

The adaptive expectations theory led to the development of the **accelerationist view** *which contends that in the longrun the Phillips curve is a vertical straight line* (such as AS_3 in Figure 24-3. It is argued that in the longrun the economy tends to operate at potential GDP with what new classical theorists call the **natural rate of unemployment.**[1] The accelerationist view holds that expansionary monetary and fiscal policies aimed at increasing aggregate output, and consequently at reducing the unemployment rate below this *natural* rate will result in an ever-increasing, or accelerating, rate of inflation. Let's see why.

---

[1] In Chapter 20 we explained NAIRU, the lowest level of unemployment consistent with no acceleration of the rate of inflation. It is a functional definition of unemployment and does not imply that everyone who is willing and able to work has a job. The accelerationist view is that in longrun equilibrium the economy will be at potential income and the unemployment rate will equal NAIRU. For this reason new classical theorists refer to NAIRU as the natural unemployment rate. The use of the term in no way implies that this level of unemployment is inevitable or desirable.

The Shortrun Trade-Off

Assume that the unemployment at potential GDP is 6.0 percent,[2] corresponding to point n_1 in Figure 26-5. However, suppose that policymakers and politicians think that a 6 percent unemployment rate is too high—that disgruntled voters will turn on them if something isn't done to reduce it. Consequently, expansionary monetary and fiscal policies are initiated, thereby increasing aggregate demand, which in turn pulls up the general price level. Given the level of money wages, if firms view the increase in the price of their own product as a rise in that product's price *relative* to the price of other goods, they will expand output and hire more labour. As a result, in the shortrun the economy moves from point n_1 to point d_1 in Figure 26-5. The unemployment rate has been reduced to 5 percent, but the inflation rate has risen from zero percent to 2 percent. Thus, there is a Phillips curve type of trade-off, at least in the shortrun, according to the accelerationist view.

---

[2]For actual estimates of the natural unemployment rate in Canada from 1946 to 1990 you might be interested in reading Chapter 3 of *Transitions for the 90s*, twenty-seventh annual report of the Economic Council of Canada. It estimated the natural unemployment rate for the 1980s at 9.3 percent. For the illustrative purposes of this chapter and in consideration of the Economic Council's suggestion that high unemployment is neither acceptable nor inevitable, we have used a slightly lower unemployment rate.

FIGURE 26-5 **The Accelerationist View**

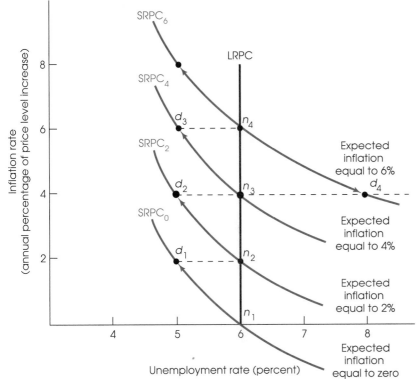

The accelerationist view holds that in the longrun the economy tends to operate at its natural rate of unemployment, here hypothetically assumed to be 6 percent. An increase in aggregate demand increases profit, and hence output and employment, in the shortrun, thereby temporarily reducing the unemployment rate below the natural rate while increasing the inflation rate (n_1 to n_2). Repetition of this process causes the inflation rate to accelerate and the shortrun Phillips curve to shift upward as workers' expected rate of inflation rises in recognition of the increases in the actual inflation rate. Hence, there is no stable longrun Phillips curve trade-off between the inflation rate and the unemployment rate.

However, the position d_1 cannot be maintained in the longrun. Adaptive expectations theory tries to explain this phenomenon by using the **asymmetrical information assumption** *which states that when aggregate demand increases, businesses become aware of it before unions or other resource suppliers.* According to adaptive expectations, as aggregate demand increases, inventories become depleted as firms sell off existing products to meet the increased demand. In addition there is an increase in backlogs of unfilled orders. Firms respond to the increased aggregate demand by increasing their prices, which pulls the general price level up. Given the level of wages and input costs, which have not yet increased, the higher level of prices for products increases profits for final goods suppliers and makes them willing to increase production. Only after firms supplying final goods have increased their prices do workers and other resource suppliers become aware of the increase in the general price level. Firms were anticipating that the general level of costs and prices was unchanged as they increased the price of their final products. In other words firms and workers have made an error in estimating the general level of prices.

For suppliers of labour this means their real wage (*defined as the money wage divided by the general price level*) has fallen. A worker gets paid the same number of dollars, but these dollars buy less. According to adaptive expectations theory, the labour force, correctly perceiving themselves as worse off, demand and receive a higher money wage in order to keep pace with the rise in the general price level. However, when the money wage has risen to restore the real wage level that initially existed at n_1, profits for final goods producers will be reduced back to their initial level. Firms therefore reduce output back to its initial level. Hence, the unemployment rate returns again to the so-called "natural" unemployment rate of 6 percent. Now, however, the inflation rate is 2 percent, so the economy is at point n_2 in Figure 26-5.

Note that at the initial point n_1 the inflation rate was zero percent, so workers and other resource suppliers had come to expect a zero-percent rate of inflation. Only after the economy has made the move to point d_1 do workers and other resource suppliers become aware that their expectation of a zero rate of inflation is no longer valid, that the inflation rate is in fact 2 percent. Along with the catch-up increase in money wages and input prices, which moves the economy to point n_2, workers and other resource suppliers revise their expected rate of inflation upward to 2 percent. Hence, according to the accelerationist view in the adaptive expectations theory there is a shortrun Phillips curve passing through points n_1 and d_1 that is stable as long as workers and other resource suppliers expect a zero rate of inflation. When they revise their expected inflation rate upward to 2 percent, the shortrun Phillips curve shifts upward until it passes through point n_2.

No Longrun Trade-Off

The whole process may be repeated. Suppose that once again, frustrated by the return of the unemployment rate to the 6 percent level, government policy-makers use expansionary monetary and fiscal policies to stimulate aggregate demand.

Adaptive expectations theory assumes that firms and workers did not learn from their past experience when expansionary government policy caused inflation to increase. In other words, adaptive expectations assumes that economic agents make systematic errors. Starting from point n_2, with the inflation rate already at 2 percent, firms and workers again get fooled by the expansionary policy of the government. When the government expands the level of aggregate demand, firms must again interpret the rise in the price of their own product as a rise in the relative price. Consequently, firms again expand output and employment. The economy moves from point n_2 to point d_2 up along the shortrun Phillips curve corresponding to a 2 percent expected rate of inflation. Again, there is a shortrun reduction of the unemployment rate to 5 percent, but the inflation rate now rises to 4 percent. Again workers and resource suppliers realize, only after it happens, that their real wages and earnings from selling inputs have fallen. In short, their expectation of a 2 percent rate of inflation is too low, since the actual inflation rate is now 4 percent. Hence, the factor costs and money wages increase to restore real compensation levels for input suppliers to their previous level. Firms would again follow their systematic readjustment, reducing output back to its previous level at potential GDP, and therefore the unemployment rate would return to the natural rate of 6 percent, corresponding to point n_3. The shortrun Phillips curve has shifted upward to a position, at point n_3, corresponding to an expected inflation rate of 4 percent. Unfortunately, the longrun consequence of policymakers' efforts to reduce the unemployment rate below the natural rate is an undesirable acceleration of the inflation rate from 2 percent to 4 percent without any reduction of the unemployment rate at all!

The process could be repeated again and again with the economy moving from n_3 to d_3 to n_4 and so forth, the inflation rate rising to ever higher levels. The downward-sloping shortrun Phillips curves through points $n_1 d_1, n_2 d_2, n_3 d_3$, and so on, correspond to successively higher expected inflation rates. Policymaker efforts to move along a shortrun Phillips curve such as $n_1 d_1$ cause it to shift upward to a less desirable position such as $n_2 d_2$. And repeated efforts result in yet higher and even less desirable positions. A stable shortrun Phillips curve representing an unchanging trade-off between inflation and unemployment simply doesn't exist according to this adaptive expectations accelerationist view. For example, in the longrun an inflation rate of 2 percent cannot be continuously maintained together with a 5 percent unemployment rate, as represented by point d_1. If policymakers wanted to keep the unemployment rate at 5 percent they would have to expand aggregate demand continuously. But such a policy would unavoidably cause the inflation rate to increase from 2 percent (point d_1) to 4 percent (point d_2) to 6 percent (point d_3), and so on.

In the longrun there can be an unchanging inflation rate only if the economy's unemployment rate is equal to the natural rate of unemployment. That is, the inflation rate can remain unchanged only if the economy is at a point on the vertical line through points n_1, n_2, n_3, and n_4. Persistent attempts by policymakers to stimulate aggregate demand to reduce the unemployment rate below the natural rate will cause an ever-increasing rate of inflation.

What happens if contractionary monetary and fiscal policies are implemented in an attempt to reduce the inflation rate? Suppose that the economy is at point n_4 in Figure 26-5 where the actual inflation rate is 6 percent and the shortrun Phillips curve through n_4 corresponds to an expected inflation rate of 6 percent. Suppose that policymakers reduce the money supply or increase taxes so that aggregate demand declines and firms now find that the growth rate of prices of their products slows down from a 6 percent to a 4 percent rate. Since workers still expect a 6 percent inflation rate they continue to push up their money wages at a 6 percent rate. Therefore, firms experience declining profits and cut back output and employment. The unemployment rate increases to 8 percent as the economy moves back down the Phillips curve to point d_4. When workers finally realize that their expected inflation rate is higher than the actual rate of 4 percent, they revise their expected inflation rate to 4 percent and become willing to settle for a 4 percent rate of increase in their money wage. Firms' profits rise, and they expand output and employment until the unemployment rate returns to the natural unemployment rate corresponding to point n_3. The Phillips curve has shifted down to the position n_3d_3.

The New Classical Theory—Rational Expectations

According to the adaptive expectations theory, policymakers can keep the unemployment rate below the natural rate, though the benefits to society of a higher level of employment can be achieved only at the cost of an ever-increasing rate of inflation. By contrast, the new classical view argues that policymaker attempts to reduce the unemployment rate below the natural rate cannot succeed—and worse yet, they still impose the costs of an ever-increasing inflation rate on society. In brief, while the accelerationist view offers the prospect of a trade-off between the benefit of lower unemployment and the cost of ever-increasing inflation, the new classical view argues there will be only the cost and no benefit. The central assumption of the new classical view is the theory of rational expectations.

Checkpoint 26-2

It might be said that the adaptive expectations view is that we must run faster and faster just to stay in the same place—if we choose the wrong place. Explain. Why might it be said that under the theory of adaptive expectations people never learn from their previous mistakes?

Rational Expectations

The **theory of rational expectations** *holds that economic agents form their expectations about the future course of economic activity (wages, prices, employment, and so forth) on the basis of their knowledge, experience, and interpretation of how the economy works, including the effects of monetary and fiscal policy. Furthermore, they make use of all relevant economic data and information available to them at the time when they form their expectations.* The theory of rational expectations implies that people do not persist in making the same mistakes; that is, economic agents do not make *systematic errors* over and over when predicting future events. Rather, they become aware of their systematic errors and alter their behaviour to eliminate them. In short, the theory of rational expectations asserts that people go about forming their expectations in a reasonable, or rational, way.

The Policy Ineffectiveness Proposition

Consider now how the theory of rational expectations would change the adaptive expectations scenario described in Figure 26-5. Recall that an increase in aggregate demand, caused by some expansionary government policy, resulted in an increase in the general price level. Given the constant input costs and money wages in the shortrun, profits increased, stimulating output and employment and thereby reducing the unemployment rate below the "natural" rate (n_1 to d_1). In the longrun workers realized that the price level had risen, hence that their real wages had fallen, and demanded and received money wage increases that restored real wages to their initial level. Thus, profits fell to their initial level and unemployment rose back to the natural rate (d_1 to n_2). The process could be repeated over and over again.

Note that in this scenario it was the fact that firms, resource suppliers, and workers expected that the inflation rate was lower than the actual inflation rate during each expansion phase (n_1 to d_1, n_2 to d_2, and so forth), which made the shortrun unemployment rate reduction possible. In addition, the asymmetrical information assumption of adaptive expectations means that workers mistakenly believed that their real wage was higher than it really was at any given time. This is because although they were immediately aware of the increase in their money wage, they were not immediately aware of the actual rate of increase in the general price level. For example, along the shortrun Phillips curve n_1 to d_1 (Figure 26-5) workers expected a zero rate of inflation, but in fact the price level rose at a 2 percent rate. Along the shortrun Phillips curve from n_2 to d_2 they expected a 2 percent rate of inflation, but the price level actually rose at a 4 percent rate.

According to rational expectations theory, firms and workers will not keep making this systematic mistake over and over. They will adjust their behaviour to avoid being economically hurt by repeating behaviour that causes them hardship. In other words, they will readjust their expectations on the basis of new information as it is revealed to them. In particular, they will come to expect that the inflation rate will increase when the monetary authority expands the money supply or when the government decreases the tax rates or increases government spending or government subsidies to reduce unemployment below the natural unemployment rate. They will thus change their interpretation of the effects of expansionary government policy. When aggregate demand increases there will be an increased tendency to interpret the rise in aggregate demand as a forerunner to impending inflation. Hence, firms will become less inclined to increase output in response to the increase in aggregate demand because they rationally interpret that the increase in the price of their product is merely a reflection of the upward movement of the general price level and not an upward movement in the price of their product relative to other prices. Consequently, there will be no reduction in the unemployment rate as aggregate demand increases. Systematic attempts to use expansionary monetary policy or fiscal policy to lower the unemployment rate will only succeed in causing an ever-increasing rate of inflation. The economy will move directly from n_1 to n_2 to n_3, and so on, in Figure 26-5. Viewed another way, rational expectations theory can be represented in Figure 26-6. As the economic agents begin to interpret expansionary policy as a cause of increased inflation, the aggregate supply curve rotates from AS_1 to AS_3. There is not even a shortrun trade-off between inflation and unemployment, and the rise in inflation can accompany any level of unemployment as long as economic agents regard the effects of expansionary government policy as more likely to increase inflation than solve unemployment.

According to the new classical interpretation of rational expectations, systematic attempts by policymakers to affect real variables in the economy, such as aggregate output and the unemployment rate, will be ineffective. This is especially true if economic agents are unsure of the intentions of policymakers or if they have difficulty in extracting clear information about the degree of change in their own prices relative to the movement of prices generally. Thus, the new classical theory implies that systematic monetary and fiscal policy efforts to smooth out the business cycle will be ineffective.

FIGURE 26-6   Rational Expectations—The New Classical View

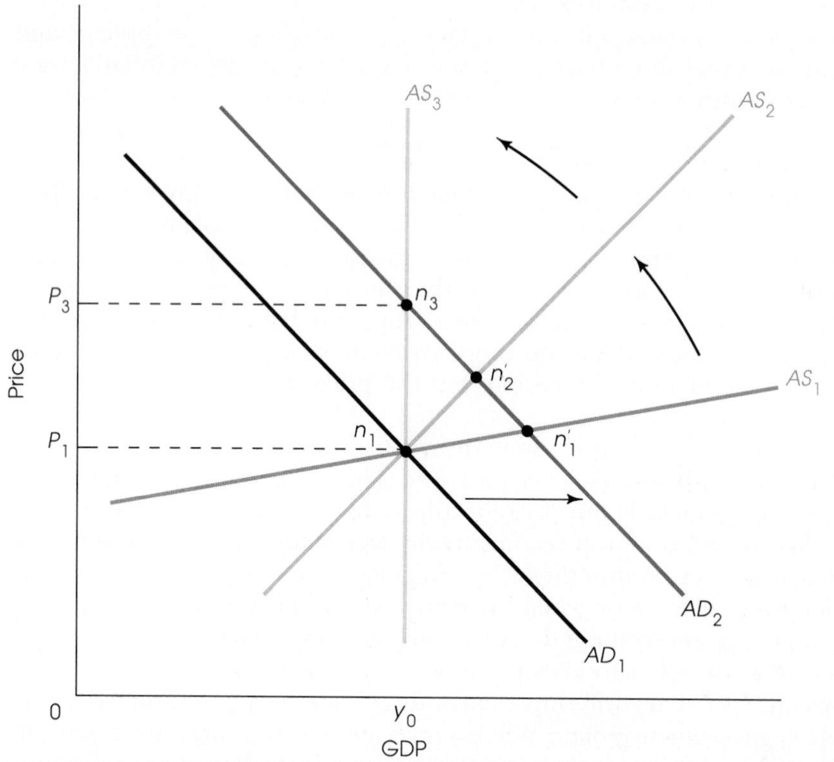

According to rational expectations theory, firms and workers will not keep making this systematic mistake over and over. They will change their interpretation of the effects of expansionary government policy. When aggregate demand increases from AD_1 to AD_2 in response to expansionary monetary policy or fiscal policy, there will be an increased tendency to interpret the rise in aggregate demand as a forerunner to impending inflation. Hence, firms will become less inclined to increase output in response to the increase in aggregate demand because they rationally interpret that the increase in the price of their product is merely a reflection of the upward movement of the general price level and not an upward movement in the price of their product relative to other prices. As a result the AS curve rotates from AS_1 to AS_3 as firms and agents receive news of the government's intention to stimulate the economy. Consequently, there will be no reduction in the unemployment rate as aggregate demand increases. The economy will move directly from n_1 to n_3.

The conclusion drawn by new classical theorists is therefore that government policy is ineffective in changing real GDP and unemployment even in the short-run. They claim that the only variable affected by policymakers is the price level.

Note that the new classical theory emphasizes that systematic policy efforts have no effect on real variables because, according to rational expectations theory, systematic policy actions are predictable, and people learn through experience how to interpret the effect of government policies—for example, by slowing money supply growth during business cycle expansions and increasing it during recessions. One implication of this is that the only policy actions that might be effective in changing real variables are those that are unpredictable. These policies would have to come as surprises—they are random events. But as some new classical theorists point out, monetary and fiscal actions that are random must be totally unrelated to the economy's performance except by chance. Such actions can hardly be said to constitute a meaningful public policy.

The New Keynesian Rebuttal—Why Policy Is Still Effective

The new classical view's conclusion that systematic monetary and fiscal policy will not affect the economy's real variables is certainly contrary to what many mainstream economists and policymakers believe. Even the most ardent supporters of the new classical view would likely agree that there are considerations that suggest why systematic monetary and fiscal policy actions are still able to affect the economy's real variables.

Learning and Lags

The theory of rational expectations (the backbone of the new classical view) assumes that people form expectations on the basis of what they have learned about the economy through experience and information gathering. If we assume an economy where there is no change in technology, institutions, laws, customs, and tastes, then it would seem that one could become fairly well informed about how the economy works. In the real world all of these things are subject to ongoing change in varying degrees. Therefore, learning about how the changes in government policies or other systematic changes to aggregate demand or aggregate supply might influence the rate of inflation or the risk of being unemployed is more difficult. Learning about change is subject to time lags, and new knowledge is already in the process of becoming obsolete.

Policymakers and politicians come and go so that predicting policymaker behaviour and knowing policymaker objectives (what they will do versus what they say they will do) is not easy. Just as history shows that no two business cycles are ever exactly alike, the responses of policymakers to such cycles (the mix of monetary and fiscal action, its magnitude, duration, and timing) is also bound to differ from one business cycle to the next. To this extent there is always a certain amount of unpredictability and surprise in any systematic policy action. Returning to Figure 26-5, for example, we see that economic agents must be able to perfectly predict the amount of monetary expansion and its effect on the price level. Having done so, they must then be capable of increasing their money wages and other input costs in unison with the price level if firms are not to experience any increase in profits that would cause them to increase employment and output. As might be expected, although it is a wonderful intellectual convenience in hypothesis creation, this assumption is the subject of much controversy concerning the empirical evidence to support it.

Rigidity of Contracts and Price Stickiness

The new classical view's policy ineffectiveness argument implicitly assumes prices and money wages are perfectly flexible. But, in fact, buyers and sellers often enter into contracts that fix the price of a good or service for some period of time. In fact prices or wages may be sticky for a number of reasons.

Checkpoint 26-3

In the theory of rational expectations it might be said that for policymakers to manage the economy their actions must be arbitrary. Explain whether this interpretation of the theory is correct. R. E. Lucas, who developed the first rational expectations model of the economy, once stated that, "it appears that policymakers, if they wish to forecast the response of citizens, must take the latter into their confidence."* Reconcile this statement with the interpretation of the policy ineffectiveness proposition that to be effective government policy must catch the public by surprise.

*R. E. Lucas, Studies in Business-Cycle Theory (Cambridge, MA: M.I.T. Press, 1981), p. 126.

A familiar example is a union contract wherein union members agree to work for some stipulated money wage over the life of the contract, typically 2 to 3 years. Suppose that the economy is initially at point n_1 in Figure 26-5 and that at least some members of the labour force have entered into such a union contract. Suppose further that the monetary authority announces that it is going to expand the money supply. In this case, there is no surprise, and despite the fact that all workers now know and may expect what is about to happen, those with a union contract cannot increase their money wage (it is fixed by the contract) in anticipation of the increase in the price level. When the price level increase occurs, those firms employing the union labour will realize increased profits, causing them to increase employment and output. Unemployment will be reduced below the natural rate, at least until the union contract expires and union workers are able to negotiate a higher money wage. In the meantime, because of the money wage fixed by contract, systematic (predictable) monetary policy or fiscal policy is able to affect real variables in the economy, such as output and unemployment.

New Keynesian theory claims that, like wage rigidity, price stickiness may also lead to systematic policy being effective in the shortrun. **Price stickiness** *means that some firms may not be able to fully adjust the price of their product in response to changes in demand.* Price stickiness may be the result of written or implied contracts between a seller and a customer or a result of what Gregory Mankiw describes as *menu costs.*[3] Mankiw and others claim that many firms have enough influence within the markets in which they sell their products that they may not respond immediately to changes in demand. Mankiw defines **menu costs** as *the administrative and related costs of firms' changing their prices.* In some cases these costs may constitute a large enough expense in relation to the gains from changing the price in the face of changing demand that a firm may delay or defer a decision to change its price. Thus, when aggregate demand increases as a result of government action, if some firms respond to the increased demand by holding their prices constant, there will be increased profits for other firms, particularly for those companies buying their raw materials from the firms who are slow in adjusting prices in response to a demand increase. This implies that a government initiative to expand aggregate demand will be effective even under the assumption of rational expectations if there is some price stickiness present in the economy.

Checkpoint 26-4

Explain why a high proportion of unionized labour in an economy might lead to systematic policy effectiveness, even if workers and resource suppliers do not suffer from making systematic errors in predicting inflation. What implications does this have for anticipated social costs of reducing unemployment rates?

Inflation and the Changing Nature of Unemployment

What level of the unemployment rate corresponds to potential GDP? It is the so-called "natural" unemployment rate, which we defined as NAIRU in Chapter 20. (You may want to reread that discussion.) There we observed that many economists believe that since the mid-1960s there has been a definite rise in Canada's natural unemployment rate. If there has been an increase in the natural unemployment rate, what are the implications for efforts by policymakers to deal with the problems of inflation and unemployment?

[3]G. Mankiw, "Small Menu Costs and Large Business Cycles," *Quarterly Journal of Economics*, vol. 100, May 1985, pp. 525–537.

The Changing Nature of Unemployment

The Economic Council of Canada has estimated that the natural unemployment rate has risen from 3 percent in the 1940s, to 4 percent in the 1950s, to 6.7 percent in the 1970s, to 9.3 percent in the 1980s. In the same study they have also stressed that these current levels of natural unemployment are neither acceptable nor unavoidable.[4] Before we look at the possible measures that can be taken to reduce the natural unemployment rate, it is useful to review those factors which may have caused the natural unemployment rate to increase over the last four decades in Canada.

As we explained in Chapter 20, the natural unemployment rate or NAIRU is a functional definition of unemployment. It is not the situation in which everyone looking for work can find a job at any wage level. Because of the functional or technical nature of this definition, the natural unemployment rate can differ from one region to another or from one time period to another.

In Chapter 24 we explained that when there is a reduction in aggregate demand there will be increased unemployment in the short term, assuming some positive slope on the aggregate supply curve as firms respond to the reduced demand by reducing output. However, the theory assumes that the natural unemployment rate does not change; instead, output adjusts to the new aggregate demand conditions through adjustments to the rational expectations of firms and workers. The changing expectations of resource suppliers will cause reductions in input costs and the economy will return to potential GDP by reemploying labour and other inputs as input costs decrease until unemployment decreases back to the same natural unemployment rate. How much of this will work and what problems will arise if the natural unemployment rate increases?

To explore this idea, we begin by examining the conditions that must be present if the natural unemployment rate does not change through time. The idea that the natural unemployment rate does not increase as a result of increases in cyclical unemployment rests on two conditions. First, and perhaps more obvious, is the assumption that the cost per unit of labour and other factors of production must be able to decrease. This is usually referred to as *downward flexibility* of wages and costs. Second, factors of production, which become unemployed because of a decrease in aggregate demand, must be reemployable as input costs decline if unemployment is to decline. This second condition requires that workers have up-to-date usable skills that can be transferred from one employer to another and from one industry to another.

Wage and Cost Rigidities

If the price per unit of labour or other input costs is not flexible for long periods of time, a decrease in aggregate demand can lead to a permanent rise in the unemployment rate. Assume that all input costs (wages, interest rates, and the prices of other raw materials) are rigid. Now assume that there is a reduction in aggregate demand. As unemployment rises in the short term in response to the reduction in aggregate demand, the cost per unit of production

---

[4]Economic Council of Canada, *Transitions For the 90s, Twenty-Seventh Annual Review* (Minister of Supply and Services Canada, 1990), pp. 33–48.

does not decrease. Because there is no reduction in the cost of production, firms have little incentive to increase production back to the previous higher levels. In other words, any increase in the rigidity of wages or other input costs will make it more difficult for unemployment to fall to its previous level after an increase in unemployment. The natural unemployment rate will increase whenever contract negotiations between firms and input suppliers or suppliers of labour result in longer periods of rigidity in input costs and wages.

In Canada and the United States it is not uncommon for firms to have multiyear contracts with their suppliers of labour. In most labour agreements the nominal wage is specified over the period of the contract. There will usually be provisions for adjustment of the nominal wage from one year to the next and sometimes a partial linkage of these adjustments to the movement in the consumer price index. However, there are very few labour contracts in Canada that explicitly tie labour compensation to the price or profits of the employer. This characteristic of labour compensation is not restricted to unionized companies or to blue-collar workers, it extends to most nonunion labour, clerical staff and middle-level managers. Thus, from the employer's point of view the cost of labour is rigid relative to changes in the demand for the product.

The situation described above for labour is also prevalent in the contracts between firms and their suppliers of other inputs. Firms will often have multiyear agreements with input suppliers of key raw materials. For example, in the 1960s it was common for steel producers to arrange agreements with their coal suppliers for purchases of ten-years' requirements at predetermined prices. Similarly, loans through credit arrangements from financial intermediaries to most firms provide mortgages and other forms of lending at nominal interest rates that are fixed for the period of the debt. For firms faced with a decrease in the price of their product there is little opportunity for lowering the costs of these key inputs once a contract with a resource supplier or lending institution has been signed. The same situation exists in the leasing arrangements between many firms and their landlords. Consequently, there is little chance of lowering their input costs in order to lower their price to maintain profitability in the face of decreasing demand.

Structural and Institutional Rigidities

The second source of natural unemployment comes from an inappropriate mix between the jobs available and the skills or geographic location of the workers available to fill these jobs. Thus the natural unemployment rate can increase if the industrial structure changes so that as old jobs disappear and new industries expand, the skills needed to enter the new jobs are substantially different from the skills needed in the declining industries. The same is true if the jobs that are disappearing are in one part of the country and the new jobs are in another region.

In Canada there is a diverse industrial mix from one region of the country to another and there has been a change in the industrial mix of employment opportunities within each region over the past two decades. Decreases in the number of jobs in the manufacturing industries of Ontario and Quebec, jobs in fisheries in Atlantic Canada, jobs in agriculture in the prairies and jobs in the resource industries of British Columbia have been replaced in varying degrees by new jobs in the service sector. This means that the mix between the jobs available in any region and the skills of the unemployed may not facilitate as easy a transition from one job to another for unemployed workers today as it did twenty years ago. For example, industrial workers laid off in southern Ontario's automobile industry or Quebec's textile industry may have few skills of immediate use to employers in an expanding financial management industry or tourism in the same area.

Canada's regional differences produce a secondary complication, since the different industries in the diverse regions expand and contract at different times and at different rates. Thus, a period of expansion in Ontario may offer increased employment opportunities in the financial services and real estate industries, putting an upward pressure on input prices and labour costs that increases inflation. At the same time, depressed conditions in Atlantic Canada's fisheries and western Canada's agricultural sector may reduce employment levels among people working in those industries and those parts of the country. The result is a rise in both unemployment and inflation at the national level, which appears as a rise in the natural unemployment rate.

Of equal concern during a time of rapidly changing technology is the fact that even jobs in the same industry in any one region start to require different skills. An accounting position in the oil industry a decade ago required much less knowledge in computer systems management than it does today. Similarly, new employment opportunities in Ontario's automobile factories—for example, controlling and serving automated industrial robots—sometimes require skills that did not even exist five or six years ago. An experienced automobile assembly line worker who becomes laid off in this environment of technological change becomes increasingly likely to lack the skills necessary to reenter the same industry, even at an entry-level job, as the period of unemployment lengthens. The reemployment of workers even in the same industry and in the same location can involve extensive and costly retraining in an environment of rapid technological change. Thus, along with reducing production costs and increasing the quality and variety of products available, technological change can cause increases in the natural unemployment rate and lead to increased costs that will be shared in varying degrees by employers, labour organizations, consumers, the government, and the unemployed.

Demographic Changes and Government Policy Changes

Several government studies over the past twenty years suggest that the natural unemployment rate has risen because of increases in the participation rate, a demographic shift toward younger participants in the labour force, and changes in unemployment insurance benefits in the 1970s.[5]

As the participation rate increased over the decades, more persons per household were seeking jobs in the marketplace. This suggests that with more individuals involved in earning income per household, the pressure on any one of these earners to stay in a job that was unrewarding in terms of financial benefits and nonfinancial rewards was reduced. Similar studies in the United States also indicate that employers may be more ready to lay off workers during tough economic times if there are other workers in the household—they may in effect

[5]*Report of the Royal Commission on the Economic Union and Development Prospects for Canada* (Ottawa: Minister of Supply and Services Canada, 1985); *Report of the Commission on Enquiry into Unemployment Insurance* (Ottawa: Employment and Immigration Canada, 1986).

POLICY PERSPECTIVE

Discretionary versus Nondiscretionary Expenditures

John Kenneth Galbraith, a noted former Harvard professor of economics, pointed out many years ago that policymakers who use demand contraction policies as a means of combatting inflation are engaged in a fool's choice— they spare people the unpleasant consequences of inflation by inflicting on them the unpleasant consequences of increased unemployment. The Economic Council of Canada recently expressed a similar view by stating that "there is one lesson to be learned from the economic policies of the 1980s, it is that fighting inflation through the exclusive use of tight monetary policy is very costly."* This has led many economists to question whether there might be a way to reduce the natural unemployment rate itself as a way of initiating reduced unemployment with reduced inflation. Much attention has been devoted to looking at those economies that have been successful in holding down

their inflation rates without having to suffer increased unemployment. By comparison with Canada, the United States, or the United Kingdom, there are economies with much better track records in this regard. During the 1970s and 1980s, Austria, Japan, Norway, and Sweden were all successful in maintaining low unemployment rates without experiencing increased inflation or reduced growth in GDP.

The search for policies that will reduce the natural unemployment rate center on changing institutional factors and laws in the labour market. If firms and labour organizations can be convinced that government policymakers place equal emphasis on the importance of maintaining high employment and low rates of inflation, they may be less likely to regard policies aimed at reducing unemployment as indications that the government is not concerned about the inflation rate. Similarly, efforts to coordinate the

monetary policies of the Bank of Canada and the fiscal policy of the Department of Finance so that they reinforce each other should produce fewer information extraction problems for economic agents trying to assess the risks of increased inflation.

Until recently it appeared that the government was using its fiscal policy almost exclusively to achieve reductions in the level of accumulated public debt. By contrast, the evidence suggested that since the mid-1970s the Bank of Canada had lowering inflation as its main goal.**

continued on next page

*Economic Council of Canada, *Transitions For the 90s, Twenty-Seventh Annual Review* (Minister of Supply and Services Canada, 1990), p. 55.

**During Parliament's review of the mandate of the Bank of Canada in the fall of 1991, John Crow, the governor of the Bank of Canada, requested that the mandate be changed to eliminate all responsibilities except controlling inflation.

feel mistakenly or otherwise that the laid-off workers will suffer less financial hardship if there are other earners in their household than if they are the only breadwinners in a family. Increased numbers of earners per household may have also increased the natural unemployment rate by reducing the mobility of the household from one region to another. This is because the opportunity cost of lost income and the actual costs of searching for a job incurred by those presently employed in the first region must be added to costs associated with the presently unemployed member moving to another part of the country in search of employment.

At the same time that demographic factors were making it harder to move workers from job to job, or increasing the willingness of firms to lay off workers, there were also some changes by the government that may have increased the natural unemployment rate. Reforms to the unemployment insurance system in the 1970s (which were discussed in Chapter 18) increased benefits to those who quit their jobs and allowed higher and more prolonged benefits to those

> **Checkpoint 26-5**
>
> Look at the data in Figure 26-4 again. Do you see any pattern in these data that might at least in part be attributable to the changing nature of the labour force?

POLICY PERSPECTIVE CONTINUED

The implication of this combination of policies was that neither of these branches of government placed a high priority on reducing unemployment. Over the same period politicians have often publicly expressed concern over unemployment and their support for policies creating more job opportunities. This lack of a coordinated policy stance by the central policymakers and shapers of public policy has undoubtedly increased the information extraction problem for private sector decision makers. If this is the case it reduces the public policymakers' ability to combat inflation and unemployment.

The Economic Council and other forecasting groups have pointed out the problem that Canada continues to use a labour market model that fosters adversarial bargaining on a company by company basis. Those countries with good records in holding down inflation while maintaining low unemployment tend to involve government as well as the private sector in labour market decisions. Norway and Sweden, for example, use tripartite bargaining on an industrywide basis. In this form of labour market, contracts for wages and working conditions tend to be short in duration. Consultation involves an employer group, a labour group, and the government. The relations between individual firms and their workers occur in an environment where national objectives concerning productivity, the costs of training and skills acquisition, inflation, international competitiveness of products, the social costs of unemployment, the cost of education, and benefits to third parties can be explicitly included in the negotiations process.

In a different way, the Japanese model of labour management fosters a cooperative behaviour between employers and employees. It recognizes and builds on the common goals of the workers and their employers within individual firms so that worker compensation is usually linked to the price and profit behaviour of the employer while production levels, technological innovation, and new product development are integrated with such issues as guaranteed employment with one employer for life and company-financed training programs. This system reduces the risk of unemployment and allows wages and other input costs to adjust in a more flexible manner to changes in aggregate demand conditions. It also fosters job training and skills upgrading paid for by the firms as a means of keeping productivity rising and unemployment low. Because economic decision makers explicitly recognize a social contract, there is an enhancement of the public good. The firms and workers experience benefits of higher employment rates, higher productivity growth rates, and lower social costs from inflation.

For Discussion

- What might be the effect on the inflation and unemployment trade-off if Canada were to institute changes in the unemployment insurance system that required firms with higher rates of labour turnover to pay higher premiums to insure their employees under the unemployment insurance scheme?
- What might be the effect on the inflation and unemployment trade-off if unemployed workers were to receive increased benefits from unemployment insurance if they enrol in retraining programs or seek further education through registering in post-secondary institutions?

who were unemployed in regions experiencing high unemployment. Some of these reforms were introduced to soften the burden of unemployment on those at greater risk of poverty because of general depressed conditions for their region of the country. In a similar way, government programs through the former Department of Regional Economic Expansion (DREE) helped to provide subsidies that reduced the pressure for firms to adopt new technologies and introduce new products in response to what appeared to be long-term reductions in demand for their products.

Policy Implications of a Rise in Natural Unemployment

Any rise in the natural unemployment rate in Canada complicates the ability of policymakers to combat inflation using traditional demand restraint measures of the type discussed in Chapters 23, 24, 25, and 31. As explained in our discussion of rational expectations theory, when policymakers decide to use demand restraint measures to combat inflation, unemployment will rise above the natural unemployment rate until the expectations of businesses, resource suppliers, and workers change so that they expect a lower inflation rate. Therefore, if there is some rise in the natural unemployment rate, the use of contractionary demand policy as a means of fighting inflation generates even higher unemployment and more widespread suffering from the effects of unemployment than would have been the case if the natural rate had not risen. It also implies less effectiveness in combatting inflation at any given level of unemployment.

Policy Ineffectiveness with a Rise in the Natural Unemployment Rate

The changing nature of unemployment has implications for the longrun aggregate supply curve and the relationship between inflation and unemployment. These implications are illustrated in the hypothetical example of Figure 26-7. The aggregate supply curve corresponding to the situation before the changes in the nature of unemployment is AS_{lr}, and AS'_{lr} is the aggregate supply curve after these changes.

Suppose that institutional changes or changes in the demographic composition of the labour market or the availability of raw materials cause a rise in the frictional and structural unemployment rates. This will cause a decrease in potential GDP and will shift the longrun aggregate supply curve to the left. The ability to provide the same level of employment is now impossible in the long-

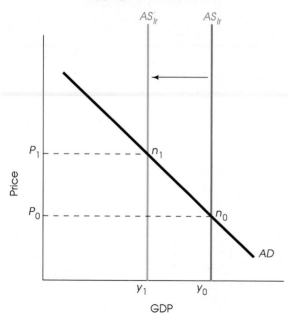

FIGURE 26-7 The Impact of Increased Natural Unemployment Rate on the Longrun Aggregate Supply Curve

When the natural unemployment rate increases, there is a shift to the left in the position of the longrun aggregate supply curve. In this case, as the natural unemployment rate increased the aggregate supply shifted from AS_{lr} to AS'_{lr}. The effect of a leftward shift in the longrun aggregate supply means that in the *longrun*, society faces lower output equilibrium production levels combined with a higher level of prices. This is illustrated through the longrun equilibrium moving from n_0 to n_1.

run, according to the policy ineffectiveness proposition developed in adaptive expectations theory and rational expectations theory.

Consider the implications for the economy resulting from a rise in the natural unemployment rate and the natural rate hypothesis on the longrun behaviour of the economy. Both the adaptive expectations and rational expectations theories have slightly different interpretations of the shifts in the shortrun aggregate supply curves that will accompany the rise in the natural unemployment rate and the sequence of events, but they both support the same longrun outcome. As the natural unemployment rate increases, the longrun aggregate supply curve will shift left. This is illustrated in Figure 26-7 by the shift from AS_{lr} to AS'_{lr}. The effect of the shift in the aggregate supply curve on the price level and output is shown by the move in equilibrium from n_0 to n_1. The price level increases from P_0 to P_1 and the output level decreases from y_0 to y_1.

Similarly, in Figure 26-8 the increase in the natural unemployment rate is shown by the shift of the longrun Phillips curve to the right from $LRPC$ to $LRPC'$. It should be remembered that the longrun Phillips curve, being vertical, indicates that there is no trade-off between unemployment and inflation in the longrun. Figure 26-8 indicates that when the longrun Phillips curve shifts to the right, all the shortrun Phillips curves shift with it, so any specific level of inflation is only sustainable at a higher unemployment rate. For example, the point n_0, which represented an inflation rate of 2 percent and unemployment of 4 percent before the rise in the natural unemployment rate, becomes n'_0 after the natural unemployment rises. For society to maintain its 2 percent inflation rate, it would now have to accept 9 percent unemployment. Furthermore, both rational expectations theory and adaptive expectations theory agree that increased aggregate demand can only temporarily reduce unemployment below the new natural unemployment rate of 9 percent. In addition, these temporary reductions in unemployment would be accompanied by higher inflation rates, as indicated by n'_2, n'_4 and n'_6. In short, this will be the unemployment rate in the longrun regardless of what rate of inflation the economy experiences.

The policy ineffectiveness proposition accepted by both theories—adaptive expectations theory and rational expectations theory—claims that government agencies will be ineffective in permanently reducing the unemployment rate to its previous level through the use of fiscal or monetary policy. In other words, the two theories suggest that the government can influence inflation, since any price level is consistent with potential GDP, but cannot permanently affect the unemployment rate, however high the natural unemployment rate. This has made some economists, and particularly the post-Keynesians, question the usefulness of a theory that seems to have as its ultimate conclusion, "unemployment will be whatever unemployment will be." They have turned their attention to investigating the changes to the economy that would reverse the process of stagflation, allowing inflation and unemployment to decrease simultaneously. Are there instruments of public policy that can reduce the natural unemployment rate itself? If they exist, then the natural rate hypothesis need not condemn policymakers to Galbraith's fool's choice.

The major focus of this recent trend has been on trying to understand why countries like Austria, Norway, Japan, and Sweden have been more successful than Australia, Canada, Germany, Italy, the United Kingdom, or the United States in holding down inflation without having to accept the consequences of higher unemployment or reduced real growth. Part of the answer appears to be to develop policies that increase the mobility of individual workers' skills from

FIGURE 26-8   **The Impact of a Rise in the Natural Unemployment Rate on the Phillips Curve**

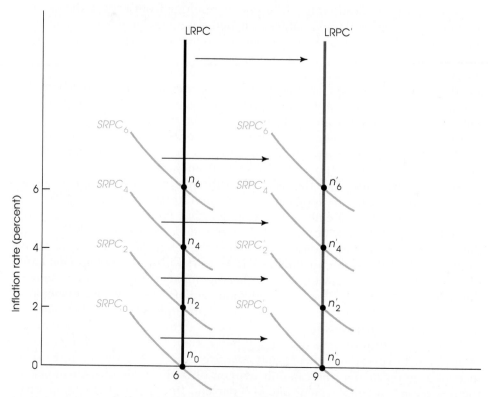

When the natural unemployment rate increases due to changes in institutional, technological, or demographic factors, the longrun Phillips curve *LRPC* shifts right from *LRPC* to *LRPC'*. At the same time each of the shortrun Phillips curves also shifts to the right, as now for each expected level of inflation the unemployment rate that will allow that inflation rate to persist without acceleration must increase. At a natural unemployment rate of 6%, $SRPC_0$ intersected the horizontal axis at 6% unemployment, indicating that if unemployment was at the natural level of 6%, inflation could remain at 0% and economic agents expected 0%. An increase in the natural unemployment rate to, say, 9% means that now 0% inflation is attainable only if the economy sustains 9% unemployment. Thus, the shortrun Phillips curve for an expected inflation rate of 0% will shift from $SRPC_0$ to $SRPC_0'$. In the same way all other shortrun Phillips curves will also shift to the right so that $SRPC_2$ shifts to $SRPC_2'$, $SRPC_4$ shifts to $SRPC_4'$, and $SRPC_6$ shifts to $SRPC_6'$. Now, for any given inflation rate to persist through time without acceleration, the level of unemployment that is suffered by members of society is higher. This is illustrated by the shift of equilibrium combinations of inflation and unemployment from n_0, n_2, n_4, and n_6 to n_0', n_2', n_4', and n_6'.

one activity to another, possibly by increasing private firms' commitment to education and training programs for employees, and by having labour organizations involved in the selection and pace of technological change in the workplace. Another part of the solution may lie in having a clear industrial strategy set out by the government and publicized so that business and labour know the social goals and can include them in their planning.

Summary

1. Economists have speculated that there is a trade-off between inflation and unemployment. The trade-off may be represented by a Phillips curve, which indicates that lowering the unemployment rate means accepting more inflation and that reducing inflation means accepting more unemployment. However, evidence suggests that movements up the Phillips curve (increasing inflation and reducing unemployment) cannot be followed by movements back down the same curve (reducing inflation while increasing unemployment). Data show that the economy has experienced an upward-spiraling inflation rate associated with a cyclical unemployment rate.

2. Increases in the price of inputs to production or in profit margins that are initiated on the supply side of the economy raise production costs and give rise to cost-push and profit-push inflation. This is represented by an upward shift of the aggregate supply curve. Given the position of the AD curve, the price level rises, output declines, and the rate of unemployment increases. Such a process underlies stagflation, wherein the economy experiences an increase in both the inflation and unemployment rates at the same time.

3. Adaptive expectations theory suggests that there is a shortrun trade-off between inflation and unemployment because suppliers of labour are assumed to have poor information, making them unaware of declining real wages until after workers are hurt by the effects of inflation. Adaptive expectations also claims that workers will adjust their expectations of inflation on the basis of past observed inflation rates so that in the longrun there is no trade-off between inflation and unemployment.

4. The policy ineffectiveness proposition says that in the longrun policymaker actions will be expected by firms, workers, and other resource suppliers so that the shortrun aggregate supply curve shifts upward in response to increases in aggregate demand. Therefore, expansionary monetary and fiscal policies intended to reduce the unemployment rate below the natural rate will cause an ever-increasing, or accelerating, rate of inflation.

5. Rational expectations theory claims that firms, resource suppliers, and workers form their expectations about the future course of economic activity on the basis of all relevant economic knowledge, experience, and data, and in such a way that they do not make repeated, or systematic, mistakes. Because of rational expectations, the new classical view forecasts that there is not even a shortrun trade-off between inflation and unemployment, and the policy ineffectiveness proposition applies to the shortrun as well as the longrun.

6. New Keynesians have adopted rational expectations methodology and have used it to suggest that if there are sticky wages or sticky prices, the policy ineffectiveness proposition does not hold. Under these circumstances, policymakers using systematic policy initiatives will influence the real variables in the economy. In addition, they argue that policymakers are never perfectly predictable or systematic, making it highly unlikely that firms and workers can anticipate policy actions so well as to render them ineffective.

7. Many economists argue that the natural unemployment rate has risen in the last twenty years. They attribute this alleged rise in natural unemployment to changes in the demographic composition of the labour force, the laws concerning government transfer payments to the unemployed, technology,

and the industrial structure of Canada. Some economists claim that as a result of these changes Canada must accept higher measured unemployment in order to maintain any given inflation rate.

8. Recent research comparing different countries' success in combatting inflation and unemployment has led to a search for policies aimed at reducing the natural unemployment rate.

Key Terms and Concepts

accelerationist view	natural rate	price stickiness
adaptive expectations	of unemployment	stagflation
asymmetrical information	new Keynesian theory	systematic errors
assumption	Phillips curve	theory of rational
menu costs	policy ineffectiveness	expectations
natural rate hypothesis	proposition	

Questions and Problems

1. Which years in Figure 26-4 most strongly suggest the possible existence of a Phillips curve? What shift in the Phillips curve is suggested by Figure 26-4? Which years in Figure 26-4 most clearly indicate this shift?

2. Classify each of the following changes according to whether you think it affects the economy's aggregate demand curve, the economy's aggregate supply curve, or both. Explain your answer in each case.
   a. An increase in personal income taxes.
   b. An increase in the employers' required portion of unemployment insurance contributions to insure employees of the firm against the risk of unemployment.
   c. A worldwide strike by dockworkers.
   d. An increase in employee absenteeism.
   e. An end to the cold war.
   f. A major discovery of oil within Ontario.
   g. A stock market crash.
   h. An announced upward revision of the Economic Council of Canada's forecast for GDP growth in the coming year.

3. Explain the natural rate hypothesis.

4. Explain the difference between the adaptive expectations view of policy ineffectiveness and the rational expectations view of policy ineffectiveness. Is there a reason why systematic policy might be effective in the shortrun in reducing unemployment according to adaptive expectations theory? Is this true for rational expectations theory?

5. According to the new classical view for rational expectations, an expected increase in the money supply will affect nominal GDP. Why is it that the adjustment of expectations that offsets any real effects of such an increase does not offset the nominal effects also?

6. How can new Keynesian theory use rational expectations methodology and still reject the policy ineffectiveness proposition?

7. How do you think each of the following would affect the shape of the aggregate supply curve and why?
   a. Increasing unemployment benefits and relaxing the requirements for eligibility.
   b. Instituting tripartite bargaining involving the government, labour groups, and employer groups.
   c. Increasing the age at which people become eligible for retirement benefits.
   d. Increasing the tax credits for firms that retrain workers whose jobs disappear because of changes in technology.

SEVEN

Money, Banking, and Monetary Policy

M

B

char
wha
hav
par
our
the
for
ho
W
pr
ti
er
th

i
p

st over two centuries ago Adam Smith
served: "When the division of labour
thoroughly established, it is but a very
a man's wants which the produce of his
n supply.... Every man thus lives by ex-
a merchant, and society itself grows to
rude ages of society cattle are said to
ommerce ... a species of shells in some
nd; tobacco in Virginia; sugar in some of
sed leather in some other countries; and
where it is not uncommon, I am told,
money to the baker's shop or the ale-
"one of humanity's finest inventions."[2]
is functioning well, this seems an appro-
ws that money and the closely related ac-
of economic instability, inflation, and un-
ems have frequently plagued our economy

ature and functions of money and bank-
why the Bank of Canada was set up to
and banking in our economy. Chapters
our banking system affects the size of the
will focus on how the money supply af-
or goods and services and on the role that
homy's equilibrium level of total output and

iam, Ont.: Penguin Books Canada Ltd, 1776 [reprinted 1986]),

nomic Activity (Don Mills, Ont.: Addison-Wesley, 1984), p. 5.

The Nature of Money

What does money do? What are the different forms of money? What determines the value of money? How is the money supply measured? Although all of us deal with money on a daily basis, few people stop to consider exactly what money is or what it does. The simplest definition is that **money** *is any substance that simultaneously performs the three functions of money.* In short, money is what money does. This definition at first appears to violate the rules of logic, which dictate that a word cannot be used to define itself. On closer inspection it raises the point that once the functions that money must perform in a society are understood, then any substance that performs these functions *is* money. Conversely, just because someone, a bank or the government, calls little metal coins *money,* if they cannot perform the functions of money, calling them money will not make them money!

What Money Does

Essentially, money does three things. It functions as a medium of exchange, a unit of account, and a store of value.

Money as a Medium of Exchange

Without money people would have to carry on trade by *barter*—the swapping of goods for goods. In Chapter 3 we saw that for trade to take place in a barter economy there must be a *coincidence of wants* between individuals. If I have good X to trade and I want to get good Y, I must find someone who not only wants to get good X but also coincidentally has good Y to give in exchange. The difficulties involved in finding a coincidence of wants tend to discourage and inhibit specialization and trade in a barter economy (recall the discussion in Chapter 3). Therefore, the total output of the economy is less than it otherwise might be. However, if money is used to carry on trade, I can sell good X to whomever wants it and accept money in exchange. Trade is now easier. Money

---

LEARNING OBJECTIVES

After reading this chapter, you will be able to:

1. Explain the nature and functions of money.
2. Describe the differences among commodity money, fiat money, bank money or chequable deposits, and near money.
3. Define the different measures used to estimate the size of the money supply.
4. State the nature of the relationship among the supply of money, prices, and the value of money.
5. Explain how banks evolved from a mere safekeeping function to a fractional reserve banking operation, creating money through their lending activities.
6. Describe the purposes and organization of the Bank of Canada.
7. Explain the functions of the Bank of Canada.
8. Describe the role of near banks, trust companies, and depository institutions as creators of money and as financial intermediaries.

is something that is generally acceptable to everyone as payment for anything. When goods are bought and sold using money as the medium of exchange, specialization and trade are encouraged, and the economy is able to be more productive.

The existence of money allows society to use its resources more efficiently because it eliminates the need for coincidence of wants. The resources that would have been used to overcome coincidence of wants in the absence of money are available to increase the production of goods and services. Thus, money allows the production possibilities frontier to shift outward.

Money as a Unit of Account

In a barter economy, comparing the relative values of different goods and services is much more complicated than in a money-using economy. For example, to get an idea of the cost of an orange in a barter economy would require a knowledge of the rate at which oranges exchange for apples, shoes, tea, bread, haircuts, and so forth. A shopping trip would entail numerous cross comparisons of the exchange rates between widely different goods and services. "Let's see, if 3 oranges will buy 8 apples and 5 apples will buy 2 pears, that must mean . . . ah . . . 15 oranges will buy 16 pears." There is no need for such complex calculations if everything is valued in terms of the same unit of account, money. In the preceding example the price of an orange is $.16, an apple is $.06, and a pear is $.15.

Money provides a common unit of account for expressing the market values of widely different goods and services. The existence of this common unit of account greatly reduces the time and effort needed to make intelligent economic decisions. More time and effort are available for use in other productive activities. This is another reason why money enables the production possibilities frontier to shift outward.

Money as a Store of Value

People can hold wealth in many forms: houses, yachts, stocks, bonds, jewelry, and so on. But no form of wealth is as readily convertible into other goods and services as is money. This ready convertibility, or **liquidity,** makes money an attractive store of value, or source of purchasing power.

If a person had to sell their new wristwatch within the next 5 minutes to get money to make purchases, they would probably only get a fraction of what they had paid for it. If they had paid $50 for it, they might only be able to get $20, a loss of $30. If instead they had $50, they could easily make $50 worth of purchases within 5 minutes. In general, people can rank assets on a scale from the most liquid to the least liquid according to the risk of possible loss, including transaction costs (such as brokerage fees, advertising costs, and time and effort searching for a buyer), that would result if they had to convert their assets into money *within a short period of time.* Money of course heads the list. A car, a house, a painting, or a piece of land might be at or near the bottom.

Forms of Money

Throughout history money has taken many forms. Many of the oldest kinds of money are still used today, while new kinds continue to be developed. In order of their historical evolution, the principal kinds of money are *commodity money, coins, paper money,* and *demand deposits.*

Commodity Money

As indicated in Adam Smith's statement earlier in this chapter, early forms of money were commodities that often had other uses besides serving as money. Shells, tobacco, sugar, hides, leather, and nails are but a few examples. Even today these items often serve as money in some economically underdeveloped regions of the world. When the German Deutschmark became worthless as a result of the German hyperinflation in the early 1920s, Germans used cognac and cigarettes as money.

Some commodities are better suited for use as money than others. The ideal commodity money would not suffer from handling or time. It should be valuable enough in small amounts, easily transportable even in very large values, easily recognizable, and easily divisible without losing value. Finally, it must be stable in value from place to place and over time. Historically, the precious metals gold and silver have been the most continuously used forms of commodity money.

Coins

The first coins were made by kings or rulers who weighed out an amount of precious metal and made a coin out of it. The coin had the amount of precious metal it contained stamped on it (its "face value") along with the ruler's seal as a guarantee of the weight. A problem with coins is that they disappear from circulation whenever the market value of the precious metal they contain exceeds the amount of the face value stamped on them. Suppose a 25-cent piece contains more than $.25 worth of silver, as Canadian quarters did in the early 1960s. Eventually, circulation will bring the 25-cent pieces into the hands of people who will melt them down for the silver rather than use each coin for purchasing $.25 worth of goods, the face value stamped on the coin. To avoid this problem most governments long ago began to issue **token coins,** coins that contain an amount of metal worth much less than the face value of the coin.

Fiat money is money that the government declares by law to be legal tender for the settlement of debts. This means that if a person owes somebody $.25 and the debtor offers the creditor a quarter to pay off the debt, the creditor must accept it or lose any legal claim on the debtor. This illustrates an important characteristic of fiat money. Fiat money is money that is not backed by or convertible into gold or any other precious metal. It is acceptable because the government declares it to be acceptable and sets the penalty, usually the loss of the right of collection, for failure to accept it as money, not because of the value of the materials contained in it. People accept it in exchange for goods and services because they know that other people will accept it and have faith in its value.

Paper Money

Paper money, the bills in a person's wallet, is also fiat money in today's economy. It, too, illustrates that money is acceptable because it will buy goods. The value of the bills themselves as a commodity is next to nothing. Indeed, the materials needed to make a $2 bill, or a $1,000 bill, cost but a tiny fraction of a cent. All paper money in Canada is issued by the Bank of Canada.

Demand Deposits

If people exchange currency (coins and paper money) for a **demand deposit** at a bank, the bank is legally obligated to give that money back to them, the moment they ask for it. Demand deposits are also called *chequing accounts* or **chequable deposits** because a person can write *cheques* against them. A cheque is nothing more than a slip of paper, a standardized form on which a person can write the bank an order to make a payment to the person or institution named on the cheque. After making this payment, the bank is then entitled to withdraw funds from the cheque issuer's account, thus reducing its indebtedness to the issuer by the amount it has paid out due to the cheque.

The receiving party (an individual, business, or other institution) has only to sign, or endorse, the cheque to receive the funds from the cheque issuer's bank out of the demand deposit. Often the party receiving the cheque will simply endorse and deposit it in his or her own chequing account, frequently in a different bank. The banks conveniently handle the transfer of funds from the cheque issuing party's chequing account to that of the receiving party.

Demand deposits function as money by virtue of the cheque writing privilege. Compared to currency they have several advantages. Lost or stolen currency is almost impossible to recover. Lost or stolen cheques are much more difficult for another party to use, so a demand deposit is relatively secure from such mishaps. In Canada, as in many other countries, it is actually illegal to send currency through Canada Post. Cheques therefore make trade possible between parties separated by great distances, adding to the transportability idea discussed earlier because they can easily and legally be sent through the mail. They also provide a convenient record of completed transactions. Given these advantages, it is not surprising that in terms of dollar value, cheques and electronic transfers account for by far the largest amount of transactions in our economy. One disadvantage of demand deposits up until the 1980s was that by law chartered banks were not allowed to pay interest on them.

Demand deposits are regarded as money because they can be converted into currency on demand and therefore represent immediate liquidity. Cheques are not considered money even though they are such a widely used medium of exchange because cheques simply represent temporary claims against the demand deposit; to count both the demand deposits and the cheques issued against demand deposits would result in counting the same money more than once.

Currency in circulation and demand deposits are the most liquid forms of money performing all the functions of money. Together their total is referred to as M1, the most narrow definition of the money supply. **M1** = *currency in circulation outside the chartered banks plus demand-deposit liabilities of the chartered banks.*

Near Money

Currency and demand deposits are regarded as money because they perform all three **functions of money** (as a medium of exchange, a unit of account, and a store of value) better than any other asset. The dividing line between what is money and what is not money is not clear-cut. M1 captures all the assets that can reasonably fulfill all three functions of money at the same time. Several other assets perform the store of value and unit of account functions of money at least as well as anything in M1. These assets are often called **near money,** since they are like money except that they are not usually regarded as a medium of exchange.

Chequable Notice Accounts

During the 1970s, spurred by the ban on interest payments on chartered bank demand deposits, the financial system began to develop other types of deposits, such as **daily interest chequing accounts,** that had limited withdrawal and chequing privileges. These accounts are technically notice accounts, which are discussed in the next section, but they have one major difference from other notice accounts. Because they can have cheques drawn on them, daily interest chequing accounts can perform all three functions of money to a limited extent set by the daily withdrawal limits and notification conditions set by any particular bank offering daily interest chequing accounts. The significance of the daily interest savings account to this investigation of money is that it bridges the gap between the narrow definition of money M1 and near money. It illustrates the point that the distinction between what is clearly money and those financial assets that are not money is unclear and exemplifies the idea given earlier that money is what money does.

Notice Accounts

Notice Accounts.   **Notice deposits** *are deposits that do not normally carry chequing privileges and may legally require the depositor to give the bank advance notice before making a withdrawal.* They pay a fixed interest rate, and often a premium of higher interest is paid if the minimum balance is maintained above some level set by the chartered bank or financial institution. Although they appear and technically are much less liquid than demand deposits, in practice financial institutions allow customers to transfer funds from one type of account to another with few or no restrictions. Money deposited in a notice account that cannot have cheques drawn against it can usually be transferred to a chequing account if the depositor wishes to spend it quickly.

Although they constitute a smaller portion of the money supply than they did before the advent of daily interest savings accounts, nonchequable savings accounts remain a good example of notice accounts. These accounts have a fixed interest rate payable monthly on the minimum average monthly balance, and although personal withdrawals can be made, and in some cases remote withdrawals up to a daily maximum amount can be made by using automated tellers, they do not provide quite the same degree of immediate liquidity in terms of access to all the funds at any location that is provided by a demand deposit.

Treasury Bill Accounts.   Many financial intermediaries now offer Treasury Bill accounts, also called *T-accounts* or *T-Bill accounts.* In this type of notice account, as long as the depositor keeps the daily balance above some relatively large figure ($10,000 or $50,000), the financial institution pays a higher interest on the account. The idea behind the account is that the financial institution has economies of scale in the administration costs associated with larger accounts and a higher degree of flexibility in investing the funds. It therefore passes on some of its higher earnings to the depositor.

Notice accounts may be deposited by individual people or they may be deposited by institutions or businesses as part of their funds management program. In the case of non-personal notice accounts, the financial institution is expected to be at lower risk of withdrawal or transfer and the notice account is considered slightly less liquid than in the case of personal notice accounts.

Fixed-Term Deposits.   **Fixed-term deposits** or *term deposits* earn a fixed rate of interest and must be held for a stipulated amount of time. Early withdrawal is penalized. Some depository institutions, such as chartered banks, trust companies, and credit unions, offer term deposits. Term deposits require that the depositor keep a minimum specified amount of money (such as $1,000 or $5,000) for a set length of time (such as 90 days or 180 days or a year). Fixed-term deposits and other notice accounts are deemed to be less liquid if they are non-personal than if the depositor is a person.

Foreign Currency Accounts of Residents Booked in Canada

Because Canada is an open economy, many firms and individuals receive income or make payments in currencies other than the Canadian dollar. While the most important foreign currency in Canada is the U.S. dollar, increasing trade across the Pacific and the growing strength of the European Community (EC) are making it increasingly convenient for many individuals and firms to maintain deposits in some Asian and European currencies. The holding of foreign currency accounts not only provides greater convenience for firms and individuals being able to quote prices to potential foreign customers in terms of either Canadian dollars or a foreign currency but also reduces the risk of a change in the exchange rate between the Canadian dollar and a foreign currency changing the profitability of a transaction involving non-residents of Canada.

The ownership of a foreign currency deposit, say pesos, in a chartered bank in Canada, will help solve some of the risks of international trade between a Canadian and a Mexican, but it will not function very well as money *inside* Canada. The owner of a peso account (or rubles, French or Swiss francs, yen, or most other foreign currencies) will find it very hard to use the foreign currency to meet all three functions of money inside Canada. Most retailers will not be able to use it effectively as a unit of account. There are of course rare exceptions— for example in Banff, it is common for retailers to post prices in both Canadian dollars and yen, but in most cities in Canada it is hard to find prices posted in foreign currency (whether Argentina's australs or India's rupees).

Guaranteed Investment Certificates, and Equity Funds

Guaranteed investment certificates (GICs) pay shareholders a rate of interest that is competitive with the highest rates of return available on large denomination ($100,000 and up) short-term government and corporate bonds and on other financial instruments typically too large for the average depositor to buy alone. These mutual funds are able to do this by pooling the relatively small deposits of the shareholders and investing them in the large-denomination financial instruments. They also typically offer the owners of relatively small deposits a higher degree of flexibility in choosing to invest in money market bonds or more risky stocks, including speculative equity funds and venture funds, which typically offer higher returns because of the higher risk of capital loss.

Broader Definitions of Money

Because of the near money nature of fixed-term deposits, T-Bill accounts, and the different kinds of registered retirement savings deposits and certificates of deposit, broader definitions of money that include these items have gained increased attention in recent years. The basic argument for including these near money assets in the broader definitions is that the near moneys are almost as liquid as currency, demand deposits, and notice deposits that carry chequing privileges. Most savings deposits without these privileges are less liquid than currency and demand deposits only because of the transaction costs (a trip to the bank, a postage stamp, or a phone call) incurred when they are transferred into currency and demand deposits. The broader definitions of money are essentially as follows:

M2 is defined as M1 plus personal savings deposits and non-personal notice deposits.

M3 is defined as M2 plus non-personal fixed-term deposits and foreign currency accounts of residents booked in Canada.

Table 27-1 provides an idea of the sizes of M1, M2, M3, along with the relative importance of the various components that make up each of these definitions of money.

TABLE 27-1   Measures of Money in Canada: M1, M2, M3
(Unadjusted Data, in Current Canadian Dollars for December 1991)*

	Total Value (in Billions) of Dollars	Percentage of M1	Percentage of M2	Percentage of M3
Currency	21.05	49.9	7.5	6.3
+ demand deposits	23.65	56.1	8.4	7.1
= M1	42.18		15.0	12.6
+ personal notice deposits and personal fixed-term deposits	239.80		85.0	71.8
= M2	281.98			84.4
+ Other non-personal fixed-term deposits and foreign currency deposits booked in Canada	52.14			15.6
= M3	334.12			

Source: Bank of Canada, *Bank of Canada Review*, June 1992 (S68, Statistical Series B2001, B2033, B2031, B2030, B2029, & B2037).

*Note percentages may not sum to 100 because of adjustment items.

Money Substitutes, Credit Cards, and Trade Credit

Credit cards and trade credit have very much the opposite properties of near money. Anything such as credit cards that serves as a medium of exchange but does not serve as a store of value is usually referred to as a **money substitute.**

If a person carries a recognized credit card, many businesses will sell goods and services on the spot in exchange for nothing more than the person's signature on a credit slip bearing the credit card number. The credit card essentially serves as a short-term medium of exchange, a substitute for a cheque or cash. It is short-term because the business ultimately expects to receive either currency or a cheque. It is also not money because although the purchaser receives the product at the time of the transaction the seller does not receive payment at that time. The seller has really made a short-term loan to the purchaser. The seller will receive payment from the company that issued the credit card to the credit card holder at some time in the future, and at a date after that the purchaser will receive a bill from the credit card company.

Businesses often extend credit to other businesses that are regular customers; a wholesaler supplying a retailer, for example. Such credit is called **trade credit.** It allows one business to buy goods from another without making immediate full payment by cheque or with currency. Like the credit card, trade credit serves as a short-term medium of exchange even though it is not a store of value. Credit cards and trade credit reduce the need for currency and chequable deposits as mediums of exchange. They cannot replace currency and chequable deposits, however, because such credit is not a store of value.

What Determines the Value of Money, or What Backs Money?

In our economy today, money is neither backed by nor convertible into gold or any other precious metal. Coins contain an amount of metal that is worth much less than their face value. Paper money is just that: pieces of paper. Both coins and paper money are money because the government declares them to be money by fiat. Chequable deposits are just bookkeeping entries. Indeed, the government has not even declared chequable deposits to be money, which only shows that general acceptability in exchange and as a store of value are more important than a government declaration. If coins, currency, and chequable deposits are not backed by gold or any other precious metal, and if they have no value in and of themselves, then what determines their purchasing power or real value? The value of money is determined by the supply and demand for liquidity and value storage.

Money Demand and Supply

Money's value derives from its scarcity relative to its usefulness in providing a unique service. The unique service lies in the fact that money can be readily exchanged for goods and services. The economy's demand for money derives from its demand for this service. Therefore, the economy's demand for money is largely determined by the total dollar volume of its current transactions as well as its desire to hold money as a relatively risk-free store of wealth.

What determines the supply of money? In the next chapter we will explain how an economy's depository institutions as a whole can create money in the form of chequable deposits. That chapter will also explain how the Bank of Canada can promote or limit this kind of money creation. Therefore, not only is the government in a position to control the supply of fiat money, through the Bank of Canada it is able to regulate the supply of money more broadly defined.

The value of a unit of money (such as a dollar) is its purchasing power, or the amount of goods and services that it will buy. The higher is the economy's price level, the smaller is the quantity of goods and services that a unit of money will buy. Conversely, the lower is the price level, the larger is the quantity of goods and services a unit of money will buy.

Determination of the Value of Money

If a person is going to the grocery store to buy four loaves of bread and the price of bread is $.50 per loaf, that person will need $2 of money to exchange for the bread. However, if the price of a loaf of bread is $1 per loaf, the person will need $4 of money. There is obviously a relationship among the total quantity of such transactions in the economy, the prices at which they take place, and the economy's demand (need) for money. Oversimplifying somewhat, the following tends to be true. Given the economy's total quantity of transactions (such as the number of bread loaves purchased) and its demand for money needed to execute these transactions, the greater the supply of money, the higher the price level at which these transactions will tend to take place. Conversely, the smaller the supply of money, the lower the price level at which these transactions will tend to take place. Thus, the supply of money and the demand for it play an important role in determining the price level in the economy. It follows that the supply and demand for money play an important role in determining the purchasing power, or value, of a unit of money.

Given the demand for money, the larger is the supply of money, the higher the price level will tend to be, and hence the less the purchasing power, or value, of a unit of money. Conversely, the smaller is the supply of money, the lower the price level will tend to be, and hence the greater the purchasing power, or value, of a unit of money. This tendency for the general level of prices and the money supply to move together has been well documented in Canada and other countries. The relationship between the growth in the money supply and the inflation rate is illustrated in Figure 27-1. In frame (a) of this figure, the percentage change in the money supply (M1) is plotted along with the percentage changes in the consumer price index (CPI), in frame (b) a broader measure of the money supply (M2) is plotted against percentage changes in the gross domestic product price deflator (P).

The Development of Banking

An examination of the nature and development of early banking practices throughout the world will enable us to better understand how modern banks

FIGURE 27-1   Growth in the Money Supply and Consumer
Prices in Canada

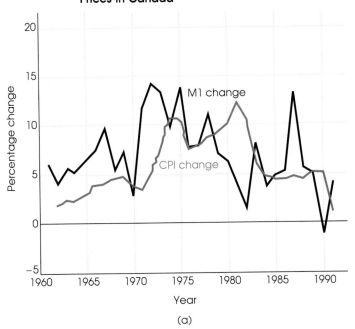

(a)

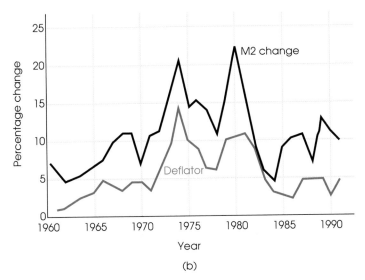

(b)

The general level of consumer prices and the money supply tend to move together.
This is illustrated by the behaviour of the Consumer Price Index (CPI) and the money
supply, defined as M1 or M2. The data suggest that the definition of the money supply
is important in determining the direction of movement in monetary aggregates. The
data do reveal that changes in the rate of inflation are linked to the growth of the
money supply. This can be seen as well in the even closer relationship between
the percentage change in the GDP deflator and M2.

POLICY PERSPECTIVE

Money and Prices: Two Cases of Hyperinflation

In the late 1750s, during the siege of Fort Louisbourg, near the present site of Glace Bay, Nova Scotia, it was very difficult for the governor of the French colony to issue sufficient gold coins to finance military and administrative operations of the colony. At the time, Fort Louisbourg was the second largest French naval base in the world and was blockaded by a British fleet attempting to prevent all trade between the fort and France. Consequently, the governor resorted to printing money (actually at one point simply having the three ranking administrators of the colony write their signatures and the denomination on playing cards), to pay for supplies, weapons, and troops.* As a result, the supply of paper money in the economy of the French outpost increased by an enormous amount between 1757 and 1759. This increase in the supply of paper money (estimated at 500 percent) greatly exceeded the growth in the economy's capacity to increase its production of goods

and services. Hence, the growth in the money supply was much larger than the growth in the quantity of transactions involving the purchase and sale of goods and services. As a result, the prices at which these transactions took place rose rapidly, and the purchasing power of a unit of money fell accordingly.**

A more recent example of hyperinflation occurred in Germany between 1921 and 1923. The German government increased the supply of currency to such an extent that the wholesale price index rose to a level in November 1923 that was 30 billion times higher than it was in January 1921! By this point the Deutschmark's value as money had been destroyed for all practical purposes. An item purchased for a mark in 1921 cost over 2 billion marks by November of 1923.*** Cases of hyperinflation like this one are relatively rare, but many governments throughout history have resorted to increasing the money supply to pay for increased spending on goods and services. This was

done in the past by minting more coins, which often resulted in debasing the value of the coins by reducing their content of precious metal. In more recent history, countries have relied less on coin than on paper currency, so they have tended to simply print more fiat money to finance their expenditures. Inflation rates on the order of 50 to 200 percent per year are not uncommon throughout history and are quite common even today among countries with a large international debt problem or a large military budget relative to the size of the economy.

*Norman Cameron, *Money Financial Markets and Economic Activity*, 2nd ed. (Don Mills, Ont.: Addison-Wesley, 1992), pp. 38–42.

**R. Schuettinger, "The Historical Record: A Survey of Wage and Price Controls over Fifty Centuries," in M. Walker, ed., *The Illusion of Wage and Price Controls* (Vancouver: The Fraser Institute, 1976), pp. 71–72.

***G. Mankiw, *Macroeconomics* (New York: Worth Publishers, 1992), pp. 162–163.

function. It will also reveal why it was felt necessary to create the Bank of Canada in order to put Canadian chartered banking on a more sound footing. In addition, we will gain further insight into the nature of money and how it functions.

Primary Functions of Banks

Modern banks have three primary functions: (1) They provide safekeeping services for all kinds of assets, not just money; (2) they make loans; and (3) as a group they create money. Originally, the provision of safekeeping services was their only function. The functions of lending and money creation developed later, although today these functions represent by far the most important role of banks in our economy.

Safekeeping: The Oldest Banking Function

Goldsmiths were the forerunners of early banks in Europe. People would often bring their own gold to the goldsmith for deposit in the goldsmith's safe, paying a fee for this safekeeping service. The depositor received a receipt designating the amount of gold deposited and attesting to the depositor's right to withdraw the gold on demand upon presentation of the receipt. When gold depositors needed their gold to purchase goods and services, they simply presented their receipts to the goldsmith, who then gave them back their gold. Perhaps the closest counterpart of the goldsmith's safe in a modern bank is the safe-deposit box a person can rent from the bank for an annual fee.

Lending: The First Banks

We might think of early banking as evolving from the original safekeeping activities of goldsmiths. Suppose that such a bank opens and accepts 1,000 ounces of gold from depositors. The depositors in turn receive receipts, which are their legal claims to the gold. The bank's balance sheet is shown in Table 27-2. Like any balance sheet, the left-hand side shows the assets of the bank, the 1,000 ounces of gold it has in its possession. The right-hand side shows the bank's liabilities, the claims on the bank's assets. The liabilities consist of the depositor's receipts, their proof of legal ownership or claim to the gold. Like all balance sheets, total assets must equal total liabilities. The bank's assets, amounting to 1,000 ounces of gold, are balanced by the liabilities, which consist of the receipts laying claim to 1,000 ounces of gold.

On a typical day the quantity of receipts turned in by depositors wishing to withdraw their gold is only a small fraction of the total 1,000 ounces of gold. Moreover, these withdrawals are often approximately offset by new deposits of gold with the bank. Hence, our early banker observes that there is usually a sizable amount of gold standing idle in the safe. The banker realizes that in addition to the fees earned for providing safekeeping services, this idle gold could be lent to people who are willing to pay the banker interest to borrow it. As long as the banker keeps enough gold in the safe to meet withdrawal demands of depositors, the depositors never need know some of their gold is lent to other people. Even if they know, they won't care if they can always get their gold back on demand.[3]

Suppose that the banker observes that depositors never withdraw more than 15 percent of the gold in the safe on any one day. The banker therefore decides

---

[3]The original practice by goldsmiths lending out gold that did not belong to them was neither legal nor ethical. However, one ounce of gold is indistinguishable from any other. Depositors are therefore only concerned about being able to get back the number of ounces of gold deposited, not the exact same particles of gold they deposited.

TABLE 27-2   Balance Sheet of an Early Bank

Assets			Liabilities	
Ounces of gold	1,000		Ounces of gold (receipts)	1,000
Ounces of total assets	1,000	=	Ounces of total liabilities	1,000

it is safe to loan out about 80 percent, or 800 ounces, of the gold. This leaves 20 percent, or 200 ounces, in the safe as a reserve to satisfy depositors' withdrawal demands, somewhat more than the banker's experience suggests is necessary. The banker receives an IOU from each individual who borrows gold. This note, a contract signed by the borrower, states the amount of gold owed to the bank, the date it must be paid back, and the interest rate that the borrower must pay the banker for the loan.

The bank's balance sheet now appears as in Table 27-3. Comparing this balance sheet with that in Table 27-2, for assets the bank now has 200 ounces of gold plus a number of pieces of paper, the IOUs, stating that various borrowers owe the bank 800 ounces of gold. For liabilities the bank still has obligations to give depositors 1,000 ounces of gold on demand, represented by paper gold receipts in the hands of depositors. The bank will have no difficulties unless depositors' demands for withdrawal exceed 200 ounces of gold in any one day. Should this happen, the bank would be unable to honor its commitment to give depositors their gold on demand.

Money Creation and the Early Banks

Given the way early banks evolved to combine safekeeping and lending functions, it is easy to see how they became creators of money as well. Suppose that merchants know their customers fairly well and that the bank has a sound reputation. Merchants are therefore willing to sell goods in exchange for customers' gold receipts. The customer simply signs the paper gold receipt and indicates that ownership of the gold has been transferred to the merchant. The merchant can either take the receipt to the bank to claim gold or use it to make purchases from someone else, transferring ownership of the gold once again in the same manner. The receipt itself is now used as money. It is acceptable in trade because people know it can be redeemed for gold on demand at the bank. It is used as money because it eliminates the need to go to the bank for gold before every shopping trip. And receipts are also easier to carry.

Expanding the Bank's Lending Activities

Once the gold receipts are being used as money, the banker sees a way to expand the bank's lending activity. If gold receipts are now acceptable as money, why not just give borrowers paper gold receipts rather than actual gold in exchange for their IOUs? The banker can now keep all 1,000 ounces of deposited gold in the safe and print up and loan out gold receipts amounting to claims on 4,000 ounces of gold. There would still be gold receipt claims on 5 ounces for every 1 ounce of actual gold reserved, just as before in Table 27-3. But now the banker can earn interest on five times as many IOUs, generated by the lending

TABLE 27-3   The Early Bank's Balance Sheet After Loaning Out 800 Ounces of Gold

Assets			Liabilities	
Ounces of gold (reserves)	200		Ounces of gold (receipts)	1,000
Ounces of gold in IOUs	800			
Ounces of total assets	1,000	=	Ounces of total liabilities	1,000

TABLE 27-4   Early Bank's Balance Sheet After Loaning Out Gold Receipts for 4,000 Ounces of Gold

Assets			Liabilities	
Ounces of gold (reserves)	1,000		Ounces of gold (receipts)	5,000
Ounces of gold in IOUs	4,000			
Ounces of total assets	5,000	=	Ounces of total liabilities	5,000

of 4,000 ounces of gold as represented by the gold receipts given to borrowers (previously the banker earned interest on IOUs for 800 ounces of gold). These receipts will have the same claim on the gold in the safe as the receipts received by the original gold depositors. Our early commercial bank's balance sheet now looks as shown in Table 27-4. All 5,000 ounces' worth of gold receipts are now circulating in the economy as money. Note, however, that there are only 1,000 ounces of actual gold.

As in the case depicted by Table 27-3, it is also true here that if all holders of these gold receipts brought them into the bank at one time and demanded gold, the bank would not be able to honor its commitments to give out gold on demand. However, as long as no more than 20 percent of the gold receipts are presented for payment at one time, there is no problem.

Bank Notes and Fractional Reserve Banking

It is now easy to see how banks got into the business of issuing paper money in the form of **bank notes.** The gold receipts of our hypothetical early bank are but a short step removed from the status of these notes. All the bank has to do is give a gold depositor bank notes instead of a receipt with the depositor's name on it.

Suppose that the bank decides to print up a bank note that says "one dollar" across the front of it and, in smaller letters below this, "This note is redeemable for one ounce of gold on demand."[4] As far as the money-using public is concerned, the important thing is that the bank note can be converted into gold at the bank on demand. Our hypothetical early bank's balance sheet now appears as shown in Table 27-5. Compare this with Table 27-4.

---

[4] Now the note could just as well have been called "one John," "one Sue," "one Klebop," or "one Mark." The term *dollar,* to designate the basic unit of accounts derives from the old German word *thal,* meaning "valley." Its early origin stems from coins used in the valley of Saint Joachim in Bohemia as early as 1519. These coins were called *Joachimsthaler* and then *thaler,* which in English became "dollar."

TABLE 27-5   Early Bank's Balance Sheet After One Dollar Bank Notes Replace Gold Receipts
(Hypothetically, $1 = 1 Ounce of Gold)

Assets			Liabilities	
Gold reserves (1,000 ounces)	1,000		Bank notes	5,000
IOUs	4,000			
Total assets	5,000	=	Total liabilities	5,000

During the nineteenth century, each bank in the colonies that later became the provinces of Canada could issue its own uniquely engraved bank note or currency. This practice was maintained after confederation. After the establishment of the Bank of Canada in 1935 and its conversion into a Crown-owned institution in 1937, the chartered banks were no longer allowed to issue their own money, but bank notes remained in circulation until 1950, when all bank notes were withdrawn from circulation. Through their lending activity the chartered banks typically ended up issuing an amount of bank notes considerably larger than the amount of gold that they had to back up the notes. That is, the banks kept only a fraction of the value of their outstanding notes in gold as backing for the notes they had in circulation, thus giving rise to the beginnings of a **fractional reserve banking system.**

The Need for Prudent Central Banking

The main difficulty with a system that combined fractional reserve banking with a convertible currency (convertible into gold) and the ability of banks to issue bank notes was that the banks could find themselves confronted with demands to exchange gold for their bank notes that exceeded the amount of gold in their safes. If this happened, a bank would be forced to close its doors. People left holding that bank's currency would really be holding only worthless pieces of paper. While this problem was not widespread or frequent in Canada it typified the "wildcat" period of banking in the United States from 1836 to 1864.[5]

Bank Panics and Economic Instability

In the United States even new legislation aimed at the problem did not put an end to that country's monetary and banking problems. Just as the banks had created bank notes when they made loans, they could also create demand deposits. When they granted a loan and received an IOU, they simply credited the amount of the loan to a demand deposit in the borrower's name. In Canada the situation was almost identical. The *Finance Act* had implemented measures that allowed the chartered banks unlimited credit from the Department of Finance provided the chartered banks could create IOUs to use as collateral. In both countries banks could use their respective national currencies as reserves, keeping them either in their own safes or possibly on deposit at another bank. The reserves typically amounted to only a fraction of the amount of their demand-deposit liabilities. The money supply could effectively grow without limit.

---

[5] A large number of note-issuing private and state banks came into existence during this time. The term *wildcat bank* was used to describe many of these banks because they often issued bank notes far in excess of the amount of gold they had on hand. They would locate in remote regions (where the wildcats were) to discourage people from trying to turn the bank notes in for gold. By 1863, there were roughly 1,600 different kinds of bank notes in circulation in the United States.

The Nature of Bank Panics

In the United States the problem, as before, was that if too many depositors attempted to withdraw currency from their demand deposits, the bank might not have enough reserves to satisfy their demands. Because of this, bank panics and financial crises were still frequent in the United States. Even a rumour that a bank had made some bad loans (an IOU on which some borrower wasn't meeting interest payments or couldn't make payments to principal) could cause people holding deposits at the bank to panic. There would then be a run on the bank as depositors rushed to withdraw currency from their accounts.

In general, bank failures caused by runs could be triggered by an adverse turn of events anywhere in the economy. Once banks started to fail, a chain reaction could set in, causing a recession throughout an economy. For example, one of the most common causes of financial crises in the United States in the last third of the nineteenth century was the growth of the economy itself. It was partially the experience south of the border during the wildcat period that caused the Canadian Parliament to pass the *Bank Act* of 1871, which established federal control and guidelines for banking.

In Canada, the problems of runs against banks and of the chronic inability of the banking system to increase the money supply quickly enough to provide for the increased liquidity needs of a growing economy were not serious because of two differences between the Canadian and American banking systems. The first reason was that Canada had evolved a **branch banking system** in which each chartered bank was allowed to have branch offices spread throughout the whole country. When a run against a particular branch of a chartered bank did occur, the branch could receive funds from other branches of the same bank. When there was a regional or sectoral slump in one region or industry, these banks had the financial muscle necessary to carry them through lean economic times. By contrast, the United States with its greater concern for competition and market forces had opted for the creation of a **unit banking system,** where each firm tended to be small and regionally specialized. The two countries therefore produced quite different systems to meet quite different goals. The United States created a unit banking system characterized by over 14,000 small, competitive, localized banks, whereas Canada developed a branch banking system, that until very recently was almost totally dominated by less than 12 very large powerful banks that operated extensive branch systems throughout the whole country.

It is interesting to note that while this has been the general case in Canadian banking, it has been suggested that part of the reason for the collapse of the Canadian Commercial Bank and the Northlands Bank, and for the failure of the Principal Group in the 1980s, was that all three of these institutions operated only on a regional basis and did not have the regional diversity to withstand a downturn in the regional economy when it developed.

Limits to Money Supply Expansion

Chartered banks in Canada could not themselves increase the total amount of the national currency available in the economy. They could of course provide credit (make loans) to feed economic expansion. The increase in deposits created by this loan expansion meant that the amount of demand deposits would get ever larger relative to the amount of currency available for bank reserves. The result was that banks might become susceptible to a sudden surge of deposit withdrawals. The bank caught short might scramble to withdraw currency from its deposit at another bank, setting off a chain of bank failures and a general financial crisis. Consumers and businesses who dealt with these banks would suffer financial losses. This would cause a general decline in aggregate demand. GDP would fall, unemployment would rise, and the economy would be plunged into recession.

While Canada had not experienced this type of liquidity shortage, these situations had developed in the United States and Canada was anxious to ensure that they did not happen here. The government instituted measures that allowed the chartered banks to create as much liquidity as was needed by borrowing from the Department of Finance and later added amendments to ensure that the Department of Finance could prevent the creation of what it felt was too much liquidity.

The Organization and Functions of the Bank of Canada

History of the Bank of Canada

The last major step in the creation of a Canadian **central bank** responsible for the control of the money supply and to serve as a banker to the chartered banks was the establishment of the **Bank of Canada** in 1935 and its conversion from a private bank to a Crown corporation in 1937. Concern that the chartered banks might create too much or too little liquidity prompted the government to set up a Royal Commission to review banking. Among other things, the commission recommended the establishment of a central bank. While much of the design was to be based on the functions and institutional structure of the Bank of England ("The Old Lady of Threadneedle Street"), the recommendations also blended with an odd American source. The Canadians used the reports of Alexander Hamilton on the formation of a national bank for the United States, which had been rejected by the Americans in the 1790s, as part of the blueprint for the Bank of Canada.

Organization of the Bank of Canada

The Bank of Canada was given a broad range of powers, and its institutional structure was specifically designed to reduce the risk that partisan political considerations might influence its activities. The Governor of the Bank of Canada and the Board of Directors are appointed by the Governor General of Canada for seven-year terms, which is longer than the term of office of the government. It is argued that because the directors are not elected, they do not have to adjust their daily activity to the whim of the electorate in order to maintain office. It is also argued that since their terms are longer than that of the government, the directors are insulated from partisan political concerns. Thus, while the conduct of monetary policy is *ultimately* under the control of the government, since it determines who the Governor General appoints, once appointed, the directors are basically free to concentrate on monetary policy without being affected by immediate political influence.

The Governor of the Bank has traditionally been chosen for his technical skills as a central banker and is not a politician or a patronage appointment. For example, the present governor, John Crow, served as Deputy Governor of the Bank before being appointed to his present position. This separation of the Bank from politics has allowed it to formulate and execute its own day-to-day monetary policy, but the close coordination of its monetary policy with that of the government's fiscal policy is accomplished by constant communication between the Department of Finance and the Bank. This communication is enhanced by such institutional arrangements as having the Deputy Minister of Finance sit on the board of the Bank.

The Functions of the Bank of Canada

The functions of the Bank of Canada are to control the size of the money supply, to act as the banker to the chartered banks, to act as the banker for the government, and to promote the smooth operation of the financial markets in Canada.[6]

Controller of the Money Supply

We have already seen that in a fractional reserve banking system the total deposits, including demand deposits, that count as part of M1 are limited by the amount of reserves available. The Bank of Canada directly controls the amount of money to act as reserves for the financial sector. The 1980 *Bank Act of Canada* required *legal reserve ratios*. All chartered banks had to keep reserves equal to 10 percent of the value of their demand-deposit liabilities, 3 percent of their notice-deposit liabilities, and 3 percent of their foreign-currency-deposit liabilities. Further, these *primary reserves* have to be kept either in the form of vault cash or as reserve deposits, which earn no interest, banked with the Bank of Canada. During the 1990s Canada, like many other Western economies, will be phasing out its required reserve ratio and adopting a system of **zero reserve requirements** under proposed amendments to the *Bank Act*. Under the proposed system the chartered banks themselves will decide the appropriate cash reserves to hold for day-to-day operations. The system will likely result in the chartered banks holding zero average reserves at the Bank of Canada.[7] Whether the reserve requirement is specified by law or the reserve ratio sits at an average

---

[6]The function of being the banker to the chartered banks excludes the responsibility for auditing the chartered banks. This function, which ensures that the equity of the stockholders is protected and that the banks operate according to sound financial practice, is fulfilled by the Superintendent of Financial Institutions. This office and its functions evolved out of the old offices of the Inspector General of Banks and other similar positions that previously regulated other financial intermediaries.

[7]"The Implementation of Monetary Policy in a System of Zero Reserve Requirements," *The Bank of Canada Review*, May 1991.

POLICY PERSPECTIVE

The Balance of Politics and Efficiency in Monetary Policy— The Coyne Affair

Generally, the separation of the Bank of Canada from daily political involvement has worked well and has allowed the Bank freedom to conduct its daily affairs without partisan political concerns. This separation does have potential drawbacks, and critics, Keynesians in particular, have argued that the conduct of monetary policy should be for the purpose of ensuring low unemployment and fostering the highest rates of investment and growth consistent with not risking undue inflation or serious disruption of the exchange rate.

To some extent, then, the conduct of monetary policy must involve political interests. Monetary policy influences the health of the whole economy. Its con-

duct, whether through a long-term steady growth for the money supply, as advocated by monetarists, or by using short-term countercyclical policies, as advocated by Keynesians, must be made in accordance with the will of the citizens of the country. This raises the problem that monetary policy is complex and difficult to administer from a technical point of view. Indeed, a discussion of which measure of the money supply (M1, M2, or M3) is most appropriate as a target variable for monitoring the Bank's own policies can be intellectually challenging, if not bewildering at times, even for professional economists. At the same time, however, in a democratic society, it is appropriate that a decision of such impor-

tance to the economy as a whole must be subject to the political will of the majority. It is a delicate balance between efficiency and professionalism on the one hand and the right of the electorate to the ultimate control over decisions of major societal importance on the other that characterizes the structure of modern central banking.

In Canada, the main instrument for ensuring the correct balance has been through the separation of the Bank's staff and directors from direct political involvement. While this delicate balance has worked

continued on next page

level of zero, the Bank of Canada can control the money supply of Canada by controlling the reserves available to financial institutions.

In addition to holding the reserve accounts of the chartered banks, it is the Bank of Canada and not the government that issues all paper currency in Canada. We will examine, in Chapters 28 and 29, exactly how the Bank decides to create or destroy dollars, but the point relevant to the present discussion is that *all dollar-denominated claims against the Bank of Canada held by the chartered banks can serve as reserves for the creation of money and the Bank of Canada controls how large these claims are.*

We will see in the next chapter that the bank has several powerful tools at its disposal with which it can virtually guarantee that it can force the money supply to increase or decrease in accordance with its policy objectives. In fact the only portion of the monetary base not controlled directly by the bank is coinage. Coins are issued by the mint, which is under the direct control of the government. The dollar value of the coins in circulation is, however, only a small fraction of the overall monetary base, and thus for all practical purposes the Bank of Canada controls the amount of money available to serve as reserves.

most of the time, there was one period in particular that epitomizes the difficulty of maintaining the correct division.

Between 1956 and 1962 two separate federal governments, one Liberal and one Conservative, became deadlocked with the Bank of Canada over monetary policy. The governments were concerned about high unemployment levels and tried to use fiscal policy to stimulate the economy. At the same time the Bank of Canada under the direction of its governor, James Coyne, was concerned about inflation. The Bank engaged in a *tight money policy* (which we will study in more detail later in this chapter and in Chapters 28 and 29), designed to restrict credit and reduce investment. Two different Ministers of Finance, Walter Harris (Liberal) and later Donald Fleming (Conservative), indicated in public statements that the Bank of Canada was responsible for the restrictive monetary policy and that the government was not in agreement with the direction the Bank was taking. After

a bitter protracted dispute between the Bank and the government, the governor resigned.

A new governor, Louis Rasminsky, accepted the appointment of governor on the understanding that under normal circumstances the Bank was autonomous in setting the short-term management and direction of monetary policy, but that the ultimate responsibility and authority for conducting monetary policy rested with the government. The resolution of this question was not left to the public declarations of good faith by the new governor.

The stalemate between the Bank and the government had been a traumatic event and the government moved to legislate changes that would guarantee the subservience of the Bank of Canada to the Government of Canada if similar disputes arose in the future. *The Bank of Canada Act* was amended to provide that in the event of a dispute over the conduct of monetary policy, the Minister of Finance in a written order can direct the Bank of Canada as to its conduct of mone-

tary policy and the Bank must comply with that order.

There have been a number of occasions since 1962 when the Bank has followed restrictive policies at the same time that the government has been stimulating the economy. In 1988 all the provincial premiers issued a public communiqué that monetary policy was restricting economic growth. From time to time federal governments have implied that monetary policy was the action of the Bank of Canada and did not necessarily reflect the will of the government. On several occasions Governor Bouey and later Governor Crow have been invited before House of Commons and Senate Committees of Finance to justify the Bank of Canada's policies. To the casual observer these spectacles seem reminiscent of the Coyne Affair. In fact the differences are substantial. While the Bank may be queried about its policies and actions, if the government is not satisfied that the Bank is moving in an appropriate direction all it needs to do is issue an order in writing!

Banker to the Chartered Banks and Financial Intermediaries

Although the Bank of Canada does not deal with the general public, it performs all the functions for the chartered banks that they perform for the public and businesses. It accepts their deposits in their reserve accounts. It arranges *clearing activities* between the members of the Canadian Payments Association when chequing and funds transfer result in a member gaining reserves from another member. But perhaps its most interesting activity as banker to the chartered banks is in its seldom-used role as *lender of last resort*.

If chartered banks have insufficient reserves to allow enough deposit creation to meet the needs of the economy, the Bank of Canada can grant them *advances* to serve as reserves. The advances are really short-term loans. The Bank of Canada lends the chartered banks reserves to prevent them from running short in return for the promise of future repayment. The function was designed to allow the Bank of Canada to provide liquidity very quickly as a bridge during times of general financial crisis or rapid growth in the economy. In practice it has served only a minor role. Advances have been employed only to help individual banks bridge short periods of reserve deficiency. It remains, however, a reassuring guaranteed potential source of credit to support the money supply in times of crisis.

Fiscal Agent for the Government of Canada

Although not involved in the formation of the government's fiscal policy, the Bank of Canada does act as the government's agent in clearing cheques involving payments to the government or by the government. Remembering the very large amounts of money which the government pays out for goods and services and transfers to individuals, corporations and other levels of government, which we studied in Chapter 25, it should be realized that the timing of withdrawal and injection of these substantial sums could easily disrupt the size of the reserves available to the chartered banks. It is part of the Bank of Canada's mandate to ensure that the collection and disbursement of federal government funds does not distort the appropriate behaviour of the money supply. Part of the job of being the banker to government is helping to arrange the most advantageous way of financing the public debt. Recall from Chapters 23 and 25 that when the government runs a deficit it must borrow the difference between its expenditures and its tax revenues. Conversely, if it has a budget surplus, it must dispose of the extra revenues that are not needed to pay for its expenditures. Remembering also that recent federal deficits have exceeded 30 billion dollars, the job of arranging the placement of government bonds so that they cause a minimum disruption through crowding out private investment, crowding out exports, and generating inflation is no easy task. As if coping with the current additions to the public debt through deficits is not a big enough job, the outstanding debt must be refinanced as it matures. Because of the decisions of the last decade to finance more of the debt with Treasury Bills and shorter-term bonds, over half the public debt must be refinanced each year.[8] Thus the Bank of Canada must help to arrange refinancing on a loan of over one hundred and fifty billion dollars a year. This function of the bank, although less important than those of controlling the money supply and acting as banker to the banks, is roughly equivalent to arranging the financing for the takeover of twenty-five firms the size of the former Canadian oil giant, Dome Petroleum, every year.

In its role as fiscal agent for the government, the Bank of Canada can lend the government money by purchasing Treasury Bills or it can assist in arranging financing for the government through foreign or domestic sources. If it lends the government money itself, to the extent that it increases the claims against the Bank of Canada, this will result in an increase in the reserves available to the chartered banks and growth in the money supply. Conversely, a decision to not offset the reduction in the liabilities of the Bank of Canada caused by the payment of taxes to the government would cause the money supply to shrink.

Intervener in Foreign Exchange Markets

As part of its responsibility to maintain the smooth functioning of the money supply of Canada, the Bank of Canada intervenes in international money markets to influence the exchange rate on the Canadian dollar.

---

[8]Department of Finance Canada, *The Fiscal Plan, Controlling the Public Debt,* April 1989, p. 115.

The exact mechanics of how the Bank of Canada influences the value of the Canadian dollar on international markets will be discussed in Chapter 34, where we will explain how exchange rates are determined. For now, all that is important is to understand that the Bank of Canada maintains holdings of foreign currency and gold that can be used to buy Canadian dollars on the international market if its value begins to decline in relation to other currencies. In this way the Bank can create an increased demand for the Canadian dollar, which will push its price up in relation to the currencies of other nations. Conversely, if the value of the Canadian dollar starts to increase relative to other currencies above a level the Bank feels is desirable, or if the rate of increase is faster than the Bank feels it should be, the Bank may intervene by supplying increased quantities of Canadian dollars to international markets until the dollar's value is returned to the desired target level.

Promoter of the Smooth Operation of Financial Markets

The Bank of Canada also has the responsibility of facilitating the efficient workings of financial markets. This function is shared with the five Stock Exchanges (Toronto, Montreal, Winnipeg, Calgary, and Vancouver) and by the regulatory laws covering trust companies and insurance companies. The function of promoter of the smooth operation of financial markets has been a relatively unimportant function of the Bank until recently. The deregulation of financial institutions in the 1980s and the increased competition between chartered banks and other financial intermediaries are beginning to reduce the clear distinction between banking and other financial intermediaries. The chartered banks have recently engaged in mergers with some of the stockbroking firms. This merger activity, combined with the chartered bank's long-established ownership of subsidiaries in the trust and mortgage businesses, suggests that banks will become financial supermarkets in the future. This broader range of increased services implies that the role of promoting the smooth operation of the financial markets will become increasingly important to the Bank of Canada in the future.

Unit Banking versus Branch Banking

Canada has roughly 65 chartered banks, divided into three schedules: A, B, and C. Of these only 8 are schedule A domestic banks, which meet the most stringent requirements of the *Bank Act* of 1980. They are large oligopolistic institutions with immense financial power, and their reserves and demand deposits collectively exceed 95 percent of the narrow definition of the money supply, M1.[9] The other 57 or so banks, which consist of the schedule B and C institutions, are obviously much smaller and of less significance collectively. These smaller banks are for the most part foreign-owned. Like the United States and many other countries, Canada has considered that the functioning

---

[9] While the deposits of the foreign-owned banks make up only about ten percent of the money supply and are an even smaller proportion of broader definitions of money, the deposits of the near banks (insurance companies, trust companies, and so forth) are excluded from the calculations of M1, M2, and M3. If they were included, they would make up approximately one third of the money supply.

> **Checkpoint 27-2**
> Why might a bank note be said to be like an IOU? When currency is convertible into gold, how does the economy put a limit on the amount of money in the economy? Describe how you think people's opinions about the soundness of banks at any particular time would affect the upper limit to the amount of the economy's money, defined as currency plus demand deposits. If bankers were to become cautious about the business outlook, how do you think this would affect the amount of IOUs on their balance sheets, and why and how would this affect the amount of money in the economy? How do you think this would affect total demand for goods and services?

of the banks is of such importance to the general well-being of the economy that tough rules limit the amount of control of the voting stock in a bank that can be owned by any individual or group and the amount of control by foreigners. These rules were loosened somewhat in 1980, and again in 1987, with measures to promote more direct competition between the banks, insurance companies, trust companies, mortgage and loan companies, and the caisses populaires.

Because of the relatively small number of institutions involved in Canada's branch banking system and the fact that they all must be federally chartered and come under one piece of federal legislation, the *Bank Act* of 1980, the job of regulating and controlling the money supply is easier than in countries like the United States with its unit system. There are approximately 14,000 commercial banks in the United States. Commercial banks in that country are divided into two classes: state banks and national banks. About one third of all commercial banks are national banks; the rest are state banks. National banks are authorized to operate by the federal government, state banks by state governments. Before 1980 this meant that all national banks, but only those state banks wishing to join, were members of the Federal Reserve System (the Fed). The number of state bank members of the Federal Reserve System declined by roughly fifty percent between 1950 and 1980, so the percentage of the banks falling under Fed control fell from about 86 percent to roughly 40 percent over this period. The main reason for the decline was that nonmember banks were subject only to state reserve requirements, which were more lenient than those imposed by the Fed.

Thus the Fed in the United States had to try to do the same job as the Bank of Canada but could directly influence only half the commercial banks in its economy, and then only by dealing with over 5,000 banks, as compared to the Bank of Canada's job of controlling one hundred percent of the banks in its economy by dealing with the eight schedule A chartered banks.

Depository Institutions as Financial Intermediaries

A **financial intermediary** is a business that acts as a middleman (intermediary) by taking the funds of lenders and making them available to borrowers, earning a profit on the difference between the interest it charges borrowers and the interest it must pay to attract the funds of lenders. When a financial intermediary accepts a lender's funds, it issues an obligation against itself, a liability, to pay the lender back. When the intermediary in turn lends these funds to a borrower, it takes on an asset in the form of the borrower's IOU, or obligation to pay the funds back. All depository institutions issuing chequable accounts are financial intermediaries.

The liabilities that a chartered bank issues are in the form of demand, savings, and time deposits. The assets of a chartered bank consist primarily of short-term loans to businesses and consumers. Until the last few years, laws required that most financial intermediaries other than chartered banks issue liabilities that were more like the savings and time deposits than demand deposits. Due to recent amendments to that legislation, trust companies, mortgage and loan companies, credit unions, savings banks, and the caisses populaires have moved into chequable accounts. The chartered banks have taken advantage of the new laws as well to move into the stockbroking activities and sale of trusts

POLICY PERSPECTIVE

A Common Misconception About the Saving and Investment Process: The Role of Banks

In the United States during the Great Depression more than 5,000 banks failed between 1929 and 1933. Many economists place at least some of the blame on the policymakers responsible for regulating the banking system at that time, arguing that they had the authority and the means to keep any bank from having to close. In Canada there were no bank failures during the Great Depression, in fact there were no bank failures from 1923, when Home Bank collapsed, until 1985, when two chartered banks, the Canadian Commercial Bank and the Northlands Bank, both failed. This lack of bank failures in Canada as compared to the United States is often attributed to the difference between our branch system with its centralized control, and the American unit banking system with its decentralized structure. While some of this may be true, it overlooks the problem that when a Canadian institution, whether a bank or some other type of financial institution, such as the Principal Group, Abacus, or Teachers' Co-op Credit Union, does fail, the failure tends to be larger on average than a corresponding failure in the United States and the impact

more damaging to the region that suffers the loss. Some might argue that the Savings and Loan collapse in the United States would alter this perspective, but this is a systemwide crisis involving many institutions and is not illustrative of the impact of the collapse of one institution.

What was not well understood in the 1930s in the United States and is of interest to us today is the exact nature of the crucial role that banks play in the economy's saving and investment process. Because of this role, either a failure of a few large financial institutions or a large number of failures by small financial intermediaries can cause severe interruptions in the saving and investment process and hence in the economy's income and expenditure flow, thereby contributing to or even causing a severe economic downturn.

The extent of the role of financial intermediaries in maintaining the income and expenditure flow was often not fully appreciated in the past because of a common misconception—namely, the idea that dollars from saving must somehow flow from the hands of savers into the hands of investors in order for investment expendi-

tures to be able to occur. But in fact, households may bury their unspent dollars in the backyard if they wish. In the Canadian economy the financial institutions and especially the chartered banks are able to create money (we shall see how in the next chapter) and lend it to businesses that want to invest in plant, equipment, and inventories or to the government for the creation of infrastructure.

The fact that dollars do not literally have to flow from the hands of savers into those of investors illustrates how much the motives and decisions of savers may be disconnected from those of investors. It also highlights an important point. If households put their savings in sugar bowls and mattresses or bury them in the backyard in coffee tins, or if the government borrows all of households' savings to finance the public debt, investment will have to be financed by the banking system. Widespread bank failures, such as those that occurred during the 1930s in the United States, remove this source of financing and cause intended investment spending to fall, thereby reducing the economy's equilibrium level of total income, output, and employment.

(RRSPs and annuities). Until the amendments, the law prevented chartered banks from taking a direct interest in the real estate market, but through the creation of subsidiaries the banks have long had an active indirect involvement in the real estate industry. Credit unions acquire assets in the form of claims against people to whom they make consumer loans. Though they are not depository institutions, insurance companies are also financial intermediaries. Insurance companies issue liabilities in the form of insurance policies. The premiums they collect from policyholders are used to acquire assets such as mortgages, various kinds of bonds, and corporate securities.

The Role of Financial Intermediaries

What special services and advantages do financial intermediaries provide for our economy? Basically, there are three.

First, financial intermediaries have expertise as credit analysts. They have the ability and experience to evaluate and compare the risk and return, or creditworthiness, of different kinds of loan opportunities. Imagine the majority of the population trying to prudently loan out their money by doing this in their spare time, after performing a day's work as a carpenter or doctor or whatever. Credit analysis is just another area of specialization in a modern, industrialized economy.

Next, financial intermediaries take the many different-sized amounts of funds that households, businesses, and other institutions want to lend and package them into the typically different-sized amounts that individual borrowers want to borrow. For example, many small depositors at a chartered bank can indirectly make a $30,000,000 loan to a business.

Finally, financial intermediaries provide an opportunity for small lenders with small amounts of money to participate in risk-reducing diversification. By depositing a small amount of money in a financial intermediary, a depositor in effect takes a proportional share of every loan the intermediary makes. The depositor has not put all of his or her eggs in one basket, and the likelihood of loss is therefore reduced.

Promoting Sound Banking and Protecting Depositors

While the Bank of Canada and the Superintendent of Financial Institutions promote sound banking practices to enhance the public confidence in banking and reduce the risk of a widespread banking panic, they are not the only institutions designed to promote safety and trust in financial intermediaries.

All the member institutions of the Canadian Payments Association have eligible deposit liabilities insured by the **Canadian Deposit Insurance Corporation (CDIC)** for the amount of $60,000 per depositor per institution. This means that an individual could have over three million dollars on deposit with the schedule A chartered banks (not to mention more in the schedule B and C chartered banks, the trust and loan institutions, and credit unions) and would be one hundred percent repaid in the event of collapse. While those with such financial assets might well find more profitable alternate ways to store their value, the members of the Canadian Deposit Insurance Corporation provide risk-free storage of wealth if consumers are careful about where they store their wealth.

As was pointed out earlier, it is not simply the number but also the size of bank failures that are important in shaking the public confidence in banking. The small number of Canadian bank failures tends to mask the fact that the value of deposits at risk can be quite large if there is a failure, and large numbers of individuals may be influenced by the loss. The failure of the two Canadian banks in 1985 caused a reserve drain of over four billion dollars; by contrast, in the United States a failure of about one hundred and twenty banks that same year caused only five hundred million dollars of claims against the American

Federal Deposit Insurance Corporation (FDIC). The fact that the Canadian and American deposits are one hundred percent insured up to their respective limits by deposit insurance corporations is seen by some as evidence that sound banking is promoted in both countries. Surely it does reduce depositor fear of loss compared to the grim experiences of American depositors during the wildcat period of the nineteenth century or the Great Depression, but there is another side to this peace of mind. Critics argue that there are two major flaws in the present deposit insurance institutions and in their supervision during periods of financial unrest.

The first problem involves the idea that in the event of bank failure, the healthy, well-run financial institutions are liable to make up the debts and honour the deposits of the failed institutions. While this reduces depositor concern, it penalizes the well-run institutions. They are in effect taxed for the sins of their competitors and are not in a position to prevent unsound financial practices by their competitors that might ultimately jeopardize their own financial health.

The second problem involves the ability to limit insurance coverage to the $60,000 limit. When a bank or other financial institution is rumoured to be in trouble, depositors begin to withdraw their funds for redeposit in an apparently more healthy institution. In the case of the Canadian Commercial Bank failure, it is argued that the institution relied very heavily on large institutional deposits over the $60,000 insured limit. These types of accounts are volatile, and they begin to desert a bank at the first hint of trouble, increasing the risk failure once a bank run begins. Politicians and regulators are hard-pressed to come up with any real solutions to runs by big institutional depositors. If they wish to prevent these institutional investors from withdrawing their funds from a troubled financial institution, they must provide guarantees that funds are safe where they are.

In addition, the argument often used by critics—that these depositors are sophisticated and do not need one-hundred-percent coverage over the $60,000 limit—overlooks the basic nature of this type of institutional deposit. Typically, large institutional deposits are using other people's money, and these people may be neither sophisticated nor wealthy. Can they be held responsible for losses when they are depositing less than $60,000 and when the institution they are depositing in assures them that they are covered by Canadian Deposit Insurance. Thus, the politicians and regulators, in an attempt to stop a bank failure by the withdrawal of large institutional deposits, and in their attempts to prevent financial damage to small depositors involved with institutional accounts, have covered all depositors to the full amount of their loss instead of to the insured limit. This has caused some critics to claim that the government's provision of deposit insurance may encourage banks to engage in riskier lending practices because bankers know that small depositors' money is protected by the CDIC in the event of failure. Since the CDIC has fully protected all depositors, regardless of the size of their deposit, critics argue that these institutions will be encouraged to engage in even riskier lending activities because of CDIC. Indeed, such actions by CDIC resulted in its own insolvency and the government had to rescue it.[10] It is therefore the taxpayers who end up footing the bill for failures of large financial intermediaries.

---

[10] W. T. Hunter, *Canadian Financial Markets* (Peterbough, N.H.: Broadview Press, 1986), pp. 170–184.

Checkpoint 27-3

How does the Bank of Canada give elasticity to the money supply? Why do you suppose the Bank of Canada is sometimes referred to as the "lender of last resort"? Some say deposit insurance is more effective in dealing with the problem of bank panics than is the depository institutions' privilege of borrowing from the Bank of Canada. Why?

There is also a double standard in the failure of financial institutions in Canada: Chartered banks and other members of the CDIC are treated one way and other financial institutions are treated differently. The failures of Abacus, (a real estate development and venture capital firm), Seaway Trust, Greymac Mortgage, London Loan, and the Principal Group all confirm that the failure of financial institutions is more likely and just as damaging for other financial intermediaries as it is for chartered banks. In the cases cited and in scores of others throughout Canada a complex maze of provincial legislation makes it difficult to unravel what the cause of failure was and which government agencies or ministers are responsible. The interests of the depositors are sometimes only guaranteed by their own actions in court and there are significant time lags between the failure and the extent of compensation is established.

Where Do We Go from Here?

In the next chapter we will examine in more detail the nature of the modern bank and how it works. We will also study how the whole banking system functions to create money and how this process is influenced by the Bank of Canada. In Chapter 30, we will examine how the money supply affects the level of aggregate demand for goods and services and the role that money plays in determining the economy's equilibrium level of total output and employment.

Summary

1. Money is anything that functions simultaneously as a medium of exchange, a store of value, and a unit of account. Money is the most liquid of all assets.
2. The basic kinds of money are commodity money, currency (fiat money consisting of coin and paper money), demand deposits (chequing accounts), and notice deposits with chequing privileges.
3. The measurements of the money supply are M1, M2, and M3. M1 is currency outside the banks and demand deposits. M2 is M1 plus personal savings deposits plus non-personal notice accounts; M3 is M2 plus non-personal fixed-term deposits plus foreign currency accounts of residents booked in Canada.
4. Near money can function as a unit of account and store of value like money, but not as a medium of exchange, though it is readily convertible into money.
5. Money in our economy is neither backed by nor convertible into gold. It has value because people have faith in it. This is because of the goods and services it will buy. The purchasing power of money depends on the price level, and this in turn depends on the Bank of Canada's management of the money supply.
6. Banks evolved from the safekeeping service provided by goldsmiths to become lenders as well. After gold receipts began circulating as money, banks were able to create money (bank notes) through the expansion of their lending activities. This eventually gave rise to present-day fractional reserve banking, with demand deposits and other chequable deposits serving as money by virtue of the cheque-writing privilege.

7. The Bank of Canada was established in 1935 to provide the economy with a formal mechanism, free from partisan political influence, that could control the growth of the money supply and ensure that the chartered banks had adequate access to reserves during financial crises.

8. The Bank of Canada serves as a clearinghouse for the collection of cheques and as the banker for the federal government, provides the economy's paper money, and supervises and regulates the banking practices of the chartered banks. The Bank of Canada's supervisory activity is supplemented and augmented by a number of other government agencies. These include the Superintendent of Financial Institutions, the various stock exchange commissions, the Canadian Deposit Insurance Corporation, and of course the federal and provincial governments with their respective laws covering the financial industry.

9. The economy's depository institutions function as financial intermediaries, accepting deposits and making loans. Depository institutions can create money by creating chequable deposits through their lending activities. Because of the Bank of Canada's control over the reserves of the chartered banks and members of the Canadian Payments Association, the Bank of Canada can influence the size of the economy's money supply and hence the level of total demand for goods and services in the economy.

Key Terms and Concepts

Bank of Canada
bank notes
branch banking
    system
Canadian Deposit
    Insurance Corp
    (CDIC)
Canadian Payments
    Association (CPA)
central bank
chequable deposits
commodity money

daily interest chequing
    accounts
demand deposit
fiat money
financial intermediary
fixed-term deposits
fractional reserve
    banking system
functions of money
liquidity
M1, M2, M3
money

money substitute
near money
notice accounts
notice deposits
savings deposit
token coins
trade credit
Treasury Bill (T-Bill)
    account
unit banking system
zero reserve
    requirements

Questions and Problems

1. What are the differences between inflation and deflation in terms of their effects on the three basic functions of money?

2. Compare and rank the different definitions of money—M1, M2, and M3—in terms of their relative merits (1) as mediums of exchange and (2) as stores of value. What difference would it make for your answer to (2) if (a) there was an inflation, (b) there was a deflation, or (c) there was neither inflation nor deflation?

3. Our money is no longer backed by nor convertible into gold or any other precious metal. Why is it still valuable?

4. What problem would be created for Canada if the Looney was made out of sterling silver instead of being minted out of cheap metal?

5. Why might fractional reserve banking be described as the "swapping of one debt obligation for another"?

6. The Western Canadian economy was largely based on fur trading in the seventeenth and eighteenth centuries. When the Hudson's Bay Company sent their first expedition to Rupert's Land to explore the feasibility of profitably trading European manufactures for North American furs, they needed to outfit two ships, *Nonsuch* and *Eaglet* for the two-way trip across the Atlantic and enough supplies to winter in Canada. In retrospect, the cost of about 1,400 pounds for the ships, their cargoes, and the sailors' wages, seems trivial as the beginning of a 300-year monopoly fur trading empire. Suppose that you were a Scottish banker in May 1668, and you heard reports of vicious storms in the North Atlantic. Would you be willing to extend credit to provisioners who hoped to sell supplies to the Hudson's Bay Company expedition as it headed out from the Orkney Islands? Would your decision be influenced if the provisioners trying to borrow from you would not be able to pay you until after the return of the expedition?

7. Why and how might central banking have greatly reduced bank panics in the nineteenth century? Why might deposit insurance also have helped?

8. Describe how the basic functions of the Bank of Canada are supposed to contribute to economic stability.

9. Why and how is financial intermediation important to our economy?

Chapter 28

Banks and Money Creation

This chapter explains how the chartered banks and other financial intermediaries, that are members of the Canadian Payments Association, operate. To begin this examination, an illustration of the balance sheet of a typical hypothetical bank will be illustrated and analyzed. The chapter will briefly discuss how financial institutions manage risk and balance it against the desire for profitability. While the profitability or risk of a particular financial intermediary failure can affect investor confidence or the willingness of an individual depositor to entrust deposits to that bank or trust company, the importance of an efficient banking system to society goes well beyond this aspect of banking. The focus of this chapter is on how the deposit multiplier process works and how the banking system can expand the deposits to a multiple of the reserves in the system.

The Banks

In the previous chapter we saw that banks create money in the process of extending credit through their lending activity (the interest received on the lending activity is their principal source of earnings). Our discussion was aided by the use of a highly simplified version of a bank's balance sheet. To understand better how modern banks operate, we need to look at the balance sheet of a hypothetical bank. We also need to consider the distinction among actual, excess, and required reserves in order to understand the deposit expansion (or contraction) process by which our banking system increases (or decreases) the economy's money supply. A chartered bank's need for liquidity on the one hand and its desire to make a profit on the other bear closely on how this deposit expansion (or contraction) process works. With this in mind, we will also consider how banks juggle the often conflicting goals of liquidity and profitability.

TABLE 28-1 Balance Sheet of Yukon Bank

Assets			Liabilities and Equity	
Building and equipment	$100,000		Equity (stock certificates of Yukon Bank)	$100,000
Total assets	$100,000	=	Total liabilities and equity	$100,000

Our discussion could be conducted in terms of any one of the different types of depository institutions that issue chequable deposits (for example, chartered banks, trust companies, savings banks, loan companies, and credit unions). However, we will focus on chartered banks because their demand deposits represent the bulk of all chequable deposits. The basic principles of deposit expansion and money creation illustrated by the chartered banks, as well as the problem of balancing liquidity against profitability, apply in similar fashion to any type of financial intermediaries offering chequable deposits.

The Balance Sheet: Assets and Liabilities

Our discussion of how a bank gets started and how it manages its assets and liabilities will be conducted in terms of the bank's balance sheet.

Starting a Bank

Suppose that a group of people decides to start a chartered bank, calling it Yukon Bank. Although the *letters patent* or *charter* granted by the government to establish a chartered bank in Canada requires a minimum capitalization and sets out restrictions on the percentage of voting shares that can be controlled by any one group, for simplicity we will assume that the group starting the Yukon Bank put $100,000 of their own money into the business. They receive in exchange shares of stock paper certificates indicating their ownership of the bank. The owners' $100,000 of capital stock is the equity, or net worth, of the bank. The $100,000 is used to buy a building and other equipment and pay fees to the Canadian Payments Association. At this point Yukon Bank's balance sheet is shown in Table 28-1. The left, or asset, side of the balance sheet shows what the bank owns, in descending order of the liquidity of the bank's assets. The right, or liability and equity, side of the balance sheet shows the claims against

---

LEARNING OBJECTIVES

After reading this chapter, you will be able to:

1. Explain the nature of the balance sheet of a bank.
2. Describe the conflict between a chartered bank's desire to make profits and its need for liquidity and security.
3. Compare and contrast the operation of an individual bank in a multibank system with the operation of the banking system considered as a whole.
4. Describe how deposit expansion and money creation take place in our banking system.
5. Define the deposit expansion multiplier.
6. Explain the factors that can reduce the size of the deposit multiplier.

TABLE 28-2 Balance Sheet of Yukon Bank

Assets		Liabilities and Equity	
Cash	$1,000,000	Demand deposits	$1,000,000
Building and equipment	100,000	Equity (stock certificates of Citizen's Bank)	100,000
Total assets	$1,100,000 =	Total liabilities and equity	$1,100,000

the bank; it, too, is arranged in descending order of liquidity. The bank's total assets equal its total liabilities and equity, because everything the bank possesses is claimed by someone.

The Bank Opens Its Doors

The bank is now ready for business. When its doors open, suppose that customers deposit $1,000,000 in currency. The bank now adds $1,000,000 in demand deposits to the liability and equity side of its balance sheet and $1,000,000 cash to the asset side. Its balance sheet now appears as shown in Table 28-2. Those who have claims on the bank, represented on the liability and equity side of the balance sheet, are divided into two groups: owners of the bank, and the non-owners. The claims of the owners represent the bank's equity, or *net worth*, amounting to $100,000 (the value of the stock certificates issued by Yukon Bank). The claims of the non-owners are represented by the $1,000,000 of demand deposits. The non-owners' claims constitute the bank's liabilities. Hence, **equity** (or **net worth**) equals the difference between total assets and the total liabilities.

Required Reserves, Actual Reserves, and Excess Reserves

Suppose that the legal **required reserves** imposed by the *Bank Act* on the chartered banks is 20 percent. This means that a bank is required by law to hold an amount of reserves equal to 20 percent of the total amount of its demand deposits. The ratio of required reserves to the total amount of demand deposits is the **required reserve ratio.** The law defines *reserves* as the cash held in the bank's vault and the deposits of the bank in a non-interest-earning reserve account at the Bank of Canada. Since Yukon Bank has $1,000,000 of demand deposits, it must hold at least $200,000 (20 percent of $1,000,000) in the form of reserves. Suppose that it deposits $200,000 of its $1,000,000 of cash in its account at the Bank of Canada. Yukon Bank's balance sheet now appears as shown in Table 28-3. While its legally required reserves amount to $200,000, its

TABLE 28-3 Balance Sheet of Yukon Bank

Assets		Liabilities and Equity	
Reserves	$1,000,000	Demand deposits	$1,000,000
On deposit at Bank of Canada	200,000		
Cash	800,000		
Building and equipment	100,000	Equity (stock certificates of Yukon Bank)	100,000
Total assets	$1,100,000 =	Total liabilities and equity	$1,100,000

total reserves actually amount to $1,000,000—that is, $200,000 on deposit at the Bank of Canada and $800,000 in the form of cash in its vault. Yukon Bank's total reserves now exceed its required reserves by $800,000. This amount is called *excess reserves*. Total (or actual) reserves are equal to required reserves plus excess reserves. Required reserves are equal to the amount of demand deposits multiplied by the required reserve ratio. **Excess reserves** are the reserves held above and beyond the amount needed for required reserves. Excess reserves are equal to total reserves minus required reserves.

Lending Out Excess Reserves

At this point Yukon Bank has excess reserves of $800,000. A bank's largest potential source of earnings is the interest it can earn by making loans and buying and holding various kinds of bonds and securities. Yukon Bank will therefore want to put these excess reserves to work rather than hold idle cash, which earns no interest at all.

Suppose that it loans out $300,000 to consumers who want to buy cars, household appliances, and perhaps bonds and stocks. Suppose that $200,000 is loaned to businesses that need money to finance their inventories of goods, raw materials, and to buy equipment. The bank holds IOUs from these consumers and businesses in the form of promissory notes (typically the IOUs of consumers and small businesses) and commercial paper (the IOUs from businesses). Suppose that the bank also purchases $100,000 worth of Government of Canada securities and $100,000 of other securities, such as corporate bonds and provincial and municipal government bonds. As a precautionary measure, Yukon Bank elects to keep $100,000 of its cash as excess reserves to meet sudden withdrawal demands by depositors or to be able to provide credit to a regular loan customer on short notice. Yukon Bank's balance sheet now appears as shown in Table 28-4.

The stages of development of our hypothetical Yukon Bank, illustrated in Tables 28-1 through 28-4, represent the basic principles of the formation of a chartered bank. The Yukon Bank balance sheet shown in Table 28-4 is now very similar to the balance sheet of a typical chartered bank except for two important items that we didn't introduce in our Yukon Bank example—namely, fixed-term deposits and notice deposits (discussed in the previous chapter). The 1980 *Bank Act* imposes a legal reserve requirement on notice and fixed-term deposits just

TABLE 28-4   Balance Sheet of Yukon Bank After Lending Out Excess Reserves

Assets		Liabilities and Equity	
Reserves	$ 300,000	Demand deposits	$1,000,000
On deposit at Bank of Canada	200,000		
Cash	100,000		
Consumer loans	300,000		
Business loans	200,000		
Government securities	100,000		
Other securities	100,000		
Building and equipment	100,000	Equity (stock certificates of Yukon Bank)	100,000
Total assets	$1,100,000 =	Total liabilities and equity	$1,100,000

like that imposed on demand deposits. The required reserve ratio for demand deposits is set at 10 percent, on notice deposits it is 3 percent, and on foreign currency deposits booked in Canada by residents of Canada it is 3 percent.[1]

Liquidity and Security versus Profit: Bank Portfolio Management

As a financial intermediary, a chartered bank primarily engages in making short-term loans to businesses and households, as well as purchasing and holding bonds and other securities. The bank's income-earning asset—its loans, bonds, and securities—together with its excess reserves constitute the bank's portfolio. A bank manages its portfolio by adjusting the relative proportions of the different income-earning assets it holds in such a way as to satisfy two often conflicting objectives: (1) the maintenance of liquidity and security, and (2) the realization of profit.

Maintenance of Liquidity and Security

In the previous chapter, we saw how banks could fail if they didn't have adequate reserves to meet depositors' demands to withdraw their funds. Modern chartered banks hold an amount of reserves equal to only a fraction of their deposit liabilities. Moreover, the largest part of a bank's reserves typically is held to satisfy the legal reserve requirement, and the bank can't really use these to satisfy depositors' withdrawals. (We shall see shortly that the main purpose of required reserves is to give the Bank of Canada control over the banking system's money creation process.) In practice, a bank will have to use its excess reserves to meet any sudden surge of deposit withdrawals. If these excess reserves are not adequate, it will then have to liquidate some of its income-earning assets—that is, convert them into funds that can be used to meet deposit withdrawals.

Therefore, a bank needs to restrict itself to holding income-earning assets that are relatively liquid and secure. As we saw in the previous chapter, the more liquid an asset is, the more easily and quickly it can be converted into money without loss. The security of an asset refers to the degree of likelihood that the contracted obligations of the asset will be met. For example, a bond is a contract stipulating that the borrower, the bond issuer, will pay the lender, or bondholder, a certain amount of interest on specified dates and return the amount of money borrowed (the principal) on the maturity of the bond. Treasury Bills are the most secure asset a bank can hold. Loans made to consumers and households are less secure, and the degree of security will of course vary from one consumer or business to the next.

In general, a bank restricts its holdings of earning assets to shorter-term loans, bonds, and securities because of the relatively higher degree of liquidity and security associated with these assets. This restriction is dictated by the large amount of deposit liabilities subject to withdrawal on demand.

---

[1] Revisions to the *Bank Act* in 1981 reduced the required reserve ratio on the first $500,000,000 worth of savings (notice) deposits to 2 percent in recognition of the difficulty a new small chartered bank has in competing with larger established banks in Canada. Canada is planning to move to a zero reserve requirement system in the 1990s. This will not fundamentally change the way the money multiplier is expected to work although it will increase the size of the money multiplier.

Checkpoint 28-1

From 1933 through 1940 banks in Europe and North America kept a considerably larger portion of their assets in the form of excess reserves than is the case today. Why do you suppose that they did this?

Answers to all Checkpoints can be found at the back of the text.

Balancing Profit Against Liquidity and Security

A chartered bank is similar to any other business in that it wants to maximize the profits realized by its owners, the stockholders. First and foremost, however, the bank is obliged to meet deposit withdrawals on demand. Whenever it is unable to do this, the bank is out of business.

Obviously, if a bank held nothing in its portfolio but vault cash, it would maximize liquidity and security. But without any earning assets in its portfolio the bank wouldn't be very profitable. Conversely, if a bank holds no excess reserves and tries to hold only those earning assets that yield the highest return, it may maximize profits, but it will run a high risk of being unable to meet a sudden surge of deposit withdrawals. Clearly, there is a conflict between the maintenance of liquidity and security on the one hand and the realization of profit on the other. The main task of bank portfolio management is to strike a balance between these conflicting objectives.

Deposit Expansion and the Banking System

In the previous chapter we saw how a chartered bank can make a loan by accepting the IOU (promissory note) of an individual or business and crediting a demand deposit in the borrower's name for the amount of the loan. The asset side of the bank's balance sheet is increased by the amount of the IOU, and the liability side is increased by the same amount in the form of a demand deposit held in the name of the borrower. The borrower may then write cheques against this demand deposit, and the bank is obliged to honour these cheques. As explained in the previous chapter, demand deposits are considered money even in the narrowest definition of money, M1. Therefore, when the borrower and a chartered bank agree on the terms of a loan and a demand deposit is increased by the amount of the loan, this new debt (loan) has resulted in the creation of new money in the economy. We will now examine how the banking system as a whole, consisting of several such banks, creates money through this process. For simplicity we will focus on chartered banks. It should be emphasized, however, that the process of money creation described applies to all financial intermediaries belonging to the Canadian Payments Association that issue chequable deposits, and that the financial system as a whole includes all of these institutions.

First, we will consider the position of an individual bank in a system containing several banks. We will then examine the process of money creation when there are several banks in the economy by considering what happens to the system as distinct from any individual bank in the system.

The Individual Bank in a System of Many Banks

Consider once again the Yukon Bank when it is in the position shown by its balance sheet in Table 28-3, reproduced here as Table 28-5a. It has $1,000,000 in demand-deposit liabilities and holds $1,000,000 of reserves. Again, assuming that the legal reserve requirement is 20 percent, the required reserves amount

TABLE 28-5a   Balance Sheet of Yukon Bank

Assets		Liabilities and Equity	
Reserves	$1,000,000	Demand deposits	$1,000,000
Required reserves	200,000		
Excess reserves	800,000		
Building and equipment	100,000	Equity	100,000
Total assets	$1,100,000 =	Total liabilities and equity	$1,100,000

to $200,000. Therefore, the bank has $800,000 of excess reserves and is in a position to make loans by creating demand deposits.

What amount of loans and, hence, demand deposits will the Yukon Bank create? It cannot create more than $800,000 worth. At this stage Yukon Bank's balance sheet appears as in Table 28-5b. The bank cannot lend out more than $800,000 because borrowers will most likely immediately spend these funds by writing cheques against the $800,000 of demand deposits that the bank has credited to them. Since Yukon Bank is just one bank in the banking system, it is likely that these cheques may be made payable to parties who deposit their money in other banks. Therefore, when all of these cheques are presented to the Yukon Bank for collection of payment, Yukon Bank will have to pay out its $800,000 of excess reserves to satisfy the cheques, which are orders to withdraw the $800,000 of deposits on demand. Assume that this happens. Yukon Bank's balance sheet will now appear as in Table 28-6.

Note that the bank is now *fully loaned up*. It has just the amount of reserves on hand to meet the legal reserve requirement ($200,000 of reserves held against $1,000,000 of demand deposits). There are no excess reserves. While the Yukon Bank now has the same amount of demand deposits it had in the beginning, it has created $800,000 more money in the economy. That money is now deposited in other banks. Although less likely, it could have happened that all of the cheques written against the $800,000 of demand deposits created by Yukon Bank in Table 28-5b were paid to parties who redeposited them at Yukon Bank. The deposits of those who wrote the cheques would then be reduced by $800,000, while the deposits of those who received the cheques would be increased by $800,000. The total amount of demand-deposit liabilities at Yukon Bank would remain unchanged at $1,000,000. Also unlikely, but possible, is that the $800,000 of demand deposits created in Table 28-5b might be withdrawn by the borrowers in the form of currency, so that the final position of the bank would be as shown in Table 28-6. *A single bank in a banking system composed of many banks cannot lend more than the amount of its excess reserves. This is true because borrowers will most likely write cheques against the deposits, which will cause the bank to lose these excess reserves, along with the deposits, to other banks.*

TABLE 28-5b   Balance Sheet of Yukon Bank After Making Loans of $800,000 but Before Cheques Are Written Against Bank

Assets		Liabilities and Equity	
Reserves	$1,000,000	Demand deposits	$1,800,000
IOUs: loans to businesses and consumers	800,000		
Building and equipment	100,000	Equity	100,000
Total assets	$1,900,000 =	Total liabilities and equity	$1,900,000

TABLE 28-6   Balance Sheet of Yukon Bank After Checks for $800,000 Are Written Against Bank

Assets		Liabilities and Equity	
Reserves	$ 200,000	Demand deposits	$1,000,000
IOUs: loans to businesses and consumers	800,000		
Building and equipment	100,000	Equity	100,000
Total assets	$1,100,000 =	Total liabilities and equity	$1,100,000

This means that a single bank cannot permanently increase the amount of its demand deposit liabilities (by making loans) beyond the amount that it initially had on deposit.

A Banking System of Many Chartered Banks

We will now see that a banking system made up of many banks can make loans and create demand deposits equal to several times the amount of total excess reserves in the system. In effect the banking system can create money.

Recall that a single bank in a banking system of many banks cannot permanently increase the amount of its demand deposits because the demand deposits it creates by lending are transferred by borrowers to other banks as cheques are written against the borrowers' accounts. As these cheques are *cleared* through the Canadian Payments Association, the demand deposits of other banks are increased. Therefore, the amount of demand deposits in the *whole* banking system is increased. Reserves and deposits cannot be lost to other banks outside the banking system because there are no banks outside the system. Let's now explore in more detail lending and deposit creation in a banking system consisting of many banks. We will see why the amount of money created is some multiple of the total amount of excess reserves.

Money Creation in a Banking System of Many Banks

Suppose that somebody deposits $1,000 of currency in a demand deposit at Bank A. Assume that the legally required reserve ratio is 10 percent, or .10, and that the bank was fully loaned up prior to the time of the $1,000 deposit. Bank A now has $1,000 more demand deposits as liabilities and $1,000 more reserves as assets, of which $100 are required reserves and $900 are excess reserves. (In the discussion to follow, we will ignore all items on the bank's balance sheet except those that change as a result of deposit expansion.) Bank A's balance sheet changes as follows:

Bank A
(Receives $1,000 in Demand Deposits)

Assets			Liabilities		
Reserves	+	$1,000	Demand deposits	+	$1,000
Required reserves	+	100			
Excess reserves	+	900			
Assets	+	$1,000	Liabilities	+	$1,000

As an individual bank, Bank A can now lend out $900 by creating $900 of new demand deposits, an amount equal to its excess reserves. At this point Bank A's balance sheet looks like this:

Bank A
(Makes $900 of Loans, Increasing Demand Deposits by $900)

Assets			Liabilities		
Reserves		$1,000	Demand deposits		$1,000
Loans	+	900	Demand deposits	+	900
Assets		$1,900	Liabilities		$1,900

Presumably, the party borrowing the $900, in whose name Bank A creates the $900 demand deposit, will soon spend that $900 by writing a cheque against the deposit for that amount. That is, the borrower will use the money to pay for some good or service. Suppose the recipient of that cheque deposits the cheque in another bank, Bank B. Since the cheque is drawn against Bank A, $900 of reserves (taken from excess reserves) will be transferred from Bank A to Bank B. At the same time Bank A will reduce its liability to the borrower by decreasing the borrower's demand deposit by the amount of the cheque. After all this, the change in Bank A's balance sheet is the following:

Bank A
(Loses $900 of Reserves and Deposits After a Cheque Is Written Against It)

Assets			Liabilities		
Reserves ($1,000 − $900)	+	$ 100	Demand deposits ($1,900 − $900)	+	$1,000
Loans	+	900			
Assets	+	$1,000	Liabilities	+	$1,000

Bank A is now fully loaned up. It has $1,000 of demand deposits and holds $100 of reserves, just the amount required by law, given that the required reserve ratio is .10. It has no excess reserves.

When the $900 cheque drawn on Bank A is deposited in Bank B, and $900 of reserves are transferred from Bank A to Bank B, the following changes are made in Bank B's balance sheet:

Bank B
(Receives $900 Deposit from Bank A, and $900 of Reserves Are Transferred to Bank B)

Assets			Liabilities		
Reserves	+	$900	Demand deposits	+	$900
Required reserves	+	90			
Excess reserves	+	810			
Assets	+	$900	Liabilities	+	$900

Bank B's demand deposits and reserves are each increased by $900. With a required reserve ratio of .10, the increase in the amount of its legally required reserves amounts to $90, while the increase in its excess reserves amounts to $810.

Suppose that Bank B now creates demand deposits by lending out $810, an amount equal to its excess reserves. Bank B's balance sheet will now change as follows:

Bank B
(Makes $810 of Loans, Increasing Deposits by $810)

Assets			Liabilities		
Reserves		$ 900	Demand deposits		$ 900
Loans	+	810	Demand deposits	+	810
Assets		$1,710	Liabilities		$1,710

Now suppose the borrower writes a cheque for $810 against this newly created demand deposit. If the recipient of the cheque deposits it in another bank, Bank C, $810 of reserves will then be transferred from Bank B to Bank C. The change in Bank B's balance sheet appears as follows:

Bank B
(Loses $810 of Reserves and Deposits After Cheque Is Written Against It)

Assets		Liabilities		
Reserves ($900 − $810)	$ 90	Demand deposits ($1,710 − $810)		$900
Loans	810	Demand deposits	+	810
Assets	$900	Liabilities		$900

Now Bank B has $900 of demand deposits and $90 of reserves. The reserves are equal to 10 percent of the amount of demand deposits, just the amount it is legally required to hold. Bank B is fully loaned up; it has no excess reserves.

The Pattern of Lending and Deposit Creation

There is a pattern to this process of lending and deposit creation. Bank A's excess reserves allow it to make loans and create new demand deposits equal to the amount of its excess reserves, which are then transferred by borrowers writing cheques to Bank B. Bank B acquires all of Bank A's excess reserves in this process. Bank B is required to hold a fraction (equal to the legally required reserve ratio) of these new reserves against its newly acquired demand deposits. The remainder are excess reserves that allow B to make loans and create new demand deposits, which are in turn transferred by borrowers writing cheques to Bank C, and so on. After borrowers write cheques transferring Bank C's newly created demand deposits, along with its excess reserves, to Bank D, the change in Bank C's balance sheet will be as follows:

Bank C
(After Borrowers Write Cheques on Newly Created Demand Deposits)

Assets			Liabilities		
Reserves	+	$ 81	Demand deposits	+	$810
Loans	+	729			
Assets	+	$810	Liabilities		$810

Repeating the same pattern another step further, the change in Bank D's balance sheet would appear as follows:

Bank D
(After the Same Pattern Repeats Again)

Assets			Liabilities		
Reserves	+	$ 73	Demand deposits	+	$729
Loans	+	656			
Assets	+	$729	Liabilities		$729

And similarly, for Bank E the change is:

Bank E
(After the Same Pattern Repeats Once More)

Assets			Liabilities		
Reserves	+	$ 66	Demand deposits	+	$656
Loans	+	590			
Assets	+	$656	Liabilities		$656

The complete process of demand-deposit expansion throughout the banking system is summarized in Table 28-7. Starting with the initial demand deposit of $1,000 at Bank A, column (1), follow the arrows and notice that the successive increases in demand deposits at Banks B, C, D, and so on become smaller and smaller. This reflects the fact that when a bank receives demand deposits and reserves from another bank, only a portion of these reserves, the excess reserves, column (2), can be passed on to yet another bank through lending and the creation of new demand deposits. The other portion must be kept as required reserves, column (3). If we want to know the total amount of new demand deposits that this process creates—that is, the total amount of money creation—we must add up the deposit increases in the banking system, as shown in column (1).

The Process of Deposit Creation Completed

When the entire process of deposit expansion is complete, all banks in the banking system are fully loaned up. At this point there are no excess reserves anywhere in the banking system. The initial $1,000 increase in reserves is totally tied up as required reserves, column (3). Including the initial increase in demand deposits of $1,000 at Bank A, the total increase in demand deposits and therefore money for the whole banking system amounts to $10,000. That is, the total increase in demand deposits, column (1), is 10 times the initial $1,000 increase in reserves at Bank A. This multiple of 10 is the reciprocal of the required reserve ratio of .10. Similarly, viewed in terms of the initial increase in excess reserves of $900 at Bank A, the total amount of new money created by the expansion process is $9,000, column (2). Again, the multiple is 10. *A single bank in a multibank system cannot permanently increase the amount of its demand deposits by lending out its excess reserves. However, the banking system as a whole can expand demand deposits to a multiple of any increase in reserves if each bank lends out its excess reserves. The expansion of demand deposits is equal to the additional reserves multiplied by the reciprocal of the required reserve ratio.*

Deposit Contraction: Destruction of Money by the Banking System

The deposit expansion or money creation process is also reversible. Suppose that the banking system is fully loaded up and a depositor at Bank A decides to withdraw $1,000 of currency. In essence this leads to a reversal of the process summarized in Table 28-7 (think of the direction of the arrows as now being reversed).

Initially, Bank A loses $1,000 of reserves in the form of cash, column (1). Since it has $1,000 less in demand deposits, it no longer needs to hold the $100 in required reserves, column (3), against these deposits. But since Bank A was fully loaded up to begin with, it is now short $900 of the amount of required reserves it must hold against its remaining deposits. Consequently, Bank A will have to get rid of $900 of other assets in its portfolio, column (2), to replenish its reserves. Suppose that it does this by selling $900 of government bonds to

TABLE 28-7   Expansion of the Money Supply by Lending and Deposit Creation by the Banking System
(Legally Required Reserve Ratio Is .10)

Bank	(1) New Reserves and Demand Deposits	(2) Excess Reserves Equal to the Amount Bank Can Lend, Equal to New Money Created (1)−(3)	(3) Required Reserves (1) × Required Reserve Ratio of .10
A	$ 1,000	$ 900	$ 100
B	900	810	90
C	810	729	81
D	729	656	73
E	656	590	66
F	590	531	59
G	531	478	53
H	478	430	48
	.	.	.
	.	.	.
(All remaining banks)	4,306	3,876	430
Total	$10,000	$9,000	$1,000

someone who holds demand deposits in Bank B. This party writes a cheque against Bank B for $900, column (1), payable to Bank A. Bank A deposits this $900 cheque in its deposit at the Bank of Canada. Since deposits at the Bank of Canada count as reserves, Bank A now has just the amount of reserves needed to satisfy its legal reserve requirement.

However, when Bank A's account at the Bank of Canada is marked up, or credited, $900, Bank B's account at the Bank of Canada is drawn down, or debited, $900. While Bank B no longer needs to hold $90 of required reserves, column (3), because it has lost $900 of demand deposits, column (1), it is now short $810 of the amount of required reserves it must hold against its remaining deposits. Therefore, Bank B sells $810 of government bonds to someone who holds demand deposits in Bank C. This party writes a cheque against Bank C for $810, column (1), payable to Bank B. Bank C then loses deposits and finds itself short of required reserves, and the whole contraction process is repeated over and over with respect to Banks D, E, F, and so forth. In the end, the total reduction in demand deposits for the whole banking system amounts to $10,000, column (1). Hence, the initial decrease in demand deposits and, therefore, reserves of $1,000 results in a total reduction in the amount of demand deposits that is 10 times greater. Note again that this multiple is the reciprocal of the required reserve ratio 1/.10 or 10. The process of multiple contraction of demand deposits is just the reverse of the process of multiple expansion of deposits.

The Deposit Multiplier

We have seen that any initial increase in reserves can result in an increase in the total amount of demand deposits, or new money, that is equal to a multiple of the amount of increase in reserves. The **deposit multiplier** is the number by which an increase in the reserves of the banking system must be multiplied in order to estimate the resulting increase in new deposits. Implicit in the working of the deposit multiplier is the assumption that the banking system is in a *loaned up* position.

Determining the Deposit Multiplier

The deposit multiplier equals the reciprocal of the required reserve ratio rr expressed as a decimal fraction.

$$\text{Deposit multiplier} = \frac{1}{rr}$$

If the required ratio is 20 percent, or .20, the deposit multiplier $1/rr$ equals 1/.20, or 5. If the required reserve ratio were 10 percent, or .10, then the deposit multiplier would equal 1/.10, or 10. In this case, for example, the maximum increase in the dollar amount of new demand deposits resulting from a $10 increase in reserves would be $100. We can express this through the following equation:

$$\$10 \times \frac{1}{.10} = \$10 \times 10 = \$100$$

In general, if ΔE is the change in reserves and ΔD is the maximum increase in demand deposits, then

$$\Delta D = \Delta E \times \frac{1}{rr}$$

Of course, the deposit multiplier is applicable to a decrease in reserves as well as to an increase. That is, if reserves are removed from the banking system when it is fully loaned up, there will be a contraction in the amount of demand deposits in the system that is equal to the amount of reserves removed multiplied by the deposit multiplier $1/rr$. For example, in our discussion of multiple deposit contraction, the reserve ratio was .10. The deposit multiplier was therefore 10. Assuming that the banking system was fully loaned up, we saw that an initial $1,000 reduction in reserves resulted in a total loss of demand deposits amounting to $10,000 for the whole banking system ($1,000 × 10).

Given the definition of the money multiplier just developed, it is not surprising that some people have concluded that an elimination of the required reserve ratio would lead to an infinitely large money multiplier. This would be the case if it were not for the other determinants of the deposit multiplier. As the legal reserve requirement is reduced to zero, these become more important in determining the size of the deposit multiplier.

Other Determinants of the Size of the Deposit Multiplier

By now you have probably been struck by the similarity between the deposit multiplier and the income or expenditure multiplier discussed in Chapter 22. Indeed, the deposit expansion process of Table 28-7 looks very similar to the income expansion process of Table 22-4. Just as the deposit expansion multiplier is equal to the reciprocal of the required reserve ratio, the expenditure multiplier is equal to the reciprocal of the marginal propensity to withdraw. Just as the expenditure multiplier reflects the fact that expenditure by one party is income for another, the deposit multiplier reflects the fact that reserves and deposits withdrawn from one bank become reserves and deposits gained by another. The size of the expenditure multiplier is determined by the amount of withdrawal into saving and taxes and imports at each round of expenditure, as determined by the size of the MPW (where $MPW = MPS + MPT + MPM$). Similarly, the size of the deposit multiplier is determined by the amount of leakage of lendable excess reserves into reserves held by banks as vault cash or on deposit at the Bank of Canada at each round of the deposit expansion process.

The similarity between the two multipliers ends here, however. While the expenditure multiplier deals with a flow, income, the deposit multiplier deals with a stock, the money supply. Moreover, money and income are completely different concepts. Nonetheless, the leakage concept is very useful to our understanding of the other determinants of the size of the deposit multiplier.

Leakages into Excess Reserves

Up to this point we have assumed that leakage into required reserves is the *only* type of leakage from the deposit expansion process. In other words, we have assumed that banks are always fully loaned up. However, as part of their portfolio management policy, banks want to keep a certain amount of vault cash reserves on hand for liquidity purposes. This is another source of leakage from the deposit expansion process in addition to the leakage into required reserves. This means that a greater portion of the reserves one bank receives from another is set aside at each round of deposit expansion, part to satisfy legal reserve requirements and part to be held as excess reserves to satisfy the liquidity objectives of a bank's self-imposed portfolio management policy. This makes the deposit multiplier equal to the reciprocal of the sum of the required reserve ratio rr plus the self-imposed vault cash reserve ratio cr.

The money multiplier = $1/(rr + cr)$. For example, if the legal reserve requirement is 10 percent and in addition banks set aside as vault cash reserves another 10 percent of any reserves received, the deposit multiplier is equal to $1/.20$ (the sum of .10 and .10), or 5. Similarly, the deposit multiplier for the deposit contraction process will be smaller if banks choose to keep vault cash reserves on hand for liquidity purposes. Why? Each bank will be able to meet deposit withdrawals out of excess reserves before it needs to start selling off assets, which would lead to further deposit withdrawals at other banks, in the manner we have already described. With the proposed amendments to the *Bank Act* the required reserve will be reduced to zero over a two-year period. This will transform the money multiplier from $1/(rr + cr)$ into $1/cr$. The chartered banks typically maintain very small vault cash reserves in excess of the required reserve ratio.[2] This fact implies that the removal of the required reserve ratio will lead to a significantly larger money multiplier once the complete adjustment is made.

Leakages Due to Cash Withdrawal

Another source of leakage from the deposit expansion process is cash withdrawal. In our discussion it was assumed that when a cheque was written against a deposit at one bank, the recipient deposited the entire amount in another bank. In reality, the recipient may deposit only part of the amount of the cheque and hold the rest in cash. Since cash in banks constitutes reserves, this means that a smaller amount of reserves ends up being transferred from one bank to the next, and the full amount of the deposit expansion process is reduced accordingly. For example, suppose that in addition to the 10 percent leakage into excess reserves there is another 10 percent leakage due to cash withdrawals by the public at each step of the deposit expansion process. The deposit expansion multiplier will now be equal to $1/.30$ (the sum of .10, .10, and .10), or 3.3.

Leakage into Non-Domestic Lending and Investment Activities

Banks may decide to take some of their excess reserves and use this to make Canadian-dollar-denomination loans or investments outside Canada. While this may be consistent with the individual bank's goals of maintaining liquidity and maximizing the return to stockholders, it also means that a portion of the reserves are moved out of the Canadian financial sector. This means that a smaller

---

[2]Norman Cameron, *Monetary Financial Markets and Economic Activity*, 2nd ed. (Don Mills, Ont.: Addison Wesley, 1992), p. 484.

amount of reserves ends up being transferred from one bank to the next *inside* Canada, and the full amount of the deposit expansion process is again reduced. For example, suppose that in addition to the total 30 percent leakage into required reserves, excess reserves, and withdrawals by the public, discussed earlier, there is another 10 percent leakage into non-domestic loans and investments in Canadian dollars at each step of the deposit expansion process. The deposit expansion multiplier will now be equal to 1/.40 (the sum of .10, .10, and .10 and .10), or 2.5.

Variation in Willingness to Lend and Borrow

Finally, the willingness of banks to lend and the eagerness of businesses and consumers to borrow tends to vary with economic conditions. At one extreme, if there is no lending and borrowing, there will be no deposit expansion at all. At the other extreme, when banks are fully loaned up there is the maximum possible amount of deposit expansion. The amount of deposit expansion usually lies somewhere between these two extremes, depending on the banks' willingness to lend and the demand for loans by borrowers. Generally, banks are more cautious and eager borrowers less numerous when the economy is in the contraction phase of a business cycle. Obviously, the amount of excess reserves banks hold will tend to vary over the course of the business cycle; consequently, so will the size of the deposit multiplier—it will tend to be larger during the expansion phase and smaller during the contraction phase of the business cycle.

In summary, the theoretical deposit multiplier calculated as the reciprocal of the required reserve ratio and vault cash reserve ratio assumes that banks are fully loaned up with respect to the amount of reserves that must be held for prudent support of their deposit liabilities. It tells us the maximum or potential amount of deposit expansion or contraction that can take place in response to a change in excess reserves under a fractional reserve system. *In reality, banks are not always fully loaned up and there are also leakages due to non-domestic bank lending and cash withdrawal by the public. Consequently, the size of the actual deposit multiplier is typically variable as well as slightly smaller than the theoretical deposit multiplier.*

Summary

1. The balance sheet of a chartered bank lists assets on the left and liabilities on the right. The columns are arranged in descending order of liquidity. To be balanced the total of assets must equal the total of liabilities and a portion of liquid assets must meet the required reserve ratios.
2. The composition of the typical bank's portfolio of earning assets reflects a compromise between two often conflicting objectives: (a) the maintenance of liquidity and security, and (b) the realization of profit.
3. A chartered bank generally restricts its holdings of earning assets to short-term loans, bonds, and securities because of their relatively high degree of liquidity and security. This restriction is dictated by the large amount of chartered bank deposit liabilities, which are subject to withdrawal on demand.
4. In general, the amount of demand deposits, or money, that a single branch of a chartered bank can create through lending cannot exceed the amount of its excess reserves. This is so because borrowers will most likely write cheques

against these newly created deposits that the cheque recipients will deposit in other banks.

5. By contrast, when each individual bank in the banking system lends out its excess reserves, the banking system as a whole can create an amount of demand deposits, or money, that is a multiple of the total amount of excess reserves in the system. While individual banks in the banking system can lose reserves and deposits to other banks in the system, the system as a whole cannot.

6. The multiple for the banking system as a whole is the reciprocal of the required reserve ratio. This multiple is called the deposit multiplier. It also applies to deposit contraction, which is just the reverse of the deposit expansion process.

7. The deposit multiplier will be smaller if there are currency drains or if the chartered banks maintain excess reserves.

Key Terms and Concepts

balance sheet (of a chartered bank)	equity	net worth
	excess reserves	required reserve ratio
deposit multiplier	money multiplier	required reserves

Questions and Problems

1. Consider the balance sheet of the following individual bank, Bank X, in a banking system of many banks: Assume that the required reserve ratio is 20 percent (.20).

Bank X

Assets			Liabilities and Equity	
Reserves	$ 220,000		Demand deposits	$ 950,000
Loans, securities and other assets	780,000		Equity	50,000
Total assets	$1,000,000	=	Total liabilities and equity	$1,000,000

a. How much excess reserves does Bank X have?

b. Suppose that Bank X creates an amount of demand deposits through lending that equals the amount of its excess reserves multiplied by the deposit multiplier. What will be the amount of the new loans it has created? What will Bank X's balance sheet look like before any cheques have been written against the new deposits?

c. Given your answer to part (b), suppose now that borrowers write cheques against the newly created demand deposit and that the recipients of these cheques deposit them in other banks. What will happen to the level of reserves in Bank X? What now will be the level of excess reserves in Bank X?

d. Given your answers to part (c), describe what Bank X must do to get its house in order. Once it has done so, how will its balance sheet look?

e. What does this example tell us about the difference between an individual bank and the banking system as a whole?

f. Starting again with the answer to part (a), if you were running Bank X, describe what you would do at this point. How would Bank X's balance sheet now look after your management strategy had been carried out?

2. It is sometimes said that there is a trade-off between bank profits on the one hand and liquidity and security on the other. Describe what is meant by this and why it is so. How does the trade-off affect the size of the deposit multiplier?

3. Suppose that Bank A's balance sheet looks as follows and that the required reserve ratio is 15 percent (.15):

Bank A

Assets		Liabilities and Equity	
Reserves	$ 200,000	Demand deposits	$ 900,000
Loans, securities	800,000	Equity	100,000
and other assets			
Total assets	$1,000,000 =	Total liabilities and equity	$1,000,000

a. What would be the maximum amount of cash that depositors could withdraw before Bank A would be forced to do something about the amount of loans, securities, and other assets it holds?

b. Suppose that Bank A decides to make loans by creating demand deposits. Assume that Bank A and all other banks in the banking system expect that 5 percent of any loans they make will be withdrawn immediately in the form of cash. What will be the maximum amount of deposit expansion, or money creation, that will take place throughout the banking system as a whole?

c. Show the deposit expansion process of part (b) in a table like Table 28-7.

4. What is the effect on the size of the actual deposit multiplier of increases and decreases in the public's desire to hold currency? What happens if the public's desire to hold currency rises during recessions and falls during the expansionary phase of the business cycle?

Chapter 29

The Instruments of Monetary Policy and the Money Market

Edwin Neave of Queen's University once wrote that "The Bank of Canada is not a full-scale financial intermediary *per se*, . . . the most important role of the Bank, however, is its function in controlling the Canada's money supply. The Bank does this by affecting the level of cash reserves available to the banking system."[1]

How do the Bank of Canada's actions affect the chartered banking system, the money supply, and the level of economic activity in general? This chapter will examine the policy instruments used by the Bank of Canada to control the process of deposit expansion, which was discussed in the previous chapter. It is through its ability to influence the availability of credit and the extent to which the financial intermediaries expand or contract deposits that the Bank of Canada conducts its monetary policy objectives. Finally, we will consider the major determinants of the demand for money and see how money demand and supply interact to determine the equilibrium level of the interest rate in the money market.

The Role of the Bank of Canada

The Executive Committee of the Bank of Canada is responsible for the conduct of monetary policy in our economy. **Monetary policy** *is deliberate action taken to affect the size of the economy's money supply for the purpose of promoting economic stability and maximum output and employment with a minimum of inflation and minimum disruption of the foreign exchange rate on the Canadian dollar.*

---

[1]Edwin H. Neave, *Canada's Financial System* (Toronto: John Wiley & Sons, 1981), p. 188.

The Bank of Canada is able to affect the size of the economy's money supply by controlling the quantity of reserves in the banking system. If the central bank increases the quantity of reserves, money creation takes place through the process of deposit expansion. If the central bank decreases the quantity of reserves, the amount of money in the economy is reduced through the process of deposit contraction. In this section we will examine the tools the Bank of Canada actually uses to conduct monetary policy. We will also look at the money market and its relationship to the way in which the Bank of Canada conducts monetary policy.

The Policy Instruments of Monetary Policy

There are five policy instruments that the Bank of Canada can use to conduct monetary policy: (1) open market operations, (2) switching operations, (3) setting the secondary reserve ratio for chartered banks and other depository institutions, (4) setting the bank rate, that is, the interest rate it charges members of the Canadian Payments Association when it lends them reserves, and (5) moral suasion, which attempts to get the financial intermediaries to act in the public interest even if this conflicts with their own best interest. Before we start it should be noted that the first two tools affect the quantity of money while the last three are qualitative instruments of public policy. In recent years the Bank of Canada has concentrated on using open market operations more than the other tools available to it partly because this instrument is relatively powerful and fairly easy to use to influence both the supply of money and the interest rate at the same time. For completeness we will consider each of these tools in turn.

We will illustrate our discussion in terms of chartered banks and we assume a required reserve ratio of ten percent. However, we again emphasize that the discussion also applies to all depository institutions that issue chequable deposits and that the conduct of monetary policy involves all such institutions. Although we will not discuss it specifically, the theory presented in this chapter is expected to apply in much the same way as the system of zero required reserve ratios, which Canada is in the process of adopting.[2]

LEARNING OBJECTIVES

After reading this chapter, you will be able to:

1. Define *open market operations* and explain how the Bank of Canada uses this instrument to change the money supply.
2. Define *switching* and explain how it can be used to change the money supply.
3. Define the *secondary reserve ratio* and distinguish it from the *primary reserve ratio*.
4. Define the *bank rate* and explain how it is used by the Bank of Canada.
5. Distinguish between the quantitative and qualitative instruments of monetary policy.
6. Explain and discuss the three components of the demand for money.
7. Define the major determinants of the demand for money.
8. Explain the equilibrium level of the interest rate in the money market.

---

[2]"Implementation of Monetary Policy in a System with Zero Reserve Requirements," *Bank of Canada Review*, May 1991.

Open Market Operations

The Bank of Canada can directly affect the amount of bank reserves by buying or selling government securities, such as Treasury Bills, in the open market where these securities are traded. Such transactions are called **open market operations**. Open market operations are the Bank's most frequently used policy instrument in conducting monetary policy. *When the Bank of Canada engages in purchases from the open market, it buys government bonds and puts additional reserves into the banking system, allowing an expansion of demand deposits and other chequable deposits and hence an increase in the economy's money supply. When the Bank of Canada engages in open market sales, it sells government bonds and takes some reserves out of the banking system, causing a contraction of demand deposits and other chequable deposits and hence a decrease in the economy's money supply.* These open market operations are now considered in more detail.

Open Market Purchases. Suppose that the Bank of Canada buys $100,000 of Treasury Bills in the open market and that the seller is a financial institution which is a member of the Canadian Payments Association. For simplicity we will consider that the seller was a chartered bank, but we must remember that the ideas presented in this section are just as easily applied to any financial intermediary that accepts chequable deposits of the public and that holds its reserves at the Bank of Canada. The Bank of Canada pays the chartered bank by increasing (crediting) the chartered bank's reserve account at the Bank of Canada by the amount of the purchase, or $100,000. Hence, the Bank of Canada has $100,000 more assets in the form of Treasury Bills and $100,000 more liabilities in the form of chartered bank reserve deposits. The changes in the Bank of Canada's balance sheet look like this:

Bank of Canada

Assets	Liabilities
Treasury Bills + $100,000	Chartered bank reserve deposits + $100,000

The chartered bank now has lost $100,000 of assets in the form of Treasury Bills sold to the Bank of Canada, but it has gained $100,000 of assets in the form of reserves in its deposit at the Bank of Canada. The changes in the chartered bank's balance sheet therefore look like this:

Chartered Bank

Assets		Liabilities
Reserves		
Deposits at the Bank of Canada	+ $100,000	
Treasury Bills	− $100,000	

Note that while the total amount of the chartered bank's assets has not changed, the chartered bank now has more reserves. If the chartered bank previously was fully loaned up, it now has $100,000 of excess reserves. It is now in a position to make new loans by creating demand deposits if it wishes. We have seen how this can lead to deposit expansion, or money creation, throughout the banking system.

Suppose that the Bank of Canada buys $100,000 of Treasury Bills in the open market, but that the seller is one individual or a business other than a bank. The Bank of Canada simply makes out a *draft* for $100,000 drawn against itself and payable to the seller of the Treasury Bills. When the seller deposits the draft in a chartered bank, the bank then presents the draft to the Bank of Canada for collection, and the chartered bank's reserve account at the Bank of Canada is increased (credited) by $100,000. The changes in the Bank of Canada's balance sheet are as follows:

Bank of Canada

Assets	Liabilities
Treasury Bills + $100,000	Chartered bank reserve deposits + $100,000

Again, the Bank of Canada has $100,000 more assets in the form of Treasury Bills and $100,000 more liabilities in the form of chartered bank reserve deposits.

The chartered bank now has $100,000 more liabilities in the form of demand deposits and $100,000 more assets in the form of reserves represented by deposits at the Bank of Canada. These changes in the chartered bank's balance sheet look like this:

Chartered Bank

Assets	Liabilities
Reserves	
Deposits at the Bank of Canada + $100,000	Demand deposits + $100,000

Again, we see that chartered bank reserves are increased by the amount of the open market purchase. Assuming that the chartered bank was initially loaned up, it now has excess reserves because it is only required to hold a fraction (say 10 percent) of its new reserves against its newly acquired $100,000 of demand deposits. Deposit expansion and money creation can take place just as before. *Chartered bank reserves are increased by the amount of Bank of Canada's open market purchases no matter whether the seller of the securities is a member of the Canadian Payments Association or an institution that is not a financial intermediary.*

Open Market Sales.   Suppose that the Bank of Canada sells $100,000 of Treasury Bills in the open market and that the buyer is a chartered bank. The Bank of Canada takes payment from the chartered bank by reducing the chartered bank's reserve deposit with Bank of Canada by $100,000. In other words, the Bank of Canada's liability to the chartered bank is reduced by $100,000, while the Bank of Canada's assets are reduced to the extent of the $100,000 of Treasury Bills it sells. The changes in the Bank of Canada's balance sheet look like this:

Bank of Canada

Assets	Liabilities
Treasury Bills − $100,000	Chartered bank reserve deposits − $100,000

POLICY PERSPECTIVE

Bank Failure and Deposit Contraction: How Serious Is the Threat?

THE HISTORICAL PERSPECTIVE

Historically, banking crises have often been identified as major contributors to economic downturns in many countries. During the Great Depression the domino effect of banking failures in the United States, where the failure of one bank triggered the failure of another, and so on, not only proved costly to depositors, shareholders, and loan customers of the banks directly affected but ultimately contributed to the length and depth of the Depression itself. It was partly as a result of Canada's observation of the American experience and concern about the safety of its own banking system that the Bank of Canada was created in the 1930s.

However there are major differences between Canada's banking system today and the American banking system of the 1930s, which is so often used as the illustration of how a reserve drainage and banking crisis can lead to a long, deep depression. In particular, the Canadian system is less likely to suffer a reserve drain because of the large oligopolistic banks which make up our system and because of the introduction of deposit insurance in the 1960s for the majority of depositors.

THE RISK OF CURRENCY DRAIN IN CANADA

As discussed in Chapter 27, Canada has a branch banking system in which the individual banks operate with a large number of branches spread over a wide geographic area. In this situation the reserve base of the bank is not dependent on business conditions in one branch or one part of the country. In addition, these banks typically engage in retail banking—they try to attract liabilities by having a large number of small accounts each deposited by one individual consumer. This results in their liabilities not being owed to a few large accounts, which tend to be mobile and which tend to move at the first sign of trouble. Instead, most of the accounts are owed in millions of small amounts to individuals who are geographically dispersed. These small accounts tend to be less mobile if there is a banking crisis, and they also provide the bank with an opportunity to support a run against one branch by using excess reserves from its other branches in other parts of the country. Finally, the point needs to be made that large depositors may at times feel safer moving their money out of the banks entirely. This type of account can buy low-risk government Treasury Bills. But even in the case where these large accounts move out of the banks and into Treasury Bills, there may not be a loss of reserves to the banking system. The institutions and individuals who sell the Treasury Bills to the funds managers who look after such large deposits may themselves redeposit the money they receive through the sale of their Treasury Bills back into the banks.

Bank runs tend to develop only when depositors in one bank fear that the bank that holds their money will be unable to meet its commitments. Under this situation the depositors panic and remove their money from the bank in which they have lost faith. This does not, however, lead to a widespread or generalized banking crisis or a reserve drainage if the money withdrawn from one institution is redeposited in another bank. *A loss in reserves to the whole banking system will happen only if the money withdrawn from one bank is not redeposited into the banking system.* In the Canadian system, when depositors lose faith in a bank and withdraw their funds from it they tend to redeposit them into some other financial intermediary that still appears solid. During the collapse of the Seaway Trust in 1984 and the failures of the Canadian Commercial Bank and the Northland Bank in 1985, depositors fearing potential loss withdrew their funds from these institutions. This undoubtedly contributed to the failure of these institutions, but because the funds reentered the banking system there was no widespread loss of reserves and thus no contraction of the money supply.

continued on next page

POLICY PERSPECTIVE CONTINUED

THE INFLUENCE OF THE CANADIAN DEPOSIT INSURANCE CORPORATION

Deposit insurance alleviates the fear of small depositors that they will not be able to convert their deposits into currency and thus eliminates a potentially major source of reserve drainage from the banking system as a whole. Since 1967, the Canadian Deposit Insurance Corporation (CDIC) has insured the vast majority of chequable deposits in Canada. Over the years, there have been amendments to the types of accounts covered by CDIC, to the limit of the coverage per depositor, and to the number of financial

continued on next page

TABLE P29-1   Distressed Member Banks and Trust Companies of CDIC

Year	Distressed Institution	Asset Size in $Millions (Year)	Method of Handling Distress	Repayment of Principal of Uninsured Deposits and GICs	Delay in Repayment of Principal of Uninsured Deposits and GICs	Repayment to Uninsured Creditors	Loss to Seniors Debtholders (if any)	Total Loss to Shareholders
1968	Security Trust	N.A.	Receivership	Full	Yes	Full	—	Yes
1970	Commonwealth Trust	N.A.	Liquidation	Full	Yes	Full	—	Yes
1980	Astra Trust	22(79)	Liquidation	84%	Yes	84%	—	Yes
1982	District Trust	67(82)	Agency agreement to wind down institution	Full	No	Full	—	Yes
1983	Amic Mortgage Investment Co. (AMIC)	42(81)	Liquidation	Partial	Yes	Partial	—	Yes
	Crown Trust	662(81)		Full	No	Full	Yes	Yes
	Fidelity Trust	851(82)		Full	No	Full	Yes	Yes
	Grey Mortgage	207(81)	Agency agreement to wind down institution	Full	No	Full	No	Yes
	Greymac Trust	74(81)		Full	No	Full	Yes	Yes
	Seaway Mortgage	391(82)		Full	No	Full	No	Yes
	Seaway Trust	391(82)		Full	No	Full	Yes	Yes
1984	Northguard Mortgage Co.	18(81)	Liquidation	Partial	Yes	Partial	—	Yes

POLICY PERSPECTIVE CONTINUED

TABLE P29-1   Distressed Member Banks and Trust Companies of CDIC *(Continued)*

Year	Distressed Institution	Asset Size in $Millions (Year)	Method of Handling Distress	Repayment of Principal of Uninsured Deposits and GICs	Delay in Repayment of Principal of Uninsured Deposits and GICs	Repayment to Uninsured Creditors	Loss to Seniors Debtholders (if any)	Total Loss to Shareholders
1985	Canadian Commercial Bank	3056(85)	Contributed to support package in March 1985; liquidation in September 1985	Full	Yes	Partial	Yes	Yes
	CCB Mortgage Investment	127(84)	Agency agreement to wind down institution	Full	Yes	Partial	—	Yes
	Continental Trust	136(84)	Liquidation	Full	No	Full	—	Yes
	London Loan	31(81)	Liquidation	Partial	Yes	Partial	—	Yes
	Northland Bank	1149(85)	Liquidation	Full	Yes	Partial	Yes	Yes
	Pioneer Trust	275(83)	Liquidation	Full	No	Partial	—	Yes
	Western Capital Trust	80(84)	Liquidation	Partial	Yes	Partial	—	Yes
1986	Bank of British Columbia	3090(8)	Assisted in merger with Hong Kong Bank of Canada	Full	No	Full	No	No
	Columbia Trust	64(81)	Liquidation	Partial	Yes	Partial	—	Yes
1987	Heritage Trust	114(84)	$275 million support package to merge trust companies	Full	No	Full	—	Yes
	North West Trust	720(87)		Full	No	Full	—	Yes
	Principle Savings and Trust	130(87)	Liquidation	Partial	Yes	Partial	—	Yes

Source: B. Smith and R. White, "The Deposit Insurance System in Canada; Problems and Policies for Change," *Canadian Public Policy*, Vol. XIV, No. 4 (Dec. 1988), pp. 331–333.

continued on next page

POLICY PERSPECTIVE CONTINUED

intermediaries belonging to CDIC. At the end of 1988 157 companies were members of the CDIC: 121 federally chartered or incorporated institutions (65 banks and 56 trust and loan companies), and 36 provincially incorporated trust and loan companies. Each firm has one-hundred-percent guaranteed coverage to a maximum of $60,000 per depositor per institution. The insurance covers all Canadian-denomination chequing accounts, savings accounts, term deposits and guaranteed investment certificates, drafts, certified drafts and certified cheques, traveller's cheques, and money orders issued by or payable by the member institutions if these were banked in Canada and are payable within five years. In addition, because the coverage allows an individual to be insured for a maximum of $60,000 in chequing accounts, savings accounts, and term deposits—and insured for a further $60,000 in RRSPs and for another $60,000 in RRIFs (registered retirement investment funds)—the individual can have $180,000 held entirely in one firm and have it 100% guaranteed against risk. Finally, joint deposits or deposits held by a spouse receive separate cover-

age. In summary, an individual in Canada has access to a relatively safe banking environment.

RECENT FAILURES AND THEIR COSTS

Since 1968 there have been 25 financial institutions in Canada which have had to rely on the Canadian Deposit Insurance Corporation to compensate their depositors and holders of term certificates. Collectively these firms cost the CDIC, and indirectly the Government of Canada which decided to support CDIC in its repayments, a total of over $11 billion!* While this was and is an impressive amount of money, the important point is that the failure of this number of firms and this large an amount of money has scarcely had any effect on Canadians' faith in the financial sector or their willingness to deposit and lend through the banks and other financial intermediaries.

Today, bank failures are much less likely to set off a chain reaction of other bank failures and ever-larger deposit losses because there is typically no loss of currency and thus no reserve drain from the banking system as a whole. Deposit insurance has largely im-

munized healthy banks from unhealthy banks, and individual large bank failures are perhaps no longer any more or less serious to the economy than the failure of any large company.

For Discussion

- Why is it that currency withdrawals can result in a multiple deposit contraction throughout the banking system?
- Why was it that a deposit withdrawal from a troubled bank in Canada in the 1930s was less likely to cause a reserve drain than a similar withdrawal from an American bank at the same time?
- Why is it that the Canadian Deposit Insurance Corporation can be said to have reduced the risk of a widespread reserve drainage but may also have contributed to depositors being less careful to bank with well-run financial institutions?

*B. Smith, and R. White, "The Deposit Insurance System in Canada: Problems and Policies for Change," *Canadian Public Policy*, December 1988.

The chartered bank has gained $100,000 of assets in Treasury Bills purchased from the Bank of Canada. But it also has had to give up $100,000 of its reserve deposits at the Bank of Canada to pay for them. The changes in the chartered bank's balance sheet look like this:

Chartered Bank

Assets	Liabilities
Reserves	
Deposits at the Bank of Canada − $100,000	
Treasury Bills + $100,000	

While the total amount of the chartered bank's assets has not been changed by these transactions, the chartered bank now has less reserves. This can set in motion the deposit contraction process, or reduction in the money supply, as we have already discussed.

What if the buyer of the $100,000 of Treasury Bills sold by the Bank of Canada is an individual or business other than a member of the Canadian Payments Association? Suppose that payment is made to the Bank of Canada with a cheque drawn against the buyer's deposit at a chartered bank. When the Bank of Canada receives the cheque, it decreases (or debits) the chartered bank's reserve deposits at the Bank of Canada by $100,000. Once again, payment to the Bank of Canada is represented by a reduction of the Bank of Canada's liability to a chartered bank. The change in the Bank of Canada's balance sheet looks like this:

Bank of Canada

Assets	Liabilities
Treasury Bills − $100,000	Chartered bank reserve deposits − $100,000

The chartered bank's demand deposit liabilities are reduced by $100,000 because of the cheque written by its depositor, the buyer of the Treasury Bills. The chartered bank's assets are likewise reduced $100,000 by the reduction in its reserve deposits at the Bank of Canada that takes place when its depositor's cheque clears. The chartered bank's balance sheet is changed as follows:

Chartered Bank

Assets	Liabilities
Reserves − $100,000	Demand deposit − $100,000

Again, we see that $100,000 of chartered bank reserves are removed from the banking system by the Bank of Canada's open market sale of $100,000 of Treasury Bills. *Bank reserves are decreased by the amount of the Bank of Canada's open market sales, regardless of whether the buyer is a member of the Canadian Payments Association or an institution that is not a financial intermediary.*

Switching Operations

As fiscal agent to the government, the Bank of Canada has the responsibility and authority to manage the funds belonging to the federal government. In this role it can place federal funds in deposits in the chartered banks or it can hold these funds in deposits banked at the Bank of Canada and payable to the government. Suppose that the Bank of Canada wished to increase the money supply. It could switch federal government funds (say, $100,000) out of the government's deposit account at the Bank of Canada and redeposit this $100,000 in a chartered bank. In this way the chartered banks would gain additional reserves and would be able to begin the process of deposit creation.

To see how this works we must look at the balance sheet of the Bank of Canada. As the Bank of Canada withdraws funds from a government account at the Bank of Canada and redeposits them in a chartered bank, it reduces its own liability to the government and transfers that liability to the chartered bank into which it has switched the government funds. The following changes occur in the Bank of Canada's balance sheet:

Bank of Canada

Assets	Liabilities
	Government of Canada deposits − $100,000
	Chartered bank reserve deposits + $100,000

The chartered bank's demand deposit liabilities are increased by $100,000 because of the increase in government funds deposited in it. The chartered bank's assets are likewise increased $100,000 by the crediting of its reserve account at the Bank of Canada that takes place when the Bank of Canada reduces its liability to the government and increases it to the chartered bank in recognition of the funds switched to the chartered bank. The chartered bank's balance sheet is changed as follows:

Chartered Bank

Assets	Liabilities
Reserves + $100,000	Demand deposit + $100,000

Again, we see that $100,000 of chartered bank reserves are gained by the switching of the government funds out of the Bank of Canada and their redeposit in the chartered bank. *Bank reserves are increased by the amount of the government funds switched out of the Bank of Canada and redeposited in a chartered bank.*

As in earlier examples, it is clear at this point, that while the chartered bank is balanced in the sense that assets and liabilities have both changed by the same amount, it is not in a loaned up position. Only a portion of the increased reserves are required (say 10 percent, with $rr = .1$), depending on the reserve ratio. The rest of the reserves are excess, and these excess reserves can support increased loan creation, leading to a multiple expansion of deposits.[3]

Conversely, if the Bank of Canada wished to engage in a tight money policy, it could switch government funds out of accounts in the chartered banks and redeposit these funds in the Bank of Canada. If the Bank of Canada switched $100,000 of government funds from a chartered bank into the Bank of Canada, it would debit the chartered bank's reserve account at the Bank of Canada and at the same time credit the government's account at the Bank of Canada. The changes in the Bank of Canada's balance sheet would look like this:

Bank of Canada

Assets	Liabilities
	Government of Canada deposits + $100,000
	Chartered bank reserve deposits − $100,000

The chartered bank's demand deposit liabilities are decreased by $100,000 because of the decrease in government funds deposited in it. The chartered

---

[3]In the event of a zero required reserve ratio, the appropriate reserve ratio to use would be cr, the vault cash reserve ratio that banks feel they must voluntarily hold as prudent security against their deposits. For a more detailed explanation of this, see the discussion in Chapters 27 and 28.

bank's assets are likewise decreased $100,000 by the reduction in its reserve account at the Bank of Canada that takes place when it loses the government deposit. The chartered bank's balance sheet is changed as follows:

Bank of Canada

Assets		Liabilities	
Reserves			
Deposits at the Bank of Canada	− $100,000	Demand deposits of government	− $100,000

At this point the chartered bank is balanced, but if it was loaned up when the government funds were switched to the Bank of Canada, it now has insufficient reserves to meet the legal requirement. Consequently, it must decrease its liabilities by calling in loans or selling off Treasury Bills or other assets to meet the legal reserve requirement. *Bank reserves are decreased by the amount of the government funds switched out of the chartered banks and redeposited in the Bank of Canada. As in earlier examples, the loss of reserves will lead to a multiple contraction of deposits in the banking system.*

Like open market operations, switching operations are a powerful way to directly influence the quantity of reserves available to the chartered banking system. They can serve as a quick and effective policy instrument for expanding or contracting the ability of the chartered banking system to expand or contract its lending but they also involve moving funds that are a part of the operation of the government in its fiscal affairs. Imagine what would happen if all the tax money raised by the government were withdrawn from the chartered banks and deposited in the Bank of Canada. The tax revenue of the federal government exceeds $100 billion per year. If this money were withdrawn from the chartered banks as taxpayers made out cheques to the federal government, it would cause a huge decrease in the money supply, which would cause disruption in the financial markets. When the government spent the money, it would cause growth in the chartered banks' reserves and consequently a huge increase in the money supply, generating another disruption. By using switching operations to counteract the cyclical effects of tax payment and government spending, the Bank of Canada can reduce the disruptions in the money supply. However, this reduces the Bank's ability to employ this policy instrument for other goals.

Changing the Primary Reserve Ratio

Earlier we saw that the size of the deposit multiplier is inversely related to the size of the reserve ratio. If the Bank of Canada could adjust the size of the primary reserve requirement it could influence the size of the banking systems' excess reserves *without changing the reserve*. This in turn would change the amount of deposit liabilities and loans which could be created by the banking system. In general terms, if a central bank increases the required reserve ratio, it causes a reduction in the excess reserves available to the banks in its system and a multiple contraction in the demand deposits. Conversely, if the primary reserve ratio was lowered, it would result in the banks in the system suddenly having excess reserves and could lead to an increase in loans and demand deposits in accordance with the deposit multiplier discussed earlier in this chapter.

Many central banks in other countries still possess the legal power to change the primary reserve ratio, but changes to legislation in 1967 removed this policy instrument from the control of the Bank of Canada and placed it under direct parliamentary control. The move was made because the Bank of Canada had used this tool very rarely and because of an acceptance of the view that this was a disruptive way of controlling the money supply. To understand why the Bank of Canada had been reluctant to use the primary reserve ratio, it is important to remember two things. First, on inspecting the deposit multiplier ($1/rr$), it becomes obvious that even a very small increase in the primary reserve ratio, say from 8 percent to 8.5 percent, will result in a large change in the money supply. However, changes of even half a percent in reserves can cause abrupt adjustment throughout the banking system as banks that are made reserve deficient by the change call in loans and sell securities to make their balance sheets conform to the new reserve requirement. This in turn can cause disruption to stock markets, housing markets, and other markets dependent on financial sector borrowing during the adjustment. Second, in order for a chartered bank to meet its *primary reserve requirement* it must hold the reserves in the form of cash in its own vault or as a *non-interest-earning account* deposited at the Bank of Canada. If the Bank of Canada wanted to decrease the money supply by increasing the primary reserve ratio, the chartered banks would have to increase the non-earning portion of their portfolio. This in turn would reduce the ability of the banks to earn profits and reduce the returns to investors in the banking sector. The decrease in bank profitability could make investing in banking less attractive than investing in other sectors of the economy and result in instability in the banking sector, which would not be in the public interest. It was in fact partly because of this second reason that the Bank of Canada supported a proposed gradual phasing in of a zero reserve ratio over a period of twenty-four months in the early 1990s.

Changing the Secondary Reserve Ratio

In addition to the primary reserve ratio, Canada has a secondary reserve ratio. The ratio must be satisfied by the member institutions of the Canadian Payments Association. The **secondary reserve ratio** *is the percentage of liquid assets that the chartered bank is legally required to hold in addition to the primary reserve.* The secondary reserve may be held as Treasury Bills or as day-to-day (call) loans to certain customers specified by the laws governing banking. The Bank of Canada has the legal authority to change the secondary reserve ratio up to a maximum of 12 percent of the value of deposit liabilities. This section will deal with the mechanics of what happens when the Bank of Canada changes the secondary reserve ratio. Again, we will view the effect of the Bank of Canada's actions on the behaviour of a chartered bank, but the same ideas would apply equally well to other members of the Canadian Payments Association.

If the Bank of Canada wishes to engage in an *easy money policy*, it can reduce the secondary reserve ratio. This reduces the percentage of liquid assets which the chartered bank must hold in Treasury Bills and approved day-to-day loans. The chartered banks can then convert some of these assets into cash or deposits at the Bank of Canada and use them as excess reserves to support new deposit creation activity. At first glace it would appear that this is just a different way of adjusting the same thing as the primary reserve ratio, but the impact is quite different under normal circumstances. A decrease in the secondary reserve requirement changes the composition of total bank lending and lets money move through the economy more easily but it does *not* increase the size of the money supply. It is a qualitative policy instrument rather than a quantitative instrument. This is because a decrease in the primary reserve rate allows the chartered banks to lend money that would otherwise be idle in reserve accounts at the Bank of Canada; by contrast, a reduction in the secondary reserve ratio does not allow the banks to do this under normal conditions. The secondary reserve is held as Treasury Bills and day-to-day loans, so the money is already in circulation although its use is restricted. When the secondary reserve ratio is lowered, the banks have a wider range of lending options open to them, but they must reduce lending to one group, those who borrow day-to-day loans or those who deal in Treasury Bills, by an amount equal to the increased amount of lending they create for other groups. Conversely, if the secondary reserve ratio is raised, the chartered banks will find it necessary to reduce lending for those things that do not count as secondary reserves (consumer loans, mortgages, and business loans) and will increase their lending for approved day-to-day loans and their purchases of Treasury Bills. Thus, the money supply will not change size but it will be restricted as to where it can flow. *A decrease in the secondary reserve ratio will make the existing money supply circulate more quickly and more widely. Conversely, an increase in the secondary reserve ratio will restrict the flow of money and make money tight without reducing the money supply.*

Changing the Bank Rate

In the previous chapter we noted that just as depository institutions make loans to the public, the Bank of Canada can make loans to members of the Canadian Payments Association. The interest rate that the Bank of Canada charges chartered banks which borrow reserves from the Bank of Canada through *advances* is called the **bank rate.**

The Bank of Canada can lend a chartered bank reserves by increasing (crediting) the chartered bank's reserve deposit with Bank of Canada by the amount of the advance. If chartered banks borrow from the Bank of Canada, these additional reserves enable them to make more loans and create more deposits. Therefore, borrowing from the Bank of Canada allows more deposit expansion and money creation to take place throughout the banking system than would otherwise be possible.

Chartered banks would naturally find it attractive to borrow from the Bank of Canada whenever the interest rates they can earn from making loans to businesses and consumers or by purchasing securities are greater than the bank rate. On the other hand, when the bank rate is higher than these interest rates, banks are discouraged from borrowing from the Bank of Canada. It follows theoretically that another possible way for the Bank of Canada to affect the amount of reserves in the banking system is by its setting of the bank rate. If the Bank of Canada raises the bank rate, the attractiveness of borrowing to cover any reserve deficiency is reduced and the amount of reserves in the banking system falls. This tends to cause deposit contraction and a reduction in the size of the money supply. If the Bank of Canada lowers the bank rate, bank borrowing rises, causing an increase in reserves and deposit expansion and hence an increase in the money supply.

While the discussion in the previous paragraph indicates that changing the bank rate is *potentially* a powerful policy instrument by which the Bank of Canada can change the money supply, in practice it has been used as an indicator or *signalling device* to make clear the intentions of the Bank of Canada with respect to the direction in which it would like to see interest rates change in the economy. This is because for many years the Bank of Canada has followed a policy of setting the bank rate *equal to one quarter of one percent above the rate of earnings on Treasury Bills.* This discourages chartered banks from borrowing reserves regardless of the level of the bank rate or its direction of movement. This and other measures have resulted in the chartered banks borrowing relatively small amounts from the Bank of Canada, and borrowing these for only short periods of time.

The bank rate remains an important monetary qualitative policy instrument to the Bank of Canada because it sends a widely publicized signal to the economy about the level of interest rates and their direction of movement. If the Bank of Canada wishes to encourage an easy money policy and wishes to see more lending, it can use open market purchases to push up the price of Treasury Bills in the money market, which in turn reduces the earnings on Treasury Bills and thus reduces the bank rate. The media will then report this downward movement in "the trend-setting bank rate," and the business community is made aware that the Bank of Canada is in favour of lower interest rates and easier lending. Conversely, if the Bank of Canada is concerned about inflationary pressures in the economy getting out of hand, by engaging in open market sales, it can push the price of Treasury Bills down and in consequence increase the earnings on Treasury Bills, which in turn pushes up the bank rate. This indicates to the financial markets that the Bank of Canada wishes "tighter" money.

The Bank of Canada uses its ability to change the bank rate as a qualitative tool to influence the financial markets instead of using it as a quantitative tool to change the money supply.

Moral Suasion

The last instrument of monetary policy that can be used to influence lending activity is **moral suasion**. As the name suggests, **moral suasion** *is the act of the Bank of Canada persuading the members of the Canadian Payments Association to alter their behaviour to better serve the public interest.* In the event that the Bank of Canada wished to decrease the risk of inflation, it might try one of two different strategies. It could try to deal with the chartered banks on a general information level, discouraging the chartered banks from lending. Alternatively, it could point out particular objectives of financial policy that need to operate more effectively and seek the cooperation of the chartered banks in arriving at a strategy for improving the situation. Ultimately, the success of moral suasion depends on two things: first, the Bank of Canada must convince the chartered banks to act in the public interest, and second, there must be few enough chartered banks that the Bank of Canada can accommodate individual chartered bank concerns in reducing their own earnings for the sake of the public interest. Convincing the chartered banks that their compliance to some strategy is in their own interest is of course a matter of discussion and works generally if the banks can see that adherence is in their own long-term interest as well as in the public interest. The second condition, that of effective communication and accommodation, becomes more difficult the larger the number of chartered banks and other depository institutions involved in the process. As the Canadian banking system has been liberalized in the last decade, the number of depository institutions that can offer chequable accounting services to the public has increased. This has undoubtedly led to a decrease in the ability of the Bank of Canada to use moral suasion as an effective an informal tool of monetary policy.

Money Demand and Supply and the Interest Rate

The demand for money interacts with the supply of money to determine the rate of interest in what is often referred to as the *money market*. We have seen how the Bank of Canada regulates the supply of money. This section will investigate the determinants of the demand for money. The demand for money and the supply of money will then be combined to examine the nature of equilibrium in the money market.

Transactions, Precautionary, and Speculative Demands for Money

Part of the demand for money stems from the service it provides as a medium of exchange. Money is needed to transact the purchase and sale of goods and services. This need is referred to as the **transactions demand** for money. The size of this demand is determined by the amount of transactions taking place in the economy. One rough measure of the amount of such transactions is the level of aggregate income, as represented by the level of money GDP. *When aggregate income rises, the transactions demand for money increases, and when aggregate income declines, the transactions demand decreases.*

Money is also needed for precautionary purposes. Hence, there is a **precautionary demand** for money. Unforeseen events or emergencies often require immediate expenditures. Money is the most liquid asset and is therefore ideally suited to meet such contingencies. For this reason people carry a little more currency with them than is needed to cover anticipated transactions for such things as lunch and bus fare or parking meters. It is probably generally true that the precautionary demand for money in the economy varies with the level of aggregate income, as does the transactions demand.

Money serves as a convenient and relatively risk-free store of wealth from a speculative point of view. If people have some sense that there is a normal interest rate, then deviations from this normal interest rate will affect the **speculative demand** for money. When people believe the interest rate is above its normal level, they will want to buy financial assets such as bonds to lock in their wealth at a high earning level. Conversely, if the interest rate is believed to be abnormally low, people will prefer to hold money and will not buy such things as bonds or investment certificates for fear of locking in their wealth earning a low interest rate. In addition, there is an inverse relationship between the price of bonds and the interest rate, so when interest rates are low, those with wealth will fear that should interest rates increase they will experience a capital loss on the market price on bonds that they presently own. Thus they will hold money and wait for the interest rates paid on bonds to increase before they will be persuaded to exchange their holdings of money for bonds. Thus money competes with all other financial assets such as bonds, stocks, and guaranteed investment certificates as a speculative store of wealth.

Money Demand and the Interest Rate

The level of aggregate income is an important determinant of money demand, primarily because of its relationship to the transactions, precautionary, and speculative motives for holding money. The interest rate is also regarded as an important influence on the demand for money.

Money in the form of currency is barren because it does not earn interest. Money in the form of demand deposits and other chequable accounts is barren to the extent that those who hold them must forgo the opportunity to earn the higher rates of return available on other assets, such as stocks and bonds. Therefore, *the opportunity cost of holding money (whether for transactions, precautionary, or speculative uses) is the forgone interest that could be earned on other assets.*

In a simplified world, where the only two assets are barren money and interest-earning bonds, the interest rate may be thought of as the price of holding money. As with any good or service, the amount of money demanded will be less when its price is high than when it is low, all other things remaining the same. That is, the higher the interest rate, the lower the quantity of money demanded, and the lower the interest rate, the greater the quantity of money demanded. This inverse relationship between the demand for money and the interest rate is illustrated by the demand curve for money *L* shown in Figure 29-1. The letter *L* is used to designate the demand curve for money simply as a reminder that money is the most liquid asset. The demand for money is really the demand for liquidity and as such is often referred to as **liquidity preference** in economic theory.

FIGURE 29-1   The Demand for Money Is Inversely Related to the Interest Rate

The demand curve for money slopes downward from left to right because the interest rate represents the opportunity cost of holding money. Therefore, a smaller quantity of money is demanded at a high than at a low interest rate.

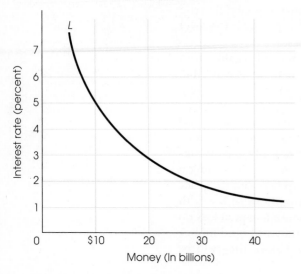

Changes in the Demand for Money

A change in the quantity of money demanded is represented by movement along the liquidity preference curve in Figure 29-1. This movement occurs when the interest rate changes, *ceteris paribus*. A change in the demand for money is represented by a shift in the position of the liquidity preference curve. Such a change occurs when one or more of the other things that could influence the demand for money changes. (To ensure that you fully understand the distinction between a change in quantity demanded and a change in demand, see Chapter 4.)

   Among the other things that can influence the preference for liquidity, the economy's nominal aggregate income (or nominal GDP) is a particularly important determinant of the transactions demand for money. It also influences the demand for money for precautionary and speculative purposes. (Recall the distinction between nominal GDP and real GDP made in Chapter 19. Hereafter, the term *aggregate income* is always taken to mean "aggregate money income" or "nominal GDP.") If aggregate income increases, the transactions, precautionary, and speculative demands for money all increase. A decline in aggregate income has the opposite effect. Therefore, a rise in aggregate income will increase the demand for money and cause the demand curve for money to shift to the right, such as from L_0 to L_1 in Figure 29-2. A decline in aggregate income would cause a shift to the left, such as from L_1 to L_0.

The Money Supply

It has been shown how, through its control over bank reserves, the Bank of Canada affects the deposit expansion or contraction process and the creation or destruction of money. Thus the Bank of Canada controls the economy's money supply.

   At any given time, the supply or stock of money available to satisfy the demand for money is fixed. The fixed supply of money may be represented by

---

FIGURE 29-2   Changes in the Demand for Money: Shifts in the Money Demand Curve

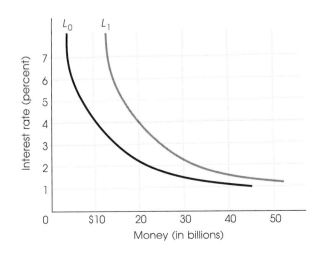

Money (in billions)

Changes in the demand for money are represented by shifts in the money demand curve (liquidity preference curve), such as from L_0 to L_1. A decrease in aggregate income would shift the liquidity preference curve to the left, such as from L_1 to L_0.

   Changes in the quantity of money demanded are represented by a movement along the liquidity preference curve. A movement along the liquidity preference curve is caused by a change in the interest rate, *ceteris paribus*.

FIGURE 29-3   The Supply Curve for Money

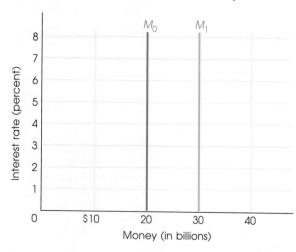

The fixed money supply or stock of money available to satisfy demand may be represented by a vertical supply curve. the fact that the supply curve for money is vertical means that the money supply does not change as a result of a change in the interest rate.

For example, M_0 represents a stock of money equal to $20 billion. If the Bank of Canada were to increase the money supply by $10 billion, the money supply curve would be shifted to the right from M_0 to M_1. A decrease in the money supply would be represented by a leftward shift in the money supply curve, such as M_1 to M_0.

a vertical supply curve such as M_0 in Figure 29-3. The vertical supply curve means that a change in the interest rate will not affect the amount of money supplied the Bank of Canada. (By contrast, it will be shown in the next section that while changes in the interest rate will not cause changes in the quantity of money supplied, changes in the supply of money will have an effect on the interest rate.) M_0 represents a stock of money equal to $20 billion. If the Bank of Canada were to increase the money supply by $10 billion, the money supply curve would be shifted rightward from M_0 to M_1 as shown in Figure 29-3. A decrease in the money supply would be represented by a leftward shift in the money supply curve.

The Money Market: The Interaction of Supply and Demand

The interaction between the demand for money and the money supply form the money market. It is important to understand that the supply of money and the demand for money are measured as stocks, not flows.

The Interest Rate and Bonds

To understand how the money market works, it is necessary to understand why interest rates and bond prices always move in opposite directions. A bond is a promissory certificate issued by borrowers (typically businesses and governments) in exchange for funds provided to them by lenders. The bond represents the borrower's promise to pay back to the lender (the bondholder) the amount of money borrowed (the principal) at the end of a certain number of years (the maturity date). The bond also promises that the borrower will make payments (coupon payments) of a set number of dollars to the lender at regular intervals (annually, for example). The coupon payments represent the rate of return, or the interest rate, that induces the lender to loan money to the borrower.

Consider a bond that promises to make coupon payments of $10 per year, year in and year out, forever. (Such bonds, called **consols**, are issued by the

British government, for example.) If you purchased such a bond for $100, you would earn a 10 percent rate of interest (the $10 coupon payment divided by the $100 purchase price), expressed as a percentage. If you paid $200 for the bond, you would earn a 5 percent rate of interest ($10 divided by $200), expressed as a percentage. The higher the price you pay for the bond, the lower the interest rate you receive. Conversely, the lower the price paid, the higher the interest rate. Calculation of the interest rate earned on a bond with a set maturity date is more complicated, but the link between the interest rate realized on the bond and the price of the bond is essentially the same. The price of a bond and its interest rate always move in opposite directions.

The exact relationship between the effective interest rate r earned on a bond, its coupon payment C, and its purchase price P_{bond} can be shown by a simple equation:

$$r = \frac{C}{P_{bond}} \times 100$$

This equation shows that for any given constant coupon value the effective interest rate varies inversely with changes in the purchase price of the bond.

Equilibrium and Disequilibrium

Suppose that demand for money and supply of money are represented by the demand curve L and supply curve M shown in Figure 29-4. The supply or stock of money made available by the Bank of Canada amounts to $30 billion. Given the demand curve L, the quantity of money demanded will equal $30 billion only if the interest rate equals 6 percent, corresponding to the intersection of L and M at point e. Hence, 6 percent is the equilibrium level of the interest rate. If the interest rate were higher or lower than this, the money market would be in disequilibrium, and market forces would move the interest rate back to the 6 percent equilibrium level.

FIGURE 29-4   The Money Market: Equilibrium and Disequilibrium

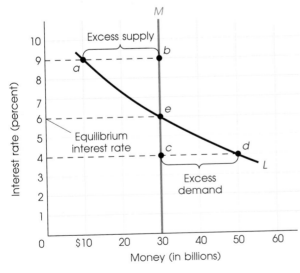

Money (in billions)

Money market equilibrium occurs at that interest rate at which the liquidity preference curve L intersects the money supply curve M at point e, corresponding to a 6 percent interest rate in this case.

At interest rates below the equilibrium level, there is an excess demand for money. For example, at a 4 percent interest rate the excess demand for money amounts to $20 billion, which is represented by the distance between c and d.

At interest rates above the equilibrium level, there is an excess supply of money. For example, at a 9 percent interest rate the excess supply of money amounts to $20 billion, which is represented by the distance between a and b.

Interest Rate Below the Equilibrium Level.

For example, if the interest rate were 4 percent, the quantity of money demanded would equal $50 billion, represented by point *d* on the demand curve. At this interest rate, there would be an excess demand for money of $20 billion (equal to the $50 billion demanded minus the $30 billion supplied). This excess demand is represented by the distance between *c* and *d* in Figure 29-4. In their attempts to obtain more money, people try to convert other assets, such as bonds, into money by selling them. While each individual thinks he or she will be able to get more money in this way, the society *as a whole* cannot increase the amount of money in this way. This is because the total money supply is determined by the central bank and, as was explained earlier, the money supply is not influenced by changes in the interest rate.

Consequently, as people try to sell bonds for money, they only succeed in pushing bond prices down. This means that the rate of return on the bond or interest rate will rise. When the interest rate rises, the quantity of money demanded declines (as represented by the movement up along the demand curve away from point *d*) and the amount by which money demand exceeds money supply gets smaller. When bond prices have fallen far enough to raise the interest rate level to 6 percent, people will demand, or be satisfied to hold, just that quantity of money that is supplied (as represented by the intersection at point *e* of the money demand curve *L* and the money supply curve *M*).

Interest Rate Above the Equilibrium Level.

Alternatively, what if the interest rate is above the equilibrium level of 6 percent? Suppose that it is 9 percent. At this level, the quantity of money demanded equals $10 billion (represented by point *a* in Figure 29-4). There is an excess supply of money amounting to $20 billion (equal to the $30 billion supplied minus the $10 billion demanded), represented by the distance between points *a* and *b*. Of course, every bit of the $30 billion of money supplied would be held by people. But at an interest rate of 9 percent, this is more than people desire to hold. While it may seem strange to imagine people having more money than they want, the key to understanding this idea is to remember that money is the most liquid asset. Therefore, people may well want to keep the *value* or wealth that the money represents but they want to store the wealth in a less liquid form so that they earn a return on it. Since money is barren, as was pointed out earlier, they naturally wish to convert out of money (M1) and buy bonds, which pay interest. Consequently, people will try to convert their excess money holdings into other assets, such as bonds. The attempts to buy bonds will cause bond prices to increase and the interest rate to fall. As the interest rate falls, the quantity of money demanded increases (represented by the movement down along the demand curve away from point *a*), and the excess supply of money gets smaller. Finally, when bond prices have risen far enough to lower the interest rate level to 6 percent, the money market will be in equilibrium. At a 6 percent interest rate, the $30 billion money supply is just the amount people desire to hold.

> **Checkpoint 29-2**
>
> Which of the following would have the greatest effect on the interest rate: (1) an increase in money demand accompanied by an increase in money supply, (2) an increase in money demand alone, or (3) an increase in money demand accompanied by a decrease in money supply? Illustrate each of these cases— (1), (2), and (3)— graphically. How do you think the demand curve for money would be affected if people became more uncertain about their jobs, say, as the result of the onset of a recession? Why?

Summary

1. The five tools used by the Bank of Canada to conduct monetary policy are (a) open market operations, (b) switching of government accounts, (c) the setting of secondary reserve requirements, (d) the setting of the bank rate,

and (e) moral suasion to persuade the chartered banks to support Bank of Canada policy.

2. Open market operations refer to the Bank of Canada buying and selling government securities in the open market. When the Bank of Canada buys government securities, it puts reserves into the banking system, causing an expansion of demand deposits and other chequable deposits, and hence an increase in the economy's money supply. When the Bank of Canada sells government bonds, it takes reserves out of the banking system, causing a contraction of demand deposits and other chequable deposits, and hence a decrease in the economy's money supply.

3. Switching operations refer to the Bank of Canada moving government accounts out of the Bank of Canada and redepositing these funds in the chartered banks or moving funds out of the chartered banks and redepositing these funds in the Bank of Canada. When the Bank of Canada moves government accounts into the chartered banks, the banking system gains reserves and can expand loans and chequable accounts. When the Bank of Canada moves government accounts out of the chartered banks, the banking system loses reserves and must contract its loans and chequable accounts.

4. The Bank of Canada lost the power to alter the primary reserve ratio in the late 1960s. This tool of monetary policy is under the direct control of Parliament. If Parliament decreased the primary reserve ratio, this would cause the banking system to have increased excess reserves and would lead to an increase in loans and chequable accounts. Conversely, if Parliament increased the primary reserve ratio, this would result in a decrease in loans and chequable accounts.

5. An increase in the secondary reserve ratio will lead to tighter credit conditions and higher interest rates for many types of loans without necessarily causing a decrease in the money supply. A decrease in the secondary reserve ratio loosens credit conditions and lowers interest rates on most types of loans without increasing the money supply. Changes in the secondary reserve ratio do not require chartered banks to change the proportion of their assets that must be held in non-interest-earning accounts at the Bank of Canada.

6. When the Bank of Canada raises the bank rate, this serves as a signal that the central bank wishes to see tighter credit conditions and higher interest rates. If the Bank of Canada lowers the bank rate, this signals the financial market that the Bank of Canada wishes to encourage more lending and lower interest rates. In recent years the Bank of Canada has followed a policy of maintaining the bank rate at one quarter of one percent above the interest rate earned on Treasury Bills. The result has been that the bank rate is determined automatically by the Bank of Canada's open market operations.

7. Moral suasion is the tool of monetary policy in which the Bank of Canada tries to get the chartered banks to agree on a course of action which places a high priority on the public interest. Because moral suasion requires close communication and coordination of the diverse interests of the chartered banks and other members of the Canadian Payments Association, as the number of members in the Canadian Payments Association increases there will likely be a decrease in the effectiveness of moral suasion as a tool of monetary policy.

8. There are three components of the demand for money: transactions demand, precautionary demand, and speculative demand. The transactions, precautionary, and speculative demands for money vary directly with the level of aggregate income.

9. Because the interest rate is the opportunity cost of holding money, the money demand curve slopes downward.

10. Because the transactions, precautionary, and speculative demands for money are directly related to income, an increase in income will shift the money demand curve to the right and a decrease in income will shift money demand to the left.

11. The money supply curve is vertical, representing the assumption that the Bank of Canada controls the money supply and that the amount of money which the Bank of Canada makes available to the banking system is not influenced by the interest rate. If the Bank of Canada increased the money supply, the money supply curve would remain vertical but would shift to the right. If the Bank of Canada decreased the money supply, the money supply curve would shift left.

12. The money supply and demand curves jointly determine the equilibrium interest rate in the money market. An increase in the money supply lowers the equilibrium interest rate, while a decrease in the money supply raises the equilibrium interest rate.

Key Terms and Concepts

bank rate
consols
monetary policy
moral suasion

open market
  operations
precautionary demand
secondary reserve ratio

speculative demand
switching
  operations
transactions demand

Questions and Problems

1. If the public's desire to hold currency rises during recessions and falls during the expansionary phase of the business cycle, over the course of the business cycle how does this affect the Bank of Canada's ability to change the money supply per dollar of any open market purchase or sale?

2. Of the five tools that the Bank of Canada can use to implement monetary policy, which one do you think is probably the least effective for controlling the amount of reserves in the banking system? Why?

3. It has been said that the Bank of Canada can be much more effective when it wants to contract the money supply than when it wants to expand the supply. Why might this be so? Explain your answer by discussing each of the Bank of Canada's five tools of monetary policy.

4. What role do the Bank of Canada's liabilities to the chartered banks play in the way that open market operations affect the economy's money supply?

5. How can it be that when there is an excess supply of money, people hold more than they want, yet when equilibrium is restored, they are content to hold the same amount? Where did the excess money or liquidity go? If there is an excess demand for money, what must be true of people's desired holdings of bonds?

6. How would the money demand curve change if people's demand for money became more sensitive to changes in the interest rate? Show how this would affect the money

demand curve L passing through point e in Figure 29-4. Would a money supply increase now have a larger or smaller effect on the equilibrium level of the interest rate? If the money demand curve shifts to the right by an amount equal to $20 billion from point e, would the rise in the interest rate be greater or less than would have been the case before the demand for money became more sensitive to changes in the interest rate?

7. Given the following equations for money demand L and money supply M_s

$$L = P(100 - .5r)$$

and

$$M_s = 95.5$$

a. Assuming $P = 1$, what is the equilibrium interest rate?
b. If the interest rate is presently 10 percent what is the demand for money?
c. Given your answer to the previous part of the question, what will happen to the price of bonds?
d. What is the equilibrium interest rate if the money supply is increased to $M_s' = 97.5$?

Chapter 30

Money and the Economy

"There cannot, in short, be intrinsically a more insignificant thing, in the economy of society, than money; except in the character of a contrivance for sparing time and labour. It is a machine for doing quickly and commodiously, what would be done, though less quickly and commodiously, without it: and like many other kinds of machinery, it only exerts a distinct and independent influence of its own when it gets out of order."[1]

In the last chapter we examined how the Bank of Canada is able to change the level of bank reserves and thereby cause the economy's money supply to expand or contract. But how and why do changes in the economy's money supply affect the general level of economic activity? In this chapter we will focus on these questions.

We should note at the outset that economists are not in complete agreement on just how and to what extent money affects the economy. In this chapter we will focus first on the Keynesian view by introducing money into the Keynesian analysis of income determination we developed in Chapters 21 and 22. Then we will examine the monetarist point of view. Finally, we will look at the new classical, or rational expectations, view, the most recent development in thinking about this issue.

Role of Money in Income Determination; The Keynesian View of the Link Between the Money Supply, Interest Rates, and Investment

We will now combine our understanding of the workings of the money market, developed in the previous chapter, with the Keynesian analysis of income

---

[1] John Stuart Mill, *Principles of Political Economy*, Rev. ed., Vol II, Bk. III (New York: The Colonial Press, 1900), p. 11.

determination that we developed in Chapters 21 and 22. We will then be able to examine the role of money in the determination of aggregate income, output, employment, and the price level from the Keynesian viewpoint.

Our first step in putting the pieces together is to show the relationships among the money market, the interest rate, and the level of investment expenditures in the economy. We will then be able to examine the relationship between the money market and the economy's aggregate demand for goods and services and, hence, the relationship between the money supply provided by the Bank of Canada and aggregate income, output, employment, and the price level.

What is the relationship between the money market and investment expenditures? To answer this question we must first recall the relationship between the interest rate and investment expenditures discussed in Chapter 22. We will then see how the interest rate serves to link the money market and the level of investment expenditures.

Investment and the Interest Rate

In Chapter 22 we argued that the interest rate is the cost to a firm of funds invested in capital goods. If such funds are borrowed from outside the firm, the cost of borrowing is the interest rate that must be paid to lenders. If the funds are generated internally, the cost is the forgone interest the firm could have earned by lending the funds to someone else.

Interest Rate versus Expected Rate of Return

When a firm considers whether or not to purchase or invest in a capital good, it must compare its expected rate of return on the capital good with the interest rate. If the firm is going to use its own funds, the two relevant choices are either to lend the funds to some other party or to invest them in the capital good. If the expected rate of return is higher than the interest rate that would be received by lending the funds to someone else, the firm can earn more by investing internally generated funds in the capital good than by lending them out. The firm will earn the difference between the expected rate of return on the capital good and the interest rate. Similarly, if the firm borrows outside funds to invest in the capital good, it will earn exactly the same amount. In this case its net expected earnings will be the difference between the expected rate

---

LEARNING OBJECTIVES

After reading this chapter, you will be able to:

1. Explain why the interest rate is a determinant of the level of investment spending.
2. Describe and explain the Keynesian view of how money affects aggregate demand.
3. Describe and explain the equation of exchange and the monetarist view of how money affects economic activity.
4. Describe the evidence on the changes in velocity of circulation in Canada.
5. Describe and explain the new classical, or rational expectations, view on the effectiveness of monetary policy.

of return on the capital good and the interest rate that must be paid on the borrowed funds. However, if the expected rate of return on the capital good is less than the interest rate, it would result in a net return lower for the firm if it invested in the new capital good than if it did not invest. Under such a circumstance the firm, assuming that it wanted to maximize its profits, would not invest in the capital good.

Expected Rate of Return on a Capital Good

The **expected rate of return** or *marginal efficiency of investment (MEI) is the amount of money a firm expects to earn per year on funds invested in a capital good expressed as a percentage of the funds invested.*

What determines the expected rate of return on a capital good? Profit, or the anticipation of profit, as noted in Chapter 22. For example, suppose that the annual revenue anticipated from the sale of goods and services produced with the aid of a capital good amounts to $500. Suppose that the anticipated annual costs of production, *excluding* the interest rate cost of the funds invested in the capital good, equal $400. The difference, in this case $100, is the amount of money the firm expects to earn per year on the funds invested in the capital good. If the price of the capital good is $1,000, the expected rate of return on the $1,000 investment in the capital good is 10 percent. This is simply the expected dollar return per time period divided by the value of the asset times 100 expressed as a percentage: $\text{MEI} = (\$100/\$1,000) \times 100$.

If the interest rate is 9 percent, the firm could borrow the $1,000 at a cost of $90 per year. Alternatively, $1,000 of internal funds could earn $90 per year if lent out at 9 percent. Either way, the firm will come out ahead $10 per year if it invests in the capital good. The capital good is therefore a profitable investment, and the firm should buy it. On the other hand, if the interest rate is 11 percent, the same calculations show that the firm will lose $10 per year if it invests $1,000 in the capital good. The good will not be a profitable investment, and the firm should not buy it. A firm will invest in a capital good if the good's expected rate of return is higher than the interest rate. It will not invest if the expected rate of return is less than the interest rate.

Inverse Relationship Between Interest Rate and Investment Spending

At any given time a typical firm has a number of investment projects it could undertake such as building a new plant, buying a new fleet of trucks, building a new loading dock, and so on. The firm forms an expectation of the rate of return it would earn on each of these projects. The lower is the interest rate, the larger is the number of these projects having expected rates of return higher than the interest rate—hence, the lower the interest rate, the greater the amount of investment expenditure by the firm. Of course, the higher is the interest rate, the smaller is the number of projects with expected rates of return above the interest rate and therefore the smaller is the amount of investment expenditure by the firm.

If we consider all the firms in the economy, the total amount of investment spending will increase as the interest rate decreases. This inverse, or negative, relationship between the interest rate and investment is illustrated

FIGURE 30-1 **The Marginal Efficiency of Investment Curve: Investment Spending Varies Inversely with the Interest Rate**

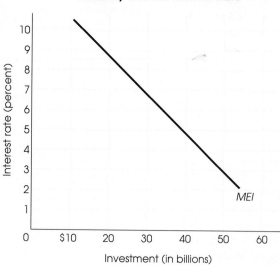

The marginal efficiency of investment curve *MEI* is downward sloping, reflecting the inverse, or negative, relationship between the level of the interest rate and the amount of investment expenditure in the economy.

    The reason for the inverse relationship between the interest rate and investment is that the lower is the interest rate, the larger is the number of investment projects that have an expected rate of return greater than the interest rate.

by the downward-sloping marginal efficiency of investment curve *MEI* in Figure 30-1. The **marginal efficiency of investment curve** *shows the total dollar amount of investment projects, or capital goods formation, that the economy's firms will demand or desire to do at each interest rate.* The marginal efficiency of investment curve is just another way of representing the relationship between the interest rate and investment spending that we discussed in Chapter 22 (Figure 22-8).

The Money Market and the Level of Investment

Now we can see how the money market and the level of investment spending in the economy are related. The connecting link between them is the interest rate. This is illustrated in Figure 30-2, where the money market is shown in frame (a), the marginal efficiency of investment curve is shown in frame (b) and aggregate expenditure is shown in frame (c).

    Suppose initially that the money supply provided by the Bank of Canada amounts to \$30 billion, represented by the money supply curve M_0 in frame (a). Given the demand curve for money, or *liquidity preference curve* L_0, the equilibrium interest rate in the money market is 6 percent, determined by the intersection of M_0 and L_0 at point a. The number of investment projects with expected rates of return greater than 6 percent is such that there will be \$35 billion of investment spending when the interest rate is at that level, corresponding to point a' on the marginal efficiency of investment curve *MEI* in frame (b).

Money, Real GDP, and the Price Level

We know from our discussion in Chapters 21 and 22 that investment spending is an important part of aggregate expenditure in the economy. We saw that in the Keynesian analysis it plays a crucial role in determining the level of the

FIGURE 30-2   Money Supply Change: Keynesian View

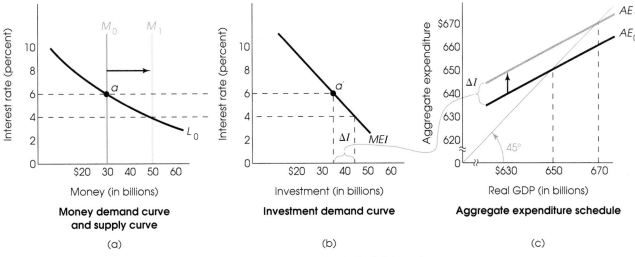

Money demand curve
and supply curve

Investment demand curve

Aggregate expenditure schedule

(a)   (b)   (c)

A $20 billion increase in the money supply causes the interest rate to fall from 6 per-
cent to 4 percent, frame (a), causing a rise in investment ΔI of $10 billion, frame (b),
which in turn causes the aggregate expenditure schedule to shift upward from $AE_0 =$
$C + I + G + X - M$ to $AE_1 = (C + I + \Delta I + G + X - M)$, frame (b). This upward shift in turn
causes real GDP to rise from $650 billion to $670 billion. This analysis is partial because
it doesn't allow for the effect of the rise in real GDP on money demand and hence on
the interest rate.

aggregate expenditure schedule, which in turn determines the equilibrium level
of real GDP, as in Figure 22-1. We are now in a position to introduce the money
market into that analysis.

The Interconnecting Links Among the Money Market, Investment, and Real GDP

Consider again Figure 30-2. The money supply curve M_0 (representing a money
supply of $30 billion) and the demand curve for money L_0 determine a 6 per-
cent interest rate. Given the position of the marginal efficiency of investment
curve, this interest rate in turn gives rise to a level of investment of $35 billion.
This amount of investment spending determines the position of the aggregate
expenditure schedule $AE_0 = (C + I + G + X - M)$, in frame (c), which in turn
determines the equilibrium level of real GDP of $150 billion. This level of real
GDP determines the position of the demand curve for money L_0 (because the
transactions, precautionary, and speculative demands for money are influenced
by the level of real GDP), which together with M_0 determines the 6 percent
interest rate.

Partial Equilibrium Analysis

Now suppose that the Bank of Canada increases the money supply by $20
billion (from $30 billion to $50 billion), represented by the rightward shift in the

money supply curve from M_0 to M_1 in frame (a). At the initial interest rate of 6 percent, there would now be an excess supply of money. This excess causes the interest rate to fall from 6 percent to 4 percent, determined by the intersection of M_1 and L_0. The decline in the interest rate from 6 percent to 4 percent means that there would be an increase in the number of investment projects having expected rates of return greater than the interest rate. The resulting increase in investment spending ΔI would amount to $10 billion (a rise from $35 billion to $45 billion), frame (b). This increase would cause the aggregate expenditure schedule to rise from $C + I + G + X - M$ to $C + I + \Delta I + G + X - M$ and real GDP to increase from $650 billion to $670 billion, frame (c).

In **partial equilibrium analysis** *we focus on a change in one market and its consequences for that market, and possibly a few others. All other markets are assumed to be unchanged. In* **general equilibrium analysis** *we consider the adjustments that a change in one market may cause in each and every other market.* Our analysis of the consequences of a money supply change in Figure 30-2 is a partial equilibrium analysis because it does not take into account the effect the rise in real GDP will have on the demand curve for money and hence on the interest rate. A general equilibrium analysis of the consequences of the $20 billion increase in the money supply from M_0 to M_1 must take account of this effect.

General Equilibrium Analysis

The general equilibrium analysis is shown in Figure 30-3. As the interest rate falls and increased investment causes a rise in real GDP, *the rise in real GDP causes the demand curve for money to shift to the right* at the same time (because of the increase in the transactions, precautionary, and speculative demands for money). This shift in the demand curve for money keeps the interest rate from falling as far as it does when the shift is ignored, as in the partial equilibrium analysis in Figure 30-2. Consequently, the rise in investment ΔI is now less, amounting to only $5 billion. The resulting upward shift in the aggregate expenditure schedule is now smaller, $AE_{r=6} = (C + I + G + X - M)$ to $AE''_{r=5} = (C + (I + \Delta I) + G + X - M)$. The rise in real GDP is therefore smaller, from $650 billion to $660 billion. The position of the demand curve for money at L_1 corresponds to (is determined by) the $660 billion real GDP level. In the general equilibrium analysis, the level of the interest rate falls to 5 percent, a higher level than the 4 percent of the partial equilibrium analysis. *According to the Keynesian view, an increase in the money supply causes a decrease in the interest rate and an increase in the level of real GDP. A decrease in the money supply will have the opposite effect, causing an increase in the interest rate and a decrease in the level of real GDP.*

Easy Money versus Tight Money

When the Bank of Canada increases the money supply, it is often said to be following an *easy money policy,* or to be "easing credit." An easy money policy stimulates the economy because it leads to a rise in real GDP. On the other hand, a *tight money policy,* or a policy of "credit tightening," refers to the opposite situation: a reduction in the money supply leading to a rise in the interest rate and a decline in real GDP.

FIGURE 30-3   Money Supply Change: Keynesian View, General Equilibrium Analysis

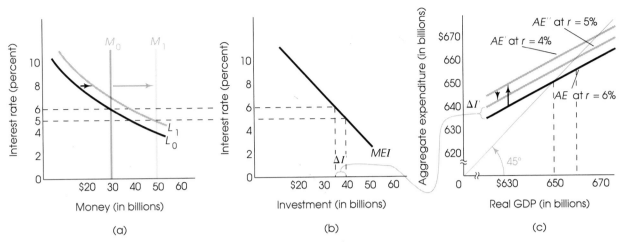

(a)   (b)   (c)

Frame (a) shows partial equilibrium analysis of the effects of a $20 billion increase in the money supply. The interest rate falls from 6 percent to 4 percent, causing a rise in investment ΔI of $10 billion which in turn causes aggregate expenditure to shift upward from $AE_{r=6}$ to $AE'_{r=4}$ in frame (c). This upward shift in AE causes real GDP to rise from $650 billion to $670 billion.

General equilibrium analysis of the effects of the same $20 billion money supply increase shown in frame (a). By comparison, here the interest rate falls a smaller amount from 6 percent to 5 percent, because of allowance for the fact that the rise in real GDP causes the demand curve for money to shift rightward from L_0 to L_1. Because of this, the rise in investment ΔI of $5 billion is smaller in frame (b). Hence, the aggregate expenditure schedule shifts upward a smaller amount, from $AE_{r=6}$ to $AE''_{r=5}$ in frame (c), and therefore the rise in real GDP is less, from $650 billion to $660 billion.

The Link Between Money and the *AD* Curve

In Figure 23-3 we saw how a shift in the aggregate expenditure schedule due to an exogenously caused change in expenditure will cause the aggregate demand curve *AD* to shift. Similarly, the increase in the money supply causing the increase in investment spending ΔI shifts the aggregate expenditure schedule upward from AE_0 to AE_1 in frame (a) of Figure 30-4, and the *AD* curve in frame (b) rightward from AD_0 to AD_1.

The Link Between Money and the Price Level

When we take account of the interaction of the *AS* curve with the *AD* curve in frame (b) of Figure 30-4, we see that the price level was initially P_0, determined by the intersection of AD_0 and *AS* at point e_0. The increase in the money supply that shifts the *AD* curve rightward from AD_0 to AD_1 causes the price level to rise to p_1, corresponding to the intersection of AD_1 and *AS* at point e_1.

In general, the response of the price level to an increase in the money supply is determined by the slope of the *AS* curve. If the *AD* curve shifts along a horizontal *AS* curve, where the economy has a great deal of excess capacity and

FIGURE 30-4A   Changes in the Money Supply Affect Real GDP and the Price Level

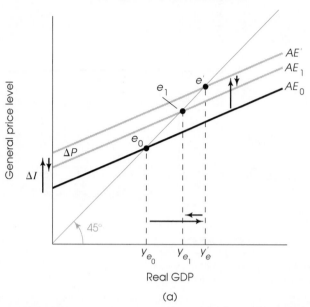

(a)

FIGURE 30-4B   The Effectiveness of Monetary Policy Depends on the Slope of the AS Curve

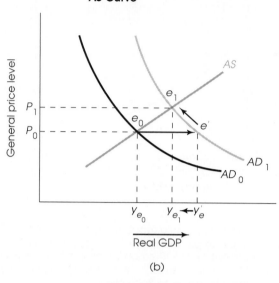

(b)

An increase in the money supply increases investment spending by $\Delta I'$, shifting the aggregate expenditure schedule upward from AE_0 to AE' in frame (a), and the aggregate demand curve rightward from AD_0 to AD_1 in frame (b). Real GDP would increase from y_{e_0} to $y_{e'}$. However at price level p_0, AD_1 now exceeds AS, so price increases from p_0 to p_1. This rise in the price level causes *crowding out*. As the price level increases, the level of aggregate expenditure decreases from AE' to AE_1 in frame (a); this corresponds to the movement to the left along AD_1 from $y_{e'}$ in frame (b). Thus the overall effect corresponds to the move from the initial equilibrium at e_0 in frames (a) and (b), to its new equilibrium, corresponding to point e_1.

unemployment, and if the information extraction problem is very small, there will be no increase in the price level and real GDP rises by the full value of the multiplier from y_{e_0} to y_{e_1}. This is illustrated by Figure 30-5, frame (a).

If the shift to the right of the AD curve is over an upward-sloping AS, as shown in frame (b) of Figure 30-5, the outcome is much different. In this case, where the economy is operating with less extra capacity or moderate information extraction problem, both real GDP and the general price level increase. The increase in aggregate demand causes the price level to rise from P_0 to P_1, which in turn causes some crowding out of expenditure. The real GDP increases from y_{e_0} to y_{e_1} but the expansion is less than in the previous case.

Figure 30-5, frame (c), indicates the effect of an increase in the money supply, which shifts AD to the right when the AS curve is vertical. This extreme case is characteristic of the classical AS curve, which assumed the economy was always at full employment in the shortrun. It also applies in the shortrun if there is a severe information extraction problem. As the AD curve shifts to the right it causes the price level to rise from P_0 to P_1. In addition, this case applies in the longrun, as the AS curve is believed to be vertical in the longrun for the reasons outlined in Chapter 26. In the cases where the AS curve is vertical, the price rises

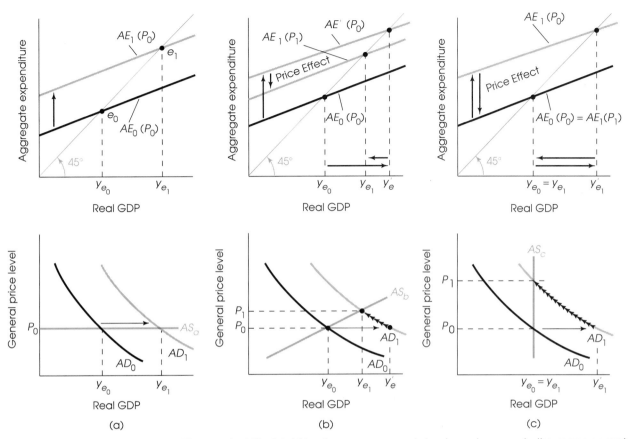

(a)   (b)   (c)

In each of the three frames the *AD* curve is shifted right by the same amount due to an increase in the money supply. How effective the increase in the money supply is in causing increases in employment and real GDP depends on the slope of the *AS* curve. In frame (a) the shift to the right in *AD* occurs in an economy with a low information extraction problem and a large amount of excess capacity. As a result the economy in frame (a) experiences no crowding out through price increases.

In frame (b) the same increase in the money supply causes the *AD* curve to shift to the right by the same amount as it did in frame (a). However, this economy has some information extraction problem, which results in an upward-sloping *AS* curve. The net increase in real GDP resulting from the shift in *AD* is smaller, shown as y_0 to y_1, because it is accompanied by some crowding out as the general price level rises from p_0 to p_1.

In frame (c) the increase in the money supply once again causes the same shift to the right in the *AD* curve. This time the economy has a severe information extraction problem, so monetary policy is ineffective. The price level rises from P_0 to P_1 and the resulting crowding out causes the *AE* curve to shift from AE_1 (P_0) all the way back down to AE_1 (P_1) which lies on top of the original *AE* curve. Thus in this case the monetary expansion caused an increase in the general price level with no increase in real GDP.

by enough to crowd out an amount of expenditure equal to the increase in expenditure that originally shifted the *AD* curve to the right. In this example, the net result of an increase in the money supply causes no change in real GDP—the level of equilibrium remains the same, with y_{e_1} equal to y_{e_0}. The effect of the money supply increase is different when it comes to the price level,

Checkpoint* 30-1

Suppose that the marginal efficiency of investment curve in Figure 30-2, frame (b), is rotated clockwise about point a' so that it is now steeper. Given the increase in the money supply from M_0 to M_1 shown in Figure 30-2, frame (a), will the resulting increase in investment spending in frame (b) now be larger or smaller than before? Suppose that the demand curve for money L in frame (a) is rotated clockwise about point a so that it is steeper. Given the money supply increase from M_0 to M_1, will the resulting increase in investment spending, given the original marginal efficiency of investment curve MEI shown in frame (b), now be larger or smaller than before?

*Answers to all Checkpoints can be found at the back of the text.

which rises from P_0 to P_1. Thus, in the case of a vertical AS curve expansionary monetary policy is just as ineffective as fiscal policy in creating increases in real GDP.

How Money Affects the Economy

A change in the money supply changes the interest rate, thereby causing a change in investment spending, which in turn shifts the aggregate expenditure schedule and hence the AD curve. The resulting change in real GDP and the general price level depends on the amount of excess capacity, the level of unemployment, and the severity of the information extraction problem in the economy, as reflected in the slope of the AS curve over which the AD curve shifts.

Monetarist View on the Role of Money

The Keynesian view of how money affects economic activity went largely unchallenged up until the 1960s when a school of thought known as **monetarism** began to assert itself. The monetarists, largely led by Milton Friedman (winner of the 1976 Nobel Prize in Economics), argue that money plays a much more important role in determining the level of economic activity than is granted to it by the Keynesian view. We now examine the monetarist view and also consider some of the main differences between it and the Keynesian view. We begin by examining the equation of exchange, a hypothesis about how the money supply affects the economy that goes back to the classical economists.

Monetarism and the Equation of Exchange

The dollar value of the purchases of final goods and services produced by the economy during a year is the economy's money GDP, the GDP expressed in terms of the prices at which the goods are actually purchased. (Recall the distinction between real GDP and money GDP made in Chapter 19.) Each purchase typically requires the buyer to give money in exchange for the good or service provided by the seller. The economy's money supply (that is, its total stock of money) is used to transact all these exchanges during the course of a year.

Money GDP, a flow, is usually several times larger than the economy's money stock. This means that the money stock must be used several times during the year to carry out all the transactions represented by the money GDP. In effect, the money stock must go around the circular flow of money exchanged for goods (discussed in Chapter 3) several times during the course of a year. This idea is given expression by the **equation of exchange,** which is written $M \times V = P \times Q$.

In this equation $P \times Q$, price times quantity, is money (nominal) GDP. For example, if the economy produces nothing but widgets, P would be the price per widget and Q the quantity of widgets produced per year. More realistically, for an economy that produces many kinds of goods, Q may be thought

Ideological Differences Among Keynesians, Monetarists, and the New Classical View

Before beginning our discussion of monetarism, it should be recognized that monetarists and proponents of the new classical view typically have differing political views and opinions than do modern-day Keynesians (sometimes called *neo-Keynesians*) on the proper role and size of government in our economy. Monetarists and new classical view proponents tend to favour a more *laissez faire* or free-market economy, with government intervening mainly to restrain monopoly and other forms of anticompetitive market practices. They believe that the market system generally does a good job of efficiently allocating resources to answer the basic economic questions of what, how, and for whom to produce. Those who adhere more to the Keynesian point of view tend to be less satisfied with the results provided by the market mechanism in a number of areas of the economy. They believe that the government can and should play a more effective and active role in correcting the shortcomings of the market mechanism. Monetarists and new classical view proponents, on the other hand, tend to view government as generally inefficient, bureaucratically cumbersome, and prone to making large mistakes when dealing with problems. Moreover, they generally fear the political implications of increasing government's control over the economy's decision-making process. They argue that increased government control poses a threat to personal freedoms and puts a damper on individual initiative.

In view of these ideological differences, it should not be surprising that monetarists and new classical view proponents are skeptical of fiscal policy as a stabilization tool. We have already discussed (in Chapters 24 and 25) the timing problems associated with discretionary fiscal policy. Quite aside from this, however, monetarists and new classical view proponents fear that fiscal policy gives rise to too much direct government intervention in the economy. On the other hand, Keynesians feel government intervention is needed to solve other kinds of social and economic problems. So, why shouldn't the government also use its spending and taxation authority to attack the problems of economic instability, unemployment, and inflation? Besides, Keynesians see the Great Depression of the 1930s and the boom of the 1960s, which was driven by government spending on social programs, as evidence that the self-regulating forces of the marketplace are not sufficient to ensure that the economy will continuously operate near its full employment capacity. For them these arguments seem to be reinforced by the recent recessions of the early 1980s and 1990s. They also argue that monetary policy alone was incapable of coping with such recessions.

In contrast, monetarists see regulation of the money supply as a much more powerful tool for affecting the economy. They argue that the Great Depression was so severe largely because the central monetary authorities in many countries, and especially in the United States, did a particularly bad job of managing monetary policy. Moreover, most monetarists feel that the linkages between the money supply and interest rates, the general price level, unemployment, and GDP are more complex than Keynesians often seemed to imply. Monetarists are therefore uncomfortable with using monetary policy to try to regulate short-term economic behaviour in the way Keynesians advocate the use of fiscal policy. Instead they propose the use of **monetary rule**. *This strategy requires that the central bank set a known publicized target for stable growth in the money supply and then stick to it.* The exact rate of increase in the money supply, they argue, is less important than that it be well publicized and that the central bank not be persuaded to deviate from it simply because of short-term fluctuations in interest rates, unemployment, or some other indicator of economic performance. This type of monetary policy doesn't require the same direct and potentially extensive government intervention in the economy as fiscal policy.

While sharing monetarists' concerns about extensive government intervention, proponents of the new classical view do not make much of a distinction between fiscal and monetary policy regarding their respective potentials for affecting economic activity. They regard both as ineffective because, according to rational expectations theory, people anticipate the effects of such policies and take actions that nullify their impact on real variables in the economy, such as real GDP and employment (as we saw in Chapter 26).

For Discussion

- Explain why Keynesians and proponents of new classical theory both opposed the use of monetary policy as a tool for stimulating the economy during the recession of the early 1980s. Were there differences in the reasons these two groups of economists might favour tax cuts as a way of stimulating the economy?

of as real GDP and P as some index of current prices, such as the consumer price index or GDP deflator, which were discussed in Chapters 19 and 20. M is a measure of the economy's money supply. V is the number of times the money stock must "turn over" during a year in order to facilitate all the purchases of final goods and services that add up to nominal GDP. In other words, *V is the number of times a typical dollar of the money stock must go around the circular flow of money exchanged for final goods and services during a year.* For this reason V is called the **velocity of circulation** of money, or simply the *velocity* of money.

For example, if the economy's money supply M is \$40 billion and its money GDP is \$640 billion, the equation of exchange would be

$$M \times V = \text{GDP}_{\text{nominal}} \quad \$40 \times 16 = \$640$$

The velocity of money V is therefore 16. This means that the money stock must turn over sixteen times per year.

The Equation of Exchange as Definition

The equation of exchange as it stands is true simply by definition. If you know the size of the money supply and the level of the money GDP, you can calculate the value of V. By definition, V has to take on whatever value is necessary to maintain the equality between the two sides of the equation $M \times V = P \times Q$. However, suppose that you took annual money GDP data and money stock data for a series of years in an economy and calculated the value of velocity for each of those years. If the calculated values of velocity didn't change much from year to year and from the earlier to the later years, your curiosity should be aroused. You should be even more curious if the same calculations for different economies revealed the same kind of stability for V.

Stability in any phenomenon is the watchword of science. When Galileo dropped objects of unequal weight from the same height on the Leaning Tower of Pisa, he discovered that they always reached the ground at the same time. He thus discovered the law of falling bodies. It is stability that leads to the formulation of theories, and often to controversy about those theories. Galileo's experiments and his formulation of the law of falling bodies went against the prevailing opinion that heavier bodies fell faster than light ones, and he was forced to resign from his position as professor of mathematics at the University of Pisa.

The story of Galileo gives us some perspective on the depth of feeling that often characterizes the clash between competing theories as explanations of scientific phenomena. This depth of feeling is not restricted to physics or astronomy and pervades most human endeavour. In macroeconomics the controversy over the behaviour and importance of the velocity of circulation makes up a major part of the conflict between monetarist and Keynesian viewpoints about the role of money. Here, too, stability is a large part of the issue. *Monetarists argue that velocity, V, in the equation of exchange is fairly stable. Those espousing the Keynesian point of view dispute this contention.* You might well ask why not settle the argument by an appeal to facts—the calculations of velocity already mentioned. As in Galileo's time, facts aren't always convincing. Also, the facts about velocity are not as clear-cut as those about falling bodies, as we shall see.

The Equation of Exchange as Theory: The Quantity Theory of Money

What does it mean to say that velocity V is stable? It means that V is more than just a symbol that takes on whatever value is necessary to ensure equality between the left-hand and right-hand sides of the equation of exchange. The classical economists contended that V was reasonably stable because it reflected the institutional characteristics of the economy. These characteristics include the frequency with which people are paid, the organization of banking, and the level of development of the transportation and communications systems. They argued that these determinants of the economy's payments mechanism were slow to change and that therefore V was stable. This view of the equation of exchange became known as the **quantity theory of money**.

With the assumption that V is stable, the equation of exchange passes from the realm of definition to that of theory because it enables us to predict the consequences of an event, namely, a change in the money supply. (You might want to review the discussion of the characteristics of a theory in Chapter 1.) If the money supply is increased by a certain percentage, then money GDP will increase by a like percentage. In the previous example—where M equals $40 billion, V equals 16, and the money GDP equals $640 billion—suppose that the money supply M is increased from $40 billion to $44 billion, a 10 percent increase. If V is stable at a value of 16, money GDP will increase by 10 percent, from $640 billion to $704 billion.

Monetarist View of the Money Transmission Mechanism

Monetarism may be viewed as a sophisticated version of the quantity theory of money. Monetarists contend that the effects of money supply changes on the economy are transmitted through a host of channels, not just via the interest rate route emphasized in the Keynesian view of the transmission mechanism. In particular, monetarists argue that an increase in the economy's money supply initially increases the money holdings of consumers and businesses, giving an excess supply of money. The excess money holdings are then spent on goods and services, directly pushing up aggregate demand and money GDP (equal to $P \times Q$). Conversely, a decrease in the economy's money supply creates an excess demand for money. In an attempt to increase their money holdings, consumers and businesses cut back on their spending. This causes aggregate demand for goods and services to fall and money GDP to decrease. Monetarists tend to believe that the cause and effect transmission from changes in the money supply to changes in money GDP is reasonably direct and tight. In terms of the equation of exchange, monetarists believe that V, the velocity of money, is quite stable. Hence, they argue that changes in the money supply have a fairly direct effect on money GDP.

An extreme version of monetarism would assume that velocity is a constant, as in the hypothetical example earlier where velocity was assumed always to equal 16. If this crude version of monetarism were true, monetary policy would indeed be a powerful and reliable tool for affecting the level of money GDP, or aggregate income. The Bank of Canada would know that it could change money GDP by any percentage amount it desired simply by changing the economy's money supply by that percentage amount. However, not even the most ardent monetarists subscribe to the view that velocity is constant.

Velocity in the Real World

What do real-world data show about the relationship between the money supply and money GDP? How does velocity actually behave?

The Money Supply and Money GDP

Figure 30-6 illustrates the behaviour of the money supply (M1, defined as currency plus demand deposits) and nominal GDP in Canada for the years since 1960. Monetarists contend that similar trends in the growth rates shown for the money supply and nominal GDP reflect a causal relationship running from the money supply to nominal GDP. However, Keynesians reply that the observed relationship is equally supportive of their point of view. They argue that the causality can also run in the other direction; that is from nominal GDP to the money supply. They point out that the economy's aggregate expenditure schedule $C + I + G + X - M$ can shift upward for a host of reasons that have nothing to do with money supply changes. Technological change, changes in profit expectations, and the development of new products can cause investment I to rise. Changes in consumer tastes, an increase in consumer optimism, population growth, and so forth can cause the consumption function C to shift upward. Government expenditures G may increase for reasons of natural disaster relief, construction of highways, schools, and so forth. Net exports, $X - M$, can increase because of increases in the incomes or relative price levels in foreign countries, or because of a decline in the external value of the Canadian dollar.

Keynesians argue that these autonomous increases in total spending in the economy lead to an increase in the demand for loans from banks, as businesses and consumers borrow to finance their spending. Banks *respond* by lending out excess reserves and thereby create money through the deposit expansion process we studied in the previous chapter. Growth in the money supply is therefore caused by the increase in the total expenditure on goods and services rather than the other way around. The ongoing debate between monetarists and Keynesians finds both sides enlisting the data from Table 30-1 and represented in Figure 30-6 as support for their points of view.

The Evidence on Velocity

Velocity can be calculated from the money supply and money GDP data given in Table 30-1 and represented in Figure 30-6. We can do this simply by recognizing that the equation of exchange:

$$M \times V = P \times Q$$

may also be expressed as

$$V = \frac{P \times Q}{M}$$

FIGURE 30-6 The Money Supply and Nominal GDP

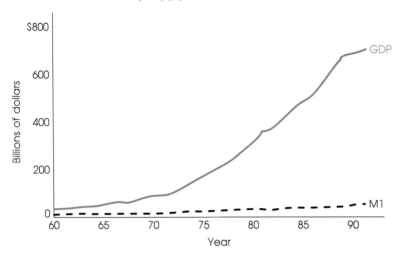

There is a direct relationship between the rate of increase of the money supply and money GDP. Monetarists cite this as evidence to support their claim that the money supply is an important causal determinant of money GDP. Keynesians claim that this relationship is equally supportive of the view that causation runs in the opposite direction—that is, from money GDP to the money supply. In addition, the issue is complicated by some monetarists pointing out that the link between money supply and money GDP is clearest and most accurate when a broad definition of the money supply such as M2 or M3 is used as the monetary aggregate. This presents a problem for central bankers because a narrow monetary aggregate such as M1 is much easier to control through policy instruments than is one more broadly defined, which is typically more susceptible to events which the central bank cannot control.

In Canada dividing nominal GDP ($P \times Q$) by money supply data (M1) and dividing nominal GDP by the broader definition of the money supply (M2) shows the respective velocities (V1) and (V2). The velocity V1 decreased from 1960 to 1961 and then experienced a relatively smooth upward trend from 1961 to 1966, moving from 7.6 to 8.9. From 1967 to 1974 it fluctuated between 9.1 and 10.4, with a lower upward trend than that experienced in the previous period. It can be seen in Figure 30-7, frame (b), that while the upward trend was lower, there was more volatility in the velocity over the 1967–1974 period than in the previous five years. From 1975 to 1982 V1 was more volatile than over the previous five-year period. Over this period V1 rose from 9.3 to 14.6. Since 1982 the upward trend on V1 has decreased slightly, with V1 rising from 14.6 to 16.0 over this period.

By contrast with the behaviour of V1 discussed in the previous paragraph, it is interesting to look at the behaviour of V2, the velocity of circulation of the broader definition of the money supply (M2). Over the period from 1960 to 1966, V2 increased from 3.2 to 3.7, moving along a trend similar to that of V1. From 1967 to 1977, V2 was stable at a value between 3.5 and 3.6. After 1977, V2 began a relatively smooth decrease in value from 3.4 until it reached 3.0 by 1988. Thus, while V1 was experiencing an increasing volatile upward trend over the period 1960 to 1991, V2 was either stable or on a very smooth downward trend.

TABLE 30-1 Macroeconomic Statistics for Canada 1960 to 1991

Year	Money Supply M1	Money Supply M2	Nominal GDP	Real GDP 1986 Dollars	Nominal GNP	Prices CPI	Prices GDP Deflator	Unemploy-ment Rate	Bank Rate	"90-Day" Commerical Rate
1960	5.2	12.3	39.5	164.1	38.8		24.0	7.0	3.54	4.00
1961	5.5	13.0	40.9	169.3	40.6	31.6	24.2	7.2	3.06	3.37
1962	5.7	13.6	44.4	181.3	40.2	32.0	24.5	6.0	4.48	4.38
1963	6.0	14.3	47.7	190.7	43.6	32.6	25.0	5.5	3.88	4.01
1964	6.3	15.1	52.2	203.4	51.3	33.2	25.7	4.7	4.04	4.20
1965	6.7	16.1	57.5	216.8	56.5	34.0	26.5	3.9	4.29	5.02
1966	7.2	17.3	64.4	231.5	63.3	35.2	27.8	3.6	5.17	6.27
1967	7.9	19.0	69.1	238.3	67.8	36.5	29.0	4.1	4.98	5.85
1968	8.3	21.1	75.4	251.1	74.2	38.0	30.0	4.8	6.79	6.82
1969	8.9	23.4	83.0	264.5	81.8	39.7	31.4	4.7	7.46	7.85
1970	9.1	25.0	89.1	271.4	87.8	41.0	32.8	5.7	7.13	7.34
1971	10.2	27.7	97.3	287.0	95.8	42.2	33.9	6.4	5.19	4.51
1972	11.7	30.8	108.6	303.4	107.2	44.2	35.8	6.3	4.75	5.10
1973	13.3	35.4	127.4	326.8	125.6	47.6	39.0	5.5	6.13	7.45
1974	14.6	42.7	152.1	341.2	149.9	52.8	44.6	5.3	8.50	10.51
1975	16.7	48.9	171.5	350.1	169.0	58.5	49.0	6.9	8.50	7.94
1976	18.0	56.5	197.9	371.7	194.4	62.9	53.3	7.1	9.29	9.17
1977	19.4	64.4	217.9	385.1	213.3	67.9	56.6	8.1	7.71	7.48
1978	21.6	71.4	241.6	402.7	235.7	73.9	60.0	8.3	8.98	8.83
1979	23.1	82.7	276.1	418.3	268.9	80.7	66.0	7.4	12.10	12.07
1980	24.5	101.3	309.9	424.5	302.1	88.9	73.0	7.5	12.89	13.15
1981	25.4	116.7	356.0	440.1	344.7	100.0	80.9	7.5	17.93	18.33
1982	25.6	127.5	374.4	426.0	361.8	110.8	87.9	11.0	13.96	14.15
1983	27.7	134.3	405.7	439.4	394.1	117.2	92.3	11.8	9.55	9.45
1984	28.6	140.3	444.7	467.2	431.2	122.3	95.2	11.2	11.31	11.19
1985	29.9	153.5	478.0	489.4	463.7	127.2	97.7	10.5	9.65	9.56
1986	31.4	169.6	505.7	505.7	489.3	132.4	100.0	9.5	9.21	9.16
1987	35.7	187.5	551.4	526.1	535.2	138.2	104.8	8.8	8.40	8.39
1988	37.6	200.9	603.4	549.2	584.5	143.8	109.9	7.8	9.69	9.66
1989	39.4	227.2	651.6	565.7	629.5	151.0	115.2	7.5	12.29	12.21
1990	38.7	251.4	671.6	567.5	647.6	158.2	117.9	8.1	13.05	13.05
1991	39.9	275.5	679.2	558.6	656.2	160.5	123.5	10.3	9.03	8.90

Year	Velocity GNP-Nom. M1	Velocity GNP-Nom. M2	Velocity GDP-Nom. M1	Velocity GDP-Nom. M2	Real Growth Rate GDP	Inflation Rate CPI	Inflation Rate GDP Deflator	Growth Rate of M1	Growth Rate of M2	% Change Velocity GDP-Nom. M1	% Change Velocity GDP-Nom. M2
1960	7.5	3.2	7.6	3.2							
1961	7.4	3.1	7.4	3.1	3.1	1.3	.8	5.8	5.7	-2.1	-2.0
1962	7.0	3.0	7.8	3.3	7.1	1.9	1.2	3.6	4.6	4.7	3.8
1963	7.3	3.1	8.0	3.3	5.2	1.8	2.0	5.3	5.1	2.1	2.2
1964	8.1	3.4	8.3	3.5	6.7	2.4	2.8	5.0	5.6	4.2	3.6
1965	8.4	3.5	8.6	3.6	6.6	3.5	3.1	6.3	6.6	3.6	3.3
1966	8.8	3.7	8.9	3.7	6.8	3.7	4.9	7.5	7.5	4.2	4.2
1967	8.6	3.6	8.7	3.6	2.9	4.1	4.3	9.7	9.8	-2.2	-2.3
1968	8.9	3.5	9.1	3.6	5.4	4.5	3.4	5.1	11.1	3.9	-1.7
1969	9.2	3.5	9.3	3.5	5.4	3.3	4.7	7.2	10.9	2.7	-.7
1970	9.6	3.5	9.8	3.6	2.6	2.9	4.5	2.2	6.8	5.0	.5
1971	9.4	3.5	9.5	3.5	5.8	4.7	3.4	12.1	10.8	-2.6	-1.4
1972	9.2	3.5	9.3	3.5	5.7	7.7	5.6	14.7	11.2	-2.7	.4
1973	9.4	3.5	9.6	3.6	7.7	7.7	8.9	13.7	14.9	3.2	2.1
1974	10.3	3.5	10.4	3.6	4.4	10.9	14.4	9.8	20.6	8.8	-1.0
1975	10.1	3.5	10.3	3.5	2.6	10.8	9.9	14.4	14.5	-1.4	-1.5
1976	10.8	3.4	11.0	3.5	6.2	7.5	8.8	7.8	15.5	7.1	-.1
1977	11.0	3.3	11.2	3.4	3.6	7.9	6.2	7.8	14.0	2.2	-3.4
1978	10.9	3.3	11.2	3.4	4.6	8.8	6.0	11.3	10.9	-.4	.0
1979	11.6	3.3	12.0	3.3	3.9	9.2	10.0	6.9	15.8	6.9	-1.3
1980	12.3	3.0	12.6	3.1	1.5	10.2	10.6	6.1	22.5	5.8	-8.4
1981	13.6	3.0	14.0	3.1	3.7	12.5	10.8	3.7	15.2	10.8	-.3
1982	14.1	2.8	14.6	2.9	-3.2	10.8	8.7	.8	9.3	4.3	-3.7
1983	14.2	2.9	14.6	3.0	3.2	5.8	5.0	8.2	5.3	.1	2.9
1984	15.1	3.1	15.5	3.2	6.3	4.4	3.1	3.2	4.5	6.2	4.9
1985	15.5	3.0	16.0	3.1	4.8	4.0	2.6	4.5	9.4	2.8	-1.8
1986	15.6	2.9	16.1	3.0	3.3	4.1	2.4	5.0	10.5	.7	-4.2
1987	15.0	2.9	15.4	2.9	4.0	4.4	4.8	13.7	10.6	-4.1	-1.4
1988	15.5	2.9	16.0	3.0	4.4	4.1	4.9	5.3	7.1	3.9	2.1
1989	16.0	2.8	16.5	2.9	3.0	5.0	4.8	4.8	13.1	3.1	-4.5
1990	16.7	2.6	17.4	2.7	.3	4.8	2.3	-1.8	10.7	4.9	-6.9
1991	16.4	2.4	17.0	2.5	-1.5	1.5	4.7	3.1	9.6	-1.9	-7.7

Data compiled from Canadian Economic Observer; Canadian Statistical Review, Bank of Canada Review, and Bank of Canada Review Supplement.

FIGURE 30-7   **The Behaviour of Velocity V1 and V2 and the Bank Rate**

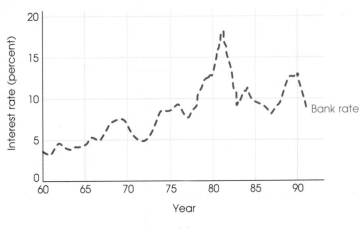

(a)

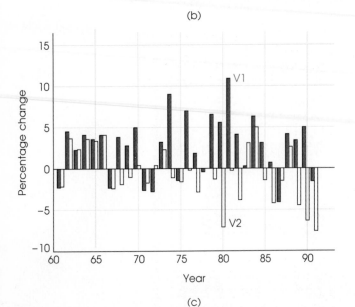

(b)

(c)

Velocities V1 and V2, plotted in frame (b), are calculated by dividing money GDP by the money supplies (M1) and (M2), respectively. The shortrun stability of these two measures of velocity is more easily judged from the year-to-year percentage changes in V1 and V2 plotted in frame (c). Monetarists believe that the evidence in frames (b) and (c), covering the period since the early 1960s, shows that velocity is reasonably stable. The more variable behaviour of the velocity V1 since 1975, and the similar increase in the variability of the velocity V2 since 1980 seems less supportive of this view. Keynesians take special note of the way that the interest rate in frame (a) moves in a parallel manner to velocity in frame (b). This is consistent with their view that velocity is sensitive to the interest rate, rising when the interest rate rises and falling when the interest rate falls.

In addition to these longrun trends in the velocities, V1 and V2 have experienced much different behaviour in their respective rates of variation on a year-to-year basis. This variation in velocity is illustrated in Figure 30-7, frame (c), which shows the year-to-year percentage change in the velocity data plotted in frame (b).

Monetarists believe that the growth in velocity has been reasonably slow and predictable. They suggest that the longrun upward trend in velocity from World War II to 1981 reflects the increased use of credit cards and the increased availability of short-term credit for consumer purchases. Both of these developments make it possible for individuals or businesses to transact any given amount of purchases of final goods and services with a smaller balance of money on hand. Hence, the economy's money supply turns over more often, or goes around the circular flow more times, during the course of a year; velocity increases.

Keynesians acknowledge the impact of these same developments on velocity. But they also note that the longrun rise in the velocity V1 has been accompanied by a longrun rise in the interest rate, shown in frame (a) of Figure 30-7. This is significant in the Keynesian view because they believe velocity is more sensitive to interest rate change than do monetarists. Keynesians claim the longrun rise in the interest rate [Figure 30-7, frame (a)] that accompanies the longrun rise in velocity up to 1981 supports their view of the link between nominal GDP and the money supply. They also can point out that the similarity in the fluctuating behaviours of both velocity (V1) and the bank rate from 1982 to 1988 [Figure 30-7, frame (b)] is consistent with their point of view. Further support for this view is found in the U.S. experience. Keynesians note that in that country the gradual decline in the interest rate from 1930 through 1946 accompanied the decline in velocity over this period and point to a similar link between the interest rate and velocity decline after 1981.

In the United States since the early 1950s, velocity has never increased by more than about 6.5 percent from one year to the next, and until 1982 it never decreased by more than about 2.5 percent. Monetarists argue that this amount of shortrun variability of velocity over this period is consistent with their view that velocity is quite stable. In Canada [as Figure 30-7, frame (c), reveals] the year-to-year fluctuations in V1 and V2 have been much less stable than the growth in the velocity in the United States. V1 in this country has grown by rates from minus 4.1 percent to rates as high as 10.1 percent from one year to the next. In addition, the growth rate in V2 has been between minus 8.4 percent to a high of 4.9 percent from one year to the next. Monetarists argue that this amount of shortrun variability of velocity is consistent with their view that velocity is relatively stable. However, Keynesians point out that in a year such as 1982, the growth rate of nominal GDP was 8.9 percent and the money supply, measured using M1, grew by only 0.8 percent. In terms of the equation of exchange $M \times V = P \times Q$ this means that almost ninety percent of the change in nominal GDP for that year must be accounted for by changes in velocity.

A Constant Money Growth Rate

Monetarists believe that there is a fairly stable relationship between the money supply and money GDP—in other words, a fairly stable *V*. *Monetarists do not, however, advocate attempts to offset recession and curb excessive economic expansion by alternately expanding and contracting the money supply.* They generally argue that such a discretionary monetary policy is more likely to aggravate economic fluctuations than to minimize them.

Time Lags in Monetary Policy

Monetarists contend that changes in the money supply affect the level of economic activity over a long and variable period of time. A change in the money supply will definitely affect the level of money GDP, but there is a time lag between the point when the money supply change occurs and the point when its effect on money GDP is fully realized. Moreover, monetarists claim that the length of this time lag is quite variable and difficult to predict. Research by the foremost monetarist, Milton Friedman, suggests that the length of this time lag may vary anywhere from roughly half a year to two and a half years. As a result, monetarists argue that it is almost impossible for policymakers to schedule expansions or contractions in the money supply so that they will have their impact on the economy at the desired time. An expansion of the money supply intended to offset a recession, may have its greatest impact a year or more down the road, after the economy has recovered and is already expanding. Hence, the money supply increase may end up adding fuel to a potentially inflationary situation rather than offsetting recession. Similarly, a contraction of the money supply intended to curb an overheated economy may end up having its greatest impact after the economy has already begun to slow down. As a result, the money supply contraction may actually contribute to an ensuing recession.

Most monetarists contend that the historical record in the United States and elsewhere suggests that discretionary monetary policy has in fact tended to destabilize rather than stabilize the economy. Therefore, monetarists claim that monetary policy mismanagement must bear some of the blame for economic instability.

Rules versus Discretion

What is the gist of the monetarist contentions? Some prominent monetarists argue that the most appropriate monetary policy is to avoid discretionary decisions to expand or contract the rate of growth of the money supply. Instead, they recommend *a constant money growth rate rule*, whereby the central bank concentrates on expanding the money supply at a constant rate, year in and year out. Monetarists argue that this will automatically tend to smooth out the business cycle. When the economy's rate of growth (the growth rate of money GDP) falls below the constant money supply growth rate, during a recession, the continually increasing money supply will automatically provide a stimulus to get the economy going again. When the economy's growth rate rises above this rate, during a boom, the slower growing money supply will automatically put a curb on the excessive economic expansion.

> **Checkpoint 30-2**
>
> What is the main distinction between the equation of exchange viewed as a definition and as a theory?

New Classical View on Monetary Policy

We have already examined the new classical view on the effectiveness of monetary policy in our discussion of the Phillips curve in Chapter 26. (You may want to reread the section titled "The New Classical View" in that chapter.) Here we briefly review that discussion merely to relate the new classical view to the debate over whether monetary policy should be discretionary, as Keynesians contend, or based on rules, as monetarists argue.

Recall that the new classical view is based on the theory of rational expectations, which holds that people form their expectations about the future course of economic activity on the basis of all relevant economic knowledge, experience, and data, and in such a way that they do not make repeated, or systematic, mistakes. In particular, people know that the economy's inflation rate will increase whenever the Bank of Canada expands the money supply in an attempt to reduce the unemployment rate below the natural rate. They immediately expect the higher inflation rate (a rise in the economy's price level) and immediately push up their money wage to maintain the level of their real wages (equal to the money wage divided by the price level). Hence, the increase in aggregate demand caused by the monetary expansion will not increase firms' profits because the increase in the price level will be offset immediately by increases in money wages. Consequently, firms will have no incentive to increase employment and output, and there will be no reduction in the economy's unemployment rate below the natural rate. The Bank of Canada's decision to increase the money supply for the purpose of increasing output and employment is translated entirely into inflation rather than into desired increases in output and employment. Acting on the expected effects of a monetary expansion, people take actions that nullify the policy's goal and result in an undesirable increase in inflation. Therefore, the new classical view shares the monetarist view that the economy is better off if monetary policy follows a constant money growth rate rule rather than following a policy of making discretionary changes in the money growth rate as Keynesians suggest.

Views Compared

Though the new classical and monetarist views both favour policy rules over discretionary actions, the reasons are quite different. The new classical view holds that discretionary policy is ineffective because of the reaction of people to its expected effects, a reaction claimed possible because people have all relevant knowledge about policy decisions and their impacts. Monetarists argue that discretionary policy doesn't work because monetary policy actions affect the economy with variable and largely unpredictable time lags. This, coupled with the general difficulty of forecasting economic activity, makes it hard for policymakers to time decisions properly. Both views, it should be noted, are consistent with the conservative philosophy that government attempts to improve the economy typically fail and cause problems unintended by policymakers. In our example of a monetary expansion intended to reduce unemployment, the ultimate result is an unintended increase in inflation.

Criticisms

The new classical view on the ineffectiveness of discretionary monetary policy is, of course, subject to all of the criticisms already pointed out in Chapter 26.

POLICY PERSPECTIVE

Canada's Brief Adoption of Monetary Gradualism 1975–1982

The monetarist idea of adopting a constant growth rate for the money supply as measured by M1 was accepted by the Bank of Canada between September 1975 and November 1982. The Bank abandoned its previous policy of controlling the nominal interest rate. The Bank set a target range for the growth of the narrow definition of the monetary base (M1) and managed to achieve this reasonably well (Figure P30-1). The policy was involved in controversy, as monetary theorists argued that structural changes in the financial markets and other considerations made M1 a poor instrument for controlling the growth of the money supply. These critics argued that the Bank of Canada should adopt M2 or M3 as the policy tool. In addition, they pointed out that the Bank should not concern itself with changes in short-term interest rates because attempting to influence short-term interest rates was inconsistent with the practice of monetarism. As explained in the chapter, monetarism claims that short-term interest rates will fluctuate over the phases of the business cycle in response to cyclical changes in the demand for money resulting from changes in aggregate income. The critics also claimed that in the theory of monetarism, attempting to influence short-term interest rates was inconsistent with the general perspective of monetarism, which views the linkages between monetary policy and income

as being complex and characterized by lagged responses of indefinite length.

THE SWITCH TO CONTROLLING MONEY GROWTH

In mid-1975, after experiencing a rapid rise in the rate of inflation (measured by the percentage change in the consumer price index) and a rapid growth in the money supply (see Figure P30-1), the Bank of Canada announced that henceforth it would concentrate much more on hitting its money growth targets and much less on controlling interest rates. The Governor of the Bank of Canada, Gerald Bouey, said from the outset that the bank would not be purely monetarist in its approach but would take other factors such as the interest rates into account when deciding how tightly to control money growth. Nonetheless, from mid-1975 until mid-1982, the Bank made its most determined effort to follow monetarist prescriptions by trying to cut back the growth rate of the money supply (see Figure P30-1).

The Liberal Government of Pierre Elliot Trudeau, the Conservative Government of Joseph Clark, and a subsequent government under Trudeau all seemed preoccupied with patriating the Canadian Constitution and with the economic effects of the two energy crises of 1973 and 1979, as well

as subsequent problems surrounding the National Energy Program. These three governments did, however, provide general support for the Bank's policy of reducing inflation by slowing the growth of the money supply. All three governments also increased the rate of increase on the government deficit in real terms during their respective terms of administration and so can be viewed as generally following an expansionary fiscal stance. It was argued that these expanded deficits enabled the economy to avoid high unemployment at the same time that inflation was declining.

WHAT HAPPENED

The government deficits increased and became structural deficits (see Chapter 25) beginning in 1975, while the Bank slowed the growth of the money supply with a vengeance during the latter part of 1975 and into 1976 (see Figure P30-1). Inflation declined gradually until 1978 and then increased slightly in 1979. At the end of 1979 the second energy crisis caused inflation to increase to double-digit levels, where it remained until 1984 (see Figure P30-1). Unemployment increased from 6.9 percent to 7.5 percent between 1975 and 1982, when it soared to almost 12 percent as the economy plunged into a deep recession (Figures P30-1 and

continued on next page

POLICY PERSPECTIVE CONTINUED

P30-2). Some economists warned of a possible depression. The supply-side contention that inflation would be cured painlessly without the throes of a recession was not accurate. Most economists said the main reason for the rapid rise in Canada's unemployment was due to the adoption of a monetarist stance by the Federal Reserve Board in the United States, which resulted in a dramatic slowing of the money growth in Canada's biggest foreign market, sending interest rates and unemployment soaring in the United States.

By July of 1982 the Federal Reserve Board in the United States, alarmed by the severity of the recession and under increasing pressure from Congress, wanted to give the economy more breathing room. The Bank of Canada,

similarly alarmed by the rise in unemployment in Canada and with little threat of increased inflation because of a sagging economy, adopted a policy of increasing the money supply to correct the downturn. Gerald Bouey announced that because of institutional factors and the changing nature of credit markets it was increasingly difficult to target the growth of M1 accurately. Henceforth the Bank would suspend its policy of focusing so heavily on controlling money supply growth, and adopt a broader, more flexible approach. The Bank eased credit and suspended pursuit of its money growth rate targets for the second half of 1982. Since then it has based its actions on a variety of factors, including interest rates, the behaviour of prices, the exchange rate

between the Canadian dollar and the American dollar, and economic growth.

AN ASSESSMENT OF THE MONETARIST EXPERIMENT

The Bank's policy during the 1975–1982 period helped bring about a reduction in the annual rate of inflation, from 10.9 percent in 1974 to 9.2 percent by 1979. The rate of inflation increased between 1979 and 1981, moving into the 12.5 percent range as the Bank let the money supply growth rate fluctuate between 11.3 and 6.1 percent. In late 1981 and into 1982, the Bank of Canada severely restricted the money supply, making M1 grow only 0.8 percent for 1982. At the same time, the American Federal

continued on next page

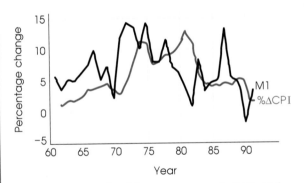

FIGURE P30-1   **Money Growth Rate and Inflation in Canada**

Percentage growth of the money supply (M1) and consumer prices (CPI). Before 1975, the trend of money supply increases and inflation was steadily upward. Under Governor Gerald Bouey, the Bank of Canada adopted the monetarist goal of slowing money growth, and inflation fell. But M1 growth became more erratic, not smoother as the monetarists wanted.

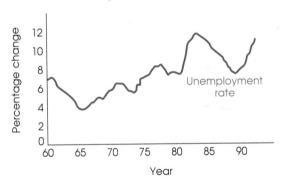

FIGURE P30-2   **The Unemployment Rate Surged**

Unemployment as a percentage of the labour force.

Reserve System adopted a policy similar to the Bank of Canada's for reducing money supply growth rates. The result was that the rate of increase in the consumer price index tumbled rapidly in Canada, from 10.8 percent in 1981 to 5.3 percent in 1983, and unemployment soared from 7.5 percent in 1981 to 11.8 percent in 1983 (see Figure P30-2). The growth rates of M1 and M2 became more erratic (see Figure P30-1 and Figure P30-4), not slow and steady as monetarists advocated.

Monetarists contend that the volatility of money growth means that monetarism was never really followed. Anna Schwartz, who collaborated with Milton Friedman in research on the relation between money supply movements and the economy, believes the Federal Reserve Board in the United States espoused monetarist principles as a smokescreen for raising interest rates (see Figure P30-3). Erratic behaviour in Canada's growth rates in the money supply have brought forth similar arguments by Tom Courchene and David Laidler in Canada (Figure P30-4). Many advocates of monetarism have claimed that erratic growth of the money supply reveals that monetarism's prescription for slow but steady money supply growth was never seriously adopted and claim that high interest rates are unfairly attributed to monetarism.

WHAT HAS MONETARISM ACCOMPLISHED?

The cause of monetarism has not always been served well even by its truest believers. In late 1983 Milton Friedman predicted a recession for the first half of 1984 and a resurgence of inflation by the second half. The sharp slowdown in M1 growth in the United States in late 1983 was the basis for the recession forecast. And he said inflation would surge because of the rapid growth of the money supply from mid-1982 to mid-1983. He was wrong. The economy experienced a strong expansion in the first half, and there was no major resurgence of inflation in the second half.

Monetarism's clout has declined in the United States and elsewhere since 1979. Overall, however, many economists contend that in future years inflation rates are likely to be lower than they would have been before monetarism focused so much attention on the importance of controlling money supply growth.

For Discussion

- Monetarists argue for slow and steady growth in the money supply because they claim no one understands the economy well enough to adjust the rate of money growth appropriately for any given time. Given this assertion, it could be said that it was inconsistent for Milton Friedman to predict the course of the economy in 1984 on the basis of the behaviour of money growth in 1982. Why?
- What evidence do you see in Figure P30-3 that the Bank of Canada relaxed its focus on controlling money supply growth and "broadened" its focus to include other factors?

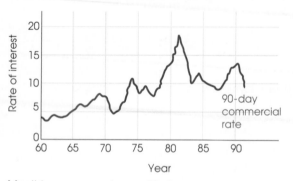

FIGURE P30-3   Interest Rates Jumped

Monthly average rates on 90-day commercial rates.

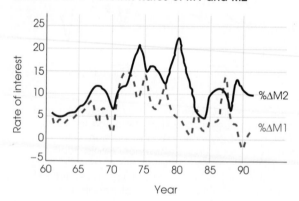

FIGURE P30-4   Growth Rates of M1 and M2

Growth rates of M1 and M2.

The theory of rational expectations assumes that expectations are formed on the basis of what people have learned about the economy through experience and information gathering. We noted in Chapter 26 that many characteristics of the economy are subject to continual change and that learning about change is subject to lags. Policymakers come and go, making it difficult to know exactly just what current "systematic" policy action is. These considerations suggest that people cannot react to the expected consequences of a monetary policy action to *completely* nullify any impact on the economy's real variables (such as real GDP and employment). We also noted in Chapter 26 that the new classical view's policy ineffectiveness argument implicitly assumes that prices and money wages are perfectly flexible. But buyers and sellers often have contracts fixing the price of a good or service over some period of time. Union contracts, rental agreements, and promises to deliver goods at a certain price in the future are but a few examples. The lack of perfect price and wage flexibility is another reason why people cannot instantly react to the expected impact of a monetary policy action to completely nullify any effect on the economy's real variables.

What is "new" about the new classical view as compared to the "old" classical view (Chapter 21) is the emphasis on the role of expectations. Both the new and the old classical views assume wage and price flexibility and that markets adjust quickly and completely. It is not surprising that critics put the same question to the new classical view as to the old. How does an advocate of such a view explain the Great Depression of the 1930s or the persistently high unemployment rates of the 1980s and the early 1990s?

> **Checkpoint 30-3**
>
> What is the shape of the aggregate supply curve in the new classical view? Why?

Summary

1. Businesses will invest in those capital goods having an expected rate of return greater than the interest rate. By this criterion, the lower is the interest rate, the larger is the amount of investment spending that is profitable. Hence, the marginal efficiency of investment curve slopes downward to the right because more investment spending will take place at low than at high interest rates.

2. According to the Keynesian view the money market is linked to the level of investment spending by the interest rate. The level of investment spending determines the level of the aggregate expenditure schedule and hence the level of real GDP. The level of real GDP in turn determines the position of the demand curve for money in the money market.

3. An increase in the money supply lowers the interest rate. According to the Keynesian view this increases investment spending, which pushes up the aggregate expenditure schedule, raising the level of real GDP. The rise in real GDP pushes the demand curve for money to the right, causing the interest rate to rise, though not enough to offset the full effects of the initial decrease in the interest rate. A partial equilibrium analysis would ignore the effect on the demand curve for money resulting from the rise in real GDP.

4. According to the Keynesian view, increasing the money supply lowers the interest rate and raises the real GDP level; this is often referred to as an easy money policy. Decreasing the money supply raises the interest rate and lowers the real GDP level; this is often called a tight money policy.

5. An increase in the money supply causes the aggregate demand curve *AD* to shift rightward, while a decrease in the money supply causes it to shift leftward. The aggregate demand curve *AD* and the aggregate supply curve *AS* determine the price level.

6. Keynesians tend to favour government intervention in the economy because they see shortcomings in the way the market system answers the economic questions of what, how, and for whom to produce. They are also doubtful that markets have the self-regulating ability to ensure economic stability and full employment without the aid of an active fiscal policy and monetary policy. Monetarists tend to see government intervention as an unnecessary and harmful interference with the market system, a threat to individual freedom, and a damper on individual initiative.

7. The equation of exchange, $M \times V = P \times Q$, is a definitional relationship between the economy's money stock M and the economy's total money income, or money GDP, which is equal to the price level P times the quantity of real output Q. V is the velocity of circulation of money. When V is regarded as stable, a reflection of institutional and behavioural characteristics of the economy, the equation of exchange becomes the expression for the quantity theory of money.

8. Monetarism may be regarded as a sophisticated version of the quantity theory of money. Monetarists argue that the cause and effect transmission from changes in the money supply to changes in money GDP is reasonably direct and tight. They argue that the effects of a money supply change are transmitted through a host of channels, not just the interest rate channel so strongly emphasized by the Keynesian view. While monetarists regard velocity as stable, Keynesians believe the velocity of money is unstable.

9. Keynesians favour discretionary monetary policy. Monetarists argue that such a policy is likely to aggravate the business cycle rather than diminish it. Therefore, some prominent monetarists argue for a constant money growth rate rule.

10. The new classical view, based on the theory of rational expectations, argues that systematic monetary policy is not able to affect the economy's real variables because people react to the expected effects of the policy, nullifying its intentions. The new classical view therefore favours policy rules over discretionary policy.

Key Terms and Concepts

equation of exchange	marginal efficiency of	monetary rule
expected rate	investment curve	partial equilibrium
of return	monetarism	analysis
general equilibrium	monetary	quantity theory of money
analysis	gradualism	velocity of circulation

Questions and Problems

1. Using a partial equilibrium analysis, start with the initial equilibrium position in Figure 30-2 (money supply M_0 equal to $30 billion) and trace through the likely effects of

each of the following (indicate the direction of changes where it is not possible to measure the precise magnitudes of changes):

a. The Bank of Canada increases the bank rate.

b. The government reduces the required reserve ratio.

c. The Bank of Canada makes an open market sale of bonds.

d. The Bank of Canada reduces the money supply by $5 billion.

e. The Bank of Canada switches $5 billion of Government of Canada deposits into chartered banks.

2. How would your answers to question 1 be affected if full adjustment in all markets is taken into account? That is, how would the answers in each case be different if a general equilibrium analysis were carried out instead of a partial equilibrium analysis?

3. In Figure 30-2, how would the slopes of the demand curve for money L_0 and the marginal efficiency of investment curve *MEI* have to be different for the $20 billion increase in the money supply to have a larger impact on real GDP? What implications do the slopes of the money demand and marginal efficiency of investment curves have for the effectiveness of monetary policy?

4. Link up the analysis in Figure 30-2 with the analysis in Figure 30-4, and describe how monetary policy affects the level of real GDP and the price level P. Do the same thing using Figure 30-3 and explain how the effect on real GDP and the price level would be different.

5. Suppose that the Bank of Canada is prone to making mistakes in its exercise of discretionary monetary policy. According to which view, Keynesian or monetarist, would the resulting fluctuations in money GDP be the greatest? Why? What bearing does this have on the Keynesian view versus the monetarist view about discretionary monetary policy?

6. Assume that the Bank of Canada decides to implement monetary policy by always keeping the interest rate at the same target level. For instance, if the interest rate falls below the target level, the Bank of Canada conducts open market sales to push it back up, while if the interest rate rises above the target level, the Bank of Canada conducts open market purchases to push it back down. Suppose that there are autonomous changes in spending, reflected in shifts in the aggregate expenditure schedule. Do you think the Bank of Canada's constant interest rate policy would tend to stabilize or destabilize the economy? Why?

7. What problems does discretionary monetary policy share with discretionary fiscal policy? (Recall the discussion of discretionary fiscal policy in Chapter 24.) In what ways would the exercise of discretionary monetary policy differ from the exercise of discretionary fiscal policy?

8. Explain the role of rational expectations theory in the new classical view that discretionary monetary policy is ineffective. Compare and contrast the arguments put forward by monetarists and the new classical view for favouring policy rules over policy discretion.

PART
EIGHT

Macroeconomic Policy Issues and Economic Growth

Chapter 31

Monetary and Fiscal Policies and Budget Deficits

On Monday, October 19, 1987, the United States and other Western economies witnessed a traumatic event that was beyond living experience for all but those who remembered 1929. The stock markets of New York, London, and Tokyo experienced drastic declines for a week, and at the end of the week the New York market collapsed. The Dow Jones average of 30 industrial stocks fell 508 points, and financial wealth on the order of $500 billion was extinguished in a single day of trading on that Monday and finished the week down 13 percent. In Tokyo, the Nikkei index declined only 2.34 percent on October 19 because of the time difference from New York, but decreased the following Tuesday and finished the week down 14.9 percent. London's FT-SE100 index dropped 10.84 percent on October 19. In Canada the TSE Composite Index, the index of equities traded on the Toronto Stock Exchange lost 407.2 points, dropping 11.3 percent on the Monday, and finished the week down 25 percent! A similar but less dramatic 9.5 percent drop was recorded on the Montreal Stock Exchange. Just as in the aftermath of the 1929 crash, market analysts and media commentators searched for an explanation. Some blamed these events on the international community's loss of confidence in the fiscal and monetary policies of the United States and on growing concern over the mounting trade deficit of the United States.

In this chapter we will first focus on why there are differing opinions on the effectiveness of fiscal policy. Then we will examine why fiscal actions that cause government budget deficits have monetary implications that make it difficult to distinguish purely fiscal from purely monetary effects. We will also examine why it is difficult in practice to coordinate monetary and fiscal policy to smooth out economic fluctuations and prod the economy closer to full employment without excessive inflation. We will then see how budget deficits can give rise to conflicts between monetary and fiscal policy.

Fiscal Policy: How Effective Is It?

The public is probably more familiar with fiscal policy than monetary policy because of the endless political arguments between the opposition parties and the government of the day over taxation, spending, and budget deficits. However, the effect of fiscal policy on economic activity and the monetary aspects of fiscal policy are a mystery to most citizens.

Why are there differing opinions about the extent to which fiscal policy can affect economic activity? How can fiscal policies that cause deficits have monetary effects? Are fiscal and monetary policies well coordinated or do they frequently work at cross-purposes with each other? Let's now consider each of these questions.

Pure Fiscal Policy and Crowding Out

The basic differences of opinion among most economists regarding the effectiveness of fiscal policy are perhaps best illustrated in terms of pure fiscal policy.[1] **Pure fiscal policy** *consists of changes in government expenditure, taxation, transfers, or all three that do not change the money supply.*

Most economists agree that an increase in government expenditure leads to some crowding out of other forms of aggregate expenditure, particularly investment spending. **Crowding out** *is the reduction in one or more of the components of aggregate expenditure as an indirect response to the increase in some other element of aggregate expenditure.* Hence, crowding out by fiscal policy occurs if any ex-

---

LEARNING OBJECTIVES

After reading this chapter, you will be able to:

1. Explain why there can be differing opinions about the extent to which fiscal policy actions affect real GDP and the price level.
2. Explain the different effects on the economy of pure fiscal policy actions as distinguished from those accomplished by money supply changes.
3. Explain why it is often difficult to coordinate monetary and fiscal policies.
4. Describe how monetary policy and government deficits can combine to give the economy an inflationary bias.
5. Describe the difference between the nominal interest rate and the real interest rate and explain how this difference complicates the conduct of monetary and fiscal policy.
6. Describe the crowding-out effect that expansionary fiscal policy has on the economy.

---

[1]Of course, strict proponents of the new classical view argue that fiscal policy is completely ineffective for reasons we examined in Chapter 26. This is not a view held by most economists.

pansionary effect on aggregate demand caused by an increase in government spending is offset to some extent by an accompanying decline in one or more of the other components of aggregate expenditure. Much disagreement exists among economists over the magnitude of this crowding-out effect. Two groups of economists, usually referred to as the *monetarist school* and the *new classical school*, have developed theoretical reasons for concluding that crowding out is almost complete. By contrast two groups identified as *Keynesians* and *New Keynesians* both claim that crowding-out effects are usually very small.

Why There Is Crowding Out

What is the explanation for the crowding-out effect and the differences in opinion regarding its size? In an open economy such as Canada's the answer hinges on two things. Any expansionary fiscal policy (increasing government expenditure for goods and services, increased transfers, or decreasing taxes) causes a rise in aggregate income. This in turn increases money demand, which leads to an increase in the interest rate. As we observed in Chapter 22, increases in interest rates result in reductions in investment spending. In addition, as we will study in Chapter 34, when the interest rate increases there is a tendency for foreign economies to try to increase their lending activity in Canada. This increase in foreign money trying to enter Canada will tend to increase the value of the Canadian dollar on international markets. The exact mechanics of why increased foreign funds flowing into our country increase the external value of our currency can wait until Chapter 34. For now we need to recognize that if the Canadian dollar increases in value relative to the currencies of other countries throughout the world, our exports will decrease and our imports from foreign economies will increase. Thus, an expansionary fiscal policy increases the interest rate, which causes a reduction in private investment and net export earnings.

Recall that increases in the economy's aggregate income cause the money demand curve to shift rightward, as illustrated in Figure 28-2. Consider now Figure 31-1, which portrays the two opposing views of the extent of crowding out. The top half of the figure, the A-view, captures the essence of the the Keynesian and New Keynesian views; by contrast the lower half, the B-view, illustrates the monetarist and new classical interpretation. The A-view portrays the money demand curve L_1 as less steeply sloped than the money demand curve L_2 in the B-view. The A-view portrays the investment demand curve I_1 as more steeply sloped than the investment demand curve I_2 in the B-view. Those who believe the slopes of these curves are in reality more like the A-view will have a different opinion about the size of the crowding-out effect than those who believe the B-view. Let's see why.

Interest Rate Crowding Out of Investment

For a *given* increase in aggregate income, there will be a certain amount of rightward shift in the money demand curve as shown in Figure 31-1. L_1 shifts to L_1' (A-view), and L_2 shifts to L_2' (B-view). The amount of this shift, equal to the distance between a and b, is of course the same in both cases, because both shifts are caused by the same given increase in aggregate income. Note,

FIGURE 31-1   **Different Views of the Effects of an Increase in Aggregate Income on Investment**

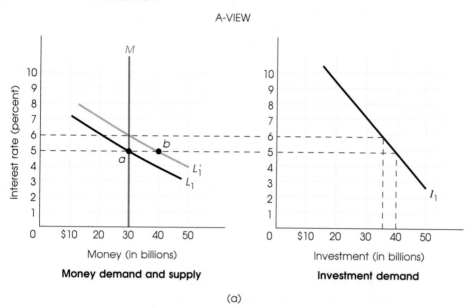

(a)

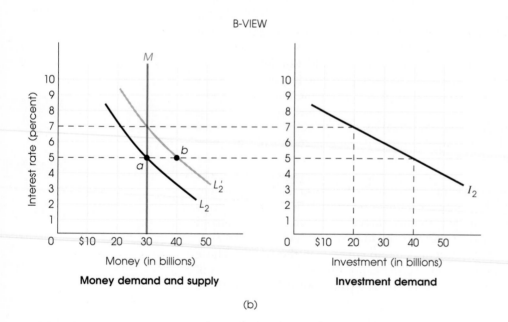

(b)

A given increase in aggregate income will shift the demand for money to the right, from L_1 to L_1' in A-view and from L_2 to L_2' in B-view. At the initial equilibrium interest rate of 5 percent, the amount of this rightward shift equals the distance from a to b. The demand curve for money is more steeply sloped in the B-view than in the A-view. Therefore, the interest rate rises further in the B-view (from 5 percent to 7 percent) than in the A-view (from 5 to 6 percent). Combined with the fact that marginal efficiency of investment curve I_2 is less steeply sloped than MEI, this means that investment spending is reduced more in the B-view than in the A-view.

however, that in the B-view the resulting rise in the interest rate is larger (from 5 to 7 percent) than in the A-view (from 5 to 6 percent). The larger rise in the interest rate, combined with the fact that I_2 has a flatter slope than I_1, results in a larger reduction in investment spending, or more crowding out of investment, in the B-view than in the A-view.

Interest Rate Crowding Out of Net Exports

Similarly any *given* increase in Canadian interest rates will put pressure on the Canadian dollar to increase in value relative to other currencies (such as the yen or the American dollar), which will cause Canadian net exports to decline. An increase in Canadian interest rates will cause the aggregate expenditure curve to shift downward by the amount of the decrease in net exports. The A-view argues that the money flows between Canada and the rest of the world are not particularly sensitive to any *given* increase in interest rates in Canada. Therefore, the A-view is that a *given* rise in the interest rate in Canada will cause a relatively small decrease in net exports and consequently only a small amount of export crowding out. The B-view is that money flows between Canada and the rest of the world are fairly sensitive to any change in Canadian interest rates, and therefore a *given* increase in Canadian interest rates will cause a large crowding out of net export demand.

Graphing the Crowding-Out Effect

Figure 31-2 shows how crowding out affects the AD curve and hence both the price level and real GDP. Suppose that the economy's AD curve is initially AD_1 so that the price level is p_1 and the equilibrium level of real GDP is GDP_0 as shown in both frames (a) and (b). Now suppose that there is an increase in government

---

FIGURE 31-2 The Crowding-Out Effect on Aggregate Demand

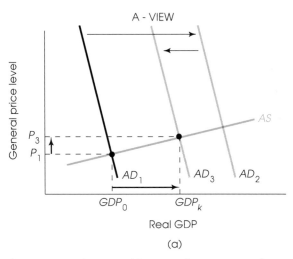

(a)

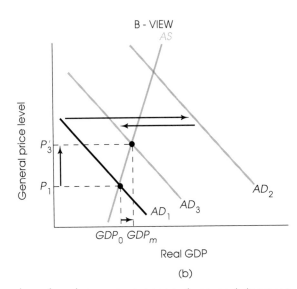

(b)

An exogenously caused increase in government spending on goods and services or an exogenously caused decrease in taxes causes less crowding out of investment spending and therefore gives rise to a larger rightward shift of the AD curve according to the A-view than according to the B-view. In addition, the A-view holds that the AS curve is fairly horizontal and consequently, when the AD curve shifts to the right it causes a relatively large increase in GDP and a fairly small increase in the general price level. By contrast, the B-view holds that the AS curve is fairly steep. In the B-view a shift right in the AD curve results in a relatively small increase in GDP and a large increase in the general price level. The B-view also holds that the longer the adjustment period the steeper the AS curve becomes, so in the longrun the overall effect of any shift to the right in the AD curve is a rise in the price level with no increase in GDP. Consequently, the A-view holds that pure fiscal policy actions cause larger changes in GDP and the general price level than is the case according to the B-view.

spending. This will shift the *AD* curve rightward, as was discussed in Chapters 24 and 26. If we momentarily ignore the effects of the resulting rise in aggregate income on money demand, the economy's *AD* curve is shifted rightward to AD_2, frames (a) and (b) of Figure 31-2. However, if we allow for the effects of the rise in aggregate income on money demand, the interest rate, investment spending, and net exports, the *AD* curve cannot shift to the position AD_2 in Figure 31-2. Why? Because the effect of the rise in government spending will be offset in part by the reduction, or crowding out, of investment and exports that results from the rise in the interest rate. According to the A-view, the crowding out of investment and exports is less than the increase in government spending, so the *AD* curve is shifted to AD_3, frame (a) of Figure 31-2, along an *AS* curve with a shallow slope and the price level rises from p_1 to p_3 as real GDP increases from GDP_0 to GDP_k. According to the B-view, frame (b) of Figure 31-2, the crowding out of investment and exports will be larger, so the *AD* curve will only shift to AD_3 along a fairly steep *AS* curve with the price level and real GDP rising by smaller amounts—from p_1 to p_3' and from GDP_0 to GDP_m, respectively.

Crowding Out and Taxation

Our illustration of the crowding-out effect has assumed that the fiscal action taken was an increase in government spending. But a tax reduction also shifts the *AD* curve rightward, as we saw in Chapters 24 and 26, and results in the same type of crowding-out effect.

In summary, there are varying views on how much fiscal policy affects the economy, ranging from those who believe fiscal policy actions have very little effect on real GDP, the price level, and employment because of the offsetting crowding-out effect, to those who hold that fiscal policy has a sizable effect because the offsetting crowding-out effect is not that significant. In addition, a strict advocate of the new classical view would argue that fiscal policy has no effect at all (as discussed in Chapters 26 and 30). But while a number of economists may agree that this might be a problem in the *longrun*, not many economists accept this view for the *shortrun* behaviour of the economy.

Fiscal and Monetary Effects Combined; Financing Budget Deficits

Fiscal policy has monetary effects whenever a fiscal action is accompanied by a change in the money supply. This may happen whenever a change in government expenditure, transfers, or taxation, or any combination of these, gives rise to a government budget deficit or surplus.

Financing Budget Deficits Without a Money Supply Change

Recall our discussion of the financing of government budget deficits in Chapter 25. There we noted that whenever government expenditure exceeds tax revenues, the government must finance the difference by issuing government bonds. If the public (businesses, individuals, and private institutions) buys the bonds, then they typically write cheques against their demand deposits or other chequable deposits. These cheques are made payable to the Receiver General of Canada for the amount of government bonds purchased. The government then spends this money, putting it right back into the hands of the public. There is no change in the supply of money in the economy when the government deficit is financed in this fashion. Hence, the only question is how much the expansionary effect of an increase in government expenditure, an increase in transfers, a decrease in taxes, or any combination of these is offset by the crowding-out effect—the same issue we discussed in connection with Figures 31-1 and 31-2.

Financing Budget Deficits with a Money Supply Increase—Monetizing the Government Debt

In Chapter 25 we observed that if the government chooses not to finance its deficit by selling bonds to the public, it can get the Bank of Canada to "print the money" it needs. This is referred to as either **monetary accommodation** or *monetizing the government debt*. Now that we've seen how the Bank of Canada can create money (Chapters 27, 28, and 29), we can see exactly how this is done.

Monetizing Government Debt

The Bank of Canada acts as the fiscal agent for the government and as the controller of the money supply. Rather than sell the deficit-financing government bonds to the public, suppose that the Department of Finance simply sells them directly to the Bank of Canada. How can the Bank pay for the bonds? Since the Bank of Canada is the government's banker, suppose that it simply credits or adds to the government's account at the Bank (the government's chequing account) the amount of funds necessary to cover the purchase of the bonds from the government. Then the government writes cheques against this account when it purchases goods and services in the economy. The cheque recipients, who provide the goods and services, deposit the cheques in their banks, and the economy's money supply is increased. In short, one arm of the government, the Bank of Canada, creates money for another arm of the government, the Treasury. When the government spends this money, it increases the entire economy's money supply.

It may have struck you that this process is very similar to what happens when the Bank of Canada makes an open market purchase of government bonds. The major difference is that in our example the Bank buys the bonds directly from the Treasury rather than from the public to finance the government deficit. In essence the government deficit is financed by the Bank of Canada's creation of extra money. *When the Bank of Canada finances the government deficit directly by increasing the money supply, it is* **monetizing the government debt**. It is turning newly issued government bonds directly into newly created money. Simply put, the Bank of Canada is "printing money." The Bank may purchase the new issue of government bonds equal only to a portion of the bonds sold by the Treasury to finance the budget deficit. In that case, only that portion of the deficit spending is financed by creating money.

When deficit spending is financed by monetizing the government debt, the money supply is increased. We know that such an increase will cause a rightward

Checkpoint* 31-1

According to a news item, the provincial premiers issue a communiqué stating that they would like the Bank of Canada to take action to lower the interest rate. But the Bank of Canada seems concerned about fighting inflation, and the staff of the bank is also concerned that the fiscal policy of the government is not helping in this fight. Describe the probable nature of the conflict in terms of Figures 31-1 and 31-2, and show why the interest rate is being driven up. Suppose that the Bank of Canada accedes to the wishes of the first ministers. What could it do to lower the interest rate? What would be the consequences of this action for inflation? Describe your answer in terms of Figures 31-1 and 31-2. Also, in terms of these figures, describe how greater discipline on fiscal policy would put less pressure on monetary policy.

*Answers to all Checkpoints can be found at the back of the text.

POLICY PERSPECTIVE

The Politics of Coordinating Fiscal and Monetary Policies

In principle, the goals of monetary and fiscal policy are the same, to smooth out economic fluctuations, to promote full employment, and to curb inflation. Those who advocate the use of discretionary, or activist, policies would argue that policymakers should coordinate monetary and fiscal actions to achieve these ends. For example, during a recession, appropriate fiscal policy should give rise to an increase in the government deficit, while appropriate monetary policy should increase the rate of expansion of the money supply. On the other hand, if the economy is operating at close to full employment and inflationary pressures are increasing, prudent fiscal policy should generate a budget surplus, or at least a decrease in the government deficit, and monetary policy should reduce the rate of expansion of the money supply. In practice, monetary and fiscal policies are not so easily coordinated.

FISCAL POLICY AND THE POLITICAL PROCESS

A major reason coordination is difficult is that the size and timing of government expenditure and tax programs are influenced by considerations in addition to those of economic stabilization. Expenditure and tax programs are a product of the political processes of Parliament and reflect the objectives and priorities of many different special interest groups and regions of the country. There is often little regard for the fiscal policy implications of expenditure and tax programs conceived under these conditions.

A typical member of Parliament finds it difficult, if not politically untenable, to consider actions taken on behalf of constituents in terms of their impact on the overall government budget. Hypothetically, a member of Parliament from Alberta who believes the Canadian Forces no longer need the Canadian Forces Radar Station at Penhold, Alberta, and votes for closing it down risks defeat at the polls. It may be true that the base closings will help trim the federal government's budget deficit. But local voters will be more concerned about the adverse impact of the base closings on the local economy.

In our parliamentary system the Prime Minister must maintain the confidence of a majority of the members of Parliament in the House of Commons in order to retain his or her position as "first among equals" on the government benches. A Prime Minister wishing to avoid a recession by initiating a tax cut or a spending program may be stymied by members of his or her own party who are concerned about the impact that this program will have on their own constituencies. The majority of the members of the Prime Minister's own party caucus may not feel that any direct benefits from the government's proposed expansionary program will be felt in their particular ridings. They may be further concerned that the public is worried about the government appearing to be spending money it does not have and they may feel that the public is generally hostile to members of Parliament who vote for such measures. Even if the Prime Minister can maintain discipline within his or her own party, with the political risks which that implies for the party's members, he or she will still have to face the possibility that the opposition members will not support the measures. Traditionally, the opposition members do their utmost to embarrass the government over any weakness in its budget document in order to win voters away from the government. The government can withstand the vote of no confidence, assuming that the governing

continued on next page

shift in the economy's *AD* curve and a rise in real GDP and the price level. This shift is an addition to the rightward shift in the *AD* curve and the rise in the price level that results from the increase in government spending, reduction in taxes, or both. Because the Bank of Canada has created additional money to finance the government's deficit, the problem of crowding out through higher interest rates is avoided. This means that monetizing the government debt makes government deficits more expansionary than deficit spending financed only by selling bonds to the public.

POLICY PERSPECTIVE CONTINUED

party has a majority in the House of Commons, and further assuming that the government can maintain party discipline during the budget vote. It may, however, lose a lot of support at the grass roots level, which weakens its chance of winning another election. The problem becomes particularly acute if the government is in a minority position to start with. Governments in Canada have been defeated on a vote of no confidence stemming from the introduction of a new budget. The problem is just as likely to occur if the Prime Minister's agenda is to fight inflation and an overheated economy. While the idea of fighting inflation may be generally popular throughout the country, it is likely to meet with hostility from the voters if they believe that they will personally face higher taxes, reduced government services in their community, or loss of their own employment due to government spending restraint.

The question is not whether or not to have fiscal policy. Whenever decisions are made about government spending and taxation, for whatever reasons, the resulting government expenditure and tax actions unavoidably affect aggregate income, output, employment, and the level of prices. All such actions amount to a fiscal policy, even when they are taken primarily in pursuit of other objectives unrelated to maintaining economic stability, reasonably full employment, and a rein on inflation. A basic difficulty with fiscal policy as a stabilization tool is

that there are so many other objectives that often take precedence in the determination of government spending and tax policy. It is largely for this reason that fiscal policy often conflicts with monetary policy.

THE PROCESS OF MONETARY POLICY

Unlike fiscal policy, monetary policy is made by a relatively small group of people: the Executive Committee of the Bank of Canada, which is a body comprised of members appointed by the government for seven-year terms. Thus, this group does not depend on the votes of any specific constituency riding to hold office; it is not elected, so it is not directly accountable to the electorate for its actions. It formulates its monetary policy without the public debates and media attention that surround the introduction of the budget speech in Parliament.

While much of the preceding discussion indicates that the Bank of Canada may have a natural advantage over Parliament in the conduct of economic stabilization, the situation is not as simple as that for two main reasons. First, the Bank is responsible for several activities besides controlling the money supply to curb inflation or unemployment. As we noted in Chapters 27 and 29 the Bank of Canada is the fiscal agent for the Government of Canada. It must help arrange financing on the government debt and must try to prevent the sizable and sometimes untimely fiscal

needs of the government from disrupting the normal healthy workings of Canada's money market. Second, the Bank of Canada monitors the external value of the Canadian dollar. The value of Canada's money relative to other world currencies, particularly the American dollar, is vital to the health and stability of our exports to foreign markets. While Canada has officially had a flexible exchange rate system for many years, the Bank of Canada intervenes in the international money markets to prevent any sudden rise or fall in the value of the Canadian dollar relative to other currencies. These two circumstances mean that the Bank of Canada's monetary policy cannot always be devoted exclusively to controlling the growth of the money supply to create stability inside Canada.

In summary, compared to fiscal policy, the process of making and carrying out monetary policy is more organized. It is also easier for monetary policy to focus more continuously on the pursuit of economic stabilization goals because, compared to fiscal policy, it is relatively less hampered by other considerations and the more direct political pressures that often dominate parliament.

For Discussion

- Even if it were possible to coordinate monetary and fiscal policy *initiatives*, what other problems might cause the *results* of such efforts to be uncoordinated?

Monetary Policy and Government Deficits

In the Policy Perspective section of this chapter we provide a discussion of some of the difficulties of coordinating monetary and fiscal policies. We will now focus more specifically on the role that the interest rate plays in the conflict between government deficit financing and the objectives of monetary policy.

Autonomous increases in consumption, investment spending, and net exports, and increases in government spending, reductions in taxes, or both, cause the *AD* curve to shift rightward. However, the resulting rise in aggregate income, or money GDP, will lead to an increase in the demand for money. This in turn will cause the interest rate to rise. The result is a cutback in any portion of aggregate expenditure that is inversely related to the interest rate and most specifically investment spending. This reduction in aggregate expenditure tends to dampen the rise in aggregate demand, as was discussed in connection with Figures 31-1 and 31-2. The only way to avoid this interest rate rise is for the Bank of Canada to increase the money supply in order to accommodate the increased money demand. Of course, if the economy is already operating at or close to full employment, such a monetary expansion will result in a rise in the price level as the *AD* curve shifts rightward along the upward-sloping aggregate supply curve *AS*.

Interest Rate Stability and Deficit Spending

Over the years, critics of the Bank of Canada have claimed that it was overly concerned with maintaining interest rate stability. As a result, such critics alleged, the bank sometimes increased the money supply to keep the interest rate from rising when the rise itself was caused by an inflationary increase in aggregate demand. These critics argued that it would have been wiser for the Bank to refrain from increasing the money supply and allow the interest rate rise to check the expansion of aggregate demand, dampening inflationary pressures. Instead, when the Bank of Canada increased the money supply in such a situation, it added further fuel to the inflationary increase in aggregate demand. Critics went on to argue that these inflationary implications of the central bank's attempts to stabilize the interest rate were of even more concern in the presence of government deficit spending. Why?

Interest Rate and Aggregate Demand

Recall the discussion of government deficit spending. There we observed that a government deficit must be financed by issuing new government bonds. Recall that when these bonds are sold to the public, there is no change in the economy's money supply. The money that the public gives to the government in exchange for the new bonds is returned to the economy when the government spends it. This government spending shifts the *AD* curve rightward, increasing real GDP and the price level, and thus the demand for money. *The interest rate rises* and cuts back investment spending and net exports (the crowding-out effect), which tends to dampen the rightward shift in the *AD* curve.

However, if the Bank of Canada does not want the interest rate to rise, it must engage in open market purchases. That is, as soon as the interest rate begins to rise, the Bank will carry out open market purchases to keep it down. But this amounts to financing the government deficit by monetizing the government debt. The money supply is increased. Government deficit spending financed in this way causes the economy's *AD* curve to shift rightward, both because of the spending increase and because of the increase in the money supply. Clearly, if the Bank of Canada does not want the interest rate to rise, the curb on the rise in aggregate demand due to the crowding-out effect is absent and inflationary pressures are greater.

The Side Effects of Monetary Policy

In the 1960s and 1970s a complaint was often made that monetary policy had an inflationary bias. Although the federal government often ran surplus budgets in the 1950s and 1960s, its budgetary position moved into large and growing deficits by the mid-1970s, and there were no surpluses after that time. More alarming, however, was the behaviour of the cyclically adjusted budget, which economists generally regard as a more accurate measure of the expansionary impact of fiscal policy (see Chapter 25). In the mid-1970s a series of tax reforms, including reductions in the effective tax rate due to the indexation on personal taxes, and increased spending by the federal government, to share the cost of provincial spending in the health and education areas, changed this. Because of these and other institutionalized changes, the federal government ran cyclically adjusted budget deficits after 1975; fiscal policy was predominantly expansionary (see Figure 25-1). To the extent that the Bank tried to keep interest rates from rising in the 1970 to 1975 period, monetary policy contributed to the inflationary pressures that plagued the economy throughout the early 1970s by monetizing some of the government debt.

The Bank of Canada adopted a policy of monetary gradualism (see Chapter 30) between 1975 and 1982. Under this policy the Bank of Canada focused on controlling the growth rate of the money supply and gave up the strategy of holding nominal interest rates constant. This reduced the impact of any inflationary bias of the government's fiscal expansion. Some critics of the Bank of Canada's monetary policy have pointed out that in spite of the Bank's adoption of monetary gradualism, it failed to regulate the right monetary aggregate (M2) and concentrated instead on M1. For this reason, they say, inflation was not really brought down by the Bank of Canada until shortly after the Federal Reserve Board in the United States adopted a policy of concentrating on controlling money supply growth south of the border. The 1981–1982 recession occurred shortly after this policy change.

The Bank of Canada formally abandoned a strict adherence to controlling monetary growth rates in 1982, as did the Federal Reserve Board in the United States. In Canada the experience since 1984 has been somewhat more complex than it has been in the United States. While the Americans have tended to concentrate on controlling nominal interest rates, the Bank of Canada has used the interest rate as a policy tool to control the exchange rate on the Canadian dollar in international trading. If the Bank of Canada keeps Canadian interest rates high, this will cause money to flow into Canada from foreign capital markets. The result will be to put upward pressure on the value of the Canadian dollar in international markets (as we will see in Chapter 34). A high international value for the dollar is politically popular among Canadian consumers wanting to purchase foreign goods and services or wanting to make investments abroad. It also reinforces the Bank of Canada in its efforts to reduce inflation because the tight money policy that is used to help keep the value of the dollar high also helps to dampen inflation. Critics of the policy have pointed out that it is also a serious problem for Canadian exporters wishing to sell goods in foreign markets. The Bank's high interest rates have reduced investment, and the high value of the dollar has resulted in lost export sales. Both of these reductions cause lower aggregate expenditure and result in higher unemployment levels than if the Bank of Canada had set a lower interest rate.

Inflation and the Interest Rate; Real versus Nominal Interest Rates

There is another important consideration that bears on the issue of interest rate stability and monetary policy: the relationship between inflation and the interest rate. Whenever there is inflation, it is necessary to recognize the existence of two distinct measures of the interest rate: the *real* interest rate and the *nominal* interest rate.

The Real Interest Rate

The **real interest rate** *is the interest rate calculated in terms of its purchasing power over goods and services.* Suppose that I agree to lend you $100 for 1 year at an interest rate of 10 percent. At the end of 1 year you will pay me back the $100 plus $10, or $110. If there is *no change in the general price level* in the meantime, I give up $100 of purchasing power over goods today in exchange for $110 of purchasing power over goods a year from now. In 1 year I will get back 10 percent more purchasing power than I originally gave up. Hence, in this example the real interest rate equals 10 percent. The real interest rate is the rate that we would actually see in the market when the general price level is stable—that is, when there is no inflation (or deflation).

The Nominal Interest Rate

The **nominal interest rate** (sometimes called the *money interest rate* or *market interest rate*) *is the interest rate calculated in terms of units of money, without any adjustment for inflation.* In other words, the interest paid and recorded as a percentage return in the market does not make an adjustment for the loss in purchasing power over goods during a period of inflation. Only when the general price level is expected to be stable is it true that the nominal interest rate equals the real interest rate. This is so because under these circumstances the purchasing power of a unit of money remains unchanged. Whenever there is anticipated inflation (or deflation), the nominal interest rate and the real interest rate will differ from each other by the amount of the anticipated inflation (or deflation). This is so because when there is a change in the general price level, the purchasing power of a unit of money changes.

Anticipated Rate of Inflation

The anticipated rate of inflation is the difference between real and nominal interest rates. To illustrate the difference between the real interest rate and the nominal interest rate, consider our $100 loan example again. To be willing to lend you $100, I again insist on getting back 10 percent more purchasing power in 1 year than I originally gave up. But now suppose that both you and I *expect* a 5 percent rate of inflation. This means that we both expect the purchasing power of a unit of money, a dollar, to decline by 5 percent over the next year. Therefore, I must charge you an additional 5 percent on the $110 ($100 × 1.10) that you will owe me at the end of the year just to compensate myself for the anticipated loss in purchasing power on each unit of money owed to me. Hence, I lend you $100 at a money rate of interest of 15.5 percent. The 15.5 percent money rate of interest equals the 10 percent real rate of interest adjusted for the anticipated rate of inflation of 5 percent ($100 × 1.10 × 1.05 = $115.50). This additional 5.5 percent may be thought of as an inflation premium on the real rate of interest. You will be willing to pay the 15.5 percent money rate of interest to borrow the $100 from me. Why? Because you will recognize that you are going to pay me back dollars that have lost 5 percent of the purchasing power of the principal and a loss of 5 percent on the purchasing power of the interest owed to me, all because of inflation.

In short, the 15.5 percent money rate of interest means that I lend you $100 of money now, and in 1 year you repay me $115.50 of money. The 10 percent real rate of interest means that I lend you $100 of purchasing power *now*, and in 1 year you repay me the equivalent amount of purchasing power *plus* another 10 percent of purchasing power.

In summary:

$$i_{\text{nominal}} = [(1 + i_{\text{real}}) \times (1 + \text{expected inflation rate}) - 1]$$

Assume that the real interest rate is to be 10 percent and the expected inflation rate is 5 percent.

$$i_{\text{nominal}} = [(1.05) \times (1.10) - 1] = .155; \text{ or } 15.5\%$$

If the anticipated rate of inflation is zero, then the nominal interest rate and the real interest rate are the same. The nominal interest rate is the one we actually observe in the market for loans and bonds. The real interest rate is unobservable unless the anticipated rate of inflation is zero. In everyday life, the interest rate that people talk about is the nominal interest rate. Now let's consider the implications of the distinction between the nominal and the real interest rate for the interest rate stabilization issue.

Interest Rate Stability and Anticipated Inflation

Critics who claim that the central bank is too preoccupied with interest rate stability are referring to the nominal interest rate, since it is the rate observed in the market. The alleged inflationary bias of such a policy seems even more likely when this fact is recognized. For example, assume that the economy is operating somewhere along a steeply sloped *AS* curve. Now suppose that there is an increase in aggregate demand (possibly due to an increase in government deficit spending or an increase in autonomous investment, net exports, and consumption spending). The resulting rise in real GDP and the price level causes money demand to increase, which in turn leads to a rise in the nominal interest rate.

Now the central bank reacts by increasing the money supply in order to bring the nominal interest rate back down (say, by making an open market purchase).

Checkpoint 31-2

If the general price level declined over a long period of time (as it did in Canada, Great Britain, and the United States during the latter part of the nineteenth century) so that people came to expect deflation, would the nominal interest rate be above or below the real interest rate? Why? Starting with the early 1960s, compare the behaviour of the nominal interest rate shown in Figure P30-3 with the annual percentage rate of change of the price level shown in Figure P30-2. How might you explain the relationship between these two measures?

But this causes a further rightward shift in the *AD* curve, which causes another increase in GDP and the price level. The increases in the price level cause people to begin to anticipate inflation. The onset of anticipated inflation causes the nominal interest rate to increase more as lenders now add on a larger inflation premium to the real interest rate, but this leads the Bank of Canada to again increase the money supply. The increase in the money supply causes another increase in aggregate demand, a further rise in real GDP and the price level, another increase in the anticipated rate of inflation and hence in the nominal interest rate, and so on for another round.

By trying to stabilize the level of the nominal interest rate, the Bank of Canada may trigger self-defeating increases in the anticipated rate of inflation, which cause the nominal interest rate to rise even more as inflation gets worse! At some point in this process, Bank of Canada critics contend, the Bank becomes alarmed at the accelerating inflation and slams the brakes on the growth of the money supply, triggering a recession and an increase in unemployment. Now the Bank of Canada feels compelled to fight the recession above all else. Once again it expands the money supply. The process repeats itself, accompanied by periodic recessions and expansions with fluctuations in the inflation rate and unemployment.

Implications for Fiscal and Monetary Policies

A pattern of conflict among policy goals seems to be a major contributing factor to the inflation, exchange rate, and unemployment process. The Bank of Canada would like to stabilize interest rates, but this goal conflicts with its desire to curb inflation and may conflict with the goal of stabilizing the exchange rate on the Canadian dollar. In addition, its goal of fighting inflation conflicts with its desire to avoid recession and unemployment and may conflict as well with the goal of stabilizing the exchange rate. When the fiscal policy stance is one of almost continual budget deficits, particularly cyclically adjusted budget deficits, the inflationary bias of a monetary policy oriented toward interest rate stabilization is accentuated by the inflationary bias of fiscal policy.

Many critics of fiscal and monetary policy make the following recommendations:

1. The central bank should worry less about interest rate stabilization. These critics contend that this would help reduce the central bank's contribution to the inflationary bias jointly shared by fiscal and monetary policy. They claim that if the central bank focused less on interest rate stabilization, it could more effectively restrain demand-pull inflation or maintain the external value of the Canadian dollar on international markets. This in turn would go far to eliminate the central bank's periodic need to tighten the money supply in an attempt to curb an acceleration of inflation or prevent the decline in the value of the Canadian dollar on international markets. The tightening of the money supply for either of these purposes can induce a recession and unemployment.

2. Governments must act more responsibly to curb excessive deficit spending, particularly during those times when the economy is experiencing inflationary expansion. At such times, a reduction or elimination of the cyclically adjusted budget deficit would make it easier for the central bank to control inflation without causing a recession. In addition a

reduction of the deficit during periods of expansion would enhance the government's ability to conduct effective expansionary fiscal policy during periods of recession.

Summary

1. There are differing opinions about the extent to which fiscal policy can affect economic activity. Some economists claim that pure fiscal policy actions have little effect on aggregate income and employment because of offsetting crowding-out effects on private spending, particularly investment and net exports. Others do not believe the crowding-out effect is that significant.
2. Fiscal policy has monetary effects whenever a fiscal action (a change in government spending, transfers, taxation, or any combination of the three) is accompanied by a change in the money supply, as may happen whenever the fiscal action gives rise to a budget deficit or surplus. Deficit spending financed by monetizing the government debt is more expansionary than deficit spending financed only by selling bonds to the public.
3. It is often difficult to coordinate fiscal and monetary policy in order to achieve economic stability and reasonably full employment with a minimum amount of inflation. A major reason is that many other considerations and political pressures affect government expenditure and tax programs, and these often take priority over economic stabilization objectives. By contrast, the monetary policymaking process is more organized, relatively more sheltered from political pressure, and therefore more easily and continuously focused on economic stabilization goals.
4. A monetary policy that is preoccupied with interest rate stability tends to have an inflationary bias, particularly in the presence of government deficit spending. This bias is accentuated by the onset of anticipated inflation, which causes the nominal interest rate to be greater than the real interest rate. Critics of such a policy argue that the inflation-unemployment problem would be lessened if monetary policymakers worried less about interest rate stability and fiscal policymakers avoided high-employment budget deficits during periods of inflationary economic expansion.
5. The nominal interest rate is the real interest rate adjusted for the expected inflation rate: $i_{\text{nominal}} = [(1 + i_{\text{real}}) \times (1 + \text{expected inflation rate}) - 1]$.

Key Terms and Concepts

crowding out	nominal interest	pure fiscal policy
monetizing the	rate	real interest rate
government debt		

Questions and Problems

1. How are Bank of Canada open market purchases similar to the financing of government deficits through money creation? How are they different?
2. It is often said that the extent of the crowding-out effect that results from a pure fiscal policy action is different when the economy is in a recession than when it is operating

at close to full employment. Explain why this might be so. Suppose a deficit is financed entirely by the government selling bonds to the Bank of Canada. Can there still be a crowding out? Explain.

3. In an open economy like Canada's, crowding out occurs through exchange rates as well as through interest rates. Explain why increases in the interest rate in Canada might lead to reductions in Canada's net exports to the United States.

4. Suppose that the economy is in a deep depression like the Great Depression of the 1930s. Suppose also that the money demand curve becomes very flat at a low level of the interest rate and that the equilibrium interest rate is at this low level. Would a pure fiscal policy action, such as a balanced budget government expenditure and tax increase, have a crowding-out effect? Under these conditions, would it make any difference whether the government resorts to a pure fiscal policy action as opposed to deficit spending financed by money creation?

5. Consider the interest rate that your local branch of a chartered bank is currently paying on savings or term deposits. Using the currently reported rate of inflation, calculate what you think is the real rate of interest earned on such deposits. Remember that the money interest rate you earn is taxable income. Taking this into account, what do you think of the real rate of interest you earn on such deposits?

6. A number of economists claim that the Bank of Canada can push the nominal interest rate down in the shortrun. That is, they say that open market purchases by the Bank of Canada have the initial effect of pushing it down but that these same purchases sow the seeds leading to a later rise in the interest rate. Explain how and why this might be so.

Chapter 32

Economic Growth

Our discussion in preceding chapters has dealt mostly with the analysis of income and employment determination in the shortrun. We have focused on the problem of how to smooth out economic fluctuations and at the same time keep the economy operating at close to its potential without generating excessive inflation. The framework of income and employment analysis that we have used throughout implicitly assumes that there is a given, unchanging quantity of resources and a given state of technology. It is those assumptions that make the analysis shortrun. In the shortrun, there is a given amount of labour, capital, and land to employ, a given state of technological knowledge, and a given population to clothe, house, and feed.

Economic growth takes place because in the longrun the quantity of available resources, the state of technology, and the size of the population all change. It is necessary to study economic growth in order to understand how and why the economy's capacity to produce goods and services changes in the longrun. When economists discuss the theory of economic growth they usually mean the growth of potential output. It is of course possible for an economy to increase its output by reducing its unemployment rate. Such increases in output normally occur when an economy recovers from a recession. It is also possible for the standard of living in an economy to improve if it develops new trade that is based upon comparative advantage. Again, this is not what economists mean in the context of growth. Therefore, we will assume that the economy is a fully employed closed economy. Alternatively we could assume that the economy is open but has exhausted all possible gains from trade.

Economic growth (or the absence of it) also has important implications for how well a society can handle many of the problems that confront its economy in the shortrun. Emphasizing the importance of the shortrun, Keynes is alleged to have once remarked that "in the longrun we are all dead." Nonetheless, the longrun phenomenon of economic growth has important consequences for how well we live in the shortrun. It is important to first-year economics students because economic growth will affect how you live for the rest of your life.

Our first concern in this chapter will be the definition and measurement of economic growth. Then we will examine the major past and present explanations of why there is economic growth. Finally, we will consider the apparent slowdown in Canadian economic growth, the issue of the benefits and costs of economic growth, and the increasing concern about the possible limits to economic growth.

Defining and Measuring Economic Growth

We can define economic growth in several different, but related, ways. Moreover, how we define economic growth largely determines how we measure it. Definition and measurement are closely related issues.

Defining Economic Growth

Economic growth *is the expansion of an economy's capacity to produce goods and services that takes place over prolonged periods of time, year in and year out, from decade to decade, from one generation to the next, or even over the course of centuries.* We have defined economic growth in this way to differentiate it from the increase in output that accompanies the movement of an economy from a point inside its production possibilities frontier to a point on its production possibilities frontier. While such a movement does result in higher output, it is a one-time change that cannot continue beyond the frontier. The process of growth is far more complex. It can involve the increase in the resources available to society, changes in technology, and even changes in social organization.

The Expanding Production Possibilities Frontier

Recall our discussion of the economy's production possibilities frontier in Chapter 2. Suppose that the economy produces two kinds of goods—consumer goods and capital goods. The production possibilities frontier PPF_1 in Figure 32-1 shows the different maximum possible combinations of quantities of capital and consumer goods that the economy can produce if it fully employs all its available resources of labour, capital, and land, given the existing state of technological knowledge. If there is an increase in the quantity or quality of

---

LEARNING OBJECTIVES

After reading this chapter, you will be able to:

1. Define the concept of economic growth.
2. Describe major components of economic growth.
3. Explain the classical view of economic growth.
4. Summarize contemporary views of the sources of economic growth.
5. Describe the circumstances underlying the slowdown of economic growth in Canada in the 1970s and the apparent recovery from those difficulties in the 1980s.
6. Explain the controversy over the benefits and costs of economic growth and the concern about possible limits to economic growth.

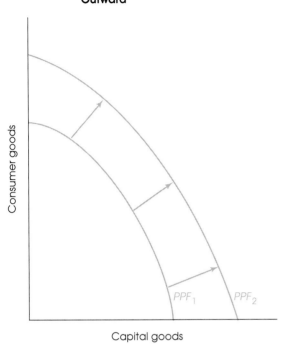

FIGURE 32-1   Economic Growth Shifts the Production Possibilities Frontier Outward

Economic growth may be represented by an outward shift of the production possibilities frontier, such as from PPF_1 to PPF_2. The shift is caused by growth in the quantity or quality, or both, of the economy's available resources, by ongoing improvement in the state of technological knowledge, or by a combination of both. To realize the full benefits of economic growth, the economy must maintain potential and avoid inefficient allocation of its resources.

Consumer goods

PPF_1 PPF_2

Capital goods

any of these resources or if there is improvement in the state of technological knowledge, the economy's production possibilities frontier will shift outward to a position such as PPF_2. As a result, the economy can produce more of both kinds of goods. This gives us an insight into the nature and causes of economic growth. Economic growth may be viewed as the continual shifting outward of the production possibilities frontier caused by growth in the quantity or quality, or both, of the economy's available resources, by ongoing improvement in the state of technological knowledge, or by some combination of both.

Staying on the Frontier

When the economy's production possibilities frontier shifts outward, the economy's *capacity* to produce increases. But the economy will not realize the full benefits of this capacity increase unless it is always on its production possibilities frontier. In Chapter 2 we saw that there are two reasons why the economy may operate inside its production possibilities frontier.

First, the economy will not operate on its production possibilities frontier if any of its resources are unemployed. Whenever part of the labour force is unemployed or whenever there is unused plant capacity, the economy operates inside its production possibilities frontier. In order to remain on the frontier, the economy's aggregate demand for goods and services must grow at a rate sufficient to utilize fully the increased productive capacity provided by economic growth.

Second, the economy will not operate on its production possibilities frontier if any of its resources are underemployed—that is, if there is not efficient resource allocation. Efficient resource allocation requires that resources be employed in those activities for which they are best suited. Only then will the economy be able to realize the maximum possible output with its available resources. (Recall from Chapter 2 the discussion of the effect on the economy's output of the inefficient use of its resources.)

In sum, if the economy is to stay on its expanding production possibilities frontier and realize the gains from economic growth, it must avoid both unemployment and underemployment. As was indicated in the discussion of the non-accelerating rate of unemployment (NAIRU) in Chapter 20, while it is not possible to eliminate unemployment completely, prudent fiscal and monetary policy should encourage aggregate demand to expand fast enough to utilize the increased productive capacity provided by economic growth. In addition, in order to minimize underemployment, markets must operate efficiently to allocate resources to those productive activities in which the value of their contribution to total output will be the greatest.

The Interdependence of Demand and Economic Growth

The rate of increase of aggregate demand for goods and services and the rate of economic growth are interrelated. If aggregate demand doesn't expand fast enough to keep the economy operating on its production possibilities frontier, the resulting unemployment will mean that a certain amount of capital goods that could be produced will not be. Capital goods not produced today will not be available to produce other goods tomorrow. Consequently, the outward expansion of the economy's production possibilities frontier will not be as great. There will be less economic growth than otherwise would have been possible had aggregate demand expanded fast enough to keep the economy continually operating on its production possibilities frontier.

For example, during the Great Depression aggregate demand declined so much that the nation's firms actually allowed their capital stock to wear out faster than they replaced it—net investment was negative. This meant that the economy's capital stock actually declined. One of the major costs of the Great Depression was the enormous quantity of capital goods that the economy never produced. This lack of capital goods production resulted in a severe decline in the rate of expansion of the economy's productive capacity, and hence in its rate of economic growth.

Measuring Economic Growth

If economic growth is represented by an outward expansion of the economy's production possibilities frontier, then one measure of economic growth is the rate of growth of the economy's potential GDP. This is the level of total output the economy can produce when it is on its production possibilities frontier. The money value of potential total output can change because of a change in prices. Since we are only interested in measurements of growth that represent an increase in the output of actual goods and services, economic growth rates must be calculated using constant-dollar, or real, measures of potential total output. An example of such a measure is potential real GDP measured in constant 1986 dollars, as was shown in Figure 20-5, frame (b).

Potential Real GDP

The rate of growth of potential real GDP is a measure of the growth in the economy's overall capacity to produce goods and services, but it tells us little about how members of the society's standard of living is changing over time. One measure of the economy's ability to provide a standard of living is output per capita, the economy's potential total output level divided by the size of its population. We can express this as

$$\text{Potential real GDP per capita} = \frac{\text{Potential real GDP}}{\text{Population}}$$

From this expression it follows that growth in potential real GDP does not necessarily mean an increase in the standard of living as measured by potential real GDP per capita. If potential real GDP (the numerator) grows faster than population (the denominator), potential real GDP per capita will grow and the economy's standard of living will increase. However, if potential real GDP grows at a slower rate than population, potential real GDP per capita declines and the standard of living goes down. Remember, however, that potential real GDP per capita is an average, and thus a very rough measure of living standards. Few economists consider it an ideal measure of the economy's standard of living. For example, it doesn't tell us anything about the actual distribution of income in the economy. (There is a discussion in Chapter 19 of what GDP does not measure.) *The rate of growth of output per capita is a measure of economic growth that provides a rough indication of change in the standard of living.*

Output per Labour Hour

Another important measure closely linked to economic growth is output per labour hour. *The conventional way of measuring* **productivity** *is in terms of output per labour hour.* This measure gives us some indication of how efficiently each labour hour combines with the capital stock and the existing state of technology to produce output. Output per labour hour is an appealing measure of productivity because it is a combined reflection of the quality of labour (education, technical skill, motivation), the quantity and quality of capital that labour uses, and the degree of sophistication of the state of technology. *The greater is the rate of growth of output per labour hour, the larger is the rate of growth of productivity, and this obviously contributes to the rate of economic growth.*

Components of Potential Total Output

The economy's potential total output Y^* may be viewed as having four components. The size of the economy's population N (the number of people) is the first component. The second is the fraction of the population that makes up the labour force. This fraction is equal to the number of labourers L divided by the size of the population N. Note that the number of labourers L may be computed as the population N multiplied by the fraction of the population in the labour force:

$$L = N \times \frac{L}{N}$$

The third component is the average number of hours H that each labourer actually works. The total number of labour hours actually worked by the entire labour force therefore equals L multiplied by H. Note that the total number of labour hours $L \times H$ may be expressed as

$$L \times H = N \times \frac{L}{N} \times H$$

The fourth component is productivity, or output per labour hour, which is equal to potential total output Y^* divided by the total number of labour hours $L \times H$:

$$\frac{Y^*}{L \times H}$$

The economy's potential total output Y^* is equal to the total number of labour hours $L \times H$ multiplied by output per labour hour $Y^*/(L \times H)$:

$$Y^* = L \times H \times \frac{Y^*}{L \times H}$$

Since

$$L \times H = N \times \frac{L}{N} \times H$$

the economy's potential total output Y^* may also be expressed as

$$Y^* = N \times \frac{L}{N} \times H \times \frac{Y^*}{L \times H} \tag{1}$$

Equation (1) shows that the economy's potential total output Y^* may be viewed as being equal to the product of the four components: the size of the population N, multiplied by the fraction of the population in the labour force L/N, multiplied by the average number of hours each labourer actually works H, multiplied by output per labour hour $Y^*/(L \times H)$. Clearly the growth of the economy's potential total output Y^* will depend on the way each of these four components in Equation (1) changes over time. [Note that the N, L, and H in the numerator of Equation (1) may be cancelled out by the N, L, and H in the denominator of Equation (1) to give $Y^* = Y^*$, which is true by definition.]

The total output of the Canadian economy, as measured by real GDP (in constant 1986 dollars), is shown in frame (a) of Figure 32-2. Between 1946 and 1990 real GDP has increased nearly sixfold. Let's examine the role that each of the four components has played in this growth.

Role of the Components of Total Output in Economic Growth

Population (N).   Population growth contributes to economic growth from both the demand side and the supply side. A growing population means a growing demand for all kinds of goods and services. On the supply side, an increasing population provides the ever-larger pool of labour needed to produce the larger quantity of output required to satisfy growing demand.

Throughout its history Canada has experienced population growth due to a high birthrate, a declining death rate, and at times substantial immigration.

FIGURE 32-2 **The Components of Economic Growth in the Canadian Economy**

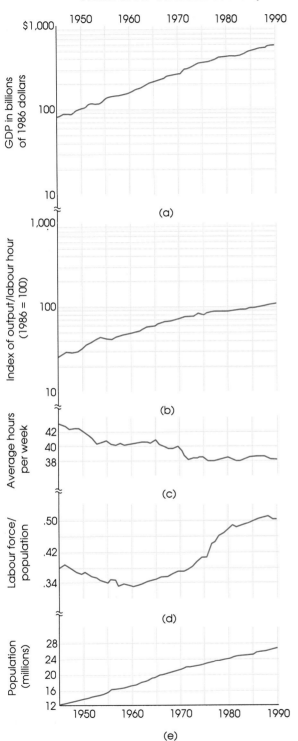

The growth of total output Y, measured by real GDP, frame (a), is the product of change in four components: population, N; the fraction of the population in the labour force, L/N; the average hours worked per labourer, H; and productivity, or output per labour hour, $Y/(L \times H)$.

Note that the vertical axes for frames (a) and (b) are a logarithmic, or ratio, scale on which equal distances represent equal percentage changes. For example, in frame (a) the distance from 60 to 90 is the same as the distance from 80 to 120, since each represents an increase of 50 percent.

The Canadian population increased from approximately 2.4 million persons in 1851 to approximately 5.4 million in 1901. By 1991 it had increased to about 27 million. In recent years the birthrate has declined somewhat, reflecting a trend toward smaller families. (This trend may be due in part to the increasing participation of women in the labour force.) Population experts project that the population will grow to somewhere between 27.9 million and 35.9 million by the year 2011. The range of possible populations reflects the difference in assumptions made about the birthrate and the level of immigration.[1] The growth in the postwar Canadian population is illustrated in frame (e) of Figure 32-2. Clearly, population growth has been a contributing factor to the growth in real GDP shown in frame (a).

Labour Force as a Fraction of the Population (L/N).   While the population provides the source of the labour pool, it is the proportion or fraction of the population that actually joins the labour force, L/N, that determines the size of the labour pool. The larger is the fraction, the larger is the labour force provided by a given size population, and hence the greater is the productive capacity of the economy.

The behaviour of this fraction in the postwar Canadian economy is shown in frame (d) of Figure 32-2. Expressing the fraction L/N as a percentage, the percentage of the population in the labour force fell from roughly 38 percent in 1946 to about 33 percent in 1962. Since that time it has increased steadily, reaching about 51 percent by 1990. In other words, the labour force has been growing faster than the population. As we observed in Chapter 20, in part this has been due to a maturing post–World War II "baby boom" that swelled the working age population during the 1960s and 1970s. Another contributing factor has been the increase in the proportion of working age women that has joined the labour force during these years.

Average Hours Worked per Labourer (H).   In the nineteenth century the length of the average workweek was roughly 60 hours.[2] During the early part of the twentieth century it declined steadily, to less than 43 hours in 1946. Since World War II, the decline has continued at a more gradual pace. By 1990 the average workweek in manufacturing in Canada was a little more than 38 hours, as is illustrated in frame (c) of Figure 32-2. The average workweek in some sectors of the economy is even less.

Obviously, a decline in the length of the average workweek tends to reduce the rate of economic growth. However, the reduction in hours worked reminds us that economic growth is certainly not the be-all and end-all of the good life. Most economists argue that the steady decline in the average workweek reflects a preference for more leisure, one of the fruits made possible by the higher standard of living provided by economic growth. Indeed, while the length of the average workweek today is much shorter than it was in 1900, real GDP per capita has grown tremendously over this time period.

Output per Labour Hour Y/(L × H).   Growth in productivity, or output per labour hour, is the principal component in economic growth. In all countries

---

[1] F. T. Denton and B. G. Spencer, "Aging and Future Health Costs," *Canadian Public Policy* IX:2, June 1983.

[2] In this context, "average workweek" refers only to full-time employees.

that have experienced sustained increases in their standard of living, productivity growth has been the wellspring. Productivity growth results from increases in the educational and skill levels of the labour force, growth in the quantity and quality of capital, and the steady advancement of the state of technological knowledge. Output per labour hour has more than tripled in the Canadian economy since 1946, as shown in Figure 32-2, frame (b). After the slowdown in the rate of increase in output per labour hour during the 1970s and again during the early 1980s, productivity growth appears to be increasing once more.

Comparing frames (b), (c), (d), and (e) of Figure 32-2, we can see that productivity growth, frame (b), has been the single most important contributor to the growth in real GDP, frame (a), since 1946, except during recent years. Next in order of importance has been population growth, frame (e). The decline in the proportion of the population in the labour force, frame (d), from 1946 to 1962 tended to work against economic growth, while the increase in that proportion since 1962 has been favourable to economic growth. The decline in average hours worked per week, frame (c), has tended to hold back growth in real GDP. But it should be stressed that if the shorter workweek represents a choice of more leisure in exchange for less growth in the output of goods, it signifies an increase in well-being.

The Significance of Growth Rates—The "Rule of 72"

What difference does it make whether an economy grows at 3 percent, 4 percent, or 5 percent? A great deal! A rule-of-thumb calculation known as the "rule of 72" readily shows why. For any growth rate in real GDP, the rule of 72 says that the number of years it will take for real GDP to double in size is roughly equal to 72 divided by the growth rate. For example, if the economy's real GDP grows at a rate of 2 percent, it will take approximately 36 years ($72 \div 2$) for real GDP to double. If it grows at a 3 percent rate, it will take 24 years to double ($72 \div 3$). A 6 percent growth rate would mean real GDP would double in only 12 years ($72 \div 6$)!

Consider the implications of different growth rates for our economy. Economists tend to agree that in the 1960s the economy could grow 4 percent each year without setting off demand-pull inflation. However, because of the slowdown in productivity growth during the 1970s and early 1980s, this figure may be more like 3, or even 2, percent. According to the rule of 72, at a 4 percent growth rate real GDP would double in roughly 18 years ($72 \div 4$). Starting from the year 1992, this doubling would occur in the year 2010. However, if the "safe growth" rate needed to avoid excessive inflation is 3 percent, real GDP would not double until approximately the year 2016, which is 24 years from 1992. If the safe growth rate is 2 percent, real GDP would not double until the year 2028.

Suppose that we start with the actual level of real GDP in 1990 and project these two different growth paths into the future, as shown in Figure 32-3. Clearly, the further into the future we go on these two different paths, the greater will be the difference in the possible levels of real GDP. In 1995 the difference will amount to roughly $34 billion (in 1986 dollars). By 2000, real GDP on the 4 percent growth path will be about $839 billion, while on the 3 percent growth path it will be about $762 billion, a difference of $80 billion. By the year 2010 the difference will amount to about $220 billion!

Checkpoint* 32-1

From 1946 to 1981 productivity in the Canadian economy roughly tripled [Figure 32-2, frame (b)]. What does the rule of 72 tell us about the rate of growth of productivity during this time period? Suppose that it is projected that productivity growth in Canada may average no more than 1.5 percent per year in coming years. What does this imply about the projected behaviour of the other three components of economic growth, given a safe growth rate of 3 percent per year? Compare frames (a) and (e) of Figure 32-2 and give a rough estimate of how much real GDP per capita has increased since 1946 in Canada.

*Answers to all Checkpoints can be found at the back of the text.

FIGURE 32-3   The Differences Between a Real GDP Growth Rate of 4 Percent and a Rate of 3 Percent

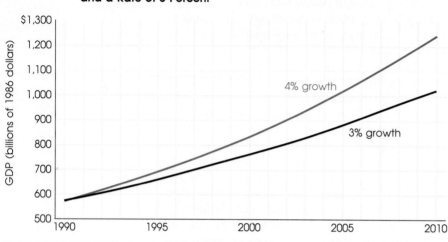

Starting from the actual level of real GDP in 1990, the difference between growing at a 3 percent and at a 4 percent rate becomes more pronounced as we proceed into the future.

Explaining Economic Growth

It has been difficult for economists to come up with a single, comprehensive theory that explains economic growth. How does a country that has experienced a low and unchanging standard of living for centuries transform itself into one that realizes a sustained, decade-by-decade increase in productivity and real GDP per capita? Part of the difficulty economists have with this question is that a good deal of the answer, no doubt, requires an explanation of the political, cultural, and sociological processes that underlie such a transformation. Classical economists, such as David Ricardo and Thomas Malthus, painted a rather gloomy picture of the prospects for economic growth. Subsequent generations of economists have had the benefit of observing economic growth on a scale that the classical economists had not anticipated. Present-day explanations of economic growth place a great deal of emphasis on such things as capital formation, technological change, and saving.

The Classical View of Economic Growth

During the late eighteenth and early nineteenth centuries the Industrial Revolution in England was just getting under way. Much of the rest of Western Europe remained untouched by this development. Observing the world around them, it is little wonder that classical economists such as Malthus and Ricardo argued that a nation's economic growth would inevitably lead to stagnation and a subsistence standard of living. In its simplest form, their argument rested on two basic premises. The first was the law of diminishing returns. The second was the proposition that the population would expand to the point where the economy's limited resources would only provide a subsistence living.

Production and the Law of Diminishing Returns

The law of diminishing returns is a proposition about the way total output changes when the quantity of one input to a production process is increased while the quantities of all other inputs are held constant. Classical economists applied this law to economic growth. *Given the state of technological knowledge, classical economists argued that as a larger and larger population works with a fixed amount of land and other resources, the increase in total output becomes less and less.* In other words, there are diminishing marginal returns in the form of successively smaller additions to total output. As a consequence, the average output per capita declines as the population grows.

The law of diminishing returns is illustrated in Figure 32-4 for a hypothetical country. We will assume that the proportion of the population that is employed remains constant. In frame (a), population N is measured on the horizontal axis and total output Y^* on the vertical axis. The total output curve Y^* shows the relationship between the size of the country's population and the quantity of total output that population can produce, assuming a fixed quantity of resources and a given state of technological knowledge. With a population of 1 million the economy is able to produce a total output of 10 million units. If the population increases by 1 million, to a total of 2 million, the level of total output rises

FIGURE 32-4 Total Output, Average per Capita, and the Law of Diminishing Returns

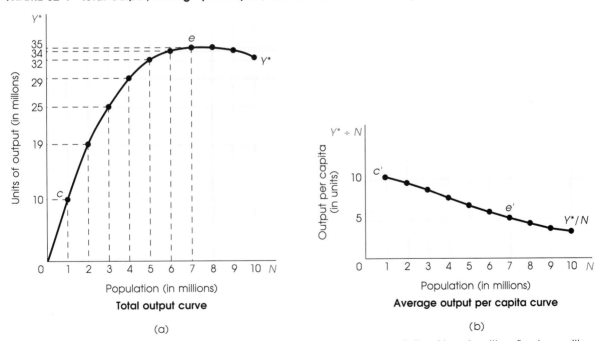

(a) Total output curve — Population (in millions)

(b) Average output per capita curve — Population (in millions)

Given an unchanging state of technology, when a larger and larger population N works with a fixed quantity of land and other resources, total output Y^*, vertical axis, frame (a), increases by successively smaller amounts, a reflection of the law of diminishing returns. Thus, the Y^* curve, frame (a), which represents the relationship between population size and total output, rises less and less steeply as population size increases. The average output per capita, vertical axis, frame (b), for each population size is calculated by dividing total output Y^* by population N. Again reflecting the law of diminishing returns, the average output per capita curve Y^*/N declines as population increases.

by 9 million units to a total of 19 million units. A population increase to 3 million results in an increase in total output from 19 million to 25 million units, or a rise of 6 million units, and so forth. Note that each successive 1 million person increase in the population results in a smaller increase in total output. The successively smaller increases in total output associated with each 1 million person increase in population reflect the law of diminishing returns. Once the population reaches 8 million, further increases in population actually cause total output to fall. That is, the Y^* curve bends over and begins to decline beyond a population of 8 million.

The consequences of diminishing returns for average output per capita are shown in Figure 32-4, frame (b). Average output per capita (vertical axis) is calculated for each population level N (horizontal axis) by dividing the total output Y^* from frame (a) by N. For example, when the population size is 1 million and total output equals 10 million units, corresponding to point c on Y^*, frame (a), average output per capita is 10 units, corresponding to point c', frame (b). The average output per capita is calculated and plotted in a similar fashion for each population size to give the average output per capita curve Y^*/N. Notice that because of the law of diminishing returns, average output per capita decreases as the population size increases, as indicated by the declining Y^*/N curve. For instance, when population is 7 million and total output equals 35 million, point e on Y^*, frame (a), average output per capita is 5 units, point e' on Y^*/N, frame (b).

The Subsistence Living Level

Another crucial ingredient of the classical theory of economic growth was the notion of a subsistence living level. *The* **subsistence living level** *may be viewed as the minimum standard of living necessary to keep the population from declining.* At the subsistence level the number of births would just equal the number of deaths. If the standard of living fell below the subsistence level, economic hardship would cause the death rate to rise above the birthrate and the population would decline. If the standard of living rose above the subsistence level, the death rate would fall below the birthrate and the population would increase.

The subsistence living level for our hypothetical economy is illustrated in Figure 32-5. The axes in frames (a) and (b) are exactly the same as those in frames (a) and (b) of Figure 32-4. Given any population size (horizontal axis), the subsistence total output curve Y_S in frame (a) indicates the minimum total output (vertical axis) necessary to maintain that population—that is, to keep it from declining. For example, the subsistence total output level necessary to sustain a population of 1 million is 5 million units of output, corresponding to point d on the curve Y_S. Similarly, the Y_S curve indicates that it would take 10 million units of output to sustain a population of 2 million, 15 million units to sustain a population of 3 million, and so forth.

The subsistence living level may also be expressed in per capita terms. The average per capita subsistence level for any size population may be obtained by dividing the corresponding subsistence total output level by the population size. For example, for a population of 1 million requiring a subsistence total output of 5 million units (corresponding to point d on Y_S,) the average per capita subsistence level is 5 units of output per person. Alternatively, observe from the Y_S curve that every additional population of 1 million requires another 5 million units of total output to maintain a subsistence level of living. Hence,

FIGURE 32-5   The Subsistence Living Level

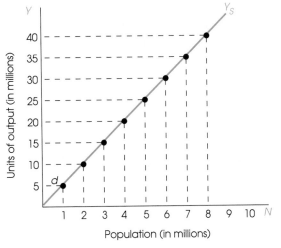

Subsistence total output curve

(a)

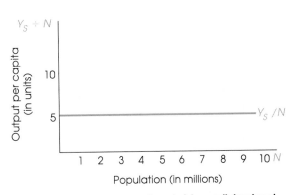

Average per capita subsistence living level

(b)

The subsistence total output curve in frame (a) shows the subsistence level of total output (vertical axis) associated with any given size population (horizontal axis) in a hypothetical economy. The subsistence level of total output for any given size population is that which provides a standard of living just sufficient to keep the total population from declining (the number of births just equal the number of deaths). The average per capita subsistence living level is equal to the subsistence level of total output for any given size population divided by the population. For the hypothetical economy shown here, the average per capita subsistence living level is 5 units of output per person, represented by the horizontal line Y_S/N in frame (b).

whatever the population size, the average per capita subsistence living level in our hypothetical economy is 5 units of output per person, represented by the horizontal line Y_S/N in frame (b).

Population Growth and Diminishing Returns

The classical view of economic growth combined the law of diminishing returns with the notion of the subsistence living level. Figure 32-6 illustrates the classical view by combining the Y^* and Y^*/N curves of Figure 32-4 with the Y_S and Y_S/N curves of Figure 32-5.

Suppose that the population is initially 1 million. Given the fixed quantity of resources and the state of technological knowledge, the economy will be able to produce a total output of 10 million units, corresponding to point c on total output curve Y^*, frame (a). However, the subsistence total output level needed for a population of 1 million is only 5 million units, point d on the subsistence total output curve Y_S, frame (a). In terms of total output, the economy's standard of living exceeds the subsistence level by 5 million units, represented by the vertical distance between points c and d in frame (a). In per capita terms, the average output per capita of 10 units [point c' in frame (b)] exceeds the per capita subsistence living level of 5 units [point d' in frame (b)] by 5 units. Consequently, the death rate will be lower than the birthrate and the population will increase.

FIGURE 32-6   The Classical View of Economic Growth

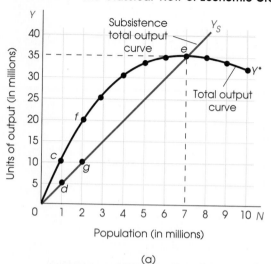

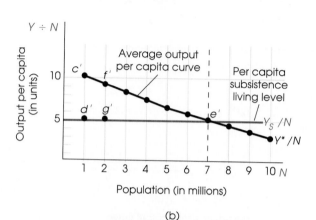

(a)   (b)

At any population size less than 7 million, the total output curve Y^* lies above the subsistence total output curve Y_S in frame (a). Because the quantity of total output produced (vertical axis) exceeds the subsistence total output level, the classical view argued that the birthrate would be higher than the death rate. Hence, both the population (horizontal axis) and total output would grow. At any population size greater than 7 million the opposite situation obtains, and both the population and total output decline. Longrun equilibrium occurs at the intersection of Y^* and Y_S, point e, where the total output level produced is just sufficient to support a population of 7 million at a subsistence living level.

The argument may also be represented in per capita terms, frame (b). To the left of point e', average output per capita, given by the Y^*/N curve, is greater than the per capita subsistence living level of 5 units of output per person, given by the horizontal line Y_S/N. Population rises, causing average output per capita to fall toward the per capita subsistence living level. To the right of point e' the opposite is true, so that population declines and average output per capita rises toward the per capita subsistence level.

Suppose that the population increases to 2 million. The economy will produce a larger total output of 19 million units [point f in frame (a)], which again exceeds the subsistence total output level of 10 million units [point g in frame (a)], this time by 9 million units. In per capita terms, the average output per capita of 9.5 units [point f' in frame (b)] again exceeds the per capita subsistence living level of 5 units [point g' in frame (b)]. Hence, the population will continue to increase.

According to the classical view, population and output will continue to grow as long as the economy's standard of living exceeds the subsistence living level. That is, population and total output will grow as long as the total output curve Y^* lies above the subsistence total output curve Y_S, frame (a). Putting it in per capita terms, they will continue to grow as long as the average output per capita curve Y^*/N lies above the per capita subsistence living level curve Y_S/N, frame (b). Once the population reaches 7 million, total output produced will be 35 million units, frame (a), which is just equal to the subsistence level of total output needed to sustain a population of 7 million. This level corresponds to the intersection of the Y_S and Y^* curves at point e in frame (a). In per capita terms, at a population of 7 million average output produced per capita is 5 units, which is just equal to the per capita subsistence living level, corresponding to the intersection of Y^*/N and Y_S at point e', frame (b). At this point population and output will cease to grow. Economic growth stops. The economy has reached a static, or unchanging, equilibrium position.

What a dismal equilibrium it is, characterized by stagnation and a subsistence standard of living. If the population were to rise above 7 million, total output produced would be less than the subsistence total output level required to sustain the larger population [to the right of point e in frame (a), the Y^* curve lies below the Y_S curve]. Average output per capita would be less than the per capita subsistence living level [to the right of point e' in frame (b), the Y^*/N curve lies below Y_S/N]. Consequently, famine and disease would cause the death rate to rise above the birthrate and the population would tend to fall back to the 7 million level. On the other hand, if the population were to fall below the 7 million level, total output produced would be more than the subsistence level required to sustain the smaller population [the Y^* curve lies above the Y_S curve, to the left of point e in frame (a)]. Living standards would rise, since the average output per capita would be above the per capita subsistence living level [the Y^*/N curve lies above Y_S/N to the left of point e' in frame (b)]. Unfortunately, according to the classical view, this would cause the birthrate to exceed the death rate. The population would tend to increase to 7 million again, and the standard of living would once again decline to the subsistence level.

The "Dismal Science"

If economic growth tended to lead society to such a dismal longrun equilibrium position, the prospects for ever improving economic well-being would seem dim indeed. It is this implication of the classical view of economic growth that earned economics its designation as the dismal science. The classical view is still relevant today in many of the third world countries. The near-subsistence living standards and the high rates of population growth that plague those countries do suggest a rush toward the dismal longrun classical equilibrium. But the classical view bears little resemblance to the spectacular rise in living standards and the sustained economic growth experienced by the present-day industrialized countries. There are a number of reasons why the dismal predictions of the early nineteenth century economists have not applied to the industrialized economies. The most obvious of these is the rapid development of new technology. A reduction in the rate of population growth has also been an important factor. Finally, the ability to substitute capital for land in the production process meant that the fixed supply of land was not as restrictive as the classical economists believed it would be. The dramatic shift of the population from agriculture to urban centers demonstrates the importance of the growth of manufacturing in the process of economic growth.

Sources of Growth and Rising Living Standards

How can the longrun classical equilibrium and a subsistence living level be avoided? One way is for the total output curve, and hence the average output per capita curve, to shift upward fast enough to stay ahead of population growth. Obviously, it would also help if population growth didn't increase every time output per capita rose above the subsistence living level.

Economic growth with rising living standards is depicted in Figure 32-7. Suppose that population is initially N_1. Total output corresponding to point b on total

FIGURE 32-7   Economic Growth with Rising Living Standards

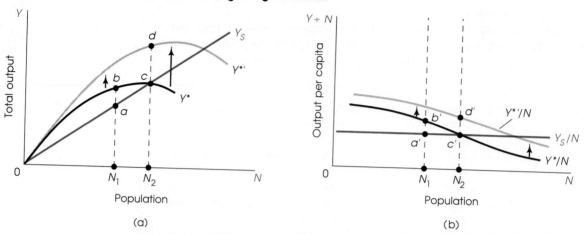

When the total output curve Y^* and hence the average output per capita curve Y^*/N shift upward rapidly enough, economic growth will be accompanied by rising average output per capita. Upward shifts in Y^*/N and Y^* are caused by capital deepening, technological change and innovation, and an increase in the quality of the labour force caused by investment in human capital.

output curve Y^* exceeds the subsistence total output level corresponding to point a on the subsistence output curve Y_S, frame (a). Hence, average output per capita corresponding to point b' on the average output per capita curve Y^*/N exceeds the per capita subsistence level Y_S/N by an amount represented by the vertical distance between b' and a', frame (b). Assume this above-subsistence standard of living causes the population to rise to N_2 in the manner suggested by the classical view. However, in the meantime suppose the total output curve shifts up to $Y^{*'}$ and hence the Y^*/N curve shifts up to the position $Y^{*'}/N$. Now, even though the population grows to N_2, the standard of living is not driven down to the subsistence level corresponding to points c and c'. Instead, total output rises to point d on $Y^{*'}$ and average output per capita rises to point d' on $Y^{*'}/N$. The standard of living has actually increased, as represented by the fact that the vertical distance between c' and d' is greater than that between a' and b'.

What would cause economic growth to take place in this fashion, rather than along the lines suggested by the classical view? In particular, what causes the increase in productivity that allows any given size population to produce more, as represented by upward shift in Y^* and Y^*/N? And what factors might inhibit the tendency for population growth to be so responsive to increases in the standard of living? While there is no hard-and-fast blueprint, most economists now agree that any list of the key elements in economic growth should include capital deepening, technological change and innovation, education or investment in human capital, rising aspirations for a better standard of living, and saving and investment.

Capital Deepening

Capital deepening *is an increase in the stock of capital (machines, tools, buildings, highways, dams, and so forth) relative to the quantities of all other resources, including labour.* Capital deepening makes it possible for any given size population to produce a larger total output, so that average output per capita is increased. This is reflected in upward shifts of the Y^* and Y^*/N curves, such as those shown in Figure 32-7. Given the size of the population, the state of technology, and the quantities of all other resources, there are diminishing returns to capital deepening just as there are to increases in the population. Increases in the quantities of the *same kinds* of machines, tools, buildings, highways, and dams beyond a certain point (that is, more of the same capital goods labour is already using) obviously will not yield further increases in total and per capita output. Why? Because there will not be enough population and quantities of other resources with which to combine them in productive activities. The emphasis on the kinds of capital brings us to the role of technological change and innovation.

Technological Change and Innovation

Invention and scientific discovery lead to technological change and innovation in production techniques. Even the most casual observer of economic life is struck by the changes that take place over time in the kinds of capital and procedures used to produce goods and services. When existing capital wears out, it is often replaced with *new kinds* of capital incorporating the new technology. Perfectly usable capital is often simply made obsolete by the development of new kinds of capital. As a result, even if the economy did not increase the quantity of resources devoted yearly to the replacement of worn-out or obsolescent capital, the productive capacity of the economy would grow. Hence, for any given size population and quantity of all other resources, total output would be larger. Again, this would be reflected in the upward shift of the Y^* and Y^*/N curves, such as that shown in Figure 32-7.

Some kinds of technological change are the result of changes in the form of a capital good. Such changes are referred to as **embodied technical change**. This is the kind of technological change that most often comes to mind. The diesel locomotive replaced the steam locomotive. Jet airliners have largely replaced the propeller variety. The electronic pocket calculator has made the slide rule obsolete. The list goes on and on.

Other kinds of technological change take the form of new procedures or techniques for producing goods and services. This type of change is referred to as **disembodied technical change**. Examples are the use of contour ploughing to prevent soil erosion on farms, the development of new management techniques in business, and the pasteurization of milk. Such technological changes are not embodied in the form of a capital good. Of course, many types of embodied technical changes make disembodied technical changes possible, and vice versa. The computer has made many new kinds of managerial procedures possible. And these procedures in turn make it possible to use new kinds of capital goods, or embodied technical changes. For example, computers enable airlines to use sophisticated procedures for scheduling and controlling the flow of passengers between airports more efficiently. This efficiency makes it practical to use certain kinds of jet aircraft.

Education and Investment in Human Capital

Just as investment in capital goods increases productive capacity, so too does investment in human beings in the form of education, job training, and general experience. It is no accident that literacy rates and average years of schooling per capita tend to be higher in developed countries than in third world countries. Improvements in the quality of the labour force shift the Y^* and Y^*/N curves upward, as in Figure 32-7, in the same way that embodied and disembodied technical changes do.

Improvements in sanitation, disease prevention, nutrition, and the general health of the population are also forms of investment in human capital. A healthier population is more capable of learning and generally gives rise to a more productive labour force less prone to absenteeism and accidents. In addition, increases in the average life-span make it possible to develop a more experienced labour force and to provide the larger pool of able managers and leaders needed to fill administrative positions.

Rising Aspirations and Population Growth

If a society is to realize both economic growth and a rising standard of living, population growth must somehow be kept from literally absorbing every increase in output per capita above the subsistence living level, as in the classical view. Countries that have experienced an industrial revolution and the progression from third world to developed status have somehow managed to escape from the drag of rapid population growth. One explanation is that once an economy realizes a rise in the standard of living above the subsistence level, the actual experience instills a taste for a high standard of living, or at least a better life. More and better food, clothing, and housing breed a keen awareness that living can be more comfortable. People aspire to a better standard of living and become more aware of the relationship between curbing family size, and hence population growth, and the ability to realize these aspirations.

The effect of a rise in the aspiration level, measured in terms of average output per capita, on population size is shown in Figure 32-8. Suppose that the aspiration level rises to Y_A/N. That is, people desire a standard of living, measured in terms of average output per capita, that exceeds the subsistence level by an amount equal to the vertical distance between Y_A/N and Y_S/N. The population will not get larger than N_a, corresponding to the intersection of Y_A/N with the average output per capita curve Y^*/N at point a. The longrun equilibrium

---

FIGURE 32-8   Effect of a Rising Aspiration Level on Population

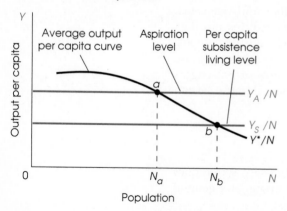

Suppose that the aspiration level, measured in terms of average output per capita, is Y_A/N. The population will not get larger than N_a, corresponding to the intersection of Y_A/N with the average output per capita curve Y^*/N at point a. The longrun equilibrium average output per capita at point a is higher than that corresponding to the classical view at point b, where a larger population N_b exists at a subsistence living level.

average output per capita at point a is higher than that corresponding to the classical view at point b, where the larger population N_b exists at a subsistence living level. Now, when capital deepening, technological change, and investment in human capital cause the Y^*/N curve to shift upward, economic growth will cause population and output per capita to tend toward equilibrium positions corresponding to the intersection of the rising Y^*/N curve with Y_A.

Another explanation of the decline in the population growth rate that tends to accompany economic development is that this decline is in part due to a change in the role of children. Such a change is brought about by the nature of economic development. The populations of third world countries are largely involved in agricultural activities, scratching out a meager living with primitive tools. It is argued that under such circumstances children are viewed as another pair of hands, useful for the work that they can perform starting at a relatively early age. In addition, they are insurance that there will be somebody to look after aging parents. As economic development progresses, an ever-larger portion of the population becomes employed in the economy's expanding industrial sector. Families earning livelihoods in factories, stores, and trades servicing a more urbanized population no longer view children as contributors to the family's economic well-being. Rather a child is primarily a dependent to be fed, clothed, and housed until he or she enters the labour force as a self-sufficient young adult. In short, in an industrial and urban setting, children are more of an economic burden on the family. The incentive to have large families that exists in a rural, agricultural setting is greatly reduced. It is therefore argued that as an increasing portion of the population moves into the industrial sector, the birthrate, and hence population growth, tends to decline.

The Role of Saving and Investment

In previous chapters we saw how saving, the refraining from consumption, makes it possible for investment to take place. Investment expenditures create new capital goods, which replace capital stock that is worn out or obsolescent, as well as increase the size of the economy's capital stock. Saving and investment are thus crucial to the capital formation and technological change that make possible economic growth and increasing output per capita.

Consider Figure 32-7 once again. The upward shift of Y^* to $Y^{*\prime}$, and hence of Y^*/N to $Y^{*\prime}/N$, requires saving and investment. When the population is N_1 and the total output curve is Y^*, there is an excess of output above that required for subsistence. This excess is represented by the vertical distance between points a and b, frame (a). In order for capital formation to shift Y^* up to $Y^{*\prime}$, the population must refrain from consuming all the excess output that the economy is able to produce. That is, some of it must be saved. What is not consumed is available for investment or the formation of the capital goods that increase the economy's productive capacity, as represented by the upward shift of the total output curve from Y^* to $Y^{*\prime}$.

Other Factors in Economic Growth

A distinguishing characteristic of third world economies is a growing specialization of labour accompanied by increases in the scale of production. In the early stages of economic development, a worker is typically engaged in many different tasks. For example, at the beginning of the Industrial Revolution in England (in the latter half of the eighteenth century), production was typically organized along the lines of the cottage industry. A family occupying a cottage on a modest parcel of land would raise a small number of farm animals, tend a few crops, and engage in crafts such as spinning, weaving, and tanning. The family supplied much of its own food and made a good deal of its own clothing. An individual worker typically performed many different tasks. With the advent of the Industrial Revolution and the advancement of production technology, greater specialization and increases in the scale of production took place, thereby reducing per unit (of output) costs of production. Lower-priced, mass-produced goods led to the expansion of markets, an integral part of the economic growth process.

Another important ingredient of economic growth is the development of extensive capital markets. In capital markets savers lend funds to borrowers who make the investment expenditures that give rise to capital formation. The growth of banking and other financial institutions that pool the savings of a large number of small savers and lend them out to investors plays a crucial role in the development of capital markets. Some economists even suggest that the state of development of a country's financial institutions provides the single most revealing indication of a country's state of economic development.

Economic growth requires a favourable cultural, social, and political environment. Legal institutions are needed to provide law and order and to enforce contracts between parties to economic transactions. Cultural attitudes toward work and material advancement are an important determinant of the incentives for economic growth. A social structure that allows reasonably fluid upward and downward mobility based on performance and merit is more conducive to economic growth than a rigid social structure that puts a premium on the station of one's birth. A society that is open to new ideas is more likely to grow than one that refuses to accept non-traditional views. Finally, economic growth rarely takes place in societies racked by political instability.

> ### Checkpoint 32-2
> Do you think that the law of diminishing returns is applicable to technological change and investment in human capital? Why or why not? What are the implications of your answer for economic growth?

Issues in Economic Growth

What are the aspects of economic growth that are currently of most concern to industrialized countries such as Canada? Policymakers were troubled by the slowing down in Canadian productivity growth that occurred during the 1970s and early 1980s. Since about 1982 productivity growth seems to have picked up. Will the revival continue? Quite aside from this issue, there has been considerable debate over whether the costs of continued economic growth in industrialized countries such as Canada are worth the benefits. Finally, there is the question of the limits to economic growth. Will we literally run out of resources? Will there be a doomsday?

Recent Problems with Economic Growth in Canada

What were the causes of the slackening of productivity growth in Canada during the 1970s and early 1980s? [See Figure 32-2, frame (b).] Economists have offered several explanations. Among the most important are inflation, changes in the composition of the labour force, inadequate investment spending, low

POLICY PERSPECTIVE

How Serious Are the Limits to Growth?

Predictions of an end to economic growth are certainly not new. Indeed, the dismal classical view, nearly 200 years old, seems very relevant in many of today's third world countries, a fact sometimes easily forgotten by those living in the industrialized or developed countries of the world. But in recent years the hard facts of pollution,* energy shortages, urban sprawl, and traffic congestion have served as increasingly insistent reminders that there may well be limits to economic growth.

RESOURCE LIMITATIONS

As we have already seen, the classical view of economic growth envisioned an inevitable tendency for countries to reach a point where both population and total output would cease to grow—a dismal longrun equilibrium of stagnation and misery. Due to the law of diminishing returns, output per capita would decline continuously until a subsistence standard of living was reached. However, capital deepening, technological change, investment in human capital, a rising aspiration level, and a favourable cultural, social, and political environment have all conspired to put off such a doomsday in the world's developed countries. But there are those who emphasize "put off." Put off for how long? It is undeniable that the earth's resources are limited. Therefore, these analysts argue that it is certainly not possible to beat the law of diminishing returns indefinitely. As the earth's resources are used up and population increases, the law of diminishing returns inevitably points to a declining per capita output.

DOOMSDAY PREDICTIONS

Among the doomsday predictions, a group known as the Club of Rome (an international business association composed of business people, academicians, and scientists) initially kicked off modern debate on this issue by constructing an elaborate computerized model of world economic growth.** The Club of Rome model assumed that population and production grow at certain historically realistic percentage rates and that there are definite limits to world resources and technological capabilities. Given these assumptions, a computer was used to generate predictions of the future trends of industrial output per capita, the quantity of the world's resources, food per capita, population, and pollution. The predictions reached the alarming conclusion that the limits to growth will be reached somewhere in the years 2050 to 2100. The Club of Rome says that this conclusion follows largely from the depletion of the earth's nonrenewable resources— coal, petroleum, iron ore, aluminum, and so forth. It is predicted that once the limit is reached, there will be an uncontrollable decline in population and productive capacity. If resource depletion does not trigger the collapse, then the precipitating factors will be famine, pollution, and disease.

What can be done to avert this doomsday prediction? Many of those who take the Club of Rome's predictions seriously argue that efforts should be made to establish zero population growth and zero economic growth. That is, establish a no-growth equilibrium. The Club of Rome suggests that by using appropriate technology, it may be possible to cut pollution, hold population growth in check, and reduce the amount of resources used per unit of output. In addition, investment in capital should be limited to the replacement of worn-out or obsolescent capital. Moreover, resources should be shifted away from the production of industrial products and toward the provision of more food and services.

PERSPECTIVE ON GROWTH AND DOOMSDAY

Many find such doomsday predictions quite unconvincing. They observe that modern doomsday predictions sound very similar to the classical view of economic growth. The economic growth of the countries of Western Europe, the United States, Canada, Japan, the former Soviet bloc countries, New Zealand, and Australia is completely at odds with the classical view. This is so largely because the classical view did not foresee the tremendous advance of technology that has taken place over the last century or more. Critics of the "doomsdayers" argue that some current doomsday predictions again vastly underestimate the potentials of science, innovation, and technological change.

This criticism may be well taken. One wonders what the classical economists of the early 1800s would have thought if one of their number had predicted that in the twentieth century people would fly to the moon, jet aircraft would cross Canada in the time it took a stagecoach to go 50 uncomfortable miles, in a split second an electronic computer would do calculations that would take a thousand clerks years, electronic communication would allow people to watch and hear a live event on the other side of the

continued on next page

*The economics of pollution is discussed in Chapters 7 and 14.

**Dennis L. Meadows et al., *The Limits to Growth* (Washington, DC: Potomac Associates, 1972).

POLICY PERSPECTIVE CONTINUED

world, or most of the populous areas of the world could be obliterated in a few seconds by nuclear explosions. The list goes on and on. Imagine how far fetched such a list would seem to someone living in 1900, let alone the classical economists of the early 1800s. This puts a perspective on the pitfalls of making predictions about economic growth in the twenty-first century.

SUSTAINABLE GROWTH

By the 1990s discussion had generally shifted from the doomsday predictions of the Club of Rome to the discussion of "sustainable growth." There is no standard definition of sustainable growth, but the idea of sustainable growth recognizes that growth is possible and necessary if the standard of living of the majority of the world's population is to ever realize anything approaching the standard of living in Canada and the other industrial countries while accepting that unlimited growth is neither possible nor desirable.

Sustainable growth emphasizes the need to manage resources to prevent their depletion. Many resources are renewable if they are properly managed. A forest can be a renewable resource. If it is selectively harvested and replanted, it can provide lumber indefinitely. However, if it is overcut, it may not be able to renew itself, even

with replanting programs. Overcutting can result in soil erosion and, if done on a large enough scale, even climate changes.

Some argue that the market provides incentives to renew resources. As overexploitation occurs the resource becomes more scarce. As it becomes more scarce its price increases and the quantity of the resources demanded drops. Buyers reduce their consumption by shifting to other resources and producers withhold production to await even higher prices expected in the future. Unfortunately there are often market failures in resources. If there are no clear ownership rights to a resource, then firms may rush in to exploit the resource before someone else does. This is exactly the problem with cod stocks off the east coast of Canada. Since there is no clear owner of the cod, individual fishermen cannot profit by conserving the declining cod stock. If one group of fishermen decide that their long-term interest is better served by reducing their catch over the next several years so that the cod population may have a chance to rebuild, another group of fishermen may rush in to harvest what is left now and sell it at the high price which the reduced supply has created. It is quite possible that all fishermen (and consumers) can benefit more by conserving the depleting stocks of cod, but no one fisherman could be assured that the others

will not continue to overfish. Individual conservation does not mean that the stocks will be replenished, but rather that someone else will get what is left. Obviously what is needed is to assign ownership, then the owner and society will profit from careful management of the stock.

Who should own the cod stock? From the standpoint of efficient use, it actually does not matter. Any rational owner will avoid overexploitation to ensure longrun profitability. However, as a practical matter it may matter. From a normative point of view, why should any particular individual or firm have the right of ownership and the profits that could be earned from the resources? On this ground alone many would argue that the property rights be assigned to society in general or, as society's representative, the government. Clearly it would be easier for a government to exercise its rights of ownership. A private company would need its own private navy to prevent poaching. A government would have the police power to ensure that there was no overfishing. The government would not have to do the actual fishing itself. It could assign (or sell) quotas to private fishermen and in the process ensure that the total stock remained viable.

continued on next page

levels of research and development expenditures, and the increased government regulation of business.

Inflation

The acceleration of inflation during the 1970s, made worse by the oil price shocks of 1973 and 1979, is widely credited with a major role in the productivity slowdown. Inflation eroded profits, reduced investment incentives, and impaired the efficiency of the market pricing system as an allocator of resources. The huge increase in energy prices increased the cost of using labour-saving machinery and fostered the use of more-labour-intensive, lower-productivity technologies.

Unfortunately even this solution has a serious limitation. What if the fish do not respect the government's jurisdiction? Fish can swim across the lake to another province or out of Canadian waters into international waters. When that happens, the provincial (or federal) government lacks jurisdiction to prevent overfishing. In the case of such a resource only international cooperation can ensure that renewable resources are not exhausted by the current generation of users.

Even if it is possible to develop policies that provide the proper incentives to ensure that the stocks of renewable resources remain viable, many reserves are not renewable. Some nonrenewable resources can be recycled. Aluminum cans, the steel in junked cars, and so on, can be and often are reused. Once again, policies must be in place that ensure that market failures do not exist that remove the incentives to recycle where it is economically efficient to do so.

There are many resources which are neither renewable or recyclable. It is not possible to bury new dinosaurs to produce new oil reserves nor is it possible to recycle the oil used as gasoline to power a car. Under these circumstances it is only a matter of time before the finite stock of oil is depleted. Just when it will run out depends upon the quantity of exploitable oil available and the rate at which is used. The stock available may of course increase because of the discovery of new fields and better technology for recovering it, but this only delays the eventual exhaustion of the finite stock. Alternatively, the date of depletion can be delayed if the rate of consumption is reduced. The farther in the future the date of depletion, the longer the time available to find suitable alternatives.

Once again it becomes vital to ensure that there is no market failure. The government must act to reflect actual market conditions so that depletion is not accelerated. Governments sometimes subsidize exploitation of resources either to create jobs or to maintain artificially low prices to placate consumers. Some, more cynical, might even suggest that on occasions some governments have given resources away at bargain prices to reward their friends. Any policy that has the effect of lowering the price of depletable resources increases their use and accelerates their depletion. Even policies that allow firms access to resources at below-market prices can be regarded as subsidies. Such policies are not compatible with sustainable growth and are not in society's long-term interests.

There are two other major concerns related to sustainable growth. One relates to the environment. It does society little good to conserve its resources if pollution makes the world uninhabitable. In effect, the environment itself is a resource that must be conserved. In many ways it is a renewable resource. The air shed can be used to dispose of unwanted wastes. However, its ability to safely absorb such wastes is limited. Indiscriminate use of this resource has lead to serious question about its viability. The dangers of global warming and ozone depletion definitely indicate that the are limits to society's exploitation of the air, if the world is to have sustainable growth.***

The other remaining concern relates to population growth. A major factor that led the classical economists to their dismal prognosis was population growth. While the rate of population growth has fallen in the industrialized world, the rate of grobal population growth is still very high. Ultimately, population growth could prove that economic is the dismal science.

For Discussion

- Of all the resources at our disposal, which seems the most abundant? Would the steps suggested to avert the doomsday predictions seem to imply more, or less, government intervention in the economy?

***The economics of the environment is discussed in the microeconomics section of this text.

Changes in the Labour Force

From the mid-1960s up through the 1970s, youths born during the postwar baby boom represented a growing portion of the labour force. Their entry into the job market is at least part of the reason for the rise in the fraction of the population composing the labour force, as shown in Figure 32-2, frame (d). (The other major cause is the increased labour force participation of women.) Many of these young entrants into the labour force initially lacked training and experience. It took several years for them to become highly productive. This influx of young workers slowed the growth of productivity, Figure 32-2, frame (b). As the baby-boom population matured during the 1980s, it became less of a drag on productivity growth.

During the 1980s the labour force grew less than half as fast as it had in the 1970s. The 15 to 24 age group actually declined about 10.7 percent in the 1980s, in contrast to a 36.6 percent growth rate in the 1970s. On average, the workforce of the 1980s was older and more experienced than that of the 1970s, and this contributed to productivity gains.

Inadequate Investment Spending

The Canadian economy has generally benefited from substantial annual additions to its capital stock. This investment has been an important factor in the growth of the Canadian economy. However, there was a drop in new capital formation during the late 1970s. A short recovery was followed by another drop in 1983 and 1984. These two periods of decline in investment contributed to the slowing of economic growth during the late 1970s and early 1980s. After 1984 investment began to increase again, and it remained strong for the rest of the decade.

A number of factors can contribute to a reduction in investment. High interest rates, low profits, and slow sales all played a role during the late 1970s and early 1980s.

Lack of Research and Development Expenditures

Research and development (R & D) expenditures sow the seeds of technological change. It is often suggested that a lack of intensity of research and development in Canada is a factor contributing to the lower productivity during our slowdown in growth. While industrial research and development started to increase in the early 1980s, Canada lags far behind other highly developed economies. Measured as a percentage of domestic product of industry, Canadian expenditure on industrial R & D rose from 0.82 in 1981 to 0.93 by 1984. At about the same time West Germany was spending 2.49 percent on R & D. The United Kingdom spent 2.02 and the United States spent 2.19. Sweden, an economy closer to Canada in size, spent 3.02 percent.[3] In spite of government declarations, Canada has not been successful in promoting private R & D. This may be due in part to the large number of branch plant operations in Canada. Public expenditure on R & D also has not fared well in recent years. In real terms, government support of universities, the National Research Council, and federal agencies that fund research has not kept up with increases in costs.

The 1980s did bring an increased awareness of the need to engage more actively in R & D. The fact that the federal and provincial governments generally had large deficits during this period may explain their relatively poor performance in funding public R & D and encouraging increased private spending.

Regulation and Pollution Control

Some economists believe that excessive government regulation hinders productivity growth. Companies had to comply with an increasing number of anti-pollution regulations and health and safety rules during the 1970s, which led to

---

[3] Statistics Canada, *Science and Technology Indicators*, 1988 (88–201).

increased spending and time devoted to these areas. Funds had to be diverted from buying productive machinery and developing more efficient operating methods. When well conceived, such regulations may make an economy more efficient by reducing external costs. Industrial accidents have undoubtedly been prevented and environmental damage reduced. But in other cases, they may mean unnecessary costs to business.

In the late 1970s a move to deregulate developed in the United States. The trend intensified and spread to Canada during the 1980s. Deregulation has had significant effects in Canada. These effects have not all been positive. For example, there have been losses in the airline and trucking industries. A number of financial institutions have gone bankrupt. On the other hand there have been a number of benefits. Many businesses are now more efficient.

Negative Factors Reversed During the 1980s

Most of the factors that had a negative impact on productivity growth in the 1970s appear to have been reversed during the 1980s. Perhaps of greatest importance has been the deceleration in the general inflation rate and the decline in energy prices since 1981. The post–World War II baby boomers, who swelled the ranks of inexperienced youthful workers in the late 1960s and the 1970s, are now passing into their prime working years. Investment spending has increased significantly since 1984. Finally, government is taking a more balanced view of regulation.

Costs and Benefits of Growth

The benefits of economic growth have always seemed quite obvious. The basic economic problem is to satisfy humanity's unlimited wants in the face of ever-present scarcity. Economic growth eases this problem by reducing scarcity. Without growth the only way one person can be made better off is by taking something away from another. With economic growth there can be more for everyone—the lot of all can be improved. However, it has become increasingly apparent in the more industrialized countries, where economic growth has been most spectacular, that there are also costs to economic growth. Among these are pollution and a possible decline in the quality of life.

Pollution and the Environment

When the economy produces goods, it also produces by-products that are "bads"—smoke, garbage, junkyards, stench, noise, traffic jams, urban and suburban congestion, polluted water, ugly landscapes, and other things that detract from the general quality of life. In fact *all* output, both goods and bads, *eventually* returns to the environment in the form of waste. The more we experience economic growth, the more obvious this fact becomes. Many people are justifiably concerned about the undesirable effects of growth on the environment and the balance of the world's ecological system. There is concern about disappearing species of wildlife and about the rising incidence of cancer related to synthetic products. There is concern about the destruction of the earth's ozone layer by

POLICY PERSPECTIVE

How We Keep Running Out of Energy—The Role of the Market

At various times in the history of the world it has appeared that we were about to run out of energy sources, important ingredients for economic growth. The alarm about an energy crisis during the 1970s and early 1980s was not the first. In the past, the dire predictions of exhausted energy reserves have always proved wrong. Why? Usually because those predictions failed to take account of the effects of rising energy prices, which encouraged people to seek out cheaper forms of energy and to develop more energy efficient technology.

For example, prior to the Industrial Revolution in the late 1700s wood was the main source of fuel. People used so much wood it was feared that the forest would soon be exhausted, resulting in energy shortages and widespread hardship. But as the forests around towns and cities were used up, the price of wood rose and coal was gradually substituted for wood. The growing demand for coal led to the development of more efficient (less costly) mining methods, and coal soon replaced wood as the primary source of energy.

During the early 1800s, in many parts of the world, lamps burning sperm whale oil were commonly used to light houses. Population growth and an expanding economy increased the demand for whale oil so much that people became concerned about the possible extinction of whales—and the world had its first "oil" crisis. The price of whale oil rose about 600 percent over a period of about 35 years. This price rise led domestic and commercial users of whale oil to seek substitute fuels such as lard oil, distilled vegetable oil, and coal gas. Eventually, by the early 1850s, kerosene made from coal oil became the dominant fuel for lighting. The whale oil crisis had passed. The discovery of petroleum in the late 1850s provided an even cheaper way to make kerosene, and petroleum replaced coal oil as the major source of kerosene.

The important point to note about the wood and whale oil "crises" is that the forces of demand and supply operated to encourage energy conservation as well as the development of alternative energy sources. For exam-

ple, as the price of whale oil rose, consumers were motivated to conserve on its use (don't leave whale oil lamps burning when they're not needed for reading or sewing, and get by with less light in hallways and porches). At the same time, consumer demand for substitute fuels increased, causing their prices to rise. The rising prices of substitute fuels made them more profitable to produce, which encouraged enterprising firms and individuals to increase the supply of these fuels. Consumer demand turned from a fuel that was becoming scarce to fuels that were becoming more plentiful. All this occurred in the absence of a national energy policy or any other form of government intervention—a stark contrast to the way we have dealt with our own energy problems in recent years.

For Discussion

- How does the market mechanism work to expand the potential for economic growth?
- How would you explain the large increase in the number of compact cars on the road over the past 15 years?

the use of aerosol spray cans. Scientists also are convinced that the large-scale burning of fossil fuels has increased the carbon dioxide content of our atmosphere to such an extent that the earth's average temperature has increased by a few degrees. The list of such worrisome by-products of economic growth goes on and on.

Critics of economic growth argue that some curbs on growth are necessary if these increasingly undesirable aspects of the quest for ever-greater income are to be controlled. Others caution that we must be careful not to confuse the control of growth with the control of pollution. They argue that the additional productive capacity made possible by growth could at least in part be devoted to pollution control efforts and the correction of past environmental damage. They point out that pollution control and a clean environment cost something, just like any other good, and that economic growth and increased productive capacity make it easier for society to incur that cost.

The Quality of Life—Progress versus Contentment

Economic growth implies change. Change is often what is most desired and needed by an impoverished population in a third world country. But many question whether continual change is as obviously beneficial in advanced industrialized economies such as Canada. Technological change, if anything, seems to have accelerated in the last half century. As a result, skills and training acquired in youth become obsolete more rapidly. There is more pressure to "keep current," to "retool," and to "update" one's skills. Fail to do so, and you may be demoted or out of a job. Such pressure creates anxiety and a sense of insecurity. It can also result in an increase in the rate of structural unemployment.

We have noted that an above-subsistence aspiration level may be necessary to avoid the tendency toward the longrun equilibrium of stagnation envisioned by the classical view. But some growth critics worry that aspiration levels in growth-oriented, industrialized countries are geared toward a "keep up with the Joneses" mentality. Goods may be valued more for the status they confer on the owner than the creature comforts they provide. ("I'd better get a new car this year or I may not look like I belong in this neighbourhood.") Consequently, people work harder, produce more, enjoy it less, and complain about smog, traffic congestion, and the rat race. What there is of contentment, or peace of mind, may come largely from the sense that you're "making it," or better yet, that you've "arrived."

Since the beginning of the Industrial Revolution, many critics have argued that industrialization forces labour into dehumanizing jobs, requiring the performance of monotonous, mind-numbing tasks. Mass production, assembly line jobs may provide bread for the table but little food for the soul. However, it has been said that those who make this criticism are not familiar with living conditions in countries where there is no industrialization.

Summary

1. Economic growth is the expansion of an economy's capacity to produce goods and services that takes place over prolonged periods of time. It may be viewed as a continual shifting outward of the economy's production possibilities frontier caused by growth in the quantity and quality of the economy's available resources (land, labour, and capital) and by ongoing improvement in the state of technological knowledge.
2. There are four major components in the growth of real GDP: labour productivity, which is influenced by workers' training and experience, technology, and the existing capital stock; population; the proportion of population in the labour force; and the average number of hours worked.
3. The classical economists such as Malthus and Ricardo believed that because of the law of diminishing returns, the maximum level of output and therefore the standard of living was limited.
4. The contemporary view of economic growth emphasizes capital deepening and technological change.

5. A number of factors resulted in the slowing of the rate of growth of the Canadian economy in the late 1970s and early 1980s. These factors included changes in the labour force, lower levels of investment spending, and low levels of R & D.

6. During the 1960s, some economists began to question the perspectives for and desirability of unrestrained economic growth. While growth has benefits in terms of a higher standard of living, it also has costs in terms of the environment and the quality of life.

Key Terms and Concepts

capital deepening	economic growth	productivity
disembodied technical change	embodied technical change	subsistence living level

Questions and Problems

1. The rate of growth of real GDP is frequently used as a measure of economic growth. If we view economic growth as an outward expansion of the production possibilities frontier, what shortcomings does this suggest are associated with the use of real GDP to measure economic growth?

2. It is technologically possible to produce the *same* quantity of total output with different combinations of quantities of capital and labour. More capital may be used and less labour, or more labour and less capital. For example, a rise in the price of capital relative to the price (wage) of labour will typically cause firms to use more of the now relatively cheaper labour and less capital. Conversely, an increase in the price of labour relative to the price of capital would typically cause firms to use more of the now relatively cheaper capital and less labour. What are the implications of these possibilities for the use of output per labour hour as a measure of productivity? What bearing do these possibilities have on the apparent slowdown of Canadian productivity growth during the 1970s, given that energy prices increased dramatically during these years?

3. Population growth can be both a blessing and a curse for economic growth. Explain.

4. It is sometimes argued that in the shortrun, low productivity growth can create jobs because more workers will be required to satisfy rising demand. But it is then said that in the longrun, low productivity growth means a slower growth of total output, which "hurts employment." Explain why you agree or disagree with this argument. What does a comparison of frames (a), (b), (c), and (d) of Figure 32-2 suggest about the validity of this argument?

5. Can you explain why it might be possible for rising aspirations to cause the growth in total output to be *negative* and the growth in average per capita output to be *positive*, while at the same time there is technological progress? What are the implications of such a situation for population growth?

6. The classical view of economic growth envisioned a longrun equilibrium in which output per capita was just equal to the subsistence living level. However, if we consider the role played by saving and investment, is it really possible for longrun equilibrium to occur at such a position? Why or why not?

7. Despite the apparent slowdown in Canadian productivity growth during the 1970s, it appears that the growth of output per capita did not experience a similar slowdown. How would you explain this? (*Hint:* Examine Figure 32-2.) What does this suggest about the relative merits of each of these measures of economic growth?

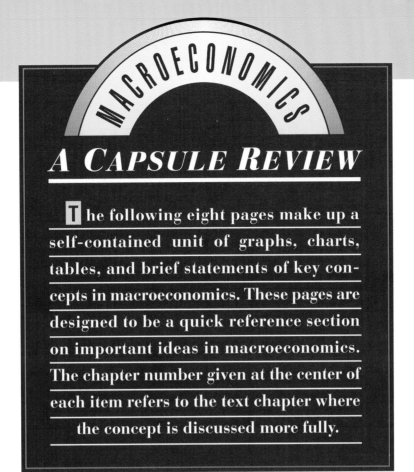

A CAPSULE REVIEW

T he following eight pages make up a self-contained unit of graphs, charts, tables, and brief statements of key concepts in macroeconomics. These pages are designed to be a quick reference section on important ideas in macroeconomics. The chapter number given at the center of each item refers to the text chapter where the concept is discussed more fully.

EXPENDITURE AND INCOME SIDES OF GDP

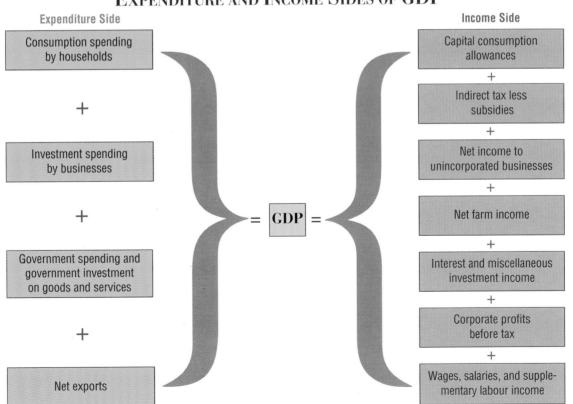

Expenditure Side	Income Side
Consumption spending by households	Capital consumption allowances
+	+
Investment spending by businesses	Indirect tax less subsidies
+	+
Government spending and government investment on goods and services	Net income to unincorporated businesses
+	+
Net exports	Net farm income
	+
	Interest and miscellaneous investment income
	+
	Corporate profits before tax
	+
	Wages, salaries, and supplementary labour income

= GDP =

THE CONSUMPTION FUNCTION AND THE SAVING FUNCTION SHOW HOW THE ECONOMY'S CONSUMPTION SPENDING AND SAVING ARE RELATED TO DISPOSABLE INCOME.

THE CONSUMPTION FUNCTION AND THE SAVING FUNCTION

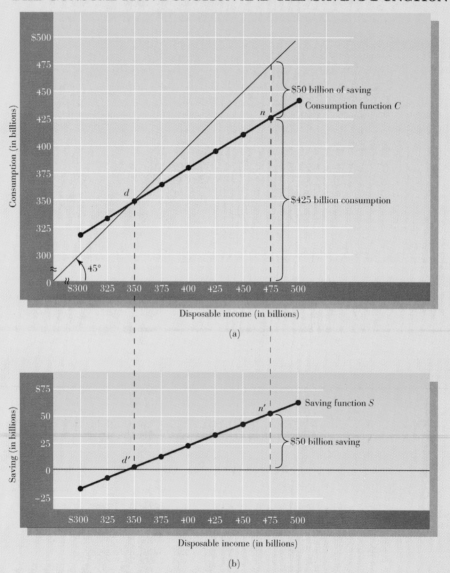

The consumption function *C* in frame (a) shows that as disposable income increases, consumption also increases, but by a smaller amount.

The amount of saving at any disposable income level is represented by the vertical distance between the consumption function and the 45° line in frame (a).

Saving also may be plotted against disposable income frame (b) to give the saving function *S*.

DETERMINING THE EQUILIBRIUM
LEVEL OF TOTAL INCOME.

INCOME–EXPENDITURE APPROACH

The economy's aggregate expenditure schedule *AE* combines with the 45° line to determine the equilibrium level of aggregate income corresponding to the intersection at point *e*. This level of aggregate income gives rise to a level of aggregate expenditure that just buys up the aggregate output that the economy's businesses produce.

At aggregate income levels lower than the equilibrium level, aggregate expenditure is greater than aggregate output. Therefore, unintended inventory reduction is necessary to satisfy the excess of aggregate expenditure over aggregate output.

At aggregate income levels greater than the equilibrium level, aggregate expenditure is less than aggregate output. There are unintended inventory increases equal to the excess of aggregate output over aggregate expenditure.

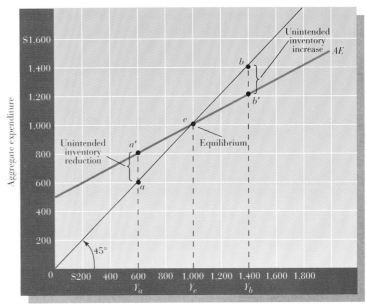

Chapter 21

WITHDRAWALS AND INJECTIONS APPROACH

The equilibrium level of aggregate income or *GDP* occurs where withdrawals equal injections or where savings plus imports plus taxes, *S + M + T*, equal intended investment plus exports plus government spending, *I + X + G*.

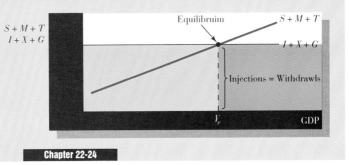

Chapter 22-24

THE MULTIPLIER

$$\text{Multiplier} = \frac{1}{MPW} = \frac{1}{1-MPE}$$

MPW = Marginal propensity to withdraw

MPE = Marginal propensity to expend which is equal to *MPC − (MPC)(MPT) − MPM*

Chapters 22-24

AGGREGATE DEMAND AND AGGREGATE SUPPLY

THE RELATIONSHIP BETWEEN AGGREGATE EXPENDITURE AND THE AGGREGATE DEMAND CURVE

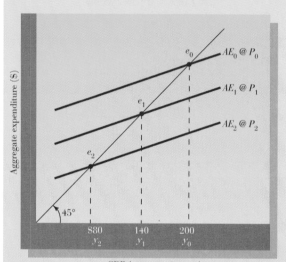

(a)

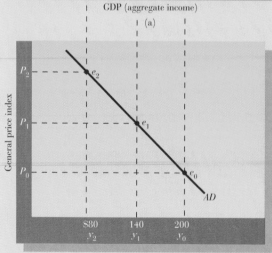

GDP (aggregate income)

(b)

A change in the general price level, *ceteris paribus*, shifts the aggregate expenditure function causing a change in equilibrium income which is shown as a movement along the aggregate demand curve.

THE EFFECT OF THE INFORMATION EXTRACTION PROBLEM ON THE SLOPE OF THE AGGREGATE SUPPLY CURVE

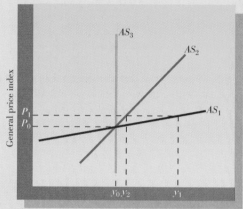

GDP (aggregate output)

If the information extraction problem is severe, a rise in the general price level will not lead to an increase in output, as shown by AS_3. In contrast if there is a small information extraction problem then AS will look more like AS_1 and a change in the general price level will be accompanied by a relatively large change in output.

THE FEDERAL GOVERNMENT'S BUDGET IS AN ITEMIZED ACCOUNT OF GOVERNMENT EXPENDITURES AND REVENUES FOR THE FISCAL YEAR.

Balanced budget: Expenditures = Government revenue

Budget surplus: Expenditures < Government revenue

Budget deficit: Expenditures > Government revenue

Chapters 23-25

THE ACTUAL BUDGET AND THE CYCLICALLY ADJUSTED BUDGET (STRUCTURAL DEFICIT) SINCE 1975

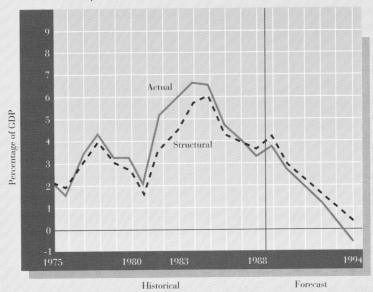

The actual budget deficit or surplus equals the difference between actual government spending (including transfers) and government revenue. The cyclically adjusted or structural budget deficit or surplus equals the difference between actual government spending and the level of government revenue that would be collected at the *average* level of economic activity that could be sustained over the cycle.

Chapter 25

MACROECONOMIC COMPARATIVE STATICS AND MONETARY EFFECTS ON THE ECONOMY'S PRICE LEVEL.

DEMAND-PULL AND COST-PUSH AGGREGATE EXPENDITURE AND THE AGGREGATE DEMAND CURVE

In a demand-pull inflation, a shift to the right in the position of the AD curve, assuming an upward-sloping AS curve, will cause increases in both real GDP and the general price level, as shown in frame (a). By contrast, frame (b) represents a cost-push inflation. In this case a leftward shift in the position of the AS curve causes an increase in general price level but a decrease in real GDP.

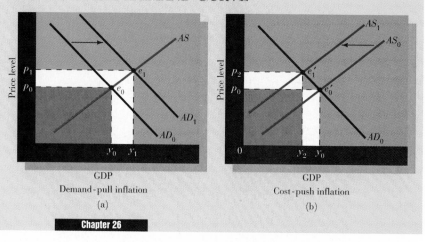

GDP
Demand-pull inflation
(a)

GDP
Cost-push inflation
(b)

Chapter 26

MONEY AND CONSUMER PRICES IN CANADA

The percent change in consumer prices and the monetary supply tend to move together. This is illustrated by the behaviour of the Consumer Price Index (CPI) and the money supply, defined as M1.

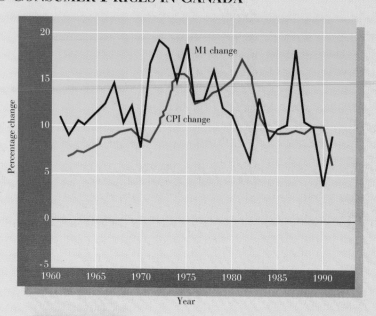

Year

Chapter 27

MONEY AND MONETARY POLICY HAVE IMPORTANT EFFECTS ON ECONOMIC ACTIVITY.

BANK OF CANADA POLICIES

Expansionary Monetary Policy

Action by Bank of Canada	Result for Chartered Banks
Buys bonds from the open market	Increased reserves and can lend more
Switches government accounts into the chartered banks	Increased reserves and can lend more
Reduces bank rate	Signalled to increase lending

Contractionary Monetary Policy

Action by Bank of Canada	Result for Chartered Banks
Sells bonds to the open market	Decreased reserves and must reduce lending
Switches government accounts out of the chartered banks	Decreased reserves and must reduce lending
Raises bank rate	Signalled to reduce lending

Chapters 27 and 28

MONEY SUPPLY CHANGE: KEYNESIAN VIEW

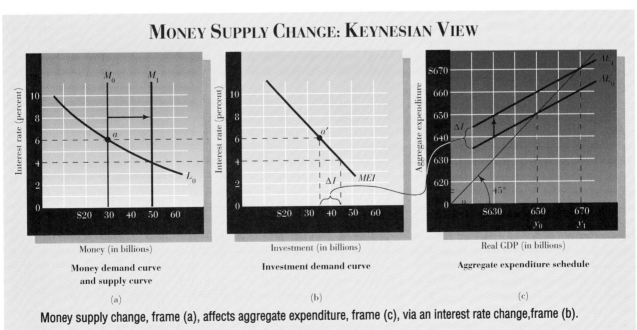

Money demand curve and supply curve (a)

Investment demand curve (b)

Aggregate expenditure schedule (c)

Money supply change, frame (a), affects aggregate expenditure, frame (c), via an interest rate change, frame (b).

Chapter 30

Different Views on How
Money Affects the Economy.

Changes in the Money Supply Affect Real GDP and the Price Level

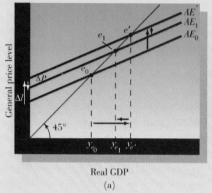

Real GDP
(a)

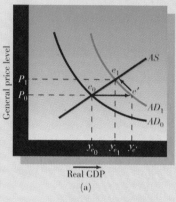

Real GDP
(a)

Chapter 30

An increase in the money supply lowers the interest rate and causes investment to increase which shifts aggregate expenditure up AE_0 to AE'. This causes aggregate demand to shift from AD_0 to AD_1. The shift in aggregate demand causes excess demand which leads to an increase in the general price level from P_0 to P_1. As prices rise aggregate expenditure decreases from AE' to AE_1 due to crowding out frame (a). The crowding out is shown by the movement left along AD_1 from e' to e_1 in frame (b). The net effect of the increase in the money supply is to increase both prices and real output.

Monetarism and the Equation of Exchange

The Equation of Exchange $MV = pQ$

Monetarists argue that the cause-effect transmission from changes in the money supply (M) to changes in money GDP (pQ) is direct and predictable. In terms of the equation of exchange, this means that V, the velocity of money, is quite stable. Therefore, changes in the money supply have a fairly direct and predictable effect on money GDP.

Chapter 30

Rational Expectations

Rational expectations theory holds that economic agents form expectations about the future course of economic events on the basis of all relevant data, experiences, and knowledge. These agents must interpret the information to decide whether a change in a particular price is a movement in that product's relative price or whether it is a move in the general price level. The more "noise" the less information extracted and the more steep the aggregate supply curve.

Chapters 26 and 30

The Policy Ineffectiveness Proposition

Most rational expectations-based theories in economics now accept, in varying degree of severity, the idea that *systematic* monetary or fiscal policies aimed at fighting unemployment or inflation will be ineffective because economic agents will learn to anticipate the effects of public policies and will change their behaviour. These behavioural changes will offset the normal effects of the policy initiative rendering them ineffective.

Chapter 30

PART
NINE

International Economics

Chapter 33

International Trade

Virtually every nation finds it advantageous to trade with other nations. To varying degrees, all are linked to one another by trade flows and financial networks that circle the globe. Canada is particularly dependent upon foreign trade. This and the next chapter will describe and analyze the nature of international trade.

In this chapter we will examine the following questions: What is the pattern of Canadian trade with the rest of the world? What are the underlying reasons why nations trade with one another? International trade is not viewed favourably by everybody. What kinds of barriers to trade do nations often erect to protect themselves from the rigors of foreign competition? What are some of the more common arguments for such barriers?

The Importance of International Trade

International trade plays a significant role in the determination of living standards throughout the world. A brief look at some of the quantitative dimensions of international trade will demonstrate how important it is for Canada.

The nations of the world differ greatly in regard to their dependence on foreign trade. This is illustrated in Figure 33-1, which shows the value of exports of selected countries as a percentage of their respective GNPs in 1989. For example, exports from the United States amounted to only 7 percent of its GNP in 1989 while exports for West Germany[1] amounted to 25.5 percent of that country's GNP. Canada's exports were about 25 percent. The differences among countries in this respect largely reflect differences in size, the extent of development of their internal markets, and the quantity and diversity of their

---

[1] At the time this text was written, information on unified Germany was not available.

FIGURE 33-1 **Exports as Percentage of GNP, Selected Countries, 1989**

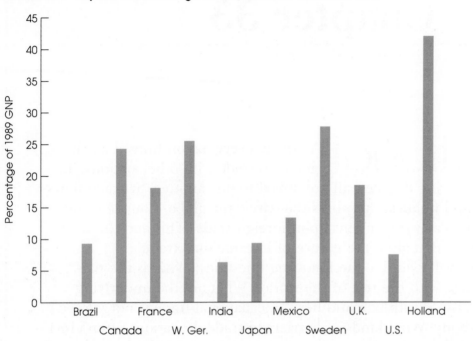

The exports of Canada to other countries represent a relatively large share of its GNP compared to many countries.

Source: The World Bank, *World Tables*, 1991 ed.,
Johns Hopkins Press

supply of resources. The United States is fortunate in each of these respects, so its economy is relatively self-sufficient. Clearly the United States is less dependent on trade (as measured by the size of total exports relative to GNP) than almost any of the other countries in Figure 33-1. While Canada is very large and well endowed with many natural resources, it has a relatively small population and consequently a low population density. As a result it is much less self-sufficient

LEARNING OBJECTIVES

After reading this chapter, you will be able to:

1. Describe briefly the geographical pattern and the industrial composition of Canadian international trade.
2. Identify the factors that are the basis for international trade.
3. Explain why specialization on the basis of comparative advantage can result in greater total output.
4. Explain how the terms of trade determine the distribution of the gains of trade between different countries.
5. State the theoretical argument for free trade.
6. Describe the various types of barriers to trade.
7. Distinguish between valid and invalid reasons for barriers to trade.
8. Outline the development of Canadian tariff policy since Confederation.
9. Discuss the arguments for and against the Canada–United States Trade Agreement.

than the United States. Again, however, the sheer size of the U.S. economy is reflected by the fact that the total value of its exports consistently exceeds that of any other country except Germany. Even though the Canadian economy is much smaller than the American and the German economies, it is still a very important trading nation. In fact, in 1991 Canada was the seventh leading exporter in the world.

The Pattern of Canadian Trade

The pattern of Canadian trade with the rest of the world is illustrated by the export and import data in Figure 33-2. There it can be seen that the total dollar value of Canadian merchandise imports ($134.3 billion), the goods purchased abroad, was somewhat less than the total dollar value of Canadian merchandise exports ($141.7 billion) in 1991. The dollar value of Canadian exports to the United States was roughly 16 percent greater than the dollar value of imports from the United States. On the other hand, Canada imported more from the European Community (EC)[2] than it exported to the EC. Canada's imports from the United Kingdom exceeded our exports by almost 40 percent, but neither exports or imports were very large. Imports from the other EC countries exceeded exports by a smaller margin. In fact, Canadian imports from the rest of the world slightly exceeded exports to the rest of the world. However, the surplus that Canada had with the United States was large enough to more than offset this deficit with the rest of the world.

The Composition of Canadian Trade

The composition of Canadian exports and imports by type of good is illustrated in Figure 33-3. Imports of machinery and equipment represented the largest share (about 33 percent) of purchases from abroad in 1991. Second in importance among Canadian imports were automobiles and parts. The third major category of imports was industrial goods. These three groups account for about 75 percent of all Canadian imports. It is probably not a surprise that Canada imports large amounts of manufactured products. You may find it more surprising that over 12 percent of our imports fall into the categories of forest, energy, agricultural, and fishery products. After all, these are areas which Canada is a major exporter. However, if you stop and think about it, there is nothing odd about it. There are the obvious imports of bananas from Central America and oranges from California. In some cases the imports are less obvious. In fact, it is quite likely that tonight someone somewhere in Canada will eat an American steak and someone in the United States will eat a Canadian steak. International trade is often like that. Italians drink French wine and the French drink German wine and Germans drink Italian wine. It makes life more interesting.

On the export side, manufactured goods accounted for well over half of Canadian sales abroad. The largest single category was automobiles and parts

---

[2]Formerly known as the European Economic Community (EEC).

FIGURE 33-2   Canadian Trade by Area, 1991

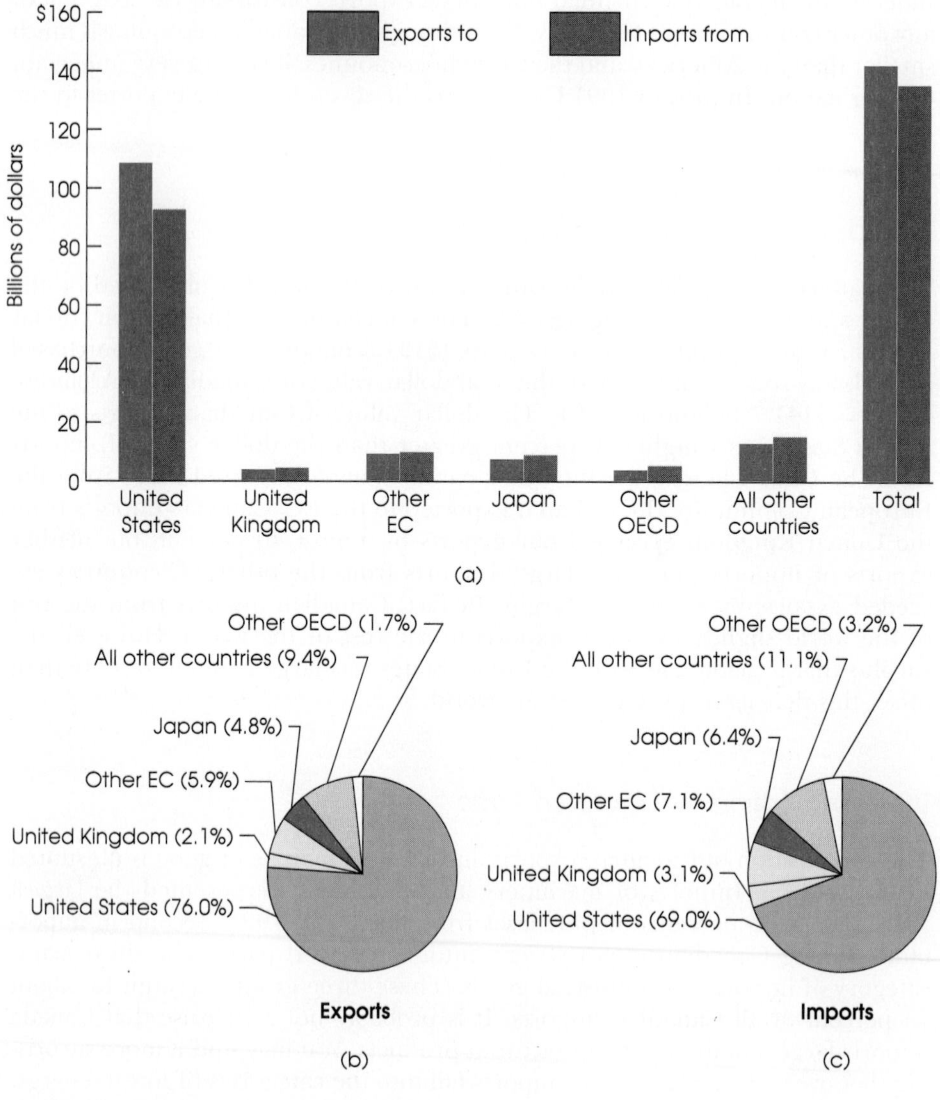

(a)

Exports

(b)

Imports

(c)

Source: Statistics Canada. *Canadian Economic Observer,*
March 1992 (11-010)

Canada's trade pattern by major geographical areas.

at 23 percent. This figure was actually down, because 1991 was in a recession and auto sales were low. Forestry, energy, and agriculture and fisheries accounted for about another 33 percent. The categories of machinery and industrial goods were just over 20 percent each. The balance of exports was in the area of consumer goods. Many Americans would be surprised to learn that their car was

FIGURE 33-3 **Distribution of Merchandise Exports and Imports for Canada, by Broad Commodity Groups, 1991**

Canadian imports consist mainly of manufactured goods: machinery and equipment, automoblies and parts, and industrial goods. This latter fact may surprise some people who still believe that Canadians are hewers of wood and drawers of water.

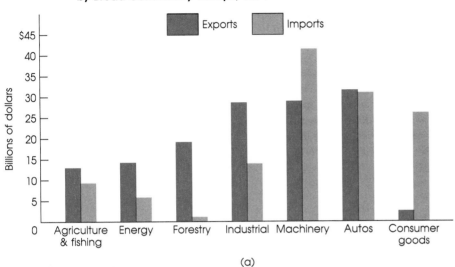

(a)

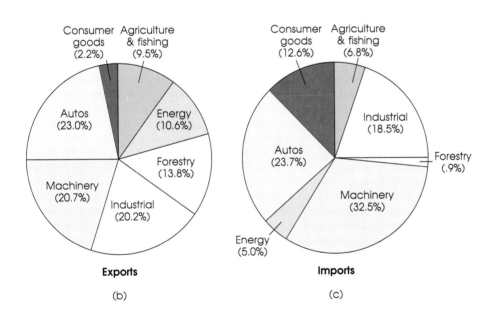

Exports

(b)

Imports

(c)

Source: Statistics Canada, *Canadian Economic Observer*, March 1992 (11-010)

made in Canada, and many Canadians would be surprised to learn how many Americans ride Canadian bikes and listen to Canadian audio components.

The preceding discussion deals with what is called *merchandise trade*. There is also what is called *non-merchandise trade*. Nations buy and sell services from one another, such as shipping services, banking services, and so forth. For example, in

1991 Canada purchased (imported) $69.9 billion of services from other nations and sold (exported) $35.7 billion of services to other nations.

The Basis for Trade—Specialization and Comparative Advantage

We now come to the question of why nations trade with one another. What is the basis for trade? In general, trade occurs because nations have different resource endowments and technological capabilities. Because of these differences, each nation can gain by specializing in those products that it produces relatively efficiently and by trading for those it produces relatively inefficiently or cannot produce at all. In short, international trade allows nations to increase the productivity of their resources through specialization and thereby to realize a higher standard of living than is possible in the absence of trade.

This general description of why nations trade sounds reasonable enough. However, to understand why it is correct requires an examination of the role of specialization and the important principle of comparative advantage. In essence, it is the principle of comparative advantage that makes it worthwhile for nations to specialize and trade. Even when Canadians and Americans trade cars, Canada is specializing in some models and the United States is specializing in other models.

In order to illustrate this principle and see why it leads to specialization and trade, let's consider the following *hypothetical* example. Suppose that there are only two countries in the world economy, Canada and Portugal. And suppose that each can produce both wheat and cloth, but with differing degrees of efficiency. The production possibilities frontier for each country is shown in Figure 33-4, frames (a) and (b). (Recall from Chapter 2 that each point on a production possibilities frontier represents a maximum output combination for an economy whose available resources are fully employed.) Metres of cloth are measured on the vertical axis and bushels of wheat on the horizontal.

Notice that each frontier is a straight line instead of a curve, as was the production possibilities frontier discussed in Chapter 2. The frontiers here are straight lines because we are assuming that costs are constant. Along a straight-line frontier, a nation must give up the same amount of production of one good in order to produce an additional unit of the other, no matter which point on the frontier is considered. In other words, we are assuming that the law of increasing costs (see Chapter 2), which causes the frontier to be curved, does not apply here. The assumption of constant costs makes our discussion simpler but still allows us to illustrate the principle of comparative advantage.

Comparative Advantage—Differences in Opportunity Costs

As we can see, the production possibilities frontiers of the two nations differ. Observe that at any point on Portugal's production possibilities frontier, frame (a), it is necessary to sacrifice 2 metres of cloth in order to have 1 more bushel of wheat. For Portugal, 1 bushel of wheat therefore has an opportunity cost

FIGURE 33-4 Production Possibilities Frontiers for Portugal and Canada (Hypothetical Data)

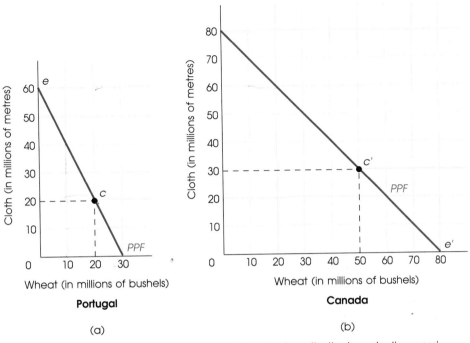

Portugal

(a)

Canada

(b)

Each nation can produce both wheat and cloth. The hypothetical production possibilities frontier are straight lines because costs are assumed to be constant. The slope of Portugal's production possibilities frontier, frame (a), indicates that 1 bushel of wheat has an opportunity cost of 2 metres of cloth, or put the other way around, 1 metre of cloth has an opportunity cost of 1/2 bushel of wheat. The slope of the Canadian production possibilities frontier, frame (b), indicates that the opportunity cost of 1 bushel of wheat is 1 metre of cloth, or the opportunity cost of 1 metre of cloth is 1 bushel of wheat. Canada has a comparative advantage in producing wheat and Portugal has a comparative advantage in producing cloth.

of 2 metres of cloth. Put the other way around, 1 metre of cloth has an opportunity cost of 1/2 bushel of wheat. For Canada, frame (b), 1 metre of cloth must be given up to have 1 more bushel of wheat. Hence, for Canada, the opportunity cost of 1 bushel of wheat is 1 metre of cloth, or the opportunity cost of 1 metre of cloth is 1 bushel of wheat. We can see from this that the opportunity cost of wheat is higher in Portugal than in Canada. While it costs Portugal 2 metres of cloth for each bushel of wheat, it costs Canada only 1. Conversely, the opportunity cost of cloth is higher for Canada than for Portugal. It costs Canada 1 bushel of wheat for each metre of cloth, while it costs Portugal only 1/2 bushel of wheat for each metre of cloth.

In short, we can say that Portugal has a *comparative advantage* (compared to Canada) in producing cloth and that Canada has a *comparative advantage* (compared to Portugal) in growing wheat. The difference in opportunity costs between the two nations reflects differences in their resource endowments, climates, and technological know-how.

Inefficiency of Self-Sufficiency—Efficiency of Specialization

As long as there is no trade between Portugal and Canada, each is isolated and must be self-sufficient. Each country is limited to choices along its own production possibilities frontier. Suppose that Portugal chooses to produce the output combination represented by point *c* on its production possibilities frontier, Figure 33-4, frame (a), a combination consisting of 20 million metres of cloth and 20 million bushels of wheat. Suppose also that the output combination Canada chooses to produce is represented by point *c'* on its production possibilities frontier [Figure 33-4, frame (b)], 30 million metres of cloth and 50 million bushels of wheat. Total "world" output is therefore 50 million metres of cloth (the sum of 20 million metres in Portugal and 30 million metres in Canada) and 70 million bushels of wheat (the sum of 20 million bushels in Portugal and 50 million bushels in Canada).

Figure 33-4 shows us that the world economy is not producing efficiently when each nation is isolated and self-sufficient, even though each nation is on its production possibilities frontier. Why do we say this? Suppose that each nation specialized in the production of that product in which it has a comparative advantage. Portugal would produce only cloth, corresponding to point *e*, frame (a), and Canada would produce only wheat, point *e'*, frame (b). Total world output would then consist of 60 million metres of cloth (Portugal) and 80 million bushels of wheat (Canada). By specializing according to comparative advantage, total world output is greater by 10 million metres of cloth and 10 million bushels of wheat as compared to what it is when each nation produces some of both products at points *c* and *c'*. This example illustrates the principle of comparative advantage. *The principle of* **comparative advantage** *states that total world output is greatest when each good is produced by that nation having the lower opportunity cost of producing the good—that is, by that nation having the comparative advantage in the production of the good.*

When Portugal produces 1 bushel of wheat, the opportunity cost is 2 metres of cloth. It is clearly an inefficient use of the world's resources for Portugal to produce wheat when Canada can produce it at an opportunity cost of only 1 metre of cloth per bushel of wheat. Similarly, it is an inefficient use of world resources for Canada to produce cloth at an opportunity cost of 1 bushel of wheat per metre of cloth when Portugal can produce a metre of cloth at an opportunity cost of only 1/2 of a bushel of wheat. If Portugal produces wheat, the world must give up more cloth than is necessary to have wheat. And if Canada produces cloth, the world gives up more wheat than is necessary to have cloth. *The allocation of world resources is most efficient when each nation specializes according to its comparative advantage.*

Since total world output of both goods is greatest when each nation specializes according to comparative advantage, clearly there can be more of both goods for both nations if each specializes and engages in trade instead of remaining isolated and self-sufficient. Let's see what particular conditions will motivate Canada and Portugal to specialize and trade.

Terms of Trade

Consider again the output combinations chosen by Portugal and Canada when each is self-sufficient, represented by points *c* and *c'* respectively in Figure 33-4.

Note that Portugal must forgo the production of 40 million metres of cloth in order to produce the 20 million bushels of wheat associated with point c, since each bushel costs 2 metres. Canada must forgo producing 30 million bushels of wheat in order to produce 30 million metres of cloth—each metre costs 1 bushel. If Portugal could get wheat by giving up *less* than 2 metres of cloth for each bushel, and if Canada could get cloth by giving up *less* than 1 bushel of wheat for each metre, each would be eager to do so.

Is this possible? Yes, because of the difference in opportunity costs between the two nations. Let us now suppose that Portugal offers to pay Canada 1 1/2 metres of cloth for each bushel of wheat it is willing to sell. For Portugal this is cheaper than the 2 metres per bushel that wheat costs if Portugal remains self-sufficient. For Canada, such a trade would mean that cloth could be obtained at a cost of 2/3 of a bushel of wheat for each metre of cloth. This is certainly cheaper than the 1 bushel of wheat per metre of cloth it costs Canada if Canada tries to be self-sufficient. Therefore, Canada agrees to the terms of Portugal's offer. The **terms of trade**, the ratio of exchange between cloth and wheat at which both nations agree to trade, would therefore be 1 1/2 metres of cloth per bushel of wheat or, equivalently, 2/3 of a bushel of wheat per metre of cloth.

Specialization and Trade

Having established the terms of trade, Portugal now specializes according to its comparative advantage in producing cloth. It produces 60 million metres of cloth, which is the maximum it can produce on its production possibilities frontier. Canada now specializes according to its comparative advantage in growing wheat, producing 80 million bushels, the maximum it can produce on its frontier. Though each nation specializes in production of one good, each nation's citizens want to consume both goods. This is possible, of course, because the nations can exchange goods at the agreed upon terms of trade. This is shown in Figure 33-5, in which each nation's production possibilities frontier (exactly the same as in Figure 33-4) is shown along with its trading possibilities frontier (TPF). The **trading possibilities frontier** shows the choices that are open to a nation if it specializes in the product in which it has a comparative advantage and trades (exports) its specialty for the product in which it has a comparative disadvantage.

When Portugal produces 60 million metres of cloth, point e in frame (a), it can trade (export) this cloth to Canada. Given the agreed-upon terms of trade of 1 1/2 metres per bushel, Portugal can trade with Canada to get (import) 1 bushel of wheat for every 1 1/2 metres of cloth it exports to Canada. Starting from point e, such trade is represented by movement down the trading possibilities frontier as Portugal gives up 1 1/2 metres for every bushel it gets. This is obviously better than the ratio of exchange along the production possibilities frontier that requires Portugal to give up 2 metres for each bushel it gets. Similarly, Canada produces 80 million bushels of wheat, corresponding to point e' in frame (a). It can then move up the trading possibilities frontier by exporting 1 bushel of wheat in trade for every 1 1/2 metres of cloth it imports from Portugal. Again, this beats the ratio of exchange along the production possibilities frontier that requires Canada to give up 1 bushel for every metre it gets.

In summary, the terms of trade ratio of exchange along the trading possibilities frontier is better than the self-sufficiency ratio of exchange along each

FIGURE 33-5   **Trading Possibilities Frontiers and the Gains from Trade**
(Hypothetical Data)

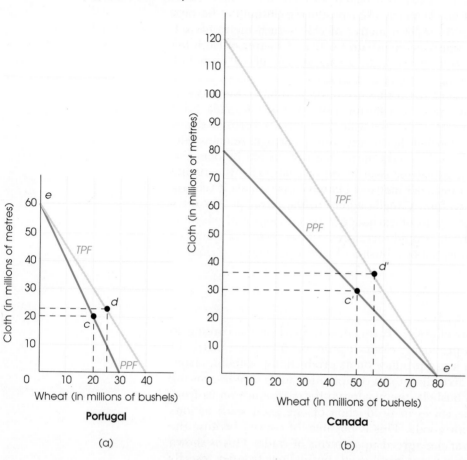

Portugal

(a)

Canada

(b)

Each nation can have more of both goods if each specializes according to its comparative advantage and trades with the other. When each nation is isolated and self-sufficient, each is forced to choose an output combination on its production possibilities frontier. Alternatively, if each nation specializes according to its comparative advantage, each can export some of its specialty in exchange for some of the other nation's specialty at terms of trade represented by the slope of the trading possibilities frontier. Each nation is then able to have more of both goods. For example, the gains from trade for Portugal amount to 4 million bushels of wheat and 4 million metres of cloth (point d compared to point c), and for Canada they amount to 6 million bushels of wheat and 6 million metres of cloth (point d' compared to point c').

nation's production possibilities frontier. Hence, Portugal can get *more* than 1 bushel of wheat for 2 metres of cloth if it specializes in cloth and trades for wheat from Canada. On this two-way street, Canada can get *more* than 1 metre of cloth for every bushel of wheat if it specializes in wheat and trades for cloth from Portugal.

The Gains from Trade

Earlier we noted that if each nation specialized according to comparative advantage, total world output would be larger than if each produced some of both goods. Now we can see how trade makes this possible by allowing the citizens of each nation to consume more of both goods despite the fact that each nation produces only one of them.

Starting from point *e*, Figure 33-5, frame (a), Portugal specializes in the production of cloth (60 million metres), which it trades to Canada for wheat. Starting at point *e'*, frame (b), Canada specializes in the production of wheat (80 million bushels), which it trades to Portugal for cloth. Given the mutually agreed upon terms of trade of 1 1/2 metres per bushel, suppose Portugal exports 36 million metres of its cloth to Canada in exchange for imports of 24 million bushels of wheat. This gives Portugal a combination of 24 million metres of cloth and 24 million bushels of wheat, represented by point *d* on its trading possibilities frontier. Compared with the self-sufficient combination of 20 million metres and 20 million bushels, represented by point *c* on its production possibilities frontier, Portugal is now able to have more of *both* goods. The 4 million more metres of cloth and 4 million more bushels of wheat represent the gains from trade to Portugal. Similarly, Canada exports 24 million bushels of its wheat to Portugal in exchange for imports of 36 million metres of cloth from Portugal. Canada thus has a combination of 36 million metres of cloth and 56 million bushels of wheat, point *d'* on its trading possibilities frontier. This is clearly superior to the self-sufficient combination of 30 million metres of cloth and 50 million bushels of wheat, point *c'* on its production possibilities frontier. The gains from trade for Canada amount to 6 million more metres of cloth and 6 million more bushels of wheat.

We noted earlier that if each nation specialized according to comparative advantage, total world output would be larger than if each produced the output combinations represented by points *c* and *c'* in Figure 33-5. Specifically, we noted that specialization would increase total world output by 10 million metres of cloth and 10 million bushels of wheat. Given the terms of trade (1 1/2 metres to 1 bushel), we now see how trade distributes this additional output—4 million metres and 4 million bushels to Portugal, and 6 million metres and 6 million bushels to Canada. *Because of specialization and trade, there is an efficient allocation of world resources in production. Each good is produced by the nation that can produce the good at the lower cost. Consequently, each nation is able to have more of both goods.*

Finally, it should be noted that Canada is more productive than Portugal in an absolute sense. The production possibilities frontiers in Figure 33-5 show that Canada can produce any combination of wheat and cloth that Portugal can, *plus* more of both goods. This highlights the fundamental point that the incentive to specialize and trade stems from the fact that Portugal and Canada have different opportunity costs in the production of wheat and cloth. For Portugal the opportunity cost of producing wheat is greater than that for Canada, while for Canada the opportunity cost of producing cloth is greater than that for Portugal. If the opportunity costs for Portugal and Canada were the same, there would be no incentive to trade. However, because nations all differ in resource endowments, climate, size, cultures, and technological capabilities, it is little wonder that there is so much specialization and trade in the world.

Some Qualifications

So far in our discussion, we have simply assumed a particular ratio of exchange as the terms of trade. But what in fact determines the terms of trade? We have also assumed constant costs throughout our discussion, so that the production possibilities frontier is a straight line. It is more realistic to assume increasing costs—that the production possibilities frontier is curved, bowed outward from the origin. How does this affect the analysis? Let's consider each issue in turn.

Determining the Terms of Trade

We have been assuming that the terms of trade ratio of exchange between Portugal and Canada is 1 1/2 metres of cloth per bushel of wheat. However, in our hypothetical example both Portugal and Canada would find trade beneficial at terms of trade lying anywhere between 2 metres per bushel, the ratio of exchange along Portugal's production possibilities frontier, and 1 metre per bushel, the ratio of exchange along the Canadian production possibilities frontier. Any terms of trade ratio of exchange lying in this range allows each nation to obtain a good at a lower cost through trade than it costs to produce the good domestically.

The actual terms of trade must fall within the range of 2 metres per bushel and 1 metre per bushel. The exact terms of trade will depend upon the circumstances of the market in which the goods are traded. The price at which trade will actually take place depends on world supply and demand conditions for the two goods. If world demand for cloth is strong relative to cloth supply and the demand for wheat is weak relative to wheat supply, the price of cloth will be high and the price of wheat low. The terms of trade will be closer to the 1 metre per bushel limit, which is more favourable to Portugal than to Canada. If world demand and supply conditions are the opposite, the price of cloth will be low and that of wheat high. Then the terms of trade will be closer to 2 metres per bushel, which is more favourable to Canada. In the absence of any government-imposed barriers, the terms of trade are determined competitively by consumers and producers in the two countries (not by their governments).

Increasing Costs

Suppose that each nation's production possibilities frontier is curved so that it bows out from the origin. That is, each nation is faced with increasing costs as it expands production of the good in which it has a comparative advantage. Suppose that Portugal is initially at the point on its production possibilities frontier at which the cost ratio is 2 metres of cloth for 1 bushel of wheat, and Canada is initially at a point on its frontier where the cost ratio is 1 metre for 1 bushel.

Now suppose that they begin to specialize and trade. As Portugal expands its production of cloth, the cost of producing it increases. That is, it will have to give up more than 1 bushel of wheat to produce 2 metres of cloth. Similarly, as Canada expands production of wheat, increasing cost will require it to give up more than 1 metre of cloth to produce 1 bushel of wheat. Hence, the cost ratio for Portugal goes from 2 metres for 1 bushel to 1.875 metres for 1 bushel to 1.75 metres for 1 bushel, and so forth, as it expands the production of cloth. The cost ratio for Canada goes from 1 metre for 1 bushel to 1.125 metres for 1 bushel to 1.25 metres for 1 bushel and so forth as it expands the production of wheat. The cost ratios of the two nations are now getting closer to each other.

At some point, after each nation has expanded the production of its specialty far enough, the cost ratios may become equal. At that point the basis for additional trade—a difference in opportunity costs between the two nations—will have been eliminated. Furthermore, at that point it is likely that each nation still produces both goods. Portugal may still produce some wheat along with its cloth, and Canada some cloth along with its wheat. When there are increasing costs, specialization may not be as complete, nor the volume of trade as large, as is the case when costs are constant.

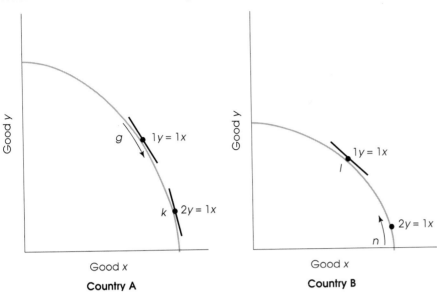

FIGURE 33-6 Trade with Increasing Costs

Country A starts at point g and moves down its production possibilities frontier as trade develops. Country B starts at n and moves up its curve as trade develops.

Figure 33-6 illustrates how opportunity costs can change as two countries trade. Assume that without any trade, country A will operate at point g on its production possibilities frontier and country B will operate at point n on its frontier. Under the circumstances 1 unit of good y will cost 1 unit of good x in country A, but 1 unit of x will cost 2y in B. Clearly there would be gains from trade. Country A would specialize in x and country B in y. As A increased its production of x it would move toward point k on its production possibilities curve. Once A reached k it would no longer have a comparative advantage in the production of x. Similarly, as B increased its production of y, it would move toward point l on its production possibility curve. After trade became established, both countries would move along the respective production possibilities curves until they had the same opportunity cost of x in terms of y. Country A would end up at some point h on its production possibilities curve and B would end up at some point m. Neither of these points are shown in Figure 33-6. They are not shown because it is impossible to say exactly where they would be. The exact location would be determined by the final terms of trade. Point h would be on A's production possibilities curve somewhere between g and k. Point m would be on B's curve somewhere between l and n. The opportunity cost of x would rise in A and fall in B until it was the same in both countries. At that point there could be no gains from additional trade. Because of increasing costs it is very common for countries to produce some of a given good and at the same time import some of that same good.

The Argument for Free Trade

We now have seen how specialization and trade lead to an efficient allocation of world resources. They make it possible for each nation to have more of all goods

Checkpoint* 33-1

Suppose that there are two pioneers in the wilderness. Each sets up a homestead, and each chops wood and grows corn. Construct an illustration showing why it would benefit both to trade with the other. Can you think of examples that illustrate the role of the principle of comparative advantage in explaining trade among various regions of Canada?

*Answers to all Checkpoints can be found at the back of the text.

than is possible in the absence of specialization and trade. While we have illustrated these points using only two nations and two goods, advanced treatments of the subject show that these conclusions hold for a multination, multiproduct world as well. Hence, it may seem odd that there are so many instances in which there is outright opposition to trade with foreign nations. The rest of this chapter will focus on the barriers to trade that nations often erect as a matter of policy. We will examine critically the arguments most often heard in favour of restricting trade. But before considering these matters, we should state the argument for free trade from a somewhat different, yet compelling perspective.

When each nation specializes in production according to its comparative advantage and trades with other nations, each nation is able to move out beyond its individual production possibilities frontier. The effect of specialization and trade is therefore the same as if each nation had gained more technological knowledge, more resources, or both. That is, the effect is the same as if each nation experienced an outward shift in its production possibilities frontier (such as we discussed in Chapter 2). It is possible for each nation to have more of all goods, thereby lessening the problem of scarcity.

Barriers to Trade and Arguments for Protection

The argument for free trade based on the principle of comparative advantage is one of the most solid cornerstones of economic analysis. No other issue seems to command such unanimous agreement among economists as the case for free trade. However, for a variety of reasons different groups in any economy are always prevailing on government to erect barriers to trade—that is, they want protection from the competition of foreign trade. We will first examine some of the more common barriers and then consider the merits of some of the more frequently used arguments for protection.

Barriers to Trade

Tariffs and quotas are the main weapons in the arsenal of protectionism. More recently, antidumping legislation has also been used as a barrier to foreign imports. There are also qualitative controls that can be used as barriers to trade. Such controls can be used to reduce either trade between countries or, in the Canadian case, between provinces. For example a complex meat inspection procedure can be used to protect the consumer against unsafe meat. It can also be used to protect domestic (provincial) producers against foreign (other provincial) producers. Finally, subsidies can be used as a barrier to trade.

Tariffs

A **tariff** (or **duty**) *is a tax on imports, most often calculated as a percentage of the price charged for the good by the foreign supplier.* For example, if the price of a tonne of imported steel were $100, a 10 percent tariff would require the domestic purchaser to pay an additional $10 per tonne. This effectively raises the price of imported steel to $110 per tonne. A tariff may obviously be used as a source of revenue for the government. However, a more common purpose of tariffs is protection against foreign competition. By raising the prices of imported goods relative to the prices of domestically produced goods, tariffs encourage domestic consumers to buy domestic rather than foreign products.

For example, suppose that Japanese steel companies can produce steel at a lower cost than Canadian producers, with the result that the price of imported Japanese steel is $100 per tonne, while the price of domestically produced steel is $102 per tonne. Domestic buyers will import the lower priced Japanese steel. Sales of domestic steel producers will suffer. Consequently, suppose that domestic producers, both company officials and steelworkers' unions, prevail on Parliament to place a 10 percent tariff on imported steel. This raises the price of imported steel to $110 per tonne, a price $8 higher than that of a tonne of domestic steel. Domestic steel users now switch from importing Japanese steel to buying the cheaper domestic steel. Steel imports decline while sales and employment in the domestic steel industry rise. Recognize, however, that while domestic steel producers are better off, the rest of the nation's citizens will have to pay higher prices for all products containing steel. Even products such as bread may be more expensive because steel is used indirectly (combines, ovens, pans) in the production of bread.

Of course, tariffs need not completely eliminate imports. As long as tariffs are not larger than the difference in production costs between domestic and foreign producers, tariffs will not completely eliminate imports. In our example, suppose that Japanese steel producers would just be able to cover costs as long as they receive a minimum of $92.73 per tonne. Suppose that Canadian producers cannot afford to sell steel at a price less than $102 per tonne. With a 10 percent tariff, Japanese producers would just be able to remain competitive with Canadian producers. Japanese steel unloaded on Canadian docks at a price of $92.73 would be taxed 10 percent by the tariff, or $9.27 (.1 × $92.73), thus costing Canadian importers $102 per tonne ($92.73 paid to Japanese producers plus $9.27 in tariff revenue paid to the government). However, if the tariff were greater than 10 percent, imports of Japanese steel would cease, because Japanese producers would suffer losses if they sold their steel at less than $92.73, and this price plus a tariff *greater* than 10 percent would increase the price of imported Japanese steel to domestic buyers so that it was above the $102 price of domestic steel, thus making Japanese steel noncompetitive. If there are increasing costs in the production of a good, then a tariff on that good will reduce but not eliminate imports.

Finally, it should be noted that the use of a tariff as a source of tax revenues runs counter to the use of a tariff for protection. A tariff generates tax revenues only to the extent that there are purchases of imported goods on which tariffs can be collected. In general, to the extent that tariffs successfully serve protectionists' objectives by cutting back imports, the tax revenues from tariffs are also reduced. A tariff so high as to effectively block out all imports, giving complete protection from foreign competition, would generate no tax revenue at all.

Import Quotas

Import quotas *limit imports by specifying the maximum amount of foreign-produced goods that will be permitted into the country over a specified period of time (per year, for example).* Import quotas are a very effective tool of protection, unlike a tariff whose effect on the volume of imports can be hard to predict. After legislating a certain level of tariffs on a particular good or class of goods, or even an across-the-board tariff on all goods, protectionists may find that imports are not limited by anywhere near the extent to which they had hoped. Import quotas remove such uncertainty. Those favouring protection simply specify in the import quota legislation the exact quantity of a particular good that may be imported over a specified period of time. An import quota on Japanese steel, for example, might limit imports of such steel to 1 million tonnes per year.

In some cases quotas are voluntary. An exporting country may agree to voluntary quotas because it fears that if it does not agree, the importing country will legislate protective barriers. In some cases exporting nations may agree to quotas on goods they export in return for voluntary quotas on goods which they import.

Antidumping Laws

Domestic producers of particular products often argue that they are unfairly victimized by competing foreign imports that are "dumped" in domestic markets. The meaning of the term **dumping** is precisely captured by a complaint once registered by U.S. coal producers. They claimed that the prices paid for imported coke (coal) were not only lower than those paid for domestic coke, they were also lower than the foreign suppliers' cost of production.

Canada, like the United States, has an antidumping law. It is the *Anti-Dumping Act* of 1968. In recent years American action against foreign producers who are alleged to have dumped exports in the United States has made the news not infrequently. In a number of cases Canadian producers have been accused. In order to understand the issue involved, it is first necessary to understand dumping. Assume that a foreign producer overproduces. It could sell the extra units in its home country by simply lowering the price. However, it cannot simply lower the price on the surplus units. It would have to lower its price on all the units it sold in the home country. Rather than do that, it ships the excess units abroad and sells them at bargain-basement prices in another country, thereby maintaining its original price in the home market.

For example, suppose the Ajax Company can sell 1,000,000 units per week of its 3G model in its domestic market for $10 each. However, it is producing 1,050,000 units per week. In order to move the extra 50,000 units, the Ajax Company must lower its price to $9. Obviously it is not interested in such a reduction. Its total revenue would fall from $10,000,000 per week to $9,450,000 per week. One of the new MBAs in marketing comes up with a solution: They could sell the excess 50,000 units per week in Canada at $6 each, which is below cost. Now their total revenue will actually increase: $10,000,000 from domestic sales and $300,000 from exports to Canada. It may not appear that there is anything wrong with this arrangement—after all, every week 50,000 Canadians pick up a real bargain. On the other hand, it is certainly not fair to Canadian producers of comparable products. Even if they can produce a good quality product at a reasonable price, they simply cannot compete with the dumped import. If this situation continues they may even be forced out of business, Canadian workers will lose their jobs, Canadian owners will lose their profits. In this case Canadian producers are not losing out to a more efficient foreign firm but to one that is dumping its surplus production. Under these circumstances the Canadian producers could (and almost certainly would) ask Ottawa to impose an antidumping tariff. If dumping were actually occurring, the Canadian government could do just that.

The U.S. antidumping law is controversial. Under U.S. law it is possible that foreign producers could be deemed to be "dumping" simply because they lower their price to meet competition from American producers or because their worldwide business is bad and they are in a shortrun-loss position. (As you will recall from Chapter 9, this means that they are covering average variable cost, but not average total cost.)

Difficulty of Detection

When domestic producers of any product cry "dumping," there is always reason to suspect they are simply campaigning for protectionist measures to shelter them from foreign competition. It may well be that foreign producers are simply more efficient than domestic producers and are not charging prices below their cost of production. That is, foreign producers can charge prices that cover their costs but yet are still below the costs of domestic producers. In that case domestic consumers reap the benefit of lower prices for imported products that cost more when produced at home. Domestic producers' claims of dumping simply amount to "crying wolf."

In the cloth and wheat example developed earlier, Canadian cloth manufacturers might claim that the Portuguese producers were dumping cloth. Similarly, Portuguese farmers might try to claim that Canadians were dumping wheat. Clearly, neither claim would be valid. Exports of both cloth and wheat were fully justified on the basis of comparative advantage, and neither Canadians nor Portuguese producers were engaging in unfair competition. Furthermore, it is hard to establish whether or not foreign producers are selling their goods at prices below their costs. It is difficult if not impossible for an outsider to determine just what foreign producers' costs are. Just such information is necessary to determine whether dumping exists.

Export Subsidies and Countervailing Duties

In addition to dumping, there are other forms of foreign competition that are unfair to domestic producers. In some nations it is not uncommon for the government to provide an **export subsidy**, or payment, to export industries to cover part of their costs of production. For example, suppose that a government pays steel producers $10 for every tonne of steel they export. If it costs the steel producers $90 to produce a tonne of steel, the $10 subsidy from the government effectively reduces their cost to $80 per tonne. Without the subsidy, the steel producers could not sell steel abroad for less than $90 a tonne. With the subsidy, they can sell exported steel for as little as $80 a tonne. Domestic steel producers in the nations importing this subsidized steel may be more efficient than the foreign producers. Let's say that they can produce steel at a cost of $85 per tonne. However, they will not be able to compete with the subsidized imported steel priced at $80 per tonne. Domestic producers in a nation importing the subsidized steel have a legitimate complaint that imported steel is unfair competition. The importing country may well wish to apply an offsetting tax to remove the unfair advantage generated by the export subsidy. Such a tax is called a **countervailing duty**.

Note that though foreign trade may increase as a result of export subsidies, it is not the kind of trade that gives rise to the world gains from trade due to specialization according to comparative advantage. In our example, the subsidized steel imports are in fact more costly to produce than the unsubsidized domestic steel. That is, the nation in which the subsidized steel is produced in fact has a comparative disadvantage in steel production relative to the nation importing the subsidized steel. The issue of export subsidies is very complicated. In the example just given the subsidy was clearly tied to the export of the steel. In many cases a government provides a subsidy for all units produced, whether they are sold domestically or exported (for example, a subsidy of $40 a tonne on wheat). Some subsidies are less obvious (for example, property tax relief given a manufacturer as an incentive to locate in a particular area). Some foreign producers have even claimed that certain Canadian social programs constitute unfair subsidies. Exactly what is an export subsidy is a matter of substantial controversy and is far too complex an issue to discuss in an introductory course. It has been (and will likely continue to be) the subject of very important multinational and bilateral negotiations.

Protecting Employment and Jobs

One of the most common protectionist arguments is that importing foreign goods amounts to "exporting jobs." It is claimed that buying foreign goods instead of domestic goods creates jobs for foreign labour that would otherwise go to domestic labour. It is charged that domestic unemployment will increase as a result. The merits of this argument depend on whether it is made with reference to the shortrun or the longrun.

The Shortrun—Adjustment Problems

There is indeed truth to this argument in the shortrun. Recall again our hypothetical example of trade between Portugal and Canada. When each was isolated and self-sufficient, each had a cloth industry and a farming industry growing wheat. However, when the two nations began to trade, Portugal's farmers could no longer compete with the wheat imported from Canada. All resources previously devoted to farming, including labour, had to be shifted into Portugal's specialty industry, cloth production. Similarly, Canada's cloth producers could no longer compete with imported Portuguese cloth. Labour and other resources in the cloth industry had to shift into Canada's specialty, wheat production.

The gains from trade *after* these shifts have occurred are clear. However, the transitional period of readjustment and reallocation of resources within each country could be painful and costly to many citizens. Workers experienced and trained in farming in Portugal and in cloth production in Canada would no longer have a market for their skills. With their old jobs eliminated, many would need retraining to gain employment in their country's expanding specialty industry. Many would have to uproot their families and move to new locations, leaving old friends and severing familiar community ties. While both nations would realize the material gains from trade in the longrun, it is understandable that those threatened with job loss and an uncomfortable and personally costly transition might well support protectionist measures.

Public policy in a number of nations recognizes that changing trade patterns typically impose transition costs on affected industries and workers. In Canada, adjustment assistance is provided to workers and firms that suffer from increased imports resulting from government actions, such as tariffs and quotas, that lower trade barriers. For example, programs have been developed to assist in the process of adjusting to the Canada–United States Trade Agreement. Not only are there special programs and payments to those workers and producers affected, there is also a phasing-in period to allow time for a more gradual transition.

The reasoning behind a policy of transitional adjustment assistance is this: The removal of trade barriers leads to increased trade. Since the whole nation realizes gains from increased trade, some of these gains can be used to compensate those citizens who suffer losses during the period of adjustment. Quite aside from any issue of "fairness," it may not be politically feasible to lower trade barriers unless those injured by such a move are compensated. As long as not all of the gains from trade are needed to compensate (or possibly bribe) the injured parties, the gains left over after compensation payments still make it worthwhile to lower barriers to trade.

The Longrun

Is there any reason why workers whose jobs have been eliminated by import competition should remain permanently unemployed? No, not as long as the economy is operating near capacity. Workers displaced by import competition will have a more difficult time making a transition to other jobs if the economy is in a recession and unemployment is high. Adjustment assistance cannot overcome a lack of alternative jobs. However, in the longrun, if the economy is operating near full employment, workers displaced by foreign competition will become employed in other areas of the economy. Hence, if the argument prevails that protection from foreign competition is needed to protect domestic jobs and avoid unemployment, in the longrun the nation will end up forgoing the gains from trade. Unemployment that results from increased foreign competition should only be transitional. Any longrun unemployment problem should be blamed on fiscal and monetary policies and other domestic policies for dealing with unemployment, not on a policy of free trade. In fact, the very high levels of unemployment during the Great Depression of the 1930s are generally believed to have been in part due to high tariffs and the resulting lack of trade.

Protection from Cheap Foreign Labour

Another popular argument for protection is that we must protect domestic industries from competition from cheap foreign labour. This argument appeals to the labour vote in particular because they view cheap foreign labour as a threat to their standard of living as well as to their jobs. The argument does not stand up, however. Let's see why.

Suppose that two countries have exactly the *same size* labour force, but one's production possibilities frontier looks like that in frame (a) of Figure 33-4 and the other's looks like that in frame (b). The labour force of frame (b) is absolutely more productive because it can produce more of both goods. Hence, compared to the country of frame (a), the country of frame (b) can pay its labourers more in both industries. Or, put the other way around, labour in the country of frame (a) is cheaper than that of the country in frame (b).

But absolute differences in productivity are not the basis of trade differences—opportunity costs are. Hence, despite the fact that labour in frame (b) is more expensive than labour in frame (a), it pays for both countries to trade, as shown in Figure 33-5. Moreover, note that despite the fact that labour is cheaper in frame (a), it would cost the country in frame (b) more to import wheat from the country in frame (a) than to produce it itself. And despite the fact that labour is more expensive in frame (b), it still costs less for the country in frame (a) to import wheat from the country in frame (b) than to produce it itself. Yes, it is true that the country in frame (b) imports cloth from frame (a) *and* that labour is cheaper in frame (a) than frame (b). But cheaper labour in frame (a) is not the reason why frame (b) imports cloth from frame (a). It does so because the opportunity cost of producing cloth in frame (a) (2 metres for each bushel sacrificed) is lower than it is in frame (b) (only 1 metre for each bushel sacrificed).

To clinch the point, suppose that the cheap labour argument prevails and insurmountable tariff barriers are erected between the two countries so that trade ceases. In each country some labour that previously worked in the industry in which the country specialized according to comparative advantage would now have to work in the less efficient industry. Real wages (the quantity of goods that can be purchased with a given money wage) would *fall* in both countries because each now has *less* output. In terms of Figure 33-5, both countries are now on their production possibilities frontiers at points such as *c* and *c'*, rather than on their trading possibilities frontiers at points such as *d* and *d'*. Living standards in both countries are reduced.

Protection for Particular Industries

Industries faced with competition from foreign imports naturally have a special interest in erecting barriers to such competition. A news item reports of warnings by Canadian steelmakers "that cut-rate imports of foreign steel 'dumped' on Canadian shores mean fewer jobs and, in the longrun, a weaker Canadian steel industry." We should be suspicious of such statements, of course. Any industry seeking protection either can't operate efficiently enough to meet the market test of foreign competition or simply wants a larger share of the domestic market and a chance to milk it by charging higher prices. In either case consumers will have to pay higher prices for the industry's products if protectionist measures are enacted into law.

The protected industry and associated special interest groups stand to gain considerably from such legislation. Hence, they organize lobbies and campaigns to pressure Parliament for tariffs, quotas, and other protective barriers. The rest of the nation's citizens are often not aware of the losses that trade restrictions imply for them. The forces that might oppose such legislation are often nonexistent, disinterested, or too disorganized to offset the industry and special interest groups who favour it. The problem is that protection provides relatively large gains to a few, while freer trade helps everybody a little. But are there circumstances that might warrant protection for a special industry because it is in the best interest of everybody? Yes, some convincing arguments have been made for protecting industries important to national defense. There is also the "infant industry" argument.

The Strategic Industries Argument

Certain industries are indispensable to any war effort—steel, transportation equipment, aircraft, mining of strategic materials, textiles, and so forth. Even though a nation may not have a comparative advantage in the production of any of these products, it may be difficult or impossible to import them when war disrupts world trade. In that case, protective tariffs and quotas may be justified to enable these industries to survive on domestic soil during peacetime. Defense considerations override the usual economic arguments. The difficulty is that many industries seek special protection in peacetime by arguing that they would be indispensable during wartime. Whether in fact they would be or not, the argument provides another vehicle for gaining protection from foreign competition. Indeed, Canadian steelmakers could make a compelling case for protection on these grounds.

This argument can be extended to industries that while not of military importance such as steel may nonetheless play an important strategic part in the independence of a nation. Canada has chosen to protect cultural industries such as television on the ground that these industries are important in developing and maintaining a sense of Canadian identity. Many Europeans feel that they must protect their farms for strategic reasons.

The Infant Industry Argument

It is sometimes argued that certain industries would develop into strong competitors in world markets if only they had a chance to get started. Unfortunately, so goes the argument, without protection from the competition of their already established counterparts in other countries, these infant industries never survive to the point where they can go head-to-head with foreign competition.

There may be some merit to this argument. However, the problem lies in correctly identifying those "infant" industries that are destined, with the aid of temporary protective measures, to mature into productive enterprises in which the nation will definitely have a comparative advantage in a world of free trade. For example, how is it to be decided when maturity has arrived and protection can be removed? Will it eventually become the case that protective measures have simply spawned a mature special interest that is more efficient at maintaining continued protection for itself than it is at producing goods? In the meantime the nation loses in two ways. First, it forgoes the gains from trade available with the purchase of more efficiently produced foreign goods. Second, domestic resources tied up in the protected industry are not available for employment in more efficient industries elsewhere in the economy.

The Diversification for Stability Argument

An economy can be highly specialized in a few products and depend to a large extent on its exports of these products for its ability to import the diversity of other goods it needs. Many developing (and some developed) nations fit this description. Brazil depends heavily on its coffee bean exports, New Zealand on exports of dairy products, and Saudi Arabia on its exported oil. Such nations often suffer from the risks inherent in having too many of their eggs in one basket. If world demand for their particular specialty fluctuates widely, real GDP and employment can be very unstable.

POLICY PERSPECTIVE

Protection and Trade Policy— The Two-Way Street

International trade is a two-way street. It requires that nations import as well as export. However, the history of trade policy among nations clearly indicates that their eagerness to export is not matched by a similar zeal for imports. While domestic producers welcome exports as a way of expanding their markets, they often view imports as a competitive threat to be stopped if at all possible. While policymakers frequently welcome exports as a way of increasing total income and employment, they may often be concerned that imports have the opposite effect (recall our analysis in Chapter 23). Add to these considerations the often emotional arguments for protection we have previously examined, and the basis for a nation's bias in favour of exports and against imports is readily apparent.

Unfortunately, if every nation indulges this bias in the longrun, international trade must cease. Why? Because every nation's exports must be another nation's imports. For example, if Canada doesn't buy goods from other nations (imports), then other nations can't earn dollars to buy goods from Canada (exports). Thus, if a nation raises tariffs, quotas, and other barriers to imports, that nation's export industries will eventually decline. Labour and other resources will have to be reallocated from the nation's shrinking export industries to its expanding industries that produce domestic goods protected by

increased trade barriers. Hence, barriers to imports shift resources away from those industries in which the nation is so efficient as to have a comparative advantage. The gains from trade are lost and the nation's standard of living is diminished. If every nation cuts imports, then every nation's exports must eventually decline as well. Everyone loses the gains from trade.

RETALIATION

The process of shrinking world trade just described could begin with one nation's attempts to cut back its imports. Others might then retaliate by erecting their own barriers to imports. This has been an all-too-common occurrence in the history of world trade. Just as the Great Depression was beginning, Parliament enacted new tariffs on imports, which imposed some of the highest duties in Canadian history. (See Figure P33-1.) If Canadian exports had remained the same, the reduction in imports caused by these tariffs would have increased net exports. This would have had an expansionary impact on total income and employment in Canada. Of course, the levels of income and employment in other nations were adversely affected, since a reduction in Canadian imports meant a reduction in their exports. Hence, other nations raised trade barriers in retaliation, and Canadian exports also declined. Overall, the resulting contraction of world trade aggravated the decline in in-

come and employment in many nations, making the Great Depression even worse.

REDUCING TRADE BARRIERS

Since the very high tariffs of the early 1930s, Canadian tariffs have declined steadily. In 1935 Canada and the United States signed a bilateral treaty reducing tariffs between the two countries. Further reductions took place in 1937. In 1947 Canada and several other nations joined together to establish the General Agreement on Tariffs and Trade (GATT). Initially 23 nations were party to GATT, but that number has expanded to the point where more than 100 nations and territories are now members of GATT. The overall effect has been that Canadian tariffs have fallen steadily since the mid-1930s. This decline has resulted from further bilateral agreements with the United States and other nations and subsequent rounds of multilateral agreements under GATT.

DEVELOPMENTS IN THE 1980s

The recessionary conditions that plagued the world economy during the 1981–1983 period created pressures in many countries to use trade barriers to ease domestic unemployment problems. Despite its formal commitment to GATT, even the United States which has

continued on next page

POLICY PERSPECTIVE CONTINUED

in recent years generally been a strong advocate of freer trade took such measures as restricting imports of Japanese cars, imposing quotas on imported sugar, and restricting imports of steel from the European Community (Belgium, Britain, Denmark, France, Greece, Ireland, Italy, the Netherlands, and West Germany). More recently an encouraging development for freer world trade has been the Uruguay round of GATT negotiations held over the four-year period from 1986 through 1990. Each of the 105 countries and territories participating in this round is committed to a "standstill" on new trade measures inconsistent with their GATT obligations and to a "rollback" program aimed at phasing out inconsistent measures. Every participant is supposed to make concessions

aimed at removing barriers to trade. However, as of the time of writing this edition, these discussions were stalemated on the issue of agricultural subsidies.

Despite substantial tariff reduction among industrialized countries since World War II, tariffs remain high in some sectors (such as textiles, footwear, steel, wood products, and shipbuilding) and among developing countries. International trade is subject to even more severe restrictions in nonmanufacturing sectors, especially in agriculture and services. An improving world economy would help provide a better political climate for the reduction of these trade barriers and the development of freer trade.

For Canada, however, the major development of the 1980s was not in the area of multinational

trade, but in bilateral trade with the United States. The **Canadian–United States Trade Agreement (CUSTA)** became effective on January 1, 1989. While this agreement is often referred to as a free trade agreement, it really fell well short of providing for free trade between the two countries. Under this agreement the remaining tariffs between the two countries are to be eliminated. The tariffs on some goods disappeared immediately. The tariffs on other goods are to be gradually eliminated in either five equal annual steps or ten equal annual steps depending upon the industry in question. This gradual phasing out of some tariffs is intended to minimize the shortrun adjustment process discussed earlier. In a very

continued on next page

FIGURE P33-1   Average Canadian Tariff Rates Since 1868

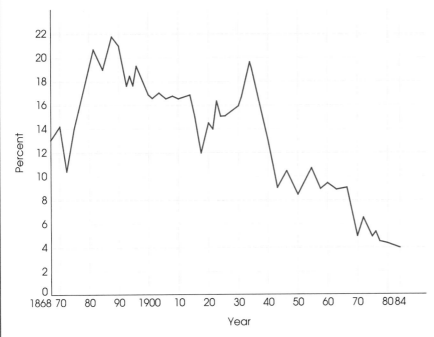

Canadian tariffs rose rapidly after 1878. They remained relatively high until World War I and then fell briefly. They rose again after the war and levelled off during the 1920s before reaching a new peak early in the Great Depression. In 1935, Canada and the United States negotiated a bilateral trade treaty. Since then Canadian tariffs have fallen steadily. In the post–World War II years they have been set at only a small fraction of the levels that prevailed throughout much of our history.

real sense, this agreement was a historic event. In another sense it was nothing more than the logical conclusion of the graduate reduction in trade barriers between the two countries over the previous fifty years.

The negotiating and subsequent signing of the *CUSTA* was one of the most controversial acts in Canadian history. It was strongly supported by many Canadians. Obviously, enough Canadians favoured it to ensure the reelection of the government of Brian Mulroney, which favoured the agreement and campaigned on a free-trade platform. On the other hand, many Canadians strongly opposed it. Both the Liberal Party under John Turner and the New Democratic Party under Ed Broadbent opposed the deal. Together they polled 53% of the votes cast, so it could be said that the majority of Canadians opposed free trade. In actual fact, we will probably never know whether the majority of Canadians favoured or opposed the pact. Other issues influenced voters, and many voters may not have seen the "free trade" issue as all that important. All we do know is that the pact is now in place. Even so, the debate on its merits continues unabated.

Many of the claims made by supporters and opponents were emotional and lacked basis in fact. However, there were thoughtful arguments presented both in favour of and in opposition to the *CUSTA*. The major argument in favour of trade liberalization was the theoretical argument presented earlier. Essentially, both Canada and the United States could benefit from the removal of trade barriers because of gains made possible by increased specialization and the more efficient use of resources. Some also argued that liberalization would allow for more rational transportation patterns. For example, trade

barriers might result in a Cleveland buyer ordering from a Salt Lake City producer and a Calgary buyer ordering from Toronto. Both the Canadian and the American producers could be efficient, but transportation cost would be far less if the Cleveland buyer could order from Toronto and the Calgary buyer could order from Salt Lake City. In general, trade barriers promote East-West trade even when North-South trade is more efficient. A last reason sometimes advanced for the *CUSTA* was the increased consolidation of the world into trading blocks. This trend led some to fear that Canada could have been left out in the cold if we did not join a trading block of our own.

Many of the arguments presented against free trade were similar to the arguments presented in the discussion earlier in this chapter. A number of Canadians were (and some still are) fearful that the *CUSTA* would result in very substantial job losses to the United States. The opponents of liberalization predicted that many branch plants would close. Some opponents took the view that Canadian manufacturing industries could not compete with American firms. Clearly there have been (and probably will continue to be) plant closings, and some Canadian manufacturing firms are not competitive with their American counterparts. The theory presented earlier predicted that some industries would contract if trade liberalization were undertaken. This does not mean that Canadian manufacturing in general will be unable to compete with American firms. Historical evidence suggests that liberalization will actually result in a growth of Canadian exports of manufactured goods. The proportion of Canadian exports that are manufactured goods as opposed to

raw materials has been growing slowly for a long time. Only time will tell what effects the *CUSTA* will have on Canadian employment. Even then, the effects may be somewhat hidden a maze of changes in other variables. In general, however, it is likely that in terms of employment, the long-term benefits of liberalization will be greater than the long-term costs.

There are those who raise a more serious objection to the *CUSTA*. The pact left certain issues to be resolved. The question of subsidies is a very complex one that was not ironed out when the pact was signed. While it should be relatively easy for negotiators to agree to drop direct export subsidies, many programs might be viewed as subsidies. Obviously, any payment to a producer that is based on output gives that producer an advantage in the export market. As such, many American and Canadian agricultural programs would qualify as subsidies. The main controversy, however, is around programs that provide more general assistance. It is possible that some Canadian regional development and social programs could be at risk. Some American producers would like their government to take a hard line on this issue. This possibility has led some Canadians to fear that programs such as unemployment insurance and medical care could be on the line. There is even some fear that general Canadian economic policy might be "harmonized" with American policy. At present the *CUSTA* does not force Canada to give up any of its general social programs. Nor is it necessary that Canada will ever agree to give up any such programs. However, it is clear that

continued on next page

POLICY PERSPECTIVE CONTINUED

there may be pressure in that direction. It is also possible that it will be more difficult for Canada (or the United States) to introduce new programs in the future. On the other hand, some Americans are now pushing for a Canadian-style health care system.

Another objection to the free trade pact is that it will in some way limit Canada's ability to prevent the exports of energy resources to the United States. This part of the treaty has lead some to predict that the government has given away the store. The latter view is a likely an overstatement. Still, it does mean that the Canadian government cannot introduce programs that would favour Canadian buyers over American buyers.

Finally, some Canadians fear that the *CUSTA* is going to result in some loss of Canadian sovereignty. In a sense this is true. Both Canada and the United States gave up a little of their sovereignty when they agreed not to erect certain barriers to the other country's goods. It is even possible that this pact could be the first step to closer economic ties and even political union. However, there is *NO* reason to believe that this is necessarily a consequence of the *CUSTA*. Nevertheless, many Canadians are fearful that Canadian economic, cultural, and/or political sovereignty is threatened.

The ink was barely dry on the *CUSTA* when the United States began pushing for a new North American Free Trade Agreement (NAFTA). Such an agreement would involve Canada, the United States, and Mexico. At the time this text was written, tripartite talks were under way. Whether or not these talks will result in a new agreement is at the time of writing hard to say. However, certain observations can be made.* At present there is relatively little trade between Mexico and Canada. In fact, in 1989 Canadian imports from Mexico accounted to less than 0.5 percent of Canadian GDP. If NAFTA is reached, it is unlikely that imports from Mexico would become very important. A doubling of imports would still mean less than 1 percent of our GDP. While it is difficult to predict the increase in trade with Mexico that would result from a NAFTA, it is unlikely that there would be much of an increase, because present Canadian tariffs on Mexican imports are low. In fact, about 34 percent of Canadian imports from Mexico enter duty free.

One frequently cited objection to a NAFTA is the very low wage levels in Mexico. However, as you already know, it is comparative advantage that determines trade and not low absolute costs. Clearly if low wages were important in determining trade given the low tariffs presently in force, Canada (and the United States) would have already been overrun by Mexican goods. It is certainly unlikely that a NAFTA would result in any significant job loss in Canada because of increased imports from Mexico. It is more likely that Mexican producers could displace some Canadian producers in markets in the United States. Even this is unlikely for the same reasons it is unlikely that Mexican exports to Canada would increase significantly. In any case, the United States is free to reach a bilateral deal with Mexico even if Canada does not join.

Further objections to a NAFTA are sometimes suggested. Mexico's record on human rights and the environment are questioned. Human rights issues may be a valid reason to withhold trade concessions. There is evidence that such a policy was effective in changing South Africa's racial policies. Obviously this objection involve sig-

nificant normative issues. However, Canada already trades with Mexico, so we to seem to feel its human rights record does not warrant economic retribution. In point of fact we have extended trade concessions to countries with far worse human rights records than Mexico.

Like many developing countries, Mexico has a poor record on environmental protection. Of course, there are those who would argue that Canada, like many developed countries, has a poor record on environmental protection. It is possible that by not protecting the environment, Mexico could gain a comparative advantage in the production of certain goods. If that were the case, it might be appropriate to impose countervailing duties.

One final word on trade liberalization. With of the international efforts to reduce trade barriers—the GATT talks, the CUSTA, and the possible NAFTA, there are still significant trade barriers between the provinces in Canada. Canada is *not* a free trade area.

For Discussion

- When a nation raises tariffs or imposes other restrictions on imports in an attempt to reduce domestic unemployment, it is said to be engaging in a "beggar-thy-neighbour" policy—literally, to make beggars of other nations. Explain why.

- Why would a recovery of the world economy make it easier for governments to resist domestic pressure for protectionist measures?

*This following discussion draws on William Watson's article, "North American Free Trade: Lessons from the Trade Data," which appeared in the March 1992 issue of *Canadian Public Policy*. This article, like many that appear in that journal, is written in a nontechnical way and as such can be highly recommended for first-year students.

Checkpoint 33-2

In a news item, coke-oven makers contend that the availability of "cheap foreign coke" is causing steelmakers to postpone "much-needed construction of new coke capacity to replace old and inefficient ovens." What do you think of the coke-oven makers' argument, and where do you think they would stand on the issue of whether or not an antidumping complaint should be filed against foreign coke producers?

It is often argued that such nations could reduce this instability by diversifying their economies—that is, by encouraging the development of a variety of industries producing largely unrelated products. To do this, it is argued, many of these industries would have to be protected from foreign competition by tariffs, import quotas, and other barriers. Otherwise, they would not be able to compete because of their relative inefficiency compared to their foreign counterparts. The main issue here is that there is presumably a trade-off between the gains from trade due to specialization according to comparative advantage on the one hand, and economic stability on the other. Some nations, like some people, prefer to have a higher *average* income level even though it means greater year-to-year income variability, rather than a lower average income with less year-to-year variability. The diversification for stability through protection argument obviously leans toward the lower average income, lower variability point of view.

Summary

1. For many countries, exports represent a sizable portion of their GDPs—for a few, as much as a half or more. Canadian exports and imports run about 25 percent of its GDP, and the absolute dollar volume of its annual exports and imports typically exceeds that of most other nations. More than half of all Canadian exports and imports consist of manufactured goods. The great majority of Canadian exports go to the United States. By the same token, most of our imports come from the United States.

2. The basis for international trade lies in the fact that nations differ in their resource endowments and technological capabilities. Differing resource endowments and technological capabilities typically make the opportunity cost of producing any given good different among nations.

3. Trade between nations is based upon specialization according to comparative advantage. By engaging in trade, nations can have a larger total output than is possible if they remain self-sufficient and isolated.

4. The terms of trade determine how the larger world output made possible by specialization and trade is distributed among nations, and the terms of trade between any two traded goods depend on world supply and demand conditions for the two goods. Increasing costs diminish the extent of specialization and trade relative to what it would be if costs were constant.

5. The argument for free trade is based on the fact that when nations specialize according to comparative advantage and trade, there is a more efficient allocation of resources. The resulting increase in world output lessens the problem of scarcity and makes possible a higher standard of living.

6. Nations often erect barriers to trade in the form of tariffs, import quotas, and antidumping laws. These measures effectively reduce the quantity of imports and allow domestic producers to sell more at higher prices. To the extent that such barriers block trade, there is a less efficient allocation of world resources and a reduced level of total world output.

7. Most of the arguments for protection are flawed. However, shortrun adjustment problems resulting from a reduction of trade barriers can cause real hardship for those in affected industries, possibly justifying shortrun adjustment assistance. In the longrun the economy must operate at near capacity so that the full gains from trade may be realized. Protection may be justified where national defense considerations are concerned.

8. Canadian tariff rates have been declining steadily ever since 1935. Initially the main decline resulted from bilateral agreements with the United States. Since World War II, world trade has been spurred by the General Agreement on Tariffs and Trade (1947).

9. In 1988 Canada and the United States signed a free trade agreement, which went into effect on January 1, 1989. The agreement was one of the most controversial policies in recent Canadian history.

Key Terms and Concepts

antidumping laws	countervailing duty	tariff (duty)
Canada–U.S. Trade	dumping	terms of trade
Agreement (CUSTA)	export subsidy	trading possibilities
comparative advantage	import quotas	frontier

Questions and Problems

1. Why is it that a doctor hires a secretary even though the doctor may be a better typist than the secretary?

2. Suppose that there are two nations, and that one is able to produce two goods, X and Y, and the other is able to produce only good X. Is there likely to be trade between these two nations? Why or why not? If you think they would trade, what do you think would be the terms of trade?

3. Is it conceivable that trade between Portugal and Canada in Figure 33-4 could lead each nation to have more of one good and less of the other—that is, say, as compared to the combinations c and c' that they have when there is no trade? If so, why is each still better off with trade than without it?

4. Suppose that one nation (such as Australia) has a lot of land relative to the size of its population and another nation (such as Japan) has a large population relative to the amount of its land. Suppose also that these two nations have similar levels of technological know-how. What do you think might be the pattern of trade between these two nations? If, on the other hand, the nation with the higher land-to-labour ratio also had a much higher level of technological know-how, how might this change your answer? Why?

5. It is sometimes argued that tariffs can force foreign exporters to provide their goods to us at a lower price. Can you explain why this is true?

6. One argument for protection runs as follows: "If I buy a car from Japan, Japan has the money and I have the car. But if I buy a car in Canada, Canada has the money and I have the car." Explain why you do or do not think this is a valid argument for putting a stiff tariff on imported cars.

7. Find news sources from 1988 that discuss the Canada–United States Free Trade Agreement. Evaluate the agreement in light of the analysis in this chapter and the empirical evidence of the intervening years.

Chapter 34

Balance of Payments, Exchange Rates, and the International Financial System

In the previous chapter we focused on the real aspects of international trade. That is, we looked at the way in which nations can have a larger quantity of goods, or more real output, by specializing according to comparative advantage and trading with one another. But international trade also has a monetary aspect, because goods are exchanged for money and each nation has its own unique money. For example, when Canadians buy goods from the United States, they must pay for them with American money (U.S. dollars). Similarly, Americans must pay for Canadian goods with Canadian dollars. (Note that even if a Canadian store accepts U.S. dollars in payment for a purchase by an American tourist, the store will eventually have to convert those U.S. dollars into Canadian funds. The Canadian store cannot pay its workers, its taxes, and so on, in U.S. dollars.) In short, every movement of goods and services or assets among nations requires a financial transaction. The flow of goods and services in one direction requires a flow of money in the other.

In this chapter we will examine how the international financial system may be organized to handle the financial transactions that accompany international trade. This requires that we become familiar with such concepts as the balance of payments, exchange rates and their determinants, and "official intervention operations." We also will examine why gold has occasionally played an important role in international trade in the past, and how and why the present system of international financial arrangements evolved.

Exchange and the Balance of Payments

When Canadians import goods and services from other nations, we must pay for these imports with foreign currencies, often called *foreign exchange*. For example, German marks must be paid for goods produced in Germany, French francs for goods produced in France, Japanese yen for goods from Japan, British pounds for goods from Great Britain, and American dollars for goods from the United States. Similarly, when Canadians export goods to other nations, Canadian suppliers want to be paid with Canadian dollars. Whatever the country, domestic producers selling goods abroad want to receive payment in domestic currency, because that is what they must use to pay wages and all other factors employed in production. Canadian workers don't want to be paid in French francs, nor do French workers want to be paid in Canadian dollars.

The fundamental point is this: If a nation wants to buy goods and services (imports) from other nations, it must somehow obtain the foreign currencies needed to make payment for these imports. For a period of time, it may be possible to borrow funds from foreigners or sell off assets such as shares of stock, oil reserves, existing factories, and so on, but ultimately the only way a nation can do this is to export some of its own goods and services to other nations and thereby earn the foreign currencies that it needs to pay for its imports. That is, to make payments for imports, a nation must use the payments received from exports—exports must finance imports. Hence, a nation's payments to other nations must be equal to, or balanced by, the payments received from other nations. It is in this sense that there is a balance of payments.

While basically correct, this is a very simplified description of how nations obtain foreign currency. The nature of the balance of payments and the way it is calculated are also considerably more complex in reality. Therefore, we need to look at currency exchange and the balance of payments in more detail.

Currency Exchange

Suppose that a Canadian firm wishes to buy an American machine. The American manufacturer ultimately will want to receive U.S. dollars from the sale of the

---

LEARNING OBJECTIVES

After reading this chapter, you will be able to:

1. Explain why there is a monetary aspect to international trade.
2. Explain the balance of payments concept and describe the major components of the balance of payments account.
3. Describe a balance of payments deficit and a balance of payments surplus.
4. Explain how flexible exchange rates eliminate balance of payments deficits and surpluses.
5. Describe how balance of payments adjustments are made under a system of fixed exchange rates.
6. Discuss the relative merits of a flexible versus a fixed exchange rate system.
7. Explain how a gold standard works.
8. Describe the Bretton Woods system.
9. Explain why the Bretton Woods system has been replaced by a mixed system of flexible exchange rates and managed floats.

machine. The Canadian firm can go to its bank, buy the amount of U.S. dollars needed to pay for the machine, and send them to the American manufacturer. (The bank typically will charge the Canadian firm a small fee for obtaining and providing the U.S. dollars in exchange for Canadian ones.) Alternatively, the Canadian firm may pay the American manufacturer in Canadian dollars. The manufacturer will then take the dollars to its own bank, where it will exchange them for U.S. dollars. Either way, Canadian dollars are exchanged for U.S. funds. The **exchange rate** *is the price of foreign currency.* It is the amount of one currency that must be paid to obtain 1 unit of another currency. Suppose, in our example, that the exchange rate between Canadian dollars and U.S. dollars is $.87 Can. for $1 U.S. Equivalently, it may be said that (approximately) $1.15 Can. can be exchanged for $1 U.S. The price of the U.S. dollar in terms of the Canadian dollar is the reciprocal of the price of the Canadian dollar in terms of the U.S. dollar. Suppose that the price of the American machine is $100,000 U.S. This means that the Canadian firm will have to give its bank $115,000 Can. to obtain the $100,000 U.S. needed to pay the manufacturer. Alternatively, the Canadian firm may give the American manufacturer $115,000 Can. In that case, the manufacturer will take the $115,000 Can. to its own bank and exchange it for $100,000 U.S. Either way the Canadian firm pays $115,000 Can. for the machine and the American manufacturer ultimately receives $100,000 U.S.

Our example illustrates that trade between nations requires the exchange of one nation's currency for that of another. The Canadian purchase of an American machine gives rise to a supply of Canadian dollars and a demand for U.S. dollars. Similarly, an American purchase of a Canadian product would give rise to a supply of U.S. dollars and a demand for Canadian dollars. Hence, international trade gives rise to the international supply and demand for national currencies, or a **foreign exchange market**. The exchange rates among different currencies are determined in the foreign exchange market. We will investigate how foreign exchange rates are determined and what these rates mean for the balance of payments later in this chapter. First, however, we must consider the balance of payments concept.

Balance of Payments

The term **balance of payments** means just what it says: *A nation's total payments to other nations must be equal to, or balanced by, its total receipts from other nations.* When Canadians supply dollars in foreign exchange markets, they are demanding foreign currencies in order to make payments to other nations. The currencies Canadians receive in exchange for their dollars are supplied by foreigners who demand dollars in order to make payments to Canada. Every dollar sold must be bought, and every dollar bought must be sold. Hence, Canadian payments to other nations must be matched exactly by payments from other nations to Canada.

We have already seen how nations keep national income accounts in order to measure domestic economic activity (Chapter 19). Similarly, nations also keep balance of payments accounts in order to keep track of their economic transactions with other nations. A nation's **balance of payments account** records all the payments that it makes to other nations, as well as all the receipts from other nations during the course of a year. The total volume of payments made to other nations is exactly equal to the total volume of receipts from other nations.

The balance of payments account divides the nation's payments to other nations into the following categories: the amount spent on foreign goods; the amount spent on foreign services; the amount paid to foreigners as investment income; the amount loaned to foreign businesses, households, and governments; and the amount invested abroad. Similarly, the account divides the receipts from other nations to show the amount of foreign purchases of the nation's goods; the amount of foreign purchases of the nation's services; the amount received as income from foreign investments; the amount of foreign lending to the nation's businesses, households, and governments; and the amount of foreign investment in the nation. While the total volume of a nation's payments to other nations must always equal the total volume of payments received from other nations, individual categories in the balance of payments accounts need not and typically do not balance. For example, in any given year Canadians may export a larger dollar volume of goods than they import or buy more services from foreigners than are sold to foreigners.

The balance of payments account for Canada is shown in Table 34-1. International transactions that give rise to payments to other nations are recorded as debit items (designated by a minus sign) in the balance of payments account. Such transactions supply dollars to the foreign exchange market and create a demand for foreign currency because Canadians must sell dollars to obtain foreign currency. The importation of a good is an example of a debit item. (Recall our example of a Canadian business importing an American machine, which gave rise to a supply of Canadian dollars and a demand for U.S. dollars.) Transactions that give rise to payments to Canada from other nations are recorded as credit

TABLE 34-1   Canadian Balance of Payments, 1991

Debits: Canadian Payments Payment to Other Nations (Millions of Dollars)		Credits: Canadian Receipts Receipts from Other Nations (Millions of Dollars)		
Current Account				
Merchandise imports	$134,323	Merchandise exports	$141,701	
Balance of trade				$ 7,378
Services	$ 34,207	Services	$ 23,427	
Investment income	31,709	Investment income	8,694	
Transfers	3,952	Transfers	3,579	
Total payments on non-merchandise (invisibles)	$ 69,867	Total receipts on non-merchandise	$ 35,701	
Balance on non-merchandise (invisibles)				−$34,167
Total payments on current account	$204,191	Total receipts on current account	$177,402	
Balance on current account				−$26,789
Capital Account				
Canadian liabilities to non-residences, net flow	$ 42,890	Canadian claims on non-residences, net flow	−$7,987	
Balance on capital account				$34,502
Statistical discrepancy				−$ 8,114
Total balance of payments				$ .00

Source: Statistical Canada. *Quarterly Estimates of the Canadian Balance of Payments*, Fourth Quarter, 1992 (67–001).

Note: Totals may not add exactly due to rounding errors.

items in the balance of payments account. Such transactions supply foreign currency to the foreign exchange market and create a demand for dollars because foreigners must sell their currency to obtain dollars. The export of a good is an example of a credit item. The credit and debit items in the balance of payments account are broadly divided into a current account and a capital account.

The Current Account

The balance of payments on current account includes all receipts during the current period from the export of goods and services and all payments made during the current period for the import of goods and services.

Imports and Exports of Goods—Visibles.   The largest portion of the current account is represented by merchandise imports and exports in the top row of Table 34-1. These are the imports and exports of goods—the "visible" items such as steel, wheat, TV sets, cars, and all the other objects that can be seen and felt. In 1991 Canadian households, businesses, and governments imported $134.3 billion worth of such merchandise and Canadian business exported $141.7 billion. The difference between merchandise exports and merchandise imports is called the **merchandise balance of trade**. When merchandise exports exceed imports, the nation has a merchandise balance of trade surplus. When imports exceed exports, the nation has a balance of trade deficit.

In 1991 Canada had a merchandise balance of trade surplus of $7.4 billion ($141.7 billion of exports − $134.3 billion of imports). As we noted before, there is no particular reason why individual categories of a nation's balance of payments should balance. In fact Canada typically runs a balance of trade surplus on merchandise. When a nation has a merchandise balance of trade surplus, it is often said to have a *favourable balance of trade*. The balance is favourable in the sense that the nation is earning more from its merchandise exports than it is spending on its merchandise imports. If a nation has a balance of trade deficit, it is said to have an *unfavourable balance of trade*. However, it is not necessarily true that it is unfavourable for a nation to get more goods from other nations than it gives in return. Besides, other categories in a nation's balance of payments will necessarily offset a balance of trade deficit, because overall the balance of payments must balance. Similar observations may be made about what is called a *favourable balance of trade* or a *balance of trade surplus*.

Imports and Exports of Services—Invisibles.   The import and export of services, or what are often called *invisibles*, are another sizable component of the current account. For example, Canadians pay for tickets to fly on foreign airlines and pay foreign shippers to carry cargo. They also buy meals and pay for hotel rooms when travelling abroad, buy consulting services from foreign firms, and pay premiums for insurance provided by foreign insurance companies. All of these transactions are examples of imports of services. Like the payments for imported goods, payments for imported services give rise to a supply of dollars in the foreign exchange market and a demand for foreign currencies because foreigners want to be paid in their own currencies. Similarly, Canadians also export services to foreigners. Like the export of goods, the export of services gives rise to a supply of foreign currencies in the foreign exchange market and a demand for dollars.

Like services, income from foreign investment in Canada is another invisible item on the current account. Such income consists of the payment of interest and dividends on Canadian bonds (both government and private) and stocks held by foreigners, as well as the income earned by foreign owned businesses on Canadian soil. It can be thought of as payment for the import of the services of the financial capital provided by foreigners to Canadian government and industry. Such payments give rise to a supply of Canadian dollars and a demand for foreign currencies in the foreign exchange market. Similarly, receipts of income on Canadian assets abroad represent payments received by Canadians (governments, firms, and households) for the services of capital exported to other nations. These payments give rise to a supply of foreign currencies and a demand for Canadian dollars in the foreign exchange market.

The third row in Table 34-1 indicates that Canada purchased more services from other nations than it sold to them in 1991. The fourth row shows that payments to other nations for the services of foreign capital were about three and one half times as large as the payments received by Canadians for providing capital to other nations. Deficits in both services and investment income are typical for Canada. These deficits generally more than offset Canada's favourable balance on merchandise trade.

Unilateral Transfers.   Unilateral transfers represent payments made to another nation for which nothing is received in exchange. Private unilateral transfers are gifts given by Canadians to foreigners. Such payments would include remittances sent home by immigrants and donations to international charities such as Oxfam. Government unilateral transfers consist primarily of foreign aid. Payments to international organizations such as the United Nations also are part of unilateral transfers. Gifts can also flow from other countries to Canada. In recent years this item has been nearly in balance.

Balance on Current Account.   Row 6 shows that the total of the debit items on invisible items ($69.9 billion) was greater than the total of the credit items ($35.7 billion) in 1991. In other words, the total payments made by Canada to other nations was greater than the total payments made by other nations to Canada by $34.2 billion. Overall, on current account Canada supplied more dollars to the foreign exchange market than other nations demanded. Or, equivalently, Canada demanded more foreign currency (to pay other nations) than other nations supplied (to get dollars to pay Canada). In short, on current account, receipts from other nations were less than sufficient to finance Canadian payments to other nations. This deficit on current account amounted to $26.8 billion dollars in 1991.

The Capital Account

There is no reason why there has to be a balance of payments on current account any more than there is a reason why merchandise imports should exactly equal merchandise exports. The current account is itself just a part of the balance of payments. Overall, however, the balance of payments must balance. Since the balance of payments is divided into the current account and the capital account, then the following is true: *If there is a deficit on current account, there must be a compensating surplus on capital account. Likewise, if there is a surplus on current account, there must be a compensating deficit on capital account.* For example, if there is an excess of payments over receipts on the current account (a deficit), then there must be a matching excess of receipts over payments on the capital account (a surplus). That is, if more foreign currency is spent (in payments to other nations) than is earned (in payments from other nations) on the current account, the difference must come from an excess of foreign currency earned over foreign currency spent on the capital account.

Alternatively, an excess of receipts over payments on the current account (a surplus) must be matched by an excess of payments over receipts on the capital account (a deficit). In that case, less foreign currency is spent than is earned on the current account, and the surplus matches the deficit on the capital account, where more foreign currency is spent than is earned. Since the balance of payments is divided into the current account and the capital account, the capital account includes all international transactions not included in the current account. Specifically, the capital account includes all purchases and sales of assets, or what is termed *capital*.

Private Imports and Exports of Capital.   When Canadian businesses and households invest and lend abroad (to foreign businesses, households, and governments), they receive IOUs from foreigners in the form of stocks, bonds, and other debt claims and titles of ownership. Such investments and loans are entered as debit items in the capital account. They represent an increase in Canadian ownership of foreign assets. Why are such transactions recorded as a debit item, just like a merchandise import? There are two basic reasons. First, these transactions represent a payment to other nations. Second, they give rise to a supply of dollars in the foreign exchange market and a demand for the foreign currencies Canadians need in order to pay for foreign stocks and bonds. Moreover, you can think of Canadians importing stock certificates and bonds, just like they import merchandise. Both types of payment represent the acquisition of a claim of ownership or property right from a foreign nation.

Similarly, foreign businesses and households also invest and make loans in Canada (to Canadian businesses, households, and governments) for which they receive Canadian stocks and bonds. These represent an increase in foreign ownership of Canadian assets and are entered as credit items in the capital account. Such transactions give rise to a supply of foreign currencies in the foreign exchange market and a demand for Canadian dollars needed by foreigners to make payment for their investments and loans. In exchange, Canada may be thought of as exporting stock certificates and bonds—that is, exporting property rights and ownership claims.

Government Imports and Exports of Capital.   Governments also make capital account transactions. These consist mostly of loans to or from other governments; the sale of federal, provincial, or local bonds to foreign citizens; changes in government holdings of official international reserve assets such as foreign currencies, gold, and reserves with the International Monetary Fund called special drawing rights (SDRs), which we will discuss later; and changes in liquid claims on official reserve assets.

Loans to other governments are debit items on the government's capital account because they represent payments to other nations for the import of their IOUs, just like lending on the private capital account. Such lending gives rise to a supply of Canadian dollars and a demand for foreign currency in the foreign exchange market. Similarly, foreign governments make loans to the Canadian government. These are recorded as credit items on the government's capital account because they represent payments received from other nations in exchange for the export of the Canadian government's IOUs (such as Canadian government bonds and Treasury Bills). Such transactions create a supply of foreign currency and a demand for Canadian dollars in the foreign exchange market.

The government capital account transactions in official reserve assets and liquid claims on official reserve assets play an accommodating role in the balance of payments. They adjust to satisfy the requirement that overall the balance of payments must balance. Therefore, they adjust because the total amount of foreign currency needed to make all payments to other nations *must* necessarily equal the total amount of foreign currency earned from all receipts from other nations.

For example, suppose that there is a deficit on current account, a deficit on private capital account, and loans to foreign governments exceed loans received from them. The volume of foreign currency received from other nations will be less than the volume of foreign currency paid to them. The difference will have to be made up either by using government holdings of official reserve assets or by giving other nations liquid claims on the government's holdings of official reserve assets. Payments out of holdings of reserve assets will, of course, reduce government holdings. Such payments are entered as a credit item on the government's capital account because they represent the export of official reserves (foreign currency, gold, or SDRs). Similarly, making payments by giving other nations liquid claims on holdings of official reserves is also a credit item. This item represents the export of an IOU, the liquid claim. The nation receiving the liquid claim may "cash it in" at any time (hence the term *liquid*) by demanding payment in official reserve assets.

Balance on Capital Account.   In 1991 Canada had a surplus on its capital account. Total credits on the capital account for that year were $42,890 million and total debits were $7,987 million. This leaves a balance of $34,902 million. Canada generally has a substantial surplus on its capital account. In theory the surplus (deficit) in the capital account should exactly offset the deficit (surplus) in the current account. However, in practice, the actual data the government has is not complete. There is no central registry of all international transactions. Consequently there are some errors and omissions. These are given in Table 34-1 as −$8,114 million. This figure compensates for the errors in data collection and the government's inability to keep track of virtually all Canadian transactions with other nations.

Balance of Payments Deficits and Surpluses

In the news we often hear or read about this or that nation's balance of payments deficit or surplus. But if the balance of payments must balance, why the talk about deficits and surpluses? Sometimes commentators are referring to the balance of trade. (To avoid confusion, they should say so explicitly.) In general, however, such references are made with respect to the balance of payments *excluding* government capital account transactions in official reserve assets (foreign currency, gold, and SDRs) and liquid claims against these reserves.

With this interpretation, a **balance of payments deficit** means that the government is reducing its holdings of official reserve assets or that the liquid claims of foreign governments against these reserves are increasing, or both. The deficit equals the excess of the nation's payments to other nations over the payments received from other nations, exclusive of government capital account transactions in official reserves and liquid claims. A **balance of payments surplus** means that the government is increasing its holdings of official reserves or its holdings of liquid claims on the official reserve assets held by foreign governments, or both. The surplus equals the excess of the payments received from other nations over the payments made to them, again exclusive of government capital account transactions in official reserves and liquid claims.

Exchange Rates and Balance of Payments Adjustments

The size of balance of payments deficits and surpluses, as well as the adjustment process for their elimination, depends on the role that exchange rates are allowed to play in international transactions. At one extreme, exchange rates between national currencies can be freely determined by the forces of supply and demand in the foreign exchange market. At the other extreme, exchange rates can be rigidly fixed by government intervention in the foreign exchange market. We will now examine each of these extremes.

Flexible Exchange Rates

When exchange rates between national currencies are freely determined by supply and demand in the foreign exchange market, they are said to be **flexible** *(or* **floating***)* **exchange rates**. They are free to change in response to shifts in supply and demand.

Currency Depreciation and Appreciation

When there is an increase in the exchange rate between Canadian dollars and a foreign currency, the foreign currency gets more expensive in terms of dollars—it takes more dollars or cents to buy a unit of foreign currency. Since this is the same thing as saying that a dollar will buy less foreign currency, we say that the value of the dollar has *depreciated* relative to the foreign currency. **Currency depreciation** means that now more units of a nation's currency will be required to buy a unit of a foreign currency.

Conversely, if there is a decrease in the exchange rate between dollars and a foreign currency, it takes fewer dollars or cents to buy a unit of foreign currency. Since a dollar will now buy more foreign currency, the value of the dollar is said to have *appreciated* relative to the foreign currency. **Currency appreciation** means that now fewer units of a nation's currency are required to buy a unit of foreign currency.

Note that an appreciation in the value of one nation's currency is necessarily a depreciation in another's. For example, suppose that the rate of exchange between dollars and Japanese yen (¥) is initially $1/¥. Suppose that the value of the dollar appreciates relative to the yen. For instance, say that the rate of exchange decreases to $.50/¥. It now takes half as many dollars to buy a given amount of yen. For the Japanese this means that the rate of exchange has risen from 1 yen per dollar to 2 yen per dollar. In other words, the value of the yen

Checkpoint* 34-1

Explain how you would classify the following international transactions on the balance of payments account and why each is a credit or a debit item: as a Canadian citizen you get a haircut in the United States to avoid paying the GST; you give a birthday present to a cousin in France; you buy a Volkswagen and finance payments on it with a loan made to you by a Canadian bank; and a Japanese company builds a new factory in Canada.

Answers to all Checkpoints can be found at the back of the text.

has depreciated relative to the dollar. It now takes twice as many yen to buy a dollar.[1]

Exchange Rates and the Price of Foreign Goods

The following example is written in terms of two countries, Canada and Sweden. (Economists traditionally discuss trade problems in terms of two countries. The student should realize that this discussion could be generalized to cover Canada and all foreign countries.)

Exchange rates allow citizens in one country to translate the prices of foreign goods and services into units of their own currency. Suppose that $1 exchanges for 5 Swedish kronor (kr) on the foreign exchange market. If the price of a Swedish-made car is 100,000 kr, its price in Canadian dollars is $20,000, or 100,000 multiplied by .20. Similarly, if the price of a tonne of Canadian wheat is $100, its price in kronor is 500 kr, or 100 multiplied by 5. If the price of the krona rose to $.25 or 4 kr for one Canadian dollar, the price of the Swedish car would increase to $25,000, but the price of Canadian wheat in kronor would decrease to 400 kr. *Changes in exchange rates alter the prices of foreign goods to domestic buyers and the prices of domestic goods to foreign buyers.*

Free-Market Determination of the Exchange Rate

In Chapter 4 we saw how supply and demand work in a freely operating market (one in which the government or some other powerful agent does not intervene) to determine the price of a good. The exchange rate is just the price of one currency stated in terms of another, and the determination of the equilibrium level of a flexible, or floating, exchange rate is determined by supply and demand just like the price of wheat or haircuts.

For example, suppose that Canada and Sweden are the only two trading countries in the world and suppose that the exchange rate between Canadian dollars and Swedish kronor is determined by supply and demand in the foreign exchange market as shown in Figure 34-1. (Our example uses hypothetical data.) The vertical axis measures the exchange rate, the price of a krona in terms of dollars. The horizontal axis measures the quantity of kronor. The equilibrium level of the exchange rate is $.20/kr, which corresponds to the intersection of the supply curve S and the demand curve D at point e.

The demand curve D shows the quantity of kronor demanded by Canadians at each possible level of the exchange rate. It comes from the desire on the part of Canadians to exchange dollars for kronor. The kronor are needed to buy Swedish goods and services and to pay interest and dividends on Swedish loans and investments in Canada. They are also needed to make unilateral transfers such as gifts and to pay for the Canadian acquisition (by government, businesses, and private citizens) of Swedish assets. In short, the demand curve D represents the Canadian demand for kronor needed to make payments to Sweden—all the transactions with Sweden that enter as debit items on the Canadian balance of payments account.

---

[1] In practice it is necessary to exchange money at a bank. Naturally they do require a profit. Therefore the price of a yen would be slightly more than $.50 and the price of a dollar would be slightly more than 2 yen. For simplicity economists often assume that there are no transaction costs for currency exchange. Similarly economists often assume that there are no transportation costs in trade.

**FIGURE 34-1   Determination of the Equilibrium
Level of a Flexible Exchange Rate**

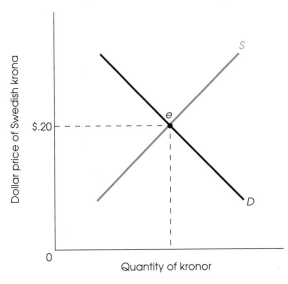

Underlying the demand curve *D*
for Swedish kronor is the desire
of Canadians to exchange
dollars for kronor needed to
buy Swedish goods and services
and to acquire Swedish assets.
Similarly, behind the supply
curve *S* for kronor is the desire
of Swedish citizens to exchange
kronor for dollars needed to buy
Canadian goods and services
and to acquire Canadian
assets.

The supply curve *S* shows the quantity of kronor supplied by Swedish citizens
at each possible level of the exchange rate. Underlying it is the desire of the
Swedes to exchange kronor for dollars needed to pay for Canadian goods and
services and for the Swedish acquisition of Canadian assets. These payments
are represented by all the credit items on the Canadian balance of payments
account.

The supply and demand curves slope in their normal directions. If the exchange rate were below the equilibrium level, the quantity of kronor demanded
would exceed the quantity supplied, and the exchange rate (the price of a krona)
would be bid up. If the exchange rate were above the equilibrium level, the
quantity of kronor supplied would exceed the quantity demanded, and the rate
would be bid down. At the equilibrium exchange rate, there is no tendency for
the rate to change, because the quantity of kronor demanded is just equal to
the quantity supplied.

Flexible Exchange Rates and the Balance of Payments

The argument for flexible exchange rates is that they automatically adjust to
eliminate balance of payments surpluses and deficits. Let's see how this happens.

The equilibrium in the foreign exchange market of Figure 34-1 (represented
by the intersection of *D* and *S* at point *e*) is reproduced in Figure 34-2. In
equilibrium there is no balance of payments deficit or surplus as we have defined
these concepts. That is, there are no government capital account transactions in
official reserves and liquid claims between the two nations. Moreover, the total
of all other Canadian payments to Sweden is exactly equal to the total of all
payments received by Canada from Sweden.

Now suppose that Canadians step up their imports of Swedish goods (say because more Canadians develop a taste for Swedish furniture and other goods).
Total payments to Sweden will now exceed total payments received from Sweden

FIGURE 34-2 **Adjustment of a Flexible Exchange Rate to Eliminate a Balance of Payments Deficit**

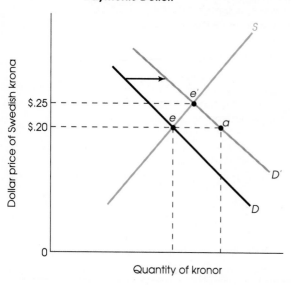

An increase in Canadian imports of Swedish goods will cause the demand curve for kronor to shift from D to D' because Canadians now need more kronor to make payments to Sweden. With a flexible exchange rate, the excess demand for kronor, equal to the distance between points e and a, will cause the rate to be bid up. This adjustment will continue until the exchange rate has risen to the new equilibrium level of $.25 per krona (corresponding to the intersection of S and D' at point e').

Canadian demand for kronor needed to make these payments will increase, as represented by the rightward shift in the demand curve for kronor from D to D' in Figure 34-2. At the initial exchange rate of $.20 per krona, there will now be a shortage of kronor. Equivalently, we can say there will be an excess demand for kronor equal to the distance between points e and a. Canada will now have a balance of payments deficit.

How will a flexible exchange rate eliminate this deficit? The excess demand for kronor will cause the exchange rate (the Canadian dollar price of kronor) to be bid up. But this will alter the prices of *all* Swedish goods to Canadians and the prices of *all* Canadian goods to Swedish citizens in the way we discussed earlier. Since Canadians will now have to pay more for kronor, the prices of Swedish goods will now be higher when translated into Canadian dollars. Therefore, as the exchange rate is bid up, Swedish goods will become more expensive for Canadian buyers and Canadian imports from Sweden will tend to decline. This decline is represented by a move from point a toward point e' along D' in Figure 34-2.

But a rise in the dollar price of kronor is the same thing as a fall in the krona price of Canadian dollars. The dollar depreciates relative to the krona, and the krona appreciates relative to the dollar. Swedish citizens will now find that they don't have to pay as much for dollars. The prices of Canadian goods and assets will therefore be lower when translated into kronor. Since Canadian goods are now less expensive for Swedish citizens, Swedish imports of Canadian goods and purchases of Canadian assets will tend to increase. This increase is represented by a move from point e toward point e' along S in Figure 34-2.

Hence, as the exchange rate rises to the new equilibrium position corresponding to e', an exchange rate of $.25 per krona, Canadian imports from Sweden decline while Canadian exports to Sweden increase. The result will be to eliminate the balance of payments deficit in Canada. *When exchange rates are flexible, or freely determined by supply and demand, balance of payments deficits and surpluses will be quickly eliminated. Indeed, it is often argued that foreign exchange markets adjust so quickly that there would be no deficits or surpluses if governments didn't interfere.* Later in this chapter we will see how governments interfere with the mechanism.

Factors Affecting Flexible Exchange Rates

We have just seen how a change in one nation's demand for the products of another can affect the exchange rate. Other factors can also cause shifts in supply and demand in foreign exchange markets, and hence changes in flexible, or floating, exchange rates. Two of the more important factors in determining exchange rates are differences in rates of inflation among nations and changes in the level of interest rates in one nation relative to the interest rates in others. Also important, but difficult to quantify, are political considerations that can influence exchange rates.

Differences in Rates of Inflation

Assume again that the equilibrium exchange rate between dollars and kronor is $.20/kr, determined by the intersection of *D* and *S* at point *e* in Figure 34-3. Now suppose that the general price level in Canada (the prices of all Canadian products) rises relative to the general price level in Sweden. Canada has a higher rate of inflation than Sweden. As a result, Swedish goods become less expensive relative to Canadian goods, *given the exchange rate of $.20/kr.* Hence, Canadians increase their demand for imports from Sweden, thereby causing their demand for kronor to increase, as indicated by the rightward shift in the demand curve for kronor from *D* to *D'*. At the same time, the rise in the Canadian price level

---

FIGURE 34-3   Differential Changes in the Price Levels of Two Nations Cause the Exchange Rate to Change

The rise in the general price level of Canadian goods relative to Swedish goods causes a depreciation of the dollar relative to the krona in the foreign exchange market.

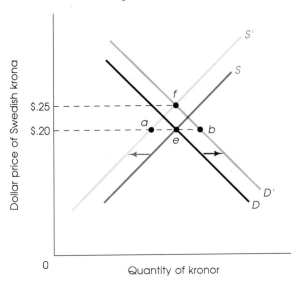

causes Swedish citizens to reduce their demand for Canadian goods. This results in a reduction of their supply of kronor (their demand for dollars), indicated by a leftward shift of the supply curve of kronor from S to S'.

At the initial exchange rate of $.20/kr, there is now an excess demand for kronor equal to the distance between points a and b. This excess demand will cause the exchange rate to be bid up from $.20/kr to $.25/kr, corresponding to the intersection of S' and D' at point f, Figure 34-3. The Canadian demand for Swedish imports will be cut back and the Swedish demand for Canadian goods will increase in exactly the manner already described in connection with Figure 34-2. In short, the rise in the general price level of Canadian goods relative to Swedish goods causes a depreciation of the dollar relative to the krona in the foreign exchange market.

Our hypothetical example illustrates a general observation about exchange rate movements in the real world. Given a sufficient length of time, the exchange rate between the nations' currencies will tend to adjust to reflect changes in their price levels, all other things remaining the same. Of course, all other things typically do not remain the same. Hence, it is usually difficult to observe real-world adjustments that are as clear-cut as our hypothetical example.

The process of exchange rate adjustment due to differential changes in national price levels operates continuously when two nations experience different rates of inflation. If two nations are each experiencing the same rate of inflation, then the relation between their general price levels remains the same. The exchange rate between their currencies will therefore remain unchanged, all other things remaining the same. *If a nation's rate of inflation is greater than that of a trading partner, the nation with the higher inflation rate will experience an increase in its exchange rate—that is, a depreciation of its currency—all other things remaining the same.* Suppose, for instance, in our example of Canada and Sweden, that the Canadian price level continued to rise relative to that of Sweden. Then the rate of exchange between the Canadian dollar and the krona would continue to rise. The dollar would continue to depreciate relative to the krona.

Changes in Interest Rates

In our discussion of the capital account of the balance of payments, we observed that money is loaned and borrowed across national borders. Some of these funds are moved around the globe almost continually in search of those highly liquid financial assets (such as short-term government bonds and commercial paper) that pay the highest interest rates. When the interest rates prevailing in one country change relative to those prevailing in another, funds tend to flow toward that country where interest rates are now highest, all other things remaining the same.

For example, suppose that the interest rate on Canadian Treasury Bills is 8 percent, the same rate as on comparable short-term Swedish government bonds. If the interest rate on Treasury Bills suddenly drops to 7.5 percent (due to Bank of Canada policies), short-term Swedish government bonds paying 8 percent interest will look relatively more attractive to Canadian investors. They will therefore increase their demand for kronor in order to buy more Swedish bonds. The demand curve for kronor will shift rightward, just as in Figure 34-3. Similarly, Swedish investors will reduce the supply of kronor, since Canadian Treasury Bills will also be relatively less attractive to them. Hence, the supply curve for kronor will shift leftward, again as in Figure 34-3. The result will be a rise in

Checkpoint 34-2

When one currency depreciates, why does another necessarily appreciate? In what sense is the supply curve in Figure 34-1 a demand curve for dollars and the demand curve a supply curve of dollars? What would happen to the exchange rate of dollars for pounds if Canadian authorities started to pursue a more expansionary monetary policy, all other things remaining the same? Why? What do you think would happen to the exchange rate of dollars for pounds if British authorities started to pursue a more restrictive fiscal policy, all other things remaining the same? Why?

the exchange rate of Canadian dollars for kronor, a depreciation of the dollar relative to the krona. *Since funds can be quickly transferred between countries, changes in the relative levels of interest rates between countries are a primary cause of day-to-day changes in flexible, or floating, exchange rates.*

Fixed Exchange Rates and the Balance of Payments

Governments have often chosen to fix, or *peg*, exchange rates, which is just the opposite of allowing the forces of supply and demand to freely determine rates in the foreign exchange market. In order to fix the exchange rate at a level above or below the equilibrium level determined by supply and demand, governments must continually intervene in the foreign exchange market. Let's see why this is so, and how governments must intervene.

Fixing the Rate Above Equilibrium

Consider the supply and demand for kronor in Figure 34-4, frame (a). If the exchange rate were flexible, or floating, it would be equal to the equilibrium rate of $.20 per krona, as determined by the intersection of the demand curve D and supply curve S at Q_e. However, suppose that the Swedish government wants to

---

FIGURE 34-4   Fixed Exchange Rates: Balance of Payments Deficits and Surpluses

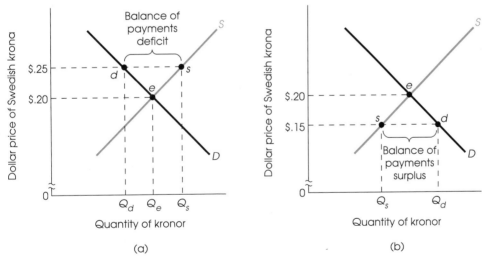

(a)   (b)

Suppose that the Swedish government wants to fix, or peg, the exchange rate above the equilibrium level at $.25 per krona, as shown in frame (a). Then it will have a balance of payments deficit equal to the excess supply of kronor, represented by the distance between points d and s. In order to maintain the exchange rate of $.25 per krona, the Swedish government will have to buy up the excess supply of kronor using dollars out of its holdings of official reserves.

Alternatively, suppose that the Swedish government wants to fix the exchange rate below the equilibrium level at $.15 per krona, as shown in frame (b). Then it will have a balance of payments surplus equal to the excess demand for kronor, represented by the distance between points s and d. In order to maintain the exchange rate $.15 per krona, the Swedish government will have to supply the foreign exchange market with a quantity of kronor equal to the excess demand.

fix, or peg, its exchange rate at $.25 per krona. At this price the quantity of kronor demanded by Canadians in order to make payments to Sweden equals Q_d. The quantity of kronor supplied by Swedish citizens in order to get dollars to make payments to Canada equals Q_s. The quantity of kronor supplied exceeds the quantity demanded—payments by Sweden to Canada are greater than payments by Canada to Sweden. Therefore, Sweden has a balance of payments deficit represented by the distance between Q_s and Q_d.

But what will keep market forces from bidding the exchange rate down to the equilibrium level of Q_e and eliminating the excess supply of kronor? The Swedish government must buy up the excess supply of kronor (equal to the distance between Q_d and Q_s) at a price of $.25/kr using dollars out of its holdings of official reserve assets (foreign currencies, gold, and SDRs). The Swedish government will be able to continue fixing the exchange rate above the equilibrium level only as long as it has reserves. Once the reserves run out, the exchange rate will fall to the equilibrium level of $.20/kr. When the price of a currency (the exchange rate) is pegged above the equilibrium level that would prevail in a free market, the currency is often said to be *overvalued*. In this case the krona is overvalued relative to the dollar.

Fixing the Rate Below Equilibrium

Now consider the opposite case, in which the exchange rate is fixed below the equilibrium level—the krona is undervalued relative to the Canadian dollar. For example, suppose that the Swedish government wants to peg the exchange rate at $.15/kr, as illustrated in Figure 34-4, frame (b). In this case, the quantity of kronor demanded by Canadians Q_d exceeds the quantity supplied by Swedish citizens Q_s. Payments by Sweden to Canada are now less than payments by Canada to Sweden. Sweden now has a balance of payments surplus equal to the distance between points Q_s and Q_d.

How will the Swedish government keep the excess demand for kronor from bidding up the exchange rate to the equilibrium level of Q_e? It will have to supply the foreign exchange market with a quantity of kronor equal to the excess demand (the distance between Q_s and Q_d). In exchange for these kronor the Swedish government will acquire Canadian dollars, which will increase its holdings of official reserves.

Policy Implications of Fixed Exchange Rates

It is generally easier for a government to keep its currency undervalued (the exchange rate is pegged below the equilibrium level) than to keep it overvalued (the exchange rate is pegged above the equilibrium level). As we have seen, a government must draw down its reserves of foreign currencies in order to keep its currency overvalued. Obviously, it can't do this indefinitely, or it will run out of such reserves. It may be able to borrow more from other nations, but again not indefinitely. By contrast, in order to keep its currency undervalued, a government only has to supply its own currency to the foreign exchange market. While this is easy to do in theory, it may not be a wise policy in the longrun. For much of the 1960s, Canada maintained the Canadian dollar at about $.925 U.S. Toward the end of this period the Bank of Canada found it very hard to hold the Canadian dollar down to this peg and eventually the Canadian dollar was allowed to float upward.

Overvalued versus Undervalued Currencies

Clearly, it is easier to keep currencies undervalued than to keep them overvalued. What are the policy implications of this fact? Suppose that all nations are trading under a system of flexible exchange rates, so that there are no balance of payments deficits or surpluses. Now suppose that they all agree to fix exchange rates at currently prevailing levels. As time passes, supply and demand curves in foreign exchange markets inevitably shift due to changing trade patterns and differing economic developments within each nation. Since exchange rates are fixed, some nations end up with overvalued currencies and balance of payments deficits while others have undervalued currencies and balance of payments surpluses.

Nations with overvalued currencies and balance of payments deficits must do something to correct their situation or they will run out of official reserves. By contrast, those with undervalued currencies and payments surpluses are not under this pressure—they need only keep supplying their own currency to the foreign exchange market. Hence, to eliminate its payments deficits and preserve its reserve holdings, a nation with an overvalued currency is often forced to allow its currency to depreciate. In a world of fixed exchange rates, this is called a **currency devaluation**—that is, the exchange rate is now officially fixed at a lower level. Of course, the problem could also be cured if nations with undervalued currencies officially allowed their currencies to appreciate, called a **currency revaluation** in a world of fixed exchange rates. Obviously, if one currency is overvalued, another must be undervalued. But the pressure on the nation with the overvalued currency to devalue is simply greater than that on the nation with the undervalued currency to revalue.

Bias Toward Contractionary Fiscal and Monetary Policy

Unfortunately, devaluing a nation's overvalued currency is not a politically popular thing for the government in office to do. It is often seen as a sign of a weakening economy and a loss of international stature. It is also likely to result in domestic inflation. As a country devalues, the price of imported goods will increase. As the price of imports rises, the producers of domestic substitutes may also increase their prices. Inflation can result in demands for increases in wages and other factor costs, leading to a vicious circle of inflation, devaluation, inflation, and so forth. Similarly, a nation with an undervalued currency faces political obstacles to revaluation because sales abroad by its export industries benefit when its currency is underpriced in the foreign exchange market.

But the nation with the overvalued currency and the balance of payments deficit must do something to avoid running out of official reserves. One possibility is to pursue a contractionary fiscal and monetary policy, thereby curbing total demand. As we saw in Chapter 23, this also will tend to reduce the nation's demand for imports, and a reduction in imports will help to reduce its balance of payments deficit. Unfortunately, curbing total demand will also increase the nation's unemployment rate and reduce its total output. Its domestic policy goals will have to be sacrificed to its international policy goal of reducing its payments deficit.

Of course, another possibility for the nation with an undervalued currency and balance of payments surplus is to pursue an expansionary fiscal and monetary policy. The nation's total demand would rise, causing an increase in its imports from the nations with overvalued currencies and payments deficits. Unfortunately, this might cause unacceptable inflationary pressures in the expanding nation. The nation is likely to be very reluctant to sacrifice its own domestic price stability for the sake of reducing another nation's balance of payments deficit, especially since this will reduce its own payments surplus as well. Consequently, the burden usually falls on the nation with the overvalued currency (the one running out of official reserves) to pursue contractionary fiscal and monetary policy in order to reduce its payments deficit. Hence, many critics of a fixed exchange rate system contend that it is biased toward enforcing contractionary fiscal and monetary policies on nations with overvalued currencies and chronic balance of payments deficits. As a result, they claim, worldwide unemployment rates are higher and worldwide output levels lower under such a system.

Finally, what if a nation with an overvalued currency and a payments deficit is neither willing to devalue nor willing to curb total demand with restrictive fiscal and monetary policy? Such a nation may simply erect tariffs and other trade barriers to curb its imports. In that event everybody loses, as we saw in the previous chapter.

Canada is a relatively small, open economy. A large proportion of its GDP is involved in foreign trade. Consequently the preceding discussion is significantly more relevant to Canada than it would be to the United States. If the American government devalued the U.S. dollar by 10 percent, the cost of imports would rise by 10 percent. However, those imports would amount to 5 percent of American purchases. Assuming that domestic prices were not affected, the price level would rise by about 0.5 percent. The same situation in Canada would result in a 10 percent increase in prices of about 25 percent of purchases or about a 2.5 percent increase in the general price level. Similarly, if the United States used fiscal and/or monetary policy to adjust an undervalued currency, the resulting unemployment would be proportionally far less than would be the case for Canada.

Flexible versus Fixed Exchange Rates

What are the advantages and disadvantages of a system of flexible exchange rates compared with a system of fixed exchange rates?

Fiscal and Monetary Policy Considerations

Under a system of fixed exchange rates, countries will run balance of payments deficits and surpluses because exchange rates cannot automatically adjust to equalize supply and demand in the foreign exchange markets. As we have just seen, countries with chronic balance of payments deficits may have to sacrifice high employment in order to reduce their payments deficits. Hence, critics argue, fixed exchange rates interfere with a nation's freedom to use fiscal and monetary policy to pursue domestic policy goals. These same critics often advocate flexible exchange rates because they automatically eliminate balance of payments problems, thus freeing fiscal and monetary policy to focus strictly on domestic objectives. However, some advocates of fixed exchange rates argue just the opposite. They claim that the fear of running large balance of payments deficits serves as a check on governments that might otherwise pursue excessively expansionary fiscal and monetary policies that cause inflation.

Stability and Uncertainty

Critics contend that flexible exchange rates inhibit international trade because of the uncertainty about their future levels. For example, suppose that a Canadian woolens wholesaler puts in an order to purchase wool blankets from a British woolen mill. Suppose that the current exchange rate is $2/£, and that a wool blanket including shipping costs £40, or $80. At this price the Canadian woolens wholesaler feels that the British blankets will be very competitive with Canadian-made blankets that sell for $90. However, suppose that the blankets are delivered to the Canadian wholesaler 3 months after the order is placed and that in the meantime the exchange rate has increased to $2.50/£. The English woolen mill contracted to sell the blankets for £40 apiece. But in dollars it will now cost the Canadian woolens wholesaler $100 per blanket ($2.50 × 40), a price that will no longer be competitive with comparable Canadian-made wool blankets selling for $90. Clearly, fluctuations in flexible exchange rates can make international business transactions risky.

Advocates of flexible exchange rates argue that it is possible to hedge against the risks of changing exchange rates by entering into futures contracts. For instance, at the time the Canadian woolens wholesaler placed the order for the wool blankets, a futures contract could have been obtained that guaranteed delivery of pounds 3 months hence to the wholesaler at a rate of $2/£. Whatever happens to the exchange rate between dollars and pounds in the meantime, the wholesaler will be assured of getting pounds at $2/£ when it comes time to pay for the blankets. Who will enter into the futures contract agreeing to supply pounds to the wholesaler at this rate of exchange? Someone needing dollars 3 months hence who wants to be sure they can be obtained with pounds at a rate of $2/£. That someone might be a British firm that has ordered goods from an Canadian firm to be delivered and paid for in 3 months.

While acknowledging the protection that hedging can offer, some critics still claim that flexible exchange rates can fluctuate wildly due to speculation—for example, the purchase of pounds at $2/£ on the gamble that the rate will rise, say to $2.25/£, yielding the speculator a profit of $.25/£. To the contrary, advocates of flexible exchange rates respond that speculative activity will tend to stabilize exchange rate fluctuations. They claim that speculators must buy currencies when they are low priced and sell them when they are high priced if they are to make money. Hence, it can be argued that speculators will tend to push the price of an undervalued currency up and the price of an overvalued currency down, thus serving to limit exchange rate fluctuations.

It can be argued that fixed exchange rates invite destabilizing speculation even more than flexible exchange rates. Suppose that a currency is overvalued, such as the krona in Figure 34-4, frame (a), and suppose that word spreads that the Swedish government is running out of the dollar reserves needed to fix the price of kronor above the equilibrium level and finance its payments deficit. Anticipating a devaluation of the krona, holders of kronor will rush to

Checkpoint 34-3

Describe what a government must do in order to fix an exchange rate. Why are balance of payments deficits and surpluses inevitable under fixed exchange rates? If a country's currency was overvalued and it decided to tighten its monetary policy, what would happen to its official reserve holdings? Why?

POLICY PERSPECTIVE

Canadian Exchange Rates

In this perspective, we will discuss the value of the Canadian dollar in terms of the U.S. dollar. It would be equally valid to discuss the value of the U.S. dollar in terms of the Canadian dollar. Someone about to take a holiday in the United States would likely want to know the Canadian value of the U.S. dollar, because that is what they would have to pay to buy U.S. dollars for their trip. However, it is common practice in Canada to quote the price of the Canadian dollar in terms of the U.S. dollar. It is also valid to discuss the value of the Canadian dollar in terms of the British pound, the French franc, or the Japanese yen. It is more common to compare the Canadian dollar with the U.S. dollar, because the United States is Canada's major trading partner. It is important to realize that when the Canadian dollar declines against the U.S. dollar, this does not necessarily mean it also declines against the pound, the franc, the yen, or in fact against any other currency. Similarly if the Canadian dollar appreciates against the U.S. dollar, it does not indicate that it is necessarily appreciating in general.

Over the last forty years the value of the Canadian dollar in terms of the U.S. dollar has varied substantially. During the 1950s the price of the Canadian dollar reached almost $1.05 U.S. At the other extreme it fell to nearly $.70 in 1986. The price of the Canadian dollar in terms of U.S. dollars for this period

is given in Figure P34-1. Not only has the value of the Canadian dollar changed during this period, so has government policy on exchange rates.

Prior to the 1950s, the Canadian dollar had been pegged or fixed in terms of the U.S. dollar. However, in the 1950s Canadian maintained a floating or flexible exchange rate policy. Under this policy the exchange rate rose and the Canadian dollar actually traded at more than $1.00 U.S. It is even reported that the New York subway made a nice profit off Canadian coins deposited by riders. However, in 1960 the value of the Canadian dollar began to fall rapidly.

In April of 1962 the Canadian dollar was again fixed. This time at about $.925 U.S. In actual practice the value of the Canadian dollar was allowed to vary slightly, but as can be seen from Figure P34-1, it remained very nearly constant throughout the balance of the decade. Near the end of the decade, strong upward pressure on the Canadian dollar developed. The government of Canada returned to a floating exchange rate.

Once the Canadian dollar was allowed to float, it quickly rose to $1.00 U.S. In fact, by 1973 it was again trading at over $1.00 U.S. In 1977 the Canadian dollar began a decade of substantial decline against the U.S. dollar. It reached a low of about $.72 U.S. in 1986 and then began to rise again. During

the earlier part of this period, the Canadian rate of inflation exceeded the American rate, so the Canadian dollar tended to fall in value. The later recovery was in part due to higher Canadian interest rates, which attracted foreign investors.

During the 1960s, when the dollar was officially pegged, it actually varied slightly. Countries never maintain absolute control of the value of their currency. It is also possible for a country to claim that its currency is floating when in fact the government is influencing its value. In some cases a government may opt for a **managed float**. Under a managed float the value of a currency is flexible. It is allowed to move up and down as dictated by the market. However, the government does intervene to maintain some order. If there is substantial downward pressure on a currency, its fall in value can be made more gradual. Similarly, in the case of appreciation, the currency can be made to increase over a period of time. If short-term conditions result in temporary speculation, the government can offset the effects of such speculation until the situation returns to normal. Seasonal variations can also be offset. There is normally downward pressure on the Canadian dollar in January as foreign-owned firms repatriate the profits, many Canadians take vacations in warmer climates, and those

continued on next page

the foreign exchange market to get rid of their kronor before their price drops. This will shift the supply curve of kronor rightward, making the excess supply even larger. With a larger payments deficit and reserves now declining faster, actual devaluation may be unavoidable. Whether the preceding argument is true is an empirical question. Moreover, it is a difficult one to disprove, since it would not necessarily always happen.

POLICY PERSPECTIVE CONTINUED

of us who stay at home eat imported fruits and vegetables. Under a managed float, the Bank of Canada might take temporary steps to counter these seasonal fluctuations.

Countries sometimes engage in a policy known as a **dirty float**. Under a dirty float, the government officially claims that it is allowing the market to establish the exchange rate for its currency but in practice is buying (or selling) its currency on the open market in order to maintain an unofficially pegged rate—or at least keep the exchange rate higher (or lower) than it would be under a freely floating policy.

Even if a country does not directly influence the exchange rate for its currency, it may do so indirectly. In the late 1980s and into the 1990s the Bank of Canada was accused of maintaining high interest rates in Canada in order to increase the flow of short-term funds from foreign investors. The effect of such a policy would be to increase the value of the Canadian dollar in terms of other currencies.

For Discussion

● One of the first economic principles to be discovered is known

as *Gresham's law*. Loosely put it states, "Bad money drives out good." It was noted earlier that when the Canadian dollar was worth more than $1 U.S., the New York city subway made a profit off Canadian coins. How do you think they made that profit? What do you think large Canadian retailers do with U.S. coins that they receive? What do you think these same Canadian retailers would do with U.S. coins if the Canadian dollar was worth $1 U.S.? How does this issue relate to Gresham's law?

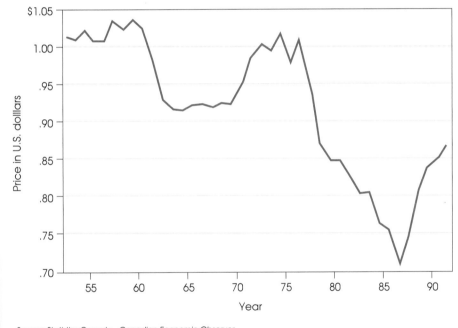

FIGURE P34-1 **Exchange Rate of Canadian Dollars**

The value of the Canadian dollar in terms of the U.S. dollar has varied substantially over the last 40 years. During the 1950s, the Canadian dollar fluctuated but remained above $1 U.S. In the 1960s the Canadian dollar was fixed at about $.925 U.S. Since then the Canadian dollar has floated.

Source: Statistics Canada. *Canadian Economic Observer,
Historical Statistical Supplement 1990/91* (11-210)
and *Canadian Economic Observer*, March 1992, (11-010)

The International Financial
System—Policies and Problems

The international financial system consists of the framework of arrangements under which nations finance international trade. These arrangements influence whether exchange rates will be fixed, flexible, or some combination of fixed and flexible, either a managed or dirty float. The arrangements also influence the way balance of payments adjustments take place and the way nations finance balance of payments deficits. We will now examine the principal ways in which the international financial system has been organized during the twentieth century. First we will briefly consider the gold standard, which prevailed during the late nineteenth and early twentieth centuries. We will then examine the Bretton Woods system, which governed international transactions from 1944 to 1971, and finally the mixed system that prevails today.

The Gold Standard

For about 50 years prior to World War II, the international financial system was predominantly on a gold standard. Canada and most other industrial nations were on a gold standard from 1879 to 1934 (except for two years, 1917–1918, during World War I).

Gold and a Fixed Exchange Rate

Under a **gold standard** gold serves as a backing for each nation's money. Each nation defines its monetary unit in terms of so many ounces of gold. The use of this common unit of value automatically fixes the rate of exchange between different currencies. For example, suppose that Canada defines a dollar as equal to 1/400 of an ounce of gold. This means Canada would pay $1 for every 1/400 of an ounce of gold to anyone who wants to sell gold to it or give 1/400 of an ounce of gold for every dollar of its currency to anyone who wants to buy gold. Alternatively, it could be said that gold is worth $400 Canadian/ounce. Canadian currency (coins and paper money) would be redeemable in gold. Suppose that Great Britain defines its monetary unit, the pound, as equal to 1/200 of an ounce of gold. The British Treasury would redeem its currency at the rate of 1/200 of an ounce of gold for every pound. This would mean that gold was worth 200 pounds/ounce. What would be the international rate of exchange between Canadian dollars and pounds?

The exchange rate would be fixed at $2/£. People who wanted pounds to buy British goods would never pay more than $2/£. Why? Simply because they could always go to the Canadian Treasury and get 1/200 of an ounce of gold for $2, then ship the gold to Great Britain, where they could exchange it at the British Treasury for a British pound. (For simplicity, we will ignore shipping costs.) Similarly, it would not be possible to buy a pound for less than $2. Why? Because no one would sell a pound for less than this when they could exchange it at the British Treasury for 1/200 of an ounce of gold and then ship the gold to Canada, where it could be exchanged for $2. In practice, under the gold standard gold bullion usually did not move, only ownership claims changed hands.

The Gold Flow Adjustment Mechanism

Now that we see why the exchange rate was rigidly fixed under a gold standard, let's see how balance of payments adjustments took place under such a system. Clearly, if Canada imported more from Great Britain than it exported,

Canada would have to pay the difference by shipping gold to Great Britain. What would eliminate Canada's balance of payment deficit and Great Britain's balance of payments surplus to ensure that Canada wouldn't eventually lose all its gold to Great Britain?

When Canada ran a payments deficit, the nation's money supply, its gold stock, would decrease, while that of its trading partner, Great Britain, would increase. Every time a Canadian bought British goods, dollars (Canadian currency) would be turned in to the Canadian Treasury in exchange for gold. The gold would then be shipped to Great Britain and exchanged at the British Treasury for the pounds needed to pay British exporters. Similarly, every time a British citizen bought Canadian goods, pounds (British currency) would be turned in to the British Treasury in exchange for gold. The gold would then be shipped to Canada and exchanged at the Canadian Treasury for the dollars needed to pay Canadian exporters. If Canadians bought more from the British than the British bought from Canadians, more gold would be flowing out of Canada than was flowing into it. The reverse would be true of Great Britain—more gold would be flowing in than out. Hence, Great Britain's money supply would increase while Canada's would decrease.

Now recall the effect of money supply changes on an economy, as was discussed in previous chapters. If Great Britain's money supply was increasing, this change in the money supply would increase its aggregate demand and income. Its price level would tend to rise and its interest rates to fall. As prices of its goods rose, they would become more expensive for Canadians and lead to a reduction of Canadian imports from Britain. Similarly, the fall in British interest rates would make British securities less attractive, so that Canadian purchases (imports) of such securities would decline. At the same time, the rise in Britain's aggregate demand and income would tend to stimulate its imports—its purchases of Canadian goods and services. All of these factors would amount to a reduction in Canadian payments to Britain and an increase in British payments to Canada. All these factors would work together to reduce the Canadian balance of payments deficit and decrease Great Britain's payments surplus.

Consider what would be happening in Canada at the same time. The Canadian money supply would be decreasing, reducing its aggregate demand and income. This would put downward pressure on its price level. The reduction in its money supply would also tend to push Canadian interest rates up. To the extent that Canadian prices fell, British citizens would find Canadian goods cheaper and would therefore buy more of them. Similarly, higher interest rates would lead British citizens to step up their purchases of Canadian securities. Finally, the reduction in aggregate demand and income would tend to reduce Canadian imports of British goods. Again, all these factors would contribute to an increase in Britain's payments to Canada and a reduction in Canadian payments to Britain.

In short, the Canadian balance of payments deficit and the British payments surplus would automatically set in motion forces that would reduce Canada's payments deficit and Britain's payments surplus. As long as a Canadian payments deficit and a British payments surplus exist, these forces would continue to operate until both the deficit and the surplus were eliminated. At that point, the flow of gold to Canada from Britain would exactly equal the flow of gold from Canada to Britain. (Of course, in actual practice gold was rarely physically shipped, it's ownership was simply transferred.) Balance of payments equilibrium would be restored. The process was slightly complicated by the fact that gold was (and still is) also a commodity that Canada produced and sold as an export. However, this complication is not serious.

To summarize, under a gold standard nations with balance of payments deficits would lose gold to nations with balance of payments surpluses. The increase in the money supplies of the surplus nations would tend to push up their price levels, reduce their interest rates, and increase their imports from deficit nations. The decrease in the money supplies of the deficit nations would tend to reduce their price levels, increase their interest rates, and reduce their imports from surplus nations. This process would continue until balance of payments equilibrium in all nations was restored.

Shortcomings of the Gold Standard

The major difficulty with a gold standard is that balance of payments adjustments operate through interest rate, output, employment, and price-level adjustments in each nation. Deficit nations may have to suffer recession and high rates of unemployment, while surplus nations experience unanticipated inflation with all the gains and losses that this bestows arbitrarily on different citizens. In short, domestic goals, such as the maintenance of high employment and output as well as price stability, are completely at the mercy of the balance of payments adjustment process. Most economists feel that this amounts to letting the tail wag the dog. While large economies like that of the United States might be able to maintain reasonable internal economic policy on the gold standard, it would be particularly difficult for smaller open economies such as Canada's.

Moreover, gold discoveries, which can happen at any time, can cause haphazard increases in money supplies and inflation. Conversely, a lack of gold discoveries can result in money supply growth lagging behind worldwide economic growth. Consequently, tightening money supply conditions may trigger recessions and put a damper on economic growth. During this century, worldwide economic activity has increased much more rapidly than the world's gold supply.

Demise of the Gold Standard

The general inflation following World War I, in particular the German hyperinflations of the 1920s and the Great Depression of the 1930s, were the undoing of the gold standard. Many nations, faced with high unemployment, resorted to protectionist measures, imposing import tariffs and quotas and exchange controls (regulations that make it difficult to exchange domestic for foreign currency). Through such measures each hoped to stimulate sagging output and employment at home by maintaining exports and reducing imports. Clearly, this was no more possible than for each participant in a foot race to run faster than everyone else. In percentage terms, world trade fell even more than world output.

As the worldwide depression deepened, nation after nation had cause to fear that if its economy began to recover while those of its trading partners remained depressed, its imports would increase while its exports remained low. Under a gold standard such a nation would lose gold, and the resulting contraction of its money supply would drag its economy back into depression. This consideration, combined with the desire to stimulate exports, led nations to devalue their currencies in terms of gold throughout the 1930s. The resolve to keep the rates of exchange between national monetary units and ounces of gold permanently fixed (and hence permanently fix rates of exchange between currencies)—the essence of an orthodox gold standard—had been broken. This state of affairs persisted until the end of World War II.

The Bretton Woods System

In 1944 the industrial nations of the world sent representatives to Bretton Woods, New Hampshire, to establish a new international financial system for international trade. They set up a system of fixed exchange rates, with the U.S. dollar serving as the key currency, called the **Bretton Woods system**. That is, the United States agreed to buy and sell gold at $35 per ounce, while the other nations agreed to buy and sell dollars so as to fix their exchange rates at agreed-upon levels. Hence, currencies of all countries that signed the Bretton Woods agreement were indirectly tied to gold. For example, someone holding German marks could exchange them for dollars at a fixed exchange rate and then exchange the dollars for gold in the United States.

The agreement seemed a logical way to set up the new system for two reasons. First, the United States had the most gold reserves. Second, the war-ravaged economies of Europe viewed the U.S. dollar as soundly backed by the productive capacity of the American economy. The Bretton Woods system (sometimes called the *gold exchange system*) clearly reflected a widespread belief that international trade would function better under a fixed exchange rate system than under one of flexible rates. It also reflected an age-old belief that money should be backed by a precious metal such as gold or silver. While the agreement provided for international exchange of currencies for gold, it did not require that internally a country necessarily had to convert its currency to gold.

Establishment of the International Monetary Fund (IMF)

Recall from our earlier discussion of fixed exchange rates that if a nation's currency is fixed above the free-market equilibrium level, it will lose holdings of official reserves. When these are gone, it simply has to devalue its currency. The International Monetary Fund (IMF) was established to deal with this problem as well as to supervise and manage the new system in general. Member nations were required to contribute funds to the IMF. Then, to bolster its ability to keep exchange rates fixed, the IMF was given the authority to lend these funds to member nations running out of reserves. For example, if the British government used up its dollar reserves purchasing pounds to fix the dollar price of pounds above the free-market equilibrium level, the IMF would lend Britain dollars to continue its support operations. The situation should be temporary, and Britain eventually should earn enough dollars in world trade to repay the IMF. A nation would be allowed to devalue relative to the dollar only if its currency were chronically overvalued, so that it continually ran a balance of payments deficit.

Problems with the Bretton Woods System

We have already examined some of the major problems that plague a fixed exchange rate system. All of these troubled the Bretton Woods system until its demise in 1971. Nations often had to compromise their domestic policy goals out of concern for balance of payments considerations. The burden of adjustment usually fell on the nations with overvalued currencies and balance of payments deficits. They often had to pursue more restrictive fiscal and monetary policies to curb total demand and income in order to reduce their imports. Deficit nations also had to devalue their currencies more often than surplus nations revalued. Deficit nations were the ones borrowing from the IMF and allegedly the source of difficulty. In addition, as it became more apparent that a currency would have to be devalued, the day of reckoning was hastened by those selling the currency to beat the fall in the exchange rate. Was a world of such sudden readjustments really more conducive to international trade than a world of flexible exchange rates? Was the uncertainty surrounding such abrupt adjustments really less than the uncertainty that would exist under flexible exchange rates? These questions were often raised. Unfortunately, politically acceptable answers were not easy to find.

End of the Bretton Woods System

As the postwar period moved into the 1960s, the fixed levels of exchange rates established after World War II became increasingly out of line with the levels that would give balance of payments equilibrium in most countries. Fixed exchange rate levels established when the Japanese and European economies were still suffering from the ravages of war became increasingly unrealistic as these nations recovered and became more competitive with the United States. As a result, during the 1960s the dollar became increasingly overvalued and the United States ran chronic and growing balance of payments deficits. At the same time countries such as Germany and Japan ran chronic balance of payments surpluses as their currencies were increasingly undervalued. They found themselves continually accepting dollar claims (IOUs) from the United States. In the meantime the United States lost more than half of its gold stock. Foreigners became increasingly nervous about holding overvalued dollars and forced the United States to honour its commitment to exchange gold for dollars at $35 per ounce.

What could be done? The American dollar, the key currency of the system, was overvalued. The United States was not willing to sacrifice domestic policy goals, such as high employment, to reduce its payments deficit. Countries with undervalued currencies often found it difficult to revalue (increase the dollar price of their currencies) because their politically powerful export industries would lose sales as their goods became more expensive to foreign customers. Finally, in 1971 the United States government announced that it would no longer buy and sell gold at the established price of $35 U.S./ounce. The link between gold and the dollar was broken and the era of the Bretton Woods system was over.

Flexible Exchange Rates and Managed Floats

Despite initial attempts by the industrial nations to restore fixed exchange rates in late 1971, the international financial system has become a mixture of flexible exchange rates and managed floats. Some nations have allowed their exchange rates to float freely. Many others operate a managed float, a system whereby exchange rates are largely allowed to float but are subject to occasional government intervention. For example, a nation with an overvalued currency may from time to time use its holdings of foreign reserves to buy its own currency, thus easing its rate of depreciation. In the spirit of Bretton Woods, some countries still attempt to peg their exchange rates more or less to the U.S. dollar.

The Declining Role of Gold

What has happened to the role of gold in the international financial system? In 1968, before the link between gold and the dollar was broken, the IMF created a paper substitute called **special drawing rights (SDRs)**. SDRs serve as an official reserve in addition to gold and currency holdings. SDRs are really special accounts at the IMF that can be swapped among member nations in exchange for currencies. Since this is exactly what nations used to do with gold, the SDRs are popularly dubbed "paper gold." Unlike gold, however, the IMF can create SDRs whenever it feels more official reserves are needed to meet the financial needs of expanding world trade. In this sense the creation of SDRs to expand official reserves in the world economy is much like a central bank's creation of member bank reserves in a national economy. Since the elimination of the fixed rate of exchange between the dollar and gold in 1971, gold has become more like any other metal bought and sold in world markets. In recent years both the U.S. Treasury and the IMF have attempted to de-emphasize the importance of gold as money by selling some of their gold holdings.

Adjustment in the New Environment

The 1970s and 1980s were turbulent years for the world economy. Oil prices quadrupled from 1973 to 1974, abruptly rose again with the revolution in Iran in 1979, and then fell throughout most the 1980s. During 1974 and 1975 and again in 1982, industrial nations experienced the most severe recession since the Great Depression of the 1930s. During the 1970s inflation was a major problem for a number of nations, including Canada. And differences in domestic inflation rates among major industrial powers changed over the decades of the 1970s and 1980s. All these factors required continual readjustment of exchange rates. Many economists feel that the more rigid exchange rate structure of the Bretton Woods system would never have survived these stresses and that the mixture of managed floats and flexible exchange rates has probably served the world economy better. However, a number of economists argue that swings in exchange rates, particularly during the 1980s, generated so much uncertainty for business decision makers that world trade was less than would have occurred under a fixed exchange rate system.

> **Checkpoint 34-4**
>
> Some economists argue that the Bretton Woods system imposed a certain amount of fiscal and monetary discipline on governments that was missing in the world economy of the 1970s and 1980s. What do they mean?

Summary

1. International trade has a monetary aspect because trade between nations requires the exchange of one nation's currency for that of another. A nation's exports of goods, services, and financial obligations (IOUs) give rise to a demand for its currency and a supply of foreign currencies in the foreign

exchange market. A nation's imports of goods, services, and financial obligations give rise to a supply of its currency and a demand for foreign currencies in the foreign exchange market.

2. A nation's balance of payments is an accounting statement that itemizes its total payments to other nations and the total payments it receives from other nations. This statement reflects the fact that total payments to other nations must be equal to (or balanced by) total payments received from other nations.

3. A nation has a balance of payments deficit when its government must draw on its official reserves, issue liquid claims (to other nations) on these reserves, or both, to finance an excess of payments to other nations over receipts from other nations. A balance of payments surplus occurs when receipts from other nations exceed payments to other nations, so that the government receives official reserves and liquid claims from other nations to finance the difference.

4. The forces of supply and demand automatically adjust flexible, or floating, exchange rates to eliminate chronic balance of payments deficits and surpluses. They do this by changing the relative attractiveness of goods, services, and assets between nations. Flexible exchange rates tend to adjust to reflect differential rates of inflation and changes in relative interest rate levels between nations.

5. Exchange rates can be fixed, or pegged, only if governments intervene in foreign exchange markets to buy and sell currencies. Fixed exchange rates give rise to balance of payments deficits and surpluses. Under fixed exchange rates deficits can be eliminated either by currency devaluation or by pursuing a restrictive fiscal and monetary policy to curb total demand and income. Conversely, surpluses can be eliminated either by revaluation or by an expansionary fiscal and monetary policy. Devaluation and revaluation are often resisted because of political considerations.

6. Critics contend that in practice a fixed exchange rate system tends to be biased toward forcing contractionary fiscal and monetary policies on nations with overvalued currencies. Advocates of fixed exchange rates argue that the uncertainty about future levels of flexible exchange rates tends to put a damper on international trade. Advocates of flexible exchange rates respond that it is possible to hedge against much of this uncertainty by entering into futures contracts. Moreover, they note, fixed exchange rates are not immune to uncertainty—namely, uncertainty about currencies that are likely to be devalued to eliminate chronic balance of payments deficits.

7. The gold standard has provided a system of fixed exchange rates in the past. However, balance of payments adjustments under this system often require severe changes in employment, income, and prices, thus sacrificing domestic policy objectives to balance of payments equilibrium.

8. The Bretton Woods system provided the financial framework for international trade from 1944 to 1971. Under this system nations fixed their exchange rates in terms of the U.S. dollar, the key currency, which was convertible into gold at a fixed rate of exchange maintained by the United States. The International Monetary Fund (IMF) was established to supervise the system, to lend official reserves to nations with temporary payments deficits, and to decide when exchange rate adjustments were needed to correct chronic payments deficits. The system eventually foundered in 1971 due to chronic and rising U.S. payments deficits that led to growing concern about the dollar's continued convertibility into gold.

9. Since the demise of the Bretton Woods system, the international financial system has been a mixture of flexible exchange rates, managed floats, and continued attempts to fix some exchange rates in terms of the dollar.

Key Terms and Concepts

balance of payments
balance of payments
 account
balance of payments
 deficit
balance of payments
 surplus
Bretton Woods system
currency appreciation

currency
 depreciation
currency devaluation
currency revaluation
dirty float
exchange rate
fixed exchange rates
flexible (floating)
 exchange rates

foreign exchange
 market
gold standard
managed float
merchandise balance
 of trade
special drawing rights
 (SDRs)

Questions and Problems

1. When a nation has a balance of payments deficit, would you say that it is exporting or importing official reserves and liquid claims? Why?

2. Tell whether each of the following generates a demand for foreign currency (any currency other than Canadian dollars) or a supply of foreign currency on foreign exchange markets.
 a. A German firm builds a plant in Nova Scotia.
 b. A British firm transfers a million dollars from its bank account in a Toronto bank to its bank account in a London bank.
 c. The Canadian government makes a foreign aid grant to Zaire.
 d. A Canadian firm transports goods from the east coast to the west coast through the Panama Canal on a Liberian freighter.
 e. Belgium has a balance of payments deficit in its transactions with Canada.
 f. A Canadian's holdings of French government bonds matures.

3. Suppose that you observe the following exchange rates: 5 French francs exchange for $1, 4 German marks exchange for $1, and 3 French francs exchange for 2 German marks.
 a. Can you think of a way to make money out of this situation?
 b. What would you expect to happen if exchange rates were flexible?
 c. What would you expect to happen if exchange rates were fixed at these levels?

4. How would a nation's exchange rate likely be affected by each of the following, all other things remaining the same?
 a. The nation's trading partners start to pursue relatively more expansionary monetary policies.
 b. The nation increases its imports.
 c. The nation experiences a decline in the growth of productivity relative to that of its trading partners, therefore weakening its competitive position in the world economy.
 d. The nation cuts its income taxes.
 e. The nation has a recession.
 f. The nation's major trading partner has a recession.
 g. The nation steps up its advertising about its tourist attractions.

5. Suppose that Great Britain and Canada were the only two trading nations in the world. Suppose also that the exchange rate between pounds and dollars is fixed so that pounds are overvalued in terms of dollars. Furthermore, suppose that Britain decides to let its currency float but Canada wants to keep the dollar pegged. Will Britain lose dollar reserves? What will Canada get for its efforts? Which country gets the "better deal" out of this situation and why?

6. Explain why exchange rates are fixed under a gold standard and describe how balance of payments adjustments take place. Explain why you never hear about balance of payments adjustment problems between Ontario and Manitoba, Quebec and Alberta, or between any of the other provinces of Canada. How does balance of payments adjustment take place between the provinces? How has balance of payments adjustment occurred between inner city slums and suburbia?

7. Compare and contrast a gold standard with the Bretton Woods system. Given that both operate under a system of fixed exchange rates, why could there be persistent balance of payments deficits and surpluses under the Bretton Woods system but not under a gold standard?

Hints and Answers to Checkpoints

Chapter 1

Checkpoint 1-1

Many items used in production are difficult to place in the categories of resources—land, labour, and capital. Dairy cattle are biological and therefore one is tempted to classify them as "land." But cattle have been genetically manipulated—that is, investment has been expended in developing the current breeds; and it may be more appropriate to classify them as capital. Trees in a tree farm are not a gift of nature. These too have a certain amount of investment expenditure in their existence. These trees may also be genetically changed. Like cattle they are better placed in the capital category. The same arguments apply to chickens. Electric power used in production is an output of another production process so it is clearly capital, as is gasoline. Money poses some interesting complications. The non-economist often talks about money or money assets when he or she refers to capital. This is clearly a misuse of the terminology as discussed in the text because capital is an output of the economy that is used in production of other outputs. Money is a medium of exchange. But money is an output of production and it does facilitate production (think how less productive the Canadian economy would be if we had to barter for everything we needed). In this sense money, as a physical entity that advances real production, does meet our definition of capital. The main point of this exercise is to emphasize that placing individual items in a classification scheme is not always clear cut, and many items are ambiguous.

Checkpoint 1-2

There is considerable leeway on what might be counted as correct in response to this question. Some statements in news items have both positive and normative elements. What should be emphasized are the (potentially, at least) *verifiable* nature of the positive statements in the paragraph and the value-judgment nature of the normative statements. The use of "loaded language" as a prop for a shortage of factual statements should be noted.

Checkpoint 1-3

These surveys suggest that young people believe that personal incomes will not keep pace with the price of housing, making single-family homes less affordable to the next generation. A hypothesis that could be made is that as house prices rise relative to incomes, fewer houses will be purchased—an inverse relationship between personal in-

come and quantity of houses bought. The endogenous variables are the price of houses and personal incomes. Important exogenous variables are the size of the population forming new households and the size of the population of households retiring (both from the labour market and the housing market). Some assumptions implied are that labour supply will be large relative to demand and depress the price of labour, while the housing supply will be small relative to the demand for housing thus increasing the price of houses. Other assumptions are made that reflect the demographics of the last three decades. The common expectation is that what has occurred in the past will continue. This is often a false perspective. In this case, for example, the last generation was commonly referred to as the "baby boom" because it formed a bulge in the demographic trends. The main hypothesis suggested could very well be correct (an inverse relationship between incomes and quantity of houses purchased, *ceteris paribus*). But the assumptions may be false. In the future, the population forming new households may decline relative to the "baby boomers" leaving the labour market and selling their houses. Incomes would then likely rise relative to house prices, making houses more affordable to the next generation. Although the hypothesis may be true, when the model is formally laid out, the predictions of young people do not seem as likely.

Testing the model would be difficult as the *ceteris paribus* condition is hard to maintain over any extensive period of time. The hypotheses in this model of an inverse relationship between incomes and quantity of housing *ceteris paribus*, a reduced price of labour with increased supply *ceteris paribus*, and increased prices of houses with increased demand *ceteris paribus* have all been supported by empirical work. But the expectation that population trends will continue to support the direction of changes in the variables is not supported and therefore the belief of young people is not supported.

Checkpoint 1-4

Some examples of cause and effect confusion might include: (1) People looking at the night sky for a longer time will see more shooting stars than people who look for a shorter time. But this does not mean that looking at the sky longer causes more shooting stars. (2) Ships can often be seen preparing to sail before high tide. But this does not mean that preparing to sail causes high tide. (3) People who read more may be more intelligent but reading does not cause intelligence. A hockey game crowd illustrates the fallacy of composition in this way: If one person stands up to watch the game, he or she will be able to see the game better. But this certainly does not remain true if everyone stands up.

Chapter 2

Checkpoint 2-1

The opportunity cost to Crusoe of choosing combination d instead of combination c in Figure 2-1 is what Clyde must give up to move from combination c to combination d, that is, 10 bushels of corn. Similarly, the opportunity cost of choosing b instead of d is what must be given up to move from d to b, namely, 10 cords of wood. The opportunity cost of choosing d instead of b is the 20 bushels of corn that must be forgone in order to move from b to d.

Checkpoint 2-2

The cost of moving from d to c is 20,000 scrubbers; the cost of moving from c to b is 30,000 scrubbers; and the cost of moving from d to a is 100,000 scrubbers. Figure 2-2 can be used to illustrate the law of increasing costs as follows: The move from e to d gains 20 million bundles of other goods (including food) at a cost of 10,000 scrubbers; the move from d to c gains 20 million bundles at a cost of 20,000 scrubbers; the move from c to b gains 20 million bundles at a cost of 30,000 scrubbers; and the move from b to a gains 20 million bundles at a cost of 50,000 scrubbers. In each step, the 20 million bundles of other goods gained has a greater opportunity cost in terms of scrubbers, thus illustrating the law of increasing costs.

Checkpoint 2-3

The questions of what to produce and for whom to produce are normative because they cannot be answered strictly by an appeal to the facts.

Checkpoint 2-4

A pure market economy would select a point on the production possibilities frontier without any government intervention, using only the price signals generated in the marketplace to determine what quantity of scrubbers and bundles would be produced and purchased. If the public desired a different quantity of scrubbers than was currently being produced, its desires would cause changes in demand for scrubbers relative to other goods, and hence would cause changes in relative prices, profits, and production of scrubbers and bundles of other goods. In a command economy, the point on the production possibilities frontier would be mandated by government, with quotas for scrubbers being assigned from a central authority in the same manner as quotas for all other goods.

For both types of economies, greater industrial development would allow greater indulgence in the "luxury" of scrubbers. Less developed economies would probably consider food, shelter, and producer goods (capital goods) necessary to survival and development rather than scrubbers.

Chapter 3

Checkpoint 3-1

A coincidence of wants is lacking here. If trade were to be carried on at all, one of the people would have to accept an unwanted good and later trade for the wanted good. For example, since C wants fish and has wheat, C can travel to A's island, trade wheat for corn, and then travel to B's island and trade the corn for the fish C desires. Substantial transport time and costs are involved, even if C knows in advance what the supplies and wants of the other people are. If A, B, and C used money, C could travel to A's island and sell his wheat for money and then transport only the money to B's island to buy fish. Coincidence of wants would no longer necessitate someone transporting goods they did not want.

Checkpoint 3-2

Let's assume you are going into the delivery business. You will need a vehicle (capital) and a driver (labour). The driver will require wages and you will need to purchase the vehicle or rent it. Some examples of other expenses are maintenance, insurance, gasoline, and oil. Your revenue will consist of the number of deliveries times the fee for delivery. If you make 10,000 deliveries per year at $5 per delivery your total revenue is $5 \times 10,000 = \$50,000$. The driver's wages are \$25,000/ year, the vehicle rental (or depreciation if you own it) is \$8,000/ year, and other expenses are \$10,000, making total expenses \$43,000. The "accounting profit" you report on your income tax statement is \$7,000. Your "economic profit" is unlikely to be this amount because your time managing this business has an opportunity cost. If the time you spend managing is worth \$5,000, the economic profit would be \$2,000 ($\$7,000 - \$5,000 = \$2,000$). As this business is quite competitive, it is likely the price of deliveries will fall when more firms enter and your total revenue will decline to \$48,000 making economic profit zero.

There are many different ways to categorize the above expenses. Some costs may be explicit, some implicit. For example, if you were to also do the driving, your "accounting profit" (revenue − explicit costs) would be \$32,000. But your opportunity costs for driving and managing may be \$30,000—the wage you could earn working for someone else. Similarly you may already own your vehicle. But if you use it for deliveries the wear and tear on it in use for this business has an opportunity cost equal to what you could receive renting it to some one else's delivery (or other) business. Some costs can be considered fixed, for example, insurance premiums, as they do not vary with the output of the firm. Other costs are variable; for example, gasoline use depends on the number of deliveries made. However, the costs are itemized, for a true sense of the economic cost, all opportunity costs—both explicit and implicit—must be included. The difference between the revenue and these costs will determine the level of economic profit. As will be shown in Chapter 9, a competitive business will be reduced to zero economic profit.

Checkpoint 3-3

The postal service is not a public good because the exclusion principle applies: only those who pay for the service can have it. Furthermore, there is a private market incentive for providing such service. Courier service is an example of a mail service provided by a private firm. On the other hand there may positive externalities—national cohesiveness—that may not be considered in a pure market approach.

Whether Canada Post should recover costs or be subsidized is a normative question and therefore there are many pro and con arguments concerning the question. The answer depends on one's views about the social value of postal service and the effect of its general availability through price rationing. More people can afford it, the lower the price at which it is provided. If it is run on a profit maximization basis the argument for it to be nationalized is weak. If it is a natural monopoly, there is an argument for it to be publicly owned but run on a break-even basis. These issues are discussed at greater length in the following chapters.

If the service were a natural monopoly there would be no need to legislate its monopoly power. The legislated monopoly power exists in order to cross-subsidize the service. All Canadians can use the service at the same price rates no matter if they live in urban centers, rural villages, or in the far reaches of the realm. If the monopoly legislation were dropped, competitors would quickly arise in the urban markets and in the market between major centers because here the costs of delivery are less than the current Canada Post price rates. But no one would want to enter the high-cost service to rural and northern customers.

Checkpoint 3-4

The nationalization of most production in China means that government produces most goods and services. This would be represented in the flow diagram of Figure 3-3 by the addition of a flow channel connecting government with the flow channel where goods and services are exchanged for money payments. Like the business sector, government would be producing and selling goods and services to households and employing most of the households' labour resources. Most capital and land resources would also be government owned and used directly in production. The price signalling of the markets for resource allocation is virtually eliminated in this situation.

Chapter 4

Checkpoint 4-1

The long gasoline lines could be shortened—that is, the quantity of gasoline demanded could be reduced—if the price of gasoline is increased.

Checkpoint 4-2

If the price of peas were to rise, this would shift the demand curve of lima beans to the right, since the two goods are substitutes, and more lima beans would be demanded at every price. If the price of pretzels were to fall, the demand curve for beer would shift to the right, since the two goods are complements. The demand curve for pretzels would remain unchanged, since we are talking about a change in the price of pretzels and this would result in a movement along the pretzel demand curve rather than a shift in the curve. If the price of hamburger buns were to go up, the demand curve for hamburgers would shift to the left, since these goods are complements, and less hamburger would now be demanded at every price.

Checkpoint 4-3

If wages go up, then supplier costs go up and a higher price must be charged at each level of production. Hence the supply curve is shifted leftward (alternatively, it can be said that at each purchase price, higher costs allow fewer units to be supplied, so that the supply curve shifts to the left). An improvement in technology, such as the improvement mentioned, will lower production costs and shift the supply curve to the right. If the price of lamb were to rise, some suppliers would begin to produce lamb instead of hamburger (since similar resources are used in producing either). This would cause a change in the supply of hamburger. Specifically, the supply curve of hamburger would shift leftward, reflecting the fact that a higher price would now have to be paid for resources that could otherwise be used to produce lamb.

Land is a resource potentially useful in both corn production and the factory production of VCRs. Suppose that the land is being used in the production of wheat, and an entrepreneur feels that it might be more profitably used in the production of VCRs. The entrepreneur can offer to buy the land at a price that reflects the potential profits in VCR production. If this price is higher than what the farmer feels the land is worth in terms of expected potential profits from wheat production, then the transaction will take place and the land will change uses.

Checkpoint 4-4

This checkpoint deals with simultaneous changes in supply and demand. If the price of hot dogs should fall, it would affect the equilibrium price and quantity of hamburger on both the demand and supply sides of the market. On the demand side, hot dogs and hamburger are substitutes, and so the fall in the price of hot dogs would reduce the demand for hamburger. This would, *ceteris paribus*, reduce both the equilibrium price and the equilibrium quantity of hamburger. But on the supply side, the same resources can be used to produce both hamburger and hot dogs, so that if the price of hot dogs falls, suppliers will tend to produce more hamburger instead, shifting the supply curve of hamburger to the right. This would, *ceteris paribus*, tend to increase equilibrium quantity and reduce equilibrium price. Therefore, equilibrium price will decrease, since both demand and supply influences push price downward. But we cannot say which way equilibrium quantity will go without knowing the relative sizes of the supply and demand influences, since they operate in opposite directions.

If hamburger bun prices fall, demand for hamburger will increase, since hamburger buns and hamburger are complementary goods. But if the cost of labour used in hamburger production falls, the supply of hamburger will increase at any given price; equilibrium quantity will tend to increase and equilibrium price will tend to decrease. Taken together with the increased demand, the net effect will be an increase in the market equilibrium quantity, with an indeterminate change in the equilibrium price.

If the price of electricity rises, then the demand for hamburger will fall, since these goods are complements. If the office rent for hamburger producers rises, then the supply of hamburger will decrease. A decrease in both demand and supply will decrease equilibrium quantity and have an indeterminate effect on equilibrium price.

If the only information that you were given was that the price of hamburger had risen, then you could not make any statement about what had happened to quantity, since it could have either risen or declined, depending on whether a shift occurred in supply or demand or both.

Chapter 5

Checkpoint 5-1

If we calculate the coefficient of price elasticity using the point method, we use the chronological order for the direction of change. Therefore the change in price is $7.50 - $7.00 = +$.50$. The change in quantity demanded is $1,010,878 - 1,055,630 = -44,752$. The original point for the calculations of percentage changes is 1991. Therefore the coefficient of price elasticity is

$$\eta = \frac{-44,752}{1,055,630} \times \frac{\$7.00}{\$.50} = -.59$$

This estimate of the price elasticity of demand is not likely to be reliable because elasticity calculations are based on the assumption *ceteris paribus*; and, for example, this year's Stampede was one of the wettest on record. Therefore the weather, an important variable for "the greatest outdoor show on earth," was not constant. Other variables may also have changed between 1992 and 1991.

Recognizing the unreliability of the estimate, but having no other measure, we will use it to predict the attendance on Sunday after the price cut. In this case we know the original quantity (1991 attendance) was 111,169, the original price (1991) was $7.00, and the change in price is $7.00 - $3.50 = 3.50. What we need to find is the expected 1992 attendance (X). Therefore, using the formula for calculating the price elasticity:

$$-.59 = \frac{X - 111,169}{111,169} \times \frac{\$7.00}{-\$3.50}$$

Rewriting to solve for X:

$$X = -.59 \times 111,169 \times \frac{-3.5}{7} + 111,169$$

$$X = 143,964$$

The predicted final Sunday attendance is 143,964. If we are to use the estimate calculated, we shouldn't be too confident in our prediction because the assumption of *ceteris paribus* was not holding. For your interest the actual attendance was just under 120,000.

Checkpoint 5-2

Using the midpoints formula, the following elasticities result: $90 to $80, 3.40; $80 to $70, 2.14; $70 to $60, 1.44; $60 to $50, 1.00; $50 to $40, .69; $40 to $30, .47; and $30 to $20, .29. As we move down the demand curve from left to right, we observe that the elasticity of demand declines (in absolute value).

If the Grey Cup game is filled to its 60,000-seat capacity and total revenue is at its maximum, then we could be at the unit elastic point on a demand curve that is to the right of the illustrated demand curve (Figure 5-4). However, it is also possible that the demand curve is so far to the right that the unit elastic point on the demand curve lies to the right of the 60,000-seat capacity point on the horizontal axis. In that case, the point on the demand curve lying directly above the 60,000-seat capacity would be in the elastic range of the demand curve. The maximum *possible* revenue would still be obtained by charging a ticket price corresponding to that point on the demand curve—still a sellout. The point lying above the 60,000-seat capacity could not be in the inelastic range of the demand curve. If it were, the unit elastic point would lie to the left of the 60,000-seat capacity, and revenue maximization would require setting the ticket price higher (at the unit elastic point) and not filling the stadium.

Checkpoint 5-3

If the demand in Kitchener is less sensitive to changes in price, then the graph of its demand would be more vertical than the demand curve for Brampton. This would show that a change in price would induce a smaller change in quantity demanded in Kitchener (the less price elastic city). Hence, Brampton would experience the greatest reduction in the quantity of electricity demanded, given an equal price increase in the two cities. If the utility companies raise the price, the longer the time people have will allow them to replace electrical heating with natural gas furnaces, replace electrical bulbs with the new low-wattage–high-output bulbs, and replace high-energy-use appliances, such as refrigerators, with new energy-efficient models.

Checkpoint 5-4

Supply elasticities are positive and demand elasticities are negative because supply curves are direct (positive-slope) relationships and demand curves are inverse (negative-slope) relationships.

Chapter 6

Checkpoint 6-1

If the marginal utility per dollar of X is greater than the marginal utility per dollar of Y, then this would mean that if the consumer took a dollar away from expenditure on Y and spent it on X instead, there would be a gain in total utility. This is so because the loss in utility from consuming a dollar's worth less of Y would be more than offset by the gain in utility from consuming an additional dollar's worth of X. This reallocation of expenditure would also mean that the marginal utility of X per dollar would decrease while that of Y would increase. We know this from the law of diminishing marginal utility. As long as the marginal utility of Y per dollar is less than that of X, the consumer's total utility can be increased by shifting expenditure away from Y and toward X. Because of the law of diminishing marginal utility, we know that eventually the marginal utility of Y per dollar would be brought into equality with the marginal utility of X per dollar.

If we begin from a point where the consumer is maximizing utility, and only the price of Y rises, then we will have a situation where the marginal utility per dollar spent on Y is less than the marginal utility per dollar spent on X, which is exactly the situation in the forgoing paragraph. And as before, the law of diminishing marginal utility will cause the consumer to shift expenditure away from Y and toward X. Thus, we have shown that an increase in the price of Y results in a decrease in the quantity demanded of it, which is a description of a demand curve that slopes downward to the right.

Chapter 7

Checkpoint 7-1

If the government removed the price ceiling on tuition fees, then the lines at universities and colleges would likely become shorter. This could be shown diagrammatically by drawing the usual supply and demand curves and placing the price ceiling line below the market equilibrium price. The distance between the supply curve and the demand curve on the price ceiling line would indicate the amount of excess demand or shortage of seats prior to the removal of the ceiling. The quantity demanded at the ceiling is greater than the equilibrium quantity. This difference is added to the lines of students wishing admission. The allocation of limited seats would now be more dependent upon ability to pay, reducing the availability of a postsecondary education to lower income groups.

Checkpoint 7-2

In terms of Figure 7-5, under both schemes the government sets a price of p_s, and the farmers, true to their supply curves, supply quantity q_s.

Under scheme 1, the farmers sell their wheat at the price that it will bring on the market, namely p_g. The entire quantity of wheat produced is bought by the public, and the government has no wheat to store. But the government pays the farmers the difference between the price they receive, p_g, and the support price p_s on each bushel of wheat sold, for a total cost of p_s minus p_g times q_s (an amount equal to the area of the rectangle $p_g b a p_s$). Now, the more elastic the demand and supply curves are, the smaller the distance from p_g to p_s will be and the less the government's cost will be. There are no storage costs associated with this scheme.

Under scheme 4, the government buys the wheat not demanded by the public at price p_s at a cost of q_s minus q_d times p_s (an amount equal to the area of rectangle $q_d q_s a c$). The more *elastic* the demand and supply curves, the greater the distance from q_d to q_s and the more the government's cost will be. In addition note that the government is the owner of q_d to q_s bushels of wheat, for which it must pay the storage costs, since it cannot sell it without affecting the price and quantity adversely. Hence, we see that the question of which scheme will cost less depends on the elasticity of the demand and supply curves and the costs of storage.

Checkpoint 7-3

If the demand curve is perfectly inelastic, then the selling price will increase by the entire amount of the tax and the entire incidence of the tax will fall on the buyer. For any given size of excise tax, the more elastic is the demand curve, the greater will be the reduction in quantity consumed.

Checkpoint 7-4

The required inspections increase the demand for service maintenance. This law might still be favoured by you even though you keep your car in top shape anyway, because it would increase the safety of the other cars on the road (some of which might not be kept in top shape without the requirement). You would realize an external benefit.

Chapter 8

Checkpoint 8-1

A limited partner has no say in the management of the firm, whereas a stockholder has some influence by virtue of his or her right to vote for a board of directors. Also, a limited partner's death would necessitate the reorganization of the partnership, while that of the stockholder would merely transfer his or her shares to heirs.

Normal profit is an economic cost because it represents the opportunity cost of the financial capital and entrepreneurial skills used by the firm.

In one store the proprietor might own the building outright. The opportunity cost of the owner's funds tied up in the building would not be included when calculating accounting profit. Suppose that the owner of the other store has borrowed funds to buy the building. Then the interest payments (opportunity cost of the funds) would be included when calculating accounting profit.

Checkpoint 8-2

If total fixed cost increased from $50 to $75, then the fixed cost line (TFC) would shift upward by $25, and the total cost curve would also shift upward by $25. The total variable curve would remain unchanged.

If wages rose from $50 to $75, the TC and TVC curves would both pivot counterclockwise about their intercepts. The TFC curve would remain unchanged.

Checkpoint 8-3

If fixed cost fell by $10, then average fixed cost would shift downward by $10 at 1 unit of output, by $5 at 2 units of output, and so on. Average total cost would shift downward in the same manner. Average variable cost would remain unchanged.

If weekly wages increase from $50 to $60, average fixed cost will not be affected, but average variable cost and average total cost will both increase, and the curves will shift upward. The new AVC and ATC columns are shown in Table A-1:

TABLE A-1

L	Q	AVC	ATC
1	1	$60.00	$110.00
2	3	40.00	56.67
3	6	30.00	38.33
4	10	24.00	29.00
5	13	23.08	26.92
6	15	24.00	27.33
7	16.5	25.45	28.48
8	17.5	27.43	30.28
9	18	30.00	32.78

Checkpoint 8-4

The change in average total cost includes the change in average fixed cost, which falls more rapidly than marginal cost over the first six units of output. If diminishing returns are larger than is the case in Table 8-2, then the slope of the marginal cost would be greater to the right of its lowest point.

Checkpoint 8-5

The longrun ATC curve represents a collection of blueprints, because each point on it corresponds to a different plant—a different-size plant. In the longrun a business can choose from a number of different sizes of plants in the planning stage. Hence, the longrun ATC is a collection of blueprints. Selection of a plant size corresponds to the selection of a particular blueprint.

Underutilizing a larger plant when production is below 1,800 units and overutilizing a smaller plant when production is over 1,800 units is necessary if the firm is to produce a given output level at the lowest possible per unit cost in the longrun—that is, if it is to operate on its longrun ATC curve.

Chapter 9

Checkpoint 9-1

As products cease to be identical, they become less substitutable for one another. The demand curve facing each firm will begin to take on some downward slope instead of being perfectly horizontal. As each firm's demand ceases to be perfectly elastic, the firm ceases to be a price taker. If the price of a competitive firm's product were to rise from $10 to $15, the TR curve in Figure 9-2, frame (a), would rotate counterclockwise around the origin until a slope of 15 was achieved. The firm's demand curve in frame (b) would shift upward to $15. This is because each unit is sold at a market price of $15, making average revenue equal to $15 and total revenue equal to $15 times the number of units sold.

Checkpoint 9-2

Table 9-1 makes it clear that the difference between total revenue and total cost is greatest at 5 units produced and sold. Figure 9-3, frame (b), was designed so that the number of profit squares shaded at 5 units of output is greater than the number shaded at 3, 4, or 6 units of output. At 5 units of output, approximately 10 squares are shaded, while at 3, 4, and 6 units of output, approximately, 3, 8, and 6 squares are shaded, respectively.

Checkpoint 9-3

Figure 9-4, frame (b), was designed so that the number of loss squares shaded at 4 units would be at a minimum. At 4 units of output, approximately 4 loss squares are shaded, while at 2, 3, and 5 units of output, approximately 8, 6, and 5 squares are shaded, respectively. The data in Table 9-2 show that the difference between price (= marginal revenue = average revenue) and average variable cost is at a maximum at 4 units of output. Figure 9-4, frame (b), shows that the shaded area of the excess of total revenue over TVC is 5 squares at 4 units (1.25×4), while the excess is 2, 4 ($= 1.34 \times 3$), and 4 ($= .80 \times 5$) squares at 2, 3, and 5 units, respectively.

Checkpoint 9-4

The shaded area would represent the loss associated with producing 4 units of output as opposed to just shutting down. The area corresponding to the vertical distance between the TC and TR_4 curves would be the area between \$4 and \$7.25 out to 4 units of output. The area representing TFC would be the area between \$7.25 and \$4.75 out to 4 units of output.

Checkpoint 9-5

An increase in the cost of raw materials would shift the $MC, AVC,$ and ATC curves upward. This would reduce the profit-maximizing output for each individual firm in the industry. This would mean less product would be offered for sale at any given price level which would shift the industry supply curve upward. If industry demand is to decrease below the level represented by D_1, then the firms would decide to produce nothing at all, and firm and industry output would fall to zero. If the demand curve were D_3, then the equilibrium price would increase, and firm and industry output would decline.

Checkpoint 9-6

When a perfectly competitive industry is in longrun equilibrium, all factors employed by the industry are earning just what they could earn if they were employed in their most profitable alternative endeavour. Hence, all factors are compensated by an amount that just equals their opportunity cost. If firms are just earning a normal profit in longrun competitive equilibrium, then the financial capital and entrepreneurial skill employed by the firms are earning an amount just equal to their opportunity cost.

Chapter 10

Checkpoint 10-1

Irving holds an equity interest in a number of newspaper companies throughout Atlantic Canada. K. C. Irving owns major refining and distribution for petroleum products in Atlantic Canada. Newspaper production using modern mass production techniques requires a major investment in fixed factors but at the same time provides for considerable economies of scale. The cash flow and profits from its petroleum empire helped to give it an advantage relative to other firms in establishing its media presence in the region. Most newspapers, in contrast to other players in the communications industry, have localized focus and appeal. This localized focus makes them ideal vehicles for advertising over localized geographic markets. The combination of economies of scale with a localized market in a relatively sparsely populated area like Atlantic Canada suggests that the industry will evolve into one where only

a few firms will dominate the market. Because these few firms control what amounts to the only vehicle for advertisers interested in sending their message to the localized markets in the Maritimes, there are considerable opportunities to earn economic profits. The large financial resources of Irving Oil provided the opportunity for successfully financing the capital costs of establishing newspapers that could realize economies of scale. In addition once established these newspapers could use the larger purchasing power of the chain to extract lower input prices from suppliers of inputs. While the overall reasons why Irving may have developed a monopoly position are many, among them are the combination of financial power available from unrelated activities, economies of scale, and a localized market that reduces the ability of other firms to compete with an established financially secure firm.

In the case of Bricklin, while the people trying to establish the firm had demonstrated expertise in the auto industry and had shown considerable innovation in design and engineering, they never had the financial backing, legal protection, or other advantages that were available to their competitors. Bricklin was unable to finance a plant large enough to realize economies of scale in automobile production. In addition, Chrysler, Ford, and General Motors had established competitive advantages in the form of patents; well-integrated sales, production, and service facilities; and well-established credit lines and consumer familiarity with their products.

Checkpoint 10-2

The relationship may be most easily demonstrated in an area around the maximum point. Between 6 and 7 units of output, marginal revenue is zero and total revenue is at a maximum (\$42). The (midpoint) elasticity of demand at this point is $1.0 = (1/6.5)/(1/6.5)$. At 1 unit of output less, between 5 and 6 units of output, total revenue is \$41 and marginal revenue is \$2. The elasticity is $1.37 = (1/5.5)/(1/7.5)$. At a point where output is one unit more than at the revenue-maximizing point (between 7 and 8 units), total revenue is \$41, marginal revenue is $-\$2$, and the elasticity of demand is $.73 = (1/7.5)/(1/5.5)$. This shows that where demand is inelastic, marginal revenue is negative, and where demand is elastic, marginal revenue is positive.

Checkpoint 10-3

An increase in fixed costs in Figure 10-3 would move ATC upward (increasing losses) but would not affect equilibrium price and output levels, since these are the loss-minimizing levels regardless of the level of fixed costs (variable costs determine loss-minimizing levels of price and output). The increase in fixed costs would increase negative economic profit (losses). Doubling a license fee paid to the federal or provincial government would constitute an increase in fixed cost and hence would not change price and output levels. If the government imposes an effective price ceiling, this could cause output to increase, since this would make the monopolist's effective demand curve horizontal, just like the perfect competitor's. The intersection of the marginal cost and marginal revenue curves would occur farther to the right of the original intersection.

Checkpoint 10-4

A monopolist can engage in noneconomic activities such as hiring discrimination, or pursuing some action that is desirable to the decision makers in the firm but not seen to be important by consumers, because there is no competitive pressure to force the monopolist to use the most economically efficient labour as there is under perfect competition. Wining and dining a monopolist can be effective for the same reasons. Without the rigorous competition of many rivals, a monopolist can afford activities that do not maximize profit. Wining and dining could influence the monopolist to buy supplies from you even if your prices were higher than those of other suppliers. Competition would force the perfect competitor to use only economic reasoning to arrive at his or her choice of supplier.

Checkpoint 10-5

If all buyers have identical demand curves, then all buyers have identical demand elasticities, and the profit-maximizing monopolist will charge the same price to all of them.

Chapter 11

Checkpoint 11-1

A list of monopolistically competitive industries could include compact disk and video sales, retail jewelry trade, video rentals, automobile service stations, construction contracting, computer peripherals, ice cream, furniture manufacturing, "variety store" retail trade, clothing retailers, hairdressers and barbershops, and restaurants. The slope of the demand curve reflects the existence of substitutes because the more close substitutes there are for a given product, the more sensitive buyers will be to a change in the price of that product. That is, buyers will more readily switch to other products in response to a change in that product's price. Hence, the more close substitutes there are for a product, the more horizontal will be that product's demand curve.

Checkpoint 11-2

If waiters and waitresses were to gain large wage increases, then the *ATC* curve for a typical restaurant would shift upward and the firm would experience losses—the typical firm's situation would look like that in Figure 11-1, frame (c). In the longrun, firms would exit the industry, (through bankruptcy or by using their resources to enter some other industry), so that the demand curves of the remaining firms would shift to the right as their market

shares increased. This would continue until the longrun equilibrium with normal profit was once again achieved—as illustrated in Figure 11-1, frame (b). Equilibrium prices would rise, and equilibrium output in the industry would fall. This would result in fewer workers, including waiters and waitresses being employed in restaurants.

Checkpoint 11-3

The popularity of publications such as *Consumer Reports, Lemon Aid*, and *Protect Yourself Magazine* implies that a substantial portion of the populace doesn't believe that the bulk of advertising is informative in nature (otherwise they would not pay for a product—accurate product information—that they could get free in advertisements). If a government agency were set up to ensure that all advertising was informative, it would raise severe difficulties concerning freedom of expression entrenched in the Canadian Charter of Rights. Distinguishing between informative and noninformative advertising would be extremely difficult. Even the limited restrictions placed on advertisers of tobacco products and alcohol advertisers by the government throughout most of Canada or the English language sign requirements in Quebec illustrate the legal complexity and deep emotions surrounding these issues.

Chapter 12

Checkpoint 12-1

The constant model changes constitute part of a policy directed at increasing product proliferation and product complexity. This helps each of the automakers to keep the others off balance and serves as a very substantial barrier to the entry of new producers. The existing auto manufacturers are quite experienced at maintaining a fairly constant stream of new and changed models. This means that a new entrant into the market must not only be able to produce autos but to produce them while constantly changing styles in order to sell to a public that has grown used to such changes. It is not at all clear that under such circumstances it would be better for the three automakers to collude in order to stop such model changes. It is even possible that the overall industry demand is being increased by this behaviour, in which case ending the constant model changes would be detrimental to the sales of all firms.

Checkpoint 12-2

Information about the relative position of the firms at the top in a concentrated industry would provide evidence of how much "in-fighting" is going on among the industry's dominant firms. For example, a highly concentrated industry might have vigourous competition—even including price competition—among the top two or three firms. But the concentration ratio method of measuring oligopoly power would count this industry the same as one that had the same concentration but a very stable (and possibly collusive) relationship among the top two or three firms. Clearly, equal concentrated ratios do not necessarily imply equal oligopoly power.

Since a merger of two firms will enable them to engage in perfectly collusive price behaviour, merger activity is almost certain to decrease price flexibility.

Checkpoint 12-3

A firm could move price to a level above the kink in the demand curve if its marginal cost curve shifted upward until it intersected the marginal revenue curve at a point to the left of the kink.

The firm would never reduce price below the kink if the demand were inelastic to the right of the kink—that is, when marginal revenue is negative to the right of the kink.

Checkpoint 12-4

It is only necessary for one of the firms in Figure 12-6 to misjudge the likely reactions of the other in order for events to lead them to the price level p_4.

Chapter 13

Checkpoint 13-1

If an industry is more concentrated than is justified by economies of scale, then it would experience higher costs per unit than if its concentration were more in accord with available scale economies. The too-concentrated industry would experience a lower profit rate than if its concentration ratio were more in line with available scale economies.

In an industry where both advertising outlays and concentration are high, one would be tempted to draw the conclusion that the high advertising outlays are responsible for the high concentration. But the nature of the product would certainly have a bearing on this conclusion. For example, the automobile and cigarette industries both have high advertising outlays and high concentration, but in the auto industry, scale economies would seem to be a much more plausible cause for high concentration. The differences among different brands of cigarettes are not as great or as complex as the differences among makes of automobiles. Cigarette advertising is less informative than automobile advertising but probably has more to do with establishing market dominance than automobile advertising.

Checkpoint 13-2

The supporters of competition legislation would say that the risk of protecting inefficient small firms from going out of business is outweighed by the risk of creating a monopoly situation if the large firms are allowed to successfully drive their small competitors out of business.

Checkpoint 13-3

Market structure might be judged a more important criterion than conduct for anti-combine enforcement because even though there may not be any misconduct, highly concentrated market structures represent a potential for misconduct. The spirit of this criterion is not whether there is a smoking gun, but rather whether there is any gun at all.

Chapter 14

Checkpoint 14-1

The CRTC's letter to the plywood makers could inform them that unless they put shields around their electronic heating machines, they might be held liable for airplane crashes attributed to interference with communication between flight-control towers and aircraft. It is likely that the plywood makers would rather incur the costs of putting shields around their machines than run the risk of incurring the potentially much larger damage costs associated with an airplane crash. Installation of the costly shields will increase the cost of making plywood. This will cause the supply curve for plywood to shift upward. Given a downward-sloping demand for plywood, the equilibrium quantity of plywood bought and sold will decline.

Checkpoint 14-2

If the marginal cost of pollution reduction were increased by $70,000 at every level of pollution reduction shown in Table 14-1, the optimal level of pollution would be 60,000 units. If pollution were reduced below this level, the marginal benefit from pollution reduction, column (3), would be less than the marginal cost, column (5).

Checkpoint 14-3

There is no unambiguously correct answer to this question. However, it might be argued that because regulations for product safety prevent or slow down the introduction of new medical drugs to the marketplace, such regulations are more restrictive of consumer choice. Regulation of deceptive advertising is less likely to restrict the introduction of products to the marketplace because its aim is to regulate what is claimed about products rather than to prevent the sale of them altogether.

Chapter 15

Checkpoint 15-1

In Figure 15-2, "the cost of labour is soaring" would be modeled by shifting the horizontal supply curve of labour upward dramatically. This would cause the equilibrium quantity of labour given by the intersection of supply and demand for labour to fall—that is, it would "trigger increasing layoffs."

Checkpoint 15-2

Changes in the firm's final product price will affect the firm's marginal revenue product curve for the factor (and hence affect D_F), because the marginal revenue product of a factor at any given output level is the marginal physical product times the output price.

If firms have managed to raise their prices more rapidly than labour costs have risen, then the MRP curve of Figure 15-2 would shift upward more than the MCF curve would, and the equilibrium quantity of labour used would increase.

Productivity gains will shift both the MPP and MRP curves upward. The first unit of variable factor will now produce more units of output, valued at more dollars than before, and so on.

Checkpoint 15-3

The tire and tube industry is by far the largest user of rubber, and rubber cost is a large proportion of final cost of tires, implying a larger elasticity for the rubber demand curve of the tire industry. Rubber is not very easily substituted for in tire production, tending to decrease the rubber demand elasticity. The demand for tires is probably inelastic, and so the tire industry's demand for rubber will tend to be inelastic. Industrial hoses, belts, and tubes use rubber and probably have an inelastic demand for rubber for the same reasons. The footwear industry uses rubber, but because it can be fairly easily substituted for in many applications, the footwear demand for rubber is probably more elastic than that of the tire or hose industries. Using "armchair averaging," it would probably be correct to say that the rubber demand, overall, is fairly inelastic.

Some inelastically demanded factor inputs (and their elasticity-determining factors) might be diesel fuel (the transportation industry's product demand is fairly inelastic, substitution of other input factors is difficult and limited, and fuel is a fairly large proportion of total transport cost), transistors (the electronics industry has a fairly inelastic product demand, substitution of other factors is difficult, and the transistor cost is a small part of total product cost), nails (although demand for wood construction might be fairly elastic, substituting for nails in the production process is difficult, and nails are a small part of the cost of the final product), crude oil (although its cost is a large part of the cost of the final products, it is difficult to substitute for, and the demand for products using crude oil seems to be quite inelastic), and fertilizer (the demand for products using it is inelastic, fertilizer is usually a fairly small cost relative to the final product cost, and it is quite difficult to substitute for).

Chapter 16

Checkpoint 16-1

If the person is consistent, he or she would not want to improve the traffic flow, since this would involve introducing new capital equipment such as traffic lights and new roads. It might eliminate some jobs, such as traffic policing, increase the productivity of truckers so that fewer would be needed, and perhaps eliminate some public transportation jobs as people decided the change made driving a more attractive choice. However, the change in traffic flow would also make the transportation of goods more efficient and reduce commuting time. Also, since most people view commuting as work related and not leisure, a reduction in commuting time would be likely to reduce worker fatigue and boost labour productivity on the job.

Checkpoint 16-2

The purpose of this question is to illustrate the fact that more unpleasant jobs will have to have a higher wage rate in order to induce someone to take them.

Checkpoint 16-3

During a recession, the demand for labour will decline. This could be modeled in Figure 16-5 by shifting the demand curve to the left. This will further increase the excess supply at the union wage, which makes it difficult for the union to push for wage increases.

The economic rationale for the Miner Owners Association is to give monopsony power to the buyers of unionized labour services to combat the monopoly power of the union.

Chapter 17

Checkpoint 17-1

Movie stars and great professional athletes earn large economic rents because they typically do not have alternative employment opportunities that are nearly as lucrative. As a proportion of earnings, the economic rents earned by corporation presidents are most likely considerably smaller than those of movie stars and great athletes because corporate presidents have more lucrative alternatives, such as other top management positions.

Checkpoint 17-2

A university education is a roundabout process because an individual typically gives up 4 years of full-time wages in order to acquire education and skills that will enable him or her subsequently to make higher wages than otherwise would be possible. One way to measure the rate of return on this investment would be to compare the lifetime earnings of university-educated and non-university-educated people and see what difference in earnings per year the 4-year university investment has made.

If people became less willing to save, the saving curve in Figure 17-6, frame (b), would shift to the left. This would decrease the longrun equilibrium stock of capital because the saving curve would intercept the vertical axis at a higher interest rate—that is, the longrun equilibrium interest rate would be higher, and therefore the longrun equilibrium capital stock would be less.

An increase in the rate of population growth would increase the rate of growth of the labour force and hence increase the potential productivity of capital. This would shift the demand for capital to the right and increase the longrun equilibrium stock of capital.

Chapter 18

Checkpoint 18-1

It would be possible to calculate per capita income for each family. For example a family of 4 with a combined income of $50,000 would become 4 individuals with $12,500 income each.

If income for families and unattached individuals were combined into one category as households, the resulting Lorenz curve would shift toward the origin indicating a less equal distribution of income. This shift would occur because single individuals tend to have lower incomes than families.

Checkpoint 18-2

**FIGURE A-1 Lorenz Curve Before and
After Taxes**

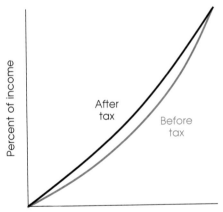

A progressive tax should result in a more equal distribution of income. The "baby boom" population began entering the work force in the late 1960s and have increased their experience and earning power with the passage of time. So one would expect the Lorenz curves for successive decades to show slightly increasing income equality *ceteris paribus*.

Checkpoint 18-3

The expected rate of return from a postsecondary education has historically been less for aborigines than whites as the result of limited job opportunities due to discrimination. Hence, the percentage of aborigines choos-

ing to make that investment is likely to be lower than among whites, *ceteris paribus*. The situation is made still worse by the fact that aboriginal students often face discrimination before they enter the postsecondary level and as a consequence are less prepared to enter colleges and universities. Some institutions have established special programs to assist aboriginal students to help offset the effects of discrimination.

Checkpoint 18-4

Social assistance and social insurance programs should result in lower incidence of poverty and therefore a more equal distribution of income. However, because they provide a safety net they may increase the level of unemployment.

Chapter 19

Checkpoint 19-1

The sales commissions are included in GDP because although the goods being sold are not considered final goods produced in the current period, the service of selling represents current productive activity.

An increase in the proportion of working wives increases GDP. This is because housekeeping and child-rearing services performed by housewives are not included in GDP. When housewives move into the labour market and take paying jobs, their work activity is measured and included in GDP.

A sample table for bread could look like Table A-2.

Checkpoint 19-2

The calculation procedure is the same as that in Table 19-3, except that the price index would be computed by dividing the current price of hamburgers by $3, which is the price in year 2. The resulting real GDP figures would be year 1, $3,000; year 2, $3,300; year 3, $3,630; year 4, $3,993; and year 5, $4,392.

A given year's real GDP will be larger than its nominal GDP if it is for a year in which prices were lower (usually true before the base year), and its real GDP will be smaller than its nominal GDP if it for a year in which prices were higher (usually true after the base year). This means that nominal GDP is "inflated" to arrive at real GDP before the base year, and it is "deflated" to arrive at real GDP after the base year.

Checkpoint 19-3

Inventories accumulate when consumers do not buy as much as businesses expect them to at the time production plans were being made. This is not as desirable as increases in consumer expenditures because unanticipated increases in inventories mean goods are accumulating faster than they are being sold, and this will very likely lead to a cutback in production, output, and employment.

Chapter 20

Checkpoint 20-1

A visual inspection of Figure 20-1, frame (a), gives the impression that the expansion phases of business cycles are a great deal longer than the recession phases because of the effect of economic growth. This impression is lessened in Figure 20-1, frame (b), which shows variations around the growth trend. The monthly seasonal adjustment factors for textbook sales would have to account for large seasonal bulges in sales in the beginning months of each term, declining dramatically until the beginning of the next semester, with a smaller increase for the beginning of summer sessions.

Checkpoint 20-2

(1) From a high to low degree of price reduction, they probably ranked as follows: agricultural commodities, food products, leather, cement, textile products, petroleum, iron and steel, automobile tires, motor vehicles, and agricultural implements. (2) From a high to low degree of output reduction, they ranked the same way as in (1).

By itself the higher level of concentration in Canada should mean that the economy is less affected by a recession, however, there are a number of other factors which could be offsetting.

Checkpoint 20-3

Based on Figure 20-5, frames (b) and (c), the unemployment rate that is associated with achieving potential GDP is about 6 percent.

Checkpoint 20-4

An unanticipated deflation would redistribute wealth from debtors to creditors, because creditors would be paid back dollars that would buy more than the dollars they originally lent. Since debtors have not anticipated the fall in the general price level, they will not have protected themselves against the fact that their borrowings will have to be paid back with more purchasing power (dollars that buy more) than the purchasing power they originally borrowed. Had borrowers anticipated the deflation, they would have entered into the loan agreement at a lower interest rate than the one at which they in fact contracted. It would have been lower by the amount of the rate of deflation. In this way borrowers would take account of the fact that they would have to pay back more valuable dollars than the ones they borrowed.

An unanticipated deflation would redistribute wealth from non-fixed-income groups to fixed-income groups. The fixed-income group would earn the same number of dollars, but these dollars would buy more as the price level fell. The non-fixed-income group would find their incomes falling right along with the general price level. Hence, they would lose purchasing power relative to the fixed-income group.

Deflation essentially gives you money by giving each dollar you have more purchasing power.

The dramatic increases and decreases in the rate of inflation may well have increased uncertainty about what the future rate of inflation would be. Fear of the consequences of unanticipated inflation may have made businesses and households more cautious about entering into loan agreements to finance investment and consumption spending. Hence, expansion in these expenditures was retarded, thus contributing to the ongoing GDP gap.

Checkpoint 20-5

The cost of alcohol and tobacco rose much more rapidly than any other component in the CPI. If you don't smoke or drink you are unaffected by these increases; but the CPI assumes that everyone uses the *average* amount of each component, so it includes the costs of "vices."

The cost of clothing rose much less than other components so it is possible that consumers tended to buy more clothing because its relatively lower price.

Chapter 21

Checkpoint 21-1

The increase in the economy's aggregate demand would cause increases in demand in the many markets making up the economy. This would lead to price increases in these markets. Attempting to increase output in response, firms

TABLE A-2

	Production Stage	Product	Sale Price of Product		Cost of Intermediate Product		Value Added (Wages, Interest, Rent, Profit)
Firm 1	Wheat farm	Wheat	$.30	−	$.00	=	$.30
Firm 2	Flour mill	Flour	.40	−	.30	=	.10
Firm 3	Baker	Bread	.65	−	.40	=	.25
Firm 4	Grocery store	Retailing service	.75	−	.65	=	.10
							$.75

(Final sale price = Sum of value added)

would increase their demand for labour. Since there is already full employment, wages would be bid up. Equilibrium would be restored with wages and prices at a higher level.

If the investment curve in Figure 21-1 shifts leftward and the interest rate for some reason cannot fall below r_e, then the savings-investment equality will break down and aggregate demand will fall (since the declining investment demand is a part of aggregate demand). The drop in the economy's aggregate demand will cause a leftward shift in the demand curves in the many markets making up the economy. Price and output will fall in these markets, and employers will be forced to lay off workers. This unemployment will cause wages to fall because unemployed labour will bid wages down in their attempts to find jobs. As long as the interest rate cannot fall below r_e, to equate saving and investment, wages and prices will continue to fall.

Checkpoint 21-2

On Crusoe's island, all saving and investment plans were made in one man's head. Hence, planned saving necessarily equaled planned investment. There could be no unemployment problem, since Crusoe was both the demander and supplier of all labour, and the quantity supplied and demanded must always have been equal. Say's Law describes such an economy perfectly, since supply (the quantity that Crusoe was *willing* and able to supply) did in fact create its own demand (the quantity that Crusoe was willing and *able* to demand). In modern industrialized economies, supply does not necessarily create its own demand because the leakage caused by saving may not be matched by the injection of investment, since savers and investors are typically different people.

Checkpoint 21-3

If interest rates decline, as the forecasters predict, then consumers will be encouraged to borrow more to finance consumption expenditures. Hence, the consumption function will shift upward and the savings function will shift downward. In other words, when one of the "other things assumed constant" as we move along a fixed consumption function or saving function changes—in this case the interest rate—it causes these functions to shift.

Checkpoint 21-4

An increase in the prices of new capital goods will cause the investment schedule to shift downward because the expected profit per dollar will be less. If labour contracts were successfully negotiated without strikes, this would reduce the uncertainty associated with future production and would make producers more willing to invest. This would in turn shift the investment schedule upward.

Checkpoint 21-5

Examining the fourth row of Table 21-3, we can explain the various columns as follows. Based on past experience

and expectations of the future, businesses expect total spending over the next period to occur at an annual rate of $800 billion, column (1). They produce $800 billion in goods and services and in the process generate exactly $800 billion in income, column (2). At this income level, consumer demand plus business demand gives a total expenditure of $900 billion, column (3). Since this dollar expenditure for goods is larger than the dollar value of goods actually produced in this period, business is forced to sell $100 billion out of inventories, column (4). Since sales have been larger than expected, businesses increase their expectation of sales for the next period and increase production accordingly. This makes total income rise, column (5).

Chapter 22

Checkpoint 22-1

Realized investment is always equal to saving because that which is produced in the current period and which *is not sold in the current period* (what consumers don't buy), businesses end up buying. Either this production forms part of planned investment (at income levels less than the equilibrium) or as unintended additions to inventories (at income levels greater than the equilibrium level). Why is it sometimes said that "this is obvious because that part of output that is not consumed must go someplace?" Because total output not consumed by households must either end up in business inventories or be purchased by businesses.

Checkpoint 22-2

At an aggregate income of $1,600 ($Y = 1,600$), in Table 22-1 the level of consumption spending is $1,000 ($C = 1,000$), and planned investment is $300 ($I = 300$). Thus the level of aggregate expenditure is $1,300 ($AE = C + I = 1,300$). In comparison with the level of output (aggregate income) it is obvious that businesses which produce $1,600 worth of goods and services cannot find buyers willing to purchase more than $1,300 worth of goods and services. The result is that $300 worth of goods and services will be left unsold. If the $300 is unsold goods it will become an undesired accumulation of inventory ($Y - AE$). Since we have assumed that prices are constant, firms will reduce their production levels to prevent further undesired accumulation of inventory. As firms reduce production, they need fewer inputs, including labour services, and consequently they lay off workers. The incomes of workers declines as production decreases.

As worker income decreases they reduce consumption *by less than* the decrease in income. In the table, as income falls from $1,600 to $1,400, consumption decreases from $1,000 to $900. This is because of the marginal propensity to consume being less than 1 ($mpc = .50$). Since planned investment is not affected by income in this table as income decreases, so $I = 300$ at $Y = 1,400$. The net effect is that the level of aggregate expenditure decreases by less than the decrease in income (*AE* decreased by 100 when *Y* decreased by 200).

As long as aggregate expenditure is less than aggregate income the process of reducing output to prevent inventory accumulation will repeat. Because of this, income will decrease from $1,600 through $1,400 and $1,200 until income equals $1,000. It is only at aggregate income level equal to $1,000 that aggregate expenditure is equal to aggregate income and the businesses can find buyers for all the output that they create.

Checkpoint 22-3

Injections are those expenditures for products which come to business from sectors of the economy *other than households*. When the injections are less than the withdrawals, it means that aggregate expenditure (*AE*) is less than total production. Under these conditions the business sector must have produced more product than is being purchased and therefore has unintended increases in inventory. The reason that firms do not simply decrease their prices to rid themselves of their unintended inventory increases is because of the assumption that prices are constant. It can also be argued that while an attempt by one firm to clear its inventory by lowering its price might be successful, if all firms lower their prices to rid themselves of unwanted inventory the effect will be lower receipts for all firms and they will still end up having to reduce production. The assumption of fixed prices provides a shortcut to the important idea that when inventory increase is *undesired*, firms will reduce output which will reduce the need to employ as many resources and may lead to increased unemployment.

Checkpoint 22-4

In order for the *APC* and the *MPC* to be equal at all levels of disposable income, the consumption function must be a straight line through the origin. In this case the *APS* and the *MPS* would also be equal at all levels of disposable income, and the saving function would be a straight line through the origin. The *APC* would increase and the

MPC would remain unchanged if the consumption function shifted upward in parallel fashion.

Checkpoint 22-5

In Figure 22-2, frame (a), the attempt by consumers to save less shifts their savings function downward, say from S_1 to S_0, but the resulting increase in aggregate income means that once equilibrium is restored, saving (the quantity actually saved) is unchanged. In frame (b) of the figure the downward shift in the saving function, from S_1 to S_0, means that once equilibrium is restored there is actually an increase in the quantity saved. As savers try to rebuild their savings, they will shift up their savings function and shift their consumption function downward. This will result in a decline in aggregate output and aggregate income and will possibly result in layoffs for auto workers and steelworkers.

Checkpoint 22-6

If there was a $200 billion upward shift in the consumption function, the aggregate expenditure curve in Figure 22-4, frame (a), would shift upward by $200 billion (note that this would look just like the shift in aggregate expenditure caused by the $200 billion upward shift in the investment function). The equilibrium level of aggregate income would increase to $1,400 billion. In frame (b) of the figure, the saving function would shift downward by $200 billion, intersecting I_0 at the new equilibrium level of $1,400 billion. If the *MPS* = 1/5, then the *MPC* = 4/5, as shown in Table A-3.

Note that the shift in consumption is downward, so that all these changes are decreases. Graphically, the consumption function shifts downward by $100 and the saving function shifts upward by $100 billion. The final change in aggregate output is a decrease of $500 billion. The slope of the consumption function (and the aggregate expenditure schedule) is 4/5, and the slope of the saving function is 1/5. The word *savings* is being used in the news item to refer to consumers' accumulated savings balances, which have been drawn on to enable consumers to "spend so heavily." In terms of a diagram like Fig-

TABLE A-3

(1) Expenditure Round	(2) Change in Income and Output	(3) Change in Consumption	(4) Change in Saving
First round	$100.00	$ 80.00	$ 20.00
Second round	80.00	64.00	16.00
Third round	64.00	51.20	12.80
Fourth round	51.20	40.96	10.24
Fifth round	40.96	32.77	8.19
Rest of rounds	163.84	131.07	32.77
Totals	$500.00	$400.00	$100.00

ure 22-4, the upward shift of the consumption function has resulted in the increased aggregate expenditure partly by a shift and partly by being further to the right along the consumption function.

Chapter 23

Checkpoint 23-1

The $100 billion increase in exports will raise total spending by $100 billion, which will increase equilibrium by $250 billion ($100 billion × 2.5, the open economy multiplier) if it occurs by itself. Viewed from the withdrawals and injections approach, the $100 billion increase in exports must be added to investment as an additional injection. This shifts the injection schedule upward by $100 billion from I to $I + X$ which increases equilibrium income by $250 billion. The increased injection of $100 billion must be absorbed by an *induced* increase in withdrawals of $100 billion in order for the economy to return to equilibrium at a new level of aggregate income. As income increases by $250 billion, it induces savings to increase by $50 billion ($MPS$ times the increase in income) and it induces imports to increase by $50 billion ($MPM$ times the increase in income). These two effects on the level of saving S and imports M will equal the increase in exports. Therefore while overall withdrawals rise to equal the increased injections, imports do not rise equal to the increase in exports. All that is important at equilibrium is that total withdrawals equal total injections.

Checkpoint 23-2

The $50 billion decrease in lump-sum taxes will raise the level of consumption by $40 billion ($MPC$ times the decrease in taxes). This increases aggregate expenditure by $40 billion and will increase equilibrium income by $100 billion ($40 billion × 2.5—the open economy multiplier) if it occurs by itself. The $50 billion decrease in government spending on goods and services will shift aggregate expenditure down by $50 billion which will tend to decrease equilibrium income by $125 billion. The net effect will be a decrease in equilibrium income of $25 billion. Viewed from the withdrawals and injections approach, the tax decrease of $50 billion will have two effects: (1) it will shift savings upward by $10 billion ($MPS \times \$50$ billion) and (2) it will shift the tax portion of the withdrawal schedule line down by the $50 billion. The net effect on the withdrawal schedule from these two effects of the tax decrease will occur in the $S + M + T$ line, which shifts down by $40 billion resulting in a tendency for equilibrium income to increase by $100 billion. The $50 billion decrease in government spending will shift the $I + X + G$ line down by $50 billion, which tends to decrease equilibrium income by $125 billion. The overall effect will therefore be a decrease in equilibrium income of $25 billion. When the government awards a tax cut

of a certain amount, ΔT, household's disposable income increases by this amount and consumption increases by some portion of the tax cut, $MPC\ \Delta T$. If the government then reduces its own spending on goods and services by the same amount that it gave to households in reduced taxes, the level of aggregate expenditure will decrease by $\Delta G = \Delta T$. The net effect on aggregate expenditure is a decrease equal to $MPS\ \Delta T$. This amount is then multiplied by the open economy multiplier $1/(MPS + MPM)$, to estimate the reduction in equilibrium income. As long as MPM is greater than zero the denominator of the open economy multiplier is less than MPS and the open economy balanced budget multiplier is less than 1 no matter what the values of MPS and MPC.

Checkpoint 23-3

With a lump-sum tax, as is depicted in Figure 23-5, frame (a), taxes do not change with changes in GDP, so that increases or decreases in investment will have no effect on the state of balance of the budget. With a proportional tax, Figure 23-5, frame (b), when investment increases and GDP increases (that is, when the economy is "heating up"), the tax revenues collected will increase. Since government spending is invariant, the government budget will be pushed toward an increased surplus. Put another way, assuming that the government had a deficit at the original GDP, if investment increases it will cause GDP to increase causing tax revenues to increase which will reduce the deficit. If the rise in GDP is large enough it could even turn a government deficit into a surplus. When investment decreases, tax revenues will decrease and the government budget will be pushed toward deficit as GDP decreases. The automatic stabilization effect works by making the budget tend more toward surplus when the economy is "heating up" and by making the budget tend more toward deficit when the economy is "cooling off."

Chapter 24

Checkpoint 24-1

An increase in the price level reduces the purchasing power of consumers' fixed-dollar assets, and hence the purchasing power of consumer wealth, thereby shifting the aggregate expenditure schedule downward, reducing the equilibrium level of real GDP. In addition, an increase in the price level, by increasing the demand for money and pushing up the interest rate, decreases both investment and consumption, hence the aggregate expenditure schedule shifts downward reducing the equilibrium level of real GDP. Finally, an increase in the general price level will make exports more expensive in foreign markets (assuming no change in the exchange rate). The reduction in exports will, like the previously explained decreases in consumption and investment, cause a reduction in aggregate expenditure and equilibrium income. The inverse relationship between the general price level and real GDP traced out in this fashion is the *AD* curve. For a given price level, any exogenously determined expenditure or tax change will cause the aggregate expenditure schedule to shift and the equilibrium level of aggregate income (GDP) to change. Given the general price level, the change in aggregate income certainly can't be represented by movement along an *AD* curve. Therefore, it must be represented by a shift of the whole *AD* curve. We know that a $100 billion increase in government expenditures financed by a $100 billion increase in lump-sum taxes gives rise to a balanced budget multiplier equal to one. Therefore, for any given price level, aggregate income will increase by $100 billion. Hence, the *AD* curve will shift rightward by $100 billion at each and every price level.

Checkpoint 24-2

According to the theory, the firm's willingness to supply a product depends on three things: the price of its own product (p_i), the price of the inputs used by the firm (in this case p_z), and the relation between its own price and the general price level. Therefore a change in the general price level by itself will make the firm readjust its profit-maximizing output decision once it is aware that the general level of prices has changed in relation to the price of its own product. Suppose that the general price level rose but the price of the firm's product remained unchanged and that the firm was aware that its product's price had now decreased in relation to other products in the economy. The firm would be aware that its input costs are likely to rise in response to its suppliers wanting to keep up with the rise in the general level of prices. Consequently the firm is likely to reduce the amount of product it will supply at a given price, p_i. This will result in a leftward shift in the position of this individual firm's supply curve. If the perception is shared by enough firms the entire *AS* curve will shift left. If the firm is aware that prices have been rising at some steady rate for a period of several years, it will make the firm more likely to respond negatively and to respond with a larger decrease in its output to a situation in which the price of its own product does not change. This is because the firm is more likely to anticipate an increase in its own price and the price of its inputs if the general price level has been increasing for many years.

Checkpoint 24-3

Given the general price level, the change in aggregate expenditure will cause the aggregate expenditure curve to shift upward at a given price level. This in turn means that if the price level were to stay constant (for example, if the *AS* curve were horizontal) then equilibrium income will increase by the open economy multiplier times the increase in aggregate expenditure. Since this would happen at any price level it means that each point on the *AD* curve must be shifted to the right by the amount of the open economy multiplier. If government spending increased by

$10 billion it would cause the *AD* curve to shift to the right by the open economy multiplier times $10 billion. Conversely if lump-sum taxes increased by $10 billion then consumption would decrease by $MPC \times \$10$ billion. Since MPC is less than 1, let us assume it is 4/5 as in the examples in the chapter. Then consumption would decrease by $8 billion. Assuming the multiplier is 2.5, the *AD* curve will shift left by 2.5 times $2, or $5 billion. Income will increase by $5 billion. Hence, the *AD* curve will shift rightward by $5 billion at each price level.

It should be noted that since we have assumed a lump-sum tax increase, it could be argued that the tax increase has not distorted the incentive to supply labour services or other factor services since it is not based on earnings. This means that the *AS* curve would be unaffected by an increase in this type of taxes.

Checkpoint 24-4

A strictly demand-side, or Keynesian, point of view would only recognize the leftward shift in the *AD* curve caused by an increase in marginal tax rates. The position of the *AS* curve would remain unchanged. However, the supply-side effects of the increase in marginal tax rates would tend to discourage work effort and reduce after-tax rates of return, thereby causing the *AS* curve to shift upward and leftward. Recognition of the leftward shift in the *AS* curve would mean that equilibrium income would fall further than is the case when only the leftward shift in the *AD* curve is taken into account. According to a strictly demand-side point of view, the general price level would fall or remain unchanged (the latter if the demand curve shift occurred along a horizontal *AS* curve). Taking account of supply-side effects, the general price level could rise or fall depending on the relative sizes of the leftward shifts in the *AD* and *AS* curves and their initial positions prior to the increase in the marginal tax rates.

Chapter 25

Checkpoint 25-1

From 1971 to 1973 the actual level of GDP was fairly close to the level of potential GDP, and the cyclically adjusted budget concept seemed to work fairly well—the cyclically adjusted budget stayed almost in balance. From 1975 onward, however, substantial cyclically adjusted deficits seem to have failed to close the gap between actual and potential GDP. For the period from 1984 to 1988, while unemployment decreased, there was no evidence that this was due to increases in the deficit. In fact, the government was attempting to reduce the deficit over this period.

Checkpoint 25-2

The effect of a cyclically adjusted deficit will be greater if the deficit is financed by the government selling bonds directly to the central bank—printing money—than it will be if it is financed by selling bonds to the private sector.

If the cyclically adjusted budget is becoming less effective, this could be due in part to increased sale of bonds to the private sector and the foreign financial markets. If a cyclically adjusted budget surplus is eliminated by holding funds from a budget surplus idle, the contractionary effect on GDP will be greater than if the funds are used to retire debt. However, if the cyclically adjusted budget is in surplus, the actual budget may not be in surplus. It is only when the actual budget is in surplus that funds can be held idle or used to retire debt, and the actual budget has not been in surplus since 1975. If taxes were cut to $100 billion, then the deficit would increase by approximately $100 billion. Canadian savings are not large enough to finance this large an increase in the government deficit at this time. If the increased deficit were financed by the sale of say an additional $50 billion in bonds to the private sector, it would result in a reduction of private investment— domestic interest rate crowding out. If the remaining $50 billion were financed by the sale of bonds on international markets, there would be upward pressure on the external value of the Canadian dollar. The result would have to be an increase in imports and a reduction in exports.

Checkpoint 25-3

Since half of the citizens would be holding the debt and receiving the interest payments on it, as the debt got larger, half of the citizens (those not holding the debt) would find themselves giving an ever larger share of their incomes in taxes to finance interest payments to the other half of the citizens holding debt. At some point the interest payments on the debt would involve such a large transfer of purchasing power from those without government bonds to those holding government bonds that political unrest would become serious. Certainly the government would be considered bankrupt when the interest payments became so large that the half of the population with no bonds were being taxed to the point that they could no longer afford a minimally acceptable standard of living on their after-tax income. No doubt there would be a tax rebellion (refusal to pay taxes) before this point was reached.

Chapter 26

Checkpoint 26-1

If the Phillips curve were to rotate counterclockwise around a 9 percent unemployment rate at zero inflation, the upper end would lie further to the left and the lower end would lie further to the right. Because of the rotation, unemployment could be reduced with a smaller increase in inflation. If the economy could have a zero percent rate of inflation with 9 percent unemployment, then the Phillips curve would intersect the horizontal axis at 9 percent unemployment.

If the Phillips curve changed to require higher increases in inflation for any given reduction in unemployment, it would have rotated clockwise. The upper end of the curve would lie further to the right and the lower end of the curve would lie further to the left.

If the Phillips curve represents a true menu of choices, then the choice of a point on the curve is normative. It cannot be decided by an appeal to facts alone. The choice of the most desired attainable combination of unemployment and inflation requires an assessment of the ethical issues surrounding the lowering of the inflation rate at the expense of higher unemployment. The effects of increasing unemployment will create burdens for some members of society and lowering inflation will create benefits for some members of society. The costs of increased unemployment include the financial and emotional suffering of the unemployed, the lower profits earned by those with lower sales due to depressed markets, and the lower standard of living measured by a decrease in gross domestic product shared by the same population. The benefits of lower inflation include: maintaining the real value of the financial assets of those with cash holdings, protection for members of society who lack the political power or opportunity to increase their nominal incomes at the rate of inflation, and decreased distortion of resource allocation into minimizing the negative effects of inflation (the "shoe-leather costs of inflation"). The optimum combination of the unemployment and inflation mix is a choice about making some groups better off at the expense of other groups. This is a problem of deciding which groups are more deserving and assessing which groups have the political influence or technical skills to improve their well-being by changing the inflation unemployment mix. It is a broad ranging social issue requiring an interdisciplinary focus which includes philosophy, political science, sociology, and many other fields. It is not a decision that economic theory is well equipped to solve alone.

Checkpoint 26-2

According to the adaptive expectations view, if policymakers want to keep the unemployment rate lower than the natural rate of unemployment, then they must unavoidably keep pushing the inflation rate to higher and higher levels. Choosing the wrong place is choosing to maintain an unemployment rate less than the natural rate. Adaptive expectations theory can be interpreted as assuming that people never learn from their mistakes because people are assumed to expect that the inflation rate which occurred in the previous time period will occur again this period. Within the theory, there is no allowance that people, having been fooled by the unanticipated effects of government policy initiatives in one time period, will learn to expect government intervention, to anticipate its effects, and to adjust their own behaviour in consequence.

Checkpoint 26-3

Rational expectations theory suggests that people do not make mistakes on average. In forming their behaviour people include in their decisions the anticipated effects of current actions and events as well as the actual behaviour of the economy over the previous period. This means that if the government behaves in a systematic way in setting policy to deal with unemployment or inflation, the people will quickly learn to anticipate the timing and effects of government policy. The result is that these people will adjust their behaviour to compensate for the government policy which renders the policy ineffective. The implication is that government policy is more effective in the shortrun if it catches people by surprise and if policy is arbitrary it is obviously difficult to forecast.

Lucas' statement implies that in the longrun governments must have publicly known goals and that the public must have confidence that the government is committed to these goals and capable of achieving them. In Lucas' view, if government can create a credibility in its policies then people will suffer less "noise" in interpreting the effects of changing prices. The result will be a reduction of the information extraction problem and the economy will more quickly adjust to equilibrium at potential gross domestic product. This will reduce the swings in output characteristic of the business cycle and, in Lucas' view, allow the price rationing mechanism to function appropriately in allocating resources.

Checkpoint 26-4

The existence of a large unionized portion of the labour force implies that unions and employers will have contracts covering the nominal wage rates and other costs of employing and laying off for a significant part of the labour force. The contracted nominal wages and other costs form rigidities which prevent input costs from adjusting over the shortrun in response to anticipated adjustments in government policy and inflation. This means that even though the workers may correctly anticipate the rate of inflation, some of them cannot adjust their wages in response to expansionary government policies. This means that expansionary policy would be effective in reducing unemployment, because the shortrun aggregate supply curve, AS_{sr}, would be fairly horizontal. The benefits of lower unemployment and a higher standard of living for other members of society would however have come at the expense of the unionized workers whose real wages, wage/general price level, has decreased. In addition, the rigidity of the wages limits the effectiveness of price rationing and increases the misallocation of resource use.

Checkpoint 26-5

The pattern of the data in Figure 26-4 suggests that the average level of the unemployment rate has increased over time. Certainly one possible explanation is the changing nature of the labour force which we have discussed previously.

Chapter 27

Checkpoint 27-1

The one that is easiest to carry. If aluminum has a higher value per pound, $10 worth of aluminum would be lighter to carry around. On the other hand, steel might be less bulky. From high to low liquidity, the items would be ranked as follows: a $10 bill, a demand deposit, a Master Charge card, a $1,000 bill, a savings deposit, a $100,000 registered retirement pension plan, a stamp collection, a real estate lot in a suburb. From high to low usefulness as a store of value, assuming a 10 percent rate of inflation, the items would be ranked as follows: a lot in a suburb, a stamp collection, a $100,000 registered retirement saving plan, a savings deposit, a $10 bill, a $1,000 bill, a demand deposit, a Master Charge card. The statement "money is acceptable because it is acceptable" means that what gives money its value as a medium of exchange is the willingness of people to accept it in exchange for goods and services. From Figure 27-1, it would appear that a dollar bill has not been a very good store of value, since a 1991 dollar bill would have bought 2/3 of the market basket that a 1980 dollar bill would have bought. This poor performance of the dollar to serve as a store of value is more dramatic if the purchasing power of the 1991 dollar is compared to the purchasing power of the 1960 dollar. In 1991 the dollar purchased only 1/5 of the amount it would purchase in 1960 (this ratio, based on the GDP deflator, is obviously somewhat simplistic, since it abstracts from changes in the quality of goods and all the other problems associated with the measurement of price level over such a long period of time).

Checkpoint 27-2

A bank note might be said to be an IOU because it is a piece of paper testifying to the bank's willingness to pay the bearer a given quantity of money that the bearer has deposited in the bank. When currency is convertible into gold, there must be enough gold to redeem the currency. This means that the rate of growth of the supply of currency is limited to the rate of growth of the gold supply. If people were to become less trusting of the soundness of banks, then they would be more likely to withdraw their money. Consequently banks would feel compelled to keep more reserves in their vaults. This would reduce their ability to create deposits through the making of loans. And this would reduce the upper limit to the economy's money supply. If bankers were to become more cautious, then they would be less willing to make loans, and this would reduce the amount of IOUs on their balance sheets. If they made fewer loans for a given level of reserves, then the money supply would be smaller. This would make money conditions "tighter," and in the aggregate, people would spend less on goods and services.

Checkpoint 27-3

The Bank of Canada makes the money supply more elastic because then it is able to create reserves at a rate commensurate with growth in the level of economic activity. The Bank of Canada is sometimes referred to as the "lender of last resort," because individual chartered banks can borrow reserves from the Bank of Canada if they find themselves in a credit squeeze due to sudden large withdrawals of deposits. It is possible that deposit insurance provided through the Canadian Deposit Insurance Corporation is more effective than the chartered banks' ability to borrow from the Bank of Canada in preventing bank panics because bank panics are essentially crises of confidence, and the deposit insurance is a very effective confidence-building measure.

Chapter 28

Checkpoint 28-1

The banks of Europe and North America held larger excess reserves from 1933 to 1940 because many banks had failed when panics led depositors to withdraw their deposits in the 1929–1932 period (the early years of the Great Depression). Surges of withdrawals had actually caused the insolvency and bankruptcy of many banks in the United States and France. Banks in Canada and other countries kept a large quantity of excess reserves on hand as they were leery of these surges in withdrawals.

Checkpoint 28-2

The resulting table is shown as Table A-4.

If a bank decided to hold all its excess reserves and make no new loans or purchase any new securities, it would stop the expansion process completely at that point. If at any point a depositor receiving one of the new loans took the entire value of his or her new loan out in cash, this would also put a stop to the expansion process. If a bank's willingness to lend increases, the bank will keep fewer excess reserves as cautionary balances, and it will become more aggressive with a larger value of loans when it is "loaned up." This will increase the money supply.

If the reserve ratio were .25 (instead of .10 or .05) the maximum effect of a $100 cash withdrawal is a decrease in the money supply of $400 (= $100 \times 1/.25$). The withdrawal will have a minimum effect if the bank was holding excess reserves, since it can pay out the cash without calling in any of its investments. In that case, M1 will be unaffected, because the only demand deposit effect will be a decrease in your balance by $100, and this will be countered by the increase in the cash component of M1 by $100.

Chapter 29

Checkpoint 29-1

The statement is true. As long as the Bank of Canada maintains its policy of setting the bank rate equal to the

TABLE A-4   Expansion of the Money Supply by Lending and Deposit Creation by the Banking System
(Legally Required Reserve Ratio Is .05)

Bank	(1) New Reserves and Demand Deposits	(2) Excess Reserves Equal to the Amount Bank Can Lend, Equal to New Money Created (1) − (3)	(3) Required Reserves (1) × Required Reserve Ratio of .10
A	$ 1,000.00	$ 950.00	$ 50.00
B	950.00	902.50	47.50
C	902.50	857.37	45.13
D	857.37	814.50	42.87
E	814.50	773.77	40.73
F	773.77	735.08	38.69
G	735.08	698.33	36.75
H	689.33	654.86	34.47
	.	.	.
	.	.	.
	.	.	.
All remaining banks	13,277.45	13,622.59	663.86
Total	$20,000.00	$19,000.00	$1,000.00

rate of return on Treasury Bills plus one quarter of one percent, then the bank rate will always move inversely with changes in the price of Treasury Bills. In the conduct of open market operations, when the Bank of Canada purchases Treasury Bills it will cause an increase in the demand for Treasury Bills which will increase the price of the Treasury Bills and lower the effective interest rate on them. With this drop in the interest rate or yield on Treasury Bills the bank rate will automatically decrease. If the Bank of Canada engages in open market sales of Treasury Bills it will increase the supply of Treasury Bills. Like an increase in the supply of any commodity, the increase in the supply of Treasury Bills will cause a decrease in the price of Treasury Bills in the open market and will increase the rate of return for those buying the Treasury Bills at this discounted price. The rise in the rate of interest earned on Treasury Bills automatically causes the bank rate to increase by the same amount.

Under normal conditions the only purpose of the bank rate is as a signalling device for the Bank of Canada. In the event of a serious and widespread financial collapse of liquidity or confidence in the chartered banks, the bank rate represents the rate of interest which would be charged by the Bank of Canada on loans—advances which it would make to the chartered banks to provide them with borrowed funds to meet their reserve requirement. It is the cost at which the chartered banks could use the Bank of Canada as a source of funds in its role as lender of last resort. When the Bank of Canada was set up in the 1930s, the commission which recommended its creation was concerned that in a severe recession there might be insufficient liquidity available for the chartered banks to function properly. The Bank of Canada was given the ability to set the bank rate low enough to make it profitable for the chartered banks to borrow from it to support their reserve needs if this were seen to be in the public interest.

Checkpoint 29-2

An increase in money demand accompanied by a decrease in the money supply would have the greatest effect on the interest rate. This can be easily demonstrated by graphs similar to Figures 29-3 and 29-4.

If people were to become more uncertain about their jobs, then they would tend to hold higher precautionary balances. This means that they would hold larger money balances at any given interest rate, and hence money demand would increase.

Chapter 30

Checkpoint 30-1

If the marginal efficiency of the investment curve in frame (b) of Figure 30-2 was made steeper, then the interest rate decrease resulting from the increase in money supply from M_0 to M_1 would cause investment spending to in-

crease by less than before. If the demand curve for money in frame (a) of Figure 30-2 became steeper, then the shift in money supply from M_0 to M_1 would result in a larger decrease in the interest rate and hence a larger increase in investment spending.

Checkpoint 30-2

Stated by itself, the equation of exchange is true by definition. It is not, however, of much significance in this form since velocity will be calculated by dividing nominal GDP by some measure of the money M1 or M2 and velocity could be any number that results and could change with each change in either the nominal GDP or the money supply. If it is postulated that the velocity of money is inherently stable, then the equation of exchange becomes a theory linking changes in the money supply to changes in nominal GDP. If the postulation that the velocity were stable is correct for a particular economy over a specified period of time, the quantity theory provides a powerful tool for predicting the impact of changes in the money supply on the rate of inflation and the level real output.

Checkpoint 30-3

In the new classical view, the shortrun aggregate supply curve is relatively horizontal if the information extraction problem is low. The more severe the information extraction problem becomes the steeper the shortrun aggregate supply curve. This is because as the information extraction problem increases, firms and other economic agents have more difficulty estimating what portion of a change in the price of their own product constitutes a change in their *relative* price.

In the longrun, new classical theory supports the view that the longrun aggregate supply curve is vertical at potential GDP. This is because shortrun deviations in the output level cause changes to the inflation rate which makes economic agents reassess the expected behaviour of prices and makes them readjust their decision making to include this anticipated inflation. The result is that they will not respond to changes in the demand levels because anticipated changes in aggregate demand only affect the price level, not the economy's output level.

Chapter 31

Checkpoint 31-1

In terms of Figure 31-2, the Bank of Canada viewed the federal government deficit spending as pushing aggregate demand rightward over a steep aggregate supply curve, such as the one illustrated in frame (b). Thus in the view of the Bank of Canada there was a high probability that the government's fiscal policy would lead to increased inflation. In terms of Figure 31-1, the Bank of Canada sees government spending as raising the interest rate because the increase in aggregate demand has increased precautionary and transactions demands for money and shifted money demand to the right. So while the provincial premiers seem to think that the Bank of Canada is causing high interest rates by keeping a tight rein on the money supply, the bank's staff thinks that the government's high spending is causing high interest rates and inflation.

If the Bank of Canada should accede to the first minister's wishes and take steps to lower the interest rate, it could buy Treasury Bills in the open market, or switch government deposits out of the Bank of Canada and redeposit them in the chartered banks. Either of these measures would increase the reserves available to the chartered banks and cause an increase in the money supply. This would shift the money supply curves to the right in both frame (a) and frame (b) of Figure 31-1. The increase in the money supply would cause a decrease the interest rate and increase investment spending. The decrease in the interest rate will also result in less willingness by non-residents to lend money to Canada which will put downward pressure on the value of the Canadian dollar on international markets. If the Canadian dollar is permitted to decrease in value there will be an increase in net exports as non-residents take advantage of the relatively lower price (in terms of their own currency) for Canadian products. In the A-view, a given money supply change would decrease interest rates and increase investment and exports less than in the B-view. The increase in investment spending and exports would increase aggregate income but would move the economy farther into the inflationary zone on the supply curve illustrated in Figure 31-2. The increase in spending would also increase precautionary and transactions demands for money, which would tend to push the interest rate back up as money demand was shifted to the right. The net effect on aggregate demand would be similar to that illustrated in Figure 31-2.

Greater discipline in fiscal policy would mean decreasing government spending. This would reverse the events pictured in Figure 31-2. Government spending would decrease and reduce aggregate demand. The reduction in aggregate demand would cause aggregate income to decrease and shift the money demand curve to the left, which would decrease the interest rate, increasing investment, offsetting some of the original government spending decline. The B-view would have the offsetting change being larger than the A-view. The leftward shift in the money demand curve due to the decrease in government spending is illustrated in Figure 31-1, which shows the larger offsetting change in investment predicted by the B-view. The net decrease in aggregate demand and aggregate income would reduce the rise of inflation by moving the economy to the left along the aggregate supply curve illustrated in Figure 31-2. The greater the policy cooperation in fighting inflation between the government with its fiscal policy and the Bank of Canada with its monetary policy, the easier it is for the Bank of Canada not to be so concerned about the necessity of fighting inflation with a tight money policy.

It should be noted that the problem with this policy is that neither fiscal policy nor monetary policy can be used to reduce the unemployment rate if both are being coordinated to counter inflation.

Checkpoint 31-2

If there was a prolonged decrease in the general price level and there was an anticipated deflation, then the money interest rate would be less than the real interest rate by an amount equal to the anticipated rate of deflation. Since borrowers would be paying back dollars that are worth more than the dollars that they borrowed, they would demand compensation for this in the form of a lower money interest rate. The interest rate shown in Figure P30-3, tends to move with the rate of inflation shown in Figure P30-1, because the anticipated rate of inflation is part of the nominal interest rate as illustrated by the equation:

$$i_{\text{nominal}} = [(1 + i_{\text{real}})(1 + \text{expected inflation rate}) - 1]$$

Chapter 32

Checkpoint 32-1

The rule of 72 allows us to approximate the growth rates based on the length of time it takes a variable to double so it cannot be applied directly to a case where productivity has tripled. However, we can use this rule to make some interesting observations. Productivity roughly doubled in the first seventeen years (1946–1963). This means that productivity was growing at an average annual rate of nearly 4.25 percent ($72 \div 17 = 4.234$). If this rate had continued, it would have doubled again by 1980. At that time it would have been 4 times the 1946 level. However, it had not tripled by 1980. Clearly the growth rate had slowed substantially. Productivity had still not redoubled by 1989. Since 1963, the average annual growth rate has been just over 2 percent.

If productivity grows only 1.5 percent, then the other components will have to grow much faster if the economy is to grow at 3 percent.

Real GDP has increased roughly sixfold, but population has only a little more than doubled so per capita income has somewhat less than tripled.

Checkpoint 32-2

Technically, an increase in any factor while other factors are held constant brings about diminishing returns for the increased factor. Historically, however, technical change and investment in human capital have tended to be the major sources of economic growth. This phenomenon would seem to suggest that technical change and investment in human capital are bound less by the law of diminishing returns than are the other factors. Hence, technical change and investment in human capital probably will have a larger impact on longrun growth than will increases in other factors of production.

Chapter 33

Checkpoint 33-1

Although the frontiersmen probably would be subject to increasing costs and hence would have nonlinear production possibility frontiers, this problem is illustrated most simply with linear production possibilities frontiers like those used in the text's Portugal and Canada example (Figure 33-4). If the two pioneers have differing abilities in the production of wood and wheat, then their production possibilities frontiers would have different slopes, reflecting different opportunity costs. Comparative advantage would lead to specialization and trade, giving rise to trading possibilities frontiers for the two frontiersmen that lie above the two production possibilities frontiers. This would allow both frontiersmen to have more of both goods than they would have in the absence of specialization and trade.

Although the Prairies can produce fruit and British Columbia can produce wheat, climatic differences give rise to a comparative advantage for British Columbia in fruit production and for the Prairies in wheat production—hence, there is specialization and trade. Similarly, Ontario specializes in steel production, whereas Newfoundland specializes in fish production. Quebec produces furniture, and Prince Edward Island produces potatoes. In each case, climate or resource endowments lead to a comparative advantage, which encourages specialization and trade. You should be able to list a number of similar examples.

Checkpoint 33-2

The steelmakers are buying more foreign coke because it is available at a cheaper price than that charged by domestic coke producers. This difference could be due to a real comparative advantage for foreign coke producers, or it could be due to the fact that foreign producers are receiving government subsidies and are able to "dump" their coke in the Canadian market at less than production cost. If foreign coke producers do have a comparative advantage in coke production, then indeed Canadian steelmakers have less incentive to invest in more efficient coke ovens (this is true whether the comparative advantage is a real one or a "false" one due to dumping). This hurts the sales of domestic producers of coke ovens. Hence, it is in their best interest to seek some protection (such as tariffs) from coke imports. Since it is very difficult to ascertain what the foreign coke production costs really are, the dumping claim might be very difficult to prove.

Chapter 34

Checkpoint 34-1

The American haircut is paid for with a Canadian payment to the United States and hence is a debit on the current account. The birthday present is a private unilateral transfer and by convention is entered as a credit item on the current account. A balancing debit entry is made under unilateral transfers. If you finance the Volkswagen domestically, then Volkswagen is paid "cash" for the car, and this constitutes a Canadian payment to Germany and is a merchandise import debit on the current account. If you buy the car and finance it with Volkswagen, then Volkswagen is "buying" your IOU for the amount of the purchase price, and this is a credit on the private capital account. As you pay off the loan, your payments will be debits on the private capital account. When a Japanese firm builds a Canadian factory, this will be recorded as a credit item on Canada's capital account.

Checkpoint 34-2

When one currency depreciates, it takes more of that currency to buy a unit of foreign currency. But, of course, this means that it takes less of the foreign currency to buy a unit of the first currency, and hence the foreign currency has appreciated.

The supply curve in Figure 34-1 is a demand curve for dollars in the sense that it is a schedule showing the quantity of kronor that the Swedish are willing and able to supply in exchange for dollars, which is the same thing as the quantity of dollars that the Swedish are willing and able to purchase in exchange for kronor. The demand curve in Figure 34-1 is a supply curve for dollars in the sense that it is a schedule showing the quantity of kronor that Canadians are willing and able to purchase in exchange for dollars, which is the same thing as the quantity of dollars that Canadians are willing and able to supply in exchange for kronor.

A Canadian expansionary monetary policy will, *ceteris paribus*, increase the exchange rate of dollars for other currencies (that is, it will take more dollars to buy a unit of any other currency). This is because an expansionary monetary policy will increase money GDP in Canada and increase the demand for imports. This will increase the demand for foreign currency to pay for these imports and will hence drive the equilibrium exchange rate upward when the demand curve for foreign goods shifts rightward.

A more restrictive British fiscal policy will, *ceteris paribus*, increase the exchange rate of dollars for pounds (that is, it will take more dollars to buy a pound). This is because a restrictive British fiscal policy will decrease GDP in Britain and decrease British demand for Canadian exports. This will decrease the supply of British pounds in the foreign exchange market, since fewer pounds are needed to be exchanged for Canadian dollars to pay for

Canadian goods. The supply curve for British pounds will decrease (shift leftward), and the equilibrium exchange rate of dollars for pounds will increase.

Checkpoint 34-3

If a government wants to fix an exchange rate, it must be prepared to use its reserves to buy up the excess supply of currency at the fixed rate when the fixed rate is above the equilibrium and to supply the foreign market with currency equal to the excess demand when the fixed rate is below the equilibrium rate (this will increase its official reserves).

Balance of payments deficits and surpluses are inevitable under fixed exchange rates since as time passes, supply and demand curves in foreign exchange markets inevitably shift because of changing trade patterns and differing economic developments within each nation. Only occasionally will the equilibrium rate and the fixed rate happen to be equal—the rest of the time balance of payments deficits and surpluses will occur as the government has to intervene to maintain the fixed rate.

If a nation's currency was overvalued, then the fixed rate of exchange would be above the equilibrium rate and the nation would have to buy up the excess supply of currency continually at the fixed rate. This would continually draw down its official reserves. If the nation were to tighten its monetary policy, then its money GDP would decline and its demand for imports of foreign goods would decline. This would decrease the supply of its currency in foreign exchange markets and hence decrease the excess supply. This would decrease the drain on the nation's official reserves.

Checkpoint 34-4

Since one of the costs of inflation to a nation is a depreciation of its currency relative to that of nations with less inflation, nations that had easy monetary and fiscal policies would experience an increased balance of payments deficit. This is because the Bretton Woods system required a member nation to use its official reserves to prevent devaluation of its currency. Hence, fiscal and monetary policies that encouraged inflation would cost a nation increased drains on its official reserves, and this would "impose a certain amount of fiscal and monetary discipline on governments," since they could not allow their official reserves to be drained continuously.

Glossary

A

abuse doctrine The concept that market conduct—the abuse of dominant position—rather than share of market control should determine guilt or innocence under the competition laws.

accelerationist view Holds that there is no stable long-run Phillips curve trade-off between the inflation rate and the unemployment rate and that persistent attempts to stimulate aggregate demand to reduce the unemployment rate below the natural rate will cause an ever-increasing rate of inflation.

accelerator principle The relationship between changes in the level of retail sales and the level of investment expenditures.

accounting profit Profit obtained by subtracting a firm's explicit costs from its total sales receipts. It does not consider any implicit costs.

actual investment See *realized investment*.

ad valorem tax Sales tax or excise tax calculated as a flat percentage of the sales price of a good.

adaptive expectations Theory based on the assumption that economic agents base their expectations of the future on the actual events of the recent past and therefore make systematic errors. See also *asymmetrical information assumption*.

agents In economics, the decision makers in the economy.

aggregate demand curve (AD) Shows the inverse relationship between the economy's aggregate demand for output and the price level of that output.

aggregate supply curve (AS) Shows the amount of aggregate output that the economy's businesses will supply at different price levels.

anti-dumping laws Laws intended to prevent unfair competition. If imported goods are priced too low, the law triggers a government investigation of possible unfair low prices—dumping.

arc elasticity Method of calculating the coefficient of price elasticity that uses the average of two points instead of the standard method of calculating percentage changes using the original point.

assumptions Things taken for granted, arbitrarily or tentatively accepted.

asymmetrical information assumption View that when aggregate demand increases, businesses become aware of it before unions or other resource suppliers.

automatic stabilizer Built-in feature of the economy that operates continuously without intervention to smooth out the peaks and troughs of business cycles.

autonomous spending Spending that is exogenously determined and that causes the aggregate expenditure schedule to shift.

average fixed cost (AFC) Cost determined by dividing total fixed cost by the number of units of output.

average product (AP) Total output divided by the number of labourers (variable factor) required to produce that output.

average propensity to consume (APC) The fraction, or proportion, of total income that is consumed.

average propensity to save (APS) The fraction, or proportion, of total income that is saved.

average revenue (AR) Total revenue divided by the number of units sold.

average total cost (ATC) Cost determined by dividing total cost by the number of units of output.

average variable cost (AVC) Cost determined by dividing total variable cost by the number of units of output.

B

balance of payments A nation's total payments to other nations must be equal to, or balanced by, the total payments received from other nations.

balance of payments account Record of all the payments made by a nation to other nations, as well as all the payments that it receives from other nations during the course of a year.

balance of payments deficit The excess of a nation's payments to other nations over the payments received from other nations, exclusive of government capital account transactions in official reserve assets. It means that the government is reducing its holdings of official reserve assets or that the liquid claims of foreign governments against these reserves are increasing, or both.

balance of payments surplus Excess of payments received from other nations over the payments made to them, exclusive of government capital account transactions in official reserves and liquid claims. It means that the government is increasing its holdings of official reserves or its holdings of liquid claims on the official reserve assets held by foreign governments, or both.

balance sheet (of a chartered bank)   Statement of the bank's financial condition that balances assets versus liabilities and equity.

balanced budget   A budget in which total government expenditures equal total revenues.

balanced budget multiplier   The ratio of the amount of change in GDP to the change in government spending financed entirely by an increase in taxes. It indicates that a simultaneous increase in government expenditures and taxes of a matched or balanced amount will result in an increase in GDP of that amount multiplied by the balanced budget multiplier.

Bank of Canada   The Canadian central bank, responsible for the control of the money supply and serving as a banker to the chartered banks and fiscal agent to the government.

bank notes   Paper money issued by a chartered bank.

bank rate   The interest rate the Bank of Canada charges chartered banks that borrow reserves from the Bank of Canada through advances.

barrier to competition   Any circumstance that makes it difficult for a new firm to enter an industry. Examples are the exclusive ownership of a unique resource, economies of scale, and government-sanctioned protection in the form of patents, licenses, copyrights, and franchises.

barter   Trading goods directly for goods.

benefit-cost analysis   An examination of the benefits and costs associated with any program, based on the principle that any program should be carried on to the point at which the last dollar spent (the last dollar of cost) on the program just yields a dollar's worth of benefit.

Bertrand model   Explanation of oligopolistic firms' behaviour that leads to a competitive price outcome.

bilateral monopoly   Market structure in which there is monopoly power on both the buyer's and the seller's side of the market.

black market   A market in which goods are traded (illegally) at prices often above a government-imposed ceiling or below a floor price.

branch banking system   System in which each chartered bank is allowed to have branch offices spread throughout the whole country.

break-even point   Point at which the quantity of output produced by a firm is such that total revenue just equals total cost or, equivalently, at which average revenue (price) equals average total cost.

Bretton Woods system   System of fixed exchange rates in which only the dollar was directly convertible into gold at a fixed rate of exchange. All other currencies were indirectly convertible into gold by virtue of their convertibility into the dollar. Also called the *gold exchange system*.

budget constraint (or **budget line**)   Straight line representing all possible combinations of goods that a consumer can purchase at given prices by spending a given money income.

budget deficit   Government expenditures are more than revenues.

budget surplus   Government expenditures are less than revenues.

bundle   Some combination of goods from all the possible goods from which a consumer expects to derive satisfaction.

burdens of the government debt   Ways in which, at least for some citizens, the public debt imposes burdens similar to those of a private debt.

business cycles   The somewhat irregular but recurrent pattern of fluctuations in economic activity and GDP.

business fluctuations   Recurring phenomena of increasing and decreasing unemployment associated with decreasing and increasing output. See also *business cycles*.

C

Canada-U.S. Trade Agreement (CUSTA)   1989 agreement providing for gradual elimination of tariffs and other trade bariers between the two countries.

Canadian Deposit Insurance Corporation (CDIC)   Institution that provides insurance up to $60,000 for qualifying types of deposits in Canadian financial institutions.

Canadian Payments Association (CPA)   Association of Canadian chartered banks and other financial intermediaries.

Canadian and Quebec Pension Plans (CPP and QPP)   Contributory pension plans for Quebec (QPP) and the rest of Canada (CPP).

capital   Goods that are used to produce other goods—a resource.

capital consumption allowance   See *capital depreciation*.

capital deepening   An increase in the stock of capital (machines, tools, buildings, highways, dams, and so forth) relative to the quantities of all other resources, including labour.

capital depreciation   The wearing out of capital, often measured by its decline in value. Also referred to as *capital consumption allowance*.

cardinal numbers   A number system that uses all of the properties of arithmetic.

cartel   A group of firms that colludes to set prices and market shares.

central bank   A bank that deals mainly with the government and other banks and assumes broad responsibilities in the national economy.

ceteris paribus Latin expression for "all other things remaining the same."

charter A franchise or license granted by the government.

chequable deposits A demand deposit or daily interest account on which a financial institution will allow chequing privileges.

circular flow model An overview of an economy showing the flows of money, goods, and resources from one economic agent to another.

classical aggregate supply curve (AS_C) Vertical aggregate supply curve under the assumption that the economy is at full employment.

closed economy An economy that does not trade with other nations.

closed shop Workplace that requires union membership as a condition of employment.

coefficient of price elasticity Number obtained by dividing the percentage change in quantity by the percentage change in price.

coincidence of wants The possibility of barter between two individuals that occurs when each has a good that the other wants.

collusion Cooperation between firms aimed to further their economic interests in opposition to the general public interest. Collusion is generally illegal in Canada.

command economy An economy in which the government answers the questions of how to organize production, what and how much to produce, and for whom to produce.

commodities Tangible goods such as food, clothing, cars, or household appliances.

commodity money Money that has other uses besides serving as money, such as shells, beaver pelts, salt, gold, silver, and so forth.

comparative advantage The ability to produce a good at a lower opportunity cost than another.

comparative statics A method of analysis that assumes the market has achieved equilibrium and then analyzes how the equilibrium changes when one or more of the exogenous variables change.

competition policy Legislation and associated administrative bureaucracy and procedures largely concerned with preventing, or at least curbing, monopoly characteristics.

complementary factors Factors of production, the use of which always increases (decreases) whenever the use of any one of them increases (decreases).

complementary good A good that tends to be used jointly with another good. The demand for one good varies inversely with the price of its complement.

composite good A bundle of goods that contains many individual goods but is treated as if it were one good.

concentration ratio A measure of the extent to which a few firms dominate an industry, computed as the percentage of total industry sales accounted for by the four (or eight) largest (in terms of sales) firms in the industry.

conglomerate A firm that produces a wide variety of goods for a number of largely unrelated markets.

conglomerate merger Merger of companies that operate in completely different markets and produce largely unrelated goods.

consol A perpetual interest-bearing obligation, such as a bond with no maturity date.

consumer price index (CPI) A commonly used and widely publicized measure of the general level of prices in the economy, constructed as a weighted average of the prices of a market basket of goods purchased by a typical family.

consumption The end purpose of the economy; the use of goods by the individuals or households in society. In macroeconomics it refers to the portion of GDP spent by private households.

consumption function The relationship between the level of disposable income and the level of planned consumption on current final output.

contestable market Market in which the incumbent firm(s) in the industry are disciplined to keep price low (close to average cost) by the threat of competition through entry.

cooperatives Corporate firms that differ from other corporations in that (1) voting is proportional to membership not ownership, and (2) returns to each member depend on patronage not ownership.

copyright Exclusive right granted to composers, artists, software programmers, and writers that gives them legal control over the production and reproduction of their work for a certain period of time.

corporation Firm that has a legal identity separate and distinct from the people who own it. This provides owners with limited liability.

countervailing duty One country's offsetting tax to remove the unfair advantage generated by another country's export subsidy.

craft union A union of skilled workers trained in a particular trade or craft.

creditors People or organizations to whom money is owed.

cross price elasticity Measures the responsiveness of the demand for one good, *A*, to a change in the price of a different good, say *B*.

crowding out The reduction in some component of aggregate expenditure, usually investment spending, that can occur as a consequence of an expansionary fiscal policy.

crown corporations Companies whose major shareholder is the government.

currency appreciation A rise in the free-market value of a currency in terms of other currencies, with the result that fewer units of the currency will be required to buy a unit of a foreign currency.

currency depreciation A fall in the free-market value of a currency in terms of other currencies, meaning that more units of a currency will be required to buy a unit of a foreign currency.

currency devaluation A lowering of the level at which the price of a currency is fixed in relation to other currencies under a fixed exchange rate system.

currency revaluation An increase in the level at which the price of a currency is fixed in relation to other currencies under a fixed exchange rate system.

cyclically adjusted budget Equals the difference between the actual level of government spending and the level of tax revenue that would be collected if the economy were operating at a high-employment level of GDP.

D

daily interest chequing accounts Chequing accounts that pay interest computed on the average daily balance during a given unit of time. These accounts may require prior notice for withdrawals above some specified amount.

debt instruments Written contracts between borrower and lender specifying the terms of a loan.

deduction Reasoning from generalizations to particular conclusions. The process of predicting specific events from theory developed from logic.

deflation A general fall in prices that causes the value of a dollar measured in terms of its purchasing power to rise. A fall in the consumer price index.

demand The various quantities of a good (resource) that households (businesses) are willing and able to take from the market at all alternative prices, *ceteris paribus.*

demand curve Graphic representation of demand.

demand deposit A deposit from which funds may be withdrawn on demand and from which funds may be transferred to another party by means of a cheque.

demand schedule Numerical tabulation of the quantitative relationship between quantity demanded and price.

demand shock A shift in the position of the entire aggregate demand curve.

deposit multiplier Assuming banks are fully loaned up, the multiplier is the reciprocal of the required reserve ratio.

depression A period of prolonged severe recession.

deregulation Reduction or elimination of government control over an industry.

derived demand Term used to characterize the demand for a productive factor because that demand is dependent upon, or derives from, the demand for the final product that the factor is used to produce.

differentiated oligopolies Oligopolies in which each firm produces a product that is somewhat different from that produced by the other firms.

diminishing marginal rate of substitution Characteristic of the behaviour of the marginal rate of substitution along an indifference curve, reflecting the fact that the more of good B a consumer has relative to good A, the more of good B the consumer is willing to part with in order to get an additional unit of good A.

direct relationship Relationship between variables in which the value of each changes in the same way (both decrease or both increase).

dirty float Situation when the government officially claims that it is allowing the market to establish the exchange rate for its currency, but in practice is buying (or selling) its currency on the open market.

discretionary fiscal policy The government's deliberate manipulation of its spending, taxing, and transfer activities to attempt to smooth out economic fluctuations to ensure maximum employment with as little inflation as possible.

diseconomies of scale Longrun average total cost of production increases with output as the size of the firm increases. It could result when a firm grows so large that it becomes cumbersome to manage.

disembodied technical change Change that takes the form of new procedures or techniques for producing goods and services.

disinvestment A decrease in the capital stock. See also *unintended inventory depletion.*

disposable income (DI) Personal income minus personal taxes.

dissolution Breaking a firm up into smaller firms.

distribution The shares of the total product of the economy that go to different individuals, or groups, in society as their incomes.

distribution effects Transfer payments from taxpayers to holders of government bonds that result in a redistribution of income.

divestiture Requiring a firm to sell some of its assets.

dividends Share of a firm's profits paid out to stockholders.

domestic bond market financing The government selling bonds to the Canadian private sector.

dumping Selling a product in a foreign market at a price below the cost of producing the product.

E

economic bad Any item that is undesired.

economic cost The alternative goods that must be forgone in order to produce a particular good. See also *opportunity cost.*

economic efficiency   Using available resources to obtain the most socially desirable maximum possible output.

economic good   Any item that is both desired and scarce.

economic growth   An outward shift in the production possibilities frontier caused by an increase in available resources and improved technological know-how.

economic policy   Proposed method of dealing with a problem or problems posed by economic reality that is arrived at through the use of economic theory and analysis.

economic problem   How to use scarce resources to best fulfill society's unlimited wants.

economic profit   Difference between the total revenue obtained for a firm's sales and the opportunity costs of all the resources used by the firm.

economic rent   Any amount of payment a factor or resource receives in excess of its supply price when there is market equilibrium.

economic resources   All the natural, human-made, and human resources used in production of goods.

economic theory   A statement about the behaviour of economic phenomena, often referred to as a law, principle, or model.

economics   A social science concerned with the study of economies and the relationships among economies. The study of the allocation of scarce resources.

economies of scale   Decrease in the longrun average total cost of production that occurs when a firm's plant size and output is increased.

economies of scope   The lower costs a firm achieves by spreading costs between a number of products.

economy   A particular system of organization for the production, distribution, and consumption of all things people use to obtain a standard of living.

elastic   Adjusting readily in response to changes.

elastic demand   Coefficient of elasticity of demand is greater than 1.

elastic supply   Coefficient of elasticity of supply is greater than 1.

embodied technical change   Technological change that is embedded in the form of the capital good itself.

endogenous   Refers to the principal variables within a model.

entrepreneur   The person who starts a business and bears the financial risk.

equation of exchange   A relationship between the economy's money supply M, the money supply's velocity of circulation V, its price level P, and total real output Q. The equation states that the total amount spent, $M \times V$, on final goods and services equals the total value of final goods and services produced, $P \times Q$. $M \times V = P \times Q$.

equilibrium income level   The level of aggregate income that will be sustained once it is achieved. At equilibrium, the aggregate income earned from production of the economy's total output corresponds to a level of aggregate spending or demand just sufficient to purchase that total output.

equilibrium price   Price at which market equilibrium is achieved.

equilibrium quantity   Quantity of the good supplied and demanded at the point of market equilibrium.

equity   The difference between a firm's total assets and its total liabilities.

excess demand   Quantity demanded for a good in excess of the quantity supplied at a price below equilibrium price.

excess reserves   Total reserves minus required reserves.

excess supply   Quantity supplied of a good in excess of the quantity demanded at a price higher than equilibrium price.

exchange rate   The price per unit of a foreign currency, or the amount of one currency that must be paid to obtain one unit of another currency.

excise taxes   Taxes levied on the sale of a particular good.

exclusion principle   Distinguishing characteristic of private goods, the benefits of which, unlike those of public goods, accrue only to those who purchase them.

exclusive dealing agreements   Manufacturers' agreements with dealers and distributors that restrict the latter's purchase, sale, or use of competing products.

exogenous   Refers to intervening variables that affect a model from outside.

expansion (or **recovery**)   The upswing of a business cycle.

expected rate of return   The amount of money that a firm expects to earn per year on funds invested in a capital good, expressed as a percentage of the funds invested.

explicit costs   Direct monetary payments a firm must make for resources not owned by the firm. See *implicit costs*.

exports   The goods a nation produces and sells to other nations.

external debt   That part of government debt held by non-residents.

external industry economies   Cost reductions a large firm obtains because its size encourages other entities to provide supporting facilities and services.

externalities   Costs or benefits related to a good that fall on others besides buyers and sellers of that particular good. Also called *spillovers, neighbourhood effects, external costs* or *benefits, spillover costs* or *benefits,* or *external economies* or *diseconomies.*

F

factors of production   The inputs (land, labour, and capital) necessary to carry on production. Also called *economic resources.*

fair return   Pricing rule under which the price of a good is determined by the intersection of the average total cost curve with the demand curve.

fallacy of composition   Error in reasoning that assumes that what is true for the part is true for the whole.

fallacy of division   Error in reasoning that assumes that what is true for the whole is true for its individual parts.

fallacy of false cause   Error in reasoning that assumes one event is the cause of another event simply because it precedes the second event in time.

fiat money   Money that is declared by the government to be legal tender. It is neither backed by nor convertible into gold or any other asset.

financial capital   Money used to purchase equipment, machinery, or other productive resources.

financial intermediary   A business that acts as an intermediary by taking the funds of lenders and making them available to borrowers, receiving the difference between the interest that it charges borrowers and the interest that it pays lenders as payment for providing this service.

financial market   Market in which lending and borrowing take place through the exchange of debt instruments at interest rates mutually determined by lenders and borrowers.

firm   A business organization that owns, rents, and operates equipment, hires labour, and buys materials and energy inputs. The firm organizes and coordinates the use of all these factors of production for the purpose of producing and marketing goods.

fiscal drag   The tendency for a progressive tax system to automatically vary taxes inversely compared to the change required by discretionary fiscal policy to move aggregate income to a desired level.

fixed-dollar assets   Assets that guarantee a repayment of the initial dollar amount invested plus some stipulated rate of interest.

fixed exchange rate   Rate of exchange of currencies that is determined ("pegged" or "fixed") by the governments involved.

fixed factor   Factor of production that cannot be changed in the shortrun.

fixed-term deposits   Deposits that earn a fixed rate of interest and must be held for a stipulated amount of time.

flexible (or **floating**) **exchange rates**   Exchange rates freely determined by supply and demand in the foreign exchange market without government intervention.

flow   A quantity per unit of time. The rate of change of the value of a variable.

foreign bond market financing   The Canadian government selling bonds to non-residents.

foreign purchases effect   Contributes to the negative slope of the aggregate demand curve because the net exports (exports minus imports) component of aggregate demand will decline (rise) as a consequence of a rise (fall) in the general price level relative to the price levels in other countries.

foreign sector   Aggregate of all the transactions between the firms, households, and governments within the domestic economy and those of other countries.

foreign-exchange market   Market in which the currencies of various countries are traded and exchange rates among different currencies are determined.

fractional reserve banking system   System in which banks are managed so that the amount of required reserves on hand is equal to a specified fraction of the amount of deposits.

free good   Something that is desired but is so plentiful that everyone can have all they want at a zero price.

free rider   Anyone who receives benefits from a good or service without having to pay for them.

fringe benefits   Any payment made by an employer for a benefit for an employee.

functional distribution of income   Method of characterizing the way income is distributed according to the function performed by the income receiver.

functions of money   What money serves as: a medium of exchange, a unit of account, and a store of value.

G

GDP gap   Potential GDP minus actual GDP, which is equal to the value of final goods and services not produced because there is unemployment.

general equilibrium analysis   Analysis of the adjustments a change in one market will cause in each and every other market.

global utility   The sum of the total utilities obtained from the consumption of a number of goods.

gold standard   A monetary system in which nations fix the rate of exchange among their currencies and gold, and hence the exchange rates among their currencies.

government   Some authority with extra economic powers (the law) to regulate production and consumption, tax and redistribute income, or generally intervene in the workings of the economy.

gross domestic product (GDP)   The market value of all final goods and services produced by the economy during a year.

gross national product (GNP)   GDP plus investment income received from non-residents minus investment income paid to non-residents.

gross private domestic investment   The total expenditures by business firms on new capital.

Guaranteed Income Supplement (GIS) A means-tested pension plan intended to augment the income of seniors with little or no other source of income other than Old Age Security.

H

horizontal merger Merger between two firms selling the same, or very similar, products in the same market.

horizontally integrated Term used to describe a firm that owns several plants, each of which produces the same or similar good.

household A social unit comprised of those living together in the same dwelling place and the economic agent making consumption decisions in the economy.

hypothesis A statement of the way we think the variables in question relate to one another; a statement of behaviour that usually implies causation; the core of any theory.

I

ideology Doctrine or way of thinking.

implicit costs Costs of resources actually owned by the firm itself. These costs are the payments such resources could have received were they employed in their next best alternative.

import quotas Limitation on imports that specifies the maximum amount of a foreign-produced good that will be permitted into a country over a specified period of time.

imports The goods a nation purchases from other nations.

impounding Action of government to hold a budget surplus in idle funds.

income effect The increasing purchase power resulting from a decrease in the price of a good a consumer was buying, allowing him or her to buy more of it even though the consumer's money income remains the same.

income elasticity Measures the responsiveness of changes in the demand for a good to changes in consumers' incomes.

increasing costs Along a production possibilities frontier, the rise in opportunity cost per additional unit of a good obtained. The longrun average cost rises with increases in output. See *diseconomies of scale*.

increasing returns to scale The gains obtained in physical output by the specialization of factors of production in larger plants.

indexing Method of keeping the purchasing power of wages, taxes, and fixed-dollar, or nominal, assets constant by adjusting their dollar-denominated values to the change in the general price level.

indifference curve A graphical representation of an indifference schedule. A curve representing all combinations of two goods that give a consumer the same level of satisfaction.

indifference map All of an individual consumer's indifference curves for two goods illustrated together.

indifference schedule A listing of all possible combinations of goods that give a consumer the same level of satisfaction.

indirect business taxes Sales and excise taxes and business property taxes.

induction Reasoning from particular facts and observations to generalizations. The process of developing theory from empirical (data) observation.

industrial union A union that seeks to organize all hourly paid workers, skilled and unskilled, in a given industry.

industry A number of firms producing the same or similar products.

inelastic Unresponsive to changing conditions. See *elastic*.

inelastic demand Coefficient (absolute value) of elasticity of demand is less than 1.

inelastic supply Coefficient of elasticity of supply is less than 1.

inferior good A good that people typically buy more of when they are at lower income levels and less of when they are at higher income levels. The demand for an inferior good is inversely related to changes in consumers' incomes.

inflation A rise in the general level of prices of all goods and services; this rise causes the purchasing power of a dollar to fall. A rise in the CPI.

information extraction problem Problem an individual firm has interpreting an increase in its price as a rise in its price relative to other prices and costs.

intended investment See *planned investment*.

interdependence Mutual dependence, as among firms in an oligopoly. The actions of one affect the other.

interest rate (or interest) The price of borrowing money, or the price received for lending money, expressed as a percentage.

interest rate effect Contributes to the negative slope of the *AD* curve because a higher (lower) price level in the economy increases (lowers) the demand for money and drives up (down) the interest rate, thereby causing a reduction (increase) in the demand for goods.

inventories Stocks of unsold goods.

inverse relationship Relationship between variables in which the value of one increases as the value of the other decreases.

investment Expenditures on new capital goods. Also called capital investment.

J

job-training programs Government-subsidized efforts aimed at improving work skills among the unemployed or underemployed.

K

Keynesian aggregate supply curve (AS$_K$) Horizontal aggregate supply curve under the special assumption that most firms in the economy are operating with a large amount of extra unused plant capacity and that most firms are not expecting the general price level to increase at all in the near future.

kinked demand model One possible explanation of price rigidity in oligopolistic industries in which there is no collusion.

L

labour Human mental and physical capabilities and skills that can be used to produce goods.

labour force All persons over the age of 15 who are employed plus all those legally eligible and actively looking for work.

Laffer curve Shows a relationship between the marginal tax rate and the amount of tax revenue that the government receives. In particular, starting from a zero marginal tax rate, tax revenues rise as the rate is increased up to some point beyond which further increases in the marginal tax rate cause tax revenue to decline.

laissez-faire capitalism An economic system which relies heavily on decentralized decision-making by households, businesses, and government agents, employing markets as the primary mechanism for production and distribution. The belief that people should be allowed to conduct their economic affairs without any interference from the government.

land All natural resources used in production.

law of demand Theory that the lower is the price of a good, the greater will be the quantity demanded and, conversely, the higher is the price, the smaller will be the quantity demanded.

law of diminishing marginal utility Given the consumer's tastes, the marginal utility associated with the consumption of additional units of any good over a given period of time eventually begins to fall as more and more units of the good are consumed.

law of diminishing returns As more and more units of a variable factor of production are used together with a fixed factor of production, beyond some point the marginal product attributable to each additional unit of the variable factor begins to decrease.

law of supply Theory that suppliers are willing and able to offer for sale larger quantities of a good at higher prices than they will at lower prices.

license Right granted by some level of government to practice certain professions or engage in a specified production activity.

lien A creditor's legal claim on a debtor's property or wages.

limit price The lowest price at which a new firm can enter an industry and just cover average total cost. Existing firms in the industry with lower average total costs can set their prices below the limit price level and discourage new entrants.

limited company See *private corporation*.

limited liability Characteristic of a corporation that makes it attractive to investors (the owners) in that financial liability extends only to the assets of the corporation, not to personal assets of the investors.

limited partner Member of a partnership who does not participate in the management of the firm or engage in business on behalf of the partners. A limited partner risks only his or her money directly invested in the firm (the limited partner's personal assets cannot be seized to satisfy the firm's debts and obligations).

liquidity The degree to which any form of wealth is readily convertible into other goods. Money is the most liquid form of wealth.

loan length The duration of time until a loan must be repaid. Also called maturity.

lockout Management prevents employees from working until they agree to a new contract.

longrun Period of time long enough that a firm can vary the quantity of all factors used to produce a particular good.

longrun supply curve The quantities of a good that firms can offer for sale at alternative prices if all factors of production can be varied. All the points formed by the intersections of all possible industry demand curves with the associated shortrun industry supply curves.

Lorenz curve Method of illustrating the extent to which actual income distribution deviates from a perfectly equal distribution of income.

low-income cut-offs Income levels below which individuals or families are considered to be living in poverty, often called poverty lines.

Lucas Critique Critique of Keynesian theory which argues that the effect of any government policy is uncertain because any new policy will cause a change in the information available to the private sector and will result in somewhat unpredictable changes to the various marginal propensities to spend throughout the economy.

M

M1 Currency in circulation outside the chartered banks plus demand deposit liabilities of the chartered banks.

M2 M1 plus personal savings and nonpersonal notice accounts.

M3 M2 plus non-personal fixed-term deposits and foreign currency accounts of residents booked in Canada.

macroeconomic comparative statics The analysis of aggregate income determination when there are changes in the aggregate price level.

macroeconomics Branch of economic analysis that focuses on the workings of the whole economy or large sectors of it.

managed float Exchange rates subject to free-market forces modified by government intervention, but without any formal commitment to fix rates at specified levels. Also called dirty float.

manager Someone who plans, administers, and coordinates production.

marginal cost (MC) Change in total cost resulting from a unit change in output.

marginal cost pricing Pricing rule under which the price of a good is set at the firm's marginal cost of producing the good.

marginal efficiency of investment curve (MEI) Graphic representation of the expected amounts of investment in capital goods at different interest rates.

marginal physical product (MPP or MP) Increase in total output associated with each one-unit increase in a variable productive factor. Also called marginal product.

marginal productivity theory of factor demand Theory that states that a profit-maximizing firm operating in a competitive factor market will increase its use of a productive factor up to the point where the factor's marginal revenue product equals the factor's price.

marginal profit The extra profit which results from producing one more unit of a product. Marginal revenue minus marginal cost.

marginal propensity to consume (MPC) The fraction or proportion of any change in income that is consumed.

marginal propensity to expend (MPE) The increase in aggregate expenditure that results from a one-dollar increase in aggregate income.

marginal propensity to import (MPM) The increase in imports that results from a one-dollar increase in aggregate income.

marginal propensity to save (MPS) Fraction or proportion of any change in income that is saved.

marginal rate of substitution (MRS) Rate at which the consumer is just willing to substitute one good for the other along an indifference curve.

marginal revenue (MR) Change in total revenue resulting from the sale of one more unit of output.

marginal revenue product (MRP) Increase in total revenue associated with the extra output produced from each one-unit increase in a variable productive factor.

marginal tax rate Indicates how much of an additional dollar of income, the marginal or last dollar earned, must be paid in taxes.

marginal utility (MU) The change in total utility that occurs with the consumption of an additional unit of a good in a given period of time.

market An institution within which buyers and sellers of a particular good or resource communicate for the purpose of exchange. The outcome of the exchange is a market price and quantity exchanged.

market demand curve Graphical representation of the sum of all the individual demand curves for a good.

market equilibrium Equilibrium established at the price where the quantity demanded of a good is just equal to the quantity supplied of the good.

market failure Condition when the market leads to a less than socially optimal allocation of resources.

market period Period of time so short that none of the factors of production used to produce a particular good can be changed.

market structure Characteristics of market organization, such as the number of buyers and sellers, the similarity of their product, and the ease of entry or exit from the industry. Also called industrial organization.

marketability Ease with which a lender may sell a debt instrument to someone else before the loan must be repaid in full. See also liquidity.

medium of exchange Money; something commonly accepted in exchange for goods and services and recognized as representing a standard of value.

menu costs The administrative and related costs to firms of changing their prices.

merchandise balance of trade The difference between merchandise exports and merchandise imports.

merit good A good that is better than the buyer realizes.

microeconomics Branch of economic analysis that focuses on individual agents or individual markets in the economy.

midpoints formula (or midpoints variation) Method of calculating the coefficient of elasticity in which the averages of the two quantities and the two prices are used as base points when computing the percentage changes in quantity and price.

minimum efficient scale (MES) The smallest level of output that achieves the lowest longrun average cost possible.

minimum-wage laws Laws that make it illegal for employers to pay workers a wage below a certain statutory level, often called the minimum wage.

misleading representation A firm's intentionally inaccurate (favourable) representation of its product(s). Prohibited by the *Competition Act*.

mixed economy An economy in which the answers to what, how, and for whom to produce are determined partly by the operation of free markets and partly by government intervention.

monetarism A school of thought that believes money is the main causal factor determining the level of economic activity.

monetary accommodation See *monetizing the government debt*.

monetary gradualism A monetary policy strategy of adopting a constant growth rate for the money supply as measured by a monetary aggregate such as M1.

monetary policy The central bank's increasing (decreasing) of the money supply to ease (tighten) credit conditions and shift the *AD* curve rightward (leftward), thereby influencing output, employment, inflation, or the exchange rate.

monetary rule Monetary policy strategy which requires that the central bank set a known publicized target for stable growth in the money supply and then stick to it.

monetizing the government debt Having the Bank of Canada finance the government deficit directly by increasing the money supply.

money Anything that is generally acceptable in trade as a medium of exchange and also serves as a unit of account and a store of value.

money GDP GDP measured in current prices or dollars. Also referred to as *nominal GDP*.

money substitute Anything (such as credit cards) that serves as a medium of exchange but does not serve as a store of value.

monopolistic competition Industry or market structure in which there is easy entry and exit, and in which there are many firms, each of which produces a product that is slightly different from that of the others.

monopoly Form of market structure in which the entire market for a good or service is supplied by a single seller or firm, and there are barriers to the entry of potential competitors.

monopsony Market structure in which one buyer purchases a good or resource from many sellers.

moral suasion Tool of monetary policy in which the Bank of Canada tries to get the chartered banks to agree on a course of action that places a high priority on the public interest instead of the self-interest of the banks.

multiplier The number of times by which the change in aggregate total income exceeds the size of the expenditure change that brought it about.

N

NAIRU The nonaccelerating inflation rate of unemployment, a level of unemployment at which there is only structural and frictional unemployment. The lowest unemployment attainable without causing an acceleration in the inflation rate. See *natural rate of unemployment*.

nationalized industries Industries owned by the government.

natural monopoly Industry in which the economies of scale make it possible for an established firm to effectively prevent rivals from entering the industry.

natural rate of unemployment The view held by some economists that the existence of frictional unemployment and a certain amount of structural unemployment constitutes a natural rate of unemployment toward which the economy automatically gravitates in the absence of other disturbances.

near money Assets that are like money except that they can't be used as a medium of exchange, though they are readily convertible into currency or demand deposits.

near-public good A good that is consumed jointly, though it is possible to exclude nonpaying customers—a movie is an example.

negative income tax Tax plan through which households with incomes below a statutory level receive a subsidy from the government equal to some fraction of the difference between the statutory income level and their earned income.

net exports The difference between the dollar value of the goods produced and sold to non-residents and the dollar value of the goods non-residents produce and sell to us.

net injections The situation at aggregate income levels less than the equilibrium level, when aggregate withdrawals (saving) will be less than aggregate injections.

net national income (NNI) NNP minus indirect taxes less subsidies.

net national product (NNP) The dollar value of GNP minus capital depreciation (capital consumption allowance).

net private domestic investment The increase (decrease) in the economy's capital stock; equals gross private investment minus depreciation.

net productivity of capital The annual percentage rate of return that can be earned by investing in capital.

net withdrawals The situation at aggregate income levels above equilibrium, when aggregate withdrawals (saving) will be larger than aggregate injections.

net worth See *equity*.

new Keynesian theory View that policymakers will influence the real variables in the economy (1) because the policy ineffectiveness proposition does not hold when wages or prices are sticky, and (2) because policy-makers are never perfectly predictable or systematic, making it highly unlikely that firms and workers can anticipate policy actions so well as to render them ineffective.

nominal interest rate   The real interest rate plus the anticipated rate of inflation.

nonpecuniary considerations   Characteristics associated with a job that will cause labour to require either a higher wage (if the characteristics are viewed as disadvantages) or a lower wage (if the characteristics are viewed as advantages).

nonprice competition   Competition among firms for sales by means other than price cutting—such as by advertising, service, and product differentiation.

normal good   A good that people typically buy more of as their income rises. The demand for a normal good varies directly with changes in consumers' incomes.

normal profit   Payments to financial capital and entrepreneurial skill that are just sufficient to keep them employed in a particular productive activity—that is, to keep them from going into some other productive activity.

normative statement   A statement of what should or ought to be that cannot be supported or refuted by facts alone; a value judgment or opinion.

notice accounts   See *notice deposits*.

notice deposits   Deposits in which the depositor may be required to give the bank advance notice before making a withdrawal.

O

Old Age Security (OAS)   A universal, noncontributory pension plan (not means tested) for all Canadian residents starting at age 65.

oligopoly   Market dominated by a few sellers.

open economy multiplier   One divided by one minus the slope of the aggregate expenditure function; $1/(1 - MPE)$. See also *multiplier*.

open market operations   The Bank of Canada's buying and selling of government securities in the open market in which such securities are traded.

opportunity cost   Cost of a unit of a good measured in terms of the other goods that must be forgone in order to obtain it.

ordinal numbers   Number designating the place occupied by any item in a numbered sequence. Use of numbers to indicate order only.

output effect   When the price of a factor falls (rises), the costs of production fall (rise), leading to a rise (fall) in the output of final product and a consequent increase (decrease) in the use of all factors.

P

paradox of thrift   If each household tries to save more, all households may end up earning and saving less.

paradox of value   Early economic puzzle—the price of a good does not correspond to its total utility; solved by the law of diminishing marginal utility.

parity   Price of an agricultural good that gives the good a purchasing power, in terms of the goods that farmers buy, equivalent to that which it had in a base period.

partial equilibrium analysis   Analysis of a change in one market and its consequences for that market and possibly a few others. All other markets are assumed to remain unchanged.

partnership   Firm owned and operated jointly by two or more individuals.

patent   Exclusive right granted to an inventor to market a product for a certain period of time.

peak (or boom)   Uppermost point in the upswing (expansion) of a business cycle.

per capita GDP   An economy's GDP divided by the size of its population.

perfect competition   Condition that exists in an industry when (1) there are many firms, (2) all firms sell a homogenous product, (3) each firm is a price taker, and (4) there is ease of entry into and exit from the industry by firms.

perfectly competitive firm   A firm operating in a perfectly competitive market which contributes such a small fraction of total industry supply that it cannot affect the market price.

perfectly elastic   Quantity of good demanded changes by an unlimited amount in response to a change in price or other variable.

perfectly inelastic   Quantity of good demanded does not change at all in response to change in price.

personal consumption (C)   Household expenditures on goods and services.

personal disposable income (PDI)   PI (personal income) less personal taxes.

personal income (PI)   NDI (net domestic income—NNI less net investment income from non-residents) plus transfer payments.

Phillips curve   An alleged inverse relationship between the rate of inflation and the rate of unemployment.

planned investment   Businesses' investment spending plans.

plant   A facility in which production takes place.

point elasticity   Method of calculating the coefficient of price elasticity; uses standard percentage changes—the difference over the original point; direction matters.

policy ineffectiveness proposition   View that in the long-run policymaker actions will be expected by firms, workers, and other resource suppliers, so expansionary monetary and fiscal policies intended to reduce the unemployment rate below the natural rate will cause an ever-increasing, or accelerating, rate of inflation.

positive statement   A statement of what is, was, or will be that can be supported or refuted by looking at empirical evidence.

potential GDP   What GDP would be if the economy were "fully" employed. The output level of the economy if the unemployment rate is equal to NAIRU.

poverty   State in which an individual's or family's income and other means of support are below some percent of average household income.

precautionary demand   The demand for money to cover unforeseen events or emergencies that require immediate expenditures.

predatory pricing   Practice whereby a large firm, operating in many markets, can afford to sell at prices below costs in some markets until competitors in those markets are driven out of business.

prediction   Description of future events.

preferences   Individual choices of one good or bundle over another. See *indifference curve*.

present value   The value today of a stream of future income.

price   The exchange value of a good in terms of other goods, most often expressed as the amount of money people will pay for a unit of the good.

price ceiling   Government-imposed legal upper limit on price.

price discrimination   Selling the same good or service at different prices to different buyers for reasons not associated with costs.

price elasticity of demand   Measure of the degree of responsiveness of quantity demanded to a change in price.

price elasticity of supply   Measure of the degree of responsiveness of quantity supplied to a change in price.

price floor   Legally imposed lower limit on a price. See *price support*.

price index   Ratio of current prices to prices in some base year.

price leadership   Informal agreement among firms in an industry that one, usually the largest, will always initiate or take the lead in price changes.

price stickiness   Tendency of prices to respond slowly to changes in demand.

price support   Government guarantee to suppliers that they will receive a specific price for a good even if the market will not pay this price. See *price floor*.

price taker   A firm that cannot influence the price of its own product by means of altering its output level.

private corporation   Privately owned firm that does not sell shares to the public.

product differentiation   Each firm's product is a close but not perfect substitute for that of every other firm in the industry.

production   The process of converting resources into goods that provide well-being to members of society.

production possibilities frontier (PPF)   A graphical representation of the maximum possible output combinations of goods for a fully employed economy.

productive efficiency   The full employment of all economic resources in a society, thereby attaining the production possibilities frontier.

productivity   The efficiency with which each labour hour combines with the capital stock and the existing state of technology to produce output—often measured as output per labour hour.

progressive tax   A tax that takes a larger percentage out of a high income than it does out of a low income.

prohibition orders   Court rulings forbidding certain activities.

proportional tax   A tax that takes the same percentage of income no matter what the income level.

proprietors' income   Income earned by the owners of unincorporated businesses.

proprietorship   See *sole proprietorship*.

public corporation   Privately owned firm that trades shares on public stock exchanges.

public goods   Goods that will not be produced in private markets because there is no way for the producer to prevent those who don't pay for the goods from using them—for example, a lighthouse beacon.

public utilities   Natural monopolies whose operation, including the setting of prices, is regulated by a government agency.

pure fiscal policy   Changes in government expenditure, taxation, transfers, or all three that do not change the money supply.

pure market economy   An economy in which the answers to what, how, and for whom to produce are determined entirely by the operation of markets.

pure public good   A good that cannot be provided to one person without being provided to others—national defense is an example.

Q

quantity theory of money   Asserts that velocity V in the equation of exchange $M \times V = P \times Q$ is stable and not just whatever number is necessary to make the equation true; therefore, changes in the money supply M are asserted to cause proportional changes in money GDP, $P \times Q$.

R

rate base Allowable capital cost used in determining the prices that may be charged by a public utility.

rate of return Ratio of the dollar measure of a capital good's net productivity to the cost of the capital good expressed as a percentage per year.

ration coupon Coupon issued by government entitling an individual or household to buy a certain number of units of a good at the set price.

real balance effect Inverse relationship between the general level of prices and consumer spending: an increase in the price level, by reducing real wealth, will shift the consumption function downward; conversely, a fall in the price level, by increasing real wealth, will shift the consumption function upward.

real GDP GDP measured in terms of prices at which final goods are sold in some base year. Changes in real GDP are due only to changes in the quantity of final goods, not changes in price.

real interest rate The annual percentage rate of increase in the lender's purchasing power on money loaned, or in other words, the interest rate calculated in terms of its purchasing power over goods.

real wage Price per unit of labour services measured in terms of the quantity of goods that can be purchased—often measured as the money wage divided by an index of the general price level.

realized investment Intended investment minus any unintended inventory reduction or plus any unintended inventory addition.

recession (or contraction) A slowing down in the growth of economic activity and GDP.

redistribution Reallocation of income through taxes and transfers or public provision of goods.

regressive tax A tax that takes a smaller percentage out of a high income than it does out of a low income.

rent Payments to those providing land resources and income received from a perfectly inelastic supply.

rent control Government-imposed price ceiling on the rental rate on housing a tenant may be charged.

required reserve ratio The ratio of required reserves to the total amount of demand deposits.

required reserves Reserves that a bank is legally required to hold against deposit liabilities—equal to the required reserve ratio multiplied by the amount of deposits.

resale price maintenance A wholesale supplier's attempt to influence retailers' prices.

resource misallocation See *underemployment*.

retained earnings Money saved by businesses out of sales revenue.

risk The likelihood that a borrower will default on a loan or that an investment may experience a capital loss.

roundabout process Taking time and effort away from the direct production of goods for current consumption and using that time to produce capital goods that will ultimately make possible a larger subsequent production of goods.

S

sales ratio Percentage of total industry sales accounted for by a firm in the industry.

sales taxes Taxes levied on the sale of any of a broad classification of goods, calculated as a percentage of price.

saving Refraining from current consumption.

saving function The relationship between the level of disposable income and the level of planned saving.

savings deposit Bank deposit drawing regular interest and payable upon some advance notice.

Say's Law The proposition that supply (in the aggregate) creates its own (aggregate) demand.

scarce The desire for or use of a good or resource exceeds the amount available at a zero price.

scarcity The social relationship between limited resources and unlimited human wants for the goods that these resources could produce.

scientific method Ongoing process of developing theory through deductive reasoning and inductive observation. Theory is used to explain and predict. These explanations and predictions are then tested against the data (evidence) and the theory is modified, continuing the cycle.

seasonal variation Regular patterns in economic data associated with custom and weather over the course of the year.

secondary reserve ratio Amount of liquid assets that the chartered bank is legally required to hold in addition to the primary reserve, expressed as a percentage of the values of deposit liabilities.

services Intangible economic goods, such as shoeshines, haircuts, doctor examinations, and so on.

shortage Less of a good is supplied than is demanded.

shortrun Period of time short enough that the quantity of one or more factors of production used to produce a particular good cannot be changed, while some others can be varied and, therefore, output can be varied.

shortrun production function Relationship between the amount of a variable factor of production used and the total quantity of output produced, while at least one factor is fixed.

shortrun shut down   Condition when a firm's total revenue is not even large enough to cover its total variable cost, so the firm minimizes its loss by producing nothing at all.

shortrun supply curve   That rising part of the perfectly competitive firm's marginal cost curve which lies above its average variable cost curve.

single-tax movement   Late-nineteenth-century movement, led by Henry George, to finance government by taxing the economic rent on land.

size distribution of income   The ranking of all families in the economy according to the size of the income received by each, lowest to highest, regardless of the source of their income.

slope   Change in the *Y*-axis variable over some range of the function divided by the change in the *X*-axis variable over that same range. Commonly expressed as "rise over run."

sole proprietorship   A firm with a single owner who makes all decisions and bears full responsibility for everything the firm does.

Special Drawing Rights (SDRs)   Special accounts that the International Monetary Fund (IMF) creates for member nations, to be used as an official reserve to finance balance of payments deficits.

specialization agreements   Agreement in which two or more firms each agree to stop production of some product and buy it exclusively from another firm in the agreement.

specialization of labour   System of production in which each worker performs only one task for which he or she is specifically trained.

specific tax   Sales tax or excise tax calculated as a fixed amount of money per unit of good sold.

speculative demand   Demand for money as a convenient and relatively risk-free store of wealth.

stagflation   The existence of high rates of inflation and unemployment at the same time.

stock   The sum total at a given point in time.

strike   Labour's refusal to work for an employer until the employer agrees to the demand for higher wages or changes in other terms and conditions of employment.

subsidy   Amount of money paid to a supplier by the government per unit of a good produced.

subsistence living level   The minimum standard of living necessary to keep the population from declining—the death rate just equals the birthrate.

substitute good   A good that can be used in place of another good because it fulfills similar needs or desires.

substitution effect   When factors are substitutable for one another in the production process, a fall (rise) in the price of one of them will to a certain extent lead to its substitution for (replacement of) the other.

supply   The various quantities of a good (resource) that businesses (households) offer for sale on the market at all alternative prices, *ceteris paribus*.

supply curve   Graphic representation of supply.

supply schedule   Numerical tabulation of the relationship between quantity supplied and price.

supply-side theory   Prediction that shifts to the right in the aggregate supply curve will tend to increase output and aggregate income, and at the same time decrease inflation and lower the unemployment rate.

surplus   More of a good is supplied than is demanded.

switching operations   Way in which the Bank of Canada directly influences the quantity of reserves available to the chartered banking system by switching government funds into or out of deposits in the chartered banks.

systematic errors   Consistent, and therefore predictable, mistakes made by economic agents.

T

tariff (or duty)   Tax on imports, most often calculated as a percentage of the price charged for the good by the foreign supplier.

tax incidence   Distribution of the burden of a tax between the buyer and the seller.

technology   The set of production methods that could be used to combine resources of all kinds, including labour, to produce goods.

terms of trade   The ratio of exchange between exported and imported goods.

theory of rational expectations   Holds that people form their expectations about future economic activity (wages, prices, employment, and so forth) on the basis of their knowledge, experience, and understanding of how the economy works (including the effects of systematic monetary and fiscal policy) and on all relevant economic data and information, and that they do not persist in making systematic mistakes when predicting future events.

TLC and CLC   Major Canadian labour organizations—The Trades and Labour Congress of Canada (TLC), and the Canadian Labour Congress (CLC).

token coins   Coins that contain an amount of metal (or other material) that is worth much less than the face value of the coin.

total cost (*TC*)   The sum of the firm's total variable cost and total fixed cost at a given output level; the sum of the opportunity costs of the inputs used to produce that output.

total fixed cost (*TFC*)   Cost of the unchangeable, or fixed, factors of production in the shortrun.

total product (*TP*) Total quantity of a good produced.

total revenue (*TR*) Quantity of a good sold multiplied by the price per unit.

total utility (*TU*) The entire satisfaction obtained from the consumption of units of a good over a given period of time. See *marginal utility*.

total variable cost (*TVC*) Costs that the firm can vary in the shortrun by changing the quantity of the variable factors of production and, hence, the quantity of output produced.

trade credit Credit extended by one business to another business, allowing the latter to buy goods from the former without making immediate full payment by cheque or with currency. Serves as a short-term medium of exchange though it is not a store of value like money.

trading possibilities frontier Graphical representation of the choices that a nation has by specializing in the product in which it has a comparative advantage and trading (exporting) its specialty for a product in which it has a comparative disadvantage.

transactions demand Demand for money for its use as a medium of exchange to transact the purchase and sale of goods and services.

transfer earnings That part of the payment to a factor that is required to induce the seller to supply that quantity of the factor.

transfer payments Payments characterized by the fact that the recipient is neither expected nor required to provide any contribution to GDP in return.

Treasury Bill (T-Bill) account A relatively liquid account on which a financial institution pays higher interest as long as the depositor keeps the daily balance above some relatively large figure ($10,000 or $50,000).

trough The lower turning point of a business cycle.

tying contract Contract whereby a firm agrees to sell one of its products only on the condition that the buyer purchases one or more of its other products as well.

U

unanticipated inflation Amount of inflation that is unexpected.

underemployment A condition in which available resources are employed in tasks for which other resources are better suited or in which the best available technology is not used in a production process. Also called resource misallocation.

undifferentiated oligopolies Oligopolies in which each firm produces the same product.

undistributed corporate profits See *undistributed profits*.

undistributed profits Profits not paid out to shareholders (but still belonging to them). Undistributed profits are usually reinvested in the firm's operation. See *retained earnings*.

unemployment A condition in which available factors of production are idle. In reference to labour, unemployment is said to exist whenever workers are actively looking for jobs but are unable to find them.

Unemployment Insurance (UI) A government-sponsored quasi-insurance plan intended to help workers who are temporarily out of work by providing them with some income. Benefit payments generally exceed the premiums paid.

unintended inventory depletion The decrease in inventories that occurs when aggregate expenditure exceeds aggregate income.

union An organization of workers that represents them collectively in bargaining with employers over wages and other terms of employment.

union shop Workplace that permits a nonunion employee to be hired provided the employee joins the union within a certain period of time after employment.

unit banking system System characterized by small, competitive, localized banks rather than a smaller number of large banks operating branches on a nationwide basis.

unit elastic The percentage change in quantity is just equal to the percentage change in price, income, or price of a related good. Coefficient of elasticity equals 1. Also called unitary elasticity.

utility The service or satisfaction a good provides to the consumer.

V

value added The difference at each stage of production between what the firm sells its product for and what it pays for all the raw materials and intermediate goods it purchases to make the product.

variable-dollar asset An asset that has no guaranteed fixed-dollar value.

variable factor Factor of production that can be changed in the shortrun.

variables Quantities subject to change.

velocity of circulation The number of times a typical dollar of the money stock must go around the circular flow of money exchanged for final goods during a year.

vertical merger Merger between a supplier and its customer.

vertically integrated   Term used to describe a firm that owns several plants, each of which handles a different stage in the production process of one good.

W

wage   Price per unit of labour services.

workable competition   Vigorous price and nonprice competition accompanied by the significant potential for the entry of new firms into an industry—may exist even in industries where there are few firms.

Y

yellow-dog contract   Signed statement whereby a worker, as a condition of employment, agrees not to join a union.

Z

zero reserve requirements   Allowing the chartered banks to hold zero reserves at the Bank of Canada and decide for themselves the appropriate cash reserves to hold for day-to-day operations.

Index

MACROECONOMIC STATISTICS FOR CANADA

1960 TO 1991

Year	Money Supply M1	Money Supply M2	Nominal GDP	Real GDP 1986 Dollars	Nominal GNP	Prices CPI	Prices GDP Deflator	Unemploy- ment Rate	Bank Rate	"90-Day" Commercia Rate
1960	5.2	12.3	39.5	164.1	38.8		24.0	7.0	3.54	4.00
1961	5.5	13.0	40.9	169.3	40.6	31.6	24.2	7.2	3.06	3.37
1962	5.7	13.6	44.4	181.3	40.2	32.0	24.5	6.0	4.48	4.38
1963	6.0	14.3	47.7	190.7	43.6	32.6	25.0	5.5	3.88	4.01
1964	6.3	15.1	52.2	203.4	51.3	33.2	25.7	4.7	4.04	4.20
1965	6.7	16.1	57.5	216.8	56.5	34.0	26.5	3.9	4.29	5.02
1966	7.2	17.3	64.4	231.5	63.3	35.2	27.8	3.6	5.17	6.27
1967	7.9	19.0	69.1	238.3	67.8	36.5	29.0	4.1	4.98	5.85
1968	8.3	21.1	75.4	251.1	74.2	38.0	30.0	4.8	6.79	6.82
1969	8.9	23.4	83.0	264.5	81.8	39.7	31.4	4.7	7.46	7.85
1970	9.1	25.0	89.1	271.4	87.8	41.0	32.8	5.7	7.13	7.34
1971	10.2	27.7	97.3	287.0	95.8	42.2	33.9	6.4	5.19	4.51
1972	11.7	30.8	108.6	303.4	107.2	44.2	35.8	6.3	4.75	5.10
1973	13.3	35.4	127.4	326.8	125.6	47.6	39.0	5.5	6.13	7.45
1974	14.6	42.7	152.1	341.2	149.9	52.8	44.6	5.3	8.50	10.51
1975	16.7	48.9	171.5	350.1	169.0	58.5	49.0	6.9	8.50	7.94
1976	18.0	56.5	197.9	371.7	194.4	62.9	53.3	7.1	9.29	9.17
1977	19.4	64.4	217.9	385.1	213.3	67.9	56.6	8.1	7.71	7.48
1978	21.6	71.4	241.6	402.7	235.7	73.9	60.0	8.3	8.98	8.83
1979	23.1	82.7	276.1	418.3	268.9	80.7	66.0	7.4	12.10	12.07
1980	24.5	101.3	309.9	424.5	302.1	88.9	73.0	7.5	12.89	13.15
1981	25.4	116.7	356.0	440.1	344.7	100.0	80.9	7.5	17.93	18.33
1982	25.6	127.5	374.4	426.0	361.8	110.8	87.9	11.0	13.96	14.15
1983	27.7	134.3	405.7	439.4	394.1	117.2	92.3	11.8	9.55	9.45
1984	28.6	140.3	444.7	467.2	431.2	122.3	95.2	11.2	11.31	11.19
1985	29.9	153.5	478.0	489.4	463.7	127.2	97.7	10.5	9.65	9.56
1986	31.4	169.6	505.7	505.7	489.3	132.4	100.0	9.5	9.21	9.16
1987	35.7	187.5	551.4	526.1	535.2	138.2	104.8	8.8	8.40	8.39
1988	37.6	200.9	603.4	549.2	584.5	143.8	109.9	7.8	9.69	9.66
1989	39.4	227.2	651.6	565.7	629.5	151.0	115.2	7.5	12.29	12.21
1990	38.7	251.4	671.6	567.5	647.6	158.2	117.9	8.1	13.05	13.05
1991	. 39.9	275.5	679.2	558.6	656.2	160.5	123.5	10.3	9.03	8.90

Data compiled from Canadian Economic Observer; Canadian Statistical Review, Bank of Canada Review, and Bank of Canada Review Supplement.